D0978769

THE COMPLETE CONCRETE, MASONRY, AND BRICK HANDBOOK

THE COMPLETE CONCRETE, MASONRY, AND BRICK HANDBOOK

J. T. ADAMS

ARCO PUBLISHING, INC.
NEW YORK

Published by Arco Publishing, Inc.
219 Park Avenue South, New York, N.Y. 10003

Library of Congress Cataloging in Publication Data

Adams, J. T.
The complete concrete, masonry, and brick handbook.

Includes index
1. Concrete construction—Handbooks, manuals, etc.
2. Bricklaying—Handbooks, manuals, etc. 3. Masonry—Handbooks, manuals, etc. I. Title.

TH1461.A3 693 77-14003
ISBN 0-668-04340-7 (Library Edition)

Printed in the United States of America

Contents

SECTION I: CONCRETE

Preface

This book has been produced to satisfy a demand for a complete handbook of concrete, masonry, and brick. It covers every phase of these subjects in a single volume.

Each of the book's seven sections describes in detail every aspect of a group of related subjects. It is written in simple, straightforward language and many actual on-the-job practices are well illustrated.

The Complete Concrete, Masonry, and Brick Handbook contains a description of all tools, equipment, and materials required for the procedures, installation, repair, and maintenance of the subject discussed in each of the 57 chapters.

Instructions for making improvements or additions to beautify and enhance the value of the home or its surroundings are also fully illustrated with detailed and dimensioned drawings, diagrams, charts, and photographs. Tables will be found throughout the book.

Every effort has been made to furnish the user of this book with authoritative information on all up-to-date materials, as well as the methods used for estimating required quantities. This information can be of inestimable value.

All the procedures and projects described here are well within the scope of any man or woman who desires to use tools and materials intelligently, and has the incentive to enhance the beauty and value of the home and its surroundings by maintaining it in proper condition at all times.

The extensive index lists page references for every tool and material of construction, and every practical operation and job.

PREFACE

In the Appendices you will also find a Glossary of Terms; Suggested Details of Concrete Masonry Construction; Patterns for Concrete Masonry; Tables; and a Suggested Method of Laying Out a Foundation.

The author hopes that the material in this book will furnish an excellent foundation for the beginner as well as giving valuable aid to the experienced worker.

J.T.A.

Acknowledgments

The author desires to acknowledge with thanks the assistance of the following national organizations, colleges, and branches of the government that have cooperated in the production of this book.

American Badminton Association; American Concrete Institute; American Face Brick Association; American National Standards Institute; American Petroleum Institute; American Society for Testing Materials; American Society of Heating, Refrigeration and Air Conditioning Engineers; American Standard Building Code Requirements of Masonry; American Standards Association; American Structural Products Co.—Owens–Illinois Glass Co.; Brick Manufacturers Association of America; British Precast Concrete Federation; Canadian Standards Association; Columbia Brick Works; Concrete Reinforcing Steel Institute; Construction Specifications Institute; Forest Products Laboratory; Henry Disston & Sons; International Masonry Industry All-Weather Council; International Masonry Institute; Iowa State College; Louisville Cement Co.; L. S. Starrett Co.; Majestic Co.; Metal Lath Manufacturing Association; Miller Falls Tools; National Association of Marble Dealers; National Building Code of Canada; National Bureau of Standards Institute; National Concrete Masonry Association; National Quartz Producers Council; National Ready Mixed Concrete Association; National Research Council of Canada; National Shuffleboard Association; Ohio State University; Parker-Kalon Corp.; Portland Cement Association; Prestreased Concrete Institute; Stanley Tools; Structural Clay Products Institute; Structural Tile Association; Thor Power Tool Co.; University of Illinois; U.S. Bureau of Naval Personnel; U.S. Bureau of Reclamation; U.S. Department of Agriculture; U.S. Department of Commerce; U.S. Department of Construction; U.S. Lawn Tennis Institute Association; U.S. Naval Bureau; U.S. Public Health Service; U.S. Table Tennis Association; U.S. Volley Ball Association.

Section 1

Concrete

As a construction material, concrete is eminently suited for many uses. It is durable, sanitary, and fire-resistant. The upkeep cost of concrete is low, and it can easily be made attractive. Because it is plastic when first mixed, concrete lends itself to the construction of diverse objects.

On the other hand, perhaps no other material depends so much upon the user for its success. Good materials, accurate proportioning, and careful control in all operations are essential to the making of good concrete.

Chapter 1

Fundamental Facts About Concrete

Concrete can be considered to be made of two components, aggregates and paste. Aggregates are generally classified into two groups, fine and coarse. Fine aggregates consist of natural or manufactured sand with particle sizes smaller than about ¼ inch (6.35 mm.); coarse aggregates are those with particle sizes greater than about ¼ inch (6.35 mm.). The paste is composed of cement, water, and sometimes entrained air. (*See* Chap. 2, Concrete Ingredients.)

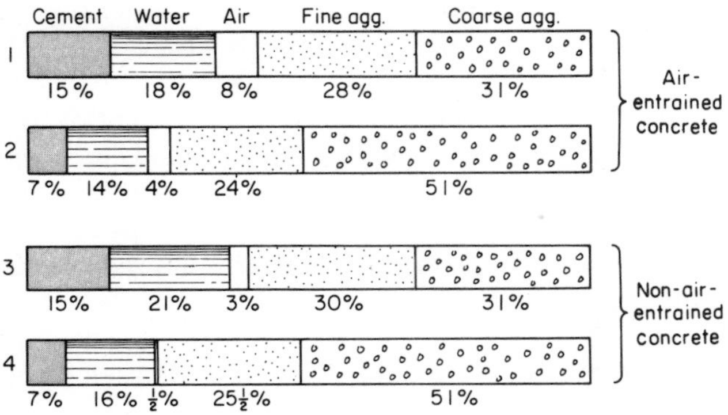

Fig. 1. Range in proportions of materials used in concrete. Bars 1 and 3 represent rich mixes with small aggregates. Bars 2 and 4 represent lean mixes with large aggregates.

Cement paste ordinarily constitutes 25 to 40 percent of the total volume of concrete. As shown in Fig. 1, the absolute volume of cement is usually between 7 and 15 percent [375 to 750 pounds per cubic yard (477.7 to 955.4 kgs. per cu. meter)] and the water from 14 to 21 percent [230 to 350 pounds per cubic

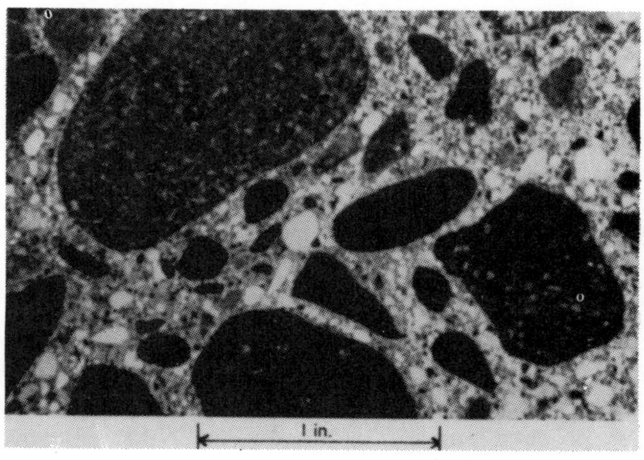

Fig. 2. Cross-section of concrete. Cement and water paste completely coats each aggregate particle and fills all of the space between particles.

yard (293 to 445.9 kgs. per cu. meter)]. Air contents in air-entrained concrete range up to about eight percent of the volume of the concrete. (*See* Chap. 3, Batching; *see also* Chap. 4, Mixing Concrete.)

Since *aggregate* makes up about 60 to 80 percent of the concrete, its selection is important. Aggregate should consist of particles having adequate strength and resistance to exposure conditions, and should not contain materials having injurious effects. A smooth gradation of particle sizes is desired for efficient use of the cement and water paste.

In properly made concrete each particle of aggregate is completely paste-coated. Also, all of the space between aggregate particles is completely filled with paste. Figure 2 shows a section cut through hardened concrete. It can be shown that the quality of the concrete is greatly dependent upon the quality of the paste. (*See* Chap. 15, Exposed Aggregate Concrete.)

Quality of paste is dependent upon the ratio of water to cement used, and the extent of curing. The cementing properties of the paste are due to the chemical reactions between cement and water. These reactions, called hydration, require time and favorable conditions of temperature and moisture. They take place very rapidly at first and then more and more slowly for a long time under favorable conditions.

More water is used in mixing concrete than is required for complete hydration in order to make the concrete plastic and workable. However, as the paste is thinned with water, its quality is lowered; it has less strength and is less resistant to weather. For successful results, a proper *proportion of water* to cement is essential.

RESISTANCE TO FREEZING AND THAWING

Concrete is used in structures and pavements that are expected to have long life and low upkeep. One requirement of such concrete is high resistance to anticipated exposure conditions. The most destructive factor of weather is freezing and thawing while the concrete is wet or moist. *Deterioration* may be caused by expansion of the water in the paste, by expansion of some of the aggregate particles, or by a combination of both. *Air entrainment* improves resistance to this deterioration. Figure 3

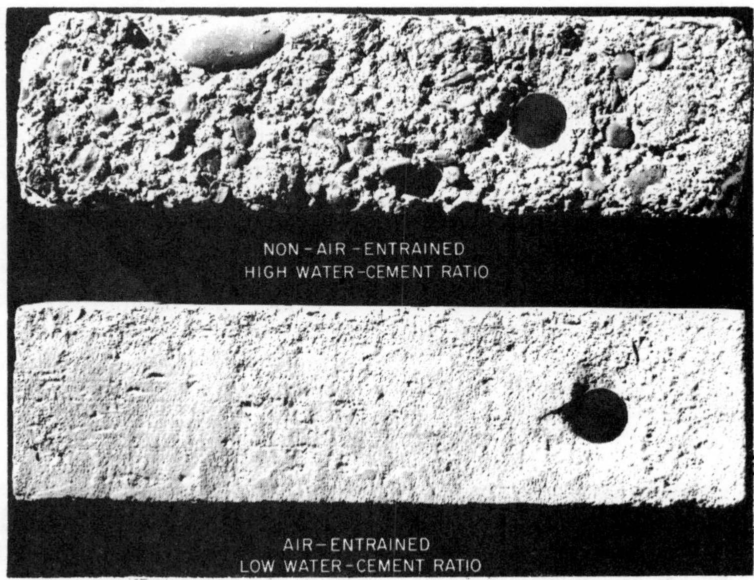

Fig. 3.

shows specimens subjected to 150 cycles of freezing and thawing. The durability of concrete exposed to freezing and thawing is effected by the quality of the paste. Air-entrained concrete with a low water-cement ratio is highly resistant to repeated freeze-thaw cycles.

Destructive expansion of water in the paste during freezing is accommodated in air-entrained concrete. Air bubbles in the paste provide chambers to relieve the expansive force.

When freezing occurs in concrete exposed to wet conditions for a sufficiently long time to saturate some aggregate particles, coarse aggregate in particular, destructive hydraulic pressures may be generated. Water displaced from these aggregate particles during the ice formation is unable to escape fast enough through the surrounding paste to prevent such pressure. However, under nearly all exposure conditions, a paste of good quality (low water-cement ratio) is able to prevent aggregate particles from becoming saturated. If this paste is air-entrained, it can accommodate the small amounts of excess water that are expelled from the aggregate, thus protecting the concrete from freeze-thaw damage.

Figure 4 illustrates that within the range of water-cement ratios normally used, air-entrained concrete is much more resistant to freeze-thaw cycles than non-air-entrained concrete. Also, concrete with a low water-cement ratio is more durable than concrete with a high water-cement ratio. *Durability* as shown in Fig. 4, is a relative measure of the number of cycles of freezing and thawing required to produce a certain amount of deterioration in test specimens. Air-entrained concrete with a low water-cement ratio will withstand a great number of cycles of freezing and thawing without showing distress.

WATERTIGHT CONCRETE

Where concrete is exposed to weather or other severe exposure conditions, it is important that it be *watertight*. Such concrete requires a *watertight paste*. Tests show that watertightness of paste depends primarily on the amount of cement and mixing water used and the length of the moist-curing period. Test re-

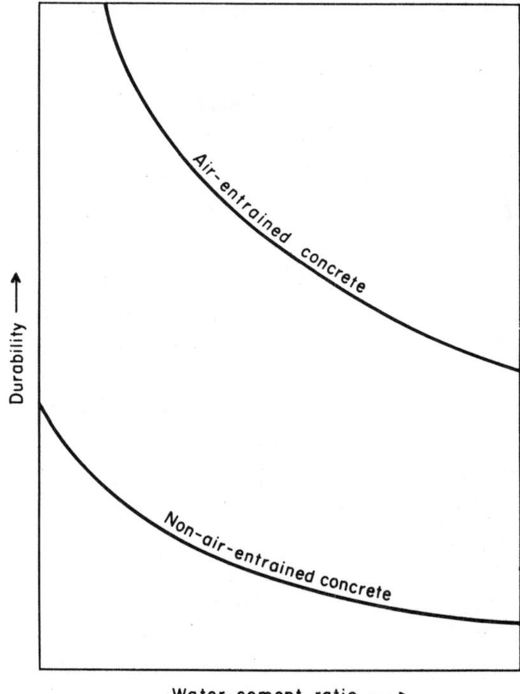

Fig. 4. High resistance to freezing and thawing is associated with entrained air and low water-cement ratio.

sults obtained by subjecting non-air-entrained mortar discs to 20 psi (1.4 kgs. per sq. cm.) water pressure as shown in Fig. 5. (*Note* in Fig. 5 that leakage is reduced as the water-cement ratio is decreased and the curing period increased.) In these tests, the mortar discs that were moist-cured for seven days had no leakage when made with a water-cement ratio of 0.50. Leakage was greater in mortars made with higher water-cement ratios. Also, for each water-cement ratio, the leakage became less as the length of curing period was increased. In the discs with a water-cement ratio of 0.80, the mortar still permitted leakage after being cured a month. (*See* Chap. 10, Curing Concrete.)

Air-entrainment improves water tightness by increasing den-

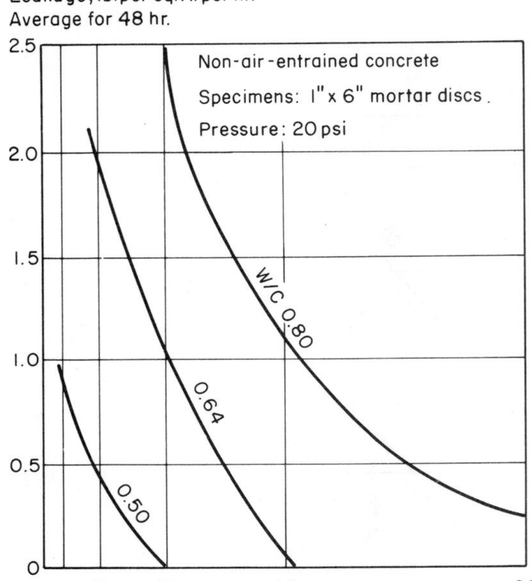

Fig. 5. Effect of water-cement ratio and curing on watertightness.

sity through improved workability and reduced segregation and bleeding. Because the total water requirement of air-entrained concrete is less, the paste will have a lower water-cement ratio and will therefore be more watertight.

To be watertight, concrete must also be free from cracks and honeycomb.

STRENGTH OF CONCRETE

The compressive strength of concrete is important in design of structures. In pavements and other slabs on ground, the flexural strength of the concrete is often used for design purposes. *Compressive strength* can be used as an index of *flexural strength*,

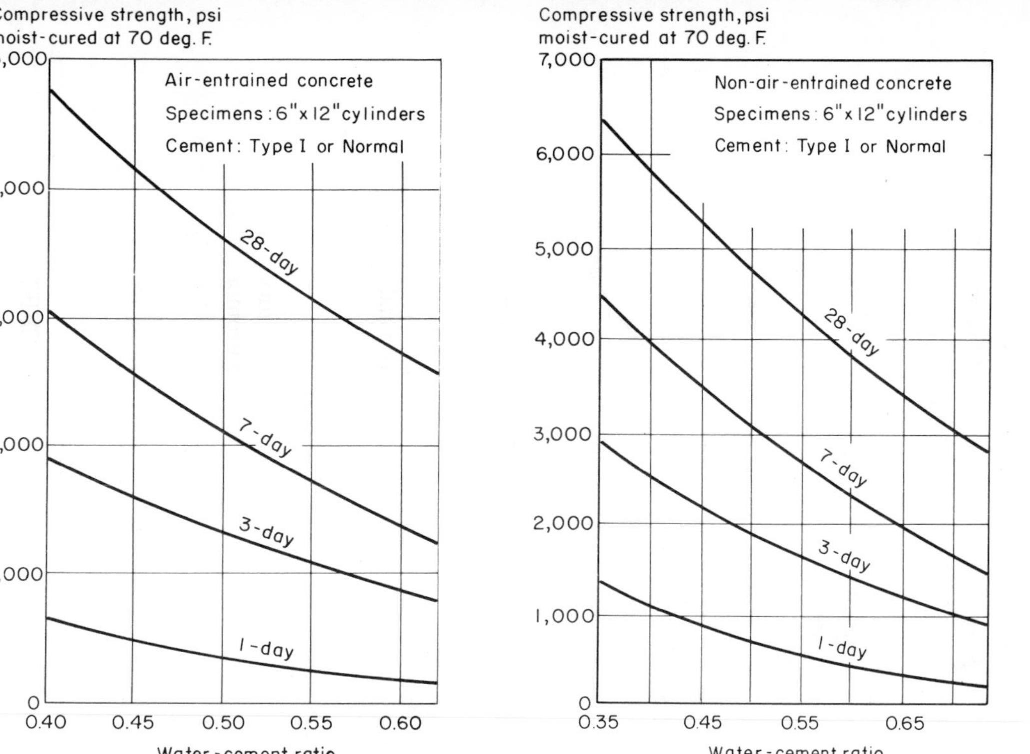

Fig. 6. Typical age-strength relationships based on compression tests of 6- × 12-inch (15- × 30-cm.) cylinders.

once the empirical relationship for the materials being used has been established. (*See* Chap. 11, Finishing Concrete Slabs; *see also* Chap. 12, Finishing Concrete Surfaces.)

The principal factors effecting strength are the water-cement ratio and the extent that hydration has progressed. Figure 6 shows the compressive strengths for a range of water-cement ratios at different ages. Tests were made on 6-inch (15-cm.) diameter specimens, 12 inches (30 cm.) in height. *Note* that strengths increase as the water-cement ratios decrease, and that strengths increase with age. Flexural and tensile strengths and bond of concrete to steel are similarly influenced by water-cement ratio.

Figure 6 also gives the typical age-strength relationships for air-entrained and non-air-entrained concretes. When more precise relationships are required, curves should be developed for the specific materials and cement contents that will be used. In general, greater strengths may be secured with lower water-cement ratios.

Air-entrained concrete requires less water than *non-air-entrained* concrete for the same workability. Hence, the water-cement ratio will be decreased when a given cement factor is maintained. Therefore, the lower water-cement ratio required for air-entrained concrete does not necessarily imply an increased cement content. This is particularly true in lean-to-medium cement content mixes.

RESISTANCE TO ABRASION

Concrete floors, pavements, and dam spillways are subjected to abrasion; hence resistance to abrasion or wear is important in these applications of concrete. Test results indicate that abrasion resistance is dependent principally upon the strength of the concrete. Strong concrete is more resistant to abrasion than weak concrete.

Figure 7 shows results of abrasion tests on concretes of different compressive strengths. The tests were conducted by rolling steel balls under pressure over the surface of concrete specimens. Each specimen was subjected to the same number of revo-

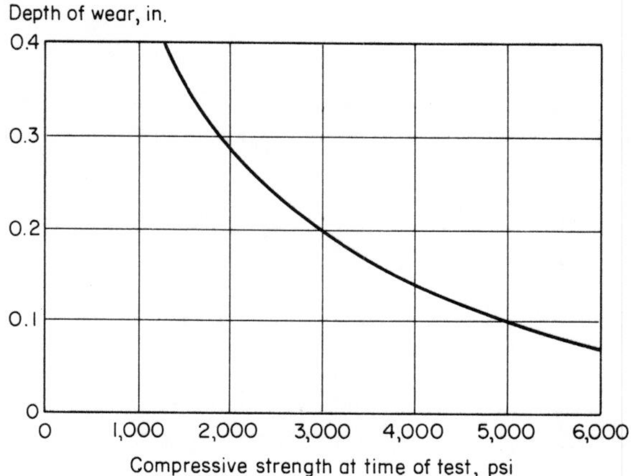

Fig. 7. Effect of compressive strength on the abrasion resistance of concrete. High-strength concrete is highly resistant to abrasion.

lutions. Since compressive strength is dependent upon water-cement ratio and curing, it is evident that a low water-cement ratio and adequate curing are necessary for abrasion resistance.

MOIST CURING

The increase in strength with age continues as long as drying of the concrete is prevented. When the concrete is permitted to dry, the chemical reactions slow down or stop. It is, therefore, desirable to keep concrete continually moist as long as possible. (*See* Fig. 8.)

When *moist curing* is interrupted, the strength increases for a short period and stops. However, if *moist curing* is resumed, the strength will again increase. Although this can be done in a laboratory, it is difficult on most jobs to resaturate concrete. It is best to moist-cure the concrete continuously from the time it is placed until it has attained the desired quality. (*See* Chap. 9, Placing and Consolidating Concrete.)

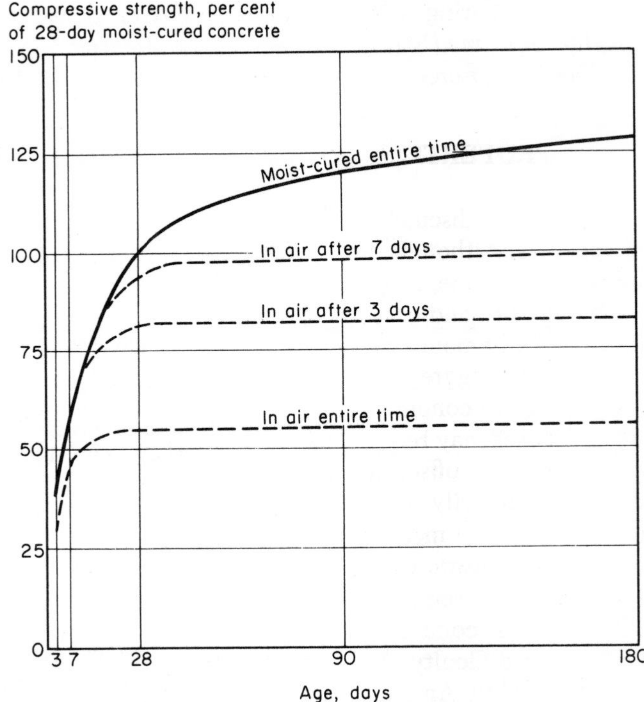

Fig. 8. Strength of concrete continues to increase as long as moisture is present for hydration of cement.

VOLUME STABILITY OF CONCRETE

Hardened concrete undergoes small changes in *volume* due to changes in temperature, moisture content, and sustained stress. These volume changes may range from about 0.01 to 0.08 percent in terms of lengths. Thermal volume changes are about the same as those for steel.

Concrete kept continually moist will remain almost constant in volume. Actually a slight expansion may occur. When permitted to dry, concrete will shrink. The amount of shrinkage depends upon several factors: amounts of mixing water and aggregate used; properties of the aggregate; size of the specimen; relative humidity and temperature of the environment; and method of curing. Concrete subjected to stress will deform elastically. *Sustained stress* will result in a deformation called *creep*. The rate of creep deformation decreases with time.

PROPERTIES OF FRESH CONCRETE

The foregoing discussion has dealt with properties of hardened concrete. Although freshly mixed concrete remains plastic for only a short time, its properties are important because they affect the quality and cost of hardened concrete.

With a given amount of water and cement paste, an increase in the amount of aggregate causes stiff mixes. Consequently, *stiff mixes* are more economical in use of materials. On the other hand, stiff mixes may require more labor in placing, and the additional cost may offset savings in materials. In general, thin members and heavily reinforced members require more plastic mixtures than large members containing little reinforcement.

Concrete of *plastic* consistency does not crumble, but flows sluggishly without segregation. Mixtures of such consistency are suitable for most concrete work.

The ease or difficulty of placing and consolidating concrete is called *workability*. An experienced workman can readily judge when fresh concrete has adequate workability for use in a given situation. Concrete should be workable but should not segregate or bleed excessively. *Bleeding* is the movement of water to the surface of freshly cast concrete. Since excessive bleeding may increase the water-cement ratio at the surface, a weak layer having poor durability may result, particularly if finishing operations take place while this excess water is present.

Generally the most economical mix is one that has the highest proportion of aggregate to cement while remaining workable at the water-cement ratio required for strength, durability, and other properties.

Chapter 2

Concrete Ingredients

The essential ingredients of concrete are cement, aggregate, and water which react chemically in a process called hydration to form another material having useful strength. Hardening of concrete is not the result of the drying of the mix as seen from the fact that fresh concrete placed under water will harden despite its completely submerged state. The mixture of cement and water is called cement paste, but such a mixture, in large quantities, is prohibitively expensive for practical construction purposes. (*See* Chap. 1, Fundamental Facts About Concrete; *see also* Chap. 13, Placing Concrete In Water.)

CEMENT

Most cement used today is *portland* cement, which is usually manufactured from limestone mixed with shale, clay, or marl. The properly proportioned raw materials are pulverized and fed into kilns, where they are heated to a temperature of 2700° F (1483.41° C.) and maintained at that temperature for a certain time. As a result of certain chemical changes produced by the heat, the material is tranformed into a clinker. The clinker is then ground down so fine that it will pass through a sieve containing 40,000 openings per square inch (16,000 per sq. cm.). (*See* Fig. 1.)

There are a number of types of portland cement, of which the most common are Types I through V and air-entrained.

Types of Cement

There are five common types of portland cement in use today. The type of construction, chemical type of the soil, economy,

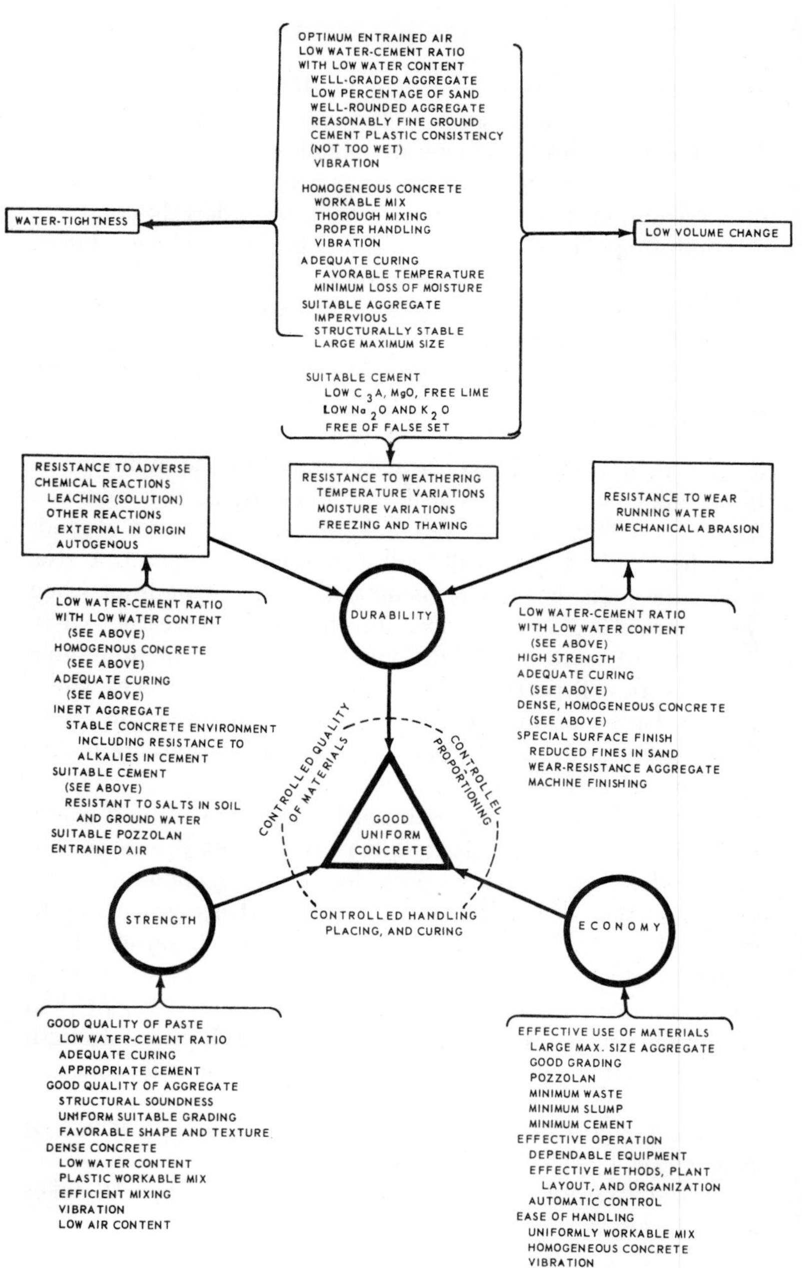

Fig. 1. The principal properties of good concrete.

and the requirements for use of the finished concrete are factors which influence the selection of the type of cement to be used. The different types of cement are as follows:

Type I (normal portland cement) is used for all general types of construction. It is used in pavement and sidewalk construction, reinforced concrete buildings and bridges, railways, tanks, reservoirs, sewers, culverts, water pipes, masonry units, and soil-cement mixtures. In general, it is used when concrete is not subject to special sulfate hazards or where the heat generated by the hydration of the cement will not cause an objectionable rise in temperature.

Type II (moderate portland cement) has a lower heat of hydration than Type I. Lower heat generated by the hydration of the cement improves resistance to sulfate attack. It is intended for use in structures of considerable size where cement of moderate heat of hydration will tend to minimize temperature rise, as in large piers, heavy abutments and retaining walls, or when the concrete is placed in warm weather. In cold weather when the heat generated is helpful, Type I cement may be preferable for these uses. Type II cement is also intended for places where an added precaution against sulfate attack is important, as in drainage structures where the sulfate concentrations are higher than normal, but not usually severe.

Type III (high-early-strength portland cement) is used where early high strengths are desired. It is used where it is desired to remove the forms as soon as possible, to put the concrete in service as quickly as possible, and in cold weather construction to reduce the period of protection against low temperatures. High strengths at early periods can be obtained more satisfactorily and more economically using high-early-strength cement than using richer mixes of Type I cement. Type III develops strength at a faster rate than other types of cement, such as follows:

Twenty-eight-day strength for Types I and II, which is reached by Type III in about seven days.

Seven-day strength for Types I and II, while Type III takes about three days.

Type IV (low-heat portland cement) is a special cement for use where the amount and rate of heat generated must be kept to a minimum. This type of cement was first developed for use on the Hoover Dam. It develops strength at a slow rate and should be cured and protected from freezing for at least 21 days. For this reason it is unsuitable for structures of ordinary dimensions, and is available only on special order from a manufacturer.

Type V (sulfate-resistant portland cement) is a cement intended for use only in structures exposed to high alkali content. It has a slower rate of hardening than normal portland cement. The sulfates react chemically with the hydrated lime and the hydrated calcium aluminate in the cement paste. This reaction results in considerable expansion and disruption of the paste. Cements which have a low calcium aluminate content have a great resistance to sulfate attack. Therefore, Type V portland cement is used exclusively for situations involving severe sulfate concentrations.

Air-entrained portland cement is a special cement that can be used with good results for a variety of conditions. It has been developed to produce concrete with a resistance to freeze-thaw action and scaling caused by chemicals applied for severe frost and ice removal. In this cement, very small quantities of air-entraining materials are added as the clinker is being ground during manufacturing. Concrete made with this cement contains minute, well-distributed, and completely separated air bubbles. The bubbles are so minute that it is estimated there are many millions of them in a cubic foot of concrete. Air bubbles provide space for freezing water to expand without damage to the concrete. Air-entrained concrete has been used in pavements in the northern states for about 25 years with excellent results. Air-entrained concrete also reduces the amount of water loss and the capillary and water-channel structure. The agent may be added to Types I, II, and III portland cement. The manufacturer will specify the percentage of air-entrainment which can be expected in the concrete. An advantage of using air-entrained cement is that it can be used and batched like normal cement. (*See* Chap. 3, Batching.)

Storage of Cement

Portland cement is packed in cloth or paper sacks, each of

which contains 94 pounds (42.6 kgs.) of cement. A 94-pound (42.6-kgs.) sack of cement amounts to about 1 cubic foot (.03 cu. meters) by loose volume.

Cement will indefinitely retain its quality if it does not come in contact with moisture. If it is allowed to absorb appreciable moisture in storage, it will set more slowly and its strength will be reduced. Sacked cement should be stored in warehouses or sheds made as watertight and airtight as possible. All cracks in roof and walls should be closed, and there should be no openings between walls and roof. The floor should be above ground to protect the cement against dampness. All doors and windows should be kept closed.

Sacks should be stacked against each other to prevent circulation of air between them, but they should not be stacked against outside walls. If stacks are to stand undisturbed for long intervals, they should be covered with tarpaulins.

When shed or warehouse storage cannot be provided, sacks that must be stored in the open should be stacked on raised platforms and covered with waterproof tarps. The tarps should extend beyond the edges of the platform to deflect water away from the platform and the cement.

Cement sacks that have been stacked in storage for long periods sometimes acquire a hardness called *warehouse pack.* This can usually be loosened up by rolling the sack around. No cement that has lumps or is not free flowing should be used.

AGGREGATE

The material combined with cement and water to make concrete is called *aggregate.* Aggregate helps to increase the strength of concrete while reducing its shrinking tendencies. Not only does aggregate strengthen concrete, it also acts as a filler for economical purposes. The aggregate is divided into *fine* (usually consisting of sand) and *coarse.* For most ordinary building concrete, the coarse aggregate usually consists of gravel or crushed stone, running not more than about 1½ inch (3.8 cm.) in size (Fig. 2). In massive structures like dams, however, the coarse aggregate may include natural stones or rocks ranging up to 6

Fig. 2. Well-graded aggregates have particles of various sizes. Shown here is 1½-inch (3.8-cm.) maximum-size coarse aggregate. Pieces vary in size from ¼ to 1½ inch (.63 to 3.8 cm.).

inches (15 cm.) or more in size. (*See* Chap. 1, Fundamental Facts About Concrete.)

What might be called the fundamental structural mechanics of a concrete mix are about as follows. The large, solid coarse aggregate particles form the basic structural members of the concrete. The voids between the larger coarse aggregate particles are filled by smaller particles, and the voids between the smallest coarse aggregate particles are filled by the largest fine aggregate particles. In turn, the voids between the largest fine aggregate particles are filled by smaller fine aggregate particles, the voids between the smaller fine aggregate particles by still smaller particles, and so on. You can see by this that the better the aggregate is *graded* (that is, the better the distribution of particle sizes), the more solidly all voids will be filled, and the denser and stronger will be the concrete.

The cement and water form a paste which binds the aggregate particles solidly together when it hardens. In a well-graded, designed, and mixed batch each aggregate particle is thoroughly coated with cement-water, paste, binding it solidly to adjacent particles when the cement-water paste hardens.

Gradation

The existing *gradation*, or distribution of particle sizes from coarse to fine, in a supply of fine or coarse aggregate is determined by extracting a representative sample of the material, screening the sample through a series of sieves ranging in size from coarse to fine, and determining the percentage of the total sample which is retained on (fine aggregate), or which passes (coarse aggregate), each sieve. This procedure is called making a *sieve analysis*.

The size of a fine aggregate sieve is designated by a number which corresponds to the number of meshes to the linear inch that the sieve contains. Obviously, then, the higher the number, the finer the sieve. The most commonly used fine-aggregate sieves are the Nos. 4, 8, 16, 30, 50, 100, and 200. Any material retained on No. 4 sieve is considered coarse aggregate, and any material which will pass the No. 200 sieve is too fine to be used in concrete. When analysis reveals the presence of a substantial percentage of material which will pass the No. 200, the aggregate must be washed before being used.

The finest coarse-aggregate sieve is the same No. 4 used as the coarsest fine-aggregate sieve. With this exception, a coarse-aggregate sieve is designated by the size of one of its openings. The sieves commonly used are the 1½ inch (3.8 cm.), ¾ inch (1.9 cm.), ½ inch (1.3 cm.), ⅜ inch (9.53 mm.), and No. 4. (*See* Chap. 6, Concrete Equipment and Tools.)

Experience and experiments have shown that for ordinary building concrete certain particle distributions consistently seem to produce the best results. For fine aggregate the recommended distribution of particle sizes from No. 4 to No. 100 is shown in Table 1.

Sieve Number	Percent retained on square mesh laboratory sieves
3/8"	0
No. 4	18
No. 8	27
No. 16	20
No. 30	20
No. 50	10
No. 100	4

TABLE 1. RECOMMENDED DISTRIBUTION OF PARTICLE SIZES.

The percentages given are *cumulative,* meaning that each is a percentage of the *total sample,* not of the amount remaining on a particular sieve. *For example,* suppose the total sample weighs 1 pound (.45 kgs.). Place this on the No. 4 sieve, and shake the sieve until nothing more will go through. If what is left on the sieve weighs 0.05 pound (.023 kgs.), then five percent of the total sample was retained on the No. 4 sieve. Place what passed through on the No. 8 sieve and shake that one. Suppose you find that what stays on the sieve weighs 0.1 pound (.045 kgs.). Since 0.1 pound (.045 kgs.) is 10 percent of 1 pound (.45 kgs.), it follows that 10 percent of the total sample was retained on the No. 8 sieve.

The nominal size of coarse aggregate to be used is usually specified as a range between a minimum and a maximum size, such as 2 inches (5 cm.) to No. 4, 1 inch (2.5 cm.) to No. 4, 2 inches to 1 inch (5 to 2.5 cm.), and so on. The recommended particle size distributions vary with maximum and minimum nominal size limits. as shown in Table 2.

A blank space in Table 2 indicates a sieve which is not required in the indicated analysis. *For example,* for the 2-inch (5.08-cm.) to No. 4 nominal size there are no values listed under the 4-inch (10.2-cm.), the 3½-inch (8.9-cm.), and the 3-inch (7.6-cm.) sieves. The reason for this is simply the fact that, since 100 percent of this material should pass a 2½-inch (6.3-cm.) sieve,

Size of coarse aggregate, inches	Percentages by weight passing laboratory sieves having square openings										
	4-in.	3 1/2 in.	3-in.	2 1/2 in.	2-in.	1 1/2 in.	1-in.	3/4 in.	1/2 in.	3/8 in.	No. 4
1.5	--	--	--	--	100	95-100	--	35-70	--	10-30	0-5
2	--	--	--	100	95-100	--	35-70	--	10-30	11	0-5
2.5	--	--	100	90-100	--	35-70	--	10-40	--	0-15	0-5
3.5	100	90-100	--	45-80	--	25-50	--	10-30	--	0-15	0-5

TABLE 2. RECOMMENDED MAXIMUM AND MINIMUM PARTICLE SIZES.

the use of sieves coarser than the 2½-inch (6.3-cm.) is superfluous. For the same size designation, there are no values listed under the 1½-inch (3.8-cm.), the ¾-inch (1.9-cm.), and the ⅜-inch (.95-cm.) sieves. Experience has shown that it is not necessary to use these sieves when making this particular analysis.

Note that when you are analyzing coarse aggregate you determine the percentage of material which *passes* a sieve, not the percentage which is retained on a sieve.

Quality Criteria

Since from 66 to 78 percent of the volume of the finished concrete consists of aggregate, it is imperative that the aggregate measure up to certain minimum quality standards. It should consist of clean, hard, strong, durable particles which are free of any chemicals which might interfere with hydration, and of any superfine material which might prevent bond between the aggregate and the cement-water paste. The undesirable substances most frequently found in aggregate are dirt, silt, clay, coal, mica, salts, and organic matter. Most of these can be removed by washing.

Aggregate may be tested for an excess of silt, clay, and the like. Proceed as follows: Fill a quart jar with the aggregate to a depth of 2 inches (5 cm.); add water until the jar is about three-fourths full; shake the jar for one minute, and allow it to stand for one hour. If at the end of that time more than ⅛ inch (3.1 mm.) of sediment has settled on the top of the aggregate as shown in Fig. 3, the material should be washed. An easily constructed rig for washing a small amount of aggregate is shown in Fig. 4.

Weak, friable (easily pulverized), or laminated (containing layers) aggregate particles are undesirable. Shale, stones laminated with shale, and most varieties of chert (impure, flinty rock) are especially to be avoided. For most ordinary concrete work, visual inspection is enough to reveal any weaknesses in the coarse aggregate. For work in which aggregate strength and durability is of vital importance (such as paving concrete) aggregate must be tested.

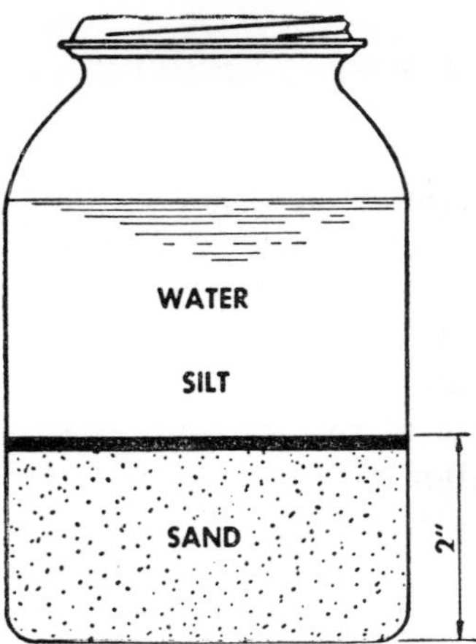

Fig. 3. Quart-jar method of determining silt content of sand.

Handling and Storing

A mass of aggregate containing particles of different sizes has a natural tendency toward *segregation,* meaning that particles of the same size tend to gather together whenever the material is being loaded, transported, or otherwise disturbed. Aggregate should always be handled and stored by a method which will minimize segregation. (*See* Chap. 5, Handling and Transporting Concrete.)

Stockpiles should not be built up in cone shapes, made by dropping successive loads at the same spot. This procedure causes larger aggregate particles to segregate and roll down the

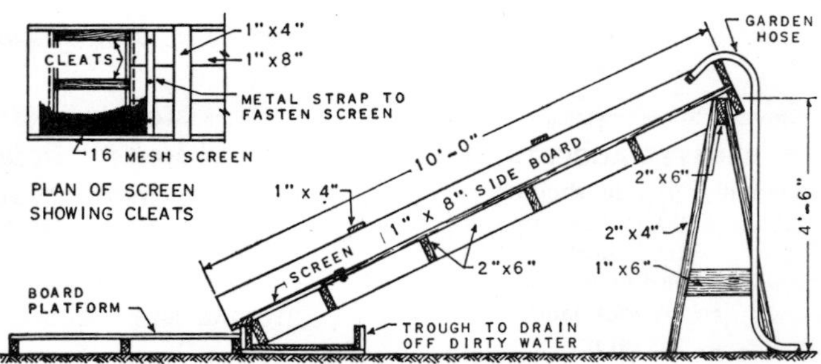

Fig. 4. Sloping rig for washing aggregate.

sides, leaving the pile with a preponderance of fine at the top and coarse at the bottom. A pile should be built up in layers, each made by dumping successive loads alongside each other. (*See* Figs. 5, 6, and 7.)

If aggregate is dropped in a free fall from a clamshell, bucket, or conveyor, some of the fine material may be blown aside, causing a segregation of fines on the lee side of the pile. Conveyors, clamshells, and buckets should be discharged in contact with the pile.

The bottom of a storage bin should always slope at least 50 degrees toward the central outlet. If the slope is less than 50 degrees, segregation will occur as the material is discharged. When a bin is being charged, the material should be dropped from a point directly over the outlet. Material chuted in at an angle, or

PREFERABLE

A crane or other equipment should stockpile material in separate batches, each no larger than a truckload, so that it remains where placed and does not run down slopes.

OBJECTIONABLE

Do not use methods that permit the aggregate to roll down the slope as it is added to the pile, or permit hauling equipment to operate over the same level repeatedly.

LIMITED ACCEPTABILITY—GENERALLY OBJECTIONABLE

Generally, a pile should not be built radially in horizontal layers by a bulldozer working with materials as dropped from a conveyor belt. A rock ladder may be needed in this setup.

A bulldozer stocking progressive layers on slope not flatter than 3:1 is also objectionable, unless materials strongly resist breakage.

Fig. 5. Stockpiling of coarse aggregate.

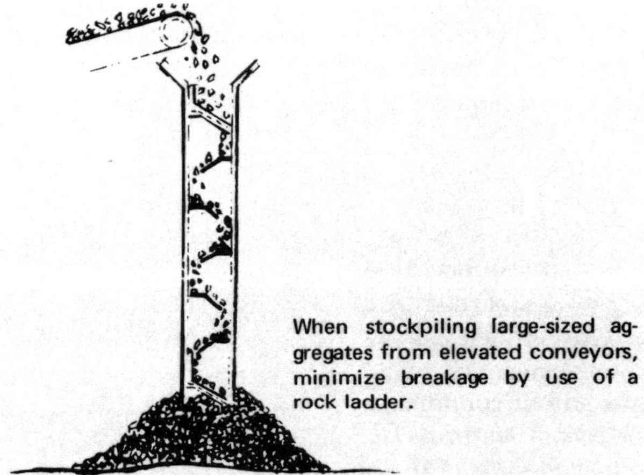

When stockpiling large-sized aggregates from elevated conveyors, minimize breakage by use of a rock ladder.

Fig. 6. Finished coarse aggregate storage.

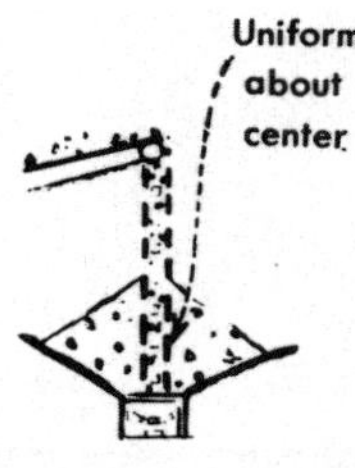

CORRECT

Chimney should surround material falling from end of conveyor, to prevent wind from separating fine and coarse materials. Openings should be provided as required to discharge materials at various elevations on the pile.

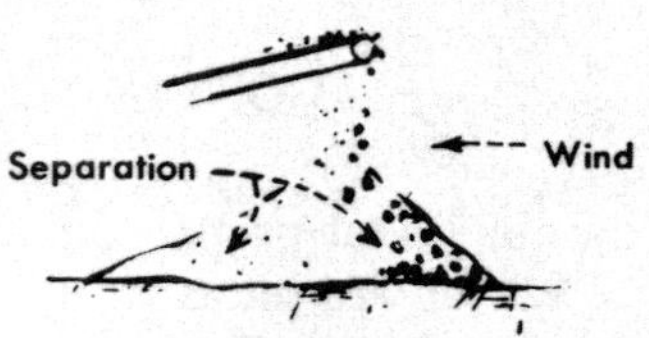

INCORRECT

Do not allow free fall of material from high end of conveyor, which would permit wind to separate fine from coarse material.

Fig. 7. Fine aggregate storage.

material discharged against the side of a bin, will segregate. Since a long drop causes both segregation and breakage of aggregate particles, the length of the drop into a bin should be minimized by keeping the bin as full as possible at all times.

WATER

The principal function of the water in a concrete mix is to bring about the hardening of the concrete through hydration of the cement. Another essential function is to make the mix workable enough to satisfy the requirements of the job at hand. To attain this result, a mix which is to be poured in forms must contain additional water over and above the amount required for complete hydration of the cement. Too much water will cause a loss of strength by upsetting the water-cement ratio. It will also cause *water gain* on the surface, a condition which leaves a surface layer of weak material called *laitance.* Also as previously mentioned, an excess of water will impair the watertightness of the concrete. (*See* Chap. 4, Mixing Concrete.)

Mixing water should be free of any acids, alkalis, or oils which would interfere with the hydration process. Water containing decayed vegetable matter is especially to be avoided. Most specifications require that the mixing water be fit for drinking, since any water fit for drinking is usually satisfactory for concrete.

CONCRETE MIX DESIGN

The ingredient proportions to be used for the concrete on a particular job are set as follows.

One of the *formulas* for 3000 psi (210 kgs. per sq. cm.) is 5.80 (bag of cement per cubic yard), 233 pounds (105.69 kgs.) of sand (per bag of cement), 297 pounds (134.72 kgs.) of coarse aggregate (per bag of cement), and the *water-cement ratio* is 6.75 gallons (25.55 liters) of water to each bag of cement. These proportions are based upon the assumption that the inert ingredients are in a *saturated surface-dry* condition, meaning that they contain all the water they are capable of absorbing, but no additional *free* water over and above this amount.

The amount of free water in the coarse aggregate is usually small enough to be ignored, but the ingredient proportions set forth must almost always be adjusted to allow for the existence of free water in the fine aggregate. Furthermore, since free water in the fine aggregate increases its measured volume or weight over that of the sand itself, the specified volume or weight of sand must be increased to offset the volume or weight of the water in the sand. Finally, the number of gallons of water used per sack of cement must be reduced to allow for the free water in the sand. *For example,* the amount of water actually added at the mixer must be the specified amount per sack, *less* the amount of free water which is already in the ingredients in the mixer.

Except as otherwise specified, concrete should be proportioned by weighing. (*See* Table 3 for Normal Concrete.)

MATERIAL ESTIMATE

A handling loss factor is added when ordering materials for jobs. An additional five percent of material is added for jobs requiring 200 or more cubic yards (153 cu. meters) of concrete, and 10 percent is added for smaller jobs. (This loss factor is based on materials estimate after requirements have been calculated.) Additional loss factors may be added where conditions indicate the necessity for excessive handling of materials before batching.

When tables, such as Table 4, are not available for determining quantities of material required for one cubic yard of concrete, the following rule, known as the 3/2's rule may be used for rough approximation. (The rule states that to produce a given volume of concrete, the combined amounts of cement, sand, and gravel are 1-½ times the volume of the concrete pour.) Since the void spaces between the coarse aggregate are filled with sand particles, and the voids between the sand particles are similarly filled with cement, the total volume occupied by the three components will be less than the sum of their individual volumes. Normally, a mix ratio of 1:2:3 is assumed when using the 3/2's rule. This means that of a total volume, one part will be

Class concrete (figures denote size of coarse aggregate in inches)	Estimated 28-day compressive strength, (pounds per square inch)	Cement factor, bags (94 pounds) of cement per cubic yard of concrete, freshly mixed	Maximum water per bag (94 pounds) of cement (gallons)	Fine aggregate range in percent of total aggregate by weight	Approximate weights of saturated surface-dry aggregates per bag (94 pounds) of cement	
					Fine aggregate (pounds)	Coarse aggregate (pounds)
(1)	(2)	(3)	(4)	(5)	(6)	(7)
B-1	1500	4.10	9.50	42-52	368	415
B-1.5	1500	3.80	9.50	38-48	376	498
B-2	1500	3.60	9.50	35-45	378	567
B-2.5	1500	3.50	9.50	33-43	373	609
B-3.5	1500	3.25	9.50	30-40	378	702
C-1	2000	4.45	8.75	41-51	329	387
C-1.5	2000	4.10	8.75	37-47	338	467
C-2	2000	3.90	8.75	34-44	338	529
C-2.5	2000	3.80	8.75	32-42	332	565
C-3.5	2000	3.55	8.75	29-39	334	648
D-0.5	2500	5.70	7.75	50-60	282	231
D-0.75	2500	5.30	7.75	45-55	288	288
D-1	2500	5.05	7.75	40-50	279	341
D-1.5	2500	4.65	7.75	36-46	287	413
D-2	2500	4.40	7.75	34-42	288	471
D-2.5	2500	4.25	7.75	32-40	287	509
D-3.5	2500	4.00	7.75	29-37	285	578
E-0.5	3000	6.50	6.75	50-58	238	203
E-0.75	3000	6.10	6.75	45-53	240	249
E-1	3000	5.80	6.75	40-48	233	297
E-1.5	3000	5.35	6.75	36-44	239	359
E-2	3000	5.05	6.75	33-41	241	410
E-2.5	3000	4.90	6.75	31-39	238	441
E-3.5	3000	4.60	6.75	28-36	237	503

TABLE 3. NORMAL CONCRETE.

cement, two parts will be sand, and three parts will be gravel. The amount of water is roughly established by assuming a ratio that assures water tightness—6 gallons (22.7 liters) per sack; additional water will be needed for wetting down forms and subgrade, washing tools, and curing the concrete. When computing quantities of concrete, the space occupied by embedded objects or steel reinforcement is ignored.

By using the 3/2's rule, you will determine the amount of cement, sand, and gravel required to construct a 45- × 10- × 2-foot (13.72- × 3.01- × .61-meters) retaining wall. Assume a mix ratio of 1:2:3.

Maximum size of aggregate, inches	Water, gallon per sack of cement	Water, gallon per cu yd of concrete	Cement, sacks per cu yd of concrete	Fine aggregate—per cent of total aggregate	Fine aggregate—lb per sack of cement	Coarse aggregate—lb per sack of cement	Fine aggregate—lb per cu yd of concrete	Coarse aggregate—lb per cu yd of concrete	Yield, cu ft concrete per sack of cement	Fine aggregate—per cent of total aggregate	Fine aggregate—lb per sack of cement	Coarse aggregate—lb per sack of cement	Fine aggregate—lb per cu yd of concrete	Coarse aggregate—lb per cu yd of concrete	Yield, cu ft concrete per sack of cement	Fine aggregate—per cent of total aggregate	Fine aggregate—lb per sack of cement	Coarse aggregate—lb per sack of cement	Fine aggregate—lb per cu yd of concrete	Coarse aggregate—lb per cu yd of concrete	Yield, cu ft concrete per sack of cement
				With Fine Sand—Fineness Modulus 2.20-2.60						With Medium Sand—Fineness Modulus 2.60-2.90						With Coarse Sand—Fineness Modulus 2.90-3.20					
¾	5	38	7.6	43	170	230	1290	1750	3.56	45	180	220	1370	1670	3.56	47	185	210	1370	1595	3.56
1	5	37	7.4	38	160	255	1185	1890	3.65	40	165	250	1220	1850	3.65	42	175	240	1295	1775	3.65
1½	5	35	7.0	34	150	300	1050	2100	3.86	36	160	290	1120	2030	3.86	38	170	280	1190	1960	3.86
2	5	33	6.6	31	150	335	990	2210	4.09	33	160	325	1055	2140	4.09	35	170	315	1120	2080	4.09
¾	5½	38	6.9	44	195	250	1345	1725	3.91	46	205	240	1415	1655	3.91	48	215	230	1480	1585	3.91
1	5½	37	6.7	39	180	285	1205	1910	4.03	41	190	275	1270	1840	4.03	43	200	265	1340	1775	4.03
1½	5½	35	6.4	35	175	320	1120	2050	4.22	37	185	315	1185	2015	4.22	39	195	305	1250	1950	4.22
2	5½	33	6.0	32	175	370	1050	2220	4.50	34	185	360	1110	2160	4.50	36	195	350	1170	2100	4.50
¾	6	38	6.3	45	225	275	1420	1730	4.29	47	235	265	1480	1670	4.29	49	245	255	1540	1610	4.29
1	6	37	6.2	40	205	305	1270	1890	4.36	42	215	295	1335	1830	4.36	44	225	285	1395	1770	4.36
1½	6	35	5.8	36	200	355	1160	2060	4.66	38	210	345	1220	2000	4.66	40	225	335	1305	1945	4.66
2	6	33	5.5	33	200	400	1100	2200	4.91	35	210	390	1155	2145	4.91	37	220	380	1210	2090	4.91
¾	6½	38	5.9	46	245	288	1445	1700	4.58	48	255	280	1505	1650	4.58	50	265	265	1560	1560	4.58
1	6½	37	5.7	41	230	330	1310	1880	4.74	43	240	320	1370	1825	4.74	45	250	310	1425	1765	4.74
1½	6½	35	5.4	37	225	380	1215	2050	5.00	39	235	370	1270	2000	5.00	41	250	355	1350	1920	5.00
2	6½	33	5.1	34	225	430	1150	2195	5.30	36	235	415	1200	2120	5.30	38	250	405	1275	2065	5.30
¾	7	38	5.4	47	280	315	1510	1700	5.00	49	290	305	1565	1650	5.00	51	300	290	1620	1565	5.00
1	7	37	5.3	42	255	355	1350	1880	5.10	44	270	340	1430	1800	5.10	46	280	330	1485	1750	5.10
1½	7	35	5.0	38	250	410	1250	2050	5.40	40	265	395	1325	1975	5.40	42	270	385	1350	1925	5.40
2	7	33	4.7	35	250	465	1175	2185	5.75	37	265	450	1245	2120	5.75	39	280	435	1315	2045	5.75
¾	7½	38	5.1	48	300	330	1530	1680	5.30	50	315	315	1605	1605	5.30	52	330	300	1685	1530	5.30
1	7½	37	4.9	43	285	380	1400	1860	5.51	45	300	365	1470	1790	5.51	47	310	355	1520	1740	5.51
1½	7½	35	4.7	39	275	430	1290	2020	5.75	41	290	415	1365	1950	5.75	43	305	400	1435	1880	5.75
2	7½	33	4.4	36	275	495	1210	2180	6.14	38	290	480	1275	2110	6.14	40	305	465	1340	2045	6.14
¾	8	38	4.8	49	330	345	1585	1655	5.63	51	345	330	1660	1585	5.63	53	360	315	1730	1510	5.63
1	8	37	4.6	44	315	400	1450	1840	5.87	46	330	385	1520	1770	5.87	48	345	370	1590	1700	5.87
1½	8	35	4.4	40	305	455	1340	2000	6.14	42	320	440	1410	1935	6.14	44	335	425	1475	1870	6.14
2	8	33	4.1	37	310	525	1270	2150	6.59	39	325	510	1330	2090	6.59	41	340	490	1395	2010	6.59

*Increase or decrease water per cu. yd. of concrete by 3% for each increase or decrease of 1 in. in slump recalculate quantities of cement and aggregate to maintain the quality of concrete. For stone sand, increase percentage of sand by 3 and water by 15 lb. per cu. yd. of concrete. For less workable concrete, as in pavements, decrease percentage of sand by 3 and water by 8 lb. per cu. yd. of concrete.

TABLE 4. SUGGESTED TRIAL MIXES FOR CONCRETE OF MEDIUM CONSISTENCY WITH A 3-INCH SLUMP (SSD CONDITION).

Volume of concrete required:

$45 \times 10 \times 2 = 900$ cubic feet = 33.3 cubic yards.
($13.2 \times 3.01 \times .61 = 25.47$ cu. meters)

Applying the 3/2's rule and allowing 10 percent handling loss, total volume required is $33.3 \times 1.10 \times 3/2$, or 55 cubic yards (42.07 cu. meters).

The required volumes needed are:

Cement: $1/6 \times 55 = 9.17$ cubic yards (7.01 cu. meters)
Sand: $2/6 \times 55 = 18.33$ cubic yards (14.02 cu. meters)
Gravel: $3/6 \times 55 = 27.50$ cubic yards (21.04 cu. meters)

Since cement is usually obtained in sacks, you should multiply the volume by 27 and round it to the next larger number.

$9.17 \times 27 = 247.59$ cubic feet (7.01 cu. meters) or 248 sacks.

The 3/2 rule is not used to estimate materials if the size of the pour is greater than 200 cubic yards (153 cu. meters).

WATER-CEMENT RATIO

The specified ingredient proportions are those which, it has been calculated, will produce an economical concrete of the strength and durability required for the project. Durability is to a large extent controlled by strength (meaning that the stronger the concrete is, the more durable it will be as well). The quality of the aggregate, the aggregate grading, and the proportion of fine to coarse aggregate also have an important effect on durability.

It has been discovered that the major factor controlling strength, everything else being equal, is the amount of water used per bag of cement. Maximum strength would be obtained by using no more than the amount of water required for the complete hydration of the cement.

As previously mentioned, a mix of this type would be too dry to be workable, and therefore a plastic concrete mix always contains more water than the amount required to attain maximum strength. Remember that the strength of the concrete decreases as the amount of this extra water increases.

The specified water-cement ratio is the happy medium between the maximum possible strength of the concrete and the necessary minimum requirements as to workability. The strength of building concrete is expressed in terms of the compressive strength in psi reached after a 7-day set and/or a 28-day set, usually referred to as *probable average 7-day strength* and *probable average 28-day strength.*

SLUMP TEST

The *slump test* may be used as a rough measure of the consistency of concrete, that is, the degree of wetness of concrete, such as stiff, medium, or wet. This test is not to be considered as an exact measure of workability, and it should not be used to compare mixes of entirely different proportions or of different kinds of aggregates. Changes in slump indicate changes in grading or proportion of the aggregates or in the water content, produced by changes in moisture content of the sand. Correction should be made immediately to get the proper consistency by changing amounts and proportion of sand and coarse aggregate, care being taken not to change the total amount of water specified for mixing with each sack of cement.

To avoid mixes that are too stiff or too wet, slumps falling within the limits given in Table 5 are recommended. This table lists a few kinds of structures as typical examples for each range of slumps. The slump test is especially useful in colored concrete work.

In making the slump test, the test specimen is made in a mold of No. 16-gage galvanized metal in the form shown in Fig. 8. The diameter at the base is 8 inches (20 cm.), the top 4 inches (10 cm.), and the height is 12 inches (30 cm.). The base and top are open. The mold is provided with foot pieces and handles as shown.

TYPE OF STRUCTURE	Slump in inches	
	Minimum	Maximum
Massive sections; pavements and floors laid on ground.	1	4
Heavy slabs, beams or walls; tank walls; posts.	3	6
Thin walls and columns; ordinary slabs or beams; vases and garden furniture.	4	8

TABLE 5. RECOMMENDED SLUMPS FOR CONCRETE.

When the slump test is made, the sample is taken immediately after the concrete has been discharged from the mixer. The mold is placed on a flat surface, such as a smooth plank or a slab of concrete, and is held firmly in place by standing on the foot pieces while filling it with concrete. The mold is filled to about one-fourth its height with concrete. The concrete is puddled with 25 strokes of a ⅝-inch (1.6 cm.) rod, bullet pointed at the lower end. The filling is completed in two more layers, rodding each 25 times without passing the rod through to the layer below. The top is struck off so that the mold is exactly filled. The mold is removed by being raised vertically immediately after being filled.

The slump of the concrete is measured immediately after the cone is removed. (*See* Figs. 9, 10, and 11.) *For example,* if the top of the slumped pile is 4 inches (10 cm.) lower than the top of the cone, the slump for this concrete is 4 inches (10 cm.); if 6 inches (15 cm.) lower, the slump is 6 inches (15 cm.), and so on.

WORKABILITY

The workability of concrete may vary with the selection and mixture of aggregates. In general, the percentage of sand should be less when it is fine than when it is coarse. There are certain objections to using very fine sand such as plaster sand or beach sand. Combined with coarse aggregate, it often produces a mixture in which it is difficult to avoid segregation. The finer the sand, the more likely it is made up predominantly of one or two sizes. It is generally accepted that coarsely graded sands are

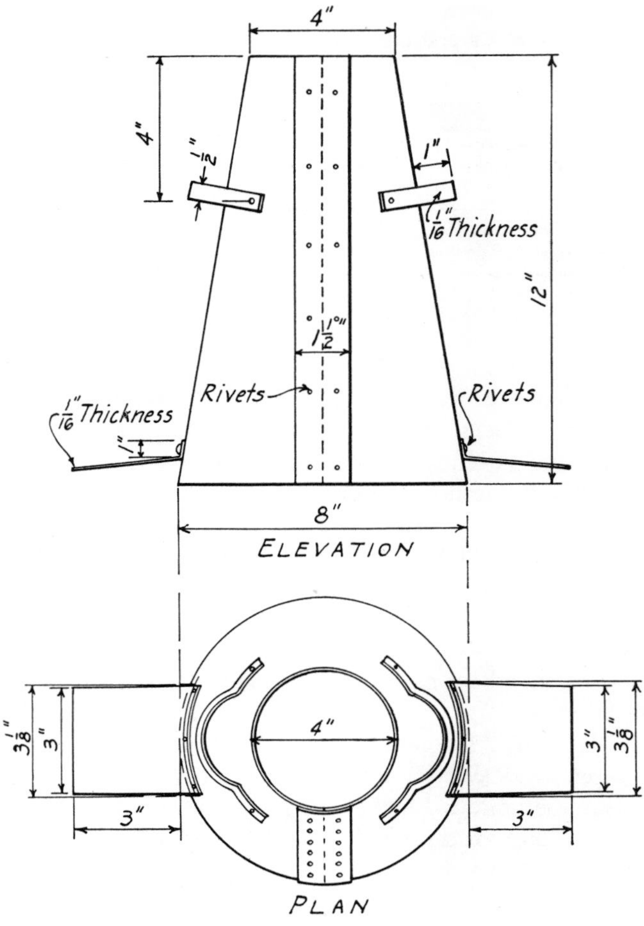

Fig. 8. Design of cone used in making slump test.

most desirable. All sands must contain sufficient fine particles to assist the cement in producing good workability. (*See* Fig. 12.)

It is desirable to select that combination of sand and coarse aggregate which will produce the largest amount of plastic, workable concrete from a given amount of paste. Experience has shown that for average sand and coarse aggregate on average jobs, this proportion is approximately 40 percent sand and 60

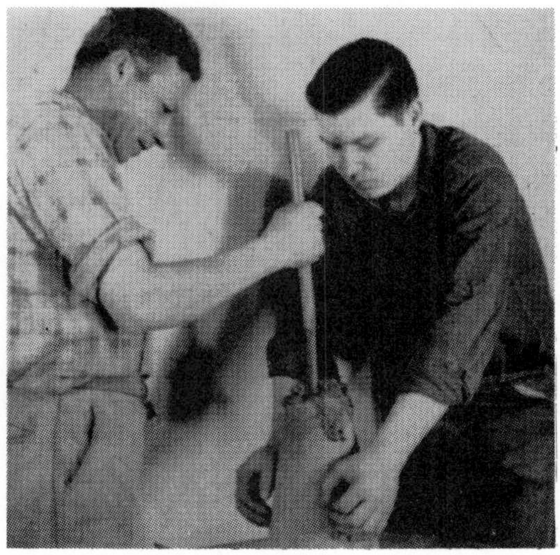

Fig. 9. Slump test shows consistency of concrete.

Fig. 10. Slump is measured from rod laid across the top of the slump of medium wet concrete mixture.

Fig. 11. Cone illustrates slump of stiff concrete.

percent coarse aggregate. Generally, a slightly over-sanded mix is the most satisfactory.

The suggested proportions given in Table 6 are for use only in trial batches. Each of these proportions may need to be corrected to get the best yield and the desired workability. Mixtures of different consistencies are shown in Figs. 13, 14, 15, and 16. For foundations, footings, walls, pavements, and similar work, a stiff consistency is recommended. A moderately wet mix is suitable for thin sections of concrete.

Fig. 12. A workable mix contains the correct amount of cement paste, sand, and coarse aggregate. With light troweling, all spaces between coarse aggregate particles are filled with sand and cement paste.

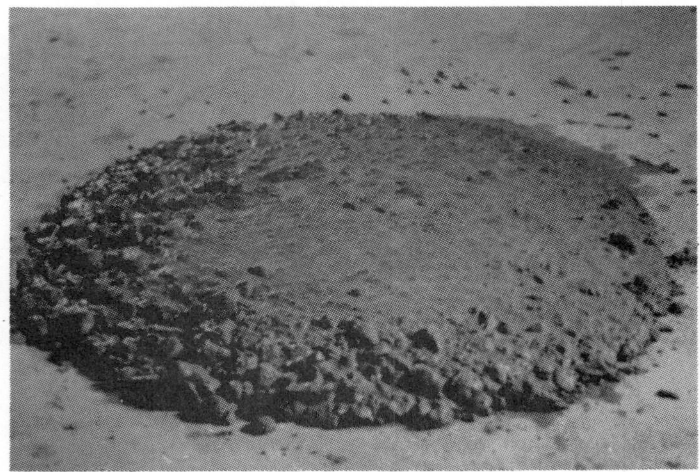

Fig. 13. This mix is too wet because it contains too little sand and coarse aggregate for the amount of cement paste. Such a mix would not be economical or durable and would have a strong tendency to crack.

Fig. 14. This mix is too stiff because it contains too much sand and coarse aggregate. It would be difficult to place and finish properly.

Fig. 15. This mix is too sandy because it contains too much sand and not enough coarse aggregate. It would place and finish easily, but would not be economical and would be very likely to crack.

KINDS OF WORK	Add U.S. gal. of water to each sack batch if sand is:			Trial mixture			Materials per cu.yd. of Concrete*		
	Very wet	Wet	Damp	Cement sacks	Aggregates: Fine, cu.ft.	Aggregates: Coarse, cu.ft.	Cement sacks	Aggregates: Fine, cu.ft.	Aggregates: Coarse, cu.ft.
5-GAL. PASTE FOR CONCRETE SUBJECTED TO SEVERE WEAR, WEATHER OR WEAK ACID AND ALKALI SOLUTIONS									
Toppings for two-course work. One-course industrial, creamery and dairy plant floors. Thin sections of dense, strong concrete.	3¾	4	4½	1	1¾	3 (Maximum size 1½ in.)	7¼	13	22
	3½	4	4½	1	2	2¼ (Maximum size ¾ in.)	8	16	18
	3½	4	4½	1	2	1¾ (Maximum size ⅜ in.)	9	18	16
6-GAL. PASTE FOR CONCRETE TO BE WATERTIGHT OR SUBJECTED TO MODERATE WEAR AND WEATHER									
Watertight floors such as industrial plant, dairy barn, basement, etc. Watertight basement walls. All watertight concrete for storage tanks, septic tanks, swimming pools, etc. Concrete subjected to moderate wear or frost action such as walks, driveways, tennis courts, etc. Reinforced structural beams, columns, slabs, etc.	4¼	5	5½	1	2¼	3½ (Maximum size 1½ in.)	6	13½	21
	4	4¾	5½	1	2½	2½ (Maximum size ¾ in.)	6½	16½	16½
	4	4¾	5½	1	2½	2 (Maximum size ⅜ in.)	7½	18¾	15
7-GAL. PASTE FOR CONCRETE NOT SUBJECTED TO WEAR, WEATHER OR WATER									
Foundation walls, footings, mass concrete, etc.	5	5½	6¼	1	2¾	4 (Maximum size 1½ in.)	5¼	14½	21
	4½	5½	6¼	1	3¼	3 (Maximum size ¾ in.)	5½	18	16½
	4½	5½	6¼	1	3¼	2¼ (Maximum size ⅜ in.)	6½	21	14¾

*Quantities are estimated on wet aggregates, using trial mixes and medium consistencies (5-in. slump). Quantities will vary according to grading of aggregate and consistency of mix. Change proportions of fine and coarse aggregate slightly if necessary to get a workable mix. Quantities are approximate. No allowance has been made for waste.

NOTE: If concrete aggregates are sold in your locality by weight, you may assume for estimating purposes that a ton contains approximately 22 cu.ft. of sand or crushed stone; or about 20 cu.ft. of gravel. For information on local aggregates consult your building material dealer.

TABLE 6. SUGGESTED PROPORTIONS OF WATER TO CEMENT FOR VARIOUS KINDS OF CONCRETE WORK AND TRIAL MIXES.

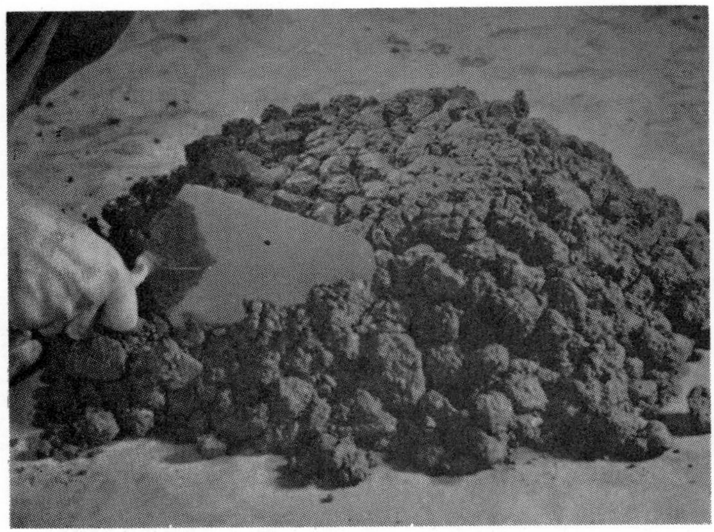

Fig. 16. This mix is too stony because it contains too much coarse aggregate and not enough sand. It would be difficult to place and finish properly and would result in honeycomb and porous concrete.

As previously mentioned, concrete consists of four essential ingredients—water, cement, sand, and coarse aggregate. A mixture of water, cement, sand, and lime is not concrete but *mortar.* Mortar, which is used chiefly for bonding masonry units together, is discussed in Section 2, Concrete Masonry, Chap. 20, Materials, section on Mortar.

The term *grout* refers to a water-cement mixture (called *neat cement grout*) or a water-sand-cement mixture (called *sand-cement grout*) used to plug holes or cracks in concrete, to seal joists, to fill spaces between machinery bed plates and concrete foundations, and for similar plugging or sealing purposes. The consistency of grout may range from stiff (about 4 gallons, or 15.1 liters, of water per sack of cement) to fluid (as many as 10 gallons, or 37.9 liters, of water per sack of cement), depending upon the nature of the grouting job at hand.

Chapter 3

Batching

When bagged cement is being used, the mix proportions are usually given in terms of designated amounts of fine and coarse aggregate per bag (per 94 pounds or per 42.6 kgs.) of cement. The amount of material which is mixed at a time is called a *batch*, and the size of a batch is usually designated by the number of bags of cement it contains, such as, a 4-bag batch, a 6-bag batch, and so on.

The process of weighing out or measuring out the ingredients for a batch of concrete is called *batching*. When mixing is to be done by hand, the size of the batch will depend upon the number of workers who are available to turn it with hand shovels. When mixing is to be done by machine, the size of the batch will depend upon the rated capacity of the mixer. The rated capacity of the mixer is given in terms of cubic feet of *mixed concrete*, not of batched ingredients.

MEASURING CEMENT

Since it is known that a bag of cement contains 94 pounds (42.64 kgs.) by weight and about 1 cubic foot (.02832 cu. meters) by loose volume, a batch formula for bagged cement is usually based upon the highest even number of bags that will produce a batch within the capacity of the workers (hand mixing) or the machine (machine mixing). (*See* Chap. 2, Table 6.)

You can use rules 38, 41, and 42, for calculating the amount of material needed for the mix without a great deal of paperwork.

The rules are used as follows. Rule 38 is used in the mixing of mortar. Rule 41 is used in calculating the quantities of materials for concrete when the size of the coarse aggregate is not over

1 inch (2.5 cm.). Rule 42 is used when the size of the coarse aggregate is not over 2½ inches (6.4 cm.). (Coarse aggregates over 1 inch or 2.5 cm. in size are termed rock in concrete work.) These three calculating rules will not give the accurate amount of required materials for large construcțiion jobs. You will have to use the absolute volume or weight formulae. In most cases you can use these rules of thumb to quickly calculate the quantities of required materials.

Rule 38 is used because it has been found that it takes about 38 cubic feet (1.08 cu. meters) of raw materials to make 1 cubic yard (.77 cu. meters) of mortar. In using the 38 calculating rule for mortar take the rule number and divide it by the sum of the quantity figures specified in the mix. *For example,* let us assume that the building specifications call for a 1:3 mix for mortar 1 + 3 = 4 – 38 ÷ 4 = 9½. You will then need 9½ bags or 9½ cubic feet (.27 cu. meters) of cement. In order to calculate the amount of fine aggregates (sand), you simply multiply 9½ by 3. The product 28½ cubic feet (.81 cu. meters) is the amount of sand you need to mix one cubic yard (.77 cu. meters) of mortar using a 1:3 mix. The sum of the two required quantities should equal the calculating rule 38. Therefore, you can always check in order to see if you are using the correct amounts. In the above example, 9½ bags of cement (.27 cu. meters) plus 28½ cubic feet (.81 cu. meters) of sand, equal 38 cubic feet (1.08 cu. meters).

Rules 41 and 42, for calculating the amount of raw materials needed to mix one cubic yard of concrete, are worked in the same manner. *For example,* let us assume that the specifications called for a 1:2:4 mix with 2-inch (5.08 cm.) coarse aggregates:

1 + 2 + 4 = 7—42 ÷ 7 = 6 (42 cu. ft. = 1.19 cu. meters—1.19 ÷ 7 = .17)—bags or cubic feet (.17 cu. meters) of cement.
6 × 2 = 12—cubic feet (.17 × 2 = .34 cu. meters) of sand.
6 × 4 = 24—cubic feet (.17 × 4 = .68 cu. meters) of coarse aggregates.
6 + 12 + 24 = 42 (.17 + .34 + .68 = 1.19 cu. meters) your calculations have been proven correct.

Frequently, it will be necessary to convert these volumes in cubic feet to weights in pounds. These conversions are very simple. Multiply the required cubic feet of cement by 94 pounds (42.64 kgs.), remembering that 1 cubic foot (.028 cu. meters) or one standard bag of cement weighs 94 pounds (42.64 kgs.). For metric conversions use the formula—cubic feet times .028 to obtain cubic meters. The average weight of dry-compacted, fine aggregate or gravel is 105 pounds (47.63 kgs.) per cubic foot, while the average weight of dry-compacted, coarse aggregate over 1 inch (2.54 cm.) in size (termed rock) is 100 pounds (45.36 kgs.). When using the rule 41 for coarse gravels or aggregates, multiply the quantity of coarse gravel in cubic feet by 105 (cubic meters by 47.63). When the calculating rule 42 is used, multiply the cubic feet of required rock by 100 (cubic meters by 47.63) in order to figure the amount of needed rock in pounds.

MEASURING WATER

The water-measuring controls on a concrete mixing machine are described in Chap. 4, Mixing Concrete. Water measurement for hand-mixing may be done with a 14-quart bucket, marked off on the inside in gallons, half-gallons, and quarts (or in a metric bucket, measuring in liters). (*See* Chap. 6, Concrete Equipment and Tools.)

Never add water to the mix without measuring it carefully, and always remember that the amount of water actually placed in the mix varies according to the amount of free water that is already in the aggregate. This means that if the aggregate is wet by a rainstorm, the proportion of water in the mix may have to be changed.

MEASURING AGGREGATE

The accuracy of aggregate measurement by volume depends upon the accuracy with which the amount of the *bulking* caused by moisture in the aggregate can be determined. The amount of bulking varies, not only with different moisture contents, but also with different gradations. Fine sand, *for example*, is bulked more than coarse sand by the same moisture content. Furthermore, moisture content itself varies from time to time, and a rather small variation causes a rather large change in the amount of bulking. For these and other reasons, aggregate should be measured by weight rather than by volume whenever possible.

To make grading easier, to keep segregation low, and to ensure that each batch is uniform, coarse aggregate should be stored in and measured from separate piles or hoppers, in each of which the ratio of maximum to minimum particle size should not exceed 2:1 for a maximum nominal size larger than 1 inch and 3:1 for a maximum nominal size larger than 1 inch and 3:1 for a maximum nominal size smaller than 1 inch (2.5 cm.). A mass of aggregate with a nominal size of 1½ inch to ¼ inch (3.8 to .64 cm.), *for example*, should be separated into one pile or hopper containing 1½ inch to ¾ inch (3.8 to 1.9 cm.), and another pile or hopper containing ¾ inch to ¼ inch (1.9 to .64 cm.). A mass with a nominal size of 3 inches to ¼ inch (7.5 to .64 cm.) should be separated into one pile or hopper containing 3 inches to 1½ inches (7.62 to 3.8 cm.), another containing 1½ inches to ¾ inch (3.8 to 1.9 cm.), and a third containing ¾ inch to ¼ inch (1.9 to .64 cm.).

BATCHING PLANT

On large jobs the aggregate is stored and weighed out in an aggregate *batching plant* (usually shortened to *batch plant*) shown in Fig. 1. A batch plant is, whenever possible, located near and used in conjunction with a *crushing* and/or *screening* plant. In a crushing and screening plant, stone is crushed into various particle sizes, which are then screened into separate piles. In a screening plant, the aggregate in its natural state is screened by sizes into separate piles.

The batch plant, which is usually a portable affair that can be knocked down and moved from site to site, is generally set up adjacent to the pile of screened aggregate. The plant may include separate hoppers for several sizes of fine and coarse aggre-

Fig. 1. Aggregate batching plant.

gate. It may include one hopper for fine aggregate and another for coarse aggregate or it may include one or more *divided* hoppers, each containing two or more separate compartments for different sizes of aggregate.

Each storage hopper or storage hopper compartment can be discharged into a *weight box*, which can in turn be discharged into a mixer or a batch truck. When a specific weight of aggregate is called for, the worker sets the weight on a beam scale, and then opens the discharge chute on the storage hopper. When the desired weight has been reached in the weight box, the scale beam rises and the worker closes the storage hopper discharge chute. The weight box discharge chute is opened, and the aggregate discharges into the mixer or batch truck. Batch plant aggregate storage hoppers are usually loaded with clamshell-equipped cranes.

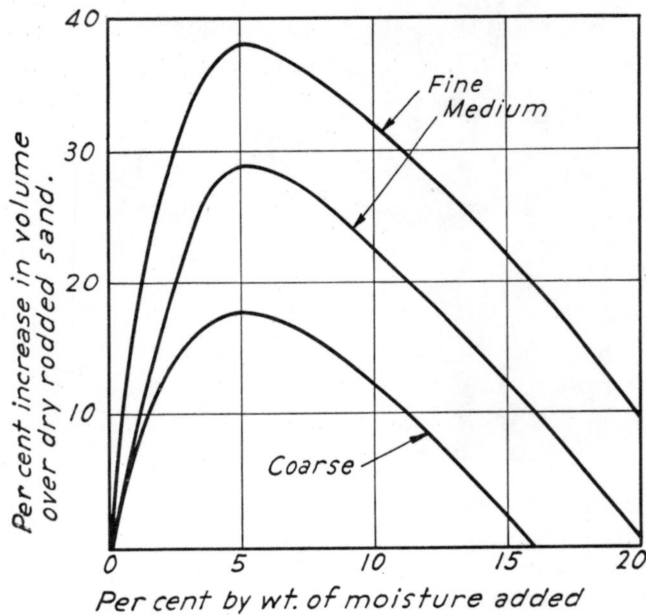

Fig. 2. Effect of moisture in bulking of sand.

Fig. 3. Making trial batch of concrete.

Continuation of Fig. 3.

STEPS IN MAKING TRIAL BATCH OF CONCRETE

Using 1½-inch (3.8-cm.) gravel and 6-gallon (22.7-liter) mix (1/5-sack batch mixer) proceed as follows (*see* Fig. 2):

Step 1. Test sand for moisture as shown in Fig. 3. If wet, use 5 gallons (18.7 liters) of water per sack of cement. (*See* Table 6.)

Step 2. Measure water. Since mixer holds 1/5 sack batch, use 1/5 of 5 gallons (18.7 liters) or 1 gallon (3.78 liters). A simple method is to measure 4 quarts which equals 1 gallon (3.78 liters) into a pail and then mark at waterline (Fig. 3). Thereafter fill to this mark.

Step 3. Measure cement. Use 1½ volume of cement for one volume of water. (*See* Table 6.) Since 4 quarts (3.78 liters) of water is used, 1½ × 4 or 6 quarts (5.68 liters) of cement is needed. Measure 6 quarts (5.68 liters) of cement into a pail, level it off, and mark at top edge of cement (Fig. 3). Thereafter fill to this mark.

Step 4. Ready for mixing. First put 4 quarts (3.78 liters) of water into mixer, as shown in Fig. 3.

Step 5. Next add part of gravel (Fig. 3). Adding gravel to water before cement is added prevents cement from sticking to drum.

Step 6. Add measured 6 quarts (5.68 liters) of cement (Fig. 3).

Step 7. Then add sand and gravel in proper proportions until a mushy workable mix is obtained (Fig. 3). In mixing a trial batch try the proportions given in Table 6.

Step 8. Mix for about two minutes after all materials have been added (Fig. 3). Run mixer at speed recommended by manufacturer.

Step 9. After all particles are coated with cement paste (about two-minute mix) dump out concrete (Fig. 3).

Chapter 4

Mixing Concrete

Mixing concrete is done by one of two methods—by hand or by machine. No matter which method is used, a well established procedure must be followed if you expect the finished concrete to be of good quality. An oversight in this phase of concrete construction, whether through lack of competence or inattention to detail cannot be overcome later. (*See* Table 7.)

Plane	Use	Remarks
Fore plane	To true surface or edge of lumber for accurate work.	Hold plane firmly, right hand on handle, left hand on knob.
Smooth plane	To smooth rough surfaces where straight edges and sides are not required.	Hold plane firmly, right hand on handle, left hand on knob.
Block plane	To make close joints, to cut across the grain or edges of small lumber.	Use with one hand. Make light cuts with short strokes toward center of work. Do not run over edge of work.
Jack plane	A substitute for fore or smooth plane. Does not do as precise work.	Hold plane firmly, right hand on handle, left hand on knob.

TABLE 7. RECOMMENDED MIXTURES FOR SEVERAL CLASSES OF CONSTRUCTION (INTENDED PRIMARILY FOR USE ON SMALL JOBS).

MIXING BY HAND

A batch which is to be hand-mixed by a couple of workers should not be much larger than about a cubic yard. The equipment required consists of a watertight metal or wooden platform, two shovels, a metal-lined measuring box, and a graduated bucket for measuring the water. (*See* Chap. 6, Concrete Equipment and Tools.)

The mixing platform should measure about 10 × 12 feet (3.048 × 3.66 meters). For a wood platform the boards should be at least 1-inch (2.5 cm.) tongue-and-groove. Tongue-and-groove joints are required for watertightness. The boards should be nailed to 2″ × 4″ (5 × 10 cm.) joists spaced not less than 2 feet (.61 meters) and not more than 3 feet (.91 meters) on center (O.C.). To prevent water or fluid flowing off the platform, a 2″ × 2″ (5.08 × 5.08 cm.) strip should be nailed along the outer edges and the platform should be level.

Mix the sand and cement together first, using the following procedure. Let us say that the batch is to consist of 2 bags of cement, 5.5 cubic feet (.16 cu. meters) of sand, and 6.4 cubic feet (.18 cu. meters) of coarse aggregate. Dump 3 cubic feet (.08 cu. meters) of sand on the platform first, spread it out in a layer, and dump a bag of cement over it. Spread the cement out in a layer, and dump the remaining 2.5 cubic feet (.07 cu. meters) of sand over it. Then dump the other sack of cement on top of the lot. Using alternate layers of sand and cement reduces the amount of shoveling required for complete mixing.

The workers doing the mixing should face each other from opposite sides of the pile, and they should work from the outside to the center, turning the material as many times as necessary to produce a uniform color throughout. When the cement and sand have been completely mixed, the pile should be leveled off and the coarse material should be added and mixed in with the necessary number of turnings.

The pile should next be troughed in the center, and the mixing water, carefully measured, should be poured into the trough. The dry materials should then be turned into the water, with great care taken to ensure that none of the water escapes. When all the water has been taken up, the batch should be mixed to a uniform consistency. At least four complete turnings are usually required.

MIXING BY MACHINE

A concrete mixer is designated as to size by its *rated capacity* expressed in terms of the volume of mixed concrete—not of batched ingredients—it can mix in a single batch. Rated capacities run from as small as 2 cubic feet (.06 cu. meters) to as large as 7 cubic yards (189 cu. ft. or 5.35 cu. meters). For most ordinary building construction the most commonly used mixer is the 16-S model (Fig. 1) with a capacity of 16 cubic feet (.45 cu. meters).

This concrete mixer is a self-contained unit capable of producing 16 cubic feet (.45 cu. meters) of concrete plus a 10 percent overload per batch. The hourly production capacity will vary from 10 to 15 cubic yards (7.65 to 11.47 cu. meters), depending on the efficiency of the personnel. Aggregate larger than 3 inches (7.62 cm.) will damage the mixer. The mixer consists of a frame which is equipped with wheels and towing tongue for easy movement, an engine, a power loader skip, mixing drum, water tank, and auxiliary water pump. The mixer may be used as a central mixing plant.

Charging the Mixer

There are two ways of charging the concrete mixers, by hand or with the mechanical skip. The mixer shown in Fig. 1 is equipped with a mechanical skip. The cement, sand, and gravel are placed in the skip and then dumped into the mixer together while the water runs into the mixing drum on the side opposite the skip. The mixing water is measured from a storage tank on top of the mixer a few seconds before the skip is dumped to wash the mixer between batches. The coarse aggregate is placed in

Fig. 1. Concrete mixer.

the skip first, the cement next, and the sand is placed on top to prevent excessive loss of cement as the batch enters the mixer.

A cement bag should be emptied onto the skip by cutting the underside of the bag lengthwise with a linoleum knife and then pulling the sack clear of the cement.

Mixing Time

The mixing time for a 1-cubic yard (.765 cu. meter) batch is 1½ minutes. Another 15 seconds should be allowed for each additional ½ cubic yard (.383 cu. meter) or fraction thereof. The water should be started into the drum a few seconds before the skip begins to dump, so that the inside of the drum will get a wash-out before the batched ingredients go in. The mixing period should be measured from the time all the batched ingredients are in, provided that all the water is in before one-fourth of the mixing time has elapsed.

Discharging the Mixer

When the material is ready for discharge from the mixer, the discharge chute is moved into place to receive the concrete from the drum of the mixer. In some cases, dry concrete has a tendency to carry up to the top of the drum and not drop down in time to be deposited on the chute. Very wet concrete may not carry up high enough to be caught by the chute. This condition can be corrected by adjusting the speed of the mixer. For very wet concrete, the speed of the drum should be increased and for dry concrete, it should be slowed down.

Cleaning and Maintaining the Mixer

The mixer should be cleaned daily when it is in continuous operation or following each period of use if it is in operation less than a day. If the outside of the mixer is kept coated with form oil, the cleaning process can be speeded up. The outside of the mixer should be washed with a hose and all accumulated concrete should be knocked off. If the blades of the mixer become worn, or coated with hardened concrete, mixing action will be less efficient. Badly worn blades should be replaced.

Hardened concrete should not be allowed to accumulate in the mixer drum. The mixer drum must be cleaned out whenever it is necessary to shut down for more than 1½ hours. Place a volume of coarse aggregate in the drum equal to one-half of the capacity of the mixer and allow it to revolve for about five minutes. Discharge the aggregate and flush out the drum with water. Do not pound the discharge chute, drum shell, or skip to remove aggregate or hardened concrete, for concrete will more readily adhere to the dents and bumps created.

For complete instructions on the operation, adjustment, and maintenance of the mixer, study the manufacturer's manual.

Chapter 5

Handling and Transporting Concrete

If mixed plastic concrete is carried by the ordinary type of vehicle (dump truck, for example) there is a strong tendency for the larger aggregate particles to segregate by settling to the bottom. To avoid this, ready-mixed concrete is usually delivered to a job by a transit mix truck.

When ready-mixed concrete is carried by the ordinary type of carrier (such as a dump truck, wheelbarrow, or buggy) any jolting of the carrier increases the natural tendency of the concrete to segregate. Carriers should therefore be equipped with pneumatic tires whenever possible, and the surface over which they travel should be as smooth as possible.

A long free fall will cause concrete to segregate. If the concrete must be discharged at a level more than 4 feet (1.21 meters) above the level of placement, it should be dumped into an *elephant trunk* as shown in Fig. 1.

Segregation also occurs whenever discharged concrete is allowed to glance off a surface, such as the side of a form or of a chute. Wheelbarrows, buggies, and conveyors should, therefore, be discharged so as to cause the concrete to fall clear.

Concrete should be transported by chute for short distances only, since it tends to segregate and also to dry out, when handled in this manner. For a mix of average workability, the best slope for a chute is about one foot of rise to 2 or 3 feet (about 30 cm. per meter rise) of run. For a mix of this type a steeper slope will cause segregation, while a flatter slope will cause the concrete to run slowly or not at all. For a stiffer mix a steeper slope will be required.

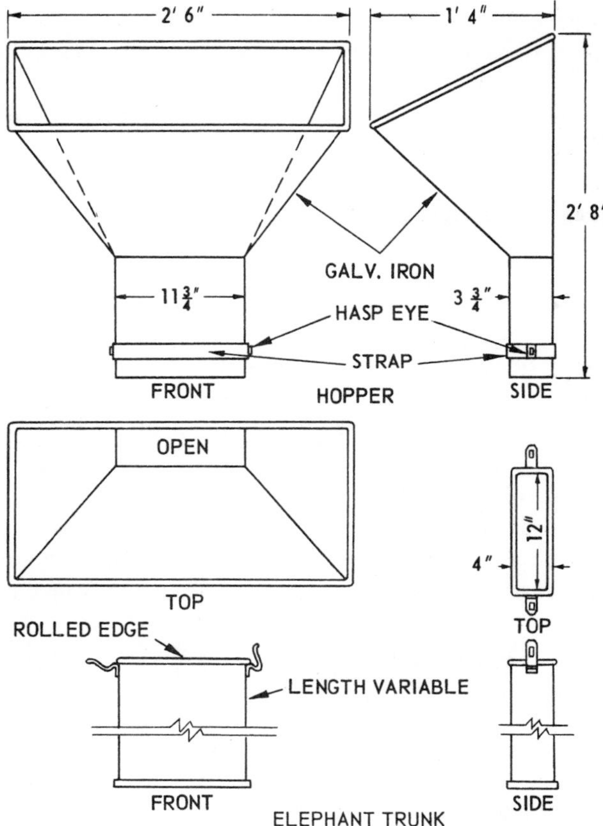

Fig. 1. Chute or down-pipe used to check free fall of concrete.

READY MIX

On some jobs, such as large highway jobs, it is possible to use a batch plant which contains its own mixer. A plant of this type discharges ready-mixed concrete into dump trucks or agitator trucks, which haul it to the construction site. An agitator truck carries the mix in a revolving chamber much like the one on a mixer. Keeping the mix agitated en route prevents segregation of aggregate particles.

A ready-mix plant is usually portable, so that it can follow the job along. It must be certain that a truck will be able to deliver the mix at the site before it starts to set. The interval between the time when the water is introduced at the mixer and the time when the truck discharges the mix into the forms must not be longer than 1½ hours.

TRANSIT MIX

A *transit mix truck* is a traveling concrete mixer. The truck carries a mixer and a water tank, from which the driver can introduce, at the proper time, the required amount of water into the mix. The truck picks up the dry ingredients at the batch plant together with a slip which tells him how much water is to be introduced into the mix. As a rule it is his best policy to wait until he arrives at the site and is sure they are ready there to receive the mix before he introduces the water and starts mixing the concrete. Usually he keeps the mixer revolving slowly en route, to prevent segregation of particles in the dry aggregate. On all but the smallest jobs the transit mix method is the most widely used of the various mixing procedures.

Chapter 6

Concrete Equipment and Tools

Good quality concrete is dependent upon the equipment and tools used. Also, accurate measurement must be used in mixing the ingredients.

STANDARD TESTING SIEVES FOR LABORATORY WORK

Standard testing sieves are made so that the openings in any screen are just half as large as those in the next larger size and twice as large as those in the next smaller size. Some variations in the manufacturer's listing of the number of meshes in the smaller sizes may mean that one manufacturer has used a larger size wire in the screen. A customary designation is ¾ inch (19.05 mm.), ⅜ inch (9.53 mm.), ⅜ inch 4, 4, 8, 14, 28, 48, 100, or 200. Soil-testing sieves with different grading may be substituted if the results are modified accordingly. (*See* Fig. 1.)

Fig. 1. Standard set of sieves.

OTHER EQUIPMENT NEEDED

Other laboratory equipment needed are as follows (*see* Figs. 2 and 3):

1. Pans
2. Graduates (500 c.c.) (*See* Fig. 3.)
3. Scales
4. 12-ounce (350 c.c.) prescription bottles
5. Quart (.95 liter) fruit jars
6. 9 × 12 inch (22.9 × 30.5 cm.) pieces of window glass
7. Slump cones

TOOLS

Most *tools* required in concrete work are simple and many of them can be homemade. The principal ones are as follows:

1. Screen
2. Mixing platform
3. Square pointed shovels
4. Measuring box
5. Water barrel
6. Pails
7. Hose
8. Tamper
9. Spading tool
10. Strikeboard
11. Wood float
12. Steel trowel
13. Edger
14. Groover
15. Wheelbarrow
16. Small wire brushes
17. Straightedge
18. Gallon and quart measures (or liter)

A *sand screen* (Fig. 2) should be about 3 × 6 feet (.91 × 1.9 meters). The frame can be made of 2-inch (5-cm.) lumber, 4 to 6 inches (10 to 15 cm.) wide. Legs should be so attached to the sides that the screen can be set at the desired angle while material is thrown upon it to separate the sand from the gravel. This angle should be about 45 degrees. A piece of wire cloth or fabric having three meshes to the linear inch (per 2.5 cm.) should be nailed to the frame. Material to be screened is thrown with a shovel against the upper portion of the screen and, as the coarse aggregate rolls down, it is separated from the fine aggregate.

Fig. 2. Typical equipment for concrete work.

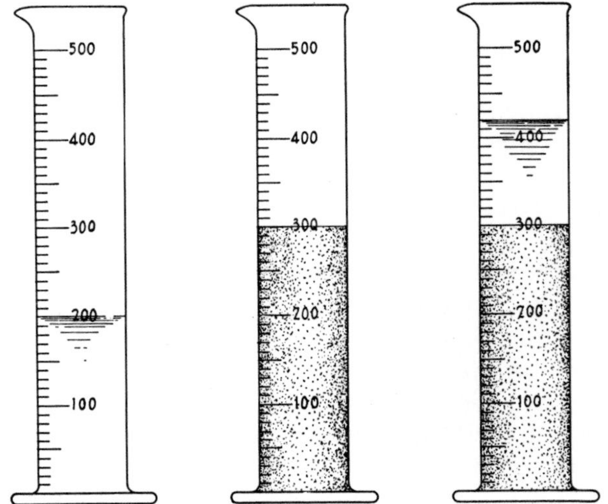

Fig. 3. Graduates (500 cc.).

For *hand-mixing*, a watertight *mixing platform* (Fig. 4) at least 7 × 12 feet (2.13 × 3.66 meters) should be provided. A platform of this size is large enough to permit two men using shovels to work upon it at one time.

The platform can be made of 1-inch (2.5-cm.) tongue-and-groove lumber nailed to 2- × 4-inch (5- × 10-cm.) stringers placed about 2 feet (.61 meters) apart. Strips of 2- × 4-inch (5- × 10-cm.) lumber nailed to three sides will keep the material from being shoveled off while being mixed. Covering the platform with galvanized sheet metal facilitates mixing and adds to the life of the platform.

The *measuring box* is necessary to measure exact quantities of sand and gravel or crushed stone. Such a box is a bottomless frame (Fig. 5) made of 1- or 1½-inch (2.5 or 3.8-cm.) material and should have a capacity of not less than 1 cubic foot (.028 cu. meters). If larger, it should be of 2- or 3-cubic foot (approximately .1 cu. meter) capacity and should be marked on the inside to show levels at which volume will equal one cubic foot, two cubic feet, and so on. (A metric box could be marked in

Fig. 4. For hand-mixing, a firm, tight platform is necessary.

Fig. 5. A bottomless measuring box.

fractions of a cubic meter.) Handles on the side of the box make lifting easier after the material required has been measured.

Ordinary *square pointed shovels* are used for mixing concrete as shown in Fig. 2.

A *wheelbarrow* (Fig. 2) facilitates transporting concrete from the mixer or platform to the place of final use. A rubber-tired, metal wheelbarrow having a body with the front higher than the back to prevent loss of concrete when the barrow handles are raised is generally used.

Concrete placed in forms must be spaded or tamped. A *tamper* (Fig. 2) is used when concrete is placed for sidewalks, floors or other flat surfaces. It may be made by boring a 1½-inch (3.8-cm.) hole in the end of an 8- × 8- × 12-inch (20- × 20- × 30-cm.) piece of timber and inserting a handle about four feet (1.22 meters) long. A metal tamper may also be used, or one can be made of concrete.

A *spading tool* of some kind is necessary to settle the material in the forms properly and also to secure a surface finish free from stone pockets. Such a spading tool may be made by flattening an ordinary garden spade or by straightening an old garden hoe. Both tools are used by working them up and down in the concrete close to the form faces to force back coarse particles and bring sand-cement mortar to the form face.

Sometimes a *chisel-edged board* 4 to 6 inches (10 to 15 cm.) wide may be used for spading concrete, the upper end being shaped to form a convenient handle. When reinforcing metal is placed in the concrete, smaller spading tools will be needed to work in the smaller spaces. *Pointed sticks, steel rods,* or *narrow chisel-edged pieces of wood* are used for this purpose.

A *strikeboard* (Fig. 6) is usually a piece of 2- × 4-inch (5- × 10-cm.) lumber, long enough to rest across the top of the form, as in sidewalk construction, so that the top of the concrete can be approximately leveled before final finish.

A *wood float* (Fig. 7) is used to finish the surface of the concrete after it is struck off, as in building walks, pavements, and floors.

A *steel hand float* or *trowel* (Fig. 8) may sometimes be required where a smoother surface is desired than can be obtained

Fig. 6. Freshly placed concrete is leveled off with a strikeboard.

Fig. 7. Wood float.

Fig. 8. Finishing trowel.

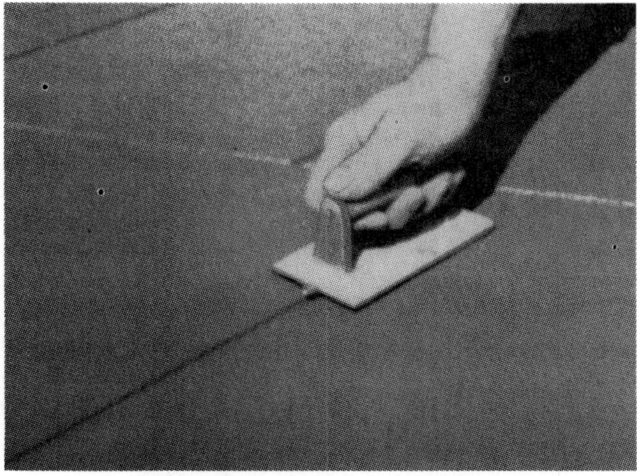

Fig. 9. Groover.

with the wood float.

For finishing joints between slabs in walks, floors, and similar concrete work, a tool known as a *groover* (Fig. 9) is used. To finish the edges of the slabs a tool known as an *edger* is used (Fig. 2).

A *water barrel* (Fig. 2) and *pails* are necessary to add the required amount of water to the correctly measured materials.

Most of the batch *mixers* in use have revolving drums with fixed blades inside, although a few have fixed drums with revolving blades or paddles. The latter type is commonly used in block manufacture where dry mixes are employed. Concrete mixers should be run at speeds recommended by the manufacturer. Batches should not be larger than the rated capacity of the mixers. (*See* Chap. 3, Batching.)

Chapter 7

Forms and Form Making

Concrete, plastic at the time of mixing, can be made to conform to almost any desired shape. The degree of success with which this may be accomplished depends very largely upon the forms used. *Forms* are the molds or receptacles in which the concrete is placed so that it will have the desired shape when hardened.

FORM REQUIREMENTS

Correctness of *shape* and *size* is the first requirement of forms for concrete. This may at times seem difficult to attain because the form must be made just the reverse of the object to be cast. Finished concrete will have no smoother surface than the forms.

Forms must be substantial enough to retain their shape when filled with wet concrete, which is fluid, heavy, and exerts great pressure on the forms. It is not sufficient that they be strong; they must also be rigid. You will be disappointed if, after placing the concrete, you find that the forms have been deformed by resulting pressures.

The forms must be tight. The escape of the water-cement paste from small openings will change the character of the remaining mixture. Forms should be easily filled and easily removed after the concrete has hardened. Double-headed nails or screws which can be withdrawn readily will assist greatly in removing forms without damaging the new concrete. Forms should be rigid enough to permit spading of the concrete.

Forms should be reasonable in cost, particularly those used only once. Greater care or expense in making forms may be justified when the work is elaborate or the forms are to be used a number of times.

TOOLS AND EQUIPMENT

Hand Tools

Claw hammer. The *carpenter's curved-claw nail hammer* (Fig. 1,A) is a steel-headed, wooden-handled tool used for driving nails, wedges, and dowels. The *claw* which is at one end of the head is a two-pronged arch used to pull nails out of wood. The other parts of the head are the eye and face.

The face may be flat, in which case it is called a *plain face.* The plain-faced hammer is easier for the beginner to learn to drive nails with, but with this hammer it is difficult to drive the head of the nail flush with the surface of the work without leaving hammer marks on the surface.

The face may be slightly rounded or convex, in which case it is called *bell-faced.* The bell-faced hammer is generally used in rough work. When handled by an expert, it can drive the nail head flush with the surface of the work without damaging the surface.

Use of claw hammer. To use the hammer, grasp the handle with the end flush with the lower edge of the palm (Fig. 1,B). Keep the wrist limber and relaxed. Grasp the nail with the thumb and forefinger of the other hand and place the point at the exact spot where it is to be driven. Unless the nail is to be purposely driven at an angle, it should be perpendicular to the surface of the work. Strike the nailhead squarely (Fig. 1,B) keeping the hand level with the head of the nail. To drive, first rest the face of the hammer on the head of the nail, then raise the hammer slightly and give the nail a few light taps to start it and to fix the aim. Then take the fingers away from the nail and drive the nail with firm blows with the center of the hammer face.

The nail can be started with one hand in either of the following ways.

Insert the nail between the claws of the hammer, with the head of the nail resting against the head of the hammer (Fig. 1,C). Start the nail with a sharp tap of the hammer held in this manner, then finish driving in the usual manner.

To pull nails, slide the claw of the hammer under the nail-

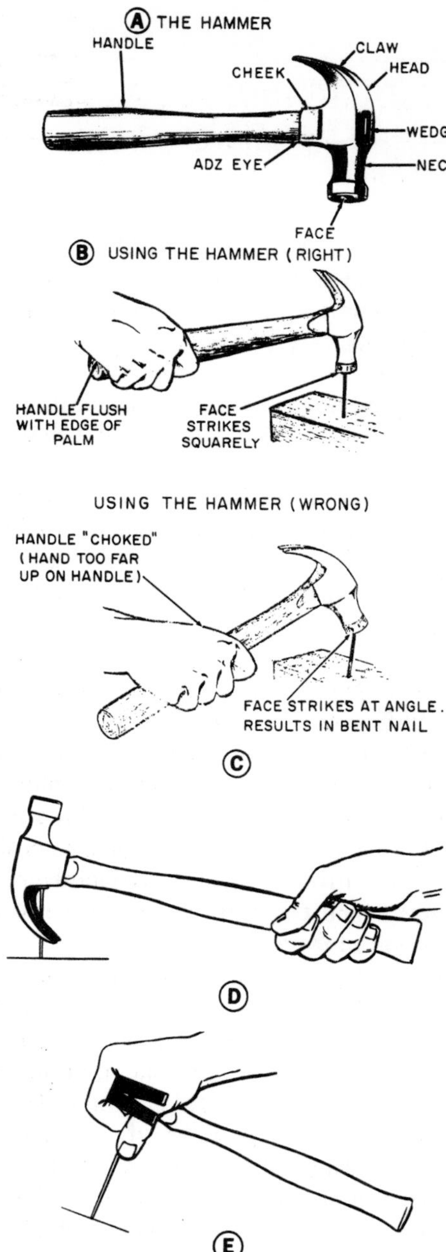

Fig. 1. Curved-claw nail hammer.

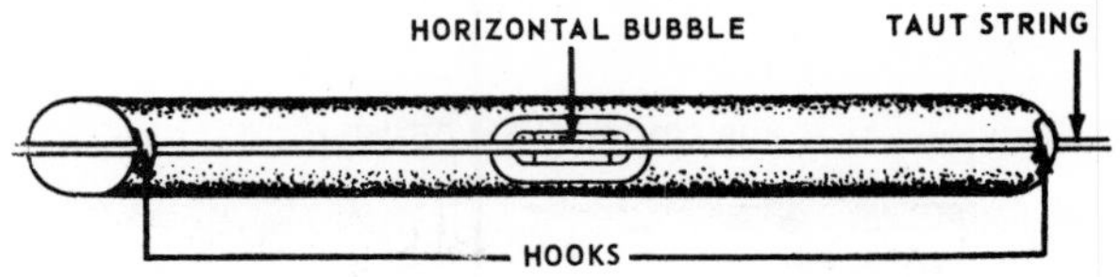

Fig. 2. Line level.

head. Pull back on the handle until the handle is nearly vertical, then slip a block of wood under the head of the hammer and pull the nail completely free (Fig. 1). The claw hammer should not be used for pulling nails larger than 8d. For larger sizes, use a wrecking bar.

Levels. The *line* level (Fig. 2) consists of a bubble tube set into a metal case with a hook at each end to permit it to be hung on a line or cord.

The line level is used to test whether a line or cord is level. It is particularly useful when the distance between two points to be checked for level is too long to permit the use of a board and the mason's level. However, the line level will show a disadvantage at a long distance because the line has a tendency to sag. To use the level stretch a cord between the two points which are to be checked for level. Hang the line level on the cord and see whether the bubble is in the middle of the tube. If it is not, raise the end of the cord which is toward the lower end of the bubble until the bubble rests in the middle of the tube. Unhook the level and turn it end for end, hang it on the cord, and retest. Continue testing until the bubble rests in the same relative position in its tube when the level is turned end for end. Remember to make the bubble rise in the tube, then lift that end of the cord which is toward the lower end of the bubble.

The line level is a delicate instrument, therefore, it must be kept in a box when not in use, to protect the bubble tube from being broken and the hooks from being bent. *Never* clean the level with water or any liquid because condensation will appear. The *mason's* level (Fig. 3) is usually a 24-inch (60-cm.) wood block with true-surface edges. There are two bubble tubes in it. One is in the middle of one of the long edges. The other is at right angles to this and parallel to the end of the level.

Bubble tubes are glass tubes nearly filled with alcohol. They are slightly curved. As a bubble of air in such a tube will rise to

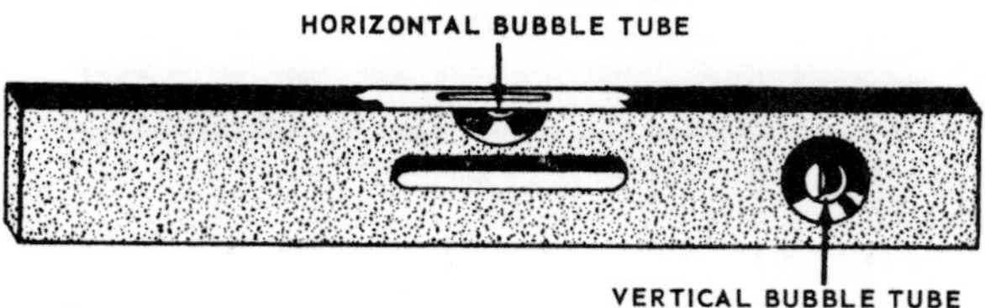

Fig. 3. Mason's level.

the highest point, the bubble will take its place in the middle of the tube when the tube is in a horizontal position.

Scratch marks of equal distances from the middle of the tube mark the proper position of the bubble when the surface on which the tube rests is level.

The mason's level is used to determine whether a surface is level. *Level* usually means a horizontal surface which throughout its extent lies on a line corresponding to that of the horizon. *Plumb* means vertical or at right angles to *level.*

Use of levels. To test the levelness of a surface, lay the mason's level on the surface and see where the bubble comes to rest. If the surface is level and the level is in adjustment, it will come to rest exactly between the two scratch marks previously mentioned. Turn the level end for end and recheck. The bubble should come to rest in the same place. If it does not, raise the end of the surface being tested toward the low end of the tube until it checks level.

To check for plumb, set the long side of the mason's level against the upright to be tested and use the bubble which is set in the end in the same way as described previously. Turn the level end for end to ensure accuracy as previously described.

Miter box. A *miter box* permits sawing a piece of stock to a given angle without laying out a line. Figure 4 shows a common type of wooden 40-degree miter box. Stock can be cut at 45 degrees by placing the saw in cuts M-S and L-F, or at 90 degrees by placing the saw in cuts A-B. The *steel miter box* (Fig. 5) can be set to cut stock at any angle.

Multiple folding rule. The *multiple folding rule* (Fig. 6) is six feet long. The sections are so hinged that it is six inches from the center of one hinge joint to the center of the next, which makes

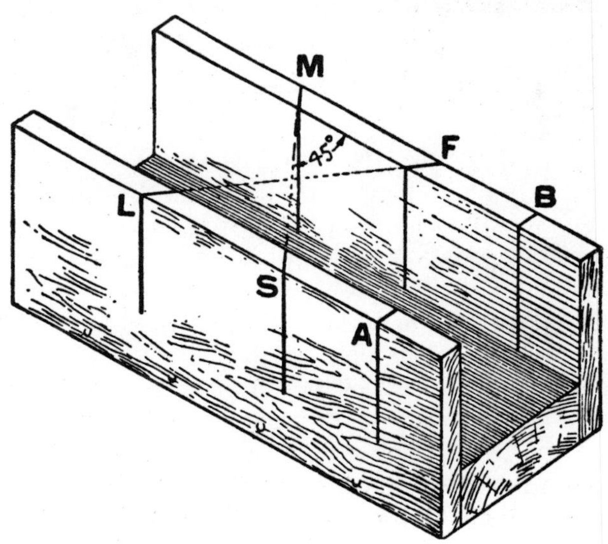

Fig. 4. Wooden miter box.

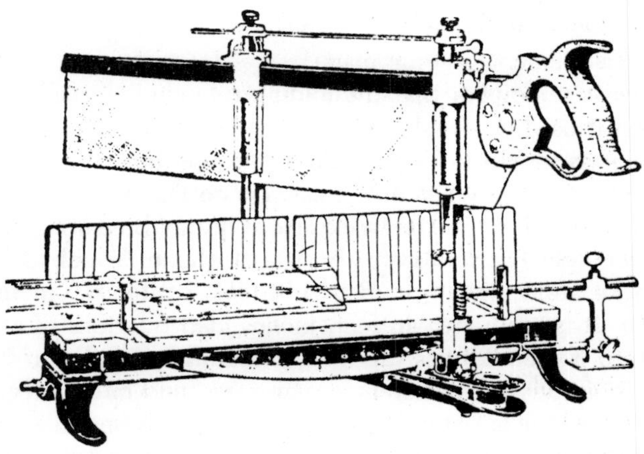

Fig. 5. Steel miter box.

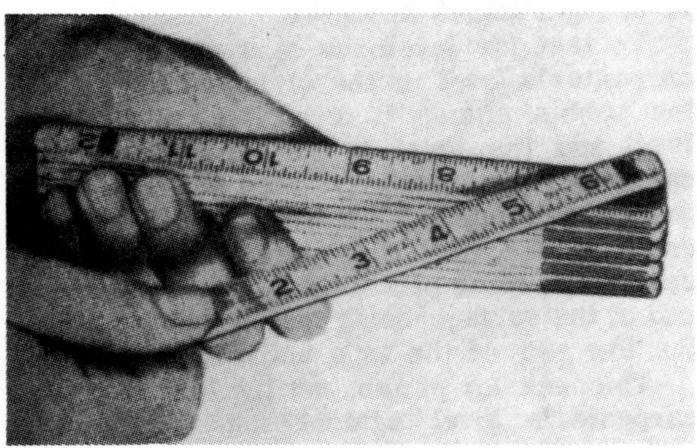

Fig. 6. Multiple folding rule.

the sections roughly eight inches in length. It is graduated in sixteenths of an inch. Metric multiple folding rules are available.

Whenever using the folding rule, hold the rule in one hand and unfold the sections one by one with the other hand until the rule is longer than the measurement to be taken.

Place the rule flat against the surface to be measured and parallel to one edge with the end at the starting point of the measurement.

Note the graduation which lines up with the point to which the measurement is being made.

Always remember that the folding rule can be easily bent or broken if used carelessly, particularly when it is being opened. Open it as shown in Fig. 6. Close the rule and keep it in your pocket or toolbox when not in use. Do not leave it lying around the workbench or on the work where it may be damaged.

Steel tape. The *steel tape* (Fig. 7) is a ribbon, ⅜ inch (3.2 mm.) in width and ranges from 6 to 100 feet (1.8 to 30.5 meters) in length. It is graduated in feet, inches, and fractions of an inch down to ⅛ inch. Metric tapes are available in lengths of 1 to 25 meters, graduated in meters, centimeters, and millimeters. One end of the tape is fastened to a reel which is housed in a leather-covered metal box provided with a slot through which the other end of the tape protrudes. This end has a metal ring attached to

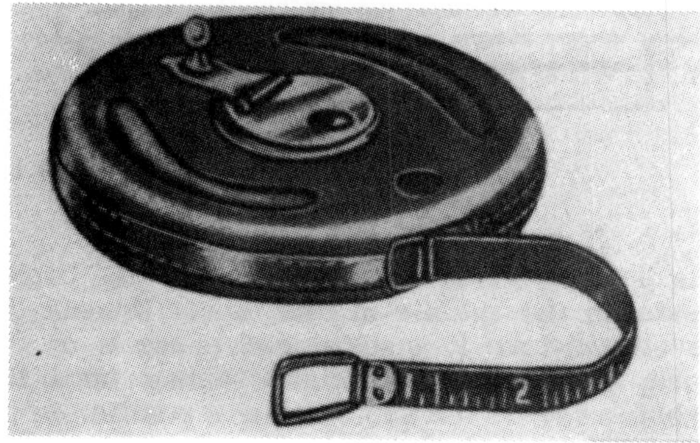

Fig. 7. Steel tape.

it. The ring will not pass through the slot in the case; thus it forms a handle by which the tape may be drawn from the case. Zero on the tape is at the inside of the end of the ring. This makes it possible to hook the ring over a nail or other projection while measuring with the tape, making it unnecessary to have another man hold the end in position. A folding crank is provided on the reel, by which the tape can be returned to the case after use.

To measure with the tape, secure the ring end at the starting point, either by slipping it over a nail or by other means. Walk in the direction to be measured, letting the tape be pulled from the case as you walk. Stretch the slack out of the tape, making sure it is parallel to the surface or edge to be measured. Read the gradation which falls at the end of the distance to be measured.

Reel the tape back into its case whenever it is not actually being used by turning the crank on the case in a clockwise direction. Do not kink the tape. It is easily kinked by being used for measuring around corners or by a vehicle running over it. Keep the tape lightly oiled. If it gets wet or damp by being used in dew-covered grass or in the rain, wipe it thoroughly dry and oil it before returning it to its case.

Chalk line. Long straight lines between distant points on surfaces are marked by snapping a *chalk line* as shown in Fig. 8.

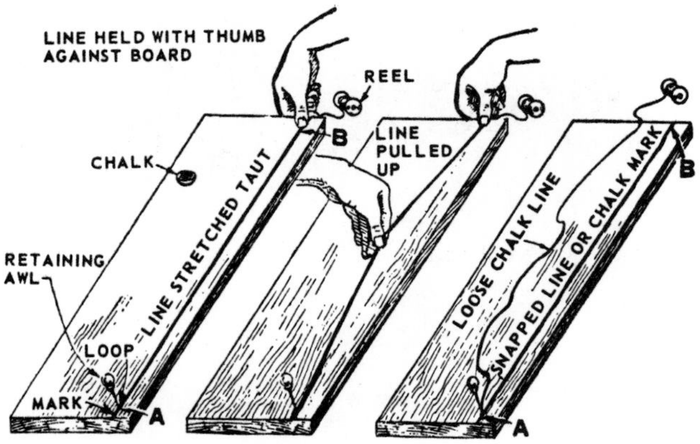

Fig. 8. Snapping a chalk line.

The line is first chalked by holding the chalk in the hand and drawing the line across it several times. It is then stretched between the points and snapped as shown in Fig. 8. For an accurate mark, never snap the chalk line over more than a 20-foot (6 meter) distance.

Handsaws. Saws are tools used for cutting wood or metal. The *handsaw* consists of a steel blade with a handle at one end. Except on the *hacksaw*, the blade is narrower at the end opposite the handle. This end of the blade is called the *point* or *toe*. The end of the blade nearest the handle is called the *heel* (Fig. 9). One edge of the blade has teeth which act as two rows of cutters. When the saw is used, these teeth cut two parallel grooves close together. The chips (called *sawdust*) are pushed out from between the grooves (the *kerf*) by the beveled part of the teeth (Fig. 10). The teeth are bent alternately to one side or the other to make the kerf wider than the thickness of the blade. This bending is called the *set* of the teeth (Figs. 10, 11, and 12). The number of teeth per inch, the size and shape of the teeth, and the amount of set depends on the use to be made of the saw and the material to be cut. Saws, except the hacksaw, are described by the number of tooth points per inch. There is always one more point than there are teeth per inch (Fig. 12). A number stamped near the handle gives the number of points of the saw.

Types of saws. The *crosscut* saw is used for cutting across the grain of wood. It has eight or more points, and the points are sharpened at a bevel so that they are like the ends of knife blades

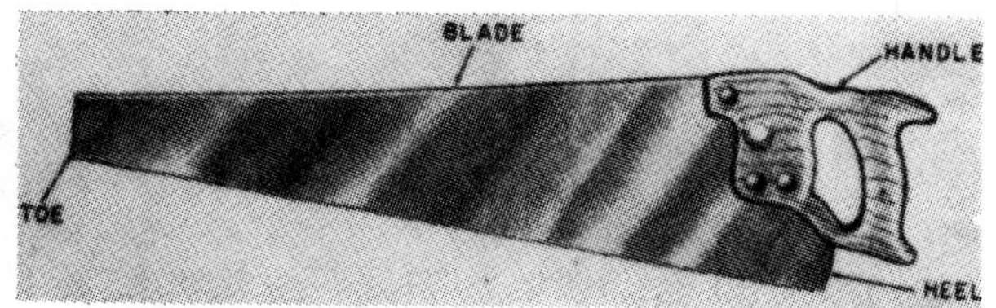

Fig. 9. Crosscut handsaw.

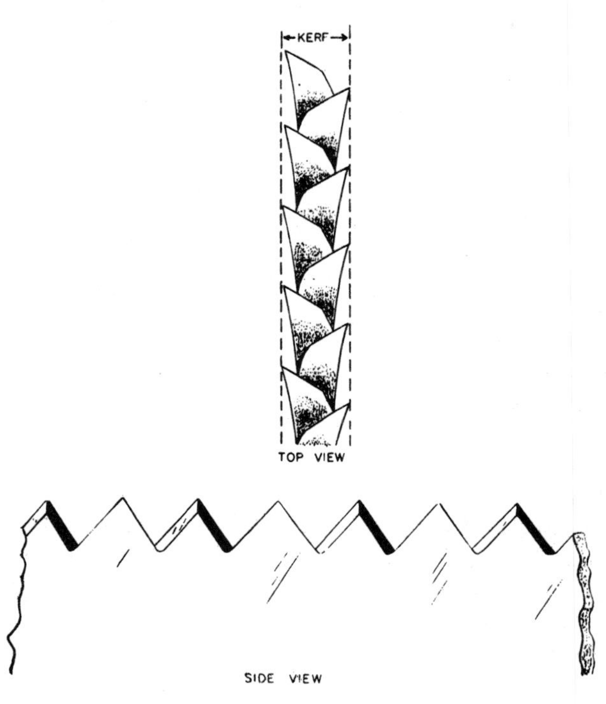

Fig. 10. Crosscut saw teeth.

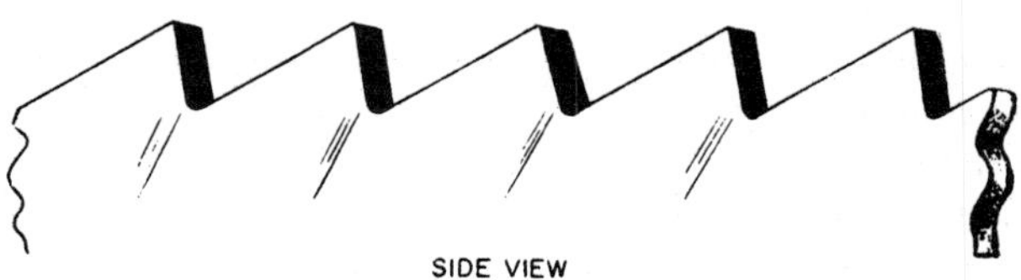

Fig. 11. Ripsaw teeth.

Figure 11—2nd part "top view"

(Fig. 10). A crosscut saw with coarse teeth and a wide set is needed for cutting green, unseasoned wood. A fine toothed saw does more accurate cutting, and is best for dry, seasoned wood.

The *ripsaw* is designed for cutting with the grain of the wood. The teeth, unlike those of the crosscut saw, are sharpened straight across the front edge, which is nearly vertical, or at right angles to the edge of the blade (Fig. 11). Thus the teeth of the ripsaw are like two rows of chisels in their action. The ripsaw in the tool set has 5½ points. Figure 12 shows angles of saw teeth.

The *nested* saws (Fig. 13) consist of a handle which is common to three blades which are a keyhole saw, a compass saw, and a plumber's saw. The handle has a thumbnut which is tightened to hold the blade securely in place. The *keyhole* saw blade is much narrower than that of the compass saw. The point is narrow enough to enter a ¼-inch (6.3-mm.) hole. It is commonly used for cutting keyholes in fitting locks in doors, and for smaller types of work. Like the compass saw, it cuts a wider kerf than either the crosscut or the ripsaw, in order that the blade may turn in making curved cuts.

The *compass* saw blade is designed for sawing curves. It is also used for starting cuts to be completed by larger saws, particularly in interior cuts. The blade is tapered to a point, and the teeth are filed in such a manner that the saw may be used either

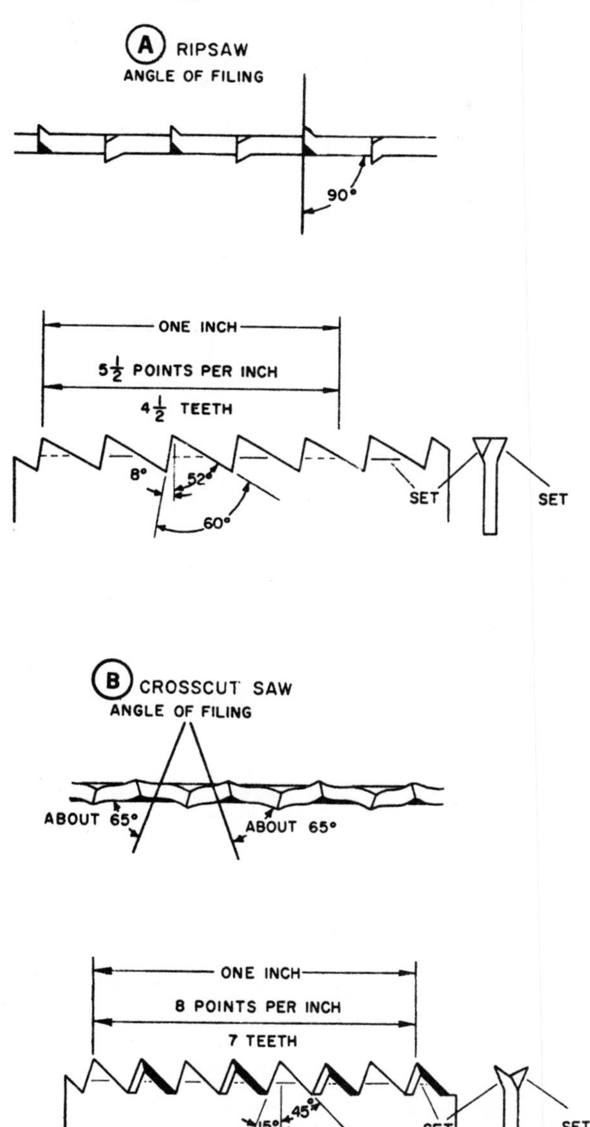

Fig. 12. Angles of saw teeth.

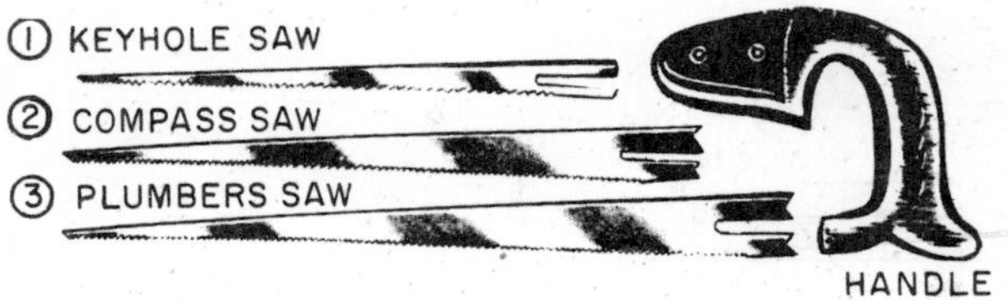

Fig. 13. Nested saws.

for crosscutting or for ripping. The kerf left by this saw is wider than that of either the crosscut or the ripsaw, in order to provide freedom for the blade to turn when cutting curves. The *plumber's* saw blade is a heavy blade with fine teeth designed for cutting nails or soft metals. The blade is thick enough to permit a woodcutting saw to pass freely through the cut it makes in a nail.

The *hacksaw* (Fig. 14) is a saw designed for cutting metal. It consists of a blade and a frame which has a handle on one end. The frame can be adjusted to hold various blade lengths at various angles. The blades have holes in each end, and are mounted on the frame by means of pins attached to the frame. The frames are of high grade tool steel, and are of two general types—*hard* which means the entire blade has been hardened in tempering, and *flexible* which means that only the teeth have been hardened. The blades furnished with the tool set should be of the *hard* type with a *pitch* (the number of teeth per inch or 2.5 cm.) of 18. This type of blade is best for brass, tool steel, cast iron, and heavy stock, and is referred to as a *general purpose* blade.

Uses of saws. In sawing with either the crosscut (Fig. 15) or the ripsaw, first draw a guideline for the saw to follow. Grasp the

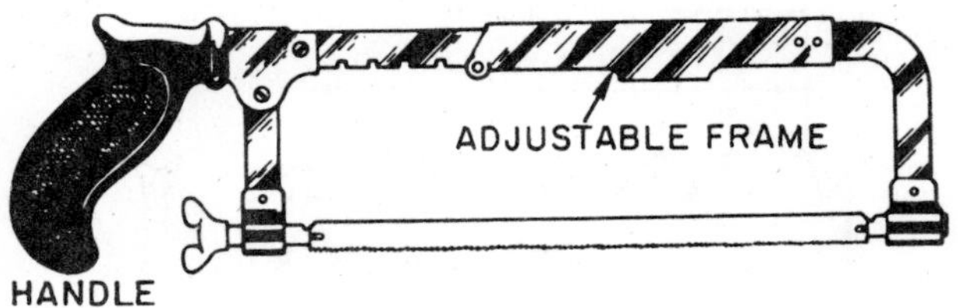

Fig. 14. Hacksaw.

saw with the right hand on the handle. Grasp the wood with the left hand (and kneel on it with one knee, if possible) to hold it securely. Guide the saw with the left thumb by resting it against the blade above the line of teeth. Keep your right shoulder directly in front of the cut to be made. This will ensure that the saw is sawing in a plane perpendicular to the surface of the wood.

Rest the teeth of the saw against the edge of the wood, with the blade on the waste side of the guideline. Start the cut by drawing the saw toward you to make an initial groove to keep the saw in place. Hold your saw lightly. Do not force it into the wood, but simply draw it back and forth, using a long stroke. If the saw tends to run off the line, or the cut is not perpendicular to the work, slightly twist or bend the blade back into place. Test a portion of the blade occasionally with a try square to ensure that the cut is being made perpendicular to the surface of the wood. The crosscut saw should make an angle of 45 degrees between the edge of the saw and the surface of the wood. The ripsaw should be used at an angle of 60 degrees.

In ripping long boards, a wooden wedge may be inserted into

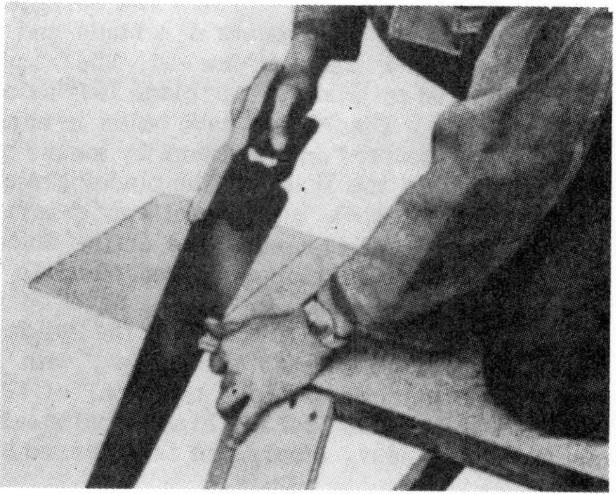

Fig. 15. Using the crosscut handsaw.

the cut to spread it apart and keep the saw from binding as shown in Fig. 16.

In using the compass saw or the keyhole saw, first bore a hole with an auger bit (Fig. 17). Insert the compass or keyhole saw into the hole and start to cut (Fig. 17) working slowly and carefully with a minimum of pressure. These narrow-bladed saws are easily bent. When the cut is long enough to permit it, remove the compass saw or keyhole saw and finish the cut with the regular crosscut or ripsaw.

The plumber's saw is used to cut through any nail encountered while sawing. The cut is then continued with the regular wood saw.

In using the hacksaw, insert the blade with the teeth pointing forward, away from the handle. Start your cut at a slight angle with a flat surface, and guide the blade with the left thumb until the cut is deep enough to allow use of both hands. Avoid starting a cut on a sharp corner as shown in Fig. 18.

An old blade will always make a narrower kerf than a new blade. Therefore, if a blade breaks before a cut is finished, it is better to start a new cut in line with the old cut, or work the blade into the cut with extreme care to prevent breaking. When cutting well away from the edge of a piece of metal, the blade may be turned in the frame as shown in Fig. 19.

Maintenance and care. Care must be taken that the saw is not

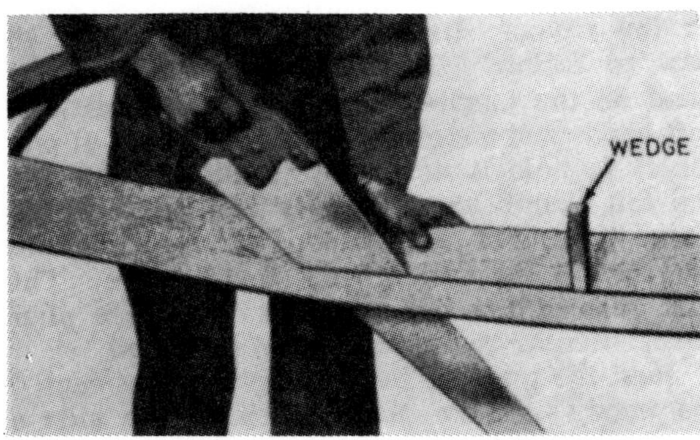

Fig. 16. Using a wedge to spread the cut.

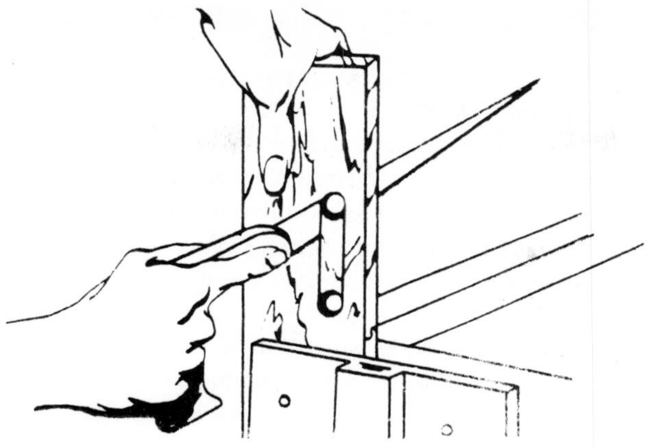

Fig. 17. Using the keyhole or compass saw.

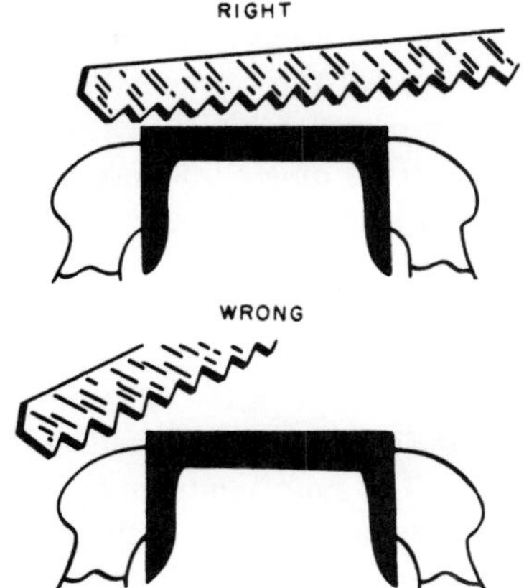

Fig. 18. Starting a hacksaw cut.

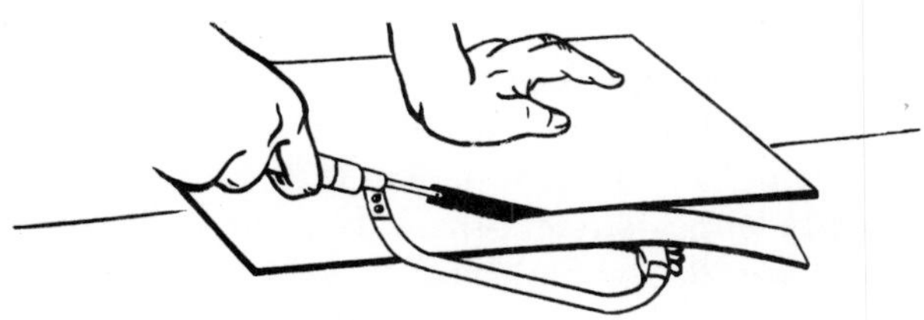

Fig. 19. Cutting deep with a hacksaw.

kinked. If the saw binds in the cut, and pressure is then applied to force it through the wood, a kink is almost certain to result. A kinked saw is useless. Make certain that nails, spikes, and other foreign objects are removed from the wood before it is sawed. When not in use, saws should be oiled and kept in a toolbox or in the rack. Saws rust easily, and a rusty saw will bind in the cut. Figure 20 illustrates some of the right and wrong ways of caring for saws.

Safety precautions. Make sure that if the saw slips from the work it will not cut your hands or other portions of your body. Lay the saw down carefully when not in use, in such a position that no one can brush against the teeth and cut themselves.

Braces and bits. Holes in wood are usually bored with *auger bits.* These bits are held and rotated by some type of *brace.* The brace has a holding device, known as a *chuck,* which clamps the square shank of the bit. A *ratchet brace* is shown with an auger bit in Fig. 21. The point of the bit does the cutting, so it is enlarged to show its important parts.

The *lips* and *nibs* of the auger bit may be sharpened with a special auger bit file. It is made thin so you can file in the narrow space between the *spur* and nib. The file has safe edges to protect the parts that are not filed. File only on the inside of nibs and lips.

The spur is a screw that pulls the bit into the wood. Do not use much pressure after the cut is started. Let the spur do the work. When you bore a hole *completely through* a piece of wood, use the *double-boring system,* as it prevents the splitting and tearing of the wood around the hole.

Auger bit sizes are stamped on the shank. If the number "6" appears on the shank, you will know it is a bit that cuts a 6/16 or ⅜-inch (9.4-mm.) diameter hole. A ½-inch (1.3-cm.) bit carries the number 8, indicating that the size is 8/16 or ½ inch (1.3-cm.). Just remember that the number on the shank indicates the bit will bore a hole that many sixteenths of an inch in diameter.

Holes having a diameter under 3/16 inch (1.6 mm.) are usually made with a straight-shank twist drill, held in a hand drill or power drill. You may have an *automatic push drill* (Fig. 22) with a set of special straight-fluted bits.

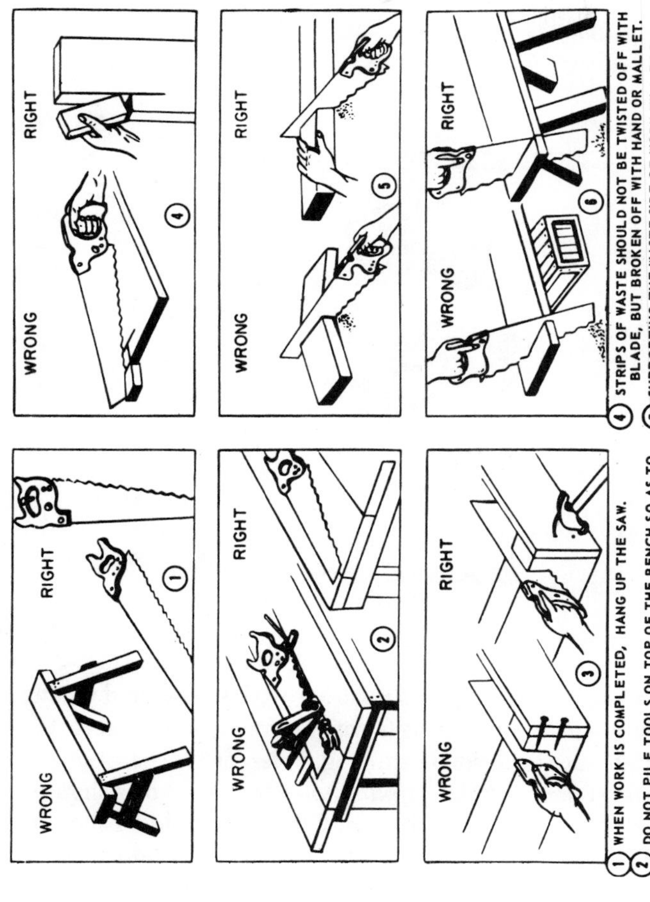
WRONG
RIGHT
1
WRONG
RIGHT
2
WRONG
RIGHT
3
WRONG
RIGHT
4
WRONG
RIGHT
5
WRONG
RIGHT
6
1 WHEN WORK IS COMPLETED, HANG UP THE SAW.
2 DO NOT PILE TOOLS ON TOP OF THE BENCH SO AS TO DISTORT BLADE
3 LOOK CAREFULLY OVER REPAIR OR ALTERATION WORK; SEE THAT ALL NAILS ARE REMOVED TO AVOID CUTTING INTO METAL
4 STRIPS OF WASTE SHOULD NOT BE TWISTED OFF WITH BLADE, BUT BROKEN OFF WITH HAND OR MALLET.
5 SUPPORTING THE WASTE SIDE OF WORK WILL PREVENT SPLITTING OFF.
6 RAISE THE WORK TO A HEIGHT SUFFICIENT TO KEEP THE BLADE FROM STRIKING THE FLOOR. IF THE WORK CANNOT BE RAISED, LIMIT THE STROKE.

Fig. 20. Care of saws.

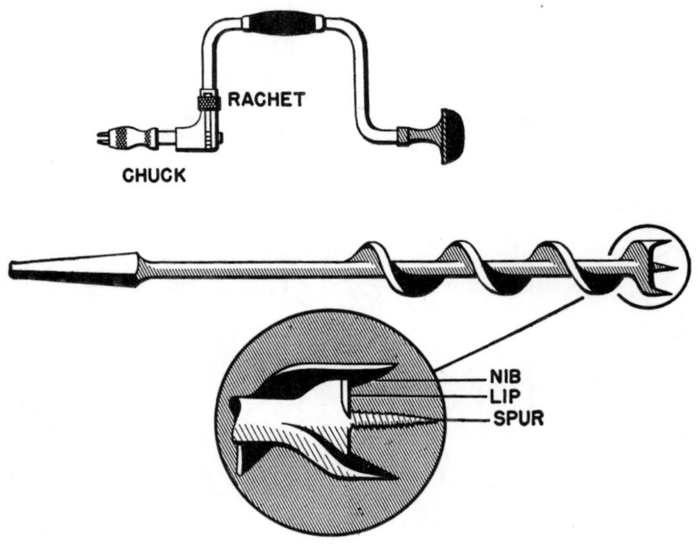

Fig. 21. Brace and auger bit.

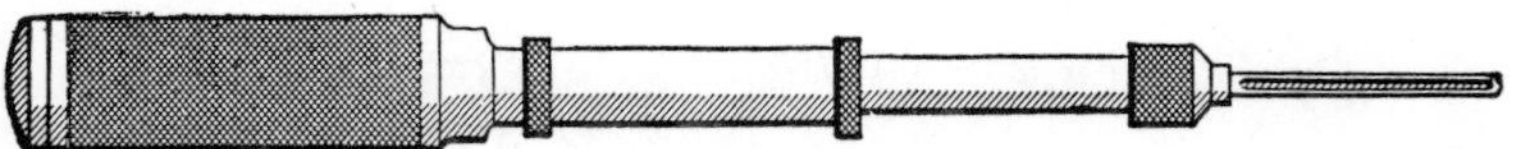

Fig. 22. Automatic push drill.

When you fasten wood pieces together with screws and when you use screws to secure hinges, hasps, locks, and braces to wood, you should drill small starting holes first. These small holes are called *anchor holes* or *pilot holes.* Anchor holes should be about *half* the diameter of the screw shank. Pilot holes should be the *same* diameter as the screw shank, or slightly larger. The chamfered recess for a flat head screw is made with the *countersink.* (*See* Fig. 23.)

Wood chisels. If you cannot do a certain job with a saw and a plane, the wood chisel may be the proper tool. For heavy work a *socket chisel* is used. Pound it with a mallet—*never* with a hammer. For light work, use the *tang type* chisel. It is not pounded but is pushed with a paring or slicing motion. Push the chisel

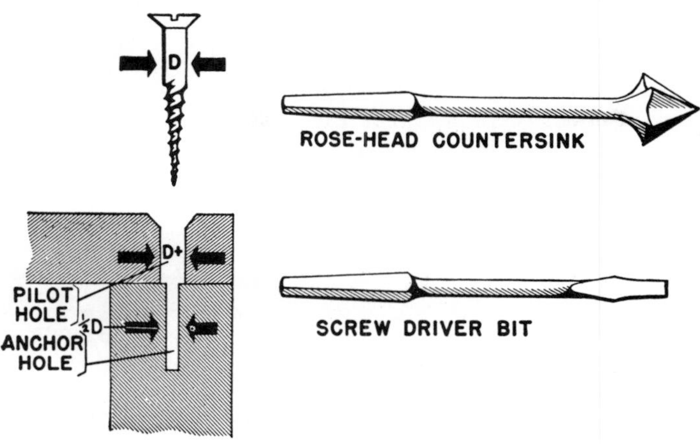

Fig. 23. Fastening with screws.

with one hand, and guide and control with the other. Both types of wood chisels are shown in Fig. 24. The size of these tools is determined by the distance across the blade. For utility work (use outside the shop), you need a set of short socket chisels, containing the ⅛, ¼, ⅜, ½, ¾, and 1-inch sizes (3–25-mm. sizes).

Chisels are used to cut and fit joints, *gain out* recesses for hinges, and to do other cutting jobs the saw and plane cannot handle.

The chisel works on the same principle as the plane, so be careful to cut *with the grain* of the wood. If you attempt to cut against the grain, the wood will probably split. Keep a razor edge on the chisel. You can grind and hone it by the same methods used for plane irons. Be especially careful not to burn the cutting edge.

You will not cut yourself if you *never allow any part of your body to get in front of the cutting edge.* Always clamp your work in a vise or secure it in some manner that permits you to keep your hands and body *back* of the sharp cutting edge.

Screwdrivers. Screwdrivers have one main purpose in life—to loosen or tighten screws. However, they are used as a substitute for everything from an ice pick to a bottle opener.

There are three main parts to a screwdriver. The portion that you grip is called the *handle,* the steel portion extending from the handle is the *shank,* and the end which fits into the slot of the screw is called the *blade.* (*See* Fig. 25.) The slim steel shank is designed to withstand considerable twisting force in proportion to its size but it will bend or crack in two if it is used as a pry or a pinch bar.

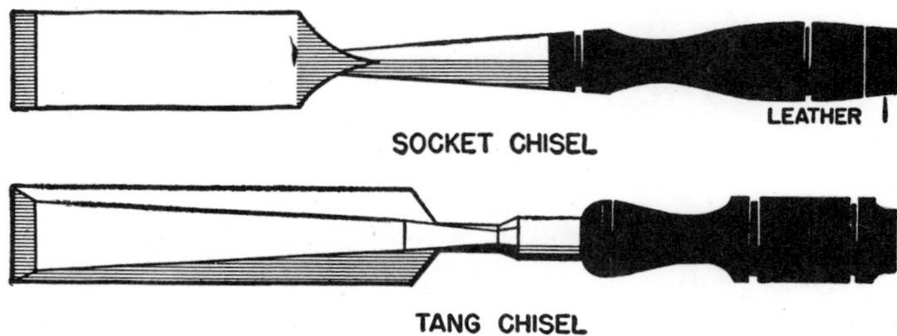

Fig. 24. Wood chisels.

Fig. 25. Parts of a screwdriver.

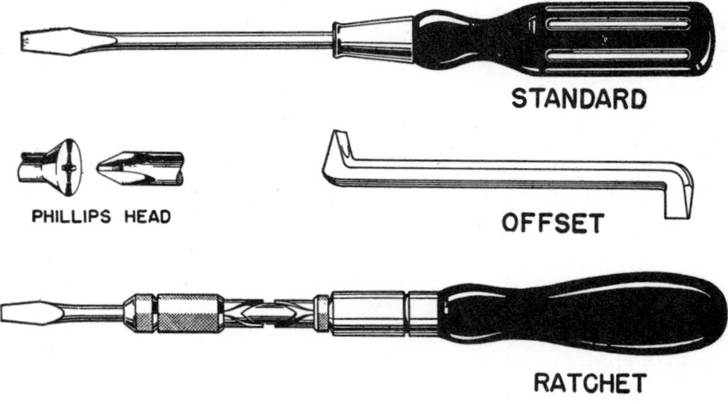

Fig. 26. Types of screwdrivers.

Another thing which may happen if the screwdriver is used for prying—*the blade may break.* The tip of the blade is hardened to keep it from wearing and the harder it is the easier it will break if much of a bending strain is applied. If the shank of the screwdriver is ever bent, it is usually difficult to get it perfectly straight again. If the shank is not straight, it is hard to keep the blade centered in the slot of the screw.

Do not hammer on the end of a screwdriver. It is not to be used in place of a cold chisel, a punch, or a drift. Hammering can break the shank, mushroom the end of the handle, or snap off the blade.

Types of screwdrivers. The most common types of screwdrivers—standard, offset, and ratchet—are shown in Fig. 26.

The *standard screwdriver* is used for most ordinary work and comes in a variety of sizes. You cannot place too much emphasis on selecting the correct size of screwdriver so that the thickness of the blade makes a good fit in the screw slot. This not only prevents the screw slot from becoming burred and the blade tip from being damaged, but reduces the force required to keep the screwdriver in the slot.

The *offset screwdriver* is a handy tool in tight corners. It has one blade forged in line with the shank or handle and the other blade at right angles to the shank. With such an arrangement, when the swinging space for the screwdriver is limited, you can change ends after each swing and work the screw in or out of the threaded hole. Use this screwdriver when there is not sufficient space to work a standard screwdriver.

The *Phillips* type screwdriver (Fig. 27) is made with a specially shaped blade that fits Phillips cross slot screws. The heads of these screws have two slots that cross in the center. This checks the tendency of some screwdrivers to slide out of the slot onto the finished surface of the work. The Phillips screwdriver will not slip and burr the end of the screw if the proper size is selected.

Safety precaution. It is dangerous to hold work in your hand while tightening or loosening a screw. If the blade slips, it can cause a bad cut. It is better to put the work in a vise or on a solid surface that will bear the pressure of the driver.

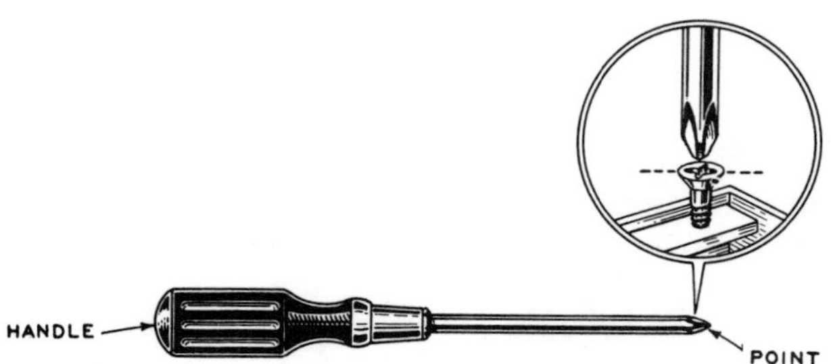

Fig. 27. Phillips screwdriver.

Planes. The smooth, fore, block, and jack planes (Fig. 28) are used for planing or roughing down the surfaces and ends of lumber.

The *smooth* plane (Fig. 28) is similar to the jack plane, but it is only nine or ten inches long, and used for planing small pieces of stock. The *fore* plane (Fig. 28) resembles the jack plane, is wider, and about 18 inches (45 cm.) long. Figure 28 shows a block and jack plane. *See* Table 8 for proper sets of jack, fore, or smooth plane. Use planes for purposes indicated in Table 8.

Snips. *Hand snips* are mighty handy instruments. *Straight hand snips* (Fig. 29) have blades that are straight and cutting edges that are sharpened to an 85-degree angle. Snips like this can be obtained in many different sizes ranging from the small 6-inch (15.2-cm.) snip to the large 14-inch (35.6-cm.) one. They are usually designed to cut sheet metal up to 1/16 inch (1.6 mm.) thick. They will also work on slightly heavier gages of aluminum alloy.

Unlike hacksaws, straight snips will not remove a certain width of metal when a cut is made. There is more danger, though, of causing minute metal fractures along the edges of the metal during the shearing process. For this reason, it is better not to cut exactly on the layout line in an attempt to avoid too much finish work.

Just cut as close to the layout line as is safe. There is no set rule for this measurement. You can proceed safely, however, on the assumption that the thinner and softer the metal is, the

Kind of Work	U.S. Gallons of Water to Add to Each 1-Sack Batch			Trial Mixture for First Batch			Maximum Aggregate Size
	Damp Sand and Pebbles	Wet Sand and Pebbles	Very Wet Sand and Pebbles	Cement	Sand	Pebbles	
				sacks	cu. ft.	cu. ft.	in.
Foundation walls which need not be watertight, mass concrete for footings, retaining walls, garden walls, etc.	6¼	Average sand 5½	4¾	1	2¾	4	1½
Watertight basement walls, walls above ground, lawn rollers, hotbeds, cold frames, etc. Well curbs and platforms, cisterns, septic tanks, watertight floors, sidewalks, steppingstone and flagstone walks, driveways, play courts, outdoor fireplace base and walls, refuse burners, ash receptacles, porch floors, basement floors, garden and lawn pools, steps, corner posts, gate posts, piers, columns, etc.	5½	Average sand 5	4¼	1	2¼	3	1½
Fence posts, grape arbor posts, mailbox posts, etc., flower boxes and pots, benches, bird baths, sun dials, pedestals and other garden furniture, work of very thin sections	4½	Average sand 4	3¾	1	1¾	2	¾

TABLE 8.

closer you can cut to the layout line. If metal is hard and thick, you can very easily fracture it in the cutting. Some fractures are so severe that they cannot be removed when the metal is dressed to size.

Leave about 1/32 of an inch (.8 mm.) for dressing. When cutting from the edge of a large sheet, you will have better luck if you cut from the left-hand side. You can get an idea of this proc-

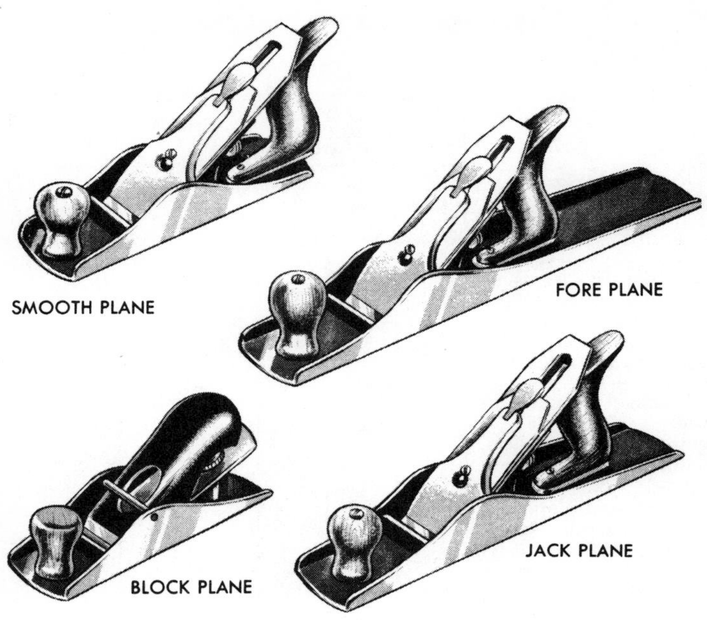

Fig. 28. Planes.

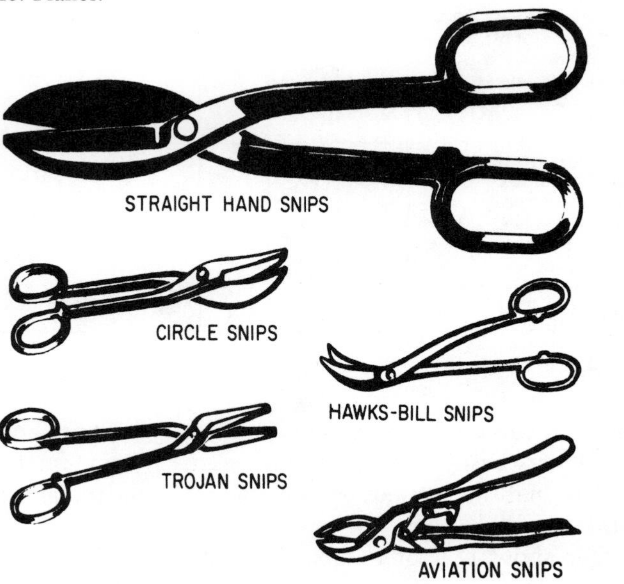

Fig. 29. Snips.

ess from Fig. 30. If the sheet is cut from the left a small section of scrap material will curl upward while the larger pieces of material will remain flat. When the left-hand portion of the material curls upward, it provides clearance for the frame of the shears to advance along the cut. The cut should never be made the full length of the blade. If the points of the snips are allowed to come together, they will tear the metal as the cut is completed. Stop the cut approximately ¼ inch (6.3 mm.) before the end of the blades have been reached and then take a new bite.

Suppose that you have to cut extremely heavy metal. This always presents an opportunity to spring the blades. Once the blades are sprung, hand snips are useless. *Use the rear portion of the blades only* when cutting heavy metal. This not only avoids any possibility of springing the blades, it gives greater leverage. Hand snips will withstand a lot of hard use but there is a limit to their endurance. *Never* use them to cut hardened steel wire or other similar objects. Such use will dent or nick the cutting edges of the blades.

It is a tough job to cut circles or arcs of small radii with straight snips. There are snips especially designed for circular cutting. They are called *circle, hawks-bill, Trojan,* and *aviation* snips (Fig. 29). Use these snips in the same manner as you would use straight hand snips and observe the same precautions. They are made in different sizes.

Circle snips have curved blades and are used for making circular cuts. They are available for either right- or left-hand use.

Hawks-bill snips can cut inside and outside circles of small

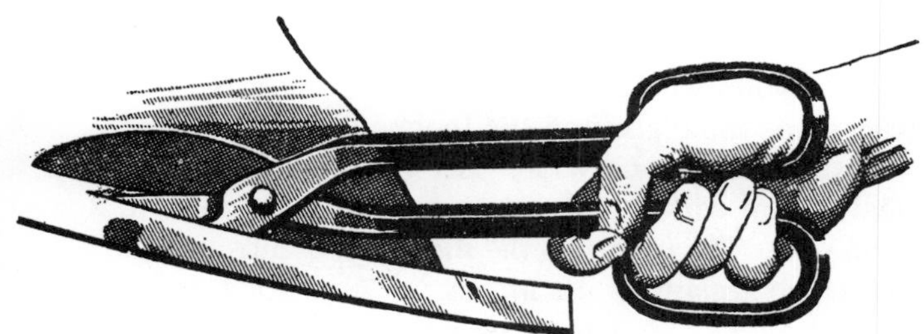

Fig. 30. Cutting from the left-hand side.

radii. The narrow curved blades are beveled enough to permit sharp turns without buckling the material.

Trojan snips are slender-bladed snips used for straight or curved cutting. The blades are small enough to permit sharp turns. They will also cut outside and inside curves.

A popular all-around hand snip, the *aviation snip,* is shown in Fig. 29. Snips of this type are known by various trade names, including Bellanca snips. They have narrow cutting blades, operated by a compound lever action. The lever action enables considerable pressure to be exerted on the blades with less effort being applied to the handles. These snips are used for cutting circles, squares, and irregular patterns. The hardened cutting blades make it easier to cut hard material.

Many snips of this type have small serrations or notches on the cutting edges which tend to prevent the snips from slipping backwards when a cut is being made. Although this feature does make the actual cutting much easier, it slightly mars the edges of the metal. You can remove small cutting marks if you allow proper clearance for dressing the metal to size.

There are many other types of hand snips used for special jobs. The snips under discussion here can be used for almost any common type of work.

Learn to use them properly. They should always be oiled and adjusted to permit ease of cutting and to produce a surface free from burrs. If the blades bind or are too far apart, the snips should be adjusted. Oil the entire length of the blade and work machine oil into the adjusting bolt. Open the snips, and tighten or loosen the nut with a small wrench until you have obtained the correct clearance.

Squares. The *steel square* is an indispensable form builder's tool. The various scales that are an integral part of this tool simplify problem layout work. The steel square consists of two parts—the body or the blade and the tongue (Fig. 31).

The *body* is the longer and wider part of a square. Figure 31 shows a steel square with a body 24 inches (60 cm.) long and 2 inches (5 cm.) wide. The tongue is the shorter and narrower part of the square and usually is 16 inches (40 cm.) long and 1½ inches (3.1 cm.) wide. The *heel* is the point at which the body

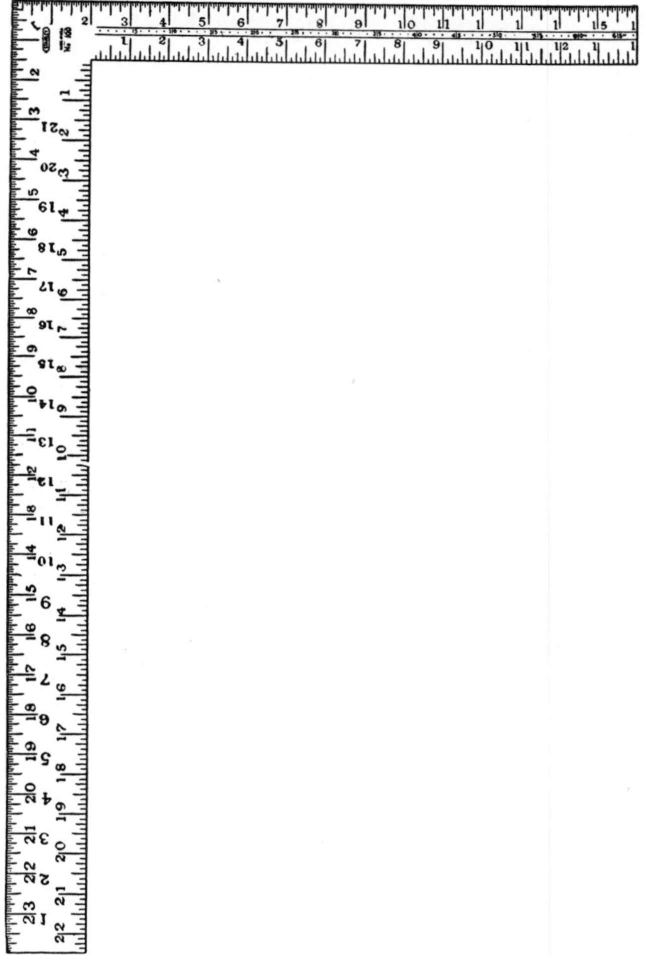

Fig. 31. Steel square.

and the tongue meet on the outside edge of the square. The intersection of the inner edges of the body and tongue is sometimes called the heel. The *face* of the square is either the side on which the name of the manufacturer is stamped, or the side that is visible when one is holding the body of the square in the left hand and the tongue of the square in the right hand. The back of the square is the side opposite to the face.

The modern square usually has two kinds of markings—scales and tables. The *scales* are the inch divisions found on the outer and inner edges of the square and the inch gradations into fractions of an inch. The square has the following scales and gradations:

Face of body	—outside edge	—inches and sixteenths
Face of body	—inside edge	—inches and eighths
Face of tongue	—outside edge	—inches and sixteenths
Face of tongue	—inside edge	—inches and eighths
Back of body	—outside edge	—inches and twelfths
Back of body	—inside edge	—inches and thirty-seconds
Back of tongue	—outside edge	—inches and twelfths
Back of tongue	—inside edge	—inches and tenths

The hundredth scale is located on the back of the tongue in the corner of the square, near the brace measure. This scale is "one inch divided into one hundred parts." With the aid of a pair of *dividers*, you can easily obtain decimal fractions of an inch. Metric squares are available also.

By using the figures in rafter tables to determine rafter lengths, you can readily convert decimal fractions to the nearest sixteenth of an inch (1.6 mm.) by means of dividers. The rafter tables (on the face of the body of the square) will help you to determine rapidly the lengths as well as the cuts of the rafters.

The octagon or eight square scale is found along the center of the face of the tongue. Using this scale you can shape a square timber into an octagon.

The brace measure table (along the center of the back of the tongue) gives the exact lengths of common braces.

The Essex board measure table (on the back of the body of the square) gives the board measure, in feet and twelfths of feet, of boards 1 inch (2.5 cm.) thick of usual lengths and widths.

A detailed description of all scales and tables and complete directions on how to read and use them are generally furnished by the manufacturer.

(Hand tools not mentioned in this chapter may be found in other chapters of this book.)

Power Tools

Your duties as a builder will also involve developing and improving your skills and techniques whenever working with power tools.

Saws. A *circular saw* has a blade which is mounted on, and spun by, a shaft called an *arbor*. Most modern saws have what is called a *motor-on-arbor* drive, meaning that the arbor and the motor shaft are one and the same member.

Like a handsaw, a circular saw blade may be a crosscut saw (usually called a *cutoff* saw blade in the case of a circular saw) or a ripsaw. The teeth of these saw blades are similar to those on the corresponding handsaws, and they cut on the same principle. A third type of circular saw blade called a *combination* or *miter* saw blade, may be used for either crosscutting or ripping.

A *tilt-arbor bench* saw is shown in Fig. 33. This saw is called a tilt-arbor saw because the saw blade can be tilted for cutting bevels and the like, by tilting the arbor. In the earlier types of bench saws the saw blade remained stationary and the table was

Fig. 32. Tilt-arbor bench saw.

tilted. A canted (tilted) saw table is hazardous in many ways, however, and most modern bench saws are of the tilt-arbor type.

For ripping stock, the *cutoff gages* are removed and the ripping fence is set a distance away from the saw equal to the desired width of the piece to be ripped off. The piece is placed with one edge against the fence, and fed through with the fence as a guide.

For cutting stock off square, the cutoff gage is set at 90 degrees to the line of the saw, and the ripping fence is set to the outside edge of the table, away from the stock to be cut. The piece is then placed with one edge against the cutoff gage, held firmly, and fed through by pushing the gage along its slot.

The procedure for cutting stock off at an angle other than 90 degrees (called miter cutting) is similar, except that the cutoff gage is set to bring the piece to the desired angle with the line of the saw.

For ordinary ripping or cutting off, the distance the saw blade should extend above the table top is ⅛ inch (3.2 mm.) plus the thickness of the piece to be sawed. The vertical position of the saw is controlled by the *depth of cut handwheel* shown in Fig. 32. The angle of the saw blade is controlled by the *tilt handwheel. The guard must be kept in place except when its removal is absolutely unavoidable.* Blade guards are shown in Figs. 32 and 33.

The slot in the table through which the saw blade extends is called the *throat.* The throat is contained in a small, removable section of the table called the *throat plate.* The throat plate is removed when it is necessary to insert a wrench to remove the saw blade. The blade is held on the arbor by a nut called the *arbor nut.* A saw is usually equipped with several throat plates, containing throats of various widths. A wider throat is required when a *dado head* is used on the saw. A dado head consists of two outside *grooving saws* (which are much like combination saws) and as many intermediate chisel-type *cutters* (called chippers) as are required to make up the designated width of the groove or dado. Grooving saws are usually ⅛-inch (3.2-mm.) thick. Consequently one grooving saw will cut a ⅛-inch (3.2-mm.) groove, and the two used together will cut a ¼-inch (6.4-

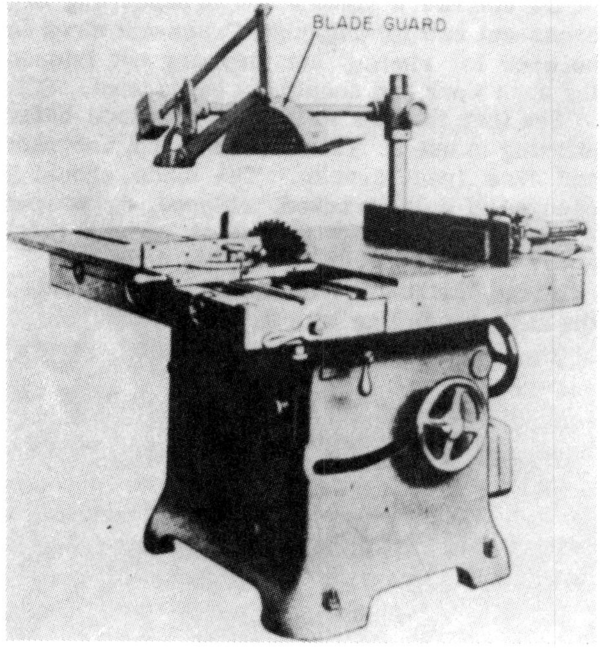

Fig. 33. Tilt-arbor bench saw with sliding table section.

mm.) groove. Intermediate cutters come in various thicknesses.

Circular saw safety. All equipment should be operated with special care, but these operating precautions are imperative for the circular saw.

1. Do not use a ripsaw for crosscutting or a cross-cut saw for ripping. Cross-cut saws can be used for ripping but they are not intended for such work and should not be so used.
2. See that the saw is in good condition before starting to use it. This means sharp, unbroken, and free from cracks. The blade should be changed if dull, cracked, chipped, or warped.
3. Be sure the saw is set at the proper height above the table to cut through the wood.
4. Avoid *kickbacks* by standing to one side of the saw—not in line with it.

5. Always use a push stick to push short narrow pieces between the saw and the gage.

6. Keep material of any kind from accumulating on the saw table and in the immediate working area.

7. *Never* reach over the saw to obtain material from the other side.

8. When cutting, do not feed wood into the saw faster than the saw will cut freely and cleanly.

9. Never leave the sawing machine unattended with the power turned on.

Radial arm saw. A *radial* arm saw is shown in Fig. 34. The motor and arbor are pivoted in a *yoke* which can be swung in any direction. The yoke slides back and forth on an *arm* (or *overarm*) which can also be swung in any direction. These arrangements make the radial saw adaptable to almost any conceivable type of saw cutting, as indicated in Fig. 35. Equipped with a grooving head, the saw can be used for *grooving* (Fig. 36) and *rabbeting* (Fig. 37). Equipped with a *shaper head* it can be used as a *shaper* (Fig. 38). Equipped with a *router bit,* it can be used for *routing* (Fig. 39). The radial saw is just about the most versatile power tool.

Radial arm saw safety. All power saws require caution.

1. Make sure the saw blade is mounted on the arbor so that the teeth of the saw point toward the operator.

2. When crosscutting stock, make sure the stock is flat on the table and that the back edge of the stock is held firmly against the fence.

3. Always make sure that the saw is back as far as it will go before starting to use it for crosscutting work.

4. When crosscutting long stock, make sure the ends are supported at the same level as the table.

5. Always keep the saw guards in place.

6. Adjust the saw for the correct depth, before starting the saw.

7. Never use a dull saw. Pinching or binding indicates a dull saw.

8. Make sure the anti-kickback guard is properly adjusted,

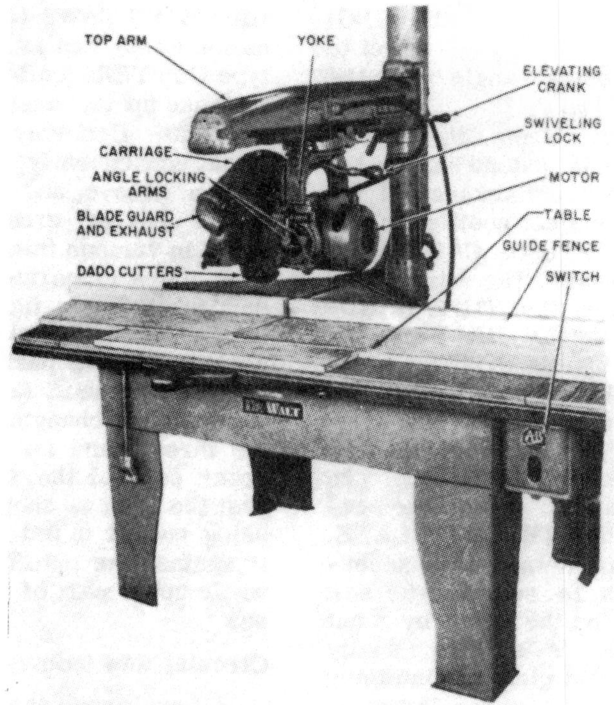

Fig. 34. Radial arm saw.

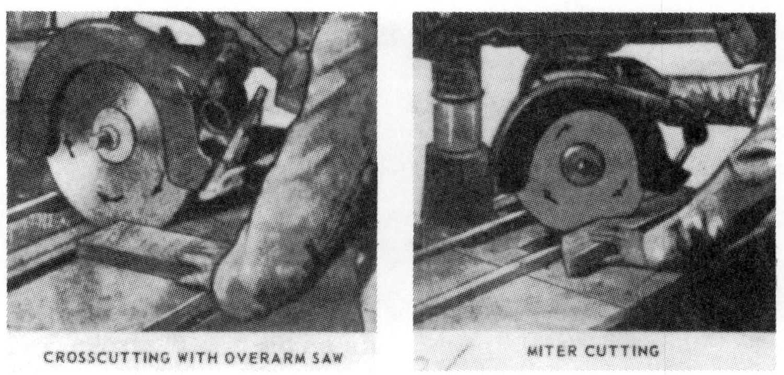

Fig. 35. Saw cutting with the radial arm saw.

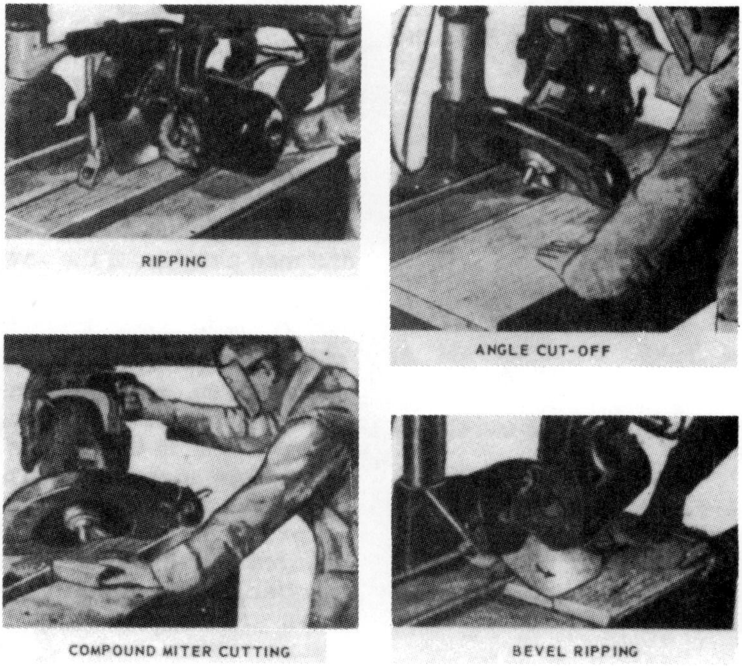

RIPPING

ANGLE CUT-OFF

COMPOUND MITER CUTTING

BEVEL RIPPING

Fig. 35. Saw cutting with the radial arm saw.

Fig. 36. Grooving with the radial arm saw.

Fig. 37. Rabbeting with the radial arm saw.

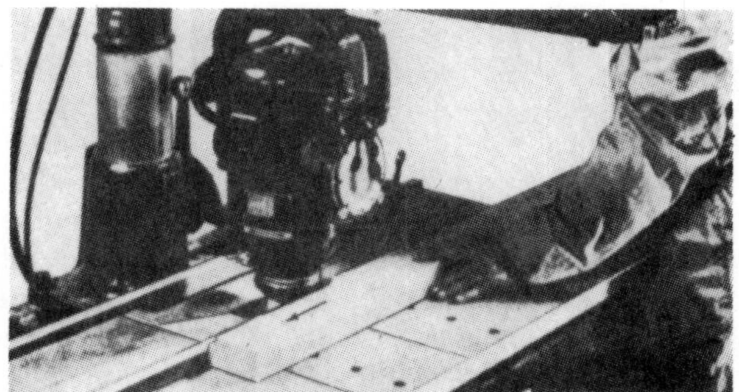

Fig. 38. Shaping with the radial arm saw.

Fig. 39. Routing with the radial arm saw.

whenever ripping stock.

9. Never rip stock unless it has a straight edge.

10. Always feed the stock to be ripped against the rotation of the saw blade.

11. Never make any adjustments while the motor is turning.

12. Always remember that the radial arm saw cuts on the *pull* stroke.

Portable circular saw. The *portable electric circular saw* is used chiefly as a great labor-saver in sawing wood framing members. The saw shown in Fig. 40 can be set to cut a piece off square (as it is set in the figure) or to cut it off at any bevel angle up to 45 degrees. To make an accurate ripping cut the *ripping guide* is set a distance away from the saw equal to the width of the strip to be ripped off, and placed against the edge of the piece as a guide for the saw. For cutting off, the ripping guide is turned upside-down, so that it will be out of the way.

The portable saw shown in Fig. 41 is being placed in the system because it seems to offer more advantages. The advantages readily detected about this portable saw are (1) the arbor can be locked whenever the blade is being changed and (2) the blade is on the opposite side to offer better visibility of the line to be cut. However, both saws are operated, basically, in the same manner.

The size of a portable circular saw is designated by the maximum diameter of the blade in inches (or centimeters) it will support within its guard.

Portable circular saw safety. All power saws require cautious use.

1. All portable, power-driven saws should be equipped with guards which will automatically adjust themselves to the work when in use, so that none of the teeth protrude above the work. The guard over the blade should be adjusted so that it slides out of its recess and covers the blade to the depth of the teeth when the saw is lifted off the work.

2. Goggles or face shields should be worn while using the saw and while cleaning up debris afterward.

Fig. 40. Portable electric circular saw.

3. Saws are to be grasped with both hands and held firmly against the work. Care should be taken that the saw does not break away, thereby causing injury.

4. The blade should be inspected at frequent intervals and always after it has locked, pinched, or burned. The electrical connection should be broken before this examination.

5. The saw motor should not be overloaded by pushing too hard or cutting stock that is too heavy.

6. Before using the saw, the material to be cut should be carefully examined and freed of nails or other metal substances. Cutting into or through knots should be avoided as far as possible.

7. The electric plug should be pulled before any adjustments or repairs are made to the saw. This includes changing the blade.

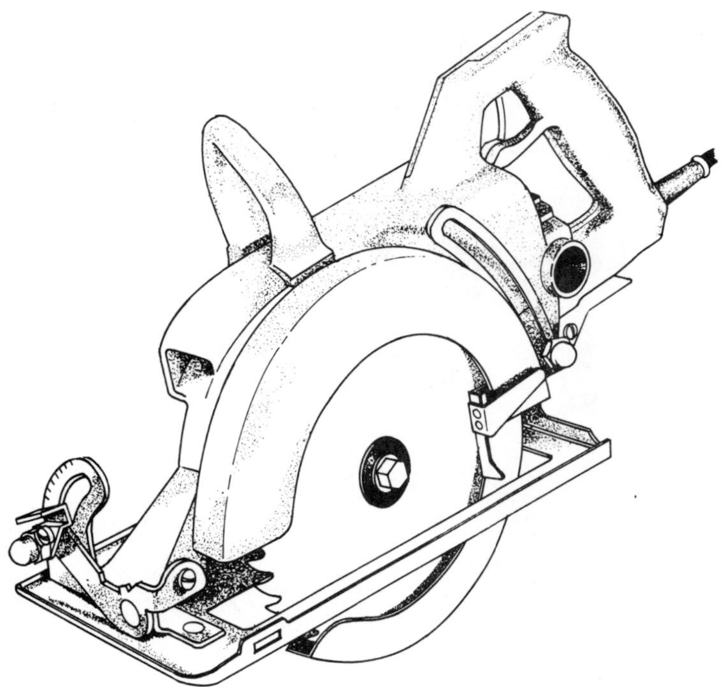

Fig. 41. Worm gear-driven portable electric circular saw.

Bandsaw. While the *bandsaw* (Fig. 42) is designed primarily for making curved cuts, it can also be used for straight cutting. Unlike the circular saws, the bandsaw is frequently used for freehand cutting.

The bandsaw has two large wheels on which a continuous narrow saw blade or *band* turns, just as a belt is turned on pulleys. The *lower wheel* located below the *working table* is connected to the motor directly or by means of pulleys or gears and serves as the driver pulley. The *upper wheel* is the driven pulley.

The saw blade is guided and kept in line by two sets of *blade guides*, one fixed set below the table and one set above with a vertical sliding adjustment. The alignment of the blade is adjusted by a mechanism on the back side of the upper wheel. *Tensioning* of the blade—tightening and loosening—is provided

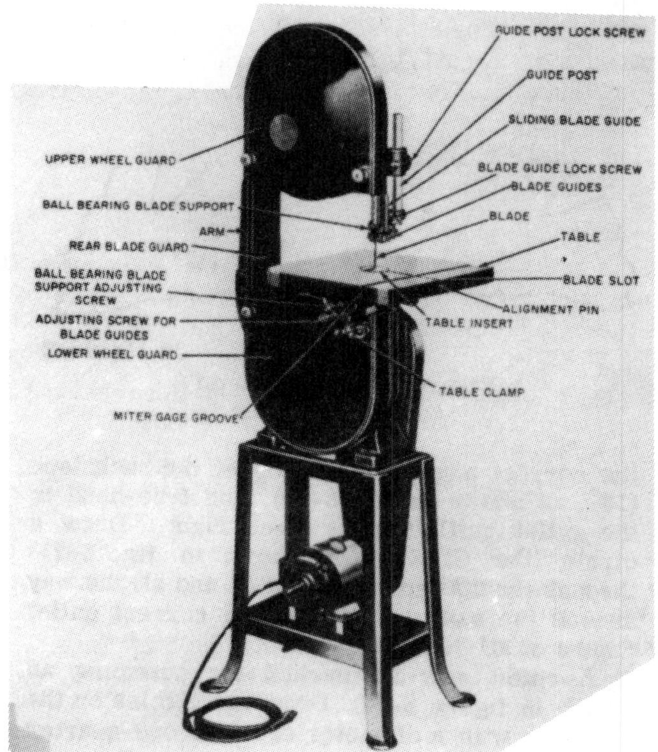

Fig. 42. Bandsaw.

by another adjustment located just back of the upper wheel.

Cutoff gages and ripping fences are sometimes provided for use with bandsaws, but you will do most of your work freehand with the table clear. With this type of saw it is difficult to make accurate cuts when gages or fences are used.

The size of a bandsaw is designated by the diameter of the wheels. Common sizes are 14- (Fig. 42), 16-, 18-, 20-, 30-, 36-, 42-, and 48-inch (35.6–122-cm.) machines. The 14-inch (35.6-cm.) size is the smallest practical bandsaw. With the exception of capacity, all bandsaws are much alike as regards to maintenance, operation, and adjustment.

Blades or bands for bandsaws are designated by *points* (tooth points per inch), *thickness* (gage), and width. The required length of a blade is found by adding the circumference of one wheel to twice the distance between the wheel centers. Length can vary within a limit of twice the tension adjustment range. Blades are set and filed much the same as with a hand ripsaw.

Bandsaw safety. Here are some safety pointers to keep in mind when you are operating a bandsaw.

1. Keep your fingers away from the moving blade.
2. Keep the table clear of stock and scraps so your work will not catch as you push it along.
3. Keep the upper guide just above the work, not excessively high.
4. Do not stand to the right of the machine while it is running and do not lean on the table at any time.
5. Bandsaw wheels should be tested by experienced men at least once a week with a small machinist's hammer to detect cracks or loose spokes. The sound of a cracked or broken wheel is dull and flat.
6. Cracked blades should not be used. If a blade develops a *click* as it passes through the work, the operator should shut off the power as the click is a signal that the blade is cracked and may be ready to break. After the saw blade has stopped moving, it should be replaced with one in proper condition.
7. If the saw blade breaks, the operator should shut off the power and not attempt to remove any part of the saw blade until the machine is completely stopped.
8. If the work binds or pinches on the blade, the operator should never attempt to back the work away from the blade while the saw is in motion since this may break the blade. He should always see that the blade is working relatively freely through the cut.
9. A bandsaw should not be operated in a location where the temperature is below 45° F. (7.2° C.) as it may break when the machine is started.
10. Using a small saw for large work or forcing a wide saw on a small radius is bad practice. The saw blade should, in all

cases, be as wide as the nature of the work will permit.

11. Bandsaws should not be stopped by thrusting a piece of wood against the cutting edge or side of the bandsaw blade immediately after the power has been shut off because the blade may break. Bandsaws 36 inches (91.4 cm.) and larger should have a hand or foot brake.

12. Particular care should be taken when sharpening or brazing a bandsaw blade to see that the blade is not overheated and that the brazed joints are thoroughly united and are finished to the same thickness as the rest of the blade. *It is recommended that all bandsaw blades be butt welded where possible, as this method is much superior to the old style of brazing.* (*See* Index for various types of Concrete Power Tools in other chapters of this book.)

FORM MATERIALS AND CONSTRUCTION

Several materials are suitable for the construction of concrete forms. Individual requirements will be the determining factors. Form material can be wood, plywood, steel, or other approved material. Forms for concrete pavement should be metal, except on curves where flexible or curved forms of metal or wood may be used. Wood forms, for surfaces exposed to view in the finished structure and requiring a standard finish, should be tongue-and-groove boards or plywood. For exposed surfaces, undressed square-edge lumber may be used. Forms for surfaces requiring special finishes should be plywood or tongue-and-groove boards, or should be lined with plywood, a non-absorptive hard-pressed fiberboard, or other approved material. Tongue-and-groove boards should be dressed to a uniform thickness, evenly matched, and free from loose knots, holes, and other defects which would affect the concrete finish. Plywood, other than for lining, should be concrete-form plywood not less than ⅝ inch (16 cm.) thick. Surfaces of steel forms should be free from irregularities, dents, and sags.

FORMWORK NOMENCLATURE

It is only those parts of the formwork which directly mold the concrete that are correctly referred to as the *forms*. The rest of the formwork consists of various bracing and tying members used to strengthen the forms and to hold them rigidly in place.

Wall, column, and floor slab forms were formerly built by joining boards edge-to-edge, but built-up forms have been largely replaced by plywood forms. Plywood forms are tighter, more warp-resistant, and easier to construct than board forms, and they can be re-used more often and conveniently.

In the following discussion of the various common types of forms, you should study the illustrations until you have learned the names of all the formwork members.

Footing Forms

When possible, the earth should be excavated to form a mold for concrete wall footings. Otherwise, forms must be constructed. In most cases, footings for columns are square or rectangular. The four sides should be built and erected in panels. The earth must be thoroughly moistened before the concrete is placed. The panels for the opposite sides of the footing are made to exact footing width. The 1-inch (2.54-cm.) thick sheathing is nailed to vertical cleats spaced on 2-foot (.61-meters) centers. Figure 43, A, shows a typical form for a large footing. Two-inch (5-cm.) dressed lumber should be used for the cleats and cleats spaced 2½ inches (6.4 cm.) from each end of the panel as shown. The other pair of panels, Fig. 43, B, have two end cleats on the inside spaced the length of the footing plus twice the sheathing thickness. The panels are held together by No. 8 or 9 soft black annealed iron wire wrapped around the center cleats. All reinforcing bars must be in place before the wire is installed. The holes on each side of the cleat permitting the wire to be wrapped around the cleat should be less than ½ inch (1.3 cm.) in diameter to prevent leakage of mortar through the hole. The panels may be held in place with form nails until the tie wire is installed. All form (duplex) nails should be driven from the out-

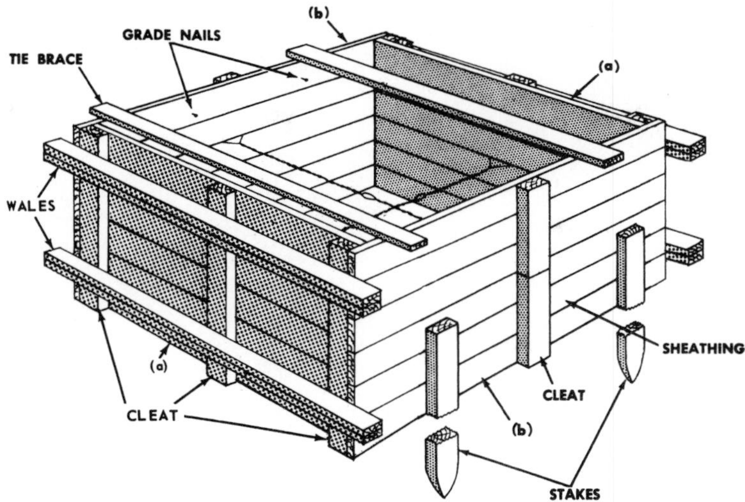

Fig. 43. Typical large footing form.

side if possible to make stripping easier. For forms 4 feet (1.22 meters) square or larger stakes should be driven as shown in illustration. These stakes and 1 × 6 (2.5 × 15 cm.) boards nailed across the top prevent spreading. The side panels may be higher than the required depth of footing since they can be marked on the inside to indicate the top of the footing. If the footings are less than 1 foot (.305 meters) deep and 2 feet (.61 meters) square, the forms can be constructed of 1-inch (2.5-cm.) sheathing without cleats. Boards for the sides of the form are cut and nailed as shown in Fig. 44. If the form can be braced no wire ties are needed.

Footing and Pier Form

Sometimes it may be necessary to place a footing and a small pier at the same time. The form for this type of concrete construction is shown in Fig. 45. The units are similar to the one shown in Fig. 43. Support for the upper form must be provided in such a way that it does not interfere with the placement of concrete in the lower form. This is accomplished by nailing a 2-

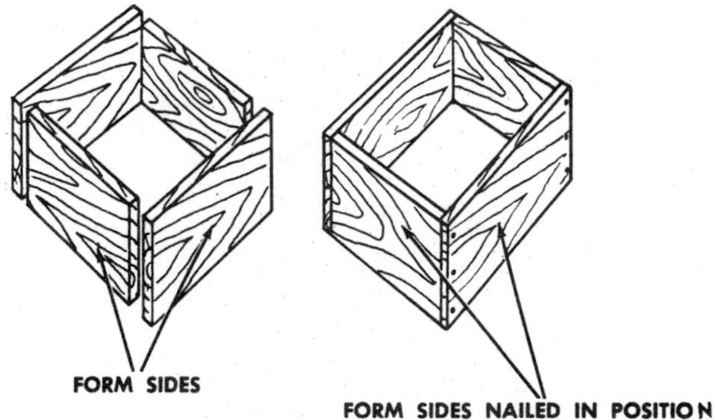

Fig. 44. Typical small footing form.

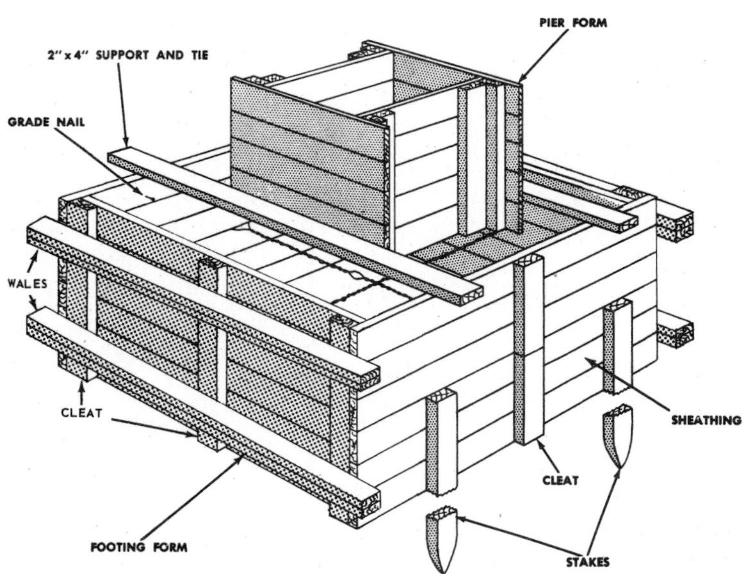

Fig. 45. Typical footing and pier form.

× 2- or 4- × 4- (5- × 5- or 10- × 10-cm.) board to the lower form as shown in Fig. 45. The top form is then nailed to these support pieces.

Wall Footing Forms

Form work for a wall footing is shown in Fig. 46 and methods of bracing the form are given in Fig. 47. The sides of the forms are made of 2-inch (5.1-cm.) lumber having a width equal to the depth of the footing. These pieces are held in place with stakes and are maintained the correct distance apart by spreaders. The short brace shown at each stake holds the form in line.

Wall Forms

Figure 48 shows a wall form without wales. The studs are usually backed by wales as shown in Fig. 49.

Wall forms are usually additionally reinforced against displacement by the use of *ties*. Two types of simple wire ties, used with wood *spreaders* are shown in Fig. 50. The wire is passed around the studs, the wales, and through small holes bored in the sheathing. The spreader is placed as close as possible to the studs, and the tie is set taut by the wedge shown at Fig. 50, A, or by twisting with a small toggle as shown at Fig. 50, B. When the concrete reaches the level of the spreader, the spreader is knocked out and removed. The parts of the wire which are inside the forms remain in the concrete; the outside surplus is cut off after the forms are removed.

Wire ties and wooden spreaders have been largely replaced by various manufactured devices in which the function of the tie and the spreader are combined. Figure 51 shows one of these, called a *snap tie*. These ties are made in various sizes to fit various wall thicknesses. The tie holders can be removed from the tie rod. The rod goes through small holes bored in the sheathing, and also through the wales, which are usually doubled for that purpose. Tapping the tie holders down on the ends of the rod brings the sheathing to bear solidly against the spreader washers. To prevent the tie holder from coming loose, drive a duplex nail in the hole provided. After the concrete has hardened, the tie

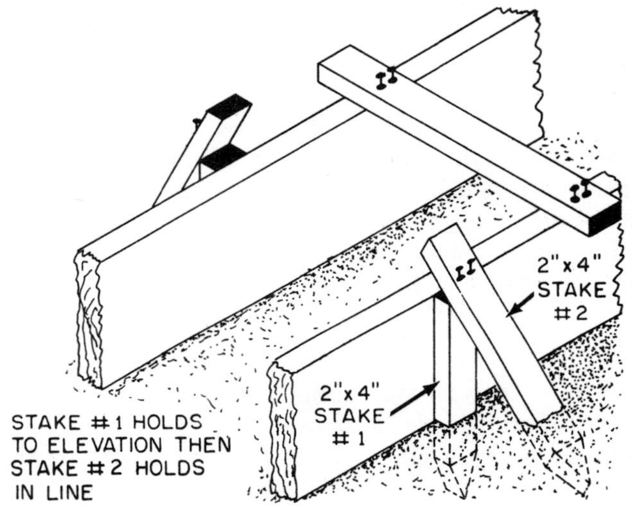

Fig. 46. Typical wall footing forms.

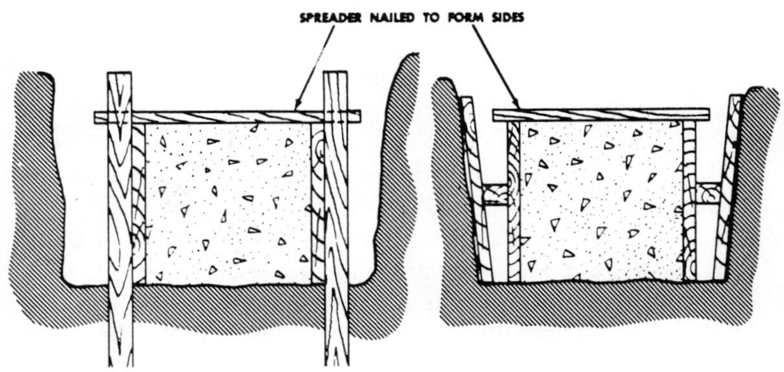

Fig. 47. Methods of bracing footing forms.

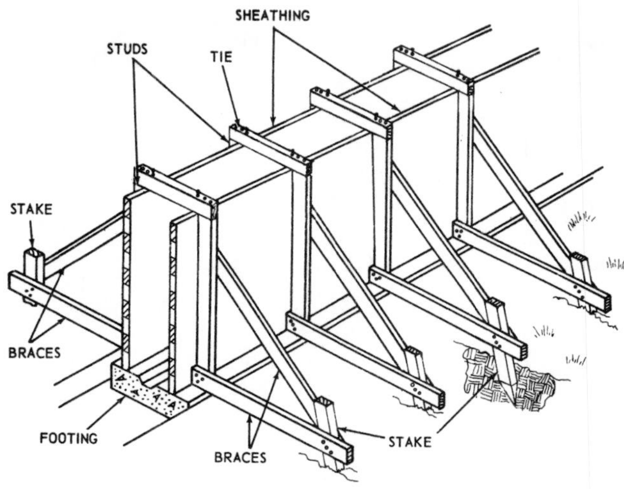

Fig. 48. Wall form without wales.

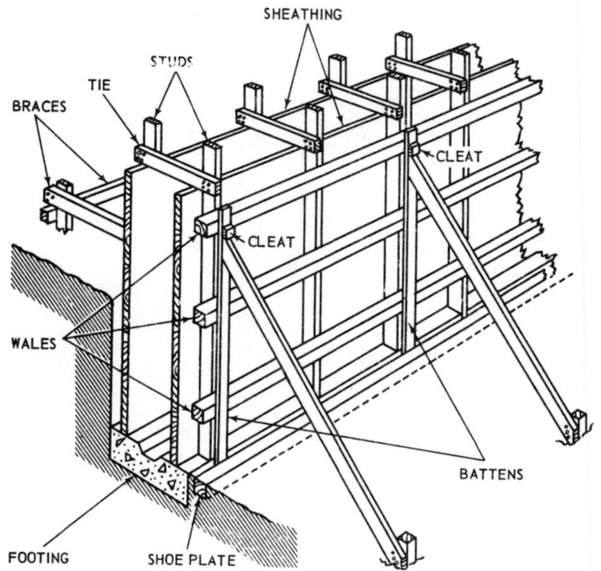

Fig. 49. Wall form with wales.

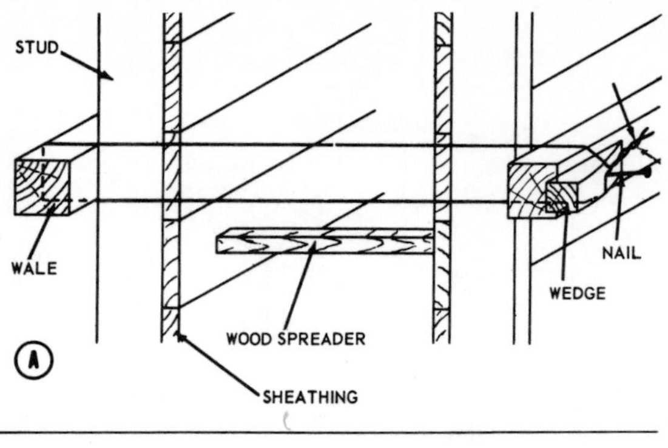

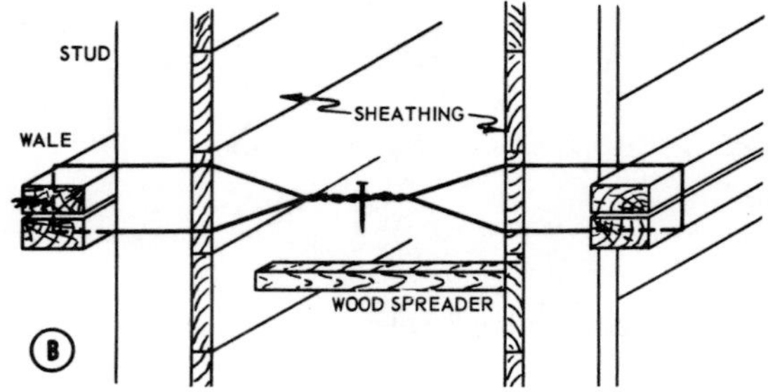

Fig. 50. Wire ties for wall forms.

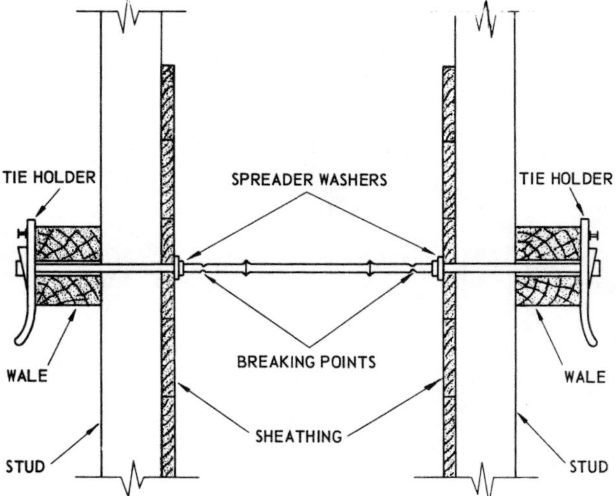

Fig. 51. Snap tie.

holders can be detached to strip the forms. After the forms are stripped, a special wrench is used to break off the outer sections of rod. These break off at the breaking points, located about 1 inch (2.5 cm.) inside the surface of the concrete. Small surface holes remain, which can be plugged with grout if necessary.

Another type of wall form tie is the *tie rod* shown in Fig. 52. The rod in this type consists of three sections—an inner section threaded on both ends, and two threaded outer sections. The inner section, with the cones set to the thickness of the wall, is placed between the forms, and the outer sections are passed through the wales and sheathing and threaded into the cone nuts. The clamps are then threaded up on the outer sections to bring the forms to bear against the cone nuts. After the concrete hardens, the clamps are loosened and the outer sections of rod are removed by threading them out of the cone nuts. After the forms are stripped, the cone nuts are removed from the concrete by threading them off the inner sections of rod with a special wrench. The remaining cone-shaped surface holes may be plugged with grout. The inner sections of rod remain in the concrete. The outer sections and the cone nuts may be re-used indefinitely.

Wall forms are usually constructed as separate panels, each made by nailing sheathing to a number of studs. Panels are joined to each other in line as shown in Fig. 53. A method of joining panels at a corner is shown in Fig. 54.

Column Form

Figure 55 shows a column form. Since the rate of placing in a column form is very high, and since the bursting pressure exerted on the form by the concrete increases directly with the rate of placing, a column form must be securely braced by the yokes shown in Fig. 55. Since the bursting pressure is greater at the bottom of the form than it is at the top, the yokes are placed closer together at the bottom than they are at the top.

The panels for the form are made up first by nailing the yoke members to the sheathing. On two panels the yoke members cone flush with the edges of the sheathing, and on the other two

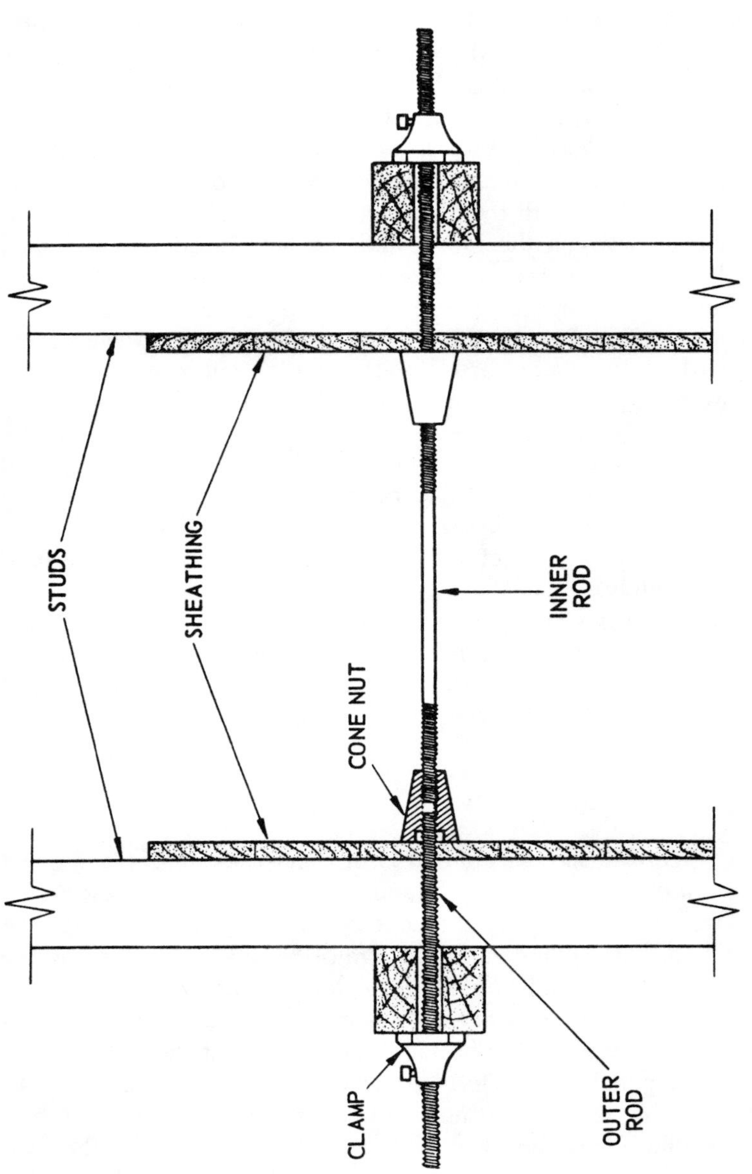

Fig. 52. Tie rod.

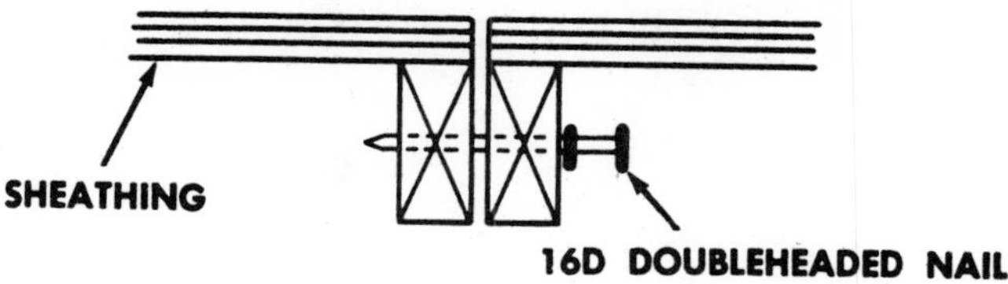

Fig. 53. Joining wall form panels together in line.

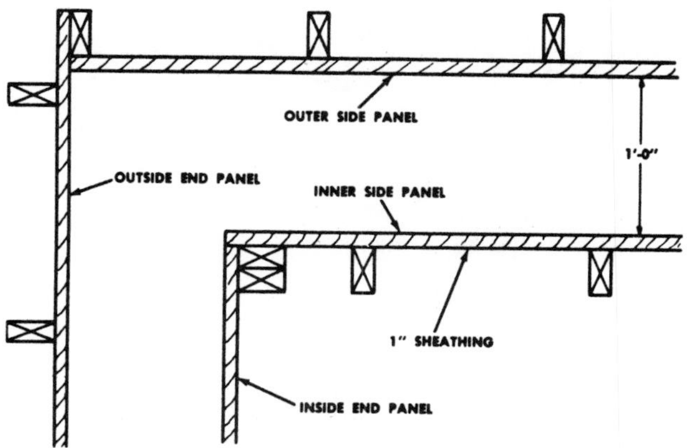

Fig. 54. Method of joining wall form panels at a corner.

they project beyond the edge as shown in Fig. 55. Bolt holes are bored in these projections as shown in Fig. 55, and bolts are inserted as shown to back up the wedges which are driven to tighten the yokes.

Beam and Girder Forms

The type of construction to be used for *beam forms* depends upon whether the form is to be removed in one piece or whether the sides are to be stripped and the bottom left in place until the concrete develops enough strength to permit removal of the shoring. The latter type beam form is preferred and details for this type are shown in Fig. 56. Beam forms are subjected to very little bursting pressure but must be shored up at frequent intervals to prevent sagging under the weight of the fresh concrete.

The bottom of the form has the same width as the beam and is

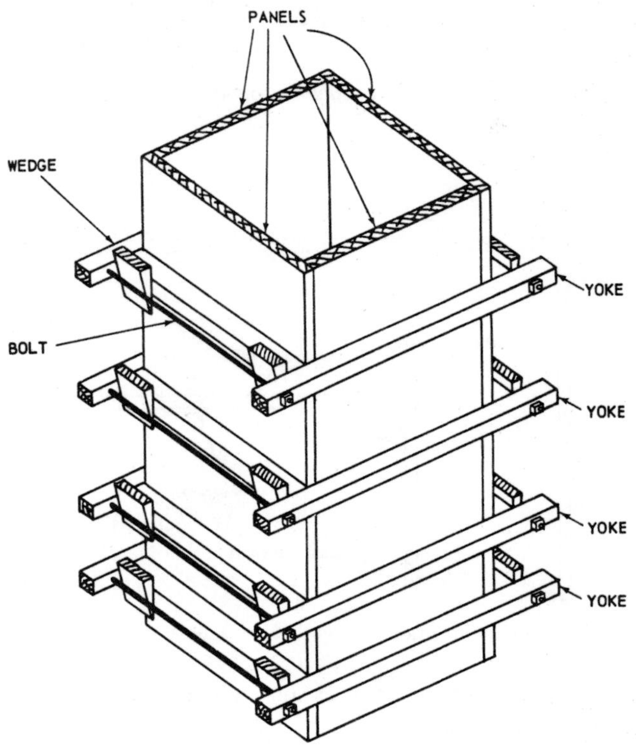

Fig. 55. Column form.

in one piece for the full width. The sides of the form should be 1-inch (2.5-cm.) thick tongue-and-groove sheathing and should lap over the bottom as shown in Fig. 57. The sheathing is nailed to 2- × 4-inch (5- × 10-cm.) struts placed on 3-foot (.91-meter) centers. A 1- × 4-inch (2.5- × 10-cm.) piece is nailed along the struts. These pieces support the joist for the floor panel, as shown in Fig. 57. The beam sides of the form are not nailed to the bottom but are held in position by continuous strips as shown in Fig. 57, E. The cross pieces nailed on top serve as spreaders. After erection, the slab panel joists hold the beam sides in position. Girder forms are the same as beam forms ex-

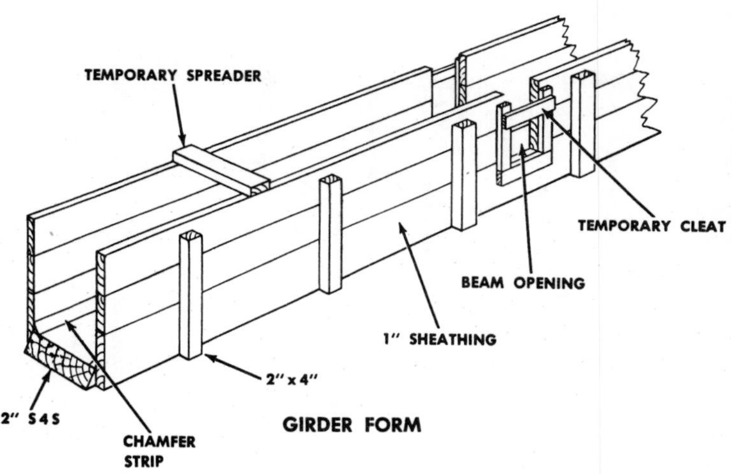

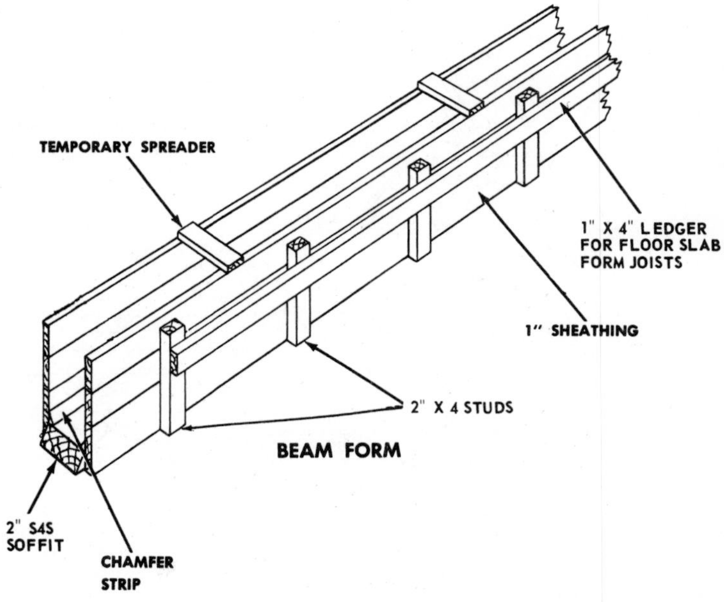

Fig. 56. Beam and girder forms.

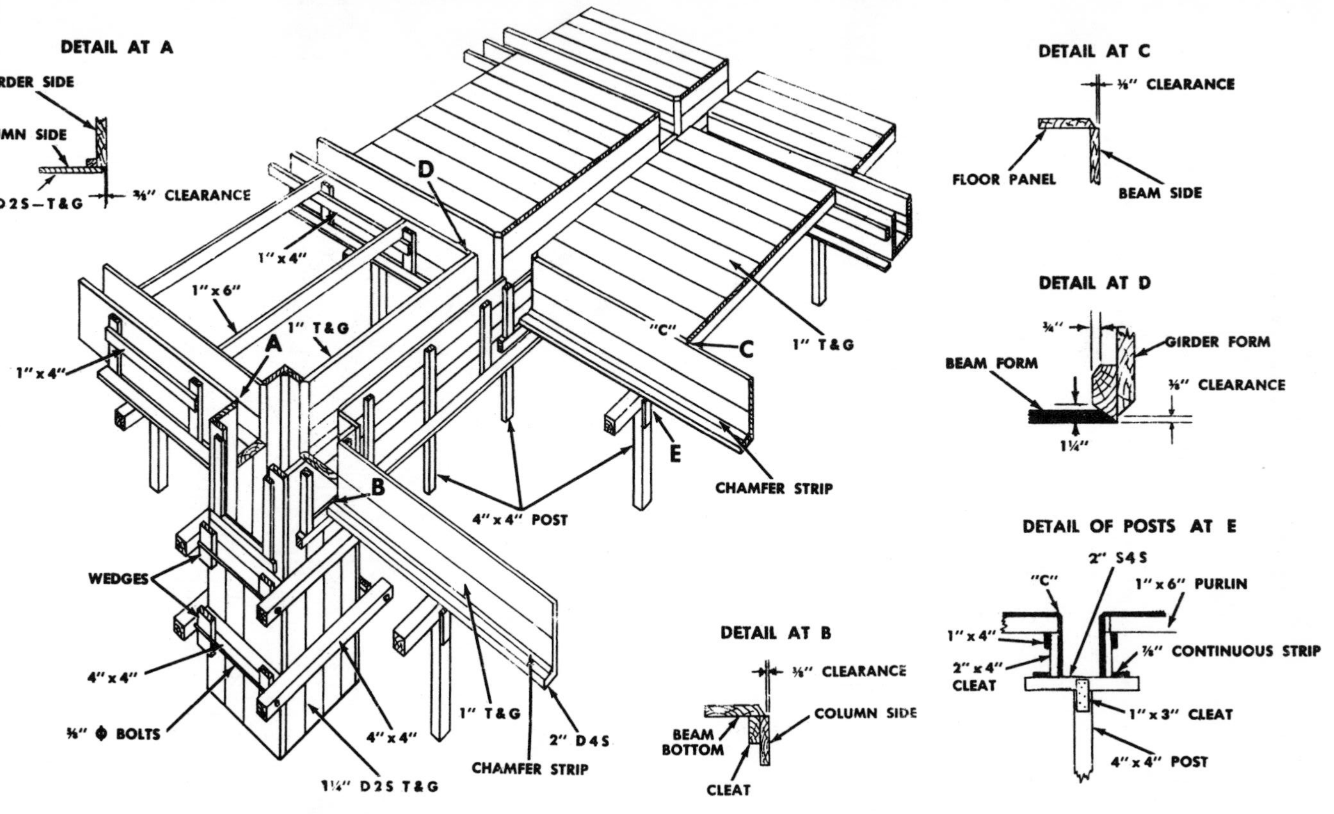

Fig. 57. Assembly details of beam and floor forms.

cept that the sides are notched to receive the beam forms. Temporary cleats should be nailed across the beam opening when the girder form is being handled.

The entire method of assembling beam and girder forms is illustrated in Fig. 57. The connection of the beam and girder is shown in Fig. 57, D. The beam bottom butts up tightly against the side of the girder form and rests on a 2- × 4-inch (5- × 10-cm.) cleat nailed to the girder side. Fig. 57, C, shows the joint between beam and slab panel and Fig. 57, A and B, show the joint between girder and column. The clearances given in these details are needed for stripping and also to allow for movement that will occur due to the weight of the fresh concrete. The 4- × 4-inch (10- × 10-cm.) posts used for shoring the beams and girders should be spaced so as to provide support for the concrete and forms and wedged as shown in Fig. 57, E.

Floor Forms

Floor panels are built as shown in Fig. 58. The 1-inch tongue-and-groove sheathing or ¾-inch (1.9-cm.) plywood is nailed to 1- × 4- (2.5- × 10-cm.) cleats on 3-foot (.91-meters) centers. These panels are supported by 2 × 6 (5 × 15 cm.) joists. Spacing of

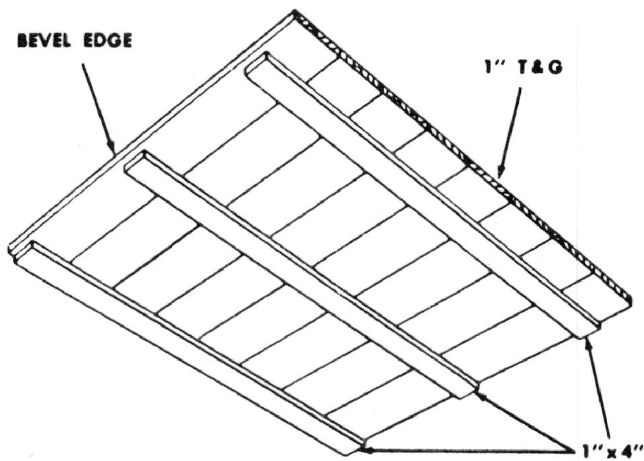

Fig. 58. Form for floor slab.

joists depends on the thickness of the concrete slab and the span of the beams. If the slab spans the distance between two walls, the panels are used in the same manner as when beams support the floor slab.

Stair Forms

Figure 59 shows a method for building stair forms up to 3 feet (.91 meters) in width. The sloping wood platform forming the underside of the steps should be 1-inch (2.54-cm.) tongue-and-groove sheathing. This platform should extend 12 inches (30.5 cm.) beyond each side of the stairs to support stringer bracing blocks. The back of the panel is shored with 4 × 4 (10.2 × 10.2-cm.) pieces as shown in Fig. 59. The 2 × 6 (5.1 × 15.2-cm.) cleats nailed to the shoring should rest on wedges to make adjustment easy and to make removal of the posts easy. The side stringers are 2 × 12 (5.1 × 30.5-cm.) pieces cut as required for the tread and risers. The riser should be 2-inch (5.1-cm.) material beveled as shown in Fig. 59.

OILING AND WETTING FORMS

Before concrete is placed in forms which are to be stripped, the forms must be coasted with a suitable form oil or other mate-

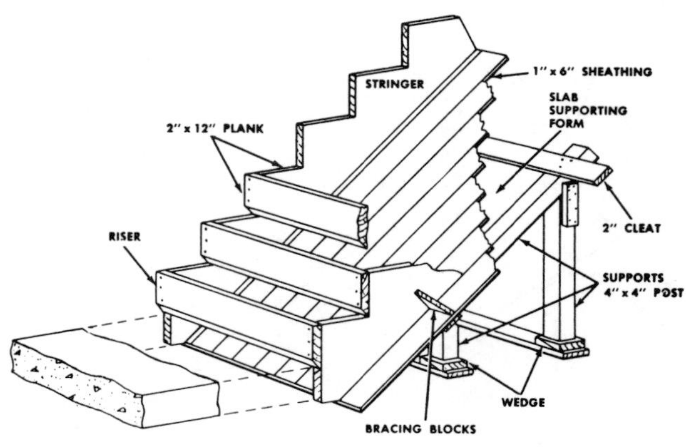

Fig. 59. Stairway form.

rial which will prevent bond between the forms and the concrete. Almost any light-bodied petroleum oil makes a satisfactory bond-preventer for wood forms. The use of oil should be avoided where finished concrete surfaces are to be painted. However, for forms which are to be re-used, a compound which will prevent bond and protect the form material is preferable.

On plywood forms, lacquer is preferred to ordinary oil. Commercial lacquers and similar preparations are also good. If the forms are to be re-used a good many times, painting is a good way to preserve them.

Ordinary petroleum oils which are satisfactory for wood forms may not prevent bond between concrete and steel forms. For steel forms certain specially compounded petroleum oils, such as synthetic castor-oil, and some types of marine engine oils should be used.

Since any form oil dropped on the reinforcing steel will prevent bond between the steel and the concrete, forms should be oiled before the steel is set in place. (*See* Chap. 8, Reinforced Concrete.) Columns panels and wall form panels must be oiled before they are erected. Surfaces which are to be oiled must be smooth, and the oil (which may be applied by brush, sprayer, or swab) must cover evenly and without holidays.

If form oil or its equivalent is not available, the forms may be thoroughly wetted to help prevent sticking. This method of bond-prevention should be used only when a suitable bond-preventing compound is unobtainable.

SAFETY PRECAUTIONS

The following safety rules apply to form construction and removal.

Construction

1. Consider protruding nails as the principal source of accidents on form work.
2. Inspect tools frequently.

3. Place mud sills under shoring that rests on the ground.
4. On elevated forms, take care to protect men on scaffolds and on the ground.
5. Do not raise large form panels in heavy wind.
6. Brace all shoring securely to prevent collapse of form work.

Stripping

1. Permit only workmen doing the stripping in the immediate area.
2. Do not remove forms until the concrete has set.
3. Pile stripped forms immediately to avoid congestion, exposed nails, and other hazards.
4. Cut wires under tension with caution to avoid backlash.

REMOVING FORMS

It is generally advantageous to leave forms in place as long as possible for better curing. However, there are times when it is desirable to remove the forms as soon as possible. *For example*, where a rubbed finish is specified, forms must be removed early to permit the first rubbing before the concrete becomes too hard. It is often necessary to remove forms quickly to permit their immediate re-use.

In any case, forms should *not* be removed until the concrete is strong enough to satisfactorily carry the stresses from both the dead load and any construction loads that may be imposed on it. The concrete should be hard enough so that the surfaces will not be injured in any way when reasonable care is used in removing forms. In general, the side forms of reasonably thick sections may be removed 12 to 24 hours after concreting. For most conditions it is better to rely on the strength of the concrete as determined by test than to arbitrarily select the time to remove the forms.

A minimum compressive strength of 500 psi (227 kgs. per sq. cm.) should be attained before concrete is exposed to freezing. The age-strength relationship should be determined from repre-

Strength, psi	Age	
	Type I or Normal cement	Type III or High-Early-Strength cement
500	24 hours	12 hours
750	1½ days	18 hours
1,500	3½ days	1½ days
2,000	5½ days	2½ days

TABLE 9. AGE-STRENGTH RELATIONSHIP OF AIR-ENTRAINED CONCRETE.

sentative samples of concrete used in the structure and cured under job conditions. Table 9 shows the ages required to attain certain strengths under average conditions, such as, air-entrained concrete made with a water-cement ratio of about 0.53. It should be remembered that strengths are affected by the materials used, temperature, and other conditions. The time required for form removal, therefore, will vary from job to job.

Forms should be designed and constructed with some thought as to their removal with a minimum of danger to the concrete. With *wood forms* the use of too large or too many nails should be avoided to facilitate removal and reduce injury to form materials.

A pinch bar or other metal tool should *not* be placed against the concrete to wedge forms loose. If it is necessary to wedge between the concrete and the form, only wooden wedges should be used. Stripping should be started at some distance away and moved toward a projection. This relieves pressure against projecting corners and reduces the chance of breaking off the edges.

Recessed forms require special attention. They should be left in place as long as possible so they will shrink away from the concrete. Wooden wedges should be driven gradually behind the form and the form should be tapped lightly to break it away from the concrete. The forms should not be jerked off after wedging has been started at one end, as this is almost certain to break the edges of the concrete.

Chapter 8

Reinforced Concrete

Concrete is strong in compression, but relatively weak in tension. The reverse is true for slender steel bars and when the two materials are used together one makes up for the deficiency of the other. When steel is embedded in concrete in a manner which assists it in carrying imposed loads, the combination is known as reinforced concrete. The steel may consist of welded wire mesh or expanded metal mesh, but commonly consists of steel bars called *reinforcing bars.*

Before placing reinforcing steel in forms, all form oiling should be completed. Oil on reinforcing bars is objectionable because it reduces the bond between the bars and the concrete. Use a piece of burlap to clean the bars of rust, scale, grease, mud, or other foreign matter. A tight film of rust or mill scale is not objectionable.

TYPES OF TIES

There are several types of ties that can be used with deformed bars—some are more effective than others. Figure 1 shows the six types used: (A) snap tie or simple tie; (B) wall tie; (C) saddle tie; (D) saddle tie with twist; (E) double strung single tie; and (F) cross tie or figure-eight tie. You will most likely only be concerned with the snap tie (Fig. 1, A) and saddle tie (Fig. 1, C).

When making the *snap tie* or *simple tie*, the wire is simply wrapped once around the two crossing bars in a diagonal manner with the two ends on top, and these are twisted together with a pair of sidecutters until they are very tight against the bars. Then the loose ends of the wire are cut off. This tie is used mostly on floor slabs.

When making the *saddle tie*, the wires pass halfway around

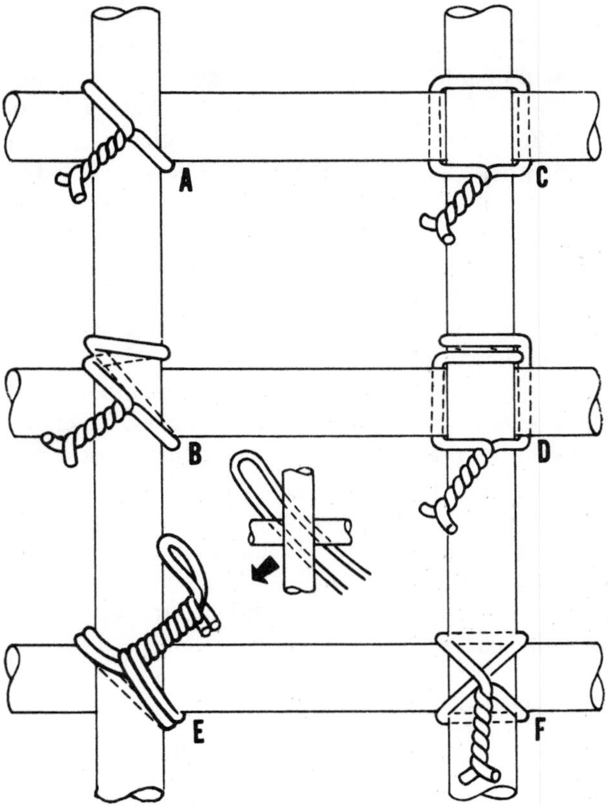

Fig. 1. Types of ties.

one of the bars on either side of the crossing bar and are brought squarely or diagonally around the crossing bar, with the ends twisted together and cut off. This tie is used on special location (walls).

When you are tying reinforcing bars you must have a supply of tie wire available. There are several ways you can carry your tie wire. One way is to make a coil 18 inches (45 cm.) in diameter, then slip it around your neck and under one arm. This leaves a free end for tying. Coil about 9 pounds of wire (4.1 kgs.).

Another way to carry the tie wire is to take pieces of wire about 9 inches (23 cm.) long, fold them and hook one end in your belt; this will enable you to pull the wires out as needed. The tools needed in trying reinforcing bars include a 6-foot (1.8-meter) folding rule, sidecutters, leather gloves, 50-foot (20-meter) tape measure, and keel crayon (yellow, red, or blue).

The proper location for the reinforcing bars is usually given on drawings. In order for the structure to withstand the loads it must carry, place the steel in the position shown. Secure the bars in position so that when the concrete is placed, they will not move. This can be accomplished by the use of the reinforcing bar supports shown in Figs. 2, 3, and 4.

Footings and other principal structural members which are against the ground should have at least 3 inches (7.6 cm.) of concrete between steel and ground. If the concrete surface is to be in contact with the ground or exposed to the weather after removal of the forms, the protective covering of concrete over the steel should be 2 inches (5 cm.). It may be reduced to 1½ inches (3.8 cm.) for beams and columns, and ¾-inch (1.9 cm.) for slabs and interior wall surfaces, but it should be 2 inches (5 cm.) for all exterior wall surfaces.

LAPPING WIRE MESH

Specifications and designs are usually used when lapping wire mesh. However, as a rule of thumb, one complete lap is usually sufficient with a minimum of 2 inches (5.08 cm.) between laps. Whenever the rule of thumb is not allowed, use the end and side lap method.

In the *end lap method* the two longitudinal side wires are placed one alongside and overlapping the other, and then are tied with a snap tie every three feet.

Where splices in reinforcing steel are not dimensioned on the drawings, the bars should be lapped not less than 30 times the bar diameter, nor less than 12 inches (30 cm.).

The stress in a tension bar can be transmitted through the concrete and into another adjoining bar by a lap splice of proper

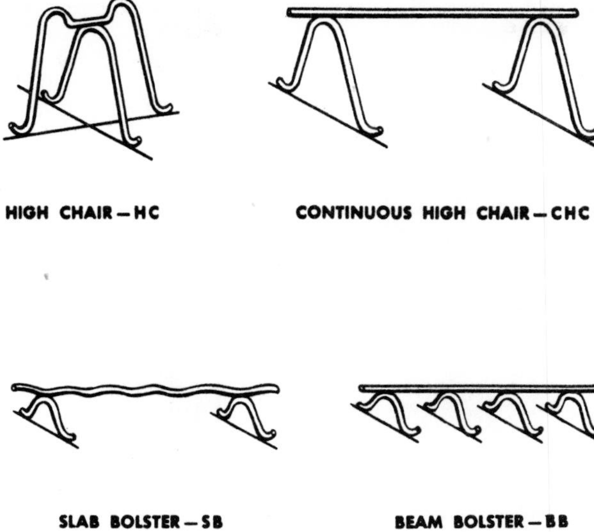

Fig. 2. Devices used to support horizontal reinforcing bars.

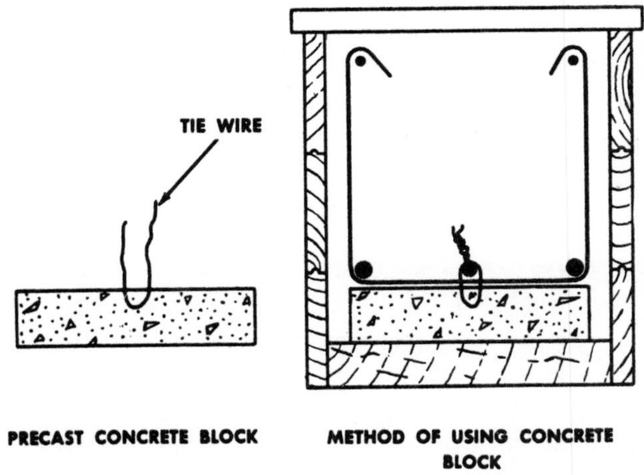

Fig. 3. Precast concrete block used for reinforcing steel support.

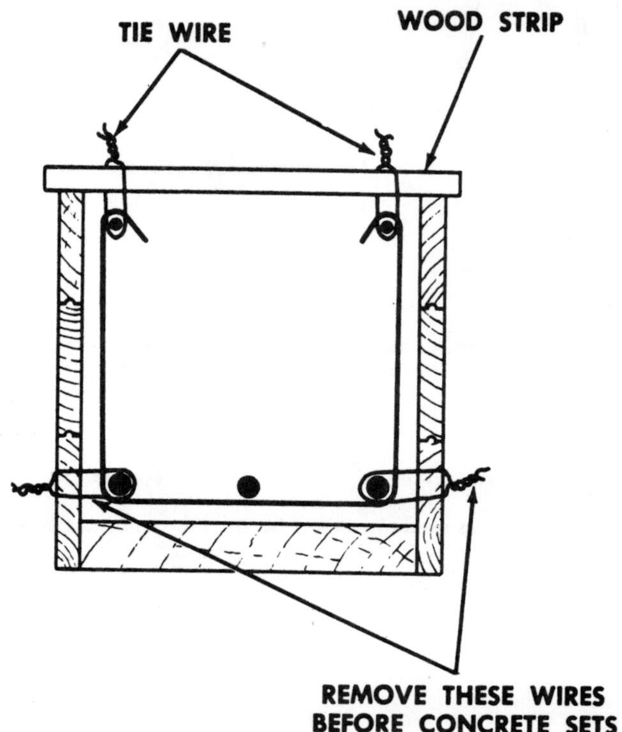

Fig. 4. Beam reinforcing steel hung in place.

length. The lap is expressed as the number of bar diameters. If the bar is #2 make the lap at least 12 inches (30 cm.). Tie the bars together with a snap tie as shown in Fig. 5.

REINFORCING STEEL FOR FLOOR SLAB

The support for reinforcing steel in floor slabs is shown in Fig. 6. The height of the *slab bolster* is determined by the concrete protective cover required. Concrete blocks made of sand-cement mortar can be used in place of the slab bolster. Wood blocks should never be used for this purpose if there is any possi-

Fig. 5. Bars spliced by lapping.

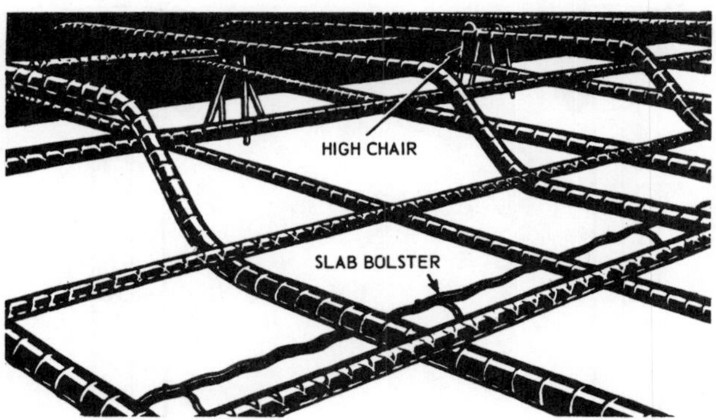

Fig. 6. Reinforcing steel for a floor slab.

bility that the concrete can become wet and if the construction is of a permanent type. *Bar chairs* of a type shown in Fig. 6 can be obtained in heights up to 6 inches (15 cm.). If a height greater than this is required, make the chair of No. 0 soft annealed iron wire. Tie the bars together at frequent intervals with a snap tie where they cross to hold the bars firmly in position.

SECURING COLUMN

Steel for column ties may be assembled with the verticals into cages, by laying the vertical bars for one side of the column horizontally across a couple of sawhorses. The proper number of ties are slipped over the bars, the remaining vertical bars are added, and then the ties are spaced out as required by the placing plans. A sufficient number of intersections are wired together to make the assembly rigid, so that it may be hoisted and set as a unit.

After the column is raised it is tied to the dowels or reinforcing steel carried up from below. This holds it firmly in position at the base. The column form is erected and the reinforcing steel is tied to the column form at 5-foot (1.5-meter) intervals as shown in Fig. 7.

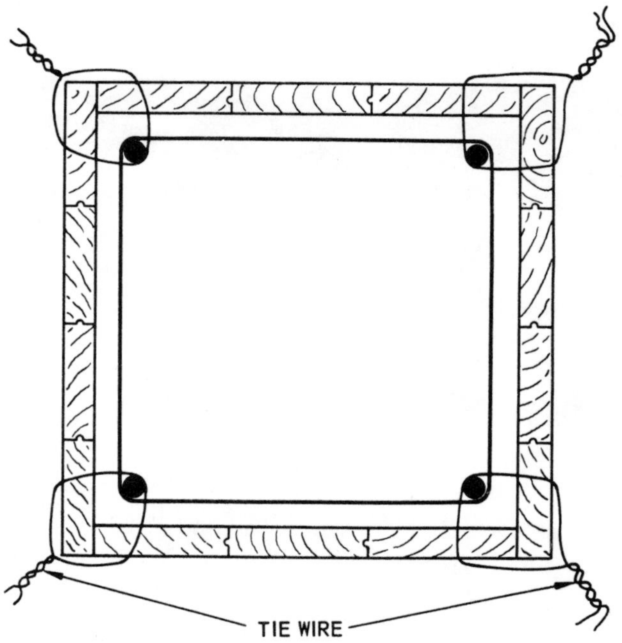

Fig. 7. Securing column reinforcing steel against displacement.

USES OF METAL SUPPORTS

The use of metal supports to hold beam reinforcing steel in position is shown in Fig. 8. *Note* the position of the beam bolster. The stirrups are tied to the main reinforcing steel with a snap tie. Wherever possible you should assemble the stirrups and main reinforcing steel outside the form and then place the assembled unit in position. Wood blocks should be substituted for the metal supports only if there is no possibility of the concrete

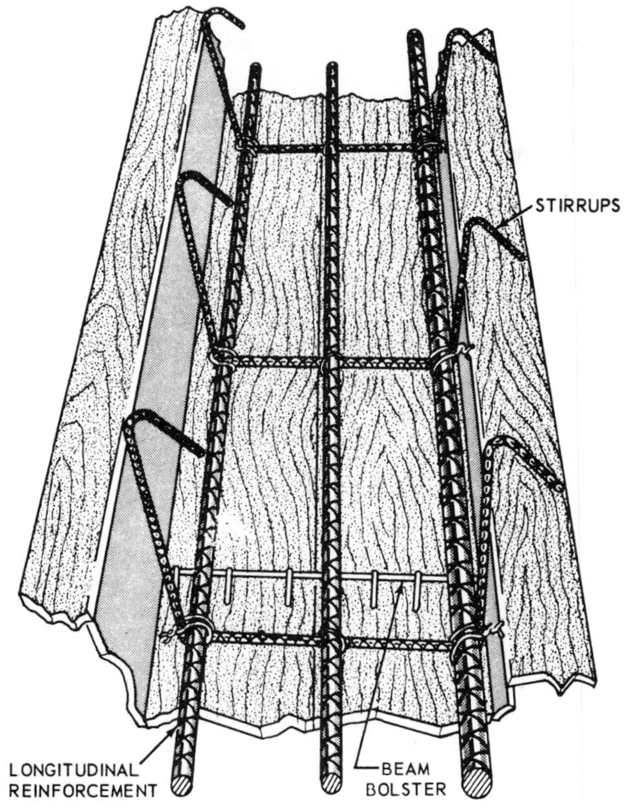

Fig. 8. Beam reinforcing steel supported on beam bolsters.

becoming wet or if the construction is known to be temporary. Precast concrete blocks, as shown in Fig. 3, may be substituted for metal supports, or if none of the types of bar supports previously described seems suitable, the method shown in Fig. 4 may be used.

PLACING STEEL IN WALLS

Steel placement in walls is the same as for columns except that the steel is erected in place and not preassembled. Horizontal steel is tied to vertical steel at least three times in any bar

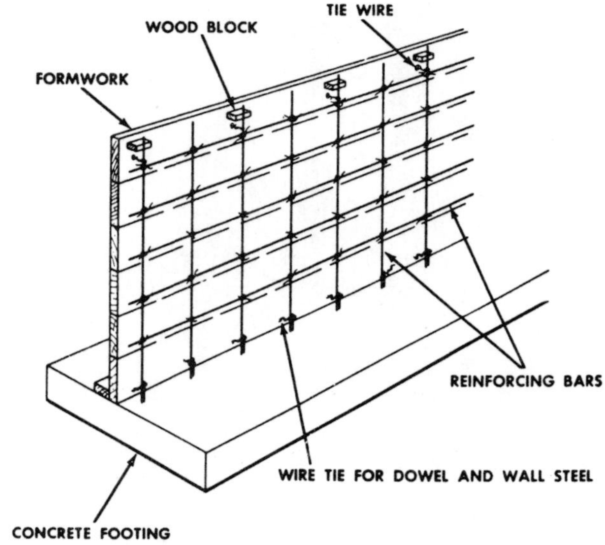

Fig. 9. Steel in place in a wall.

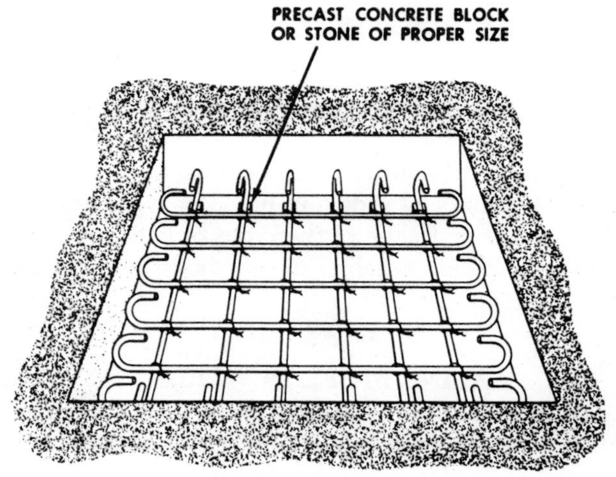

Fig. 10. Steel in place in a footing.

length. Steel placed in a wall is shown in Fig. 9. The wood block is removed when the form has been filled up to the level of the block. For high walls, ties in between the top and bottom should be used.

PLACING STEEL IN FOOTINGS

Steel is placed in footings very much as it is placed in floor slabs. Stones rather than steel supports may be used to support the steel at the proper distance above the subgrade. Steel mats in small footings are generally preassembled and placed after the forms have been set. A typical arrangement is shown in Fig. 10. Steel mats in large footings are constructed in place.

Chapter 9

Placing and Consolidating Concrete

Preparation prior to concreting includes compacting, trimming, and moistening the subgrade; erecting the forms; and setting the reinforcing steel. A moist subgrade is especially important in hot weather to prevent extraction of water from the concrete. Where concrete is to be deposited on rock, all loose material should be removed before concrete is placed. When rock must be cut out, the surfaces in general should be vertical or horizontal rather than sloping.

Forms should be clean, tight, adequately braced, and constructed of materials that will impart the desired texture to the finished concrete. Sawdust, nails, and other debris should be removed before concrete is placed. Wood forms should be moistened before placing concrete, otherwise they will absorb water from the concrete and swell. Forms also should be treated with a parting agent such as oil or lacquer to facilitate their removal. For architectural concrete, lacquer or emulsified stearates are used since they are non-staining.

Reinforcing steel should be clean and free of loose rust or mill scale at the time concrete is placed. Mortar coatings need not be removed from reinforcing steel and other items to be embedded in the concrete if a lift is to be completed within a few hours. However, loose dried mortar should be removed from items that extend outward for later lifts of concrete. (*See* Chap. 7, Forms and Form Making; *see also* Chap. 8, Reinforced Concrete.)

PREPARING HARDENED CONCRETE

When fresh concrete is placed on hardened concrete, certain

precautions should be taken to secure a well-bonded watertight joint. The hardened concrete should be clean, moist, fairly level, and reasonably rough, with some coarse aggregate particles exposed. Any laitance or soft mortar should be removed from the top surface of the hardened concrete.

At horizontal construction joints the surface of the lower layer can be prepared either before or after the concrete hardens. In some types of construction, such as dams, the surface of the concrete is cut with a high-velocity air-water jet to expose a clean surface of sound concrete before final setting of the concrete has occurred. This work is usually done four to twelve hours after placing. Such a surface should be protected until concreting is resumed, usually with a 2-inch (5-cm.) layer of wet sand or wet burlap. Sandblasting is another method of preparing the surface of hardened concrete. When the surface is prepared after the concrete has hardened, it is cleaned by wet sandblasting and washing.

For two-course floors, the top of the lower course may be broomed, just before it sets, with a steel or stiff fiber broom. The surface should be level but heavily scored and free of laitance. It must then be protected and thoroughly cleaned just before the grout coat and top course are placed. The *grout*, which is a mixture of portland cement and water, should be scrubbed into the surface of the slab a short distance ahead of the top course.

The surface of old concrete, upon which a topping is to be placed, must be thoroughly roughened and cleaned of all dust, loose particles, grease, oil, or other material. In most cases it is necessary to remove the entire surface. Chipping the surface with pneumatic tools or using other mechanical means are satisfactory methods for exposing sound concrete.

In wall construction and other reinforced concrete work, it may not be convenient to sandblast or to use water jets for cleaning joint surfaces. Good results have been obtained by constructing the forms to the level of the joint, overfilling the forms 1 to 2 inches (2.5 to 5 cm.), and then removing the excess concrete just before setting occurs. The concrete then can be finished with stiff brushes. (*See* Chap. 8, Reinforced Concrete.)

Hardened concrete should be moistened thoroughly before

new concrete is placed on it. However, its surface should be completely free of shiny spots that indicate free moisture. Although laboratory studies indicate that a better bond is obtained on a dry surface, experience with large projects has shown that a damp *but not wet* surface, free of standing water, gives better construction control.

PLACING MORTAR AT BOTTOM OF LIFT

Where concrete is to be placed on hardened concrete or on rock, a layer of mortar is needed on the hard surface to provide a cushion against which the new concrete can be placed. The fresh mortar prevents stone pockets and assists in securing a tight joint. The mortar should have a slump of less than 6 inches (15 cm.) and should be made of the same materials as the concrete, but without the coarse aggregate. It should be placed to a thickness of about ½ inch (1.3 cm.), and worked well into the surface irregularities.

PLACING CONCRETE

Concrete should be placed as near as possible to its final position. In slab construction, placing should be started around the perimeter at one end of the work with each batch dumped against previously placed concrete. The concrete should not be dumped in separate piles and the piles then leveled and worked together. Nor should the concrete be deposited in big piles and then moved horizontally to its final position. This practice results in segregation because mortar tends to flow ahead of coarser material. (*See* Chap. 11, Finishing Concrete Slabs.)

In general, concrete should be placed in horizontal layers of uniform thickness, each layer being thoroughly consolidated before the next is placed. Layers should be 6- to 20-inches (15- to 50-cm.) thick for reinforced members, 15- to 20-inches (38- to 50-cm.) thick for mass work. The thickness depends on the width between forms and the amount of reinforcement.

Concrete should not be moved horizontally over too long a

distance within forms or in slabs. In some work, such as against sloping wingwalls or beneath openings in walls, it is necessary to move the concrete horizontally within forms. The horizontal distance should be minimized since excess water and mortar are forced ahead of the moving concrete. This produces a poorer quality of concrete where increased water-cement ratio finally occurs. (*See* Fig. 1.)

In walls, the first batches in each lift should be placed at either end of the section, and the placing should then progress toward the center. This method also should be used in placing beams and girders. In all cases, water should be prevented from collecting at the ends and corners of forms and along form faces. In sloping wingwalls water may collect along the sloping top surface, an area most vulnerable to weathering. However, if the top form boards of the sloping face are omitted, the concrete can be placed directly in this section of the wall. If necessary, boards forming the sloping surface may be placed as concreting progresses.

Fig. 1. Pumping is a point-to-point delivery system in which concrete is deposited in its final position in the forms with little necessity for further handling of the mix. With pumping there is less chance for segregation.

Drop chutes will prevent incrustation of dried mortar on reinforcement and forms. If the placement can be completed before mortar dries, drop chutes may not be needed. The height of free fall of concrete need not be limited unless separation of coarse particles occurs, in which case a limit of 3 to 4 feet (.9 to 1.2 meters) may be adequate.

Concrete is sometimes placed through openings, referred to as *windows*, in the sides of tall narrow forms. When a chute discharges directly through the opening there is danger of segregation. A collecting hopper outside the opening permits the concrete to flow more smoothly through the opening and there is much less tendency to segregate.

When concrete is placed in tall forms at a fairly rapid rate, there is likely to be some bleeding of water to the top surface, especially with non-air-entrained concrete. Bleeding can be reduced by more slowly placing concrete of a stiffer consistency. When practicable, the concrete should be placed to a level about a foot (30 cm.) below the top in high walls and an hour or so should be allowed for settling. Concreting should be resumed before setting occurs to avoid formation of cold joints. It is a good practice to overfill the form by an inch (2.5 cm.) or so and to cut off the excess concrete after it has partly stiffened. Another means of controlling this accumulation of bleed water is to increase the amount of coarse aggregate in the mixture as the placement approaches the top of the lift.

To avoid cracking due to settlement, concrete in columns and walls should be allowed to stand for at least two hours, and preferably overnight, before concrete is placed in slabs, beams, or girders framing into them. Hauches and column capitals are considered as part of the floor or roof and should be placed integrally with them.

CONSOLIDATING CONCRETE

Consolidation is the process of compacting fresh concrete to mold it within the forms and around embedded parts and reinforcement, and to eliminate voids other than entrained air. It may be accomplished by hand or by mechanical methods. The method chosen depends on the consistency of the mix and the placing conditions, such as intricacy of the form, amount of reinforcement, and the like.

Plastic, flowing mixes may be consolidated by hand, thrusting a rod or other suitable tool into the concrete. The rod should be long enough to reach the bottom of the form or lift being placed, and thin enough to pass between the reinforcing steel and forms. A mix that can be consolidated readily by hand tools should not be consolidated by mechanical methods because the concrete is likely to segregate under this action. (*See* Fig. 2.)

Proper use of mechanical consolidation methods makes possible the placement of stiff mixes with low water-cement ratios and higher coarse aggregate contents, resulting in a reduction in concrete costs. The most popular mechanical methods include: pneumatic ramming used to compact very stiff mixes in precast units; spinning or centrifugation used in making pipes, poles, and piles; shock or drop tables used in the manufacture of architectural precast units; and vibration.

Vibration is the most widely used method (*see* Fig. 3). When concrete is vibrated, the internal friction between the coarse aggregate particles is temporarily destroyed and the concrete behaves like a liquid, and settles in the forms under the action of gravity. Friction is reestablished as soon as vibration stops.

Vibrators are usually characterized by their frequency of vibration, expressed as the number of vibrations per minute, and by the amplitude of vibration, which is the deviation in inches from the point of rest. They may be of the internal or external type.

Internal or *immersion-type vibrators* are commonly used to consolidate concrete in walls, columns, beams, and slabs. These vibrators consist of a vibrating head connected to a driving motor by a flexible shaft. Inside the head an unbalanced weight rotates at high speed, causing the head to revolve in a circular orbit. The motor may be electric, gasoline, or air-powered. The vibrating head is usually cylindrical and its diameter may range from ¾ to 7 inches (2 to 18 cm.). Some vibrators have the motor built into the head, which is then generally at least 2 inches (5.08 cm.) in diameter. The performance of a vibrator is affected by

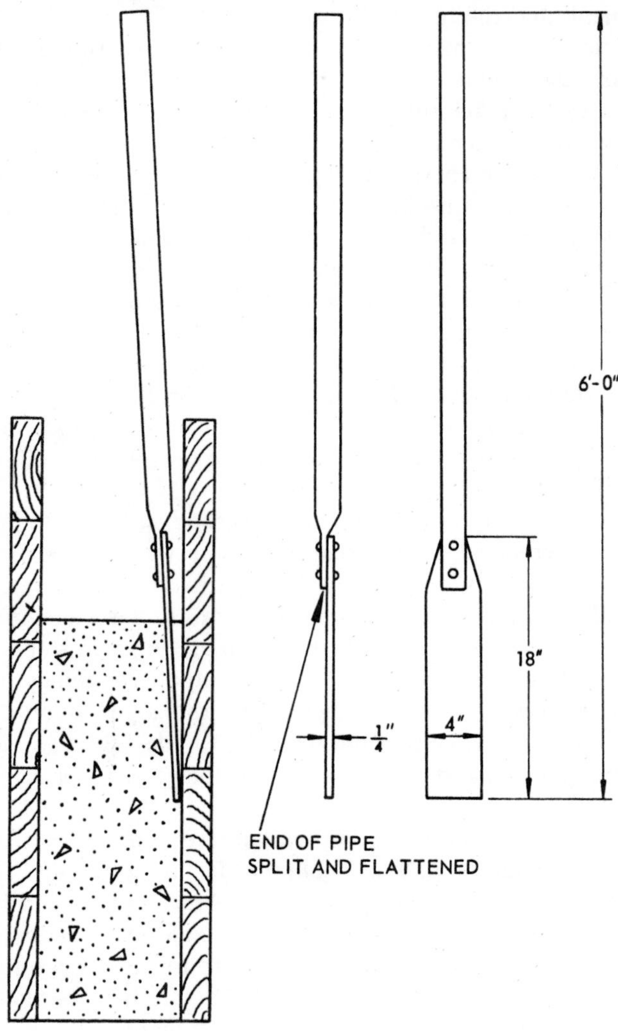

Fig. 2. Consolidation by spading and the spading tool.

Fig. 3. Vibration of such low-slump concrete, even in narrow forms, results in smooth surfaces and clean lines.

the dimension of the vibrator head as well as its frequency and amplitude.

Small-diameter vibrators have high frequencies, ranging from 10,000 to 15,000 vpm (vibrations per minute) and low amplitudes ranging between 0.015 and 0.03 inches (.38 to .76 mm.). As the diameter increases, the frequency decreases and the amplitude increases. The effective radius of action increases with increasing diameter. Vibrators with a diameter of ¾ to 1½ inches (2 to 3.8 cm.) have a radius of action ranging between 3 and 6 inches (7.6 and 15.2 cm.), whereas the radius of action for vibrators of 2- to 3½-inches (5 to 9-cm.) diameter ranges between 7 and 14 inches (17.8 and 36 cm.).

Proper use of internal vibrators is important for the best result. Whenever possible vibrators should be lowered vertically into the concrete at regular intervals and allowed to descend by gravity. The vibrator should penetrate to the bottom of the layer being placed and at least 6 inches (15 cm.) into any preceding layer. (In thin slabs the vibrator should be inserted at an angle or horizontally, if need be, so that the head is fully embedded.) The distance between insertions should be about one and one-half times the radius of action so that the *spheres of influence* overlap a few inches. The vibrator should be held stationary for five to fifteen seconds until adequate consolidation is attained. This can be recognized by a leveling of the top surface, the appearance of a thin film of glistening paste, and the cessation of large bubbles of entrapped air escaping at the surface.

Leaving a vibrator immersed in concrete after the paste accumulates over the head results in nonuniformity. The length of time that a vibrator should be left in the concrete is a function of the slump of the concrete; high-slump concrete requires little or no vibration. Vibrators should not be used to move concrete horizontally since this causes segregation.

Revibration or delayed vibration of previously compacted concrete may be done intentionally or it may occur when the underlying layer has partially hardened. This practice has been used to improve bond between concrete and reinforcing steel. In general, if concrete becomes plastic under revibration, this action is not harmful and may be beneficial.

External vibrators may be form vibrators, vibrating tables, or surface vibrators, such as vibrating screeds, plate vibrators, vibratory roller screeds, or vibratory hand floats or trowels.

The form vibrators, which are designed to be securely attached to the outside of the forms, are especially useful for consolidating concrete in members that are very thin or congested with reinforcement. In many situations they are used to supplement internal vibration, and they are very well suited for stiff mixes where internal vibrators cannot be used.

Form vibrators may be either electrically or pneumatically operated. They should be spaced so as to distribute the vibration uniformly over the form—the most adequate spacing is best found by experimentation. Sometimes it may be necessary to operate some of the form vibrators at a different frequency for better results. Therefore, it is recommended that form vibrators be equipped with controls to regulate their frequency and amplitude. The duration of vibration is generally between one and two minutes.

Form vibrators should not be applied within the top few feet of vertical forms. Vibration of the top of the form, particularly if the form is thin or inadequately stiffened, causes an in-and-out movement that can create a gap between the concrete and the form. Accordingly, internal vibrators are recommended for use in this area of vertical forms.

In heavily reinforced sections where an internal vibrator cannot be inserted, it is sometimes helpful to vibrate the reinforcing bars by attaching a form vibrator to their exposed portions. This practice eliminates air and water entrapped underneath the reinforcing bars and increases the bond between the bars and the surrounding concrete, provided the concrete is still mobile under the action of vibration. Internal vibrators should not be used for this purpose because they may be damaged.

Vibrating tables are used mainly in precasting plants. They should be equipped with controls so that the frequency and amplitude can be varied according to the size of the element to be vibrated and the consistency of the concrete. Plastic mixes will generally require higher frequencies than stiff mixes. Increasing the frequency and decreasing the amplitude as vibration progresses may improve consolidation.

Surface vibrators such as vibrating screeds are used to consolidate concrete in floors and other flatwork. Vibrating screeds give positive control of the strikeoff operation and save a great deal of labor. However, this equipment should not be used on concrete with slumps in excess of 3 inches (7.5 cm.). Surface vibration of such concrete will result in an excess accumulation of mortar and fine material on the surface and thus reduce wear resistance. For the same reason, surface vibrators should not be operated after the concrete has been adequately consolidated.

Vibrating screeds are recommended for consolidating slabs up to 6 inches (15 cm.) thick, provided such slabs are nonreinforced or only lightly reinforced (light welded-wire fabric). Nonreinforced slabs 6 to 8 inches (15 to 20 cm.) thick may be consolidated by either internal vibrators or vibrating screeds. Internal vibration is recommended for all slabs over 8 inches (20 cm.) thick and any slab of lesser thickness with reinforcing steel, conduit, or other embedded items.

Chapter 10

Curing Concrete

Properties of concrete such as resistance to freezing and thawing, strength, watertightness, wear resistance, and volume stability improve with age as long as conditions are favorable for continued hydration of the cement. The improvement is rapid at early ages but continues more slowly for an indefinite period as shown in Fig. 1 for strength. Two conditions for such improvement in quality are required: (1) the presence of moisture and (2) a favorable temperature.

When moist curing is interrupted, the strength increases for a short period and stops. However, if moist curing is resumed, the strength will again increase. Although this can be done in a laboratory, it is difficult to resaturate concrete on most jobs. It is best to moist-cure the concrete continuously from the time it is placed until it has attained the desired quality. (*See* Chap. 1, Fundamental Facts About Concrete.)

Excessive evaporation of water from newly placed concrete can significantly retard the cement hydration process at an early age. Loss of water also causes concrete to shrink, thus creating tensile stresses at the drying surface. If these stresses develop before the concrete has attained adequate strength, surface cracking may result. All exposed surfaces including exposed edges and joints must be protected against moisture evaporation.

Hydration proceeds at a much slower rate when the concrete temperature is low. Temperatures below 50° F. (10° C.) are unfavorable for the development of early strength; below 40° F. (4.5° C.) the development of early strength is greatly retarded; and near or below freezing temperatures (0 to −1° C.) little or no strength develops. It follows that concrete should be protected so that the concrete temperature remains favorable for

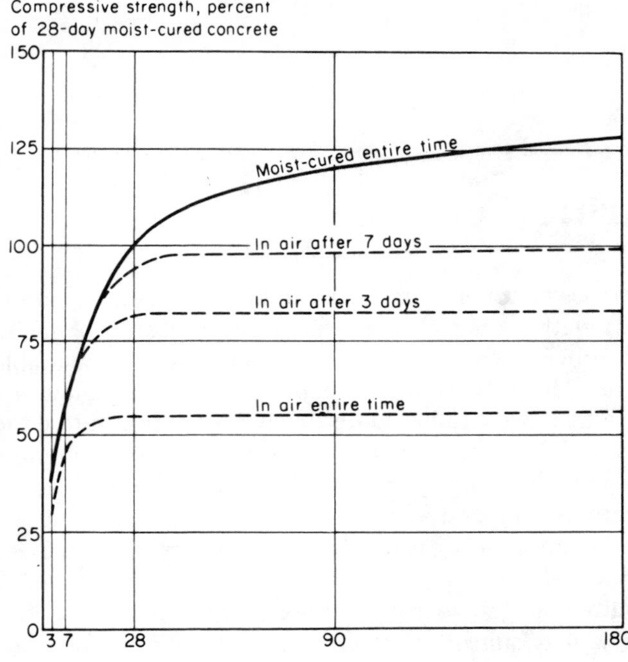

Fig. 1. Strength of concrete continues to increase with age as long as there is moisture and a favorable temperature present for hydration of cement.

hydration and moisture is not lost during the early hardening period.

CURING METHODS

Concrete can be kept moist (and, in some cases, at a favorable temperature) by a number of *curing methods* that may be classified as follows:

1. Methods that supply additional moisture to the surface of the concrete during the early hardening period. These in-

clude ponding or immersion, sprinkling or fogging, and using wet coverings. Such methods afford some cooling through evaporation, which is beneficial in hot weather.

2. Methods that prevent loss of moisture from the concrete by sealing the surface. This may be done by means of waterproof paper, plastic film, curing compounds, and forms left in place.

3. Methods that accelerate strength gain by supplying heat and moisture to the concrete. This is usually accomplished with live steam or heating coils.

The method or combination of methods chosen depends on factors such as availability of curing materials, complexity and size of the concrete surface, esthetic appearance, and economics.

Ponding or Immersion

On *flat surfaces* such as pavement, sidewalks, or floors, concrete can be cured by *ponding*. Earth or sand dikes around the perimeter of the concrete surface retain a pond of water within the enclosed area. An efficient method for preventing loss of moisture from the concrete, ponding is also effective for maintaining a uniform temperature in the concrete. However, the curing water should not be more than about 20° F. (7° C.) cooler than the concrete to prevent thermal stresses that could result in cracking. Since ponding generally requires considerable labor and supervision, the method is often impractical except for small jobs. Ponding is undesirable if fresh concrete will be exposed to early freezing.

The most thorough but seldom used method of curing with water consists of total immersion of the finished concrete element. This method has been used to some extent in precast concrete plants but it is more common in the laboratory for curing concrete test specimens. Where appearance is important, the water used for curing by ponding or immersion should be free of substances that will stain or discolor the concrete. (*See* Chap. 14, Precast Concrete.)

Sprinkling or Fogging

Continuous *sprinkling* or *fogging* with water is an excellent method of curing when the temperature is well above freezing. A fine spray of water may be applied continuously through a system of nozzles or a soil-soaker hose. Ordinary lawn sprinklers are effective if good coverage is provided and water runoff is of no concern.

A disadvantage of sprinkling or fogging may be its cost. The method requires an adequate supply of water and careful supervision. If sprinkling or fogging is done at intervals, care must be taken to prevent the concrete from drying between applications of water. Alternate cycles of wetting and drying may cause crazing or cracking. Care must also be taken that water erosion of newly finished concrete does not occur.

Wet Coverings

Wet coverings such as burlap, cotton mats, or other moisture-retaining fabrics are extensively used for curing. *Treated burlaps* that reflect light and are resistant to rot and fire are available.

Burlap must be free of sizing or any substances that are harmful to concrete or cause discoloration. *New burlap* should be thoroughly rinsed in water to remove soluble substances and make the burlap more absorbent.

Wet, moisture-retaining fabric coverings should be placed as soon as the concrete has hardened sufficiently to prevent surface damage. Care should be taken to cover the entire surface, including the edges of slabs such as pavements and sidewalks. The coverings should be kept continuously moist so that a film of water remains on the concrete surface throughout the curing period.

Wet coverings of earth, sand, or sawdust from most woods are effective for curing but in recent years have been largely discontinued due to their high cost. (Sawdust from oak and other woods that contain tannic acid should *not* be used since deterioration of the concrete may occur. However, sawdust from most woods is acceptable.) This method is often useful on small jobs. The moist earth, sand, or sawdust should be evenly distributed over the previously moistened surface of the concrete in a layer about two inches thick. It should be kept continuously wet.

Moist hay or straw can be used to cure flat surfaces. This method has been largely outmoded by labor-saving curing procedures. If straw or hay is used, it should be placed in a layer at least 6 inches (15 cm.) thick, covered to prevent being blown off by wind, and kept continuously wet.

A major disadvantage of moist earth, sand, sawdust, hay, or straw coverings is the possibility of discoloration of the concrete. The effect of discoloration on surface appearance should be considered.

Waterproof Paper

Waterproof paper for curing concrete consists of two sheets of kraft paper cemented together by a bituminous adhesive with fiber reinforcement. Such paper is an efficient means of curing horizontal surfaces and structural concrete of relatively simple shapes. One important advantage of this method is that periodic additions of water are not required. Curing paper assures suitable hydration of cement by preventing loss of moisture from the concrete (Fig. 2).

The widest curing paper practical should be applied as soon as the concrete has hardened sufficiently to prevent surface damage, and after the concrete has been thoroughly wetted. Edges of adjacent sheets should be overlapped several inches and tightly sealed with sand, wood planks, pressure-sensitive tape, mastic, or glue. The sheets should be weighted to maintain close contact with the concrete surface during the entire curing period.

Curing with waterproof paper may cause patchy discoloration, especially if the concrete contains calcium chloride and has been finished by hard steel troweling. This discoloration is experienced when the paper becomes wrinkled. It is difficult and time-consuming on a project of significant size to smooth out the wrinkles that are apt to form. The discoloration may be prevented by occasionally flooding the surface under the covering, but other means of curing should be used when uniform color is important.

Fig. 2. Waterproof curing paper.

Curing paper provides some protection to the concrete against damage from subsequent construction activity as well as protection from the direct sun. It should be inspected for rips and holes that would permit loss of moisture and thus destroy its effectiveness. It should also be light in color and nonstaining. Paper with a white upper surface is preferable during hot weather. (*See* Chap. 16, section on Hot-Weather Concreting.)

Plastic Film

Certain plastic sheet materials such as *polyethylene film* are used to cure concrete (Fig. 3). Polyethylene film is a lightweight, effective moisture barrier and easily applied to complex as well as simple shapes. Its application is the same as described pre-

Fig. 3. Curing with plastic sheeting.

viously for waterproof paper. As with waterproof paper, curing with polyethylene film may cause patchy discoloration if the film is not kept flat on the concrete surface.

Black film is satisfactory under some conditions. Although white should be used during hot weather to reflect the sun's rays, black can be used during cool weather or for interior locations. The clear film has little effect on heat absorption.

The specifications referred to here also include a sheet material consisting of burlap impregnated on one side with white opaque polyethylene film. Combinations of polyethylene film bonded to absorbent fabric such as burlap help retain moisture on the concrete surface.

Curing Compounds

Liquid membrane-forming compounds consisting of waxes, resins, chlorinated rubber, and solvents of high volatility may be used to retard or prevent evaporation of moisture from concrete. *Curing compounds are not recommended* during late fall in the northern states and Canada where deicers are used to melt ice and snow. Use of curing compounds under these conditions may prevent proper air-drying of the concrete, which is necessary to enhance resistance to scaling caused by use of deicers. They are suitable not only for curing fresh concrete, but also for further curing of concrete after removal of forms or after initial moist curing.

Curing compounds are of two general types: clear or translucent and white-pigmented. Clear or translucent compounds may contain a fugitive dye that fades out soon after application. This helps assure complete coverage of the exposed concrete surface. During hot, sunny days, white-pigmented compounds are most effective since they reflect the sun's rays, thereby reducing the concrete temperature. Pigmented compounds should be kept agitated in the container to prevent the pigment from settling out.

Curing compounds are applied with hand-operated or power-driven spray equipment immediately after the disappearance of the water sheen and the final finishing of the concrete. Normally, the concrete surface should be damp when the coating is applied so that the compound will not be absorbed into the surface pores. However, during hot, dry, windy days or during other periods of adverse weather when conditions could result in plastic shrinkage cracking, formation of cracks may be prevented by applying the curing compound immediately after final finishing and before all the free water on the surface has evaporated. Power-driven spray equipment is recommended for uniform application on large paving projects. Spray nozzles and windshields on such equipment should be arranged to prevent wind-blown losses of curing compound.

Normally only one even coat is applied, but two coats may be necessary to ensure complete coverage. A second coat, when used, should be applied at right angles to the first. Complete coverage of the surface must be attained because even small holes in the membrane will permit evaporation of moisture from the concrete.

Curing compounds can prevent bond between hardened and fresh concrete, and they should not be used if bond is necessary.

For example, a curing compound should not be applied to the base slab of a two-course floor since it may prevent the topping from bonding. Similarly, some curing compounds affect the adhesion of paint or resilient flooring materials to concrete floors. Curing compound manufacturers or dealers should be consulted to determine if their product is in this category.

Forms Left in Place

Forms provide satisfactory protection against loss of moisture if the top exposed concrete surfaces are kept wet. A soil-soaker hose is excellent for this. The forms should be left on the concrete as long as practicable.

Wood forms left in place should be kept moist by sprinkling, especially during hot, dry weather. If not kept moist, wood forms should be removed as soon as practicable and another method of curing started without delay. (*See* Chap. 7, Forms and Form Making.)

Steam Curing

Steam curing is advantageous where early strength gain in concrete is important or where additional heat is required to accomplish hydration—as in cold-weather concreting.

Two methods of steam curing for a gain in early strength are used today. Curing in live steam at atmospheric pressure (for enclosed cast-in-place structures and manufactured precast concrete units), and curing in high-pressure steam autoclaves (for small manufactured units).

A *steam-curing cycle* consists of (1) an initial delay prior to steaming, (2) a period for increasing temperature, (3) a period for holding the maximum temperature constant, and (4) a period for decreasing temperature. A typical atmospheric steam-curing cycle is shown in Fig. 4. In many cases the time lapse from casting to steam shutoff remains nearly constant at 18 hours.

Steam curing at atmospheric pressure is generally done in a steam chamber or other enclosure to minimize moisture and heat losses. Tarpaulins are frequently used to form the enclosure. Application of steam to the enclosure should be delayed at

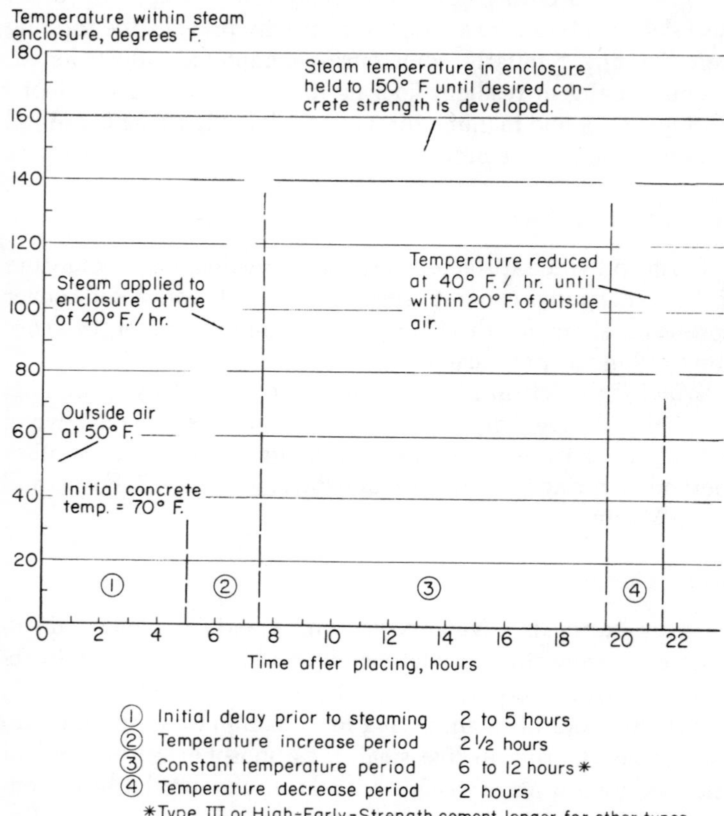

Fig. 4. Atmospheric steam-curing cycle.

least two hours after final placement of concrete to allow for some hardening of the most recently placed concrete. However, a 4- to 5-hour delay period prior to steaming will achieve maximum early strength as shown in Fig. 5. Strength will not increase significantly if the maximum steam temperature is raised from 150 to 175° F. (66° C.–80° C.). Maximum steam temperatures above 180° F. (83° C.) should be avoided as they are uneconomical and may result in undue reduction in ultimate strength.

Excessive rates of heating and cooling during atmospheric

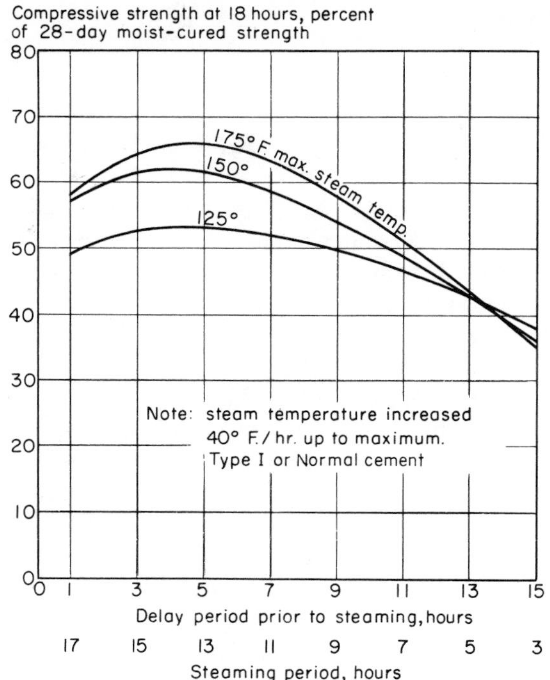

Fig. 5. Compressive strength of steam-cured cement.

steam curing should be avoided to prevent volume changes damaging to the concrete. Temperatures in the enclosure surrounding the concrete should not be increased or decreased more than 40° F. (5° C.) per hour.

The maximum steam temperature in the enclosure should be held until the concrete has reached the desired strength. The time required depends on the concrete mix and steam temperature.

High-pressure steam curing in autoclaves takes advantage of temperatures in the range of 325 to 375° F. (163° C. to 191° C.), and corresponding pressures of about 80 to 170 psig (pounds per square inch gauge) (5.6 to 11.9 kgs. per sq. cm.). Hydration is greatly accelerated and the elevated temperatures and pressures may produce additional beneficial chemical reactions between the aggregates and/or cementitious materials that do not occur under normal steam curing.

LENGTH OF CURING PERIOD

The length of time that concrete should be protected against loss of moisture is dependent upon the type of cement, mix proportion, required strength, size and shape of the concrete section, weather, and future exposure conditions. This period may be three weeks or longer for lean concrete mixtures used in structures such as dams. It may be only a few days for richer mixes, especially if Type III or high-early-strength cement is used. Steam-curing periods are normally much shorter.

Since all the desirable properties of concrete are improved by curing, the curing period should be as long as practicable in all cases. For concrete in slabs on the ground (floors, highway and airfield pavements, canal linings, parking lots, driveways, sidewalks, and the like) and for structural concrete (cast-in-place walls, columns, slabs, beams, small footings, piers, retaining walls, bridge decks, and so on), the length of the curing period for ambient temperatures above 40° F. (5° C.) should be a minimum of seven days or the time necessary to attain 70 percent of the specified compressive or flexural strength, whichever period is less. If strength tests are made, the representative concrete cylinders or beams should be kept adjacent to the structure or pavement and cured by the same methods.

Since the rate of hydration is influenced by cement composition and fineness, the curing period should be prolonged for concretes made with cements possessing slow strength gain characteristics. For mass concrete (most frequently used in large piers, locks, abutments, dams, heavy footings, and massive columns and transfer girders) containing no pozzolan as part of the cementitious material, curing of unreinforced sections should continue for at least two weeks. If the mass concrete contains a pozzolan, the minimum curing time for unreinforced sections should be extended to three weeks. Heavily reinforced mass concrete sections should be cured for a minimum of seven days.

During cold weather, additional heat is often required to maintain favorable curing temperatures (50 to 70° F. or 10° C. to 21° C.). This can be supplied with vented gas- or oil-fired heaters, heating coils, or live steam. In all these cases, take care to avoid the loss of moisture from the concrete. (*See* Chap. 17, section on Cold-Weather Concreting.)

High-early-strength concrete may also be used during cold weather to speed up setting time and strength development. This can reduce the curing period from seven to three days, but a minimum temperature of 50° F. (10° C.) must be maintained in the concrete for the three days.

For adequate scale resistance to chemical deicers, the minimum curing period generally corresponds to the time required to develop the design strength of the concrete. A period of air drying, which enhances resistance to scaling, should then elapse before application of deicing salts. This drying period should be at least one month if possible.

Chapter 11

Finishing Concrete Slabs

Concrete slabs may be finished in many ways, depending on the effect desired. Various colors and textures, such as an exposed-aggregate surface, may be called for. Some surfaces may require only screeding to proper contour and elevation, while in other cases a broomed, floated, or troweled finish may be specified. (*See* Chap. 15, Exposed Aggregate Concrete.)

One of the principal causes of surface defects in concrete slabs is finishing while bleed water is on the surface. *Any finishing operation performed on the surface of a concrete slab while bleed water is present will cause serious dusting or scaling.* The use of low-slump, air-entrained concrete having an adequate cement content and properly graded fine aggregate will minimize bleeding and will help ensure maintenance-free slabs.

Mixing, transporting, and handling of concrete for slabs should be carefully coordinated with the finishing operation. Concrete should not be placed on the subgrade or forms more rapidly than it can be spread, struck off, consolidated, and bullfloated and darbied. In fact, concrete should not be spread over too large an area before strikeoff, nor should a large area be struck off and allowed to remain before bullfloating or darbying.

CONCRETE FINISHING TECHNIQUES

Screeding

Screeding is the process of striking off the excess concrete to bring the top surface to proper grade. The templet used is known as a straightedge. The lower edge of the templet may be straight or curved, depending on the surface requirements. It should be moved across the concrete with a sawing motion and advanced forward a short distance with each movement. (*See* Fig. 1.) There should be a surplus of concrete against the front face of the straightedge to fill in low areas as the tool passes over the slab. However, allowing too great a surplus may tend to leave hollows. Straightedges are sometimes equipped with vibrators that consolidate the concrete and assist in reducing the work of screeding. (Vibrating screeds are discussed in Chap. 9 in the section on Consolidating Concrete.)

Bullfloating or Darbying

To eliminate high and low spots and to embed large aggregate particles, a *bullfloat* or *darby* is used immediately after screeding. Generally, the bullfloat is used on areas too large to reach with a darby. For normal-weight concrete, these tools should preferably be made of wood.

Bullfloating or *darbying* must be completed before any excess bleed water accumulates on the surface. Care must be taken not

Fig. 1. The surface of a slab under construction is brought to final grade by screeding.

to overwork the concrete. Overworking will result in a less durable surface.

Although sometimes no further finishing is required, in most cases bullfloating or darbying is followed by one or more of the following operations—edging, jointing, floating, troweling, and brooming. A slight hardening of the concrete is necessary before proceeding further. When the water sheen is gone and the concrete will sustain foot pressure with only about a ¼-inch (6.3-mm.) indentation, the final finishing operations should begin.

Edging and Jointing

Edging is not required for most floor slabs, but it is common practice for outdoor slabs such as walks, drives, and patios. Edging produces a neat, rounded ege that prevents chipping or damage, especially when forms are removed. Edging also compacts and hardens the concrete surface next to the form where floating and troweling are less effective.

In the *edging operation,* the concrete should be cut away from the forms to a depth of 1 inch (2.5 cm.), using a pointed mason trowel or a margin trowel. Then an edger should be held flat on the surface and run with the front slightly raised to prevent digging into the surface. Caution is necessary to prevent the edger from leaving too deep an impression. Edging may be required after each subsequent finishing operation.

Immediately after or during the edging operation, the slab should be jointed or grooved. Proper jointing practices can eliminate unsightly random cracks. Control joints are made by using a hand groover or saw, or by inserting strips of wood, metal, or premolded joint material into the concrete. (*See* Making Joints in Floors and Walls later in this chapter for additional information.)

Floating

After the concrete has been edged and jointed, it should be floated with wood or metal hand floats or with a finishing machine using float blades.

The purpose of *floating* is threefold: (1) to embed aggregate particles just beneath the surface; (2) to remove slight imperfections, humps, and voids, and; (3) to compact the concrete at the surface in preparation for other finishing operations. The concrete should not be overworked while it is still plastic as this may bring an excess of water and fine material to the surface and result in subsequent surface defects.

Floating is used as a final finish, especially for exterior slabs, because it produces a relatively even (but not smooth) texture with good slip resistance. Where such a finish is desired, it may be necessary to float the surface a second time after it has partially hardened.

Marks left by edgers and hand groovers are normally removed during floating unless desired for decorative purposes. In that case those tools should be rerun after final floating.

Troweling

Where a smooth, hard, and dense surface is desired, floating is followed by *steel troweling.* No troweling should ever be done on a surface which has not been floated. Troweling after bullfloating or darbying is not sufficient.

It is customary when hand-finishing large slabs to float and immediately trowel an area before moving the knee-boards. These operations should be delayed until after the concrete has hardened enough that water and fine material are not brought to the surface. The tendency in a majority of cases is to float and trowel the surface while the concrete is too soft and plastic, as too long a delay will result in a surface too hard to float and trowel. Premature floating and troweling may cause scaling, crazing, or dusting and will result in a surface with reduced wear resistance.

Spreading dry cement on a wet surface to soak up excess water is a bad practice because it may cause crazing. Such wet spots should be avoided, if possible, by adjustments in gradation, mix proportions, and consistency. When wet spots do occur, the excess water should be removed with a squeegee or finishing operations should be delayed until the water evaporates. If a squeegee is used, cement should not be removed with the water.

The first troweling may be sufficient to produce the desired surface free of defects. Surface smoothness, density, and wear resistance can all be improved by timely additional trowelings. There should be a lapse of time between successive trowelings to permit the concrete to become harder. As the surface stiffens, each successive troweling should be made with smaller trowels, using progressively more tilt on the trowel blade. The final pass should make a ringing sound as the trowel moves over the hardening surface.

When the first troweling is done by machine, at least one additional troweling by hand is required to remove small irregularities. (*See* Fig. 2.) If necessary, tooled edges and joints should be rerun after troweling to maintain uniformity and true lines.

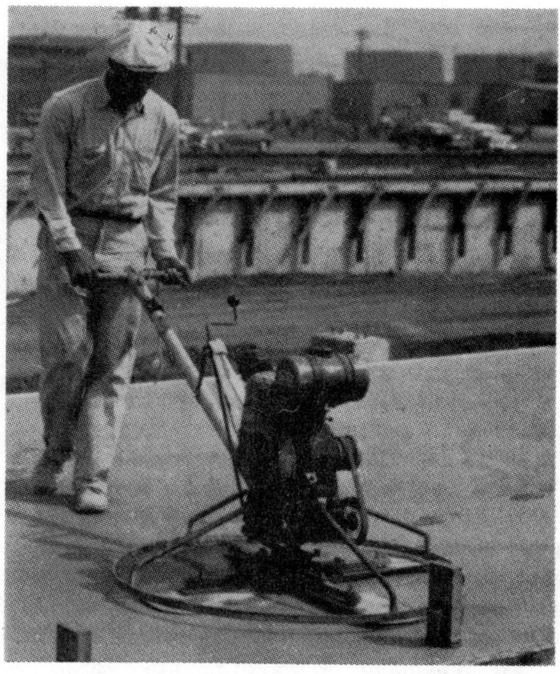

Fig. 2. Power troweling is properly timed here, as evidenced by the not-too-deep footprints.

Brooming

A slip-resistant surface may be produced by *brooming* before the concrete has thoroughly hardened, but it should be sufficiently hard to retain the scoring. Rough scoring is achieved by the use of a steel wire or stiff, coarse, fiber broom. Such brooming usually follows floating. If a finer texture is desired, the concrete is troweled to a smooth surface and then brushed with a soft-bristled broom. Best results are obtained using a broom specially made for texturing concrete. Slabs are usually broomed transversely to the main direction of traffic.

Patterned and Textured Finishes

A variety of patterns and textures can be used to produce decorative finishes. *Patterns* are formed with divider strips or by scoring or stamping the surface just before the concrete hardens. *Textures* can be produced with little effort and expense by using floats, trowels, and brooms. More elaborate textures can be achieved with special techniques using a mortar dash coat or rock salt. (*See* Chap. 12, Finishing Concrete Surfaces.)

An exposed-aggregate finish provides a ruggedly attractive surface. Select aggregates, usually of uniform size such as ⅜ or ½ inch (10 or 13 mm.) or larger, are evenly distributed on the surface immediately after the slab has been bullfloated or darbied. Flat or elongated aggregate particles should not be used since they may become dislodged while being exposed.

Aggregates to be exposed should be washed thoroughly before use to assure satisfactory bond. The aggregate particles must be completely embedded in the concrete. This can be done by lightly tapping them with a wooden hand float, darby, or the broad side of a piece of 2 × 4 (5 × 10 cm.) lumber. When the concrete can support a finisher on knee-boards, the surface should be hand-floated with a magnesium float or darby until the mortar completely surrounds and slightly covers all the aggregate particles. When the concrete has hardened sufficiently, the aggregate is exposed by simultaneously brushing and flushing with water.

Since *timing* is important, test panels are usually made to determine the correct time for exposing the aggregate without dislodging the particles. On large jobs a reliable retarder may be sprayed or brushed on the surface immediately after floating, but on small jobs this may not be necessary. (*See* Chap. 12, Finishing Concrete Surfaces.)

MAKING JOINTS IN FLOORS AND WALLS

Three basic types of joints are commonly used in concrete construction:

Isolation joints are used to separate different parts of a structure to permit both horizontal and vertical differential movements. *For example,* such joints are provided around the perimeter of a floor on ground and around columns (Fig. 3) and machine foundations.

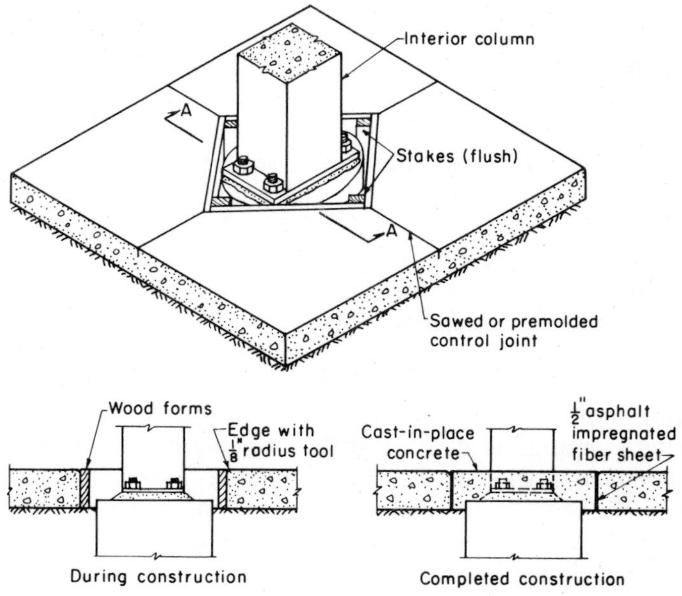

Fig. 3. Complete isolation of column and slab is provided by this jointing procedure.

Control joints provide for differential movement in the plane of a slab or wall. They are used to allow for contraction caused by drying shrinkage. Control joints should be constructed so as to permit transfer of loads perpendicular to the plane of the slab or wall. If no control joints are used in slabs on the ground or in lightly reinforced walls, random cracks will occur when drying shrinkage produces tensile stresses in excess of the concrete's tensile strength.

Construction joints allow for no movement across the joint. They are merely stopping places in the process of casting due to the impracticability of placing and finishing large areas of concrete in one operation. Construction joints, however, can be made to perform as control joints.

These joints are frequently referred to by other names. Isolation joints are sometimes called *expansion joints*. Control joints are often called *contraction* or *dummy joints*. Construction joints are also called *bonded joints*.

Construction joints are described in Chap. 9, Placing and Consolidating Concrete. Suggestions are given on preparing the hardened concrete at horizontal construction joints and on using a cushion of mortar when concreting is resumed. If these suggestions are followed, joints will be well bonded and free of stone pockets and voids. On most structures it is desirable to have joints that will not detract from appearance. When properly made, they can be inconspicuous and the joints themselves may be hidden by use of rustication strips. They thus may be an architectural as well as functional feature of the structure.

Joints should be straight, exactly horizontal or vertical, and should be placed at suitable locations. In walls, horizontal construction joints can be made straight by nailing a 1-inch (2.5-cm.) wood strip to the inside face of the form. Concrete is then placed to a level about ½ inch (1.3 cm.) above the bottom of the strip. After the concrete has settled and just before it becomes hard, any laitance which has formed on the top surface is removed. The strip is then removed and irregularities in the joint are leveled off.

The *forms* are usually removed at construction joints and then re-erected for the next lift of concrete as shown in Fig. 4. A

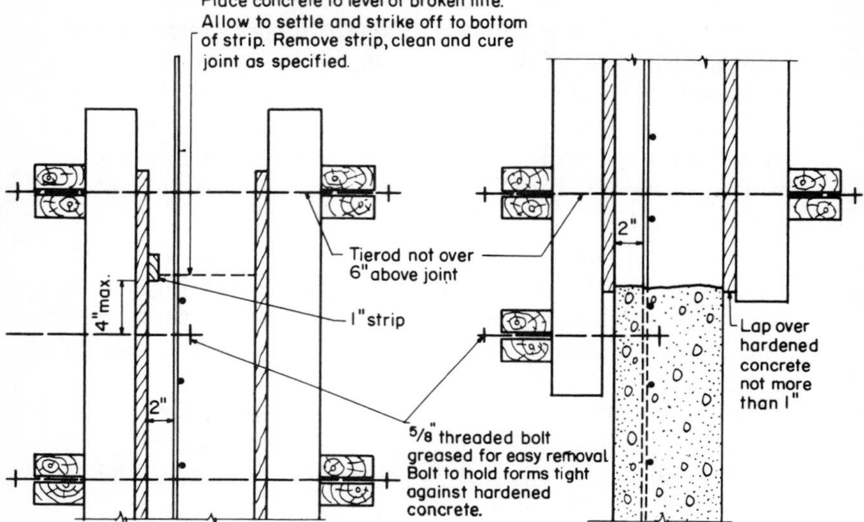

Fig. 4. A straight horizontal construction joint is provided by this detail.

variation of this procedure is to use a rustication strip instead of the 1-inch (2.5-cm.) wood strip and to form a groove in the concrete for architectural effect. Rustication strips may be V-shaped, rectangular, or slightly beveled. If V-shaped, the joint should be made at the point of the V. If a rectangular or slightly beveled strip is used, the joint should be made at the top edge of the inner face of the strip.

Control joints *in floor on ground* should be spaced at intervals of 15 to 25 feet (4.6 to 7.6 meters) in both directions, depending on the type of coarse aggregate used in the concrete. Unless reliable data indicate that more widely spaced joints are feasible, these intervals should be used with gravel or slag in the mix, 15 feet (4.6 meters); crushed limestone, 20 feet (6 meters); crushed granite, 25 feet (7.6 meters). The resulting panels should be approximately square. Panels with excessive length-to-width ratio (more than 1½ to 1) are likely to crack.

Control joints *in slabs on ground* can be made in several ways. One of the most economical types is made by sawing a continuous straight slot in the top of the slab (Fig. 5). This forms a

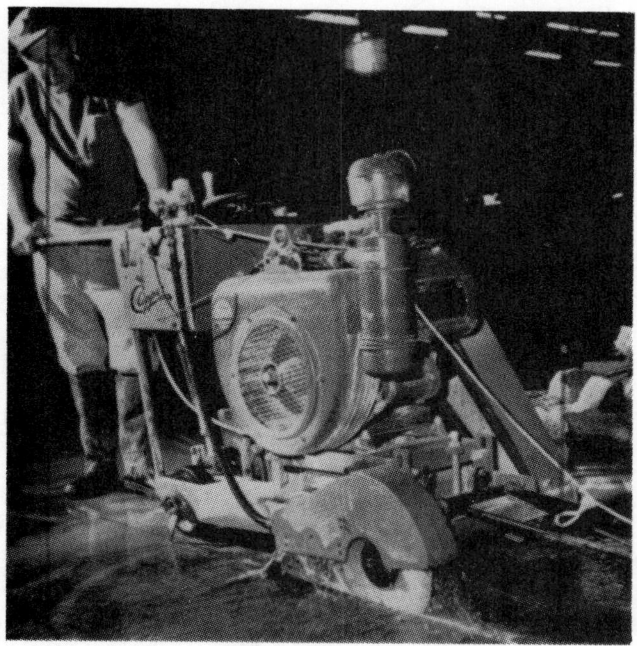

Fig. 5. Sawed control joints provide weakened planes helpful in controlling cracking.

plane of weakness where a crack will form. Vertical loads can be transmitted across the joint by contact through the cracked surfaces. Control joints also can be formed in the fresh concrete with hand groovers or by placing strips of wood, metal, or premolded joint material at the joint locations. The top edge of the strips should be flush with the concrete surface. Control joints, whether sawed, grooved, or premolded, should extend into the slab to a depth of from one-fifth to one-fourth the slab thickness.

Control joints *in cast-in-place walls* are planes of weakness that permit differential movements in the plane of the wall. In lightly reinforced walls, half of the horizontal steel bars should be cut at the joint. Care should be taken to cut alternate temperature bars precisely at the joint. Control joints in walls should be spaced not more than about 20 feet (6 meters), and also should be made where abrupt changes in thickness or height occur. Furthermore, a control joint should be located near a corner, if possible, as close as 5 feet (1.2 meters).

Isolation joints are used to ***separate slabs on ground*** from walls, columns, or footings. The joint material may be as little as ¼ inch (6.3-mm.) thick or less. Care must be taken to ensure that all the edges of the slab are isolated from adjoining construction to avoid cracking. (*See* Chap. 7, Forms and Form Making, section on Removing Forms.)

PATCHING, CLEANING, AND FINISHING FORMED CONCRETE

After forms are removed, bulges, fins, and small projections must be removed by chipping or tooling. The surface should then be rubbed or ground. Any cavities such as tie-rod holes should be filled unless they are to remain unfilled for decorative purposes. Also, honeycombed areas must be repaired and stains cleaned to present a concrete surface of uniform color. All of these operations can be minimized by exercising care in construction of formwork and during concrete placement. In general these repairs should be made as soon as practicable, preferably as soon as the forms are removed.

Patches for Bolt Holes and Defects

Patches usually appear darker than the surrounding concrete. Therefore, some white cement should be mixed in the patching mortar or concrete where appearance is important. Samples should be applied in an inconspicuous location, perhaps a basement wall, several days in advance to determine the most suitable proportions of white and gray cements. Steel troweling should be avoided since this makes the match appear dark in color. Trial patches should be cured as described later in this chapter.

Bolt holes, tie-rod holes, and *other cavities* that are small in area but relatively deep should be filled with a dry-pack mortar.

The mortar should be mixed as stiff as practicable, using 1 part portland cement to 2½ parts sand passing a No. 16 sieve, and just enough water to form a ball when the mortar is squeezed gently in the hand. After the cavity has been cleaned of oil and loose material and kept damp for several hours, the mortar should be tamped into place in ½-inch (1.3-cm.) thick layers. Vigorous tamping and adequate curing will ensure good bond and minimum shrinkage of the patch. (*See* Chap. 20, Masonry Materials.)

Honeycombed and ***other defective concrete*** must be cut out to expose sound material. If defective concrete is left adjacent to a patch, moisture may get into the voids and, in time, weathering action will cause the patch to spall. The edges should be cut or chipped straight and at right angles to the surface, or slightly undercut, to provide a key at the edge of the patch. No featheredges should be permitted.

Before the patching concrete is applied, the surrounding concrete should be kept wet for several hours. A grout (1 part portland cement, 1 part fine sand passing a No. 30 sieve, and sufficient mixing water for a creamy consistency) should be scrubbed with a brush into the surfaces to which the new material is to be bonded. The area should be damp when the grout is applied ***but not wet*** with free moisture. (*See* Chap. 2, Concrete Ingredients.)

Shallow patches may be filled with stiff mortar similar to that used in the concrete. This should be placed in layers not more than ½ inch (1.3 cm.) thick, with each layer given a scratch finish to improve bond with the subsequent layer. The final layer can be finished to match the surrounding concrete by floating, rubbing, or tooling, or on formed surfaces by pressing the form material against the patch while still plastic. ***Deep patches*** may be filled with concrete held in place by forms. Such patches should be reinforced and doweled to the hardened concrete.

Following patching, good curing is essential. Curing should be started as soon as possible to avoid early drying. Damp burlap, wet sand, or tarpaulins can be used. In locations where it is difficult to hold these materials in place, an application of two coats of membrane curing compounds is often the most convenient method. (*See* Chap. 10, Curing Concrete.)

Grout Cleandown of New Concrete

Concrete surfaces are not always uniform in color when forms are removed. They may have a somewhat blotchy appearance, and there may be a slight film of parting agent in certain areas due to an excess on the forms. There may be mortar stains from leaks in the forms or there may be rust stains. The latter are best removed by lightly sandblasting the surface. Where appearance is important, all surfaces should be cleaned with grout after construction has progressed to the stage where there will be no discoloration from subsequent construction activities.

Since a clean surface is necessary to establish good bond between grout and the concrete surface, any keel marks, oil stains, laitance, or other material that will adversely affect the bond must be removed prior to the grout application. The cleaning should begin at the top and progress down. Wherever necessary, the surface should be stoned by hand or machine. If a power grinder is used, very smooth or polished surfaces should be avoided. (*See* Chap. 12, Finishing Concrete Surfaces.)

Grout must be used within 1 to 1½ hours of the time of original mixing. Therefore, the amount to be mixed at any one time is limited. It should consist of water and 1 part sand to 1 part portland cement. The sand should be clean and able to pass a No. 30 sieve; the cement should be a mixture of gray and white to match the color of the existing concrete. Small trial samples should be made at least a day ahead to determine the exact mix. To start with, the following trial mixes may be made: 2 parts sand to 1 part gray cement and 1 part white cement; 3 parts sand to 1 part gray cement and 2 parts white cement; and 3 parts sand to 2 parts gray cement and 1 part white cement. These dry materials should be mixed in a clean container and enough water added to bring the grout to a workable mortar consistency. The sand supply and brands of gray and white cement should not be changed during the grout cleandown.

Before use, the grout should be allowed to stand for 20 to 30 minutes, depending on ambient temperatures. Then, just before application, the grout should be remixed without adding any additional water. The concrete surface should be thoroughly water-soaked at least 15 minutes ahead of the grout application and again just prior to it. In fact, the surface must be kept wet during grouting.

Grouting should begin at the top of any particular area and proceed down. The grout may be applied with a plasterer's trowel or a sponge rubber float in long, sweeping arcs (from the bottom up), or by wielding a brush or spray gun. Immediately after application, the grout must be vigorously floated with a sponge rubber float. This procedure will fill all small air holes and remove some excess grout. The grout remaining on the surface should be allowed to stand undisturbed until it loses some of its plasticity but not its damp appearance. Then the surface must be rubbed with clean, dry burlap to remove all excess grout. All air holes should be filled but no visible film of grout should remain after the rubbing. Since grout remaining on the surface overnight is too difficult to remove, any section being cleaned with grout must be completed in one day. (*See* Chap. 32, Stucco Materials and Tools, section on Tools.)

If possible, work should be done in the shade and preferably during cool damp weather. During hot or dry weather, the concrete may be kept moist during the grout cleandown by using a fine fog spray.

The completed surface should be *moist-cured* by keeping the area wet the entire day following the cleandown. When completely dry, the surface should have a uniform color and texture.

Paints and Clear Coatings

Concrete can be finished with many types of paints and clear coatings. Among the principal paints used are portland cement base, latex modified portland cement, and latex (acrylic and polyvinyl acetate) paints. (*See* Chap. 16, Mineral Pigments for Use in Coloring Concrete.)

Portland cement base paints can be used on either interior or exterior exposures. The surface of the concrete should be *damp* at the time of application and each coat should be dampened as soon as it can be done without disturbing the paint. *Damp curing of portland cement paint is essential.* On open-textured surfaces the paint should be applied with stiff-bristle brushes such as scrub brushes. Paint should be worked well into the surface. For concrete of smooth or sandy surface, whitewash or Dutch-type calcimine brushes are best.

The *latex materials* used in modified portland cement paints retard evaporation, thereby retaining the necessary water for hydration of the portland cement. Moist curing is unnecessary with the latex modified paint and, in fact, may be undesirable.

Latex paints are resistant to alkali and may be applied to new concrete after 10 days of good drying weather. The preferred method of application is by long-fiber, tapered nylon brushes 4 to 6 inches (10 to 15 cm.) wide. However, application may also be made by roller or spray. The paints may be applied to damp, but not wet, surfaces and if the surface is moderately porous or extremely dry conditions prevail, prewetting of the surface is advisable.

Other paints used on concrete include styrene-butadiene, chlorinated rubber, oil base, and alkyd coatings; epoxies; polyesters; and urethanes.

Clear coatings are frequently used on concrete surfaces to prevent soiling or discoloration of the concrete by air pollution, to facilitate cleaning the surface if it does become dirty, to brighten the color of the aggregates, and to render the surface water-repellent and thus prevent darkening due to water absorption. Many clear coatings cause permanent discoloration of the concrete surface. The better coatings often consist of methyl methacrylate forms of acrylic resin. The methyl methacrylate coatings should have a higher viscosity and solids content when used on smooth concrete. The original appearance of smooth concrete is more difficult to maintain than the original appearance of exposed-aggregate concrete.

Tooled Finishes

Mechanical spalling and chipping of concrete to produce a finish similar to some finishes used on cut stone can be accomplished with a variety of hand and power tools. The technique is usually called *bushhammering.* Pneumatic tools are available with combs, chisels, or multiple points. Hand tools are used for small areas, corners, and places where power tools cannot reach. (*See* Chap. 24, Stone Masonry.)

Basically, all methods of tooling concrete involve removing a layer of hardened concrete matrix while fracturing the aggregate at the surface (Fig. 6). The finishes attained can vary from a light *scaling* to a deep, bold texture achieved by jackhammering with a single pointed chisel.

Concrete should not be tooled until it has reached a strength of at least 3,750 psi (262.5 kgs. per sq. cm.). Although tooling has been done as early as two weeks after casting, a more uniform surface will be achieved after three weeks.

Exposed-Aggregate Finishes

Various methods may be used to produce exposed-aggregate finishes on concrete. (*See* Chap. 12, Finishing Concrete Surfaces, section on Exposed-Aggregate Finishes for Slabs.) Precast wall

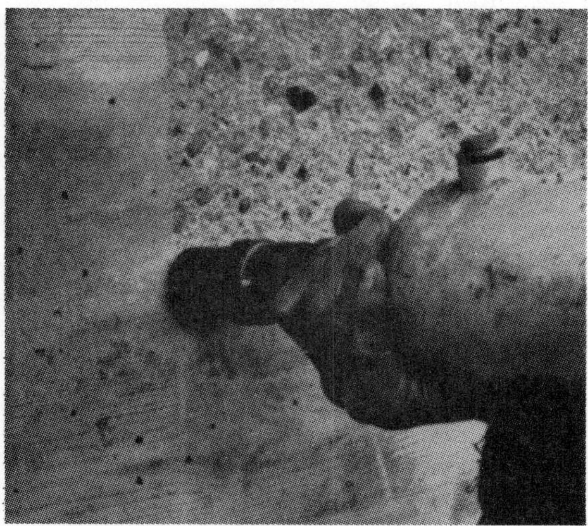

Fig. 6. An interesting stonelike texture is achieved by bushhammering.

panels are often cast face down for exposure of aggregates on the face. If large aggregate particles (1 inch and larger or 2.5 cm. and greater) are to be exposed, the sand-bedding technique is frequently used. In this procedure, aggregates are placed in a layer of sand and concrete is cast directly over them. If smaller size particles are to be exposed, they are generally incorporated into the concrete mixture and the forms are treated with a retarder. It leaves a retarded mortar that must be scrubbed away from the hardened concrete surface to expose the aggregates.

Rather than use a retarder on the forms, muriatic acid may be used to etch the surface and expose the aggregates, which in this case must be siliceous or other acid-resistant types. Small-sized particles are generally used because only a thin layer of mortar can be removed economically by acid etching. This method is applicable if aggregates must be exposed on more than one surface of a panel. Another method frequently used for the removal of surface mortar to expose the aggregates is abrasive blasting (Fig. 7).

Three basic techniques are used to distribute the aggregates uniformly for a pleasing appearance when casting exposed-aggregate surfaces on cast-in-place concrete walls, beams, and columns. They involve the use of (1) low-slump, gap-graded concrete mixes, (2) preplaced aggregate concrete, or (3) aggregate transfer. (*See* Chap. 14, Precast Concrete.)

Low-slump, gap-graded concrete mixes are used most frequently to produce an attractive exposed-aggregate finish on cast-in-place structures. These mixes contain a maximum amount of coarse aggregate, with the particles of one size or having a very narrow size range. The use of continuously graded coarse and fine aggregates in the percentages usual in conventional concrete mixtures results in nonuniform distribution of the exposed aggregate. Mixes that satisfy architectural requirements usually contain a large percentage of coarse aggregate and a small percentage of fine aggregate, sufficient for workability—with no aggregate in the intermediate-size range. This is known as gap-grading (sometimes skip or jump grading). Aggregate exposure is accomplished by the use of chemical retarders, abrasive blasting, or tooling.

Fig. 7. Colorful aggregates in a white cement matrix were exposed on this precast unit by sandblasting. Exposed-aggregate finishes impart a ruggedly handsome texture to concrete surfaces.

Preplaced aggregate concrete is named for its unique placement procedure. Forms are filled with coarse aggregate and then structural quality grout is moved, either under pressure or by vibration, into the voids among the aggregate particles to produce concrete. This technique avoids the main disadvantage of exposing aggregate in conventional cast-in-place concrete—an irregular surface texture caused by uneven distribution of coarse aggregate. When the forms are stripped, the surface appears as normal, off-the-form concrete, but when the aggregate is exposed, usually by tooling or abrasive blasting, the distribution of the coarse aggregate particles over the surface is uniform.

With the *aggregate-transfer method* aggregates are held in an adhesive on form liners; the liners are installed in forms; and the concrete is placed and cured. When the forms and liners are removed, the aggregates are firmly embedded in the concrete and exposed to view. This method is applicable for cast-in-place formed concrete, and has been used for precast panels.

Off-the-Form Finishes

Many formed concrete surfaces require little or no additional treatment. They can be obtained by proper use of certain forming materials or form liners. These surfaces may be divided into two general classes—smooth and textured or patterned. The *smooth surfaces* are produced by using plastic-coated forms, steel forms, fiberglass reinforced plastic forms, formica forms, or tempered hardboard forms. *Textured* or *patterned surfaces* are achieved by using rough-sawn lumber, special grades and textures of plywood, or form liners, or by fracturing the projections of a striated surface. (*See* Chap. 12, finishing Concrete Surfaces, sections on Textured and Patterned Finishes for Slabs.)

Chapter 12

Finishing Concrete Surfaces

TEXTURED FINISHES FOR SLABS

Variation in texture of concrete surfaces is limited only by the imagination and skill of the craftsman. Many interesting and functional textured finishes can be produced with less effort and expense than a smooth-troweled surface.

Finish texture can be varied as desired, from a smooth, polished appearance to the roughness of a gravel path. The smoothest finish is produced by a finisher with a steel trowel; the final troweling taking place when the surface is quite hard.

Practical decorative textures can be produced by using floats, trowels, and brooms. More elaborate textures are possible with special techniques using a mortar dash coat or rock salt.

Float and Trowel Textures

A swirl float or trowel finish makes for visual interest as well as surer footing. To produce a *swirl float texture,* the concrete is struck off, bull-floated (or darbied), and then hand-floated in the usual manner, except that the float should be worked flat on the surface in a swirling motion, using pressure. Patterns are made by using a series of uniform arcs or twists. Coarse textures are produced by wood floats, and medium textures by aluminum, magnesium, or canvas resin floats.

To produce a *swirl trowel texture* the concrete is finished as previously described and then troweled in the usual manner. Some time after the first troweling, a trowel should be worked flat on the surface, using a swirling motion and pressure. An older trowel works best, since the blade of a *broken in* tool has a slight curvature allowing it to be worked flat without the edges digging into the concrete.

Timing is important. After the first troweling, whether by hand or power, there should be a lapse of time—the length depending on such factors as temperature, humidity, and the like—to allow the surface to become harder. Do not wait too long because the swirl should be applied while it is still possible to work a small amount of fine mortar to the surface. This material creates a *drag* on the trowel, leaving the surface with a fine-textured, matte-like finish. Care should be taken to allow the concrete to set sufficiently so that the texture is not marred during curing.

Broomed Textures

Broomed finishes are attractive, nonslip textures secured by pulling damp brooms across freshly floated or troweled surfaces. Coarse textures suitable for steep slopes or heavy traffic are produced by stiff-bristle brooms on newly floated concrete (Fig. 1). Medium to fine textures are obtained by using soft-bristle brooms on floated or steel-troweled surfaces. For best results, the broom should be rinsed in water after each pass and tapped to remove excess water. Sharp, uniform textures are obtained when using a broom that is specially made for texturing concrete as shown in Fig. 2. The broom shown in Fig. 2 has 2¼-inch (6-cm.) plastic bristles set into an 18-inch wide (45-cm.), ⅞-inch (2-cm.) thick wood holder. Other models up to 4 feet (1.2 meters) wide, with extendable handles are available.

A *broomed texture* can be applied in many ways—straight lines, curved lines, wavy lines, or sawtooth patterns. A close-up view of a wavy broomed texture is shown in Fig. 3. Driveways and sidewalks are usually broomed at right angles to direction of traffic. Each pass of the broom can be contiguous to the previous one, or an area of unbroomed concrete can be left between passes. To create a checkerboard effect, the slab is divided into square panels by control joints, and each panel is broomed at a 90-degree angle to the brooming of immediately adjacent panels.

Fig. 1. A coarse-textured broomed finish.

Fig. 2. A fine-textured broomed finish.

Fig. 3. A wavy broomed texture.

Travertine Texture

A *travertine finish,* sometimes called keystone, requires a more elaborate procedure. After the concrete slab has been struck off, darbied, and edged in the usual manner, the slab is broomed with a stiff-bristle broom to ensure bond when the finish (mortar coat) is applied.

The finish coat is made by mixing one bag of white portland cement and 2 cubic feet (.06 cu. meters) of sand with about ¼ pound (.1 kg.) of color pigment. Yellow is generally used to tint the mortar coat, but any mineral oxide color may be used. Care must be taken to keep the proportions exactly the same for all batches. Enough water should be added to make a soupy mixture with the consistency of thick paint.

This mortar is placed in pails and thrown vigorously on the slab with a dash brush to make an uneven surface with ridges and depressions. The ridges should be about ¼ to ½ inch (6 to 13 mm.) high. The mortar is allowed to set enough to permit the worker to work on the surface with kneeboards. The slab is then steel-troweled to flatten the ridges and spread the mortar. This leaves the surface smooth in some places with voids and rough, low areas resembling travertine marble when the mortar is made with white cement and yellow pigment. By varying the amount of mortar thrown on the slab and the extent of troweling many interesting texture variations can be produced (Figs. 4 and 5). The slab may then be scored into random geometric designs before curing.

A *stimulated travertine finish* may also be created using a factory-prepared dry-shake material that is applied to the concrete surface just when it is ready for the first floating. This material is applied in two applications, wood floated after each application, and then troweled after a proper lapse of time to allow the surface to become harder.

Rock Salt Texture

A *rock salt texture* is frequently used as an economical, decorative surface finish for concrete slabs (Fig. 6). This texture is produced by scattering rock salt over the surface after floating, troweling, or brooming. The salt grains are rolled or pressed into the surface with only the tops of the grains left exposed. After five days of curing under waterproof paper, the surface is washed and brushed, dislodging and dissolving the salt grains and leaving pits or holes. The surface between the holes may be left slightly rough to give better traction in outdoor applications. The swirl float, swirl trowel, or broomed texture may be used.

The salt crystals used are ordinary sodium chloride (kiln-dried water softener salt) with a coarse gradation that permits 100

Fig. 4. Travertine texture.

Fig. 5. Random-scored travertine finish.

Fig. 6. Rock salt texture.

percent to pass a ⅜-inch (9-mm.) sieve and 85 percent to be retained on a No. 8 sieve. An extra coarse gradation may be used to obtain a greater percentage of larger holes in the finished surface texture. Holes larger than ¼ inch (6 mm.) are not desirable for foot traffic.

Normally, the salt grains are distributed at a rate of about 5 pounds per 100 square feet (2.3 kilos per 10 sq. meters) of slab surface, but a range of 3 to 12 pounds per 100 square feet (1.4 to 5.4 kilos per 10 sq. meters) may be used to create a light to heavy pattern. The heavier concentrations produce textures that resemble travertine.

A 90-pound (41-kgs.) floor tile roller has been found to work best, but hand tools or pipes may be used to press or roll the salt grains into the surface. The grains must be spread and worked into the surface before the concrete becomes too hard.

Curing compounds may be used in lieu of waterproof curing paper, but the salt-dissolving operation will be more difficult. A water cure is not satisfactory for use with the rock salt procedure. Plastic sheeting may cause discoloration if it is not kept flat and wrinkle-free on the concrete surface.

Neither the rock salt nor the travertine finish is recommended for use in areas subject to freezing weather. Water trapped in the recesses of these finishes tends, when frozen, to spall the surface.

PATTERNED FINISHES FOR SLABS

Many pleasing decorative finishes can be built into concrete slabs during construction. One increasingly popular method of embellishing sidewalks, driveways, patios, and other slabs is the use of *incised patterns* which are stamped or tooled into the concrete to resemble stone, brick, or tile paving. Other interesting patterns are obtained by using divider strips of wood, plastic, metal, or masonry to form panels of various sizes and shapes—rectangular, square, or diamond. Straight-line designs can also be scored into the surface of slabs by using hand groovers or concrete saws. (*See* Fig. 7.)

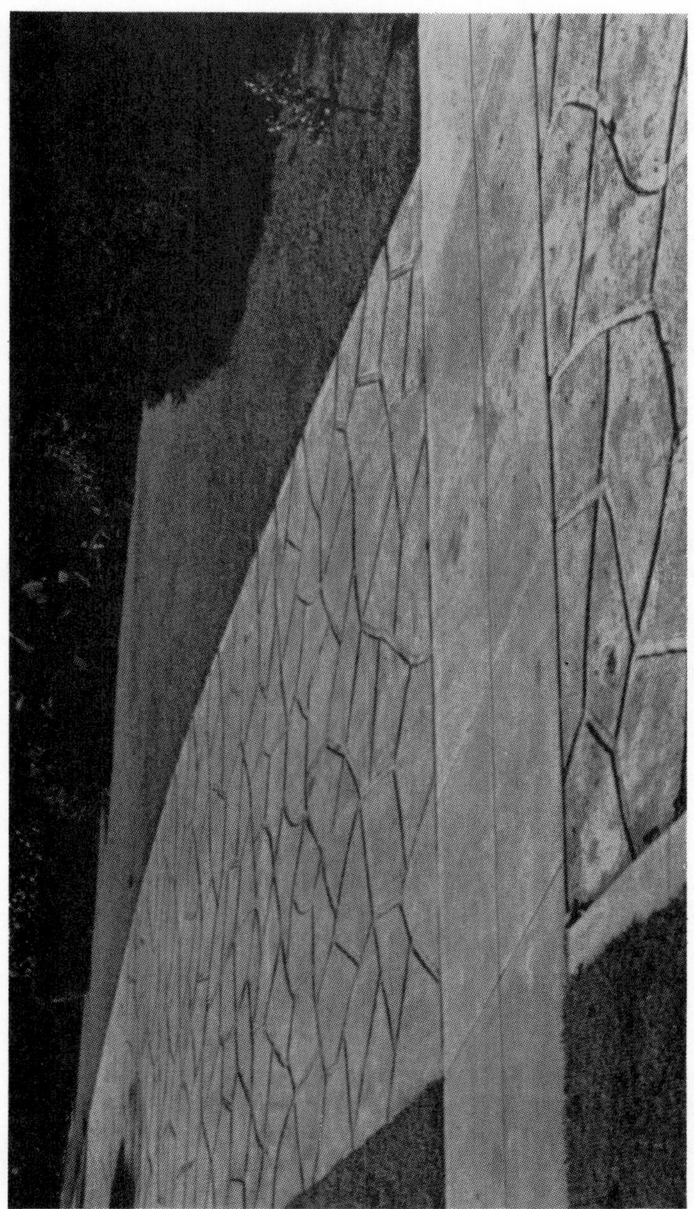

Fig. 7. Driveway finished with a float texture and a random flagstone pattern.

Incised Patterns

Random flagstone or *ashlar patterns* make an attractive finish for patio, sidewalk, driveway, or poolside slabs. Such patterns are made easily by embedding prepared *joints* made of wood or felt, which are removed after the slab has hardened. Wood lattice stock (¼- × 1½-inch or 6- × 13-mm.) or 15-pound (7-kgs.) roofing felt (1 inch or 25 mm. wide) are cut into lengths varying from 4 to 32 inches (10 to 81 cm.). Individual pieces are finished by cutting the sides into irregular jagged shapes to resemble the edges of paving stones. When wood is used, edges must be undercut to ease removal and prevent locking of the wood into the slab surface (Fig. 8). Curling of wood strips may be prevented by thoroughly soaking them in water prior to use or by waterproofing with two complete coats of good varnish.

After the slab has been struck off and bull-floated or darbied, it is allowed to set until ready for finishing. In this case somewhat sooner than is usual. The strips are laid out on the slab in the desired pattern (Fig. 9). Very small or complex shapes should be avoided.

As soon as the pattern is laid out, the strips are pressed into the concrete and the surface is floated. Felt strips, if used, may

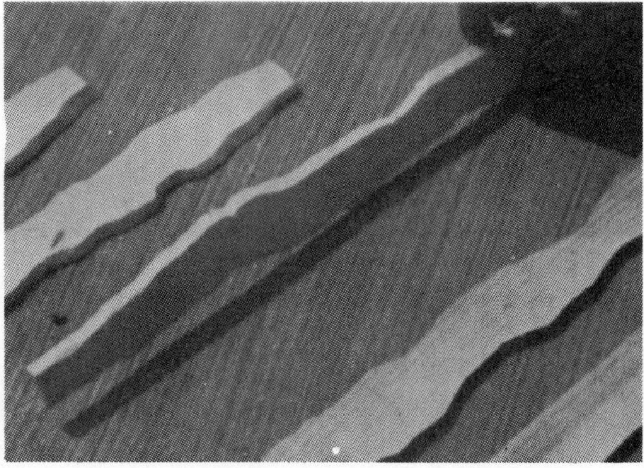

Fig. 8. Wood "joint" forms for flagstone or ashlar patterns.

Fig. 9. Laying out flagstone pattern with strips.

be patted into the surface using a hand float. The top of the strips should be just flush with the surface of the concrete (Fig. 10). The concrete may then be finished in its normal color, or, if desired, a different color can be added at this time, using a dry-shake.

The dry-shake method consists of applying a factory-prepared dry-color material over the concrete surface after preliminary floating. Two applications of the dry-shake are made, the first using about two-thirds of the total amount specified by the manufacturer. The surface is floated thoroughly after each application to make sure the color is uniformly worked into the concrete. After floating the second application the tops of the strips are cleaned of any paste that may have been carried over them. A patching trowel or putty knife can be used to scrape the strips clean (Fig. 11). If a smooth, hard surface is desired, troweling follows floating in the usual manner. A final steel troweling will then bring the strips and concrete to a uniform surface, which can be left smooth or be lightly broomed.

Felt strips are carefully removed before the slab is cured. Wood strips are removed the following day. The curing cover

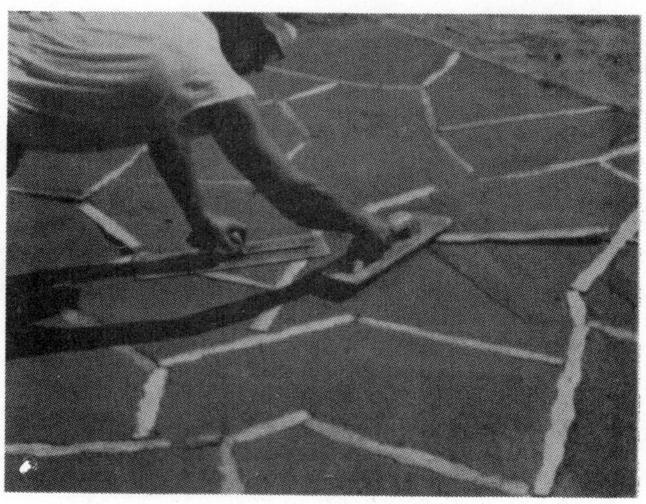

Fig. 10. Floating in wooden strips.

Fig. 11. Cleaning wooden strips.

can be taken off and the wooden strips removed by lifting with a patching trowel (Fig. 12). The slab may be left with depressed joints or with the joints filled in with a contrasting mortar. A natural gray slab with white mortar joints is very attractive. A colored slab looks good with natural gray joints.

Before filling the joints the slab should be flooded with water to keep the slab cool and the joints damp. Immediately before troweling in the mortar, the joints should be brushed with a paste of portland cement and water, mixed to the consistency of thick paint (Fig. 13). Care must be taken to prevent smearing mortar outside the joint area. A large coarse synthetic sponge and a bucket of water will be useful in cleaning the joint edges. In this operation it is best for two finishers to work together, with one painting in the cement grout ahead of the mortar and cleaning up the joint edges, while the other concentrates on packing in the mortar firmly and neatly.

Another way to produce the previous pattern makes use of an 18-inch (45-cm.) long piece of ½- or ¾-inch (13- or 19-mm.) copper pipe bent into a flat S-shape. After the concrete has been struck off and bull-floated or darbied, and after excess moisture has left the surface, the slab is scored in the desired pattern. This tooling must be done while the concrete is still quite plastic as the coarse aggregate must be pushed aside when the tool is pressed into the surface (Fig. 14).

The first tooling will leave burred edges. After the water sheen has completely disappeared the entire area should be floated and the joining tool run again to smooth the joints. Floating produces a texture that has good skid resistance and is relatively even (but not smooth). It is often used as a final finish. In such cases, it may be necessary to float the surface a second time after some hardening has taken place to impart the desired final texture. If a smooth, hard surface is desired, a careful steel troweling follows (Fig. 15). The final operation is a light brooming of the troweled surface, along with a careful touching-up of the joints with a soft-bristle paint brush (Fig. 16).

Cobblestone, brick, and tile in a variety of sizes and patterns can be cut deeply into partially set concrete with special platform stamping tools. The concrete may be colored integrally by

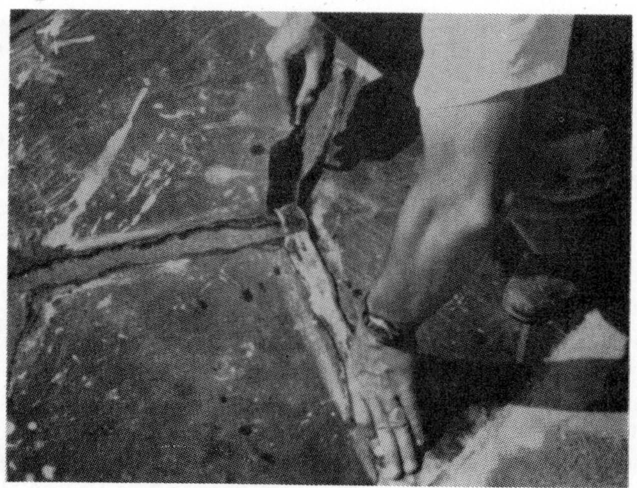

Fig. 12. Removing strips after concrete hardens.

Fig. 13. Filling joints with contrasting mortar.

Fig. 14. Tooling joints in slab.

Fig. 15. Troweling after jointing and floating.

Fig. 16. Touching up joints with soft brush.

the dry-shake method, or by both methods. The joints can be filled with plain or colored mortar to create any number of striking effects.

Concrete to receive a stamped pattern should contain small coarse aggregate such as pea gravel. Finishing follows the usual procedures. *Do not* trowel the surface more than once (Fig. 17). After the surface is floated or troweled to the desired texture, platform stamping pads are used. One pad is placed next to the other on the slab so that the pattern is accurately aligned. Eight pads were used for the driveway shown in Fig. 18, at least two are required. The user simply steps from one pad to the next, stamping the design to a depth of about 1 inch (2.5 cm.).

In addition to the weight of the workman, a hand tamper is sometimes used (as shown in Fig. 19) to ensure proper indentation of the stamping pad. After stamping, a tool similar to a brick mason's jointer is used to dress edges and cause some artificial imperfections (Fig. 20). (*See* Chap. 26, Bricklaying Tools and Equipment.) A small hand stamp is used to complete the pattern next to the slab edges (Fig. 21). Light tapping with a hand hammer may be required. This operation can be eliminated or greatly minimized by choosing slab sizes that are equal

Fig. 17. Finishing slab in preparation for stamped pattern.

Fig. 18. Pattern is stamped while concrete is still in plastic stage of set.

Fig. 19. A 25- to 35-pound (11.3- to 15.9-kgs.) hand tamper may be required to ensure indentation.

Fig. 20. Dressing edges and creating artificial imperfections.

Fig. 21. Completing pattern along edges with small hand stamps.

to even multiples of the platform stamping tool dimensions. On the driveway shown in Fig. 22 stamping nears completion five hours after concrete placement. Timing is critical since all stamping must be completed before the concrete sets too hard.

Other interesting relief patterns can be stamped into the surface of concrete slabs to resemble the wood grain of a boardwalk, basket weaving, or sea shells. Attractive geometric patterns can be produced by marking circles on the slab after the final smooth finish has been completed. This can be done without special stamping tools by using a variety of sizes of tin cans in a random pattern, or by using one or more sizes in a definite regular pattern. Large metal cookie cutters of various shapes may also be used for this purpose.

Wherever a large area is to be finished in this fashion several workers will be required. Immediately after the final troweling the surface will be quite hard but still easily marked (Fig. 23). As the slab continues to harden it will become more and more difficult, and finally impossible, to make impressions of the same depth and appearance. When more than one worker is involved, all must carefully coordinate their efforts so that the finished pattern will be uniform. Production of a sample pattern on a

Fig. 22. After curing, stamped impressions may be left open or grouted with a contrasting mortar.

Fig. 23. Making geometric pattern with a can.

nearby driveway or sidewalk is a good method of obtaining uniformity in the design layout. This can be done by dipping the cans in powdered chalk and marking an area large enough to serve as a guide. The sample can easily be washed away later. If no slab is convenient a large sheet of wallboard may be used.

A pattern giving a *fossil effect* can be produced by pressing leaves into the slab surface either singly as a border, or in groups or sprays as a focus of interest. Fresh leaves are carefully pressed into the surface immediately after it has been floated and troweled (Fig. 24). The leaves should be so completely embedded that they may be troweled over without being dislodged, but no mortar should be deposited over the leaves. After the concrete has set sufficiently, the leaves are removed. (*See* Chap. 11, Finishing Concrete Slabs.)

Fig. 24 Making fossil effect leaf impressions.

DIVIDER STRIPS

Divider strips and *borders of wood, plastic, metal,* or *masonry* serve a number of purposes. Unusual patterns and designs can be created with rectangles, squares, and diamonds. Concrete work can be segmented into small areas for better control of placing and finishing. Combinations of various surface finishes are possible, and random cracks are greatly reduced or eliminated because divider strips act as control joints.

Wood divider strips and side forms which are to remain in place permanently for decorative purposes are usually made of 1 × 4 or 2 × 4 (2.5 × 10 or 5 × 10 cm.) rot-resistant lumber such as redwood, cypress, or cedar (Fig. 25). For further resistance to weathering these woods should be primed with a clear wood sealer. Also, it is a good practice to mask the top surfaces with tape to protect the wood from abrasion and staining by concrete during construction (Fig. 26). Miter corner joints neatly and join intersecting strips with neat butt joints. Anchor outside forms to the concrete with 16-penny galvanized nails driven at 16-inch (40-cm.) intervals horizontally through the forms at mid height. Divider strips should have nail anchors similarly spaced but driven from alternate sides of the board (Fig. 27,C). Drive all nail heads flush with the forms. Never drive nails through the top of side forms or divider strips. All stakes that are to remain in place permanently must be driven or cut off 2 inches (5 cm.) below the surface of the concrete.

Plastic strips are difficult to install straight in concrete unless they are nailed or stapled to the top of wood strips securely staked to the subgrade.

Another method of dividing a slab into patterns is with metal strips like those used for terrazzo. All-metal or combination plastic top-metal bottom strips are available in brass or zinc in widths from 20 gage (.032 inch or .8 mm.) up to ½ inch (1.3 cm.) and from 1¼ to 1½ inches (3.1 to 3.8 cm.) deep. For rigidity the plastic top strips are mounted on metal bases in such a way that only the plastic shows in the finished surface.

Divider strips of the type used in terrazzo are suitable only for two-course construction where the topping varies from ½ to ¾ inch (1.3 to 1.9 cm.) thick. In slabs finished by troweling rather than grinding, care must be exercised to set the strips at the exact finished level.

Concrete masonry, brick, or stone divider strips and borders may be set in a sand bed with or without mortared joints. For more permanent work masonry units should be set in a mortar bed with all joints mortared. For the most permanent installa-

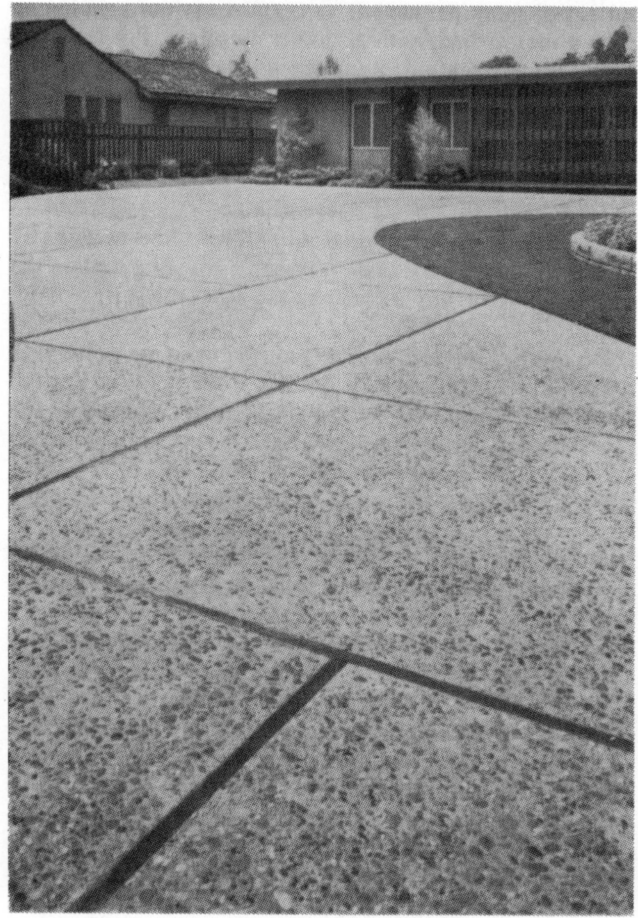

Fig. 25. Use of wood divider strips in driveway. Exposed aggregate surface obtained with Mexican beach pebbles.

Fig. 26. Masking the top surfaces of wood divider strips.

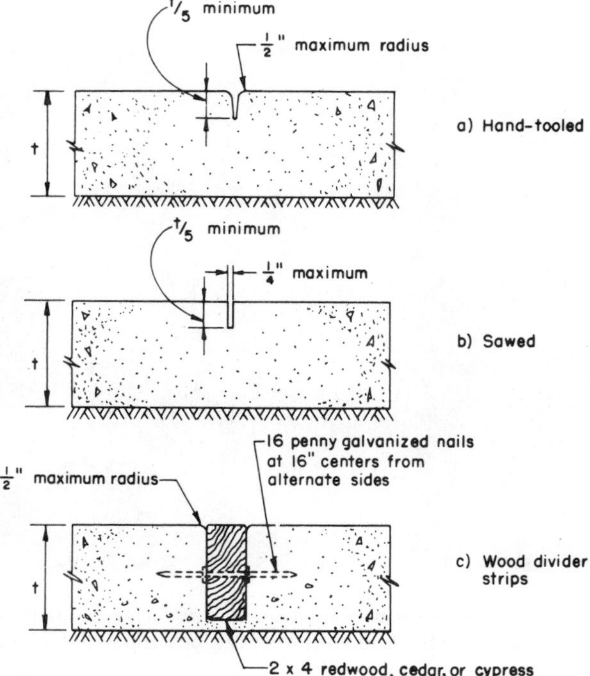

Fig. 27. These methods of producing patterns in concrete slabs also act as control joints, eliminating unsightly random cracking.

tion units should be bedded in mortar spread on a concrete base slab and all joints mortared. (*See* Chap. 22, Concrete Masonry Units.)

Scoring and Sawing

Concrete slabs may be *scored* into straight-line patterns by the use of an ordinary cement mason's grooving tool on the fresh concrete or with a concrete saw after the surface hardens. (*See* Chap. 21, Masonry Tools and Equipment.)

Decorative scoring with a groover must be done with care or this operation may detract from the final appearance of the concrete. To get a straight line, use a straightedge, such as a 1-inch (2.5 cm.) thick board at least 6 inches (15 cm.) wide, to serve as a guide (Fig. 28).

Hand groovers are made of stainless steel and other metals and are available in various sizes and styles. The radius of a groover should be ¼ to ½ inch (6 to 13 mm.). The bit (cutting edge) should be deep enough to cut the slab to a depth of about ¼ inch (6 mm.) for decorative work. If the groove is also to serve

Fig. 28. Proper use of straightedge while scoring a slab with a hand groover.

as a control joint, a groover with a bit deep enough to cut the slab a minimum of one-fifth, and preferably one-fourth, of its depth is mandatory (Fig. 27,A). Groovers with worn-out or shallow bits should not be used for making control joints but may be used for decorative scoring of the surface.

Instead of being hand-grooved, patterns can be cut with a concrete saw. For small jobs an electric handsaw equipped with a masonry cutting blade can be used. A diamond blade produces a narrow ⅛-inch (3-mm.) wide cut while an abrasive blade makes a ¼-inch (6-mm.) wide cut. For decorative sawing the depth of cut need not be more than about ¼ inch (6 mm.). However, to function as a control joint the blade must cut as deep as a hand-tooled control joint—one-fifth to one-fourth of the slab thickness (Fig. 27,B).

Sawing should be done as soon as the surface is firm enough not to be torn or damaged by the blade. This is normally four to twelve hours after the concrete hardens. Light raveling of the sawed edges is permissible and indicates proper timing of the sawing operation. If sawing is delayed too long the concrete may crack before it is sawed, or cracks may develop ahead of the saw.

Combinations

When concrete is used decoratively, striking effects can be obtained by combining colors and textures with one or more of the patterns described in this chapter. *For example,* alternate areas of exposed aggregate can be eye-catching when combined with plain, colored, or textured concrete. Ribbons and borders of concrete masonry or brick add a distinctive touch when combined with exposed aggregate. Light-colored strips of exposed aggregate may divide areas of dark-colored concrete or vice versa. Scored and stamped designs are enhanced when combined with integral or dry-shake color.

These are just a few combinations. The possibilities are unlimited. With a little imagination a concrete driveway, sidewalk, plaza, floor, patio, or pool deck can be tailored to fit the mood and style of any architecture or landscape.

EXPOSED-AGGREGATE FINISHES FOR SLABS

Exposed aggregate offers a wide range of textures and an unlimited color selection making it one of the most popular and attractive decorative finishes for concrete slabs. *Exposed-aggregate finishes* can be rugged, slip-resistant, and highly immune to wear and weather. They are ideal for sidewalks, driveways, patios, pool decks, tilt-up panels, and other applications where flat concrete slabs are cast horizontally (Fig. 29).

Construction Procedures

There are a number of methods for obtaining exposed-aggregate finishes on flatwork. One of the most practical and commonly used is the *seeding* method.

Figures 30 to 41 illustrate the construction procedure used to produce exposed-aggregate panels.

Fig. 29. An entry walk combines wood divider strips to separate bands of smooth colored concrete and expanses of exposed-aggregate texture.

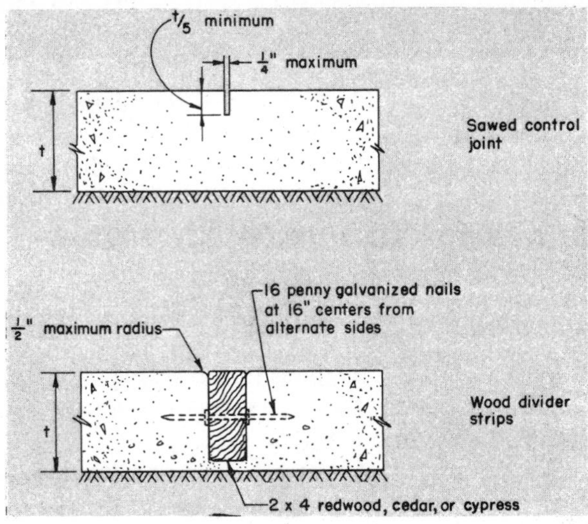

Fig. 30. Types of control joints used in exposed-aggregate walks, drives, patios, and other flatwork.

Fig. 31. Concrete to receive a seeded exposed-aggregate finish should have a slump of between two and four inches.

Fig. 32. The slab is struck off in the usual manner except that the level of the surface should be left ⅛ to 7/16 inches (3.2 to 11.1 mm.) lower than the top of forms to accommodate the seeded aggregate.

Fig. 33. After strikeoff, the surface is leveled and smoothed with a wood darby.

Fig. 34. The select aggregate is spread uniformly by shovel and hand. A mixture of black and white crushed stone is used.

Fig. 35. The entire surface is completely covered with one layer of select stone.

Fig. 36. The aggregate is initially embedded by tapping with a wood darby. A hand float or straightedge may also be used.

Fig. 37. Further embedment of aggregate is done with a bullfloat.

Fig. 38. Final embedment is done with a hand float until appearance of the surface is similar to that of a normal slab after floating.

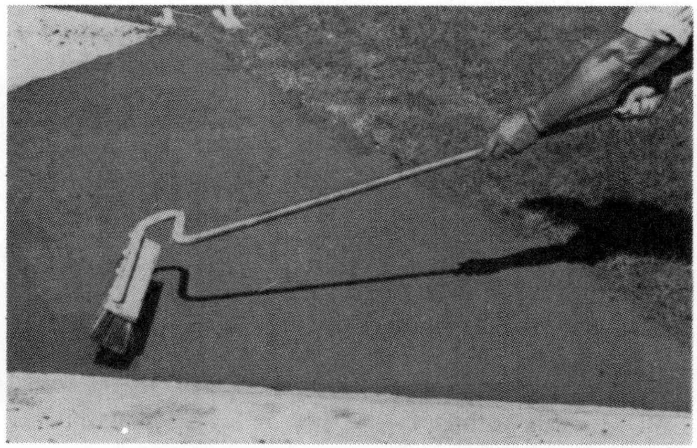

Fig. 39. In exposing the aggregate, timing is critical. Work should begin as soon as the mortar can be removed without over exposing or dislodging the aggregate. The first step is to brush the surface lightly with a stiff nylon-bristle broom to remove excess mortar.

Fig. 40. Fine spray the surface with water while brushing. Special exposed-aggregate brooms with built-in water jets are available.

Fig. 41. Continue washing and brushing until flush water runs clear and there is no noticeable cement film left on aggregate.

General

Sample panels should be made to assess the workability and finishing properties of the mix and to determine the appearance of the finished surface and depth of exposure that will be the basis for the work. Normally, the worker selects the aggregate source and specifies its size within one or more of the following gradations: ¼ to ½ inch (.6 to 1.3 cm.), ⅜ to ⅝ inch (.9 to 1.6 cm.), ½ to ¾ inch (1.3 to 1.9 cm.), ⅝ to ⅞ inch (1.6 to 2.2 cm.), ¾ to 1 inch (1.9 to 2.5 cm.), 1 to 1½ inch (2.5 to 3.8 cm.), 1½ to 2 inches (3.8 to 5 cm.). Depth of exposure should not exceed one-third of the average diameter of the aggregate and not more than one-half the diameter of the smallest aggregate.

When the two smaller gradations are used—¼ to ½ inch or ⅜ to ⅝ inch (.6 to 1.3 cm. or .9 to 1.6 cm.)—a two-course method of slab placement is suggested, using in the top course a specially designed gap-graded mix of the selected aggregate and masonry sand instead of normal concrete sand. Use of a surface retarder is advisable with these small aggregate sizes.

Concrete

Concrete requirements are covered under ASTM C94 specifications for ready mixed concrete. A maximum size of ¾-inch (1.9-cm.) coarse aggregate for the base concrete mix is specified to assist in embedment of the select seeding aggregate. Sometimes an oversanded mix is used for the same reason. Care should be taken to ensure that No. 4 and smaller sizes of coarse aggregate are eliminated from the base mix when crushed stone or an aggregate whose color is not compatible with the select seeding aggregate is specified. Scheduling of concrete trucks for a smooth operation should be carefully controlled.

Seeding Aggregate

Selection of the aggregate to be exposed must be made carefully in order to avoid aggregates that contain deleterious materials or staining substances such as iron oxides and iron pyrites. The select seeding aggregate may be specified as a rounded river gravel, cubical-shaped stone, or crushed stone; a particular source may be specified.

Caution: When crushed stone is specified, additional cost in labor can be expected. Crushed stone has more of a tendency to stack during the seeding operation than rounded aggregate. Also, the exposed surfaces can have sharp edges that would be undesirable in some applications, such as pool decks.

Forms

Forms are usually set for a minimum slope of ¼ inch per foot (2 cm. per meter) to allow for drainage of slabs. Permanent forms (left in place) are generally made of 1 × 4 or 2 × 4 (2.5 × 10 or 5 × 10 cm.) redwood, cypress, or cedar.

Joints

In driveways and sidewalks *control joints* should be spaced at intervals about equal to the slab width. Drives and walks wider than about 10 to 12 feet (3 to 3.7 meters) should also have a longitudinal control joint down the center. Joint spacing in patios should not be over 10 feet (3 meters) on center in either direction.

If possible the panels formed by control joints should be approximately square. Panels with excessive length-to-width ratio (more than 1½ to 1) are likely to crack. As a general rule, the smaller the panel the less likelihood of random cracking. Joints should be continuous, not staggered or offset.

Control joints can be sawed or formed with wood divider strips as shown in Fig 30. Hand-tooled control joints are not practical for use with exposed-aggregate finishes. Sometimes 1 × 2 or 2 × 2 (2.5 × 5 cm. or 5 × 5 cm.) wood divider strips are used, particularly if welded-wire fabric (mesh) is specified for slab reinforcement.

Aggregate Preparation

In washing the seeding aggregate, it is recommended that the screening used be one with openings one size smaller than the minimum specified aggregate size.

Aggregate Quantities

The quantity of select seeding aggregate required per square foot of slab surface will vary from approximately 3 pounds for ⅜-inch (3-mm.) aggregate to 6 pounds (.9 kg.) for 2-inch (5-cm.) material. It is very important to have a sufficient supply of the seeding aggregate available to complete the work.

Placement of Concrete

The work output per worker for exposed-aggregate finishes will vary greatly, according to the individual's skill, weather conditions, and the workability of the mix. In general, a finisher can produce only about one-third of the area that he would normally finish for a steel-troweled surface. The strike-off operation on the base slab should be such that a level surface is obtained ⅛ to 7/16 inch (3 to 11 mm.) below the desired final finish grade to allow the addition of the seeding aggregate. Allow approximately ⅛ inch (3 mm.) for aggregate sizes ⅜ to ⅝ inch (3 to 16 mm.), 3/16 inch (9.5 mm.) for aggregate sizes ½ to ¾ inch (13 to 19 mm.), ¼ inch (6 mm.) for aggregate sizes ¾ to 1 inch (19 to 25 mm.), 5/16 inch (8 mm.) for aggregate sizes 1 to 1½ inches (25 to 38 mm.), and 7/16 inch (11 mm.) for aggregate sizes 1¼ to 2 inches (32 to 58 mm.).

Seeding and Embedment

The seeding operation is usually started immediately after the concrete has been placed, struck off, and darbied or bullfloated. It is important that the slump of the base concrete be not less than 2 inches (5 cm.) when the concrete temperature is 70° F. (21° C.) or lower so that the seeded aggregate can be worked into the slab. This minimum slump should be increased as the concrete temperature increases above 70° F. (21° C.), but the maximum slump should not exceed 4 inches (10 cm.) in any case.

The select aggregate is carefully seeded by shovel or by hand to completely cover the entire surface with one layer of stone. Seeding by hand may be necessary in difficult locations such as corners and along edges. Care must be taken to see that stacked stone and flat or slivered particles are removed.

The seeded aggregate is normally embedded in the concrete by tapping with a wooden hand float, a darby, or a straightedge. Sometimes a rolling device such as a large diameter pipe is used. Final embedment can be obtained with a magnesium float or darby until all the aggregate is entirely embedded and mortar completely surrounds and slightly covers all particles. Appearance after final embedment should be similar to a normal slab after floating, with all voids and imperfections removed. Special care must be taken to see that the aggregate is not overembedded and that the finished surface is not deformed. If too high a slump is used in the base mix, the seeded aggregate will settle and the completed surface may be below the final finish grade and below the top of any permanent left-in-place forms.

A layer of mortar about 1/16 inch (1.6 mm.) thick over all embedded aggregate is desired. Care should be taken that none of the seeding aggregate is mixed with the base concrete in order to get sufficient mortar to complete the embedment. If this happens the color of the coarse aggregate in the base concrete will show up on the finished surface. The need for additional mortar is generally due to an improper mix design or too long a delay in the seeding and embedment operation. When very small areas require additional mortar, excess mortar from nearby areas may be used.

Exposing the Aggregate

Timing of the start of the aggregate exposure operation is critical and is usually based on previous experience. In general, this operation should be delayed until the slab will bear the weight of a man on knee-boards with no indentation. At this time the slab is lightly brushed with a stiff nylon-bristle broom to remove excess mortar. If aggregate is dislodged, the operation must be delayed until none of the aggregate is dislodged. (To test for the proper time of exposure when large areas are involved, a sample panel, let us say, 2 × 2 feet (.6 × .6 meters) can be prepared at the same time that the project is cast.)

Next, brushing combined with a fine water spray can begin.

Adequate delay is required between each pass, the length of delay depending upon the slab's rate of set. As the slab sets, washing and brushing can proceed at a more vigorous pace. Soft and hard bristle brooms and special exposed-aggregate brooms with water jets are available to complete the job. Occasionally, wire-bristle brooms may be needed for a particularly stubborn area, but such brooms should be used with caution as they may stain the aggregate. It is extremely important that the aggregate have a uniform exposure at the end of the washing and brushing operations. Some areas may need special attention. Several passes will be required before the proper exposure is obtained. Continue washing and brushing until exposure is uniform at the proper depth, the flush water runs clear, and there is no noticeable cement film on the aggregate.

Surface Retarders

Surface retarders may be used to advantage in some cases, but they are not generally needed. *For example*, because of placing conditions it may be necessary, on large jobs, to delay the time of washing and brushing. Also, when using the smaller aggregate sizes, it is desirable to delay the time of set of the surface matrix to allow the base concrete to attain its initial set. This procedure will help prevent dislodgment of the small aggregates. When using surface retarders the following tips will be found helpful.

1. Choose a reliable surface retarder.
2. Make certain that the surface retarder is compatible with the concrete materials to be used (*see* No. 6).
3. Apply the surface retarder uniformly—this is essential for good results.
4. Know the effects of concrete temperature on length of delay of set for the particular retarder used (*see* No. 6).
5. Read the instructions and literature issued by the manufacturer for any brand of retarder being used for the first time.
6. Make sample panels under job conditions.

Curing

Standard moist-curing procedures should be followed. The

use of ponding, sprinkling, covering with waterproof paper or plastic sheeting, or continuous saturation of burlap coverings are all acceptable. It is better not to use a curing compound on this type of work. Also avoid curing with damp sand that contains silt and clay because of the difficulty of cleaning the slab afterwards.

Acid Wash

The use of an *acid wash* is not a necessity, but it is often helpful to brighten the appearance of an exposed-aggregate surface, especially those made with the darker aggregates.

For best results acid washing should be delayed a *minimum* of two weeks after the concrete has been placed, but a longer delay is better. Caution should be exercised when using acid on some aggregates such as limestones, dolomites, and marbles that may discolor and dissolve in muriatic acid. Workers should be protected as well as adjacent areas and materials. Residue from acid washing should be flushed with clear water and drained away from areas that might be damaged.

The surface to be cleaned with a five to ten percent solution of muriatic acid should be thoroughly saturated with water and any excess water removed before application of the acid.

Sealer

Clear coatings often bring out the true color of the aggregate and help keep the exposed matrix from discoloring with use. Care is needed in selection of a coating material. Some coating materials may darken the matrix and some may oxidize from exposure to sunlight and become a dirty yellow or possibly brown. Many of the better coatings consist of methyl methacrylate forms of acrylic resin.

Weather Conditions

During hot, dry, windy days, the surface may set prematurely (sometimes called crusting). Covering the slab with damp burlap, waterproof paper, or plastic sheeting immediately after embedding the select aggregate will prevent this and will help retain surface moisture until the start of washing and brushing.

Chapter 13

Placing Concrete in Water

If placement of concrete underwater is necessary, it should be done by the best methods available.

METHODS USED

Concrete can be placed under water by several methods. For best results, concrete should not be placed in water having a temperature below 45° F. (7.2° C.), and should not be placed in water flowing with a velocity greater than 10 feet (3 meters) per minute, although sacked concrete may be used for water velocities greater than this. If the water temperature is below 45° F. (7.2° C.), the temperature of the concrete when it is deposited should be above 60° F. (15.6° C.) but in no case above 80° F. (26.7° C.). If the water temperature is above 45° F. (7.2° C.), no temperature precautions need be taken. Cofferdams or forms must be tight enough to reduce the current to less than 10 feet (3 meters) per minute through the space to be concreted. Pumping of water should not be permitted while concrete is being placed or for 24 hours thereafter.

Tremie Method

The *tremie method* involves a device shown in Fig. 1. A tremie is a pipe having a funnel-shaped upper end into which the concrete is fed. The pipe must be long enough to reach from a working platform above water level to the lowest point at which the concrete is to be deposited. Frequently the lower end of the pipe is equipped with a gate, permitting filling before insertion in water. This gate can be opened from above at the proper

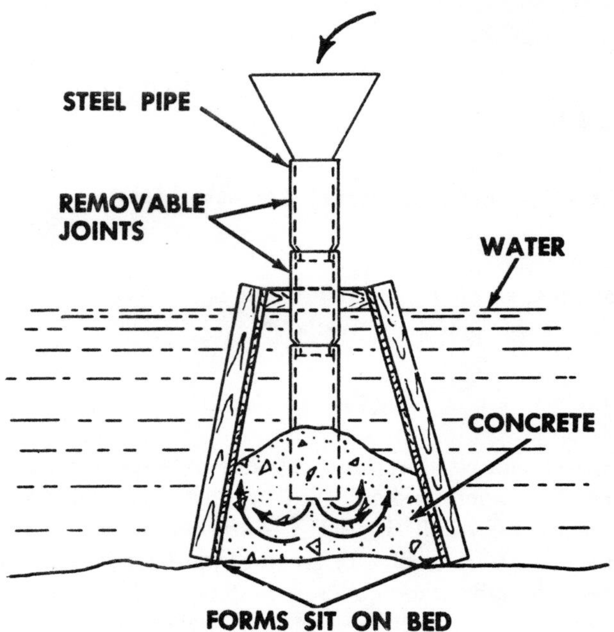

Fig. 1. Placing concrete under water with a tremie.

time. The bottom or discharge end is kept continuously buried in newly placed concrete. Air and water are excluded from the pipe by keeping it constantly filled with concrete. The tremie should be lifted slowly to permit the concrete to flow out. Care must be taken not to lose the seal at the bottom. If lost, it is necessary to raise the tremie, plug the lower end, and lower the tremie into position again. The tremie should not be moved laterally through the desposited concrete. When it is necessary to move the tremie, it should be lifted out of the concrete and moved to the new position, keeping the top surface of the concrete as level as possible. A number of tremies should be used if the concrete is to be deposited over a large area. They should be spaced on 20- to 25-foot (6.1- to 7.6-meter) centers. Concrete should be supplied at a uniform rate to all tremies with no interruptions at any of them. Pumping from the mixer is the best method of supplying the concrete. Large tremies can be suspended from a crane boom and can be easily raised and lowered with the boom. Concrete that is placed with a tremie should have a slump of about 6 inches (15 cm.) and a cement content of seven sacks per cubic yard (.77 cu. meters) of concrete. About 50 percent of the total aggregate should be sand and the maximum coarse aggregate size should be from 1½ to 2 inches (3.8 to 5 cm.).

Bucket Method

Concrete can be placed at considerable depth below the water surface by means of the open-top *bucket method.* This bucket has a drop bottom. Concrete placed by this method can be slightly stiffer than that placed by the tremie method, but it should still contain seven sacks of cement per cubic yard (.77 cu. meter). The bucket is completely filled and the top covered with a canvas flap. The flap is attached to one side of the bucket only. The bucket is lowered slowly into the water so that the canvas will not be displaced. Concrete must not be discharged from the bucket before the surface, upon which the concrete is to be placed, has been reached. Soundings should be made frequently so that the top surface is kept level.

Sack Method

In an emergency, concrete can be placed under water by the *sack method.* Jute sacks of about 1-cubic foot (.03 cu. meter) capacity, filled about two-thirds full, are lowered into the water, preferably shallow water. These sacks are placed in header and stretcher course, interlocking the entire mass. A header course is placed so that the length of the sack is at right angles to the direction in which the stretcher-course sacks are laid. Cement from one sack seeps into adjacent sacks and they are thus bonded together. No attempt should be made to compact concrete under water, for experience has shown that the less the concrete is disturbed after placement, the better it will be.

Chapter 14

Precast Concrete

Precasting is the fabrication of a structural member at a place other than its final position of use. It can be done anywhere although this procedure is best adapted to a factory or yard. Jobsite precasting is not uncommon for large projects. *Precast concrete* can be produced in several different shapes and sizes, including piles, girders, and roof members. *Prestressed concrete* is especially well adapted to precasting techniques.

Generally, structural members including standard highway girders, poles, electric poles, masts, and building members are precast by factory methods unless the difficulty or impracticability of transportation makes jobsite casting more desirable.

PRECAST CONCRETE FLOOR AND ROOF SLABS, WALLS, AND PARTITIONS

The most commonly used precast slabs or panels for *floor* and *roof decks* are the channel and double-T types (Fig. 1).

Channel slabs (Fig. 1) vary in size with a depth ranging from 9 to 12 inches (22.9 to 30 cm.), width 2 to 5 feet (.6 to 1.5 meters), thickness 1 to 2 inches (2.5 to 5 cm.), and have been used in spans up to 50 feet (15.2 meters). If desired or needed, the legs of the channels may extend across the ends, and if used in combination with the top-slab it may be stiffened with occasional cross-ribs. Wire mesh may be used in the top slab for reinforcement. The longitudinal grooves located along the top of the channel legs may be grouted to form keys between adjacent slabs.

The *double-T slab* (Fig. 1) vary in size from 4 to 6 feet (1.2 to 1.8 meters) in width, 9 to 16 inches (22.9 to 40.6 cm.) in depth, and have been used in spans as long as 50 feet (15.2 meters).

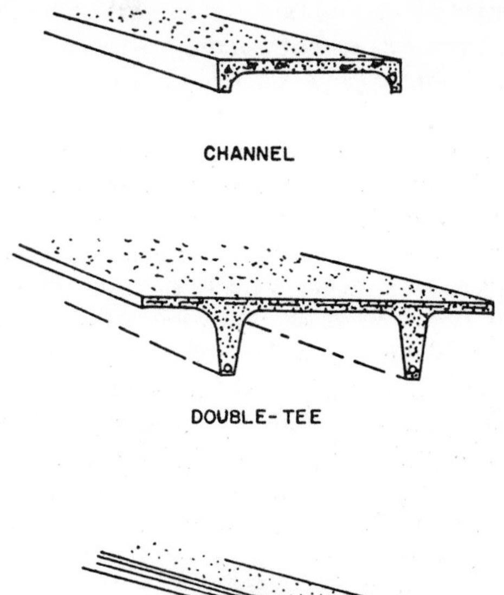

Fig. 1. Typical precast planks.

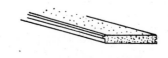

When the top slab sizes range from 1½ to 2 inches (3.8 to 5 cm.) in thickness, it should be reinforced with wire mesh.

Welded matching plates are ordinarily used to connect the supporting members to the floor and roof slabs.

Panels precast in a horizontal position, in a casting yard or on the floor of the building, are ordinarily used to make up bearing and nonbearing *walls* and *partitions.* These panels are placed in their vertical position by cranes or by the tilt-up procedure.

Usually these panels are solid reinforced slabs 5 to 8 inches (12.7 to 20 cm.) thick, and the lengths vary according to the distances between columns or other supporting members. When windows and door openings are cast in the slabs, extra reinforcements should be installed around the openings.

A concrete floor slab with a smooth regular surface can be used as a casting surface. When casting on the smooth surface, the casting surface should be covered with some form of liquid or sheet material to prevent bonding between the surface and the wall panel. The upper surface of the panel may be finished as regular concrete is finished by troweling, floating, or brooming.

Sandwich panels are panels that consist of two thin, dense, reinforced concrete face slabs separated by a core of insulating material such as lightweight concrete, cellular glass, plastic foam, or some other rigid insulating material. These panels are sometimes used for exterior walls to provide additional heat insulation. The thickness of the sandwich panel varies from 5 to 8 inches (12.7 to 20.3 cm.) and the face slabs are tied together with wire, small rods, or in some other manner. Welded or bolted matching plates are also used to connect the wall panels to the building frame, top and bottom. Calking on the outside and grouting on the inside should be used to make the points between the wall panels watertight.

PRECAST CONCRETE JOISTS, BEAMS, GIRDERS, AND COLUMNS

Small closely spaced beams used in floor construction are usually called *joists.* However, these same beams whenever used in roof construction are called *purlins.* The cross sections of these beams are shaped like a T or an I. The ones with the inverted T-sections are usually used in composite construction where they support cast-in-place floor or roof slabs.

Beams and *girders* are terms usually applied to the same members, but the one with the longer span should be referred to as the girder. Beams and girders may be conventional precast design or prestressed. Most of the beams will be I-shaped unless the ends are rectangular. The T-shaped ones can also be used.

Precast concrete *columns* may be solid or hollow. If the hollow type is desired, heavy cardboard tubing should be used to form the core. A looped rod is cast in the column footing and projects upward into the hollow core to help hold the column upright. An opening should be left in the side of the column so that the column core can be filled with grout; this way the looped rod becomes embedded to form an anchor. (The opening is dry-packed.)

Advantages

Precast concrete has the greatest advantage when there are identical members to be cast, because the same forms can be used several times. In addition to using the same forms, precast concrete has other advantages such as the following:

1. Control of the quality of concrete.
2. Smoother surfaces, and plastering is not necessary.
3. Less storage space is needed.
4. Concrete member can be cast under all weather conditions.
5. Better protection for curing.
6. Weather conditions do not affect erection.
7. Faster erection time.

Handling

Precast concrete should not be lifted or otherwise subjected to strain until the concrete has cured for the specified period. Except as otherwise specified, casting forms should not be removed earlier than 24 hours after placing the concrete. Precast concrete moved prior to completion of the curing period or before the concrete has attained specified strength, should be handled according to an approved procedure, with equipment of an approved type. Care should be taken to ensure that the precast member is not overstressed or otherwise damaged during the specified curing period. Precast members, including piles, should not be skidded, rolled, driven, or subjected to full design load until they have attained their 28-day strengths as indicated by cylinders made from the same concrete, at the same time as the precast concrete, and cured in the same manner. Handling of cured precast members should be either as specified or indicated, or as approved.

Chapter 15

Exposed Aggregate Concrete

Exposed aggregate concrete is concrete in which sufficient surface matrix has been removed to expose the coarse aggregate or concrete in which the coarse aggregate has been carefully placed at the surface.

Exposed aggregate textures can be obtained on all surfaces of precast or cast-in-place concrete of practically any shape using a variety of techniques. The wide range of colors and textures, and the demonstrated durability that can be obtained have led to the use of exposed aggregate concrete in all types of structures.

Producing exposed aggregate concrete is neither a difficult nor an overly simple procedure for the concrete man. Proper attention to details and basic knowledge of concrete are essential. The element of artistry in the selection of aggregates and matrix makes it impossible to lay down firm rules, but certain key factors must be considered for successful production of *exposed aggregate surfaces.* (*See* Chap. 12, Finishing Concrete Surfaces.)

AGGREGATES

Aggregates should be selected on the basis of color, hardness, size, shape, gradation, method of exposure, durability, cost, and availability. Popular decorative aggregates are natural materials such as quartz, granite, marble, limestone, gravel, and manufactured materials such as glass and ceramics.

Color

The *colors* of natural aggregates vary considerably according to their geological classification and even vary among rocks of one type.

Quartz aggregates are generally available in several varieties—clear, white, yellow, green, gray, and light pink or rose. Clear quartz is used widely as a sparkling surface to complement the color effect created by the use of pigmented concrete. Clear quartz is also used in combination with other colored aggregates to emphasize the color of the matrix. White quartz ranges from a translucent white verging on clear to a deep milky white. Rose quartz gives finishes ranging from a delicate pink to a warm rose color.

Granite, long known for its durability and beauty, is available in shades of pink, red, gray, dark blue, black, and white. Trap rocks such as basalt can provide gray, black, or green. Among the natural aggregates, *marble* probably offers the widest selection of colors ranging from green, yellow, red and pink to gray, white, and black. Crushed limestone is available in white, gray, or pink.

Certain *gravels*, after being washed and screened, can be used to provide attractive brown or reddish-brown finishes. Yellow ochers, umbers, and sandy shades are abundant in river bed gravels. An almost pure white gravel comes from several sedimentary rock formations. Gravels vary widely in color depending upon the area in which the pits are situated.

Ceramic aggregates and *vitreous materials* such as glass offer the most brilliant and varied colors available for exposed aggregate work. Almost any color can be produced. Producers of glass aggregates should warrant low reactivity of their materials with portland cement. While the colors of ceramic aggregates are bright and clear, they are characteristically soft.

Expanded shale lightweight aggregates may be used to produce reddish-brown, yellow, gray, or black colors. These materials are porous and crushable, resulting in a dull surface with soft colors. These aggregates should be tested for iron-staining characteristics.

A producer of exposed aggregate concrete should select an aggregate that is decidedly darker than the color specified by the customer. The reason given is that the general appearance of large areas after installation tends to be lighter than indicated by the trial samples.

The relative importance of aggregate versus cement in determining the color of exposed aggregate concrete depends largely upon the treatment given to the face of the concrete. In most exposed aggregate finishes, the color of the cement is less important because a major part of the visible area is covered by the aggregate. Nevertheless, the cement has an effect on the general tone value of the element and for this reason it should be considered when the aggregate is chosen. While gray cement can be combined very effectively with a number of aggregates, the use of white cement, with or without color pigments, greatly extends the range of possible color combinations.

Hardness

Aggregate hardness and density must be compatible with structural requirements and with durability under anticipated weathering conditions. Quartz aggregates are very hard, with a hardness rating of 7 on Moh's scale—about equal to carbon steel. Granite composed of 30 percent quartz and 70 percent feldspar, has a rating nearly as high as quartz. Gravel and marble may vary from 3 to 7 on Moh's scale. Vitreous aggregates rate at approximately 5.5. Ceramic aggregates have not been tested for hardness but are believed to be about equal to hard-grade gravel.

Size

Aggregates may vary from ¼ inch (6 mm.) gravel up to stones and rubble 6 to 7 inches (15.2 to 17.76 cm.) in diameter and larger. The extent to which they are exposed or *revealed* is largely determined by their size. Reveal should be no greater than one-third the average diameter of the aggregate particle.

Aggregate size is selected on the basis of the total area to be cast and the distance from which it is to be viewed. Larger aggregates are required on large areas for any degree of apparent relief. When surfaces are some distance from the main flow of traffic, large aggregate is required for a rough-textured look. A suggested visibility scale is given in Table 10.

Aggregate size	Distance at which texture is visible
¼"—½"	20'— 30'
½"— 1"	30'— 75'
1"— 2"	75'—125'
2"— 3"	125'—175'

TABLE 10. SUGGESTED VISIBILITY SCALE.

Shape

Aggregate shape will affect surface pattern and texture and may slightly affect color. Large irregularly-shaped aggregate may permit more of the concrete matrix to show, changing the overall effect. Cubical or rounded aggregates will give the best area coverage. Flat pieces and slivers do not hold well in the concrete matrix and should not be used.

Aggregates with a rough surface have better bonding properties than those with slick glassy surfaces. *For example,* bond problems have occured with some milky white quartz aggregates. Bond is more important in cases where small aggregates are used. In that case, some of the aggregate pieces may be only half embedded in the cement matrix. With aggregate sizes ½ inch (1.3 cm.) or larger, enough of each piece will be embedded to insure against loss of bond, even in the case of glossy, smooth aggregates.

Aggregate shape affects the tone of a surface after weathering. Rounded aggregates are largely self-cleaning while angular aggregates of rough texture tend to collect dirt, but this dirt pickup is generally confined to the matrix. For this reason, as well as architectural appearance, the area of exposed matrix between the pieces of stone should be minimized. It may be advisable for the matrix to be darker than the aggregate for structures subjected to considerable atmospheric pollution. Protection of exposed aggregate concrete from airborne contaminants is discussed in this chapter under Clear Coatings.

Gradations

Close control over *gradation* of aggregates is essential to avoid variations in the surface texture of the finished product. Sieve analysis tests are required to insure uniformity of materials received and to check consistency of gradation with the aggregate supplier's reported sieve analysis (taking into account expected changes in gradation that may be caused by rough handling in shipment). Sieve analyses are advisable once weekly when receiving more than one carload per week of a given aggregate type and size, or for each car when receiving less than a carload per week.

Exposure Technique

The method used to expose the aggregate in the finished product should be considered when selecting the type of aggregate. Natural gravels are inclined to shatter, leading to bond failure and loss of aggregate particles when bushhammered. Certain aggregates such as granite and quartz are difficult to bushhammer uniformly because they are very hard. Aggregates such as marble, calcite, and limestone are softer and more suitable for bushhammered surfaces. The comb chisel is suitable only for use with softer aggregates. For sand blasting, hard aggregates such as quartz, granite, and siliceous gravels are generally used although limestones are also suitable. For grinding and polishing the softer aggregates such as marble should be used.

When an acid-etched finish is employed, or a solution of muriatic acid is used to wash an exposed aggregate surface to bring out its full color, only acid-resistant aggregates, such as quartz or granite, are recommended. Aggregates with a high calcium content such as limestones, dolomites, and marbles will discolor and dissolve in muriatic acid. Even a relatively mild acid solution may affect the color of marbles or limestones and may cause crumbling or popping of the chips. If acid must be used, it should be applied with care and thoroughly washed off immediately with plenty of water to remove all traces of acid.

Durability

Any aggregate for exterior use should be thoroughly evaluated for the climatic conditions to which it will be exposed.

Moisture absorption rates for quartz, granite, marble, and gravel generally vary from 0.05 to 1.50 percent, a negligible amount. Moisture absorption rates of vitreous aggregates are too low to measure accurately. The moisture absorption qualities of ceramic aggregates are related to their chemical composition and length of burning.

Exposed aggregate panels, although not exposed to salting or intense freezing and thawing as concrete in highways, are exposed to strong wet-dry cycling. Wet-dry sensitive coarse aggregates may crumble and may be noticeable even if used in small quantities. Aggregates that have a wet-dry sensitivity, such as some shales, are generally detected in the unconfined aggregate freeze-thaw test.

The mineralogical and physical properties of the aggregate play important roles in providing restraint against shrinkage. Aggregate type will affect concrete shrinkage. Generally speaking, hard dense aggregates with low absorption and high modulus of elasticity produce concrete with minimum shrinkage.

Cost and Availability

Cost is a factor when selecting an aggregate and cost comparisons must be made on a consistent basis. *For example,* do not compare cost per ton of a dense aggregate with cost per ton of a lightweight aggregate. Instead, compare volume cost in dollars per cubic yard.

Natural aggregates vary in price according to their availability. Marble aggregates are generally available throughout the United States and are relatively low in price for most types. Quartz and granite are slightly higher since their hardness makes them more difficult to quarry and crush, while gravel is the lowest priced of all aggregates since they require only washing and screening. Manufactured aggregates cost more to produce than natural aggregates. Ceramic aggregates are three to five times the cost of marble, while vitreous materials are 10 to 20 times as much. Transportation charges also figure heavily in the final cost of any aggregate. However, even the most expensive aggregates are often practical in exposed aggregate concrete especially when they are used only in thin facing mixes.

In general, aggregates used in concrete of any type represent only a small part of the cost of concrete in place. Any mistakes made through use of an inferior aggregate cannot readily be corrected. It is often wiser to use high quality aggregates from a distant source, if need be, rather than a local material of questionable quality.

MIX DESIGNS

Concrete mix designs used in exposed aggregate work, both precast and cast-in-place, are different from those that most concrete users are familiar with. However, many of the same theories and technology apply.

Precast

Two types of mixes are generally used in precast exposed aggregate work—facing mixes and backup mixes. *Facing mixes* use special decorative aggregates and are frequently combined with white portland cement and sometimes a pigment. *Backup mixes* are composed of more conventional aggregates with gray cement and are used to reduce material costs in large units employing facing mixes. In precast units of complicated shape the facing type mix may be used throughout the member if procedures for separating the facing and backup mixes become too cumbersome. Backup mixes are usually normal weight concrete or structural-grade light weight concrete. Facing and backup mixes should be designed for a minimum compressive strength of 6,000 psi (420 kgs. per sq. cm.) at 28 days.

The strength of facing concrete is usually determined by using 6 × 12 inch (15 × 30 cm.) standard cylinders. If fabrication of cylinders is impractical, 4-inch (10-cm.) cubes may be used. The measured cube strength should be reduced 20 percent to obtain an estimate of cylinder strength. It may be impractical to prepare a standard test cylinder, *for example*, in the case of a facing mix containing a high percentage of coarse aggregate. Often such mixes are placed with greater than the desired water content to achieve proper consolidation. An extremely dry backup concrete is used to remove excess water. The 4-inch (10-cm.) cube will provide an adequate size for practically all facing mixes. Such cubes may be prepared as individual specimens or they may be sawed from 4-inch (10-cm.) thick slabs. The latter may be more convenient and are probably more representative of the final product.

Mix proportions for facing mixes are determined by considerations of appearance and weathering. The facing concrete will absorb some moisture, the amount depending upon the mix proportions, type of aggregate used and the final surface treatment. This absorption is harmless unless excessive. The Prestressed Concrete Institute recommends a maximum 24-hour absorption of six percent based on oven-dried 28-day samples no smaller than 4- × 4-inch (10- × 10-cm.) cubes or 3- × 6-inch (7.6- × 15.2-cm.) cylinders.

The proportion of cement to fine aggregate used in facing mixes should be at least 1:3 but not greater than 1:1, regardless of the technique used for producing the exposed aggregate finish. With mixes leaner than 1 part cement to 3 parts sand, there is some danger of pieces of coarse aggregate being dislodged during handling.

The proportion of total aggregate to cement in the backup and facing mixes should be sufficient to produce, as nearly as possible, the same shrinkage factors and thermal coefficient of expansion throughout an element.

The ratio of volume of fine aggregate to coarse aggregate for facing mixes usually is about 1:2½ or 3. This is due to the need for a high concentration of coarse aggregate to achieve a uniformly textured finish. Backup mixes more nearly approach 1:1½.

In addition it is desirable to use coarse aggregates that are composed of particles nearly all the same size. Some common sizes of coarse aggregates are ½ × ¾ inch (1.3 × 1.9 cm.), ⅜ × ½ inch (.9 × 1.3 cm.), and ¼ × ⅜ inch (.6 × .9 cm.). Some common fine aggregate (white silica sand) sizes are 30 to 50 mesh and 16 to 30 mesh. However, graded silica is better for its bleeding characteristics. These so-called *gap-graded* combinations of fine and coarse aggregates produce less segregation of particle sizes and a more uniform and pleasing finish.

Gradation standards for aggregates for precast exposed aggregate products have varied widely. In the past, each producer of aggregates has more or less established his own sizing schedule or used standards of the terrazzo industry. In 1967, the National Quartz Producers Council was formed primarily to establish uniform standards for sizing hard aggregates used in exposed aggregate work. These size specifications are given in Table 11.

The water/cement ratio for precast exposed aggregate is usually limited to a maximum 0.49 by weight. This may be too much for some applications. Excess water in the facing mix may be removed prior to initial set by using a very low or zero slump backup mix, certain highly absorptive materials, or a vacuum process.

It is difficult to recommend a slump for concrete used in precast exposed aggregate. Very stiff mixes require more labor to place and special vibration techniques. Horizontally cast panels can be produced successfully by using a 4-inch (10-cm.) slump facing mix backed up with a no-slump structural-grade concrete. In this case the backup mix absorbs excess water from the facing.

	Percent Passing			
Size Designation	1⅜" x ⅞" "D"	⅞" x ½" "C"	½" x ¼" "B"	¼" x 3/32" "A"
1½	100			
1⅜	95-100			
1	30- 60	100		
⅞	20- 40	95-100		
⅝	0- 10	30- 50	100	
½		10- 25	95-100	
⅜		0- 10	40- 70	100
¼			10- 20	95-100
⅛			0- 10	15- 35
3/32				0- 10

TABLE 11. NATIONAL QUARTZ PRODUCERS COUNCIL SIZE SPECIFICATIONS.

Therefore, the slump and workability of a mix should be suitable for the conditions of each individual job. This usually relates to the shape of the unit, the amount and complexity of reinforcing, and the method of consolidation.

Admixtures other than air-entraining agents are not recommended. Air-entraining admixtures will improve the workability of harsh gap-graded facing mixes and increase resistance to freezing and thawing. The addition of normal amounts of an air-entraining agent to a harsh, high-strength concrete mix typical in exposed aggregate units significantly improves the frost resistance of the concrete even though only a small amount of air is usually entrained. A *normal* amount of agent may be defined as that which would result in 19 ± 3 percent air in a 1:4 standard sand mortar tested.

Sometimes other admixtures are used for a specific effect. Unnecessary or excessive use of admixtures, or combinations of admixtures, can complicate successful production and introduces problems affecting the entire project. Calcium chloride, or admixtures containing it, are not recommended for precast exposed aggregate work. Its use can lead to nonuniformity in color and may disrupt the efficiency of surface retarders.

Color in exposed aggregate concrete is generally obtained by aggregate selection, both coarse and fine, but occasionally small amounts of pigments are added to the mix to enhance or vary the color and appearance of the background matrix. (*See* Chap. 16, Mineral Pigments for Use in Coloring Concrete.)

When pigments are added, the amount should be less than 10 percent of the weight of the cement. White portland cement will produce cleaner, brighter colors and is usually used for the light pastels such as the buffs, creams, and ivories, as well as the bright, pale pink, and rose tones.

The concentrations of pigment used in pastel work are surprisingly low, a fact that helps mitigate the cost of white cement. *For example,* buffs, creams, and ivory tints used with white aggregate and white cement seldom require more than 1 pound of pigment per 100 pounds (11 gms. per kilo) of cement. Frequently the requirement is as low as 2 ounces per 100 pounds (1.4 gms. per kilo), depending upon the depth of pastel desired.

For deep color tones about 6 pounds of pigment per 100 pounds (65 gms. per kilo) of cement may be required.

Cast-In-Place

The mix design discussion up to this point has been concerned with precast concrete. High quality exposed aggregate surfaces can also be produced for cast-in-place structural elements such as walls, columns and beams, and flatwork such as walks, drives, and patios.

Low-slump gap-graded mixes. Any exposed aggregate surface has a more pleasing appearance if it contains a maximum amount of coarse aggregate of one size or has a narrow size range. The use of continuously-graded coarse and fine aggregates in the usual percentages generally results in non-uniform distribution of the exposed aggregate. Thus mixes which satisfy architectural requirements contain a large percentage of coarse aggregate and a small percentage, sufficient for workability, of fine aggregate, with no aggregate in the intermediate size range. This results in what is known as gap-grading (sometimes called *skip* or *jump* grading).

For cast-in-place work, typical gap-graded aggregates consist of only one size of coarse aggregate with all particles of the sand being able to pass through the voids in the compacted coarse aggregate. Maximum size of aggregate is limited by the spacing of reinforcing steel, but for structural elements, the maximum size usually is about 1½ inches (3.8 cm.) depending on architectural considerations. For driveways, sidewalks, and patios ⅜-inch (.95-cm.) pea gravel is commonly used.

For an aggregate of ¾-inch (1.9 cm.) maximum size, the No. 4 to ⅜-inch (.95-cm.) particles can be omitted without making the concrete unduly harsh or subject to segregation. In the case of 1½-inch (3.8-cm.) aggregate the No. 4 to ¾-inch (1.9-cm.) sizes should be omitted. Eliminating the material under ¾ inch (1.9 cm.) prevents separation of sizes in the bins, thus giving a more uniform product.

Fine aggregate generally consists of material passing the No. 8 screen. The percentage of sand should be chosen carefully. A wrong choice—too low, for example—may result in segregation or honeycombing due to an excess of coarse aggregate. An excess of sand results in a less desirable architectural appearance. Concrete with a low density and high water requirement can also result from too much sand. Sand is usually 25 to 35 percent by volume of the total aggregate. The lower percentage is used with rounded-aggregates and the higher with crushed material. The sand cement content depends upon the cement content, type of aggregate, and workability.

Since low-slump gap-graded mixes use a lower percentage of sand producing harsh mixes, air entrainment is a standard requirement for workability with added durability. Workability and placeability generally require a minimum of 564 pounds of cement per cubic yard of concrete (334 kgs. per cu. meter). On the job 425-pound (192.8-kgs.) mixes are almost impossible to consolidate properly and honeycombing will occur. A water/cement ratio of 0.50 by weight should be considered the maximum. Any water used above the absolute minimum needed for placing may cause segregation and paste accumulations which in turn may result in imperfections in the exposed aggregate surface.

For adequate consolidation of the concrete, the desirable range of matrix (air, water, cement, and sand) is about 45 to 51 percent by volume depending on the angularity of the one-size coarse aggregate. Rounded aggregate such as gravel requires about 45 to 48 percent matrix, while crushed limestone requires slightly higher values such as 48 to 51 percent. Most continuously graded concrete have matrix percentages of 55 or more.

Segregation must be prevented by restricting the slump to the lowest value consistent with good consolidation. This may vary from 0 to 3 inches (0 to 7.6 cm.) depending on the thickness of the section, amount of steel, height of casing, and so on. *For example,* a thin, heavily reinforced wall might require a 3-inch (7.6-cm.) slump, whereas ½-inch (1.3-cm.) slump or less would be sufficient for a massive section with a lower percentage of reinforcing steel. A 2-inch (5-cm.) slump would be right for a sidewalk or driveway. Because of their low sand volumes and low water/cement ratio, gap-graded mixes might be considered as unworkable for cast-in-place construction. *When properly proportioned, however, these concretes are readily consolidated with vibration.* (*See* Chap. 9, Placing and Consolidating Concrete, section on Consolidating Concrete.)

The standard slump test is inadequate as a measure of the workability of concretes with such high proportions of coarse aggregate. A better measure of consistency than slump for such concrete is obtained with the Vebe consistometer. The Vebe apparatus subjects the concrete to a slump test on a vibrating table. The criterion of this test is the time in seconds required to consolidate the slump cone into a 9⅜-inch (23.8-cm.) diameter cylindrical mass. Concretes that require a Vebe time of more than 6.5 seconds may be difficult to consolidate properly with internal vibration. Concretes with Vebe times of less than 4.5 seconds may be judged as having excellent consolidation characteristics.

Preplaced aggregate. Proprietary techniques, such as Arbeton and Naturbetong, are used to produce exposed aggregate surfaces for walls, columns, and beams. These are *preplaced aggregate systems* developed both in the United States and in Norway. Concrete in the usual sense is not used. Dry, coarse aggregate is pre-positioned in the forms before mortar is moved into the voids by high frequency vibration or pressure grouting.

Seeding method. Seeding of select aggregates is commonly used for exposed aggregate surfaces on cast-in-place flatwork as well as precast panels. The base concrete to receive an exposed aggregate surface by the *seeding method* should contain a minimum of 564 pounds of cement per cubic yard (334 kgs. per cu. meter), and a water/cement ratio no greater than 0.53 by weight. The maximum slump should not exceed 4 inches (10 cm.) and air entrainment should be 6 percent ±1 percent. The maximum size of coarse aggregate in the base mix should be ¾-inch (1.9 cm.) to assist in embedment of the special seeded aggregate. Sometimes an oversanded mix is used for the same reason. If oversanding is used, the water/cement ratio previously mentioned should govern the mix design and the cement content should be increased accordingly. No. 4 and smaller sizes of coarse aggregate should be eliminated from the base mix when crushed stone or an aggregate whose color is not compatible with the select seeding aggregate is specified.

The method of seeding and additional information on preplaced aggregate techniques are discussed later in this chapter in the section on Casting and Placing.

Mixing

Mixing exposed aggregate concrete varies from one plant or job to the next. The type of mixer used and the characteristics of the concrete have a bearing on the mixing procedure used. However, there are a few basic guidelines that are accepted as good practice.

It is not unusual for some precast manufacturers to gather sufficient aggregates to complete an individual job. They then blend the whole quantity together since aggregate can differ in coloring from face to face within the same quarry. By blending aggregates any color difference is spread throughout all the panels and thus goes unnoticed.

The quality of mix will depend very much on a suitable mixer. This is particularly true of low-slump or no-slump mixes which are used to a large extent for exposed aggregate precast concrete. For these mixes, pan-type or rapid countercurrent mixers are a definite asset.

The mixer should be in operation while materials are being charged. Ribbon feeding of aggregates, cement, and water is recommended, if possible. All admixtures should be premixed with the mixing water prior to entering the mixer. Normally, for mixers of less than 1 cubic yard (.765 cu. meter) capacity, aggregates are placed into the mixer first followed by cement and water, at the same time. This procedure should be revised when heated water or aggregates are used during cold weather. In this case, introduction of cement into the mixer should be delayed until after all aggregates and water have been charged and mixed for at least one minute.

Most lightweight aggregates are absorptive and should be prewetted, but not soaked, before mixing. This will eliminate the possibility of loss in workability due to rapid absorption of mixing water.

Exposed aggregate concrete requires good mixing. Mixing should continue for at least one minute after all materials have been charged or as recommended by the mixer manufacturer. Mixing can be considered complete when all ingredients are thoroughly distributed and the mixture is uniform in appearance. This time will vary with the characteristics of the concrete and the mixer.

Uniformity of mixing time should be carefully controlled from batch to batch to obtain uniformity of color in the end product. This is particularly important when using white cement with or without color pigments and when colors of sand and cement differ. Mixers should never be loaded beyond rated capacity.

Good clean equipment is essential. Special attention should be given to prevention of contamination of the mix by oil, grease, dirt, and chucks of hardened concrete that may break loose from the mixer blades. When colored or white concrete is used in conjunction with normal gray concrete, for example, with facing and backup mixes, separate mixers and handling arrangements are required.

When using low-slump gap-graded concrete for cast-in-place exposed aggregate, the transit mix truck must be selected carefully. Many older concrete mixer trucks will not discharge concrete with less than a 2-inch (5-cm.) slump.

CASTING AND PLACING

There are several good ways of *casting* and *placing* exposed aggregate concrete, and the techniques employed depend upon many factors. The final assessment of any technique should be the quality of the end product.

Exposed aggregate concrete is precast either horizontally or vertically at the plant, or at the job site, or is cast in place at the job site.

Precasting Temperatures

Concrete temperature should be maintained above 55° F. (12.8° C.) during mixing, transporting, and placing. Temperatures of 80° F. to 85° F. (26.7° C. to 29.5° C.) are preferable with form temperature about the same. An optimum of 75° F. to 80° F. (23.9° C. to 26.7° C.) is recommended for forms and can be achieved by heating the form or by placing it in a temperature controlled building. Constant temperatures throughout the project are more important than temperatures near the upper or lower level.

Horizontal Precasting

Horizontal casting, both in plant and jobsite precasting, is the most common method.

Face-up methods. Face-up methods usually involve embedding the coarse aggregate in the surface of the concrete by tamping or rolling. Then the aggregate is exposed by washing away the surface layer of mortar with water. Large aggregate can be hand placed in the matrix if a third or less of the diameter of the individual pieces is left exposed. The face-up method is used widely for exposed surfaces with aggregates from ¾ to 1 inch (1.9 to 2.5 cm.) though its use with larger aggregates in panels previously cast face down on a sand bed is becoming more popular.

A cage of reinforcement is fixed in the form and a backing mix of regular or lightweight concrete is placed around it, allowing the required cover, and vibrated. The backup concrete is leveled below the top of the form sufficiently to allow for the top surface layer. Then a facing mix or matrix is placed, vibrated, and screeded. If aggregate seeding is used the screeding operation should produce a level surface ⅛ to 7/16 inch (3.2 to 11 mm.) below the desired finish to allow for the volume of select aggregate to be seeded. About ⅛ inch (3.2 mm.) should be allowed for aggregate sizes ⅜ inch to ⅝ inch (9.5 to 15.9 mm.); 3/16 inch (4.8 mm.) for aggregate sizes ½ inch to ¾ inch (12.7 to 19 mm.); ¼ inch (6.3 mm.) for aggregate sizes ¾ inch to 1 inch (19 to 25.4 mm.); 5/16 inch (7.9 mm.) for aggregate sizes 1 inch to 1½ inch (25.4 to 38 mm.), and 7/16 inch (11 mm.) for aggregate sizes 1¼ inches to 2 inches (31.8 to 50.8 mm.).

Seeding is usually started immediately after the base concrete has been placed, screeded, and smoothed. The select aggregate is carefully seeded by shovel or hand to completely cover the surface with a layer of stone. Quantity of select aggregate required per square foot of surface will vary from about 3 pounds for ⅜-inch aggregate to 6 pounds for 2-inch material (14.65 kgs. of 9.5-mm. aggregate to 29.3 kgs. of 50.8 mm.-aggregate per sq. meter). Apply only one layer of stone, removing stacked stone and flat or slivery particles. Handwork may be necessary at difficult locations including corners and along edges.

Next embed the aggregate into the concrete by tapping with a wood float, a darby, or the broad side of a piece of 2- × 4-inch (5- × 10-cm.) lumber. Sometimes a rolling device can be used. The aggregate should be well tamped in the fresh concrete without lateral displacement. Use a magnesium float or darby for final embedding—mortar completely surrounds and slightly covers all particles. Appearance then is similar to a normal slab after floating with all voids and imperfections removed. On large panels or jobs, or when small-size aggregates are seeded, a surface retarder may be desirable. The timing and technique of aggregate exposure is discussed later in this chapter in the section on Exposure Techniques.

Crushed stone for seeding means additional finishing labor costs. Also, it has a tendency to stack during the seeding operation, and exposed surfaces have sharp edges that may be undesirable.

Face-down methods. When aggregate to be exposed is 1 inch (2.5 cm.) or more in diameter, the *sand embedment technique* is frequently used. Stones ranging from 1 to 8 inches (2.5 to 20 cm.) in diameter produce walls that look bold and massive. Flagstone has also been used.

One method is to spread a layer of fine sand over the bottom of the form to a depth of about one-third the diameter of the uniform size aggregate used. Aggregate is pushed close together into the sand for dense coverage. Extreme care is necessary in distributing the aggregate evenly and densely. A fine spray of water is used to settle the sand around the aggregates yet leave about one-third to one-half of each piece embedded in the sand.

An alternate method is to spread a layer of aggregate on the panel form and pack it closely. Then sprinkle fine dry sand over the aggregate and allow it to sift down around the pieces until its depth is one-third to one-half the aggregate size. Excess sand on the rocks is pushed down around the aggregates with a soft-bristle brush and an air blast. The surface is moistened with a fine spray of water to settle the sand firmly into place.

If a white matrix is desired, a white mortar, consisting of one part white cement to two and one-half parts well-graded white or light-colored sand with sufficient water to make a creamy mixture, may be placed over the aggregate.

Now the panel is ready for placement of reinforcement with bolting and welding inserts attached. These items may be supported on plastic or galvanized chairs, the mortar mix or part of the backup concrete may be placed and screeded to a flat surface before the steel is placed. Care should be taken not to dislodge any of the aggregate when placing the first layer of mortar or concrete.

If a mortar facing mix is used, usually the backup mix is of a low slump, a maximum of 1 inch (2.5 cm.), to absorb excess water from the facing mix. Otherwise, the backup mix is standard structural concrete with a slump of 3 to 5 inches (7.5 to 12.5 cm.). After placing the backup mix, a vibrating screed or spud vibrator is used to compact the concrete. Care must be exercised during vibration not to disturb the sand or aggregates causing uneven aggregate distribution.

When the panels have cured they are raised and any clinging sand removed by brushing, air blasting, or washing with a stream of water. Some sand bonds to the concrete. Therefore, the color of the bedding sand should be carefully chosen to harmonize with the aggregate to be exposed.

Many precasters use facing and backup mixes with horizontal face-down casting. Production techniques vary widely from plant to plant. The type of facing and backup mix used depends largely upon the method of consolidation. Some precasters use vibrating tables, while others use shocking tables or vibrators externally mounted on the forms. Internal spud type vibrators are also used in the conventional manner and special plate vibrators are available for low slump mixes.

The use of a facing mix and a subsequent backup concrete, or the alternate use of a uniform mix throughout an element, depends on the practice of the particular plant or the size and type of unit being produced. Generally speaking, units with intricate shapes and deep, narrow sections require a uniform mix throughout.

Facing concrete should be carefully placed and worked into all details of the form. This is particularly important in external and internal corners for true and sharp casting lines. This is accomplished by either external or internal vibration, surface vibration, tamping, impact, or a combination of these methods. The methods used are normally based on individually developed techniques and will vary with type of form, shape or product, mix proportions and plant preference. The end objective is to consolidate the concrete into a dense, uniform product with an imperfection-free surface. Casting of a unit should continue uninterrupted to avoid cold joints. (*See* Chap. 9, Placing and Consolidating Concrete.)

When horizontally cast panels require an exposed aggregate finish on both sides, the face-up and face-down methods are both used on the panel.

Vertical Precasting

Greater care is required with *vertical precasting* than with horizontal. Vertical casting can use battery type forms that require less floor space than horizontal casting. Vertical casting for interior wall units forms both faces against the mold, reducing finishing and enabling control of unit thickness. Handling is simplified and only nominal reinforcement is required because units are lifted vertically. However, form stripping within four to five hours is impractical as are methods of finishing exposed aggregate surfaces that require early form stripping such as washing and brushing.

Cast-In-Place

There are four basic construction methods for casting exposed aggregate concrete in place: (1) low-slump gap-graded concrete;

(2) preplaced aggregate concrete; (3) aggregate transfer; and (4) aggregate seeding. The first three are applicable for formed concrete—walls, beams, and columns—while the first and last are used for unformed concrete—walks, drives, and patios.

Low-slump, gap-graded concrete. The aggregates and mix design for low-slump gap-graded concretes were discussed previously in this chapter. These mixes, when used in walls, beams, and columns, must be considered for workability and freedom from segregation in relation to the method of placing and consolidating.

Ease of placement is an important consideration. Gap-graded mixes do not flow readily down a long chute or from a Georgia buggy. Construction methods should allow the concrete to be dropped vertically in all handling operations, since the mixes can be dropped considerable distances without segregation.

Once in the forms, the 0- to 3-inch (0- to 7.5-cm.) slump concrete can be consolidated easily with internal vibration but requires ample vibration to assure proper compaction and elimination of honeycomb areas. The concrete should be placed in lifts of not more than 18 inches (45 cm.) with the vibrator inserted into each lift at intervals not to exceed 18 inches (45 cm.) in any direction. Vibrators should be placed in the concrete rapidly to penetrate approximately 3 inches (7.5 cm.) of the previous layer and withdrawn slowly. This will minimize entrapped air between the concrete and the form and blend the two layers. Insufficient vibration rather than over-vibration is more often the problem, provided forms are designed to withstand longer periods of high frequency vibration.

Vibrators should not be used any closer than 3 inches (7.5 cm.) from the formed surface that will be exposed or the coarse aggregate will be driven away from the form face causing a mortar line on the visible surface. A small diameter vibrator should be used in thin sections.

Placing low-slump, gap-graded concrete in flatwork follows conventional placing methods with a few exceptions. The slump must be low—from 1 to 3 inches (2.5 to 7.5 cm.)—to keep coarse aggregate at the surface. Spread, compact, screed, darby, or bullfloat in the usual manner but do not overdo the last two operations. Too much working of the surface with these tools may depress the one size coarse aggregate too far below the surface.

Preplaced aggregate concrete. Preplaced aggregate concrete is named from its unique placement procedure. Forms are filled with coarse aggregate, then structural quality grout is moved, either under pressure or by vibration, into the voids of the aggregate to produce concrete. Some registered trade names are Prepski, Colcrete, Naturbetong, and Arbeton. These techniques avoid one of the main disadvantages of exposing the aggregate in conventional cast-in-place concrete—the irregular surface texture caused by uneven distribution of the coarse aggregate.

For the first three techniques, the reinforcing steel and forms are erected in the usual manner and the forms are filled with aggregate to be exposed. (*See* Chap. 7, Forms and Form Making; *also see* Chap. 8, Reinforced Concrete.) The aggregate is essentially one-sized coarse, usually ⅝ to 1½ inch (1.5 to 3.75 cm.), so that grout can flow between the particles. A rich grout is mixed and pumped through holes in the forms or through tubes previously placed within the forms to fill the voids in the preplaced aggregate. When the forms are stripped, the surface appears as normal, off-the-form concrete, but when treated to expose the aggregate the distribution of coarse aggregate over the surface appears uniform.

In the Arbeton process, the reinforcing steel is erected in the usual manner and wire mesh tied around it. Mesh openings are smaller than the aggregate to be exposed. Forms are erected and the space between the mesh and the forms is filled with the aggregate, also one-sized coarse ⅝ to 1½ inch (1.5 to 3.75 cm.). A specially-designed mix of structural concrete with a surplus of mortar is placed within the space enclosed by the mesh. Surplus mortar from this mix is moved through the mesh and into the voids of the face aggregate by means of high frequency vibration. The finished surface is treated to expose the aggregate. Sections to be cast should be relatively large with facing thickness generally about 2½ inches (6.4 cm.), determined by the size of the aggregate used in the facing. Minimum thickness of a section, be it a wall, beam, or column, should be 10 to 12 inches (25.4 to 30.5 cm.), including the facing, to effectively use the process. This method is best utilized for columns.

Aggregate transfer. Aggregate transfer has been used as a method for placing exposed aggregate surfaces on cast-in-place concrete but is being replaced by newer and less expensive techniques. However, it has the advantage of providing positive means of developing distinct patterns and sculptured effects not available by other means.

A pattern can be defined by small wooden strips on a liner panel of ¼-inch (6.4-mm.) plywood. Spread a layer of adhesive on this liner. The adhesive can be made of dammar gum and acetate, or any water-resistant, high-solid (15 to 20 percent) lacquer. Next comes a layer of select aggregate. It is very important to get a thorough covering to the very edges of the liner. At this point the liner is vibrated thoroughly in a horizontal direction. After the adhesive has hardened, the liner may be attached to the forms using finishing brads so that forms may be stripped without damage to the liner. Usually the liners can be taken off after five days, but it may be necessary to allow more delay in cool weather. A mixture of one-half perlite and one-half adhesive by volume may be used to achieve greater aggregate reveal. Brushing or washing the perlite from the surface is then the only finishing required.

Aggregate seedings. Aggregate seeding is used extensively for exposed aggregate flatwork—sidewalks, driveways, and patios. The mix design of base concrete for the seeding methods is important and was discussed previously in this chapter under Mix Designs. The placing operation is the same as discussed under Face-up Methods.

FORMS

Both precast and cast-in-place exposed aggregate concrete require quality form workmanship. Forms must withstand the vibration normally associated with placing exposed aggregate concrete. For cast-in-place work, the use of light steel forms that vibrate as concrete is vibrated may cause nonuniform aggregate distribution near the surface of the concrete.

Forms must be tight and accurately aligned at butt joints,

since the slightest misalignment at form joints may be visible in the exposed surface, showing up under certain lighting and shadow conditions.

Seal or caulk joints in formwork to prevent leakage of water and fines. Thin, plastic, pressure-sensitive tape is preferred. If joints are not sealed, a dark line will appear on the finished surface—sometimes even after heavy texturing by bushhammering or abrasive blasting.

Joints between forms for cast-in-place work may be disguised by rustication strips. The strips are also used to hide tie rod holes. A commonly used size is 1 inch wide, 1 inch (2.5 × 2.5 cm.) deep with a slight taper for easy removal.

An important consideration in cast-in-place, exposed concrete is the treatment of form ties to prevent rusting of the ties and subsequent staining of the wall. Form ties can be the type that are withdrawn from the concrete or have plastic cones so that the ties break off at least 1½ inches (3.8 cm.) from the surface of the concrete, leaving a hole no more than ⅞ inch (2.2-cm.) in diameter. The rod holes may be left exposed in carefully predetermined patterns to eliminate patching (if stainless steel ties are used) or patched immediately after stripping the forms.

FORM STRIPPING

Precast units should remain in the form until the concrete has reached sufficient handling strength. The duration of this period will vary considerably from a few hours, when additional heat is employed for curing, to an extended period, when low curing temperatures exist. Most plants are set up on a 24-hour cycle, with initial curing taking from 16 to 18 hours before the forms are stripped.

Stripping time for cast-in-place work depends on several factors, such as safety, resulting effect on the concrete, and the most favorable time to expose the aggregate with a particular exposure technique. The first requirement is that stripping be done at a time that will insure complete safety of the structure. Forms for elements not supporting the weight of the concrete may be stripped as soon as hardening has progressed sufficiently to resist damage from stripping. This may be as early as four hours if the aggregate is to be exposed by early washing, or under more normal conditions 12 to 24 hours after casting if temperatures of surrounding air are above 50° F. (10° C.). Formwork for elements that support the weight of concrete should remain in place until the specified 28-day strength is reached, unless otherwise specified or permitted. (*See* Chap. 7, Forms and Form Making.)

CURING

Curing requires time, a favorable temperature, and moisture. In the production of precast, exposed aggregate, the initial curing usually takes place in the form with final curing accomplished after the forms are stripped. Many plants use a 16- to 18-hour initial curing period at temperatures not less than 70° F. (21° C.). During this period all exposed areas of a precast element should be covered to prevent loss of moisture from the concrete. A uniform moisture content should be maintained over the whole member. Curing materials or methods that permit one portion of an element to cure or not dry out as fast as other portions produce color variation in the finished product. Complete immersion in water for 24 hours immediately after stripping gives effective curing and extremely uniform color.

Accelerated curing with live steam at atmospheric pressure can produce high early strength for rapid reuse of forms. This method provides both heat and moisture.

Other accelerated curing methods may utilize heat supplied by pipes carrying steam, hot water, or oil. Electric heating is also used to some extent. When only heat is applied, positive means should be used to prevent loss of moisture from the concrete. Surface retarders should not be used with accelerated curing methods.

After stripping, precast units should be kept in a surface-damp condition until they reach a strength of 3,500 psi (245 kgs. per sq. cm.). Then they may be subjected to outside weather conditions without further curing. However, they should air dry before being exposed to freezing temperatures or rapid temperature changes, which can cause cracking.

Cast-in-place formed concrete to receive an exposed aggregate finish should be cured by established standard procedures. Curing of exposed aggregate flatwork should begin as soon as the washing operation ceases, and the surface should be kept wet continuously for five days in warm weather—70° F. or higher (21° C. or higher)—or seven days in cooler weather—50° F. to 70° F. (10° to 21° C.). The temperature should be kept above 50° F. (10° C.) during the curing period. Curing compounds are not recommended for this type of work.

EXPOSURE TECHNIQUES

Exposure of the aggregate is accomplished by removing the surface matrix through a number of *techniques,* including washing and brushing, acid etching, abrasive blasting, tooling, and grinding.

Washing and Brushing

The simplest and perhaps the most inexpensive way to expose aggregates is by washing and brushing of the surface. If the operation is done before the concrete has gained much strength it is not necessary to use a surface retarder. A stiff brush together with flushing of water is all that is needed.

Treatment of concrete should begin as soon as possible upon removal from the form. In the face-up method, some precasters prefer to expose the aggregate by washing while the product is still in the form, but the concrete should be sufficiently set to prevent aggregate from being dislodged. The concrete is allowed to stiffen until the water sheen disappears and the surface can bear the weight of a man with no indentation. At this time, which corresponds roughly to initial set of the concrete, the surface layer of mortar is carefully washed away by using a light spray of water and brushing until the desired exposure is achieved. Timing of this operation is critical since the environmental conditions have a considerable bearing on the time of set. Depth of exposure will vary with the size of the aggregate and hardness of the matrix. Several passes may be required before the proper exposure is obtained. The aggregate should have a uniform exposure at the end of each washing operation. Once uniform exposure is obtained the washing can cease when the flush water is clear and there is no noticeable cement film on the aggregate.

Soft and hard bristle brushes and special exposed aggregate flush brooms are available for this type work. Plastic bristle brushes are preferred because they will not soften in water. Wire brushes may be required occasionally for particularly stubborn areas. Care should be taken to remove any pieces of wire that become embedded in the surface to prevent future rust stains. Power brushes may burnish the aggregate or damage the surface and should be used only after experimentation on sample panels.

On large flatwork or panel jobs, it may be necessary, because of placing considerations, to delay the washing and brushing 12 to 18 hours. With small aggregate sizes it may also be desirable to delay the time of set of the surface matrix to allow the base concrete to attain its initial set. Surface retarders may be advantageous in such cases.

Retarders. Chemical surface retarders delay the set of the surface cement paste so that the aggregate can be exposed easily by brushing away the retarded cement paste with or without applied water. Some retarders are effective for long periods of time while others are active for only a few hours. A water-insoluble type retarder is generally used when retardation to a depth of ⅛ to 3/16 inch (3 to 4.7 mm.) is desired. Water soluble retarders result in penetrations in excess of 3/16 inch (4.7 mm.) and are used to advantage for aggregates ¾ inch (1.9 cm.) and larger.

Surface retarders can be applied by roller, brush, or air-less spray and are usually clear liquids with a dye added to facilitate even application. Dyes are also used for color codifying to indicate retarders of varying strengths. The strength or degree of reveal of a retarder can be varied by the manufacturer by increasing the amount of active material in the retarder, by using a stronger retarding agent, or by varying the ability of active material to be dissolved by the water of the concrete mixture. Drying times are variable and most users agree that the faster a retarder dries the better its performance. Retarders possess various degrees of resistance to abrasion. This is important for built-in resistance to abrasion by the concrete during placing into forms coated with a retarder. Retarders are formulated so that the retarded matrix either remains on the concrete unit or stays on the forms. The choice depends upon the individual operation under consideration. The presence of an accelerator in concrete or the heating of concrete to accelerate strength gain will reduce the time during which the retarder is effective.

Best results are obtained by removing the retarded surface matrix when concrete strength is in the range of 1000 to 1500 psi (70 to 105 kgs. per sq. cm.). When using retarders, follow the manufacturers' recommendations closely. Forms normally are stripped within 24 hours in precasting work. At this time retarded matrix should be removed immediately. Extended stripping time can offset a surface retarder's action and the matrix will harden and become difficult to remove.

Retarders used to obtain exposed aggregate finishes can leave visible blemishes from over- or under-retardation that stand out prominently, especially on large surfaces.

Use of surface retarders is not recommended for vertical casting. It is difficult to obtain an even effect. Deep elements cast vertically require particular care to prevent over-retarded areas at the bottom and under-retarded areas at the top. Concrete can brush against the formwork during placing and carry the retarder with it to the bottom. One solution is to place a plastic sheeting over the form and withdraw it as the level of the concrete rises. Also, the bleed water may carry the retarder to the top or in small channels along the surface.

If forms are exposed to sunlight too long before placing, a retarder's action may be nullified and large under-retarded areas may result. The same may happen if rain falls on forms treated with a retarder prior to placing concrete.

It is important to achieve an even coating of retarder for best results. Retarders are more successful when applied to an absorbent surface such as hardboard but retarders are available for use on nonabsorbent surfaces such as steel forms. A retardant form liner such as commercially available retarder-impregnated cloth produces the most uniform results and simplifies form cleaning. A profiled surface also causes difficulties. If exposure is required all over the surface the retarder should be capable of uniform spread without collecting in corners and the bottom of any grooves. Also, it should dry before the concrete is placed in order to avoid scuffing. A retarder applied only to a part of a form face may not be very successful because of the ragged effect produced at the edge of the treated area.

Acid Etching

An acid etched finish is sometimes used in precasting where a fine texture is desired, usually with ¼-inch (6.4-mm.) aggregate. Only acid resistant siliceous aggregates such as quartz and granite should be used. Carbonate aggregates—dolomite and marble—will discolor or be severely damaged by the acid.

Acid etching may be accomplished by immersing the unit in a tank containing from 5 to 35 percent hydrochloric acid at 70° F. (21° C.). Best results are obtained when the concrete is at least several weeks old. Surfaces to be left unexposed may be coated with acrylic lacquer. The acid should be agitated and/or heated to improve its effectiveness. The surface of the unit should be lightly brushed while immersed. Once the etching is complete, the unit should be neutralized in an alkaline bath, then thoroughly flushed with water. Before etching, all exposed metal surfaces should be protected with acid-resistant coatings.

In working with acid, safety precautions should be followed to protect personnel and equipment. Protective clothing, breathing masks, and eye protection are mandatory. Used acid must be carefully disposed of or neutralized.

Acid etching is similar to but should not be confused with acid cleaning of exposed aggregate. (*See* the section on Patching and Cleaning later in this chapter.) Much stronger acid solutions are used to etch; therefore, it is generally more hazardous. Know the effect of various concentrations of acid used for etching.

Abrasive Blasting

Abrasive or *sandblasting* is used extensively for exposing aggregates. The depth of reveal may vary from a light *once over* to a depth of ¾ inch (1.9 cm.) or more. Surfaces with exposed aggregates as large as 2½ to 3 inches (6.3 to 7.5 cm.) have been deeply abrasive blasted with satisfactory results.

It is not always possible to determine in advance what the appearance of any given concrete will be after it is abrasive blasted. Blasting may give some aggregates a muted or frosted effect, which tends to lighten the color and subdue the luster of aggregate. A noticeable difference between abrasive blasted and washed concrete is that in washed concrete the coarse aggregate near the surface retains its smooth surface permitting the color in the aggregate to be more pronounced. Also, when blasting a white cement matrix, abrasive grits should be used that do not cause any color contamination. With certain types of colored abrasives, it is possible to impart color to the surface of concrete. Consequently, when abrasive blasting is proposed, it is desirable to cast and abrasive blast one or more 2-foot (60 cm.) square sample panels to check texture and color tone. Use of several abrasive materials may be experimented with at this time. *Abrasive materials* commonly used for blasting are silica sand, certain hard angular sands, boiler slag, and crushed chat, a waste by-product of lead mining.

The proper *time* for blasting is mostly a question of economics. The concrete matrix will be easier to cut in the first 24 to 72 hours after casting. As the concrete cures and gains strength, it becomes more difficult to blast to any appreciable depth, increasing the cost of the operation. Also, concrete with soft aggregate will have a flatter appearance if blasted at late stages. The higher cost of deferred blasting may be justified by the avoidance of job scheduling problems. Blasting also may be deferred to avoid accidental damage to finished surfaces from subsequent construction activities. However, all surfaces should be blasted at the same age for uniform results.

When blasting, the operator should hold the nozzle perpendicular to the surface and about 2 feet (60 cm.) away. The actual distance depends on the pressure used, hardness of the concrete matrix, and the cutting rate of the abrasive. An experienced operator can quickly determine the exact nozzle position to produce the specified surface finish. The matrix may be removed to a maximum depth of about one-third the average diameter of the coarse aggregate. Uniformity is essential in abrasive blasting as in all other exposure techniques and is a function of the skill and experience of the operator.

Sandblasting is usually done with dry abrasive in a stream of compressed air. *Wet blasting* by a jet of water is preferred in some areas because it presents less of a health hazard. Safety precautions are necessary to protect operating personnel, especially against silicosis.

Tooling

Mechanical spalling and chipping to produce an exposed aggregate texture can be accomplished with a variety of hand and power tools. The technique is usually called *bushhammering.* Pneumatic tools are available with combs, chisels, or multiple points. Hand tools are used for small areas, corners, and where power tools cannot reach.

Basically all methods of tooling concrete remove a layer of hardened concrete matrix while fracturing the aggregate at the surface. Surfaces attained can vary from a light *scaling* to a deep bold texture achieved by jackhammering with a single pointed chisel.

Concrete should not be tooled until it has reached a strength of at least 3,750 psi (262.5 kgs. per sq. cm.)—generally three weeks when using a low-slump gap-graded mix as described previously. Tooling has been done as early as two weeks after casting, but a more uniform surface will be achieved after three weeks.

Exposing aggregates by tooling can cause unsightly corners because of excessive material removal. Mask off and stop tooling 1 to 2 inches (2.5 to 5 cm.) from sharp corners to avoid this problem. Best results are possible with chamfered corners.

Tooling removes a certain thickness of material (3/16 inch or

4.7 mm. on the average) from the surface of the concrete and may fracture particles of aggregate, allowing moisture to penetrate the depth of the aggregate particle. For this reason, the minimum cover to the reinforcement should be somewhat greater than normally required. It is sometimes recommended that from 2 to 2½ inches (5 to 6.3 cm.) of cover be provided for all cast-in-place exposed aggregate work to be tooled or blasted.

Grinding

Grinding produces smooth exposed aggregate surfaces. Grinding is also called honing and polishing depending on the degree of smoothness of the finish. In general, honed finishes are produced by grinding tools varying from about No. 24 coarse grit to a very fine grit of about No. 300. Polishing is usually accomplished after honing and is done with a polishing compound and a buffer. In most instances, a honed finish is smooth enough for precast work. Grinding elements may consist of carborundum particles bonded together with a resin, or diamonds set in a cutting surface. Diamond elements, initially more expensive, are used more widely because they cut much faster. Equipment may vary from a simple hand grinder to a very elaborate multihead machine.

Honing consists of several successive grinding steps, each employing a finer grit than the preceding step. Air voids in the concrete surface must be filled before each of the first few grinding operations using a sand-cement mixture that matches the matrix in the precast unit. Careful filling and curing are required and the next grinding operation must be delayed until the fill material has reached sufficient strength. Rough grinding, filling, and fine grinding is similar to terrazzo work.

Surface grinding hardened concrete requires more labor than most other aggregate exposure techniques. Vertical and overhead surfaces are especially difficult. Grinding costs depend upon the hardness of the aggregate and depth of exposure required.

Samples

Wherever possible it is desirable to specify an exposed aggregate finish by reference to a sample; this sample to be acceptable to both the producer and the architect. The sample can be the first unit produced or a completed building readily accessible for inspection. The sample which the contractor must match may be a full-sized mock-up constructed in the manner proposed for the project. Small samples done in the laboratory may not be duplicated under job conditions, particularly exposed aggregate concrete.

PATCHING AND CLEANING

Despite the care exercised most projects have some blemishes. Repair is a highly skilled business requiring more than ordinary care if the remedial measures are not to prove more unsightly than the original defects. *Patching* is routinely performed prior to delivery and after installation when necessary. This discussion will be concerned with precast exposed aggregate concrete but the procedures are little different for cast-in-place work.

Patching

It is easier to patch exposed aggregate than plain smooth concrete elements. First, the damaged area should be chipped out and cut back to a depth a little deeper than the maximum size of exposed aggregate. *For example,* with ¾-inch (1.9-cm.) aggregate go down 1 inch (2.5 cm.). The sides of the hole should be at right angles to the surface. It is not necessary to undercut. Then the area must be thoroughly soaked with water to assure the patch has a good bond. A good practice is to use a scrubbing brush with this operation. If a bonding agent is used, the area is left dry. After the patching area is well soaked with no free water, brush in a mixture of cement and water to the consistency of a thick paint. The damaged area is now ready to receive the patching mix.

The patching concrete must contain the same materials as

used in the unit minus the coarse aggregates exposed. If the matrix was made with gray cement a small amount of white cement or silica flour must normally be added to the patching mix. This is because the lower water-cement ratio of the patch causes it to dry darker than the original concrete. The amount of white material to add varies but about 25 percent is average. On the other hand, if the original concrete matrix is white a small amount of gray cement may have to be added to match the slight gray tint imparted to white concrete while mixing due to drum wear. Trial mixes are essential to determine the exact quantities. These mixes should be allowed to age for 7 to 14 days before final judgment. Small sample panels—12 inches (30.5 cm.) square—should be cast during production and later broken for use as guides in matching mix color. The patching mix must be stiff but not so stiff that the exposed aggregates cannot be pressed into it.

The patching mix should be compacted into the hole immediately after the neat cement slurry coat is applied (or if a bonding agent is used any time during the agent's period of tackiness). The mix should be vigorously hand tamped then struck off level with the surrounding matrix.

On horizontal surfaces the aggregate to be exposed is next spread on the surface of the new patch to match the surrounding area. The stones are patted into the surface with a small wood block. On vertical surfaces or overhead work each piece of aggregate must be hand placed. After a few minutes set, a wet sponge can be dabbed against the surface of the patch to remove any matrix from the aggregate so it matches surrounding areas. Finally, the patch should be cured with water and acid cleaned if the rest of the unit was so treated.

When producing exposed aggregate elements with small size aggregates, about ⅛ to ¼ inch (3.2 to 6.4 mm.), it is often difficult to obtain uniform exposure with retarders. To restore the surface, wet it, then smear and brush a grout coat of cement, sand and water into the surface to match the original concrete matrix. This operation also fills small voids that occur in the surface. Shortly after it has set, excess grout is carefully brushed off the aggregate.

Precast panels patched after erection get similar treatment

from the precasters' patching specialist at the jobsite. Frequently a broken-off piece can be *glued* back in place using an epoxy bonding agent. Broken surfaces of panel and piece should both be painted with the adhesive.

Cleaning

Various techniques and materials to clean exposed aggregate concrete include plain water, hot water with detergents or other commercial cleaners, steam, light abrasive blasting, and dilute hydrochloric (muriatic) acid. The last method is most commonly used, especially in the precasting plant.

Exposed aggregates can be brightened by washing with a 5 to 10 percent concentration of hydrochloric acid, which removes the dull cement film remaining from some exposure techniques, especially washing and brushing. Normally, the acid is applied to a prewetted surface by brush but it can be sprayed. The surface is wetted to reduce acid penetration. As soon as possible, and before the panel dries, all traces of acid should be removed by flushing with plenty of clean water. The best procedure is to use two men, one applying acid while the other hoses the surface.

Acid cleaning is best used after a one or two week delay but often is done immediately after initial curing to reduce handling operations. Acid washing too soon contributes to formation of white deposits on units with a gray cement matrix or with dark colored aggregates. The white deposit is an insoluble silica gel. The reaction of hydrochloric acid and portland cement results in the formation of a somewhat soluble silica gel that soon becomes insoluble and extremely difficult to remove. Hydrofluoric acid is effective in removing deposits but is extremely dangerous for inexperienced personnel. Such cleaning is definitely not suggested for use by regular plant employees.

Plant practices have some effect on this situation. If hydrochloric acid is used too soon after grouting the surface, a white deposit may result. The units and/or surface must have at least three or four days of moist curing. Delaying the acid wash significantly reduces chances of forming these deposits because of more complete hydration. The acid and brush must be kept clean. When acid is brushed on to the surface the brush may build up a concentration of insoluble silica gel in the bucket that may then be picked up by the brush and smeared over the surface.

CLEAR COATINGS

Clear coatings are frequently used on exposed aggregate surfaces to prevent attack, soiling or discoloration of the concrete by air pollution, to facilitate cleaning the surface if it does become dirty, to brighten the color of the aggregates, and to render the surface water repellent and prevent darkening due to water absorption.

Commercial coatings were recently evaluated both in the laboratory and outdoor exposure tests to determine their ability to maintain the initial surface appearance of exposed aggregate concrete. Many of the better coatings consist of methyl methacrylate forms of acrylic resin. The use of the proper coating permits relatively easy cleaning of surface dirt. However, many coating materials cause permanent discoloration of the concrete surface.

Recommendations on the use of clear coatings on exposed aggregate concrete are as follows: (1) coating use may be inadvisable in areas of little or no air pollution; (2) if used, coatings of the methyl methacrylate form of acrylic resin are recommended; (3) any coating used should be guaranteed by the manufacturer not to stain, soil, darken or discolor the exposed aggregate finish; and, finally, (4) strictly follow the manufacturer's directions for application of a coating.

Chapter 16

Mineral Pigments for Use in Coloring Concrete

Only commercially pure mineral pigments should be used, as other pigments are likely to fade or reduce the strength of the stucco, mortar, or concrete in a marked degree.

COLORING MATERIALS

The amount of *coloring materials* added should not exceed 10 percent by weight of the cement, as larger quantities may affect the strength of the mortar or concrete to an injurious degree. Deep shades can generally be produced with less than this amount of color by judicious choice of pigments. Different shades of color can be secured by varying the amount of coloring material used or by mixing together two or more pigments. The full coloring value of pigments can be obtained only with white portland cement. White cement must be used to obtain the more delicate shades of the lighter colors and for white finishes. When clear white is desired, white sand and white cement should be used. The use of white portland cement with yellow and brown sand will produce varying shades of cream, yellow, and buff. If the colors desired can be secured without pigments, such practice is to be recommended.

Variations in the color of the materials are such as to make color formulas only approximate. Best results are obtained by experiment or trial. After selecting the primary color desired, the exact shade may be determined by preparing a number of small panels which should be made of the same materials and proportions as are intended to be used in the actual work, varying the ratio of pigment to cement. Store the samples for about five days under conditions similar to the actual work. Panels will have a darker shade when damp than when dry.

MIXING MATERIALS

Carefully weigh out the aggregate and cement. Add to this the predetermined amount of pigment, by weight. The whole mixture should then be uniformly mixed dry until the entire batch is of uniform color. Then, add water to bring the mixture to the proper consistency.

Another method which has been successfully used is to grind the cement and pigment in the desired proportions in a small ball mill. This mixture is then added to the aggregate and the batch thoroughly mixed dry to a uniform color before adding water.

The intensities of shades produced by mineral pigments will be slightly increased by thorough mixing of the mortar or concrete.

MATERIALS USED IN COLORING

A general guide to the selection of colors and coloring materials to obtain various effects follows:

For *blues* use cobalt oxide.
For *browns* use brown oxide of iron.
For *buffs* use synthetic yellow oxide of iron.
For *greens* use chromium oxide.
For *reds* use red oxide of iron.
For *grays* and *slate* effects use black iron oxide or carbon black, preferably black iron oxide. Common lampblack should not be used.

TESTS TO DETERMINE QUALITY

Most architects and builders depend upon the reputation of

the manufacturer of pigments for assurance that the quality of the material is satisfactory. There are, however, a few simple tests that can easily be made which will often be of assistance in determining the suitability of pigments, although a complete examination would involve extensive physical and chemical tests.

The finer a pigment is ground, the greater is its coloring ability and the less the amount required to produce a given shade.

The ability to resist the action of lime can be tested by mixing a sample pat of twenty parts cement and one part pigment and observing it for several days, while keeping the specimen moist. Any pronounced fading indicates that the pigment is not limeproof.

To test the durability of a color under the influence of light takes some time, unless a special artificial light is at hand. Pronounced fading of a colored mortar on exposure to sunlight for one month is evidence that the pigment is unsuitable.

Chapter 17

Hot- and Cold-Weather Concreting

Weather conditions existing at a jobsite—hot or cold, windy or calm, dry or humid—may be vastly different from the optimum assumed at the time the concrete mix was specified, designed, and selected.

HOT-WEATHER CONCRETING

Conditions during hot weather that otherwise did not exist can create such difficulties as premature stiffening (false set), plastic cracking, thermal shock, or loss of strength. However, by taking precautions in anticipation of these adverse hot-weather conditions, concrete work can proceed smoothly.

When to Take Precautions

The most favorable temperature for fresh concrete in hot weather is usually lower than can be obtained without artificial cooling. A concrete temperature of 50° F. to 60° F. (10° C. to 16° C.) is desirable, but not always practical. For massive concrete structures the concrete temperature is often specified at less than 50° F. (10° C.). Many specifications require that concrete, when placed, should have a temperature of less than 85° F. or 90° F. (29° C. to 32° C.).

For most concrete work in hot weather it is impractical to limit the maximum temperature of the concrete when placed because circumstances vary widely. A limit that would serve successfully at one jobsite could be highly unsatisfactory at another. *For example,* flatwork done under the roof and with exterior walls in place could be completed at a concrete temperature that would cause much difficulty were the same concrete being placed outdoors on the same day.

Accordingly, the effects of a higher concrete temperature should be anticipated and the concrete placed at a temperature limit that will allow best results in hot-weather conditions, probably somewhere between 75° F. and 100° F. (24° C. and 38° C.). The limit should be established for conditions at the jobsite based on concrete tests at the limiting temperature, not at 70° F. (21° C.).

EFFECTS OF HIGH CONCRETE TEMPERATURES

As the concrete temperature increases there is a loss in slump, which is usually compensated for by adding more water at the jobsite. At a higher concrete temperature a greater amount of water is required to hold slump constant than is needed at a lower temperature. Adding water *without* adding cement results in a higher water-cement ratio, thereby lowering the strength and adversely affecting other desirable properties of the hardened concrete.

As shown in Fig. 1, if the temperature of fresh concrete is increased from 50° F. to 100° F. (10° C. to 38° C.), about 33 pounds (15 kgs.) of additional water is needed per cubic yard (0.765 cu. meters) of concrete to maintain the same 3-inch (76-mm.) slump. The 33-pound (15-kg.) increase in water content could reduce strength by 12 to 15 percent, nullify the strength overdesign required by standard deviation strength test data, and give a compressive strength cylinder test break less than the specified f'_c.

Figure 2 shows the effect of high concrete temperatures on compressive strength. The temperatures of the concrete at the time of mixing, casting, and curing were 73° F., 90° F., 105° F., and 120° F. (23° C., 32° C., 40° C., and 49° C.) respectively. After 28 days the specimens were moist cured at 73° F. (23° C.) until the age of test. These tests, using identical concretes of the same water-cement ratio, show that while higher concrete temperatures give higher early strength than concrete at 73° F.

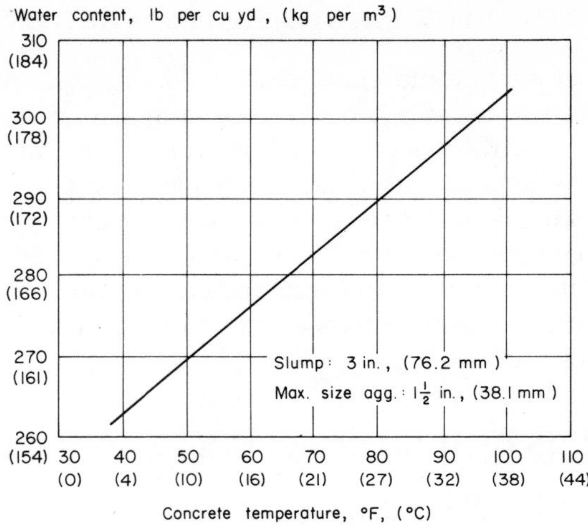

Fig. 1. The water requirement of a concrete mix increases with an increase in temperature.

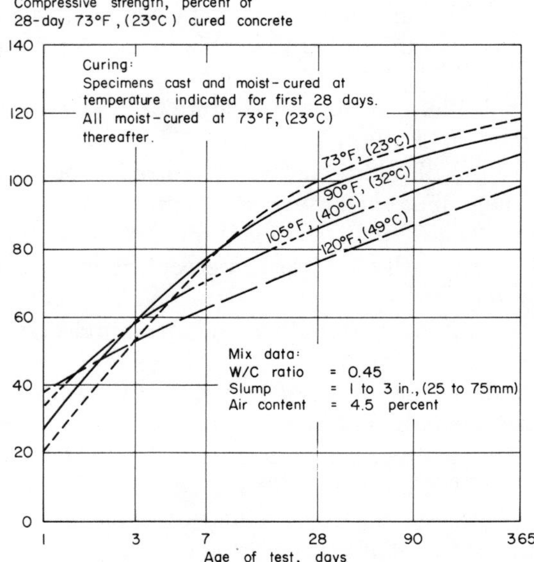

Fig. 2. Effect of high temperature on concrete compressive strength at various ages.

(23° C.), at later ages lower ultimate strength is recorded. If the water content had been increased to maintain the same slump (without changing the cement content), the reduction in strength would have been even greater than shown in Fig. 2.

Besides reducing the strength and increasing the mixing water requirement, high temperatures of fresh concrete have other harmful effects. Setting time is reduced, and high temperatures increase the rate of concrete hardening and shorten the length of time within which the concrete can be transported, placed, and finished. Concrete should remain plastic for a sufficiently long period of time so that each layer can be placed without development of cold joints or discontinuities in the concrete. Retarding admixtures meeting ASTM C494, Type B, may be beneficial in offsetting the accelerating effects of high temperatures.

In hot weather the tendency for cracks to form is increased both before and after hardening. Rapid evaporation of water from hot concrete may cause plastic shrinkage cracks before the surface has hardened. Cracks may also develop in the hardened concrete because of increased shrinkage due to higher water content, or volume changes due to cooling down from the initial high temperature at placement to the low temperature in service.

Air entrainment of concrete is also affected in hot weather. At elevated concrete temperatures an increase in the amount of air-entraining admixture is required to produce a given air content.

Because of the detrimental effects of high concrete temperatures, operations in hot weather should be directed toward keeping the concrete as cool as practicable.

Cooling Concrete Materials

The most practical method of maintaining low concrete temperatures is to control the temperature of the concrete materials. One or more of the ingredients may be cooled before mixing. In hot weather the aggregates and water should be kept as cool as practicable.

The contribution of each material in a concrete mixture to the

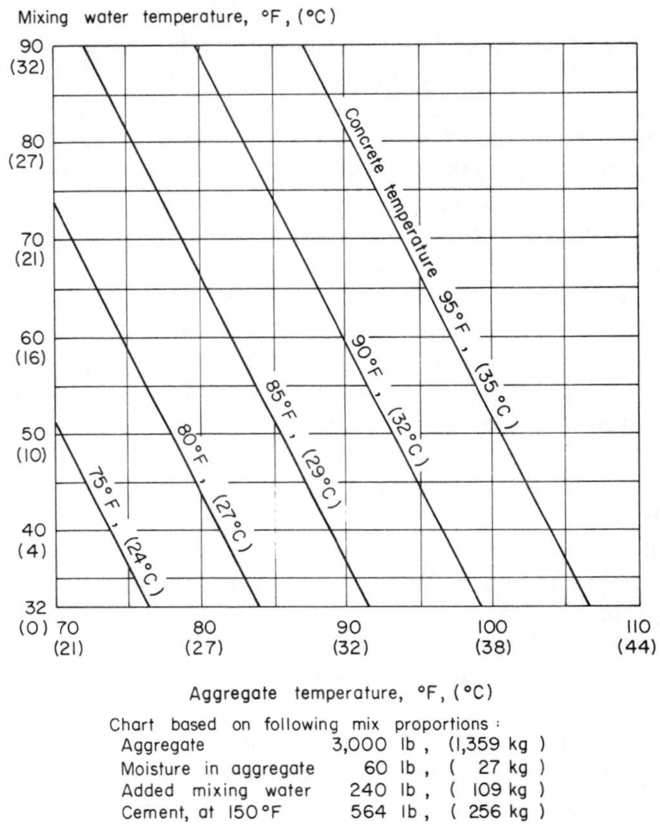

Fig. 3. Temperature of fresh concrete as affected by temperature of materials.

temperature of concrete is related to the temperatures, specific heat, and quantities of the materials used. Figure 3 shows graphically the effect of temperature of materials on the temperature of fresh concrete. It is evident that although concrete temperature is primarily dependent upon the aggregate temperature, it can be effectively lowered by cool mixing water. The chart is based on the particular concrete mix shown, but is reasonably accurate for most ordinary concrete mixtures. It conforms to the following general formula (without ice; U.S. Customary and SI Units).

$$T = \frac{0.22(T_a W_a + T_c W_c) + T_f W_f + T_m W_m}{0.22(W_a + W_c) + W_f + W_m}$$

where T = temperature (Fahrenheit or Celsius) of the freshly mixed concrete.

T_a, T_c, T_f, and T_m = temperature of the aggregates, cement, free moisture in aggregates, and added mixing water, respectively.

W_a, W_c, W_f, and W_m = weight (pounds or kilograms) of the aggregates, cement, free moisture in aggregates, and added mixing water, respectively.

Of the materials in concrete, water is the easiest to cool. Even though it is used in smaller quantities than the other ingredients, cold water will effect a moderate reduction in the concrete temperature. A 4° F. (2° C.) change in water temperature will lower the concrete temperature 1° F. (0.56° C.). Mixing water from a cool source should be used. It should be stored in tanks that are not exposed to the direct rays of the sun. Tanks and pipelines carrying the mixing water should be buried, insulated, shaded, or painted white to keep water at the lowest practical temperature.

Water may be cooled by refrigeration, the use of liquid nitrogen, or by adding crushed ice. Ice can also be used as part of the mixing water provided it is completely melted by the time mixing is completed. When using crushed ice care must be taken to store it at a temperature below 28° F. (−2° C.) to prevent lumps from forming by refreezing of the ice particles.

The formula for temperature of the fresh concrete is modified as follows (where W_i is the weight in pounds or kilograms of ice):

(with ice; U.S. Customary Units)

$$T = \frac{0.22(T_a W_a + T_c W_c) + T_f W_f + T_m W_m - 112 W_i}{0.22(W_a + W_c) + W_f + W_m + W_i}$$

(with ice; SI units)

$$T = \frac{0.22(T_a W_a + T_c W_c) + T_f W_f + T_m W_m - 79.6 W_i}{0.22(W_a + W_c) + W_f + W_m + W_i}$$

Crushed or flaked ice is more effective than chilled water in reducing concrete temperature. As the cement and aggregates are cooled, the temperature of the cooling water from ice is consequently raised. One pound (0.453 kg.) of the ice in melting absorbs 144 Btu (151,928 J.). However, 1 pound (0.453 kg.) of water heated 1° F. (0.56° C.) absorbs only 1 Btu (1055 J.). For instance, 1 pound (0.453 kg.) of ice heated from 32° F. to 73° F. (0° C. to 23° C.) absorbs a total of 185 Btu (195,185 J.); 1 pound (0.453 kg.) of water absorbs only 40 Btu (42,202 J.) when its temperature is raised from 33° F. to 73° F. (0.56° C. to 23° C.). Therefore, if 75 pounds (34 kgs.) of ice replaces an equal weight of water per cubic yard (0.765 cu. meters) in a concrete mix with a temperature of 90° F. (32° C.), the temperature would drop to about 75° F. (24° C.). The amount of water and ice used must not exceed the total requirements for mixing water. Crushed ice is charged into a transit-mix truck prior to the addition of other materials. By substituting ice for part of the mixing water, the concrete temperature can be substantially lowered.

Aggregates have a pronounced effect on the fresh concrete temperature because they represent 60 to 80 percent of the total weight of concrete. To lower the temperature of concrete 10° F. (5.6° C.) requires only a 15° F. (9.4° C.) reduction in the temperature of the aggregates. There are several simple methods of keeping aggregates cool.

Stockpiles should be shaded from the sun and kept moist by sprinkling. Since evaporation is a cooling process, sprinkling provides effective cooling, especially when the relative humidity is low.

Sprinkling of coarse aggregates should be adjusted to avoid producing excessive variation in the surface moisture and thereby causing loss of slump uniformity. Refrigeration is another method of cooling materials. Aggregates can be immersed in cold water tanks, or cooled air can be circulated through storage bins or insulated tunnels. Vacuum cooling can reduce aggregate temperatures to as low as 34° F. (1° C.).

Cement temperature has only a minor effect on the temperature of the freshly mixed concrete because of cement's low specific heat and the relatively small amount of cement in the mix. A change in cement temperature of 10° F. (5.6° C.) generally will change the concrete temperatures by 1° F. (0.56° C.). Because cement loses heat slowly during storage, it may be warm when delivered. (This heat is produced in grinding the cement clinker during manufacture.) Since the temperature of cement does affect the temperature of the fresh concrete to some extent, some specifications place a limit on its temperature at time of use. This limit varies depending on conditions from 150° F. to 180° F. (66° C. to 82° C.). However, test results indicate that it is desirable to specify a maximum temperature for freshly mixed concrete rather than place a limit on the temperature of ingredients.

Preparation Before Concreting

Before concrete is placed certain precautions can be taken during hot weather to help lower the concrete temperature. Mixers, chutes, belts, hoppers, pump lines, and other equipment for handling concrete can be shaded, painted white, or covered with wet burlap to reduce the effect of the sun's heat.

Forms, reinforcing steel, and subgrade should be fogged with cool water just before the concrete is placed (Fig. 4). Fogging the area cools the contact surfaces and surrounding air and increases its relative humidity. This not only reduces the temperature rise of the concrete but also minimizes evaporation of water from the concrete during placement. For slabs on ground, it is a good practice to dampen the subgrade the evening before concreting. There should be no standing water or puddles on the subgrade at the time that concrete is placed.

During extremely hot periods improved results can be obtained by restricting concrete placement to the evening hours or nighttime, especially in arid climates. On thick slabs and pavements this has resulted in less thermal shrinkage and cracking.

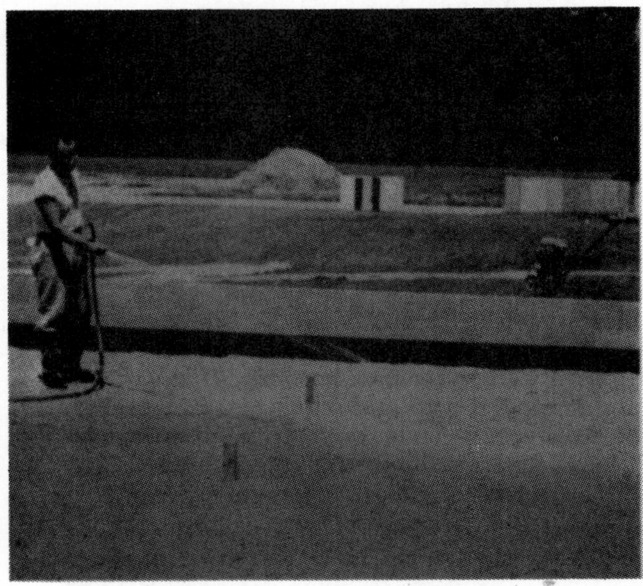

Fig. 4. Sprinkling subgrade and forms before placing concrete.

Transporting, Placing, and Finishing

Transporting and placing concrete should be done as quickly as practicable during hot weather. Delays contribute to loss of slump and an increase in concrete temperature. Enough workmen and equipment should be available to handle and place concrete immediately upon delivery.

Prolonged mixing, even at agitating speed, should be avoided. If delays occur, the heat generated by mixing can be minimized by stopping the mixer and then agitating intermittently. Specifications for ready mixed concrete (ASTM C94 or CSA A23.1) require discharge of concrete to be completed within one and one-half hours or by the time the drum has revolved 300 times, whichever occurs first. During hot weather the time limit could reasonably be reduced to one hour or possibly 45 minutes. (*See* Chap. 5, Handling and Transporting Concrete.)

Since concrete hardens more rapidly in hot weather, extra

care in placing techniques is required to avoid cold joints. For placement of walls, shallower layers may be required to assure consolidation with each previous lift. Temporary sunshades and windbreaks help to minimize cold joints.

All steps in finishing should be done promptly after the water sheen disappears or after the concrete can support the weight of a man. Finishing on hot, dry, and windy days requires extra care. The rapid drying of the concrete at the surface may cause plastic shrinkage cracking and cold joints in slabs.

Plastic Shrinkage Cracking

Plastic shrinkage cracking can occur at any time, but is usually encountered on hot and windy days when the humidity is low. Water will evaporate from the surface faster than it can bleed (rise naturally to the surface). This will create overly rapid drying shrinkage and growing tension stresses in the surface that often cause short, irregular, plastic shrinkage cracks to appear. These cracks can be practically eliminated and positively minimized when the following simple precautions are taken.

Cool the air and lessen the rapid evaporation from the surface with a fog spray. Spread and remove polyethylene sheeting between finishing operations or apply a spray-on monomolecular film to the surface. Erect sunshades and windbreaks to reduce temperatures and wind velocity on the surface. Sometimes, in more massive placements, revibration prior to floating will prevent the development of plastic shrinkage cracking. And if the cracks do appear prior to final set, they can be closed by striking the surface on each side of the crack with a float. However, the cracking can recur unless the causes are corrected.

Curing and Protection

Curing and *protection* are more critical in hot weather than in cooler periods. Forms cannot be considered a satisfactory substitute for curing in hot weather. They should be loosened as soon as this can be done without damage to the concrete. Water should then be applied on the top exposed concrete surfaces and allowed to run down inside the forms. Wood forms should be sprayed with water while still in place, since otherwise they may absorb part of the mixing water. On hardened concrete, and on flat concrete surfaces in particular, curing water should not be excessively cooler than the concrete. This will minimize cracking caused by stresses due to temperature change.

In order to prevent the drying of exposed concrete surfaces, moist curing should commence as soon as the surfaces are finished and continue for at least 24 hours. During hot weather, continuous moist curing is preferred. The need for adequate moist curing is greatest during the first few hours after finishing. If moist curing is not continued beyond 24 hours, the concrete surfaces should be protected from free circulation of drying air with curing paper or heat-reflecting plastic sheets while the surfaces are still damp. Moist-cured surfaces should be allowed to dry out slowly after the curing period to reduce the possibility of surface crazing and cracking.

White-pigmented curing compounds can be used on horizontal slabs. Application of a curing compound during hot weather should be preceded by 24 hours of moist curing. If this is not practical, the compound should be applied immediately after the final finishing of the concrete. The concrete surfaces should be moist.

Admixtures

Admixtures should be used to supplement the basic properties of a concrete mix rather than to replace any of the basic ingredients. For unusual cases during hot weather and where careful inspection is maintained, a retarding admixture may be beneficial in delaying the setting time while increasing somewhat the rate of slump loss.

Retarding admixtures should conform to the requirements of ASTM C494, Type B. Admixtures should be tested with job materials under job conditions, including temperature, in advance of construction to determine their compatibility with the basic concrete ingredients and their ability under these particular conditions to produce the desired properties.

COLD-WEATHER CONCRETING

Concrete can be placed safely throughout winter months if certain precautions are taken. For successful winter work, adequate protection must be provided when temperatures of 40° F. (4.5° C.) or lower occur during placing and the early curing period.

General Requirements

Fresh concrete must be protected against the disruptive effects of freezing. This danger exists until the degree of saturation of the concrete has been sufficiently reduced by the withdrawal of mix water in the process of hydration. If no water is available from outside the concrete (for example, curing water) the time at which this reduction is accomplished will correspond approximately to the time at which the concrete attains a compressive strength of about 500 psi (35 kgs. per cu. cm.).

Furthermore, protection sometimes must be afforded until the concrete has attained minimum properties required by the environment and loading to which it will be exposed. Often, resistance of the surface to damaging effects of saturated freezing and thawing is the governing property. Sometimes protection to assure freeze-thaw durability may not be adequate for structural safety.

To protect fresh concrete, plans should be made well in advance. Appropriate equipment should be available for heating the concrete materials, for constructing enclosures, and for maintaining favorable temperatures after concrete is placed. Heated enclosures are the most effective means of protecting concrete during severe and prolonged cold weather (Fig. 5).

To prevent freezing until protection can be provided, the temperature of concrete *as placed* should not be less than shown in Table 12, line 4. In addition to the recommended minimum temperatures of concrete *as mixed,* shown in Table 12, lines 1, 2, and 3, thermal protection may be required. This is to assure that subsequent concrete temperatures do not fall below the minimums shown in Table 12, line 4, for the periods shown in Table 13 to ensure durability or to develop strength.

Fig. 5. During severe cold weather a heated enclosure is the most effective means of protecting concrete.

Air-Entrained Concrete

It is desirable to use *air-entrained concrete* during cold weather to reduce the possibility of freeze-thaw damage. All concrete that will be exposed to freezing and thawing in service should contain the proper amount of entrained air. Concrete that may be frozen before having had an opportunity to dry out (after curing) should also be air-entrained even though its later service environment may not involve freezing and thawing. Extra protection should be provided after placement if air-entrained concrete is not used during cold weather.

High-Early-Strength Concrete

High strength at an early age is frequently desired during winter construction to reduce the length of time protection is required. The value of *high-early-strength concrete* during cold

Line	Condition of placement and curing		Very thin sections**	Thin sections	Moderately massive sections	Massive sections
1	Min. temp. fresh concrete *as mixed* for weather as indicated, deg. F.	Above 30 deg. F.	60	55	50	45
2		Zero to 30 deg. F.	65	60	55	50
3		Below 0 deg. F.	70	65	60	55
4	Min. temp. fresh concrete *as placed*, deg. F.		55	50	45	40
5	Max. allowable *gradual* drop in temp. after end of protection	For first 24 hours	50	40	30	20
6		In any 1 hour	5	4	3	2

*Adapted from Recommended Practice for Cold-Weather Concreting (ACI 306-66), American Concrete Institute.

**Canadian Standards Association (CSA) Standard A23.1-73, Concrete Materials and Methods of Concrete Construction, uses the following four classifications to delineate size of section: least dimension less than 12 in.; 12 to 36 in.; 37 to 72 in.; and greater than 72 in.

TABLE 12. RECOMMENDED CONCRETE TEMPERATURES FOR COLD-WEATHER CONSTRUCTION* (AIR-ENTRAINED CONCRETE).

Degree of exposure to freezing and thawing in service	Protection for durability at temperature indicated in line 4 of Table 1, days	
	Conventional concrete**	High-early-strength concrete†
No exposure	2	1
Any exposure	3	2

*Adapted from Recommended Practice for Cold-Weather Concreting (ACI 306-66), American Concrete Institute.

**Made with ASTM Type I or II (CSA Normal or Moderate) cement.

†Made with ASTM Type III (CSA High-Early-Strength) cement, or an accelerator, or an extra 100 lb. of cement per cubic yard.

TABLE 13. RECOMMENDED DURATION OF PROTECTION FOR CONCRETE PLACED IN COLD WEATHER* (AIR-ENTRAINED CONCRETE).

weather is often realized through early re-use of forms and removal of shores, savings in the cost of additional heating and protection, earlier finishing of flatwork, and earlier use of the structure. High early strength may be obtained by using one or a combination of the following:

1. Type III, IIIA, or high-early-strength cement.
2. Lower water-cement ratios (that is, additional cement) with any type of portland cement.
3. Higher curing temperatures (by steam curing or use of heated enclosures, for example).
4. Chemical accelerators.

Small amounts of an accelerator such as calcium chloride (a maximum of two percent by weight of cement) may be used to accelerate the setting and early-age strength development of concrete in cold weather. Precautions are necessary when using accelerators containing chlorides where there is an in-service potential for corrosion as, for example, in prestressed concrete, or where aluminum or galvanized inserts are contemplated. Chlorides are not recommended for concretes exposed to soil or water containing sulfates or for concretes subjected to alkali-aggregate reaction.

Accelerators should not be used as a substitute for proper curing and frost protection. Also, the use of so-called antifreeze compounds or other materials to lower the freezing point of concrete should not be permitted. The quantity of these materials needed to appreciably lower the freezing point of concrete is so great that strength and other properties are seriously affected.

Effect of Low Temperatures

Temperature affects the rate at which hydration of cement occurs—low temperatures retard concrete hardening and strength gain. Figure 6 shows the age-compressive strength relationship for concrete that has been mixed, placed, and cured at temperatures between 40° F. (4.5° C.) and 73° F. (22.8° C.). At temperatures below 73° F. (22.8° C.) strengths are lower at early ages but higher at later periods. Concrete made with Type I or normal cement and cured at 55° F. (12.8° C.) has relatively low strengths for the first few days, but after 28 days has slightly higher strengths than concrete made and cured at 73° F. (22.8° C.).

The higher early strengths that may be achieved through use of Type III or high-early-strength cement are illustrated by Fig. 7. Principal advantages occur prior to seven days. At 40° F. (4.5° C.) curing temperature, the early advantages of this type of mixture are more pronounced and persist longer than at higher temperatures.

It should be remembered that strength gain practically stops when moisture required for curing is no longer available. Concrete that is placed at low temperatures (but above freezing) may develop higher strengths than concrete placed at high temperatures, but curing must be continued for a longer period. It is not safe to expose concrete to freezing temperatures at early periods. If freezing is permitted within 24 hours, much lower strength will result.

Concrete of low slump is particularly desirable for cold-weather flatwork. During cold weather, evaporation is slowed, therefore, minimizing bleed water will lessen delays in finishing.

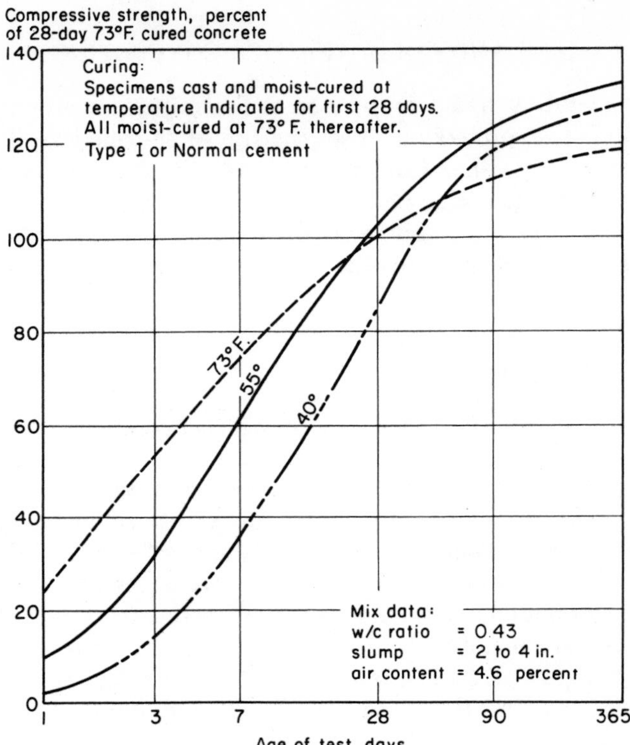

Fig. 6 Effect of low temperatures on concrete compressive strength at various ages.

Temperature of Fresh Concrete

The temperature of fresh concrete *as mixed* should not be less than shown in Table 12, lines 1, 2, and 3. Note that lower concrete temperatures are recommended for heavy mass concrete sections because heat generated during hydration is dissipated less rapidly as the concrete section becomes more massive. Furthermore, at lower air temperatures more heat is lost from concrete during transporting and placing, and the recommended concrete temperatures shown in Table 12, lines 1, 2, and 3 are higher for colder weather.

It is rarely necessary to use fresh concrete at a temperature much above 70° F. (21° C.). Higher concrete temperatures do not afford proportionately longer protection from freezing be-

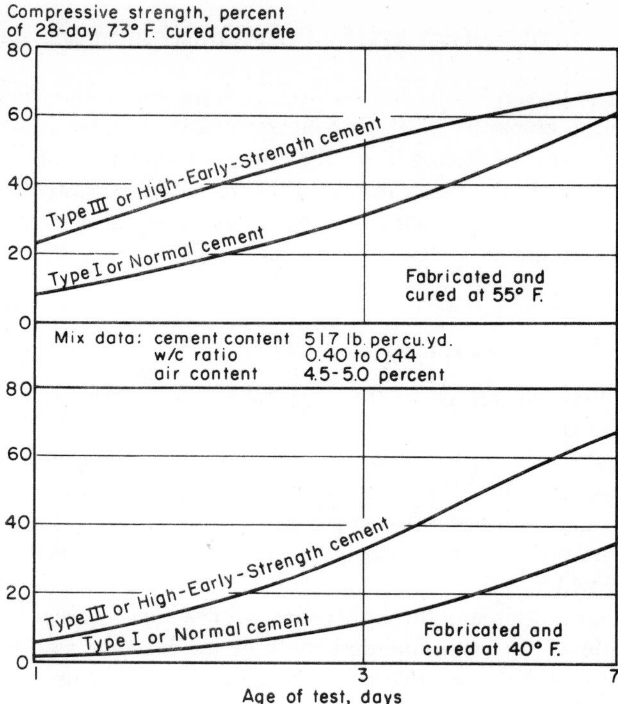

Fig. 7. Early compressive strength relationships involving portland cement types and low curing temperatures.

cause the loss of heat is greater. Also, high concrete temperatures are undesirable since they increase thermal shrinkage, require more mixing water for the same slump, and contribute to the possibility of plastic shrinkage cracking (moisture loss through evaporation is greater). Therefore, the temperature of the concrete *as mixed* should be maintained at not more than 10° F. (5.6° C.) above the minimums recommended in Table 12. Temperatures as high as 20° F. (11° C.) above the values in Table 12 should be rare.

HEATING CONCRETE MATERIALS

The temperature of cement and aggregates varies with the weather and type of storage. Since aggregates usually contain moisture, frozen lumps and ice are often present when the temperature is below freezing. Frozen aggregates must be thawed to avoid pockets of aggregate in the concrete after placing and, if thawing does take place in the mixer, to avoid excessively high water contents. Thawing frozen aggregates also facilitates proper batching.

Aggregate Temperatures

At temperatures above freezing it is seldom necessary to heat aggregates. At temperatures below freezing, often only the fine aggregate is heated to produce concrete of the required temperature, provided the coarse aggregate is free of frozen lumps. If aggregate temperatures are above freezing, the desired concrete temperature can usually be obtained by heating only the mixing water.

Circulating steam through pipes over which aggregates are stockpiled is a recommended method for heating aggregates. Stockpiles should be covered with tarpaulins to retain and distribute heat and to prevent the formation of ice. Live stream, preferably at high pressure (75 to 125 psi or 5.3 to 8.8 kgs. per cu. cm.), can be injected directly into the aggregate pile to heat it, but variable moisture content in aggregates might result in erratic mixing water control.

On small jobs aggregates are sometimes heated by stockpiling over metal culvert pipes in which fires are maintained. Care should be taken to prevent scorching the aggregates. The average temperature of the aggregates should not exceed about 150° F. (65° C.) which is considerably higher than necessary for obtaining recommended concrete temperatures.

Temperature of Mixing Water

Of the ingredients used for making concrete, mixing water is the easiest and most practical to heat. The weight of aggregates and cement in the average mix is much greater than the weight of water. However, water can store five times as much heat as the same weight of solid materials. The average specific heat (heat units required to raise the temperature of one pound of material 1° F. or −17.2° C.) of the solid materials in concrete (cement and aggregates) may be assumed as 0.22 Btu (232 J.) per pound per degree F. compared to 1.0 (1055 J.) for water.

Figure 8 shows graphically the effect of temperature of materials on temperature of fresh concrete. The chart is based on the formula:

$$T = \frac{0.22(T_a W_a + T_c W_c) + T_f W_f + T_m W_m}{0.22(W_a + W_c) + W_f + W_m}$$

In the formula:

T = temperature in deg. F. of the fresh concrete.

T_a, T_c, T_f, and T_m = temperature in deg. F. of the aggregates, cement, free moisture in aggregates, and mixing water, respectively; generally, $T_a = T_f$.

W_a, W_c, W_f, and W_m = weight in pounds of the aggregates, cement, free moisture in aggregates, and mixing water, respectively.

Figure 8 is based on the particular mix shown; however, it is reasonably accurate for other mixes.

If the weighted average temperature of the aggregates and cement is above 32° F. (0° C.), the proper mixing water temperature for the required concrete temperature can be selected from the chart. The range of concrete temperatures corresponds with recommended values given in Table 12, lines 1, 2, and 3. To avoid the possibility of causing a quick or *flash* set of the concrete when either water or aggregates are heated to above 100° F. (37.8° C.), they should be combined in the mixer first (before the cement is added) to obtain a temperature not to exceed 100° F. (37.8° C.) for the aggregates-water mixture. Ac-

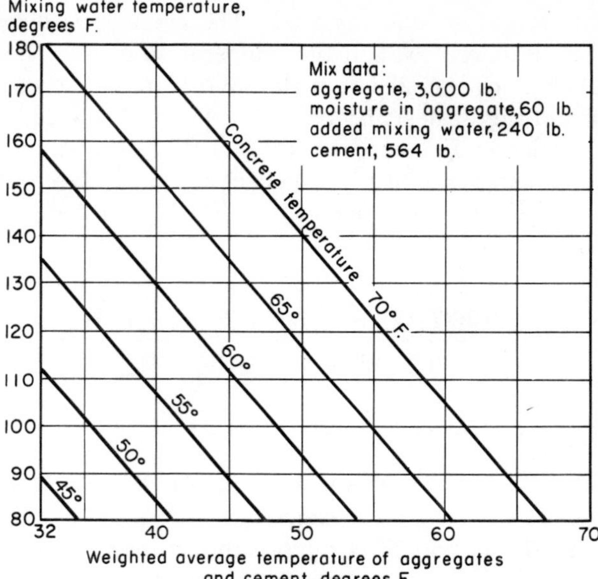

Fig. 8. Temperature of mixing water needed to produce heated concrete of required temperature. Although illustration is based on the mixture shown, it is reasonably accurate for other typical mixtures.

tually, the temperature should rarely exceed 60° F. to 80° F. (15.6° C. to 26.7° C.). If this mixer-loading sequence is followed, water temperatures up to the boiling point may be used, provided the aggregates are cold enough to reduce the final temperature of the aggregates-water mixture to appreciably less than 100° F. (37.8° C.).

In some cases both the aggregates and water must be heated, as indicated in Fig. 8. *For example,* if a concrete temperature of 70° F. (21° C.) is required and the weighted average temperature of aggregates and cement is below about 39° F. (3.9° C.), the aggregates must be heated in order to limit the water temperature to 180° F. (82.3° C.).

Appreciable mixing water temperature fluctuations from batch to batch should be avoided. The temperature of the mixing water may be adjusted by blending hot and cold water.

COLD-WEATHER PLACING

Concrete should never be placed on a frozen subgrade because uneven settlement may occur when the subgrade thaws. This can cause cracking. Also, heat will flow from the concrete, retarding its rate of hardening and creating the possibility that the lower part of the slab may freeze. Ideally, the temperature of the subgrade should be as close as practicable to the temperature of the concrete to be placed on it.

When the subgrade is frozen for a depth of only a few inches, the surface may be thawed by (1) steaming; (2) spreading a layer of hot sand, gravel, or other granular material where the grade elevations allow it; or (3) burning straw or hay if local air pollution ordinances permit it. Concrete placing should be delayed until the ground thaws and warms up sufficiently to ensure that it will not freeze again during the curing period.

The inside of forms, reinforcing steel, and embedded fixtures should be free of snow and ice when concrete is placed.

COLD-WEATHER CURING

Concrete in forms or covered with insulation seldom loses enough moisture at 40° F. to 55° F. (4.5° C. to 12.8° C.) to impair curing. However, moist curing is needed during winter to offset drying when heated enclosures are used. It is important that concrete be supplied with ample moisture when warm air is used.

Live steam exhausted into an enclosure is an excellent method of curing concrete because it provides both heat and moisture. Steam is especially practical during extremely cold weather because the moisture provided offsets the rapid drying that occurs when very cold air is heated.

Early curing with liquid membrane-forming compounds may be used on concrete surfaces within heated enclosures. It is a better practice, however, to moist-cure the concrete first and then apply a curing compound after protection is removed and air temperature is above freezing. The heat liberated during hy-

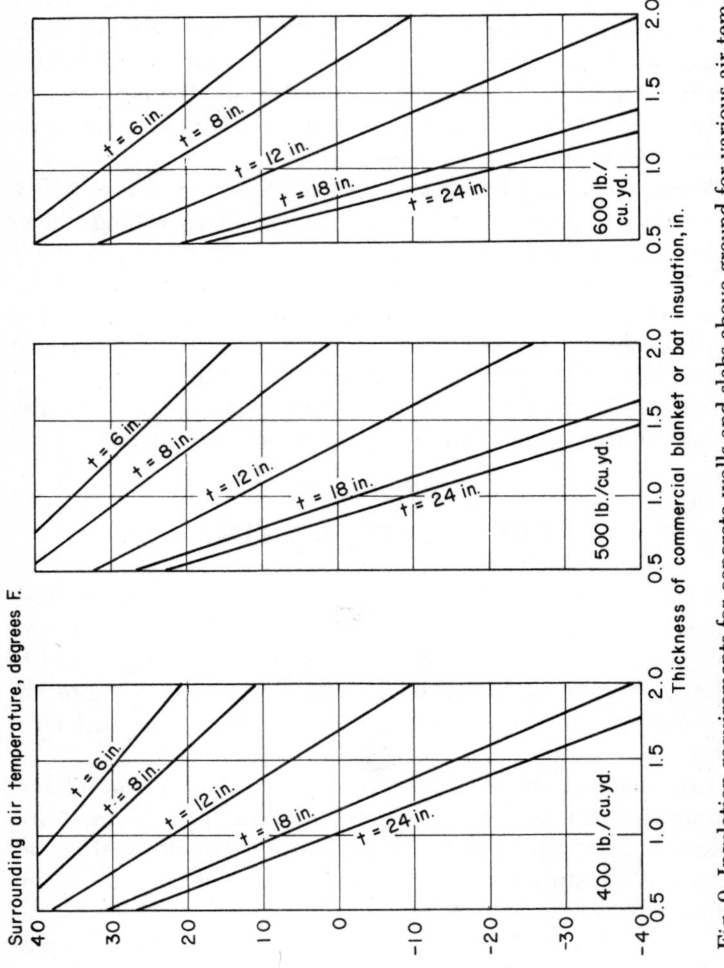

Fig. 9. Insulation requirements for concrete walls and slabs above ground for various air temperatures, concrete section thicknesses, and cement contents (placed at 50° F. or 10° C.).

dration of cement will offset to a considerable degree the loss of heat during finishing and early curing operations.

Insulating Materials

Heat may be retained in the concrete by use of commercial insulating blanket or bat insulation. The effectiveness of insulation can be determined by placing a thermometer under the insulation in contact with the concrete. If the temperature falls below the minimum required, additional insulating material should be applied. Corners and edges of concrete are most vulnerable to freezing and should be checked to determine effectiveness of the protection.

Estimates of insulation requirements for protection of various types of concrete work exposed to various temperature conditions are shown in Figs. 9 and 10. The insulation should be kept in place for the period of time shown in Table 13 to assure that the heat generated during cement hydration is conserved within the concrete. This heat is generally sufficient to prevent the temperature of the concrete from falling below that at which it was placed. The curves in Figs. 9 and 10 are based on blanket-type insulation with an assumed conductivity of 0.25 Btu (263.8 J.) per square foot per hour per degree F. per inch thickness. The values are for still air conditions and will be different where air infiltration due to wind occurs. Equivalent thicknesses for other commonly used insulating materials can be determined from Table 14 or by consulting manufacturer's literature. For maximum efficiency, insulating materials should be kept dry and in close contact with either concrete or form surfaces.

Forms built for repeated use can often be economically insulated. Commercial blanket or bat insulation used for this purpose should have a tough moistureproof covering to withstand handling abuse and exposure to the weather.

Concrete pavements can be protected from cold weather by using 6 to 12 inches (15 to 30 cm.) of dry straw or hay as the insulation material. Tarpaulins, polyethylene plastic film, or waterproof paper should be used as a protective cover to inhibit infiltration of wind, to keep the straw or hay dry, and to prevent it from blowing away.

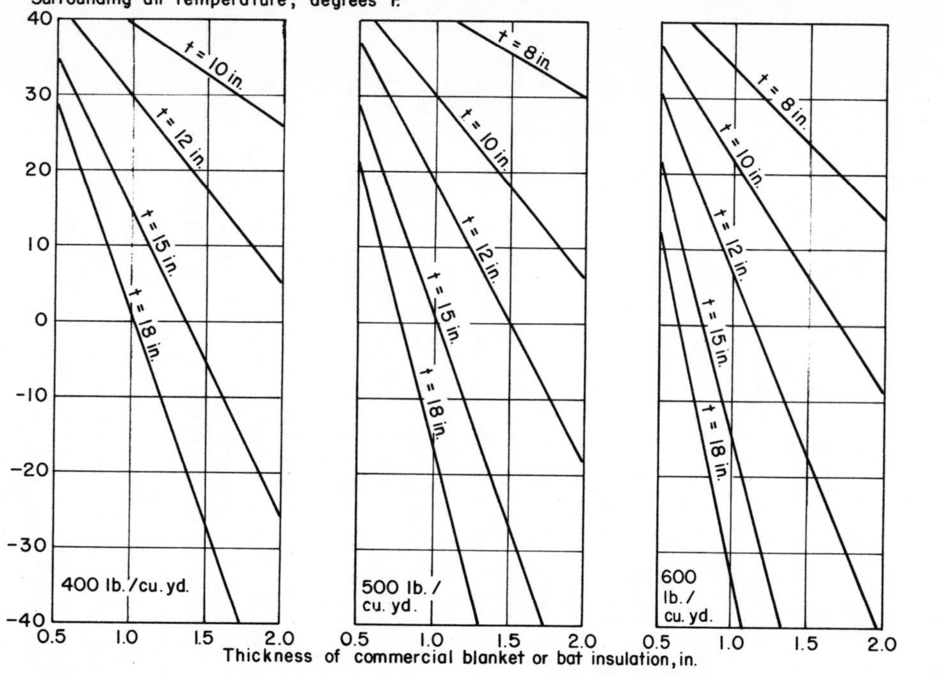

Note: Thicknesses of less than 8 to 10 in. are not shown in this chart because insulation alone will not maintain the temperature of concrete at the required 50 deg. F. due to the influence of cold subgrades on thin slabs. In such cases it will be necessary to supply additional heat by using higher concrete placing temperatures, preheated subgrades, electrical heating wires under the insulation, or heated enclosures, depending on the severity of the weather.

Fig. 10. Insulation requirements for concrete slabs on ground for various air temperatures, slab thicknesses, and cement contents (concrete at 50° F. placed on ground at 35° F., 10 and 1.7° C., respectively).

Type	Description	k*	Equivalent thickness, in.
Blanket	Mineral fiber, processed rock, slag, or glass	0.25	1.00
Board	Expanded polyurethane	0.16	0.64
	Expanded polystyrene, regular (extruded)	0.19	0.76
	Expanded rubber (rigid)	0.22	0.88
	Glass fiber	0.25	1.00
	Cork board	0.28	1.12
	Mineral fiber (resin binder)	0.29	1.16
	Building fiberboard	0.38	1.52
	Cane or wood fiber	0.38	1.52
	Cellular glass	0.40	1.60
	Wood shredded (cemented)	0.60	2.40
	Lumber	0.80	3.20
Fill	Wood pulp	0.27	1.08
	Wood fibers	0.30	1.20
	Mineral wool	0.37	1.48
	Perlite	0.37	1.48
	Sawdust	0.45	1.80
	Vermiculite	0.47	1.88

*k is the conductivity in Btu/sq.ft./hr./deg.F./in. of thickness according to manufacturers' literature and *ASHRAE Handbook*

TABLE 14. RELATIVE EFFECTIVENESS OF INSULATION.

Heating Enclosures

Heated enclosures are commonly used for protecting concrete when air temperatures are near or below freezing. They can be made of wood, canvas, building board, plastic film, waterproof paper, or other suitable material.

Wood or metal framework is commonly covered with tarpaulins or plastic film. Such enclosures should be safe for wind and snow loadings and reasonably airtight, with ample space provided between concrete and enclosure to permit free circulation of the warmed air.

Enclosures may be heated by live steam, steam in pipes, hot-air blowers, salamanders, or other heaters of various types. Control of the enclosure temperature is easiest with live steam, although ice may form on the enclosure. Steam is also advantageous because of the ever-present hazard of fire in heated enclosures. Strict fire prevention measures should be enforced.

Hot-air blowers fired by oil, natural gas, or liquefied petroleum gas are perhaps the next best source of heat for enclosures, provided the units are of the type in which exhaust gases can be vented to the outside air (Fig. 11). Ideally, such heaters should be located outside the enclosure while blowing hot air into it.

Oil- or coke-burning salamanders are easily handled and inexpensive to operate. They are convenient for small jobs but have several disadvantages. They produce a dry heat, so care must be taken to prevent drying of the concrete, especially near the heating element. When placed on floor slabs they should be elevated and the concrete near them protected with damp sand.

Salamanders and other fossil fuel-burning heaters produce carbon dioxide, which combines with calcium hydroxide in fresh concrete to form a weak layer of calcium carbonate on the surface. When this occurs, unformed surfaces such as floors will

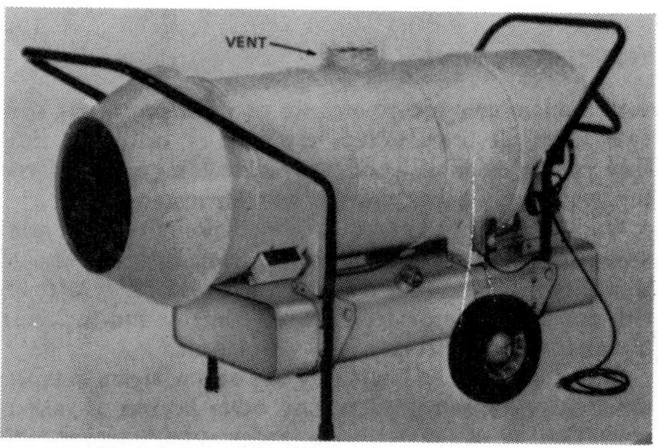

Fig. 11. Oil-fired heater with blower.

dust under traffic. For this reason, salamanders or other heaters that produce carbon dioxide as a by-product should not be permitted in a building or enclosure during the casting operations or for the following 36 hours unless properly vented.

Since considerable variations in temperature within a heated enclosure can occur in very cold weather, care must be taken to minimize such differences. They may be caused by cold air circulation due to a poor seal in the enclosure, poor location of heaters, or an insufficient number of heaters.

Rapid cooling of the concrete at the end of the heating period should be avoided. Sudden cooling of the concrete surface while the interior is still warm may cause cracking, especially in massive sections such as bridge piers, abutments, dams, and large structural members. Cooling should be gradual so the maximum drop in temperature throughout the first 24 hours and during any one hour will not be more than that given in Table 12, lines 5 and 6. Gradual cooling can often be accomplished by simply shutting off the heat and allowing the enclosure to cool to outside air temperature.

Curing Period

After concrete is in place, it should be kept at a favorable curing temperature until it gains sufficient strength to withstand subsequent exposure to low temperatures and anticipated environment and service loads. For durability, the concrete should be kept at the temperature shown in Table 12, line 4 for the period of time shown in Table 13. For the development of sufficient strength to carry imposed loads, the judgment of the structural engineer may be guided by strength tests of job-cured cylinders. If strength-time curves similar to those in Figs. 6 and 7 have been developed for the materials to be used in the job, such curves may also assist the decision of the structural engineer.

Curing or protection time will vary according to type and amount of cement, use of accelerators, size and shape of concrete mass, required strength, and future use of the structure. The concrete should not be subjected to freezing in a saturated condition before reaching the design strength.

FORM REMOVAL AND RESHORING

It is good practice during cold-weather concreting to leave forms in place as long as job schedules permit. Even within heated enclosures, forms serve to distribute heat more evenly and help prevent drying and local overheating.

Without careful simultaneous reshoring, it is hazardous in freezing weather to remove shores even temporarily before suitable tests shown conclusively that the specified strength has been attained. Ordinarily, for temporary removal of support from an entire panel during reshoring, attainment of 55 to 65 percent of the design strength is sufficient.

Reshores should be left in place as long as necessary to safeguard each member and, consequently, the entire structure. The number of tiers reshored below the tier being placed and the length of time reshores remain in place are dependent on the development of sufficient strength to carry dead loads and any construction loads with adequate factors of safety.

FROZEN CONCRETE

Temperatures below freezing are harmful to fresh concrete. Concrete that is allowed to freeze soon after placing gains very little strength and some permanent damage is certain to occur. Concrete that has been frozen just once at an early age may be restored to nearly normal strength by providing favorable curing conditions. Such concrete, however, is neither as resistant to weathering nor as watertight as concrete that has not been frozen.

The critical period after which concrete is not seriously damaged by one or two freezing cycles is dependent upon concrete ingredients and conditions of mixing, placing, curing, and subsequent drying. *For example,* air-entrained concrete is less susceptible to damage by early freezing than concrete without entrained air. Also, all concrete should be allowed to undergo some drying before exposure to freezing temperatures because new concrete in a saturated condition is vulnerable to freezing.

Chapter 18

Efflorescence

Efflorescence is a crystalline deposit, usually white, that may develop on the surfaces of masonry or concrete construction. Often it appears just after the structure is completed when the owner, the builder, and the architect are most concerned with the appearance of the new structure. Although unattractive, in general, efflorescence is harmless. However, deposits can occur within the surface pores of the material causing expansion that may disrupt the surface.

A combination of circumstances causes efflorescence. First, there must be soluble salts in the material. Second, there must be moisture to pick up the soluble salts and carry them to the surface. Third, evaporation or hydrostatic pressure must cause the solution to move. If any one of these conditions is eliminated, efflorescence will not occur.

All masonry and concrete materials are susceptible to efflorescence. Water-soluble salts that appear in chemical analyses as only a few tenths of one percent are sufficient to cause efflorescence when leached out and concentrated at some point on the surface. The amount and character of the deposits vary according to the nature of the soluble materials and the atmospheric conditions. Efflorescence is particularly affected by temperature, humidity, and wind. In the *summer*, even after long rainy periods, moisture evaporates so quickly that comparatively small amounts of salt are brought to the surface. Usually efflorescence is more common in the *winter* when a slower rate of evaporation allows migration of salts to the surface. With the passage of time, efflorescence becomes lighter and less extensive unless there is an external source of salts. Light-colored surfaces show the deposits much less than darker shades.

Efflorescence-producing salts are usually sulfates of sodium, potassium, magnesium, calcium, and iron (ferrous); carbonates of sodium, potassium, and calcium; or sodium bicarbonate or silicate. However, almost any soluble salt that finds its way into the material may appear as efflorescence; consequently chlorides, nitrates, and salts of vanadium, chromium, molybdenum, and others are occasionally found. Chloride salts are highly soluble in water, so the first rain will often wash them off.

In most cases, salts that *cause* efflorescence come from beneath the surface. But, chemicals in the materials can react with chemicals in the atmosphere to form the undesired efflorescence. In concrete, mortar, stucco, or concrete masonry, the hydrated cement contains some calcium hydroxide (soluble) as an inevitable product of the reaction between cement or lime and water. When this calcium hydroxide is brought to the surface by water, it combines with carbon dioxide in the air to form calcium carbonate (very slightly soluble), which then appears as a whitish deposit.

Surface discoloration or mottling of concrete slabs can be caused by the migration of chloride salts toward the drying surface. Discoloration is increased by hard troweling, calcium chloride admixtures, or poor curing. Immediate and thorough washing with water of the concrete surface is the easiest way to remove the discoloration. Special chemical treatments are also beneficial.

Another source of salts is the soil in contact with basement and retaining walls. If the walls are not protected with a good moisture barrier, the salts may migrate 1 to 2 feet (30 to 60 cm.) above grade.

HOW TO PREVENT EFFLORESCENCE

Since many factors influence the formation of efflorescence, it is difficult to predict if and when any will appear. As previously mentioned, efflorescence will not occur if (1) the soluble salts are eliminated, (2) moisture is eliminated, or (3) water passage through the mass is prevented.

Eliminating the Salts

In the selection of materials, all component parts of the construction should be considered for their soluble salt content. To eliminate efflorescence-producing soluble salts:

1. Never use unwashed sand. Sand should meet the requirements of ASTM C33 or CSA A23.1 for concrete; ASTM C144 for mortar; or ASTM C35 for plaster and stucco.
2. Never use masonry units known to effloresce while stockpiled. Use only masonry units of established reliability that pass the efflorescence tests in ASTM C67. There is at present no standard test for evaluating the efflorescing potential of masonry mortars or concrete masonry units.
3. Use clean mixing water free from harmful amounts of acids, alkalies, organic material, minerals, and salts. In some areas the drinking water may contain sufficient quantities of dissolved minerals and salts to adversely affect the resulting construction.
4. If walls of hollow masonry units are to be insulated by filling the cores, the insulating material must be free of harmful salts.
5. Be absolutely certain that mixer, mortar box, and mortarboards are not contaminated or corroded. Never deice this equipment with salt or antifreeze material.
6. Tools should be clean and free of rust, salts, and other harmful material. *For example,* do not use a shovel for any salt and then use it for sand without first thoroughly washing the shovel.
7. Lime used for mortar or stucco should be hydrated lime free from calcium sulfate.

Water-repellent surface treatments such as silicones decrease surface efflorescence by causing the dissolved salts to be deposited beneath the treated surface. Localized accumulation of salts and their crystallization beneath the treated surface may cause surface spalling or flaking of pourous and soft masonry units. When there are large amounts of salts in the masonry, use of a surface treatment therefore may cause problems.

Eliminating Moisture and Water Passage

Low absorption of moisture is the best assurance against efflorescence. Concrete, mortar, stucco, or concrete masonry will have maximum watertightness when made with properly graded aggregates, an adequate cement content, and a low water-cement ratio. These products must be consolidated to produce maximum density and must be thoroughly cured. *Air entrainment* also improves watertightness by increasing workability and reducing segregation and bleeding, thereby increasing density.

To eliminate moisture or moisture passage through the structure, the following steps are recommended:

1. Prevent inadequate hydration of cementitious materials caused by cold temperatures, premature drying, or improper use of admixtures.
2. Give proper attention to design detailing for correct installation of waterstops, flashings, and copings to prevent entry of water.
3. During construction, cover the top course of masonry at the completion of each day's work, particularly when rain is expected.
4. Curing concrete masonry units in the presence of carbon dioxide gas appears to be beneficial in changing calcium hydroxide to calcium carbonate. The carbonate seems to be formed in the pores at or just below the surface. The pores are thus partially filled, reducing the passage of water.
5. Install vapor barriers in exterior walls or apply vapor-proof paint to interior surfaces.
6. Apply paint or other proven protective treatment to the outside surfaces of porous masonry units.
7. Tool all mortar joints with a V- or concave-shaped jointer to compact the mortar at the exposed surface and create a tight bond between mortar and masonry units. Weeping, raked, and untooled struck joints are not recommended except in dry climates.
8. Carefully plan the installation of lawn sprinklers or any other water source so that walls are not subjected to excess water.

HOW TO REMOVE EFFLORESCENCE

Where there is efflorescence, the source of moisture should be determined and corrective measures taken to keep water out of the structure.

Most efflorescence can be removed by dry-brushing or light sandblasting followed by flushing with clean water. If this is not satisfactory, it may be necessary to wash the surface with a dilute solution of muriatic acid (5 to 10 percent). (*Caution:* Rubber gloves, glasses, and other protective clothing should be worn by workers using an acid solution. All precautions on labels should be observed because muriatic acid can affect eyes, skin, and breathing.) For integrally colored concrete, a more dilute solution (two percent) may be necessary to prevent surface etching that may reveal the aggregate and change colors and textures. Before an acid treatment is used on any masonry wall, the solution should be tested on a small, inconspicuous portion to be certain there is no adverse effect.

Before applying an acid solution, always dampen the wall surface with clean water to prevent the acid from being absorbed deeply into the wall where damage may occur. Application should be to small areas of not more than 4 square feet (.37 sq. meters) at a time, with a delay of about five minutes before scouring off the salt deposit with a stiff bristle brush. After this treatment the surface should be immediately and thoroughly flushed with clean water to remove all acid. If the surface is to be painted, it should be thoroughly flushed with water and allowed to dry.

Since an acid treatment may slightly change the appearance, the entire wall should be treated to avoid discoloration or mottled effects.

A green stain sometimes appears on buff or gray face brick or tile from vanadium or molybdenum compounds in the clay. *Never* treat such stains with acid, because the acid will react with these compounds and produce an insoluble brown stain that is extremely difficult to remove.

To remove the green stain, first dampen the surface by spraying with clean water; then wash with a solution of 1 part, by volume, sodium hydroxide crystals (lye) and 10 parts water; and thoroughly flush with clean water.

Chapter 19

Concrete Brick Veneers

Residential builders and developers want to create buildings that will have and maintain market appeal—buildings that will give people homes they will enjoy for years to come. A brick residence symbolizes traditional strength, security, warmth, and beauty. Therefore, brick masonry is a favorite veneer for single-family and high- or low-rise apartment buildings and townhouses.

TYPES AND SIZES

Today strong, durable, and attractive concrete brick can be used to advantage as a cladding for residential structures. High-quality concrete brick are now produced in concrete masonry plants through the United States and Canada (Fig. 1) in the same colors and sizes as clay brick to match what is accepted as most pleasing for residential building wall veneers. It is often impossible to distinguish high-quality concrete brick from clay brick. Although this chapter concerns concrete brick for veneers, most of what is covered also applies to through-the-wall concrete brick.

Concrete brick are available in a wide range of colors. Not only are they manufactured in red, white, brown, yellow, and other solid colors, but in any blend or mingle desired, according to the color ranges or percentages selected by the user. Blends and mingles are recommended by their beauty as well as to accommodate natural small color variations in individual units. Antiqued units are also available to give walls that popular *antique brick* appearance.

As shown in Fig. 1 concrete brick are manufactured in a variety of sizes sometimes called modular, normal, module, queen, and oversize. They can be made to any size desired. Some companies have created different sizes for their localities to enable local masons to clad walls more economically. Basically, concrete brick match the size and scale of clay brick. They are laid in the same way and require no new skills for their installation. (*See* Chap. 25, Brick.)

It is important to note that the overall scale of a building can change with the size of concrete brick used as veneer. *For example,* long, low brick such as the normal size (Fig. 1) can make an apartment building appear longer and more horizontal. Local dealers should be checked for the sizes in a particular area.

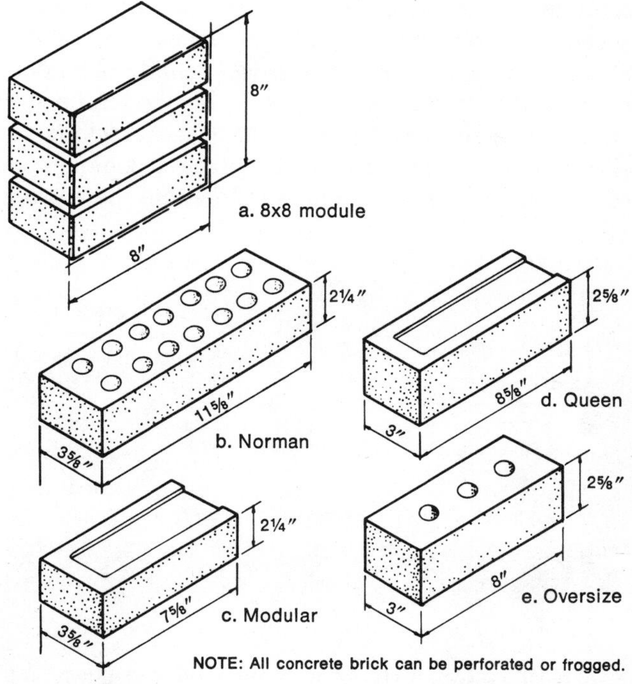

Fig. 1. Concrete brick.

LOW MAINTENANCE

Concrete brick veneers result in beautiful, long-lasting, low-maintenance walls. Manufactured to modern standards, concrete brick are strong, durable materials with permanent finishes that do not require painting. They need very little maintenance over a long period of time.

Concrete brick producers, realizing that their products will be used on exposed surfaces and thus be subject to careful scrutiny and to the vagaries of the weather, have developed new manufacturing equipment and procedures to achieve high quality. As shown in Table 15, the ASTM compressive strength requirements for concrete brick are *higher* than those for regular concrete block, and concrete brick producers have chosen to manufacture their products well in excess of the ASTM standards. Many of these producers also manufacture concrete brick to exceed the applicable ASTM requirements for clay brick.

In achieving the higher compressive strengths of modern concrete brick, the producers also obtain higher tensile strengths and thus a greater resistance to shrinkage cracking. Special shrinkage control procedures and storage techniques are followed in concrete brick manufacture to attain these properties.

ASTM designation	Grade	Compressive strength*	
		Average of Units	Individual Unit
C90-70, hollow load-bearing units	NI and NII	1,000	800
	SI and SII	700	600
C145-71, solid load-bearing units	NI and NII	1,800	1,500
	SI and SII	1,200	1,000
C55-71, concrete building brick	NI and NII	3,500	3,000
	SI and SII	2,500	2,000

*Measured in pounds per square inch on gross area.

TABLE 15. COMPARISON OF REQUIRED UNIT STRENGTHS OF MASONRY UNITS.

SPECIAL TIPS FOR QUALITY

Control During Manufacture

As with any product that has virtually limitless possibilities for color and size, it is recommended that local concrete brick producers be checked to verify availability of colors, blends and mingles, and sizes.

Using either conventional block-making machinery or the new machines designed for making brick-sized units, modern concrete brick producers follow rigid in-plant quality control procedures. They have developed accurate and consistent means for proportioning concrete mixtures and a systematic plan to monitor production and assure the properties desired for their products. Knowing that strength and durability are not the only performance criteria since their products will be used for architectural veneers, concrete brick producers pay special attention to appearance. Proportioning of colors is especially important to them and to their customers.

Colors are obtained by using natural or synthetic iron oxides, chromates, or other compounds. Manufactured *synthetic colors* are most popular since their intensity can be controlled better and thus the results are more consistent. Reds, browns, and other earth colors that are obtained through the use of iron oxide compounds are the most durable.

While not essential, most concrete brick producers begin with an integrally colored concrete and obtain a customer's selected blend or mingle by applying added colors to the fresh concrete with a spray device. In this way the colors actually become part of the concrete when it is cured. *Antique slurries* also are added by a spray device after application of the main colors and are cured as part of the brick units. The concrete brick are cured by various accepted methods to accelerate strength gain, allow for early automatic handling in the plants, and reduce the moisture content and potential shrinkage of the units.

Moisture Control

As with all cementitious products, concrete brick will shrink with age, principally as a result of drying. The shrinkage resulting in a wall can be reduced by using concrete brick that are as dry as possible when laid in the wall. ASTM C55-71 specifies the allowable moisture content for concrete brick based on the atmospheric conditions under which the brick will be used and the total shrinkage potential of the concrete mixture used for the brick. (*See* Table 16.) The average relative humidity for an area is the criteria for establishing allowable moisture content. This can be obtained by contacting a local weather station.

A positive method for controlling moisture content should be used for concrete brick in storage and on the jobsite as it is during their production. Quality concrete brick are properly cured to the lowest possible moisture content (expressed as a percent of the total absorption as defined by ASTM C140-70). Further drying is accomplished if the producer permits the brick to air-dry in yard storage. Where weather conditions are such that the concrete brick can pick up moisture from rain or snow, covered storage is used by producers—and should be used by builders. Covering the brick with polyethylene and keeping the brick raised off the ground are probably the most economical ways to protect concrete brick at the jobsite.

ASTM designation	Grade	Maximum water absorption* for oven-dry weight classification		
		105 lb.	105 to 125 lb.	125 lb.
C90-70 and C145-71, hollow and solid load-bearing units	NI and NII SI and SII	18 20**	15 —	13 —
C55-71, concrete building brick	NI and NII SI and SII	15 18	13 15	10 13

*Average of three units in pounds per cubic foot.
**Requirement based on lightweight units with less than 85 pcf density.

TABLE 16. COMPARISON OF WATER ABSORPTION LIMITS FOR CONCRETE MASONRY UNITS.

Mortar Selection

The use of Type N mortar as specified in ASTM C270-71 is recommended for concrete brick veneers. (*See* Table 17.) High-strength mortars are not required. Extensible mortars such as Type N are better suited to this kind of application where wall movements exist.

From an esthetic standpoint, the color of the mortar used with the concrete brick can change the overall appearance of the concrete brick wall. *For example,* a dark mortar against light-colored concrete brick may be used to emphasize the bond pattern; conversely a white mortar against a dark antique concrete brick enhances the rustic colors.

Sequence of Removing Brick from Cubes

Most concrete brick are manufactured and cubed automatically. When they have a color blend, mingle, or antique finish, the sequence of removing brick from their cubes can affect the distribution of colors in the wall. Prior to laying a wall on a production basis, the mason should check with the concrete brick producer to ascertain the best way to remove them from their cubes or he should build a trial wall to determine which way to

Mortar type**	Portland cement or portland blast-furnace slag cement	Masonry cement	Hydrated lime or lime putty
M	1	1 (Type II)	—
	1	—	¼
S	½	1 (Type II)	—
	1	—	Over ¼ to ½
N	—	1 (Type II)	—
	1	—	Over ½ to 1¼

*Adapted from proportion specification of ASTM C270-71. The aggregate, measured in a damp, loose condition, shall be not less than 2¼ and not more than three times the sum of the volumes of the cements and lime used.

**Mortar type designations A-1, A-2, B, C, and D are the former type designations in effect prior to 1954.

TABLE 17. MORTAR PROPORTIONS, PARTS OF VOLUME.*

go. Working *down* a cube, a corner at a time, is generally best when laying up a wall. It is also recommended that several cubes be used simultaneously so that subtle variations in tones, resulting from aggregate variations and the manufacturing process, are used to the best advantage.

Correction of Floating

Floating is a term that describes shifting or other movement of a brick wall as the wall is laid up and before the mortar has set. It is generally attributed to low absorption of the units, reducing bond and thus resulting in undesired movement. In most instances floating can be eliminated or minimized by adjusting the mortar mix.

The problem of floating can also be alleviated by the use of *frogs,* which are small indentations in the mortar bed face of a unit. Sometimes core holes are manufactured into the concrete brick to work like frogs in reducing floating.

Crack Control

Control of wall movements is essential for crack-free construction. Shrinkage due to moisture loss and temperature changes will cause wall movements, and tensile forces due to these changes must be relieved to prevent cracking. This can be accomplished most effectively with *control joints* (Fig. 2).

Where control joints are used, they should be spaced at intervals that are close enough to prevent the development of damaging stresses. Generally they should be located at pilasters, at changes in wall heights and thicknesses, over openings, under openings, and at wall intersections. Where possible the brickwork should be divided into rectangular panels whose width is about twice the height, with a maximum spacing of 40 feet (12.2 meters).

Crack control can also be accomplished with control joints in conjunction with joint reinforcement. The diameter of joint reinforcement should be no greater than one-half the thickness of the joint. Usually reinforcement is made with two No. 9 longitudinal wires linked with transverse wires.

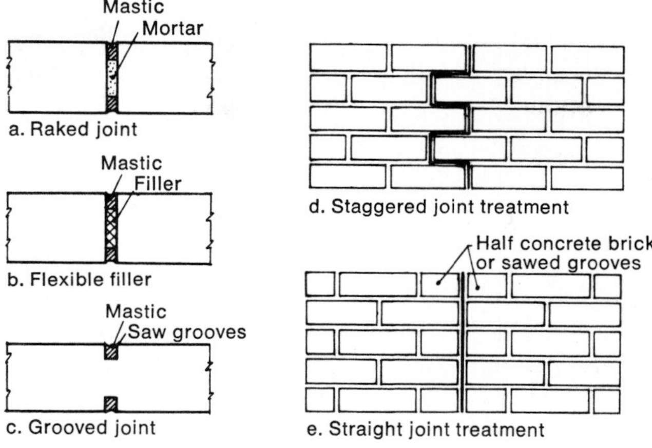

Fig. 2. Methods of forming control joints.

Where joints are not provided at openings in the wall, reinforcement should be provided in two joints under and over the opening, extending at least 2 feet (.6 meters) beyond that opening.

Cleaning

As with all quality brickwork, care should be taken to construct the wall with a minimum of smearing or damage to the exposed face. *Note* that the use of muriatic acid (hydrochloric acid) is *not* recommended for cleaning down concrete brick walls. Scrubbing with clean water after the mortar is set is the best way to clean a concrete brick wall. A detergent may be added to the water.

Waterproofing

When manufactured in accordance with the requirements of ASTM C55, concrete brick are almost impermeable in normal weather conditions. This cannot be said for mortar joints. As with all brick walls, moisture penetration through joints can be minimized by the use of full mortar bedding, tight head joints, and proper workmanship. For additional resistance to moisture penetration, clear acrylic coatings can be applied to the finished walls. The manufacturer's directions should be followed to obtain the maximum benefits of the coating selected. (*See* Section 3, Brick Masonry.)

Section 2

Concrete Masonry

IMPORTANT TECHNOLOGICAL DEVELOPMENTS in the manufacture and utilization of concrete units have accompanied the rapid increase in the use of concrete masonry. Concrete masonry walls properly designed and constructed will satisfy varied building requirements including fire, safety, durability, economy, appearance, utility, comfort, and good acoustics.

The use of *exposed concrete masonry* for finer types of buildings has opened up new fields of construction to the masonry craft.

Concrete masonry construction is a term commonly used to denote an assembly of *precast concrete units* in building construction.

Chapter 20

Masonry Materials

The American Standard Building Code Requirements for Masonry defines masonry as "a built-up construction or combination of building units of such materials as clay, shale, glass, gypsum, or stone, set in mortar or plain concrete." However, for our purpose, the commonly accepted definition of masonry, or unit masonry as it is sometimes called, is a construction made up of prefabricated masonry units (*for example,* concrete blocks, structural clay tile, and brick) laid in various ways and joined together with mortar.

MORTAR

There are two common types of masonry mortar—lime mortar and portland cement-lime mortar. *Lime mortar* is normally used only in temporary work, from which the masonry units are to be salvaged for re-use. It is a mixture of sand, hydrated lime, and water proportioned so as to produce a plastic, workable paste. If the mortar sticks to the tools, add more sand; if it lacks cohesion and fails to adhere to the units, add more lime. If it is too stiff for easy mixing and troweling, add water.

Portland-cement-lime mortar is used for permanent masonry structures. Mortar can be made with portland cement, sand, and water only (leaving out the lime), but mortar of this type is hard to work. The addition of lime greatly increases the workability and *fatness* of the mortar.

Type A portland cement-lime mortar is a strong mortar, intended primarily for use in reinforced masonry structures. The ingredient proportions for this type are approximately as follows:

1 sack cement
3 cubic feet (.08 cu. meters) damp sand
13 pounds (5.9 kgs.) hydrated lime

Type B portland cement-lime mortar should not be used for reinforced masonry, but is strong enough for almost all other purposes. The ingredient proportions for this type are approximately as follows:

1 sack cement
6 cubic feet (.16 cu. meters) damp sand
50 pounds (22.72 kgs.) hydrated lime

Sufficient mixing water should be added to obtain the desired consistency. If a large quantity of mortar is required, it should be mixed in a drum-type mixer similar to those used for mixing concrete. The mixing time should not be less than three minutes. All dry ingredients should be placed in the mixer first and mixed for one minute before adding the water.

Unless large amounts of mortar are required, the mortar is mixed by hand using a mortar box like the one shown in Chap. 21, Masonry Tools and Equipment, Fig. 4. Care must be taken to mix all the ingredients thoroughly to obtain a uniform texture. As in machine mixing all dry material should be mixed first. A steel drum filled with water should be kept close to the mortar box for the water supply. A second drum of water should be available for shovels and hoes when not in use.

Mortar for masonry is designed not only to join masonry units into an integral structure with predictable performance properties, but also to (1) effect tight seals between units against the entry of air and moisture; (2) bond with steel joint reinforcement, metal ties, and anchor bolts, if any, so that they perform integrally with the masonry; (3) provide an architectural quality to exposed masonry structures through color contrasts or shadow lines from various joint-tooling procedures; and (4) compensate for size variations in the units by providing a bed to accommodate tolerances of units.

Properties

Good mortar is necessary for good workmanship and proper structural performance of masonry construction. Since mortar must bond masonry units into strong, durable, weathertight walls, it must have the following properties.

Workability. Probably the most important quality of plastic masonry mortar is *workability,* because of its influence on other important mortar properties in both the plastic and hardened states. Workability is difficult to define because it is a combination of a number of interrelated properties. The properties considered as having the greatest influence on workability are consistency (flowability), water retentivity, setting time, weight, adhesion, and penetrability.

Mortar of good workability should spread easily on the masonry unit, cling to vertical surfaces, extrude readily from joints without dropping or smearing, and permit easy positioning of the unit without subsequent shifting due to its weight or the weight of successive courses (Fig. 1). Mortar consistency should change with weather to help in laying the units. A good workable mix should be softer in summer than in winter to compensate for water loss.

Water retentivity. Mortar having this property resists rapid loss of mixing water (prevents loss of plasticity) to the air on a dry day or to an absorptive masonry unit. Rapid loss of water causes the mortar to stiffen quickly, making it practically impossible to obtain good bond and weathertight joints.

Water retentivity is an important property and is related to workability. A mortar that has good water retentivity remains soft and plastic long enough for the masonry units to be carefully aligned, leveled, plumbed, and adjusted to proper line without danger of breaking the intimate contact or bond between the mortar and the units. When low-absorption units such as split block are in contact with a mortar having too much water retentivity, they may float. Consequently, the water retentivity of a mortar should be within tolerable limits.

Entrained air, extremely fine aggregate or cementitious materials, or water add workability or plasticity to the mortar and

Fig. 1. Mortar of proper workability is soft, but with good body. It spreads readily and extrudes without smearing or dropping away.

increase its water retentivity.

Consistent rate of hardening. The *rate of hardening* of mortar due to hydration (chemical reaction) is the speed at which it develops resistance to an applied load. Too rapid hardening may interfere with the use of the mortar by the mason. Very slow hardening may impede the progress of the work because the mortar will flow from the completed masonry. During winter construction slow hardening may also subject mortar to early damage from frost action. A well-defined, consistent rate of hardening assists the mason in laying the masonry units and in tooling the joints to the same degree of hardness. Uniform color of masonry joints reflects proper hardening and consistent tooling times.

Hardening is sometimes confused with a stiffening caused by rapid loss of water, as when low-water-retention mortar is used with highly absorptive units. Also, during very hot, dry weather mortar may tend to stiffen more rapidly than usual. In this case, the mason may find it advisable to lay shorter mortar beds and fewer units in advance of tooling.

Bond. The term *bond* refers to a specific property that can be subdivided into (1) extent of bond, or degree of contact of the mortar with the masonry units; and (2) tensile bond strength, or force required to separate the units. A chemical and a mechanical bond exist in each category.

Good extent of bond (complete and intimate contact) is important to watertightness and tensile bond strength. Poor bond at the mortar-to-unit interface may lead to moisture penetration through the unbonded areas. Good extent of bond is obtained with a workable and water-retentive mortar, good workmanship, full joints, and masonry units having a medium initial rate of absorption (suction).

Tensile bond strength is perhaps the most important property of hardened mortar. Mortar must develop sufficient bond to withstand the tensile forces brought about by structural, earth, and wind loads, expansion of clay brick, shrinkage of concrete masonry units or mortar, and temperature changes.

Many variables affect bond, including (1) mortar ingredients, such as type and amount of cementitious materials, water retained, and air content; (2) workmanship, such as pressure applied to the mortar bed during placing; and (3) curing conditions, such as temperature, relative humidity, and wind. The effects of these variables on bond will be briefly discussed.

All other factors being equal, mortar bond strength is related to mortar composition, especially the cement content. The bond strength of the mortar increases as the content of cement increases.

Bond is low on smooth, molded surfaces, such as glass or die skin surfaces of clay brick or tile. On the other hand, good bond is achieved on concrete block or on wire-cut or textured surfaces of clay brick. The suction rates of concrete masonry units are low enough that they never require wetting prior to laying of mortar. Some clay brick units have such high suction rates that poor bond will result unless the brick are wetted, and surfaces of the wetted brick should be dry.

There is a distinct relationship between mortar flow (water content) and tensile bond strength. For all mortars bond strength increases as water content increases. The optimum bond strength is obtained by using a mortar with the highest water content compatible with workability, even though mortar compressive strength decreases.

Workmanship is paramount in ensuring bond strength. The time lapse between mortar spreading and the placing of the masonry units should be kept to a minimum because the water content of the mortar will be reduced through suction of the masonry unit on which it is first placed. If too much time elapses before a unit is placed, the bond between the mortar and the unit will be reduced. The mason should not realign, tap, or in any way move units after initial placement, leveling, and alignment. Movement breaks the bond between unit and mortar, after which the mortar will not readhere well to the masonry units.

Portland cement requires a period in the presence of moisture to develop its full strength. In order to obtain optimum curing conditions, the mortar mixture should contain the maximum amount of water possible with acceptable workability, considering maximum water retention, and lean, oversanded mixtures should be avoided. Freshly laid masonry should be protected from the sun and drying winds. With severe drying conditions, it may be necessary either to wet the exposed mortar joints with a fine water spray daily for about four days or to cover the masonry with a polyethylene plastic sheet or both.

Durability. The *durability* of masonry mortar is its ability to endure the exposure conditions. Although harsh environments and use of unsound materials may contribute to the deterioration of mortar joints, the major destruction is from water entering the masonry and freezing.

In general, damage to mortar joints and to mortar bond by frost action has not been a problem in masonry wall construction above grade. For frost damage to occur, the hardened mortar must first be water-saturated or nearly so. After being placed, mortar becomes less than saturated due to the absorption of some of the mixing water by the units. The saturated condition does not readily return except when the masonry is in continuous contact with saturated soils, downspout leaks, there are heavy rains, or horizontal ledges are formed. Under these conditions the masonry unit and mortar may become saturated and undergo freeze-thaw deterioration.

High-compressive-strength mortars usually have good durability. Because air-entrained mortar will withstand hundreds of freeze-thaw cycles, its use provides good protection against localized freeze-thaw damage. Mortar joints that have deteriorated due to freezing and thawing present a maintenance problem generally requiring tuckpointing.

Strength. The principal factors affecting the compressive strength of masonry structures are the compressive strength of the masonry unit, the proportions of ingredients within the mortar, the design of the structure, the workmanship, and the degree of curing. Although the compressive strength of masonry may be increased with a stronger mortar, the increase is not proportional to the compressive strength of the mortar. Tests have shown that compressive strengths of concrete masonry walls increase only about 10 percent when mortar cube compressive strengths increase 130 percent. Composite wall compressive strengths increase 25 percent when mortar cube compressive strengths increase 160 percent.

Compressive strength of mortar is largely dependent on the type and quantity of cementitious material used in preparing the mortar. It increases with an increase in cement content and decreases with an increase in air entrainment, lime content, or water content.

Low volume change. A popular misconception is that mortar shrinkage can be extensive and cause leaky structures. Actually the maximum shrinkage across a mortar joint is miniscule and therefore not troublesome. This is even more true with the weaker mortars because they have greater creep (extensibility) and so are better able to accommodate shrinkage.

Appearance. Uniformity of color and shade of the mortar

joints greatly affects the overall appearance of a masonry structure. Atmospheric conditions, admixtures, and moisture content of the masonry units are some of the factors affecting the color and shade of mortar joints. Others are uniformity of proportions in the mortar mix, water content, and time of tooling the mortar joints.

Careful measurement of mortar materials and thorough mixing are important to maintain uniformity from batch to batch and from day to day. Control of this uniformity becomes more difficult with the number of ingredients to be combined at the mixer. Pigments, if used, will provide more uniform color if premixed with a stock of cement sufficient for the needs of the whole project. In some areas colored masonry cements are available. (*See* Chap. 16, Mineral Pigments for Use in Coloring Concrete.)

Tooling of mortar joints at like degrees of setting is important to ensure a uniform mortar shade in the finished structure. A darker shade results if the joint is tooled when the mortar is relatively hard than if the joints are tooled when the mortar is relatively soft. Some masons consider mortar joints ready for tooling after the water sheen is gone and the mortar has stiffened but is still thumb-print hard.

White cement mortar should never be tooled with metal tools because the metal will darken the joint. A glass or plastic joint tool should be used.

SPECIFICATIONS AND TYPES

Current specifications for mortars for unit masonry are shown in Tables 18 and 19. Mortar types are to be identified by either proportion or property specification but not both.

The proportion specification (Table 18) identifies mortar type through various combinations of portland cement with masonry cement, masonry cement singly, and combinations of portland cement and lime. The proportion specification governs when ASTM C270 (Standard Specification for Mortar for Unit Masonry) or CSA Standard A179 (Mortar for Unit Masonry) is re-

Specification	Mortar type	Parts by volume		
		Portland cement or portland blast-furnace slag cement	Masonry cement**	Hydrated lime or lime putty
For plain masonry, ASTM C270, CSA A179	M	1 1	1 —	— 1/4
	S	1/2 1	1 —	— Over 1/4 to 1/2
	N	— 1	1 —	— Over 1/2 to 1-1/4
	O	— 1	1 —	— Over 1-1/4 to 2-1/2
	K	1	—	Over 2-1/2 to 4
For reinforced masonry, ASTM C476†	PM PL	1 1	1 —	— 1/4 to 1/2

*Aggregate ratio to be noted: Under the proportion specifications, the total aggregate shall be equal to not less than 2-1/4 and not more than 3 times the sum of the volumes of the cement and lime used. Also note that:

1. Under ASTM C270, Standard Specification for Mortar for Unit Masonry, aggregate is measured in a damp, loose condition and 1 cu ft of masonry sand by damp, loose volume is considered equal to 80 lb of dry sand.
2. Under CSA A179, Mortar of Unit Masonry, aggregate is proportioned on a dry basis and adjusted for bulking.

**Under CSA A179, masonry cement is to be Type H, except that it may be Type L for Type O mortar.

†Standard Specification for Mortar and Grout for Reinforced Masonry.

TABLE 18. PROPORTION SPECIFICATION FOR MORTAR.

ferred to without noting which specification—proportion or property—should be used.

Mortar type classification under the property specification (Table 19) is dependent on the compressive strength of 2-inch (5-cm.) cubes using standard laboratory tests per ASTM C270 or CSA A179. These laboratory test cubes are prepared with less water than will be used on the job. Similar test cubes are not intended to be made on the job. Instead, mortar may be tested in the field according to Standard Method for Preconstruction and Construction Evaluation of Mortars for Plain and Reinforced Unit Masonry (ASTM C780).

The ratio of cementitious material to aggregate in the mixture

Specification	Mortar type	Compressive strength of 2-in. cubes, psi	
		At 7 days	At 28 days
For plain masonry, ASTM C270, CSA A179	M S N O K	– – – – –	2,500 1,800 750 350 75
For reinforced masonry, ASTM C476	PM PL	1,600** 1,600**	2,500 2,500

*The total aggregate shall be equal to not less than 2-1/4 and not more than 3-1/2 times the sum of the volumes of the cement and lime used. For the property of water retention, allowable initial flow tests range from 100% to 115% (or in the case of ASTM C476 mortars, to a flow of 130% ± 5%), and the flow-after-suction test must exceed 70% or 75%.

**If the mortar fails to meet the 7-day requirement but meets the 28-day requirement, it shall be acceptable.

TABLE 19. PROPERTY SPECIFICATION FOR MORTAR.*

under the property specification may be less than under the proportion specification. This is to encourage preconstruction mortar testing. An economic reward is possible if less cement is required when selecting a mix to meet the strength requirement of the property specification. The testing portion of both specifications is limited to preconstruction evaluation of the mortars.

In both the property and proportion specification, the amount of water to be used on the job is the maximum that will produce a workable consistency during construction. This is unlike conventional concrete practice where the water-cement ratio must be carefully controlled.

Another physical requirement of both specifications is the water retention limit. In the laboratory it is measured by a flow-after-suction test (described in ASTM C91, Standard Specification for Masonry Cement, and CSA A8, Masonry Cement), which simulates the action of absorptive masonry units on the plastic mortar. While performing a flow test before and after absorptive suction a truncated cone of mortar is subjected to twenty-five ½-inch (1.3-cm.) drops of a laboratory flow table plate. The diameter of the disturbed sample is compared to the original diameter of the conical sample. Allowable initial flow tests range from 100 to 115 percent (or in the case of ASTM C476 mortars, to a flow of 130 percent ± 5 percent), and the flow-after-suction test must exceed 70 or 75 percent. These values are specified for laboratory test purposes, while flow values of 130 to 150 percent are common for mortar in actual construction.

An interplay of property and proportion specification is not intended or recognized by specifications for plain masonry, but is mandatory for reinforced masonry under ASTM C476.

Once the design loads, type of structure, and masonry unit have been determined, the mortar type can be selected. No one mortar type will produce a mortar that rates highest in all desirable mortar properties. Adjustments in the mix to improve one property often are made at the expense of others. For this reason, the properties of each mortar type should be evaluated and the mortar type chosen that will best satisfy the end-use requirements.

In the *United States,* for plain (nonreinforced) masonry, mortar type is selected by the user on the basis of Table 20. For reinforced masonry, the job specification may simply state that the mortar shall meet the requirements of ASTM C476. This allows the mason or mason contractor the option of selecting the individual mixture, PM or PL, that will be used, since either type must meet the same strength requirement. This freedom of selection of individual mixtures is favored since workability of mixtures and availability of cementitious materials vary with geographical area.

In *Canada,* the selection of mortars for plain and reinforced masonry depends on whether or not the masonry is based on engineering analysis of the structural effects of the loads and forces acting on the structure. For masonry that is based on engineering analysis, Type M, S, or N mortar is permitted. For masonry *not* based on engineering analysis, Type M, S, N, O, or K is permitted, except that Types O and K are not allowed where the masonry is to be (1) directly in contact with soil, as in a founda-

Kind of masonry	Type of mortar
Foundations:	
Footings	M, S,
Walls of solid units	M, S, N
Walls of hollow units	M, S
Hollow walls	M, S
Masonry other than foundation masonry:	
Piers of solid masonry	M, S, N
Piers of hollow units	M, S
Walls of solid masonry	M, S, N, O
Walls of solid masonry, other than parapet walls or rubble stone walls, not less than 12 in. thick nor more than 35 ft in height, supported laterally at intervals not exceeding 12 times the wall thickness	M, S, N, O, K
Walls of hollow units, load-bearing or exterior, and hollow walls 12 in. or more in thickness	M, S, N
Hollow walls less than 12 in. thick where assumed design wind pressure:	
1. exceeds 20 psf	M, S
2. does not exceed 20 psf	M, S, N
Glass block masonry	M, S, N, O
Linings of existing masonry, either above or below grade	M, S
Masonry other than above	M, S, N

*Adapted from National Bureau of Standards Misc. Pub. 211 (Ref. 1). Mortar types have been changed to ASTM C270 designations.

TABLE 20. GUIDE TO THE SELECTION OF MORTAR TYPE (UNITED STATES).*

tion wall, or (2) exposed to the weather on all sides, as in a parapet wall, balustrade, chimney, and steps and landings.

From the preceding paragraphs it can be seen that a choice of mortar type still exists. Where an analysis of structural stresses is required, the type of mortar selected will, in conjunction with the compressive strength of the concrete masonry units, determine the allowable stresses for the wall. It is not always necessary to use a Type M mortar for high strength because many building codes rate Type S in the wall as giving equally high allowable strengths. [Per ACI Committee 531 (Ref. 2) and the National Building Code of Canada (Ref. 3). On the other hand, some codes permit higher stresses with Type M than with Type S.] Moreover, mortar of Type S or N has more workability, water retention, and extensibility.

WHITE AND COLORED MORTAR

Pleasing architectural effects with color contrast or harmony between masonry units and joints are obtained through the use of white or colored mortars.

White mortar is made with white masonry cement, or with white portland cement and lime, and white sand. For *colored mortars* the use of white masonry cement or white portland cement instead of the normal grey cements not only produces cleaner, brighter colors but is essential for making pastel colors such as buff, cream, ivory, pink, and rose.

Integrally colored mortar may be obtained through use of color pigments, colored masonry cements, or colored sand. Brilliant or intense colors are not generally attainable in masonry mortars. The color of the mortar joints will depend not only on the color pigment, but also on the cementitious materials, aggregate, and water-cement ratio.

Pigments must be dispersed throughout the mix. To determine if mixing is adequate, some of the mix is flattened under a trowel. If streaks of color are present, additional mixing is required. For best results, the pigment should be premixed with the cement in large, controlled quantities. Colored masonry cement produced by cement plants is available in many areas. (*See* Chap. 16, Mineral Pigments for Use in Coloring Concrete.)

As a rule, color pigments should be of mineral oxide composition and contain no dispersants that will slow or stop the portland cement hydration. Iron, manganese, chromium, and cobalt oxides have been used successfully. Zinc and lead oxides should be avoided because they may react with the cement. Carbon black may be used as a coloring agent to obtain dark grey or almost black mortar, but lampblack should not be used. Carbon black should be limited to three percent by weight of the portland cement. Durability of this mortar may be deficient.

It is recommended to use only those pigments that have been found acceptable by testing and experience. The following is a guide to the selection of coloring materials.

Red, yellow, brown, black	Iron oxide
Green	Chromium oxide

Blue	Cobalt oxide
Black or grey	Carbon pigments

Only the minimum quantity of pigment that will produce the desired shade should be used. An excess of pigment, more than 10 percent of the portland cement by weight, may be detrimental to the strength and durability of the mortar. The quantity of water used in mixing colored mortar should be accurately controlled; the more water, the lighter the color. Retempering or the addition of water while using colored mortar should be avoided. Thus, any mortar not used while plastic and workable should be discarded.

Variations in the color of the materials are such that any color formula is only approximate. Best results are obtained by experiment. Test panels should be made with the same materials and proportions intended for use in the actual work, and the panels stored for about five days under conditions similar to those at the jobsite. When wet, panels will have a darker shade than when dry.

Fading of colored mortar joints may be caused by efflorescence, the formation of a white film on the surface. Efflorescence is more visible on a colored surface. The white deposits are caused by soluble salts that have emerged from below the surface, or by calcium hydroxide, liberated during the setting of the cement, that has combined with atmospheric carbon dioxide to form carbonate compounds. Good color pigments do not effloresce or contribute to efflorescence. Efflorescence may be removed with a light sandblasting or stiff-bristle brush. (*See* Chap. 18, Efflorescence.)

MORTAR COMPONENTS

Cementitious materials. Foremost among the factors that contribute to good mortar is the quality of the mortar ingredients. The following material specifications of the American Society for Testing and Materials (ASTM) or the Canadian Standards Association (CSA) are applicable.

Masonry cement—ASTM C91, CSA A8 (Type H or L)
Portland cement—ASTM C150 (Types I, IA, II, IIA, III, or IIIA), CSA A5 (Normal, Moderate, or High-Early-Strength)
Portland blast-furnace slag cement—ASTM C595 (Types IS or IS-A)
Portland pozzolan cement (for use in mortar property specification only)—ASTM C595 (Type IP or IP-A when fly ash is the pozzolanic material)
Hydrated lime for masonry purposes—ASTM C207 (Type S or N), CSA A82.43
Quicklime for structural uses—ASTM C5, CSA A82.42

Masonry sand. Since the quantity of sand required to make 1 cubic foot (.028 cu. meters) of mortar may be as much as 0.99 cubic foot (.027 cu. meters), the sand has considerable influence on the mortar properties. *Masonry sand* for mortar should comply with the requirements of ASTM C144 (Standard Specification for Aggregate for Masonry Mortar) for masonry construction within the United States and CSA A82.56 (Aggregate for Masonry Mortar) within Canada. These specifications include both natural and manufactured sands. Sand should be clean, well-graded, and meet the gradation requirements listed in Table 21.

Sands with less than 5 to 15 percent passing the Nos. 50 and 100 sieves generally produce harsh or coarse mortars which possess poor workability and result in mortar joints with low resistance to moisture penetration. On the other hand, sands finer than those permitted by the specifications in this section yield mortars with excellent workability, but they are weak and porous.

For mortar joints that are less than the conventional ⅜-inch (9.5-mm.) thickness, 100 percent of the sand should pass the No. 8 sieve and 95 percent the No. 16 sieve. For joints thicker than ⅜ inch (9.5 mm.), the mortar sand selected should have a fineness modulus approaching 2.5 or a gradation within the limits of concrete sands (fine aggregate) shown in ASTM C33, Standard Specification for Concrete Aggregates, or CSA A23.1, Concrete

	Gradation specified, percent passing		
	ASTM C144*		
Sieve size No.	Natural sand	Manufactured sand	CSA A82.56**
4	100	100	100
8	95 to 100	95 to 100	95 to 100
16	70 to 100	70 to 100	60 to 100
30	40 to 75	40 to 75	35 to 80
50	10 to 35	20 to 40	15 to 50
100	2 to 15	10 to 25	2 to 15
200	—	0 to 10	—

*Additional requirements: Not more than 50% shall be retained between any two sieve sizes, nor more than 25% between No. 50 and No. 100 sieve sizes. Where an aggregate fails to meet the gradation limit specified, it may be used if the masonry mortar will comply with the property specification of ASTM C270 (Table 2).

**Fine aggregate shall be so graded that neither the proportion of particles finer than a No. 16 sieve and coarser than a No. 30 sieve nor the proportion of particles finer than a No. 30 sieve and coarser than a No. 50 sieve exceeds 50%.

TABLE 21. AGGREGATE GRADATION FOR MASONRY MORTAR.

Materials and Methods of Concrete Construction. (Fineness modulus equals the sum of the cumulative percentages *retained* on the standard sieves, divided by 100. The higher the fineness modulus, the coarser the sand.) (*See* Chap. 6, Concrete Equipment and Tools.)

All cementitious materials and aggregates should be stored in such a manner as to prevent wetting, deterioration, or intrusion of foreign material. Brands of cementitious materials and the source of supply of sand should remain the same throughout the entire job.

Water. *Water* intended for use in mixing mortar should be clean and free of deleterious amounts of acids, alkalies, and organic materials. Some potable waters contain appreciable amounts of soluble salts such as sodium and potassium sulfate. These salts may later contribute to efflorescence. Also, a water containing sugar would retard the set. Thus, the water should be fit to drink but investigated if it contains alkalies, sulfates, or sugars.

Admixtures. Although water-reducers, accelerators, retarders, and other admixtures are used in concrete construction, their use in masonry mortar may produce adverse effects on the normal chemical reaction between cement and water, especially during the early periods after mixing and when the water is available for hydrating the portland cement. Whenever admixtures are considered for use in masonry and experience or performance records are not available, it is recommended that the admixture be laboratory-tested in the construction mortars at the temperature extremes requiring their use and then jobsite-inspected to ensure their satisfactory performance under the prevailing conditions.

Materials that retard the hydration process are particularly undesirable because they reduce strength development and increase the possibility of efflorescence.

The best known and most commonly used accelerator is calcium chloride. Although calcium chloride is used in concrete, its use in masonry is controversial because of possible adverse side effects, such as increased shrinkage, efflorescence, and corrosion of embedded metal. Calcium chloride should not be permitted in masonry containing metal ties, anchors, door bucks, or joint reinforcement because it may produce corrosion failures. Soluble chromates and sodium benzoate have been proposed as corrosion-inhibiting compounds. Their value in cold-weather masonry has not been fully determined, and so they are not recommended. Where corrosion is not involved, the maximum recommended amount of calcium chloride to be used is two percent by weight of portland cement or one percent of masonry cement, added in solution form.

Although air-entraining agents may be added at the mixture to increase workability and freeze-thaw durability at later ages, their effect on masonry mortars subjected to *early* freezing has not been established. In practice, both masonry cements (which entrain air) and air-entraining cements perform satisfactorily in mortars for use during winter construction.

MEASURING MORTAR MATERIALS

Measurement of masonry mortar ingredients should be completed in a manner that will ensure the uniformity of mix proportions, yields, workability, and mortar color from batch to batch. Aggregate proportions are generally expressed in terms of loose volume, but experience has shown that the amount of sand can vary due to moisture bulking.

Figure 2 shows how loose sand with varying amounts of surface moisture occupies different volumes. Figure 3 has the same data in another form for the fine and coarse sands, and shows the density of the sand. Loose, damp sand may consist of from 76 to 105 pcf (1219 to 1685 kgs. per cu. meter) of sand itself, plus the weight of the water. CSA A179 requires that the volume of sand be adjusted to the amount of bulking. ASTM C270 merely states that a cubic foot (.028 cu. meters) of loose, damp sand contains 80 pounds (36.4 kgs.) of dry sand.

Ordinary sands will absorb water amounting to 0.4 to 2.3 percent of the weight of the sand. In the field, damp sands usually have 4 to 8 percent moisture, and so most of the water is on the surface of the sand.

Mortar ingredients other than sand are often sold in bags la-

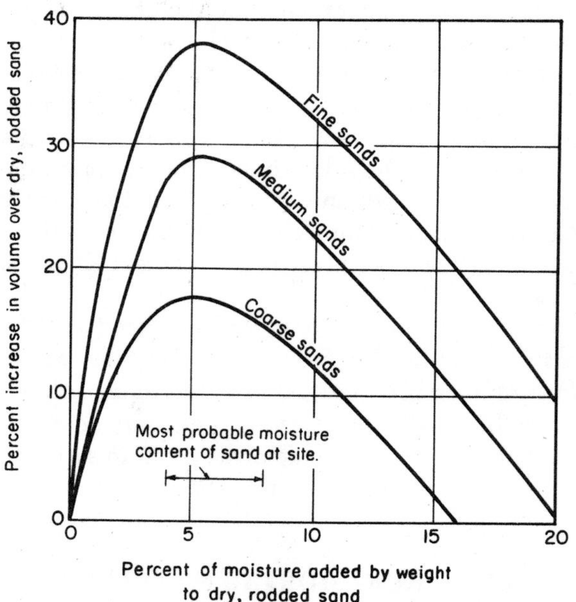

Fig. 2. Volume of loose, damp sand.

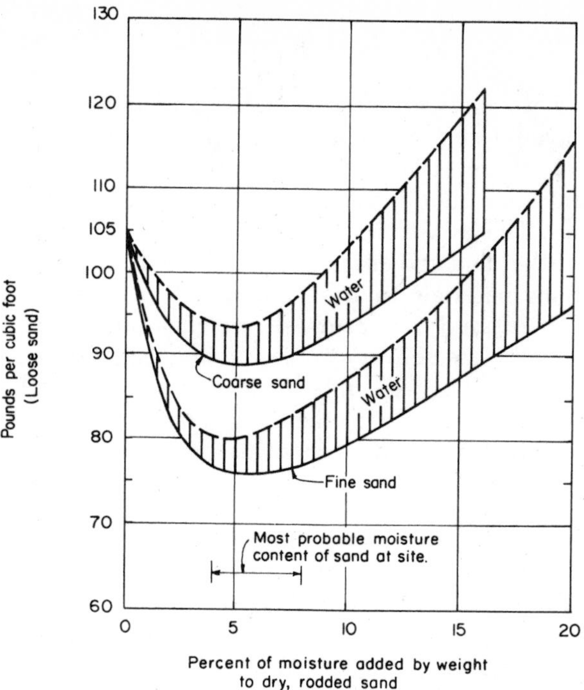

Fig. 3. Weight of loose, damp sand.

beled only by weight. Since mortar is proportioned by volume, it is necessary to know the following data.

	Unit weight, pcf
Portland cement	94
Masonry cement	70
Hydrated lime (dry)	40
Hydrated lime (putty)	80

The usual practice of measuring sand by the shovel can result in oversanding or undersanding the mix. For more positive control, the following method is suggested. Construct one or two wooden boxes, 12 inches square and 6 inches deep (30 cm. square and 15 cm. deep), and use them to measure the sand required in a batch. Add the cement or lime by the bag. Then add water, measuring by the pail. When the desired consistency of mix is attained, mark the level of the mortar in the mixing drum.

Use that as the mark for later batches when sand will be added by the shovelful. Repeat the measuring process halfway through the day, or whenever it is necessary or the inspector requests it.

A recent innovation is the process of dry-batching all mortar ingredients. This avoids the need to adjust the mix for moisture content of the sand and ensures consistent portions of sand and cementitious materials. In dry-batching, the cementitious materials and dried sand are accurately weighed and blended at a central plant before delivery to the site in a sealed truck, where the mixtures is conveyed into a sealed, weathertight hopper. When the mason is ready for the mortar, he has only to add the water and mix. It is apparent that this method offers great convenience and can result in very uniform mortar mixes. (*See* Chap. 3, Batching.)

MIXING

To obtain good workability and other desirable properties of plastic masonry mortar, the ingredients must be thoroughly mixed.

Mixing by machine. With the possible exception of very small jobs, mortar should be machine-mixed. A typical mortar mixer has a capacity of 4 to 7 cubic feet (.112 to .196 cu. meters) (Fig. 4). Conventional mortar mixers are of rotating-spiral or paddle-blade design with tilting drum. After all batched materials are together, they should be mixed for three to five minutes. Less mixing time may result in nonuniformity, poor workability, low water retention, and less than optimum air content. Longer mixing times may adversely affect the air content of mortars containing air-entraining cements, particularly during cool or cold weather. Longer mixing times may also reduce the strength of the mortar.

Batching procedures will vary with individual preferences. Experience has shown that good results can be obtained when about three-fourths of the required water, one-half of the sand, and all the cementitious materials are briefly mixed together. The balance of the sand is then charged and the remaining water

Fig. 4. Power mortar mixer.

added. The amount of water added should be the maximum that is consistent with satisfactory workability.

Mixing is carried out most effectively when the mixer is charged to its design capacity. Overloading can impair mixing efficiency and mortar uniformity. The mixer drum should be completely empty before charging the next batch.

Mixing by hand. When hand-mixing of mortar becomes necessary, as on small jobs, all the dry materials should first be mixed together with a hoe, working from one end of a mortar box (or wheelbarrow), then from the other. Next, two-thirds to three-fourths of the required water is mixed in with the hoe and the mixing continued as previously mentioned until the batch is uniformly wet. Additional water is carefully mixed in until the desired workability is attained. The batch should be allowed to stand for approximately five minutes and then thoroughly remixed with the hoe. (*See* Chap. 4, Mixing Concrete.)

Retempering. Fresh mortar should be prepared at the rate it is used so that its workability will remain about the same throughout the day. Mortar that has been mixed but not used immediately tends to dry out and stiffen. Loss of water by absorption and evaporation on a dry day can be reduced by wetting the mortar board and covering the mortar in the mortar box, wheelbarrow, or tub.

If necessary to restore workability, mortar may be retempered by adding water; thorough remixing is then necessary (Fig. 5). Although small additions of water may slightly reduce the compressive strength of the mortar, the end result is acceptable. Masonry built using plastic mortar has a better bond strength than masonry built using dry, stiff mortar.

Mortar that has stiffened because of hydration hardening should be discarded. Since it is difficult to determine by sight or feel whether mortar stiffening is due to evaporation or hydration, the most practical method of determining the suitability of mortar is on the basis of time elapsed after mixing. Mortar should be used within two and one-half hours after mixing.

If colored mortar is used, no retempering should be permitted. Additional water may cause a significant lightening of the mortar.

Fig. 5. To restore workability, mortar may be retempered.

Cold-weather construction. When masonry construction is carried on during periods of freezing weather, proper facilities should be available for preparing the mortar and protecting the fresh masonry work against frost damage. The most important consideration is that sufficient heat be provided to ensure hydration of the cement. After combining all ingredients, mortar temperature should be within the range of 40° F. to 120° F. (4.5° C. to 49° C.). In Canada, the range is 70° F. to 120° F. (21° C. to 49° C.). If the air temperature is falling, a minimum temperature of 70° F. (21° C.) is recommended. Mortar temperatures in excess of 120° F. (49° C.) may cause excessively fast hardening with resultant loss of compressive and bond strength. Table 22 gives requirements at various cold-weather temperatures for heating of materials and protection of construction (*See* Chap. 17, Hot- and Cold-Weather Concreting.)

Air temperature, deg. F.	Construction requirements	
	Heating of materials	Protection
Above 40	Normal masonry procedures. No heating required.	Cover walls with plastic or canvas at end of work day to prevent water entering masonry.
Below 40	Heat mixing water. Maintain mortar temperatures between 40°F and 120°F until placed.	Cover walls and materials to prevent wetting and freezing. Covers should be plastic or canvas.
Below 32	In addition to the above, heat the sand. Frozen sand and frozen wet masonry units must be thawed.	With wind velocities over 15 mph, provide windbreaks during the work day and cover walls and materials at the end of the work day to prevent wetting and freezing. Maintain masonry above 32°F using auxiliary heat or insulated blankets for 16 hours after laying units.
Below 20	In addition to the above, dry masonry units must be heated to 20°F.	Provide enclosure and supply sufficient heat to maintain masonry enclosure above 32°F for 24 hours after laying units.

*Adapted from recommendations of the International Masonry Industry All-Weather Council (Ref. 4).

TABLE 22. RECOMMENDATIONS FOR COLD-WEATHER MASONRY CONSTRUCTION.*

The use of an admixture to lower the freezing point of mortars during winter construction should be avoided. The quantity of such materials necessary to lower the freezing point of mortar to any appreciable degree would be so large that mortar strength and other desirable properties would be seriously impaired.

ESTIMATING THE REQUIRED MATERIALS

You will be able to use rule 38 for calculating the amount of raw material needed to mix 1 yard (.765 cu. meters) of mortar without a great deal of paper work. This calculating rule will not give the accurate amount of required raw materials for large masonry constructions jobs—you will have to use the absolute volume or weight formulae. However, in most cases, particularly in advanced base construction, you can use the rule of thumb to quickly estimate the quantities of required raw materials.

Workers have found that it takes about 38 cubic feet of raw materials to make 1 cubic yard (.765 cu. meters) of mortar; therefore, take the rule number and divide it by the sum of the quantity figures specified in the mix. *For example,* let us assume that the specifications call for a 1 : 3 mix for mortar 1 + 3 = 4 then 38 ÷ 4 = 9½. You will then need 9½ sacks or 9½ cubic feet (.27 cu. meters) of cement. In order to calculate the amount of fine aggregates (sand), you simply multiply 9½ by 3. The product, 28½ cubic feet (.8 cu. meters), is the amount of sand you need to mix 1 cubic yard (.765 cu. meters) of mortar using a 1 : 3 mix. The sum of the two required quantities should always equal the calculating rule 38. Therefore, you can always check in order to see if you are using the correct amounts. In the previous example, 9½ sacks of cement, plus 28½ cubic feet (.8 cu. meters) of sand, equal 38.

Chapter 21

Masonry Tools and Equipment

The mason's tools shown in Fig. 1 include trowels, bolster, hammer, and jointer.

The mason's *trowel* may be a *brick*, a *buttering*, or a pointing trowel. The trowel is used for mixing, placing, and spreading mortar. (*See* Chap. 26, Bricklaying Tools and Equipment, section on Trowel Practice.) The hammer is used for tapping masonry units into the beds where necessary, and for chipping and rough-cutting. For smoother cutting the bolster (also called a *brickcutting chisel* or *brick set*) is used. Breaking into bats and closures is done with the chisel peen on the mason's hammer. Splitting and rough breaking is done with the head or flat of the hammer.

The *jointer*, of which there are several types, besides the one shown in Fig. 1, is used for making various joint finishes. They are described in Chap. 22, Concrete Masonry Units, section on Joint Finishing; *see also* Chap. 26, Bricklaying Tools and Equipment.

The mason must maintain a constant check on his courses to ensure that they are level and plumb; otherwise the courses will appear wavy and the plane surfaces warped. The equipment for this vital purpose consists of a length of line, carpenter's or framing squares (Fig. 2) and level and plumb bob (Fig. 3), and a straightedge shown in Fig. 4. The square is used to lay out cor-

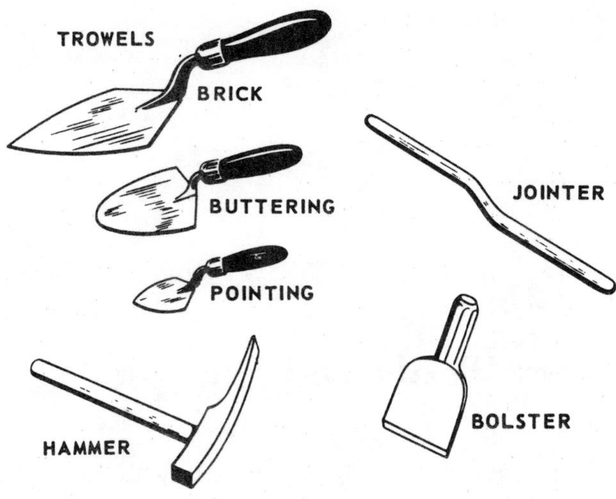

Fig. 1. Mason's tools.

ners and for other right-angle work. The mason's level is used exactly as the carpenter's level is in wood construction. The straightedge is used in conjunction with the level for leveling or plumbing long stretches.

A *mortar board* for holding a supply of ready-to-use mortar should be constructed as shown in Fig. 5. If mortar is to be mixed by hand, it should be mixed in a *mortar box* like the one shown in Fig. 6. However, if the box is expected to be used over a period of time, it should be lined with some type of metal. The metal will make mixing easier and also prolong the life of the box. Other required equipment includes shovels, mortar hoes, wheelbarrows, and buckets. (*See* Chap. 6, Concrete Equipment and Tools; Chap. 7, Form and Form Making, section on Tools and Equipment; and Chap. 26, Bricklaying Tools and Equipment.) For most large jobs a *power mortar mixer* may be required. (*See* Chap. 20, Masonry Materials, Fig. 4.)

In a sawed type of control joint, a vertical groove is produced by cutting with a *masonry saw* as shown in Fig. 7. A board nailed to the wall serves as a straightedge.

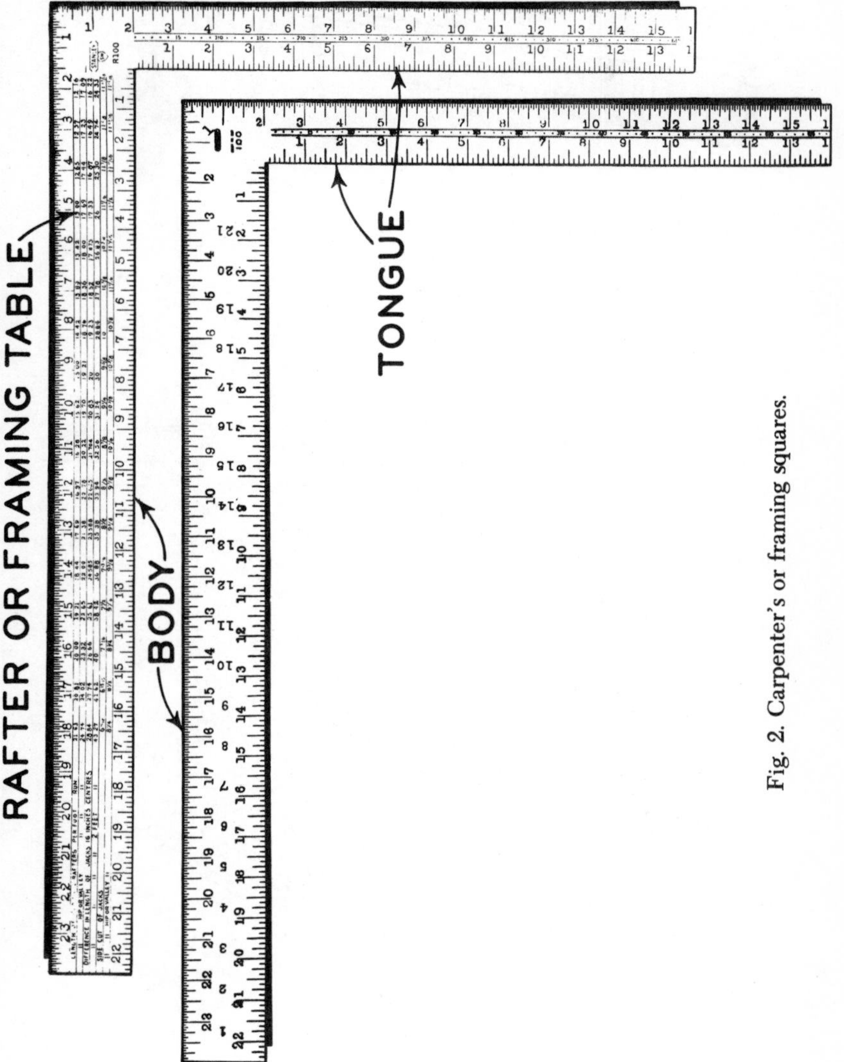

Fig. 2. Carpenter's or framing squares.

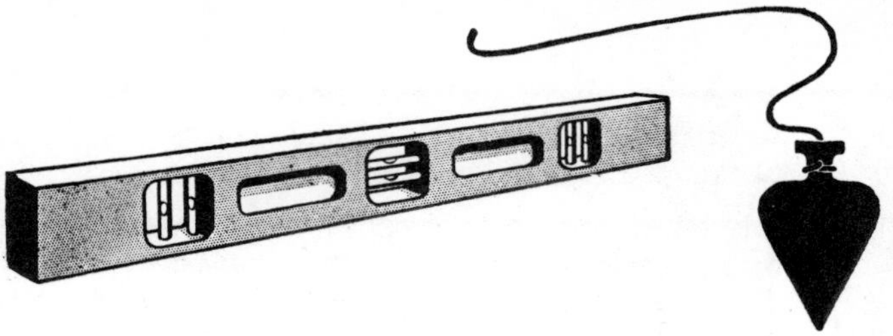

Fig. 3. Level and plumb bob.

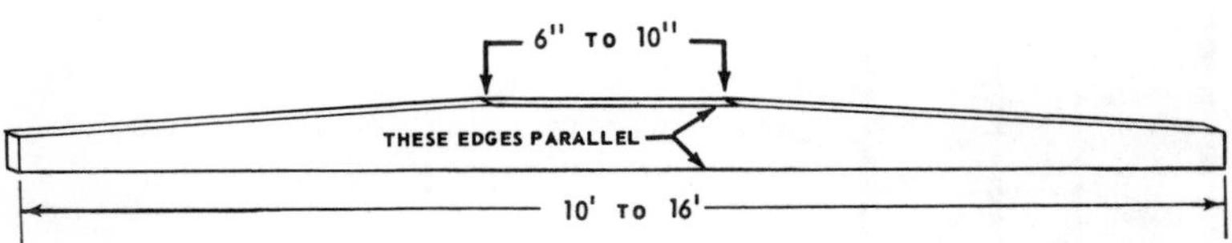

Fig. 4. Mason's straightedge.

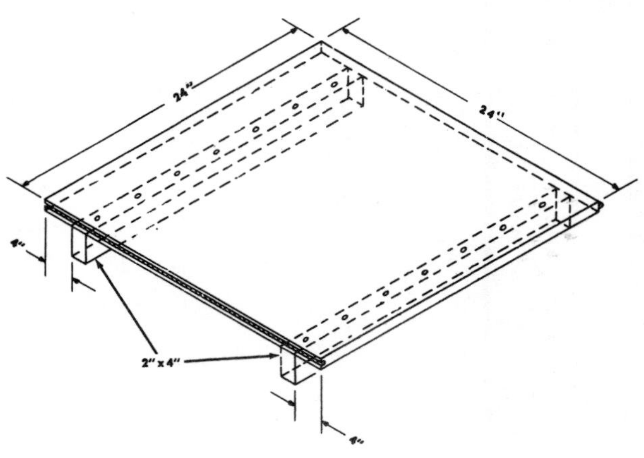

Fig. 5. Mortar board.

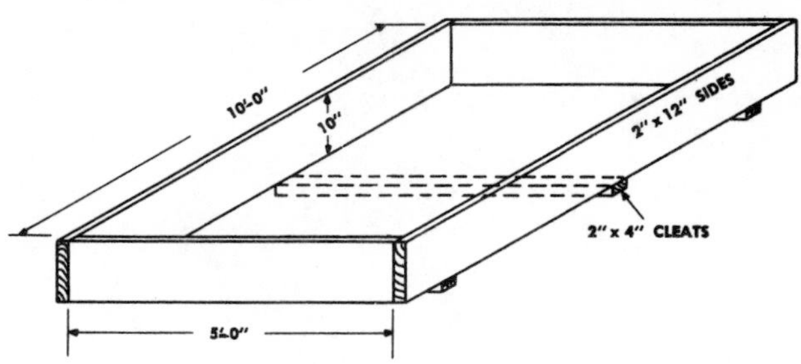

Fig. 6. Mortar box.

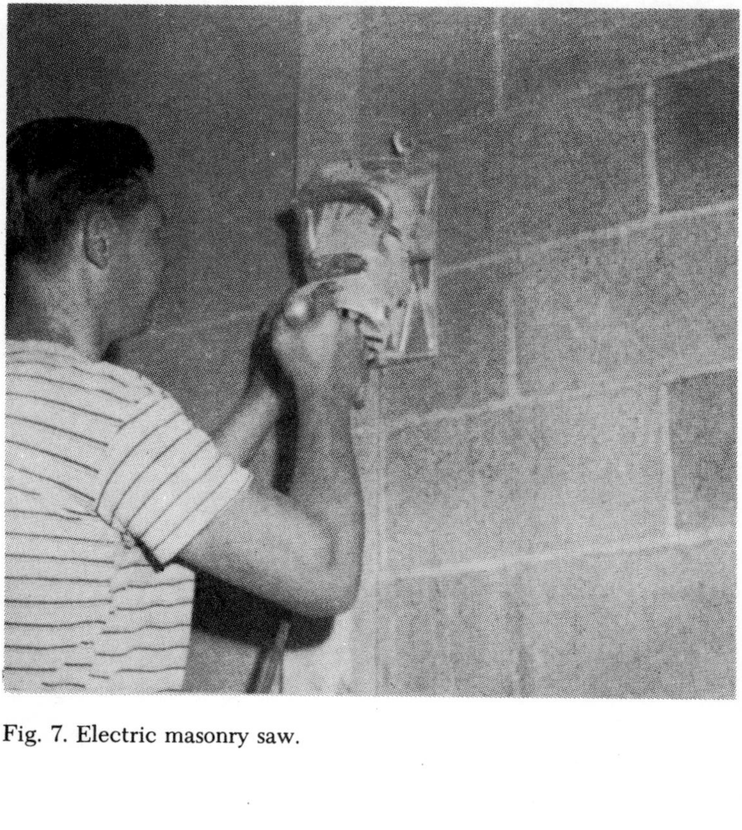

Fig. 7. Electric masonry saw.

Fig. 8. Electric unit cutting saw.

Masonry saws (Fig. 8) are used for fast, neat cutting of units to fit special job conditions. Units must be cut dry so as not to raise their moisture content.

You will find various useful tools and equipment throughout the book. For quick referral turn to the Index.

Chapter 22

Concrete Masonry Units

Concrete masonry units were at one time made only with cinder or slag, small-diameter aggregate, but they are now made for the most part like any other lightweight concrete, except that the maximum diameter of the coarse aggregate is about ⅝ inch (1.6 cm.). Concrete for units which will be exposed to the weather should contain at least six sacks of cement per cubic yard (.765 cu. meters).

Concrete units may be manufactured either by machine or by hand. A concrete block machine feeds a *dry* mix from a hopper into a mold and tamps it hard enough to allow the mold to be removed at once, and the block to be put aside for setting without losing its shape. In the hand method, a plastic mix is poured into sets of iron molds which are stripped after the concrete has set.

Blocks can be steam-cured to 70 percent of 28-day strength in about 15 hours. They can be ordinary damp-cured in about seven days.

BLOCK SIZES AND SHAPES

Concrete building units are made in sizes and shaped to fit different construction needs. Units are made in full and half-length sizes as shown in Fig. 1. Concrete unit sizes are usually referred to by their nominal dimensions. A unit measuring 7⅝ inches wide, 7⅝ inches high, and 15⅝ inches long (19.3 × 19.3 × 39 cm. respectively) is referred to as an 8- × 8- × 16-inch (20- × 20- × 40-cm.) unit. When it is laid in a wall with ⅜-inch (9.4-mm.) mortar joints, the unit will occupy a space exactly 16 inches long and 8 inches high (40 cm. and 20 cm. respectively). Besides the basic 8- × 8- × 16-inch (20- × 20- × 40-cm.) units, the illustration shows a smaller partition unit and other units which are used much as cut brick are in brick masonry.

The corner unit is laid at a corner or at some similar point where a smooth rather than a recessed end is required. The header unit is used in a backing course placed behind a brick face tier header course. Part of the block is cut away to admit the brick headers. The uses of the other specials shown are self-evident. Besides the shapes shown in Fig. 1, a number of smaller shapes for various special purposes are available. Units may be cut to desired shapes with a bolster or, more conveniently and accurately, with a power-driven masonry saw such as that shown in Fig. 2.

BLOCK MORTAR JOINTS

The sides and the recessed ends of a concrete block are called the *shell,* and the material which forms the partitions between the cores is called the *web.* Each of the long sides of a block is called a *face shell,* and each of the recessed ends is called an *end shell.* Bed joints on first courses and bed joints in column construction are mortared by spreading a one-inch layer of mortar. This is called *full mortar bedding.* For most other bed joints, only the upper edges of the face shells need to be mortared. This is called *face shell mortar bedding.*

The vertical ends of the face shells, on either side of the end shells, are called the *edges.* Head joints may be mortared by buttering both edges of the block being laid, or by buttering one edge on the block being laid and the opposite edge on the block already in place.

MODULAR PLANNING

Concrete masonry walls should be laid out to make maximum use of full- and half-length units, thus minimizing cutting and fitting of units on the job. Length and height of wall, width and height of openings, and wall areas between doors, windows, and

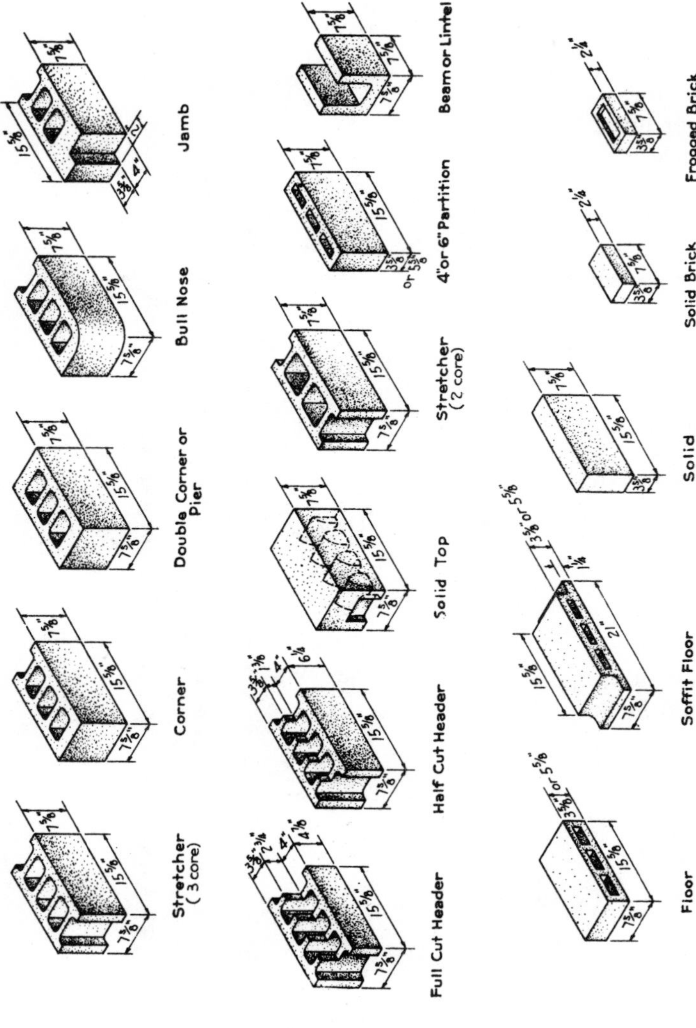

Fig. 1. Typical sizes and shapes of concrete masonry units.

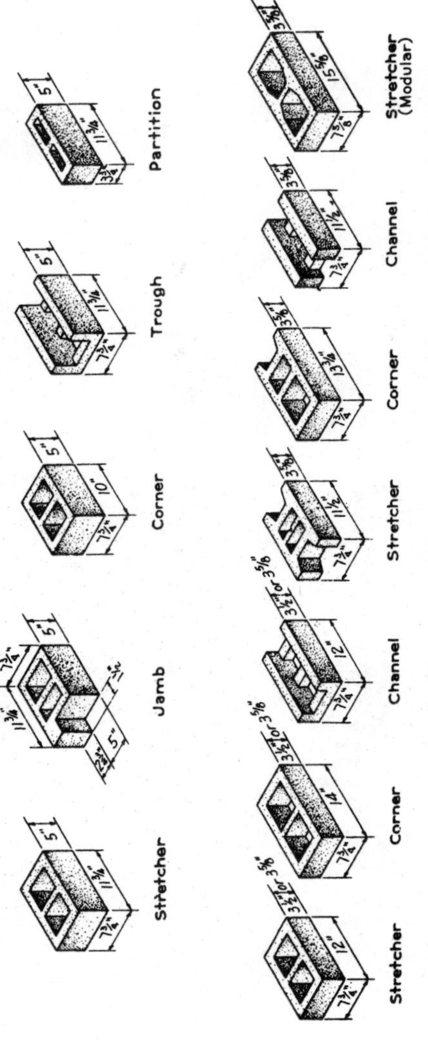

(Dimensions shown are actual unit sizes. A 7⅝″ x 7⅝″ x 15⅝″ unit is commonly known as an 8″ x 8″ x 16″ block.)

Fig. 1. Typical sizes and shapes of concrete masonry units (continued).

Fig. 2. Masonry saw.

corners should be planned to use full-size and half-size units which are usually available (Fig. 3). This procedure assumes that window and door frames are of modular dimensions which fit modular full- and half-size units. Then, all horizontal dimensions should be in multiples of nominal full-length masonry units and both horizontal and vertical dimensions should be designed to be in multiples of eight inches. Table 23 lists nominal length of concrete masonry walls by stretchers and Table 24 lists nominal height of concrete masonry walls by courses. When units 8 × 4 × 16 inches (20 × 10 × 40 cm.) are used, the horizontal dimensions should be planned in multiples of 8 inches (20 cm.)—half-length units—and the vertical dimensions in multiples of 4 inches (10 cm.). If the thickness of the wall is greater or less than the length of a half unit, a special length unit is required at each corner in each course.

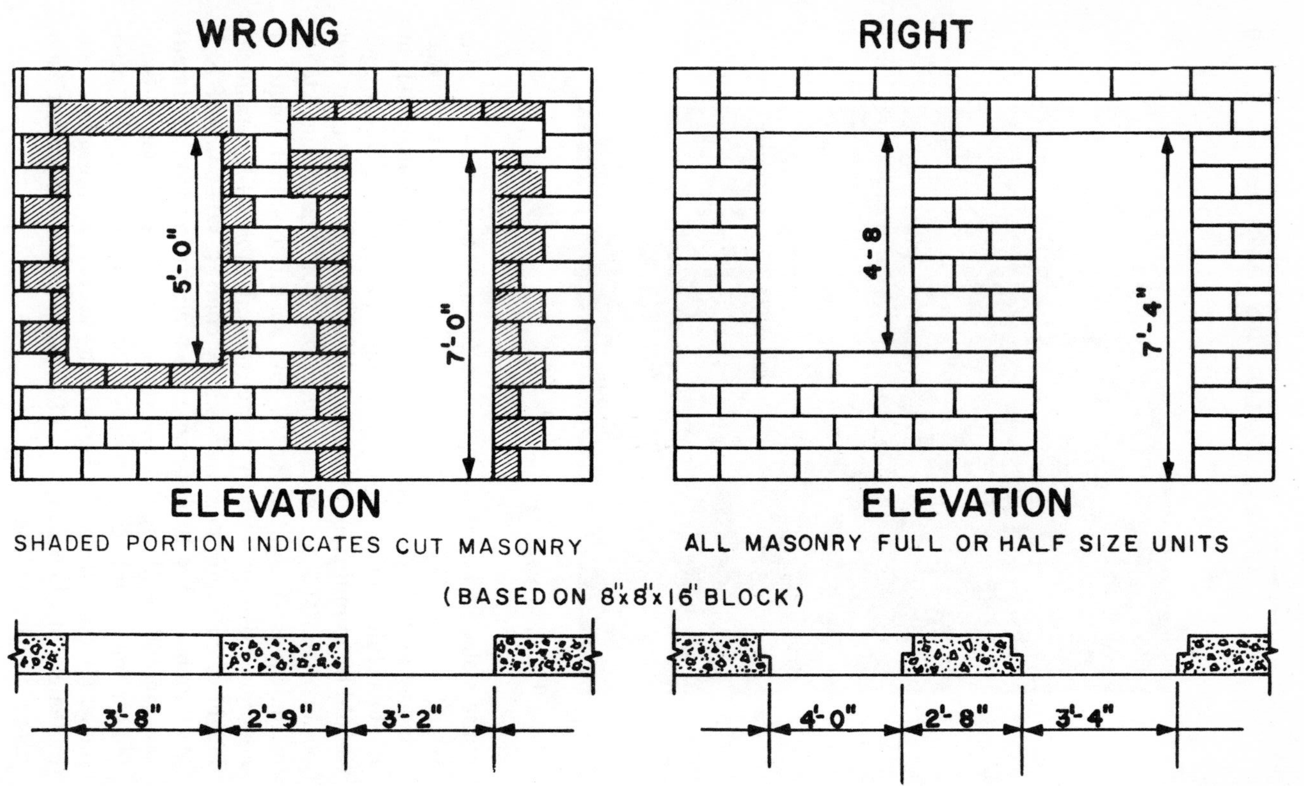

Fig. 3. Planning concrete masonry wall openings.

No. of stretchers	Nominal length of concrete masonry walls	
	Units 15⅝″ long and half units 7⅝″ long with ⅜″ thick head joints.	Units 11⅝″ long and half units 5⅝″ long with ⅜″ thick head joints.
1	1′ 4″	1′ 0″.
1½	2′ 0″	1′ 6″.
2	2′ 8″	2′ 0″.
2½	3′ 4″	2′ 6″.
3	4′ 0″	3′ 0″.
3½	4′ 8″	3′ 6″.
4	5′ 4″	4′ 0″.
4½	6′ 0″	4′ 6″.
5	6′ 8″	5′ 0″.
5½	7′ 4″	5′ 6″.
6	8′ 0″	6′ 0″.
6½	8′ 8″	6′ 6″.
7	9′ 4″	7′ 0″.
7½	10′ 0″	7′ 6″.
8	10′ 8″	8′ 0″.
8½	11′ 4″	8′ 6″.
9	12′ 0″	9′ 0″.
9½	12′ 8″	9′ 6″.
10	13′ 4″	10′ 0″.
10½	14′ 0″	10′ 6″.
11	14′ 8″	11′ 0″.
11½	15′ 4″	11′ 6″.
12	16′ 0″	12′ 0″.
12½	16′ 8″	12′ 6″.
13	17′ 4″	13′ 0″.
13½	18′ 0″	13′ 6″.
14	18′ 8″	14′ 0″.
14½	19′ 4″	14′ 6″.
15	20′ 0″	15′ 0″.
20	26′ 8″	20′ 0″.

TABLE 23. NOMINAL LENGTH OF CONCRETE WALLS BY STRETCHERS. (ACTUAL LENGTH MEASURED FROM OUTSIDE EDGE TO OUTSIDE EDGE OF UNITS AND IS EQUAL TO THE NOMINAL LENGTH MINUS ⅜-INCH OR ONE MORTAR JOINT.)

No. of courses	Nominal height of concrete masonry walls	
	Units 7⅝" high and ⅜" thick bed joint	Units 3⅝" high and ⅜" thick bed joint
1	8"	4".
2	1' 4"	8".
3	2' 0"	1' 0".
4	2' 8"	1' 4".
5	3' 4"	1' 8".
6	4' 0"	2' 0".
7	4' 8"	2' 4".
8	5' 4"	2' 8".
9	6' 0"	3' 0".
10	6' 8"	3' 4".
15	10' 0"	5' 0".
20	13' 4"	6' 8".
25	16' 8"	8' 4".
30	20' 0"	10' 0".
35	23' 4"	11' 8".
40	26' 8"	13' 4".
45	30' 0"	15' 0".
50	33' 4"	16' 8".

TABLE 24. NOMINAL HEIGHT OF CONCRETE MASONRY WALLS BY COURSES. (FOR CONCRETE MASONRY UNITS 7⅝ INCHES AND 3⅝ INCHES IN HEIGHT LAID WITH ⅜-INCH MORTAR JOINTS. HEIGHT IS MEASURED FROM CENTER TO CENTER OF MORTAR JOINTS.)

CONCRETE MASONRY WALL

After locating the corners of the wall, the worker usually checks the layout by stringing out the blocks for the first course without mortar (Fig. 4). A chalked snapline is useful to mark the footing and align the block accurately. A full bed of mortar is then spread and furrowed with the trowel to ensure plenty of mortar along the bottom edges of the face shells of the block for the first course (Fig. 5). The corner block should be laid first and carefully positioned (Fig. 6). All block should be laid with the thicker end of the face shell up to provide a larger mortar-bed-

Fig. 4. Stringing out blocks.

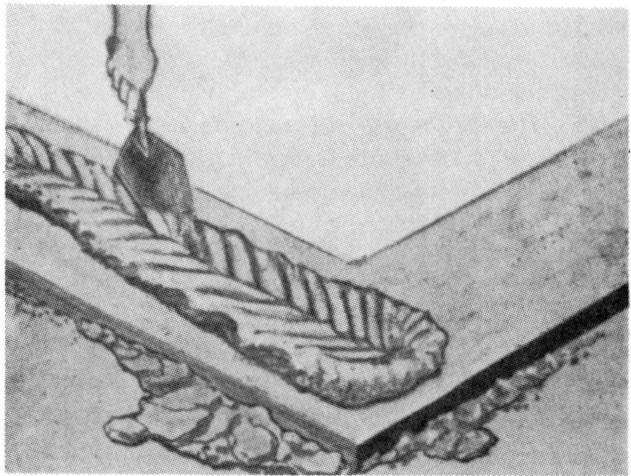

Fig. 5. Spread and furrow mortar bed.

Fig. 6. Position corner block.

ding area (Fig. 7). Mortar is applied only to the ends of the face shells for vertical joints. Several blocks can be placed on end and the mortar applied to the vertical face shells in one operation. Each block is then brought over its final position and pushed downward into the mortar bed and against the previously laid block to obtain a well-filled vertical mortar joint (Fig. 8). After three or four blocks have been laid, the mason's level is used as a straightedge to assure correct alignment of the blocks. Then the blocks are carefully checked with the level and brought to proper grade and made plumb by tapping with the trowel handle (Fig. 9). The first course of concrete masonry should be laid with great care, to make sure it is properly aligned, leveled, and plumbed, and to assure that succeeding courses, and finally the wall, are straight and true.

After the first course is laid, mortar is applied only to the horizontal face shells of the block (face-shell mortar bedding). Mortar for the vertical joints may be applied to the vertical face shells of the block to be placed or to the block previously laid or both, to ensure well-filled joints (Fig. 10). The corners of the wall are built first, usually four or five courses higher than the center of the wall. As each course is laid at the corner, it is checked with a level for alignment, for levelness, and for plumbness as shown in Fig. 11. Each block is carefully checked with a level or

Fig. 7. Blocks buttered for vertical joints.

Fig. 8. Positioning block.

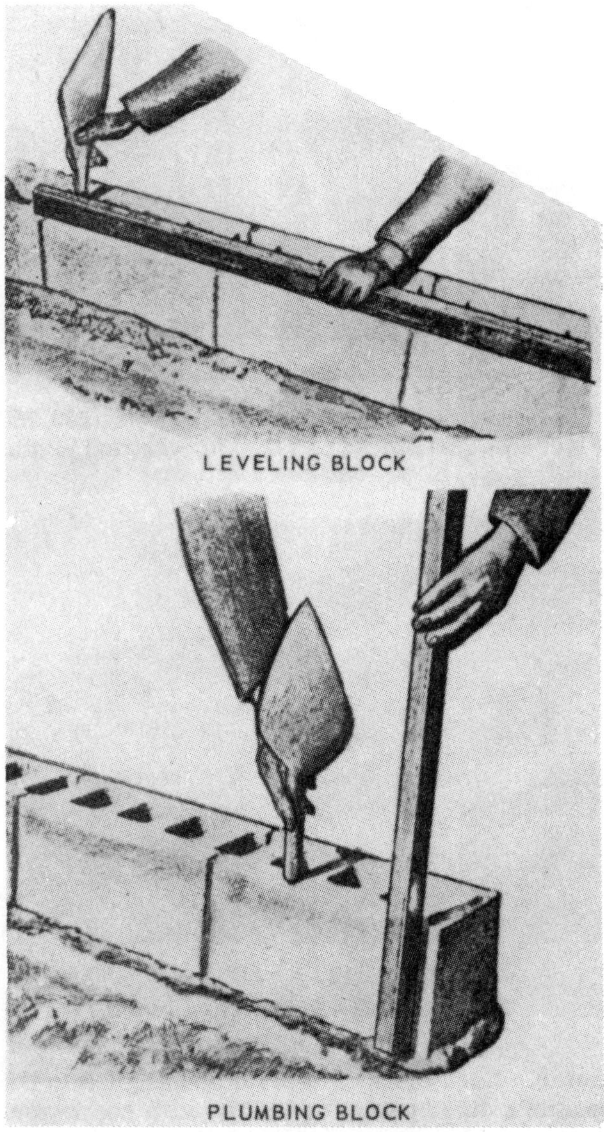

Fig. 9. Checking first course of blocks.

Fig. 10. Vertical joints.

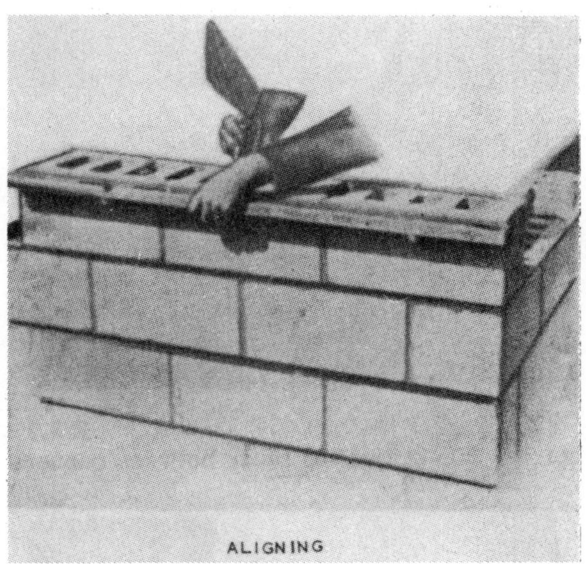

Fig. 11. Checking each course.

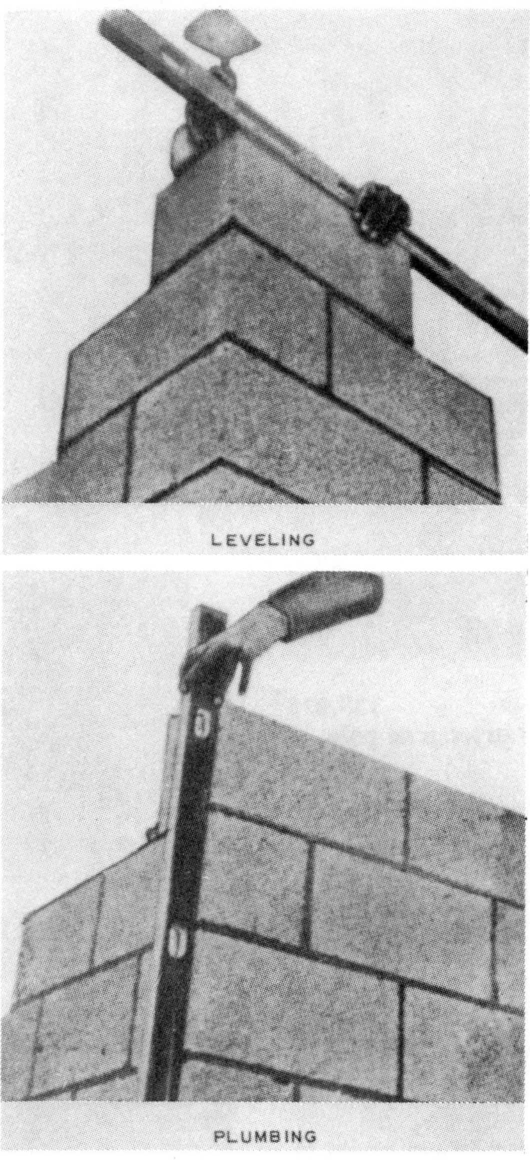

Fig. 11. Checking each course (continued).

straightedge to make certain that the faces of the block are all in the same plane to ensure true, straight walls. The use of a story or course-pole, a board with markings 8 inches (20 cm.) apart, provides an accurate method of determining the top of the masonry for each course (Fig. 12). Joints are ⅜-inch (9.4-mm.) thick. Each course in building the corners is stepped back a half block and the worker checks the horizontal spacing of the block by placing his level diagonally across the corners of the block (Fig. 13).

When filling in the wall between the corners, a mason's line is stretched from corner to corner for each course and the top outside edge of each block is laid to this line. The manner of gripping the block is important. It should be tipped slightly toward the worker so he can see the edge of the course below, enabling him to place the lower edge of the block directly over the course below (Fig. 14). All adjustments to final position must be made while the mortar is soft and plastic. Any adjustments made after the mortar has stiffened will break the mortar bond and allow the penetration of water. Each block is leveled and aligned to the mason's line by tapping lightly with the trowel handle. The use of the mason's level between corners is limited to checking the face of each block to keep it lined up with the face of the wall.

To assure good bond, mortar should not be spread too far ahead of actual laying of the block or it will stiffen and lose its plasticity. As each block is laid, excess mortar extruding from the joints is cut off with the trowel (Fig. 15), and is thrown back on the mortar board to be reworked into the fresh mortar. Dead mortar that has been picked up from the scaffold or from the floor should not be used.

When installing the closure block, all edges of the opening and all four vertical edges of the closure block are buttered with mortar and the closure block is carefully lowered into place (Fig. 16). If any of the mortar falls out, leaving an open joint, the block should be removed and the procedure repeated.

Weathertight joints and neat appearance of concrete block walls are dependent on proper tooling. The mortar joints should be tooled after a section of the wall has been laid and the mortar

Fig. 12. Use of story or course pole.

Fig. 13. Checking horizontal spacing of block.

Fig. 14. Adjusting block between corners.

Fig. 15. Cutting off excess mortar.

Fig. 16. Installing closure block.

has become *thumb-print* hard. Tooling (Fig. 17) compacts the mortar and forces it tightly against the masonry on each side of the joint. All joints should be tooled either concave or V-shaped. Horizontal joints should be tooled first, followed by striking the vertical joints with a small S-shaped jointer. Mortar burrs remaining after tooling is completed should be trimmed off flush with the face of the wall with a trowel or removed by rubbing with a burlap bag or soft bristle brush. (*See* Chap. 21, Masonry Tools and Equipment.)

Wood plates are fastened to tops of concrete masonry walls by anchor bolts ½ inch (1.3 cm.) in diameter, 18 inches (45 cm.) long and spaced not more than 4 feet (1.2 meters) apart. The bolts are placed in cores of the top two courses of block with the cores filled with concrete or mortar. Pieces of metal lath placed in the second horizontal mortar joint from the top of the wall and under the cores to be filled (Fig. 18) will hold the concrete or mortar filling in place. The threaded end of the bolt should extend above the top of the wall.

CONTROL JOINTS

Control joints are continuous vertical joints built into concrete masonry walls to control cracking resulting from unusual

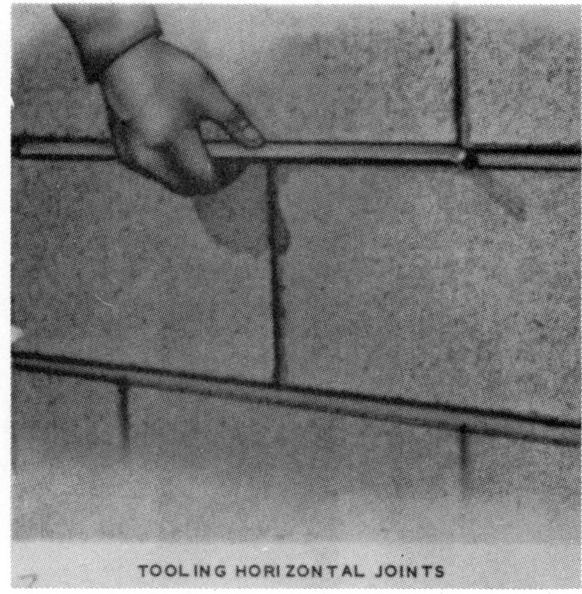

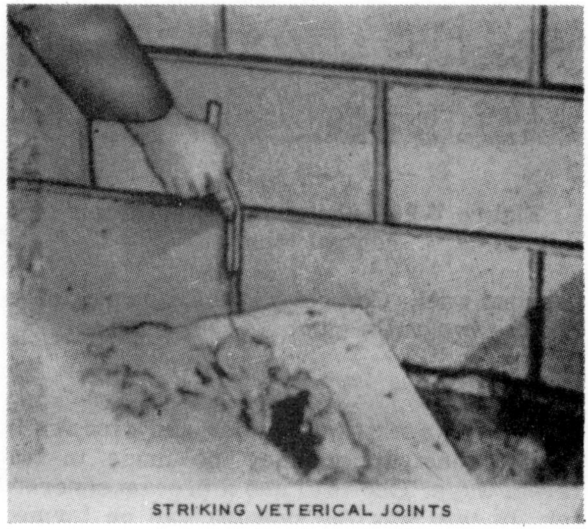

Fig. 17. Tooling mortar joints.

PLACING METAL LATH

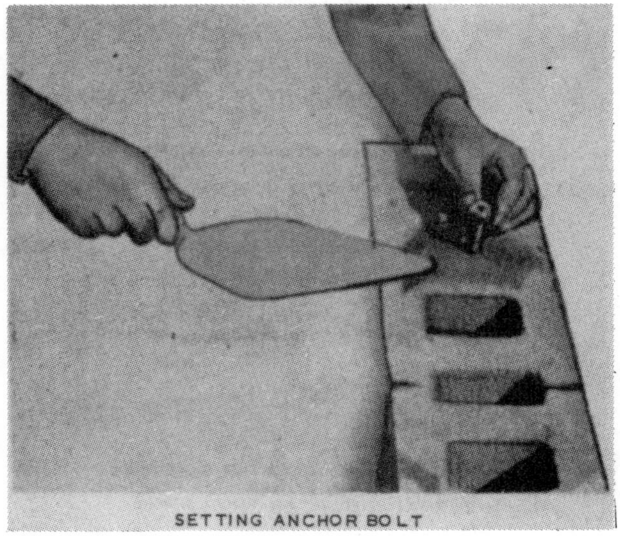
SETTING ANCHOR BOLT

Fig. 18. Installing anchor bolts on top of wall.

stresses. The joints are intended to permit slight wall movement without cracking. Control joints should be laid up in mortar just as any other joint. Full- and half-length block are used to form a continuous vertical joint (Fig. 19). If they are exposed to the weather or to view, they should be caulked. After the mortar is quite stiff, it should be raked out to a depth of about ¾ inch (1.9 cm.) to provide a recess for the caulking material. A thin, flat caulking trowel is used to force the caulking compound into the joint. Another type of control joint can be constructed with building paper or roofing felt inserted in the end core of the block and extending the full height of the control joint (Fig. 20). The paper or felt, cut to convenient lengths and wide enough to extend across the joint, prevents the mortar from bonding on one side of the joint. Sometimes control joint blocks are used if available.

To provide lateral support, metal ties can be laid across the joint in every other horizontal course.

INTERSECTING WALLS

Intersecting concrete block bearing walls should not be tied together in a masonry bond, except at the corners. Instead, one wall should terminate at the face of the other wall with a control joint at the point. Bearing walls are tied together with a metal tiebar ¼ × 1¼ × 28 inches (.64 × 3.1 × 70 cm.), with 2-inch (5-cm.) right angle bends on each end (Fig. 21). Tiebars are spaced not over 4 feet (1.2 meters) apart vertically. Bends at the ends of the tiebars are embedded in cores filled with mortar or concrete. Pieces of metal lath placed under the cores support the concrete or mortar filling as shown in Fig. 18.

To tie nonbearing block walls to other walls, strips of metal lath of ¼-inch (6.3-mm.) mesh galvanized hardware cloth are placed across the joint between the two walls (Fig. 22), in alternate courses in the wall. When one wall is constructed first, the metal strips are built into the wall and later tied into the mortar joint of the second wall. Control joints are constructed where the two walls meet.

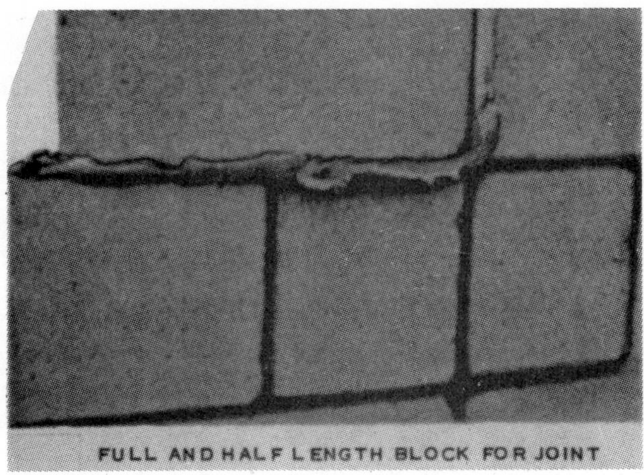

Fig. 19. Control joint.

Fig. 20. Paper or felt used for control joints.

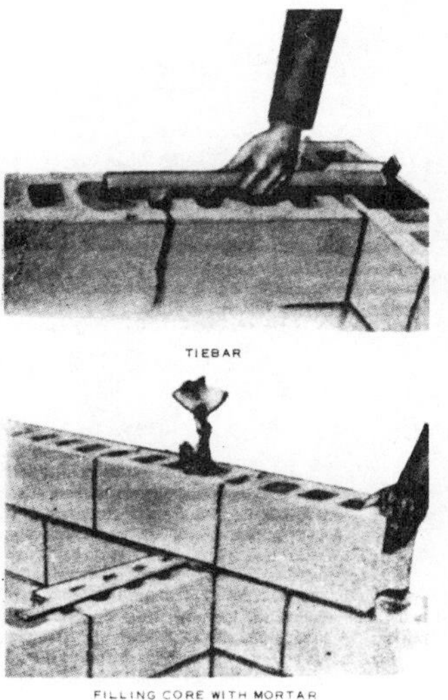

Fig. 21. Tying intersecting bearing walls.

Fig. 22. Tying intersecting nonbearing walls.

LINTELS

The top of openings for door and windows in masonry construction may be made in two different ways: (1) Use a precast concrete lintel so the opening can be formed before the door or window frame is set; (2) use the lintel block like that shown in Fig. 23. Here the frame is set in place and the block wall built around it. Lintel blocks are used across the top. Reinforcing bars and concrete are placed in the lintel blocks. Window and door openings in masonry should be planned to bring the top or bottom of a course in line with the openings.

PATCHING AND CLEANING BLOCK WALLS

Any patching of the mortar joints or filling of holes left by nails or line pins should be done with fresh mortar.

Hardened, embedded mortar smears cannot be removed, and paint cannot be depended on to hide smears, so particular care should be taken to prevent smearing mortar into the surface of the block. Concrete block walls should not be cleaned with an acid wash to remove smears or mortar droppings. Mortar droppings that stick to the block wall should be allowed to dry before removal with a trowel (Fig. 24, A). Most of the mortar can be removed by rubbing with a small piece of concrete (broken) block after the mortar is dry and hard (Fig. 24, B). Brushing the rubbed spots will remove practically all of the mortar (Fig. 24, C).

CUTTING CONCRETE BLOCKS

Concrete blocks are usually made in half-sizes, as well as full-length units. However, it is sometimes necessary to cut a block to fit a particular location. This can be done in two ways. The block may be scored with a bolster and broken along the score lines. Blocks may also be cut with a masonry saw as shown in Chap. 21, Figs. 7 and 8. The saw shown in Fig. 8 is particularly useful when only a portion of the block is to be cut. For instruc-

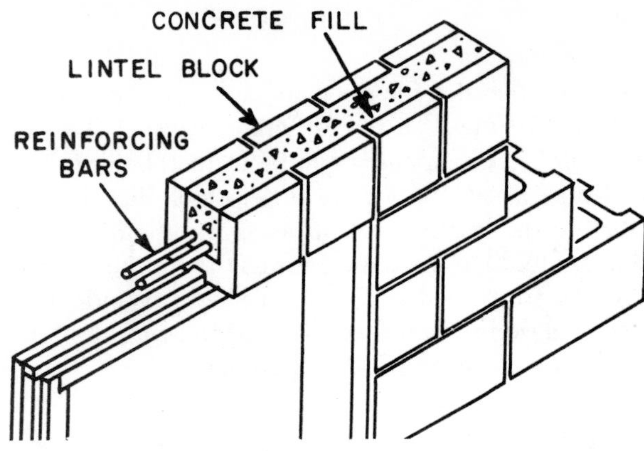

Fig. 23. Lintel made from blocks.

tion on the operation and maintenance of the concrete saw, study the manufacturer's manual.

REINFORCED BLOCK WALLS

Block walls may be reinforced vertically or horizontally. To reinforce vertically, place reinforcing rods into the cores at the specified spacing and fill the cores with a relatively high slump concrete. Rebars (studs) should be placed at each corner and at both sides of each opening. The vertical rebars should generally be spaced a maximum of 32 inches (80 cm.) O.C. in walls. Where splices are required, the bars should be lapped 40 diameters. The concrete should be placed in one continuous pour from foundation to plate line. A cleanout block may be placed in the first course at every rebar (stud) for cleanout of excess mortar and to ensure proper alignment and laps of rebars.

Horizontal rebars should be placed in bond beam units which are laid with the channel up and then filled with concrete. Bond beams may be installed both below windows and at the top of the wall at the plate line. Typically, the reinforcing rebars used may be two ⅜-inch (.94-cm.) diameter deformed bars (lapped 40 diameters at splices). Lintels formed by placing bond beam

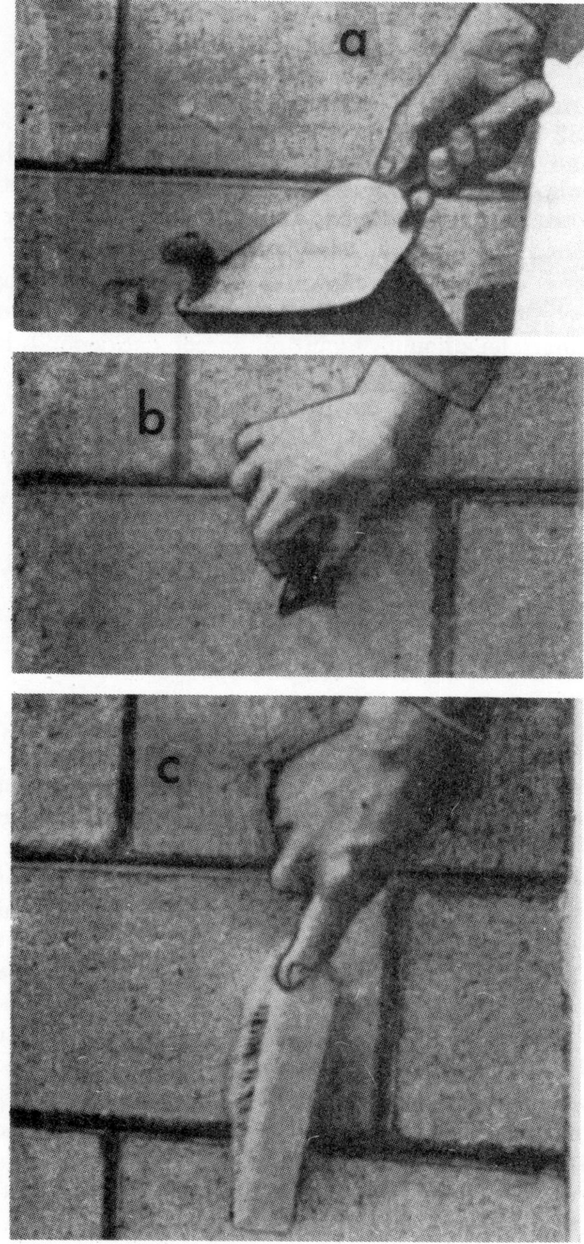

Fig. 24. Patching and cleaning block.

blocks are usually extended 8 inches (20 cm.) past each opening. You should always check the specifications carefully for the size and number of rebars to be used. A pilaster block may be used for lateral strength and to provide greater bearing area for beam ends carried on the wall. One type of pilaster is shown in Fig. 25.

Practical experience indicates that control of cracking and wall flexibility can be achieved with the use of horizontal joint reinforcing. The amount of joint reinforcement depends largely upon the type of construction. Horizontal joint reinforcing, where required, should consist of not less than two deformed longitudinal No. 9 (or heavier) cold drawn steel wires. Truss type cross wires should be ⅛-inch (3-mm.) diameter (or heavier) of the same quality. Figure 26 shows joint reinforcement at a vertical spacing of 16 inches (40 cm.).

The location and details of bond beams, control joints, and joint reinforcing should all be shown on drawings.

WATERTIGHT BLOCK WALLS

To ensure that block walls below grade will be watertight, they should be covered with plaster and sealed. Plastering consists of applying two ¼-inch (6.3-mm.) coats of plaster, using 1:2½ mortar mix. The wall should be dampened before applying the plaster in order to get a good bond. The first coat should extend from 6 inches (15 cm.) above the grade line down to the footing. When it is partially set up, roughen the surface with a wire brush and then allow at least 24 hours. Dampen the wall again before the second coat is applied. After the second coat is applied the wall should be kept damp for 48 hours.

In poorly drained or heavy wet soils the plaster should be covered with two coats of an asphalt waterproofing, brushed on. The wall may be further protected by laying a line of drainage tile around the outside of the footing. Cover the tile joints with pieces of building paper, and cover the tile with about 12 inches (30 cm.) of washed gravel before the back filling is done.

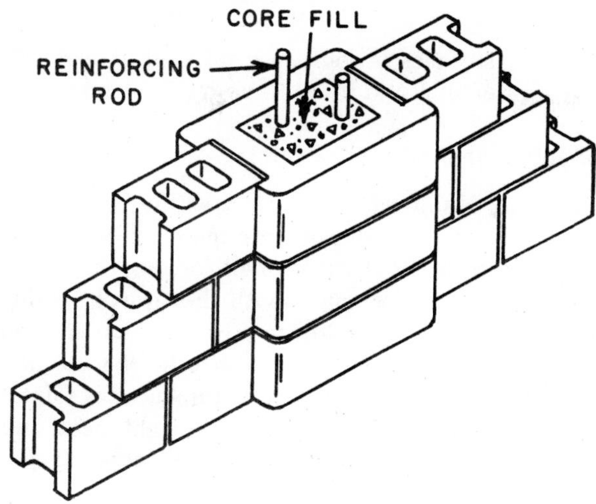

Fig. 25. One type of pilaster.

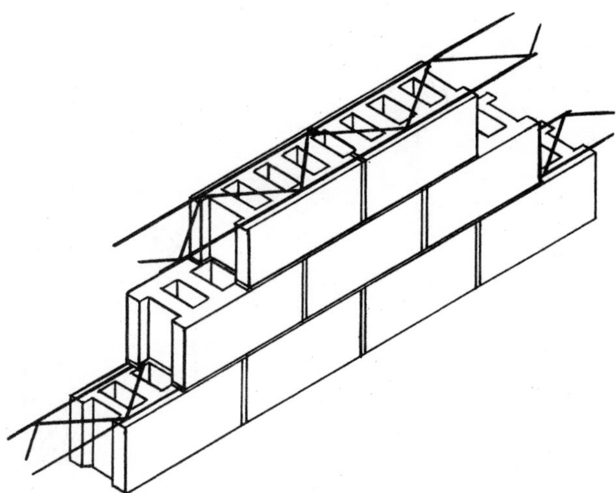

Fig. 26. Masonry wall horizontal joint reinforcement.

JOINT FINISHING

The exterior surfaces of joints are finished to make the masonry more watertight and to improve its appearance.

Concave and V-Shaped Mortar Joints

Concave and *V-shaped mortar joints* (Fig. 27) are recommended for walls of exterior concrete masonry in preference to struck or raked joints that form small lodges which may hold water. Some joints can be made with the trowel, while others have to be made with the jointer. With modular-size masonry units mortar joints will be approximately ⅜-inch (9.3-mm.) thick. Experience has shown that this thickness of joint, where properly made, helps to produce a weathertight, neat, and durable concrete masonry wall. (*See* Chap. 6, Concrete Equipment and Tools.)

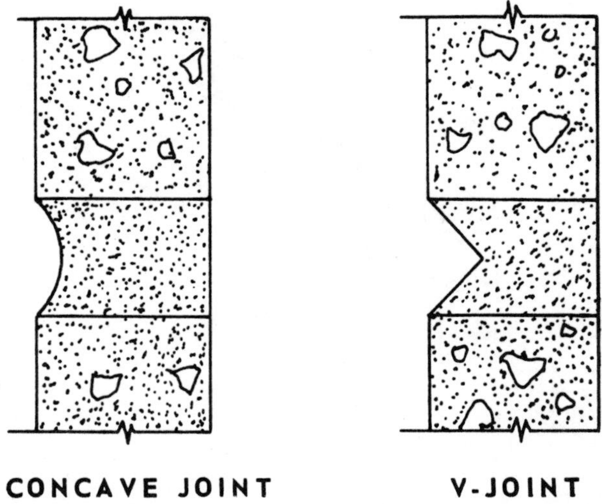

Fig. 27. Tooled mortar joints for watertight concrete.

Pointing

There is a process called *pointing* that may have to be done after jointing has occurred. Pointing is the process of inserting mortar into horizontal and vertical joints after the unit has been laid. Basically, pointing is done to restore or replace deteriorated surface mortar in old work. Pointing of this nature is called *tuck* pointing. However, pointing may be necessary for filling holes or correcting defective joints in freshly laid masonry.

Chapter 23

Structural Clay Tile Masonry

Hollow masonry units made of burned clay or shale are called structural tiles, building tiles, hollow tiles, structural clay tiles, structural clay hollow tiles, and structural clay hollow building tiles. Let us call them building tiles in this book. In building tile manufacture, plastic clay is pugged through a die and the shape which emerges is cut off into units. The units are then burned much as bricks are burned.

The apertures in a building tile, which correspond to the cores in a brick or a concrete block, are called *cells.* The solid sides of a tile are called the *shell* and the perforated material enclosed by the shell is called the *web.* A tile which is laid on one of its shell faces is called a *side-construction* tile; one which is laid on one of its web faces is called an *end-construction* tile. Figures 1 and 2 show the sizes and shapes of basic side- and end-construction building units. Special shapes for use at corners and openings, or for use as closures are also available.

USES FOR STRUCTURAL CLAY TILE

Structural clay tile may be used for exterior walls of either the load-bearing or non-load-bearing type. It is suitable for both below-grade and above-grade construction.

Non-load-bearing partition walls of from 4- to 12-inch (10- to 30-cm.) thickness are frequently made of structural clay tile. These walls are easily built, light in weight, and have good heat- and sound-insulating properties.

Figure 3 illustrates the use of structural clay tile as a backing unit for a brick wall. Figure 3 also shows the use of header brick to tie the brick tier to the tile used for backing.

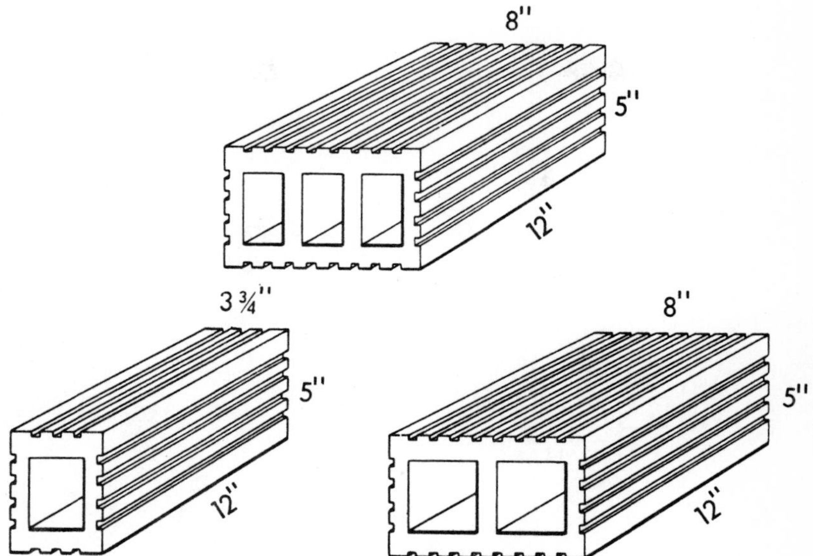

Fig. 1. Standard shapes of side construction building tiles.

MORTAR JOINTS FOR STRUCTURAL CLAY TILE

In general, the procedure for making mortar joints for structural clay tile is the same as for concrete block. (*See* Chap. 22, Concrete Masonry Units.)

The bed joint for the end-construction is made by spreading a 1-inch (2.5-cm.) thickness of mortar on the shell of the bed tile but not on the webs. The mortar should be spread for a distance of about 3 feet (.9 meters) ahead of the laying of the tile. The position of the tile above does not coincide with the position of the tile below since the head joints are to be staggered as shown in Fig. 4. The web of the tile above will not contact the web of the tile below and any mortar placed on these webs is useless.

The head joint for the end-construction is formed by spreading plenty of mortar along each edge of the tile as shown in Fig. 4, and then pushing the tile into its proper position in the mortar

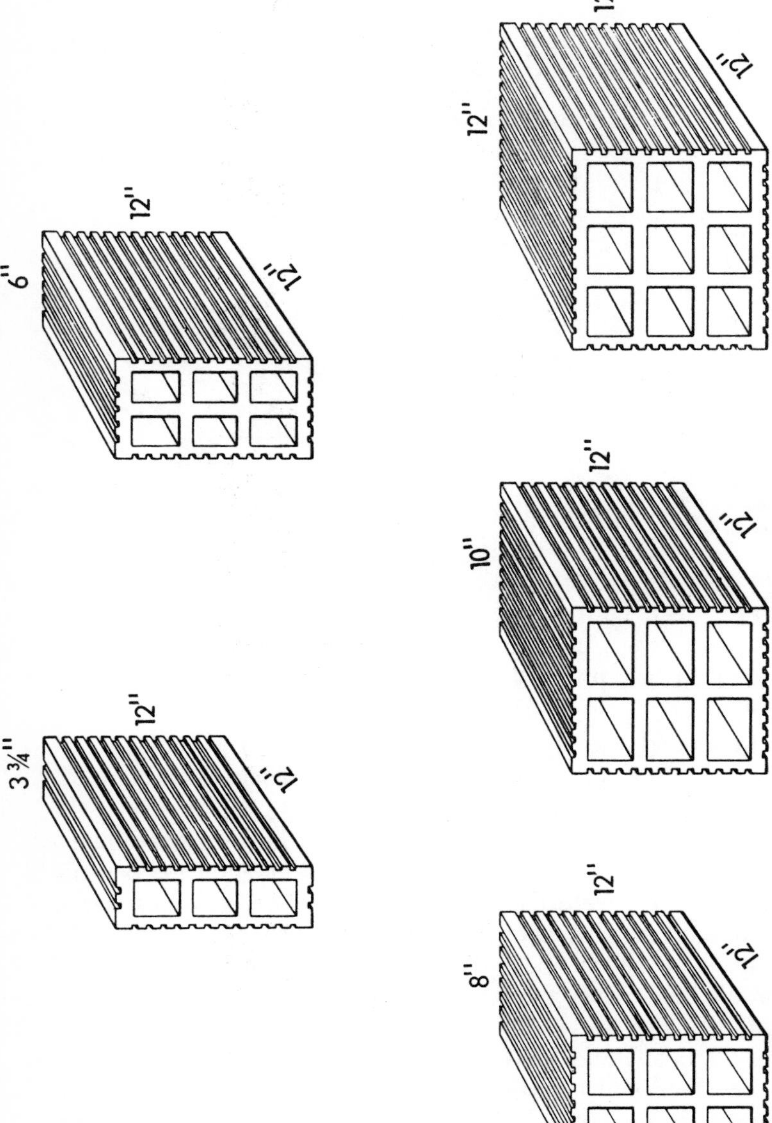

Fig. 2. Standard shapes of end construction building tiles.

Fig. 3. Structural clay tile used as a backing unit.

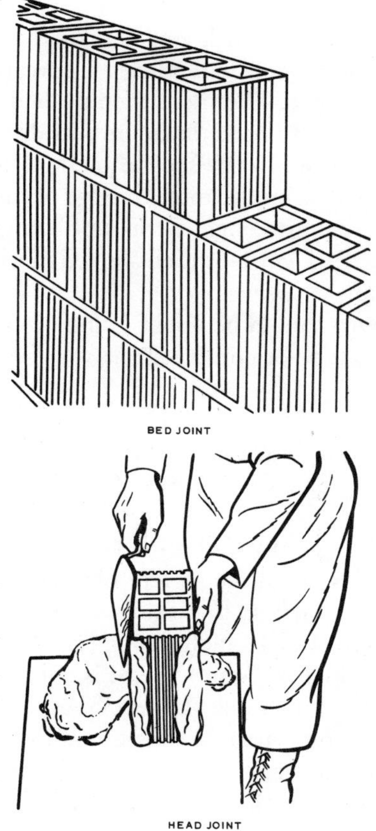

Fig. 4. Laying end-construction tile.

bed. Enough mortar should be used to cause excess mortar to squeeze out of the joints. This excess mortar is cut off with a trowel. The head joint need not be a solid joint as recommended for head joints in brick masonry unless the joint is to be exposed to the weather. Clay tile units are heavy, making it necessary to use both hands when placing the tile in position in the wall. The mortar joint should be about ½-inch (1.3-cm.) thick, depending upon the type of construction.

The bed joint for the side-construction is made by spreading the mortar to a thickness of about 1 inch (2.5 cm.) for a distance of about 3 feet (.9 meters) ahead of the laying of the tile. A furrow need not be made.

There are two methods of laying the head joint. In the first method, as much mortar as will adhere is spread on both edges of tile as shown in Fig. 5. The tile is then pushed into the mortar bed against the tile already in place until in its proper position. Excess mortar is cut off. In the second method, as much mortar as will adhere is placed on the interior edge of the tile already in place and on the opposite edge of the unit being placed. This is also shown in Fig. 5. The tile is then shoved in place and the excess mortar cut off.

The mortar joints should be about ½ inch thick (1.3 cm.), depending upon the type of construction.

EIGHT-INCH WALL WITH FOUR-INCH STRUCTURAL CLAY TILE BACKING

For the 8-inch (20-cm.) wall with 4-inch (10-cm.) structural clay tile backing there will be six stretcher courses between the header courses. The backing tile is side-constructed tile, 4 inches wide, 5 inches high, and 12 inches long (10 × 6.3 × 30 cm., respectively). The 5-inch (6.3-cm.) height is equal to the height of two brick courses and a ½-inch (1.3-cm.) mortar joint. These tiles are laid with a bed joint such that the top of the tile will be level with every second course of brick. The thickness of the bed joint therefore depends upon the thickness of the bed joint used for the brick.

METHOD A FOR MAKING HEAD JOINT

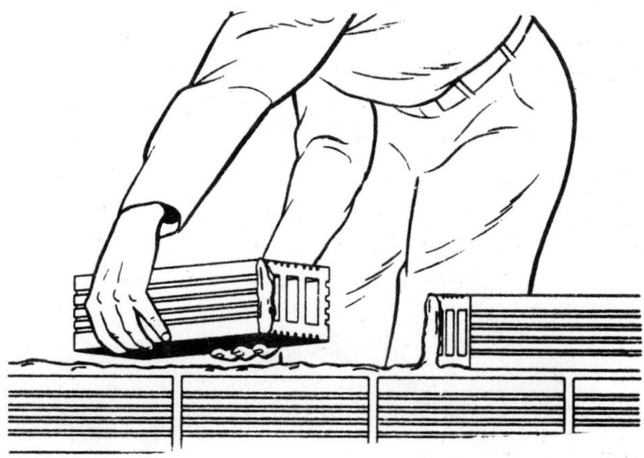

METHOD B FOR MAKING HEAD JOINT

Fig. 5. Laying side-construction tile.

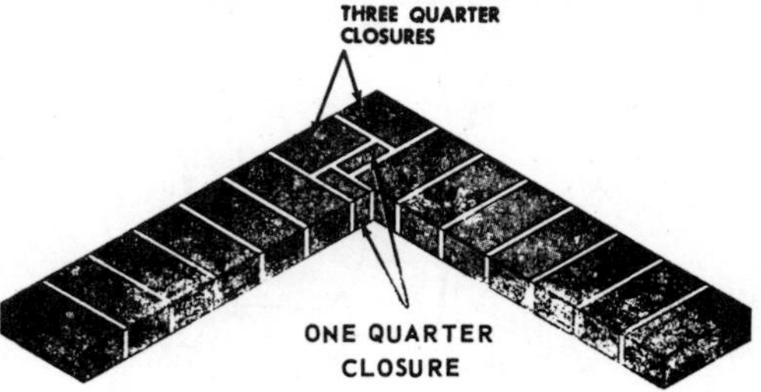

FIRST COURSE OF CORNER LEAD, HOLLOW TILE BACKING

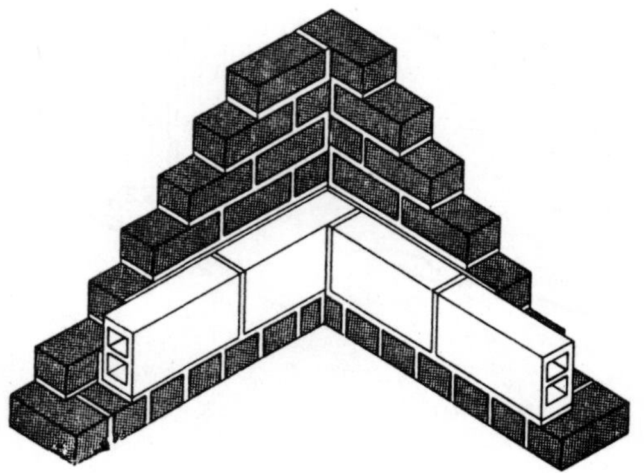

FIRST COURSE OF TILE, HOLLOW TILE BACKING

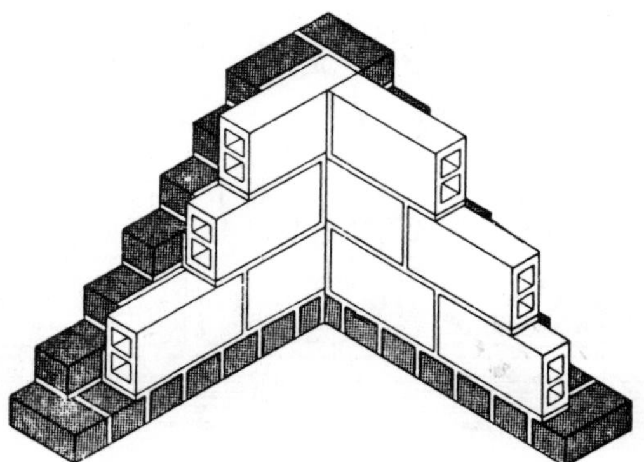

COMPLETE CORNER LEAD, HOLLOW TILE BACKING

Fig. 6. Corner lead hollow tile backing.

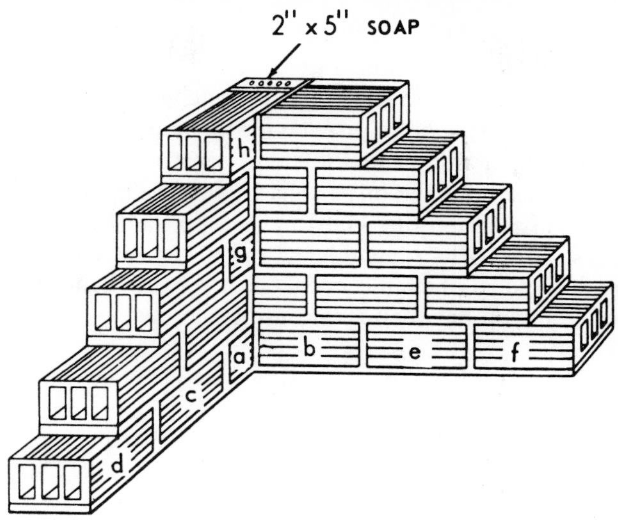

Fig. 7. Eight-inch (20-cm.) structural clay tile wall.

The first course of the wall is temporarily laid out without mortar as recommended for solid brick walls. This will establish the number of brick required for one course.

As shown in Fig. 6 the first course of the corner lead is identical to the first course of the corner lead for a solid 8-inch (20-cm.) brick wall except that one more brick is laid.

All the brick required for the corner lead are laid before any tile is placed. The first course of tile and the completed corner lead are also shown in Fig. 6.

EIGHT-INCH STRUCTURAL CLAY TILE WALL

The 8-inch (20-cm.) structural clay tile wall is constructed of 8- × 5- × 12-inch (20- × 12.5- × 30-cm.) tile. The length of the tile is 12 inches (30 cm.), the width is 8 inches (20 cm.), and the height is 5 inches (12.5 cm.). A 2- × 5- × 8-inch (5- × 12.5- × 20-cm.) soap is used at the corners as shown in Fig. 7. Half-lap bond is used as indicated.

Figure 7 also illustrates laying the corner leads by showing that tiles a and b are laid first, then c and d. The level is checked as they are laid. Tiles e and f are laid and their level checked. Tile b must be laid so that it projects 6 inches (15 cm.) from the inside corner, as shown, to provide for the half-lap bond. Corner tiles such as b, g, and h should be end-construction tile in order to avoid exposure of the open cells at the face of the wall, or a thin end-construction tile, known as a *soap,* may be used at the corner as shown. The remainder of the tile in the corner is then laid, and the level of each is checked. After the corner leads are erected, the wall between is laid using the line.

Chapter 24

Stone Masonry

Stone masonry is masonry in which the units consist of natural stone. In *rubble* stone masonry the stones are left in their natural state without any kind of shaping. In *ashlar* masonry the faces of stones which are to be placed in surface positions are squared, so that the surfaces of the finished structure will be more or less continuous plane surfaces. Both rubble and ashlar work may be either *coursed* or *random.*

Random rubble is the crudest of all types of stonework. Little attention is paid to laying the stones in courses as shown in Fig. 1. Each layer must contain bonding stones that extend through the wall as shown in Fig. 2. This produces a wall that is well tied together. The bed joints should be horizontal for stability but the *builds* or head joints may run in any direction.

Coursed rubble is assembled of roughly squared stones in such a manner as to produce approximately continuous horizontal bed joints as shown in Fig. 3.

MATERIALS USED

The *stone* used in stone masonry should be strong, durable, and cheap. Durability and strength depend upon the chemical composition and physical structure of the stone. Some of the more commonly found stones that are suitable are limestone, sandstone, granite, and slate. Unsquared stones obtained from nearby ledges or quarries, or even fieldstones, may be used. The size of the stone should be such that two men can easily handle it. A variety of sizes is necessary in order to avoid using large quantities of mortar.

The *mortar* for use in stone masonry may be composed of

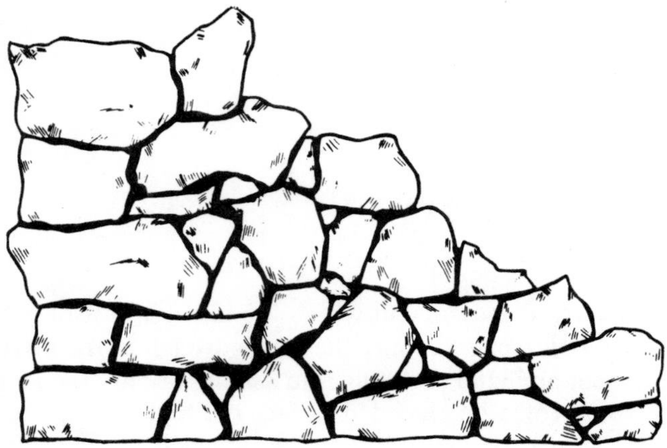

Fig. 1. Random rubble masonry.

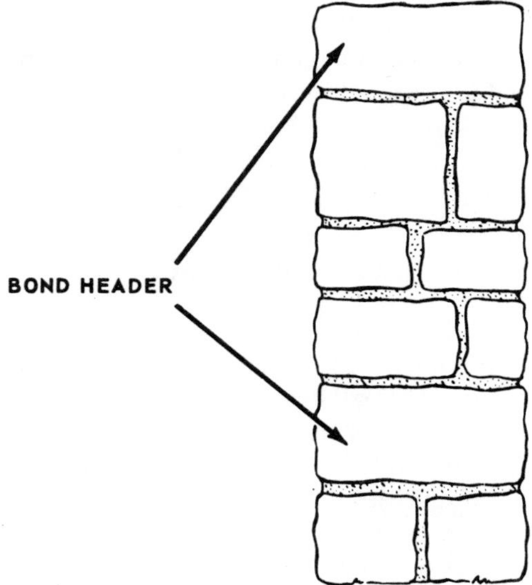

Fig. 2. Bond stones.

Fig. 3. Coursed rubble masonry.

portland cement and sand in the proportions of one part cement to three parts sand by volume. Such mortar shrinks excessively and does not work well with the trowel. A better mortar to use is portland cement-lime mortar. (*See* Table 25.) Mortar made with ordinary portland cement will stain most types of stone. If staining must be prevented, non-staining white portland cement should be used in making the mortar. Lime does not usually stain the stone.

LAYING STONE MASONRY

The wall proper should be laid on a footing of large stones, each of which should be as long as the footing is wide. Some general rules for laying stones are as follows:

1. Each stone should be laid on its broadest face.
2. If appearance is a factor, the larger stones should be laid in the lower courses and the size of stones should gradually diminish toward the top of the wall. An exception to this is work in which the stones are deliberately arranged to form an ornamental pattern, as is the case in much ashlar work.
3. Masonry stone is classified as absorbent or nonabsorbent. The absorbent type stone must be wetted before placing, to prevent absorption of water and consequent weakening of the mortar. The nonabsorbent type does not need wetting at all.

Proportions by Volume

Type of service	Cement	Hydrated lime	Mortar sand, in damp, loose condition
For ordinary service.	1—masonry cement*	----------	2¼ to 3.
	or 1—portland cement.	½ to 1¼--	4½ to 6.
Subject to extremely heavy loads, violent winds, earthquakes, or severe frost action. Isolated piers.	1—masonry cement* plus 1—portland cement	----------	4½ to 6.
	or 1—portland cement.	0 to ¼---	2¼ to 3.

*ASTM Specification C 91 Type II.

TABLE 25. RECOMMENDED MORTAR MIXES.

4. Stones should be selected and placed so as to make the spaces between stones as small as possible. If large spaces are unavoidable, they must be filled with small stones embedded in mortar.

5. If a stone must be moved after it has been set in bed mortar, it must be lifted out entirely and reset.

6. The thickness of bed joints depends upon the size and type of the stone to be set. The only general rule is that the mortar must be thick enough to fill all the spaces between stones.

7. Head joints are not made by buttering, as with brick, but by slushing with mortar, and if necessary, filling with small stones after three or four stones have been laid on bed joints.

8. There should be a bond stone like those shown in Fig. 2 in every 6 to 10 square feet (.56 to .93 sq. meters) of wall.

JOINTS AND POINTING

There are two classifications for horizontal joints between stones and they are ***bed joints*** and simply ***beds.*** Vertical joints are classified as ***head joints*** or ***builds.***

The joints in rubble masonry are neither constant in direction nor uniform in thickness because they are used to fill the spaces between stones of irregular shape.

The joints in ashlar or cut-stone masonry do not exceed ½ inch (1.3 cm.) in thickness because the stones are accurately dressed to shape. A joint thickness of ¼ inch (6.3 mm.) is commonly used whenever ashlar facing is used and a joint thickness of ⅛ inch (3.2 mm.) is used for interior stonework.

Pointing is whenever the mortar in the horizontal and vertical joints of ashlar masonry is raked out to a depth of about ¾ inch (1.9-cm.). Sometimes a special mortar may be used to make a tighter and more attractive joint. The pointing process should not be performed while the wall is being constructed. This process must be done after the mortar has fully set and the wall has received its full load.

Rubble masonry does not require the pointing process. Therefore the joints are usually considered finished whenever the stones are set. Sometimes the joints of rubble masonry are made flush with the surface of the stones, enabling the worker to run a narrow bead of colored mortar on the wide joints to give the effect of narrow joints. The wide joint is usually the same color as the stone and the narrow joint a contrasting color. (This operation is also carried on after the mortar has set.)

Section 3

Brick Masonry

WHILE THE CHEMICAL and physical properties of individual brick are important, the properties of brick masonry are those with which we are most concerned.

The principal properties or requisities of *brick masonry* are compressive and transverse strengths, resistance to fire, weathering, moisture penetration, heat transmission, and sound transmission. A pleasing appearance is frequently an important consideration, particularly in exposed surfaces.

Chapter 25

Brick

Brick masonry is that type of construction in which units of baked clay or shale of uniform size, small enough to be placed with one hand, are laid in courses with mortar joints to form walls of virtually unlimited length and height. Brick are kiln-baked from various clay and shale mixtures. The chemical and physical characteristics of the ingredients vary considerably—these and the kiln temperatures combine to produce brick in a variety of colors and hardnesses. In some regions, pits are opened and found to yield clay or shale which, when ground and moistened, can be formed and baked into durable brick. In other regions, clays or shales from several pits must be mixed.

The dimensions of a United States standard building brick are 2½ × 3¾ × 8 inches (6.3 × 9.4 × 20 cm.). The actual dimensions of brick may vary a little because of shrinkage during burning.

BRICK TERMINOLOGY

Frequently the worker must cut the brick into various shapes. The more common of these are shown in Fig. 1. They are called half or bat, three-quarter closure, quarter closure, king closure, queen closure, and split. They are used to fill in the spaces at corners and such other places where a full brick will not fit.

The six surfaces of a brick are called the face, the side, the cull, the end, and the beds as shown in Fig. 2.

BRICK CLASSIFICATION

A finished brick structure contains *face* brick (brick placed on the exposed face of the structure) and *back-up* brick (brick

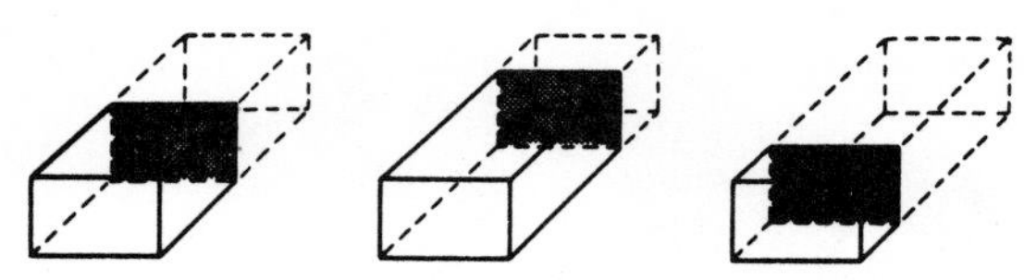

Fig. 1. Nomenclature of common shapes of cut brick.

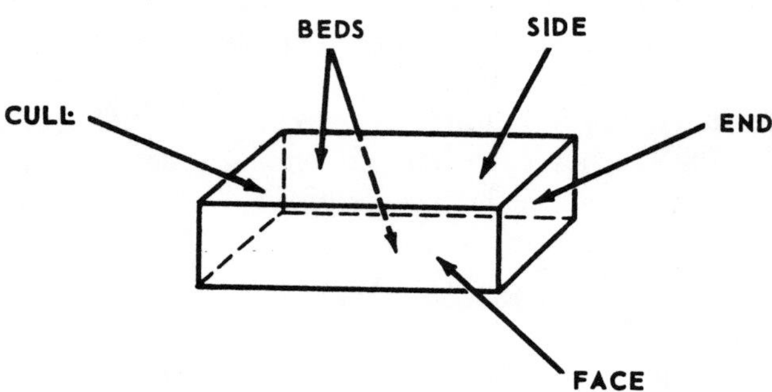

Fig. 2. Names of brick surfaces.

placed behind the face brick). The face brick is often of higher quality than the back-up brick. However, the entire wall may be built of *common* brick. Common brick is brick which is made from pit-run clay, with no attempt at color control and no special surface treatment like glazing or enameling. Most common brick is red.

Although any surface brick is a face brick as distinguished from a back-up brick. The term face brick is also used to distinguish high-quality brick from brick which is of common brick quality or less. Applying this criterion, face brick is more uniform in color than common brick, and it may be obtained in a variety of colors as well. It may be specifically finished on the surface, and in any case it has a better surface appearance than common brick. It may also be more durable as a result of the use of select clay and other materials, or as a result of special manufacturing methods.

Back-up brick may consist of brick which is inferior in quality even to common brick. Brick which has been underburned or overburned, or brick made with inferior clay or by inferior methods, is often used for back-up brick.

Still another type of classification divides brick into grades in accordance with the probable climatic conditions to which it is to be exposed.

Grade SW is brick designed to withstand exposure to below-freezing temperatures in a moist climate like that found in the northern regions of the United States.

Grade MW is brick designed to withstand exposure to below-freezing temperatures in a drier climate than that mentioned in the previous paragraph.

Grade NW is brick primarily intended for interior or back-up brick. It may be used exposed, however, in regions where no frost action occurs, or in regions where frost action occurs but the annual rainfall is less than 15 inches (37.5 cm.).

TYPES OF BRICK

There are many types of brick. Some are different in formation and composition while others vary according to their use. Some commonly used types of brick are as follows:

Building brick, formerly called common brick, is made of ordinary clays or shales and burned in the usual manner in the kilns. These bricks do not have special scorings or markings, and are not produced in any special color or surface texture. Building brick is also known as hard and kiln run brick. It is used generally for the backing courses in solid or cavity brick walls. The harder and more durable kinds are preferred for this purpose.

Face brick are used in the exposed face of a wall and are higher quality units then back-up brick. They have better durability and appearance. The more common colors of face brick are various shades of brown, red, gray, yellow, and white.

When bricks are overburned in the kilns, they are called *clinker* brick. This type of brick is usually hard and durable and may be irregular in shape. Rough hard brick corresponds to the clinker classification.

The dry press process is used to make this class of brick, which has regular smooth faces, sharp edges, and perfectly square corners. Ordinarily, all *press* brick are used as face brick.

Glazed brick has one surface of each brick glazed in white or other color. The ceramic glazing consists of mineral ingredients which fuse together in a glass-like coating during burning. This type of brick is particularly suited for walls or partitions in hospitals, dairies, laboratories, or other buildings where cleanliness and ease of cleaning is necessary.

Fire brick is made of a special type of fire clay which will withstand the high temperatures of fireplaces, boilers, and similar usages without cracking or decomposing. Fire brick is generally larger than regular structural brick and is often hand molded.

Cored brick are brick made with two rows of five holes extending through their beds to reduce weight. There is no significant difference in strength between the strength of walls constructed with cored brick and those constructed with solid brick. Resistance to moisture penetration is about the same for both types of walls. The most easily available brick that will meet requirements should be used whether the brick is cored or solid.

Sand-lime brick are made from a lean mixture of slaked lime and fine silicious sand molded under mechanical pressure and hardened under steam pressure.

Chapter 26

Bricklaying Tools and Equipment

The tools and equipment explained for various operations in Chap. 21, Masonry Tools and Equipment, may also be used when working with brick, concrete block, structural clay tile, and stone.

TOOLS

The mason's tools include trowels, brick hammer, bolster, and jointer. (*See* Chap. 21, Masonry Tools and Equipment, Fig. 1.)

Trowels. The mason's *trowel* may be a *brick* (Fig. 1), a *buttering*, or a *pointing* trowel (Fig. 2). The trowel is used for mixing, placing, and spreading mortar. The brick trowel is the largest and the one most generally used (Fig. 1). The buttering trowel is shorter, with a blunt point. It is used on very small joints where its shape is more convenient than the larger brick trowel. It derives its name from the fact that it is used for buttering or spreading the mortar on the brick singly as it is laid. The pointing trowel is much smaller than either of the other two, and is used to point up or shape the joints.

Trowel practice. When laying up a wall, use the fewest possible motions in order to increase efficiency and conserve energy. Before starting the actual laying of brick, the inexperienced bricklayer can quickly acquire the technique of efficiently handling the trowel by proceeding as follows.

Secure a used, worn, broken-in trowel. Grasp the handle of the trowel between the thumb and first finger, with the thumb resting on top and well forward toward the end of the handle. The second, third, and fourth fingers should be bent around the handle (not rigidly) to assist in stabilizing the tool in the hand.

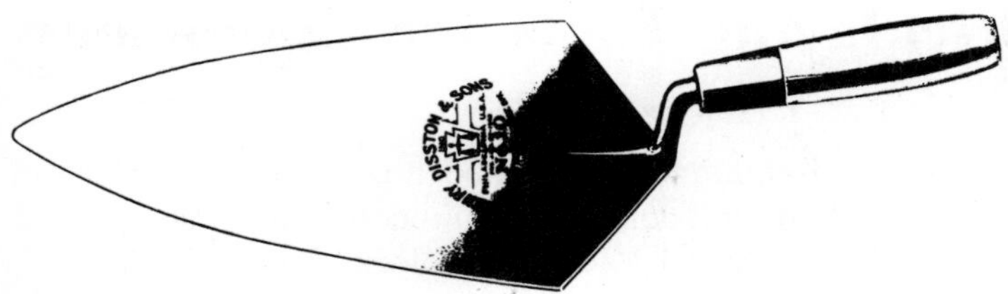

Fig. 1. Brick trowel.

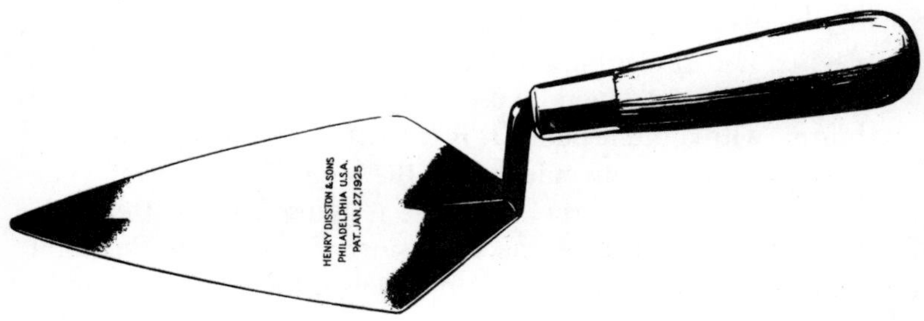

Fig. 2. Pointing trowel.

The muscles of the hand and forearm must remain relaxed so that the trowel may be manipulated freely and properly. Free movement of the wrist is essential in acquiring the knack of handling the trowel.

Manipulate the trowel in the mortar by cutting and working the mortar around on the mortarboard. Care should be taken not to splash the mortar onto the floor, clothing, or body. Practice the proper method of handling the trowel in picking up a quantity of mortar. This procedure is known as *cupping and picking up the mortar.* Practice this procedure until the mortar can be cupped and picked up without effort. Lay four or five bricks end to end in a straight line upon the floor about 2 feet (60 cm.) away from the board. Keep the brick pile and mortar at least 2 feet (60 cm.) away from the wall at all times. Cup and pick up a small amount of mortar and spread it upon the brick laid out on the floor. When spreading mortar, keep the elbow of the trowel hand away from the body, as this posture permits unrestricted freedom of action. Using the trowel, pick up the mortar from the brick and return it to the mortarboard. Use the trowel to work the mortar again. Cup and pick up another small quantity of mortar (enough to cover or bed two bricks) and spread it on the brick. Pick up the mortar and return it to the mortarboard.

Repeat this operation until you master the knack of handling the trowel so that you pick up the correct quantity of mortar to spread the two bricks with one sweep of the trowel and with little or no mortar thrown over the edge of the bricks. Continue repeating this operation, picking up enough mortar to spread three bricks, and finally four bricks. This is the customary amount of mortar to be spread at a time. Proper spreading of mortar makes the difference between good and poor workmanship.

Cup, pick up, and spread mortar over the four bricks. The mortar that extends on either side of the bricks should be trimmed off evenly and neatly. When trimming mortar that overhangs the wall, hold the blade of the trowel horizontally so that the mortar will not fall from the trowel to the floor or scaffold. Mortar trimmed from the wall may be placed upon the newly spread bed joint or returned to the mortarboard. Make a shallow furrow in the middle of the bed joint with the point of the trowel. The freshly spread mortar is furrowed to provide more equal distribution of the mortar from the next bed joint. Deeply furrowed bed joints must be avoided since they result in leaky masonry walls. A shallow furrow in the bed joint provides a space for a little movement of the mortar whereby it adjusts itself to an even and uniform bedding for the brick placed upon it.

Keep practicing the handling of the trowel by cupping and picking up the mortar, and spreading, trimming, and furrowing the mortar joint, until you can manipulate the trowel with reasonable speed and proficiency.

Brick hammer. The *brick hammer* (Chap. 21, Fig. 1) is a combination hammer and pick, and is used for breaking brick, tapping brick into the beds where necessary, and for chipping and rough-cutting.

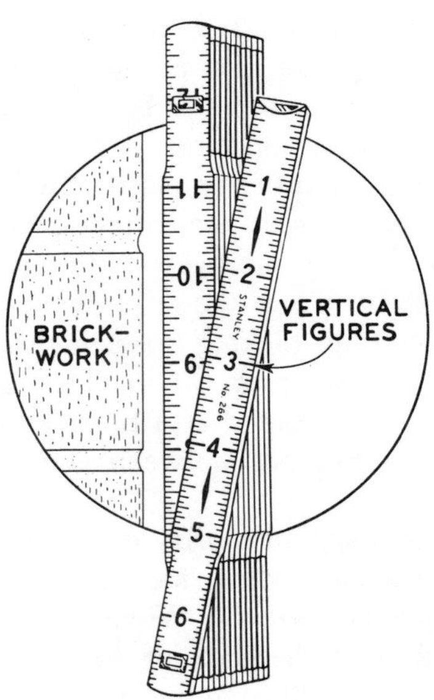

Fig. 3. Zig-zag rule for masonry work.

Bolster. For smooth cutting the *bolster* [also called a *brickcutting chisel* or *brick set* (Chap. 21, Fig. 1)] is used. Breaking into bats and closures is done with the chisel peen on the *mason's hammer* shown in Chap. 21, Fig. 1.

EQUIPMENT

Equipment used by the bricklayer are levels made of either wood or metal, a plumb line, a zigzag rule with vertical figures (*see* Fig. 3), a mortar box, a mortarboard, and carpenter's or framing squares. (*See* Chap. 21, Figs. 2, 3, 4, 5, and 6; Chap. 6, Concrete Equipment and Tools; Chap. 7, Forms and Form Making, section on Tools and Equipment; Chap. 21, Masonry Tools and Equipment; and Chap. 32, Stucco Materials and Tools.)

Chapter 27

Scaffolding

As the working level on a structure rises above the reach of workers standing on the ground, temporary elevated platforms called *scaffolds* are erected to support the craftsmen, their tools, and materials.

There are several types of wood scaffolds in use today, but they are rapidly being replaced by the ready-made steel bracket type. Of the wood type scaffolds in use, there is the one which is suspended from above and called a swinging scaffold, whereas the one supported below is called a pole scaffold. Now, let us take a look at the construction of the various scaffolds that you may use from time to time.

SPECIFICATIONS FOR SCAFFOLD MEMBERS

The poles on a job-built pole scaffold should not exceed 40 feet (13 meters) in height. If higher poles than this are required, the scaffolding must be specially designed.

For a light-duty (not over 25 pounds per square foot or 120.7 kilos per sq. meter) scaffold, either single-pole or double-pole, the minimum lumber dimensions are as follows:

Poles:	24 feet (7 meters) or less; 2 × 4 (5 × 10 cm.); 24 to 40 feet (7 to 12 meters); 2 × 6 (5 × 15 cm.)
Putlogs:	2 × 6 (5 × 15 cm.) on edge
Ledgers:	2 × 6 (5 × 15 cm.)
Braces:	1 × 4 (2.5 × 10 cm.)
Planking:	2 × 10 (5 × 25 cm.)
Guardrails:	2 × 4 (5 × 10 cm.)

For a heavy-duty (25 to 75 pounds per sq. ft. or 122 to 366 kgs. per sq. meter) single-pole scaffold the minimum dimensions are as follows:

Poles:	24 feet (7 meters) or less, 2 × 6 (5 × 15 cm.); 24 to 40 feet (7 to 12 meters), doubled 2 × 4 (5 × 10 cm.)
Putlogs:	doubled 2 × 4 (5 × 10 cm.) or 2 × 8 (5 × 20 cm.) on edge
Ledgers:	2 × 8 (5 × 20 cm.)
Braces:	1 × 6 (2.5 × 15 cm.)
Planking:	2 × 10 (5 × 25 cm.)
Guardrails:	2 × 4 (5 × 10 cm.)

For a heavy-duty double-pole scaffold the minimum lumber dimensions are as follows:

Poles:	24 feet (7 meters) or less, 2 × 6 (5 × 15 cm.); 24 to 40 feet (7 to 12 meters); for load from 25 to 50 pounds per square foot (122 to 244 kgs. per sq. meter) double 2 × 4 (5 × 10 cm.) for load from 50 to 75 pounds per square foot (122 to 366 kgs. per sq. meter), double 2 × 6 (5 × 15 cm.)
Putlogs:	2 × 8 (5 × 20 cm.) on edge
Ledgers:	2 × 8 (5 × 20 cm.)
Braces:	1 × 6 (2.5 × 15 cm.)
Planking:	2 × 10 (5 × 20 cm.)
Guardrails:	2 × 6 (5 × 15 cm.)

The longitudinal maximum pole spacing for a light-duty scaffold is 7 feet 6 inches (2.3 meters). For a heavy-duty scaffold it is 7 feet (2.1 meters).

The transverse maximum pole spacing for a light- or heavy-duty independent-pole scaffold with poles up to 24 feet (7 meters) is 6 feet 6 inches (2 meters). For a light-duty independent-pole scaffold with poles 24 to 40 feet (7 to 12 meters) the transverse maximum pole spacing is 7 feet (2.1 meters). For a heavy-duty independent-pole scaffold with poles 24 to 40 feet (7 to 12 meters) the transverse maximum spacing is 10 feet (3 meters).

For a single-pole light- or heavy-duty scaffold the pole spacing from the wall should be from 3 to 5 feet (.9 to 1.5 meters).

For a light-duty scaffold the maximum ledger vertical spacing is 7 feet (2.1 meters). For a heavy-duty scaffold the maximum ledger vertical spacing is 4 feet 6 inches (1.3 meters).

SCAFFOLD CONSTRUCTION REQUIREMENTS

Construction requirements for *pole scaffolds* are as follows:

1. All poles must be set up perfectly plumb.
2. The lower ends of poles must not bear directly on a natural earth surface. If the surface is earth, a board footing 2-inches (5-cm.) thick by from 6- to 12-inches (15- to 30-cm.) wide (depending on the softness of the earth) must be placed under the poles.
3. If poles must be spliced, splice plates must not be less than 4 feet (1.2 meters) long, not less than the width of the pole, and each pair of plates must have a combined thickness not less than the thickness of the pole. Adjacent poles must not be spliced at the same level.
4. A ledger must be long enough to extend over two pole spaces, and it must overlap the poles at the ends by at least 4 inches (10 cm.). Ledgers must be spliced by overlapping and nailing *at poles*—never between poles. If platform planks are raised as work progresses upward, the ledgers and putlogs on which the planks previously rested must be left in place to brace and stiffen the poles. For a heavy-duty scaffold, ledgers must be supported by cleats nailed or bolted to the poles, as well as by being themselves nailed to the poles.
5. A single putlog must be set with the longer section dimension vertical, and putlogs must be long enough to overlap the poles by at least 3 inches (7.5 cm.). They should be both face nailed to the poles and toenailed to the ledgers. When the inner end of the putlog butts against the wall (as it does in a single-pole scaffold), it must be supported by a 2 × 6 (5 × 15

cm.) bearing block not less than 12 inches (30 cm.) long, notched out the width of the putlog and securely nailed to the wall. The inner end of the putlog should be nailed to both the bearing block and the wall. If the inner end of a putlog is located in a window opening, it must be supported on a stout plank nailed to a building stud and must rest on a cleat of the same thickness as the putlog, nailed to the stud.

6. A platform plank must never be less than 2 inches (5 cm.) thick. Edges of planks should be close enough together to prevent tools or materials from falling through the opening. A plank must be long enough to extend over three putlogs, with an overlap of at least 6 inches (15 cm.), but not more than 12 inches (30 cm.).

SWINGING SCAFFOLDS

The simplest type of *swinging scaffold* is one which consists simply of a stout plank (minimum thickness 2 inches or 5 cm.) with a couple of transverse *horns* nailed or bolted to the under side near the ends. The stage hangs from a couple of lines (minimum size 2 inches or 5 cm.) which lead up and over or through some supporting device (such as a pair of shackles secured to outriggers at the roof line) and back to the stage.

Figure 1 shows the method of bending a bowline to a stage by means of a *scaffold hitch.* A stage provides a convenient means for working down from upward (painting down a wall from roof line to ground level), but since you cannot hoist yourself aloft on a stage, it is no good for working from down upward.

When the rig shown in Fig. 2 is hooked to the tackles, you can move up or down at will, simply by heaving in or slacking out on the tackles. The two projecting timbers to which the tackles will be attached are called *outriggers.*

Figure 3 shows you a single-pole wood scaffold. Study the illustration closely until you have learned the names of the various parts. Figure 4 shows you a double-pole wood scaffold, and Fig. 5 shows you a double-pole steel scaffold being constructed. The double-pole scaffold (steel or wood) which is completely independent of the main structure, is used for the erection of

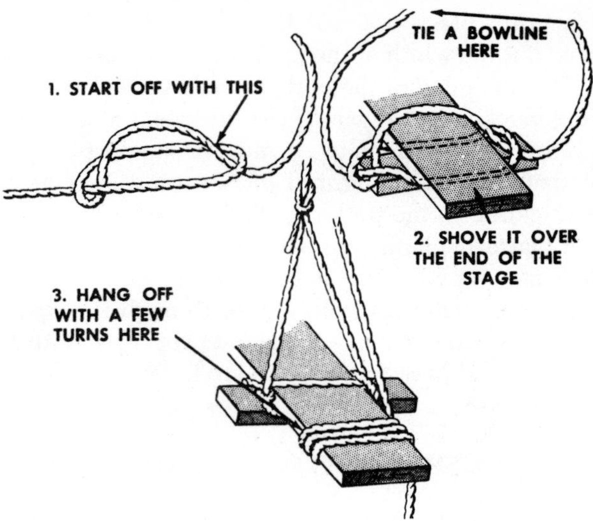

Fig. 1. Making a scaffold hitch.

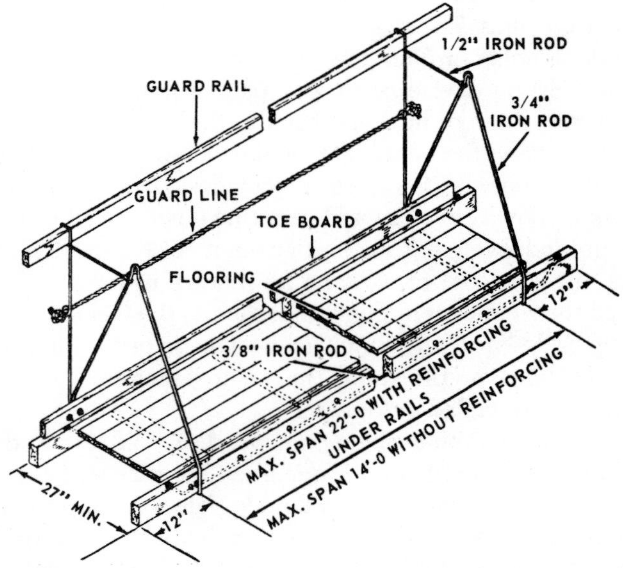

Fig. 2. Swinging scaffold.

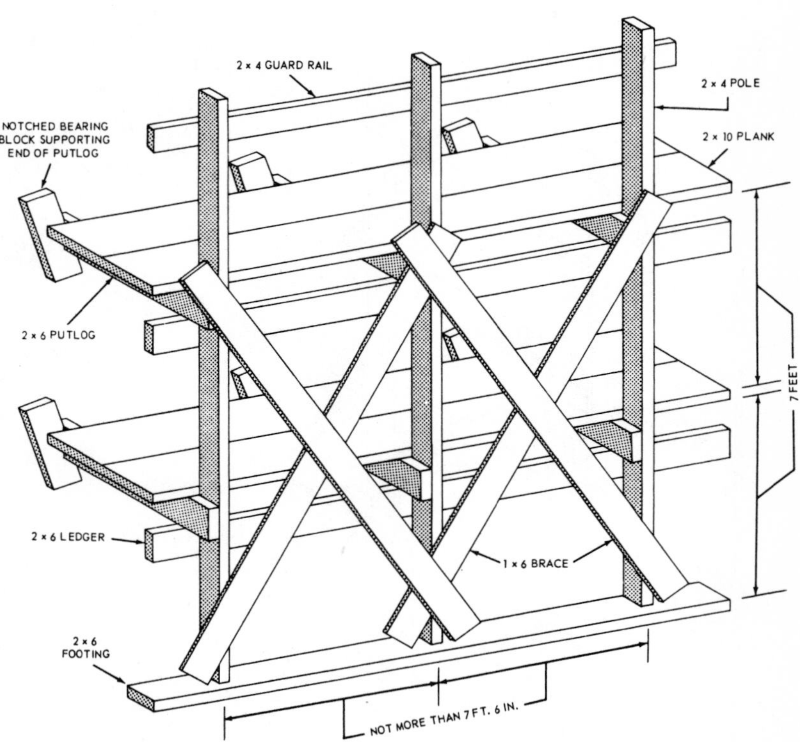

Fig. 3. Single-pole scaffold.

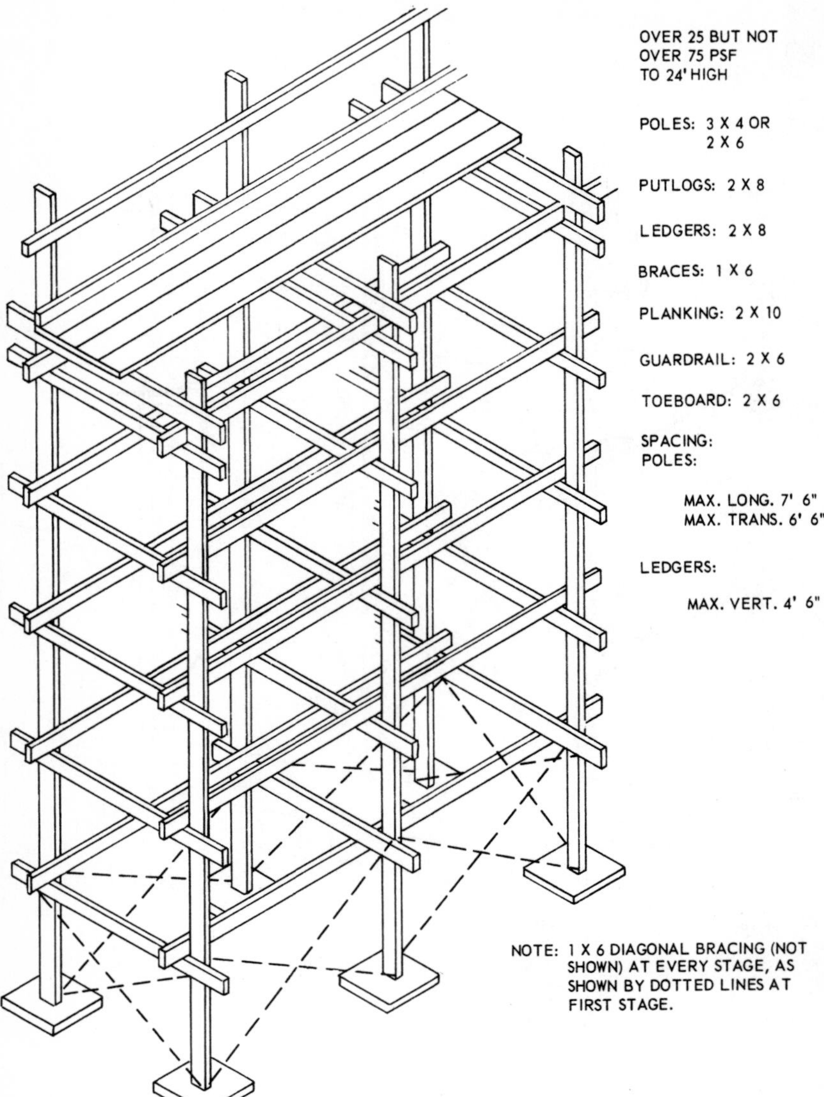

OVER 25 BUT NOT
OVER 75 PSF
TO 24' HIGH
POLES: 3 X 4 OR
2 X 6
PUTLOGS: 2 X 8
LEDGERS: 2 X 8
BRACES: 1 X 6
PLANKING: 2 X 10
GUARDRAIL: 2 X 6
TOEBOARD: 2 X 6
SPACING:
POLES:
MAX. LONG. 7' 6"
MAX. TRANS. 6' 6"
LEDGERS:
MAX. VERT. 4' 6"
NOTE: 1 X 6 DIAGONAL BRACING (NOT
SHOWN) AT EVERY STAGE, AS
SHOWN BY DOTTED LINES AT
FIRST STAGE.

Fig. 4. Heavy-duty independent-pole scaffold. (Diagonal bracing not shown.)

Fig. 5. Assembling prefabricated independent scaffolding.

sheathing, siding, and the like. (A light-duty scaffold, designed for loads not more than 25 pounds per square foot (122 kgs. per sq. meter), is used by masons, builders, painters, and others using relatively light materials. A heavy-duty scaffold designed for loads from 25 to 75 pounds per square foot (122 to 366 kgs. per sq. meter) is used by masons and other workers in heavy materials.) Several types of patent independent scaffolding are available for simple and rapid erection as shown in Fig. 5. The scaffold uprights are braced with diagonal members as shown in Fig. 6, and the working level is covered with a platform of planks. All bracing must form triangles and the base of each column requires adequate footing plates for bearing area on the ground. The patented steel scaffolding is usually erected by placing the two uprights on the ground and inserting the diagonal members. The diagonal members have end fittings which permit rapid locking position. The first tier is set on steel bases on the ground. A second tier is placed in the same manner on the first tier with the bottom of each upright locked to the top of the lower tier. A third and fourth upright can be placed on the ground level and locked to the first set with diagonal bracing. The scaffolding should be tied in to the main structure.

NAILING POLE SCAFFOLDS

The safety of a wood scaffold (or of any wood structure) depends on the nails as well as on the timbers selected. Nails smaller than 8d common should not be used in scaffolds. (*See* Fig. 7.) All nails should be driven full length, and in directions which will ensure that the pull is across, not along, the length of the nail. Nails should be placed not less than half their lengths from the ends of boards, and not less than one-quarter their lengths from the edges of boards.

FRAMED PORTABLE-SUPPORTED SCAFFOLD

An excellent scaffold can be constructed to provide three elevated platforms in order to expedite the erection of 40- × 100-foot (12- × 30-meter) Quonset huts or similar buildings. (*See* Fig. 8.)

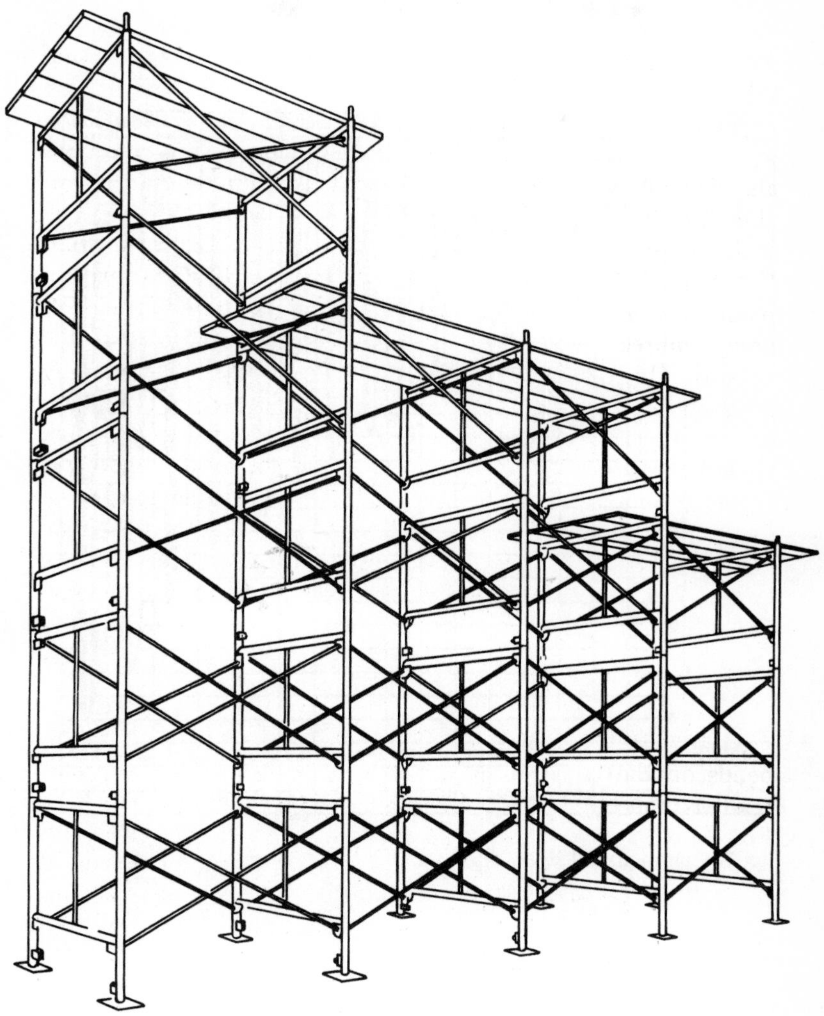

Fig. 6. Prefabricated independent scaffolding.

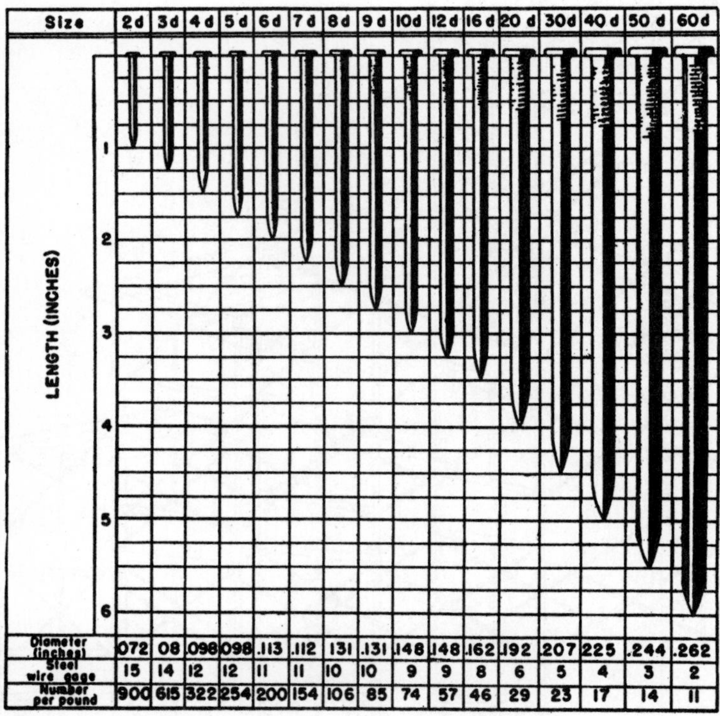

Size	2d	3d	4d	5d	6d	7d	8d	9d	10d	12d	16d	20d	30d	40d	50d	60d
Diameter (inches)	072	08	.098	098	.113	.112	131	.131	148	148	.162	192	.207	225	.244	.262
Steel wire gage	15	14	12	12	11	11	10	10	9	9	8	6	5	4	3	2
Number per pound	900	615	322	254	200	154	106	85	74	57	46	29	23	17	14	11

Fig. 7. Common nail sizes.

In order to make the framed portable-supported scaffold, a rectangular frame is constructed with four skids, 12 feet long (3.7 meters). Make the skids of 2- × 8-inch (5- × 20-cm.) material and fasten them to two foundation pieces of 2- × 6-inch (5- × 15-cm.) material, 24 feet (7.3 meters) in length. The four skids (Fig. 8, B) are fastened to the foundation pieces (A) so that their ends extend 1 foot (30 cm.) on each side of the foundation pieces. This increases the stability of the scaffolding. The two center skids are spaced 12 feet (3.7 meters) apart, and the two end skids, 6 feet (1.8 meters) from the center skids.

Four 4- × 4- inch (10- × 10-cm.) uprights with diagonal cross braces are then nailed to the foundation pieces at their intersection with the center skids. These uprights should be 16 feet (4.8 meters) long. To make these uprights even more secure use 90-degree angle irons and lag screws to fasten them to the foundation. The diagonal braces should be of 1- × 4-inch (2.5- × 10-cm.) or 1- × 6-inch (2.5- × 15-cm.) material. Four outriggers or supports are secured to the uprights to which planking of 2- × 12-inch (5- × 30-cm.) material is made fast to form the horizontal elevated deck.

Four 4- × 4-inch (10- × 10-cm.) uprights (two on each side) with diagonal braces are then nailed to the foundation pieces at their intersection with the end skids. These uprights should be

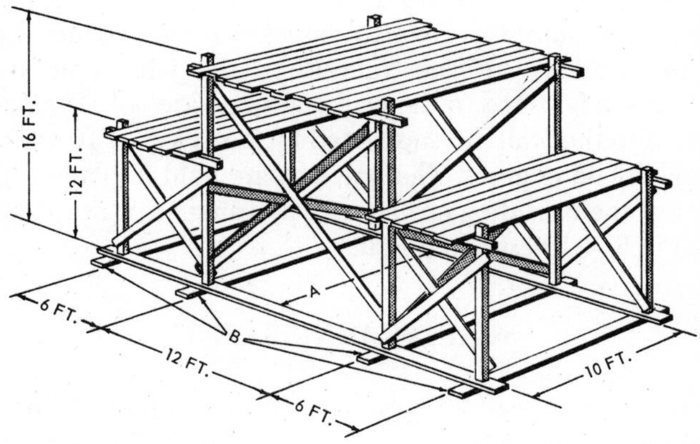

Fig. 8

cut 12 feet (3.7 meters) in length and may be secured by fastening them to the foundation pieces with 90-degree angle irons and lag screws. The diagonal braces should be of 1- × 4-inch (2.5- × 10-cm.) or 1- × 6-inch (2.5- × 15-cm.) material. The two end platforms are constructed in the same manner as the center platform. All planking must be securely nailed to the horizontal outriggers or supports.

BRACKET SCAFFOLDING

Bracket scaffolding has certain advantages over the ones previously discussed. This type of scaffolding is easier to erect, involves less labor, and requires less material. It can be easily constructed of wood, and in some areas is readily available in prefabricated steel.

Caution is a must when fastening steel bracket scaffolding in place with nails, because the nails must be driven as not to break the heads. Nails with broken heads are definitely unsafe for scaffolds. Some brackets are even fastened to the wall with spikes while others may be hooked around a stud. The latter type of bracket is safe, but requires the making of a hole in the sheathing for withdrawal of the bracket. To fasten another type steel bracket you need to bore a hole in a 2- × 4-inch (5- × 10-cm.) crosspiece nailed to the inside of a stud.

The most simple, yet sturdy, bracket is the wooden bracket and the worker can construct it on the job. Some wooden brackets are fastened to the wall and some are not. The ones not fastened to the wall are supported by 2 × 4's (5 × 10 cm.) set at an angle of 45 degrees. The brackets are held in place and kept from tipping or sliding on the wall by using cross braces of 1- × 6-inch (2.5 × 15-cm.) material.

SCAFFOLDING SAFETY

The following scaffolding safety precautions must be observed by all men working on scaffolds, or tending other men who are working on the scaffolds.

Standard scaffolds suitable to the work on hand must be provided and used.

All scaffolds must be maintained in a safe condition, and a scaffold must not be altered or disturbed while in use. Do *not* use damaged or weakened scaffolds.

Structural members supporting lines and tackles and other scaffold equipment must be inspected daily before work on scaffolding is started.

When men working on a scaffold are directly below other men working above, the men below must be sheltered against possible falling objects by a protective covering. The men below *must* wear protective headgear.

If the frequent presence of personnel directly under a scaffold is unavoidable, a protective covering should be set up under the scaffold. A passageway or thoroughfare under a scaffold must have both overhead and side protection.

Access to scaffolds must be by standard stairs or fixed ladders only.

The erection, alteration, and dismantling of scaffolds must be done carefully.

When scaffolding is being dismantled it should be cleaned, and ready for storage or use. Scaffolding that is not ready for use should never be stored.

Work on scaffolds should be secured during storms or high winds, or when scaffolds are covered with ice or snow.

Unstable objects, such as barrels, boxes, loose brick, or building blocks, must not be used to support scaffold planking.

No scaffold may be used for the storage of materials in excess of those currently required for the job.

Tools not in immediate use on scaffolds must be stowed in containers, to prevent tools left adrift from being knocked off. Tool containers must be lashed or otherwise secured to the scaffolds.

Scaffolds must be kept clear of accumulations of tools, equipment, materials, and rubbish.

If part of a scaffold must be used as a loading or landing stage for materials, the scaffold must be additionally braced and reinforced at and around the landing stage area.

Do *not* throw objects to scaffolds or drop them from scaffolds. Hand lines must be used for raising or lowering objects which cannot be passed hand-to-hand.

A standard guardrail and toeboard should be provided on the open side of the platform on all single-pole and independent-pole scaffolds.

If the space between the scaffold and building is more than 18 inches (45.7 cm.), a standard guardrail should be erected on the building side.

No person should remain on the rolling scaffold while it is being moved.

When a light-duty portable scaffold is formed of planks supported or hitched on trestle ladders, the base of the ladder should be secured against opening up to the full spread before laying on the planks.

A scaffold must *never* be overloaded. Scaffolds are built in the following strength categories (1) extra-heavy-duty, (2) heavy-duty, (3) light-duty, and (4) an intermediate category between light and heavy, for scaffolds used by stucco workers and by lathers and plasterers. The maximum uniform safe working load per square foot of platform for each of these categories is as follows:

Extra-heavy-duty (stone mason's scaffold) (36.6 kgs. per sq. meter)	75 pounds
Heavy-duty (stone setters and bricklayers) (24.4 kgs. per sq. meter)	50 pounds
Light-duty (carpenter's and miscellaneous) (12.2 kgs. per sq. meter)	25 pounds
Intermediate (stucco workers and plasterers) (14.6 kgs. per sq. meter)	30 pounds

To get the load per square foot of platform of a pile of materials on a platform, divide the total weight of the pile by the number of square feet (square meters) of platform it covers.

Chapter 28

Mortar for Brick Masonry

Mortar is used to bond the brick together and unless properly mixed and applied will be the weakest part of brick masonry. Both the strength and resistance to rain penetration of brick masonry walls are dependent to a great degree on the strength of the bond. Water in the mortar is essential to the development of bond and if the mortar contains insufficient water the bond will be weak and spotty. When brick walls leak it is usually through the mortar joints. Irregularities in dimensions and shape of bricks are corrected by the mortar joint.

Mortar should be plastic enough to work with a trowel. The properties of mortar depend largely upon the type of sand used in it. Clean, sharp sand produces excellent mortar. Too much sand in mortar will cause it to segregate, drop off the trowel, and weather poorly.

SELECTION OF MORTAR

The *selection of mortar* for brick construction depends on the use requirements of the structure. *For example,* the recommended mortar for use in laying up interior non-load-bearing partitions would not be satisfactory for foundation walls. In many cases, the builder relies upon a fixed proportion of cement, lime, and sand to provide a satisfactory mortar.

TYPES OF MORTAR

The following *types of mortar* are proportioned on a volume basis.

Type M is 1 part portland cement, ¼ part hydrated lime or lime putty, and 3 parts sand, or 1 part portland cement, 1 part type II masonry cement, and 6 parts sand. This mortar is suitable for general use and is recommended specifically for masonry below grade and in contact with earth, such as foundations, retaining walls, and walks.

Type S is 1 part portland cement, ½ part hydrated lime or lime putty, and 4½ parts sand, or ½ part portland cement, 1 part type II masonry cement, and 4½ parts sand. This mortar is also suitable for general use and is recommended where high resistance to lateral forces is required.

Type N is 1 part portland cement, 1 part hydrated lime or lime putty, and 6 parts sand, or 1 part type II masonry cement and 3 parts sand. This mortar is suitable for general use in exposed masonry above grade and is recommended specifically for exterior walls subjected to severe exposures.

Type O is 1 part portland cement, 2 parts hydrated lime or lime putty, and 9 parts sand, or 1 part type I or type II masonry cement and 3 parts sand. This mortar is recommended for load-bearing walls of solid units where the compressive stresses do not exceed 100 pounds psi (7 kgs. per sq. cm.) and the masonry will not be subjected to freezing and thawing in the presence of excessive moisture.

RESISTANCE TO WEATHERING

The *resistance of masonry walls* to weathering depends almost entirely upon their resistance to water penetration because freezing and thawing action is virtually the only type of weathering that affects brick masonry. With the best workmanship, it is possible to build brick walls that will resist the penetration of rain water during a storm lasting as long as 24 hours accompanied by a 50- to 60-mile-per-hour (80- to 96-kilometers-per-hour) wind. In most construction, it is unreasonable to expect the type of workmanship required to build a wall that will allow no water penetration. It is advisable to provide some means of taking care of moisture after it has penetrated the brick masonry. Properly designed flashing and cavity walls are two ways of handling

Normal wall thickness (inches)	Type of wall	Material	Ultimate fire-resistance period. Incombustible members framed into wall or not framed in members		
			No plaster (hours)	Plaster on one side* (hours)	Plaster on two sides* (hours)
4	Solid	Clay or shale	1¼	1¾	2½
8	Solid	Clay or shale	5	6	7
12	Solid	Clay or shale	10	10	12
8	Hollow rowlock	Clay or shale	2½	3	4
12	Hollow rowlock	Clay or shale	5	6	7
9 to 10	Cavity	Clay or shale	5	6	7
4	Solid	Sand-lime	1¾	2½	3
8	Solid	Sand-lime	7	8	9
12	Solid	Sand-lime	10	10	12

*Not less than ½ inch of 1:3 sanded gypsum plaster is required to develop these ratings.

TABLE 26. FIRE RESISTANCE OF BRICK LOAD-BEARING WALLS LAID WITH PORTLAND CEMENT MORTAR.

moisture that has entered the wall.

Important factors in preventing the entrance of water are tooled mortar joints and caulking around windows and door frames.

The joints between the brick must be solidly filled, especially in the face tier. Slushing or grouting the joints after the brick has been laid does not completely fill them. The mortar joint should be tooled to a concave surface before the mortar has had a chance to set up. In tooling, sufficient force should be used to press the mortar tight against the brick on both sides of the mortar joint.

Mortar joints that are tightly bonded to the brick have been shown to have greater resistance to moisture penetration than joints not tightly bonded to the brick.

FIRE RESISTANCE

Fire-resistance tests conducted upon brick walls laid up with portland-cement-lime mortar have made it possible to give fire-resistance periods for various thicknesses of brick walls. A summary is given in Table 26. The tests were made using the American Society for Testing Materials standard method for conducting fire tests. (*See* Chap. 2, Concrete Ingredients, section on Workability.)

Chapter 29

Bricklaying

Good bricklaying procedure depends on good workmanship and efficiency. Means of obtaining good workmanship are described in this chapter. Efficiency involves doing the work with the fewest possible motions. The mason studies his own operations to determine which motions are unnecessary. Each motion should have a purpose and accomplish a definite result. After learning the fundamentals, every worker develops his own methods for achieving maximum efficiency. The work must be arranged in such a way that the mason is continually supplied with brick and mortar. The scaffolding required must be planned before the work begins. (*See* Chap. 27, Scaffolding.)

GENERAL CHARACTERISTICS OF BRICK MASONRY

Solid brick masonry walls provide very little insulation against heat and cold. A cavity wall or a brick wall backed with hollow clay tile has much better insulating value.

Because brick walls are exceptionally massive, they have good sound-insulating properties. In general, the heavier the wall, the better its sound-insulating value will be. However, there is little difference in sound insulation between a wall more than 12 inches (30 cm.) thick as compared to one 10 to 12 inches (25 to 30 cm.) thick. The expense involved in constructing a thicker wall merely to take advantage of the slight increase is too excessive to be worthwhile. Dividing the wall into two or more layers, as in the case of a cavity wall, will increase its resistance to the transmission of sound from one side of the wall to the other. Brick walls are poor absorbers of sound originating within the walls and reflect much of it back into the structure. Sounds caused by impact, as when the wall is struck with a hammer, will travel a great distance along the wall.

Brick masonry expands and contracts with temperature change. Walls up to a length of 200 feet (61 meters) do not need expansion joints. Longer walls need an expansion joint for every 200 feet (61 meters) of wall. The joint can be made as shown in Fig. 1. A considerable amount of the expansion and contraction is taken up in the wall itself. For this reason, the amount of movement that theoretically takes place does not actually occur.

The resistance of brick to abrasion depends largely upon its compressive strength, related to the degree of burning. Well-burned brick are heavier than under-burned brick.

TYPES OF BONDS

The word bond when used in reference to masonry may have three different meanings.

Structural bond is the method by which individual masonry units are interlocked or tied together to cause the entire assembly to act as a single structural unit. Structural bonding of brick and tile walls may be accomplished in three ways. First, by overlapping (interlocking) the masonry units; second, by the use of metal ties imbedded in connecting joints; and third, by the adhesion of grout to adjacent wythes of masonry.

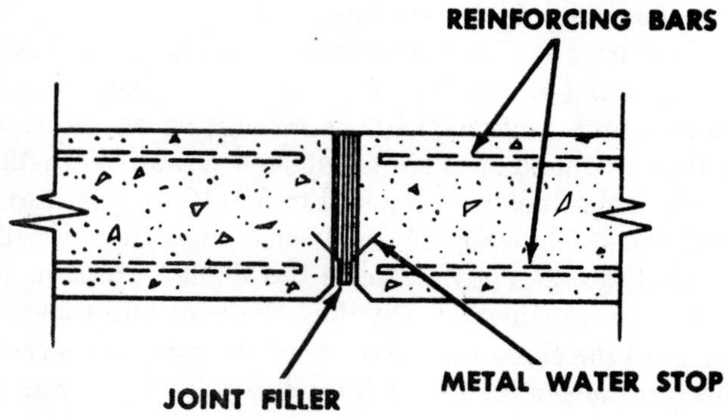

Fig. 1. Expansion joint for wall.

Mortar bond is the adhesion of the joint mortar to the masonry units or to the reinforcing steel.

Pattern bond is the pattern formed by the masonry units and the mortar joints on the face of a wall. The pattern may result from the type of structural bond used or may be purely a decorative one in no way related to the structural bond. There are five basic pattern bonds in common use today as shown in Fig. 2. Running bond, common or American bond, Flemish bond, English bond, and block or stack bond.

Running bond is the simplest of the basic pattern bonds, and consists of all stretchers. Since there are no headers used in this bond, metal ties are usually used. Running bond is used largely in cavity wall construction, veneered walls of brick, and, often, in facing tile walls where the bonding may be accomplished by extra width stretcher tile.

Common or *American bond* is a variation of running bond with a course of full-length headers at regular intervals. These headers provide structural bonding as well as pattern. Header courses usually appear at every fifth, sixth, or seventh course depending on the structural bonding requirements. In laying out any bond pattern it is very important that the corners be started correctly. For common bond a *three-quarter* brick must start each header course at the corner. Common bond may be varied by using a Flemish header course.

Flemish bond is made up of alternate stretchers and headers, with the headers in alternate courses centered over the stretchers in the intervening courses. Where the headers are not used for the structural bonding, they may be obtained by using half brick, called *blind-headers.* There are two methods used in starting the corners. Figure 2 shows the so-called *Dutch* corner, in which a three-quarter brick is used to start each course, and the *English* corner, in which 2-inch (5-cm.) or quarter-brick closures must be used.

English bond is composed of alternate courses of headers and stretchers. The headers are centered on the stretchers and joints between stretchers. The vertical (head) joints between stretchers in all courses line up vertically. Blind headers are used in courses which are not structural bonding courses.

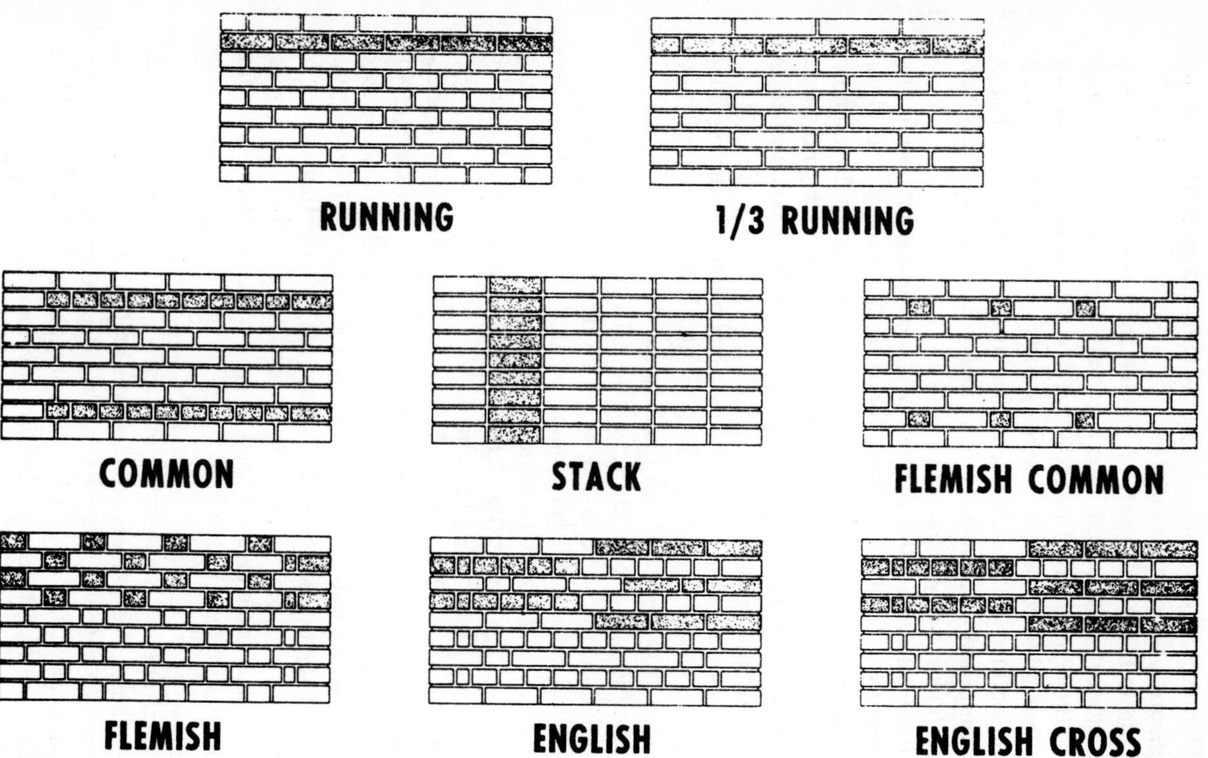

Fig. 2. Various types of brick masonry bond.

Block or *stack bond* is purely a pattern bond. There is no overlapping of the units, all vertical joints being aligned. Usually this pattern is bonded to the backing with rigid steel ties, but when 8-inch (20-cm.) thick stretcher units are available they may be used. In large wall areas and in load-bearing construction it is advisable to reinforce the wall with steel pencil rods placed in the horizontal mortar joints. The vertical alignment requires dimensionally accurate units, or carefully prematched units, for each vertical joint alignment. Variety in pattern may be achieved by numerous combinations and modifications of the basic patterns shown.

English Cross or *Dutch bond* is a variation of English bond and differs only in that vertical joints between the stretchers in alternate courses do not line up vertically. These joints center on the stretchers themselves in the courses above and below.

MASONRY TERMS

Specific terms are used to describe the various positions of masonry units and mortar joints in a wall in Fig. 3. (*See* Appendix 1, Glossary of Terms.)

METAL TIES

Metal ties can be used to tie the brick on the outside face of the wall to the backing courses. These are used when no header courses are installed. They are not as satisfactory as header courses. Typical metal ties are shown in Fig. 4.

FLASHING

Flashing is installed in masonry construction to divert moisture, which may enter the masonry at vulnerable spots, to the outside. Flashing should be provided under horizontal masonry surfaces such as sills and copings, at intersections of masonry walls with horizontal surfaces such as roof and parapet or roof and chimney, over heads of openings such as door and windows,

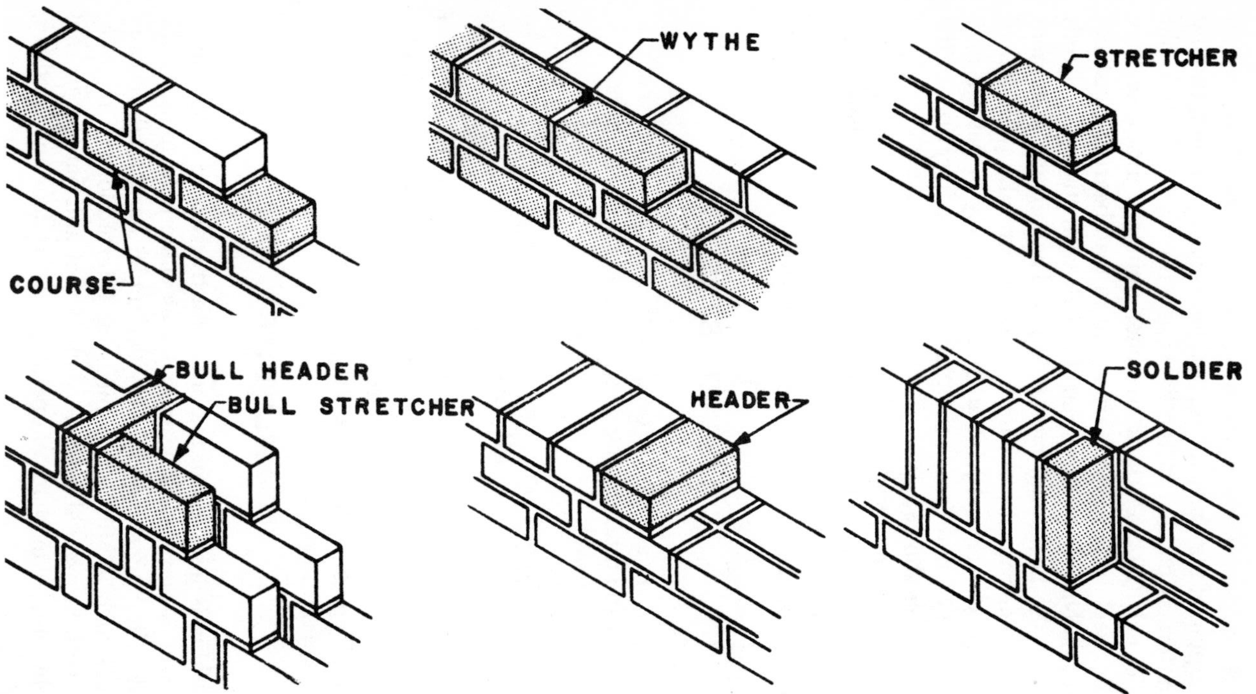

Fig. 3. Masonry units and mortar joints.

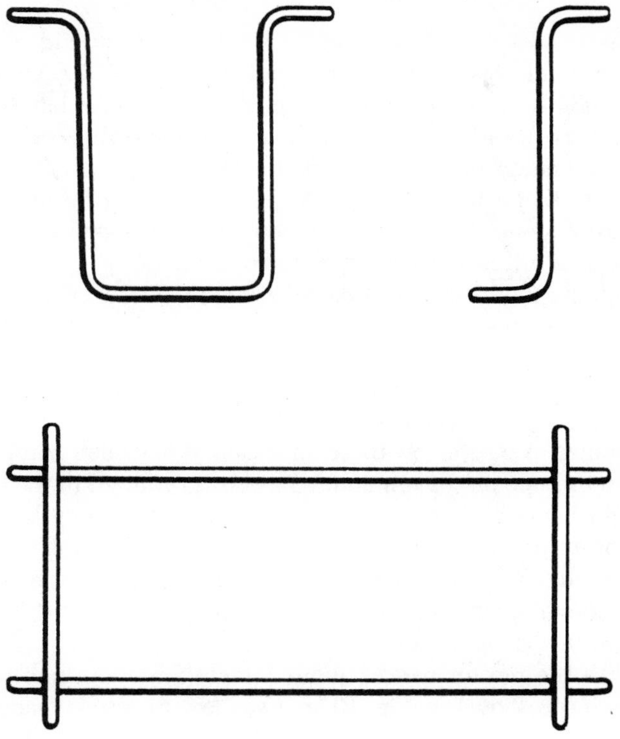

Fig. 4. Metal ties.

and frequently at floor lines, depending on the type of construction. To be most effective the flashing should extend through the outer face of the wall and be turned down to form a drop. Weep holes should be provided at intervals of 18 inches to 2 feet (45 to 60 cm.) to permit the water which accumulates on the flashing to drain to the outside. If because of appearance it is necessary to stop the flashing back of the face of the wall, weep holes are even more important than when the flashing extends through the wall. Concealed flashings with tooled mortar joints will frequently retain water in the wall for long periods, and by concentrating moisture at one spot may do more harm than good.

MORTAR JOINTS AND POINTING

The trowel should be held in a firm position (Fig. 5). The thumb should rest on top of the handle and should not encircle it. A right-handed mason picks up mortar with the left edge of the trowel from the outside of the pile (Fig. 6). He picks up the correct amount to spread for one to five bricks, according to the wall space and his skill. A pickup for one brick forms a small windrow along the left edge of the trowel. A pickup for five bricks is a full load for a large trowel (Fig. 7).

Holding the trowel with its left edge directly over the centerline of the previous course, the mason tilts the trowel slightly and moves it to the right, dropping a windrow of mortar along the wall until the trowel is empty, as shown in Figs. 8 and 9. In some instances mortar will be left on the trowel when the spreading of mortar on the course below has been completed. When this occurs the remaining mortar is returned to the board. A right-handed mason works from left to right along the wall.

Mortar projecting beyond the wall line is cut off with the trowel edge (Fig. 10, 1) and thrown back on the mortar board, but enough is retained to *butter* the left end of the first brick to be laid in the fresh mortar.

With the mortar spread about 1 inch (2.5 cm.) thick for the bed joint as shown in Fig. 10, 1, a shallow furrow is made (Fig. 10, 2) and the brick pushed into the mortar (Fig. 10, 3). If the furrow is too deep, there will be a gap left between the mortar and the brick bedded in the mortar. This gap will reduce the resistance of the wall to water penetration. The mortar for a bed joint should not be spread out too far in advance of the laying. A distance of four or five bricks is advisable. Mortar that has been spread out too far will dry out before the brick is bedded in it. This results in a poor bond as can be seen in Fig. 11. The mortar must be soft and plastic so that the brick can be easily bedded in it.

The next step after the bed joint mortar has been spread is the laying of the brick. The brick to be laid is picked up, as shown in Fig. 12, with the thumb on one side of the brick and the fingers on the other. As much mortar as will stick is placed on the end of

Fig. 5. One way to hold a trowel.

Fig. 6. Proper way to pick up mortar.

Fig. 7. Trowel full of mortar.

Fig. 8. Mortar thrown on brick.

Fig. 9. Mortar spread for a distance of three to five brick.

Fig. 10. Bed joint and furrow.

Fig. 11. A poorly bonded brick.

Fig. 12. Proper way to hold a brick.

the brick. The brick should then be pushed into place so that excess mortar squeezes out at the head joint and at the sides of the wall as indicated in Fig. 13. The head joint must be completely filled with mortar. This can be done only by placing plenty of mortar on the end of the brick. After the brick is bedded, the excess mortar is cut off and used for the next end joint. Surplus mortar should be thrown to the back of the mortar board for retempering if necessary. The proper position of the brick is determined by the use of a cord which can be seen in Fig. 10, 1.

The method of inserting a brick in a space left in a wall is shown in Fig. 14. A thick bed of mortar is spread (Fig. 14, 1) and the brick shoved into this deep bed of mortar (Fig. 14, 2) until it squeezes out at the top of the joint at the face tier, and at the header joint (Fig. 14, 3) so that the joints are full of mortar at every point.

The position of a cross joint is illustrated in Fig. 15. These joints must be completely filled with mortar. The mortar for the bed joint should be spread several brick widths in advance. The mortar is spread over the entire side of the header brick before it is placed in the wall (Fig. 15, 1). The brick is then shoved into place so that the mortar is forced out at the top of the joint and the excess mortar cut off as shown in Fig. 15, 2.

Figure 16 shows the method of laying a closure brick in a header course. Before laying the closure brick, plenty of mortar

Fig. 13. Head joint in a stretcher course.

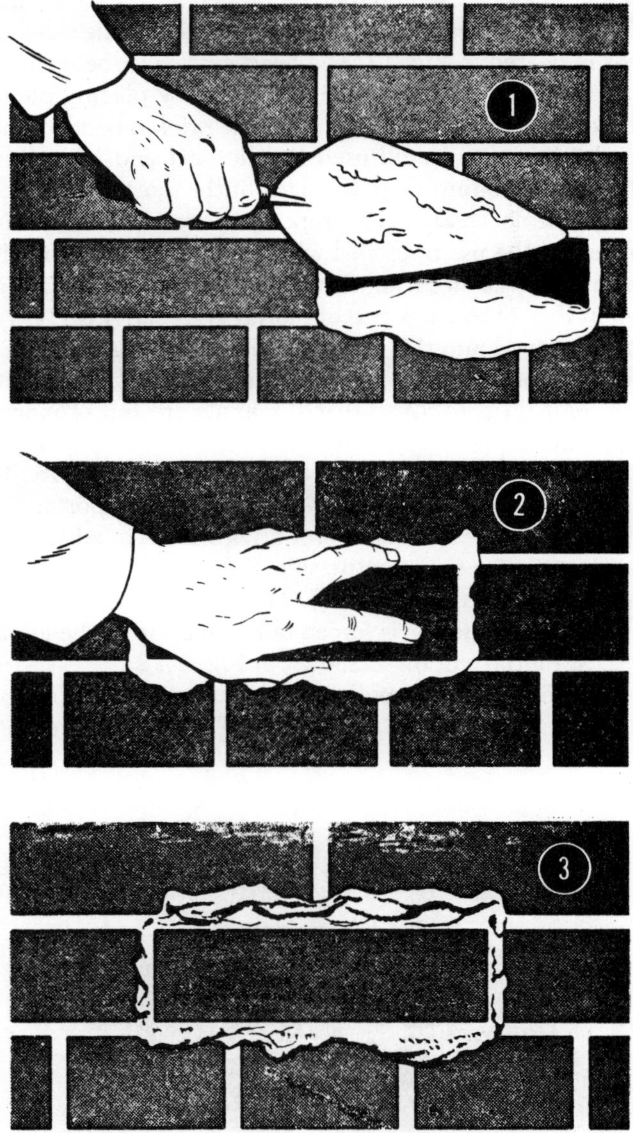

Fig. 14. Laying inside brick.

Fig. 15. Making cross joints in header courses.

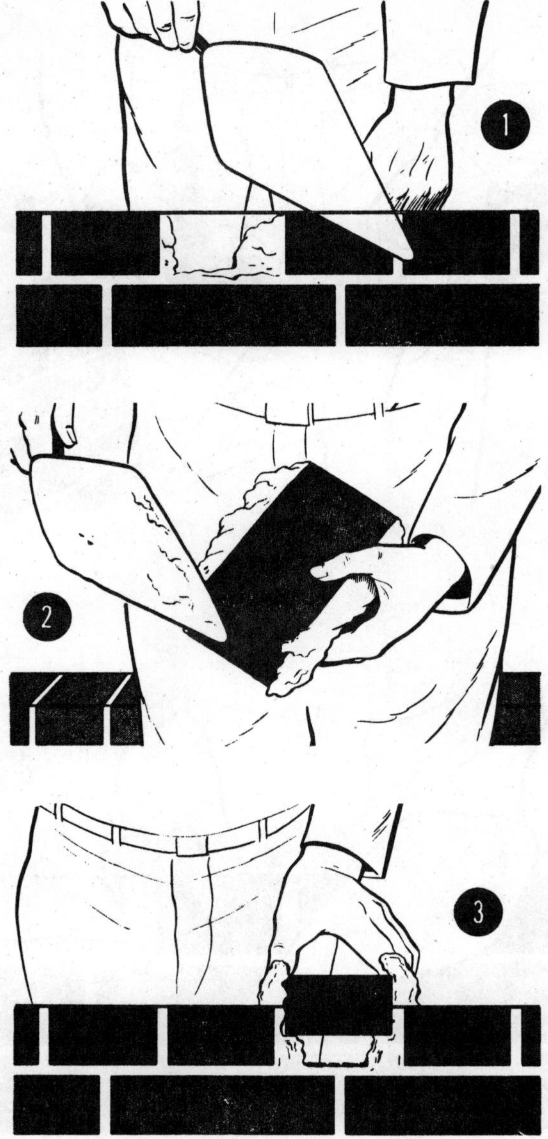

Fig. 16. Making closure joints in header courses.

should be placed on the sides of the brick already in place (Fig. 16, 1). Mortar should also be spread on both sides of the closure brick to a thickness of about 1 inch (2.5 cm.) (Fig. 16, 2). The closure brick should then be laid in position without disturbing the brick already in place (Fig. 16, 3).

Before laying a closure brick for a stretcher course, the ends of the brick on each side of the opening to be filled with the closure brick should be well covered with mortar (Fig. 17, 1). Plenty of mortar should then be thrown on both ends of the closure brick (Fig. 17, 2), and the brick laid without disturbing those already in place (Fig. 17, 3). If any of the adjacent brick are disturbed they must be removed and relaid. Otherwise, cracks will form between the brick and mortar, allowing moisture into the wall.

There is no hard and fast rule regarding the thickness of the mortar joint. Brick that are irregular in shape may require mortar joints up to ½-inch (1.3-cm.) thick. All brick irregularities are taken up in the mortar joint. Mortar joints ¼-inch (6.3-mm.) thick are the strongest and should be used when the bricks are regular enough to permit it.

Slushed joints are made by depositing the mortar on the head joints in order that the mortar will run down between the brick to form a solid joint. *This should not be done.* Even when the space between the brick is completely filled, there is no way to compact the mortar against the faces of the brick and *a poor bond will result.*

Filling exposed joints with mortar immediately after the wall has been laid is called *pointing.* Pointing is frequently necessary to fill holes and correct defective mortar joints. The pointing trowel is used for this purpose. (*See* Chap. 21, Masonry Tools and Equipment, Fig. 7.)

CUTTING BRICK

If a brick is to be cut to exact line, the bolster or brick set should be used. When using these tools, the straight side of the cutting edge should face the part of the brick to be saved and also face the mason. One blow of the hammer on the brick set

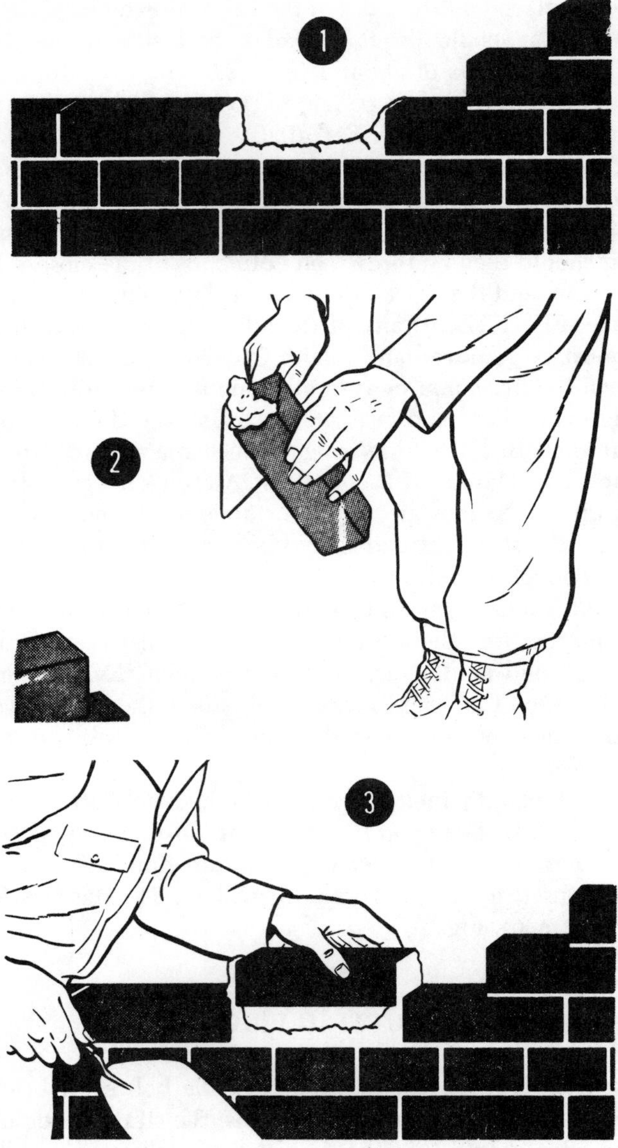

Fig. 17. Making closure joints in stretcher courses.

should be enough to break the brick. Extremely hard brick will need to be cut roughly with the head of the hammer in such a way that there is enough brick left to be cut accurately with the brick set (Fig. 18).

For normal cutting work, such as is required for making the closures and bats required around openings in walls and for the completion of corners, the brick hammer should be used. The first step is to cut a line all the way around the brick with light blows of the hammer head (Fig. 19). When the line is complete, a sharp blow to one side of the cutting line will split the brick at the cutting line. Rough places are trimmed using the blade of the hammer, as shown in Fig. 19. The brick can be held in the hand while being cut.

JOINT FINISHES

Exterior surfaces of mortar joints are finished to make the brickwork more waterproof and to improve the appearance. There are several types of joint finishes, as shown in Fig. 20. The more important of these are discussed. When joints are cut flush with the brick and not finished, cracks are immediately apparent between the brick and the mortar. Although these cracks are not

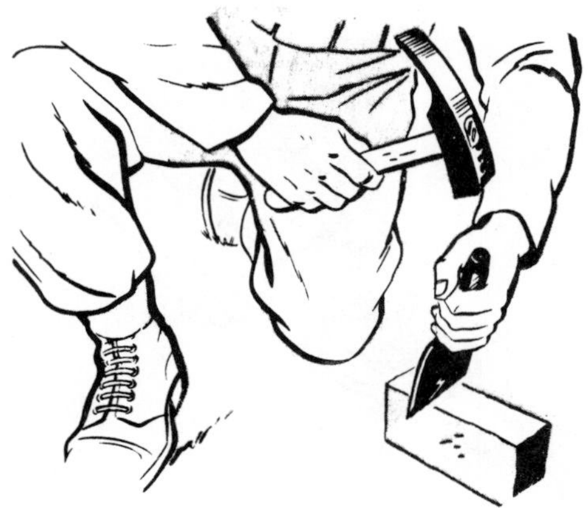

Fig. 18. Cutting brick with a bolster.

deep, they are undesirable and can be eliminated by finishing or tooling the joint. In every case, the mortar joint should be finished before the mortar has hardened to any appreciable extent. The jointing tool is shown in Chap. 21, Masonry Tools and Equipment, Fig. 1.

The best joint from the standpoint of weather-tightness is the *concave* joint. This joint is made with a special tool after the excess mortar has been removed with the trowel. The tool should be slightly larger than the joint. Force is used to press the mortar tight against the brick on both sides of the mortar joint.

The *flush* joint (Fig. 20) is made by keeping the trowel almost parallel to the face of the wall while drawing the point of the trowel along the joint.

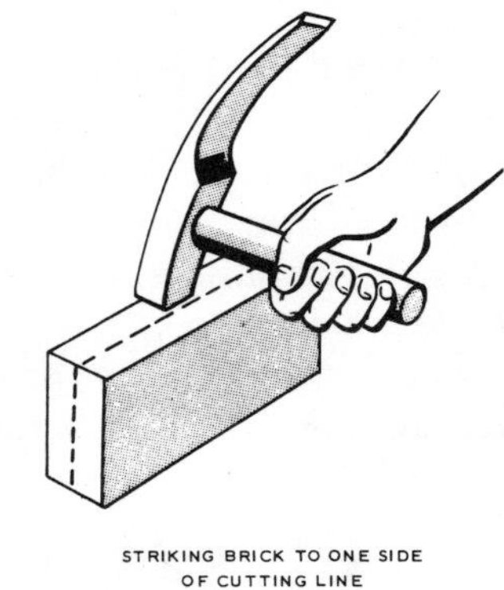

STRIKING BRICK TO ONE SIDE OF CUTTING LINE

TRIMMING ROUGH SPOTS

Fig. 19. Cutting brick with a hammer.

A *weather* joint sheds water more easily from the surface of the wall and is formed by pushing downward on the mortar with the top edge of the trowel.

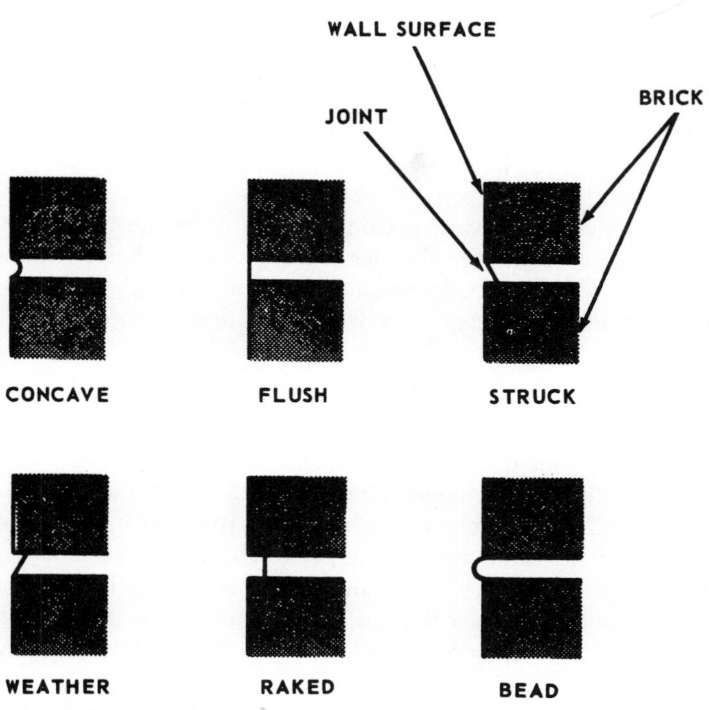

Fig. 20. Joint finishes.

Chapter 30

Brick Construction

An attractive brick construction depends upon the interpretation of the plans and the abilities of the mason and helper (if one is needed). Whether building an 8- or 12-inch wall they must be able to work together and carry out their duties properly.

HELPER'S DUTIES

The helper mixes the mortar, carries brick and mortar to the mason laying brick, and keeps him supplied with these materials at all times. He fills the mortar board and places it in a position convenient for the mason laying brick. He assists in the laying out, and at times such as during rapid backup bricklaying, he may lay out brick in a line on an adjacent course so that the mason needs to move each brick only a few inches in laying backup work. (*See* Chap. 28, Mortar for Brick Masonry.)

Wetting brick is also done by the helper. This is done when bricks are laid in warm weather. There are four reasons for wetting brick just before they are laid.

1. There will be a better bond between the brick and the mortar.
2. The water will wash dust and dirt from the surface of the brick. Mortar adheres better to a clean brick.
3. If the surface of the brick is wet, the mortar spreads more evenly under it.

4. A dry brick may absorb water from the mortar rapidly. This is particularly bad when mortar containing portland cement is used. In order for cement to harden properly, sufficient moisture must be present to complete the hydration of the cement. If the brick robs the mortar of too much water, there will not be enough left to hydrate the cement properly.

MASON'S DUTIES

The mason does the actual laying of the brick. It is his responsibility to lay out the job so that the finished masonry will be properly done. In construction involving walls, he must see that the walls are plumb and the courses level.

FOOTINGS

A *footing* is required under a wall when the bearing capacity of the supporting soil is not sufficient to withstand the wall load without a further means of redistribution. The footing must be wider than the thickness of the wall as shown in Fig. 1. The required footing width and thickness for walls of considerable height or for walls that are to carry a heavy load should be determined by a qualified mason. Every footing should be below the frost line in order to prevent heaving and settlement of the foundation. For the usual one-story building with an 8-inch (20-cm.) thick wall, a footing 16 inches (40 cm.) wide and approximately 8 inches (20 cm.) thick is usually enough. Although brickwork footings are satisfactory, footings are normally concrete, leveled on top to receive the brick or stone foundation wall. As soon as the subgrade is prepared, the mason should place a bed of mortar about 1-inch (2.5-cm.) thick on the subgrade to take up all irregularities. The first course of the foundation is laid on this bed of mortar. The other courses are then laid on this first course.

A column footing for a 12- × 16-inch (30- × 40-cm.) brick column is shown in Fig. 2. The construction method for this footing is the same as for the wall footing.

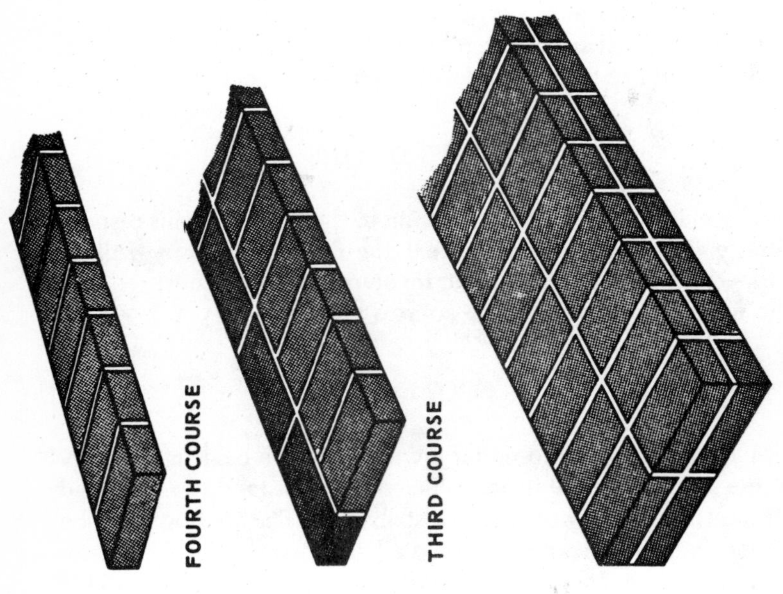

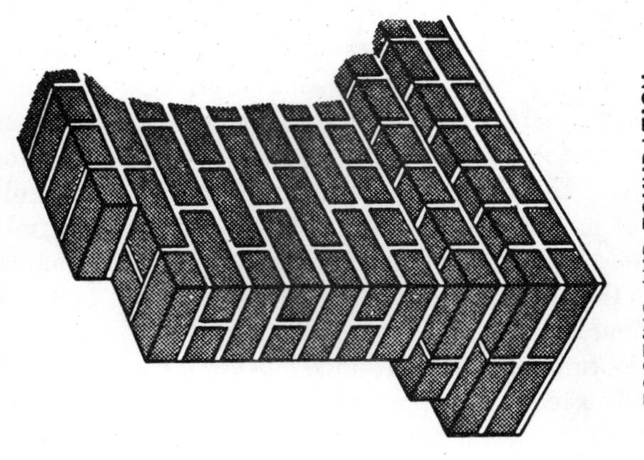

Fig. 1. Wall footing.

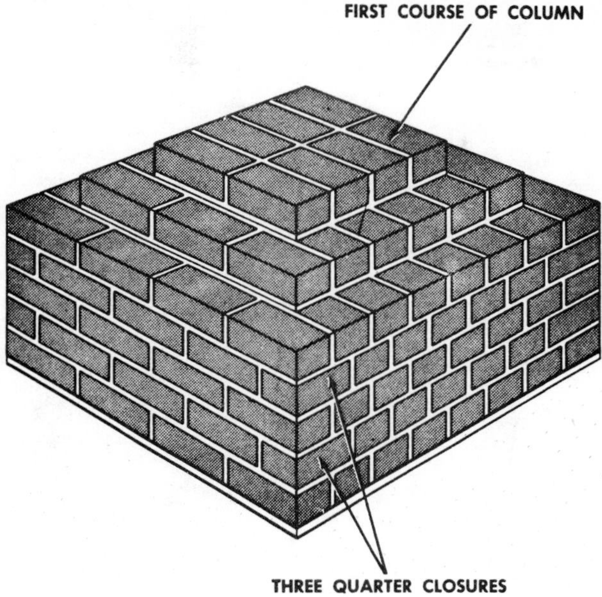

Fig. 2. Column footing.

EIGHT-INCH COMMON BOND BRICK WALL

For a wall of given length, the mason makes a slight adjustment in the width of head joints so that some number of brick, or some number including one half-brick, will just make up the length. The mason first lays the brick on the foundation without mortar as shown in Fig. 3. The distance between the bricks is equal to the thickness of the head mortar joints. Tables 27, 28, and 29 give the number of courses and horizontal joints required for a given wall height.

The *corners* are erected first. This is called *laying of leads.* The mason will use these leads as a guide in laying the remainder of the wall.

Laying a corner lead is shown in Fig. 4, step 1. Two three-quarter closures are cut and a 1-inch (2.5-cm.) thick mortar bed is laid on the foundation. The three-quarter closure marked by *a*

Courses	Height	Courses	Height	Courses	Height	Courses	Height	Courses	Height
1	0′ 2⅝″	21	4′ 7⅛″	41	8′ 11⅝″	61	13′ 4⅛″	81	17′ 8⅝″
2	0′ 5¼″	22	4′ 9¾″	42	9′ 2¼″	62	13′ 6¾″	82	17′ 11¼″
3	0′ 7⅞″	23	5′ 0⅜″	43	9′ 4⅞″	63	13′ 9⅜″	83	18′ 1⅞″
4	0′ 10½″	24	5′ 3″	44	9′ 7½″	64	14′ 0″	84	18′ 4½″
5	1′ 1⅛″	25	5′ 5⅝″	45	9′ 10⅛″	65	14′ 2⅝″	85	18′ 7⅛″
6	1′ 3¾″	26	5′ 8¼″	46	10′ 0¾″	66	14′ 5¼″	86	18′ 9¾″
7	1′ 6⅜″	27	5′ 10⅞″	47	10′ 3⅜″	67	14′ 7⅞″	87	19′ 0⅜″
8	1′ 9″	28	6′ 1½″	48	10′ 6″	68	14′ 10½″	88	19′ 3″
9	1′ 11⅝″	29	6′ 4⅛″	49	10′ 8⅝″	69	15′ 11⅛″	89	19′ 5⅝″
10	2′ 2¼″	30	6′ 6¾″	50	10′ 11¼″	70	15′ 3¾″	90	19′ 8¼″
11	2′ 4⅞″	31	6′ 9⅜″	51	11′ 1⅞″	71	15′ 6⅜″	91	19′ 10⅞′
12	2′ 7½″	32	7′ 0″	52	11′ 4½″	72	15′ 9″	92	20′ 1½″
13	2′ 10⅛″	33	7′ 2⅝″	53	11′ 7⅛″	73	15′ 11⅝″	93	20′ 4⅛″
14	3′ 0¾″	34	7′ 5¼″	54	11′ 9¾″	74	16′ 2¼″	94	20′ 6¾″
15	3′ 3⅜″	35	7′ 7⅞″	55	12′ 0⅜″	75	16′ 4⅞″	95	20′ 9⅜″
16	3′ 6″	36	7′ 10½″	56	12′ 3″	76	16′ 7½″	96	21′ 0″
17	3′ 8⅝″	37	8′ 1⅛″	57	12′ 5⅝″	77	16′ 10⅛″	97	21′ 2⅝″
18	3′ 11¼″	38	8′ 3¾″	58	12′ 8¼″	78	17′ 0¾″	98	21′ 5¼″
19	4′ 1⅞″	39	8′ 6⅜″	59	12′ 10⅞″	79	17′ 3⅜″	99	21′ 7⅞″
20	4′ 4½″	40	8′ 9″	60	13′ 1½″	80	17′ 6″	100	21′ 10½″

TABLE 27. HEIGHT OF COURSES: 2¼-INCH BRICK, ⅜-INCH JOINT.

Courses	Height	Courses	Height	Courses	Height	Courses	Height	Courses	Height
1	0′ 2¾″	21	4′ 9¾″	41	9′ 4¾″	61	13′ 11¾″	81	18′ 6¾″
2	0′ 5½″	22	5′ 0½″	42	9′ 7½″	62	14′ 2½″	82	18′ 9½″
3	0′ 8¼″	23	5′ 3¼″	43	9′ 10¼″	63	14′ 5¼″	83	19′ 0¼″
4	0′ 11″	24	5′ 6″	44	10′ 1″	64	14′ 8″	84	19′ 3″
5	1′ 1¾″	25	5′ 8¾″	45	10′ 3¾″	65	14′ 10¾″	85	19′ 5¾″
6	1′ 4½″	26	5′ 11½″	46	10′ 6½″	66	15′ 1½″	86	19′ 8½″
7	1′ 7¼″	27	6′ 2¼″	47	10′ 9¼″	67	15′ 4¼″	87	19′ 11¼″
8	1′ 10″	28	6′ 5″	48	11′ 0″	68	15′ 7″	88	20′ 2″
9	2′ 0¾″	29	6′ 7¾″	49	11′ 2¾″	69	15′ 9¾″	89	20′ 4¾″
10	2′ 3½″	30	6′ 10½″	50	11′ 5½″	70	16′ 0½″	90	20′ 7½″
11	2′ 6¼″	31	7′ 1¼″	51	11′ 8¼″	71	16′ 3¼″	91	20′ 10¼″
12	2′ 9″	32	7′ 4″	52	11′ 11″	72	16′ 6″	92	21′ 1″
13	2′ 11¾″	33	7′ 6¾″	53	12′ 1¾″	73	16′ 8¾″	93	21′ 3¾″
14	3′ 2½″	34	7′ 9½″	54	12′ 4½″	74	16′ 11½″	94	21′ 6½″
15	3′ 5¼″	35	8′ 0¼″	55	12′ 7¼″	75	17′ 2¼″	95	21′ 9¼″
16	3′ 8″	36	8′ 3″	56	12′ 10″	76	17′ 5″	96	22′ 0″
17	3′ 10¾″	37	8′ 5¾″	57	13′ 0¾″	77	17′ 7¾″	97	22′ 2¾″
18	4′ 1½″	38	8′ 8½″	58	13′ 3½″	78	17′ 10½″	98	22′ 5½″
19	4′ 4¼″	39	8′ 11¼″	59	13′ 6¼″	79	18′ 1¼″	99	22′ 8¼″
20	4′ 7″	40	9′ 2″	60	13′ 9″	80	18′ 4″	100	22′ 11″

TABLE 28. HEIGHT OF COURSES: 2¼-INCH BRICK, ½-INCH JOINT.

Courses	Height	Courses	Height	Courses	Height	Courses	Height	Courses	Height
1	0′ 2⅞″	21	5′ 0⅜″	41	9′ 9⅞″	61	14′ 7⅜″	81	19′ 4⅞″
2	0′ 5¾″	22	5′ 3¼″	42	10′ 0¾″	62	14′ 10¼″	82	19′ 7¾″
3	0′ 8⅝″	23	5′ 6⅛″	43	10′ 3⅝″	63	15′ 1⅛″	83	19′ 10⅝″
4	0′ 11½″	24	5′ 9″	44	10′ 6½″	64	15′ 4″	84	20′ 1½″
5	1′ 2⅜″	25	5′ 11⅞″	45	10′ 9⅜″	65	15′ 6⅞″	85	20′ 4⅜″
6	1′ 5¼″	26	6′ 2¾″	46	11′ 0¼″	66	15′ 9¾″	86	20′ 7¼″
7	1′ 8⅛″	27	6′ 5⅝″	47	11′ 3⅛″	67	16′ 0⅝″	87	20′ 10⅛″
8	1′ 11″	28	6′ 8½″	48	11′ 6″	68	16′ 3½″	88	21′ 1″
9	2′ 1⅞″	29	6′ 11⅜″	49	11′ 8⅞″	69	16′ 6⅜″	89	21′ 3⅞″
10	2′ 4¾″	30	7′ 2¼″	50	11′ 11¾″	70	16′ 9¼″	90	21′ 6¾″
11	2′ 7⅝″	31	7′ 5⅛″	51	12′ 2⅝″	71	17′ 0⅛″	91	21′ 9⅝″
12	2′ 10½″	32	7′ 8″	52	12′ 5½″	72	17′ 3″	92	22′ 0½″
13	3′ 1⅜″	33	7′ 10⅞″	53	12′ 8⅜″	73	17′ 5⅞″	93	22′ 3⅜″
14	3′ 4¼″	34	8′ 1¾″	54	12′ 11¼″	74	17′ 8¾″	94	22′ 6¼″
15	3′ 7⅛″	35	8′ 4⅝″	55	13′ 2⅛″	75	17′ 11⅝″	95	22′ 9⅛″
16	3′ 10″	36	8′ 7½″	56	13′ 5″	76	18′ 2½″	96	23′ 0″
17	4′ 0⅞″	37	8′ 10⅜″	57	13′ 7⅞″	77	18′ 5⅜″	97	23′ 2⅞″
18	4′ 3¾″	38	9′ 1¼″	58	13′ 10¾″	78	18′ 8¼″	98	23′ 5¾″
19	4′ 6⅝″	39	9′ 4⅛″	59	14′ 1⅝″	79	18′ 11⅛″	99	23′ 8⅝″
20	4′ 9½″	40	9′ 7″	60	14′ 4½″	80	19′ 2″	100	23′ 11½″

TABLE 29. HEIGHT OF COURSES: 2¼-INCH BRICK, ⅝-INCH JOINT.

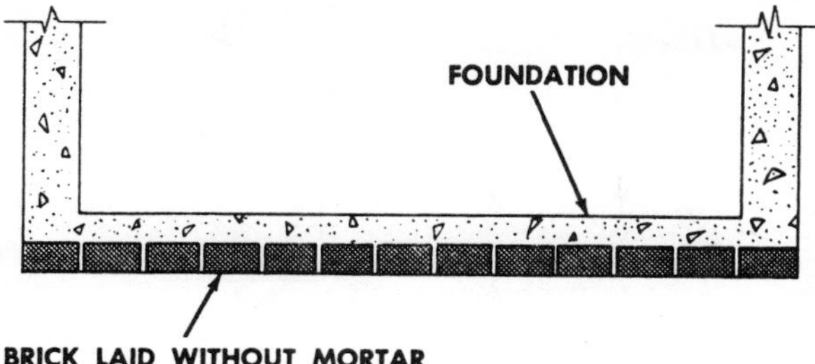

Fig. 3. Determination of vertical brick joints and number of bricks in one course.

Fig. 4, step 2) is pressed down into the mortar bed until the bed joint becomes ½-inch (1.3-cm.) thick. Next, mortar is placed on the end of three-quarter closure *b* and a head joint is formed as described previously in Chap. 29, Bricklaying. The head joint between the two three-quarter closures should be ½-inch (1.3-cm.) thick also. Excess mortar that has been squeezed out of the joints is cut off. The level of the two three-quarter closures should now be checked by means of the plumb rule placed in the positions indicated by the heavy dashed lines (Fig. 4, step 2). The edges of both these closure bricks must be even with the outside face of the foundation. Next mortar is spread on the side of brick *c*, and it is laid as shown in Fig. 4, step 3. Its level is checked using the plumb rule in the position given in Fig. 4, step 3. Its end must also be even with the outside face of the foundation. Brick *d* is laid and its level and position checked. When brick *d* is in the proper position, the quarter closures *e* and *f* should be cut and placed according to the recommended procedures for laying closure brick. All excess mortar should be removed and the tops of these quarter closures checked to see that they are at the same level as the tops of surrounding brick.

Brick g (Fig. 4, step 4) is now shoved into position after mortar has been spread on its face. Excess mortar should be removed. Bricks *h*, *i*, *j*, and *k* are laid in the same manner. The level of the brick is checked by placing the plumb rule in the positions indicated (Fig. 4, step 4). It will be noted that six header bricks are required on each side of the three-quarter closures *a* and *b*.

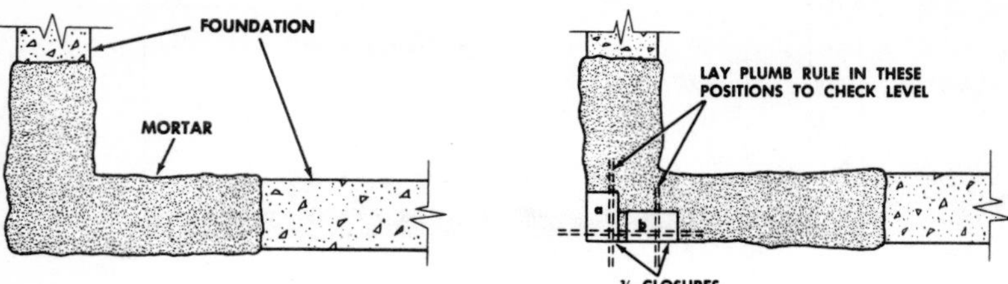

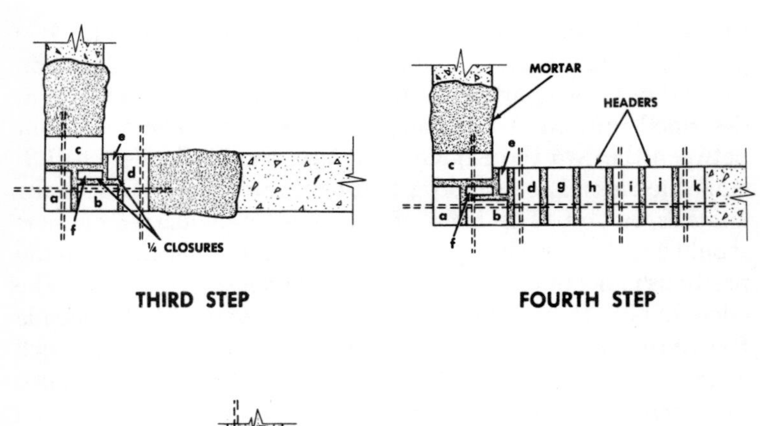

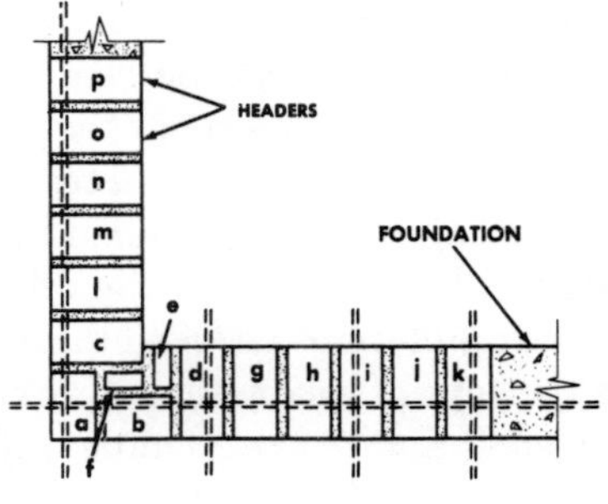

Fig. 4. First course of corner lead for 8-inch (20-cm.) common bond brick wall.

The second course, a stretcher course, is now laid. Procedure is shown in Fig. 5, step 1. A 1-inch (2.5-cm.) thick layer of mortar should be spread over the first course and a shallow furrow made in the mortar bed. Brick *a* (Fig. 5, step 2) is then laid in the mortar bed and shoved down until the mortar joint is ½-inch (1.3-cm.) thick. Brick *b* may now be shoved into place after mortar has been spread on its end. Excess mortar is removed and the joint checked for thickness. Bricks *c, d, e, f,* and g are laid in the same manner and checked to make them level and plumb. The level is checked by placing the plumb rule in the position indicated in Fig. 5, step 2. The brick are plumbed by using the plumb rule in a vertical position as shown in Fig. 6. This should be done in several places. As may be determined from Fig. 5, step 3, seven bricks are required for the second course. The remaining brick in the corner lead are laid in the manner described for the brick in the second course.

Since the portion of the wall between the leads is laid using the leads as a guide, the level of the courses in the lead must be checked continually, and after the first few courses the lead is plumbed. If the brickwork is not plumb, bricks must be moved in or out until the lead is accurately plumb. It is not good practice to move brick much once they are laid in mortar; therefore care should be taken to place the brick accurately at the start. Before the mortar has set the joints are tooled or finished.

A corner lead at the opposite end of the wall is built in the same manner. It is essential that the level of the tops of corresponding courses be the same in each lead. That is, the top of the second course in one corner lead must be at the same height above the foundation as the second course in the other corner lead. A long 2- × 2-inch (5 × 5-cm.) pole can be used to mark off the heights of the different courses above the foundation. This pole can be used to check the course height in the corner leads. The laying of leads should be closely supervised and only skilled masons should be employed in this work.

With the corner leads at each end of the wall completed, the face tier of brick for the wall between the leads is laid. It is necessary to use a line as shown in Fig. 7.

Knots are made in each end of the line to hold it within the

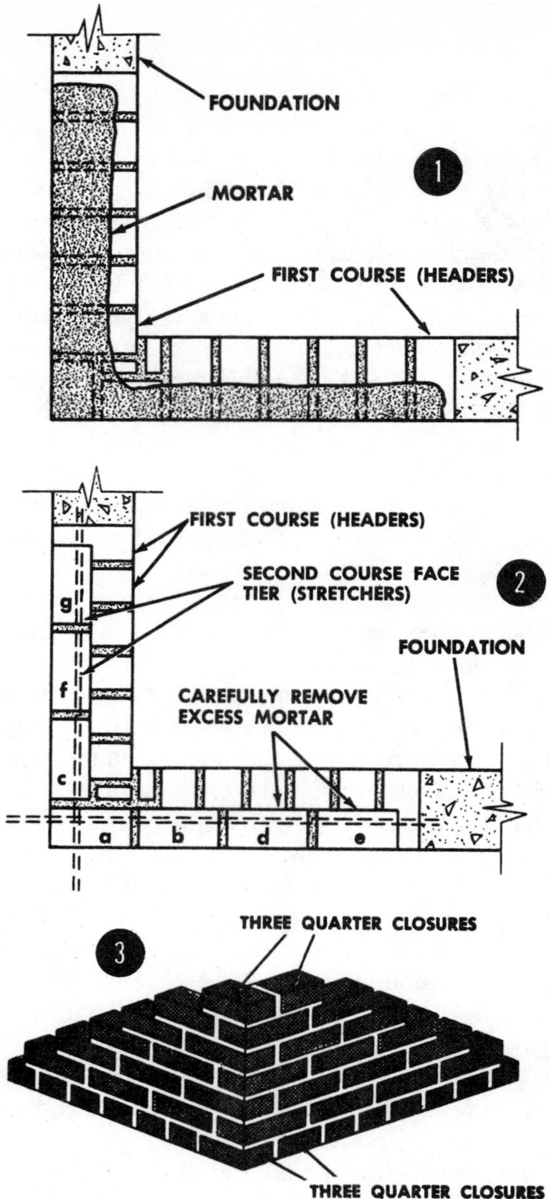

Fig. 5. Second course of corner lead for 8-inch (20-cm.) common bond brick wall.

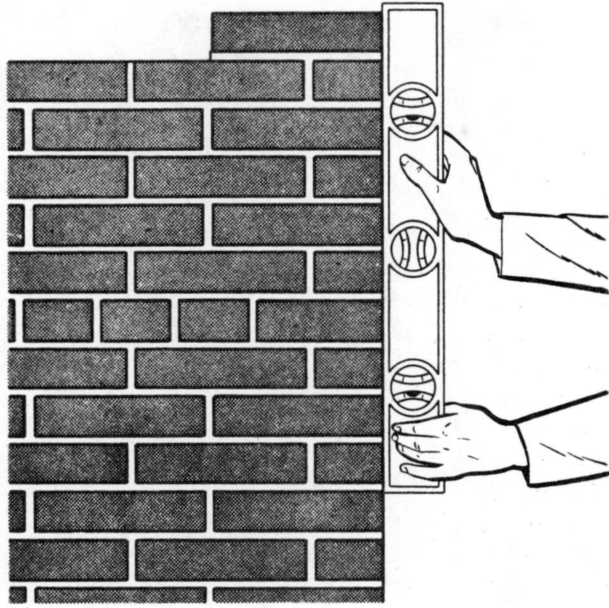

Fig. 6. Plumbing a corner.

slot of the line block as shown in Fig. 7. The line can be made taut by hooking one of the line blocks to each end of the wall.

The line is positioned 1/16 inch (1.6 mm.) outside the wall face level with the top of the brick.

With the line in place, the first or header course is laid in place between the two corner leads. The brick is shoved into position so that its top edge is 1/16 inch (1.6 mm.) behind the line. Do not crowd the line. If the corner leads are accurately built, the entire wall will be level and plumb. It is not necessary to use the level on the section of the wall between the leads. However, it is advisable to check it with the level at several points. For the next course the line is moved to the top of the next mortar joint. The brick in the stretcher course should be laid as described in Chap. 29, Bricklaying. Finish the face joints before the mortar hardens.

When the face tier of brick for the wall between the leads has

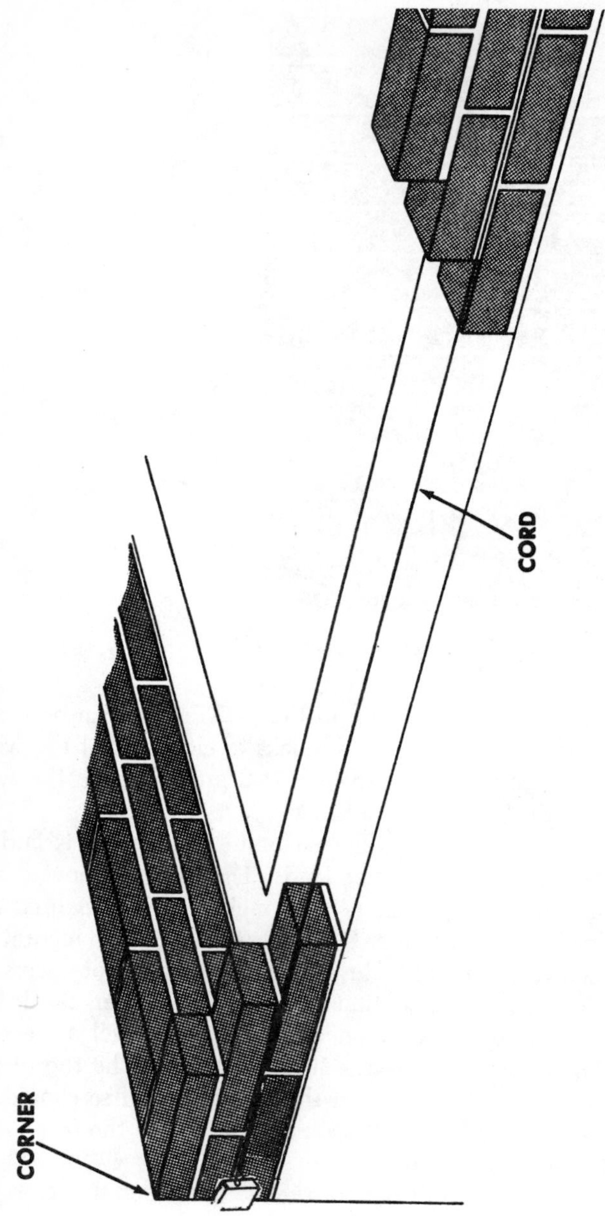

Fig. 7. Use of the line.

been laid up to, but not including the second header course, normally six courses, the backup tier is laid. Procedure for laying backup brick has already been described in Chap. 29, Bricklaying. The backup brick for the corner leads are laid first and the remaining brick afterwards (Fig. 8). The line need not be used for the backup brick in an 8-inch (20-cm.) wall. When the backup brick have been laid up to the height of the second header course, the second header course is laid.

The wall for the entire building is built up to a height including the second header course at which time corner leads are continued six more courses. The wall between the leads are continued six more courses. The wall between the leads is constructed as before and the entire procedure repeated until the wall has been completed to the required height.

TWELVE-INCH COMMON BOND BRICK WALL

The 12-inch (30-cm.) thick common bond brick wall is laid out as shown in Fig. 9, step 3. Note that construction is similar to that for the 8-inch (20-cm.) wall with the exception that a third tier of brick is used. The header course is laid (Fig. 9, step 1) first and the corner leads built. Two tiers of backing brick are required instead of one. The second course is shown in Fig. 9, step 2, and the third course in Fig. 9, step 3. Two header courses are required and they overlap as shown in Fig. 9, step 1. A line should be used for the inside tier of backing brick for a 12-inch (30-cm.) wall. (*See* Chap. 22, Concrete Masonry Units.)

PROTECTION OF BRICKWORK AND USE OF A TRIG

The tops of all brick walls should be protected each night from rain damage by placing boards or tarpaulins on top of the wall and setting loose bricks on them.

When a line is stretched on a long wall, a *trig* is used to prevent sagging and to keep it from being blown in or out from the

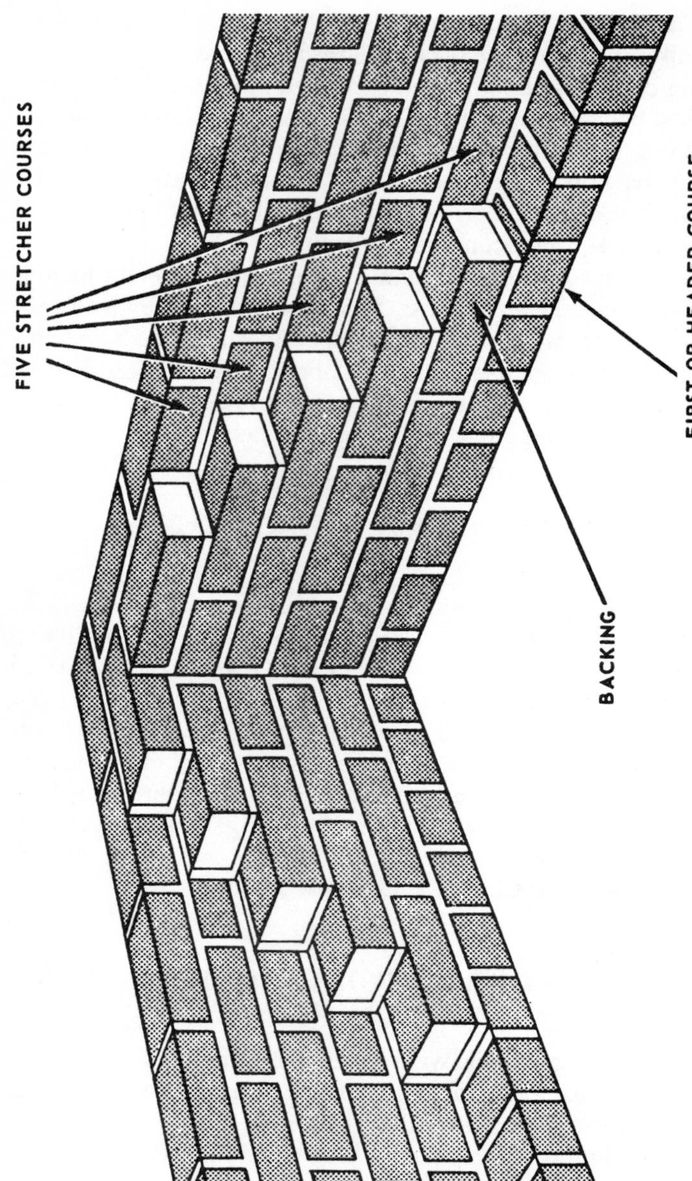

Fig. 8. Backing brick at the corner—8-inch (20-cm.) common bond brick wall.

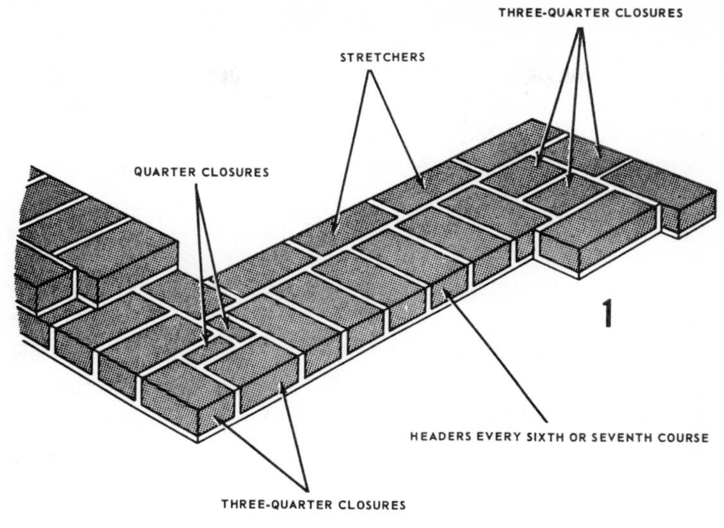

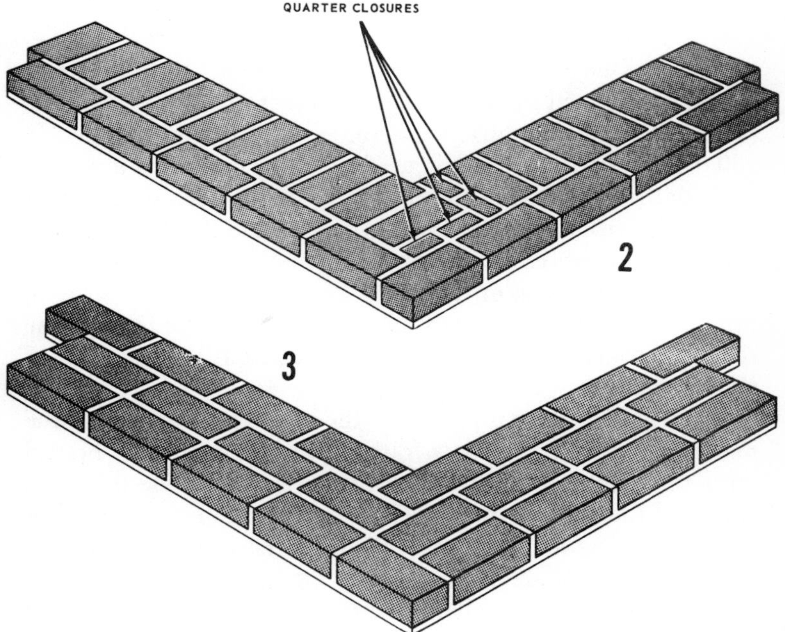

Fig. 9. Twelve-inch (30-cm.) common bond wall.

face of the wall by the wind. The trig consists of a short piece of line looped around the main line and fastened to the top edge of a brick that has been previously laid in proper position. A lead between the corner leads must be erected in order to place the trig brick in its proper location.

WINDOW AND DOOR OPENINGS

If windows are to be installed in the wall, openings are left for them as the bricklaying proceeds. The height to the top of one full course should be exactly the height of the window sill. When the distance from the foundation to the bottom of the window sill is known, the mason can determine how many courses are required to bring the wall up to that height. If the sill is to be 4 feet 4¼ inches (130.6 cm.) above the foundation and ½-inch (1.3-cm.) mortar joints are to be used, 19 courses will be required. (Each brick plus one mortar joint is 2¼ + ½ = 2¾ inches or 6.9 cm.) One course is thus 2¾-inches (6.9-cm.) high. Four feet 4¼ inches divided by 2¾ is 19, the number of courses required. [This also works in metric measurements. The height of the sill, 130.6 cm., divided by 6.875 cm. (brick plus mortar) is also 19.]

With the brick laid up to sill height, the rowlock sill course is laid as shown in Fig. 10. The rowlock course is pitched downward. The slope is away from the window and the rowlock course normally takes up a vertical space equal to two courses of brick. The exterior surface of the joints between the brick in the rowlock course must be carefully finished to make them watertight.

The window frame is placed on the rowlock sill as soon as the mortar has set. The window frame must be temporarily braced until the brickwork has been laid up to about one-third the height of the window frame. These braces are not removed for several days in order that the wall above the window frame will set properly. Now the mason lays up the brick in the rest of the wall in such a way that the top of the brick in the course at the level of the top of the window frame is not more than ¼ inch (6.3 mm.) above the frame. To do this he marks on the window frame

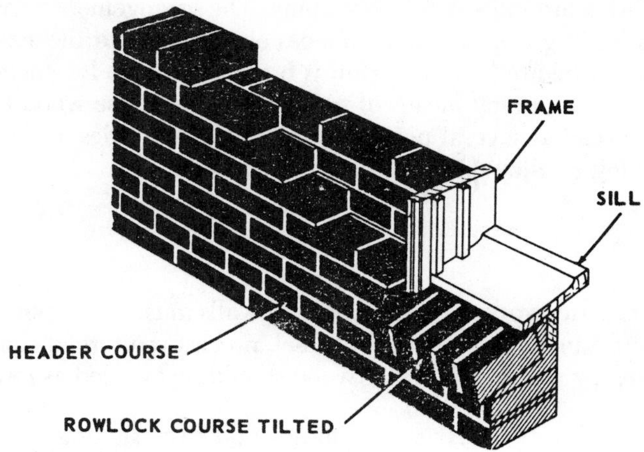

Fig. 10. Construction at a window opening.

with a pencil the top of each course. If the top course does not come to the proper level, he changes the thickness of the joints slightly until the top course is at the proper level. The corner leads should be laid up after the height of each course at the window is determined.

The mortar joint thickness for the corner leads is made the same as that determined at the window opening. With the corner leads erected, the line is installed as already described and is stretched across the window opening. The brick can now be laid in the rest of the wall. If the window openings have been planned properly, the brick in the face tier can be laid with a minimum of brick cutting.

Lintels are placed above windows and doors to carry the weight of the wall above them. They rest on the brick course that is level or approximately level with the frame head, and are firmly bedded in mortar at the sides. Any space between the window frame and the lintel is closed with blocking and weather-stripped with bituminous materials. The wall is then continued above the window after the lintel is placed.

The same procedure (including placement of the lintel) can be used for laying brick around a door opening as was used for laying brick around a window opening. The arrangement at a door opening is given in Fig. 11. Pieces of wood cut to the size of a half closure are laid in mortar as brick to provide for anchoring the door frame by means of screws or nails. These wood blocks are placed at several points along the top and sides of the door opening to allow for plumbing the frame.

LINTELS

The brickwork above openings in walls must be supported by lintels. Lintels can be made of steel, precast reinforced concrete beams, or wood. The use of wood should be avoided as much as

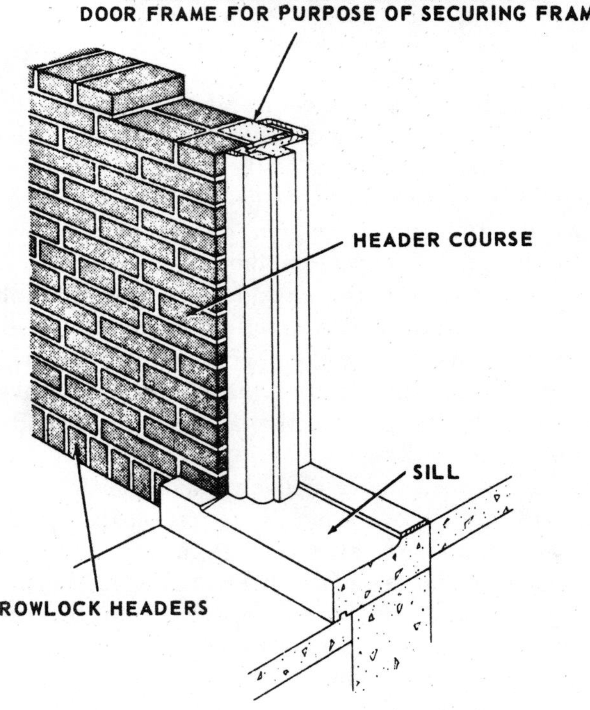

Fig. 11. Construction at a door opening.

possible. If reinforced brick masonry is employed, the brick above the wall opening can be supported by the proper installation of steel reinforcing bars. This will be discussed in Chap. 31, Reinforced Brick Masonry. Figures 12 and 13 illustrate some of the methods of placing lintels for different wall thicknesses. The relative placement and position is determined both by wall thickness and the type of window being used.

Usually the size and type of lintels required are given on drawings for the structure. When not given, the size of double-angle lintels required for various width openings in an 8-inch (20-cm.) and 12-inch (30-cm.) wall can be selected from Table 30. Wood lintels for various width openings are also given in Table 30.

Installation of a lintel for an 8-inch (20-cm.) wall is shown in Fig. 12. The thickness of the angle for a two-angle lintel should be ¼ inch (6.3 mm.). This makes it possible for the two-angle legs that project up into the brick to fit exactly in the ½-inch (1.3-cm.) joint between the face and backing-up ties of an 8-inch (20-cm.) wall.

Fig. 12. Lintels for an 8-inch (20-cm.) wall.

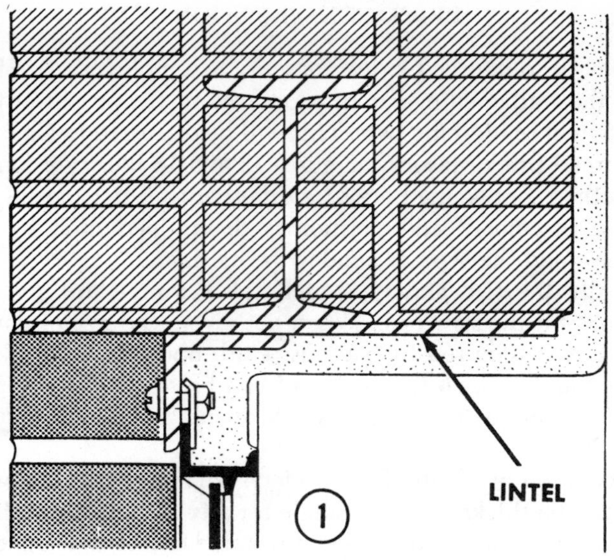

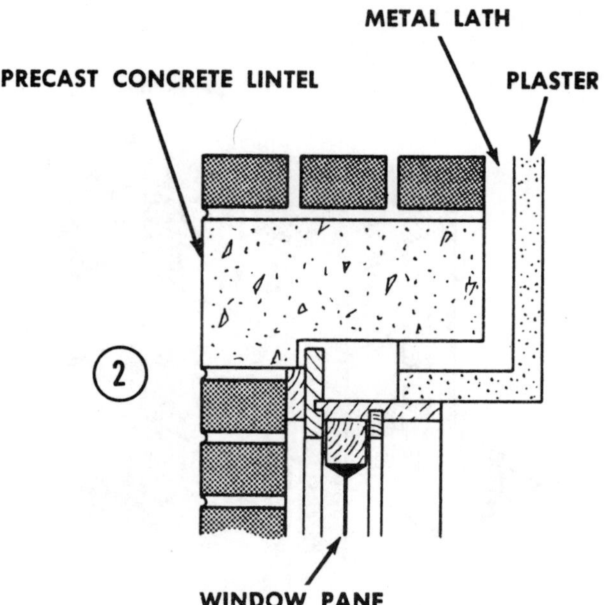

Fig. 13. Lintels for a 12-inch (30-cm.) wall.

Wall thickness	Span						
	3 feet		4 feet* steel angles	5 feet* steel angles	6 feet* steel angles	7 feet* steel angles	8 feet* steel angles
	Steel angles	Wood					
8''----------	2–3 x 3 x ¼	2 x 8 2–2 x 4	2–3 x 3 x ¼	2–3 x 3 x ¼	2–3½ x 3½ x ¼	2–3½ x 3½ x ¼	2–3½ x 3½ x ¼
12''----------	2–3 x 3 x ¼	2 x 12 2–2 x 6	2–3 x 3 x ¼	2–3½ x 3½ x ¼	2–3½ x 3½ x ¼	2–4 x 4 x ¼	2–4 x 4 x 4¼

*Wood lintels should not be used for spans over 3 feet since they burn out in case of fire and allow the brick to fall.

TABLE 30. LINTEL SIZES.

CORBELING

Corbeling consists of courses of brick set out beyond the face of the wall in order to form a self-supporting projection. This type of construction is shown in Fig. 14. The portion of a chimney that is exposed to the weather is frequently corbeled out and increased in thickness to improve its weathering resistance. In corbeling, headers should also be used as much as possible. It is usually necessary to use various-sized bats. The first projecting course may be a stretcher course if necessary. No course should

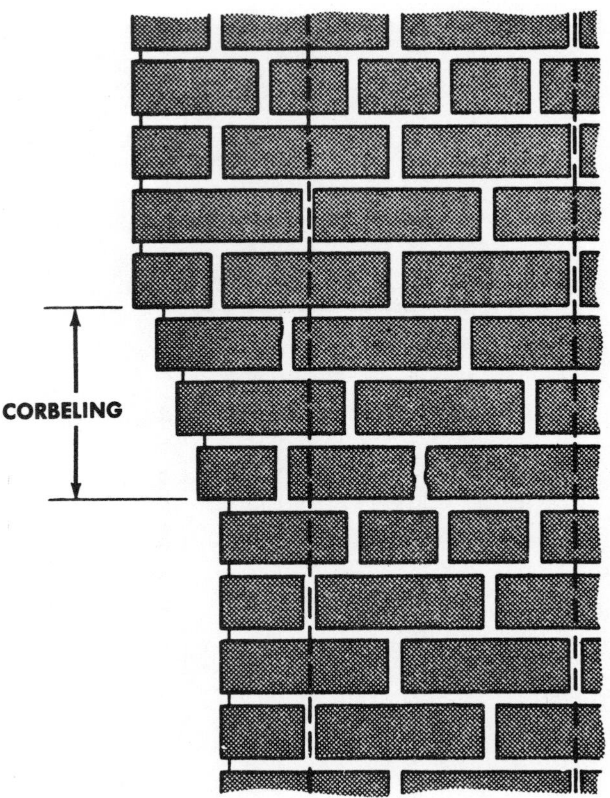

Fig. 14. Corbeled brick wall.

extend out more than 2 inches (5 cm.) beyond the course below it and the total projection of the corbeling should not be more than the thickness of the wall.

Corbeling must be done carefully for the construction to have maximum strength. All mortar joints should be carefully made and completely filled with mortar. When the corbeled-out brick masonry is to withstand large loads, you should consult your local authority.

BRICK ARCHES

If properly constructed, a brick arch can support a heavy load. The ability to support loads is derived primarily from its curved shape. Several arch shapes can be used—the circular and elliptical shapes are most common (Fig. 15). The width of the mortar joint is less at the bottom of the brick than it is at the top, and it should not be thinner than ¼ inch (6.3 mm.) at any point. Arches made of brick must be constructed with full mortar joints. As laying progresses, care must be taken to see that the arch does not bulge out of position.

A brick arch is constructed on a temporary support that is left in position until the mortar has set. The temporary support is made of wood as shown in Fig. 16. The dimensions required are obtained from drawings. For arches up to 6 feet (1.8 meters) in span, ¾-inch (1.9-cm.) plywood should be used for temporary supports. Two pieces cut to the proper curved shape are made and nailed to 2 × 4's (5 × 10 cm.) placed between them. This will provide a surface wide enough to adequately support the brick.

The temporary support should be held in position with wedges that can be driven out when the mortar has hardened enough for the arch to be self-supporting.

Construction of an arch is begun at the two ends or abutments of the arch. The brick is laid from each end toward the center or crown. The key, or middle brick, is to be placed last. There should be an odd number of brick in order for the key or middle brick to come at the exact center of the arch. The arch should be

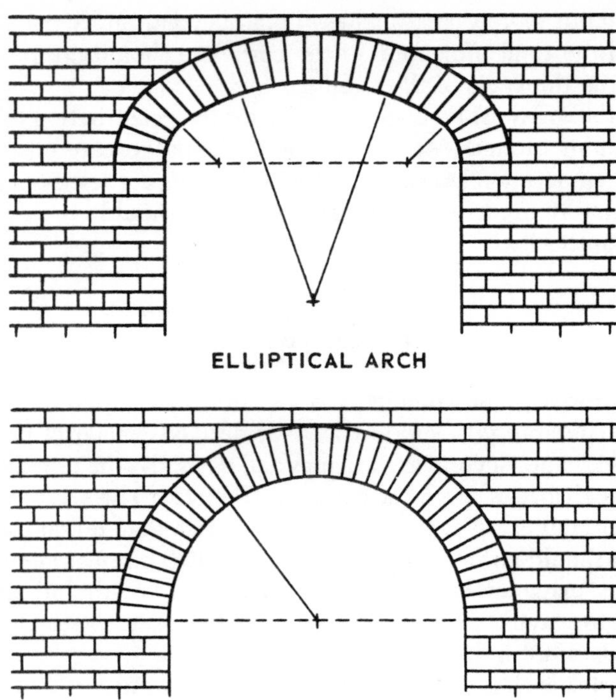

Fig. 15. Types of arches.

Fig. 16. Use of a templet in arch construction.

laid out in such a way that no brick need be cut.

The best way to determine the number of brick required for an arch is to lay a temporary support on its side on level ground and set brick around it. Adjust the spacing until the key brick comes at the exact center of the arch. When this has been done, the position of the brick can be marked on the temporary support, to be used as a guide when the arch is actually built.

WATERTIGHT WALLS

The water that passes through brick walls does not usually enter through the mortar or brick but through cracks between brick and mortar. Sometimes these cracks are formed because the bond between the brick and mortar is poor. They are more apt to occur in head joints than in bed joints. To prevent this some brick must be wetted. If the position of the brick is changed after the mortar has begun to set, the bond between the brick and mortar will be destroyed and a crack will result. Shrinkage of the mortar is also frequently responsible for the formation of cracks.

Both the size and number of cracks between the mortar and the brick can be reduced if the exterior face of all the mortar joints is tooled to a concave finish. All head joints and bed joints must be completely filled with mortar if watertightness is to be obtained.

A procedure found effective in producing a leakproof wall is shown in Fig. 17. The back of the brick in the face tier is plastered with not less than ⅜ inch (9 mm.) of rich cement mortar before the backing brick are laid. This is called *parging* or back plastering. Since parging should not be done over mortar protruding from the joints, all joints on the back of the face tier of bricks must be cut flush.

Membrane waterproofing, installed in the same way as specified for concrete walls, should be used if the wall is subject to considerable water pressure. The membrane, if properly installed, is able to adjust to any shrinkage or settlement without cracking. If the wall is to be subjected to considerable ground

Fig. 17. Parging.

water or the surrounding soil is impervious, tile drains, or French drains if drainage tile is not available, should be constructed around the base of the wall (Fig. 18). (*See* Chap. 52, Building Watertight Concrete Masonry Walls; *see also* Miscellaneous Concrete Wall Jobs.)

For a foundation wall below ground level two coats of bituminous mastic applied to the outside surface of the brick will yield satisfactory results. Asphalt or coal-tar pitch may be used and applied with mops.

The watertightness of brick walls above ground level is improved by the application of transparent waterproof paints such as a water solution of sodium silicate. Varnish is also effective. When used these paints should be applied as specified by the manufacturer. Certain white and colored waterproofing paints are also available. Good results have been obtained by the use of high-quality oil base paints.

Portland cement paint generally gives excellent results. The brick wall should be at least 30 days old before the portland cement paint is applied and all efflorescence must be removed from the surface to be painted. Manufacturer's instructions for mixing and applying the paint are to be followed. Surfaces must be damp when the paint is applied. A water spray is the best means of wetting the surface. Whitewash or calcimine type brushes are used to apply the paint. Portland cement paint can be applied with a spray gun but its rain resistance will be reduced.

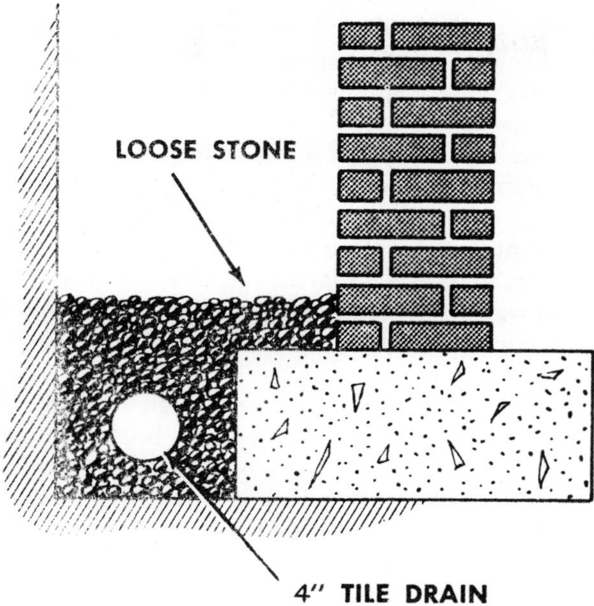
LOOSE STONE
4" TILE DRAIN
WHEN TILE DRAIN IS OMITTED, THE DRAIN IS CALLED A FRENCH DRAIN

Fig. 18. Drain around foundation.

FIRE-RESISTANT BRICK

Fire brick are manufactured for such uses as lining furnaces and incinerators. Their purpose is to protect the supporting structure or outer shell from intense heat. This outer shell may consist of common brick, or, in some cases, steel, neither of which has good heat resistance. There are two types of fire-resistant brick.

Firebricks are made from a special clay known as fireclay. They will withstand high temperatures and are heavier and usually larger than common brick. The standard size is 9 × 4½ × 2½ inches (22.5 × 11.3 × 6.3 cm.).

Silica brick should be used if resistance to acid gases is required. Silica brick should not be used if it is to be alternately heated and cooled. Most incinerators, therefore, should be lined with fire brick rather than silica brick. (*See* Chap. 54, Fireplaces, Barbecues, and Incinerators.)

Thin joints are of the utmost importance in laying fire brick. This is especially true when the brick are exposed to the high temperatures occurring in incinerators or the like. The brick should be kept in a dry place until they are used.

The mortar to be used in laying fire brick consists of fire clay mixed with water. The consistency of the mortar should be that of thick cream. Fireclay can be obtained by grinding used fire brick.

The brick is dipped in the mortar in such a manner that all faces except the top face are covered. The brick is then tapped firmly in place with a bricklayer's hammer. The joint between the brick should fit tightly together. Any cracks between the fire brick will allow heat to penetrate to the outside shell of the incinerator or furnace and damage it. The fire brick in one course lap those in the course below by one-half brick. Thus, the head joints are staggered in the same way as they are staggered in the usual type of brick construction.

Silica brick are laid without mortar. They fit so closely that they fuse together at the joints when subjected to high temperatures. The head joints for silica brick are staggered as for fire brick.

SPECIAL TYPES OF WALLS

Many different types of walls may be built of brick. The solid 8- and 12-inch (20- and 30-cm.) walls in common bond are the ones usually used for solid wall construction in the United States. The most important of the hollow walls are the cavity wall and rowlock-type wall.

Cavity walls provide a means of obtaining a watertight wall that may be plastered without the use of furring or lathing. From the outside they appear the same as solid walls without header courses (Fig. 19). No headers are required because the

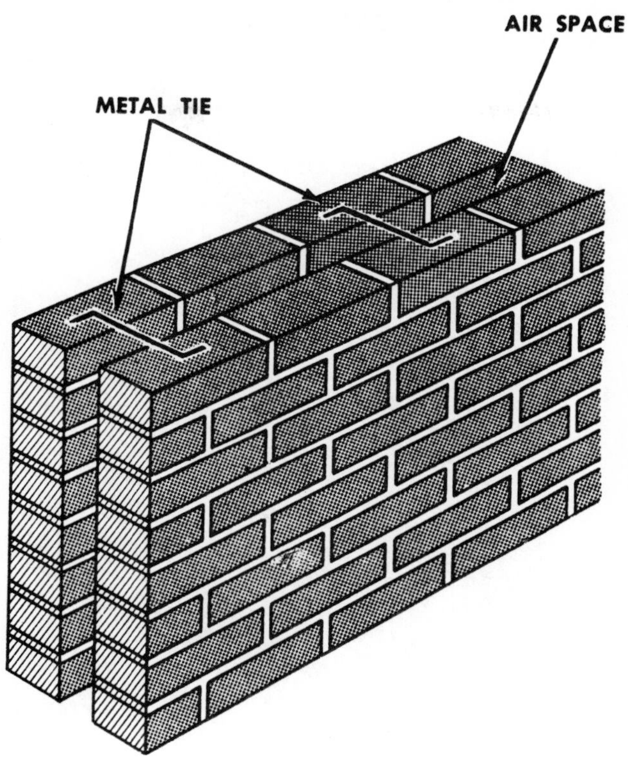

Fig. 19. Details for a cavity wall.

two tiers of brick are held together by means of metal ties installed every sixth course and on 24-inch (60-cm.) centers. To prevent waterflow to the inside tier, ties must be angled in a downward direction from the inside tier to the outside tier.

The 2-inch (5-cm.) cavity between the two tiers of brick provides a space down which water that penetrates the outside tier may flow without passing through to the inside of the wall. The bottom of the cavity is above ground level and is drained by weep holes placed in the vertical joints between two bricks in the first course of the outer tier. These holes may be formed by leaving the mortar out of some of the vertical joints in the first

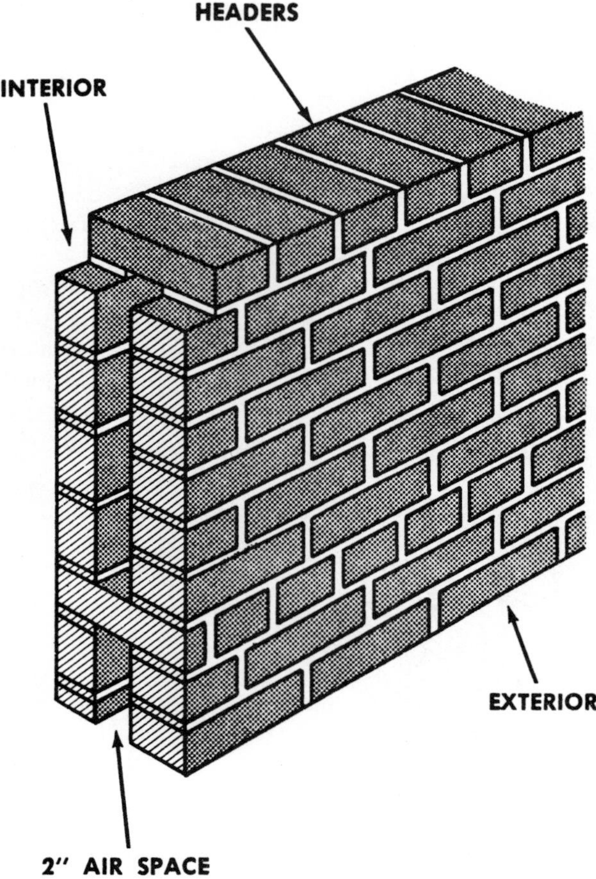

Fig. 20. Details of a rowlok backwall.

course. The holes should be spaced at about 24-inch (60-cm.) intervals. The air space also gives the wall better heat- and sound-insulating properties.

One type of *rowlock wall* is shown in Fig. 20. The face tier of this wall has the same appearance as a common bond wall with a full header course every seventh course. The backing tier is laid with the brick on edge. The face tier and backing tier are tied together by a header course as shown. A 2-inch (5-cm.) space is provided between the two tiers of brick, as for a cavity wall.

An all-rowlock wall is constructed with brick in the face and backing tier both laid on edge. The header course would be installed at every fourth course—three rowlock courses to every header course. A rowlock wall is not as watertight as the cavity wall. Water is able to follow any crack present in the header course and pass through the wall to the inside surface.

Partition walls that carry very little load can be made using one tier of brick only. This produces a wall 4-inches (10-cm.) thick. A wall of this thickness is laid up without headers.

Brick are laid in cavity walls, and partition walls according to the procedure given for making bed joints, head joints, cross joints, and closures. The line is used the same as for a common bond wall. Corner leads for these walls are erected first and the wall between is built up afterward.

Chapter 31

Reinforced Brick Masonry

Because the strength of brick masonry in tension is low, as compared with its compressive strength, reinforcing steel is used when there are tensile stresses to be resisted. In this respect brick masonry and concrete construction are identical. The reinforcing steel is placed in the horizontal or vertical mortar joints. *Reinforced brick masonry* may be used for beams, columns, walls, and footings in the same manner as reinforced concrete is used. Structures built of reinforced brick masonry have successfully resisted the effect of earthquake shocks intense enough to damage unreinforced brick structures severely. The design of reinforced brick masonry structures is similar to the design of reinforced concrete structures.

Brick used for reinforced brick masonry is the same as that used for ordinary brick masonry. It should, however, have a compressive strength of at least 2,500 psi (175 kgs. per sq. cm.). (*See* Chap. 29, Bricklaying; *see also* Chap. 30, Brick Construction.)

The reinforcing steel is the same as the steel used to reinforce concrete and it is stored and fabricated in the same way. Hard-grade steel should not be used except in emergencies because many sharp bends are required in this type of construction.

Type N mortar is used because of its high strength.

Wire for tying reinforcing steel should be 16-gage soft annealed iron wire.

CONSTRUCTION METHODS FOR REINFORCED BRICK MASONRY

Bricklaying is the same as for normal brick masonry. Mortar joint thickness is ⅛ inch (3.2 mm.) more than the diameter of the steel bar used for reinforcing. This will allow 1/16 inch (1.6 mm.) of mortar between the surface of the brick and the bar. When large steel bars are used, the thickness of the mortar joint will exceed ½ inch (1.3 cm.).

All reinforcing steel must be firmly embedded in mortar. (*See* Chap. 28, Mortar for Brick Masonry.)

Horizontal bars are laid in a bed of mortar and pushed down into position. More mortar is spread on top of the rods and smoothed out until a bed joint of the proper thickness can be made. The next course of brick is then laid in this mortar bed according to the procedure outlined for laying brick without reinforcing steel.

In order to place them in the mortar joints, stirrups for most reinforced brick beams must be of the shape shown in Fig. 1. The lower leg is placed under the horizontal bars and in contact with them. Note that a thicker joint may be required at this point.

Vertical bars are placed in the vertical mortar joints. They are held in position by wood templets in which holes have been drilled at the proper bar spacing or by wiring to a horizontal bar. The brick is laid up around the vertical bars.

Horizontal and vertical bars need not be wired together as was recommended for reinforcing steel in concrete walls.

The minimum center-to-center spacing between parallel bars is 1½ times the bar diameter.

Reinforced brick beams require form work for the same reason that reinforced concrete beams need form work. The form will consist only of a support for the bottom of the beam. No side form work is required. The form for the bottom is the same and is supported in the same way as recommended for concrete beams. No form work is required for walls, columns, or footings. (*See* Chap. 7, Forms and Form Making.)

Where the beam joins a wall or another beam, the form should be cut ¼-inch (6.3-cm.) short and the gap filled with mortar to allow for swelling of the lumber and to permit easy removal of the forms. (At least ten days should elapse before the bottom form work for beams is removed.)

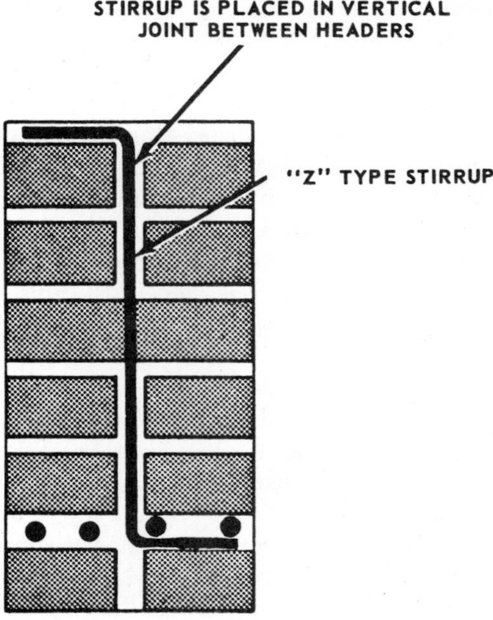

Fig. 1. Reinforced brick masonry beam.

Reinforced Brick Masonry Beams

The width and depth of beams depend upon brick dimensions, thickness of the mortar joints, and the load that the beam is required to support. Beam widths are usually the same as the wall thicknesses, that is, 4, 8, 12, and 16 inches (10, 20, 30, and 40 cm., respectively). The depth should not exceed approximately three times the width.

The first course of brick is laid on the form with full head joints but without a bed joint (Fig. 1).

A bed of mortar about ⅛ inch (3.2-mm.) thicker than the diameter of the horizontal reinforcing bars is spread on the first course of brick and the bars embedded in it as already described.

If stirrups are required, the leg of the stirrup is slipped under the horizontal bars as shown in Fig. 1. Care must be taken to get the stirrup in the center of the vertical mortar joint in which it is to be placed.

After the stirrups and the horizontal bars are in the proper position, spread additional mortar on the bed joint if necessary, and smooth the surface of the mortar. The mortar bed is now ready for the remaining courses which are laid in the usual way.

All the brick in one course are laid before any brick in the next course are placed. This is necessary to ensure a continuous bond between the mortar and steel bars. It is frequently necessary to have three or four workers working on one beam in order to get the bed joint mortar for the entire course spread, reinforcing steel placed, and brick laid before the mortar sets up.

The proper placement of reinforcing steel in the brick wall above a window or door opening will serve the purpose of a lintel.

The steel bars should be ⅜ inch (9.5 mm.) diameter or less if it is necessary to maintain a ½-inch (1.25-cm.) thick mortar joint. The bars should extend 15 inches (37.5 cm.) into the brick wall on each side of the opening and should be placed in the first mortar joint above the opening and also in the fourth joint above the opening (Fig. 2). The lintel acts as a beam and needs a bottom form. The number and size bars required for different width wall openings are as follows:

Width of wall opening in feet	Number and size of bars
6 (1.83 meters)	2¼-inch (5.6-cm.) diameter bars
9 (2.7 meters)	3¼-inch (8.1-cm.) diameter bars
12 (3.7 meters)	3⅜-inch (8.4-cm.) diameter bars

Reinforced Brick Masonry Foundations

In large footings, reinforcing steel is usually needed because of the tensile stresses that develop. As in all brick foundations, the first course of brick is laid in a bed of 1-inch (2.5-cm.) thick mortar that has been spread on the subgrade.

A typical wall footing is shown in Fig. 3. The dowels extend above the footing. Their purpose is to tie the footing and brick wall together. The No. 3 bars shown running parallel to the direction of the wall are used to prevent the formation of cracks

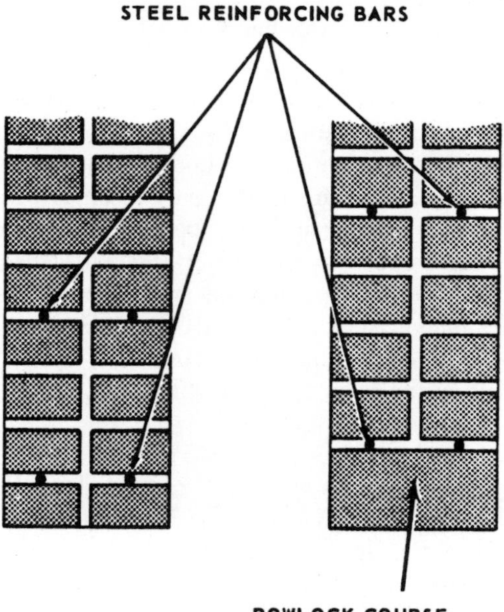

Fig. 2. Reinforced brick masonry lintels.

perpendicular to the wall.

Column footings are usually square or rectangular and are reinforced as shown in Fig. 4. The dowels are needed to anchor the column to the footing and to transfer stress from the column to the footing. Note that both layers of horizontal steel are placed in the same mortar joint. This is not necessary, and if large bars are used one layer of steel should be placed in the second mortar joint above the bottom. If this is done the spacing between the bars in the upper layer of steel must be reduced.

Reinforced Brick Masonry Columns and Walls

The load-carrying capacity of brick columns is increased when they are reinforced with steel bars. There should be at least 1½ inches (3.8 cm.) of mortar or brick covering the reinforcing bars and these bars should be held in place with ⅜-inch

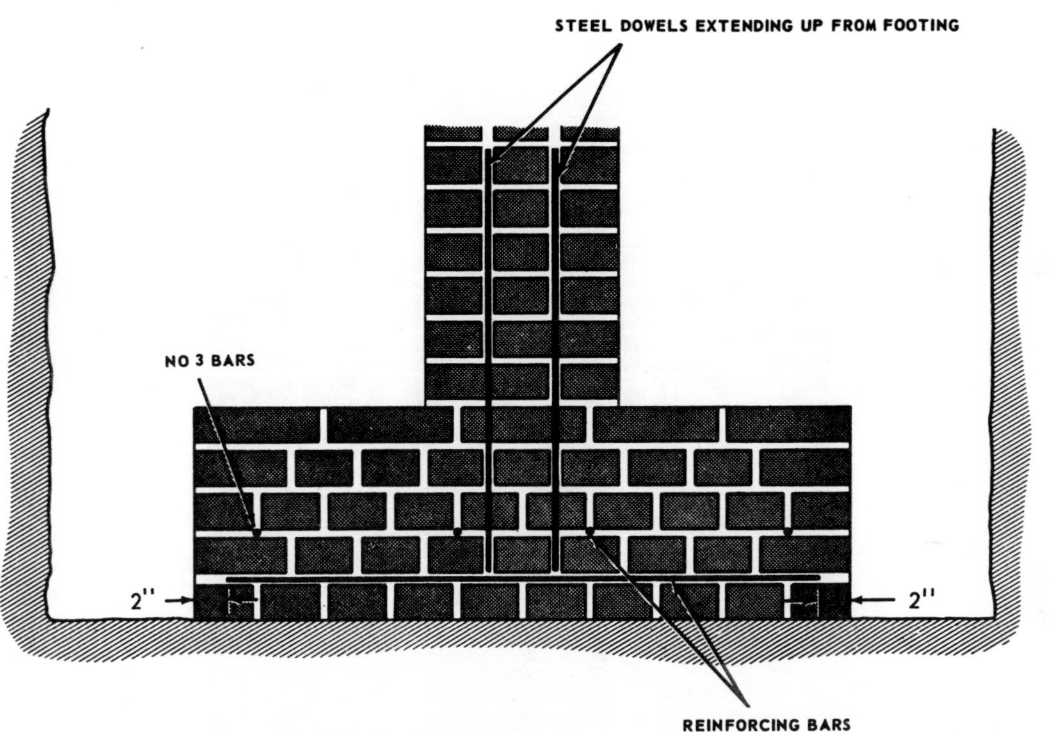

Fig. 3. Reinforced masonry wall footing.

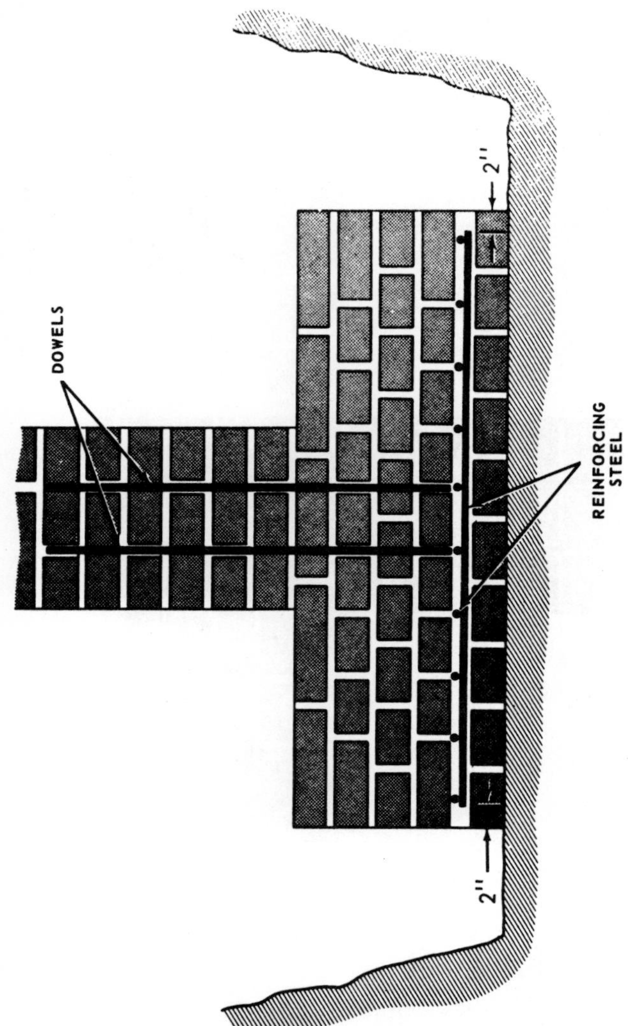

Fig. 4. Reinforced masonry column footing.

(9-mm.) diameter steel hoops or ties as shown in Fig. 5. When possible, the hoops or ties should be circular rather than rectangular or square. The ends of the hoop or tie should be lap-welded together or bent around a reinforcing bar. Hoops should be installed at every course of brick.

After the footings are completed, the column reinforcing steel is tied to the dowels projecting from the footing. The required number of hoops is then slipped over the longitudinal reinforcing bars and temporarily fastened to these bars some distance above the level at which brick are being laid but within reach of the mason laying the brick. It is not necessary for the hoops to be

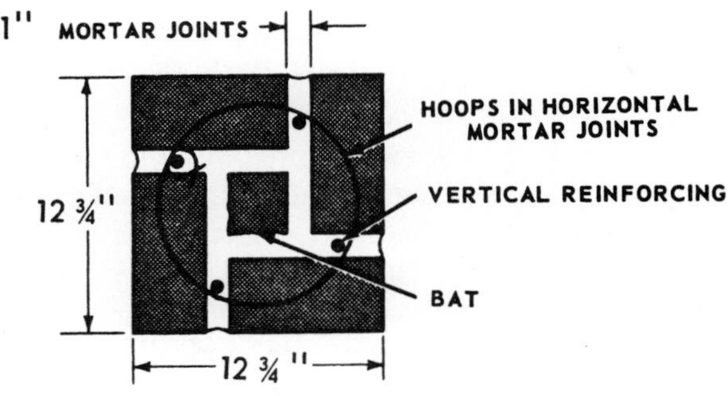

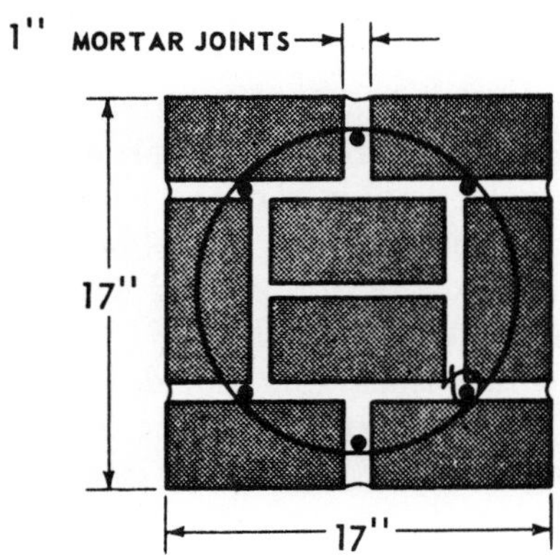

Fig. 5. Reinforced brick masonry columns.

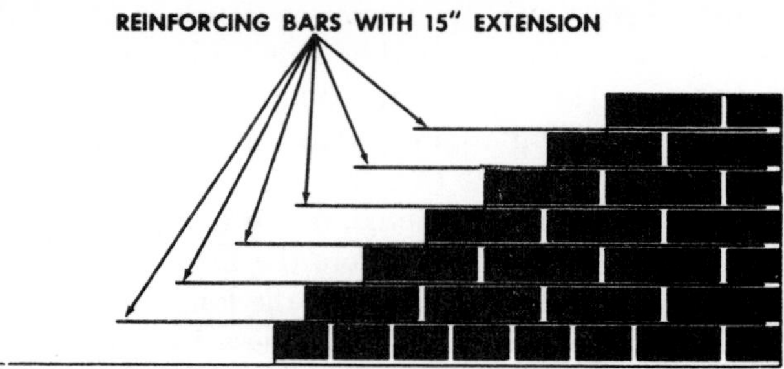

Fig. 6. Corner lead for reinforced brick masonry wall.

held in position by wiring them to the longitudinal reinforcing. The tops of the longitudinal reinforcing bars are held in position by means of a good templet or by securely tying them to a hoop placed near the top of the column.

The brick are laid as described previously in Chap. 30, Brick Construction. The hoops are placed in a full bed of mortar and the mortar smoothed out before the next course of brick is laid. Brick bats may be used in the core of the column or where it is inconvenient or impossible to use full-size brick. After all the brick in a course are laid, the core, and all remaining space around the reinforcing bars, is filled with mortar. Any bats required are then pushed into the mortar until completely embedded. The next mortar bed is now spread and the process repeated.

Reinforcing steel for walls consists of both horizontal and vertical bars and is placed as discussed previously. The vertical bars are wired to the dowels projecting up from the footing below and are placed in the mortar joint between tiers of brick. As the brick are laid, all space around the bars is filled with mortar. Otherwise, the wall is constructed as specified.

In the construction of corner leads, bars should be placed in the corner as shown in Fig. 6. The extension is 15 inches (37.5 cm.) and the bar size should be the same as that used for horizontal bars in the rest of the wall. The horizontal bars in the remainder of the wall lap these corner bars by the same 15 inches (37.5 cm.). As for beams, all the brick in one course between corner leads are laid before any other brick are laid. This is necessary since the entire reinforcing bar must be embedded in mortar at the same time.

Section 4

Stuccoing

STUCCO IS THE term given to plaster whenever it is applied on the exterior of a building or structure. Stucco can be applied over wood frames or masonry structures. The end product has all the desirable properties of concrete. It is hard, strong, fire resistant, weather resistant, does not deteriorate after repeated wetting and drying, resists rot and fungus, and retains colors.

Chapter 32

Materials and Tools

Stucco is a mixture of portland cement, hydrated lime, aggregate, and water used as an exterior wall covering. When properly mixed and applied it has durability combined with satisfactory appearance. Stucco hardens and sets slowly enough to permit texturing or finishing the final coat in any desired fashion. It is decorative and is a fairly good insulator against heat or cold. Properly mixed and applied stucco increases in strength and density with age. Its cost is moderate. (*See* Chap. 2, Concrete Ingredients.)

COMPOSITION OF STUCCO

Stucco is made with portland cement, hydrated lime, aggregate of a suitable size, and clean water. Other materials that may be required for specific types of stucco work are mineral pigments for tinting or color, hair or fiber for the scratch coat, and plasticizing materials added to the mixture when increased workability of the finish coat is desired.

Portland cement. The *portland cement* must be of standard, uniform quality and free from any lumps.

Aggregate. *Aggregate* should be clean natural sand, or prepared from stone or blast furnace slag, free from harmful amounts of loam, silt, soluble salts, and vegetable matter and should conform to the requirements for concrete sand, except that it should be graded within the following limitations.

Passing No. 4 sieve, 100 percent
Passing No. 8 sieve, 80 to 98 percent
Passing No. 16 sieve, 60 to 90 percent
Passing No. 30 sieve, 35 to 70 percent
Passing No. 50 sieve, 10 to 30 percent
Passing No. 100 sieve, not more than 10 percent

As in other forms of concrete work, the importance of proper grading of aggregate for portland cement stucco cannot be overemphasized. The coarser the aggregate in the base coats (scratch and brown), within the screen sizes previously indicated, the better. Care should be taken to select sands meeting these grading requirements that are at the same time well-graded from fine to coarse without a preponderance of particles retained between any successive screen sizes. This precaution applies particularly to the percentage of particles retained between the No. 30 and No. 50 standard screens. Where local concrete fine aggregates are deficient in the smaller sizes of fines, blending with available plaster sands may provide suitable grading.

For finish coats, it may be necessary to use a somewhat finer aggregate, but it should be kept in mind that excessive fineness is one of the principal causes of crazing and cracking. Aggregate such as that used to obtain a fine sand-finish on interior plaster is not suitable for use in portland cement stucco.

Water. Use only *water* that is fit to drink. It should be free from oil, acid, alkali, and vegetable matter.

Plasticizing agents. Materials (excepting cement) used as *lubricators* or *fatteners* to increase workability of the mortar are referred to as *plasticizing agents.* Diatomaceous earths, finely divided clays, asbestos flour or fiber, hydrated lime or lime putty, and the like, or small amounts of admixtures known as *wetting agents* are common plasticizing agents. Some portland cements prepared for use in stucco contain the proper amounts of plasticizing materials ground in with the cement by the manufacturer at the mill. The use of such cement makes it unnecessary to add a plasticizing admixture on the job. Where such cements are not used and where admixtures are added on the job, care should be taken to use only the highest quality materials and then only in limited amounts. Use minimum quantity that will produce required workability. Excessive amounts reduce strength and increase porosity.

Mineral pigments. Use only high-grade mineral pigments for coloring stucco. Such pigments have the highest color values and are most economical since less pigment is required to produce a desired effect. Do *not* use aniline base colors, other organic or vegetable dyes, or ordinary mortar colors. (*See* Chap. 16, Mineral Pigments for Use in Coloring Concrete.)

Mix pigments in finish coat materials on the job *only* when factory-made portland cement stucco is not available. It is possible to attain accuracy in measurement and thorough mixing of portland cement and mineral pigments in a factory-made product which ordinarily cannot be approached on the job.

In the event that factory-made portland cement stucco is not available, the use of colored cement, a commercial product obtainable in most markets, will be found best. If colored cement is not obtainable, then it will be necessary to mix the cement and mineral pigment on the job.

Coloring materials. A general guide for the selection of coloring materials follows:

For maximum brightness and clearness of color and for light shades, use white portland cement.

For *white,* use white portland cement.

For *brown,* use burnt umber or brown oxide of iron. Yellow oxide of iron may be added to obtain modification of this color.

For *buff,* use yellow ocher or yellow oxide of iron. Red oxide of iron may be added in limited quantities.

For *gray,* use small quantities of black iron oxide, manganese black, or Germantown lampblack.

For *green,* use chromium oxide. Yellow oxide of iron may be added.

For *pink,* use small quantity of red oxide of iron.

For *rose,* use red oxide of iron.

For *cream,* use yellow oxide of iron in small quantities.

PROPORTIONING AND MIXING

Each coat of stucco should be not richer than 1 part of portland cement to 3 parts damp, loose aggregate. Where aggregate is well graded with a good proportion of coarse particles a 1:3½ or 1:4 mix may be found satisfactory. If necessary, a plasticity agent may be used to increase workability of the mortar. Some portland cements prepared for use in stucco contain the proper amount of plasticizing material ground in with the cement by the manufacturer at the mill. The use of such cements makes it unnecessary to add a plasticizing admixture on the job. Where a plasticizing agent is added on the job, the amount required will vary with the kind of agent used, the grading of the aggregate, proportion of cementing materials and aggregate, and other factors. The kind and amount of plasticizing agent necessary for proper workability should be determined in advance of starting the job. Use the smallest amount possible to secure desired plasticity. The use of rich mixes or a large amount of admixtures will likely result in crazing or other damage.

To secure the desired strength and durability properties of portland cement stucco, the minimum average compressive strength of the stucco at 28 days of age should be 2,000 psi (140 kgs. per sq. cm.) when molded and tested as 2-inch (5-cm.) cubes. Portland cement stucco should not absorb more than 10 percent of its weight of water.

Determine proper proportion of mineral pigments in finish coat stucco by experiment. In general, see that the amount of coloring material does not exceed six percent of the weight of the cement. To obtain maximum clearness and brightness in colored finishes, white portland cement should be used. White finishes are obtained by using white cement and light-colored aggregate. A general guide to the selection of mineral pigments was described previously.

Measure materials accurately and proportion all batches exactly alike. Because variations in moisture content of aggregates cause changes in volume due to bulking, use only aggregates of uniform moisture content.

Mix materials to a uniform color before water is added; then wet mix them to the desired consistency. Thorough mixing is essential. Hand-mixing is satisfactory if done thoroughly, but machine-mixing usually gives greater uniformity. Run the mixer at least five minutes after all ingredients are in the drum. In hand-mixing, hoe the batch back and forth 10 to 15 minutes after the water is added. Stucco mortar made with normal portland cement is not injured by standing 2½ to 3 hours if it is remixed frequently without adding water. Let stucco stand at least one hour before using it. *Never* use stucco after it has hardened due to setting of the cement. Do not use admixtures to hasten set.

TOOLS

Tools similar to those used for general plastering are also used for cement stucco.

- Standard plastering trowel
- Round-point trowel
- Small leaf tool
- Carpet covered wood float
- Sheepskin glove
- Jointing tool
- Combing tool
- Rubber sponge
- Rubber glove
- Wire brush
- Dutch brush
- Cork float

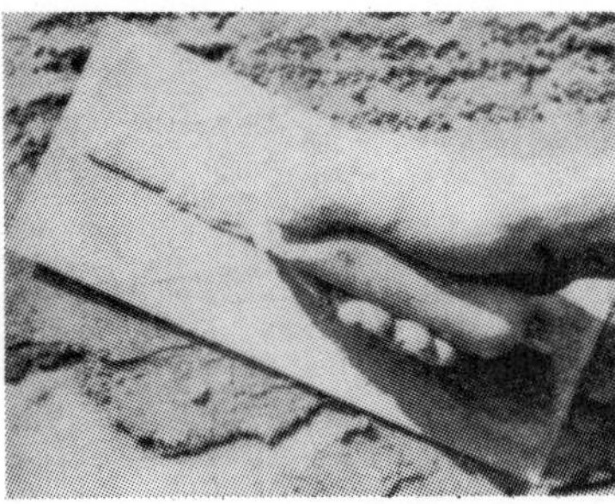

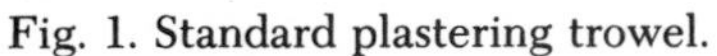

Fig. 1. Standard plastering trowel.

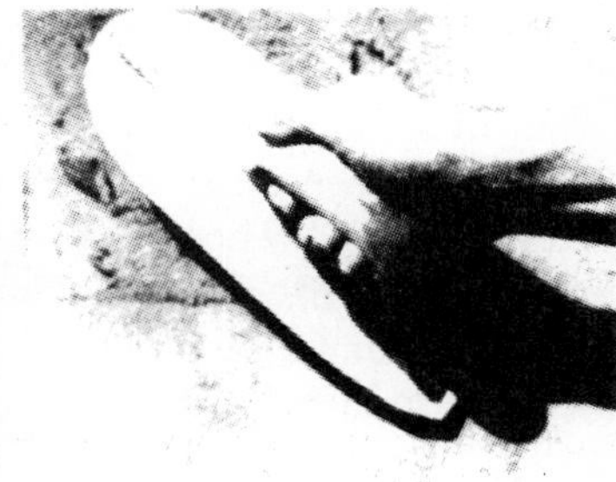

Fig. 2. Round-point trowel.

Fig. 3. Small leaf tool.

Fig. 4. Wood float.

For application of the first and second coats, use a standard plastering trowel and the round-point trowel (Figs. 1 and 2). The small leaf tool is for fine pointing (Fig. 3). A wood float covered with carpet produces a sanded finish (Fig. 4). When it is necessary to rub down heavy-textured stucco, use a sheepskin glove (Fig. 5). A jointing tool is used for marking off surfaces to resemble masonry (Fig. 6). After the surface of the concrete is marked off with the jointing tool, a combing tool (Fig. 7) produces the effect of a tooled stone finish. Rubber sponges (Fig. 8) produce pleasing surfaces. A rubber glove is used in making hand or palm textures (Fig. 9). The wire brush is used in making the *Travertine* texture (Fig. 10). Use the Dutch brush (Fig. 11) for applying washes or for softening rough textures. A cork float (Fig. 12) is used to produce finishes.

(*See* Chaps. 6, 7, 21 and 26 for tools and equipment used for Concrete, for Forms and Form Making, for Masonry, and for Bricklaying.)

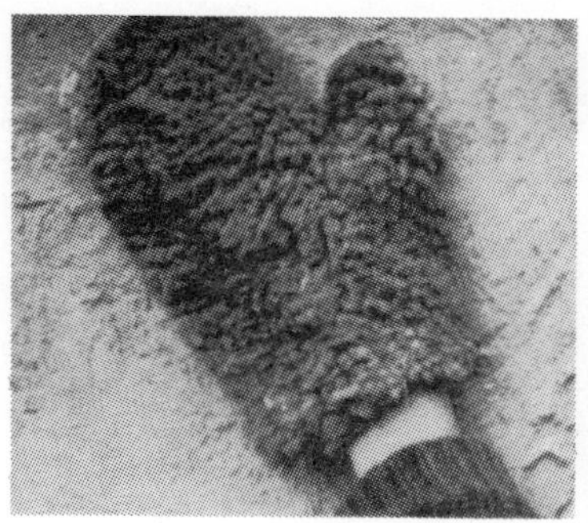

Fig. 5. Sheepskin glove.

Fig. 6. Jointing tool.

Fig. 7. Combing tool.

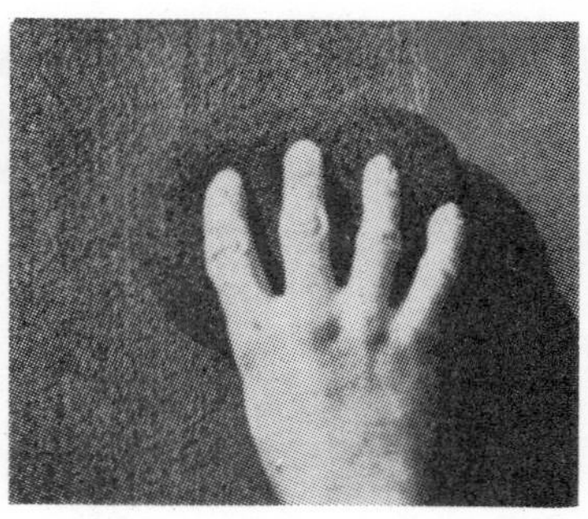

Fig. 8. Rubber sponge.

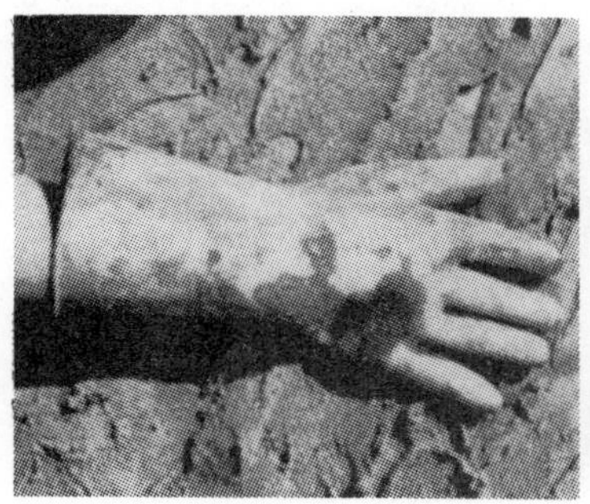

Fig. 9. Rubber glove.

Fig. 10. Wire brush.

Fig. 11. Dutch brush.

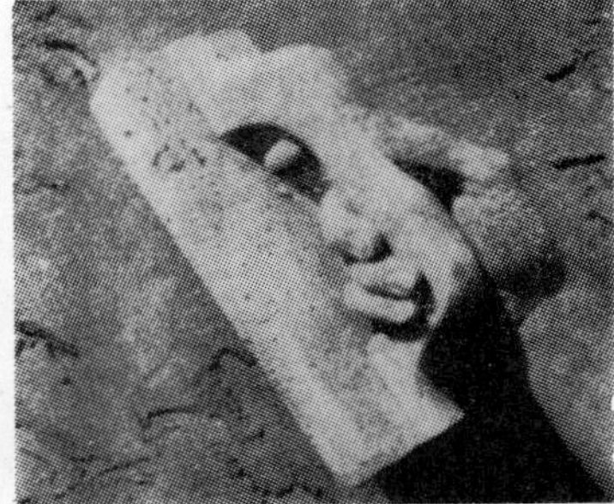

Fig. 12. Cork float.

SUCTION

Suction is absolutely necessary in order to get the proper bond of stucco on masonry or cast-in-place concrete. It is also necessary in first and second coats so that succeeding coats will bond properly.

Uniform suction helps to obtain uniform color. If one part of the wall draws more moisture from the stucco than another, the finish coat may be spotty.

Obtain uniform suction by dampening, but not soaking, the wall evenly before applying the stucco. If the surface becomes dry in spots, dampen these areas again to restore uniform suction. A fog spray (Fig. 13) is recommended for this work. Work on the shady side of buildings when possible, for it is hard to keep walls damp when they are exposed to the sun. If water-

Fig. 13. Fog spray.

proofing is used in base coat mortar, dampening the first and second coats to obtain uniform suction may not be required except in hot, dry weather.

CURING

To develop maximum strength and density, it is necessary to cure portland cement stucco properly. *Keep brown and finish coats damp continuously for at least two days.* Begin moistening each coat as soon as the stucco has hardened sufficiently not to be injured, applying the water in a fine fog spray. Avoid soaking the wall. Give it only as much water as will be readily absorbed. To prevent excessive evaporation in hot, dry weather, hang tarpaulins over the outside.

After the damp-curing period, allow the stucco coat to dry thoroughly before the next is applied. The practice of doubling coats is not a good construction practice.

When stucco is applied during cold weather, longer curing periods are necessary. In freezing weather, do not apply stucco unless special methods are employed to keep the materials at a temperature above 50°F. (10°C.) for at least 48 hours.

Chapter 33

Preparation of Base and Application of Stucco

Proper application of portland cement stucco requires that it be used either (1) as a material that is bonded to and becomes an integral part of the base to which it is applied, such as stucco on masonry, or (2) as a thin reinforced concrete slab anchored to the structure but not itself forming an integral part of the backing, such as stucco applied on metal reinforcement. (*See* Chap. 32, Stucco Materials and Tools.)

MASONRY WALLS AS STUCCO BASE

Concrete masonry walls are excellent bases for the direct application of portland cement stucco. (*See* Fig. 1.) The surfaces of masonry units should be rough to provide good mechanical key and should be free from paint, oil, dust, dirt, soot, or any material that might prevent satisfactory bond.

It is recommended that masonry cement or portland cement mortar be used in laying up masonry walls that are to be stuccoed. Joints may be struck off flush or slightly raked.

Old masonry walls softened by weathering, surfaces that cannot be cleaned thoroughly, such as painted brickwork, and *all chimneys*, must be covered with metal reinforcement before applying stucco. (*See* Figs. 2 and 3.) (*See* section on Metal Reinforcement later in this chapter; *see also* Chap. 2, Concrete Ingredients; Chap. 20, Masonry Materials.)

Fig. 1. Scratch coat applied directly to masonry walls having a coarse texture.

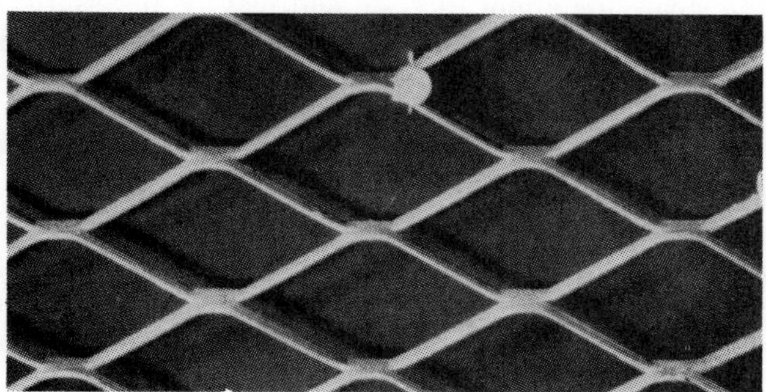

Fig. 2. Type of expanded metal reinforcement.

Fig. 3. Type of welded wire fabric reinforcement.

CAST-IN-PLACE CONCRETE

Cast-in-place concrete walls having coarse or roughened surfaces are suitable bases for direct application of portland cement stucco. Such surfaces should be free from paint, oil, dust, dirt, soot, or any material that might prevent satisfactory bond. When surfaces are not rough enough, prepare them as follows:

1. Roughen old cast-in-place concrete walls with bushhammers or other special tools; wash thoroughly with water; let wall dry until suction is restored.
2. Acid-washing (Fig. 4) using a solution of one part muriatic acid to six parts water, is another method. First wet the wall with water so that the acid will act on the surface only. More than one application of acid may be necessary. After this treatment wash the wall thoroughly with water to remove all acid. Let wall dry until suction is restored. If wall is not roughened sufficiently, use bushhammers.
3. New cast-in-place concrete can be roughened with a heavy wire brush or a special scoring tool if forms are removed early, but do not remove forms before the concrete is hard enough to be self-sustaining. *Never* coat forms with oil or soap, as these are likely to remain on the concrete, interfering with stucco bond. Oil on the surface of concrete can be removed by washing with soap and water.
4. Dashing on the first coat of portland cement stucco is another method when concrete walls are not sufficiently rough (Fig. 5).
5. Cast-in-place concrete surfaces also can be roughened by special compounds painted on the form faces (Fig. 6). These retard hardening of the surface concrete. Roughness is obtained by brushing off surface material after forms are removed. (*See* Chap. 7, Forms and Form Making.)

METAL REINFORCEMENT

Metal reinforcement must be used for stucco applied on wood or steel frame structures of open or sheathed type, on masonry

Fig. 4. Acid-washing cast-in-place concrete will improve the bond between dash coat and concrete surface.

Fig. 5. If concrete wall isn't sufficiently rough, dash on first coat of portland cement stucco.

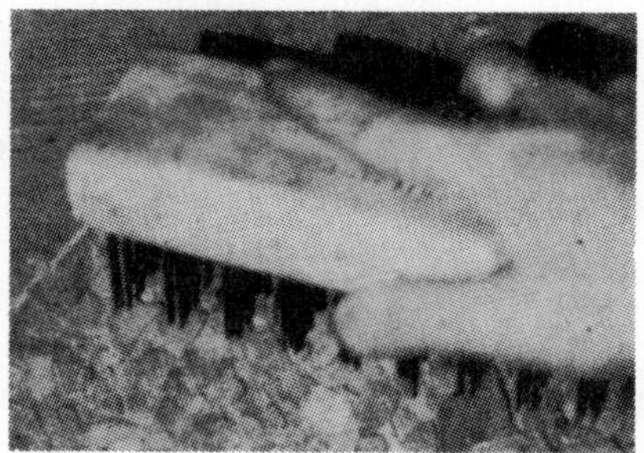

Fig. 6. Roughness obtained by brushing off surface material after forms are removed.

structures that do not provide satisfactory bond (chimneys and disintegrating surfaces), and on many old stucco surfaces. (*See* section on Refinishing Old Stucco Jobs later in this chapter.) Metal reinforcement is also used wherever stucco is to be carried over flashing.

Structures to receive stucco on metal reinforcement should be well braced and rigid. In sheathed construction, see that studs are not more than 16 inches (40 cm.) on center, are tied together below floor joists, and bridged at least once every story height.

Diagonal bracing at all corners, let into the studs, is recommended to give additional rigidity. Place the sheathing horizontally and nail it well on each stud. In open wood-frame construction, studs should be not over 12 inches (30 cm.) on center. Brace them even more rigidly than in sheathed construction.

Cover surfaces to receive metal reinforcement (excepting areas to be back-plastered) with waterproof building paper. On open construction the paper serves as a backing for the scratch coat. In sheathed construction and on masonry surfaces requiring metal reinforcement, paper prevents absorption of moisture from fresh mortar. Attach paper with large-headed galvanized nails. Make upper strips overlap lower strips at least 3 inches (7.5 cm.). Lap vertical joints at least 6 inches (15 cm.). To support the paper and prevent tearing on open-frame construction, fasten wires (usually No. 18 gage) tightly across the faces of the studs in single strands at 6- or 8-inch (15- or 20-cm.) intervals.

Use large-mesh metal reinforcement—expanded metal, welded wire, or stucco netting of minimum net weight, 1.8 pounds per square yard or 20 pounds per 100 square feet (.98 kgs. per sq. meter). For some jobs, a heavier product is desirable. Openings should not be less than ¾ inch (1.9 cm.) in the small dimension nor larger than 3 inches (7.5 cm.) in the large dimension and not exceed 4 square inches (26 cm.) in area. For back-plaster construction, metal reinforcement weighing 3.4 pounds per square yard (1.9 kgs. per sq. meter) is recommended.

Large openings in the reinforcement are desirable so that mortar will be pushed through to backing, completely embedding the metal. Where there is no backing, as in work to be back-plastered, reinforcement of relatively small mesh (metal lath or wire lath) is necessary. Complete coverage of the metal in the latter case is obtained when back-plaster coat is applied. (*See* Chap. 34, Flashing and Overcoating Construction Details.)

Attach reinforcement securely. Do not nail or staple it flat against the face of studs or sheathing. Have it furred out at least ¼ inch (6.3 mm.) so that stucco can be forced behind the metal. Use furring nails or other furring devices that will not reduce the thickness of the stucco (Fig. 7). Nails should penetrate supports no less than 1 inch (2.5 cm.). Solid furring strips which cut into

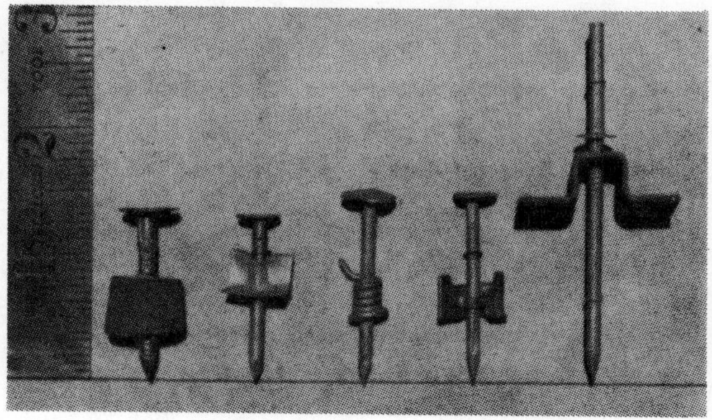

Fig. 7. Several types of furring nails.

the stucco slab are objectionable. They make lines of weakness and may cause cracking.

Reinforcement should form a continuous network of metal over the entire surface as shown in Fig. 8. Laps at ends and sides of large mesh reinforcement should be at least one mesh and not less than 2 inches. For small mesh types, laps should be at least 1 inch (2.5 cm.). Laps should be wired securely. Lapping at the ends of the reinforcement should be staggered. Carry sheets of reinforcement around corners with at least one stud spacing on open-frame construction, and at least 4 inches (10 cm.) on other types.

Overcoating

In refinishing old buildings having weatherboard or shingle siding, weatherboards or shingles may be removed or left in place. In the latter case, re-nail any loose pieces and build out trim to provide proper projection. Waterproof paper and metal reinforcement must be applied. (*See* Chap. 34, Flashing and Overcoating Construction Details.)

APPLICATION OF STUCCO

Stucco should be applied in three coats. The first coat is called the *scratch* coat; the second the *brown* coat; and the final coat

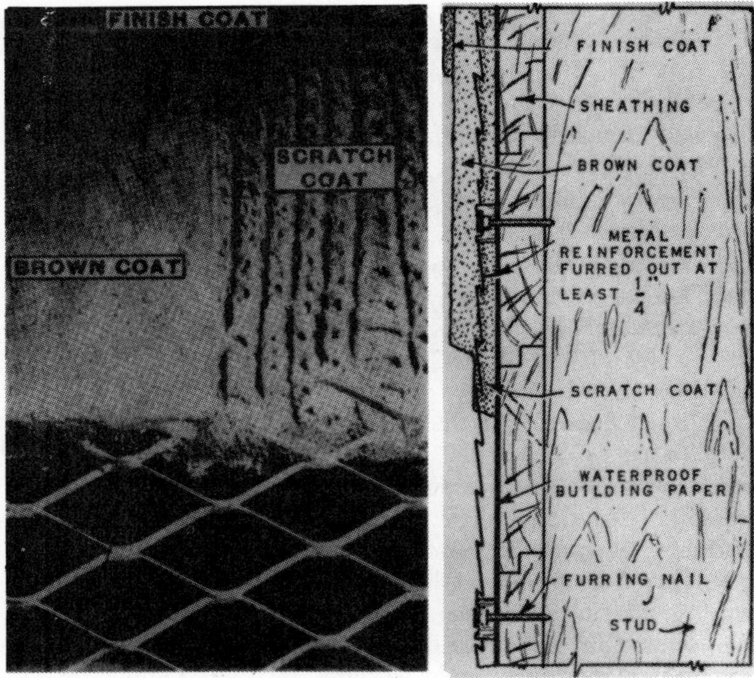

Fig. 8. Proper construction for stucco on metal reinforcement. Note the backing of waterproof building paper, metal reinforcement held at least ¼ inch away from the backing with furring nails, and scratch coat filled in solidly behind metal.

the *finish* coat. However, on masonry, where no reinforcement is used, two coats may be sufficient. Start at the top and work down the wall. This will prevent balls of mortar falling on completed work.

Scratch Coat

Make the scratch coat approximately ⅜-inch (.94-cm.) thick; (measured from the face of the backing) carry it the full length of the wall or to natural breaking points like doors or windows. Before the scratch coat hardens, cross-scratch it to provide mechanical key for the brown coat. The type of scratcher, shown in Fig. 9, not only makes broad impressions but when used at an angle also roughens the surface between furrows. Scratching

Fig. 9. Scratcher.

should be done horizontally so that when moisture is applied it will be retained in the wall to aid curing.

Masonry walls on which stucco is to be applied direct should be clean and dry. But, before applying the scratch coat, dampen the surface evenly to control suction. (*See* section on Suction in this chapter.) Apply the scratch coat with heavy pressure.

On cast-in-place concrete walls, dash the first coat on unless the surface is sufficiently rough to insure adequate bond for a scratch coat applied with a trowel. Rough surfaces that permit successful application with the trowel are produced by mechanical roughening or through the use of special compounds. (*See* section on Cast-in-place Concrete previously described.) Surfaces treated by acid-washing generally are not rough enough, in which case a dash coat is necessary. Dashing on the first coat aids in getting good bond by excluding air which might otherwise be trapped behind the stucco.

Apply the dash coat with a whisk broom or fiber brush, using a strong whipping motion at right angles to the face of the wall, or with a stucco machine or cement gun. In either case, project it with considerable force. Use mortar of a mushy consistency, composed of 1 part portland cement to 1½ parts aggregate. Keep damp for at least two days immediately following its application. Then allow it to dry thoroughly.

Completely embed *metal reinforcement* in mortar. This is easy when the large-mesh type of reinforcement is used, for openings are large enough to permit scratch coat mortar to pass through readily. Metal which is not embedded completely is likely to rust out within a few years. In back-plastered construction, the back-plaster coat assures complete coverage of the metal. This is ⅜-inch (9.4-mm.) mortar applied to the back of the reinforcement after the scratch coat has hardened enough so pressure will not break the plaster keys.

Second or Brown Coat

Before starting to apply the *brown coat,* dampen the surface of the scratch coat evenly as described in the section on *Suction.* Make the brown coat about ⅜-inch (9.4-mm.) thick. This coat may be applied in two thin coats, one immediately following the other. Such a method may prove helpful in applying sufficient pressure to insure a proper bond with the base coat. Bring it to a true even surface, then roughen with a wood float or cross-scratch it lightly to provide bond for finish coat. Damp-cure the brown coat for at least two days, and allow it to dry.

Finish Coat

There should be at least a seven-day interval between application of the brown coat and finish coat. Before applying the finish coat, dampen the brown coat evenly as described in the section on *Suction.* Whenever possible, apply texture coat from top to bottom in one operation to eliminate joining marks. If the finish coat is factory-made material, follow manufacturer's directions closely.

TEXTURES AND TEXTURING

The plasticity of stucco makes it possible for many attractive textures to be produced on the finish coat. The most popular textures are Colonial, Spanish, Californian, Modern American, English Cottage, Italian, and Italian Travertine. (*See* Chap. 32, Stucco Materials and Tools.)

The *Colonial texture* is a smooth, sand-floated surface (Fig. 10). The lighter tints—white, ivory, buff, or, occasionally, a pale cream yellow—are generally used for this finish. Use a square trowel and the method shown for applying the brown coat to produce this finish (Fig. 11). To insure a regular, even surface, rub the brown coat with a wood float (Fig. 12). Use a circular motion to produce an even but comparatively coarse texture. For the finish coat apply the mortar in a very thin, hard layer (Fig. 13). Allow it to harden sufficiently so that it does not rub off when work is continued. Wetting the finish coat with a brush may be necessary so the wall can be rubbed with a carpet float. (*See* Figs. 14 and 15.) Finish by carpet floating the surface. Use a circular rubbing motion to produce a smooth, evenly sanded finish.

The Spanish texture is a wavy, trowel-marked finish, with the stucco compacted and the surface pores closed (Fig. 16). The first two coats are applied in the usual way. (*See* Figs. 17 and 18.) For the finish coat apply heavy layers using a round-point trowel. Use a full trowel of fairly stiff mortar for each stroke. Make strokes in all directions, curving and varying them to form rolling ridges and hollows in the finished surface. Make a left horizontal stroke (Fig. 19) to produce this texture. Note that uniform dampening of the brown coat helps spread this finish. This procedure makes the mortar stand as placed. Irregular overlapping (Fig. 20) helps to produce a pleasant effect. Avoid excessive troweling in producing any portland cement stucco texture. Finish by smoothing out rough edges with a round-point trowel (Fig. 21) before mortar hardens to a point where workability is lost.

The *Californian texture* is a rubbed, troweled finish (Fig. 22)—like plaster over an irregular surface with the added touch of highlights. Use full sweep spreading, as in creating the Spanish texture, stroking full trowels of mortar in all directions (Fig. 23). Make curved strokes with a rounded trowel (Fig. 24) as there are no straight-line markings. Apply full trowels of mortar and leave in place without additional smoothing (Fig. 25). Before the mortar hardens, rub its surface down with a wadded piece of burlap to produce a wavy, irregular, coarse surface (Fig.

Fig. 10. Colonial texture.

Fig. 11. Use a square trowel to apply the brown coat.

Fig. 12. Rub the brown coat with a wood float to insure an even texture.

Fig. 13. Apply a thin, hard layer of mortar for the finish coat.

Fig. 14. Wetting the wall with a brush.

Fig. 15. Finish by carpet floating the surface. Use a circular rubbing motion.

Fig. 16. Spanish texture.

Fig. 17. First coat.

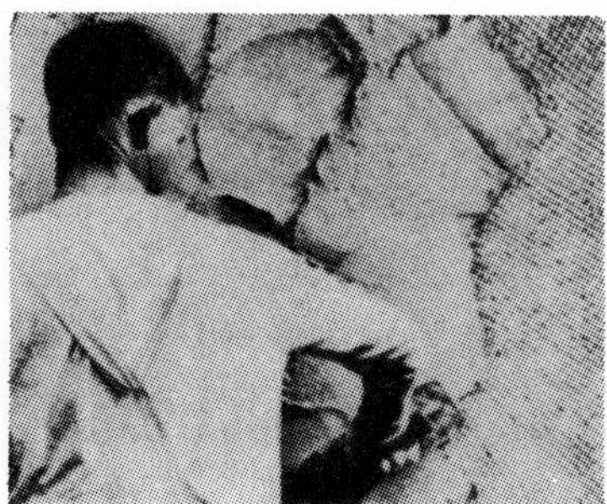

Fig. 18. Second coat.

Fig. 19. Apply heavy layers using a round-point trowel for finish coat.

Fig. 20. Irregular overlapping produces the wavy finish characteristic of the Spanish texture.

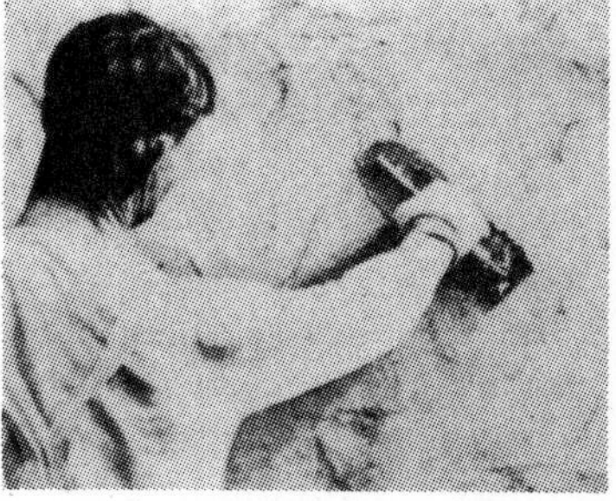

Fig. 21. Finish by smoothing out rough edges with round-point trowel.

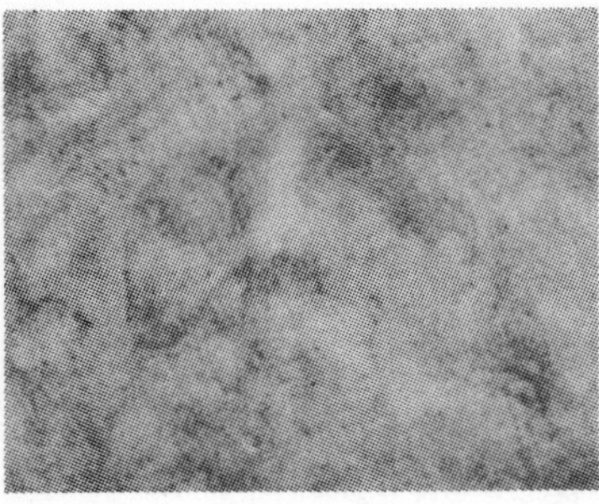

Fig. 22. California texture.

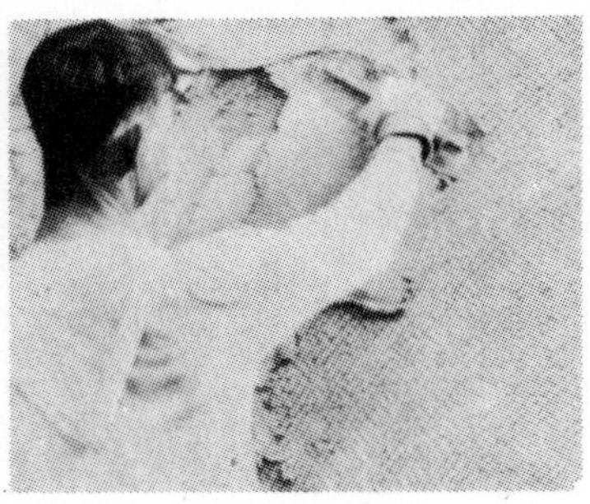

Fig. 23. Use full-sweep spreading, stroking full trowels of mortar in all directions.

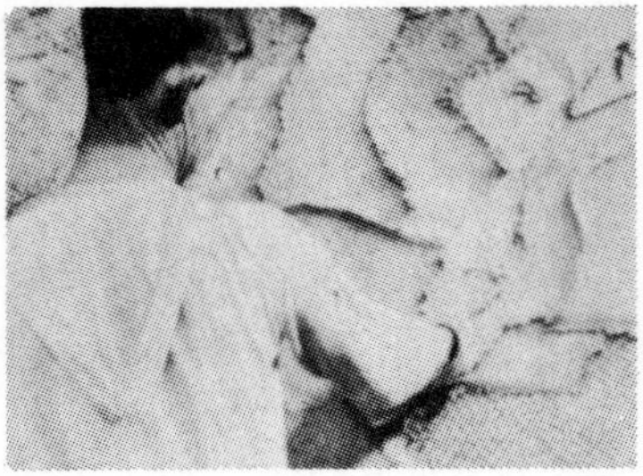

Fig. 24. Make curved strokes with a rounded trowel.

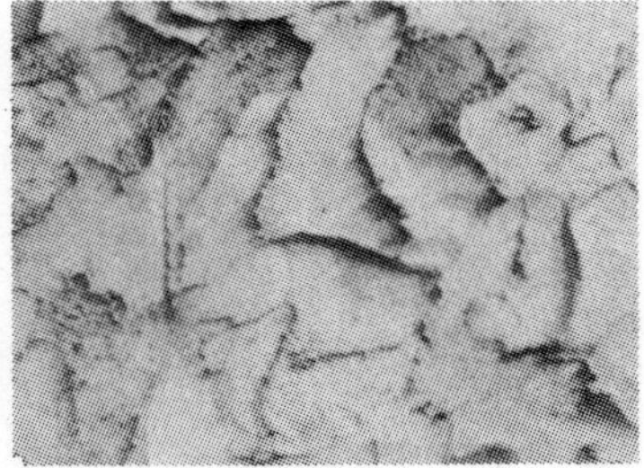

Fig. 25. Apply full trowels of mortar and leave in place without additional smoothing.

26). To finish this texture (Fig. 27), trowel the entire area creating highlights. Force the sand particles into the mortar, compacting the surface.

The *modern American texture* is a tapestry finish (Fig. 28). Its surface may be lightly brushed with a color pigment different from the one used in the mortar. To produce this rough-torn texture, make the final mortar coat rather heavy, about ¼-inch (6.3-mm.) thick (Fig. 29); this will permit roughening later. To produce the preliminary finish, use the full spread placing of the mortar (Fig. 30). Make no special effort to remove the trowel marks. The preliminary finish should be rough-torn by drawing the edge of a wood block up the face of the wall (Fig. 31). To

Fig. 26. Rub surface down with burlap before it hardens.

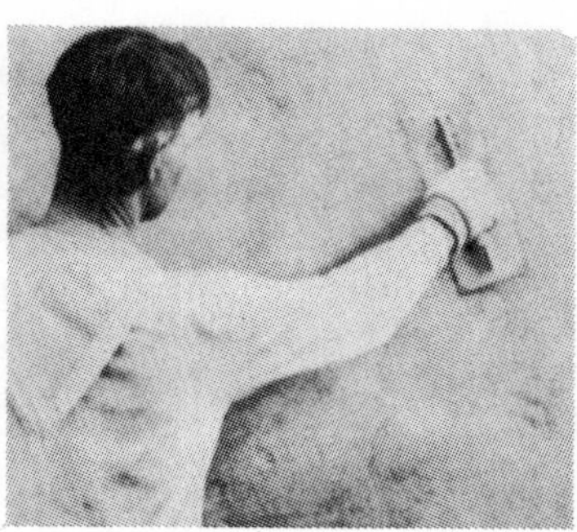

Fig. 27. Rub surface down with trowel to create highlights.

Fig. 28. Modern American texture.

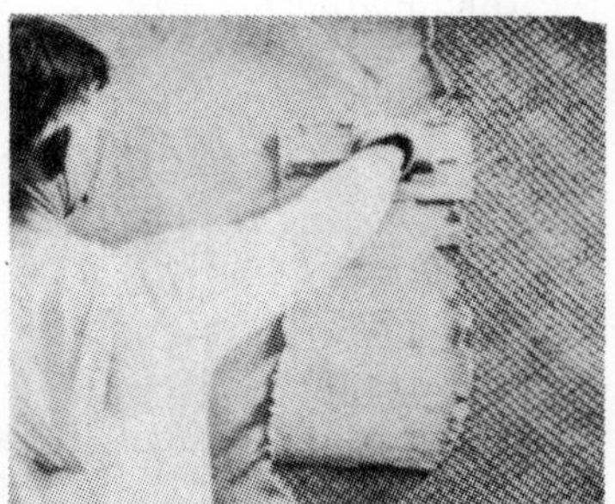

Fig. 29. Final coat should be heavy, about ¼-inch (6.3-mm.) thick.

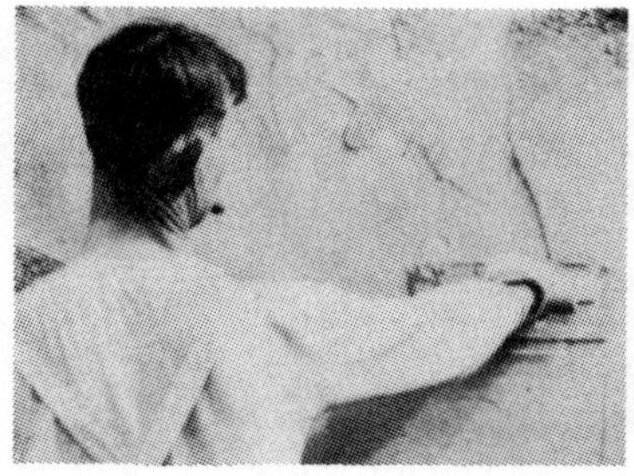

Fig. 30. Use full spread placing of the mortar.

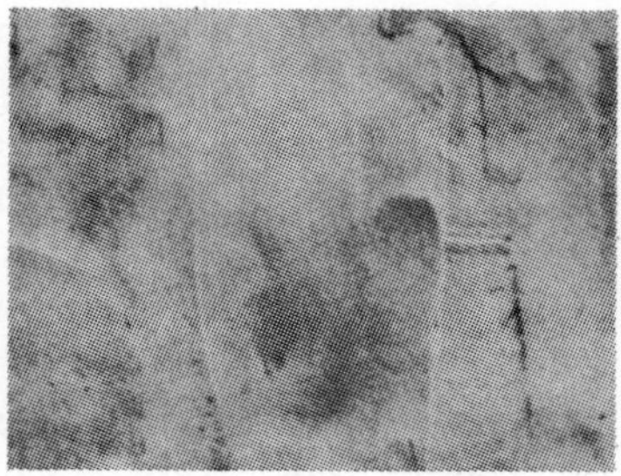

Fig. 31. Preliminary finish.

produce a lightly torn surface, tilt the block at an angle as it is drawn up (Fig. 32). Never use a downward stroke. To tear the surface lightly, hold the board in one hand. If a heavier texture is desired, use both hands (Fig. 33).

The *English Cottage texture* (Fig. 34) is a fine, leaflike finish. This texture is produced by applying a thin backing coat about ⅛-inch (3.1-mm.) thick (Fig. 35). Portions of this are exposed in final texture; other portions provide a base for added mortar. Continue by feathering with a square trowel (Fig. 36) as you add small amounts of the mortar with short, twisting strokes at varying angles to the wall. Pinch off the stucco in all directions (Fig. 37). Avoid vertical or nearly vertical strokes when feathering with the square trowel. When producing this texture, use a twisting, feathering application (Fig. 38). Twisting the trowel in this manner as you apply a pat of mortar will form slightly curved ridges. Variations of this texture are obtained by varying the amount of mortar, the directions and length of the strokes, and the twisting motion (Fig. 39).

The *Italian texture* (Fig. 40) is a troweled, spatter-dash finish. To produce this attractive and popular finish, apply a thin backing coat over the entire surface to insure uniform color (Fig. 41). Proceed by dashing small quantities of mortar with quick strokes of a whisk broom (Fig. 42). This texture may be a different color, if a polychrome effect is desired. Holding a bucket for spatter-dash work, cover only 30 square feet (2.8 sq. meters) of the wall at a time with a whisk broom (Fig. 43). A bundle of reeds may be used instead of a whisk broom. Allow the spatter-dash coat of mortar to set partially before beginning the final finishing operation (Fig. 44). To finish this texture, place the trowel flat against the dash coat, and draw it evenly across the wall, left to right (Fig. 45). Smoothing the return stroke erases possible trowel marks.

The *Italian Travertine texture* (Fig. 46) is a stippled, troweled finish. Greater pressure on the trowel will give a finer veining. You can cut joints in this texture to simulate masonry by using the jointing tool. Apply a very thick coat of mortar (about ⅜ inch or 6.3-mm. thick) to a well-dampened brown coat to retard hardening and permit texturing operations (Fig. 47). Trowel the

Fig. 32. Use the edge of a wood block to produce rough-torn finish.

Fig. 33. Use both hands to hold the board if a heavier texture is desired.

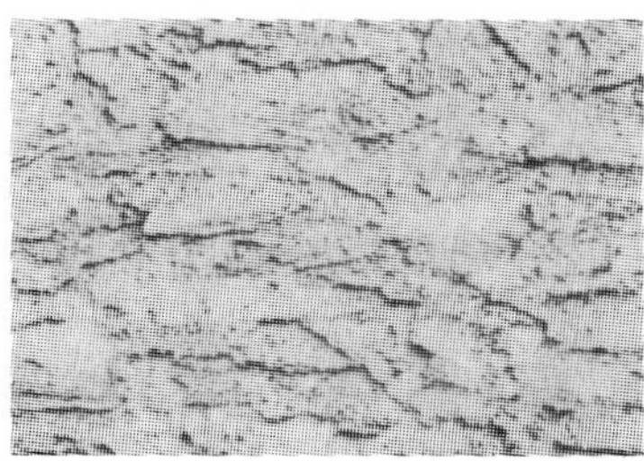

Fig. 34. English cottage texture.

Fig. 35. Apply a thin backing coat, about ⅛-inch (3.2-mm.) thick.

Fig. 36. Feather with a square trowel.

Fig. 37. Pinch off the stucco in all directions.

Fig. 38. Use twisting, feathering application to form slightly curved ridges.

Fig. 39. Varying the amount of mortar, the direction and length of the strokes, and the twisting motion will vary the texture.

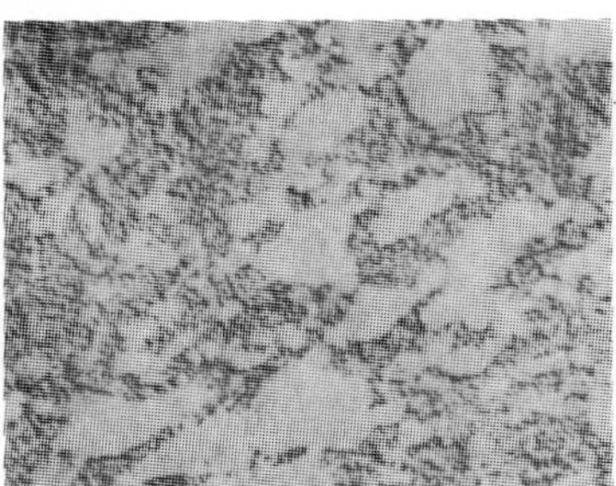

Fig. 40. Italian texture.

Fig. 41. Apply a thin backing coat over the entire surface.

Fig. 42. Dash small quantities of mortar with quick strokes of a whisk broom.

Fig. 43. Carry a bucket and cover only about 30 square feet (2.8 sq. meters) at a time.

Fig. 44. Allow the spatter-dash coat to partially set before finishing.

Fig. 45. Draw the trowel (held flat) evenly across the wall.

finish coat fairly smooth (Fig. 48), then stipple deeply, and, using a whisk broom or a wire brush, pull up an irregular texture. Hold the brush at an angle as shown in Fig. 49. Stippling should be irregular in appearance as shown in Fig. 50, and later troweled while it is still plastic and workable. Depressions made by stippling remain rough and furnish a veined effect (Fig. 51).

REFINISHING OLD STUCCO JOBS

Old stucco jobs may be resurfaced to renew finish and change color or texture, or both. The new stucco may be applied directly, provided the old stucco is sound. If original stucco is

Fig. 46. Italian travertine finish.

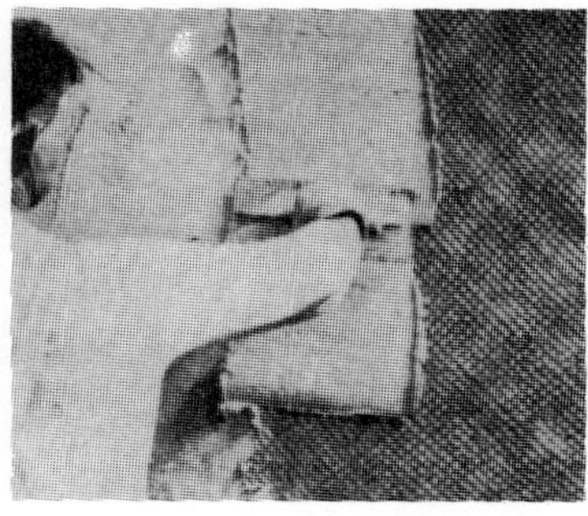

Fig. 47. Apply a very thick coat of mortar (⅜-inch or 9.3-mm.) to well-dampened brown coat.

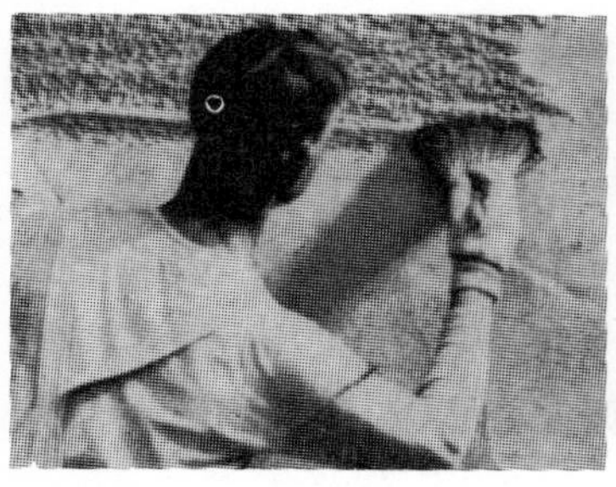

Fig. 48. After troweling the surface fairly smooth, stipple it deeply using a whisk broom or wire brush.

Fig. 49. Hold the brush at an angle.

Fig. 50. Stippling should be irregular in appearance.

Fig. 51. The surface should be troweled while it is still plastic.

unsound, it is necessary to remove the old material entirely and apply a new three-coat job.

Where old stucco is not removable, it is necessary to cover the old surface with paper and metal reinforcement and then apply the standard three coats.

Hard to Prepare Surface

Prepare sound stucco surfaces for refinishing as follows:

Wet the entire area; then clean it with a solution of one part muriatic acid and six parts water. After the acid-treatment, wash the area thoroughly with water to remove all traces of acid. Allow the wall to dry thoroughly; then moisten it just prior to applying the new coat. On surfaces of coarse or rough texture, the new finish may be a single coat applied with the trowel. If the old surface lacks roughness, apply two coats, dashing on the first to establish bond.

After the dash coat is properly cured, as previously described in Chap. 32, Stucco Materials and Tools, in the section on Curing, trowel on the finish coat.

Never apply portland cement stucco directly over lime, gypsum, or magnesite stucco. These materials either should be removed entirely or covered first with waterproof paper and metal reinforcement. (*See* section on Metal Reinforcement in this chapter.)

In either case, apply the standard three coats of portland cement stucco.

CAUSES OF DISCOLORATION

The most common causes of discoloration are:

1. Failure to have uniform suction in either of the base coats.
2. Improper flashing and corrosion of flashing or metal attachments. (*See* Chap. 34, Flashing and Overcoating Construction Details, for Flashing Details.)
3. Poor mixing of finish coat materials and use of inferior pigments.

4. Changes in materials or in proportions during a job.
5. Variations in amount of mixing water.
6. Failure to provide drips and washes on sills and projecting trim.
7. Use of additional water to retemper mortar.

Chapter 34

Flashing and Overcoating Construction Details

Flashing is vital to satisfactory results. Design and place it so water will not get behind the stucco. Place continuous flashing under all copings, cornices, belt courses, and multiple-piece sills to prevent entry of water. Use only high-grade rust-resisting material for flashing. Do not use a short-lived metal with a permanent wall covering such as portland cement stucco. Lead-covered copper is preferable, as pure copper has a tendency to turn green and stain the stucco finish. All flashings must be designed and placed to prevent water seepage behind the stucco.

For suggested designs and construction details for flashings see Figs. 1 through 6.

Overcoating. In refinishing old buildings that have weatherboard or shingle siding, you may either remove weatherboards and shingles or leave them in place. In the latter case, renail any loose pieces and build out trim to provide proper projection. Waterproofing paper and metal reinforcement must be applied as shown in detail in Fig. 3. (*See* Chap. 12, Stucco Materials and Tools; *see also* Chap. 33, Preparation of Base and Application of Stucco.)

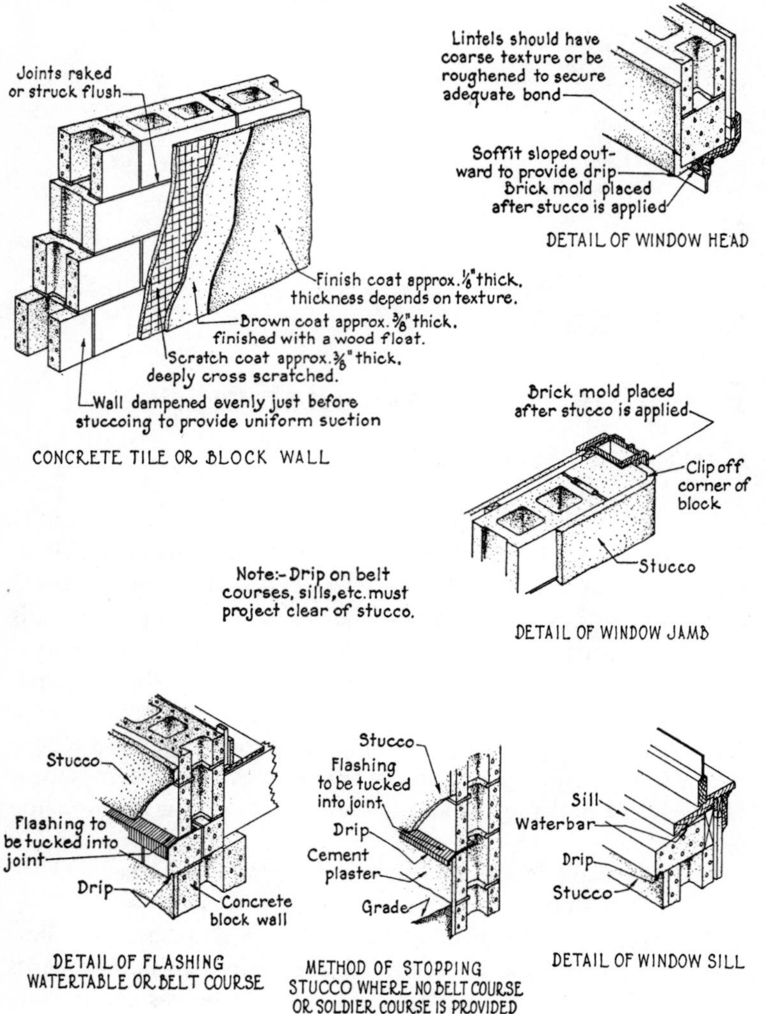
Joints raked or struck flush
Finish coat approx. 1/8" thick. thickness depends on texture.
Brown coat approx. 3/8" thick. finished with a wood float.
Scratch coat approx. 3/8" thick. deeply cross scratched.
Wall dampened evenly just before stuccoing to provide uniform suction
CONCRETE TILE OR BLOCK WALL
Lintels should have coarse texture or be roughened to secure adequate bond
Soffit sloped outward to provide drip
Brick mold placed after stucco is applied
DETAIL OF WINDOW HEAD
Brick mold placed after stucco is applied
Clip off corner of block
Stucco
Note:- Drip on belt courses, sills, etc. must project clear of stucco.
DETAIL OF WINDOW JAMB
Stucco
Flashing to be tucked into joint
Drip
Concrete block wall
DETAIL OF FLASHING WATERTABLE OR BELT COURSE
Stucco
Flashing to be tucked into joint
Drip
Cement plaster
Grade
METHOD OF STOPPING STUCCO WHERE NO BELT COURSE OR SOLDIER COURSE IS PROVIDED
Sill
Waterbar
Drip
Stucco
DETAIL OF WINDOW SILL

Fig. 1. Stucco on concrete masonry.

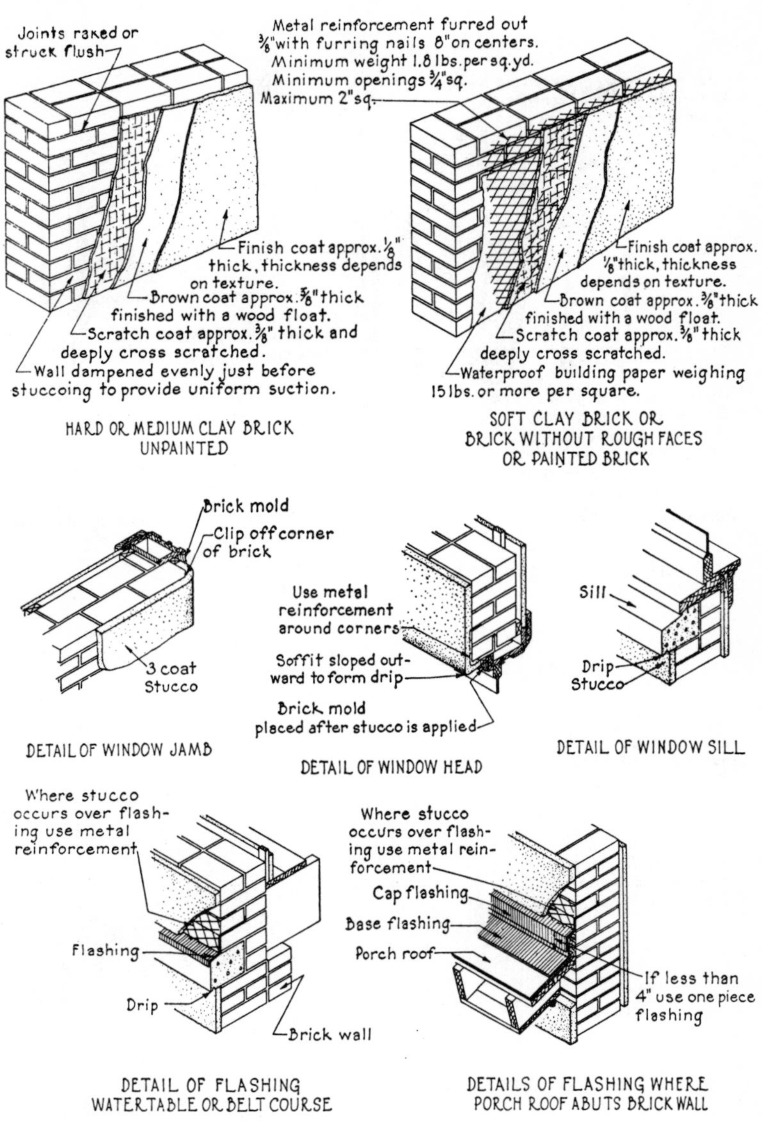
Joints raked or struck flush
Metal reinforcement furred out 3/8" with furring nails 8" on centers. Minimum weight 1.8 lbs. per sq. yd. Minimum openings 3/4" sq. Maximum 2" sq.
Finish coat approx. 1/8" thick, thickness depends on texture.
Brown coat approx. 3/8" thick finished with a wood float.
Scratch coat approx. 3/8" thick and deeply cross scratched.
Wall dampened evenly just before stuccoing to provide uniform suction.
Finish coat approx. 1/8" thick, thickness depends on texture.
Brown coat approx. 3/8" thick finished with a wood float.
Scratch coat approx. 3/8" thick deeply cross scratched.
Waterproof building paper weighing 15 lbs. or more per square.
HARD OR MEDIUM CLAY BRICK UNPAINTED
SOFT CLAY BRICK OR BRICK WITHOUT ROUGH FACES OR PAINTED BRICK
Brick mold
Clip off corner of brick
3 coat Stucco
DETAIL OF WINDOW JAMB
Use metal reinforcement around corners
Soffit sloped outward to form drip
Brick mold placed after stucco is applied
DETAIL OF WINDOW HEAD
Sill
Drip
Stucco
DETAIL OF WINDOW SILL
Where stucco occurs over flashing use metal reinforcement
Flashing
Drip
Brick wall
DETAIL OF FLASHING WATERTABLE OR BELT COURSE
Where stucco occurs over flashing use metal reinforcement
Cap flashing
Base flashing
Porch roof
If less than 4" use one piece flashing
DETAILS OF FLASHING WHERE PORCH ROOF ABUTS BRICK WALL

Fig. 2. Stucco on brick.

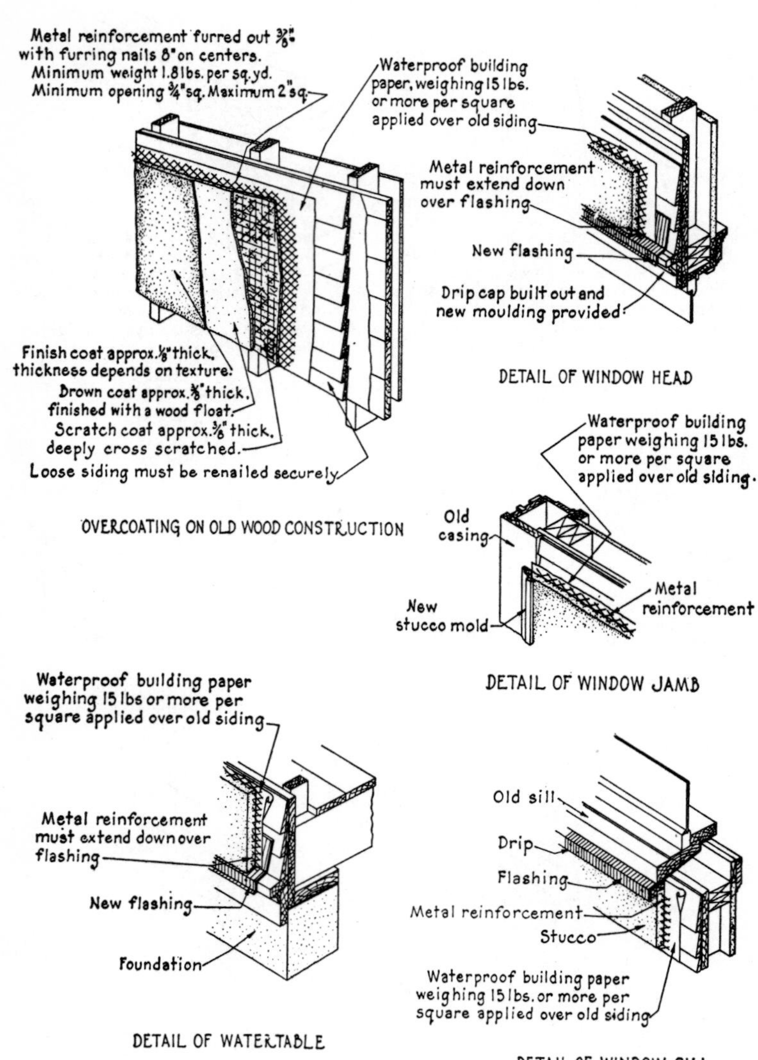
Metal reinforcement furred out 3/8" with furring nails 8" on centers. Minimum weight 1.8 lbs. per sq. yd. Minimum opening 3/4" sq. Maximum 2" sq.
Waterproof building paper, weighing 15 lbs. or more per square applied over old siding
Finish coat approx. 1/8" thick, thickness depends on texture.
Brown coat approx. 3/8" thick, finished with a wood float.
Scratch coat approx. 3/8" thick, deeply cross scratched.
Loose siding must be renailed securely
OVERCOATING ON OLD WOOD CONSTRUCTION
Metal reinforcement must extend down over flashing
New flashing
Drip cap built out and new moulding provided
DETAIL OF WINDOW HEAD
Waterproof building paper weighing 15 lbs. or more per square applied over old siding.
Old casing
New stucco mold
Metal reinforcement
DETAIL OF WINDOW JAMB
Waterproof building paper weighing 15 lbs or more per square applied over old siding
Metal reinforcement must extend down over flashing
New flashing
Foundation
DETAIL OF WATERTABLE
Old sill
Drip
Flashing
Metal reinforcement
Stucco
Waterproof building paper weighing 15 lbs. or more per square applied over old siding
DETAIL OF WINDOW SILL

Fig. 3. Stucco overcoating on wood frame.

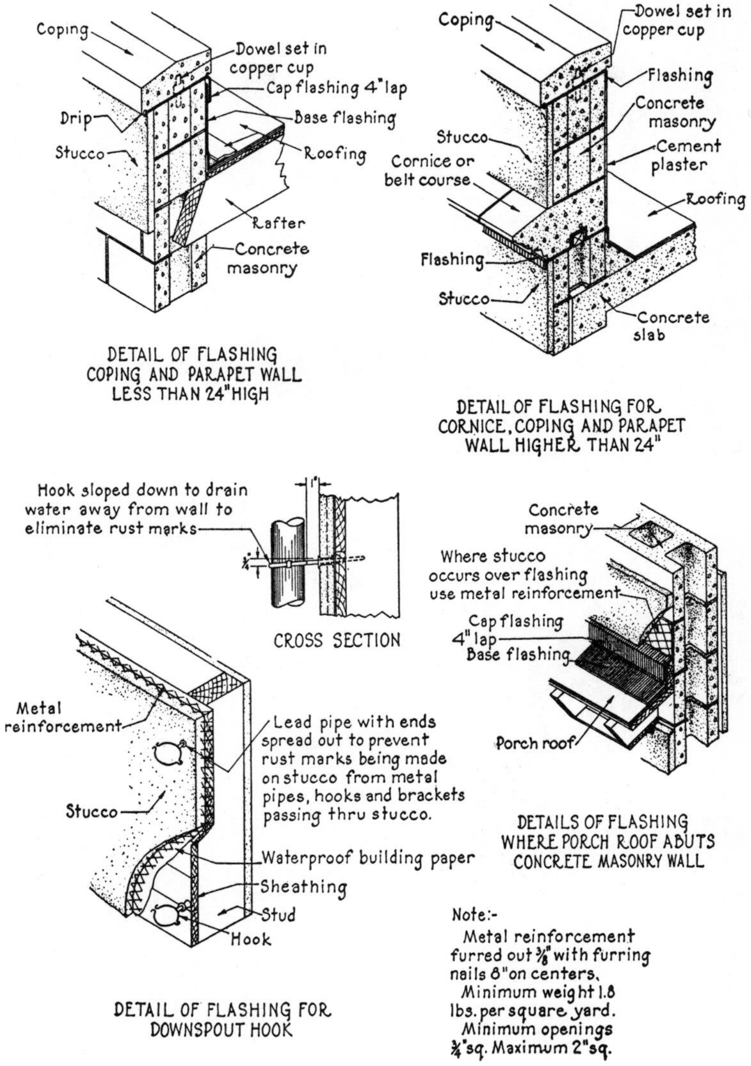
Coping
Dowel set in copper cup
Cap flashing 4" lap
Drip
Base flashing
Stucco
Roofing
Rafter
Concrete masonry
DETAIL OF FLASHING COPING AND PARAPET WALL LESS THAN 24" HIGH
Coping
Dowel set in copper cup
Flashing
Concrete masonry
Stucco
Cement plaster
Cornice or belt course
Roofing
Flashing
Stucco
Concrete slab
DETAIL OF FLASHING FOR CORNICE, COPING AND PARAPET WALL HIGHER THAN 24"
Hook sloped down to drain water away from wall to eliminate rust marks
1"
¾"
CROSS SECTION
Concrete masonry
Where stucco occurs over flashing use metal reinforcement
Cap flashing 4" lap
Base flashing
Porch roof
DETAILS OF FLASHING WHERE PORCH ROOF ABUTS CONCRETE MASONRY WALL
Metal reinforcement
Lead pipe with ends spread out to prevent rust marks being made on stucco from metal pipes, hooks and brackets passing thru stucco.
Stucco
Waterproof building paper
Sheathing
Stud
Hook
DETAIL OF FLASHING FOR DOWNSPOUT HOOK
Note:-
Metal reinforcement furred out ⅜" with furring nails 8" on centers.
Minimum weight 1.8 lbs. per square yard.
Minimum openings ¾" sq. Maximum 2" sq.

Fig. 4. Miscellaneous flashing details.

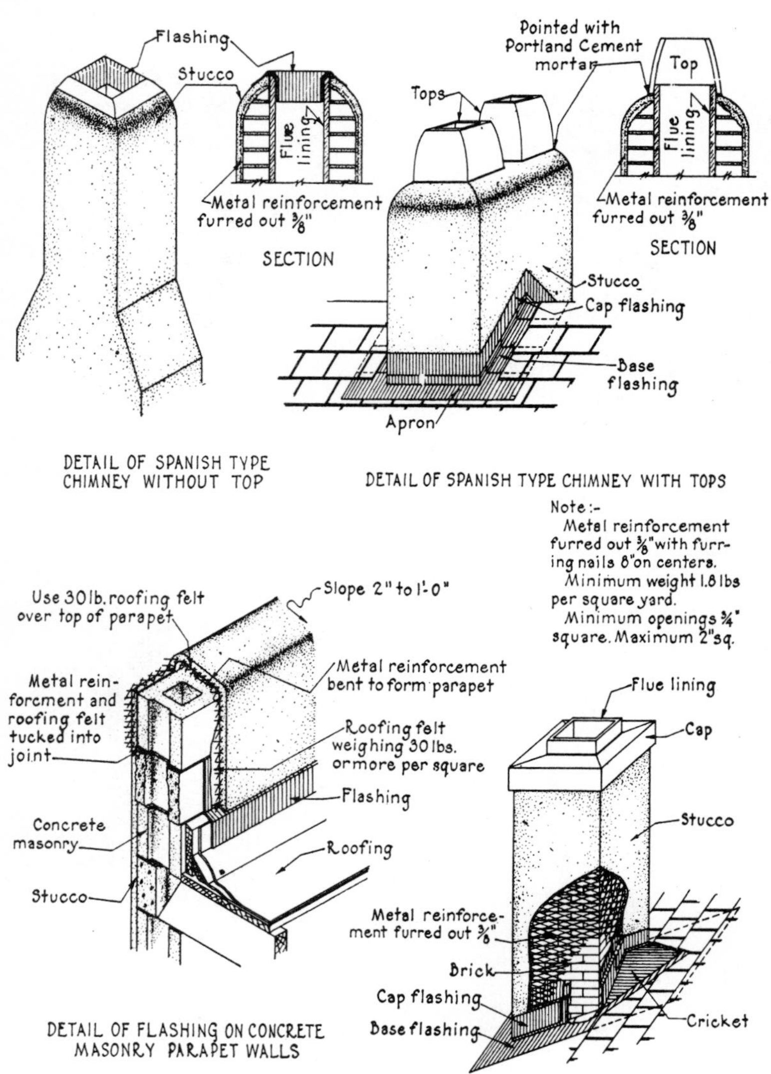
Flashing
Stucco
Flue lining
Metal reinforcement furred out 3/8"
SECTION
DETAIL OF SPANISH TYPE CHIMNEY WITHOUT TOP
Pointed with Portland Cement mortar
Tops
Top
Flue lining
Metal reinforcement furred out 3/8"
SECTION
Stucco
Cap flashing
Base flashing
Apron
DETAIL OF SPANISH TYPE CHIMNEY WITH TOPS
Note:- Metal reinforcement furred out 3/8" with furring nails 8" on centers. Minimum weight 1.8 lbs per square yard. Minimum openings 3/4" square. Maximum 2" sq.
Use 30 lb. roofing felt over top of parapet
Slope 2" to 1'-0"
Metal reinforcement and roofing felt tucked into joint
Metal reinforcement bent to form parapet
Roofing felt weighing 30 lbs. or more per square
Flashing
Concrete masonry
Roofing
Stucco
DETAIL OF FLASHING ON CONCRETE MASONRY PARAPET WALLS
Flue lining
Cap
Stucco
Metal reinforcement furred out 3/8"
Brick
Cap flashing
Base flashing
Cricket
DETAIL OF FLASHING AROUND CHIMNEY

Fig. 5. Flashing details chimney and roof.

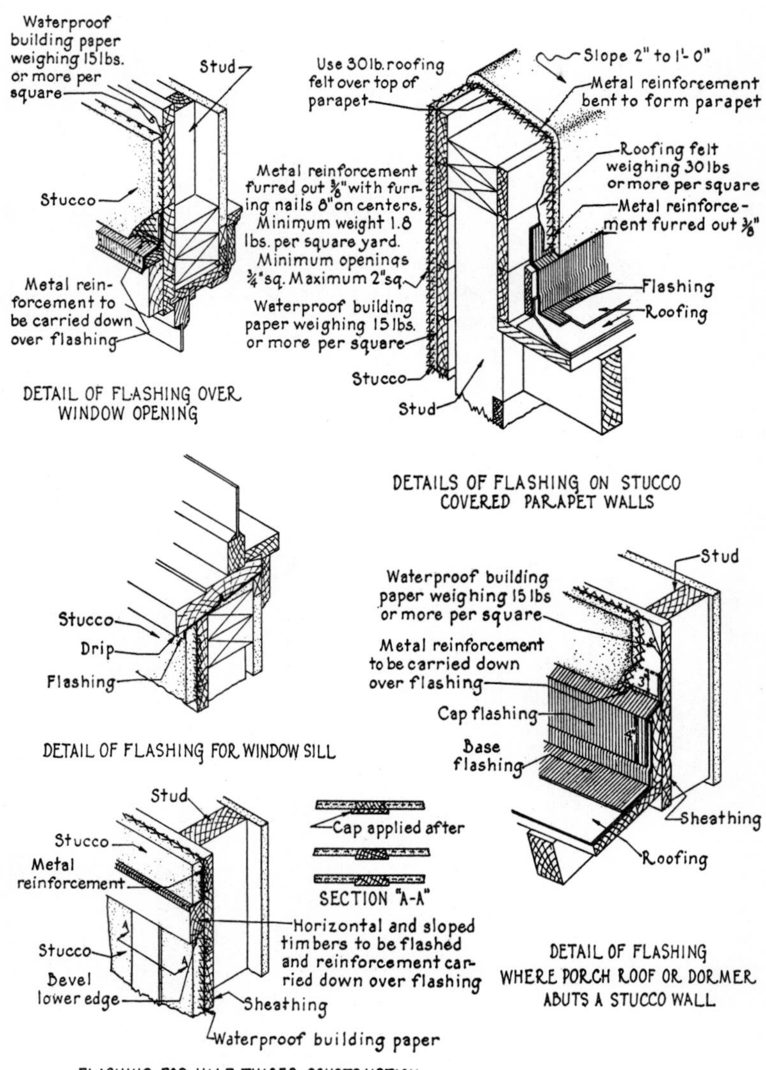
Waterproof building paper weighing 15 lbs. or more per square
Stud
Stucco
Metal reinforcement to be carried down over flashing
DETAIL OF FLASHING OVER WINDOW OPENING
Use 30 lb. roofing felt over top of parapet
Slope 2" to 1'-0"
Metal reinforcement bent to form parapet
Roofing felt weighing 30 lbs or more per square
Metal reinforcement furred out 3/8"
Metal reinforcement furred out 3/8" with furring nails 8" on centers. Minimum weight 1.8 lbs. per square yard. Minimum openings 3/4" sq. Maximum 2" sq.
Waterproof building paper weighing 15 lbs. or more per square
Flashing
Roofing
Stucco
Stud
DETAILS OF FLASHING ON STUCCO COVERED PARAPET WALLS
Stucco
Drip
Flashing
DETAIL OF FLASHING FOR WINDOW SILL
Stud
Waterproof building paper weighing 15 lbs or more per square
Metal reinforcement to be carried down over flashing
Cap flashing
Base flashing
Sheathing
Roofing
DETAIL OF FLASHING WHERE PORCH ROOF OR DORMER ABUTS A STUCCO WALL
Stud
Stucco
Metal reinforcement
Stucco
Bevel lower edge
Cap applied after
SECTION "A-A"
Horizontal and sloped timbers to be flashed and reinforcement carried down over flashing
Sheathing
Waterproof building paper
FLASHING FOR HALF-TIMBER CONSTRUCTION

Fig. 6. Flashing for stucco on wood frame.

Section 5

Concrete Projects and Improvements

IN TOWN OR country, concrete finds a wide range of usefulness for making improvements around the home that enhance the beauty and increase the utility and value of the property.

It may be feasible in some cases for the homeowner to do all or part of the job. Placing and finishing concrete is hard work, but if the homeowner is a fair do-it-yourselfer (and has some capable and willing friends), he or she should be able to do a respectable job.

Chapter 35

Design and Layout

The best time to plan and build a concrete drive, walk, patio, or step project is early in the construction season before the hot days of summer. Following are a few pointers on design and layout that homeowners and builders should consider before construction begins. (*See* Chap. 38, Forms for Drives, Walks, and Patios.)

DRIVEWAYS

Driveways for single-car garages or carports are usually 10 to 14 feet (3 to 4.3 meters) wide (Fig. 1) with a 14-foot (4.3-meters) minimum width for curving drives. In any case, a driveway should be 36-inches (91-cm.) wider than the widest vehicle it will serve.

Long driveway approaches to two-car garages may be single-car width, but must be widened near the garage to provide access to both stalls. Short driveways for two-car garages should be 16 to 24 feet (4.9 to 7.3 meters) wide.

How thick a driveway should be depends primarily upon the weight of the vehicles that will use it. For passenger cars 4 inches (10 cm.) is sufficient, but if an occasional heavy truck uses the driveway, a thickness of 5 or 6 inches (12.5 or 15 cm.) is recommended.

If the garage is considerably above or below street level and is located near the street, the driveway grade may be critical. A grade of 14 percent is the maximum recommended. That is, *for example,* a vertical rise of 1¾ inches for each running foot (14.4 cm. for each running meter). The change in grade should be gradual to avoid scraping the car's bumper or underside. The

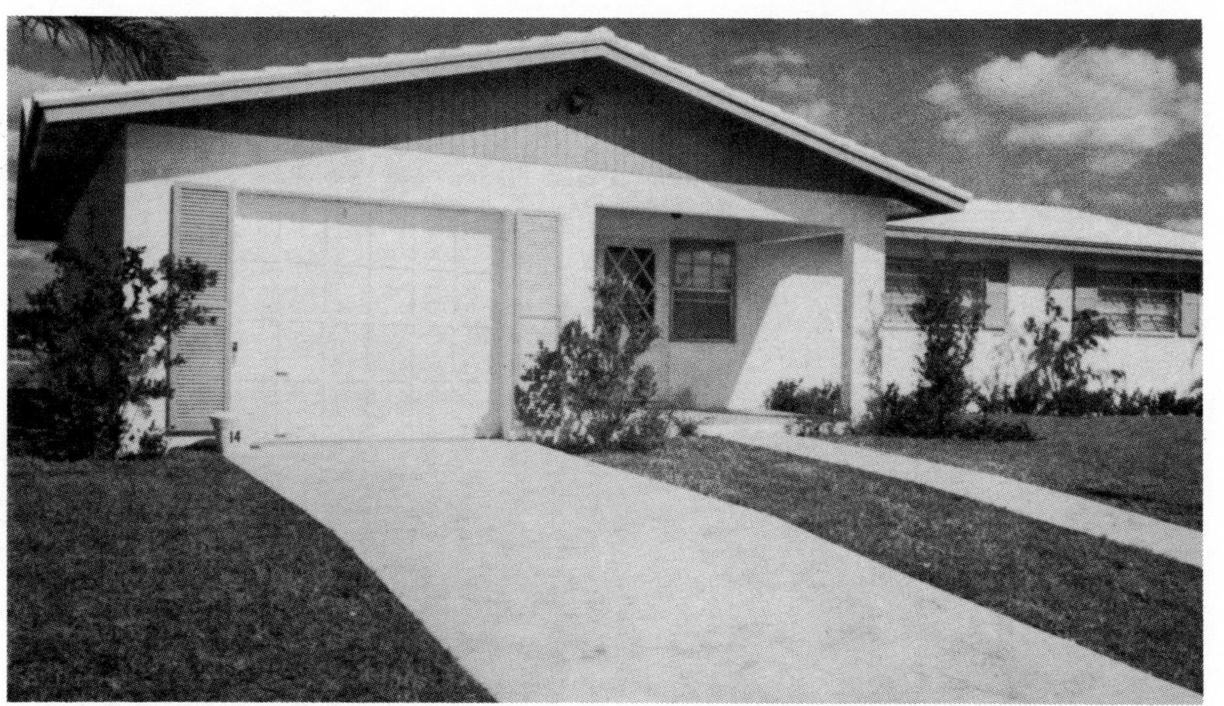

Fig. 1. Driveways for single-car garages. A travertine texture was used on both drive and walk.

most critical point occurs when the rear wheels are in the gutter as a vehicle approaches a driveway from the street (Fig. 2).

The driveway should be built with a slight slope so that it will drain quickly after a rain or washing. A slope of ¼ inch per running foot (20.8 mm. per running meter) is recommended. The direction of slope will depend on local conditions, but usually it should be toward the street. A crown or cross-slope may be used for drainage instead (Fig. 3).

The part of a driveway between the street and public sidewalk is usually controlled by the local municipality. It should be consulted when a driveway is built after the street, curbs, and public walks are in place. If curb and gutter have not been installed, it is advisable to end the driveway temporarily at the public sidewalk or property line. An entry of gravel or crushed stone can be used until curbs and gutter are built. At that time, the drive entrance can be completed to meet local requirements. A typical driveway entrance is shown in Fig. 4.

If the driveway is built before the public walk, it should meet the proposed sidewalk grade and drop to meet the gutter (if no curb is planned) or the top of any low curb.

While in the planning stage, consideration should be given to other elements that can make a driveway a beautiful approach to a home rather than just a pathway to the garage (Fig. 5). *For example*, consider off-street parking, turnaround areas for safe head-on street entry, multi-use paved areas for games, and the like. (*See* Figs. 6 and 7.) More information, ideas, and plans for these and other methods of creating an out-of-the ordinary concrete driveway, sidewalk, patio, and steps will be found in Chaps. 36, 37, 38, 39, and 40.

SIDEWALKS

Private walks leading to the front entrance of a home should be 3 to 4 feet (.9 to 1.2 meters) wide. Service walks connecting the back entrance may be 2 to 3 feet (.6 to .9 meters) wide.

Public walks should be wide enough to allow two people walking abreast to pass a third person without crowding. The width will vary with the amount of pedestrian traffic expected.

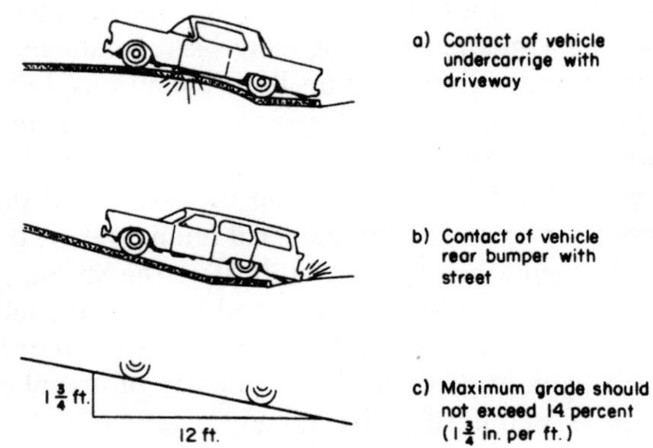

Fig. 2. The driveway slope should be planned carefully.

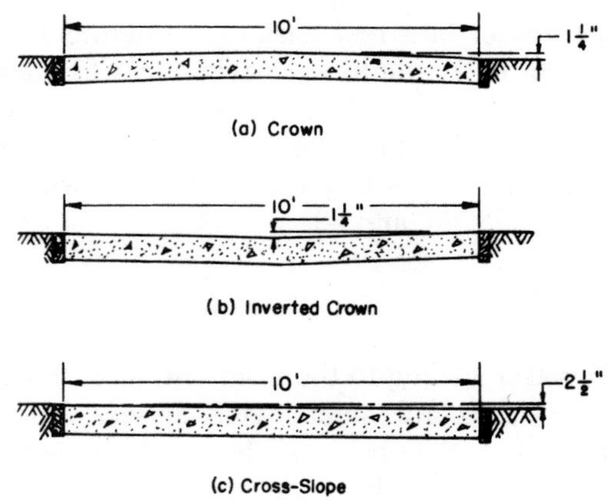

Fig. 3. Methods of obtaining side drainage.

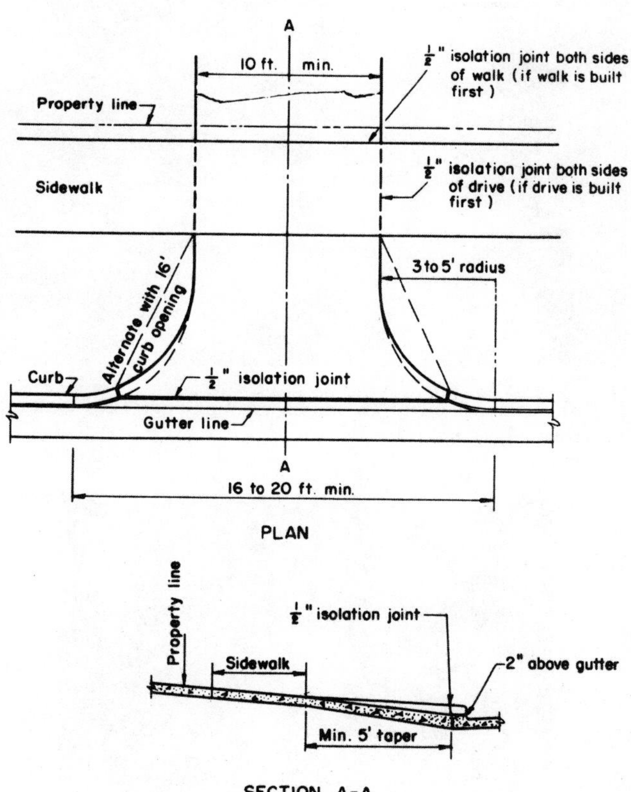

Fig. 4. Details of a typical entrance.

Fig. 5. This driveway combines exposed-aggregate concrete with brick borders.

Fig. 6. A broad front walk makes an imposing, attractive entry to any home.

Fig. 7. This driveway has ample room for guest parking and turnaround area for safe head-on street entry.

A width of 4 to 5 feet (1.2 to 1.5 meters) is advisable for areas with single-family housing. A greater width is required near schools, shopping centers, churches, and other areas where walks are used by a great number of people. Walks serving predominately apartment-dwelling areas should be at least 8-feet (2.4-meters) wide. Those in commercial shopping areas should be 12-feet (3.6-meters) wide. Walks along rural highways may be 4-feet (1.2-meters) wide.

At other buildings where vehicles frequently receive and discharge passengers and where there is a grass plot between walk and curb, narrow courtesy walks are sometimes used. Such walks may be 18- to 30-feet (5.5- to 11-meters) wide.

In some neighborhoods, sidewalks are built adjacent to the street curb. This allows larger lawns and proper footing for people alighting from vehicles. However, such sidewalks give pedestrians less protection from street traffic than walks set back from the curb. For pedestrian safety, public walks in residential areas should be set back from the street curb a minimum of 7 feet (3.8 meters) where trees are planted between the curb and the walk; a minimum of 3 feet (.9 meters) if there are no trees.

Private residential walks should be not less than 4-inches (10-cm.) thick. Walks in commercial or business areas are generally 5 or 6 inches (12.5 to 15 cm.) thick.

The usual practice is to build walks with one-course construction. That is, the full thickness of concrete is placed at one time with the same mixture used throughout. Terrazzo sidewalks are an exception. Terrazzo is placed in three layers consisting of a base course of conventional concrete, an underbed of mortar, and a terrazzo topping.

It is customary to slope walks ¼ inch per foot (13.2 cm. per running meter) of width for drainage. Where walks abut curbs or buildings, the slope should be toward the curb and away from the building over the full width of the walk. In some areas where side drainage permits, walks built with a crown or slope from center to edge are desirable. Certain conditions may require that a slope other than ¼ inch per foot (2 cm. per running meter) be used (*for example*, where a new walk meets an existing driveway or alley). In such cases, the cross-slope of the walk may be increased to ½ inch per foot (4 cm. per running meter).

For the convenience of pedestrians, sidewalk approaches at street intersections can be planned to eliminate steps by providing a gentle ramp from walk to street. This is ideal for housewives with baby buggies, elderly pedestrians, cyclists, and roller skaters.

Sidewalk design is closely linked with street pavement and curb and gutter design. Quite often all are constructed at the same time. By coordinating sidewalks with streets, curbs, and gutters, a pleasing effect can be obtained.

Public walks adjacent to private properties are generally controlled by the municipality. These walks perform a valuable service by enhancing the value of the private properties. Accordingly, it has been traditional for municipalities to charge abutting properties for all or part of the cost of construction and maintenance of public walks.

PATIOS

A carefully planned patio is a valuable extension of the living and entertainment area of any home (Fig. 8). Patio planning should include consideration of a number of factors such as the view, the climate, traffic flow to the house and kitchen, weather and insect protection, privacy, and outdoor cooking and entertaining.

Location of the patio will be determined by the lot size and

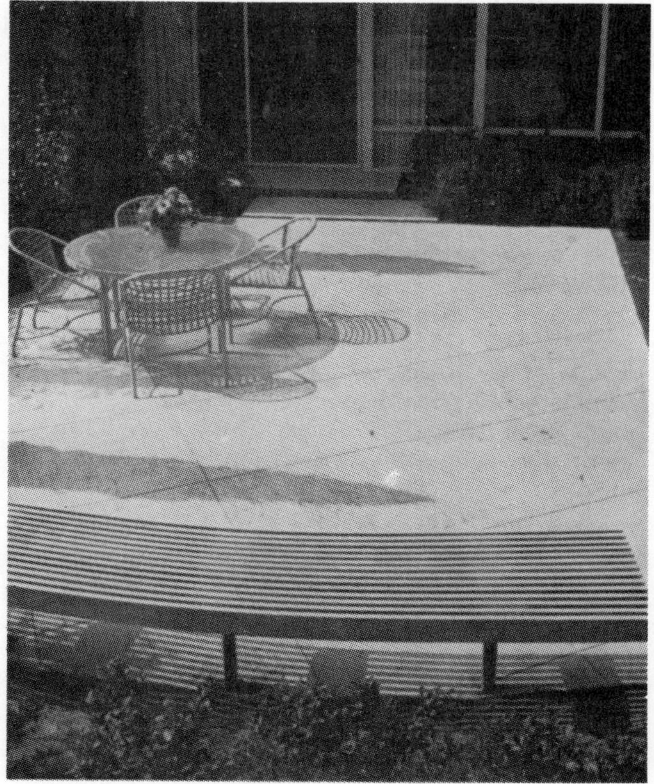

Fig. 8. A patio of this size is excellent for outdoor dining and entertaining.

how the house is set on the lot. If the lot has a beautiful view of the city or surrounding countryside, the patio should be located to take advantage of the view.

Outdoor living must be oriented to the sun and general climate of the region. A patio facing south will never be deserted by the sun. It dries quickly after rains and warms readily in winter months. Patios exposed to the west are likely to be very hot in the afternoon and cool and damp in the morning. They are not as pleasant during the winter months as patios with southern exposures. Patios facing east are desirable for hot climates because they cool off in the afternoon. And even better for hot climates are patios with northern exposure: they never receive direct sun.

The patio should be designed as part of the house (Fig. 9). Location of the doors and windows with consideration of traffic flow from the house to the patio will help bring the outdoors indoors and vice versa. If the floor of the house is a few steps above ground level, think about building the patio slab up to the level of the house floor.

Fig. 9. This patio was designed level with the floor of the house and convenient to the kitchen and living room.

If you live where insects are a serious problem, then consider enclosing part of the patio with screening. Also, the outdoor living season can be prolonged with a roof for sun or rain protection over part of the patio.

The distance to the nearest neighbor usually determines the type of privacy screen needed for a patio. Privacy can be obtained with walls, fences, or other visual barriers such as shrubbery or growing vines. Concrete masonry screen walls are very decorative and ideally suited for this purpose. (*See* Chap. 36, Preparation of Subgrade.)

Entertaining, cooking, and dining outdoors are among the most enjoyable uses of a patio. The patio should be spacious if considerable entertaining is anticipated. A good rule is to make the patio larger than the largest room in the house. The food-serving area should be convenient to the kitchen. Also, the location of any future barbecue should be carefully thought out.

The shape of a patio is limited only by the imagination. Square and rectangular patios are commonly used, but any shape can be built with concrete. A curved or free-form patio can be particularly attractive, especially when it complements the contour of the lawn and is accented with proper plantings (Fig. 10).

Cast-in-place patios should be a minimum of 4 inches thick and built with a ¼ inch per foot (2 cm. per running meter) slope for drainage away from the house.

STEPS

Steps at entranceways must conform to the provisions of local building codes. These codes establish critical dimensions such as (1) width, (2) height of flights without landings, (3) size of landings, (4) size of risers and treads, and (5) relationship between riser and tread size.

Steps for private homes are usually 48 inches (1.2 meters) wide. Some codes allow 30- and 36-inch (76- and 91-cm.) widths. However, steps should be at least as wide as the door and walk they serve.

A landing is desirable to divide flights of more than 5 feet (1.5

Fig. 10. A curved patio.

meters) and it should be no shorter in direction of travel than 3 feet (.9 meters). The top landing should be no more than 7½ inches (19.1 cm.) below the door threshold. (*See* Fig. 11.)

For flights less than 30 inches (75 cm.) high, maximum step rise is usually 7½ inches (18.8 cm.) and has a minimum tread width of 11 inches (27.5 cm.). For higher flights, step rise may be limited to 6 inches (15 cm.), with a minimum tread width of 12 inches (30 cm.). Choice of riser and tread size should depend on how the steps are to be used. For esthetic reasons, steps with risers as low as 4 inches (10 cm.) and treads as wide as 19 inches

Fig. 11. Concrete steps make the approach to a home safe and attractive.

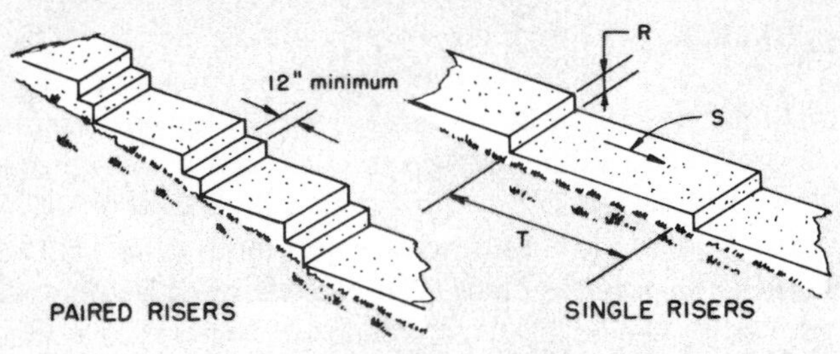

	PAIRED RISERS		SINGLE RISERS	
	Min.	Max.	Min.	Max.
Riser Height (R)	4"	6"	4"	6"
Tread Length (T)*	3'0"	8'0"	5'6"	5'6"
Tread Slope (S)	$\frac{1}{8}$"/ft.	$\frac{1}{4}$"/ft.	$\frac{1}{8}$"/ft.	$\frac{1}{4}$"/ft.
Overall Ramp Slope	$2\frac{1}{8}$"/ft.	$3\frac{1}{4}$"/ft.	$\frac{15}{16}$"/ft.	$1\frac{7}{16}$"/ft.

*May be optional. Recommended values given provide 1 or 3 easy paces between paired risers and 2 easy paces between single risers.

Fig. 12. Details for stepped ramps.

(47.5 cm.) are sometimes built. On long, sloping approaches, a stepped ramp can be used as shown in Fig. 12.

Many studies have been made to find the best combination of riser and tread for optimum comfort and safety. One study concludes that the sum of riser and tread should equal 17½ inches (43.8 cm.). This is a good combination for most steps. However, more generous steps may be desirable in leisure areas—patios, gardens, and terraces—or for esthetic purposes (Fig. 13). In these instances the following combinations of riser to tread dimensions (in inches) can be used: 4 to 19 (10 to 48); 4½ to 18 (11.5 to 45 cm.); 5 to 17 (12.5 to 45 cm.); 5½ to 16 (13.8 to 40 cm.); or 6 to 15 (15 to 37.5 cm.). (*See* Chap. 39, Building Exterior Steps of Unreinforced Cast-in-Place Concrete; *see also* Chap. 40, Precast Concrete Units.)

Fig. 13. In these concrete and stone steps, low-profile risers, wide treads, and intermediate landings are combined to complement the sloping landscape.

BUILDING REGULATIONS

Before construction begins on a driveway, sidewalk, patio, or steps, it is advisable to check with the local city or county building department. Most communities require a building permit to ensure that work is done in accordance with the building code. Laws regulating building methods vary with localities. Building permits are especially important for driveways and sidewalks that cross a public way (that strip of land on either side of a street extending from your property line to the curb and reserved for public sidewalks, grass, and trees). Some cities will set permissible sidewalk grades when a sidewalk permit is obtained.

Chapter 36

Preparation of Subgrade

The first step in building a walk, drive, or patio is preparation of the subgrade. This is an essential step for building any slab on ground. *Serious cracks, slab settlement,* and *structural failure can very often be traced to a poorly compacted subgrade.* The subgrade should be uniform, hard, free from foreign matter, and well-drained.

Remove from the site all organic matter—grass, sod, roots, and the like—and grade the ground (Fig. 1). Dig out soft or mucky spots, and fill them with soil similar to the rest of the subgrade, or with granular material such as sand, gravel, crushed stone, or slag, and compact thoroughly. Loosen and tamp hard spots to provide the same uniform support as the rest of the subgrade. All fill materials should be uniform, free of vegetable matter, large lumps or stones, and frozen soil.

Granular fills of sand, gravel, crushed stone, or slag are recommended for bringing the site to uniform bearing and final grade (Fig. 2). Compact these fills in layers not more than 4-inches (10-cm.) thick. It is best to extend the fill at least 1 foot (30 cm.) beyond the slab edge to prevent undercutting during rains.

Cover poorly drained subgrades that are water-soaked most of the time with 4 to 6 inches (10 to 15 cm.) of granular fill. The bottom of these granular fills must not be lower than the adjacent finished grade. This prevents the collection of water under the slab.

Unless fill material is well compacted, it is advisable to leave the subgrade undisturbed. Undisturbed soil is superior as support for a concrete slab to soil that has been dug out and poorly compacted. Subgrade compaction can be done with hand tampers (Fig. 3), rollers (Fig. 4), or vibratory compactors (Fig. 5).

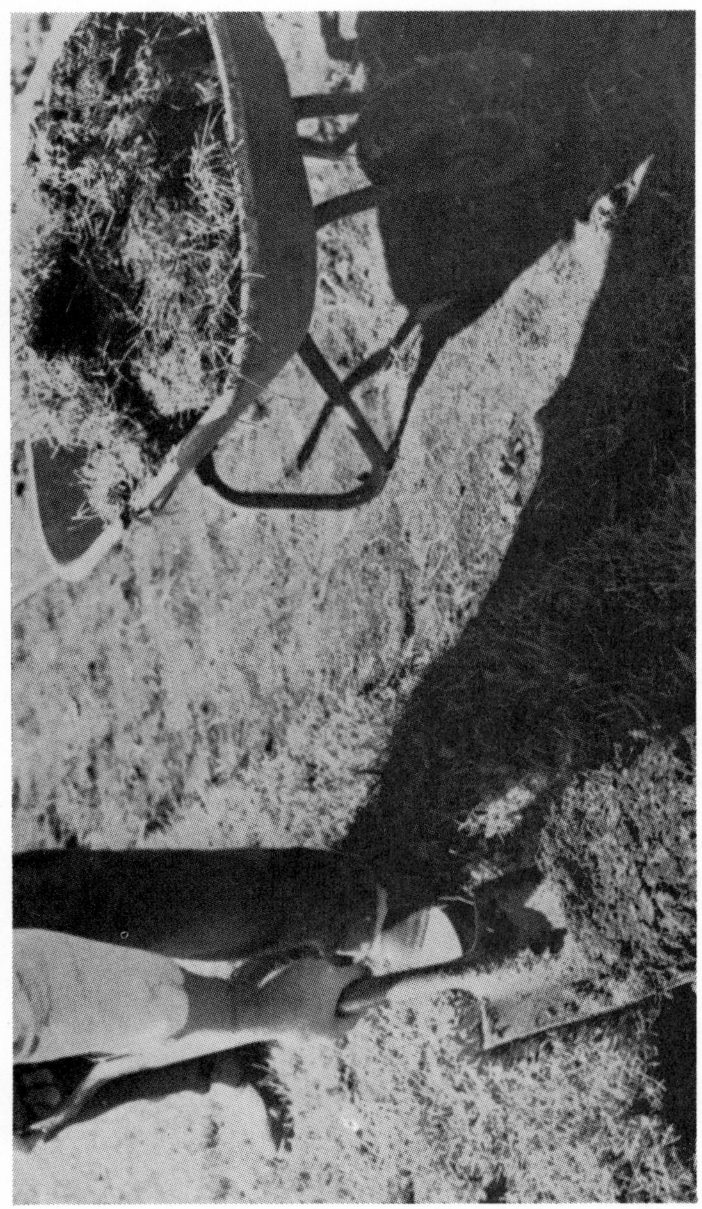

Fig. 1. To prepare a subgrade for a walk, drive, or patio, first remove all sod, roots, and debris.

Fig. 2. Workman preparing site with fill to final grade.

Fig. 3. Use hand tampers for small jobs.

Fig. 4. Use mechanical rollers for large projects.

Fig. 5. Vibratory compactor.

Fig. 6. Spraying subgrade with water.

For a small job, hand tampers may be used, but for a major undertaking, such as a large driveway, sidewalk, or patio project, mechanical rollers or vibratory compactors are strongly recommended.

The subgrade should be uniformly moist at the time of concreting. If necessary, dampen it by spraying with water (Fig. 6). However, there should be no standing water on the subgrade, nor should there be any muddy or soft spots when the concrete is placed. A dry spot on the subgrade absorbs more water from the concrete slab than does an adjacent moist one. This in turn may result in dark and light spots in the concrete finish.

Chapter 37

Decorative and Special Finishes

Many pleasing decorative finishes can be built into concrete during construction. Color may be added to the concrete through use of white cement, pigments, and by exposing colorful aggregates. Textured finishes can be as varied as desired, from a smooth polished appearance to the roughness of a gravel path. Geometric patterns can be scored or stamped into the concrete to resemble stone, brick, or tile paving. Other interesting patterns are obtained by using divider strips (commonly redwood) to form panels of various sizes and shapes—rectangular, square, or diamond. Special techniques are available to render concrete slip-resistant and sparkling. The possibilities are unlimited. Figure 1 shows a striking walk of random-size stepping stones with white cement and exposed beach pebbles.

COLORED CONCRETE

Concrete can be colored during construction by three different methods: (1) one-course, (2) two-course, and (3) dry-shake.

One- and Two-Course Methods

The one- and two-course methods are similar. In both the concrete mix is integrally colored by addition of a mineral oxide pigment especially prepared for use in concrete. The amount of pigment used should never exceed 10 percent by weight of cement. White portland cement will produce brighter colors or light pastel shades when used with light-colored sand. White cement should be used in preference to normal gray portland cement, except for black or dark gray colors. All materials in the

Fig. 1. Walk with random size stepping stones with white cement and exposed beach pebbles.

mix must be carefully controlled by weight to maintain a uniform color from batch to batch. Mixing color pigments and cement should always be done in the dry state. To prevent streaking, separate mixers and thoroughly clean finishing tools are required for colored concrete. When using the *one-course method*, uniform moistening of the subgrade is important for uniform color results. The best means to accomplish this is to soak the subgrade thoroughly the evening before placing concrete or to use a moisture barrier under the slab.

The only difference between the one- and two-course methods is that the latter uses a base course of conventional concrete. The surface of the base course is left rough to help provide good bond for the topping. After the base stiffens slightly and the surface water disappears, the top course of ½ to 1 inch (1.3 to 2.5 cm.) of colored concrete is placed.

Dry-Shake Method

The *dry-shake method* consists of applying a factory-prepared dry color material over the concrete surface after preliminary floating, edging, and grooving. Two applications of the dry-shake are made, the first using about two-thirds of the total amount specified by the manufacturer (Fig. 2). The surface is floated, edged, and grooved thoroughly after each application to make sure the color is uniformly worked into the concrete. If a smooth, hard surface is desired, troweling follows floating in the usual manner. (*See* Chap. 16, Mineral Pigments for Use in Coloring Concrete; *see also* Chap. 6, Concrete Equipment and Tools.)

EXPOSED AGGREGATE

Exposed aggregate is one of the most popular decorative finishes. It offers unlimited color selection and a wide range of textures. Exposed-aggregate finishes are not only attractive, but they can be rugged, slip-resistant, and highly immune to wear and weather.

There are a number of ways to obtain exposed-aggregate finishes. One of the most practical and commonly used techniques,

Fig. 2. Applying a black-colored dry-shake material to a side-walk slab.

called the seeding method, is described and illustrated in Figs. 3 through 8. With the seeding method, a surface retarder may be used for better control of the exposing operations, but this step is not essential.

Base concrete to receive a seeded exposed-aggregate finish should have a maximum 3-inch (7.5-cm.) slump. Place, strike off, and bull-float or darby in the usual manner (Fig. 3), except that the level of the surface should be ⅜- to ½-inch (.93- to 1.3-cm.) lower than the forms to accommodate the extra aggregate. As shown in Fig. 4 spread aggregate uniformly by shovel and hand so that the entire surface is completely covered with a layer of stone. Embed the aggregate initially by tapping with a wood hand float, a straightedge, or a darby (Fig. 5). For final embedding (Fig. 6), use a bull float or hand float until the appearance of the surface is similar to that of a normal slab after floating.

Timing of the start of the aggregate exposure operation is critical. In general, wait until the slab can bear the weight of a man on knee-boards with no indentation. Then brush the slab lightly with a stiff nylon-bristle broom (Fig. 7) to remove excess mortar.

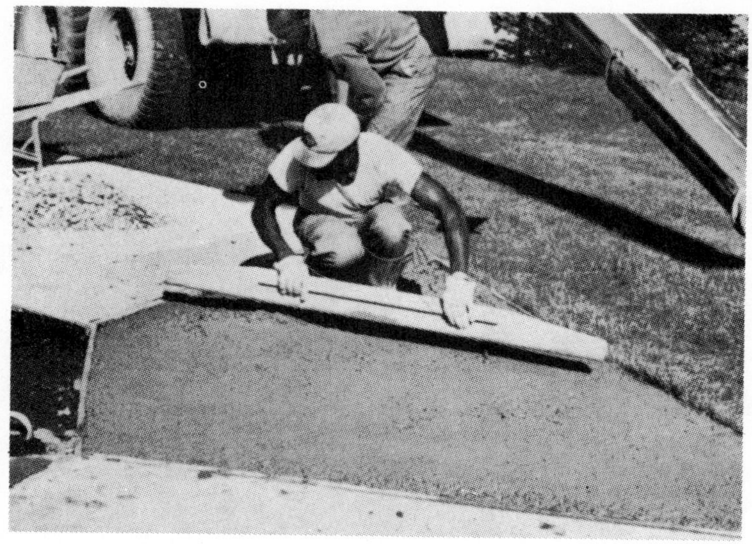

Fig. 3. Place, strike off, and bull-float so that the level of the surface is ⅜- to ½-inch (.93- to 1.3-cm.) lower than the forms to leave room for the extra aggregate.

Fig. 4. Spread the aggregate uniformly over the entire surface by shovel and hand.

Fig. 5. Embed the aggregate initially by tapping with a wood hand float, a straightedge, or a darby.

Fig. 6. For final embedding, use a bull float or hand float.

Fig. 7. Begin aggregate exposure by brushing lightly with a stiff broom to remove excess mortar.

Next fine-spray with water along with brushing (Fig. 8). Special exposed-aggregate brooms with water jets are available. If aggregate is dislodged, delay the operation. Continue washing and brushing until flush water runs clear and there is no noticeable cement film left on the aggregate.

In an *alternate method* the aggregates are exposed in conventionally placed concrete. For success with this method the mix should contain a high proportion of coarse to fine aggregate. The coarse aggregate used should be uniform in size, bright in color, closely packed, and properly distributed. The concrete slump must be low—1 to 3 inches (2.5–7.5 cm.)—so that the coarse aggregate remains near the surface. In placing, striking off, bullfloating, or darbying, the usual procedures are followed. Care should be taken not to overdo floating, as this may depress the coarse aggregate too deeply. The aggregate is ready for exposing when the water sheen disappears, the surface can support a man's weight without indentation, and the aggregate is not

Fig. 8. Special exposed-aggregate broom with water jets.

overexposed or dislodged by washing and brushing.

In still another method of producing exposed-aggregate finishes, a thin topping course of concrete containing special aggregates is placed over a base slab of conventional concrete. Terrazzo construction uses this technique. Terrazzo toppings for outdoor work are ½-inch (1.3-cm.) thick and contain decorative aggregates such as marble, quartz, or granite chips. The colorful aggregates are exposed by brushing and washing with water. Brass or plastic divider strips set in a bed of mortar are used to eliminate random cracking. They also permit the use of different colored terrazzo mixtures in a wide variety of patterns. This type of terrazzo is called rustic or washed terrazzo. Only a qualified terrazzo contractor should attempt this kind of work. (*See* Chap. 15, Exposed Aggregate Concrete.)

TEXTURED FINISHES

Interesting and functional decorative textures can be produced on a concrete slab with little effort and expense by using floats, trowels, and brooms. More elaborate textures are possible with special techniques using a mortar dash coat or rock salt. (*See* Chap. 11, Finishing Concrete Slabs; *see also* Chap. 12, Finishing Concrete Surfaces.)

A swirl finish lends visual interest as well as surer footing (Fig. 9). To produce this texture, the concrete is struck off, bull-floated, or darbied, and a hand float is worked flat on the surface in a semicircular or fanlike motion, using pressure. Patterns are made by using a series of uniform arcs or twists. Coarse textures are produced by wood floats, and medium textures by aluminum, magnesium, or canvas resin floats. A fine-textured swirl is obtained with a steel trowel. Take care to allow the concrete to set sufficiently that these textures are not marred during curing.

Broomed finishes are attractive, nonslip textures secured by pulling damp brooms across freshly floated or troweled surfaces. Coarse textures suitable for steep slopes or heavy traffic are produced by stiff-bristle brooms on newly floated concrete (Fig. 10). Medium to fine textures are obtained by using soft-bristle

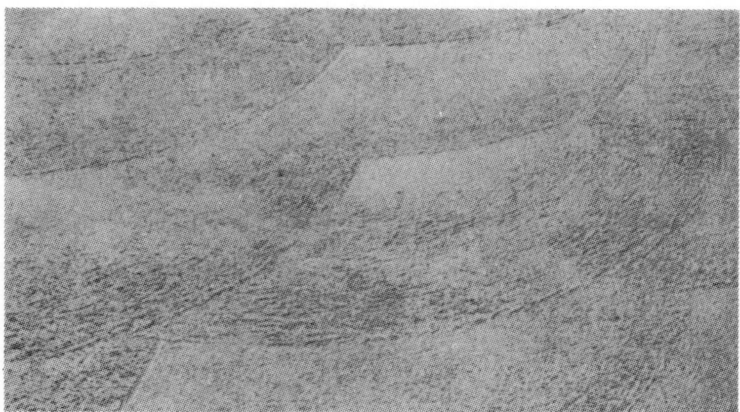

Fig. 9. Swirl finish.

Fig. 10. Coarse texture suitable for steep slopes or heavy traffic.

brooms on floated or steel-troweled surfaces. Best results are obtained when using a broom that is specially made for texturing concrete (Fig. 11). A broomed texture can be applied in many ways—in straight lines, curved lines, or wavy lines (Fig. 12). Driveways and sidewalks are usually broomed at right angles to the direction of traffic.

A *travertine finish* (sometimes called keystone) is created by applying a dash coat of mortar over freshly leveled concrete. The dash coat is mixed to the consistency of thick paint and usually contains a yellow pigment. It is applied in a splotchy manner with a dash brush so that ridges and depressions are formed. After allowing the coating to harden slightly, the surface is flat-troweled to flatten the ridges and spread the mortar. The resulting finish is smooth on the high areas and coarse grained in the depressed areas, resembling the appearance of travertine marble (Fig. 13). Many interesting variations of this finish are possible, depending upon the amount of dash coat applied, the amount of color used, and the amount of troweling.

A similar texture can be produced by scattering rock salt over the surface after hand floating or troweling. The salt is rolled or pressed into the surface so that only the tops of the grains are

Fig. 11. Best results are obtained when using a broom specially made for texturing concrete.

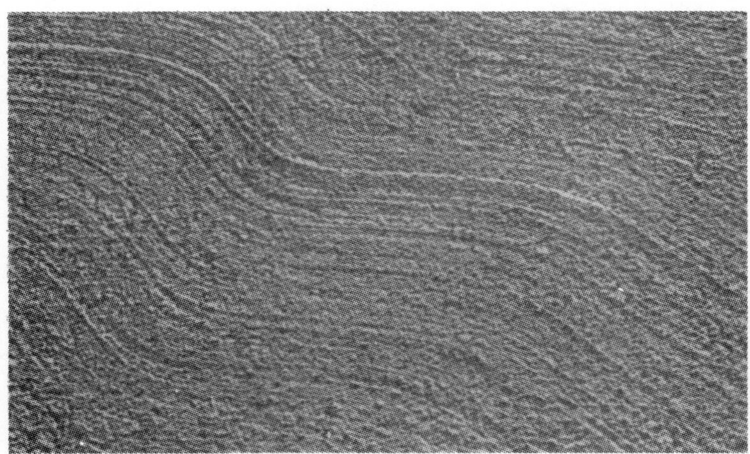

Fig. 12. Wavy broomed texture.

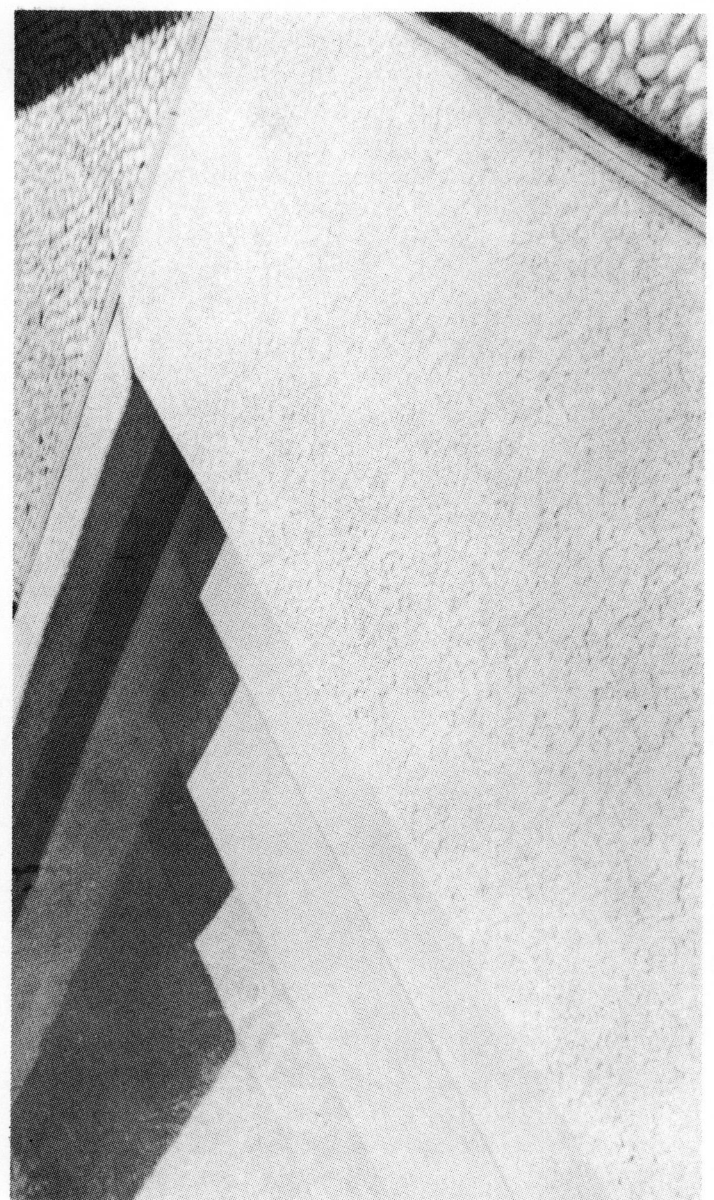

Fig. 13. Travertine texture.

exposed. After the concrete has hardened, the surface is washed and brushed, dislodging and dissolving the salt grains and leaving pits or holes in the surface (Fig. 14). The salt distribution and grain size should be such that holes of about ¼-inch (6.3-mm.) in diameter are created.

Neither the rock salt nor the travertine finish is recommended for use in areas subject to freezing weather. Water trapped in the recesses of these finishes tends, when frozen, to spall the surface.

GEOMETRIC PATTERNS

A wide variety of geometric designs can be stamped, scored, or sawed into a concrete slab to enhance the beauty of walks, drives, and patios. Random flagstone or ashlar patterns may be produced by embedding 1-inch (2.5-cm.) strips of 15-pound (6.8-

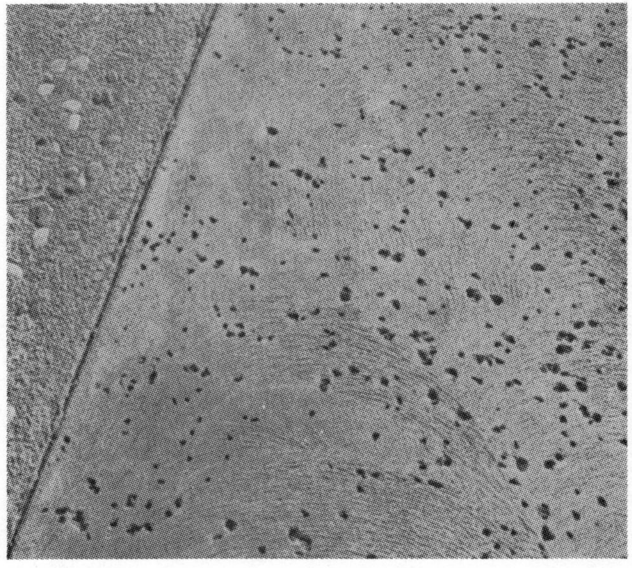

Fig. 14. Rock salt texture.

kgs.) roofing felt in concrete. After floating, the strips, precut to the pattern desired, are laid on the surface, patted flush, and floated over. At this time, a color dry-shake can be applied or the slab can be finished in its natural color. The strips are carefully removed before the slab is cured.

An *alternate method* of producing these patterns makes use of an 18-inch (45-cm.) long piece of ½- or ¾-inch (1.3- or 1.8-cm.) copper pipe bent into a flat S-shape. The slab shown in Fig. 15 was scored with this tool. Scoring must be done while the concrete is still plastic, since coarse aggregate must be pushed aside. The best time is soon after darbying (or bull-floating). A second scoring to smooth the joints is done after hand-floating.

Stone, brick, tile, and other patterns can be deeply cut into partially set concrete with special stamping tools, as described and illustrated in Figs. 16 through 21.

Concrete to receive a stamped pattern should contain small

Fig. 15. Random flagstone pattern on a sidewalk slab.

coarse aggregate such as pea gravel. Finishing follows the usual procedures; however, do not trowel the surface more than once (Fig. 16). After the surface is floated or troweled to the desired texture, stamping pads are used. One pad is placed next to the other on the slab so that the pattern is accurately aligned. Eight pads were used for the driveway shown in Fig. 17—a minimum of two are required. The worker steps from one pad to the next, stamping the design to a depth of about 1 inch (2.5 cm.). A handtamper is used to ensure proper identation of the stamping pad (Fig. 18). A tool similar to a brick mason's jointer (Fig. 19) is used to dress edges and cause some artificial imperfections. A small hand stamp (Fig. 20) is used to complete the pattern next to the pavement edges. Light tapping with a hand hammer may be required. Five hours after placing concrete, stamping nears completion (Fig. 21). Timing is critical since all stamping must be completed before the concrete sets too hard. (*See* Chap. 9, Placing and Consolidating Concrete.)

The concrete may be colored integrally or by the dry-shake method and the joints filled with plain or colored mortar to create any number of striking effects.

Divider strips and borders of wood, plastic, metal, or masonry serve a number of purposes: unusual patterns and designs can be

Fig. 16. Concrete to be stamped should only be troweled once.

Fig. 17. Use of stamping pads.

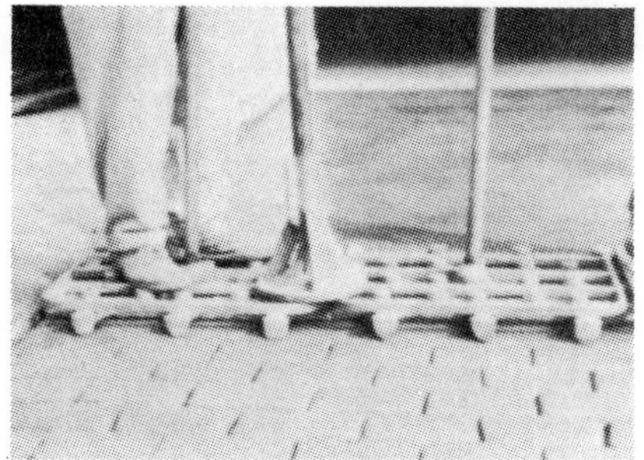

Fig. 18. Stamping the design.

Fig. 19. A tool similar to a brick mason's jointer is used to dress edges and cause artificial imperfections.

Fig. 20. Completing pattern next to pavement edges.

Fig. 21. Stamping nears completion.

created with rectangles, squares, and diamonds; concrete work can be segmented into small areas for better control of placing and finishing; combinations of various surface finishes are possible; and very important random cracks are greatly reduced or eliminated because divider strips act as control joints. Wood divider strips should be made of rot-resistant lumber such as redwood, cedar, or cypress. (*See* Chap. 38, Forms for Drives, Walks, and Patios, the section on Permanent Forms.)

Plastic strips are difficult to install straight in concrete unless they are nailed or stapled to the top of wood strips securely staked to the subgrade.

Concrete masonry, brick, or stone divider strips and borders may be set in a sand bed with or without mortared joints. For more permanent work, masonry units should be set in a mortar bed, with all joints mortared.

NONSLIP AND SPARKLING FINISHES

Surfaces that are frequently wet or that would be dangerous if slippery can be given special nonslip finishes. These finishes are most commonly achieved with hand tools—floats, trowels, or brooms—or with dry-shake applications of abrasive grains. The latter method provides a long-lasting, nonslip surface suitable for areas with heavy foot traffic.

The two most widely used abrasive grains are silicon carbide and aluminum oxide. Silicon carbide grains are sparkling black in color and are also used to make "sparkling concrete." The sparkle is especially effective under artificial light. Aluminum oxide may be gray, brown, or white, and is used where the sparkle of silicon carbide is not required. Application of the abrasive grains follows essentially the same procedure as for a color dry-shake. The grains should be spread uniformly over the surface in a quantity of from ¼ to ½ pound per square foot (1.2 to 2.4 kgs. per sq. meter) and lightly troweled (Fig. 22). The manufacturer's directions should be followed if given.

COMBINATIONS

In using concrete decoratively, striking effects can be obtained by combining colors, textures, and patterns. *For example,* alternate areas of exposed aggregate can be eye-catching when combined with plain, colored, or textured concrete. Ribbons and

Fig. 22. Troweling silicon carbide grains into the surface of sidewalk.

Fig. 23. Exposed aggregate contrasts nicely with rock salt texture.

borders of concrete masonry or brick add a distinctive touch when combined with exposed aggregate. Figure 23 shows exposed aggregate in foreground combines well with rock salt texture for this poolside patio. Also, light-colored strips of exposed aggregate may divide areas of dark-colored concrete or vice versa. Scored and stamped designs are enhanced when combined with integral or dry-shake color. These are just a few possibilities. With a little imagination, concrete driveways, sidewalks, and patios can be tailored to fit the mood and style of any architecture or landscape.

Chapter 38

Forms for Drives, Walks, and Patios

Forms for drives, walks, and patios may be lumber or metal, braced by wood or steel stakes driven into the ground. All forms should be straight, free from warping, and of sufficient strength to resist concrete pressure without bulging. Stake and brace the forms firmly to keep them in horizontal and vertical alignment. Setting forms to proper line and grade is normally accomplished by use of a string line as shown in Figs. 1 through 6.

The finished grade of a concrete slab depends on accurate setting of the side forms (Fig. 1). This should be done with a leveling device. A builder's level can be used, as shown in Fig. 1. Sight the level on a measuring rod or rule that is set on an established grade and take a reading. Move the rule (Fig. 2) to where a form is to be set and a stake has been driven. Place the rule against the stake and adjust it up or down until the desired grade is read through the level. Put a mark on the stake at the bottom of the rule, and attach a string line tightly to the stake at this mark. Using the level, mark additional stakes and string the line tightly from stake to stake (Fig. 3). Drive intermediate stakes in line with the string. Check the distance from string to subgrade to make sure there is enough depth to place the forms.

Set forms so that their tops are level with the string line (Fig. 4). If there is insufficient room under the string for the form, dig out the subgrade. Attach forms to stakes with nails (Fig. 5). Nails should be driven through the stake and into the form as shown. Hold the form tightly against the stake and level it with the string by foot pressure. Double-headed nails are recommended for easy form stripping. For added security stakes can be braced

Fig. 1. Setting of side forms.

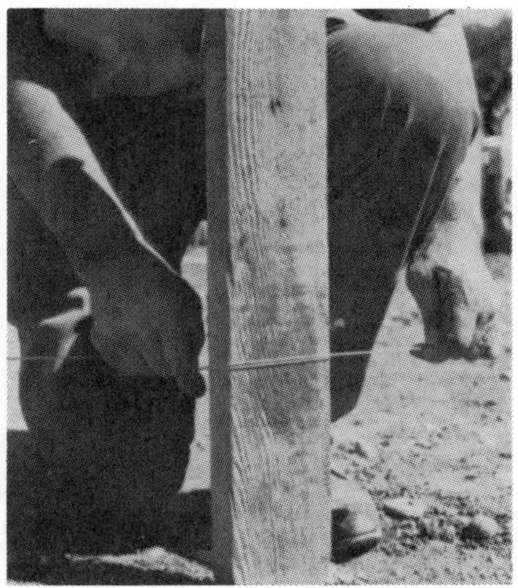

Fig. 2. Attach string to stake at desired level.

Fig. 3. Drive intermediate stakes in line with string.

Fig. 4. Setting forms.

Fig. 5. Attach forms to stakes with nails.

Fig. 6. Bracing stakes.

as shown in Fig. 6. This is good practice when forming 5- or 6-inch (12.5- to 15-cm.) slabs. To prevent the brace from slipping, drive a nail through the brace into the stake.

FORMING AND CONSTRUCTION OF DRIVEWAY OR SIDEWALK

Forming and other construction details for a simple driveway or sidewalk and for a typical free-form patio are shown in Figs. 7 and 8.

Materials

For a 4-inch (10-cm.) thick slab, 1 × 4 or 2 × 4 (2.5 × 10 or 5 × 10 cm.) lumber may be used. A 5-inch (12.5-cm.) slab can be formed with 2 × 4's (5 × 10 cm.), but 2 × 6's (5 × 15 cm.) are preferable. Slabs of 6-inch (15-cm.) thickness require at least 2 × 6 (5 × 15 cm.) forms.

Lumber used for formwork is generally *dressed*, that is, surfaced in a planing machine to attain smoothness and uniformity of size. Dressing reduces the size of lumber, consequently the 4-inch (10-cm.) dimension of a nominal 1 × 4 or 2 × 4 (2.5 × 10 or 5 × 10 cm.) is actually 3½ to 3 9/16 inches (8.8 to 8.9 cm.), and the 6-inch (15-cm.) dimension of a 2 × 6 (5 × 15 cm.) will be between 5½ and 5⅝ inches (13.75 to 14 cm.). Accordingly the final grade should be slightly lower than the bottom of the form when using dressed 1 × 4 or 2 × 4 (2.5 × 10 or 5 × 10 cm.) forms for 4-inch (10-cm.) slabs. The same applies when using 2 × 4's (5 × 10 cm.) for 5-inch (12.5-cm.) slabs and 2 × 6's (5 × 15 cm.) for 6-inch (15-cm.) slabs. A little backfilling outside the forms will prevent the concrete from running under them (Fig. 9).

On large-volume work such as public walks and housing projects, metal forms may be less expensive than wood. They permit the work to proceed faster and can be reused more often. Also, they may produce a better job.

Wood stakes are made from 1 × 2, 1 × 4, 2 × 2, or 2 × 4 (2.5 × 5, 2.5 × 10, 5 × 5, or 5 × 10 cm.) lumber. They may be hand cut or purchased precut. Space stakes at 4-foot (1.2-meter) intervals for 2-inch (5-cm.) thick formwork. With 1-inch (2.5-cm.) lumber, space the stakes more closely to prevent budging. A maximum interval of 2 to 3 feet (.6 to .9 meters) is suggested.

Reusable steel stakes for use with wood forms are available in

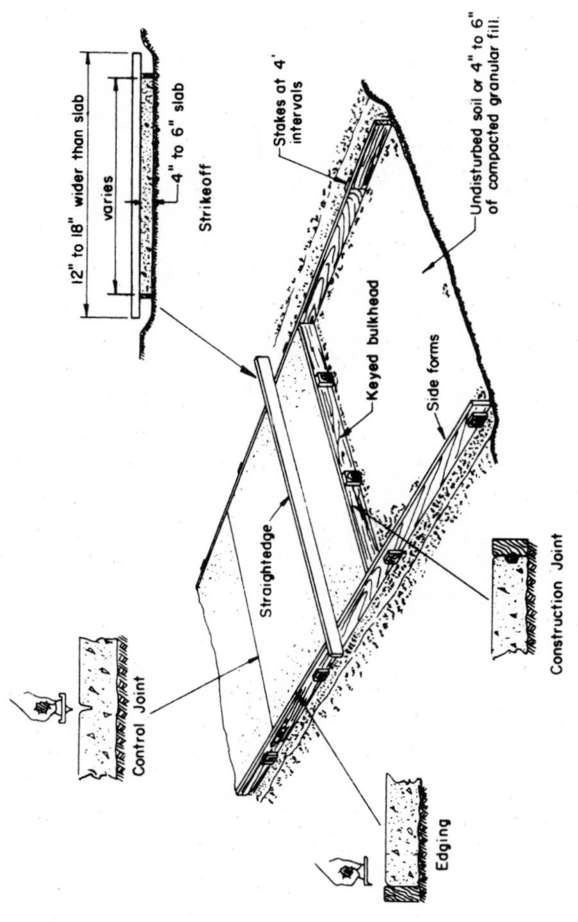

Fig. 7. Details for forming and construction of a typical concrete driveway or sidewalk.

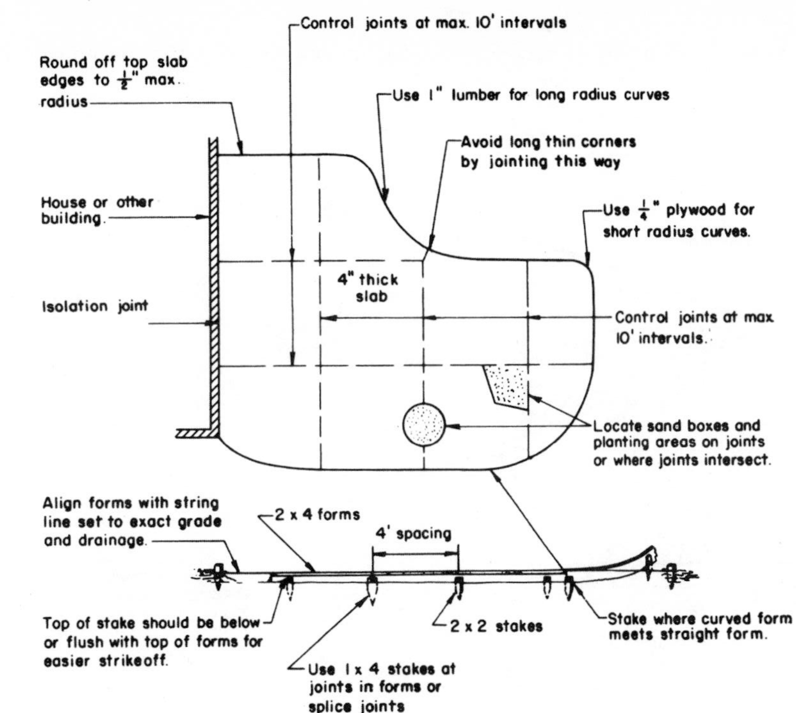
Control joints at max. 10' intervals
Round off top slab edges to $\frac{1}{2}$" max. radius
Use 1" lumber for long radius curves
Avoid long thin corners by jointing this way
House or other building.
Use $\frac{1}{4}$" plywood for short radius curves.
4" thick slab
Isolation joint
Control joints at max. 10' intervals.
Locate sand boxes and planting areas on joints or where joints intersect.
Align forms with string line set to exact grade and drainage.
2 x 4 forms
4' spacing
Top of stake should be below or flush with top of forms for easier strikeoff.
2 x 2 stakes
Stake where curved form meets straight form.
Use 1 x 4 stakes at joints in forms or splice joints

Fig. 8. Details for forming and construction of a typical free-form patio.

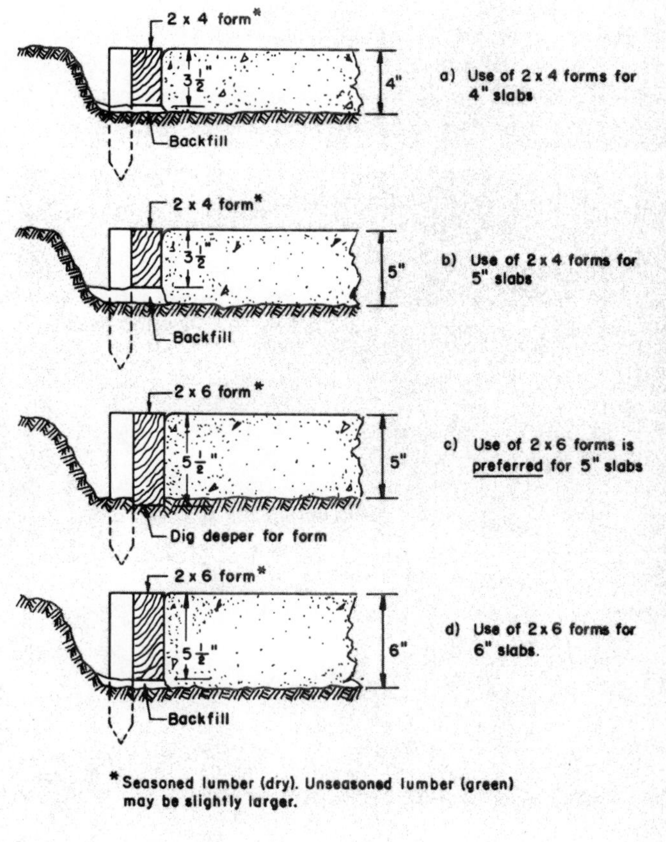

Fig. 9. The subgrade must be carefully fine-graded to ensure proper slab thickness when using dressed lumber for formwork.

various lengths and styles. They have closely spaced nailing holes and are easier to drive and pull than wood stakes. Despite higher initial cost, with many reuses steel stakes can bring substantial economies for volume work.

For ease in placing and finishing concrete, drive all stakes slightly below the top of the forms. Wood stakes can be sawed off flush. All stakes must be driven straight and true if forms are to be plumb. For easy stripping, use double-headed nails driven through the stake into the form (Fig. 5) and not vice versa.

Forming Curves

Horizontal curves may be formed with 1-inch (2.5-cm.) lumber (Fig. 10), ¼- to ½-inch (6.3- to 12.5-mm.) thick plywood,

Fig. 10. Forming curves with 1 × 4 (2.5 × 10 cm.) lumber. Inside stakes are pulled out after outside stakes are nailed firmly to the forms.

hardboard, or sheet metal. Short-radius curves are easily obtained by bending plywood with the grain vertical. Two-inch (5-cm.) thick wood forms may be bent to gentle horizontal curves during staking or to shorter-radius curves by saw kerfing (Fig. 11, D). Wet lumber is easier to bend than dry lumber. Additional information on forming horizontal curves is given in Fig. 11.

Gentle vertical curves can sometimes be formed by bending a 2 × 4 (5 × 10 cm.) during staking. When the change in slope is

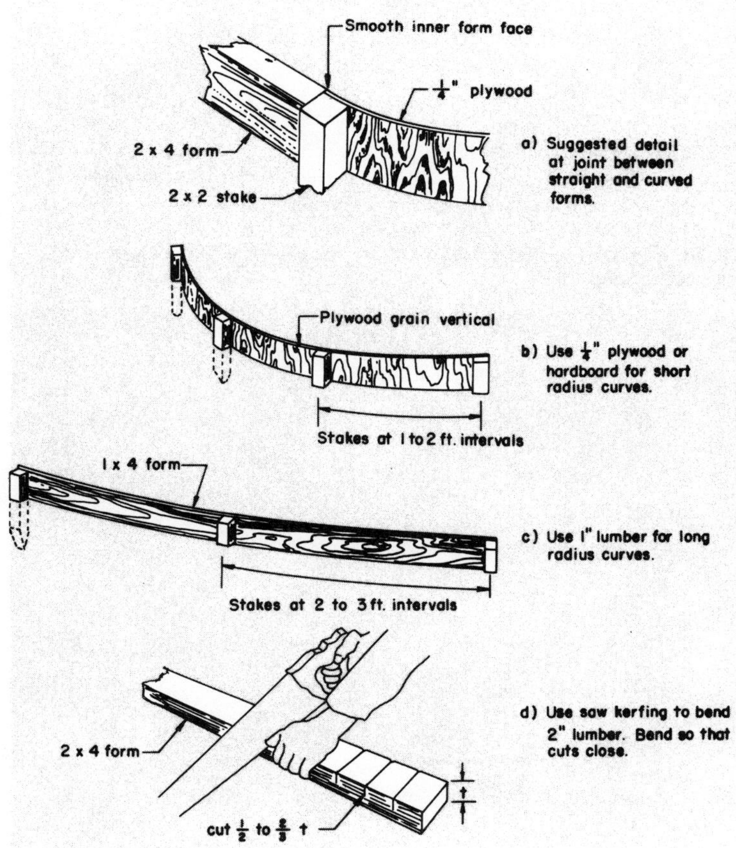

Fig. 11. Details for forming horizontal curves.

sharper, short lengths of forming may be used. The curve is laid out with a string line tied to temporary stakes. The line is adjusted up or down on the stakes to give a smooth curve; then short lengths of forming are set to the string line and securely staked. Vertical curves may also be formed by saw kerfing.

To hold forms at the proper grade and curvature, set stakes closer on vertical and horizontal curves than on straight runs.

Permanent Forms

Wood side forms and divider strips may be left in place permanently for decorative purposes and to serve as control joints.

Fig. 12. Divider strips stained to match deck, fence, and screen, carrying out landscape theme.

(*See* Fig. 12.) Such forms are usually made of 1 × 4 or 2 × 4 (2.5 × 10 or 5 × 10 cm.) redwood, cypress, or cedar that has been primed with a clear wood sealer. It is a good practice to mask the top surfaces with tape to protect them from abrasion and concrete staining (Fig. 13). Miter corner joints neatly and joint intersecting strips with neat butt joints. Anchor outside forms to the concrete with 16-penny galvanized nails driven at 16-inch (40-cm.) intervals horizontally through the forms at midheight. Interior divider strips should have nail anchors similarly spaced but driven from alternate sides of the board. Drive all nail heads flush with the forms. Never drive nails through the top of permanent forms. All stakes that are to remain in place permanently must be driven or cut off 2 inches (5 cm.) below the surface of the concrete.

Fig. 13. Covering permanent divider strips and outside forms with masking tape.

Fig. 14. Checking slab thickness and smooth subgrade with wood templet.

Final Check

Before concreting give all forms a final check for trueness to grade and proper slope for drainage. Check the subgrade with a wood templet (Fig. 14) or a string line to ensure correct slab thickness and a smooth subgrade. Finally, dampen forms with water or oil them for easier form removal. Motor oil may be used for small jobs. A regular form release agent applied by hand-spray equipment is preferred for volume work.

Chapter 39

Building Exterior Steps of Unreinforced Cast-in-Place Concrete

Whether the steps desired are elaborate (Fig. 1) or just simple entry steps with three or four risers (Fig. 5), the methods of construction are the same. Exterior steps of unreinforced cast-in-place concrete are used primarily at entryways to buildings and for changing levels in patios, gardens, and terraces. (*See* Chap. 35, Design and Layout, section on Steps; *also see* Chap. 40, Precast Concrete Units, section on Steps.)

FOOTINGS

Footings for steps should be placed at least 2 feet (60 cm.) deep in firm, undisturbed soil and, in areas where freezing occurs, 6 inches (15 cm.) below the prevailing frost line. Steps with more than two risers and two treads should be supported on unit masonry, concrete walls, piers at least 6 inches (15 cm.) thick (Fig. 2), or should be cantilevered from the main foundation walls. Steps should be securely tied to foundation walls with anchor bolts or tierods. On new construction step footings should be cast integrally with foundation walls (Fig. 3). (*See* Chap. 42, Foundation Walls and Piers.)

When new steps are added to an existing building, the following economical procedure will prevent their sinking. Two or more 6- to 8-inch (15- to 20-cm.) diameter postholes should be dug beneath the bottom tread and filled with concrete. The holes should extend to the depth indicated above. The top step

Fig. 1.

Fig. 2. Footings.

Fig. 3. Brackets cast integrally with basement walls.

or landing should be tied into the foundation wall with two or more metal anchors. (*See* Chap. 41, Footings.)

FORMWORK

Forms for steps must be rigidly braced to prevent bulging (Fig. 4) and tight to prevent leaking. They must be built for easy stripping without damage to the concrete. Forming materials should be straight, true, and free from imperfections that would be visible in the hardened concrete. Wood containing protruding or missing knots, bent nails, or other blemishes makes finishing more difficult and the final appearance less attractive.

Before proceeding further, it is important to outline the two methods of finishing steps, since the method used affects how the

Fig. 4. Riser and sidewall forms.

forms are built.

In one method, stripping of riser forms begins 30 minutes to several hours after placing concrete, depending on weather conditions and how fast the concrete sets. At this point, the steps should be strong enough to support their own weight. Rough edges and formed surfaces are rubbed with a float to bring mortar to the surface, and additional mortar can be plastered and troweled onto the surface in a thin layer. After some stiffening, the mortar is troweled and brushed.

In another method, treads and landings are finished soon after placing, and all forms are left in place for several days until curing is completed. After stripping any necessary chipping, handstoning, or patching is done, and risers and sidewalls are given a grout cleandown by which all voids are filled and no mortar is left on the surface.

Step sidewalls can be formed with plywood or hardboard panels (Fig. 4) or with board materials (Fig. 5). When using panels, riser forms must be cut to fit inside dimensions.

Installation of riser forms should start at the top to eliminate

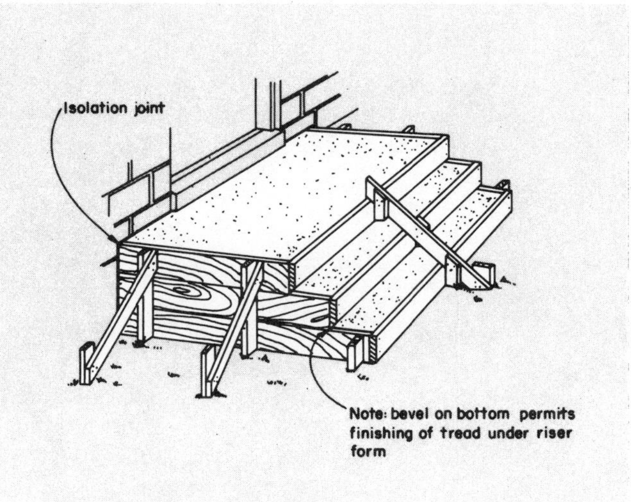

Fig. 5. Details of forming and bracing for typical entry steps.

unnecessary traffic on previously placed risers. Risers should be checked with a hand level (Fig. 6) and positioned to allow a ¼-inch (6.3-mm.) slope on each tread for drainage. A bevel on the lower edge of the riser form will permit finishing the full width of the tread. Riser forms are sometimes tilted or battered about 1 inch (2.5 cm.) to increase the width of the treads. Riser forms must be securely fastened to the sidewall forms and well-braced to prevent bending under pressure of the concrete. Wood cleats are the best way to attach riser forms to plywood sidewall forms (Fig. 4). Wood wedges should be used for holding risers between solid concrete or masonry walls (Fig. 7). Braces are usually centered on the risers and staked and nailed outside the formwork (Fig. 5).

During forming, provision should be made for any recesses needed for the attachment of ironwork or railings. Also, an isolation joint is required where the top tread or landing meets the building. A thin layer of building paper will do the job. If this is

Fig. 6. Leveling and positioning risers.

not done the concrete may bond to the wall and some day cause a crack. (*See* Chap. 7, Forms and Form Making.)

FILL MATERIALS

Brick, stone, or broken concrete can be used inside the formwork as fill to reduce the amount of concrete needed (Fig. 2). Soil or granular fill placed in well-compacted layers may also be used. There should be no fill material any closer than 4 inches (10 cm.) from the face of any form.

Falsework (inside forms) may be used to reduce the concrete required in large steps. When falsework of any absorbent material such as wood is to remain in place permanently, it should be no closer than 6 inches (15 cm.) from the face of any outside form. If falsework is protected with a moisture-proof membrane such as plastic sheeting, the concrete thickness may be reduced

Fig. 7. Technique for attaching and bracing riser forms between concrete or masonry walls.

to 4 inches (10 cm.). Improperly protected falsework will absorb water from the concrete and swell. This swelling coupled with normal drying shrinkage in concrete can cause severe cracking.

PLACING CONCRETE

Concrete suitable for steps is the same as that required for driveways, sidewalks, and patios, except that the maximum size of coarse aggregate should not exceed 1 inch (2.5 cm.), and slump should not exceed 3 inches (7.5 cm.). (*See* Chap. 9, Placing and Consolidating Concrete.)

Before placing concrete, forms should be wetted with water or coated with a form-release agent such as oil. Forms to be removed the same day may be wetted, and those to stay in place several days should be oiled.

Placing should begin with the bottom step and continue upward filling against sidewall forms as work progresses. The concrete should be carefully spaded or vibrated, especially next to form faces. Each tread should be floated off as it is filled. The top step or landing is filled last, then struck off with a straightedge and darbied (Fig. 8). Forms should be tapped lightly to release air bubbles.

FINISHING STEPS

It is common practice in some areas to strip forms early so that risers and treads can be finished before concrete sets firmly. With this method, finishing starts at the top and continues down the steps, one at a time. After the top landing is struck off, darbied, and edged, it is hand-floated and given its first troweling. Each tread is floated, then edged along the riser form, usually with a ¼- to ½-inch (6.3- to 12.5-mm.) radius tool (Fig. 9). This is followed by the first troweling.

After these operations there is normally a waiting period until the steps set sufficiently to hold their shape when the riser boards are removed. At the proper time each riser form should be carefully removed (Fig. 10). The riser is floated (Fig. 11) and an inside step tool is used where the riser meets the tread below

Fig. 8. Darbying the top step landing.

Fig. 9. Edging along a riser form.

Fig. 10. Removing riser forms.

Fig. 11. Floating riser with a rubber float.

(Fig. 12). The radius of this tool is usually the same as that used at the top of the riser. Matching inside and outside step tools are available for this purpose (Fig. 13).

If sufficient mortar cannot be worked out of the concrete for proper finishing, a little mortar consisting of 1 part cement to about 1½ parts fine sand should be applied. After troweling a damp brush should be drawn across the riser and tread to obtain a fine-textured, nonslip surface. These operations are repeated for the next lower riser, and so on. Fast and careful work is es-

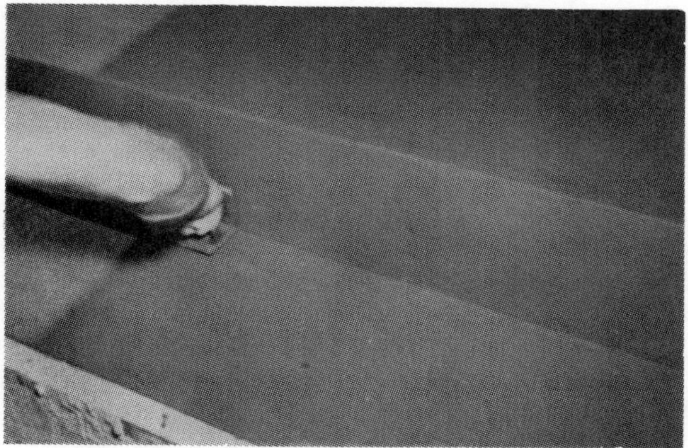

Fig. 12. Finishing an inside edge with a step tool.

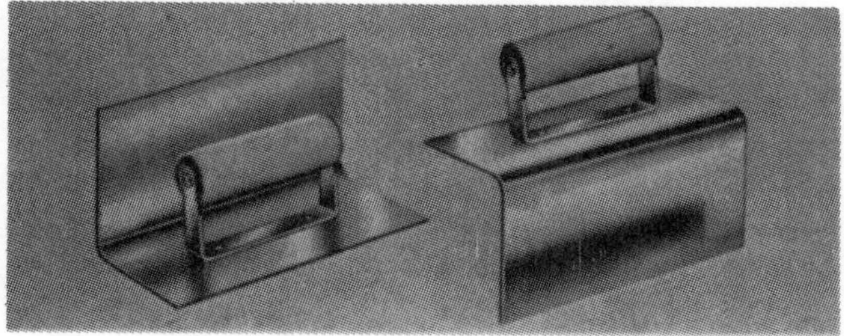

Fig. 13. Matching inside and outside step tool.

sential since too much time on any one step may cause the others to set too firmly for proper finishing.

Side forms can be removed the same day, and the sidewalls first floated, than plastered with a ⅛- to ¼-inch (3.2- to 6-mm.) layer of mortar. The mortar should be spread with a trowel, then floated with a cork or sponge rubber float. This finish is suitable for most step sidewalls (Fig. 14). If a smooth finish is desired, troweling should follow. A brushed or swirl finish may be used after floating or troweling.

Side forms may be left in place several days while the steps are cured. In this case, sidewalls should be given a grout cleandown.

In the other method of finishing steps, the treads and landings are floated, edged, troweled, and brushed in the usual manner with all forms left in place for several days while the steps are cured. After forms are stripped, small projections should be removed by chipping and hand-stoning. Honeycomb areas, if any, should be chipped out and patched with a stiff mortar to match that used in the concrete. These operations can be minimized if care is exercised in forming and placing the concrete. If risers and sidewalls are not uniform in color when forms are stripped, a grout cleandown may be used. Surfaces to be cleaned should

Fig. 14. These sidewalls were finished with a cork or rubber float to complete steps.

be saturated with water and a grout (1 part portland cement and 1½ to 2 parts fine sand) applied by brushing or rubber float. The grout should be vigorously floated to fill all voids and excess grout scraped off. After the surface has dried thoroughly, it should be rubbed with clean, dry burlap to remove all fried grout.

CURING

Steps must be cured the same as driveways, sidewalks, or patios. (*See* Chap. 10, Curing Concrete.) Care should be taken to cure sidewalls after forms are removed. Methods that use water are most satisfactory.

NONSLIP FINISHES

Nonslip finishes for better safety on steps can be obtained in a number of ways. Brushing, swirl-floating, and swirl-troweling produce a satisfactorily rough texture, but these finishes may wear smooth under heavy foot traffic. A more permanent nonslip tread can be obtained by using a dry-shake of abrasive grains such as silicon carbide or aluminum oxide. The most permanent nonslip steps are built with special abrasive strips and nosings that are embedded in the surface of the treads.

Chapter 40

Precast Concrete Units

Precast concrete units in a wide range of sizes, styles, colors, and textures are readily available from local precast or concrete masonry producers, building materials suppliers, or nurserymen. They can be used for building walks, drives, patios, and steps. The units are easy to handle and install, requiring only a few tools and little special knowledge of concrete. (*See* Fig. 1.)

PAVING SLABS

Precast concrete paving slabs are machine-made or precast by conventional methods. Slabs are commonly available in square and other rectangular shapes measuring from 12 to 36 inches (30 to 90 cm.), with thicknesses of 2, 2½, and 3 inches (5, 6.3, and 7.5 cm.). The 2-inch (5-cm.) thickness is suitable for residential walks and patios, while the 2½- or 3-inch (6.3- or 7.5-cm.) thickness should be used for driveways and municipal walks. Other sizes and shapes are also manufactured. Some of the more popular special shapes are round, triangular, diamond, hexagonal, and Spanish tile. (*See* Fig. 2.)

The slabs may be a natural gray, white cement color, or pigmented in tones of red, black, brown, green, or yellow. Exposed-aggregate finishes are available in some areas (Fig. 3).

Combinations of plain and colored or exposed-aggregate slabs are a pleasing contrast in walks, drives, and patios. One popular decorative feature for sidewalks makes use of a row of charcoal-colored units every sixth row. This strip feature in combination with staggered joints changes the entire appearance of a walk.

Installation of precast paving slabs can begin in spring as soon

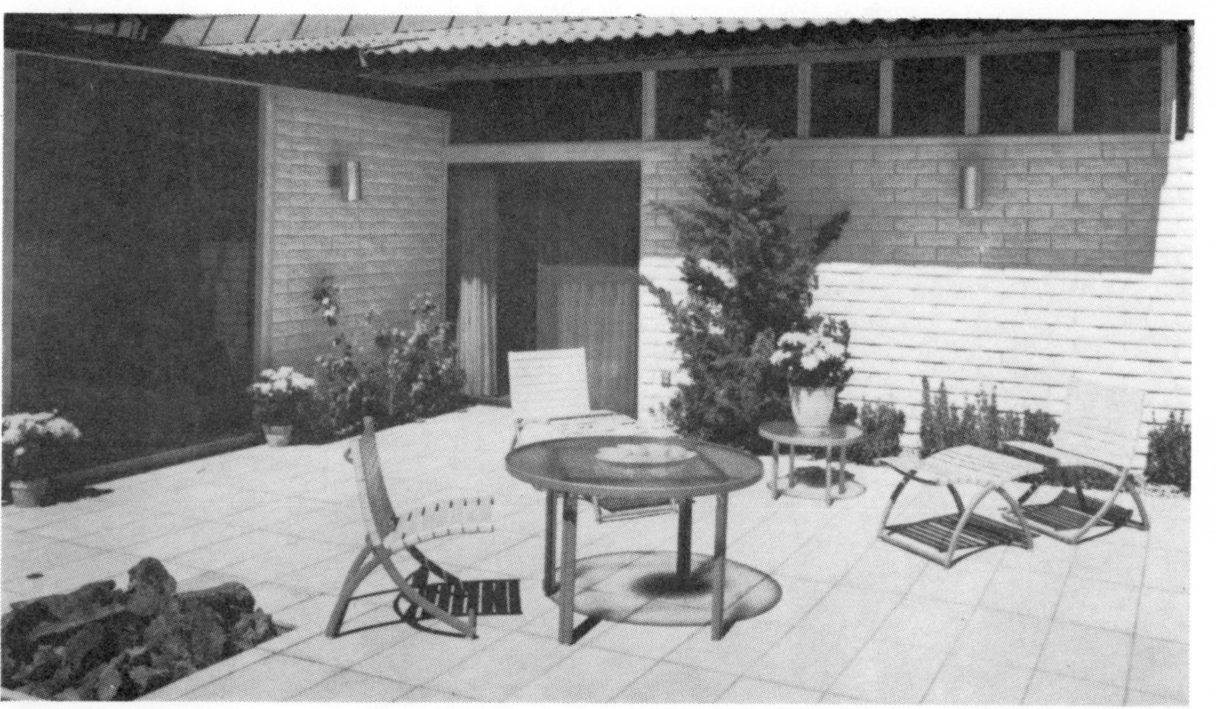

Fig. 1. This patio is built entirely of rectangular precast concrete paving slabs with mortared joints.

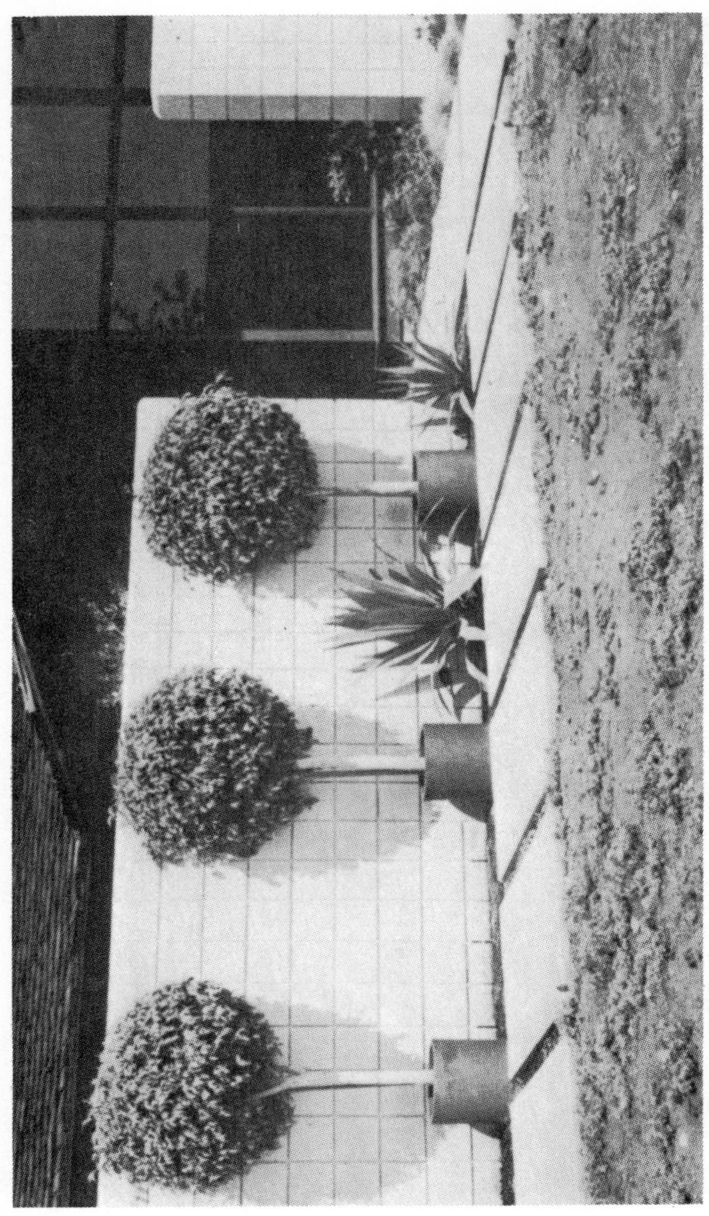

Fig. 2. Precast concrete paving slabs make an attractive walk for this contemporary home.

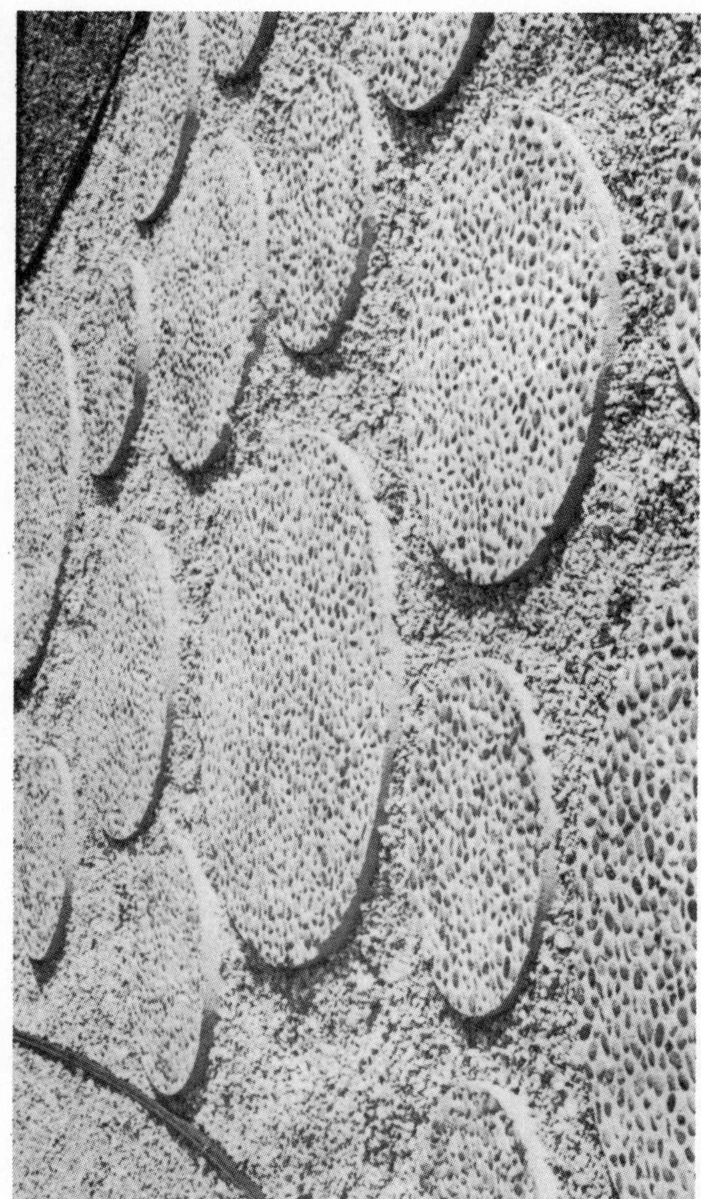

Fig. 3. Precast rounds (stepping stones) with exposed-aggregate finish are popular for garden walks.

as the frost is gone and ground conditions permit. In the fall, installation can continue until frozen ground prevents proper compaction of the subgrade material. Slabs are bedded either in sand or mortar. Regardless of the method used the final job will be only as stable as the subgrade underneath the sand or mortar. Accordingly, subgrade preparation should be done as carefully for precast work as for cast-in-place work. (*See* Chap. 36, Preparation of Subgrade.)

For residential work paving slabs are usually bedded in 2 to 3 inches (5 to 7.5 cm.) of sand as illustrated in Figs. 4 through 8. Sand bedding can give satisfactory and long-lasting results. The sand-bedding method is ideally suited for the do-it-yourselfer in such applications as walks and patios, or it may be used for temporary pathways. Precast slabs used in temporary locations can easily be lifted and reused.

Stake off the desired area, keeping outside dimensions in even increments of stock-size precast units. String a line between stakes and excavate to the required depth. Allow 2 to 3 inches (5 to 7.5 cm.) for sand in addition to the slab thickness (Fig. 4).

Replace the soil with slightly damp sand and compact firmly. Embed straight boards in the sand to establish a level, smooth bed. Allow ¼-inch per foot of slope (2-cm. per running meter) for drainage (Fig. 5). Level the sand by running a strike board over the leveling boards (Fig. 6). After leveling and smoothing, remove the boards.

Starting in a corner, set precast slabs on the sand bed with the joints butted together (Fig. 7). Plan the job to avoid use of special-cut sizes if possible. Continue laying slabs until the area is covered (Fig. 8). Then sweep sand into the joints to complete the job. Mortaring of joints is not required. Growth of grass or weeds through the joints can be controlled by use of soil poison.

Bedding of slabs in a layer of mortar is recommended for driveways and municipal walks. Screeds of 2 × 4 (5 × 10 cm.) lumber set to grade on both sides of the area to be paved are recommended to ensure good alignment and a level surface. When a curb is used in combination with a sidewalk or driveway, the curb may serve as one screed. A second screed should be set to grade at the proper distance, depending on the width desired.

Fig. 4. Stake off desired area and excavate to required depth.

Fig. 5. Embed straight boards in the sand to establish a level, smooth bed.

Fig. 6. Level the sand by running a strike board over the leveling boards.

Fig. 7. Begin laying precast slabs in a corner.

Fig. 8.

The width can be any dimension from 12 inches (30 cm.) up, in 6-inch (15-cm.) modules. *For example,* a 4-foot (1.2-meter) walk may use a combination of 18 × 24 and 30 × 24-inch (45 × 60 and 75 × 60-cm.) slabs.

Screeds should be set about 3¼ inches (8.1 cm.) above the compacted subgrade when using 2½-inch (6.3-cm.) thick slabs. Next, a ¾-inch (1.9-cm.) layer of air-entrained cement-sand mortar (1 part cement: 6 to 8 parts sand) should be placed on the subgrade. The mortar bed should be struck off 2½ inches (6.3 cm.) below finished grade with a straightedge containing a row of nails about 1 inch (2.5 cm.) apart in the bottom edge. When drawn over the mortar bed, the nails leave a series of ridges and valleys in the mortar which ensures even support over the full area of each slab when it is tamped into place.

Slabs 2½-inches (6.3-cm.) thick weigh about 32 pounds per square foot (156.3 kgs. per sq. meter). Many of the smaller precast slabs can be lifted and placed by hand. When too heavy for hand lifting, slabs may be lifted by means of a vacuum pad with handles. With this device, two men can butt the largest slabs tightly together without having to place their hands under or between the slabs (Fig. 9). A vacuum lifting device may be available from the precast slab manufacturer. A straight plank should be placed across the screeds and a tamper used to set the slabs to grade. Traffic should be kept off the slabs until the mortar bed has firmly set.

Where manholes, hydrants, poles, or other obstructions occur, a slab should be left out and the area filled with smaller slabs, brick, or a combination of the two. When water or gas valve stems are located in the paved area, holes through the slabs are required. Holes up to 6 inches (15 cm.) in diameter can be drilled or cut with a hammer and chisel. The valve stem cover should be set flush with the slab and the surrounding space grouted. The radius at intersections of streets and sidewalks requires slabs that are sawed to fit flush with the curb.

Machine-made paving slabs, which have perfectly true edges and corners, can be laid with very close tolerances by using tight butt joints. Sealing of the joints is not required. It is advisable to stagger the joints each time a slab is laid (Fig. 10).

Fig. 9. Vacuum lifting device for placing precast paving slabs.

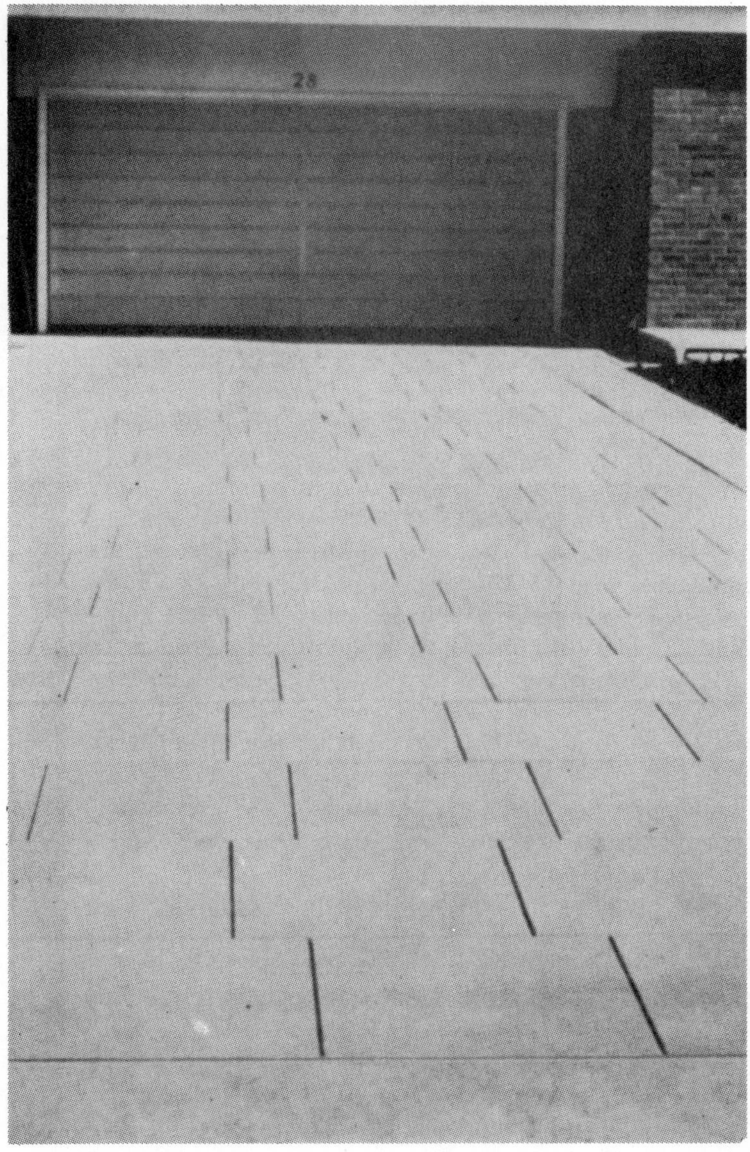

Fig. 10. Staggered joints in a precast driveway.

When paving large areas it is recommended that 1/16-inch-per-foot (5-mm.-per-meter) allowance be made for particles of sand or mortar that may cling to the sides of the slabs. *For example,* in a 24-foot (7.3-meters) wide area requiring twelve 24-inch (60-cm.) slabs an allowance of 1½ inches (3.8 cm.) should be made.

STEPS

Complete or partial use of precast concrete units can simplify step construction. Precast steps with treads, risers, sidewalls, and porch all cast as one piece are available in a wide variety of styles and sizes. Widths of 3 to 6 feet (.9 to 1.8 meters) with any number of risers up to 6 and porches up to 6-feet (1.8-meters) deep are commonly available from manufacturers of precast steps (Fig. 11).

To meet the need for wide entryways step units can be used in multiples. Also separate precast porches (Fig. 12) are available in some areas in heights up to 42 inches (1.1 meters) and varying lengths and widths to meet the requirements of wide entryways.

Precast steps are used for new construction and as step replacements for older homes. The units are delivered by the manufacturer ready for installation. Often the manufacturer can install the units quickly with special trucks and hoists (Fig. 13). Railings are bolted to inserts cast into the steps during manufacture.

There are several methods of installing precast steps. In one method, units are bolted directly onto the building's foundation wall. The steps cantilever from the wall and do not depend on the ground for any support. In another method, steps are supported on simple slab footings that are cast by the manufacturer and supplied with the steps. The slabs are placed at the desired depth on a leveling bed of sand. In some cases, builders use the sidewalk as a base for supporting precast steps. In these instances, the sidewalk should be placed up to the foundation walls. The manufacturer should be consulted as to the best method of installing the steps, particularly in areas subject to

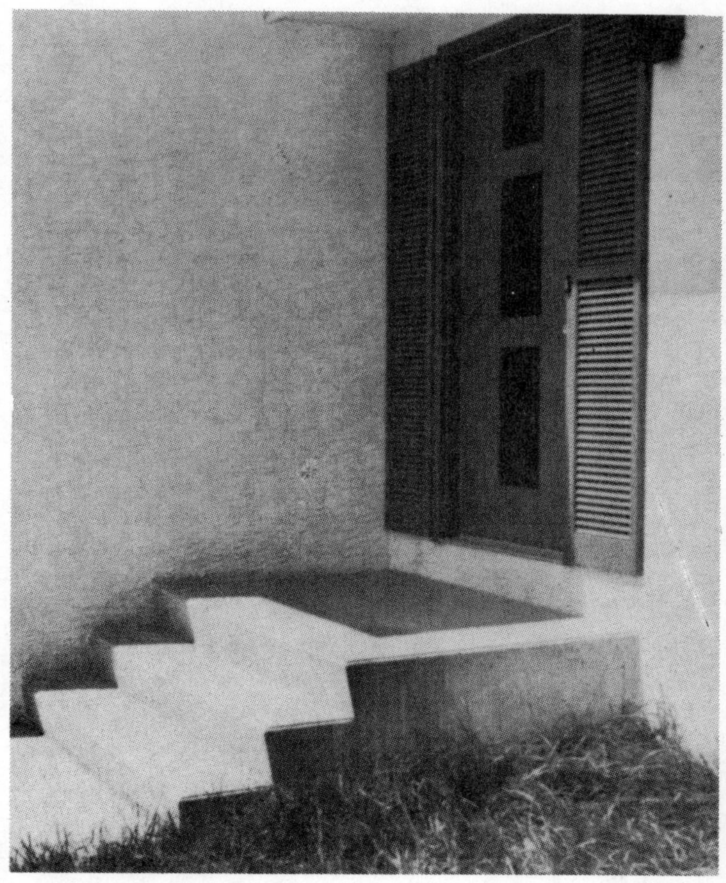

Fig. 11. Unit steps are precast all in one piece in a factory.

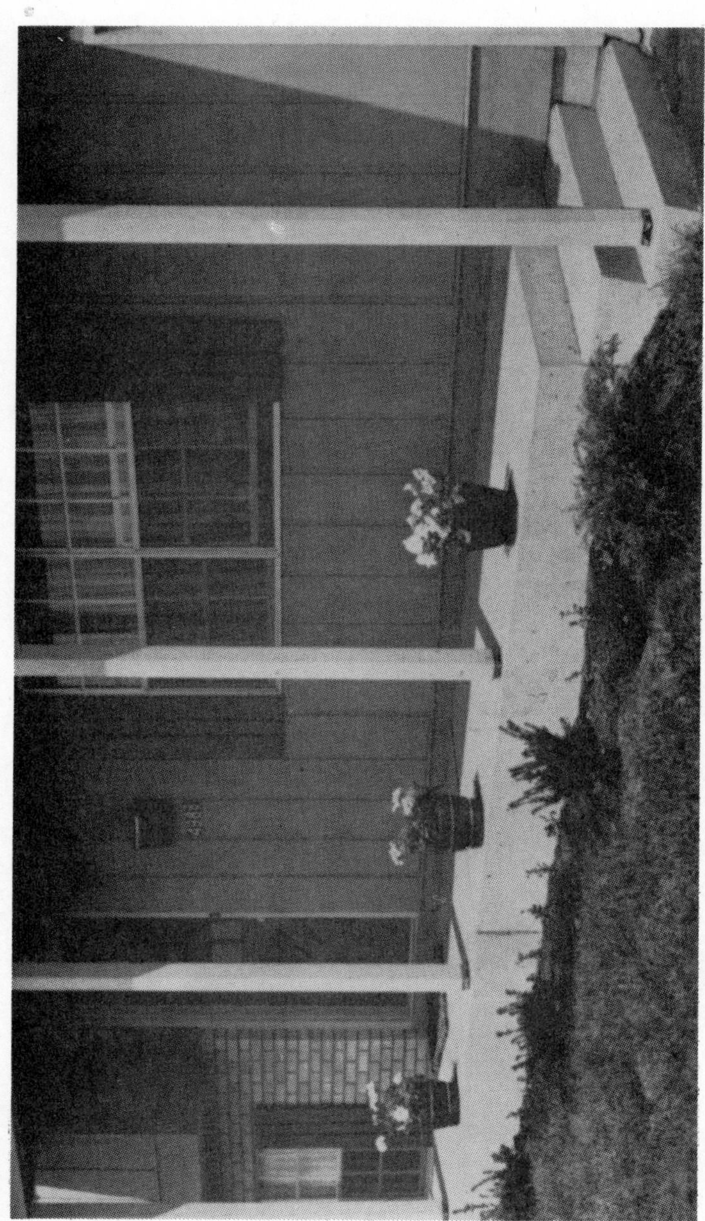

Fig. 12. Precast concrete porches can be used in combination with precast steps to fit the requirements of any entryway.

Fig. 13. With special equipment, precast steps are lifted from the truck into position in a short time.

movements of the soil by frost action.

A cast-in-place or concrete block footing is generally best especially in cold climates. The method described in Chap. 39, Building Exterior Steps of Unreinforced Cast-in-Place Concrete, for adding new cast-in-place steps to an existing building is also suitable for precast steps; or the method may be modified as follows. Attach two 5/16-inch (8-mm.) steel angles or precast concrete brackets to the foundation wall with power-driven studs or large bolts through the wall. If the foundation wall is made of concrete masonry, two blocks can be set in the wall so that they project 4 inches (10 cm.) from the surface. The back of the precast steps will be supported on this shelf. For the front footing two 6-inch (30-cm.) diameter post-holes are dug, going below

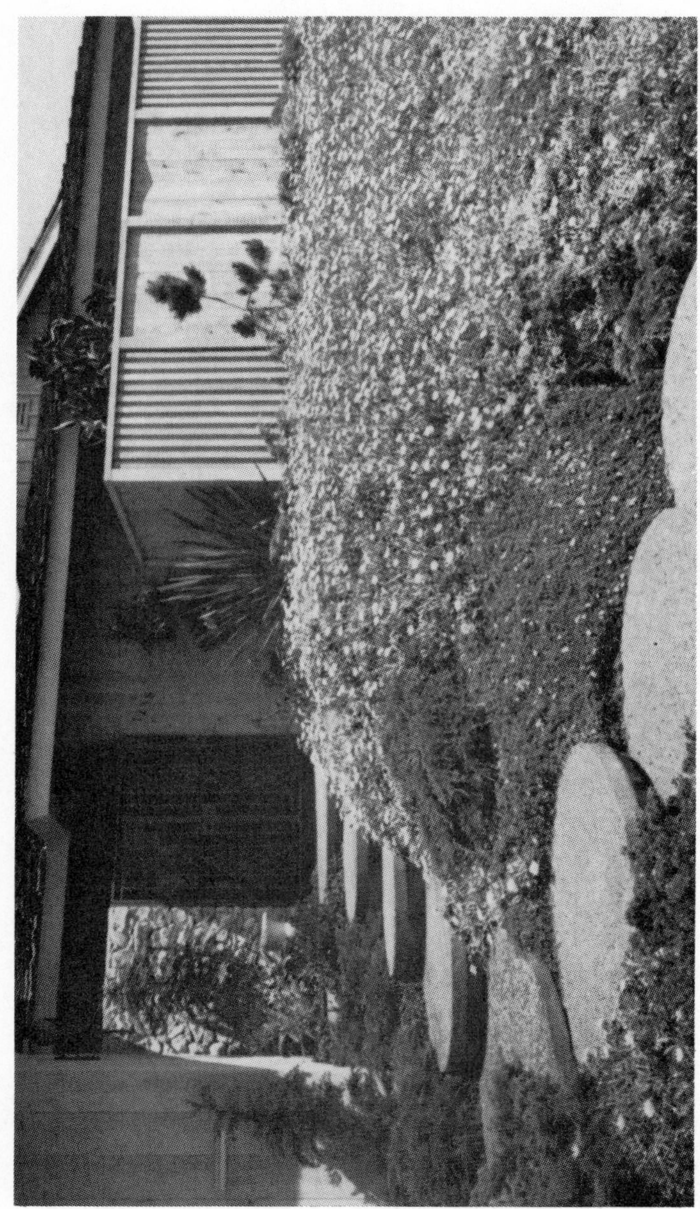

Fig. 14. Precast rounds make a novel stepped ramp approach to this lovely home.

frost level. Precast concrete piers are then inserted into the holes and adjusted so that the steps will be level when lowered onto the piers and wall supports. It is important that these piers be on firm support in the ground. To ensure this, 3 inches (7.5 cm.) of wet concrete may be placed in the bottom of each hole. After the precast steps have been lowered onto the supports, grading up to the bottom of the unit completes the installation.

In addition to the one-piece or unit steps previously described, individual treads or combination tread-riser units are available. These vary considerably in design and style—they can be supported at both ends, cantilevered from one end, or double cantilevered from a center support. Precast paving slabs in square, rectangular, or round shapes also may be used for steps (Fig. 14). With a wide variety of units to choose from, the most demanding architectural requirements can be met.

DURABILITY

It is important that precast units be durable in service. Good-quality concrete is required to provide durability for paving slabs and steps subject to freezing-thawing and deicers used for melting ice and snow. Some manufacturers do not recommend the use of deicers on their products. It is suggested that the purchaser obtain information on durability (field performance) from the manufacturer of the precast units. (*See* Chap. 14, Precast Concrete.)

Chapter 41

Footings

The *footings* act as the base of the foundation and transmit the superimposed load to the soil. The type and size of footings should be suitable for the soil condition, and in cold climates the footings should be far enough below ground level to be protected from frost action. Local codes usually establish this depth, which is often 4 feet (1.2 meters) or more in northern sections of the United States.

Poured concrete footings are more dependable than those of other materials and are recommended for use in home foundations. Where fill has been used, the foundations should extend below the fill to undisturbed earth. In areas having adobe soil or where soil moisture may cause soil shrinkage, irregular settlement of the foundation and the building it supports may occur. Local practices that have been successful should be followed in such cases.

WALL FOOTINGS

Well-designed wall footings are important in preventing settling or cracks in the wall. One method of determining the size, often used with most normal soils, is based on the proposed wall thickness. The footing thickness or depth should be equal to the wall thickness (Fig. 1, A). Footings should project beyond each side of the wall one-half the wall thickness. This is a general rule as the footing bearing area should be designed to the load capac-

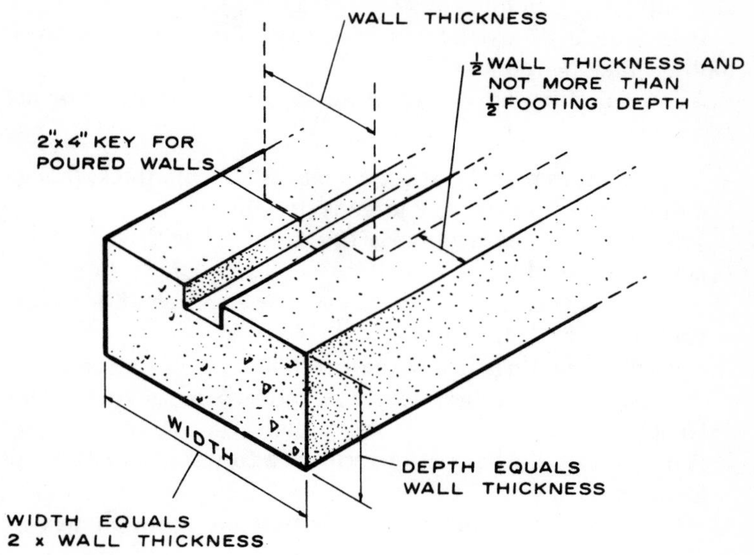

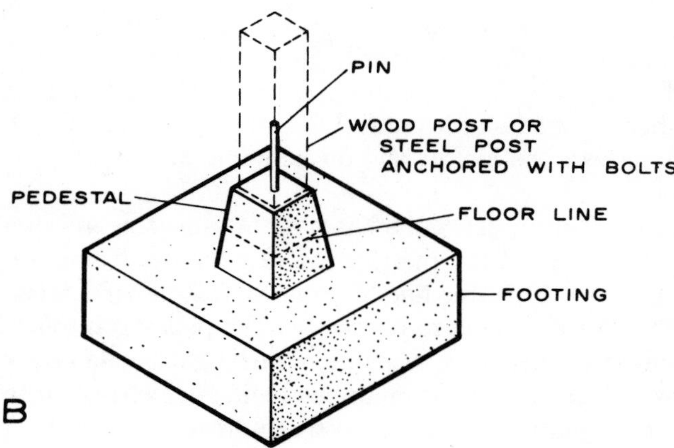

Fig. 1. Concrete footing. (A) Wall footing; (B) post footing.

ity of the soil. Local regulations often relate to these needs. This also applies to column and fireplace footings.

If the soil is of low load-bearing capacity, wider reinforced footings may be required.

A few rules that apply to footing design and construction are as follows:

1. Footings must be at least 6 inches (15 cm.) thick, though a thickness of 8 inches or more is preferable.
2. If footing excavation is too deep, fill with concrete—never replace dirt.
3. Use formboards for footings where soil conditions prevent sharply cut trenches.
4. Place footings below the frostline.
5. Reinforce footings with steel rods where they cross pipe trenches.
6 Use key slot for better resistance to water entry at wall location.
7. In freezing weather, cover with straw or supply heat.

PIER, POST, AND COLUMN FOOTINGS

Footings for *piers, posts,* or *columns* (Fig. 1, B) should be square and include a *pedestal* on which the member will bear. A protruding steel pin is ordinarily set in the pedestal to anchor a wood post. Bolts for the bottom plate of steel posts are usually set when the pedestal is poured. At other times, steel posts are set directly on the footing and the concrete floor poured around them.

Footings vary in size depending on the allowable soil pressure and the spacing of the piers, posts, or columns. Common sizes are 24 × 24 × 12 inches and 30 × 30 × 12 inches (60 × 60 × 30 and 75 × 75 × 30 cm., respectively). The pedestal is sometimes poured after the footing. The minimum height should be about 3 inches (7.5 cm.) above the finish basement floor and 12 inches (30 cm.) above finish grade in crawl-space areas.

Footings for fireplaces, furnaces, and chimneys should ordinarily be poured at the same time as other footings.

STEPPED FOOTINGS

Stepped footings are often used where the lot slopes to the front or rear and the garage or living areas are at basement level. The vertical part of the step should be poured at the same time as the footing. The bottom of the footing is always placed on undisturbed soil and located below the frostline. Each run of the footing should be level.

The vertical step between footings should be at least 6 inches (15 cm.) thick and the same width as the footings (Fig. 2). The height of the step should not be more than three-fourths of the adjacent horizontal footing. On steep slopes more than one step may be required. It is a good practice, when possible, to limit the vertical step to 2 feet (60 cm.). In very steep slopes special footings may be required.

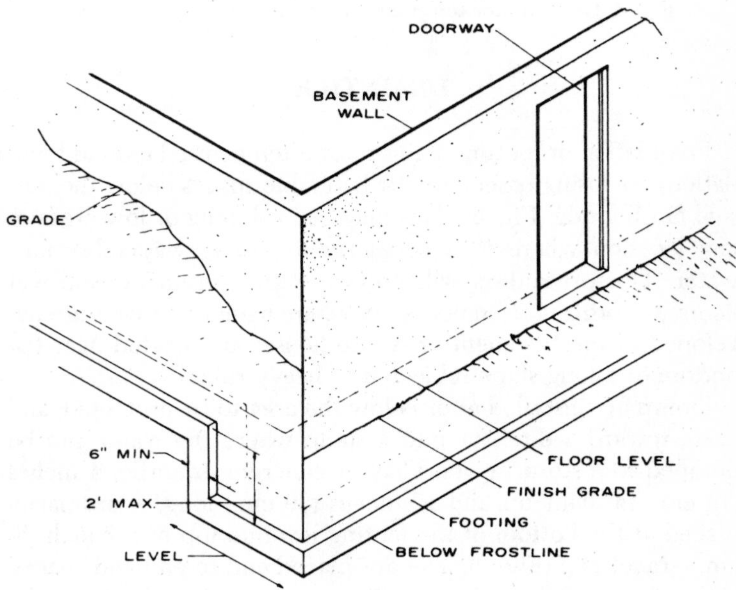

Fig. 2. Stepped footings.

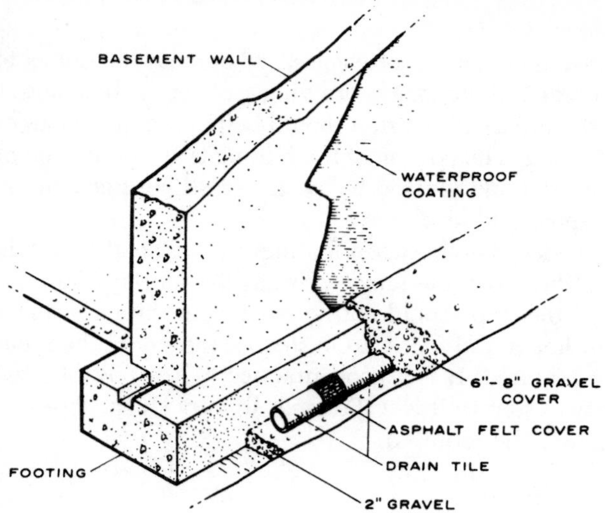

Fig. 3. Draintile for soil drainage at outer walls.

DRAINTILE

Foundation or footing drains must often be used around foundations enclosing basements, or habitable spaces below the outside finish grade (Fig. 3). This may be in sloping or low areas or any location where it is necessary to drain away subsurface water. This precaution will prevent damp basements and wet floors. *Draintile* is often necessary where habitable rooms are developed in the basement or where houses are located near the bottom of a long slope subjected to heavy runoff.

Drains are installed at or below the area to be protected, and drain toward a ditch or into a sump where the water can be pumped to a storm sewer. Clay or concrete draintile, 4 inches (10 cm.) in diameter and 12 inches (30 cm.) long, is ordinarily placed at the bottom of the footing level on top of a 2-inch (5-cm.) gravel bed (Fig. 3). Tile are placed end to end and spaced about ⅛ inch (3.2 mm.) apart. The top of the joint between the tile is covered with a strip of asphalt felt or similar paper, and 6 to 8 inches (15 to 20 cm.) of gravel is used over the tile. Drainage is toward the outfall or ditch. Dry wells for drainage water are used only when the soil conditions are favorable for this method of disposal. Local building regulations vary somewhat and should be consulted before construction of a drainage system is started.

Chapter 42

Foundation Walls and Piers

Foundation walls form an enclosure for basements or crawl spaces and carry wall, floor, roof, and other building loads. The two types of walls most commonly used are *poured concrete* and *concrete block*. Treated wood foundations might also be used when accepted by local codes.

Preservative-treated posts and poles offer many possibilities for low-cost foundation systems and can also serve as a structural framework for the walls and roof.

Wall thicknesses and types of construction are ordinarily controlled by local building regulations. Thicknesses of poured concrete basement walls may vary from 8 to 10 inches (20 to 25 cm.) and concrete block walls from 8 to 12 inches (20 to 30 cm.) depending on story heights and length of unsupported walls.

Clear wall height should be no less than 7 feet (2.1 meters) from the top of the finish basement floor to the bottom of the joists. Greater clearance is usually desirable to provide adequate headroom under girders, pipes, and ducts. Many contractors pour 8-foot (2.4-meters) high walls above the footings, which provide a clearance of 7 feet 8 inches (2.3 meters) from the top of the finished concrete floor to the bottom of the joists. Concrete block walls, eleven courses above the footings with 4-inch (10-cm.) solid cap-block, will produce about a 7-foot 4-inch (2.2-meters) height to the joists from the basement floor.

POURED CONCRETE WALLS

Poured concrete walls (Fig. 1) require forming that must be tight and also braced and tied to withstand the forces of the pouring operation and the fluid concrete.

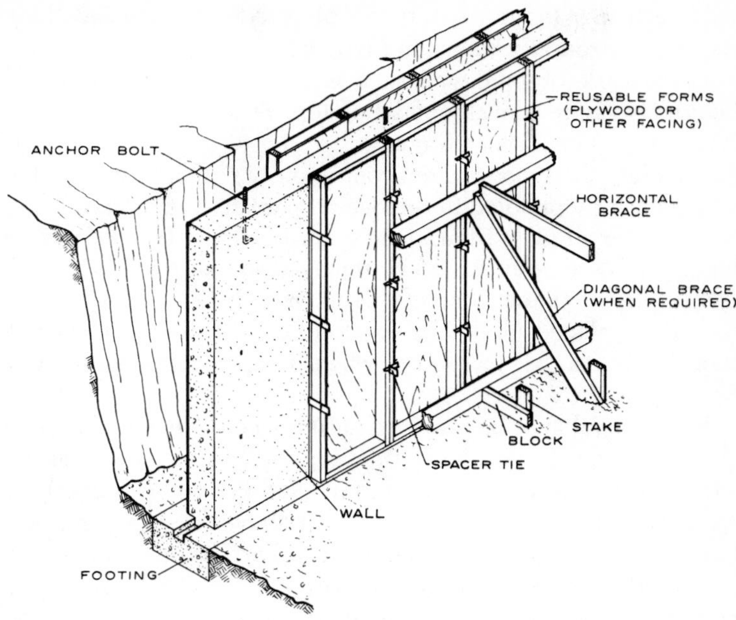

Fig. 1. Forming for poured concrete walls.

Poured concrete walls should be double-formed (formwork constructed for each wall face). Reusable forms are used in the majority of poured walls. Panels may consist of wood framing with plywood facings and are fastened together with clips or other ties (Fig. 1). Wood sheathing boards and studs with horizontal members and braces are sometimes used in the construction of forms in small communities. As in reusable forms, formwork should be plumb, straight, and braced sufficiently to withstand the pouring operations. (*See* Chap. 7, Forms and Form Making.)

Frames for cellar windows, doors, and other openings are set in place as the forming is erected, along with forms for the beam pockets which are located to support the ends of the floor beam.

Reusable forms usually require little bracing other than horizontal members and sufficient blocking and bracing to keep them in place during pouring operations. Forms constructed with vertical studs and waterproof plywood or lumber sheathing require horizontal whalers and bracing.

Level marks of some type, such as nails along the form, should be used to assure a level foundation top. This will provide a good level sill plate and floor framing.

Concrete should be poured continuously without interruption and constantly puddled to remove air pockets and work the material under window frames and other blocking. If wood spacer blocks are used, they should be removed so that they do not become buried in the concrete. Anchor bolts for the sill plate should be placed while the concrete is still plastic. Concrete should always be protected when temperatures are below freezing.

Forms should not be removed until the concrete has hardened and acquired sufficient strength to support loads imposed during early construction. At least two days (and preferably longer) are required when temperatures are well above freezing, and perhaps a week when outside temperatures are below freezing.

Poured concrete walls can be dampproofed with one heavy cold or hot coat of tar or asphalt. It should be applied to the outside from the footings to the finish gradeline. Such coatings are usually sufficient to make a wall watertight against ordinary seepage (such as may occur after a rainstorm), but should not be applied until the surface of the concrete has dried enough to assure good adhesion. In poorly drained soils, a membrane (as previously described for concrete block walls) may be necessary.

CONCRETE BLOCK WALLS

Concrete blocks are available in various sizes and forms, but those generally used are 8, 10, and 12 inches (20, 25, and 30 cm.) wide. Modular blocks allow for the thickness and width of the mortar joint so are usually about 7⅝ inches (19.1 cm.) high by 15⅝ inches (39.1 cm.) long. This results in blocks which measure 8 inches (20 cm.) high and 16 inches (40 cm.) long from centerline to centerline of the mortar joints.

Concrete block walls require *no* formwork. Block courses start at the footing and are laid up with about ⅜-inch (9.4-mm.) mortar joints, usually in a common bond (Fig. 2). Joints should be tooled smooth to resist water seepage. Full bedding or mortar should be used on all contact surfaces of the block. When *pilasters* (column-like projections) are required by building codes or to strengthen a wall, they are placed on the interior side of the wall and terminated at the bottom of the beam or girder supported.

Basement door and window frames should be set with keys for rigidity and to prevent air leakage (Fig. 2).

Block walls should be capped with 4 inches (10 cm.) of solid masonry or concrete reinforced with wire mesh. *Anchor bolts* for sills are usually placed through the top two rows of blocks and the top cap. They should be anchored with a large plate washer at the bottom and the block openings filled solidly with mortar or concrete (Fig. 2).

When an exposed block foundation is used as a finished wall for basement rooms, the *stack bond pattern* may be employed for a pleasing effect. This consists of placing blocks one above the other, resulting in continuous vertical mortar joints. However, when this system is used it is necessary to incorporate some type of joint reinforcing every second course. This usually consists of small diameter steel longitudinal and cross rods arranged in a grid pattern. The common bond does not normally require this reinforcing, but when additional strength is desired, it is good practice to incorporate this bonding system into the wall.

Freshly laid block walls should be protected in temperatures below freezing. Freezing of the mortar before it has set will often result in low adhesion, low strength, and joint failure.

To provide a tight, waterproof joint between the footing and wall, an elastic caulking compound is often used. The wall is waterproofed by applying a coating of cement-mortar over the block with a cove formed at the juncture with the footing (Fig. 2). When the mortar is dry, a coating of asphalt or other waterproofing will normally assure a dry basement.

For added protection when wet soil conditions may be encountered, a waterproof membrane of roofing felt or other material can be mopped on, with shingle-style laps of 4 to 6 inches (10 to 15 cm.), over the cement-mortar coating. Hot tar or hot

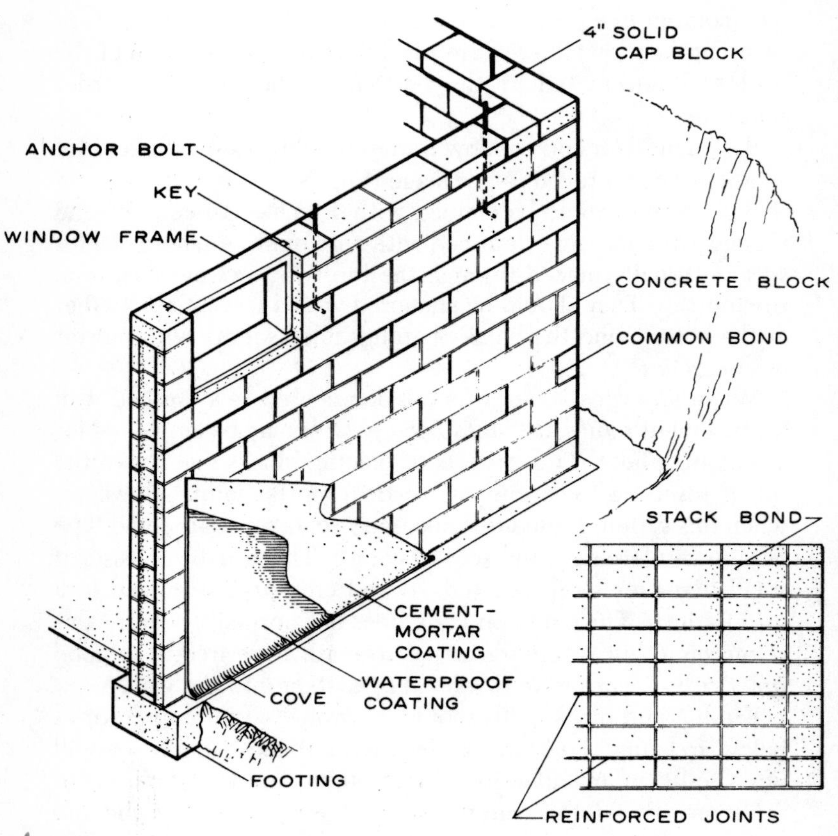

Fig. 2. Concrete block walls.

asphalt is commonly used over the membrane. This covering will prevent leaks if minor cracks develop in the blocks or joints between the blocks. (*See* Chap. 22, Concrete Masonry Units.)

MASONRY CONSTRUCTION FOR CRAWL SPACES

In some areas of the country, the crawl-space house is often used in preference to those constructed over a basement or on a concrete slab. It is possible to construct a satisfactory house of this type by using (1) a good soil cover, (2) a small amount of ventilation, and (3) sufficient insulation to reduce heat loss.

One of the primary advantages of the crawl-space house over the full basement house is the reduced cost. Little or no excavation or grading is required except for the footings and walls. In mild climates the footings are located only slightly below the finish grade. However, in the northern states where frost penetrates deeply, the footing is often located 4 (1.2 meters) or more feet below the finish grade. This requires more masonry work and increases the cost. The footings should always be poured over undisturbed soil and never over fill unless special piers and grade beams are used.

The construction of a masonry wall for a crawl space is much the same as those required for a full basement (Figs. 1 and 2), except that no excavation is required within the walls. Waterproofing and draintile are normally *not* required for this type of construction. The masonry pier replaces the wood or steel posts of the basement house used to support the center beam. Footing size and wall thicknesses will vary somewhat due to location and soil conditions. A common minimum thickness for walls in single-story frame house is 8 inches (20 cm.) for hollow concrete block and 6 inches (15 cm.) for poured concrete. The minimum footing thickness is 6 inches and the width is 12 inches (30 cm.) for concrete block and 10 inches (25 cm.) for the poured foundation wall for crawl-space houses. However, in well-constructed houses, it is common practice to use 8-inch (20-cm.) walls and 16- × 8-inch (40- × 20-cm.) footings.

Poured concrete or concrete block piers are often used to

support floor beams in crawl-space houses. They should extend at least 12 inches (30 cm.) above the groundline. The minimum size for a concrete block pier should be 8 × 16 inches with a 16- × 24- × 8-inch (40- × 60- × 20-cm.) footing. A solid cap block is used as a top course. Poured concrete piers should be at least 10 × 10 inches (25 × 25 cm.) in size with a 20- × 20- × 8-inch (50- × 50- × 20-cm.) footing. In height, unreinforced concrete piers should be no greater than ten times their least dimension. Concrete block piers should be no higher than four times the least dimension. The spacing of piers should not exceed 8 feet (2.4 meters) on center under exterior wall beams and interior girders set at right angles to the floor joists, and 12 feet (3.7 meters) on center under exterior wall beams set parallel to the floor joists. Exterior wall piers should not extend above grade more than four times their least dimension unless supported laterally by masonry or concrete walls. As for wall footing sizes, the size of the pier footings should be based on the load and the capacity of the soil.

SILL PLATE ANCHORS

In wood-frame construction, the *sill plate* should be anchored to the foundation wall with ½-inch (1.3-cm.) bolts hooked and spaced about 8 feet (2.4 meters) apart (Fig. 3, A). In some areas sill plates are fastened with masonry nails, but such nails do not have the uplift resistance of bolts. In high-wind and storm areas, well-anchored plates are very important. A *sill sealer* is often used under the sill plate on poured walls to take care of any irregularities which might have occurred during the curing of the concrete. (*See* Chap. 10, Curing Concrete.) Anchor bolts should be embedded 8 inches (20 cm.) or more in poured concrete walls and 16 inches (40 cm.) or more in block walls with the core filled with concrete. A large plate washer should be used at the head end of the bolt for the block wall. If termite shields are used, they should be installed under the plate and sill sealer.

Although not the best practice, some contractors construct wood-frame houses without the use of a sill plate. Anchorage of

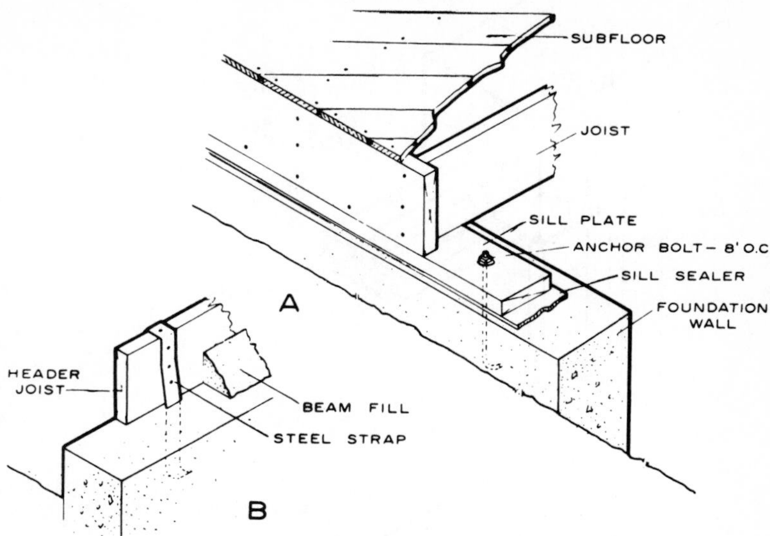

Fig. 3. Anchoring floor system to concrete or masonry walls. (A) With sill plate; (B) without sill plates.

the floor system must then be provided by the use of steel strapping, which is placed during the pour or between the block joints. Strap is bent over the joist or the header joist and fastened by nailing (Fig. 3, B). The use of a concrete or mortar beam fill provides resistance to air and insect entry.

REINFORCING IN POURED WALLS

Poured concrete walls normally do not require steel *reinforcing* except over window or door openings located below the top of the wall. This type of construction requires that a properly designed steel or reinforced-concrete *lintel* be built over the frame (Fig. 4, A). In poured walls, the rods are laid in place while the concrete is being poured so that they are about 1½ inches (3.8 cm.) above the opening. Frames should be prime painted or treated before installation. For concrete block walls, a similar reinforced poured concrete or a precast lintel is commonly used.

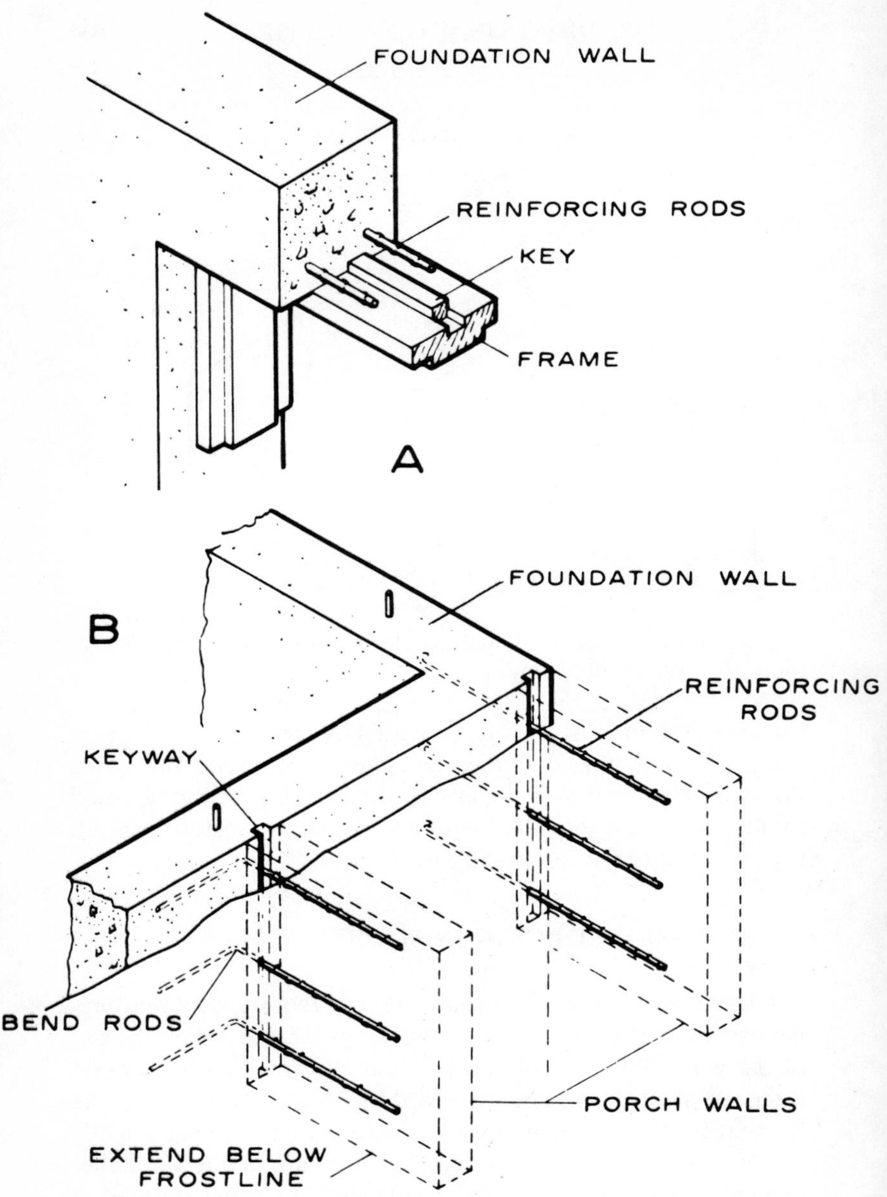

Fig. 4. Steel reinforcing rods in concrete walls. (A) Rods used over window or doorframes; (B) rod ties used for porch or garage walls.

(*See* Chap. 8, Reinforced Concrete; *see also* Chap. 14, Precast Concrete.)

Where concrete work includes a connecting porch or garage wall not poured with the main basement wall, it is necessary to provide reinforcing-rod ties (Fig. 4, B). These rods are placed during pouring of the main wall. Depending on the size and depth, at least three ½-inch (1.3-cm.) deformed rods should be used at the intersection of each wall. Keyways may be used in addition to resist lateral movement. Such connecting walls should extend below normal frostline and be supported by undisturbed ground. Wall extensions in concrete block walls are also of block and are constructed at the same time as the main walls over a footing placed below frostline. (*See* Chap. 41, Footings.)

MASONRY VENEER OVER FRAME WALLS

If *masonry veneer* is used for the outside finish over wood-frame walls, the foundation must include a supporting ledge or offset about 5 inches (12.5 cm.) wide (Fig. 5). This results in a space of about 1 inch (2.5 cm.) between the masonry and the sheathing for ease in laying the brick. A base flashing is used at the brick course below the bottom of the sheathing and framing, and should be lapped with sheathing paper. To provide drainage, weep holes are also located at this course and are formed by eliminating the mortar in a vertical joint. Corrosion-resistant metal ties (spaced about 32 inches, or 80 cm., apart horizontally and 16 inches, or 40 cm., vertically) should be used to bond the brick veneer to the framework. Where other than wood sheathing is used, secure the ties to the studs.

Brick and stone should be laid in a full bed of mortar. Avoid dropping mortar into the space between the veneer and sheathing. Outside joints should be tooled smooth for maximum resistance to water penetration.

Masonry laid during cold weather should be protected from freezing until after the mortar has set. (*See* Chap. 29, Bricklaying.)

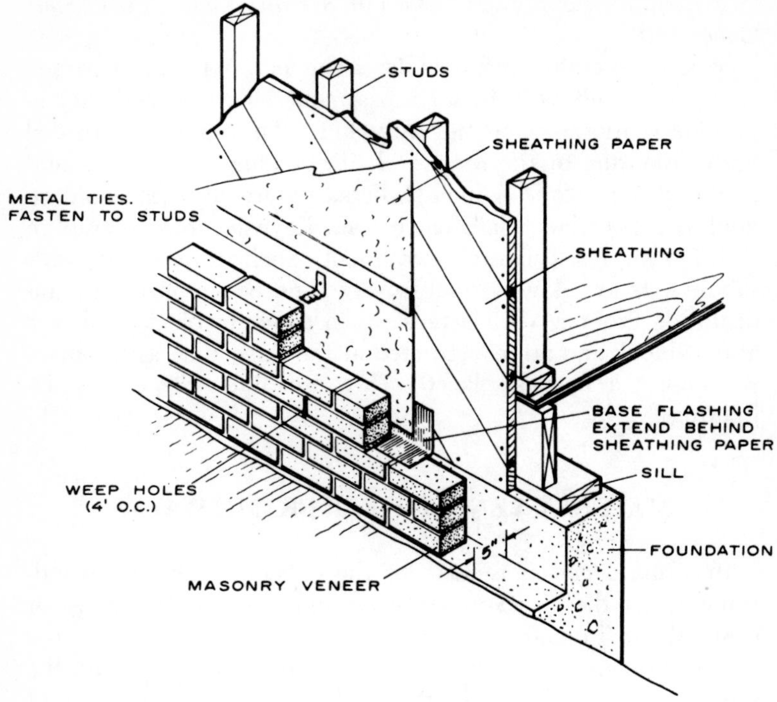

Fig. 5. Wood-frame wall with masonry veneer.

PROTECTION AGAINST TERMITES

Certain areas of the country, particularly the Atlantic Coast, Gulf States, Mississippi and Ohio Valleys, and southern California, are infested with wood-destroying termites. In such areas, wood construction over a masonry foundation should be protection by one or more of the following methods:

1. Poured concrete foundation walls. (*See* Chap. 42, Foundation Walls and Piers.)
2. Masonry unit foundation walls capped with reinforced concrete. (*See* Chap. 22, Concrete Masonry Units, section on Reinforced Block Walls.)

3. Rust-resistant metal shields. (Metal shields are effective only if they extend beyond the masonry walls and are continuous, with no gaps or loose joints. This shield is of primary importance under most conditions.)

4. Wood-preservative treatment. (This method protects only the members treated.)

5. Treatment of soil with soil poison. (This is perhaps one of the most common and effective means used.)

Chapter 43

Concrete Floor Slabs on Ground

The number of new one-story houses with full basements has declined in recent years, particularly in the warmer areas of the United States. This is due in part to lower construction costs of houses without basements and an apparent decrease in need for the basement space.

In the past, the primary function of a basement has been to provide space for a central heating plant and for the storage and handling of bulk fuel and ashes. It can also house a laundry and utilities. With the wide use of liquid and gas fuels the need for fuel and ash storage space has greatly diminished. Because space can be compactly provided on the ground floor level for the heating plant, laundry, and utilities, the need for a basement often disappears.

TYPES OF FLOOR CONSTRUCTION

One common type of *floor construction* for basementless houses is a concrete slab over a suitable foundation. Sloping ground or low areas are usually not ideal for slab-on-ground construction, because structural and drainage problems would add to costs. Split-level houses often have a portion of the foundation designed for a grade slab. In such use, the slope of the lot is taken into account and the objectionable features of a sloping ground become an advantage.

The finish flooring for concrete floor slabs on the ground was initially asphalt tile laid in *mastic* directly on the slab. These concrete floors did not prove satisfactory in a number of instances, and considerable prejudice has built up against this method of construction. The common complaints are that the floors are cold and uncomfortable and that condensation sometimes collects on the floor, near the walls in cold weather, and elsewhere during warm, humid weather. Some of these undesirable features of concrete floors on the ground apply to both warm and cold climates; others only to cold climates.

Improvements in methods of construction based on experience and research have reduced the common faults of the slab floor, though increased their cost.

Floors are cold principally because of loss of heat through the floor and the foundation walls, with most loss occurring around the exterior walls. Suitable insulation around the perimeter of the house will help to reduce the heat loss. *Radiant floor heating* systems are effective in preventing cold floors and floor condensation problems. Peripheral warm-air heating ducts are also effective in this respect. Vapor barriers over a gravel fill under the floor slab prevent soil moisture from rising through the slab.

BASIC REQUIREMENTS

Certain basic requirements should be met in the construction of concrete floor slabs to provide a satisfactory floor. They are as follows:

1. Establish finish floor level high enough above the natural ground level so that finish grade around the house can be sloped away for good drainage. Top of slab should be no less than 8 inches (20 cm.) above the ground and the siding no less than 6 inches (15 cm.)
2. Top soil should be removed and sewer and water lines installed, then covered with 4 to 6 inches (10 to 15 cm.) of gravel or crushed rock well-tamped in place.
3. A vapor barrier consisting of a heavy plastic film, such as 6-mil polyethylene, asphalt laminated duplex sheet, or 45-pound (14.5-kgs.) or heavier roofing, with minimum of ½-perm rating should be used under the concrete slab. Joints should be lapped at least 4 inches (10 cm.) and sealed. The barrier should be strong enough to resist puncturing during placing of the concrete.

4. A permanent, waterproof, nonabsorptive type of rigid insulation should be installed around the perimeter of the wall. Insulation may extend down on the inside of the wall vertically or under the slab edge horizontally.

5. The slab should be reinforced with 6 × 6 inch (15- × 15-cm.) No. 10 wire mesh or other effective reinforcing. The concrete slab should be at least 4-inches (10-cm.) thick. A monolithic slab (Fig. 1) is preferred in termite areas.

6. After leveling and screeding, the surface should be floated with wood or metal floats while concrete is still plastic. If a smooth, dense surface is needed for the installation of wood or resilient tile with adhesives, the surface should be steel troweled.

COMBINED SLAB AND FOUNDATION

The combined slab and foundation, sometimes referred to as the ***thickened-edge slab,*** is useful in warm climates where frost penetration is not a problem and where soil conditions are especially favorable. It consists of a shallow perimeter reinforced footing poured integrally with the slab over a vapor barrier (Fig. 1). The bottom of the footing should be at least 1 foot (30 cm.) below the natural gradeline and supported on solid, unfilled, and well-drained ground. (*See* Chap. 41, Footings, the section on Draintile.)

INDEPENDENT CONCRETE SLAB AND FOUNDATION WALLS

When ground freezes to any appreciable depth during winter, the walls of the house must be supported by foundations or piers which extend below the frostline to solid bearing on unfilled soil. In such construction, the concrete slab and foundation wall are usually separate. Three typical systems are suitable for such conditions (Figs. 2, 3, and 4). (*See* Chap. 42, Foundation Walls and Piers.)

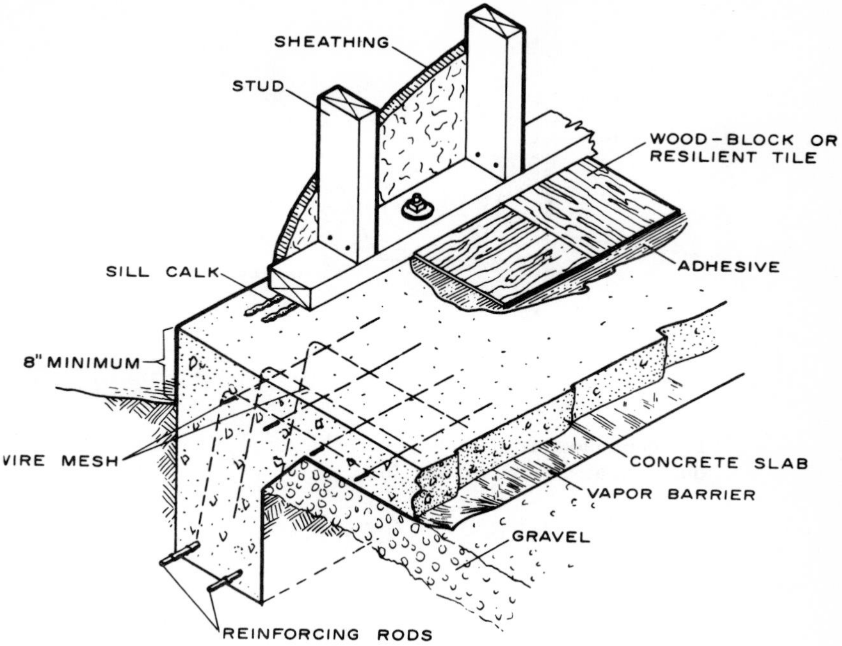

Fig. 1. Combined slab and foundation (thickened edge slab).

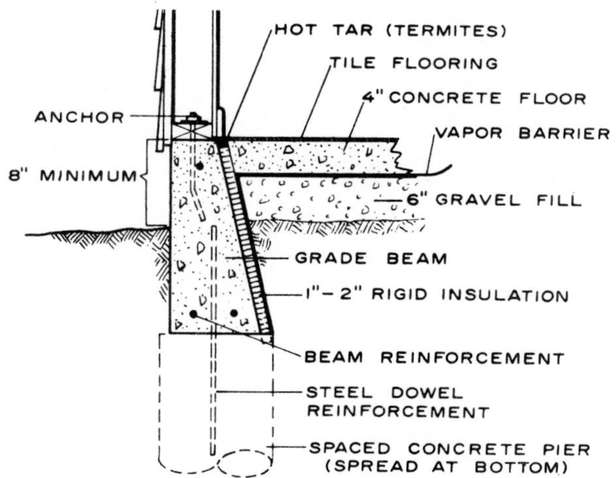

Fig. 2. Reinforced grade beam for concrete slab. Beam spans between concrete piers located below frostline.

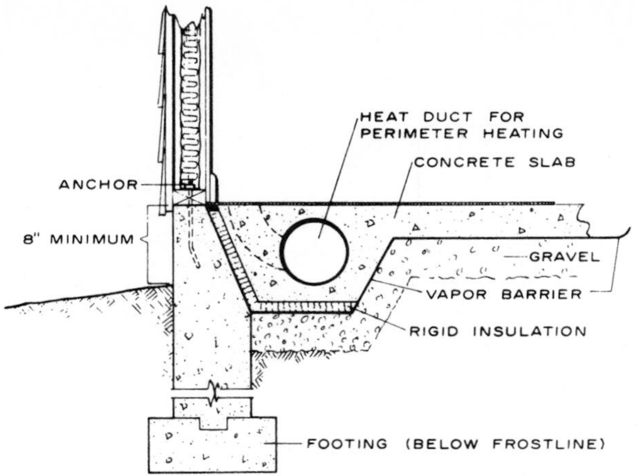

Fig. 3. Full foundation wall for cold climates. Perimeter heat duct insulated to reduce heat loss.

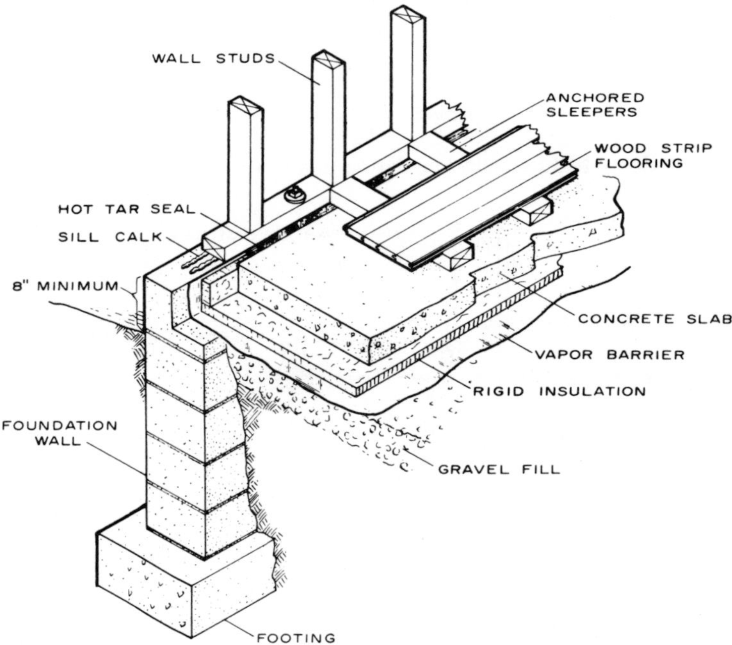

Fig. 4. Independent concrete floor slab and wall. Concrete block is used over poured footing which is below frostline. Rigid insulation may also be located along the inside of the block wall.

VAPOR BARRIER UNDER CONCRETE SLAB

The most desirable properties in a vapor barrier to be used under a concrete slab are: good vapor-transmission rating (less than 0.5 perm); resistance to damage by moisture and rot; and ability to withstand normal usage during pouring operations. Such properties are included in the following types of materials:

1. 55-pound (24.9-kgs.) roll roofing or heavy asphalt laminated duplex barriers.
2. Heavy plastic film, such as 6-mil or heavier polyethylene, or similar plastic film laminated to a duplex treated paper.
3. Three layers of roofing felt mopped with hot asphalt.
4. Heavy asphalt impregnated and vapor-resistant rigid sheet material with sealed joints.

INSULATION REQUIREMENTS FOR CONCRETE FLOOR SLABS ON GROUND

The use of perimeter insulation for slabs is necessary to prevent heat loss and cold floors during the heating season, except in warm climates. The proper locations for this insulation under several conditions are shown in Figs. 2 through 4.

The thickness of the insulation will depend upon requirements of the climate and upon the materials used. Some insulations have more than twice the insulating value of others. The resistance (R) per inch (2.5 cm.) of thickness, as well as the heating design temperature, should govern the amount required. Perhaps two good general rules to follow are:

1. For average winter low temperatures of 0° F. (−17.8° C.) and higher (moderate climates), the total *R* should be about 2.0 and the depth of the insulation or the width under the slab not less than 1 foot (30 cm.)
2. For average winter low temperatures of −20° F. (−28.9° C.) and lower (cold climates), the total *R* should be about 3.0 without floor heating and the depth or width of insulation not less than 2 feet (60 cm.). Table 31 shows these

Low temper-atures	Depth insulation extends below grade	Resistance (R) factor	
		No floor heating	Floor heating
°*F.*	*Ft.*		
−20	2	3.0	4.0
−10	1½	2.5	3.5
0	1	2.0	3.0
+10	1	2.0	3.0
+20	1	2.0	3.0

TABLE 31. RESISTANCE VALUES USED IN DETERMINING MINIMUM AMOUNT OF EDGE INSULATION FOR CONCRETE FLOOR SLABS ON GROUND FOR VARIOUS DESIGN TEMPERATURES.

factors in more detail. The values shown are minimum and any increase in insulation will result in lower heat losses.

INSULATION TYPES

The properties desired in insulation for floor slabs are (1) high resistance to heat transmission; (2) permanent durability when exposed to dampness and frost; and (3) high resistance to crushing due to floor loads, weight of slab, or expansion forces. The slab should also be immune to fungus and insect attack, and should not absorb or retain moisture. Examples of materials considered to have these properties are as follows:

1. *Cellular-glass insulation board* available in slabs 2, 3, 4, and 5 inches (5, 7.5, 10, and 12.5 cm.) thick. *R* factor, or resistivity, 1.8 to 2.2 per inch (2.5 cm.) of thickness. Its crushing strength is approximately 150 pounds per square inch (10.5 kgs. per centimeter). It should be easily cut and worked. The surface may spall (chip or crumble) away if subjected to moisture and freezing. It should be dipped in roofing pitch or asphalt for protection. Insulation should be located above or inside the vapor barrier for protection from moisture (Figs. 2 through 4). This type of insulation has been replaced to a large extent by the newer foamed plastics such as polystyrene and

polyurethane.

2. *Glass fibers with plastic binder* coated or uncoated, and available in thicknesses of ¾, 1, 1½, and 2 inches (1.9, 2.5, 3.8, and 5 cm.). *R* factor, 3.3 to 3.9 per inch (2.5 cm.) of thickness. Crushing strength about 12 pounds per square inch (.8 kgs. per sq. cm.). Water penetration into coated board is slow and inconsequential unless the board is exposed to a constant head of water, in which case this water may disintegrate the binder. Use a coated board or apply coal-tar pitch or asphalt to uncoated board. Coat all edges. Follow manufacturer's instructions for cutting. Placement of the insulation inside the vapor barrier will afford some protection.

3. *Foamed plastic* (polystyrene, polyurethane, and others) insulation in sheet form, usually available in thicknesses of ½, 1, 1½, and 2 inches (1.3, 2.5, 3.8, and 5 cm.). At normal temperatures the *R* factor varies from 3.7 for polystyrenes to over 6.0 for polyurethane for a 1-inch (2.5-cm.) thickness. These materials generally have low water-vapor transmission rates. Some are low in crushing strength and perhaps are best used in a vertical position and not under the slab where crushing could occur.

4. *Insulating concrete.* Expanded mica aggregate, 1 part cement to 6 parts aggregate, thickness used as required. *R* factor, about 1.1 per inch (2.5 cm.) of thickness. Crushing strength, adequate. It may take up moisture when subject to dampness, and consequently its use should be limited to locations where there will be no contact with moisture from any source.

5. *Concrete made with lightweight aggregate,* such as expanded slag, burned clay, or pumice, using 1 part cement to 4 parts aggregate, and thickness used as required. *R* factor about 0.40 per inch (2.5 cm.) of thickness. Crushing strength, high. This lightweight aggregate may also be used for foundation walls in place of stone or gravel aggregate.

Under service conditions, two sources of moisture that might affect insulating materials are (1) vapor from inside the house, and (2) moisture from soil. Vapor barriers and coatings may retard but not entirely prevent the penetration of moisture into the insulation. Dampness may reduce the crushing strength of insulation, which in turn may permit the edge of the slab to settle. Compression of the insulation, moreover, reduces its efficiency. Insulating materials should perform satisfactorily in any position if they do not change dimensions and if they are kept dry.

PROTECTION AGAINST TERMITES

In areas where termites are a problem, certain precautions are necessary for concrete slab floors on the ground. Leave a countersink-type opening 1-inch (2.5-cm.) wide and 1-inch (2.5-cm.) deep around plumbing pipes where they pass through the slab, and fill the opening with hot tar when the pipe is in place. Where insulation is used between the slab and the foundation wall, the insulation should be kept 1 inch (2.5 cm.) below the top of the slab and the space should also be filled with hot tar (Fig. 2).

FINISH FLOORS OVER CONCRETE SLABS ON THE GROUND

A natural concrete surface is sometimes used for the finish floor, but generally is not considered wholly satisfactory. Special dressings are required to prevent dusting. Moreover, such floors tend to feel cold. Asphalt or vinyl-asbestos tile laid in mastic in accordance with the manufacturer's recommendations is comparatively economical and easy to clean, but it also feels cold. Wood tile in various forms or wood parquet flooring may be used, also laid in mastic (Fig. 1) in accordance with the manufacturer's recommendations. Tongued-and-grooved wood strip flooring 25/32 inch (2 cm.) thick may be used but should be used over pressure-treated wood sleepers anchored to the slab (Fig. 4). For existing concrete floors, the use of a vaporproof coating before installation of the treated sleepers is a good practice.

Chapter 44

Outdoor Home Improvements

A large part of the pleasure to be derived from an outdoor improvement comes from the planning and actual construction of its many features. The things you will want to plan and build will, of course, depend on your own tastes and their uses.

CHIMNEY CAPS

A concrete chimney cap protects the top of the chimney where deterioration most frequently starts. Figure 1 shows typical details for precasting a *concrete cap.* A No. 2 (¼-inch or 6.3-mm.) reinforcing bar is bent to form a rectangle and is placed in the center of the concrete section. Lap the bar ends at least 10 inches (25 cm.). Use a concrete mix of approximately 1:2:2¼

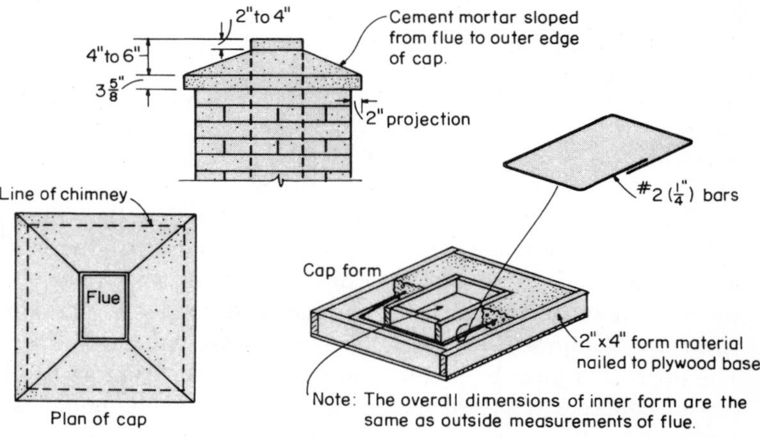

Fig. 1. Chimney cap.

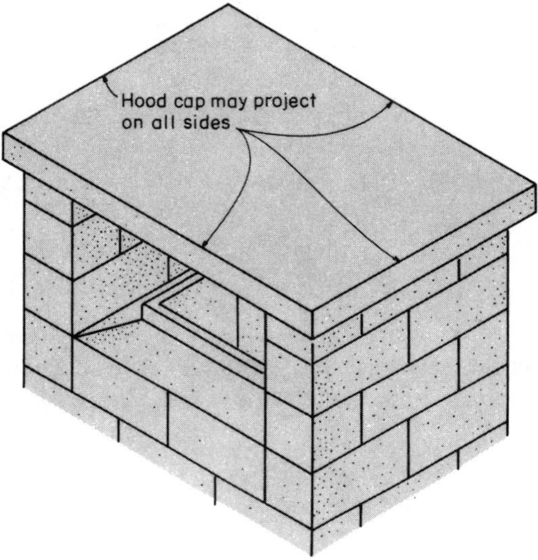

Fig. 2. Chimney hood.

proportions (1 part portland cement, 2 parts sand and 2¼ parts gravel). The coarse aggregate in the mix should not be larger than ¾ inch (1.9 cm.) in diameter. In setting a chimney cap, mortar should be used. Mortar is made of 1 part masonry cement to 3 parts mortar sand, with enough water to give a smooth, workable mix.

CHIMNEY HOODS

Chimney hoods of concrete give a finished touch to the silhouette of the modern house. They prevent downdrafts when the house is located below adjoining buildings, trees, and other obstacles. A hood also protects the chimney and fireplace from rain and snow. Chimney hoods must have at least two sides open. The open area must be larger than the flue area. A simple hood cap of concrete is shown in Fig. 2. Chimney hoods should be reinforced with reinforcing bars or welded wire fabric (wire mesh).

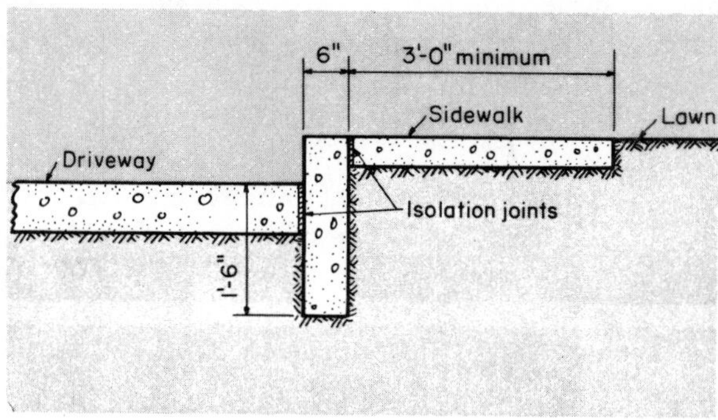

Fig. 3. Curb and sidewalk details.

CONCRETE CURBS

Attractive approaches beautify and enhance a home. A *concrete curb* provides a neat divider between the lawn and driveway. Figure 3 illustrates typical construction details for a curb, sidewalk, and driveway.

Ready-mixed concrete can be used for these improvements, or you can mix the concrete yourself using a 1:2¼:3 mix. The sidewalk and driveway should be prevented from bonding to the curb by inserting premolded joint material as shown in Fig. 3. Control joints should be cut in the curb at 10- to 15-foot (3.1- to 4.5-meter) intervals. These should match the joint locations in the driveway or sidewalk. (*See* Chap. 38, Forms for Drives, Walks, and Patios, the section on Forming Curves.)

SIDEWALKS

Concrete walks provide easy access to the house in all weather and give the children a hard-surfaced play area. They are serviceable in all types of weather. Further, concrete walks, either plain, patterned, or colored, lead the eye to the center of interest—your home.

The construction of a high-quality, durable concrete walk is surprisingly simple. You can place sections of the walk in easy stages at your convenience. If ready-mixed concrete is ordered, you will want to complete the job at one time. This may mean getting extra help so that all the concrete can be properly placed and finished.

Careful preparation of the area is most important if the finished job is to be done right. The main walk should be at least 3-feet (91-cm.) wide, and service walks a minimum of 2-feet (60-cm.) wide.

All sod and debris must be removed to the depth of the walk. A subbase of crushed stone is used where the soil is spongy or the area low and wet. Two-by-four-inch (5- × 10-cm.) form boards are used. These are held in place by stakes as shown in Fig. 4.

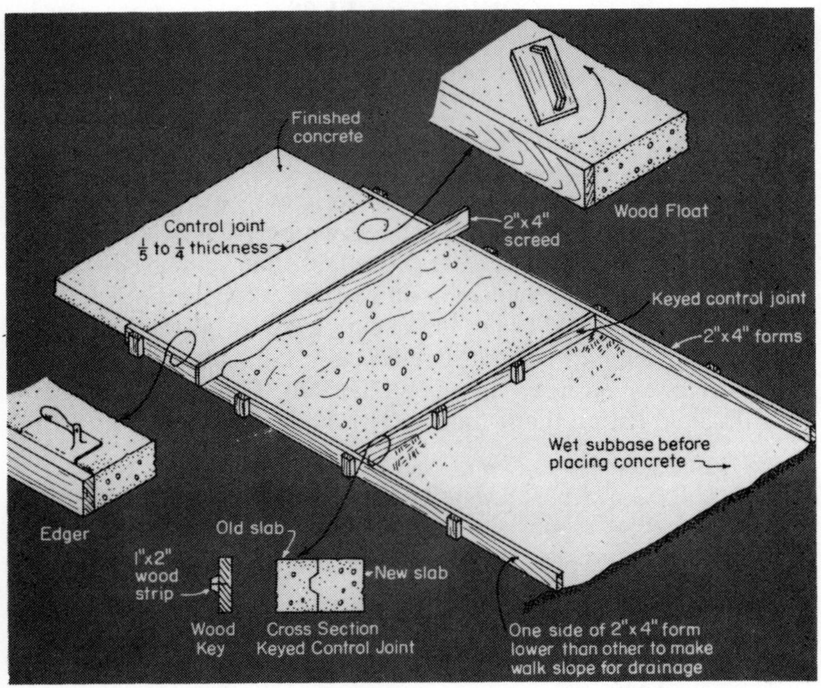

Fig. 4. Detail for forming and construction of concrete walks.

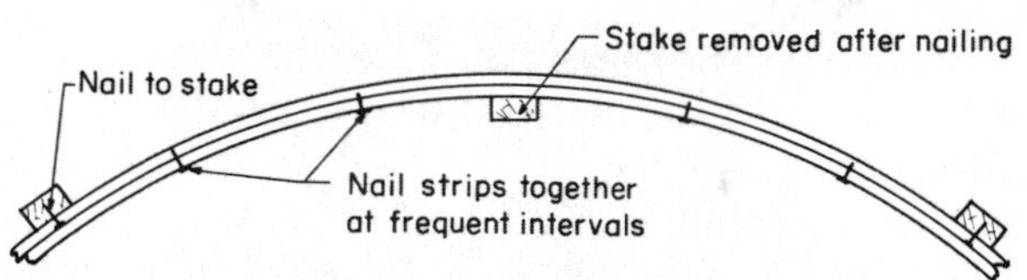

THIN STRIPS OF WOOD FOR FORMING CURVES

Fig. 5. Concrete sidewalks provide a welcome mat for your home.

The cross-slope should be ⅛-inch per foot (1-cm. per meter) to drain away from the house or buildings.

For laying out pleasing curves in walks, a flexible garden hose can be used to mark off the curvature. Curved forms are easily made with two thin strips of plywood or hardboard as shown in Fig. 5. Bend the first strip to the proper radius by setting outside and inside stakes. Nail through the strip to the outside stakes, then place the second strip inside the first and nail the two together. Remove the inside stake and the form will hold its curved shape.

For walks, use quality concrete as described in Chap. 2, Concrete Ingredients, and Chap. 4, Mixing Concrete. Mixing water should be limited to not more than 6 gallons (22.71 liters) of water per bag of cement. For a 4-inch (10-cm.) thick sidewalk, 1 cubic yard (.765 cu. meters) of concrete will be enough for 27 linear feet (8.3 meters) of walk, 3-feet (91-cm.) wide. Use asphalt-impregnated joint material where the slab abuts foundations, curbs, or steps. Control joints, weakened planes to control cracking, are cut with a groover 4 to 5 feet (1.2 to 1.5 meters) apart to a depth of one-fifth to one-fourth the slab thickness.

A wood bulkhead is placed where concrete work must be stopped before the walk is completed. The bulkhead is made with a 2- × 4-inch (5- × 10-cm.) piece cut to the inside dimension of the walk forms. A beveled 1- × 2-inch (2.5- × 5-cm.) strip nailed the length of the 2 × 4 (5 × 10 cm.) will form a keyed control joint so that future sidewalk slabs will always remain level with the previously cast slabs.

Place the concrete in forms after wetting the subbase. Screed the surface even with the top of the forms. Finish off with a wood or light metal float to give a gritty, nonslip surface. Use an edger on all open edges to give long-wearing edges. Pattern the walk, if desired, before the concrete hardens.

Cover the walk with a sheet of plastic, sand, burlap, or other materials and damp-cure it. (*See* Chap. 35, Design and Layout, the section on Sidewalks.)

DRIVEWAYS

All-weather driveways are a necessity today. Attractive approaches show off the home to best advantage and provide year-round access under all conditions. The availability of ready-mixed concrete makes the installation of a drive easier than ever before. Order ready-mixed concrete containing not more than 6 gallons (22.71 liters) of water per bag of cement, with 6 bags of cement per cubic yard (.765 cu. meters) and 6 percent entrained air.

Driveways for single cars should be 8 to 10 feet (2.4 to 3 meters) wide to allow passengers to step from the car onto the driveway (Fig. 6). Where only passenger car traffic is expected, a concrete driveway 4 inches (10 cm.) thick is all that is needed. When heavier vehicles such as trucks use the drive it should be 6 inches (15 cm.) thick.

Fig. 6. A concrete driveway affords all-weather access to your home and adds to its beauty.

Concrete is placed on firm earth or gravel subbase using 2- × 4- or 2- × 6-inch (5- × 10- or 5- × 15-cm.) forms as shown in Fig. 7. The cross-slope or pitch should be a minimum of ⅛-inch for each foot (1-cm. per meter) of width. A long 2 × 4 (5 × 10 cm.) strike-off board riding on side forms is used to level the concrete. Control joints cut to a depth of one-fifth to one-fourth the thickness of the slab every 10 to 15 feet (3 to 4.6 meters) will control cracking of the concrete. Moist-cure the concrete at least five days.

Attractive patterns can be built right into the driveway surface. Light brooming makes a skid-resistant surface. Many of the ideas described later in this chapter on concrete patterns can be successfully applied to beautify driveways and approaches.

CONCRETE STEPS

Concrete steps make a home approach safer and more attractive. Concrete will not rot, so steps will not sag or become a haz-

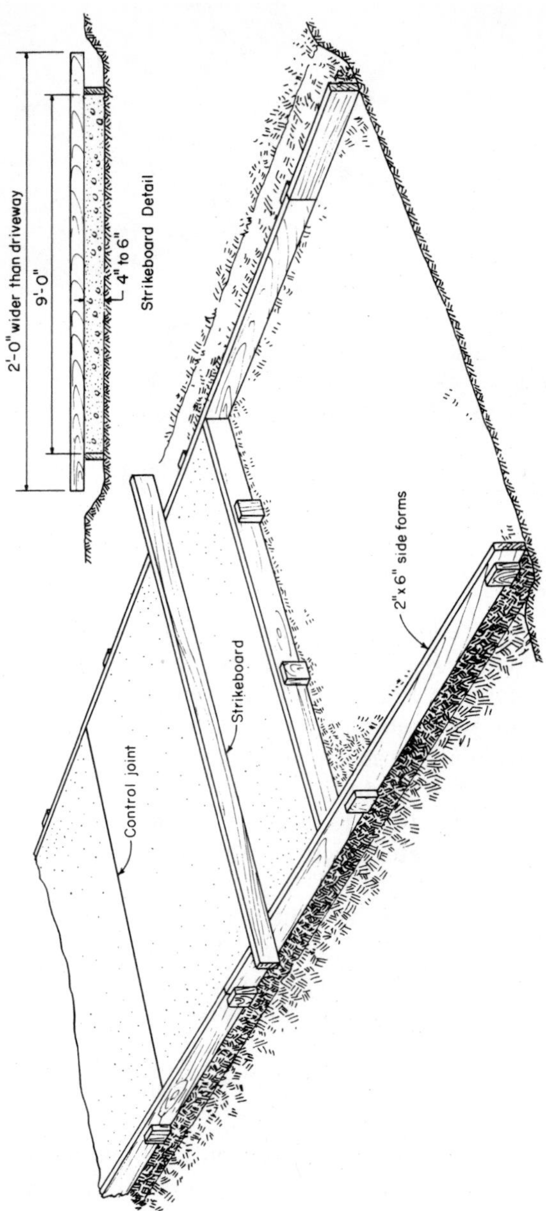

Fig. 7. Forming and construction procedures for a concrete driveway.

ard. Concrete steps are easy to keep clean by sweeping or hosing down. Properly built, they are slip-proof in wet weather and do not require painting or other maintenance.

Steps should be at least as wide as the sidewalk, and all risers should be exactly the same height. A landing is desirable to divide flights more than 5 feet (1.5 meters) high. For safety and convenience, the tread should be at least 11 inches (27.5 cm.). All treads should be of the same width. The rise for each step should be not more than 7½ inches (18.8 cm.). Allow a ⅛-inch (3-mm.) pitch on each tread for drainage.

A stepped ramp shown in Fig. 8 is often used on a long slope. Ramps should have a tread length to provide two easy paces between the risers.

A simple form for steps is shown in Fig. 9. Steps with long treads will require 2-inch (5-cm.) thick riser forms to keep from bending or bulging. (*See* Fig. 10.)

An economical way to keep steps from sinking is to dig two 6- or 8-inch (15- or 20-cm.) diameter postholes beneath the bottom tread. The holes extend below the frostline and are filled with concrete. The top step or platform is tied to the existing wall with two or more metal anchors. Forms are placed as shown, braced, then oiled for easy removal. Well-tamped soil or granular fill may be used inside the forms to reduce the amount of concrete needed for the steps.

Quality concrete should be used. Place the mix in postholes and in the forms starting at the bottom. Spade the concrete thoroughly around the form edges. Tap the forms lightly to release air bubbles. Screed off the concrete at tread level. Finish the treads with a float and then broom to make a nonskid step surface. Use an edging tool to round the front edge of the treads. Moist cure at least five days. Remove the forms and wire brush the steps to clean them.

High-quality precast concrete steps are available from many manufacturers. These steel-reinforced units may be obtained in several types. They are quickly installed and usually have built-in lugs to hold railings and grill work. (*See* Chaps. 35, 39, and 40, the sections on Steps.)

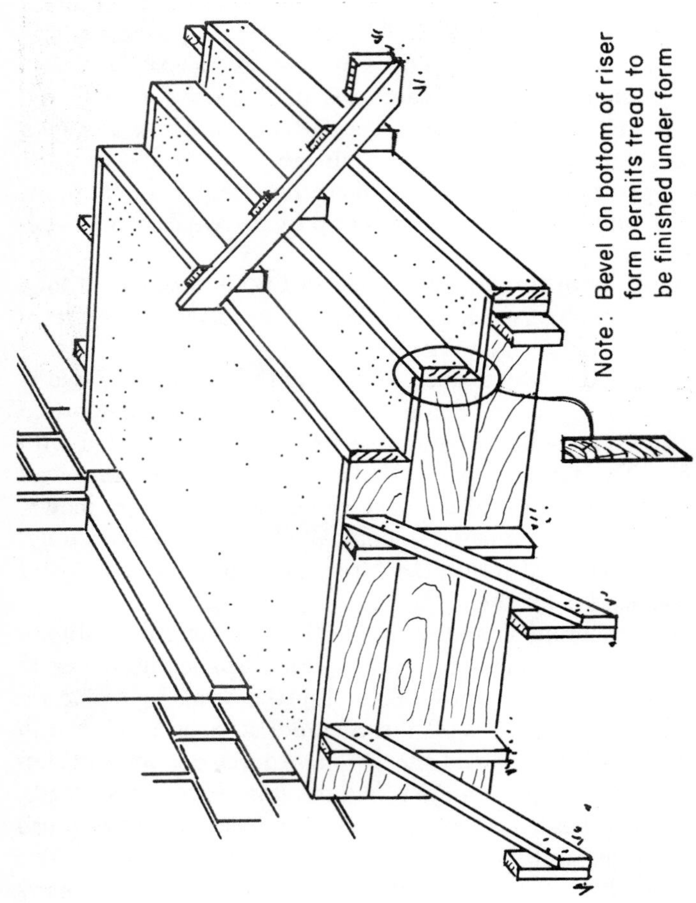

Fig. 8. Forming for concrete steps.

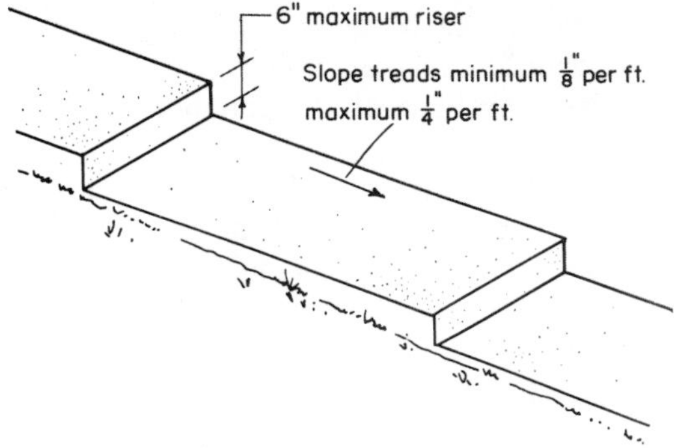

Fig. 9. Stepped ramp for long slopes.

Fig. 10. Concrete steps and patio make a lovely setting for this attractive home.

GREENHOUSES

A most enjoyable way to start plants, flowers, and vegetables is in a home greenhouse. Many people have found owning and keeping a greenhouse a relaxing hobby and a source of added income. Complete prefabricated greenhouse roofs are now available.

Regardless of what you choose for the roof, durable concrete or concrete masonry should be used for the foundation and sidewalls. Concrete will not rot or decay under the severe conditions of high moisture.

Orientate your greenhouse with the long sides almost due east and west. Select a location for maximum winter sunlight. Where small greenhouses are built, some people attach them to the garage or house, close to water, heat, and electricity.

As Fig. 11 shows, foundation walls should be below the frostline and extend at least 2½ feet (75 cm.) above grade level. A concrete floor or concrete center aisle will help keep the greenhouse serviceable at all times. Tops of benches are usually level with the top of the foundation wall. In building a wall or slab, follow suggested practices described in Chap. 11, Finishing Concrete Slabs; Chap. 12, Finishing Concrete Surfaces; Chap. 14, Precast Concrete; and Chap. 42, Foundation Walls and Piers.)

CONCRETE ROOF TILE

Your home quickly takes on new exterior beauty with a roof of concrete tile. Tiles are now manufactured in many textures and colors and will harmonize, contrast, or blend with any architectural style. A high-fashion, durable *concrete tile roof* will increase the value of your home. Local concrete tile manufacturers can provide application advice and information.

CONCRETE SPLASH BLOCK

An easy way to protect your lawn from erosion is by use of *precast concrete splash block* (Fig. 12). By carrying water col-

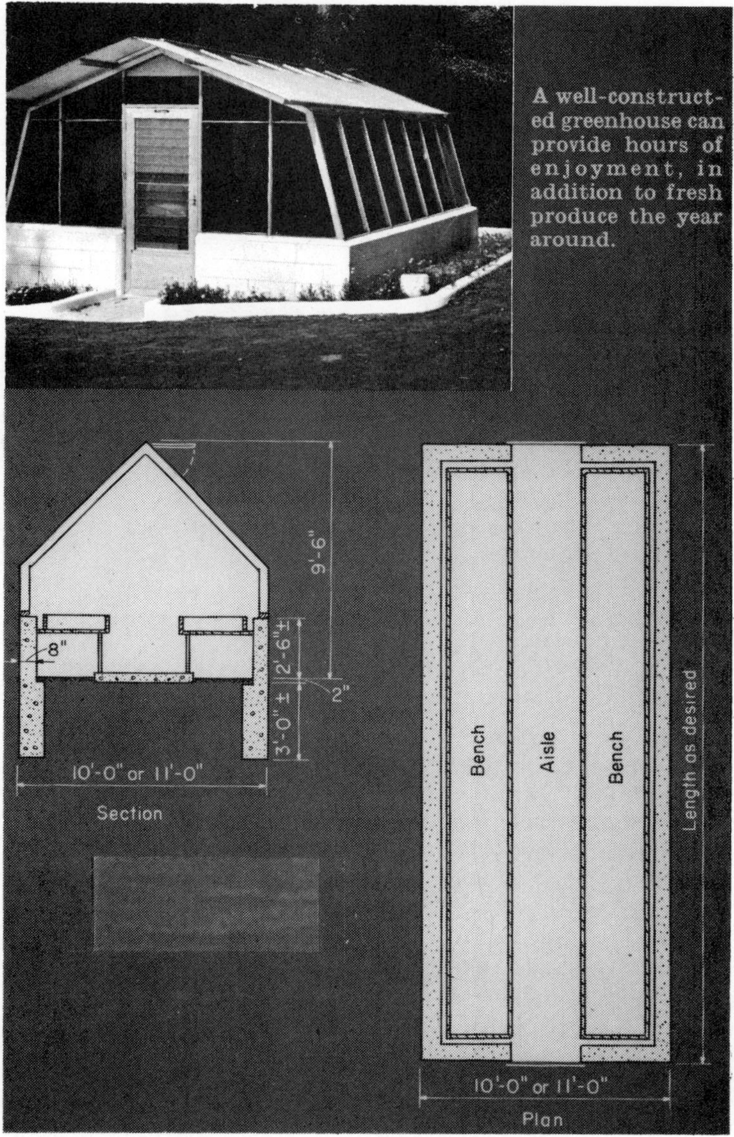

Fig. 11. Typical greenhouse construction details.

Fig. 12. Concrete splash block at downspout.

lected from downspouts away from the foundation and spreading it over a wide area, splash block help assure a dry basement.

Precast products plants and lawn or garden shops around the country usually carry splash block. These handy precast items are ready to use, and they need only to be set under the downspout to start serving their purpose.

TORNADO AND FALLOUT SHELTERS

Tornadoes occur in every part of the country. Wind velocities as high as 500 miles (800 kilometers) per hour have been reported. Tornadoes strike with a sudden ferocity leaving a path of destruction. A *concrete storm shelter* will furnish a place of safety when one of these devastating freaks of nature strikes. The flat roof area may serve as a useful, attractive patio for barbecues and picnics. (*See* Figs. 13, 14, and 15.)

By careful planning and a few more materials, you can also

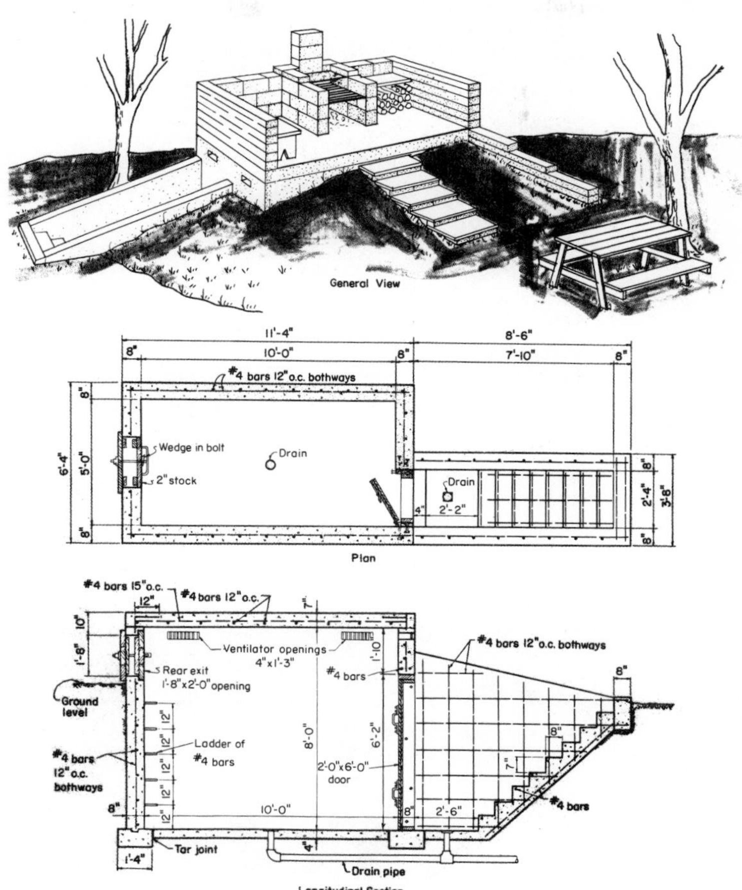

Fig. 13. Detailed drawing and cross-sections of a storm shelter and patio combination.

Fig. 14. Detail of fallout shelter.

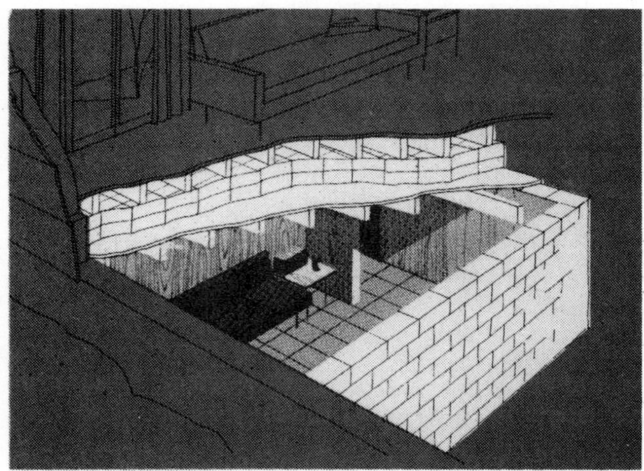

Fig. 15. Detail of fallout shelter.

secure a shelter that will give protection against nuclear fallout and radiation. For family shelters, allow at least 10 square feet (9 sq. meters) per person. This is for an extended period of occupancy. A 5- × 10-foot (1.5- × 3-meter) shelter is the smallest size to build for a family of five.

The main difference between fallout and storm shelters is that an exterior fallout shelter has 2 or 3 feet (60 or 90 cm.) of earth covering the roof and the entrance has at least one right angle turn or a baffle wall to protect from radiation.

In some areas precast concrete shelters may be purchased from local products or ready-mixed concrete plants.

CONCRETE CURBS AND COMBINED CURBS AND GUTTERS

Curbs or combined curbs and gutters should consist of air-entrained portland cement concrete constructed on a prepared subgrade.

The cement factor should not be less than 520 pounds per cubic yard (308 kgms. per cubic meter) and the water-cement ratio should not exceed 0.53. In areas of frequent freeze-thaw and deicer use, however, the cement factor should not be less than 560 pounds per cubic yard (332 kgs. per cu. meter) and the water-cement ratio should not exceed 0.45.

The concrete should have a uniform consistency and slump. The slump should be 1 to 3 inches (2.5 to 7.5 cm.) for hand-vibrated concrete, 2 to 4 inches (5 to 10 cm.) for hand-tamped or spaded concrete, and ½ to 2 inches (1.3 to 5 cm.) for concrete placed by a slipform/extrusion machine. (*See* Chap. 2, Concrete Ingredients.)

SUBGRADE PREPARATION

The subgrade should be excavated or filled with suitable material to the required grades and lines. All soft, yielding, and otherwise unsuitable material should be removed and replaced with suitable material. Filled sections should be compacted and extend a minimum of 1 foot (30 cm.) outside the form lines. The subgrade should be reasonably dense, firm, trimmed to a uniform smooth surface, and in a moist condition when the concrete is placed. (*See* Chap. 36, Preparation of Subgrade.)

CONCRETE PLACEMENT

The concrete should be placed either by an approved slipform/extrusion machine, by the formed method, or by a combination of these methods.

Machine Placement

The slipform/extrusion machine approved should be so designed as to place, spread, consolidate, screed, and finish the concrete in one complete pass in such a manner that a minimum of hand finishing will be necessary to provide a dense and homogeneous concrete section. The machine should shape, vibrate, and/or extrude the concrete for the full width and depth of the concrete section being placed. It should be operated with as nearly a continuous forward movement as possible. All operations of mixing, delivery, and spreading concrete should be so coordinated as to provide uniform progress, with stopping and starting of the machine held to a minimum.

Formed Method

The forms should be of wood, metal, or other suitable material that is straight and free from warp, having sufficient strength to resist the pressure of the concrete without displacement and sufficient tightness to prevent the leakage of mortar. Flexible or rigid forms of proper curvature may be used for curves having a radius of 100 feet (30.5 meters) or less. Division plates should be metal.

The front and back forms should extend for the full depth of the concrete. All of the forms should be braced and staked so that they remain horizontally and vertically aligned until their removal. They should be cleaned and coated with an approved form-release agent before concrete is placed against them.

The concrete should be deposited into the forms without segregation and then tamped and spaded or mechanically vibrated for thorough consolidation. Low roll or mountable curbs may be formed without the use of a face form by using a straightedge and templet to form the curb face. When used, face forms should be removed as soon as possible to permit finishing. Front and back forms should be removed without damage to the concrete after it has set. (*See* Chap. 9, Placing and Consolidating Concrete.)

FINISHING

The plastic concrete should be finished smooth, if necessary, by means of a wood float and then it should be given a final surface texture using a light broom or burlap drag. Concrete that is adjacent to forms and formed joints should be edged with a suitable edging tool to the dimensions. (*See* Chap. 12, Finishing Concrete Surfaces.)

JOINTING

Contraction Joints

Transverse weakened-plane contraction joints should be constructed at right angles to the curb line at intervals not exceeding 15 feet (4.6 meters). Joint depth should average at least one-fourth of the cross section of the concrete.

Contraction joints may be sawed, hand-formed, or made by ⅛-inch (3.2-mm.) thick division plates in the formwork. Sawing should be done early after the concrete has set to prevent the formation of uncontrolled cracking. The joints may be hand-formed by either (1) using a narrow or triangular jointing tool or a thin metal blade to impress a plane of weakness into the plastic concrete, or (2) inserting ⅛-inch (3.2-mm.) thick steel strips into the plastic concrete temporarily. These steel strips should be removed before final finishing of the concrete. Where division plates are used to make contraction joints, the plates should be removed after the concrete has set and while the forms are still in place.

Expansion Joints

Expansion joints should be constructed at right angles to the curb line at immovable structures and at points of curvature for short-radius curves.

Expansion joints in a slipformed curb or curb-and-gutter should be constructed with an appropriate hand tool by raking or sawing through partially set concrete for the full depth and width of the section. The cut should be a snug fit for the joint filler. After the filler is placed, open areas adjacent to the filler should be filled with concrete, then troweled and edged.

Alternately, an expansion joint may be installed by removing a short section of freshly extruded curb-and-gutter immediately, installing temporary holding forms, placing the expansion joint filler, and replacing and reconsolidating the concrete that was removed. Contaminated concrete should be discarded.

Other Jointing

Construction joints may be either butt- or expansion-type joints. Curbs or combined curbs and gutters constructed adjacent to existing concrete should have the same type of joints as in the existing concrete, with similar spacing. However, contraction joint spacing should not exceed 15 feet (4.6 meters).

PROTECTION

The homeowner or contractor should always have materials available to protect the surface of the plastic concrete against rain. These materials should consist of *waterproof paper* or *plastic sheeting.* For slipform construction, materials such as wood planks or forms to protect the edges should also be required.

When concrete is being placed in cold weather and the temperature may be expected to drop below 35° F. (1.7° C.), suitable protection should be provided to keep the concrete from freezing until it is at least 10 days old. Concrete injured by frost action should be removed and replaced at the contractor's expense, if the work is done by him.

CURING

Concrete should be cured for at least three days after placement to protect it against loss of moisture, rapid temperature change, and mechanical injury. Moist burlap, waterproof paper, white polyethylene sheeting, white liquid membrane compound, or a combination thereof may be used as the *curing material. Membrane curing* should not be permitted in frost-affected areas when the concrete will be exposed to deicing chemicals within 30 days after completion of the curing period. (*See* Chap. 10, Curing Concrete.)

BACKFILLING

After the concrete has set sufficiently, the spaces in front and back of curbs should be refilled with suitable material to the required elevations. The fill material should be thoroughly tamped in layers.

CONCRETE PATTERNS AND FINISHES

Exposed aggregate. Patios, walks, flagstones, and other outdoor improvements may be made more decorative, or rugged in appearance by exposing the surface aggregate of the concrete. Selection of the proper aggregate is the key to getting the color desired. Use ½- to ¾-inch (1.3- to 1.9-cm.) aggregate such as marble chips, granite screenings, slag, garnet sand, or colored rock materials. (*See* Chap. 15, Exposed Aggregate Concrete; *see also* Chap. 37, Decorative and Special Finishes.) (*See* Table 32.)

To obtain exposed-aggregate concrete, mix and place ordi-

Color desired	Materials to use
White	White portland cement, white sand
Brown	Burnt umber, or brown oxide of iron (Yellow oxide of iron will modify color)
Buff	Yellow ocher, yellow oxide of iron
Grey	Normal portland cement
Green	Chromium oxide (yellow oxide of iron will shade)
Pink	Red oxide of iron (small amount)
Rose	Red oxide of iron
Cream	Yellow oxide of iron

TABLE 32. COLOR GUIDE.

nary concrete in the usual manner. As soon as the slab has been screeded (struck off) and floated (Fig. 16), scatter the colored aggregate evenly over the surface of the concrete (Fig. 16). Push the colored aggregate just below the surface of the concrete by patting with a wood float (Fig. 16). After the concrete firms up, use a magnesium float to be sure that all the aggregate is embedded below the surface. After the concrete starts to harden, take a stiff brush and carefully work the cement-sand mortar away from the top portion of the colored aggregate. A fine water spray used in a limited amount will help (Fig. 16).

Finishes from forms. Unique finishes may be imparted to concrete work from the inner surfaces of forms. (*See* Fig. 17.) A glassy smoothness is obtained by using polyethylene or plastic liners.

Rough texture or patterned textures. These are obtained by use of paneling, rough lumber, or insert strips placed on the forms.

Patterns of Flat Work

Geometric designs make decorative patterns in concrete surfaces. Random patterns may be made in concrete by the use of a bent piece of ¾-inch (1.9-cm.) copper pipe about 18-inches (45-

Fig. 16. The slab is struck off and floated, then the aggregate is scattered evenly over the surface of the concrete. After a suitable period a stiff brush and water are used to work the excess mortar away from the top of the aggregate.

Fig. 17. Finishes can be imparted by the forms.

Fig. 18. Random patterns can be made in concrete with a bent piece of ¾-inch (1.9-cm.) copper pipe.

Fig. 19. Use a stiff-bristle broom to texture the concrete.

cm.) long (Fig. 18). Circles, squares, ovals, and other designs may be made with household cans of various sizes by impressing the can surface in the semi-hardened concrete.

Wavy broom finishes can be used to give variety to concrete surfaces. These textures also assure a nonslip surface (Fig. 19).

Leaf impressions result in interesting and decorative patterns. Press the leaves stem side down into freshly troweled concrete. Embed the leaf completely, but do not allow the concrete to cover the top of the leaf. Carefully remove the leaf after the concrete sets.

Special instructions regarding forming, number and size of reinforcing bars, and finishing methods are given in various chapters in the book. (*See* Contents and/or Index.) By getting the proper equipment ready, by preparing the forms correctly, and by mixing quality concrete in the correct proportion, you can complete your home improvement projects in less time with less labor and worry. Useful concrete improvements will make living more comfortable and convenient, and your finished concrete projects will be an attractive addition to your home and yard. (*See* Chap. 35, Design and Layout; *see also* Chap. 37, Decorative and Special Finishes.)

Chapter 45

Courts and Recreation and Play Areas

CHILDREN'S PLAY EQUIPMENT

A few pieces of outdoor play equipment will serve the double purpose of keeping the peppiest youngsters happy and giving them the required amount of physical exercise.

Sandboxes

Keep your children happy with a smart-looking sandbox they can call their own. A sandbox 5 × 15 feet (1.5 × 4.5 meters) long will accommodate several children playing at the same time, but you do not need to build your *concrete sandbox* this particular size. Construct it to fit the space and design of the play area.

Figure 1 shows how to construct a sandbox with 8-inch (20-cm.) thick concrete walls. A wall this thick forms a comfortable seat for the children playing. Dig the trench 18-inches (45-cm.) deep and 8-inches (20-cm.) wide, following lines laid out in your yard. Use 1- × 8-inch (2.5- × 20-cm.) lumber and form the sides so that the wall of the box will extend above ground 6 inches (15 cm.). Make both sides of the wall forms level at the top and stake in position. Coat the form boards with oil before placing the concrete.

For a box 15-feet (4.5-meters) long and 5-feet (1.5-meters) wide, with walls 2-feet (60-cm.) high, you need about 1⅔ cubic yards (.05 cu. meters) of concrete. To complete the job quickly, consider using ready-mixed concrete.

Place the mix in the forms. Work along the sides of the wall forms with a trowel to remove air bubbles. Use a straightedge to

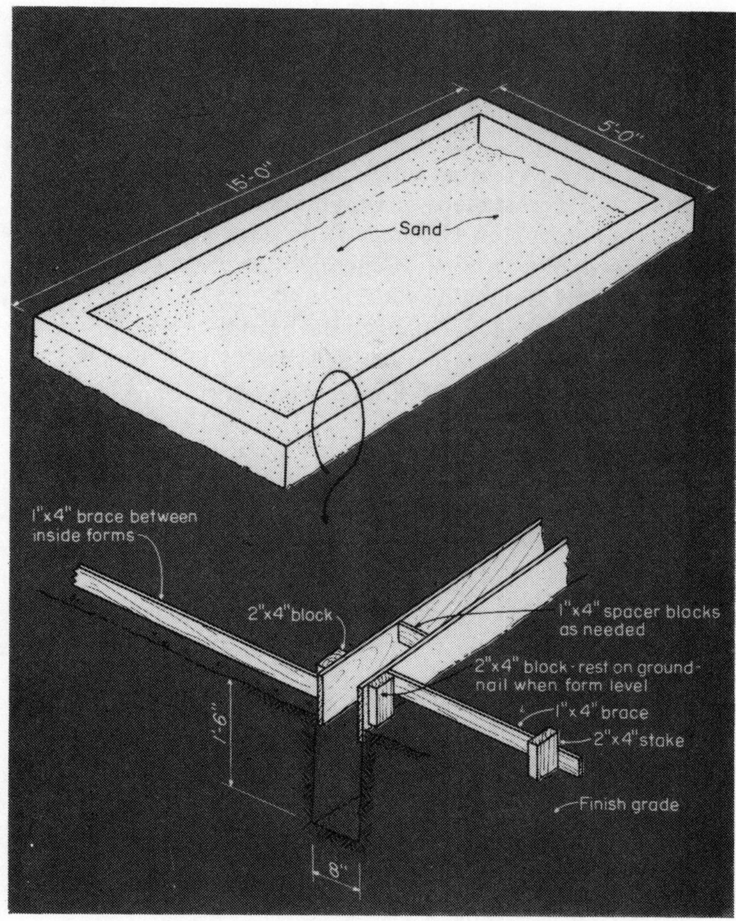

Fig. 1. Details of forming a concrete sand box.

strike off the concrete level with the top of the forms.

Wood-float the concrete. Use an edger and steel trowel to give a smooth surface and edge. Cover the top of the forms and leave them in place for five days. After stripping the forms, fill in around the wall with earth and sod. The box is then ready to fill with sand. (*See* Chap. 6, Concrete Equipment and Tools.)

You may also build an attractive sandbox with concrete block. Blocks are laid on a footing and foundation as described in Chap. 39, Building Exterior Steps of Unreinforced Cast-in-Place Concrete, in the section on Footings. For a concrete block sandbox you will need 48 8- × 8- × 16-inch (20- × 20- × 40-cm.) block plus 8 8- × 8- × 16-inch (20- × 20- × 40-cm.) end corner block. To prevent cutting of block, make the outside dimensions of the box 5 feet 4 inches (1.6 meters) wide by 14 feet 8 inches (4.5 meters) long. (*See* Chap. 22, Concrete Masonry Units.)

Play Area

Children can spend many happy hours outdoors, even in wet weather, with a concrete play area as shown in Fig. 2. (*See* Chap. 9, Placing and Consolidating Concrete.)

Fig. 2. Concrete play area.

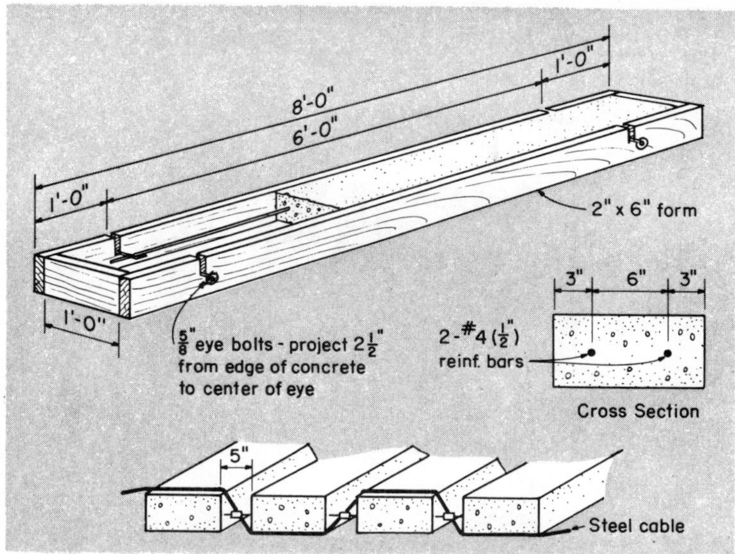

Fig. 3. Movable boat launching ramp using precast concrete planks.

BOAT LAUNCHING RAMPS AND DOCKS

For individual boat owners or for boating clubs, one of the major problems is a satisfactory ***boat launching ramp.*** Concrete is the best construction material for use in such water projects.

To overcome the problem of having to build a long solid ramp to take care of fluctuating water levels, a series of concrete planks linked together by steel cables may be used (Fig. 3). This corrugated concrete roadway is flexible and will fit the existing contours of the lake bank. Concrete planks will withstand the rough wave action of the water and need not be anchored to the lake bottom (Fig. 4). The planks should be used over sand or on a base that provides uniform bearing. A broom finish should be applied to the surface of the planks to provide traction for cars and to back into the water. (*See* Chap. 12, Finishing Concrete Surfaces.) The cables hold the planks in place and serve as a ***back-up*** guide.

Fig. 4. Precast concrete retaining wall along a boat dock.

HOME SHUFFLEBOARD COURT

A concrete shuffleboard court is installed in almost the same manner as a sidewalk. The exceptions are that no joints are used in the shuffleboard court. Reinforcing bars help reduce the cracking and keep the surface of the court continuous and smooth. (*See* various chapters in the book for procedures used, tools and materials; *also see* Index.)

The overall size of the court is 52 feet (15.8 meters) long and 6 feet (1.8 meters) wide (Fig. 5). Form boards of 2 × 4's (5 × 10 cm.) are placed on firm soil excavated to the proper depth. Place No. 3 (⅜-inch or 9.5-mm.) bars on 12-inch (30-cm.) centers the full length of the court. The bars must lap at least 1 foot (30 cm.) where they meet, and be wire tied together. Use a concrete mix as shown in Table 33 with air entrainment. Steel must be as close to the center of slab depth as possible. Lift the bars when placing the concrete. The concrete is steel-troweled for a dense, smooth surface. Curing is most important. Premature drying will cause surface cracks. Damp-cure or cover the concrete with plastic for six days.

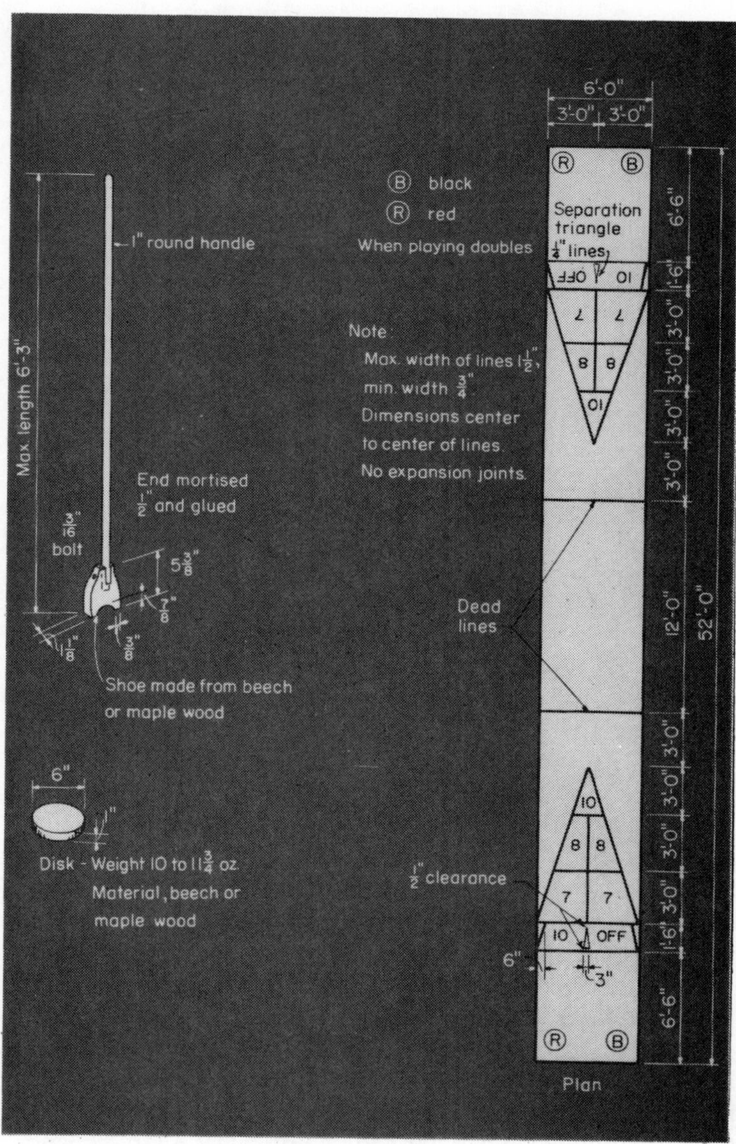

Fig. 5. Details for outdoor shuffleboard court.

A 1:2¼:3 mix=1 part cement to 2¼ parts sand to 3 parts 1-in. max. aggregate.

Concrete Required cu.ft.	Cement* lb.	Max. Amount of Water to Use gal. U.S.	Imperial	Sand lb.	Coarse Aggregate lb.
1	24	1¼	1	52	78
3	71	3¾	3⅛	156	233
5	118	6¼	5¼	260	389
6¾ (¼ cu. yd.)	165	8	6¾	350	525
13½ (½ cu. yd.)	294	16	13½	700	1,050
27 (1 cu. yd.)	588	32	27	1,400	2,100

*U.S. bag of cement weighs 94 lb. Canadian bag of cement weighs 80 lb.

TABLE 33. MATERIALS NEEDED FOR CONCRETE.

SWIMMING POOL

Once you have decided that you want a swimming pool, you must decide who will build it. Although you can do the job yourself, the safest and best way is to have a professional pool builder do it for you.

It takes a great deal of skill to successfully build a pool and the problems which can result from lack of knowledge can cause many heartaches and much loss of money. The professional will secure all the necessary permits, plans, and specifications and will take care of unusual problems.

There are five basic ways to build concrete pools—using cast-in-place concrete, shotcrete, hand-packed concrete, concrete masonry, or precast concrete. All five have advantages, but the home owner who decides to build his own pool will find that building with masonry block permits construction over an extended period of time. A formed pool involves a large quantity of concrete and requires professionals to move it around quickly.

Cast-In-Place Concrete

Cast-in-place concrete pools are built in a manner similar to that in which a concrete basement is constructed. Vertical forms for the walls of the pool, outside and inside, are positioned for the proper wall thickness, with steel reinforcement between forms. (*See* Chap. 14, Precast Concrete; and Chap. 40, Precast Concrete Units.) The forms can be either curved or straight, or a combination of both. Concrete is placed in the space between the forms; then the floor is cast. After removal of the forms, the pool can be painted with white portland cement plaster.

Shotcrete

Shotcrete (sometimes referred to in the pool industry by the trade name Gunite) is pneumatically placed concrete. A shotcrete pool is built by first excavating to the exact size and shape of the pool, placing steel reinforcing bars within the excavation, and spraying (shooting) concrete into place with pneumatic equipment. While the concrete is still workable (plastic), finishes smooth it with wooden floats. After this, the concrete can be painted with portland cement base paint or, as is most often done, coated with white portland cement plaster. (*See* Chap. 8, Reinforced Concrete, the section on Types of Ties.)

Hand-Packed Concrete

A *hand-packed* (also called dry-packed) concrete pool is a cast-in-place type, but is constructed somewhat like a shotcrete pool. The excavation is dug to the exact size and shape of the pool, and then steel reinforcing bars are set in place, with the excavation serving as the outside form. Up to this point, the construction of the hand-packed pool is the same as that of the shotcrete pool. But from here on, the two methods differ.

Pneumatic equipment is not used to place the concrete. Instead, a stiff concrete mixture (low water content) is mixed and placed in the excavation. Then the concrete is shoveled and tamped into place, completely encasing the steel reinforcement. The still plastic surface is finished with wooden floats. The pool can be coated with either portland cement base paint or white portland cement plaster. (*See* Chap. 6, Concrete Equipment and Tools.)

Concrete Masonry

A *concrete masonry* pool features concrete block walls with a solid cast-in-place concrete floor. Placed first, the floor provides a stable base for the masonry walls. The walls are strengthened with steel reinforcing bars running vertically through the core holes of the block. To complete the wall construction, the surface is coated with either portland cement base paint or white portland cement plaster. (*See* Section 2, Concrete Masonry.)

Precast Concrete

Precast concrete pools are made with large wall sections of reinforced concrete that have been hauled to the pool site for placement within the excavation. The sections are anchored to precast concrete buttresses and the joints are sealed. The concrete floor is cast in place, and the pool can then be coated with either portland cement base paint or white portland cement plaster. (*See* Chap. 14, Precast Concrete.)

POOLSCAPE

Now that you are more familiar with the various methods by which concrete pools are built, consider the area surrounding the new pool. Elements that complete the poolscape are the deck, patio, walks, landscaping, and privacy walls. Each of these features is important to the total environment of a home swimming pool. (*See* Figs. 6 through 14.)

The *deck*, which is the paved apron surrounding the pool, must be wide enough to allow for foot traffic and the placement of outdoor furniture. Regardless of the pool shape, a graceful free-form concrete deck can do the job nicely. It can be wide where necessary, narrow in less used areas. A *patio* adjoining the deck provides an area for family pleasure as well as for entertaining. Give it your careful consideration.

Fig. 6. An indoor or outdoor swimming pool.

Concrete offers you a great variety of finishes for the pool deck, patio, and access walk; it can be made smooth, textured, colored, patterned, or a pleasing combination of these finishes. As with the pool itself, these features can be cast in any size and shape to fit your particular site and your style of home. You will appreciate the compatibility of concrete. (*See* various chapters throughout the book; *also see* the Index.)

Figure 7 shows an excellent example of a designer's ability to create a unique pool within a modest budget in this relatively small, free-form concrete pool with its charming, natural pool-scape. The exposed-aggregate concrete deck adds interest because of its texture and shape.

Concrete masonry retaining walls (Fig. 8) form an interesting background for this delightful free-form concrete pool; smooth-face concrete block units at the left contrast with rugged-texture concrete split-block units at the right. The circular raised deck area of exposed-aggregate concrete serves as a planter as well as a base for the pool slide.

A beautiful garden enhances the classic beauty of the concrete pool shown in Fig. 9. Two gargoyle heads, mounted on the rough-textured concrete retaining wall, add the excitement of splashing water. Water is supplied to the gargoyles by the pool's recirculation system.

Fig. 7. Free-form pool.

It is very handy to have shower and dressing rooms for pool use, especially to serve your guests. The double-unit pool structure shown in Fig. 10 accommodates the shower and dressing rooms as well as the pool's water heater and filtration equipment. It is a very practical and handsome structure, made even more interesting by the vertically combed stucco wall surfaces. (*See* Chap. 33, Preparation of Base and Application of Stucco.)

Landscaping should be carefully planned to perform its esthetic and utilitarian functions. In selecting and positioning the plantings, keep in mind that an abundance of falling leaves and other debris can become a nuisance if they litter the pool.

Walls around the pool should afford privacy, serve as barriers to neighborhood toddlers who might otherwise make their way into the pool, and enhance the appearance of the poolscape.

Concrete masonry is the perfect material for your privacy walls. Concrete masonry units (concrete block, split block, slump block, and screen block) are available in a variety of sizes, shapes, textures, patterns, and colors. (*See* Chap. 23, Concrete Masonry Units.) Concrete masonry walls offer the additional advantage of having an attractive finished surface on both sides.

Accessories for Your Pool

To make your pool function properly, several accessories are

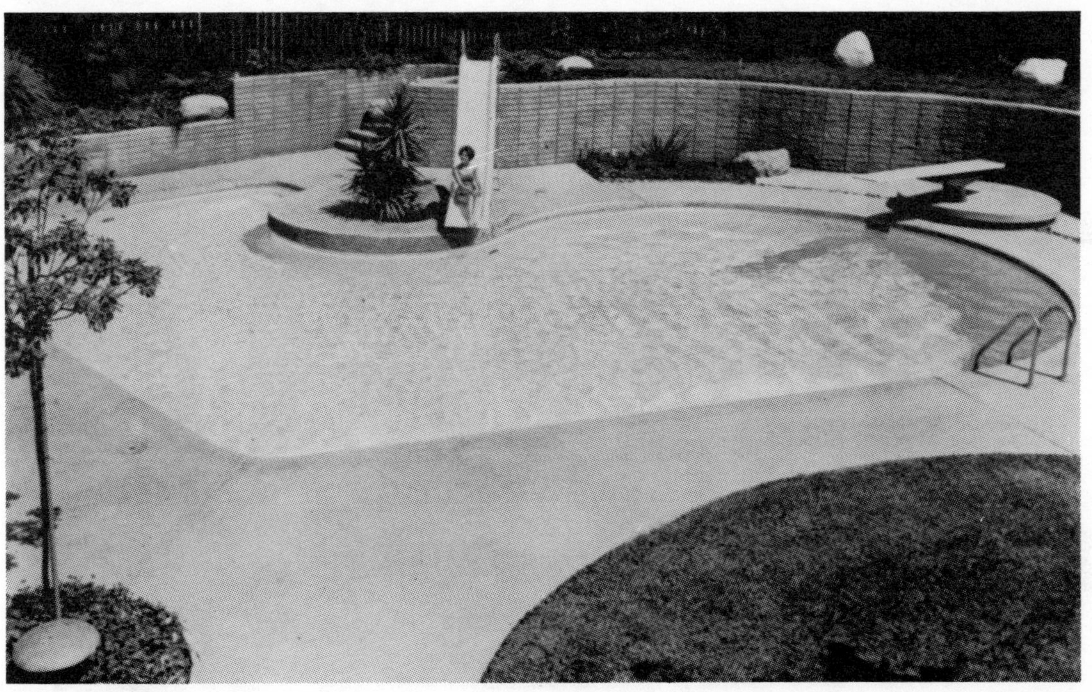

Fig. 8. The concrete block retaining wall is an interesting background for this free-form pool.

Fig. 9.

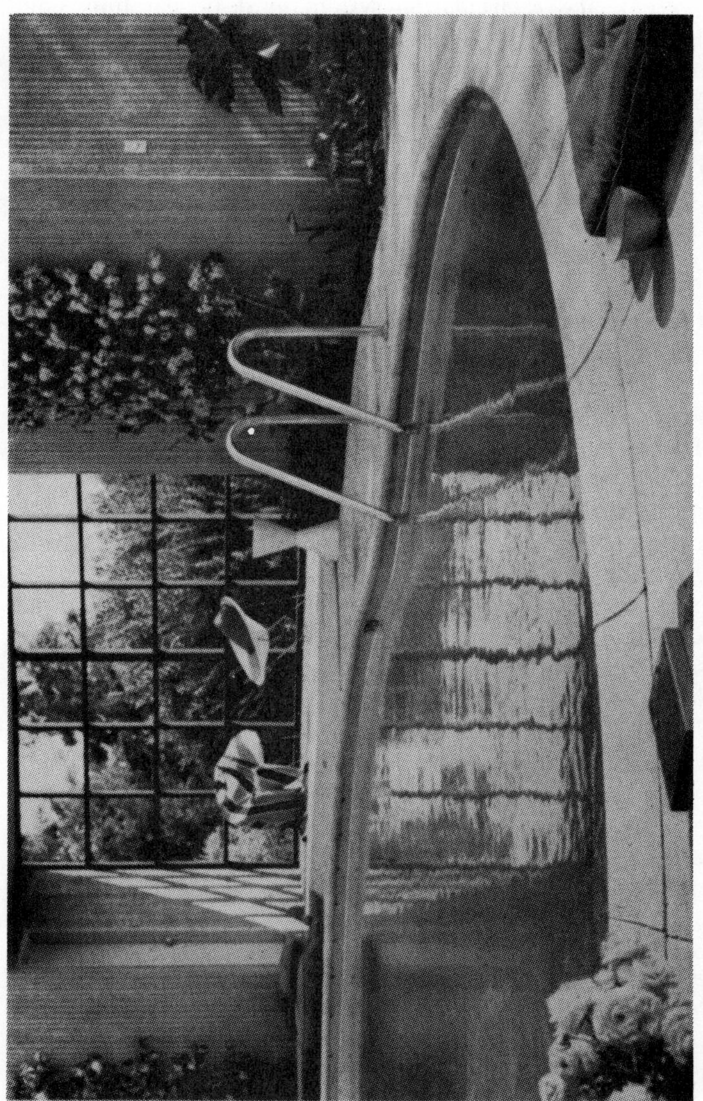

Fig. 10. Double unit pool structure accommodates shower and dressing rooms.

necessary. A good filter and recirculation system is vital. The filter, pump, and recirculation system must be carefully engineered to provide proper filtration for the pool. In addition to being filtered, the water must be treated with purification chemicals for it to remain sparkling clear and perfectly sanitary. The recirculation system can include mechanical equipment which will dispense chemicals automatically, or they can be added to the pool by hand. Either method produces satisfactory results.

The pool must have a vacuum cleaner that operates either in conjunction with the recirculation system or as a self-functioning piece of equipment. The cleaner removes foreign matter that clings to the pool surface. The walls should be brushed down and the floor vacuumed about once each week under normal conditions.

Because of the filtration, vacuuming, and water-purifying chemicals, it is unnecessary to drain and refill the pool during a swimming season. However, the water must be tested regularly to ensure that proper sanitary conditions are maintained.

A pool water heater is an optional item that both increases the length of the swimming season and keeps the pool water at a comfortable temperature during cool periods of the normal swimming season. Even in northern areas, the normal swimming season of three or four months' duration can be almost doubled with the use of a water heater.

Underwater lighting is another optional feature that can add many hours of pool enjoyment. It creates an attractive nighttime scene and provides a safety factor by clearly defining the edges of the pool. Low-voltage systems offer complete safety for swimmers should a short circuit occur. And while you are considering lighting, give thought to patio and garden lighting, too.

Diving boards and pool slides (Fig. 11) add fun to any pool scene. The pool, however, must be at least 30 feet (9.1 meters) long and 7½ feet (2.2 meters) deep in the diving area to permit use of a diving board. A pool of this size will accept a board 10 to 12 feet (3 to 3.6 meters) in length. Larger and deeper pools will handle longer boards. Slides can be used with small pools as long as the depth of water is at least 2½ feet (76 cm.). Slides are available in several sizes and models to fit your pool and deck layout. (*See* Fig. 12.)

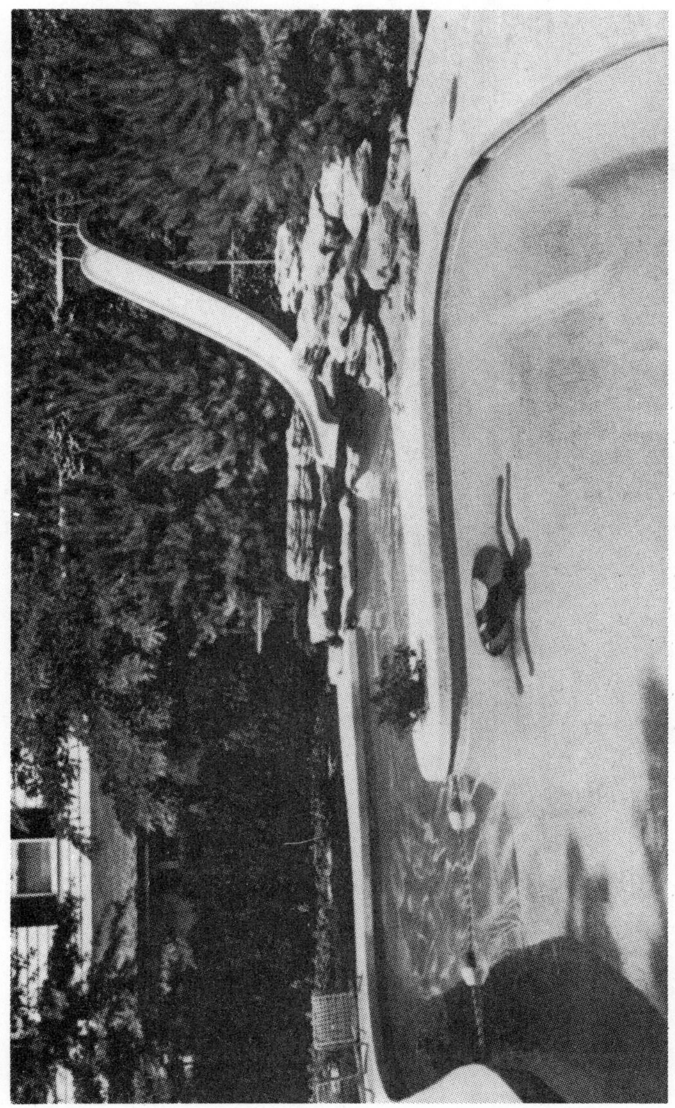

Fig. 11. Fun pool. The slide plunges a swimmer into the deep end of the pool, and the hole in the wall provides an underwater route from the deep end to shallow water.

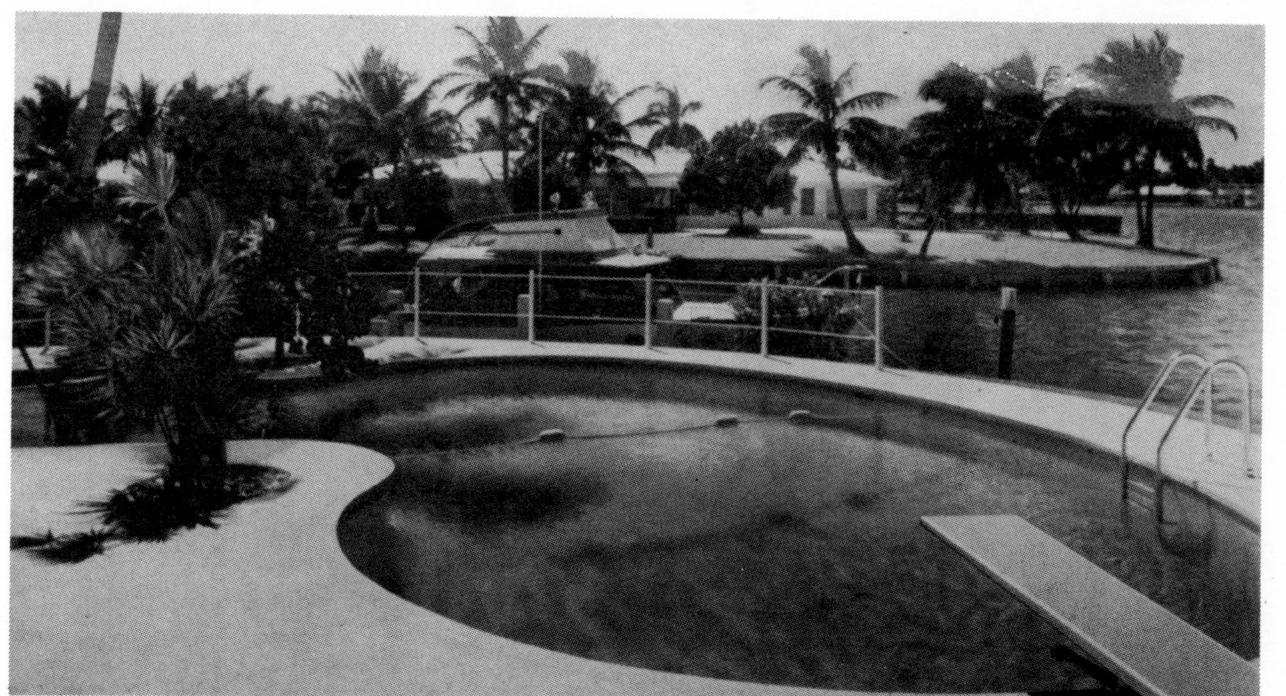

Fig. 12. Pool built at water's edge, with a pool heater.

The pool shown in Fig. 13 is more than just a pool—it is a magnificent sculpture, particularly intriguing because it takes on a different form and shape from each different vantage point. The tail section is a pool slide.

The poolscape shown in Fig. 14 includes a companion wading pool, which complements the projection of the main pool stairway. The design is well integrated by the liberal deck area of exposed-aggregate concrete which provides a safe, nonskid surface.

TENNIS COURTS

The fast, uniform surface of a concrete tennis court has, in the opinion of experts, contributed more than any other one factor toward the development of championship tennis players. The true, even surface assures a consistently accurate bounce of the ball, a feature so essential to superior play.

Reinforced concrete is equally well adapted to both private and public courts, as little or no attention is required to keep the surface in playing condition.

Good materials are necessary and other conditions must be satisfactory, but no matter how good the materials may be, or how adequate other conditions are, expert finish workmanship is essential in obtaining a good court.

Subgrade

It is very important that the *subgrade* be properly tamped, free from deleterious materials or soft spongy areas. (*See* Chap. 36, Preparation of Subgrade.)

Where a court is built on a heavy clay soil such as adobe, or any soil having appreciable expansive characteristics, it is recommended that the subgrade be thoroughly soaked down several days in advance of concreting, and a minimum of 2 inches (5 cm.) of sand or rock dust fill be used. The subgrade should then be maintained in a moist condition until the concrete is placed.

In areas subject to severe ground freezing, granular subbases have been found to be the best protection against frost heaving.

Fig. 13. A sculptural pool. The tail section is a pool slide.

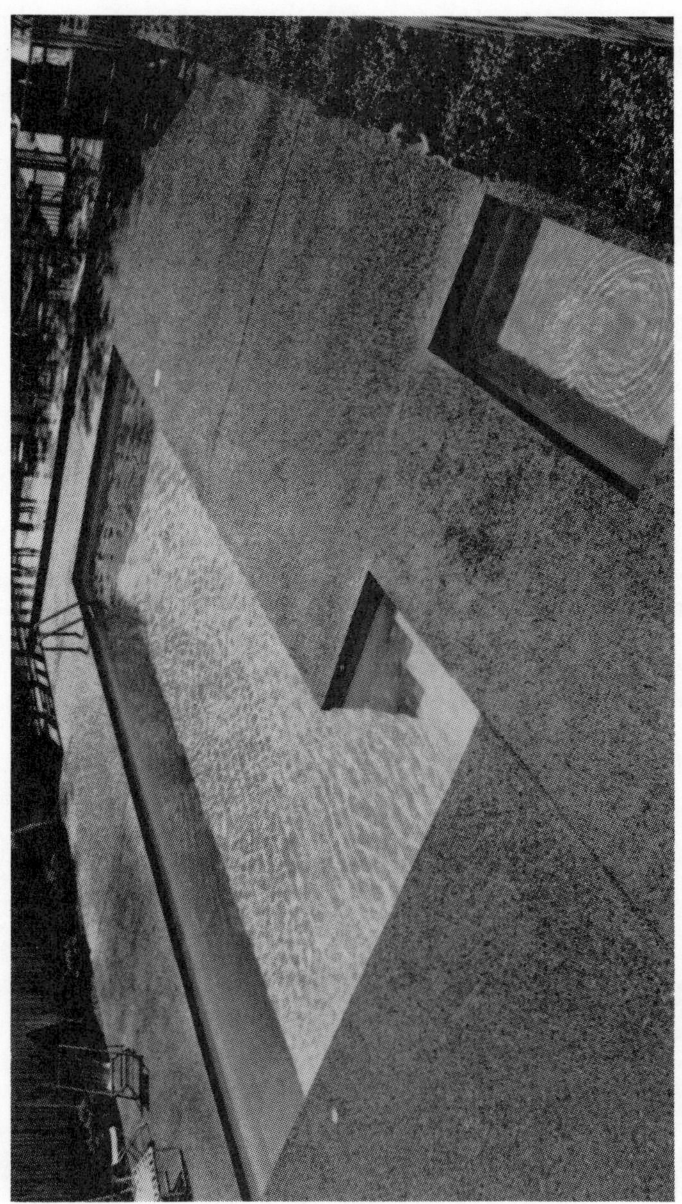

Fig. 14. Poolscape includes a companion wading pool.

The thickness of the subbase will depend upon the severity of the climate and the type of soil encountered.

Design and Construction

A 4-inch (10-cm.) thickness of concrete should be specified. An expansion joint should be placed across the court under the net to separate the two halves of the court. Each half of the court must be placed in one continuous operation to produce a continuous slab without contraction, construction, or expansion joints.

A concrete beam 6-inches (15-cm.) thick and 18-inches (45-cm.) wide should be cast in a trench across the center of the court (Fig. 15). This beam is for support of the two slabs at the expansion joint under the net. The top of the beam should be at the elevation of the bottom of the court slab. The beam should be cast a day or two in advance of the court concrete. Bond between the beam and the court concrete should then be prevented by painting the top of the beam with an asphaltic material. This beam is thickened to 12 inches (30 cm.) at the steel net posts to provide additional stability at these points.

A 2 × 4 (5 × 10 cm.) has been rigidly braced and staked (Fig. 16) in place over the center of the trench in which the concrete beam is to be cast. The top of this header is set accurately to the elevation of the finished slab. After the concrete beam has been

Fig. 15. A concrete beam should be cast across the center of the court.

Fig. 16. A 2 × 4 (5 × 10 cm.) is rigidly placed over the center of the trench. The top of the header is set to the elevation of the finished slab.

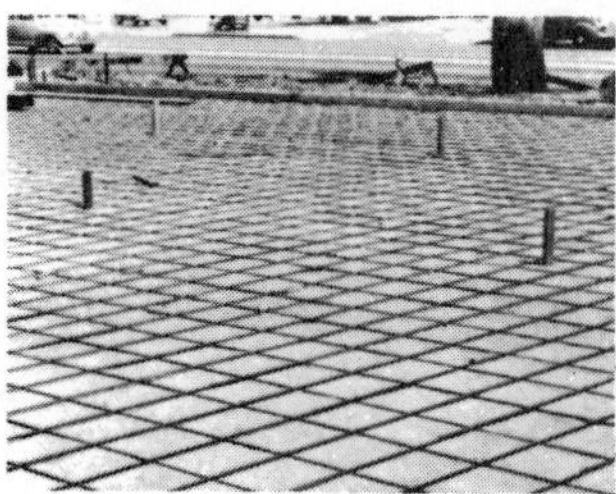

Fig. 17. Continuous bar reinforcement.

Fig. 18. Screed board support stakes driven to accurate grade.

placed, 1 inch (2.5 cm.) of expansion joint material is attached to this header. If the entire court is placed in one operation, the header should be removed as soon as the concrete is placed on both sides of the joint.

The steel net post sleeve is supported in the thickened section of the trench prior to casting the concrete beam.

Either bars or wire mesh may be used as reinforcement. Continuous bar reinforcement is shown in Fig. 17.

Screed board support stakes are driven to accurate grade so that the lower edge of the supported 2 × 4 (5 × 10 cm.) screed board will be at the exact elevation of the surface of the finished court (Fig. 18).

Reinforcement is adjusted to the center of the slab during placement of concrete (Fig. 19).

Proper elevation of the court surface is obtained by pulling the strike-off templet along the previously set screed boards.

After the concrete has been struck off to the proper elevation,

Fig. 19. Reinforcement is adjusted to the center of the slab during concrete placement.

Fig. 20. Using a grid tamp to force coarse aggregates below the surface.

Fig. 21. Long-handled metal float.

Fig. 22. Mechanical rotary finisher.

the larger particles of the coarse aggregate are forced slightly below the surface through the use of a grid tamp (Fig. 20). Caution must be exercised to use the grid tamp only enough to accomplish the purpose, as overuse will bring an undesirable amount of fine sand, cement, and water to the surface.

The surface is then floated with a long handled metal float (Fig. 21) to work out high and low spots.

A mechanical rotary finisher should be used as soon as the concrete has hardened sufficiently (Fig. 22). The purpose of the rotary finisher is to further level the surface and to compact the concrete to the most even surface possible.

One of the most serious errors in concrete finishing is the practice of overworking and overtroweling. Overmanipulation in the floating and rotary finishing draws to the surface excess water, cement, and fine sand particles resulting in a less durable surface. Another undesirable practice which should not be permitted is that of sprinkling on a mixture of fine sand and cement to *dry up* areas still too wet for proper finishing.

The final playing finish is obtained with a steel trowel. By using the flat of the trowel in small circular movements, a *swirl* pattern will be produced, thus providing a uniform nonglassy surface texture.

Suggested Specifications for Reinforced Concrete Tennis Courts

Location. The long axis of the court should be in a north and south direction.

Subgrade. (1) the subgrade should be uniformly and thoroughly compacted. When fills are required, they should be placed in layers not exceeding 6 inches (15 cm.) in thickness and each layer should be properly compacted at optimum moisture content. (2) Where expansive type soils are encountered, they should be thoroughly soaked down at least five days in advance of concreting and covered with a 2-inch (5-cm.) blanket of moist sand or rock dust which should be kept in a moist condition until concrete is placed. (3) In areas subject to severe ground freezing, granular subbases should be constructed to the thickness required by the contract. Such subbase material should have a plastic index of less than two and should contain less than three percent by weight of material passing a 270 sieve.

Grade. Provision should be made so that surface water from surrounding areas will not drain on to the court. Provision should also be made to drain away runoff water from the court.

Design. (1) There should be no cross slope in the court, but a continuous slope of 1 inch in 20 feet (2.5 cm. in 6 meters) may be permitted from one end of the court to the other. (2) Each full half of the court should be placed in one continuous operation without expansion, contraction or construction joints. (3) A 1-inch (2.5-cm.) thick expansion joint should be placed under the net and between courts when they are constructed in batteries. (4) The thickness of the finished slab should be 4 inches (10 cm.). A concrete beam should be cast under the expansion joint at the net line as shown in Fig. 23. An alternative to this rule—the thickness of the finished slab should be 4 inches (10 cm.). The edges of the court should be thickened and a concrete beam cast under the expansion joint at the net line as shown in Fig. 23.)

Reinforcement. (1) Reinforcement may be reinforcing bars or wire mesh. Equal cross-section area of reinforcement should be

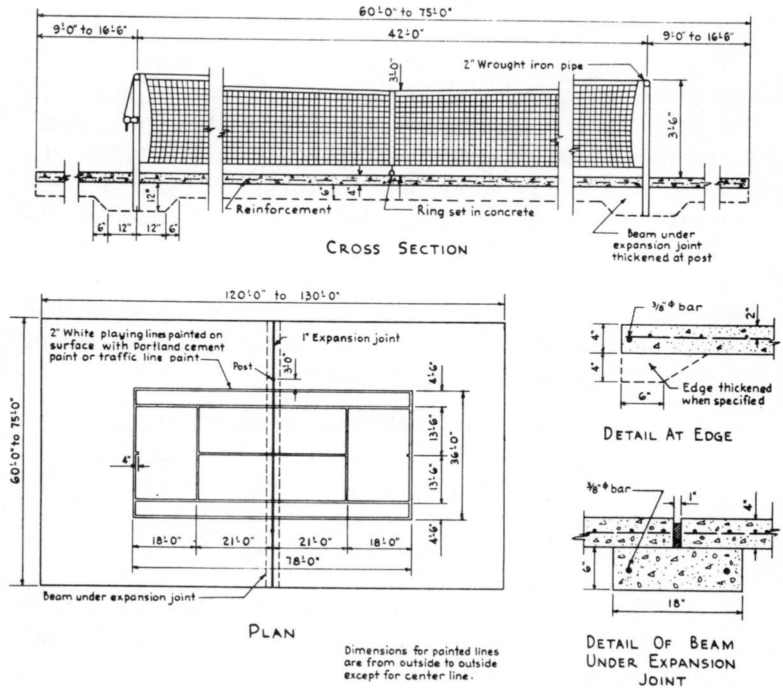

Fig. 23. Detailed reinforced concrete tennis court.

placed in both direction and should be continuous in each half of the court. (2) When reinforcing bars are used, they should be ⅜-inch (9.5-mm.) round bars, spaced at 12-inch (30-cm.) centers in both directions. (3) When wire mesh reinforcement is specified, a mesh composed of No. 6 gage wire spaced at 4-inch (10-cm.) centers should be used. (4) Reinforcement should be placed in the center of the 4-inch (10-cm.) slab. (*See* Chap. 8, Reinforced Concrete.)

Concrete materials. (1) Portland cement should comply with the standard specifications for portland cement. (2) Fine and coarse aggregate should be obtained from an approved source and should be clean, durable, and well-graded. The maximum size of coarse aggregate should be ¾ inch (1.9 cm.). (3) Water suitable for drinking should be considered satisfactory. (*See* Chap. 2, Concrete Ingredients, Chap. 3. Batching, and Chap. 4, Mixing Concrete.)

Proportioning. (1) Water per sack of cement, including moisture in the aggregate, should not exceed 6 gallons (22.7 liters). (2) The proportions of the fine and coarse aggregates should be adjusted to produce concrete that will work readily without requiring excessive floating and manipulation and without permitting the materials to segregate or water to collect on the surface.

Placing. When concreting is once started, it should be carried on as a continuous operation until the placing of at least one-half of the court is completed. In constructing the slab, the following sequence of operations should be followed:

1. Adjust the reinforcing steel accurately to the proper elevation when depositing the concrete on the subgrade.
2. Strike off the concrete to the elevation established by the screed boards.
3. Remove the screed boards and stakes.
4. Use the grip tamp sparingly.
5. Float the surface to even out apparent irregularities.
6. Allow the concrete to stand until it has hardened sufficiently to permit the proper use of a mechanical rotary finisher. From two to four passes of this finisher are usually

required to compact and level out the concrete to a true, even surface.

7. Obtain the final finish by using the flat of a steel trowel in small circular movements to produce a *swirl* pattern. A uniform nonglassy surface texture is required. (*See* Placing and Consolidating Concrete.)

Curing. As soon as the concrete has hardened sufficiently to prevent damage thereby, it should be cured by keeping it wet for at least three days. The usual method of curing is through the use of a fog spray of water. Any method of curing which will stain, mar, or blemish the surface should be avoided.

Color. After all dark moisture spots have disappeared from the concrete (usually from one to two months) the surface may be colored by an inorganic chemical stain which reacts with the cement. (*See* Chap. 16, Mineral Pigments for Use in Coloring Concrete.)

Chapter 46

Home Water Supply and Sewage Disposal

Today, the conveniences of modern plumbing are available to most American farm and suburban families. Running water in the kitchen and bathroom increases comfort and makes life more enjoyable. Plenty of water on tap at the barn, poultry house, hog house, and other buildings saves time and labor. But the only practical way to assure a pure water supply is to build wells and other water supply structures so that they keep out contamination. The health of many farm and suburban families is endangered by polluted water from unprotected wells. The fact that water tastes good and looks clean is no proof that it is pure and safe to drink.

Proper disposal of sewage from the home is closely associated with the protection of the water supply. For most farms and suburban homes without sewer connections the safest and most efficient method of disposing of household wastes is the septic tank sewage disposal system. Only when a septic tank sewage disposal system is installed can the full advantages of running water be enjoyed by the majority of rural residents.

WATER REQUIREMENTS

Table 34 will help you determine your *water requirements.* To estimate the capacity of water system needed in gallons (or liters) per hour, divide the total daily use by two. When you improve or expand your water system or when you build a new system, consider the water supply and well recharge capacity. A large pressure tank will help build sufficient reserve capacity if

Home:	
Each member of the family	50 gal.
Automatic washers	45 gal.
Automatic driers (condenser type)	40 gal.
Shower	15-30 gal.
Dishwasher	9 gal.
Lawn or Garden Sprinkling (per hour)	300 gal.
Farm Production:	
Each cow producing milk	35 gal.
Each dry cow or beef animal	15 gal.
Each hog	4 gal.
Each sheep	2 gal.
Each 100 chickens	4 gal.

TABLE 34. WATER NEEDED PER DAY.

well yield is low. A pump large enough to handle the capacity is necessary. Drilled wells of larger diameter, 6 inches or more (15 cm.), will help keep pace with modern household water demands. Install pipe of ample size as undersized pipe systems limit the flow.

PROTECTING DUG AND BORED WELLS

Concrete well casings or concrete-lined watertight seals around casings will help protect your water supply from surface contamination. Well platform and covers make it possible to maintain clean, sanitary conditions around pumps and wells. Clean, fresh, healthful water in adequate supply will allow your family maximum convenience.

Figure 1 shows a suggested method of protecting driven or drilled wells. Cement grout prevents surface water from running down along the casing and entering the water supply.

PUMP HOUSES AND WELL PLATFORMS

Figure 2 shows protection of dug or bored wells. Concrete is cast around concrete pipe well casings. The well platform

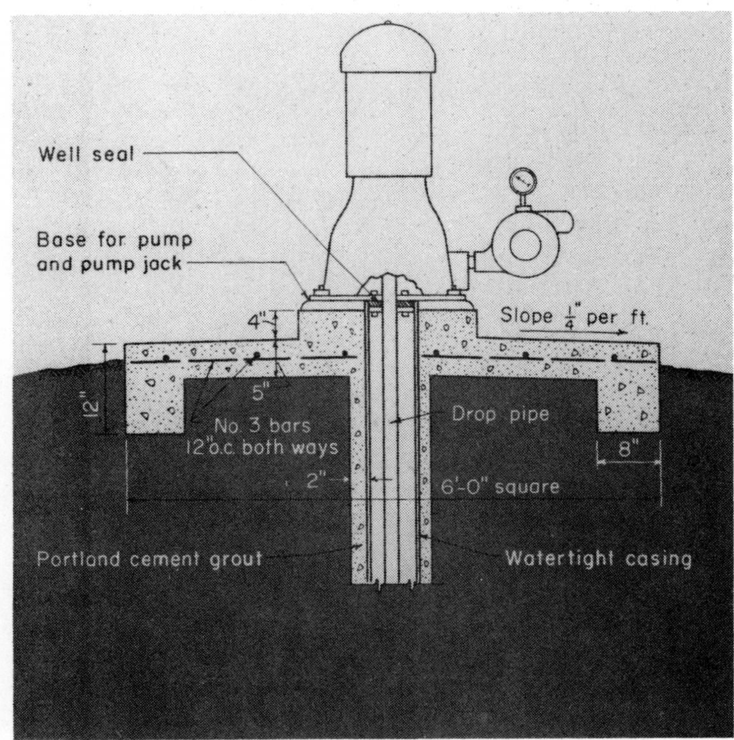

Fig. 1. Method of protecting driven or drilled wells with cement grout.

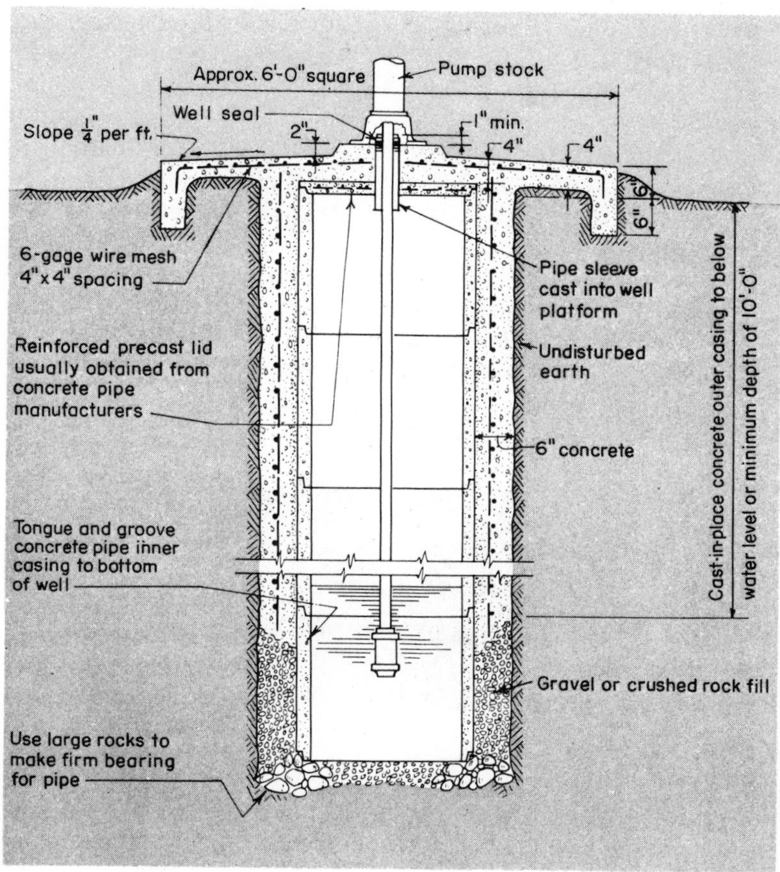

Fig. 2. Method of protecting dug or bored wells with concrete casings.

should be sloped at least ¼-inch per foot (1.3-cm. per meter) for drainage.

Concrete masonry pump houses will protect valuable equipment and pumps from serious weather and dirt damage. An electric light or a heat lamp in the pump house (Fig. 3) will usually furnish enough heat to prevent freeze-up in cold weather.

A *pump pit* such as the one shown in Fig. 4 is sometimes used instead of a pump house. Often the pit is placed adjacent to the basement of the house. Local regulations should be checked before installing a pump pit.

A treating system for pond water similar to that shown in Fig. 5 utilizes concrete settling basins, filters, and cisterns. Many state agricultural colleges have detailed plans and suggestions for setting up pond water treatment systems for farm use.

Fig. 3. A concrete masonry pump house provides ideal protection for equipment.

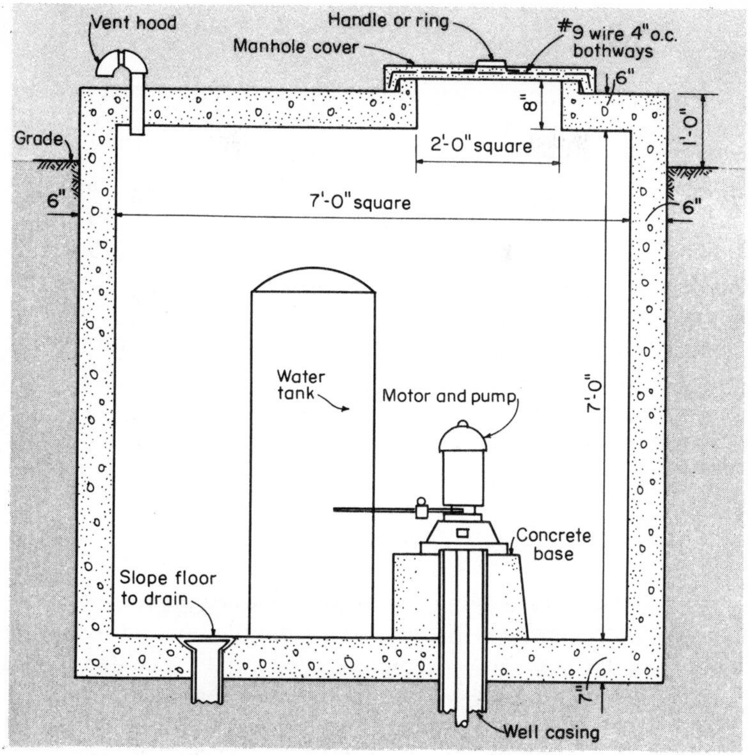

Fig. 4. Cross-section of a pump pit.

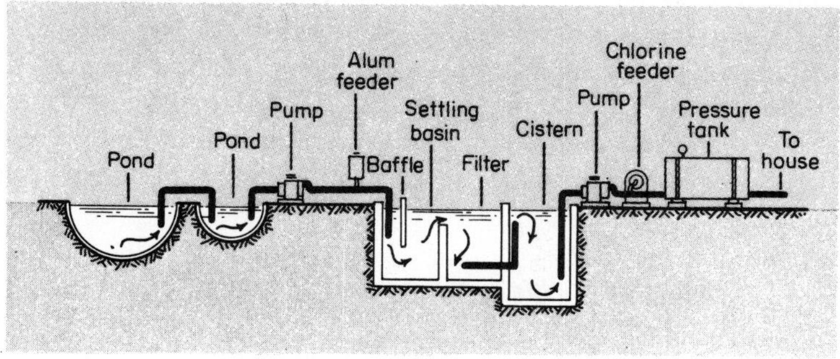

Fig. 5. Typical water-treating system for the farm home.

FIRE CISTERNS

One way to improve fire protection is to build a *concrete fire cistern* and keep it filled. The fire cistern should be about 100 feet (30.48 meters) from the service buildings and the house to allow free movement of fire equipment. A location near the driveway is preferred. The cistern shown in Fig. 6 will hold 3,600 gallons (13,626 liters). In constructing the cistern, the earth bank may be used as the outside form for the concrete. Wire mesh and No. 4 (½-inch, or 1.3-cm.) bars are used for reinforcement. Precast concrete joists are constructed to support cover slabs. A 10-inch (25-cm.) tile riser is placed conveniently to receive the fire suction hose. The completed tank is covered with 1 foot (30 cm.) of earth, leaving only the riser exposed. (*See* Chap. 11, Finishing Concrete Slabs; and Chap. 14, Precast Concrete.)

DRAIN TILE

The first step in making a basement watertight is to use concrete drain tile around the wall. Place the tile beside the footing to carry away any water that might accumulate. The line should lead away from the foundation to an outlet that always remains open. When the line empties into a ditch or stream, the outlet should be above the high-water mark to prevent a reverse flow. The drain tile line should be placed with a slope of 1 inch per 20 feet (4.2 mm. per meter). Place the tile ¼-inch (6.3-mm.) apart and cover the top half of each joint with a strip of building paper to keep out silt and fine particles of earth. A layer of coarse granular material should be placed to a depth of 6 to 8 inches (15 to 20 cm.) over the drain tile line to aid water movement into the line. (*See* Chap. 52, Building Watertight Concrete Masonry Walls; *see also* Chap. 53, Miscellaneous Concrete Masonry Wall Jobs.)

CISTERNS FOR RAINWATER STORAGE

Figure 7 shows a plan for a household cistern with a roof filter. Large quantities of soft water can be collected in such a cis-

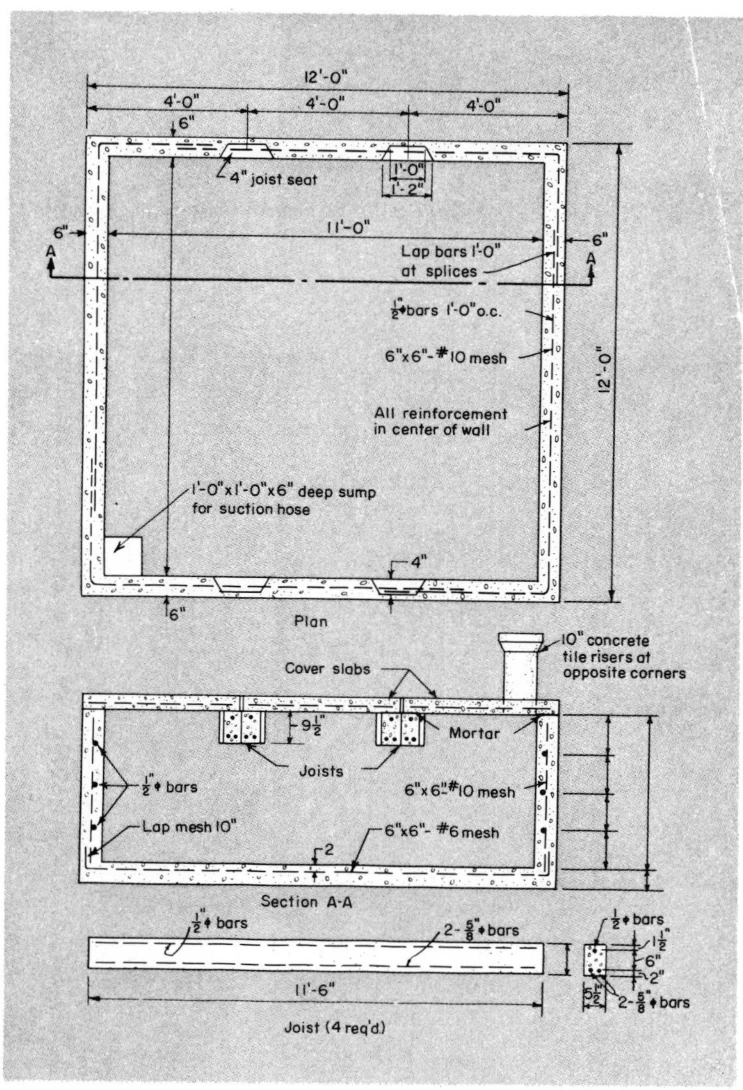

Fig. 6. Longitudinal and transverse cross-sections of concrete fire cisterns.

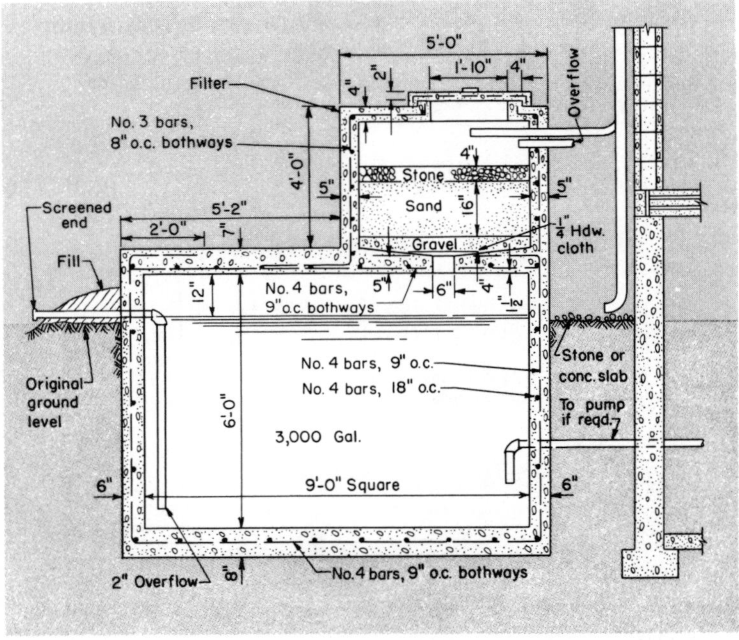

Fig. 7. Cross-section of household cistern with gravel filter.

tern. Filtering water does not necessarily make it fit for drinking; it only removes sediment from the water. (*See* Fig. 8.)

SEPTIC TANKS AND SEWAGE DISPOSAL

Modern plumbing is a *must* today. A *septic tank system* properly designed, correctly built, and reasonably operated provides a safe and convenient method of disposing of household wastes in areas not served by community or municipal sewage treatment facilities.

A typical *sewage disposal system* is illustrated in Fig. 9. The system consists of (1) a house drain, (2) a house sewer line, (3) a septic tank, (4) an outlet line, (5) a distribution box, and (6) tile properly placed in a disposal field. Some regulations permit omission of the distribution box.

Precast concrete septic tanks are readily available in most areas. Table 35 shows suggested septic tank capacities based on recommendations of the U.S. Public Health Service.

Fig. 8. Cover top half with asphalt paper to keep dirt out of line.

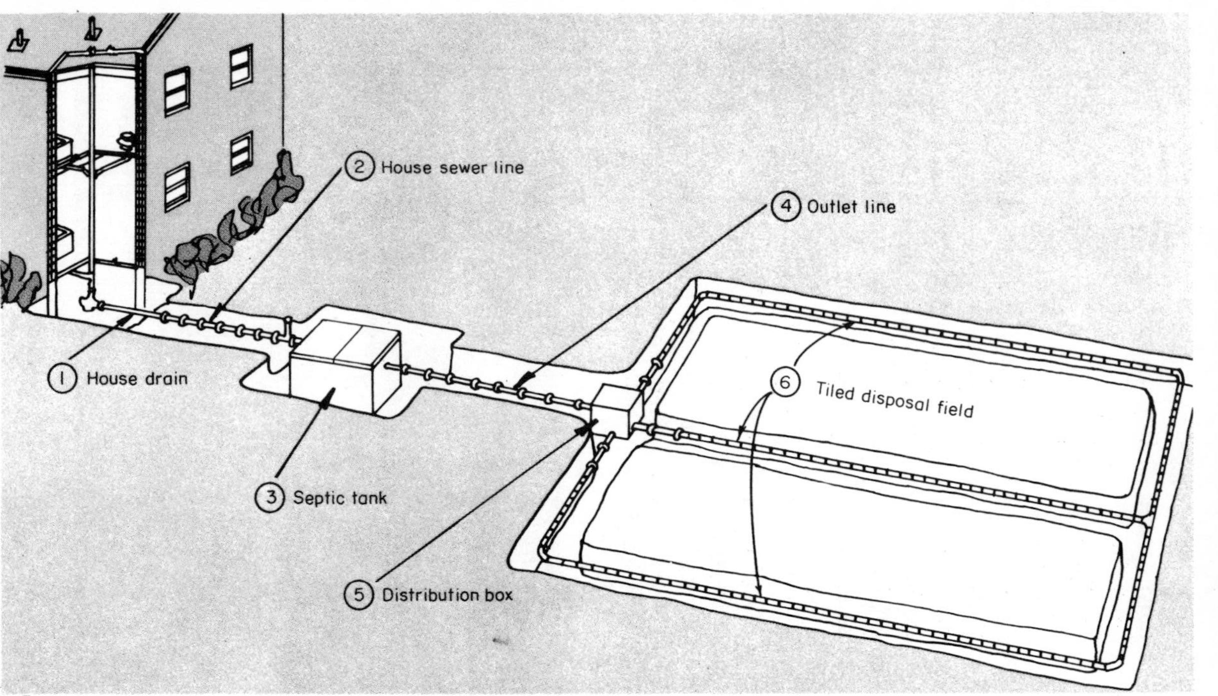

Fig. 9. Typical septic tank system showing the six main parts of the system.

No. of bedrooms in dwelling	Capacity per bedroom in gallons	Required total tank capacity in gallons	Tank size			
			Inside width	Inside length	Liquid depth	Total depth
2 or less	375	750	3 ft. 6 in.	7 ft. 6 in.	4 ft. 0 in.	5 ft. 0 in.
3	300	900	3 ft. 6 in.	8 ft. 0 in.	4 ft. 6 in.	5 ft. 6 in.
4	250	1,000	4 ft. 0 in.	8 ft. 0 in.	4 ft. 6 in.	5 ft. 6 in.
5	250	1,250	4 ft. 0 in.	9 ft. 0 in.	4 ft. 6 in.	5 ft. 6 in.

*U.S. Public Health Service Recommendations. Check local health authorities for recommendations in your area.
Above sizes provide for use of garbage grinders, automatic washers, and other household appliances.
Some regulations permit sizes 150 gal. smaller if garbage grinders are not used.

TABLE 35. RECOMMENDED SEPTIC TANK CAPACITIES.*

The efficiency of a disposal field depends upon the capacity of the soil to absorb liquid from the septic tank. The minimum number of tile lines for each system is two, and the maximum length of each line is 100 feet (30.48 meters). Septic tanks should be drained periodically. Consult your county agent or county sanitarian on the construction of septic tank systems. Many states and counties have codes that *must* be followed in the installation.

Chapter 47

Outdoor Living

We hope that this chapter will show you how to make leisure-time living more rewarding. The entire family can enter into most of these projects with enthusiasm.

Skillfully planned outdoor living space makes older houses fit into modern living patterns and turns newer houses into a homeowner's dream. Kids share the pleasure when you plan space for outdoor games. A sandbox, basketball court, concrete strip for shuffleboard or badminton play area will increase the appeal of any home.

Get your dream terrace out of the planning stage and turn it into a reality that will give years of lasting enjoyment to you, your family, and friends. Colorful and spacious, or subdued and private, your outdoor living area can be designed to your taste.

Make an overall plan or sketch of your available area similar to the one shown in Fig. 1. You may not be able to do the entire job at once but make those improvements first that you need the most. A *patio* is a natural place to start. It can be connected to the house or built as a special area in the lawn. Attractive and interesting effects using cast-in-place concrete or precast patio units can lead to modern yard improvements that will be the envy of all your neighbors. (*See* Chap. 14, Precast Concrete; and Chap. 22, Concrete Masonry Units.)

After the patio is finished, perhaps you will want to make a worthwhile improvement, such as concrete edging strips, to eliminate the necessity of clipping around borders, beds, and rows. Also, you may want to consider building screen walls or garden walls for privacy and protection. And, a barbecue pit or fireplace may be constructed for a wonderful world of savory outdoor cooking.

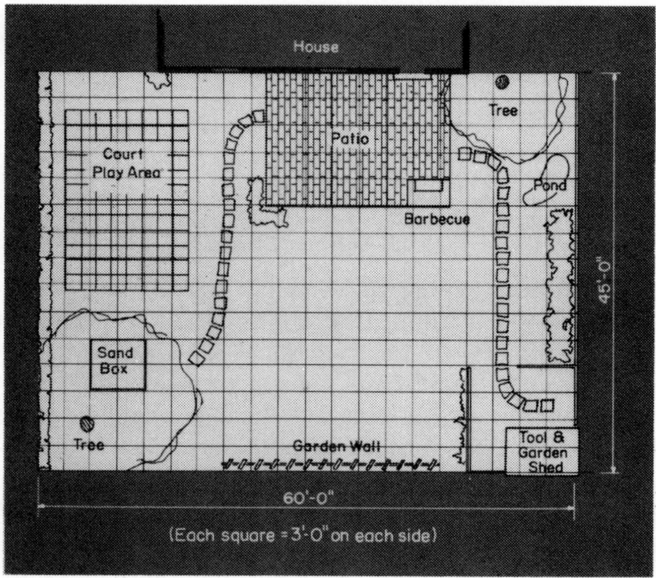

Fig. 1. Plan of outdoor living area.

Many worthwhile projects can be accomplished by devoting a few weekends to leisurely developing lawn, garden, and home improvements such as those shown in the illustrations.

BARBECUE AND OUTDOOR FIREPLACE

Pleasant evenings and outdoor cooking mean fun for all. You will enjoy the exciting experience of entertaining family and friends at meals cooked in your own backyard. Here is how inexpensive, serviceable fireplaces for outdoor cooking can be built with minimum labor and time.

Concrete masonry block and split block used singularly or in combination make attractive outdoor fireplaces. Build on a good foundation (*see* Fig. 2). (*See* Section 2, Concrete Masonry.)

For a simple slab foundation used in areas free from severe frost damage, excavate sod, loose earth, and other materials to a

Fig. 2. An outdoor fireplace and a concrete work area.

depth slightly below ground suface. Level and tamp earth. Place 2- × 4-inch (5- × 10-cm.) form boards so that the final surface of the slab will be at least 1 inch (2.5 cm.) above ground level. Make the slab base at least 2 inches (5 cm.) wider on all sides than the fireplace. If the soil in your yard does not have good drainage or is subject to frost heave, the slab should be placed on a 4-inch (10-cm.) layer of gravel or crushed stone. (*See* Fig. 3.)

The masonry fireplace shown in Fig. 4 is lined with standard fire brick for increased durability. These units come 9 × 4½ × 2½ inches (22.5 × 11.3 × 6.3 cm.) and are laid so that the wide face is exposed to the flame. Four bricks will cover approximately 1 square foot (.09 sq. meters). For best results, use air-setting high temperature cement mortar. Thirty-five pounds

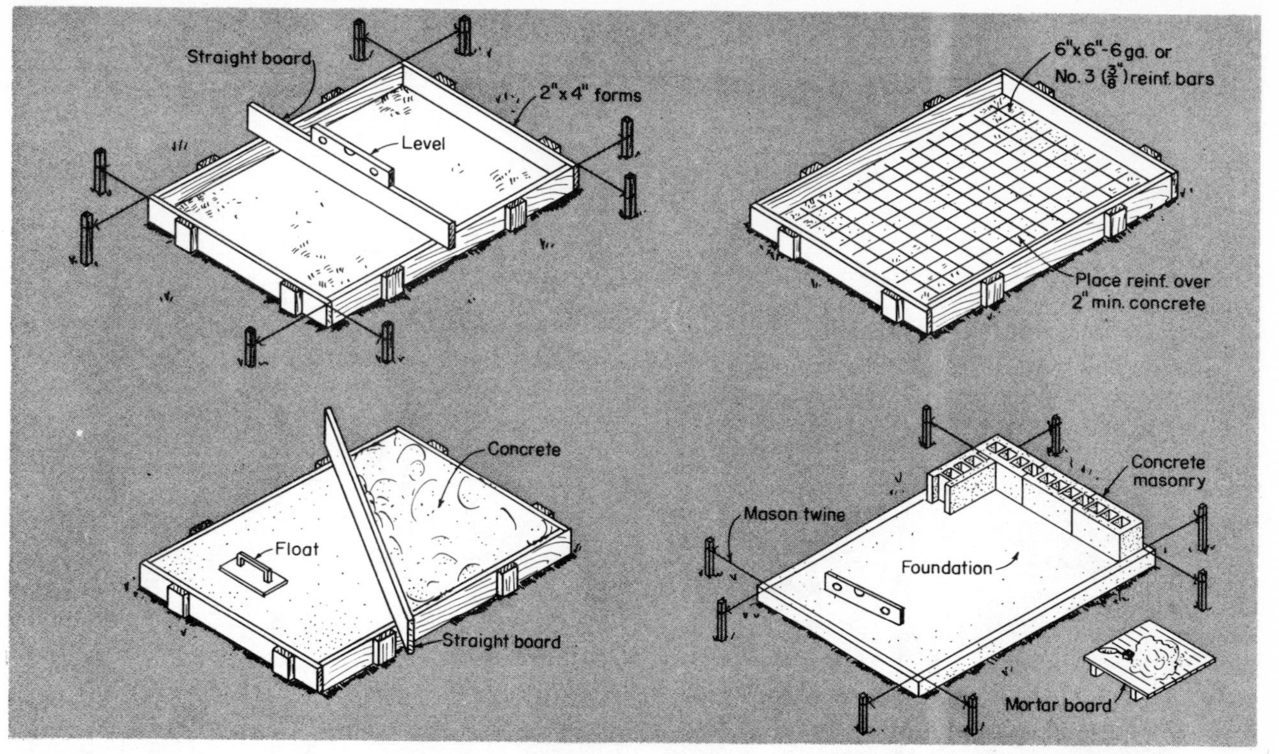

Fig. 3. Forming and construction procedures for constructing a simple foundation slab for an outdoor fireplace.

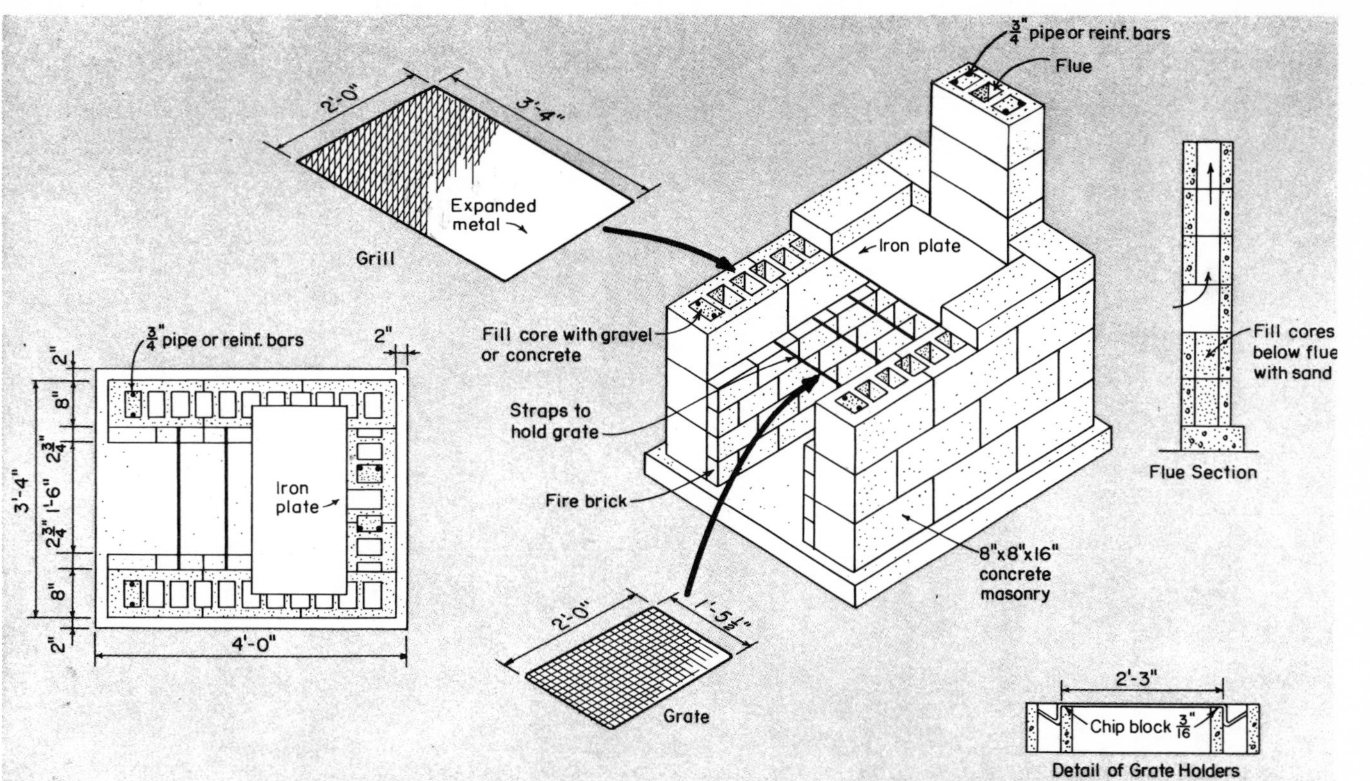

Fig. 4. Details and cross-sections of a typical outdoor fireplace.

(15.9 kgs.) will be needed for 100 bricks. (*See* Section 3, Brick Masonry.)

If you do not want an upright fireplace, a fire pit can be a welcome addition to your patio. Youngsters and adults enjoy an evening of fun around the fire. In winter this handy pit can be used as a warming area.

PATIO STONES AND STEPPING STONES

Concrete patio stones add a touch of color to outdoor improvements. Placed close together they form any size patio or walk. Entrance areas, outdoor terraces, and recreation and play areas can be covered with these durable concrete units.

Precast patio units available from local product plants or dealers make ideal units for building walks and patios. The design, pattern, arrangement, and colors are unlimited and the ultimate beauty of the finished area is as varied as the individual taste.

For the construction of walks and patios proceed as follows:

Prepare the area. All soil, sod, and debris must be removed to a depth about twice the thickness of the stone. Where there are soft, spongy areas, remove the soil and replace with 4 to 6 inches (15 cm.) of gravel fill, well tamped.

Place sand bed. After cleaning the walkway or patio area, place a 2-inch (5-cm.) sand bed. Wet the sand and tamp thoroughly in place. Level the sand bed using a 2- × 4-inch (5- × 10-cm.) straightedge.

Place concrete patio units. Lay patio units flat to the pattern desired. Leave a ¼- or ½-inch (6.3-mm. or 1.3-cm.) space between units which will later be filled with sand. Edge or trim block or precast concrete strips may be used to hold the patio in place. Redwood divider strips may be placed to divide a patio into larger, eye-catching units.

Patio units can be precast in forms built to your particular pattern. Such a job can be done at your leisure and the finished product stacked until ready for installation. Or the forms may be put in an area where the sod has been removed to the proper depth and the concrete patio units are cast in place. Precast patio units are usually 2 inches (5 cm.) thick, an economical size that is easy to handle.

Place concrete of proper mix in forms using the proportion of 1:2:2¼. Level with a straightedge then wood-float, leaving a textured surface. Fill in the strips between the cast stones with strips of sod.

For quantities, the form shown in Fig. 5 is most successful. Reverse the form when repeating the pattern to get varied effects. Colors and patterns may be varied to suit individual taste. (*See* Chap. 16, Mineral Pigments for Use in Coloring Concrete; and Chap. 44, Outdoor Home Improvements, the section on Patterns on Flat Work.) For attractive patterns, divider strips may be inserted. (*See* Fig. 6.)

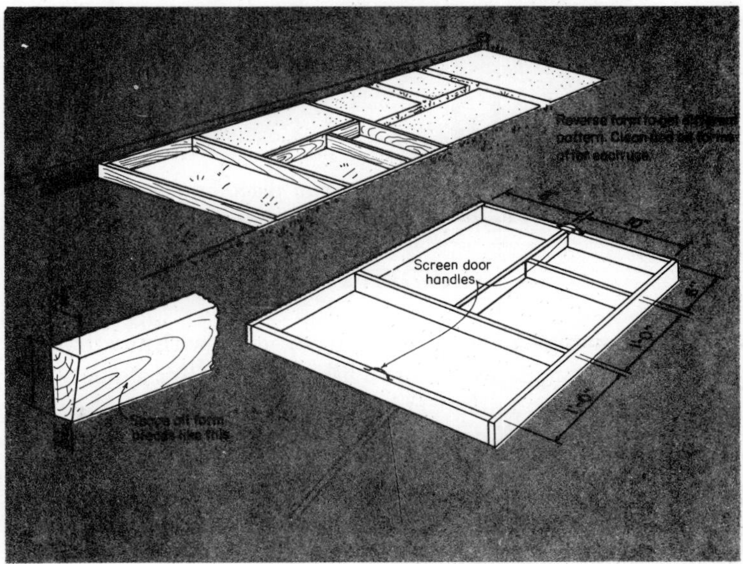

Fig. 5. Reusable forms for flagstones. Dividers are beveled for easy removal.

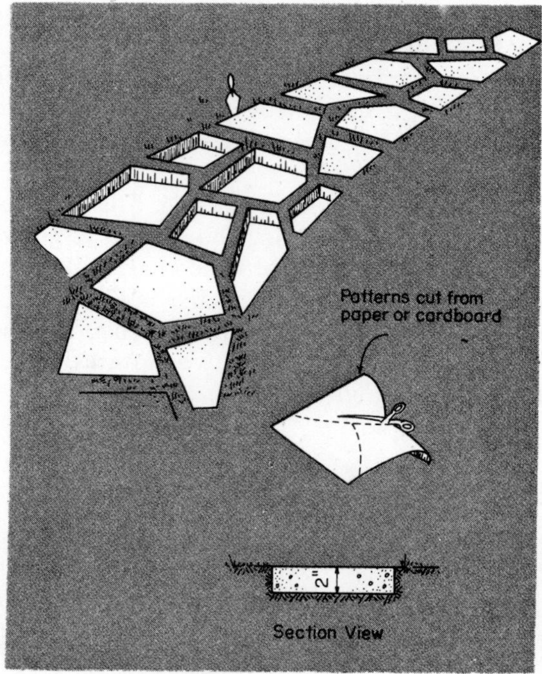

Fig. 6. Flagstones can be cast in place by digging away earth to the shape desired.

GARDEN POOLS

Outdoor living can be made more enjoyable with an attractive pool. Aquatic plants and colorful fish can make this a quiet, restful corner in your outdoor area. (*See* Figs. 7 and 8.)

A 6- × 10-foot (1.8- × 3-meter) pool is not hard to build and it provides ample space for fish and plants. Pools can be as simple or as elaborate as you care to make them. A simple bowl-shaped pool is readily made by scooping out a small depression in the ground, setting mesh or bars for reinforcement, and then placing overflow pipe to the proper height.

Place concrete about 6 inches (15 cm.) thick. Be sure that the

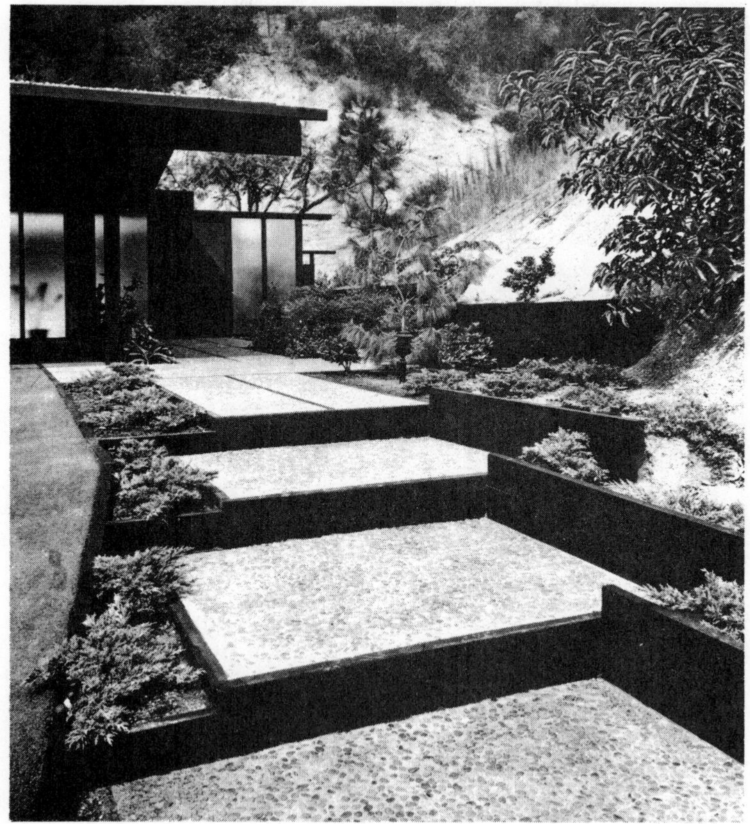

Fig. 7. Boxed squares of exposed aggregate make steps and floor of terrace for this home. Aggregates come in a variety of shapes and colors.

wire mesh is centered in the concrete. Smooth the concrete with a wood float. Cure by filling the pool with water as soon as the concrete is hard enough to avoid marring.

A pool of this kind is usually about 3 feet (91 cm.) deep at the center. If fish are to be kept in a new pool, the water should be changed several times at weekly intervals to remove the excess alkalies before putting in the fish. Plants placed in soil boxes or baskets can be easily removed when you want to clean the pool.

Fig. 8. A garden pool is the center of this outdoor living scheme.

Precast patio stones may be used to edge the pool by placing them on a sand bed so that the top is level with the concrete pool wall as shown in Fig. 9.

If you have sloping terrain, two pools may be used in combination to give a waterfall effect. The inlet pipe for the water supply is in the upper pool while the outlet pipe for drainage is in the lower pool.

GARDEN WALLS AND SCREEN WALLS

Outdoor living areas are greatly enhanced by well-engineered, tastefully designed garden walls. Attractive walls can be built in many designs, and are limited only by your imagination.

Concrete and *concrete masonry walls* offer a new dimension in wall design. From the simple 8- × 8- × 16-inch (20- × 20- × 40-cm.) concrete block to the newest screen wall unit and grille block, concrete gives the beauty, the appeal, and the pleasing backdrop for a beautiful garden setting. Also, concrete maintains its beauty—it will not peel, warp, rot, or decay in adverse weather. Colorful concrete can be used in almost every item in your outdoor living plan.

Garden walls furnish privacy for your outdoor living area and

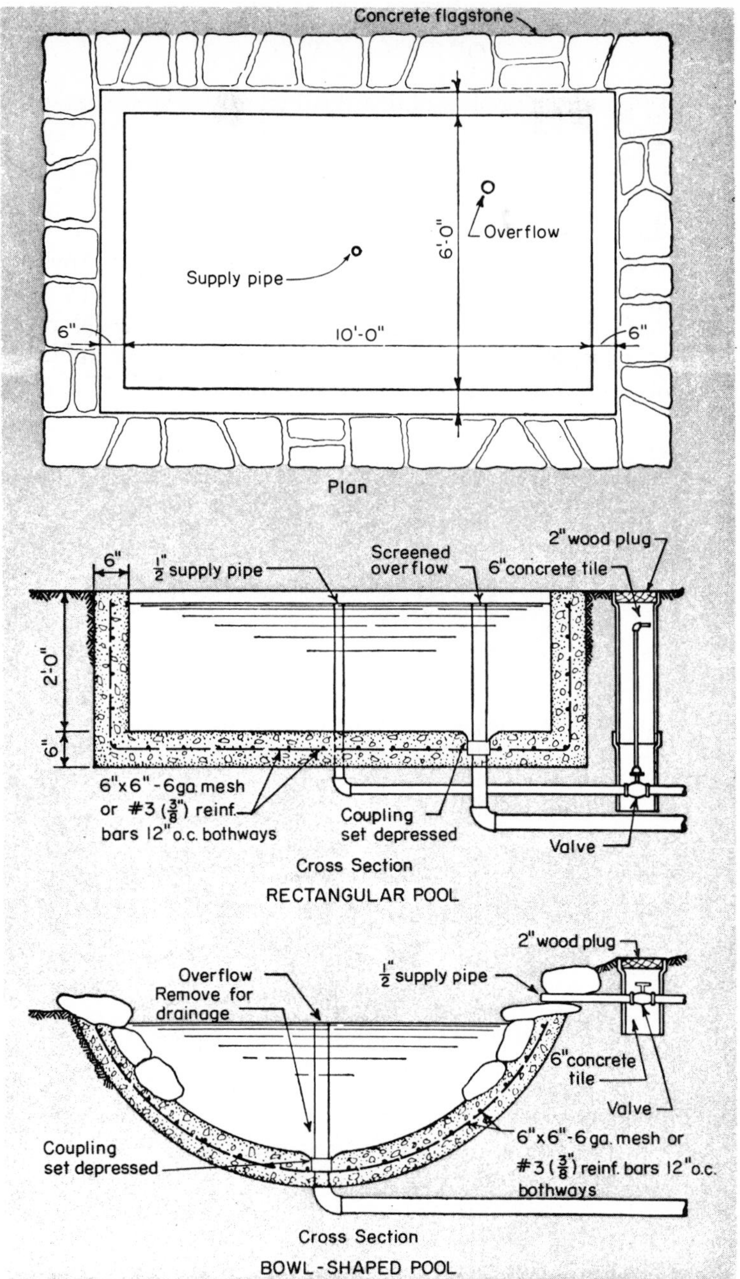

Fig. 9. Details of rectangular or bowl-shaped garden pool.

around swimming pools. Solid walls (Fig. 10) of block can protect your area from chilling winds, yet with very little design change, block can be placed so air circulates freely through the wall.

Outdoor space is designed to be appealing to the eye as well as functional in use. Do not forget the versatile outdoor area for night parties, picnics, and social gatherings for family and friends. A new touch of glamour is added when well-planned lighting is included in the outdoor living area. White lights on colorful walls of concrete add a three-dimensional charm. Sub-

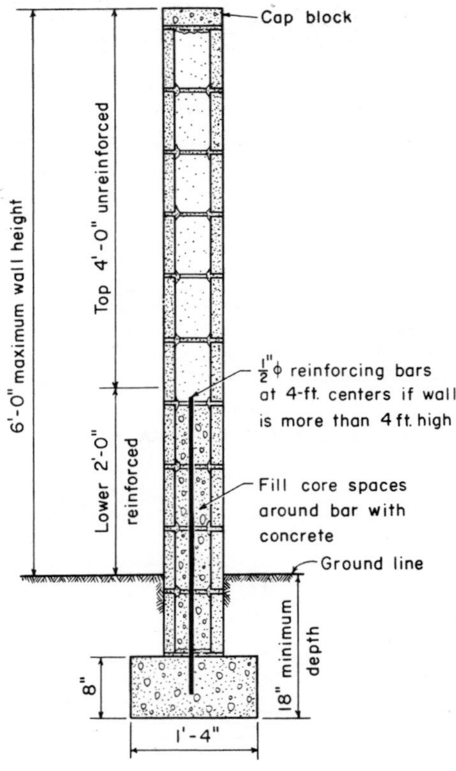

Fig. 10. Easy method for construction of a solid masonry wall.

dued colored lights behind plantings and properly arranged in other areas, will add beauty to your leisure hours.

Both solid and open-type garden walls are used as needs dictate. The many textures and patterns available in concrete help you dramatize your landscaping ideas. Patterns of squares, rectangles, and strong diagonal lines add a feeling of movement to ordinary garden walls. Lacy intricate patterns of screen block walls add beauty and an air of grandeur (Fig. 11). Walls can be painted with cement paint or left unpainted. Split block and textured block capture shadows and highlights creating ever-changing shadow patterns and designs.

For a rugged appearance extruded mortar or offset block in the garden wall lends a feeling of security.

Large panels that afford year-round protection can be easily obtained in precast units (Fig. 12) or asbestos-cement. Asbestos-cement panels are often framed with divider strips. Panels can be set vertical, angular, and even pivoted on center pins to allow movement.

Garden walls need good foundations to keep them attractive for years of service. Lay out the wall in the desired line and dig a

Fig. 11. Many striking patterns are available in screen block.

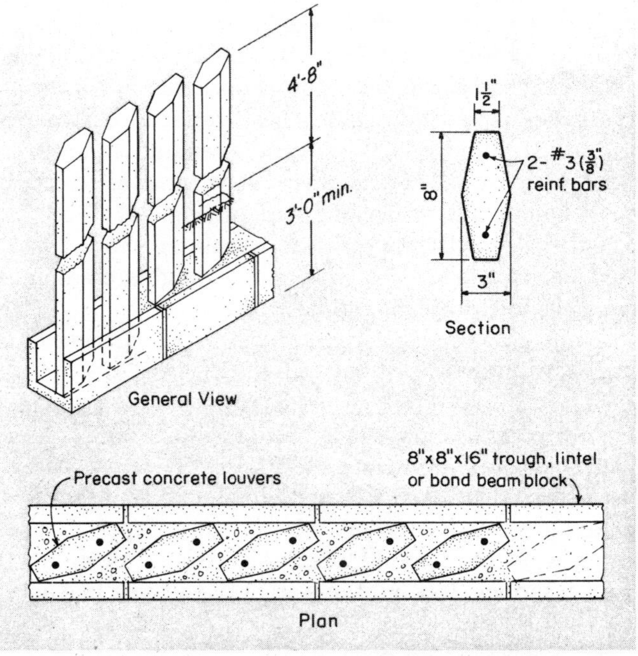

Fig. 12. Screen wall. Walls can be painted with cement paint or left unpainted.

trench slightly more than twice the thickness of the proposed wall. The trench should be a minimum of 18 inches (45 cm.) deep or below the frostline in colder areas. Make the footing twice the width of the wall, and the same depth as the wall width. Thus for an 8-inch (20-cm.) block wall, the concrete footing should be 16 inches (40 cm.) wide and 8 inches (20 cm.) thick.

The below-grade portion of the wall can be built of regular 8 × 8 × 16 inches (20 × 20 × 40 cm.) block or with the same block as the wall above grade. Follow the practices recommended in Chap. 22, Concrete Masonry Units.

CAST-IN-PLACE PATIO

There is a saying that, "Where you have the walls of a house, you have the start of a patio." This means that you already have exciting possibilities for a garden terrace or an outdoor living room. Outdoor living may mean only a small place to relax or it may mean a large, spacious area with swimming pool and play courts. Whatever the size of the area, patios are convenient and often add that extra room that you have always wanted. (*See* Figs. 13 and 14.)

To build a cast-in-place patio, mark off the area and remove sod and soil to the depth desired (Fig. 15). Most patios are formed with 2 × 4 (5 × 10 cm.) wood forms (Fig. 16). For circular borders, drive stakes on desired arcs and place two thin strips of wood around the stakes. By nailing the strips together, an arc is formed and can be held in place by outside stakes. (*See* Fig. 17.)

For dividers to be left in the concrete, use redwood or treated

Fig. 13. Attractive patios can be built using precast concrete sections.

Fig. 14. This patio area is conveniently on the same level as the den.

Fig. 15. All sod and debris must first be carefully removed from patio area.

Fig. 16. Setting forms to proper grade. Redwood forms may be left in as dividers.

Fig. 17. Placing sand to a depth of 2-inch (5-cm.) over patio area.

lumber placed to give the desired patterns (Fig. 16). Sand should be placed to a depth of 2 inches (5 cm.) over the patio area (Fig. 17). Where this is done, you will want to protect dividers by covering the top edge with masking tape before concrete is placed (Fig. 18). Set the forms with a slight pitch to keep water away from the house and to aid water run-off when hosing down. For special surfaces and coloring *see* Table 32; *also see* Chap. 16, Mineral Pigments for Use in Coloring Concrete, and Chap. 37, Decorative and Special Finishes.

One cubic yard (.765 cu. meters) of concrete will place 81 square feet (7.5 sq. meters) of 4-inch (10-cm.) thick patio (Fig. 19). To allow for waste and irregularities in excavation, order 5 to 10 percent more concrete than actually calculated. Order a mix of 6 bags of cement per cubic yard (.765 per cu. meter) with not more than 6 gallons (22.7 liters) total water. Specify six percent air entrainment.

Be certain all forming is ready before concrete is delivered. Check forms and have finishing tools and enough labor on hand. If you have never finished concrete, consider hiring a concrete finisher, or ask a friend who knows. Spade the concrete well into the corners of the forms. (*See* Fig. 20.) Overfill the forms slightly, then screed with a straightedge. Screeding merely levels the concrete with the top of forms. *Do not* try to use the screed to

Fig. 18. Redwood forms covered with masking tape to preserve their rich color during construction.

Fig. 19. Placing and consolidating concrete. Note consistency of concrete.

Fig. 20. Striking off concrete with a long 2 × 4 (5 × 10 cm.). Form stakes were cut off to aid strike-off.

Fig. 21. After strike-off, concrete surface is floated with a wooden float.

get a smooth surface.

Check the concrete frequently to determine when it is ready for finishing. Wood floating will give the concrete a rough texture (Fig. 21). Steel troweling is used for a dense smooth surface. (*See* Fig. 22.)

Moist-cure the concrete at least five days (Fig. 23).

A screened-in patio or terrace doubles as a comfortable living-eating area where you may relax without bother from flies and other insects. If you protect the patio with overhead shelter, it can be used in bad weather.

Where precast patio block are used they are laid on a smooth sand bed to the pattern desired. Follow the suggestions given previously in this chapter on patio walks.

FLOWER BEDS AND BORDERS

You know what a chore it can be to keep flower borders neat and attractive. With concrete you can easily build borders that are inexpensive, serviceable, and long-lasting.

The reusable form shown in Fig. 24 is for making 4-inch (10-cm.) thick units for flower bed facing. Units can be stacked to the height desired.

Place the assembled forms on oiled boards or on a plastic sheet spread on a concrete floor or walk. Use the concrete mix shown in Table 33. Using a screed board, strike off level and wood-float the concrete surface. Round the edges with an edging tool.

Forms may be removed after 24 hours and reused. Keep the concrete units under waterproof paper or a plastic sheet at least six days before using. Concrete placed on plastic such as polyethylene will harden to a glass-like surface where it is in contact with plastic.

The units can be made in a variety of colors and patterns. Old, weathered wood used in the forms will give an interesting texture to the sides of the concrete block. Wrinkling the plastic sheeting or placing it over a gravel bed will give the block surface a random pattern.

Fig. 22. Using a fine-bristle broom to give texture to the surface.

Fig. 23. A plastic film weighted at the edges seals in moisture for curing.

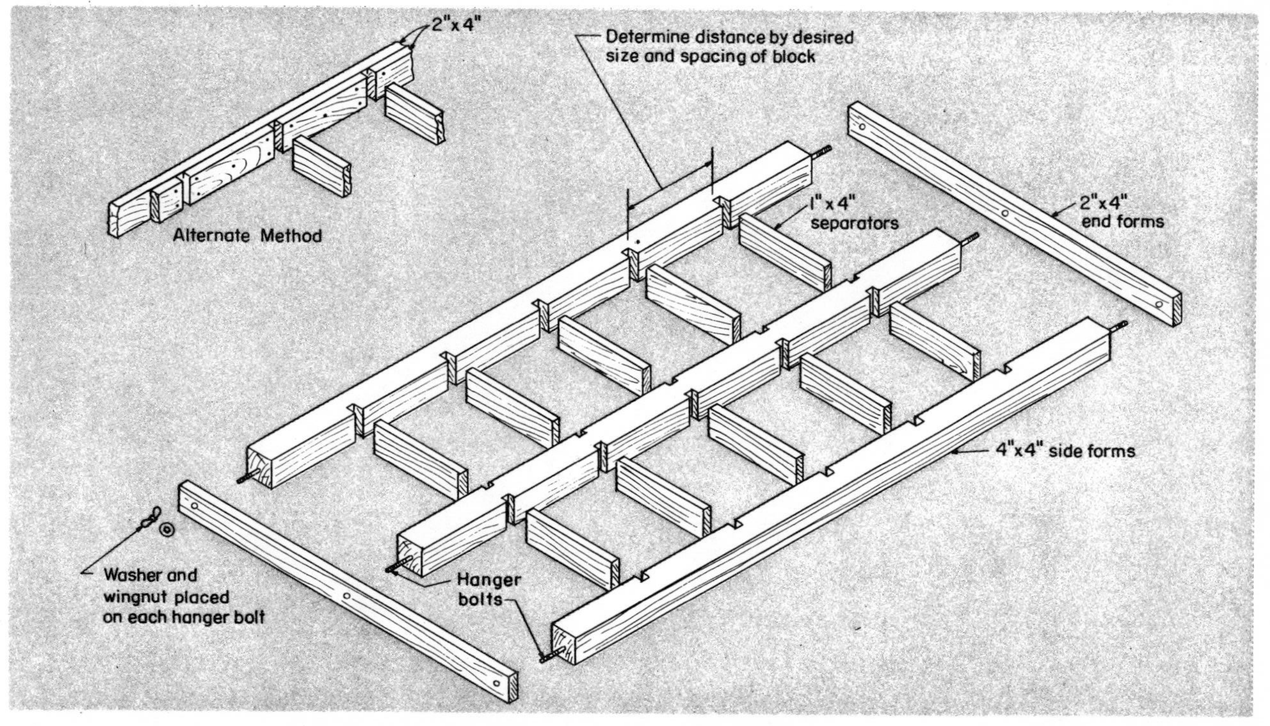

Fig. 24. Forms for casting 4-inch (10-cm.) thick block for flower bed edging.

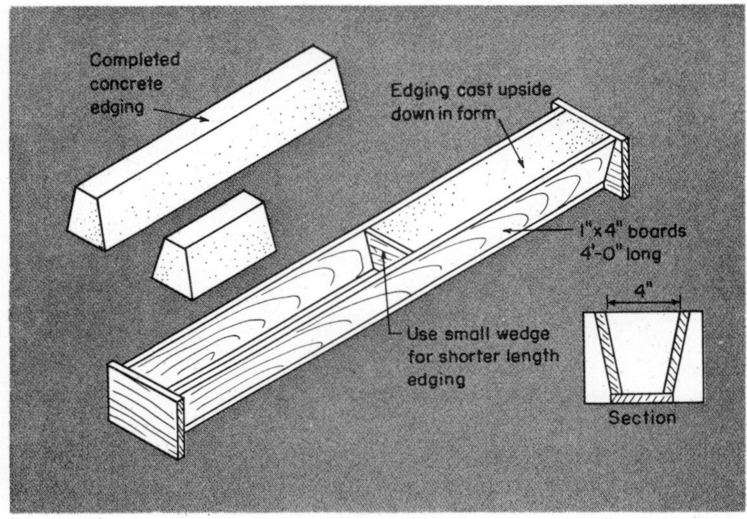

Fig. 25. Concrete edging strips can be precast in short sections.

Fig. 26. Corrugated asbestos cement strips along a flower bed simplify maintenance.

Another type of border strip can be made as shown in Fig. 25. Decorative and serviceable units are also available from local concrete products plants. These precast units are generally available in various lengths and shapes to fit your needs.

Corrugated asbestos-cement also makes a serviceable edging strip (Fig. 26). Cut large sheets into strips of the desired depth. Place the strips in a prepared trench and backfill with dirt.

Chapter 48

Outside Ornaments

Small, decorative objects of concrete add a touch of friendliness to your lawn and garden. Forms of steel, wood, aluminum, and plastic are available from many commercial firms. The forms may be used over and over to obtain the same item. In addition, many ready-made precast items are available at concrete products plants.

Items such as sundials, figurines, lamps, ashtrays, small animals, and other objects are easy to make. Any special design that can be copied with a plaster mold can be made with concrete. If the mold is painted or oiled on the inside and handled with care, it may be used again.

First, make a plaster cast of the model. To prevent bond, use several coats of shellac on the original model. Objects may be formed in two or more parts to permit the plaster mold to be removed. After the model is removed the mold is reassembled and filled with concrete.

The use of white portland cement for ornaments and other decorative uses should be considered. White cement used with light-colored aggregates produces attractive white surfaces that never need painting.

BIRD BATHS

One of the most popular outdoor lawn ornaments is a *bird bath* (Fig. 1). Inexpensive precast concrete bird baths are available in many sizes and shapes from concrete products producers. Often colored concrete is used to add to their attractiveness.

If you wish to cast your own *bird bath*, one can be built in three separate parts—the bowl, the pedestal, and the base.

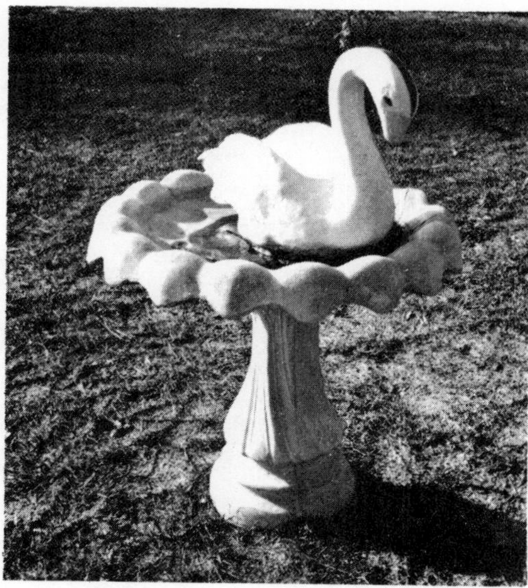

Fig. 1. Precast concrete bird bath.

The *bowl* is cast bottom side up over a clay core, disk, or any similar convex surface as shown in Fig. 2. Place a low slump concrete mix over the dried, oiled core to a depth of about 1 inch (2.5 cm.), then place wire mesh reinforcement. Follow this with another layer of 1-inch (2.5-cm.) thick concrete which is shaped using the bowl template. Set a ½- × 3-inch (1.3- × 3.8-cm.) bolt in the exact center with the threaded end projecting out about 2 inches (5 cm.). Cure the concrete. (*See* Chap. 10, Curing Concrete.)

A *rectangular pedestal* may be formed by using the flat forms as shown in the illustration. Pieces of ¾-inch (1.9-cm.) cove molding should be placed in the corner of the mold. A ⅝-inch (1.6-cm.) greased dowel is centered and set 3 inches (3.8 cm.) deep in the top of the pedestal after the concrete is placed. The dowel is removed after the concrete sets, leaving a hole to receive the bolt projecting from the bowl.

A 10- × 3½-inch (25- × 8.8-cm.) thick *base* may be used for

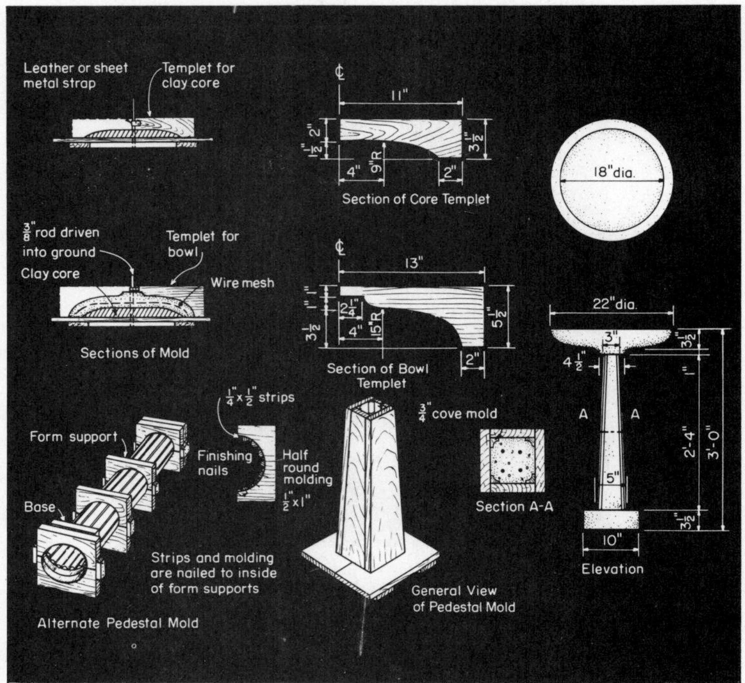

Fig. 2. Details for forming a concrete bird bath in three parts.

the pedestal. Or, the pedestal form can be set over a posthole dug below frostline. Use a 1:2:2¼ mix for this project. (*See* Chap. 4, Mixing Concrete; *also see* Table 33.) After parts have been covered and cured, assemble the bowl to the pedestal.

FLOWER BOXES

A concrete flower box is a durable item that will withstand the damaging effects of soil organisms and high moisture.

In constructing a *concrete flower box,* you need an inside and outside form. Any width or length may be chosen to fit your plans. Figure 3 shows one method of forming using standard

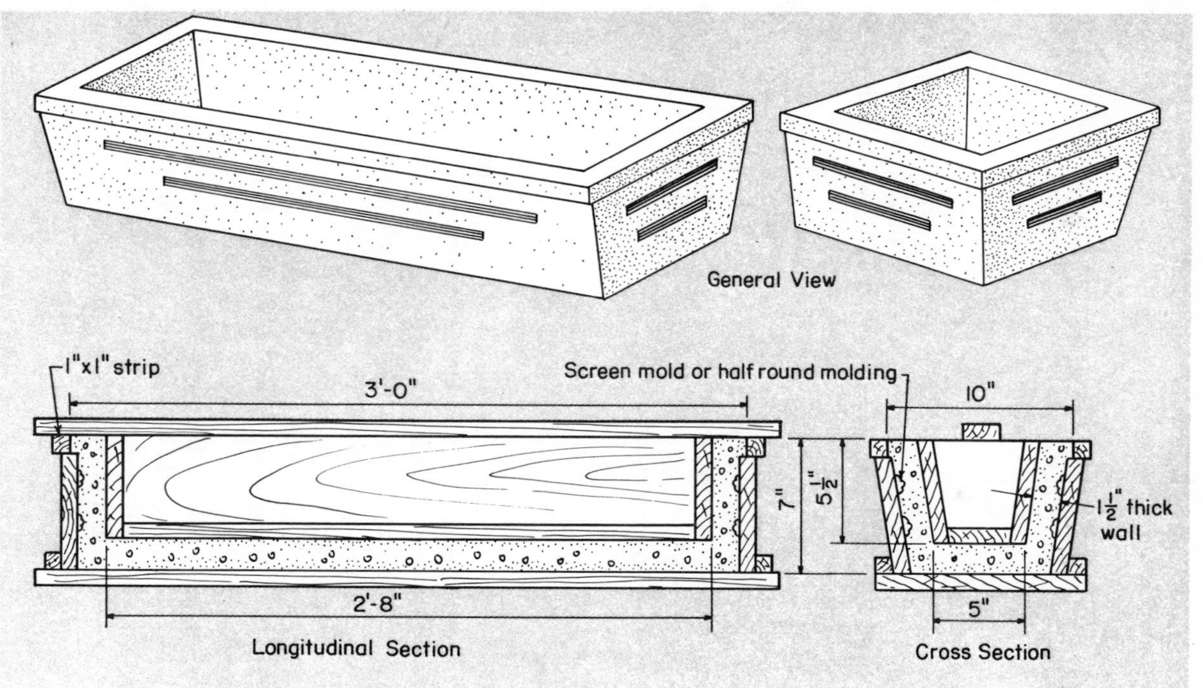

Fig. 3. Forming for concrete flower box.

lumber with screen mold or half round molding for patterns and decorative fluting. More elaborate patterns may be placed on the form side if desired.

By careful selection of special aggregates, or by choosing harmonizing colors, distinctive and unusual combinations of flower pots and boxes can be obtained. These strong and attractive units will do much to make your outdoor living area a pleasant summer showplace.

Be sure to sand the inside face of the forms and coat them with shellac or clear plastic spray to give a smooth concrete surface. Use white portland cement for a durable white finish. Mix concrete to the approximate proportions of 1:2:2¼. Gravel size should not exceed ¾ inch (1.9 cm.). The fresh concrete must be well spaded in the forms. Tap the forms lightly as you work. Cure the box by leaving the forms in place for 24 hours.

Patch any irregularities with a mixture of cement and water mixed to a creamy consistency. Cure for five days under a plastic sheet or a plastic drop cloth.

BENCHES

Lawn or garden benches lend an inviting, restful air to your outdoor living area. Precast concrete benches of many designs are sold by precast product producers.

You can also make your own *garden bench* as shown in Fig. 4. Use straight, dressed 2- × 4-inch (5- × 10-cm.) lumber for forming. Reinforcement is needed for the seat section. Use three No. 3 (⅜-inch, or 9.3 mm., round) reinforcing bars lengthwise and wire them to three reinforcing bars 16 inches (40 cm.) long crosswise.

A suggested mix is 1:2:2¼ parts of cement, sand, and gravel, in that order. Gravel should be screened to ¾-inch (1.9-cm.) diameter but no larger. Five cubic feet (3.8 cu. meters) of concrete will make the seat slab and two end supports.

Assemble oiled forms on an oiled wood base or on concrete slab that has been covered with a polyethylene sheet. Place a 2-inch (5-cm.) layer of concrete in the seat form. Work the con-

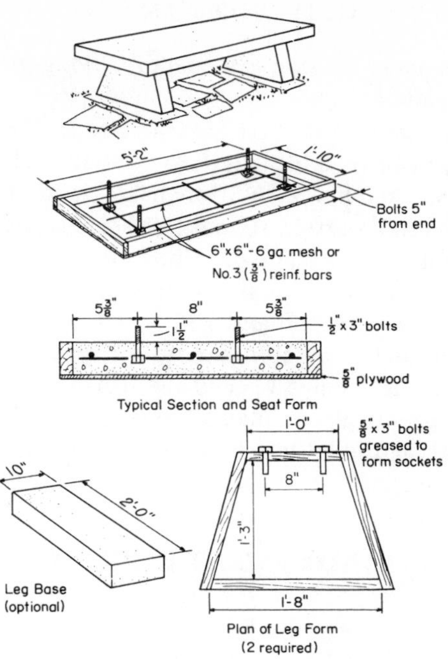

Fig. 4. Forms for casting a simple lawn bench in three parts.

crete carefully along the inside edge of the form with a trowel so that it is tight against the form. Level the concrete, then place the reinforcing bars as shown in Fig. 4. Add concrete to the top of the forms and strike it off level with a 2 × 4 (5 × 10 cm.), using a sawing motion. Smooth the surface with a wood float. Allow the mixture to stiffen, and after the watery sheen has gone, use a steel trowel for the finish. Use an edging tool around the form to obtain a smooth dense well-rounded edge.

PLANTERS

For all-year use or just for a season, attractive concrete masonry or concrete split block planters add a dramatic, colorful touch to living enjoyment.

Indoors or out, versatile concrete gives a handsome, rugged appearance that fits in well with decorating plans. A planter near your doorway (Fig. 5) is a friendly, living greeting to your friends and guests.

Choose the design that best fits your needs. The long, low silhouette of split block adds length to the outward appearance of your home. Stacked 8- × 8- × 16-inch (20- × 20- × 40-cm.) block can be placed in a pattern to make either vertical or horizontal lines stand out. Screen block or grille block in combination with regular units of concrete make interesting patterns and unique arrangements. (*See* Figs. 6 and 7.)

In constructing a *planter box,* make sure you have a firm foundation strong enough to hold the weight of the planter and the soil it contains. If live plants are placed in the box, provide *weep holes* along the bottom of the planter to allow excess moisture to run out.

SAND-CEMENT PAINTINGS

Sand paintings were produced hundreds of years ago by Indians of the Southwest as a visual history of great events. Today's modern art trend is *painting on a mortar base.* For an original work of art that will be the center of conversation for you and

Fig. 5. Slump block planter with decorative tree adds life to entrance area.

Fig. 6. Cone-shaped planters provide geometric interest in colorful corner.

Fig. 7. Flowers, shrubs, even small trees can be grown in planters around your home.

Fig. 8. Place the mix in the form and smooth with trowel.

Fig. 9. Use tools or fingers to form a picture outline.

Fig. 10. Moist cure for at least six days, then paint with oil colors.

your friends, try this unique hobby. You will quickly see how much fun it is and how easy it is to express your artistic feeling in concrete. Just follow these simple steps (*see* Figs. 8, 9, and 10):

1. Nail metal lath (expanded metal) to a sheet of ½-inch (1.3-cm.) plywood cut to the size of the finished picture.
2. Frame with wood molding to form a shallow tray to hold the wet concrete.
3. Use one part white portland cement, one-quarter part lime, and three parts sharp, clean white sand with water for a stiff, workable mix.
4. Place the mix in the form and smooth it with a trowel.
5. Use fingers, spoons, or modeling tools to form a picture outline for a three-dimensional view. For special effects, embed stones, wood, cloth, and other materials in the fresh concrete mix.
6. Moist cure the concrete for at least six days. When it is dry, use regular artists' oil colors to finish the painting.

Chapter 49

Miscellaneous Concrete Projects

It doesn't matter how modest the home is or limited the space in lawn or garden, concrete finds practical application. Furthermore, utilitarian and decorative improvements made with concrete are decidedly economical in first cost, durable, rotproof, firesafe—and practically maintenance-free.

COLD FRAMES AND HOTBEDS

Garden and flower transplants can easily be raised right at home in your own hotbed or cold frame. The two structures are very similar. However, hotbed walls usually extend about 3 feet (91 cm.) below the ground level to hold a deep layer of manure as in Fig. 1. No manure is used in cold frames but the soil should be a sandy loam.

Simple concrete construction such as precast panels or cast-in-place walls and floors makes a lasting structure which is free

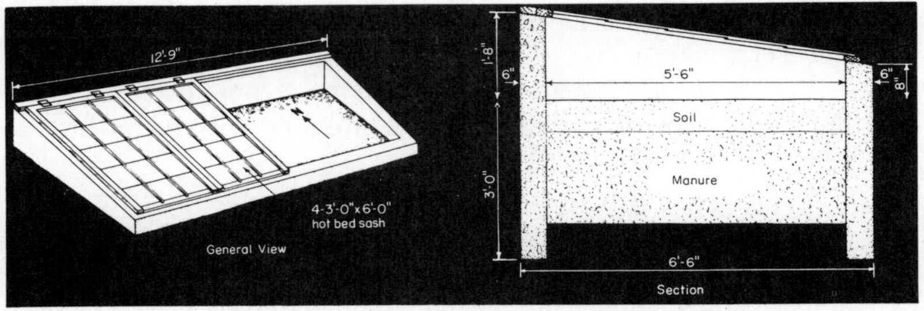

Fig. 1. Cross-section of hotbed made of cast-in-place concrete.

from decay and insect damage. (*See* Chap. 14, Precast Concrete.)

A southern exposure to full sunlight is recommended and protection from the wind as well as good drainage must be provided. Make the pits in multiples of 3 feet (91 cm.) which is the width of a standard hotbed sash. For a four-sash bed, the outside dimensions would be 6 feet 6 inches by 12 feet (1.9 × 3.7 meters). Check with a local supply house for available sizes of storm or barn and utility sash. A wood strip anchored in the top edge of the frame permits hinging of the sash.

The sides of a hotbed or cold frame may be precast on a flat surface in forms as shown in Fig. 2. Sub-surface watering can be economically accomplished by making grooves in the concrete bottom with a piece of 2-inch (5-cm.) pipe.

A ½-inch (1.3-cm.) elbow is set into the concrete with the open end directed toward the groove. An 8-inch (20-cm.) length of ½-inch (1.3-cm.) pipe is screwed into the upright opening of the elbow. Use a funnel to pour water into the top of the ½-inch (1.3-cm.) pipe.

INCINERATORS

Unsightly trash and rubbish can be removed easily if you follow these simple plans for a *cast-in-place concrete incinerator.*

Make the burner at least 2 feet 8 inches (8.5 cm.) square. Place

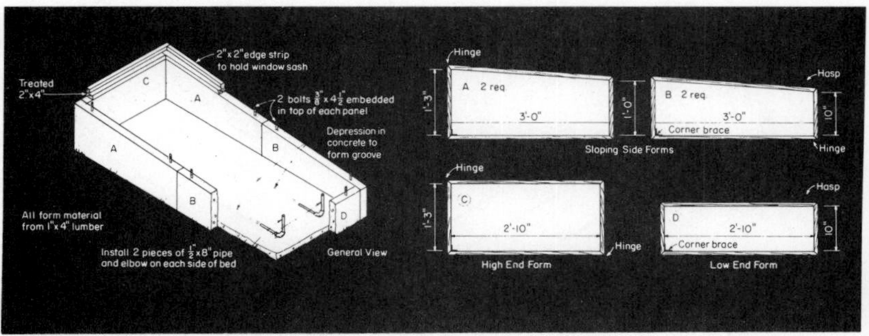

Fig. 2. Form details for precast concrete wall panels for cold frame.

bolts to hold the grate at the desired level. Use a heavy metal grating. By making provision for a grate near the top of the burner, the burner can sometimes double as a barbecue pit. (*See* Fig. 3.)

SIGN POSTS AND CLOTHESLINE POSTS

Part of Americana may be found in unique names of farms, ranches, and homes. Show off your place with an attractive sign on a sturdy concrete post. Your entryway is often the first view your friends and neighbors get of your place. Make this a memorable occasion with a colorful, descriptive sign. Posts are 11 feet 6 inches (3.5 meters) long to allow at least 3 to 3½ feet (.9 to 1.1 meters) to be put in the ground for firm anchorage. Often, a sign

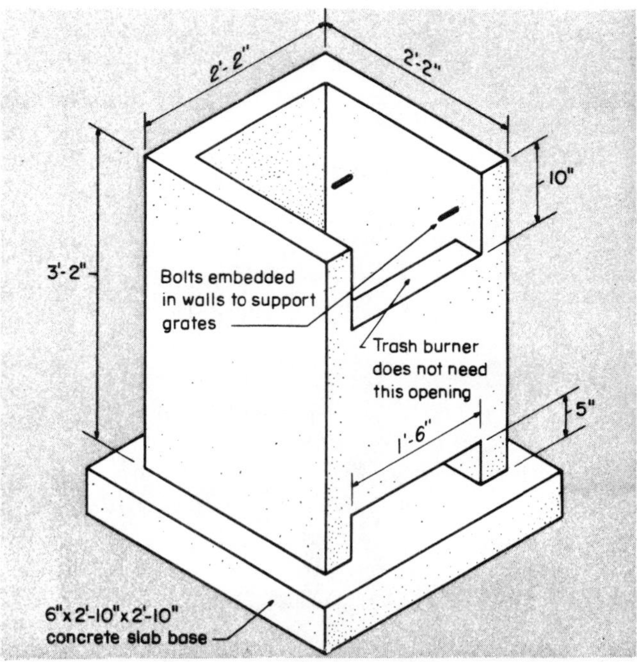

Fig. 3. Details of concrete trash burner.

with an RFD or house number can be combined with an outdoor lamp post. For suggestions on lamp posts see the section later in this chapter.

Concrete sign posts (Fig. 4) and *backyard clothesline posts* (Fig. 5) can be made with the same forms. Only the length differs, with the clothesline post being 10 feet (3 meters) overall.

Forms of 1- × 6- or 2- × 6-inch (2.5- × 15- or 5- × 15-cm.) lumber are used to make a 5⅝-inch (14-cm.) square post. Four No. 3 (⅜-inch or 9.3 mm.) reinforcing bars are placed in the forms as shown in Figs. 4 and 5. For a pleasing appearance, quarter-round molding or triangular strips rounded at the ends may be placed in the corner of the forms extending the length of the upper 8 feet (2.4 meters) of the forms. This gives a beveled edge to the post.

Holes for the hanger arms or cross-arms are formed in the concrete posts at the location shown by inserting (¾-inch or 1.9-cm.) dowels in the forms. Mortise the 4- × 4-inch (10- × 10-cm.) wooden cross pieces as shown, and when the post is ready, assemble it with ½-inch (1.3-cm.) galvanized machine bolts.

Use a concrete mix of the approximate proportions of 1:2:2¼. Use gravel of ½-inch (1.3-cm.) maximum size. White portland cement with white aggregates are often used to get a pure white post that needs no painting. Use a reasonably stiff mix, placing it carefully in the oiled forms. Be sure not to dislocate the reinforcing bars during placing. Spade the concrete well along the sides of the forms and around all corners. Tap the forms lightly with a hammer to release any trapped air bubbles. Leave the post forms in place for at least 24 hours.

After stripping forms, any imperfections in the post can be fixed by working a cement-sand mortar into the imperfection with a wood float. Wrap the post with polyethylene or waterproof paper and moist-cure for at least six days.

MAILBOX POST

Many attractive *concrete mailbox posts* dot the countryside giving evidence to the long-lasting qualities of concrete. The

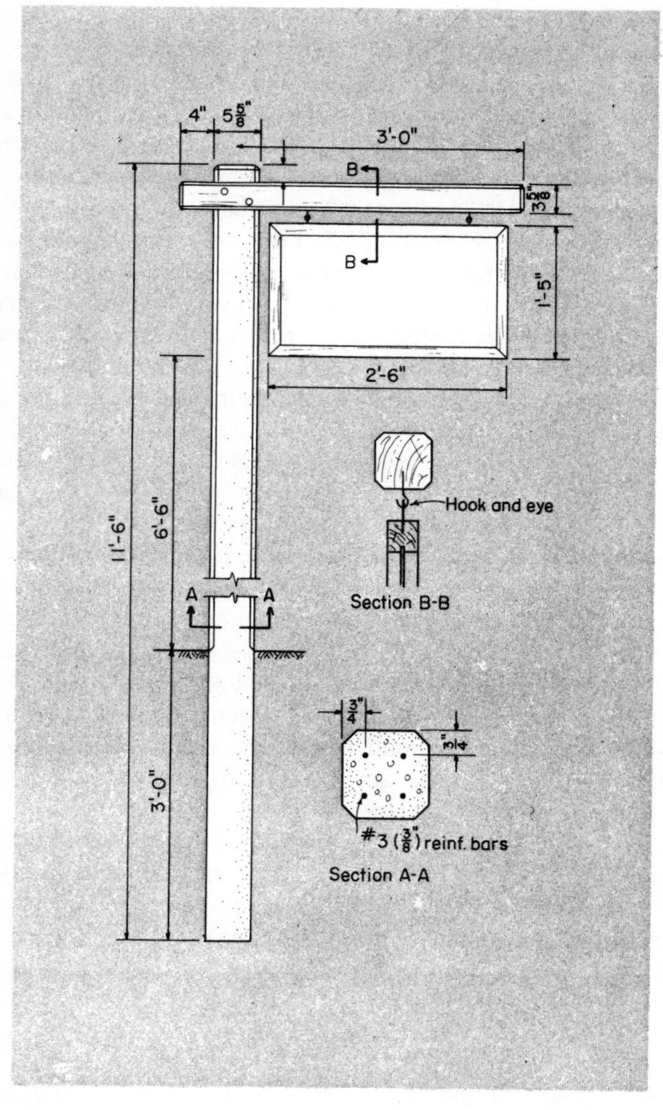

Fig. 4. Concrete sign post.

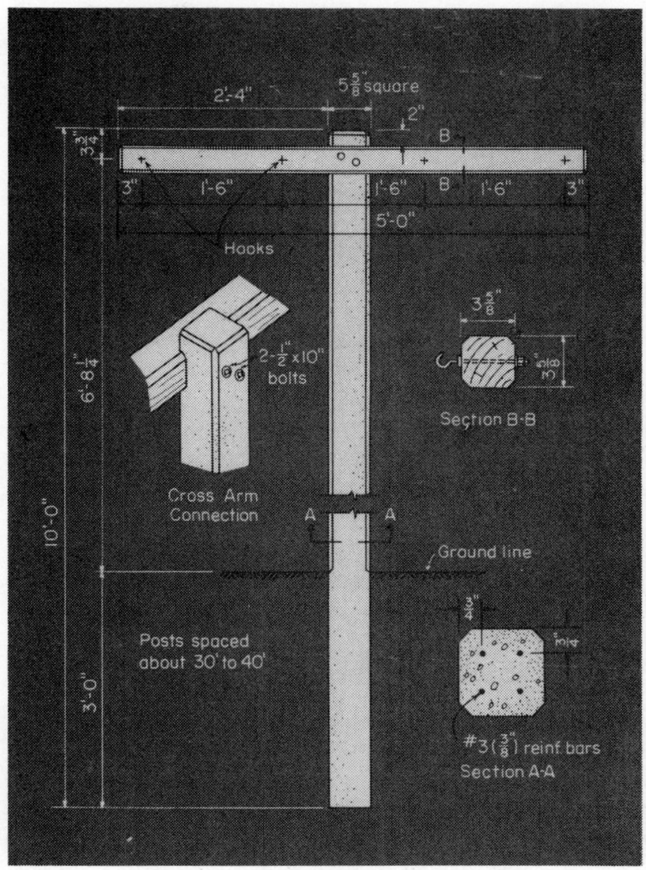

Fig. 5. Concrete clothesline post.

mailbox post shown in Fig. 6 can be moved from place to place.

One or several posts may be made at a time depending upon the form assembly. Use 2 × 4 (5 × 10 cm.) end and side forms on an oiled wood base supported by 2 × 6 (10 × 15 cm.) cleats. (*See* Fig. 6.) Use four pieces of No. 2 (¼-inch or 6.3-mm.) reinforcing bars, two pieces 4 feet 4 inches (1.3 meters) long, and two pieces

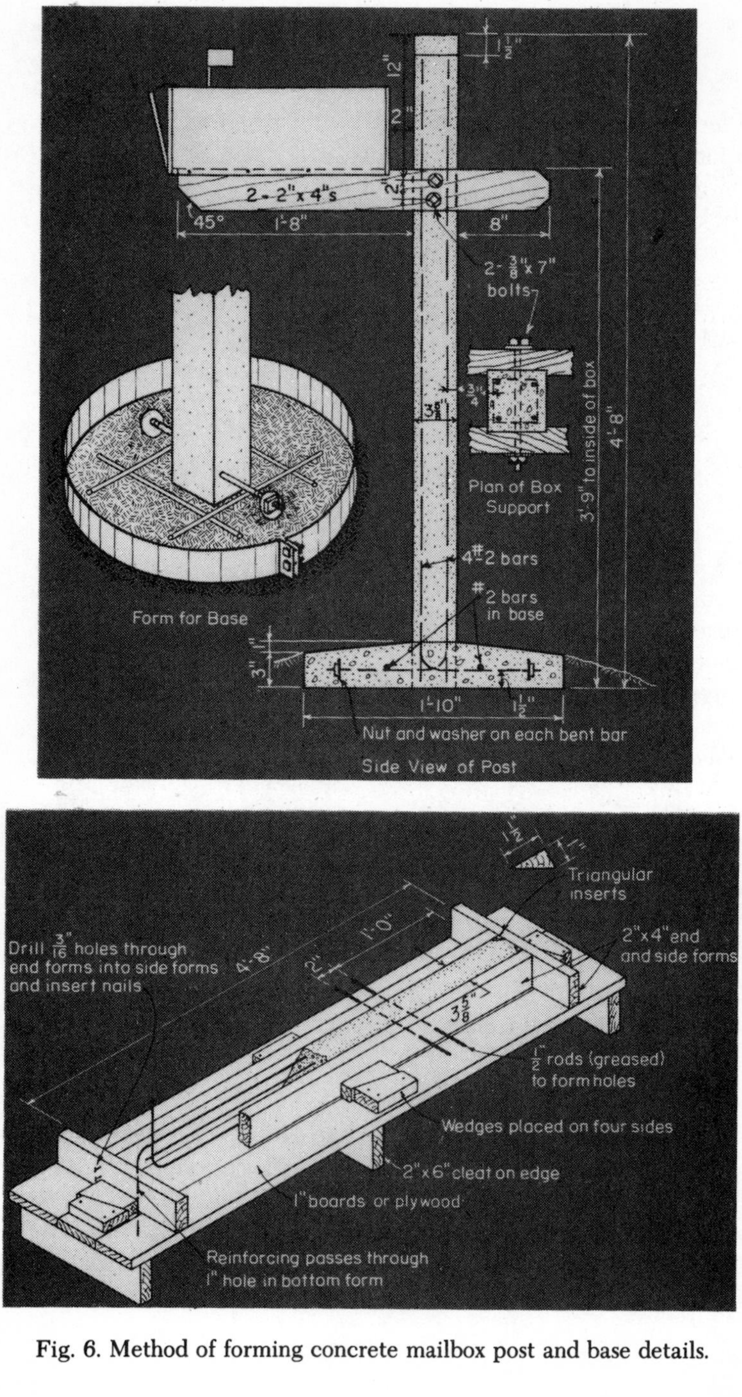

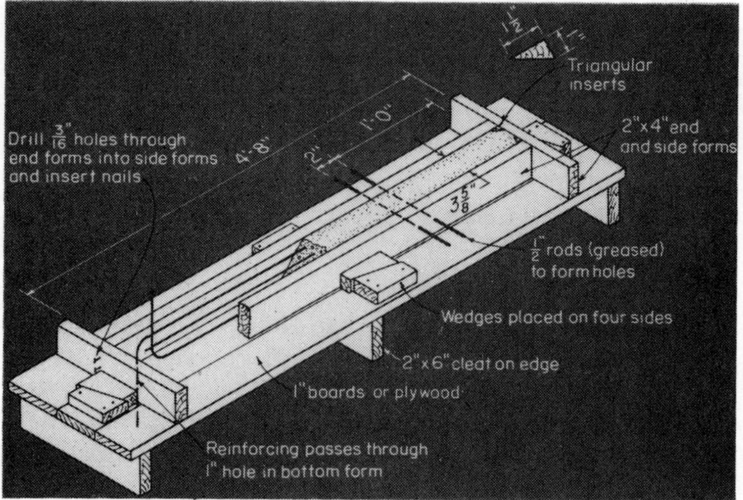

Fig. 6. Method of forming concrete mailbox post and base details.

4 feet 11 inches (1.5 meters) long. Each of the longer pieces has a 9-inch (22.5-cm.) right angle bend at one end. One bent bar goes through a hole in the form in the down position, and the other sticks up as shown in Fig. 6. Place the straight pieces as illustrated.

Follow the procedure for casting the post as previously described in the section on Sign Posts. Note the position of the steel rods which form holes for cross-arms to support the mailbox. These are greased and removed after the concrete stiffens. Moist-cure the post for six days.

If a circular base is desired, set the cured post in a base form as shown in Fig. 6. Position No. 2 (¼-inch or 6.3-mm.) 1 foot 4 inch (41 cm.) reinforcing bars on four sides of the bar as shown in Fig. 6. Mark the post 1 inch (2.5 cm.) up from the top of the base form so that the concrete will slope from this point to the edge. Center and plumb the post in the circular base. Use concrete mixed to the same proportions as that used for the post, and fill the base to a point marked on the post. Slope the concrete to the edge of the circular form. Wet-cure the base for at least six days. Cut and mortise the wooden supports as shown in Fig. 6, and fasten them to the post after curing.

Mailbox flanges fit over the outside of the wooden supports. Your name, address, and box number painted on the box completes the project. The post and stand weigh approximately 150 pounds (68 kgs.) and can be rolled into position near the road. Remove the sod if you desire to set the base flush with the ground level.

ORNAMENTAL LAMP POST

With the resurgence of decorative yard lights for rural and suburban homes, the *ornamental lamp post* has gained wide favor.

A warm and friendly greeting of light is made possible with this concrete improvement. A light to show steps, walks, and entryways at night is an important safety precaution for your family and friends.

With a minimum of effort, you can have a distinctive, useful lamp post which will be serviceable for years to come. It can be easily formed with clean, sharp, modern lines, or made as decorative as you like.

Forms of 1- × 6-inch (2.5- × 15-cm.) lumber are cut to the length of post desired. Heavy grained wood forms leave a pleasing pattern on the finished concrete post. For a more refined appearance, the upper portion of the form should have triangular strips rounded on the ends nailed to the inside of the form as shown in Fig. 7.

A ¾-inch (1.9-cm.) diameter pipe is centered to extend the length of the lamp post. No other reinforcement is needed. A shoulder and collar are formed on the post to receive the orna-

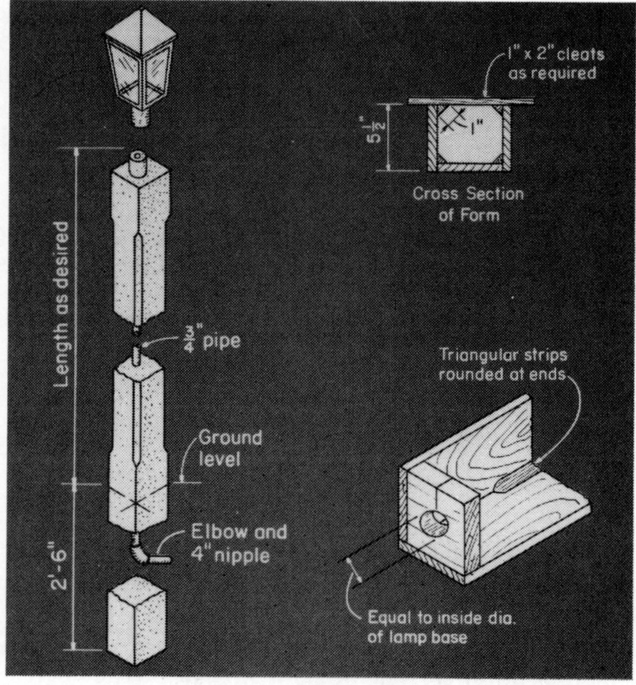

Fig. 7. Concrete lamp post for either electrical or gas connection.

mental lamp base.

Follow the procedures for placing and curing posts as previously outlined in the section on Sign Posts.

CONCRETE LOADING RAMPS

Loading and unloading of cattle and hogs, heavy machinery, and implements can be greatly simplified and speeded if a *loading ramp* is available. Construction of a permanent and practical loading ramp is shown in Fig. 8. If the ramp is to be used principally for loading and unloading livestock it is most convenient to build it in, or adjacent to, one of the fenced lots in the barnyard. In such cases the ramp is usually fenced as shown in Fig. 9.

Where the ramp is to be used only for loading of livestock it may be built 6 feet (1.8 meters) wide, outside dimensions, which provides a clear passage about 4 feet (1.2 meters) wide. Where

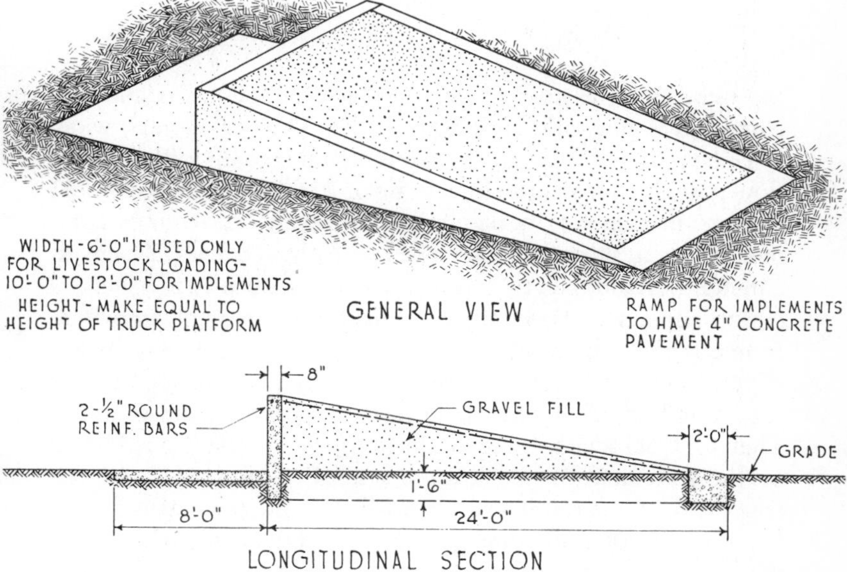

Fig. 8. Method of building concrete loading ramp. If the ramp is used for loading livestock it is usually fenced as shown in Fig. 9.

Fig. 9. A fenced ramp.

the ramp is to be used for loading heavy implements and machinery it is generally built 10 to 12 feet (3 to 3.6 meters) wide.

To be most convenient, the ramp should be built with a gentle slope, usually not steeper than a rise of 1 foot in a length of 6 feet (16 cm. in a meter) horizontally. However, farm ramps commonly vary in slope from one foot vertically in 8 feet (12.5 cm. in a meter) horizontally, to slopes of one foot vertically in 5 feet (20 cm. in a meter) horizontally. Height of ramp may be anywhere from 36 to 48 inches (90 to 120 cm.) depending upon the height of the truck platform. The ramp is usually made of such height that it will accommodate the largest trucks which are to use it. Then for trucks with lower platforms pieces of plank may be laid on the pavement on the loading side of the ramp to raise the truck floor to the ramp level. A small concrete pavement for the loading side of the ramp as shown in Fig. 8 prevents truck wheels from bogging down under heavy loads or in soft earth. Construction of forms and placing and finishing of concrete for the ramp walls are accomplished in much the same manner as described in Chap. 41, Footings, and Chap. 42, Foundation Walls and Piers.

SMALL FARM BRIDGES

A makeshift bridge is dangerous at best and requires constant and annoying repairs. It should be replaced with a strong, dependable concrete structure as shown in Fig. 10. A *farm bridge* should be designed to take loads up to 6 tons (5.45 metric tons). This is adequate for most farm requirements, such as trucks, livestock, and farm machinery. It is especially important to extend the bridge abutments to a depth of about 2 feet (60 cm.) below the level of the creek bed or ditch bottom to prevent undermining by washing.

Concrete for the deck slab is supported on a platform of 1-inch (2.5-cm.) form boards fastened to 2 × 6 (5 × 15 cm.) joists. The joists are supported on 4 × 4's (10 × 10 cm.) or larger timbers. (*See* Table 36.) These timbers in turn are supported on shoring which is wedged and braced firmly in position. Building forms for the concrete abutments is much the same procedure as described for foundation walls in Chap. 7, Forms and Form Making. (*See* Fig. 11.) Construction of the bridge should be completed during dry weather, if possible, when the stream or ditch water level is low.

CONCRETE FENCE POSTS

Making *concrete posts* is an interesting job and one which produces useful, economical, lasting improvements. Concrete posts cannot burn, rot, or rust. A fence built with concrete posts is virtually free from upkeep expense. Millions of concrete posts are in use on farms and other areas in this country.

Concrete posts last indefinitely. This is attested to by the fact that hundreds of concrete posts are in excellent condition after more than 25 years of service and promise to give good service for many more years. (*See* Figs. 12 and 13.)

Metal molds are most satisfactory for casting concrete posts if large numbers are to be built.

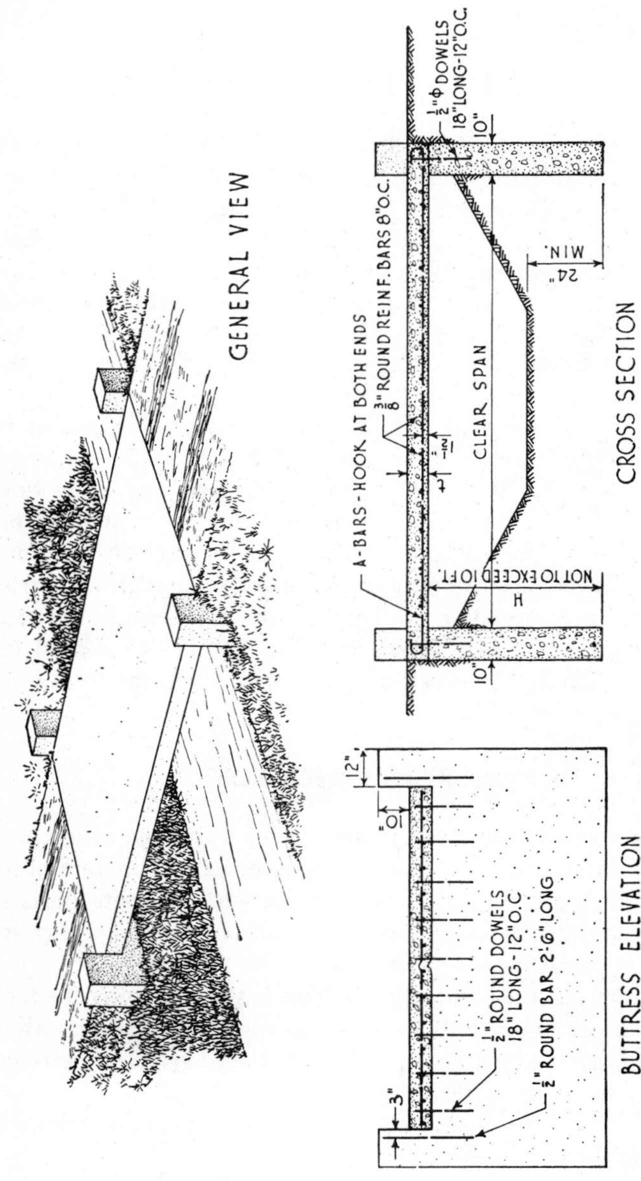

Fig. 10. Suggested plans for a small farm bridge.

Clear span in feet	Thickness of slab in inches	Size and spacing of "A" bars required in slab
6	5½	⅝-in. round reinf. bars 8 in. o.c.
9	6½	⅝-in. round reinf. bars 7 in. o.c.
12	7	¾-in. round reinf. bars 8 in. o.c.
15	8	¾-in. round reinf. bars 7 in. o.c.

*All transverse reinforcing bars are ⅜-in. rounds placed 8 in. on centers.

TABLE 36. DIMENSIONS AND REINFORCEMENT FOR SMALL FARM BRIDGE.*

Fig. 11. This slab bridge is typical of many farm bridges which provide lasting repair-free service.

Fig. 12. Concrete posts.

Fig. 13. Concrete posts for heavily laden grape vines.

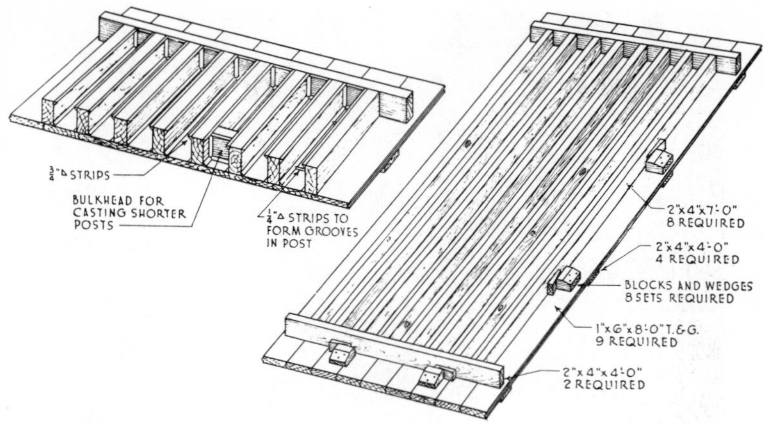

Fig. 14. Details of mold for concrete fence posts.

Where only a moderate number of posts are being built, however, a simple gang mold as shown in Fig. 14 will prove satisfactory. A one-sack batch of concrete makes seven of the 7-foot (2.1-meters) posts; thus a gang mold for casting seven posts is convenient. Shorter posts are made by inserting bulkheads in the form as shown in Fig. 14.

Molds should be assembled on a flat surface which has been painted with oil or covered with two or three layers of heavy, waterproof paper. Molds should be thoroughly coated with clean, thin oil before and after each use.

For a heavy-duty concrete post, four ¼-inch (6.3-mm.) round reinforcing bars are used, one placed near each corner. (*See* Fig. 15.) However, a post which will meet average requirements may be reinforced with four No. 6 wires. The reinforcing bars or wires should be covered with not less than ¾ inch (1.9 cm.) of concrete. If placed closer to the surface, reinforcement may rust, causing the concrete to spall and thus shorten the life of the post.

Two of the reinforcing bars or wires for each post are cut 12 inches (30 cm.) shorter than the length of the post and placed with the ends 6 inches (15 cm.) from the top and bottom ends of the post. The other two bars or wires need to be only 3 feet (91 cm.) long, placed to extend from a point 18 inches (45 cm.)

Fig. 15. These massive concrete entrance posts provide permanent support for the gate and enhance the beauty of the grounds.

below the ground line to a point 18 inches (45 cm.) above it. Bars of equal length should be placed diagonally opposite each other.

The ¼-inch (6.3-mm.) triangular strips to form grooves in the post should be placed as required, depending upon fence wire spacing to be used (Fig. 16). Where posts should be adaptable to various wire spacings, the groove strips may be placed on 9-inch (22.5-cm.) centers from the ground line (2 feet 6 inches—76 cm.—from the lower end) to a point 18 inches (45 cm.) above the ground line, and then on 3-inch (7.5-cm.) centers to the top of the post.

In erecting a *fence*, the wire ties hold the fence wires securely in the grooves (Fig. 17). Line posts should be set at least 2 feet (60 cm.) into the ground; 2 feet 6 inches (76 cm.) is better. Corner posts should be well braced and set at least 3½ feet (1.1 meters) into the ground.

Posts are set in two ways—in holes dug to receive them or, if of small diameter, they can be driven with a special driving sleeve made from a piece of pipe of somewhat larger diameter

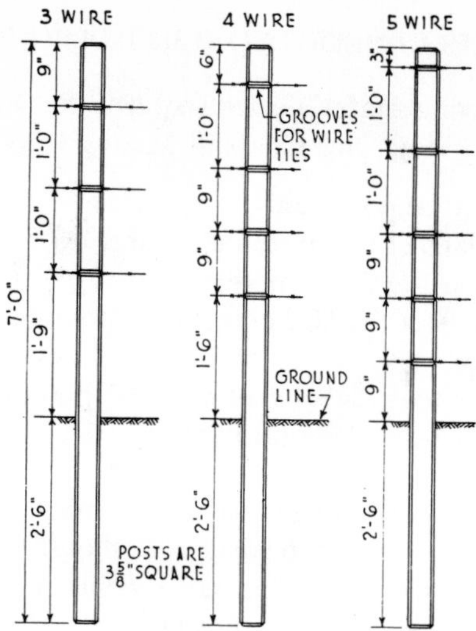

Fig. 16. Standard wire spacing for barbed wire fences.

Fig. 17. Method of fastening fence wire in the grooves in concrete posts.

than the post and about 3 feet (91 cm.) long. One end of the pipe is capped and cushioned by inserting an oak driving block. This method saves much time and labor in setting posts, particularly in soft or wet soils. Concrete fence posts are usually spaced one rod (16½ feet or 5.03 meters) apart.

The suggested concrete mix is 1 sack portland cement to 4 gallons (15.14 liters) water to 1¾ cubic feet (.05 cu. meters) average wet sand to 2 cubic feet gravel (¾-inch or 1.9-cm. maximum size). The following materials are required for 100 posts each 7 feet (2.1 meters) long. (*See* Chap. 4, Mixing Concrete.)

21 sacks portland cement
1⅓ cubic yard (1.04 cu. meters) sand
1½ cubic yard (1.2 cu. meters) gravel
1,800 linear feet (548.6 meters) (177 pounds or 80.3 kgs. No. 6 wire) or
1,800 linear feet (548.6 meters) (300 pounds or 136.1 kgs.) ¼-inch (6.4-mm.) round bars

After concrete in the forms has been struck off and troweled lightly to make a smooth top surface, it should be left to harden for at least 48 hours, longer in cold weather. Molds are then taken apart and the new concrete posts are stored in a shaded place where they should be kept constantly wet by sprinkling for at least ten days. Posts should be at least one month old before being hauled away and set in place.

CORNER POSTS AND GATE POSTS

Corner posts, end posts, and *gate posts* are made heavier and stronger than other posts to resist the greater strains imposed upon them. Corner post construction is shown in Fig. 18. End posts and corner posts may be of similar design except that the concrete brace is needed on only one side of the end post.

In most soils the earth walls of the excavation may be used for forms below ground level. The trench for the concrete brace and the hole for the post should be dug at least 3½ feet (1.1 meters) deep. The trench can usually be kept narrow and true if dug with a tiling spade or other narrow spade. Forms needed above ground level are shown in Fig. 18. The ¾-inch (1.9-cm.) triangular strips for lining corners of the form help make an attractive post with smooth beveled corners. If desired, quarter-round molding or cove molding may be used for this purpose. Decorative fluting for gate posts at the entrance may be provided by fastening triangular strips to the form faces in any one of a variety of patterns.

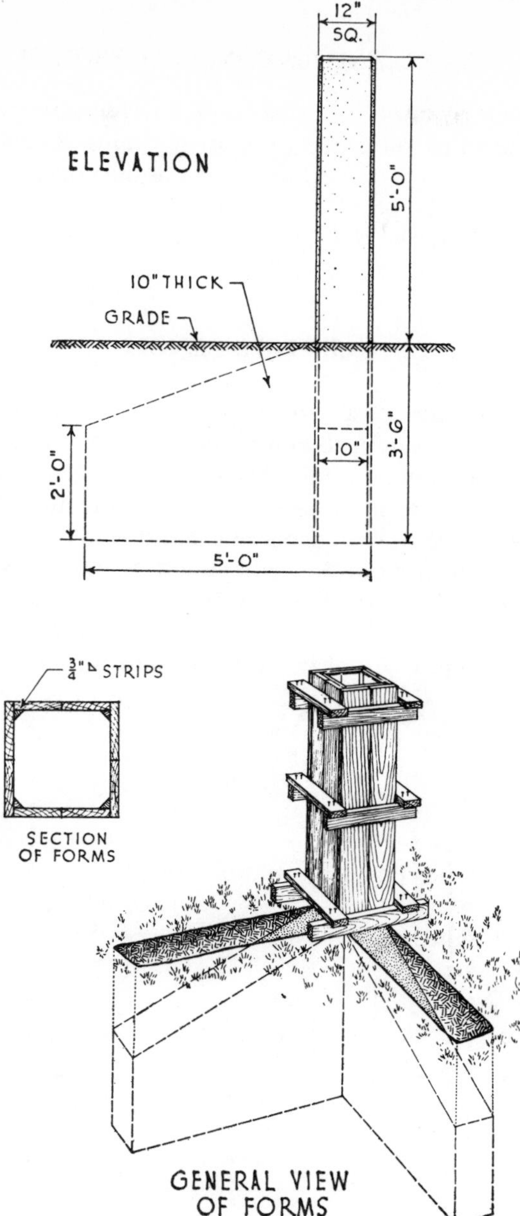

Fig. 18. Form construction for concrete corner posts and end posts.

Heavy corner posts ordinarily do not need reinforcement, but if they are to be subjected to unusual strains, ½-inch (1.3-cm.) round reinforcing bars may be placed in the concrete, one near each corner of the post. There should be at least 1 inch (2.5 cm.) of concrete between the reinforcing bars and the surface of the concrete.

ELECTRIC FENCES

Concrete fence posts are well suited for one- or two-wire *electric fences.* As with all other types of posts, the electric fence wire must be insulated from the post. A satisfactory method for fastening the wire is shown in Fig. 19. Insulators of the type shown in Fig. 18 are not expensive and should be used to assure dependable operation. A single strand of barbed wire is generally most satisfactory, the wire being placed at a height equal to three-fourths the height of the animal to be fenced in. Posts for electric fences are of two types as shown in illustration.

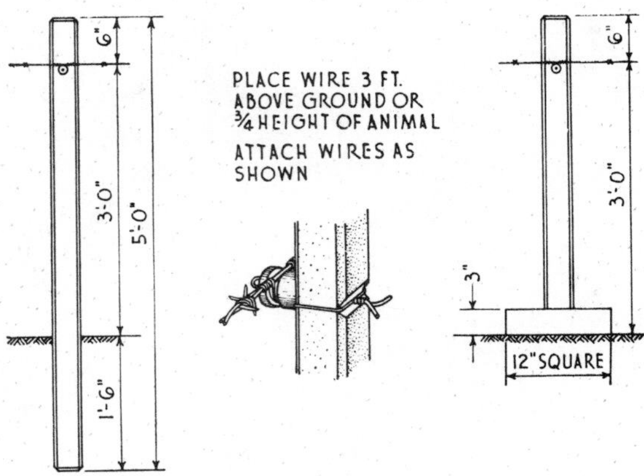

Fig. 19. Concrete posts for electric fences. Electric fence wire should be insulated from posts in this manner.

VINEYARD POSTS

Concrete posts for vineyards may also be made in gang molds of the type shown in Fig. 14. Length of posts and materials required are the same as for all standard fence posts except end posts (Fig. 20). Line posts are provided with holes through which smooth wires are threaded. The holes are formed (about 14 inches or 35 cm. on centers) by inserting ¼-inch (6.3 mm.) greased dowels or bolts in the fresh concrete when the posts are cast. End posts should be well braced and reinforced with four ⅜-inch (9.5 mm.) round bars. Vineyard posts are commonly set about two feet (60 cm.) in the ground and 12 to 16 feet (3.7 to 4.9 meters) apart.

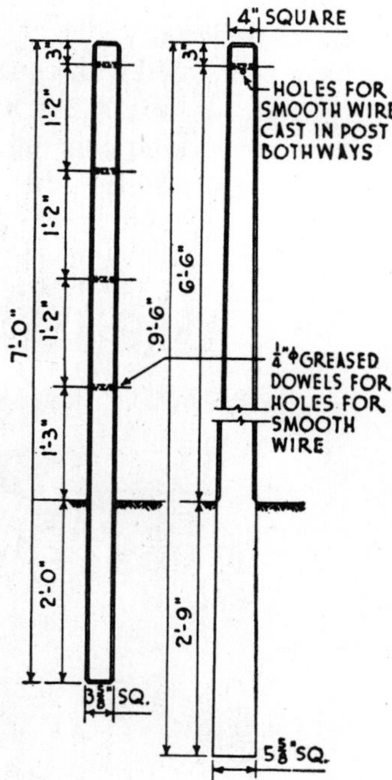

Fig. 20. Common dimensions of vineyard posts.

MILK COOLING TANKS

An *insulated milk cooling tank* (Fig. 21) is usually employed where milk regulations specify that milk be cooled rapidly to 50° F. (10° C.) or lower. Size of tank required may be determined from Table 37.

Construction of the insulated cooling tank is illustrated in Fig. 22. The concrete base slab 4 inches (10 cm.) thick is placed, then tank forms and insulation are installed. The overflow pipe and other pipes are placed before concreting begins. In northern areas, drain pipes should be laid below frost level. Only high-quality insulation board 3 inches (7.5 cm.) thick put up in vaporproofed packages should be used. When necessary to cut a package, exposed edges should be dipped repeatedly in hot asphalt to secure a thoroughly waterproof seal. Every caution must be taken to keep insulation dry.

When wall forms have been filled with concrete, anchor bolts for attaching the rim planks and the 2 × 2 (5 × 5 cm.) angle irons are set. Forms may be removed after concrete hardens for 24 to 48 hours. The new concrete should then be moist cured for at least 10 days.

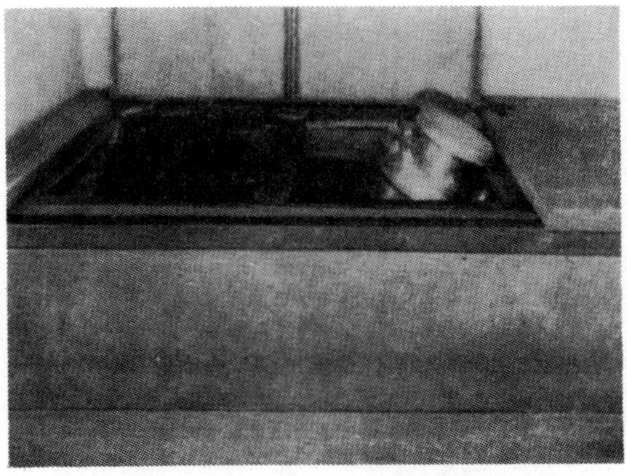

Fig. 21. The insulated cooling tank is economical to build and helps cool milk efficiently.

No. of 10-gal. cans tank holds	Inside length	Outside length
4	4 ft. 0 in.	5 ft. 8 in.
6	6 ft. 0 in.	7 ft. 8 in.
8	8 ft. 0 in.	9 ft. 8 in.

For each additional 2 cans, increase inside and outside length of tank 2 ft.

TABLE 37. DIMENSIONS OF INSULATED MILK COOLING TANKS.

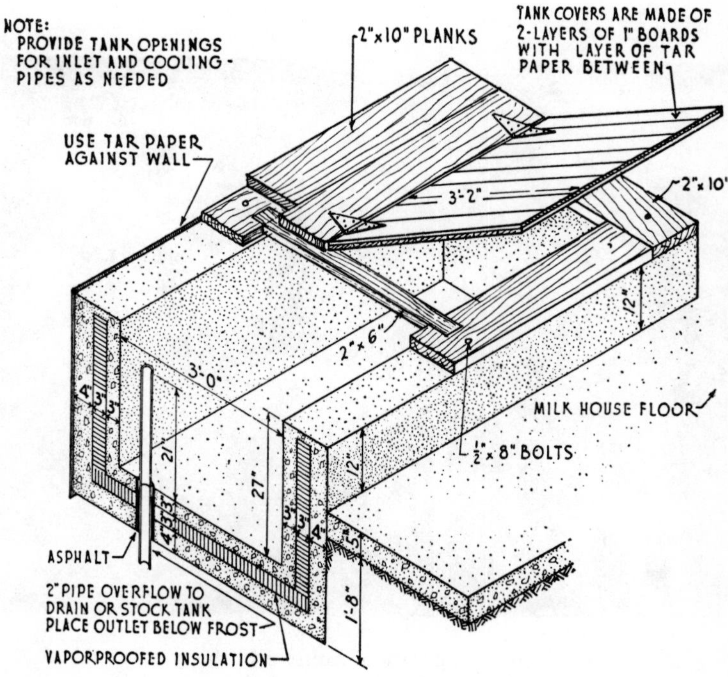

Fig. 22. Construction of insulated milk cooling tanks.

BULL PENS

A substantial *bull pen* or *paddock* which permits sunlight, exercise and safe confinement for the herd bull is considered a necessity on the modern dairy farm. General practice is to enclose a space about 20 × 80 feet (6 × 24.4 meters). Construction may be as shown in Figs. 23 and 24. Concrete posts are usually 8 or 10 inches (20 or 25 cm.) square and 8 feet (2.4 meters) long; ¾-inch (1.9-cm.) triangular strips are used to line corners of the post forms. The posts are set about 8 feet apart (2.4 meters) and 2½ feet (76 cm.) into the ground. Rails of 1½-inch (3.8-cm.) galvanized pipe are fastened to the posts with U bolts, or the pipes may better be cast in place along the centerline of the post as shown in Fig. 24.

Fig. 23. The herd sire gets plenty of exercise in this yard attached to a concrete masonry bull barn. The fence is solidly supported by concrete posts.

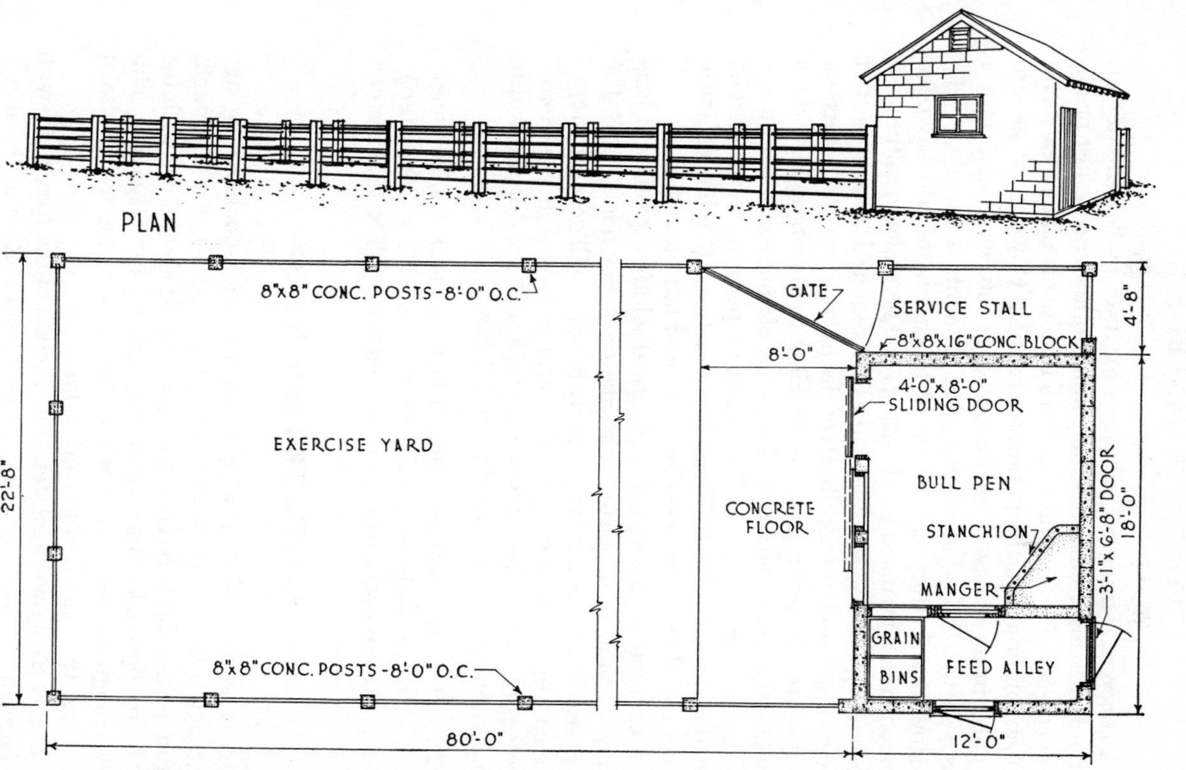

Fig. 24. Method of building a safe bull pen.

CONCRETE MANURE PITS

A *concrete manure pit* soon pays for itself by helping to conserve fertilizing elements which would otherwise be lost or destroyed. (*See* Fig. 25.) Farm manure is valuable chiefly for its nitrogen, phosphorus, and potassium content. However, if manure is piled in an unpaved yard exposed to sun, wind, and rain a large part of the valuable fertilizing elements is lost.

How this fertility can be saved to enrich the soil has been demonstrated by many good farmers and several agricultural experiment stations. Only two things are required to save most of the nitrogen and practically all of the phosphorus and potassium in manure: (1) generous use of bedding to absorb liquids which contain the larger part of the fertilizing elements, and (2) storage of manure in damp, well-compacted piles in a watertight, weather-protected pit. These two practices, if followed faithfully, will double the fertilizing value of farm manure.

A concrete manure pit is a practical solution to efficient handling of manure. Suggested construction is shown in Fig. 26. The increased value of manure properly handled will generally repay the cost of the pit during the first year or two of its use. A concrete pit is built 4 feet (1.6 meters) high with lengths and widths to accommodate the size of herd as follows:

10 cows—16 feet wide, 16 feet long (4.9 × 4.9 meters)
20 cows—18 feet wide, 26 feet long (5.5 × 7.9 meters)
40 cows—24 feet wide, 40 feet long (7.3 × 12.2 meters)

CONCRETE TRENCH SILOS

A generous and dependable supply of high-quality roughage through winter months and through periods of severe drought often makes the difference between success and failure with the dairy or livestock enterprise. Corn, hay, or cane silages are valuable roughages which can readily be put into the trench silo at low cost to assure ample feed supplies.

Figure 27 shows suggested construction of the *trench silo* with a permanent concrete lining for best preservation of the silage.

Fig. 25. Fertilizing value of farm manure can be increased 100 percent by proper storage and handling.

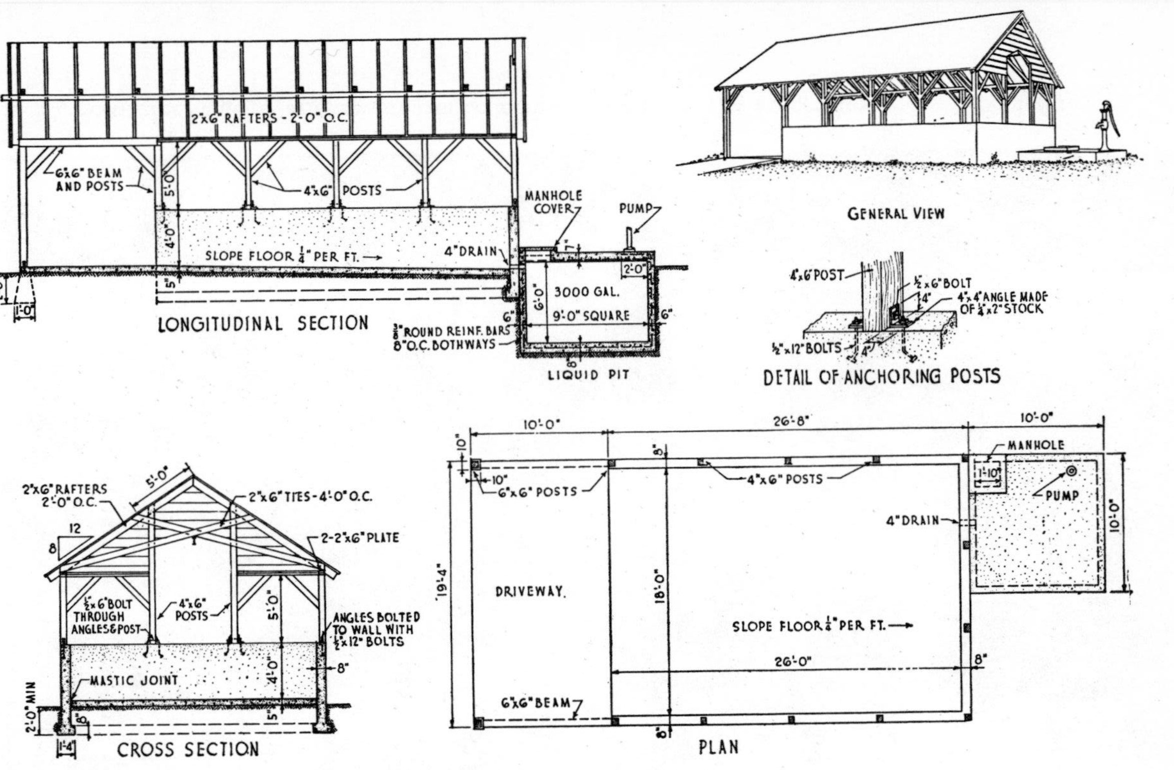

Fig. 26. Plans for concrete manure pit with liquid tank.

Fig. 27. Typical trench silo with cast-in-place concrete walls.

Although the trench silo is often used without lining, experience shows that in most silos it is necessary to install a concrete or other masonry lining within a few seasons. Otherwise the earth banks begin to slough away causing spoiled feed and great inconvenience in handling the silage.

Where underground drainage is excellent some prefer to apply a 3-inch (7.5-cm.) coating of portland cement plaster to the sides of the trench, this coating being reinforced with heavy hog wire or ¼-inch (6.3-mm.) round reinforcing bars spaced 12 inches (30 cm.) on centers each way. (*See* Fig. 28.) A concrete floor is almost a necessity, to permit convenient hauling out of the trench during wet weather. A roof is not ordinarily considered necessary where the trench is lined with concrete. Common practice is to cover the silage in the trench, first with 4 to 6 inches (10 to 15 cm.) of wet straw, then with about the same thickness of dirt. Well-compacted silage of proper moisture content keeps in good condition with this covering.

If possible the trench silo should be located on well-drained sloping ground near the barn or feed lots. Drainage around the trench is further improved by filling and sloping the banks of the trench as shown in Fig. 29. Earth is usually excavated and moved with a slip scraper or Fresno. The concrete floor of the

Fig. 28. A trench silo with portland cement plastered walls.

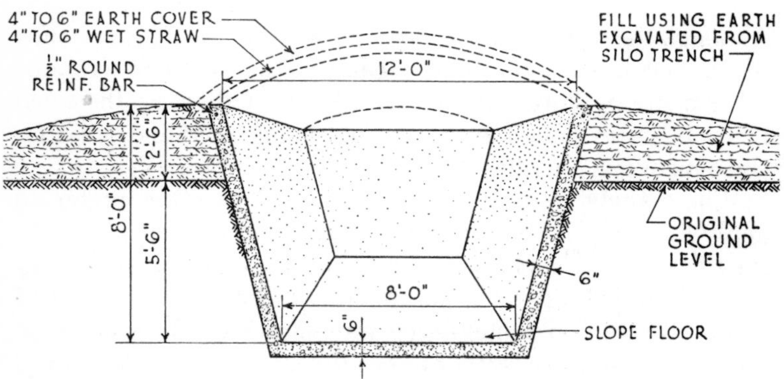

Fig. 29. Cross-section of typical concrete trench silo.

trench silo should be sloped at least ¼ inch per foot (2 cm. per meter) to drain.

Size of trench silo to build may be determined from Table 38. Trench silo capacities in this table are based on filling with mature corn silage of average moisture content which when compacted weighs about 35 pounds per cubic foot (560.6 kgs. per cu. meter). The amount of silage needed, as shown in Table 38, is on the basis of feeding 35 pounds (15.9 kgs.) of silage per animal per day for a season of 180 days. In figuring the size of trench to build, however, it should be remembered that young stock often require additional tonnage equal to about one-half the amount provided for mature cattle. It may also be necessary to increase the size of the trench if it is planned to keep a reserve supply of feed in the silo to meet emergencies such as a severe drought.

Where silage is made from overly-mature corn put up rather dry, the size of the trench must be increased 10 to 20 percent to obtain required tonnages shown in Table 38. In case of immature corn, which is very well eared, the size of silo can be decreased 10 to 15 percent for tonnages shown in Table 38.

No. of cows or 2-year-old steers	Tons of silage needed	Width in feet		Length in feet
		Top	Bottom	
5	16	8	6	22
10	32	10	7	27
20	63	12	8	45
30	95	13	9	61
40	126	14	10	75
50	158	15	11	95
75	236	16	12	97
100	315	17	12	124

All silos to be 8 ft. deep except 5-cow size which is 6 ft. deep and silos for 75 and 100 head which are 10 ft. deep.

*Young stock often require additional tonnage equal to about one-half the amount provided for mature cattle. In such cases increase size of silo accordingly.

TABLE 38. SIZE OF TRENCH SILO TO BUILD* (ON BASIS OF CORN SILAGE, FEEDING 35 POUNDS OF SILAGE PER ANIMAL PER DAY FOR 180 DAYS AND WITH SILAGE AVERAGING 35 POUNDS PER CUBIC FOOT).

SMALL RETAINING WALLS

Retaining walls (Fig. 30) must be safe against overturning and sliding forward. The pressure under the toe (front bottom edge of the base) should not exceed the bearing power of the soil. The friction between the base and the soil on which it rests plus the pressure of the earth in front of the wall must be sufficient to keep it from sliding forward. In addition, the wall must be sufficiently strong to prevent failure at any point in its height due to pressure of the retained material. (*See* Table 39.)

It is desirable to have an engineer familiar with local conditions check the design of even small walls and where especially unfavorable soil conditions obtain, such as silt or quicksand or where piles are required under the wall, the services of an engineer are essential both in design and construction.

Types of retaining walls suitable for comparatively low heights are as follows: (1) The simple vertical face gravity wall,

Fig. 30. Concrete retaining walls give the property a trim, neat appearance as well as protect the land from costly and unsightly soil erosion.

Height in feet H	Width of footing in feet B	Cu.yd. concrete required per lin.ft. of wall
3	2½	0.2
4	3	0.3
6	4	0.6
8	5½	1.0

TABLE 39. DIMENSIONS OF RETAINING WALLS.

Fig. 31,A and B; (2) the backward leaning gravity wall, Fig. 32,A and B, Fig. 33,A and B; (3) the cantilever reinforced wall, Fig. 34,A and B.

The choice of type depends on a number of factors peculiar to the location that affect the cost, efficiency, and suitability of the different types. The relative cost of materials and labor in a given locality may determine the selection of a gravity or reinforced type. The reinforced type has a slightly lower toe pressure which may make it desirable where soil-bearing values are low. The gravity wall has, however, greater resistance to sliding because of its greater weight. The backward leaning wall is economical as to materials, but reduces the usable surface back of the wall. Retaining walls built at property lines or where their bases are fixed by physical conditions and where a maximum of usable surface area back of them is desired, should have a vertical face. The appearance of a backward leaning and vertical face may also influence the choice of type.

Construction

A footing offset of 6 inches (15 cm.) at the base is sufficient to support forms for the stem, and allows a close approach of the face of the wall to the property line.

Resistance to horizontal movement of the retaining wall by sliding is obtained by frictional resistance between base and foundation. Often a lug or offset under the base slab is provided to assist in resisting any tendency to slide. The same effect is achieved by requiring that the base slab be well below the ground surface. This requirement applies particularly to walls higher than 7 feet (2.1 meters) above the base. The base of the wall should be below the frostline.

Since gravity walls are stable because of their weight, no reinforcement is required in them. It is not necessary, therefore, to dowel the stem to the base with bars. It is satisfactory simply to form a *key-way* by casting a *V* groove in the base.

The stepped back as shown in Fig. 31 has the advantages of providing more openings for placement of concrete, and also does away with the tendency of the forms to *float.* The *treads* of the *steps* need not be formed. Quantities of materials are practically the same for both types.

Backward leaning walls having great enough inclination to cause them to tip backward before the filling is placed require a longer heel than vertical walls to make them stable. For inclinations greater than 20 degrees the length of heel required will be greater than those shown in Figs. 32 and 33. The forms should be braced to prevent backward tipping while the concrete is being placed and maintained in position until the concrete has thoroughly hardened.

Where the ground surface back of the wall is level, or nearly so, the wall should carry a railing for safety and appearance. Railings vary greatly and may be either precast or cast in place. Cast-in-place railing posts are anchored to the wall with reinforcement dowels. Precast posts may be anchored in the same manner, except that the dowels are cast in the posts and anchored in holes which are cast or drilled into the top of the wall and filled with mortar when the posts are set. Precast posts may also be anchored by means of flange plates held to the posts by bars or bolts embedded in them—the flange plates being anchored to the wall by means of anchor bolts or cinch anchors.

Excavation should be carried to firm ground and below the frostline. A depth of 3 feet (30 cm.) should be sufficient in moderate climates to eliminate the possibility of *heaving.*

Proper drainage of retaining walls should be provided. A layer of coarse stone 12 inches (30 cm.) thick should be placed against the back of the wall, and weep holes through the stem installed at frequent intervals along the base. Four-inch (10-cm.) diameter tile drains spaced about 10 feet (3 meters) apart are usually sufficient.

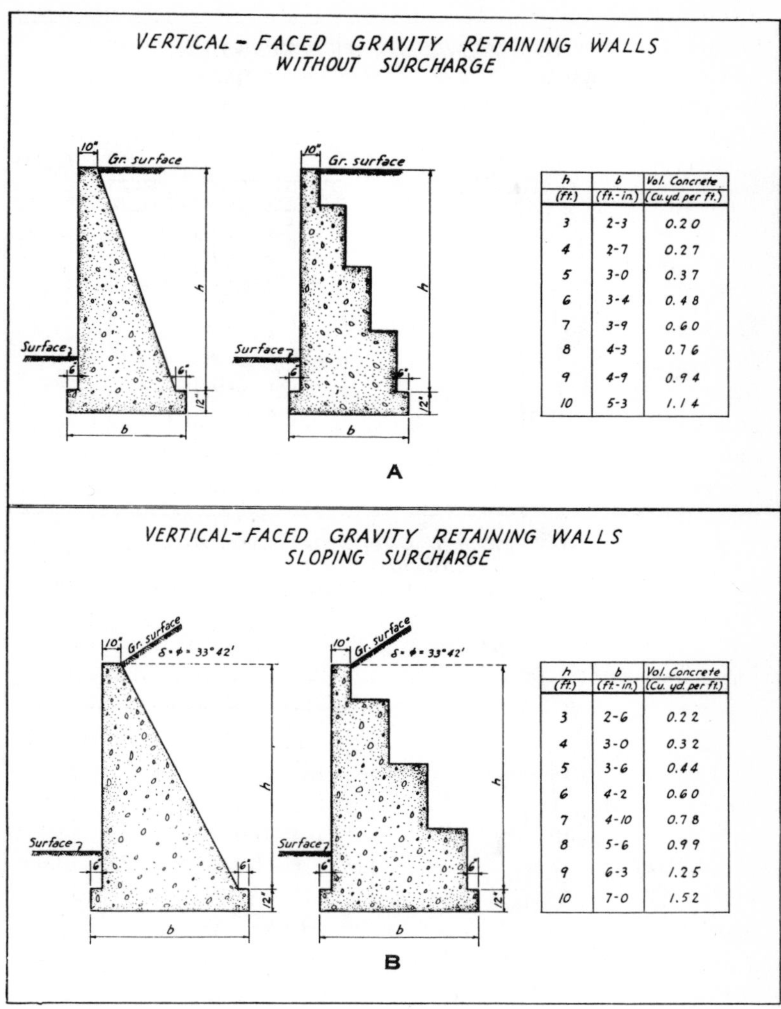

h (ft.)	b (ft.-in.)	Vol. Concrete (Cu. yd. per ft.)
3	2-3	0.20
4	2-7	0.27
5	3-0	0.37
6	3-4	0.48
7	3-9	0.60
8	4-3	0.76
9	4-9	0.94
10	5-3	1.14

h (ft.)	b (ft.-in.)	Vol. Concrete (Cu. yd. per ft.)
3	2-6	0.22
4	3-0	0.32
5	3-6	0.44
6	4-2	0.60
7	4-10	0.78
8	5-6	0.99
9	6-3	1.25
10	7-0	1.52

Fig. 31. Simple vertical face gravity wall.

BACKWARD INCLINED GRAVITY RETAINING WALLS WITHOUT SURCHARGE

(Inclination from 0° to 10° -- Vertical back to inclination of 1 horizontal to 6 vertical.)

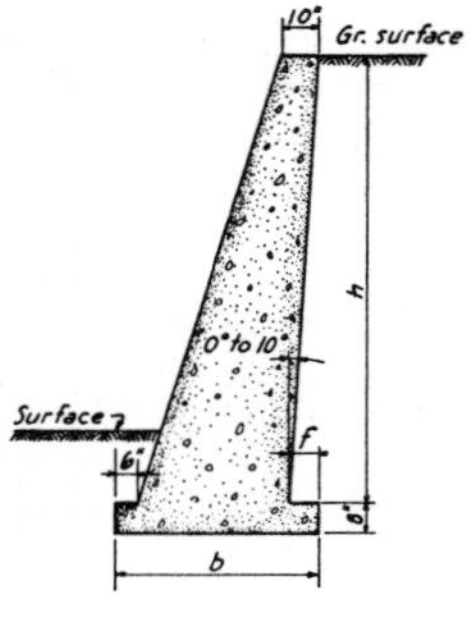

h (ft.)	f (in.)	b (ft.-in.)	Vol. Concrete (Cu. yd. per ft.)
3	6	2-0	0.15
4	6	2-4	0.22
5	6	2-8	0.30
6	6	3-0	0.39
7	6	3-4	0.49
8	7	3-9	0.61
9	7	4-1	0.74
10	8	4-6	0.88

A

BACKWARD INCLINED GRAVITY RETAINING WALLS SLOPING SURCHARGE

(Inclination from 0° to 10° -- Vertical back to inclination of 1 horizontal to 6 vertical)

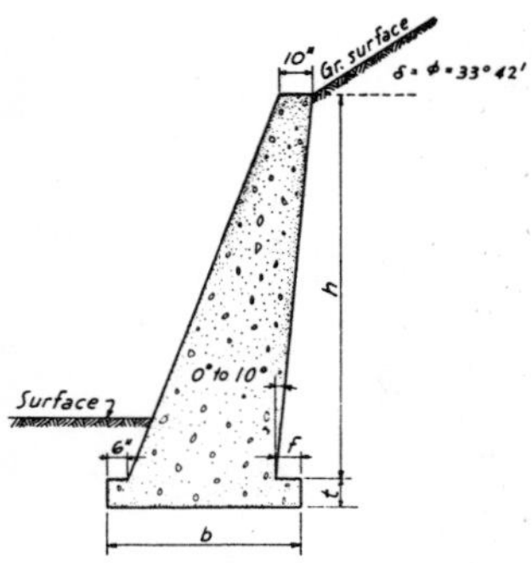

h (ft.)	f (in.)	b (ft.-in.)	t (in.)	Vol. Concrete (Cu. yd. per ft.)
3	6	2-4	8	0.18
4	6	2-8	8	0.25
5	6	3-0	8	0.34
6	6	3-4	8	0.43
7	7	3-9	8	0.55
8	8	4-2	8	0.67
1	8	4-6	8	0.80
10	9	5-0	9	0.99

B

Fig. 32. Backward leaning gravity wall.

BACKWARD INCLINED GRAVITY RETAINING WALLS
WITHOUT SURCHARGE

(An inclination varying from 10° to 20°—from 1 horizontal-6 vertical to 1 horizontal-3 vertical)

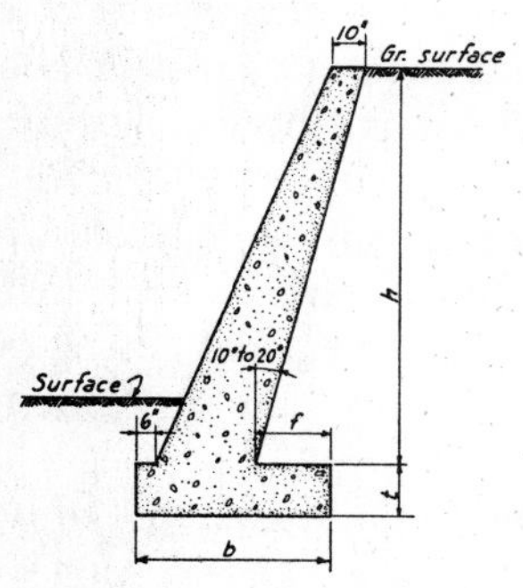

h (ft.)	f (in.)	b (ft.-in.)	t (in.)	Vol. Concrete (Cu. yd. per ft.)
3	8	2-0	8	0.14
4	10	2-4	8	0.19
5	12	2-9	8	0.26
6	14	3-2	12	0.38
7	16	3-7	12	0.47
8	18	4-0	12	0.57
9	20	4-5	16	0.73
10	22	4-10	16	0.86

A

BACKWARD INCLINED GRAVITY RETAINING WALLS
SLOPING SURCHARGE

(An inclination varying from 10° to 20°-- from 1 horizontal-6 vertical to 1 horizontal-3 vertical.)

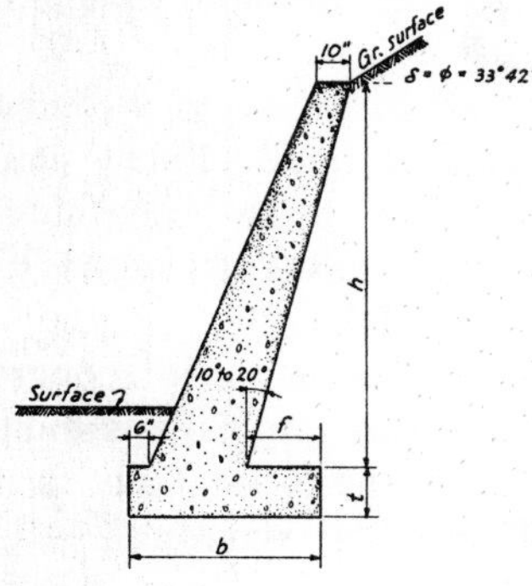

h (ft.)	f (in.)	b (ft.-in.)	t (in.)	Vol. Concrete (Cu. yd. per ft.)
3	10	2-2	8	0.15
4	12	2-6	8	0.20
5	14	3-0	8	0.27
6	16	3-6	12	0.41
7	18	3-10	12	0.49
8	20	4-3	14	0.62
9	22	4-8	14	0.73
10	23	5-0	16	0.88

B

Fig. 33. Backward leaning gravity wall.

Concrete when used in retaining walls is usually subject to quite severe exposure so the mixture should be based on six gallons total water per sack of portland cement. For a mix of medium consistency with gravel aggregate graded up to 2-inch (5-cm.) size the proportions will be about 220 pounds (100 kgs.) damp sand and 425 pounds (192.8 kgs.) gravel per sack of cement. The water to be added for each sack of cement is about 4.7 gallons (17.8 liters). This allows 5 percent by weight of free moisture in the sand.

From these data it is found that 1 cubic yard of concrete (.765 cu. meters) requires 5.3 sacks of cement, 1165 pounds (528.4 kgs.) of damp sand, and 2250 pounds (1020.6 kgs.) of gravel. (*See* Chap. 1, Fundamentals of Concrete, and Chap. 2, Concrete Ingredients.)

The quantities of materials required to build any type of wall are easily determined. *For example,* a gravity type retaining wall with level fill (Fig. 31,A), according to the table requires 0.76 cubic yard concrete per linear foot (1.9 cu. meters per linear meter) for a wall of h = 8 feet (2.4 meters). The materials necessary are 4.0 sacks cement, 885 pounds (401.4 kgs.) damp sand, and 1710 pounds (775.6 kgs.) of gravel for each foot (30 cm.) of wall.

Retaining walls are usually exposed to public view and for best appearance require care in form construction. Forms should be substantial so that bulging does not occur, and sheathing of uniform quality should be driven up tight so that leakage is prevented. (*See* Chap. 7, Forms and Form Making.)

Several types of surface textures are available for concrete walls. Board marked surfaces show the grain impressions and the joint lines of rough or dressed lumber in the forms. Smooth surfaces are produced with plywood lining. Materials and methods for producing various textures are described in Chap. 12, Finishing Concrete Surfaces. Vertical contraction joints should be placed in the wall at 20- to 30-foot (6- to 9-meter) intervals to prevent the occurrence of unsightly cracks due to temperature change and shrinkage. A tongue-and-groove key should be provided to aid in maintaining alignment of adjacent sections. It is advisable to cover contraction joints with a strip of membrane waterproofing on the back of the wall to prevent seepage through the joint.

The back filling should be placed in such a manner as not to produce impacts, as from large stones rolling down a slope against or dropping on the wall, nor undue variations of pressure against it. It is good practice to bring up the filling material along the wall at a rate as nearly uniform as practicable.

FIGURES AND TABLES

The tables accompanying Figs. 31 through 34 are based on unit weights of earth and concrete of 100 and 150 pounds per cubic foot (1601.7 and 2402.5 kgs. per cu. meter) respectively. If the filling material or the method of placement used is such as to produce much higher thrusts than from ordinary filling of earth, sand, and gravel, the tables do not apply.

The reinforced walls in the tables were all designed so that the resultant of the weight of the wall, the weight of the filling material, and the thrust of the retained material will pass through the outside edge of the middle third of the bottom of the footing. Under this condition the foundation pressure at the toe will be twice the average. The gravity walls are designed so that the resultant will be within the middle third of the bottom of the footing but close to the outside edge.

When the surface back of a wall slopes upward, or where it is level but carries a load—as from a road or building—the wall is said to have a surcharge. Surcharge increases the thrust against the back of the wall and requires a heavier wall than otherwise. The tables give dimensions and quantities for surcharged walls supporting an upward sloping fill and for an unloaded level fill. If the latter carries an external load, such as a building or roadway that will carry heavy loads, the dimensions—but not the quantities—may be taken from the tables for a level fill, by considering the load per square foot as additional depth of fill, and taking the base slab width and thickness as for a wall having a height increased by the surcharge load. Thus, if the surcharge load on the level fill amounts to 200 pounds per square foot

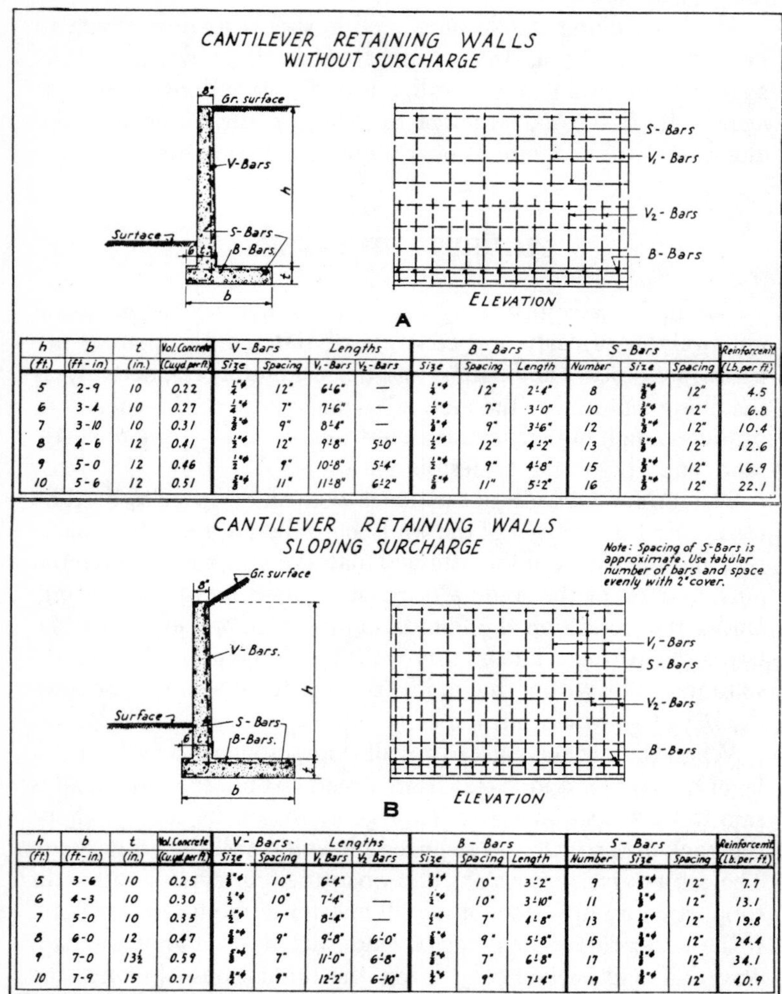

h	b	t	Vol. Concrete	V-Bars		Lengths		B-Bars			S-Bars			Reinforcem't
(ft.)	(ft-in)	(in.)	(Cu yd per ft.)	Size	Spacing	V_1-Bars	V_2-Bars	Size	Spacing	Length	Number	Size	Spacing	(Lb. per ft.)
5	2-9	10	0.22	$\frac{1}{4}$"φ	12"	6'-6"	—	$\frac{1}{4}$"φ	12"	2'-4"	8	$\frac{3}{8}$"φ	12"	4.5
6	3-4	10	0.27	$\frac{1}{4}$"φ	7"	7'-6"	—	$\frac{1}{4}$"φ	7"	3'-0"	10	$\frac{3}{8}$"φ	12"	6.8
7	3-10	10	0.31	$\frac{3}{8}$"φ	9"	8'-4"	—	$\frac{3}{8}$"φ	9"	3'-6"	12	$\frac{3}{8}$"φ	12"	10.4
8	4-6	12	0.41	$\frac{1}{2}$"φ	12"	9'-8"	5'-0"	$\frac{1}{2}$"φ	12"	4'-2"	13	$\frac{3}{8}$"φ	12"	12.6
9	5-0	12	0.46	$\frac{1}{2}$"φ	9"	10'-8"	5'-4"	$\frac{1}{2}$"φ	9"	4'-8"	15	$\frac{3}{8}$"φ	12"	16.9
10	5-6	12	0.51	$\frac{5}{8}$"φ	11"	11'-8"	6'-2"	$\frac{5}{8}$"φ	11"	5'-2"	16	$\frac{3}{8}$"φ	12"	22.1

h	b	t	Vol. Concrete	V-Bars		Lengths		B-Bars			S-Bars			Reinforcem't
(ft.)	(ft-in.)	(in.)	(Cu yd per ft.)	Size	Spacing	V_1 Bars	V_2 Bars	Size	Spacing	Length	Number	Size	Spacing	(Lb. per ft.)
5	3-6	10	0.25	$\frac{3}{8}$"φ	10"	6'-4"	—	$\frac{3}{8}$"φ	10"	3'-2"	9	$\frac{3}{8}$"φ	12"	7.7
6	4-3	10	0.30	$\frac{1}{2}$"φ	10"	7'-4"	—	$\frac{1}{2}$"φ	10"	3'-10"	11	$\frac{3}{8}$"φ	12"	13.1
7	5-0	10	0.35	$\frac{1}{2}$"φ	7"	8'-4"	—	$\frac{1}{2}$"φ	7"	4'-8"	13	$\frac{3}{8}$"φ	12"	19.8
8	6-0	12	0.47	$\frac{5}{8}$"φ	9"	9'-8"	6'-0"	$\frac{5}{8}$"φ	9"	5'-8"	15	$\frac{3}{8}$"φ	12"	24.4
9	7-0	$13\frac{1}{2}$	0.59	$\frac{5}{8}$"φ	7"	11'-0"	6'-8"	$\frac{5}{8}$"φ	7"	6'-8"	17	$\frac{3}{8}$"φ	12"	34.1
10	7-9	15	0.71	$\frac{3}{4}$"φ	9"	12'-2"	6'-10"	$\frac{3}{4}$"φ	9"	7'-4"	19	$\frac{3}{8}$"φ	12"	40.9

Fig. 34. Cantilever reinforced wall.

TABLE 40. BEARING POWER OF SOILS

Material	Bearing power (pounds per square foot)
Clay	2,000
Sand and Clay Mixed	4,000
Alluvium and Silt	5,000
Hard Clay and Firm Compressed Sand	8,000
Fine Sand	9,000
Sand, Compacted and Cemented	10,000

(976.5 kgs. per cu. meter), base slab dimensions and stem thickness at top of base should be taken for a wall 2 feet (30 cm.) higher than the actual height of the wall (assuming weight of filling material to be 100 pounds per cubic foot or 488.3 kgs. per cu. meter).

Safety against overturning or forward rotation about the front edge of the base is attained only if the pressure on the earth under the toe does not exceed its bearing power. The approximate maximum pressure on the soil under the vertical-faced walls without surcharge shown in the tables may be obtained by adding together the weight per foot (or meter) of length of wall and the filling vertically over the base, dividing by the width of the base in feet (or meters), and multiplying the quotient by two. Table 40 gives safe bearing power values for different soils. If the computed pressure exceeds the value shown for the soil in question, the toe or heel or both must be extended.

For walls leaning backward the thickness can be decreased proportionately to the amount of backward leaning. It is evident that if the wall leans backward at an angle equal to the angle of repose of the earth (a slope such that the earth will stand alone) it is not needed to retain the material back of it and becomes simply a revetment (protection for the slope). It is evident, also, that the theoretical dimensions would change with each change in the backward inclination. The tables are computed for the *least backward inclination in each group. Therefore, Fig. 32,A is applicable to a wall with a vertical back and inclined face and for all backward inclinations of the back* up to 10 degrees (about one horizontal to six vertical).

The tables for cantilever walls give the reinforcement in standard bar sizes. The length of the V_2 bars was determined from the bending moments in the vertical stem of the wall and the ordinary requirement for length to provide anchorage by bond.

Section 6

Concrete Masonry Projects and Improvements

CONCRETE MASONRY HAS become increasingly important as a construction material. Along with the rapid increase in use of concrete masonry there have been important technological developments in the manufacture and utilization of the units.

In all buildings, firesafety, durability, and economy are of supreme importance. Additional requirements may be beauty, comfort, utility, quietness, and good acoustics. Concrete masonry walls properly designed and constructed will satisfy these varied requirements.

Chapter 50

Laying Concrete Block

Use of concrete masonry is experiencing one of the most remarkable growths of any modern building material. (*See* Chap. 20, Masonry Materials.)

Concrete masonry units are made with such aggregate as sand, gravel, crushed stone, air-cooled slag, coal cinders, expanded shale or clay, expanded slag, volcanic cinders, pumice, and scoria. In some localities, the term *concrete block* has been used to designate only those units, usually of 8- × 8- × 16-inch (20- × 20- × 40-cm.) dimensions, made with aggregate such as those shown in Fig. 1.

Some concrete block may not be available in all areas. Local concrete masonry manufacturers should be consulted as to shapes and sizes available. (*See* Chap. 22, Concrete Masonry Units.)

MORTAR

Good *mortar* is necessary to good workmanship and good wall performance. It must bond the masonry units into a strong, well-knit wall. The strength of the bond is affected by various factors—the type and quantity of cementing material, the workability or plasticity of the mortar, the surface texture of the mortar-bedding areas, the rate of suction of the masonry units, the water retentivity of the mortar—and always the quality of workmanship in laying up the units.

Mortar that has stiffened on the mortar board because of evaporation should be retempered to restore its workability by thorough remixing and by the addition of water as required (Fig. 2). Mortar stiffened by hydration (setting) should be discarded.

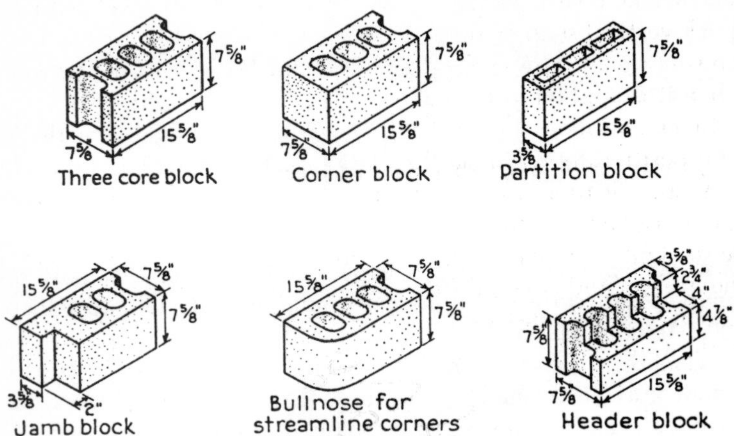

Fig. 1. Common shapes and sizes of concrete masonry units.

Fig. 2.

Since it is difficult to distinguish between these two causes of stiffening, the practical method of determining suitability of mortar is on the basis of time elapsed after initial mixing. Mortar should be used within 2½ hours after original mixing when the air temperature is 80° F. (26.7° C.) or higher or within 3½ hours when the air temperature is below 80° F. (26.7° C.). Mortar not used within these time limits should be discarded. Mortar must also be sticky so that it will adhere to the concrete block when it is laid into the wall. When taking a trowel full of mortar from the mortar board, workers will often shake the trowel with a quick vertical snap of the wrist to make the mortar stick to the trowel (Fig. 3). This keeps the mortar from falling off the trowel when it is applied to the edges of the block. (*See* Table 41.)

Block and mortar should be placed on the scaffold near their final position to minimize the mason's movements (Fig. 4).

As specifications limit the moisture content of concrete block, care must be taken to keep the block *dry* on the job. They should be stockpiled on planks or other supports free from contact with the ground and covered for protection against wetting (Fig. 5). Concrete block must *never* be wetted before and during laying in the wall.

FIRST COURSE

In order to check the layout (Fig. 6), the mason, after locating the corners, will often string out the block for the first course without mortar. A chalked snap-line is sometimes used to mark the footing, thus helping to align the block accurately. A full mortar bed is then spread and furrowed with a trowel to insure plenty of mortar along the bottom edges of the face shells of the block for the first course (Fig. 7). The corner block should be laid first and carefully positioned (Fig. 8).

All block should be laid with the thicker end of the face shell up, as this provides a larger mortar-bedding area. For vertical joints, only the ends of the face shells are buttered. By placing several block on end, the mason can apply mortar to the vertical face shells of three or four block in one operation (Fig. 9). Each block is then brought over its final position and pushed down into the mortar bed and against the previously laid block, thereby producing well-filled vertical mortar joints (Fig. 10).

After three or four block have been laid, the mason's level is used as a straightedge to assure correct alignment of the block (Fig. 11). Block are then carefully checked with the level and brought to proper grade (Fig. 12) and made plumb (Fig. 13) by tapping with the trowel handle.

The first course of concrete masonry should be laid with great

Fig. 3.

Type of service	Cement	Hydrated lime or lime putty	Mortar sand in damp, loose condition
For ordinary service	1—masonry cement*	—	2 to 3
	or		
	1—portland cement	1 to 1¼	4 to 6
Subject to extremely heavy loads, violent winds, earthquakes or severe frost action. Isolated piers.	1—masonry cement* plus 1—portland cement	—	4 to 6
	or		
	1—portland cement	0 to ¼	2 to 3

*Federal Specifications SS-C-181c, Type II.

TABLE 41.

Fig. 4.

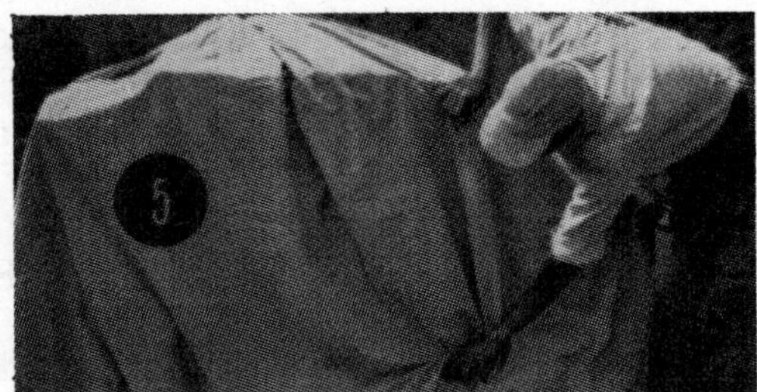

Fig. 5.

Fig. 6.

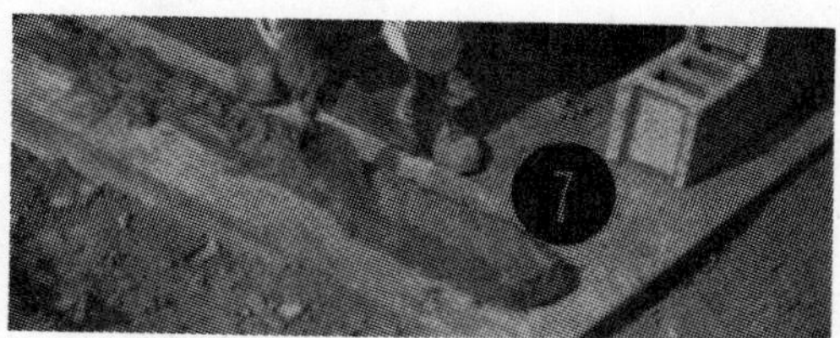

Fig. 7.

Fig. 8.

Fig. 9.

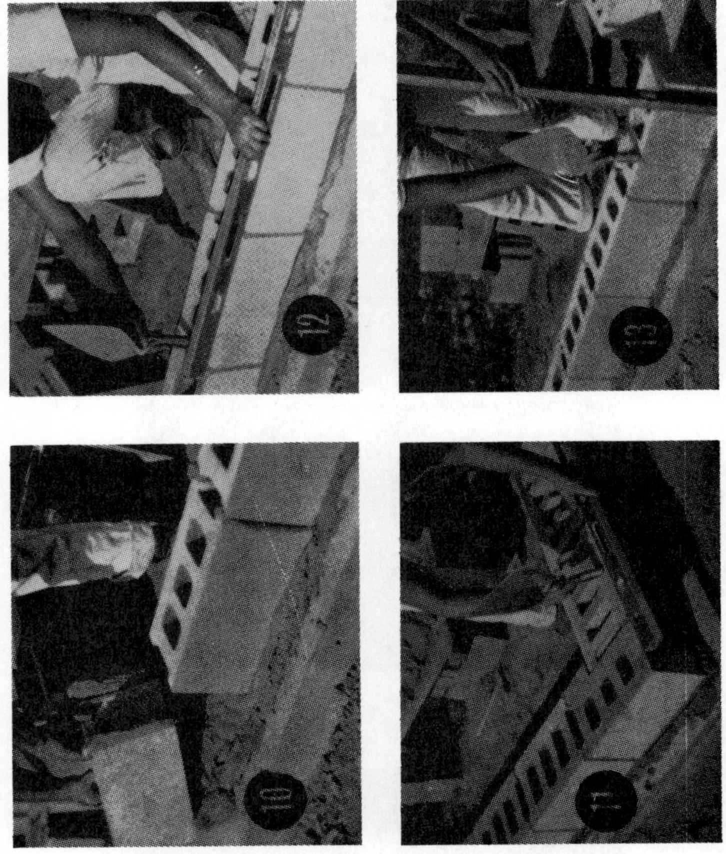

Figs. 10-13

care. Make sure it is properly aligned, leveled, and plumbed, as this will assist the mason in laying succeeding courses and in building a straight, true wall.

LAYING UP THE CORNERS

After the first course is laid, mortar is usually applied only to the horizontal face shells of the block. This is called face-shell mortar bedding (Fig. 14). Mortar for the vertical joints can be applied to the vertical face shells of the block to be placed or to the vertical edges of the block previously laid. Some masons butter the vertical face shells of the block previously laid as well as the block to be laid to insure well-filled joints.

The corners of the wall are built first, usually four to five courses higher than the center of the wall. As each course is laid at the corner, it is checked with a level for alignment (Fig. 15), for being level (Fig. 16), and for being plumb (Fig. 17). Each block is carefully checked with a level or straightedge to make certain that the faces of the block are all in the same plane (Fig. 18). This precaution is necessary to insure true, straight walls.

The use of a story- or course-pole, which is simply a board with markings 8 inches (20 cm.) apart, provides an accurate method of finding the top of the masonry for each course (Fig. 19). Mortar joints for concrete masonry should be ⅜ inch (6.3 mm.) thick. Each course, in building the corners, is stepped back a half block and the mason checks the horizontal spacing of the block by placing his level diagonally across the corners of the block (Fig. 20).

LAYING BLOCK BETWEEN CORNERS

When filling in the wall between the corners, a mason's line is stretched from corner to corner for each course and the top outside edge of each block is laid to this line.

The manner of handling or gripping the block is important. Practice will determine the most practical way for each individual (Fig. 21). Tipping the block slightly toward him, the mason

Fig. 14.

Fig. 15.

Fig. 16.

Fig. 17.

Fig. 18.

Fig. 19.

Fig. 20.

Fig. 21.

can see the upper edge of the course below, thus enabling him to place the lower edge of the block directly over the course below (Fig. 22).

By rolling the block slightly to a vertical position and shoving it against the adjacent block, it can be laid to the mason's line with minimum adjustment. *All adjustments to final position must be made while the mortar is soft and plastic. Any adjustments made after the mortar has stiffened will break the mortar bond.* By tapping lightly with the trowel handle, each block is leveled and aligned to the mason's line (Fig. 23). The use of the mason's level between corners is limited to checking the face of each block to keep it lined up with the face of the wall. (*See* Chap. 21, Masonry Tools and Equipment.)

To assure good bond, mortar should not be spread too far ahead of actual laying of the block or it will stiffen and lose its plasticity. As each block is laid, excess mortar extruding from the joints is cut off with the trowel (Fig. 24) and is usually thrown back on the mortar board to be reworked into the fresh mortar. If the work is progressing rapidly, some masons apply the extruded mortar cut from the joints to the vertical face shells of the block just laid (Fig. 25). Should there be any delay long enough for the mortar to stiffen on the block, the mortar should be removed to the mortar board and reworked. The application of mortar to the vertical joints of the block already in the wall and to the block being set insures well-filled joints (Fig. 26). Dead mortar that has been picked up from the scaffold or from the floor should not be used. In some localities, a full mortar bed may be specified on all concrete block construction. This requires mortar on the cross webs as well as on the face shells (Fig. 27).

CLOSURE BLOCK

When installing the *closure block*, all edges of the opening and all four vertical edges of the closure block are buttered with mortar (Fig. 28). The closure block should be carefully lowered into place (Fig. 29). If any of the mortar falls out, leaving an

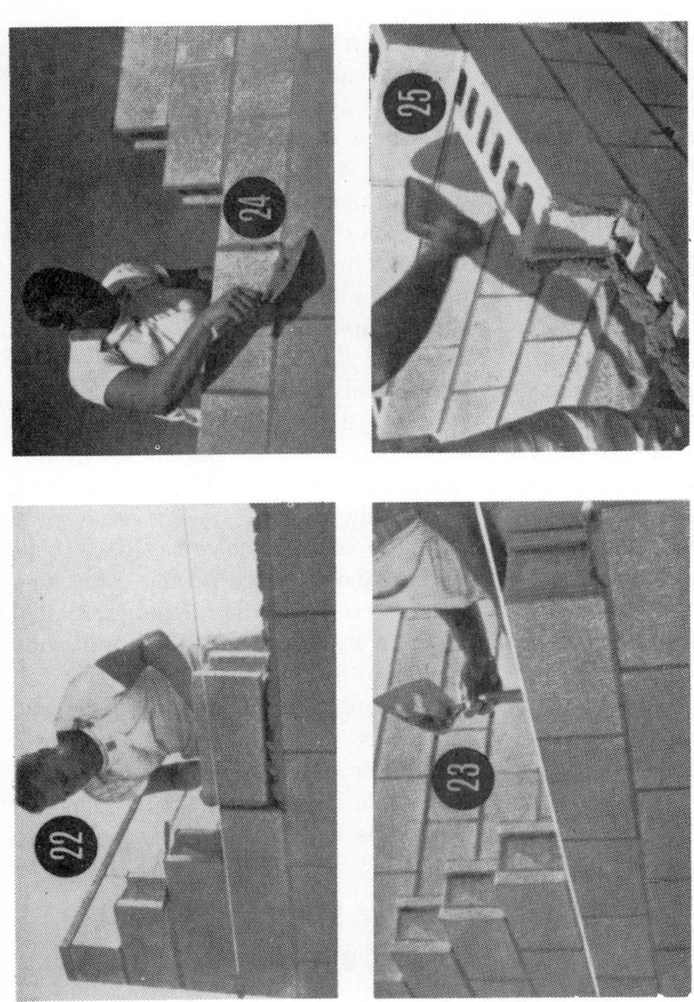

Figs. 22-25

Fig. 26.

Fig. 27.

Fig. 28.

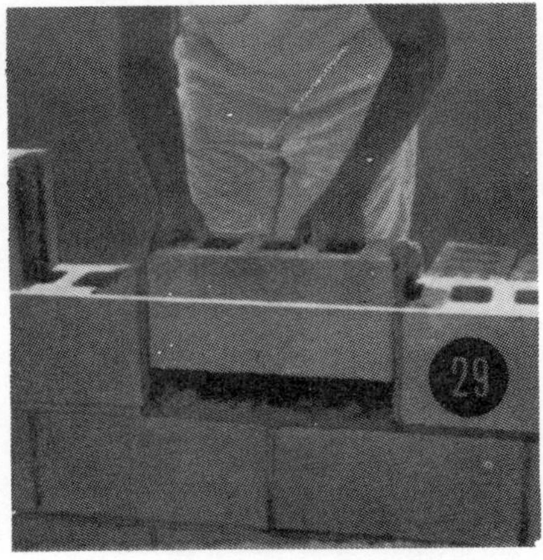

Fig. 29.

open joint, the closure block should be removed, fresh mortar applied, and the operation repeated.

TOOLING

Weathertight joints and neat appearance of concrete block walls depend on proper tooling. After a section of the wall has been laid and the mortar has become *thumb-print* hard, the mortar joints should be tooled. The tooling operation compacts the mortar and forces it tightly against the masonry on each side of the joint. Proper tooling also produces joints of uniform appearance with sharp, clean lines. Unless otherwise specified, all joints should be tooled either concave or V-shaped.

The jointer for tooling horizontal joints should be at least 22 inches (55 cm.) long, preferably longer, and upturned on one end to prevent gouging the mortar. A suitable handle should be located approximately in the center for ease in handling. For concave joints, a tool made from a ⅝-inch (1.6-cm.) round bar is satisfactory (Fig. 30). For V-shaped joints, a tool made from a ½-inch (1.3-cm.) square bar is generally used (Fig. 31). Tooling of the horizontal joints should be done first, followed by striking the vertical joints with a small S-shaped jointer (Fig. 32). After the joints have been tooled, any mortar burrs should be trimmed off flush with the face of the wall with a trowel (Fig. 33) or removed by rubbing with a burlap bag.

Do not move or straighten the block in any manner once the mortar has stiffened, or even partly stiffened. Final positioning of the block must be done while the mortar is soft and plastic. Any attempt to move or shift the block after the mortar has stiffened will break the mortar bond (Fig. 34) and allow the penetration of water.

ANCHOR BOLTS

Wood plates are fastened to tops of concrete block walls by *anchor bolts* ½-inch (1.3-cm.) in diameter, 18-inches (45-cm.) long, and spaced not more than 4 feet (1.2 meters) apart. These anchor bolts are placed in cores of the top two courses of block with the cores filled with concrete or mortar. Pieces of metal lath placed in the second horizontal mortar joint from the top of the wall and under the cores to be filled (Fig. 35) will hold the concrete or mortar filling place. The threaded end of the bolt should extend above the top of the wall (Fig. 36). When the filling has hardened, the wood plate can be securely fastened to the wall.

CONTROL JOINTS

To curb movements in masonry walls from various kinds of stresses, *control joints* are being used more and more. Control joints are continuous vertical joints built into concrete masonry walls at places where stresses might concentrate. To keep control joints as unnoticeable as possible, care must be taken to build them plumb and of the same thickness as the other mortar joints. If the control joint is to be exposed to the weather or to view, it should be sealed with a knife-grade caulking compound. Edges of the masonry in the control joint may have to be primed before caulking to prevent the dry masonry from absorbing oils

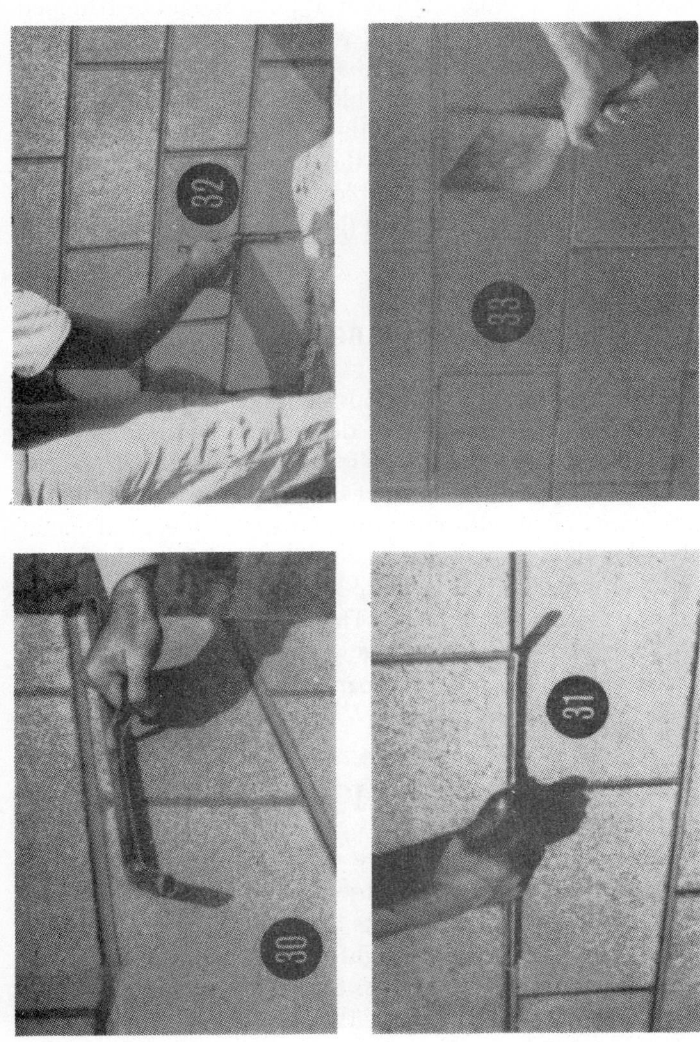

Fig. 30–33

Fig. 34.

Fig. 35.

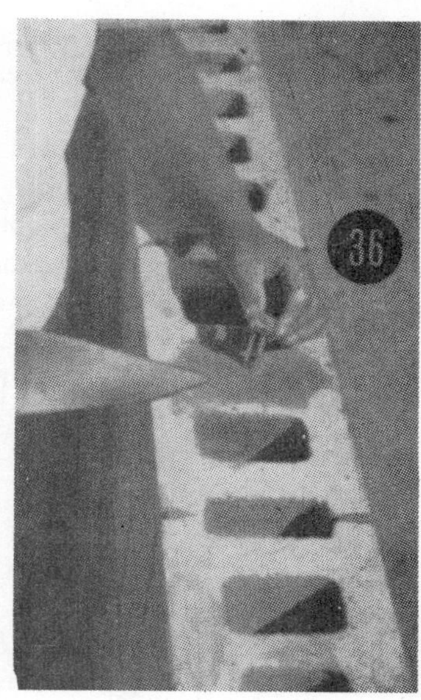

Fig. 36.

from the compound. Recommendations of manufacturers of caulking materials regarding priming should be followed.

All control joints should be laid up in mortar just as any other vertical joint. If the control joint is to be caulked, a recess should be provided for the caulking material by raking out the mortar to a depth of about ¾ inch (1.6 cm.) after the mortar has become quite stiff (Fig. 37). A thin, flat caulking trowel is used to force the caulking compound into the joint (Fig. 38).

One type of control joint can be built with stretcher block. Placing a noncorroding metal Z-tiebar 2 inches (5 cm.) narrower than the width of the wall in every other horizontal joint will provide lateral support to wall sections on each side of the control joint (Fig. 39). To form a continuous vertical joint, full- and half-length block are used (Fig. 40). Sometimes offset jamb block are used at control joints, with a noncorroding metal tie bent in the form of an open Z laid across the joint (Fig. 41). Another type of control joint can be constructed with building paper or roofing felt inserted in the end core of the block and extending the full height of the control joint. The core is then filled with mortar for lateral support (Fig. 42). The paper or felt, cut to convenient lengths and wide enough to extend across the joint, prevents the mortar from bonding on one side of the joint, thus permitting the control joint to function (Fig. 43).

A control joint block available in some areas provides lateral support by means of tongue-and-groove shaped ends of the block (Fig. 44). These control joint blocks are also made in full- and half-length units (Fig. 45).

INTERSECTING BEARING WALLS

Intersecting concrete block bearing walls should not be tied together in a masonry bond, except at the corners. Instead, one wall should terminate at the face of the other wall with a control joint at that point. For lateral support, bearing walls are tied together with a metal tiebar ¼ inch (6.3 mm.) thick, 1¼ inch (3.1 cm.) wide, and 28 inches (70 cm.) long, with 2-inch (5-cm.) right angle bends on each end (Fig. 46). These tiebars are spaced not

Fig. 37.

Fig. 38.

Fig. 39.

Fig. 40.

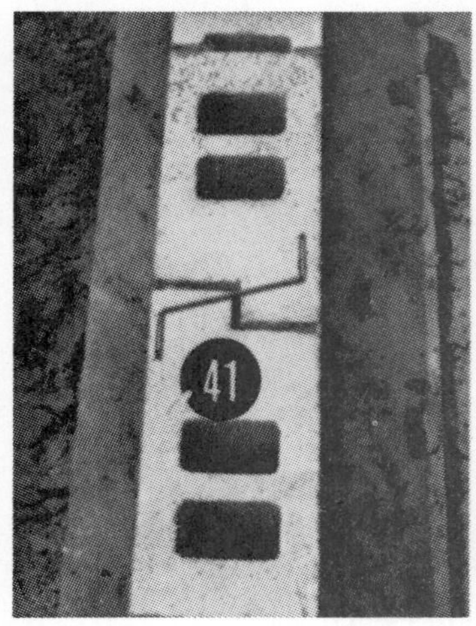

Fig. 41.

Fig. 42.

Fig. 43.

Fig. 44.

Fig. 45.

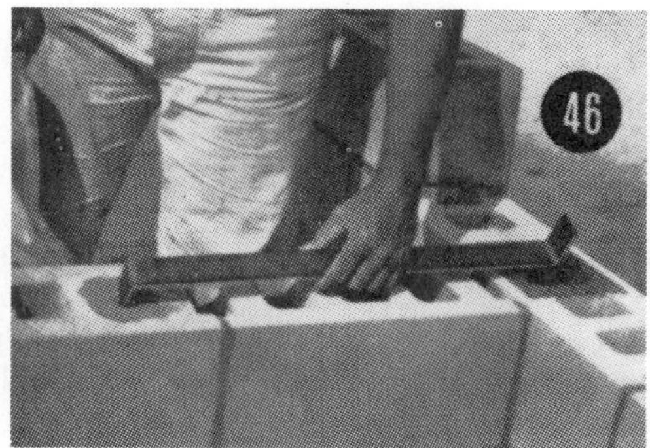

Fig. 46.

over 4 feet (1.2 meters) apart vertically. The bends at the ends of the tiebars are embedded in cores filled with mortar or concrete (Fig. 47). Pieces of metal lath placed under the cores support the concrete or mortar filling (Fig. 48).

If the control joint at the intersection of the two bearing walls is to be exposed to view or the weather, it should be constructed and sealed with a caulking compound as previously described under Control Joints.

INTERSECTING NONBEARING WALLS

For tying nonbearing block walls to other walls, strips of metal lath or ¼-inch (6.3-mm.) mesh galvanized hardware cloth are placed across the joint between the two walls (Fig. 49). The metal strips are placed in alternate courses in the wall. When one wall is constructed first, the metal strips are built into the wall and later tied into the mortar joint of the second wall (Fig. 50).

Where the two walls meet, the vertical mortar joint is raked out to a depth of ¾ inch (1.6 cm.) if it is exposed to view in the finished building, and caulking compound is packed into this recess as previously described under Control Joints.

LINTELS AND SILLS

Precast concrete lintels are often used over door and window openings (Fig. 51). For modular window and door openings, precast concrete lintels are designed with an offset on the underside (Fig. 52). Steel angles are also used for lintels to support block over openings. To fit modular openings the steel lintel angles must be installed with an offset on the underside (Fig. 53). A noncorroding metal plate, placed under the ends of lintels where control joints occur, will permit lintels to slip and the control joints to function properly (Fig. 54). A full bed of mortar should be placed over this metal plate to distribute the lintel load uniformly. After the mortar in the vertical control joint, at the end of the lintel and under the lintel has hardened sufficiently, it should be raked out to a depth of ¾ inch (1.6 cm.) and then filled with a caulking compound (Fig. 55) as previously described under Control Joints. *Precast concrete sills* are usually installed after the masonry walls have been built (Fig. 56). Joints at the ends of the sills should be tightly filled with mortar or with a caulking compound.

SPECIAL CORNERS

Where L-shaped corner block are available for walls thicker than 8 inches (20 cm.), they should be used in constructing the

Figs. 47-50.

Fig. 51.

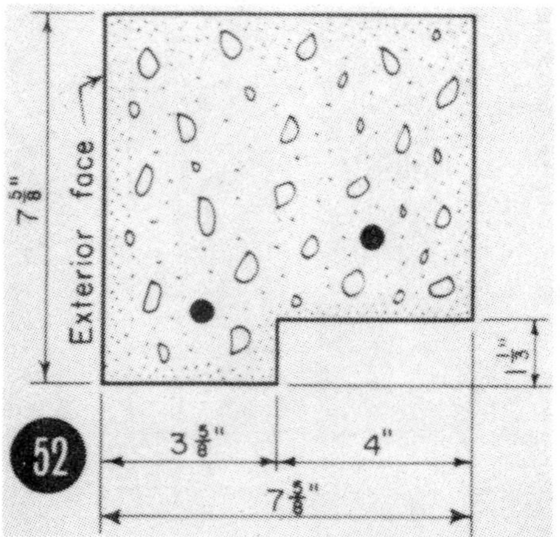

Fig. 52.

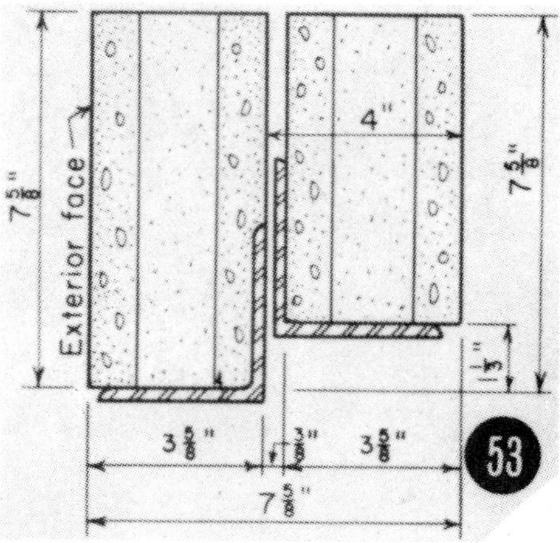

Fig. 53.

Fig. 54.

Fig. 55.

Fig. 56.

corners (Fig. 57). Where they are not available, the corner can usually be laid up with an 8- × 8- × 16-inch (20- × 20- × 40-cm.) corner block on the outside corner and a concrete brick on the inside corner (Fig. 58). The concrete brick, well buttered with mortar, can be slid into place to complete the corner detail (Fig. 59).

FOUNDATION WALLS

Foundation walls of hollow concrete block must be capped with a course of solid masonry to help distribute the loads from floor beams and to act as a termite barrier. Solid top block, in which the top 4 inches (10 cm.) is of solid concrete, are available in some areas (Fig. 60). When stretcher block are used, a strip of metal lath wide enough to cover the core spaces is placed in the mortar joints under the top course (Fig. 61). The cores are then entirely filled with concrete or mortar and troweled smooth (Fig. 62). Sometimes 4-inch (10-cm.) solid units are used to cap concrete block foundation walls (Fig. 63). All vertical joints must be completely filled, and slushing of joints should not be permitted.

CAVITY WALLS

A *cavity wall* consists of two walls separated by a continuous air space and securely tied together with noncorroding metal ties embedded in the mortar joints. Ties should be rectangular in shape, made from No. 6 gage wire and placed every 16 inches (40 cm.) vertically and every 32 inches (80 cm.) horizontally (Fig. 64). When weepholes are required at the bottom of cavity walls, approved flashings should be used to keep any moisture which might collect in the cavity away from the inner wall (Fig. 65). Weepholes can be formed by placing well-greased sash cord or rubber tubing in the horizontal mortar joints and pulling them out after the mortar has hardened. To keep the cavity clean, a 1- × 2-inch (2.5- × 5-cm.) board is laid across a level of wall ties to catch mortar droppings (Fig. 66). The board can then be raised, cleaned, and laid in the wall at the next level (Fig. 67).

Fig. 57.

Fig. 58.

Fig. 59.

Fig. 60.

Fig. 61.

Fig. 62.

Fig. 63.

Fig. 64.

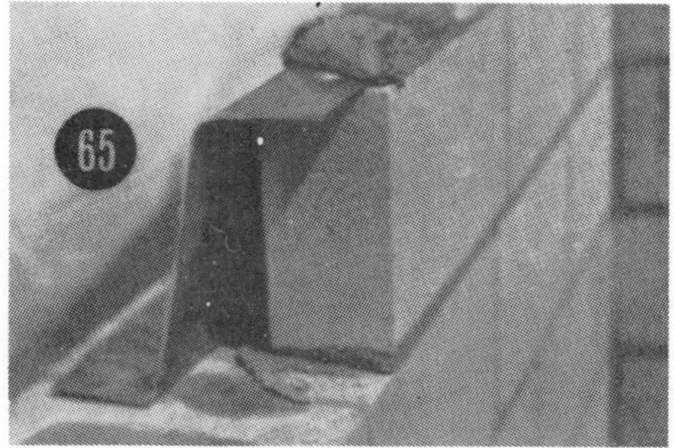

Fig. 65.

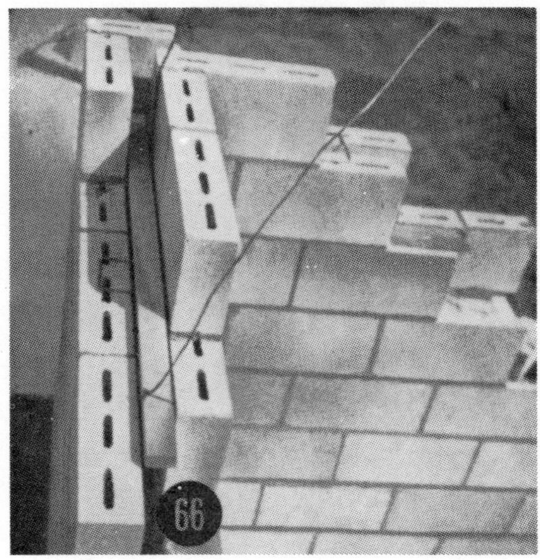

Fig. 66.

Fig. 67.

EIGHT-INCH WALL WITH CONCRETE BLOCK BACKUP

Concrete block is commonly used as *backup* for various facing materials such as brick and stone. (*See* Chap. 24, Stone Masonry; and Chap. 30, Brick Construction.) In an 8-inch (20-cm.) wall the first course of facing can either be a header (Fig. 68) or a stretcher course. All facing courses should be laid in a *full* mortar bed and with head joints *completely* filled. Extruded mortar joints on the back face of the facing units should be cut flush before the mortar has a chance to harden (Fig. 69); otherwise, any parging done over the hardened mortar may break the bond in the mortar joints and result in a leaky wall (Fig. 70). When parging the facing, a level is often used to prevent the facing from becoming dislodged and breaking the bond in the mortar joints (Fig. 71). If the concrete masonry backup is laid first, the face of the block should be parged before the facing is laid (Fig. 72).

In an 8-inch (20-cm.) wall, facing headers are laid every seventh course to bond the facing with the backup (Fig. 73).

TWELVE-INCH WALL WITH CONCRETE BLOCK BACKUP

If the brick facing is laid up first, the back of the facing should be parged with mortar (Fig. 74). Some masons apply hand pressure to hold the brick facing in place when parging. With sixth-course bonding, the brick headers bond with the 8-inch (20-cm.) concrete header block (Fig. 75). The concrete block backup is laid in vertical and horizontal face-shell mortar bedding. To insure straight, plumb walls, the block backup, as well as the facing, should be carefully checked with the level when building up the corners (Fig. 76). A mason's line stretched tightly between corners will serve as a guide when filling in between corners. Brick facing must be laid in a full mortar bed with *full* head joints. Mortar joints, when *thumb-print* hard, should be compacted firmly by tooling. If the block backup is laid up first, parging of the block will help to insure weather-

Fig. 68.

Fig. 69.

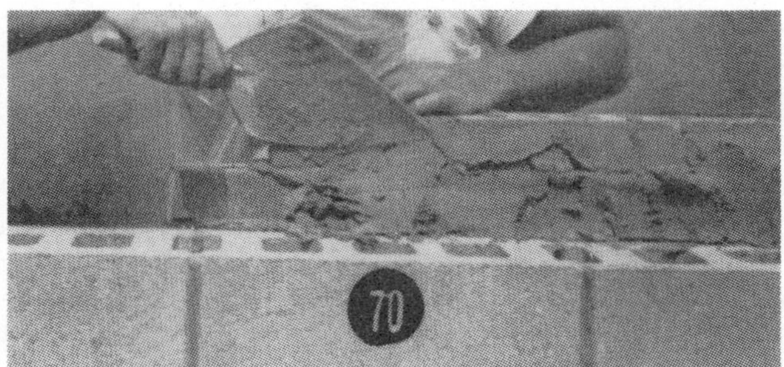

Fig. 70.

Fig. 71.

Fig. 72.

Fig. 73.

Fig. 74.

Fig. 75.

Fig. 76.

tight construction (Fig. 77). The notched shape of the concrete header block permits bonding of the facing headers and the backup (Fig. 78).

Sixth-course bonding—header up—Concrete header block can be laid in sixth-course bonding with the recessed notch either up or down, depending upon job conditions. In sixth-course bonding, header up, the brick facing, as always, is laid in full mortar bedding and full head joints (Fig. 79). Block backup is laid in horizontal and vertical face-shell mortar bedding (Fig. 80). Whichever is laid up first, the facing or the backup, parging should be applied to insure weathertightness.

Seventh-course bonding—In a 12-inch (30-cm.) wall using seventh-course bonding, the block backup consists of stretcher block only. Concrete brick should be used as backup to the brick headers (Fig. 81).

PATCHING AND CLEANING BLOCK WALLS

Any *patching* of the mortar joints or filling of holes left by nails or line pins should be done with fresh mortar.

Particular care should be taken to prevent smearing mortar into the surface of the block. Once hardened, embedded mortar smears can never be removed and they detract from the neat appearance of the finished wall. Paint cannot be depended upon to hide mortar smears. As concrete block walls should not be cleaned with an acid wash to remove mortar smears or mortar

Fig. 77.

Fig. 78.

Fig. 79.

Fig. 80.

Fig. 81.

Fig. 82.

Fig. 83.

Fig. 84.

Fig. 85.

Fig. 86.

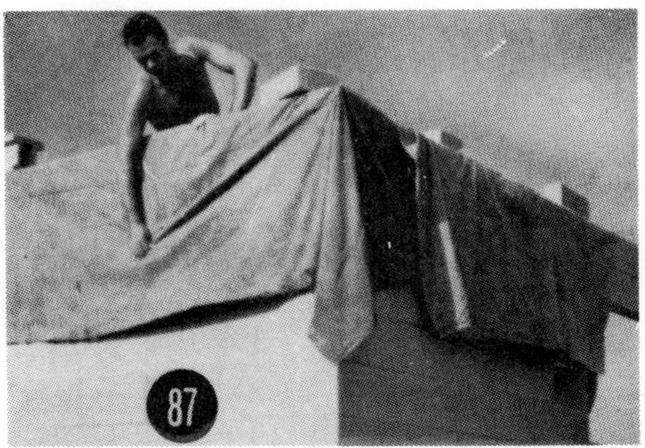

Fig. 87.

droppings, care must be taken to keep the wall surface clean during construction. Any mortar droppings that stick to the block wall should be allowed to dry before removal with a trowel (Fig. 82). The mortar may smear into the surface of the block if it is removed while soft. When dry and hard most of the remaining mortar can be removed by rubbing with a small piece of block (Fig. 83). Brushing the rubbed spots removes practically all of the mortar (Fig. 84).

CUTTING BLOCK

Concrete masonry units are usually available in half- as well as full-length units. However, to fit special job conditions it is sometimes necessary to cut a block with a brick hammer and chisel. The block is scored on both sides to obtain a clean break (Fig. 85). For fast, neat cutting, masonry saws are often used (Fig. 86). Block should be cut *dry* when masonry saws are used so as not to increase the moisture content of the block.

PROTECTION

Boards, building paper, or tarpaulins are used for coverings for the top of the block walls at the end of the day's work to prevent rain or snow from entering the cores (Fig. 87).

Chapter 51

Concrete Masonry Basements

A warm, dry, light basement provides valuable additional living space to a home. It can be a place for hobbies and recreation. You can use it for a workshop and space to repair or paint household items; a play area; or storage space for garden tools, flower bulbs, lawn furniture, and bulky household articles.

PLANNING

During the planning stage of a home, consideration should be given to whether basement windows will be below the grade of the lawn to give the home a ground-hugging silhouette or above grade to provide more daylight and ventilation.

Sometimes both results can be achieved by grading only the front of the yard up to about the floor level and using areaways with the front basement windows. At the sides and rear, the basement windows then would be at or above ground level.

Sloping yards or sidehill locations permit interesting variations in basement planning. *For example,* where the ground slopes down toward the back of the lot, after a little regrading of the yard, the basement floor at the rear could be placed at grade (Fig. 1). With the addition of full-sized windows or sliding glass doors, an attractive room leading directly to the garden area could be provided in the basement for family living. Similar arrangements could be made for the sides of a house with yards sloping in the same direction as the street. Sloping lots (Fig. 2) are ideal for split-level or split-foyer houses where the entrance to the home is located between floor levels or where the garage is built as part of the basement.

The elevation of the street sewer will have a bearing on the

Fig. 1. A sloping lot provides an opportunity for an interesting house with a basement garage or a basement family room opening directly to the garden.

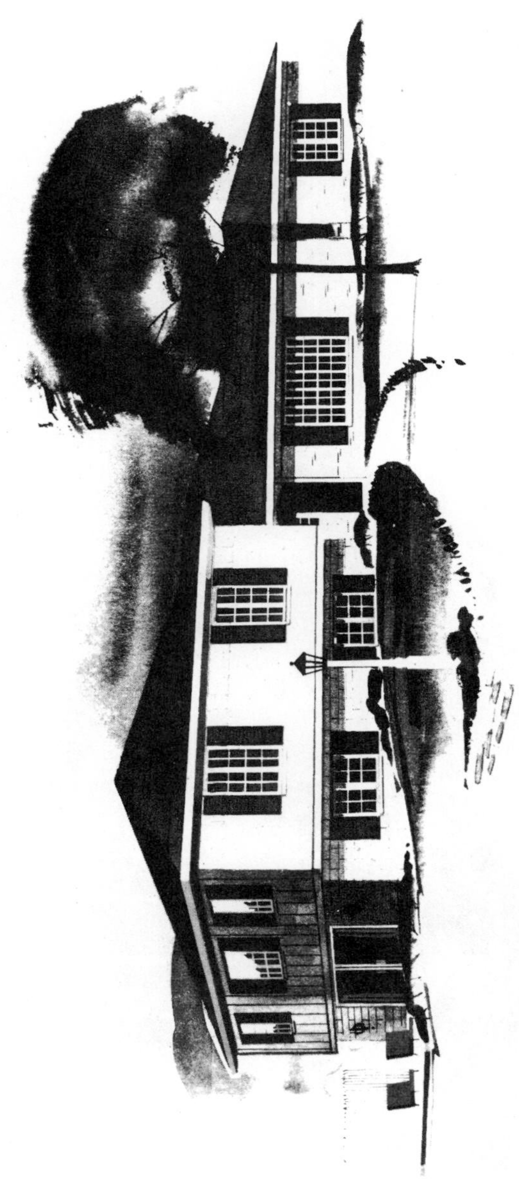

Fig. 2. Front yard is graded up, giving the home a low silhouette. Basement windows at sides and rear are at or above grade level.

elevation of the basement floor for proper drainage.

Plans should also include considerations for a direct entrance to the basement such as a separate outside stairway or a combined entrance (Fig. 3) serving both the basement and the first-floor area at approximately grade level. Direct entrances make the basement more easily accessible and usable without the necessity of tracking through the house (Fig. 4).

Fig. 3. Outside basement stairway gives easy access to basement from yard.

Fig. 4. Combination back door and basement entrance.

LAYOUT

Usually residential areas have ordinances limiting the location of a house with respect to property lines. These requirements help ensure light, air, and privacy to abutting properties.

Surveying instruments should be used to locate the corners of the basement accurately and to establish the grade of the top of the basement wall. Batter boards with string lines set to proper line and grade assist in preserving reference points during excavation, setting the forms for the footing, and locating the basement walls. (*See* Appendix V, Suggested Method of Laying Out a Foundation.)

For economical construction, the height of *basement walls* should be in multiples of concrete masonry course heights. *For example,* with 8-inch (20-cm.) high block (actually 7⅝ inch plus

⅜ inch for the mortar joint or 19.1 and .9 cm., respectively) the dimension from the top of the footing to the top of the basement wall should be a multiple of 8 inches (20 cm.). Should special units be used for the top course, their dimensions must be considered. Similarly, the horizontal outside dimensions of the basement should be in multiples of full- or half-block lengths. With block 16 inches (40 cm.) long (actually 15⅝ inches plus ⅜ inch for mortar or 39.1 and .9 cm., respectively) these dimensions should be in multiples of 16 or 8 inches (40 or 20 cm.). (*See* Chap. 41, Footings.)

EXCAVATION

All organic materials such as sod, bushes, trees, roots, and the like within the limits of the excavation should be removed. Topsoil should be stripped and stockpiled for use later in grading and landscaping the property.

Excavation for footings should extend down to at least 6 inches (15 cm.) into firm, undisturbed bearing soil and at least 6 inches (15 cm.) below the prevailing frostline. In case the excavation has been made too deep, no backfilling should be permitted, since uneven settlement of the house would likely occur. Such excessive excavations should be filled instead with concrete as part of the footing. Where footings would bear partially on rock, which would probably cause uneven settlement, the rock should be removed to approximately 6 inches (15 cm.) below the bottom of the proposed footing and replaced with a cushion of compacted sand or soil.

On property that has recently been regraded and filled, it is recommended that the footings extend down into the original undisturbed soil unless soil tests prove that the fill has been sufficiently compacted.

FOOTINGS

Cast-in-place concrete should be used for all *footings.* It readily conforms to any subgrade irregularities and ensures uniform bearing on the soil. If possible, the concrete should be placed continuously so the footing will have no construction joints. Where construction joints must be used, two No. 6 reinforcing bars 3 feet (91 cm.) long should be embedded in the concrete across the joint to transfer the loads.

As various loads are added to the structure during construction, the footing compresses the average subgrade soil, causing a slight settlement. Sometimes there may be two or more different subsoils under various parts of the same house, which may result in unequal settlement because of some differences in compressibility of the soils. Also, in most homes, the roof and floor joists frame on two of the four walls, bringing most of the loads to bear upon only two sides of the continuous concrete footing and presenting another chance of unequal settlement. It is advisable, therefore, that footings be wide enough to minimize any of these differences in possible settlements.

The dimensions of the footings can be determined from a structural analysis of the loads involved and the load-bearing value of the subsoil. If such an analysis is not made, the recommended dimensions for residential footings shown in Fig. 5 may be used. They are based on average soils having about 2,000

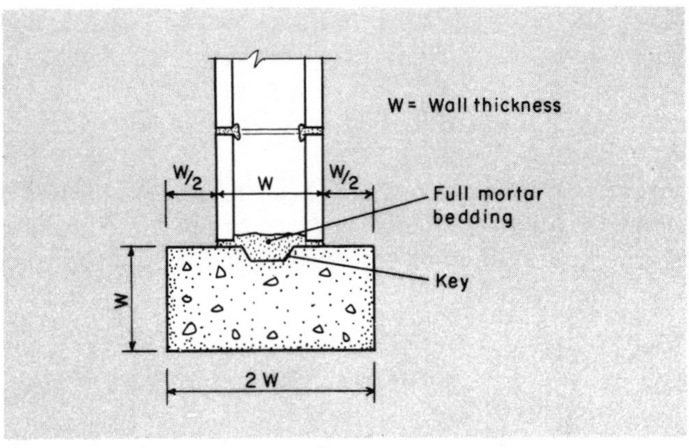

Fig. 5. Recommended dimensions for residential footings.

pounds per square foot (9765.3 kgs. per sq. meter) load-bearing value.

Longitudinal reinforcement consisting of two No. 6 bars placed 2 inches (5 cm.) from the bottom may be necessary in footings placed (1) over soft, poorly drained soils, (2) where subsoils are not uniform, or (3) over backfilled utility trenches. In all cases, the addition of continuous longitudinal reinforcing bars in the footings could be good insurance in providing additional stability and useful life to the house.

Chimneys on the outside wall of the house should have footings that are wider but cast integrally with the wall footings. Separate footings are needed for interior columns (Fig. 6), fireplaces, and chimneys, with the tops of such footings placed below the concrete basement floor slab. Separate footings should be rectangular or square and for one-story construction they should have a minimum thickness of 8 inches (20 cm.) with a minimum projection of 5 inches (12.5 cm.) beyond the face of the column or masonry. For two-story homes, minimum thickness should be 12 inches (30 cm.) with a minimum projection of 7 inches (17.5 cm.).

On sidehill locations stepped footings may be required. Footings must be placed horizontally and the height of the vertical step should not be more than three-quarters of the distance between the steps.

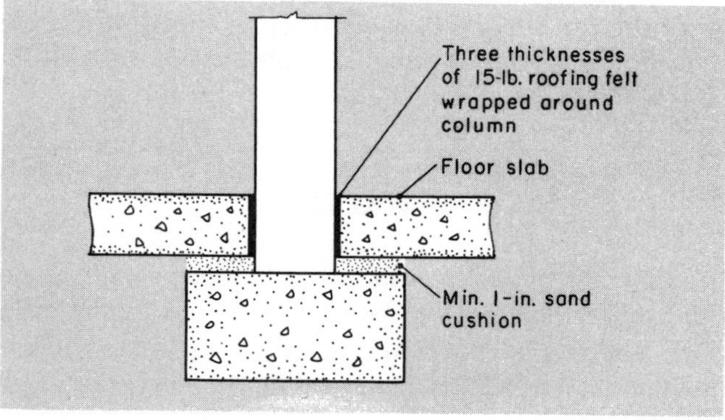

Fig. 6. Separate footings for interior columns.

Surveying instruments should be used in setting forms for footings to proper alignment and grade. The forms for the footings should be carefully staked and securely braced. The top of each footing must be horizontal to help the mason in laying the first course of masonry to correct grade and alignment. This in turn will help in laying succeeding courses and maintaining a straight, true wall. (*See* Chap. 50, Laying Concrete Block.)

The subgrade inside the footing forms should be clean of all scrap lumber, debris, water, and the like, that would not provide good uniform bearing for the concrete footing. In freezing temperatures the concrete for the footing should not be placed on a frozen subgrade. It should be placed as soon as possible after excavation or the subgrade should be covered and protected from freezing until the concrete is placed. (*See* Chap. 36, Preparation of Subgrade.)

Concrete for footings must have *both* a minimum compressive strength of 3,000 psi (210 kgs. per sq. m.) and a minimum cement content of five bags—470 pounds per cubic yard (278.7 kgs. per cu. meter). The concrete should be well mixed, workable, and placed as near as possible to its final position to prevent segregation. The use of chutes or buggies is recommended. The concrete should then be spaded along the faces of the forms and struck off level with the top of the forms, leaving the surface in a roughened condition.

A notch or depression sometimes called a key, formed in the center of the top surface of the footing as shown in Fig. 5, will provide additional lateral stability at the base of the wall. A beveled 2 × 4 (5 × 10 cm.) can be used to form this key.

WALLS

The thickness of *concrete masonry basement walls* is dependent on the vertical loads to be supported and the lateral earth pressure. Building codes usually specify a minimum thickness at various depths below grade, depending on local soils. Table 42 shows recommendations for minimum thicknesses based on conventional residential construction and average soils. The dimen-

Type of unit	Minimum wall thickness, in. (nominal)	Maximum height of unbalanced fill, ft.**	
		Frame superstructure	Masonry and masonry veneer superstructure
Hollow load-bearing	8†	5	5
	10	6	7
	12	7	7
Solid load-bearing	8†	5	7
	10	7	7
	12	7	7

*Basement walls should be at least as thick as the walls supported immediately above except as noted below.

**Heights shown may be increased to 7 ft. with approval of building official if justified by soil conditions and local experience.

†If the 8-in. basement wall supports an 8-in. wall, the combined height should not exceed 35 ft. If it supports brick veneer on wood frame or a 10-in. cavity wall, it may be corbeled out a maximum of 2 in. with solid units; but the total height of wall supported, including the gable, should not exceed 25 ft. Individual corbels should not project more than ⅓ the height of the unit. If a concrete first floor is used, it helps provide adequate bearing for these walls and corbeling can be omitted.

TABLE 42. MINIMUM THICKNESS OF BASEMENT WALLS.*

sions given for wall thickness are nominal. The height of the unbalanced fill is measured from the outside finished grade of the lawn to the basement floor.

Strength and Stability

The *strength* and *stability* of a masonry basement wall to resist earth pressure depends on its height and thickness, the bond of the mortar, vertical loads on the wall, support from basement crosswalls, pilasters or wall stiffeners, and especially the support provided by the first-floor framing. Earth pressure will vary with soil conditions from practically zero to an amount equal to the hydrostatic pressure of a liquid with the density of mud.

When local experience indicates strong earth pressures are to be expected, pilasters can be used to help strengthen the wall (Figs. 7 and 8). Pilasters must be built at the same time as the foundation wall and laid in a strong masonry bond with the wall. Pilaster block are often used for such construction. Pilasters

Fig. 7. Pilaster is laid in a masonry bond with the wall and with full mortar bedding.

Fig. 8. Alternate course in pilaster.

should have a minimum width of 16 inches (40 cm.), with a projection of 8 inches (20 cm.) from the inside basement face for 8-inch (20-cm.) walls and 6 inches (15 cm.) for 10-inch (25-cm.) walls.

Another method of strengthening the walls is to use wall stiffeners. For instance, place a No. 4 bar in one core of the block from the top of the wall to the footing and fill that core space with mortar or grout.

With 12-inch (30-cm.) concrete masonry foundation walls, pilasters or wall stiffeners are not usually needed. In walls 10 inches (25 cm.) thick and over 36 feet (10.9 meters) long, the distance between pilasters or between pilasters and endwalls or crosswalls should not be greater than 18 feet (5.5 meters). In 8-

inch (20-cm.) thick walls over 30 feet (9.1 meters) long, this distance should be not greater than 15 feet (4.6 meters). With wall stiffeners the spacing should not exceed 15 feet (4.6 meters) for 10-inch (25-cm.) walls and 12 feet (3.7 meters) for 8-inch (20-cm.) walls.

The use of continuous horizontal steel joint reinforcement placed in the mortar joints at not more than 16 inches (40 cm.) vertically will provide additional lateral strength to the basement walls.

With wood-frame construction, the supporting basement walls should extend at least 8 inches (20 cm.) above the finished grade. Wood sills should be anchored to the basement walls on approximately 8-foot (2.4-meters) centers with ½-inch (1.3-cm.) bolts at least 15 inches (38 cm.) long and 2-inch (5-cm.) washers. At least two anchor bolts should be used for each sill piece (Fig. 9). The bolts and washers should be placed in the cores of the top two courses of masonry, and the cores containing bolts filled with mortar or concrete. A piece of metal lath or other similar material should be used to support the filling in the cores (Fig. 10).

At least two cores should be similarly filled to a minimum

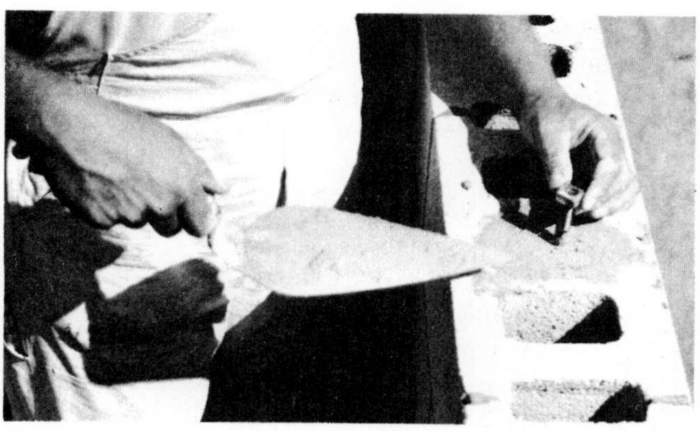

Fig. 9. Anchor bolts to hold sills to the basement wall.

Fig. 10. Piece of metal lath is used under core to be filled.

depth of 6 inches (15 cm.) in the top course or courses of masonry where ends of girders bear on the foundation wall. Sometimes pilasters bonded into the wall are used for additional support for girders, and the cores in their top course should also be filled to a minimum depth of 6 inches (15 cm.).

The concrete masonry units should meet the applicable specifications, of the American Society for Testing and Materials, such as hollow load-bearing, solid load-bearing, or brick. These units should be laid up in mortar composed of one of the proportions shown in Table 43. (*See* Chap. 29, Bricklaying.)

MORTAR

Mortar should be made with a good-quality, well-graded sand. Power mixers should be used to blend and mix the ingredients thoroughly. This is particularly important when using masonry cements that contain air-entraining agents since power mixers provide the churning and mixing action needed to entrain air in the mortar. Mixing should continue for a minimum of five minutes, using as much mixing water as practicable to attain the de-

Type of soil	Cement	Hydrated lime or lime putty	Mortar sand in damp, loose condition
Ordinary	1—masonry cement*	—	Not less than 2¼ and not more than 3 times the sum of the volumes of the cement and lime used.
	1—portland cement	1 to 1¼	
Wet, heavy, fluid-like	1—masonry cement* plus 1—portland cement	—	
	1—portland cement	¼	

*ASTM Specification C91, Type II.

TABLE 43. RECOMMENDED MORTAR MIXES.

sired workability. (*See* Chap. 20, Masonry Materials.)

Mortar that has been mixed and not used right away will tend to stiffen and dry out. The workability of the mortar can be restored by thorough spading with a trowel and, if necessary, by the addition of water. The mortar should be used within two and one-half hours after mixing since it tends to stiffen by hydration. It should be discarded if not used within this time.

The top of the footing should be clean. All dirt, mud, water, and the like must be removed to provide good bond with the mortar. After the corners of the basement have been accurately located on the footing, a chalked snap line is sometimes used to mark the line for the wall.

A full bed of mortar should be placed on the footing to receive the first course of masonry (Fig. 11). On succeeding courses face-shell mortar bedding should be used; like mortar covers only the vertical and horizontal face shells (Fig. 12).

Mortar joints should be ⅜ inch (9.3 mm.) thick. With block 7⅝ inches (19.1 cm.) high (actual dimension) and this thickness of mortar joint, the top of each masonry course is located at some multiple of 8 inches (20 cm.) above the top of the footing.

LAYING UNITS

The corners of the basement should be built first about five or

Fig. 11. Full mortar bed is placed on footing for first course of masonry.

Fig. 12. Face-shell mortar bedding is used on both vertical and horizontal face shells.

six courses high in a true masonry bond and then the wall filled in between the corners (Figs. 13 and 14). This method helps ensure straight, plumb walls. Basement walls other than 8 inch (20 cm.) thick require special corner-construction details together with specially shaped block to maintain a running bond pattern. Several methods of building such corners are shown in Figs. 15 through 20. (*See* Chap. 22, Concrete Masonry Units.)

Final positioning of the block *must* be done while the mortar is soft and plastic. No attempt should be made to move or

Fig. 13. Corners are built first, about five or six courses high. The wall is then filled in between corners.

Fig. 14. L-shape block may be used at corners of walls more than 8-inches (20-cm.) thick.

Fig. 15. Another method of preserving the 8- × 16-inch (20- × 40-cm.) masonry pattern at corners with walls thicker than 8 inches (20 cm.).

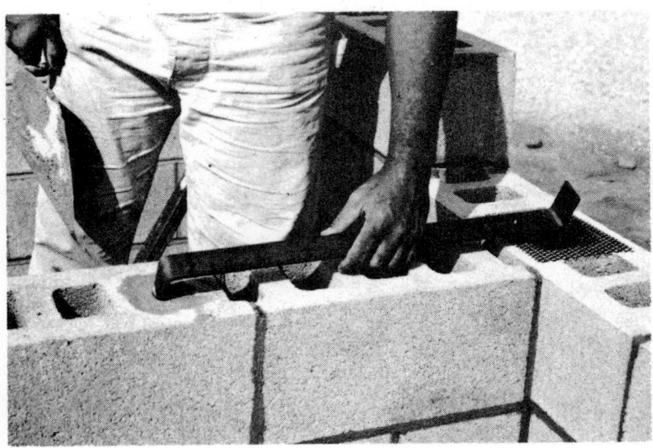

Fig. 16. Load-bearing crosswalls are tied to basement walls with metal tiebars.

Fig. 17. Solid-top block (top 4-inch or 10-cm. solid) capping top of basement walls.

Fig. 18. Four-inch (10-cm.) solid masonry units for top course.

Fig. 19. Cores in top course are completely filled.

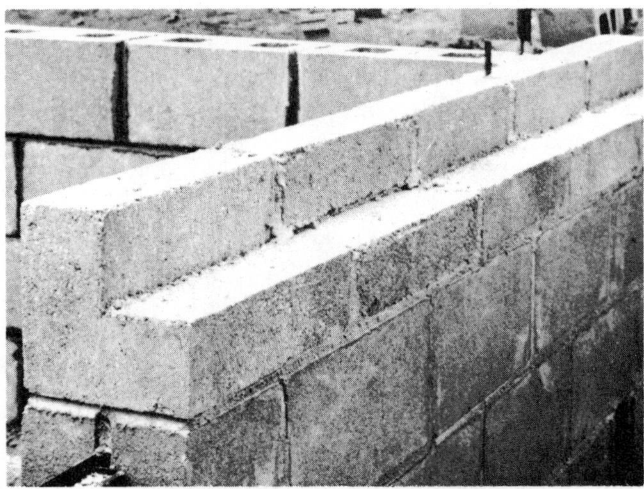

Fig. 20. L-shape solid block for top course provides ledge for brick veneer.

straighten any block once the mortar has stiffened. Any movement of the block after the mortar has stiffened will break the bond of the mortar, which would tend to weaken the wall and possibly cause future moisture problems.

On basement wall surfaces that will not be parged or plastered, the mortar joints should be firmly compacted, after the mortar has stiffened, with a round or V-shape tool. The jointer for tooling the horizontal mortar joints should be at least 22 inches (59 cm.) long to produce neat, straight joints. On the side of the basement wall that is to be parged or plastered, the mortar joints are cut flush and not tooled.

Load-bearing crosswalls in the interior of the basement should not be tied to the basement walls in a masonry bond. Instead they should be anchored with metal tiebars ¼ inch (6.3 mm.) thick, 1¼-inches (3.1-cm.) wide, and at least 28 inches (70 cm.) long, with 2-inch (5-cm.) right-angle bends on each end. The ends of the tiebar should be embedded in cores filled with mortar or concrete. Pieces of metal lath should be placed under the cores to support the concrete or mortar filling.

To distribute the floor loads uniformly, the top course of concrete masonry supporting the first floor and the walls of the structure should be capped by (1) solid-top block, in which the hollow cores do not extend up into the top 4 inches (10 cm.) of the block; (2) 4 inches (10 cm.) of solid masonry; (3) reinforced concrete masonry bond beam; or (4) cores in the top course filled with concrete or mortar after a strip of metal lath or other material has been placed in the mortar joint under the top course to hold this core filling. Capping may be omitted when a wood sill is used that bears on both inner and outer face shells.

Where a concrete porch, entrance slabs, or precast concrete window areaways are to be used, a 4-inch (10-cm.) wide masonry ledge should be provided to support them at the face of the wall.

TERMITE PROTECTION

For *termite protection* the wall should be capped with at least 4 inches (10 cm.) of concrete reinforced longitudinally with two No. 3 bars or equivalent. Such capping should be placed in one continuous operation and extend across the full width of the wall. An alternate method is to use a continuous concrete masonry bond beam reinforced with two No. 3 bars or equivalent for the top course, with the concrete filling placed on one operation. There are other methods of termite protection such as metal shields and soil treatment with poison chemicals.

DAMPPROOFING

Downspouts should never discharge water at or near the face of the wall. If the surrounding soil is dense and nonporous, most of the water will collect around the outside of the basement wall in the newly placed backfill and probably find its way into the basement. All downspouts should be either connected to a sewer or discharged away from the wall and backfill area. They must never be connected to the tile drains around the footing.

With proper grading, surface water should be drained away from the basement wall. On sidehill locations the ground on the uphill side should be graded to drain surface water around the house.

Except in areas of dry climate or where the subsoil is well drained, a line of drain tile 4 or 6 inches (10 or 15 cm.) in diameter should be placed around the outside of the footing and connected to a sewer or other suitable outlet. The tile can be laid without any grade (level) as it must not be lower than the bottom of the footing. Joints between tiles should be covered with pieces of building paper or felt to prevent the backfill from entering the tile. At least 8 inches (20 cm.) of coarse gravel or crushed stone should be placed over the tile prior to backfilling.

Various practices are used to dampproof concrete masonry basement walls, depending on the climate and the surface and subsurface drainage. In well-drained or ordinary soils, the earth side of the wall should be coated by one of the following methods (*see* Fig. 21):

1. Parging (plastering) with a ½-inch (1.3-cm.) coat of plaster, preferably applied in two ¼-inch (9.3-mm.) coats (Fig. 22). Either the mortar used in laying up the block or a portland ce-

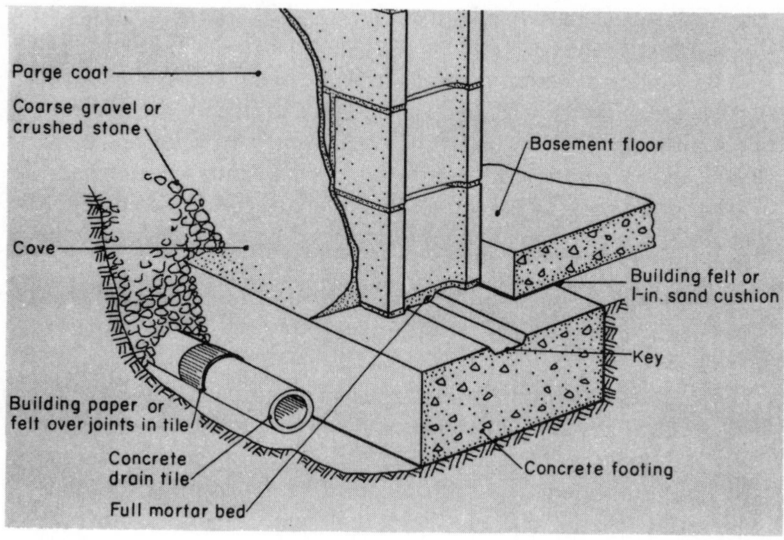

Fig. 21. Details of basement walls.

Fig. 22. Parging (plastering) the earth side of masonry basement wall. Note that surface to be parged has been sprayed with water to control suction.

ment plaster (1 part portland cement and 2½ parts mortar sand by volume) should be used.

The concrete masonry surface must be clean and then sprayed with water (but not soaked) just before applying the parging. This prevents the dry masonry units from absorbing excessive water too rapidly from the parge coat and assures better bond.

When the parging is applied in two coats, the first coat should be firmly troweled over the masonry and horizontally scored or scratched to provide additional bond through good mechanical key with the second coat. The second coat should be applied as soon as the first coat has set up sufficiently to hold the weight of both coats.

If there is a delay in applying the second coat, the first coat will tend to dry out. This should be prevented by keeping the first coat moist with occasional fine sprays of water until the second coat is applied. The first coat must be moist but without any free surface water when applying the second coat to assure good bond and to control the rapid suction that would make the application difficult. For maximum water-resistant qualities of the parge coats, the last coat should be moist-cured for at least 48 hours after application.

Parge coats should not be applied by the mason at the same time he is laying up the wall. The pressure needed to apply the plaster properly would tend to move the freshly laid units and, therefore, would likely break the bond of the mortar joint. This mortar joint bond must not be disturbed—the strength and watertightness of the wall depend upon good bond.

The parge coats should be troweled to a dense, tight surface and formed into a cove at the base of the wall on the footing (Fig. 21). This cove helps to seal the joint from water penetration. The parging should extend from the footing to 6 inches (15 cm.) above the finished ground line, where the top edge should be cut off neatly and beveled to form a wash.

2. Scrubbing two heavy (thick) cement-grout coats well into the surface with a stiff-bristle brush, such as an ordinary floor scrub brush. The grout should be made with equal parts by volume of portland cement and fine sand (passing No. 30 sieve) mixed with water to a consistency of heavy cream. The grout

should be stirred frequently to maintain uniform consistency.

The masonry wall must be clean and then sprayed with water, as described previously for parge coats, before applying the first grout coat. This coat should be cured by being kept moist for at least 24 hours. Before the second grout coat is applied, the surface must be dampened again and the second coat similarly moist-cured.

3. Applying two coats of cement-based paints, commercially prepared specifically for dampproofing basements. Manufacturers' recommendations should be followed.

In poorly drained and wet soils the earth side of concrete masonry basement walls should always be parged as described previously, under method 1. In addition, the parge coat should be given the additional protection previously described for methods 2 or 3. It is also advisable to secure advice on local conditions and necessary construction details such as adding one or more of the following: (1) sump pump; (2) reinforcement of floor slab against uplift by groundwater pressure; (3) membrane waterproofing; or (4) check valve in floor drain, and the like.

BRACING AND BACKFILLING

In some areas with poor soil conditions, masonry walls must be braced from the inside of the basement until the first floor and backfill are in place (Fig. 23). In other areas the support provided by the first floor framing is sufficient. (*See* Figs. 24 and 25.)

Whether or not bracing is needed depends on the nature of the soil, the width of the excavation to be backfilled, the presence of water or a fluid-type soil, the length of the wall, and the like. If there is no water present, a narrow trench when backfilled will exert less pressure on the wall than a widely excavated trench with slanting back slope.

All debris—trash, pieces of lumber, and sod—should be removed from the excavation before backfilling. The backfill should be made with soil from the excavation and should be free of large boulders, large frozen chunks of earth, sod, and material

Fig. 23. Parging should extend down to footing and form a cove at the base.

Fig. 24. Wood bracing supports basement wall until first floor and backfill are in place.

that can rot. Care should be taken to place the backfill evenly around the excavation to uniformly build up the pressure on the wall. Heavy earth-moving equipment must not operate too close to the wall because the pressure may become excessive. The backfill must not be watersoaked to hasten compaction, as the hydrostatic pressure on the wall could become excessive.

The top of the backfill should be placed above the adjacent grade to allow for anticipated settlement and to provide surface drainage away from the wall. [*See* Fig. 26 for concrete masonry basement wall construction (on right), and cast-in-place concrete basement wall construction (on left).]

FLOORS

Concrete for the basement floor is usually placed directly on firmly compacted soil. If the soil is dry, it should be dampened with water to prevent absorption of too much mixing water from the fresh concrete. However, in the case of poorly drained soils, a fill of coarse gravel or crushed stone 4 to 6 inches (10 to

Fig. 25. Cement-grout coats are scrubbed into the basement wall surface.

15 cm.) thick should be placed over the soil. This fill must be provided with a tile drain connected to a positive outlet to remove any water that would tend to accumulate under the floor slab; otherwise the fill should not be used.

The base for the concrete slab, whether it is the soil or the gravel or stone fill, should be thoroughly compacted to prevent any settlement of the slab and should be sloped toward the floor drains to ensure a uniform slab thickness. The floor slab should have a minimum thickness of 4 inches (10 cm.). (*See* Chap. 43, Concrete Floor Slabs on Ground.)

Floor drains should be placed at the proper elevations and the top of the slab sloped to the drains. Temporary screeds or string lines will help in placing the concrete surface to proper grade.

If there is danger of considerable groundwater and water pressure, the building site should be tiled and the water drained to a positive outlet. Where this is not possible, the floor slab should contain reinforcing steel designed by a competent engineer to withstand the uplift pressure. As an added precaution, the concrete for the slab should be placed in two layers having a bituminous built-up membrane between them for waterproofing.

Fig. 26. Metal bracing frame supporting basement wall.

When the first layer or base of the concrete floor has hardened and dried, it should be mopped with hot bituminous material. As the mopping proceeds, and before the application has time to cool and harden, a layer of roofing felt should be placed on the bituminous coating with edges of the felt lapped a minimum of 2 inches (5 cm.). Two layers of roofing felt are recommended. Hot bituminous material should be mopped between layers and also on top of the second felt. The membrane should be continuous over the entire floor area and carried up the inside of the foundation walls to the basement floor level.

Concrete for floors as well as footings must have both a minimum compressive strength of 3,000 psi (210 kgs. per sq. cm.) and a minimum cement content of 5 bags (470 pounds or 213.2 kgs.) per cubic yard. The concrete should be placed by chutes or other means as near to its final position as practicable. It should not be dumped at widely spaced intervals and allowed to flow horizontally to its final place.

After being placed, the concrete should be screeded or struck off to grade and immediately darbied, before any water bleeds to the surface, to bring the surface to an even plane. If water tends to bleed to the surface, all finishing operations should stop until the water has disappeared.

After the water sheen has disappeared and the concrete surface has stiffened enough to bear a man's weight with only a slight indentation, the surface should be floated with hand tools or power-driven float. (*See* Chap. 6, Concrete Equipment and Tools, and Chap. 21, Masonry Tools and Equipment.)

The purpose of floating is: (1) to embed the large aggregate just beneath the surface; (2) to remove any slight imperfections, humps, and voids to produce a plane surface; and (3) to consolidate mortar at the surface in preparation for final steel-troweling.

Immediately after floating, the surface should be steel-troweled with hand tools or by power to produce a smooth, dense surface. A second and third troweling are usually required, with adequate time lapses between operations.

Moist-curing of the concrete slab is one of the most important construction operations. Curing prevents rapid loss of moisture that might cause the concrete to shrink and form cracks. Concrete must attain sufficient tensile strength to resist such stresses and curing develops rapid strength gain. In addition, curing increases wear resistance and watertightness—necessary properties in floor slabs. (*See* Chap. 10, Curing Concrete, and Chap. 11, Finishing Concrete Slabs.)

Concrete can be moist-cured by covering with (1) burlap or canvas that is kept continuously wet, (2) waterproof paper, or (3) plastic sheets. Sometimes liquid membrane-curing compounds are used, but they may interfere later with bonding any floor tile or floor paint. If such curing compounds are to be used, the manufacturer should be consulted first.

To prevent any dusting (the appearance of a powdery material on the surface of concrete), care must be taken that all surface water and water sheen have disappeared before any floating or steel-troweling operations are begun. If any tempering heating units are used during cold-weather operations, they must be properly vented. Dusting will also occur because of carbon dioxide absorbed by the fresh concrete from unvented heaters.

Bond between the floor slab and all footings under basement walls and interior columns must be broken by use of building felt or a 1-inch (2.5-cm.) sand cushion (Figs. 6 and 7). In addition, a sleeve consisting of about three layers of building felt should be placed between the columns and the floor slab.

Contraction joints can be installed in the slab to help control any tendencies for shrinkage cracking. They should be placed in line with the interior columns, at changes in width of the floor slab or at maximum spacings of about 20 feet (6.1 meters). Such joints are formed by cutting grooves in the freshly placed concrete with a jointing tool. (*See* Chap. 21, Masonry Tools and Equipment, Fig. 1.) They also can be cut into the slab with a power saw as soon as the surface is firm enough not to be torn or damaged by the saw blade. The depth of these joints or grooves should be at least one-fourth the thickness of the slab. (*See* Chap. 22. Concrete Masonry Units, the section on Joints; *see also* Chap. 26, Bricklaying Tools and Equipment.)

Many basement floors are constructed without contraction

joints. Some homeowners and builders believe any random shrinkage cracking that may occur is not objectionable.

COLD-WEATHER CONSTRUCTION

Concrete should never be placed on frozen ground. It should have a temperature when placed of not less than 50° F. nor more than 70° F. (10° C. and 21° C., respectively). It should be kept and protected at that temperature range for three to five days by adequate covers such as tarpaulins or even loose straw.

Heating the mixing water to not more than 180° F. (82.3° C.) is a good method of raising the temperature of the concrete. If either the water or aggregates are heated to above 100° F. (37.8° C.), they should be combined in the mixer first before the cement is added. This will prevent any chance for flash set. If early high strengths are obtained with either high-early-strength portland cement or calcium chloride (in amounts up to two percent by weight of the portland cement), the protection period can be reduced to two or three days.

For additional information on cold-weather construction, *see* Chap. 17, Hot- and Cold-Weather Concreting, the section on Cold-Weather Concreting; *see also* Chap. 20, Concrete Masonry Construction in Cold Weather.

Chapter 52

Building Watertight Concrete Masonry Walls

Leaky masonry walls are sources of vexation to homeowners, architects, builders, masons, and to manufacturers of masonry units and mortars.

Leaky walls are not confined to any one type of masonry construction. Leaks have occurred and are occurring in walls built of the best materials and apparently with special care. The fact is often overlooked, however, that the percentage of those that leak is small compared with the large number of masonry walls that are watertight. Unfortunately the occasional important building that has leaky walls usually receives unfavorable attention, with the masonry units or the mortar erroneously being blamed for the leakage.

LEAKS IN MASONRY WALLS

A logical explanation for the leaks in masonry walls is the haste with which our modern buildings are erected. Workmanship is frequently sacrificed for speed. Perfection in design and materials cannot make up for this sacrifice.

The prevention of leaky walls must begin with the design of the building, follow through the selection of materials and the supervision of the workmanship, and continue with the maintenance of the structure after its completion.

FLASHING

Flashing should be placed under all vertical joints in sills, coping, and caps or other horizontal surfaces which may permit the accumulation of water on or the passage of water through them. Projecting soldier courses and water tables, walls corbelled back, and recessed panels with projecting horizontal courses at the bottom are frequently used without consideration for the more severe exposure resulting therefrom. As a result water seeps through the vertical joints into the wall. Snow and ice melting on these surfaces greatly increases the possibility of water entering the wall. Flashing over horizontal surfaces may be necessary. There is no alternative for adequate flashing. (*See* Chap. 34, Flashing and Overcoating Construction Details.)

Parapet walls should be flashed through just above the roof level and also under the coping. Only permanent, rust-resisting metal or bituminous, asphaltic or pitch preparations should be used for flashing.

Copings, caps, cornices, and sills should be provided with projections having drips. Overflowing gutters and leaky downspouts are a common source of trouble. Gutters and drains (Fig. 1) should be ample to carry away the heaviest rains. Metal from gutters should extend up under the roofing far enough to eliminate any possibility of water getting back of it.

MORTAR JOINTS

Raked joints greatly increase the chance for the development of leaks. In making these joints, there is a tendency to open up the body of the mortar and draw it away from the masonry unit, forming small ledges upon which water can collect. Cut joints also are likely to be torn and drawn away from the units. If these joints are used, adequate means of waterproofing or parging should be provided, or special attention given to the selection of materials and tooling of joints. (*See* Chap. 51, Concrete Masonry Basements.)

Concave and V joints afford the best protection against leaks and are recommended in preference to other types. Each of these provides an excellent surface for shedding water. Their formation requires an amount of pressure sufficient to compress the mortar and create a firm bond between the mortar and the units at the face of the wall.

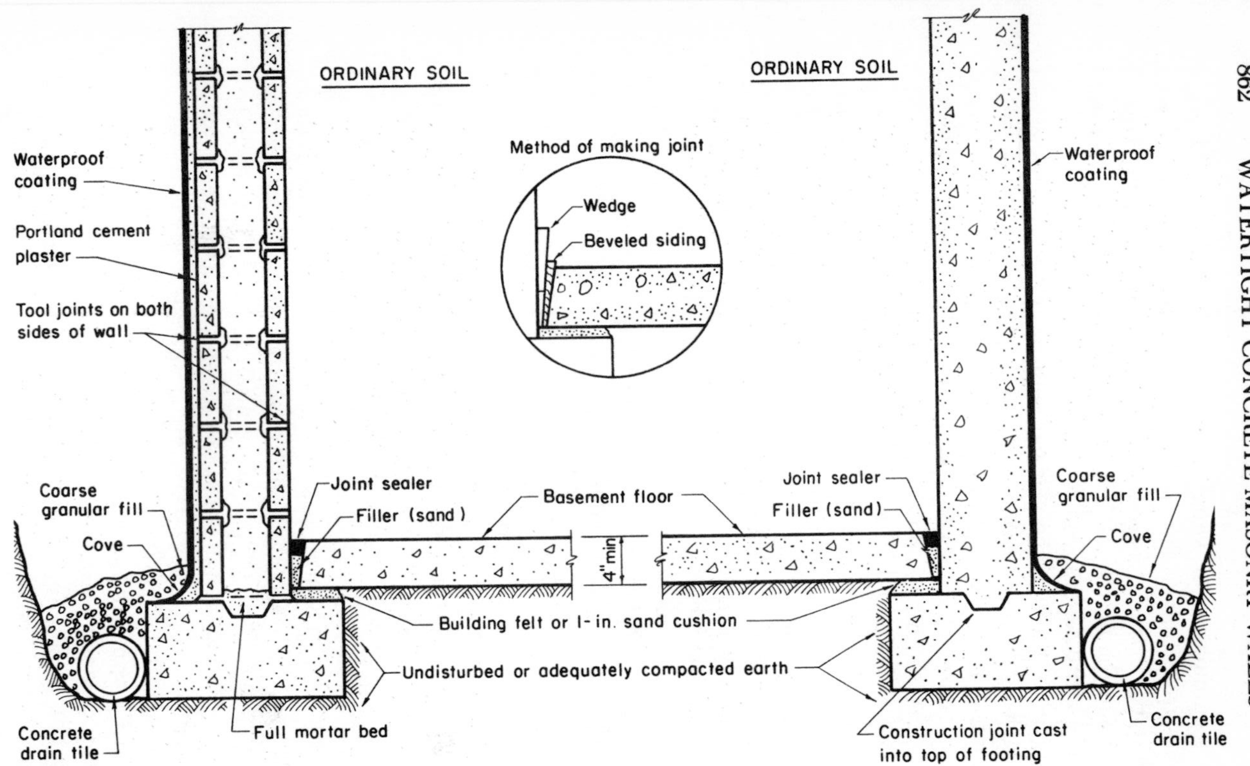

Fig. 1. Concrete drain tile laid with open joints around outside of basement wall.

Thin mortar joints are best, because it is known that such joints produce a stronger, more watertight wall. Thick joints may be desirable for architectural effects, but unless precautions are taken to make the wall surface tight, when the joints are more than ½-inch (1.3-cm.) thick, watertightness may be sacrificed for appearance.

An important requirement of a mortar is that it be workable for the job at hand. Workability is obtained by proper grading of the sand, by good water retentivity, and by thorough mixing rather than by use of excessive amounts of cementitious material.

Water retentivity is the property of a mortar that resists rapid loss of water to masonry units which may possess high absorption. Loss of moisture because of poor water retention results in rapid loss of plasticity and may seriously reduce the effectiveness of the bond. Water retention requirements of the current specifications for mortar for unit masonry specify that mortar of the materials and proportions to be used in the construction should have a flow after suction of not less than 70 percent. As concrete masonry units should be kept dry until they are built into the wall, they should never be wetted to control suction before the application of mortar. It may be necessary to use mortars having water retentivities of more than 70 percent when the air and concrete masonry units are exceedingly hot and dry.

No mortar, however good, can make up for defective design and poor workmanship. While some mortars are better adapted than others for particular jobs, the differences in the watertight properties are minor compared with design and workmanship.

Tight joints are essential to watertight masonry. Hollow concrete masonry units should have full mortar coverage of the face shells in both the horizontal and vertical joints. Furrowing of the mortar should not be permitted. If all the joints in the exposed face of the wall are tightly filled, there is little possibility of leakage.

Tool finishing of the joint should be delayed until the mortar has stiffened sufficiently to hold its shape. A careful tooling at this time is frequently the final touch required to make the joints watertight.

While workmanship is the most important element, the mason cannot fairly be held wholly responsible for leaks arising from poor workmanship. The homeowner, architect, and builder share the responsibility because they hire the mason and govern the type of workmanship desired. Most masons are capable of doing good work, but the economic necessity of getting a large number of units laid per day frequently works against painstaking craftsmanship. Some homeowners are able to do this work themselves.

Good workmanship, good materials, and good design will add but a small percentage to the original cost of a structure. Any additional cost entailed in obtaining good workmanship will be measurably less than the expense of repairing leaks that are likely to result from attempts to save money by violating principles of good construction. (*See* Chap. 53, Miscellaneous Concrete Masonry Wall Jobs.)

REPAIR OF LEAKY MASONRY

Where leaky masonry walls are encountered, the cause must be determined before any intelligent steps to correct this condition are undertaken. The following construction features should be checked:

1. Was thorough flashing placed under all copings, cornices, sills, and other horizontal surfaces where water might collect and enter the wall?
2. Are gutters and downspouts properly installed?
3. Were suitable materials used for flashing, gutters, and downspouts?
4. Were drips provided on all projecting surfaces?
5. Are mortar joints well filled?
6. Are there any ledges on mortar joints where water can collect and subsequently seep into the wall?
7. Have cracks developed where mortar joins the masonry units?
8. Are the mortar joints thin or thick? If thick, this fact may be causing leakage. Thin joints are best.

9. Are mortar joints of the type which are most readily watertight—that is, concave or V joints? These two are best.

10. If raked joints were used, was adequate waterproofing or parging provided? If not, this fact may be causing leakage.

11. Are there any cracks in the wall due to settlement or faulty design?

The results of this examination will largely determine the methods to be used to satisfactorily recondition the walls.

Faulty flashing and horizontal surfaces should always be repaired prior to treating vertical wall surfaces. A plastic caulking compound or similar material should be used around cased window openings or where the masonry joins other types of material.

All openings in the wall proper which tend to leak should be repointed or filled. In this connection, vertical joints should receive particular attention as they are often improperly filled during the original construction. In most instances, adequate treatment of flashing, horizontal surfacing, and around openings will prevent water from passing through the masonry wall. Where it is evident that water passes through the masonry units a waterproofing treatment of the vertical wall surfaces may be necessary.

The application of two coats of portland cement paint to concrete masonry walls has proved to be an effective and durable treatment for waterproofing this type of wall. In instances where repointing and exterior wall treatment costs appear to be excessive, the application of three coats of portland cement stucco may prove to be the most economical and satisfactory method for maintaining the exterior masonry wall. (*See* Section 4, Stuccoing.)

Chapter 53

Miscellaneous Concrete Masonry Wall Jobs

DESIGNING WALLS TO AVOID CUTTING UNITS ON JOB

To achieve economy in construction, concrete masonry walls should be laid out to make maximum use of full- and half-length units. This minimizes cutting and fitting of units on the job—operations which slow up construction. All dimensions such as overall length and height of wall, width and height of door and window openings and wall areas between doors, windows and corners should be planned to use full- and half-sized units which are commonly carried in stock (Fig. 1). Full advantage of modular design for concrete masonry requires that window and door frames be of modular dimensions which fit modular full- and half-size units. All horizontal dimensions will then be in multiples of nominal half-length units, and all vertical dimensions will be multiples of nominal full-height units. Therefore, with the nominal 8- × 8- × 16-inch (20- × 20- × 40-cm.) block, both horizontal and vertical dimensions should be designed to be in multiples of 8 inches (20 cm.). In those sections of the country where units nominally 8-inches wide, 4-inches high, and 16-inches long (20- × 10- × 40-cm.) are used, the horizontal dimensions should be planned to be in multiples of 8 inches (20 cm.) (half-length units) and the vertical dimensions in multiples of 4 inches (10 cm.). Where the thickness of the wall is greater or less than the length of a half unit, a special length unit is required at each corner in each course. (*See* Appendix 2, Suggested Details of Concrete Masonry Construction.) It is recommended that the designer obtain schedules of the sizes of concrete masonry units locally available. (*See* Section 2, Concrete Masonry.)

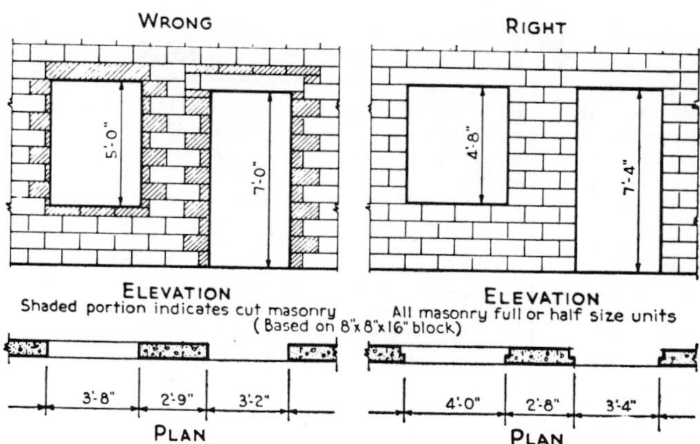

Fig. 1. Examples of wrong and right planning of concrete masonry wall openings.

In modular planning the dimensions used on working drawings are nominal and are from center to center of mortar joints. With concrete masonry units all mortar joints are designed to be ⅜-inch (9.3-mm.) thick. (*See* Appendix 3, Patterns of Concrete Masonry.)

DIMENSIONING CONCRETE MASONRY WALLS

Tables 44 and 45 show the number of full- and half-length masonry units required to obtain given dimensions. Dimensions are in accordance with modular planning. The location as well as the width and height of openings should fit these dimensions. With metal sash it may be necessary to provide metal surrounds to fit them into modular concrete masonry openings.

DRY UNITS

When delivered to the job, concrete masonry units should be dry enough to comply with the specified limitation for moisture content. They should be maintained in this dry condition by

No. of stretchers	Nominal length of concrete masonry walls	
	Units 15⅝″ long and half units 7⅝″ long with ⅜″ thick head joints.	Units 11⅝″ long and half units 5⅝″ long with ⅜″ thick head joints.
1	1′ 4″	1′ 0″
1½	2′ 0″	1′ 6″
2	2′ 8″	2′ 0″
2½	3′ 4″	2′ 6″
3	4′ 0″	3′ 0″
3½	4′ 8″	3′ 6″
4	5′ 4″	4′ 0″
4½	6′ 0″	4′ 6″
5	6′ 8″	5′ 0″
5½	7′ 4″	5′ 6″
6	8′ 0″	6′ 0″
6½	8′ 8″	6′ 6″
7	9′ 4″	7′ 0″
7½	10′ 0″	7′ 6″
8	10′ 8″	8′ 0″
8½	11′ 4″	8′ 6″
9	12′ 0″	9′ 0″
9½	12′ 8″	9′ 6″
10	13′ 4″	10′ 0″
10½	14′ 0″	10′ 6″
11	14′ 8″	11′ 0″
11½	15′ 4″	11′ 6″
12	16′ 0″	12′ 0″
12½	16′ 8″	12′ 6″
13	17′ 4″	13′ 0″
13½	18′ 0″	13′ 6″
14	18′ 8″	14′ 0″
14½	19′ 4″	14′ 6″
15	20′ 0″	15′ 0″
20	26′ 8″	20′ 0″

TABLE 44. NOMINAL LENGTH OF CONCRETE MASONRY WALLS BY STRETCHERS.

No. of courses	Nominal height of concrete masonry walls	
	Units 7⅝″ high and ⅜″ thick bed joint	Units 3⅝″ high and ⅜″ thick bed joint
1	8″	4″
2	1′ 4″	8″
3	2′ 0″	1′ 0″
4	2′ 8″	1′ 4″
5	3′ 4″	1′ 8″
6	4′ 0″	2′ 0″
7	4′ 8″	2′ 4″
8	5′ 4″	2′ 8″
9	6′ 0″	3′ 0″
10	6′ 8″	3′ 4″
15	10′ 0″	5′ 0″
20	13′ 4″	6′ 8″
25	16′ 8″	8′ 4″
30	20′ 0″	10′ 0″
35	23′ 4″	11′ 8″
40	26′ 8″	13′ 4″
45	30′ 0″	15′ 0″
50	33′ 4″	16′ 8″

TABLE 45. NOMINAL HEIGHT OF CONCRETE MASONRY WALLS BY COURSES.

stockpiling them on planks or other supports free from contact with the ground and covering them with roofing paper or a tarpaulin for protection against wetting. Moreover, any time work stops, the top of the wall should be covered with tarpaulins or boards to prevent rain or snow from entering the cores of the block. Concrete masonry units should *never* be wetted prior to laying in the wall, a practice customary with some masonry materials. It is necessary to observe these precautions and lay only dry units to minimize shrinkage in the finished wall. (*See* Chap. 22, Concrete Masonry Units.)

In some cases, it may be advisable to dry block below the moisture content given in most specifications. This applies particularly where exposed concrete masonry walls are to be used in buildings where relatively high temperatures and low humidities are likely to occur over extended periods of time, as during the winter heating season. Experience has shown that damp concrete masonry units can be artificially dried to the air-dry condition which they will attain in service. This can be done by blowing heated air through the cores and the spaces between units stacked to facilitate drying. Generally, this drying will not require more than 48 hours with the equipment and method shown in Fig. 2. With larger capacity drying equipment the time can be shortened.

FOOTINGS

Footings for masonry walls should be of ample width and thickness to carry the expected loads in accordance with local building code requirements. Inadequate footings are to be avoided since they may result in uneven settlement which may cause cracking in the walls. Footings should be placed on firm, undisturbed soil of adequate load-bearing capacity and below frost penetration. In areas where there are no applicable local building codes, it is general practice to make footings for small buildings twice as wide as the thickness of the walls which will bear on them. The thickness of such footings is made equal to one-half their width (Fig. 3). (*See* Chap. 41, Footings.)

SUBSURFACE DRAINAGE

Unless the groundwater level in wet seasons is well below the footing or the basement floor, the placing of a line of drain tile along the outer side of footings is recommended. The tile line should have a fall of at least ½ inch in 12 feet (3.5 mm. per meter) and should drain to a suitable outlet. Pieces of roofing felt placed over the joints prevent sediment from entering the tile during backfitting. The tile line should be covered to a depth of 12 inches (30 cm.) with a permeable fill of coarse gravel or crushed stone ranging from 1 to 1½ inch (2.5 to 3.8 cm.) in size after which the balance of the trench can be filled with earth from the excavation after the first floor is in place.

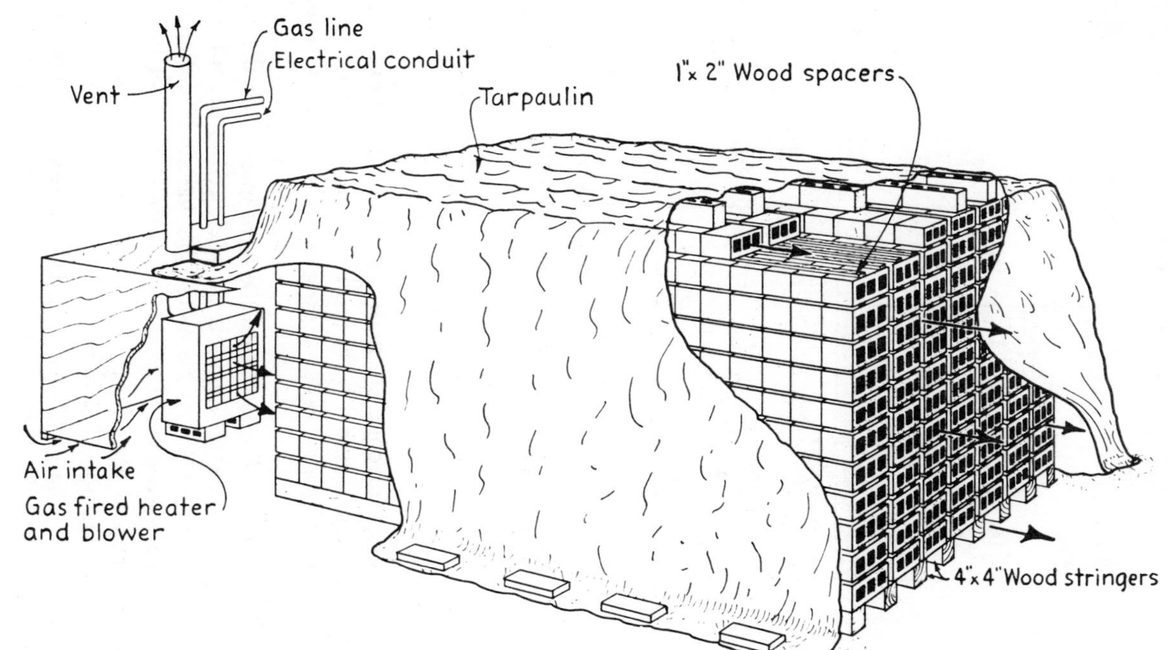

Fig. 2. A suggested method for drying concrete block. It can be used indoors or outdoors at plant or jobsite.

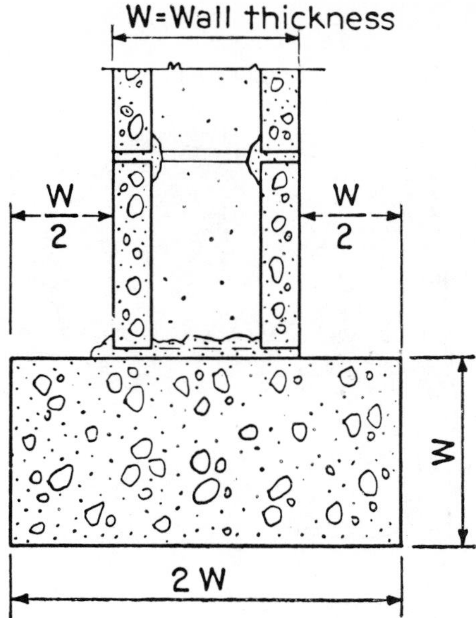

Fig. 3. Recommended footing dimensions for small buildings.

ANCHORING THE WALLS

Lateral support for concrete masonry walls is commonly obtained by the floors and roof. Cast-in-place concrete floor or roof slabs bearing on masonry walls are considered as providing sufficient anchorage.

When wood joists or wood beams bear on masonry walls, the ends of the joists or beams are securely anchored to the walls at maximum intervals of 6 feet (1.8 meters) in one- and two-family dwellings and a maximum of 4 feet (1.2 meters) in other buildings. Metal anchors at least 16 inches (40 cm.) long having a minimum cross section of ¼ × 1¼ inches (.9 × 3.1 cm.) are fastened securely to the ends of the joists or beams and are provided with split and upset ends or other approved means for building into masonry.

When masonry walls are parallel to wood joists or wood beams the walls must be anchored to the floor or roof joists with metal anchors spaced at maximum intervals of 8 feet (2.4 meters) in one- and two-family dwellings and 6 feet (1.8 meters) in other buildings. Such anchors should engage at least three joists or beams and be provided with upset or T-ends which develop the full strength of the anchor strap.

SETTING DOOR AND WINDOW FRAMES

Jamb block (Fig. 4) are commonly used in laying up the sides of window and door openings. The offset design of these block and of precast concrete lintels permit window or door frames to be inserted after the walls have been laid (Fig. 5). This method is preferred over the method of setting and bracing the frames in position on the wall and then building the walls up around them.

SILLS AND LINTELS

Most concrete sills are precast. However, concrete sills may be cast-in-place. Figure 6 shows sills for use with either wood or metal window frames. The sills are sloped to drain water away quickly. A drip ledge causes the water to fall free and not run down the face and stain the wall.

Precast sills are usually installed after the masonry walls are laid. When installed as the wall is laid up they should be protected against possible breakage or staining during construction. Joints under sills should be completely filled with mortar and tightly tooled. Joints at ends of sills should be filled with mortar or with an elastic caulking compound.

Lintels over door and window openings carry either the wall load or both the wall and floor loads as the design of the structure may require. Reinforced concrete lintels, one- or two-piece, are suitable for use. They may be precast in a products plant or can be cast-in-place. Figure 7 shows one-piece and split lintels (two-piece) with Tables 46 and 47 for supporting wall loads only. Figure 8 and Table 48 are for lintels supporting both wall

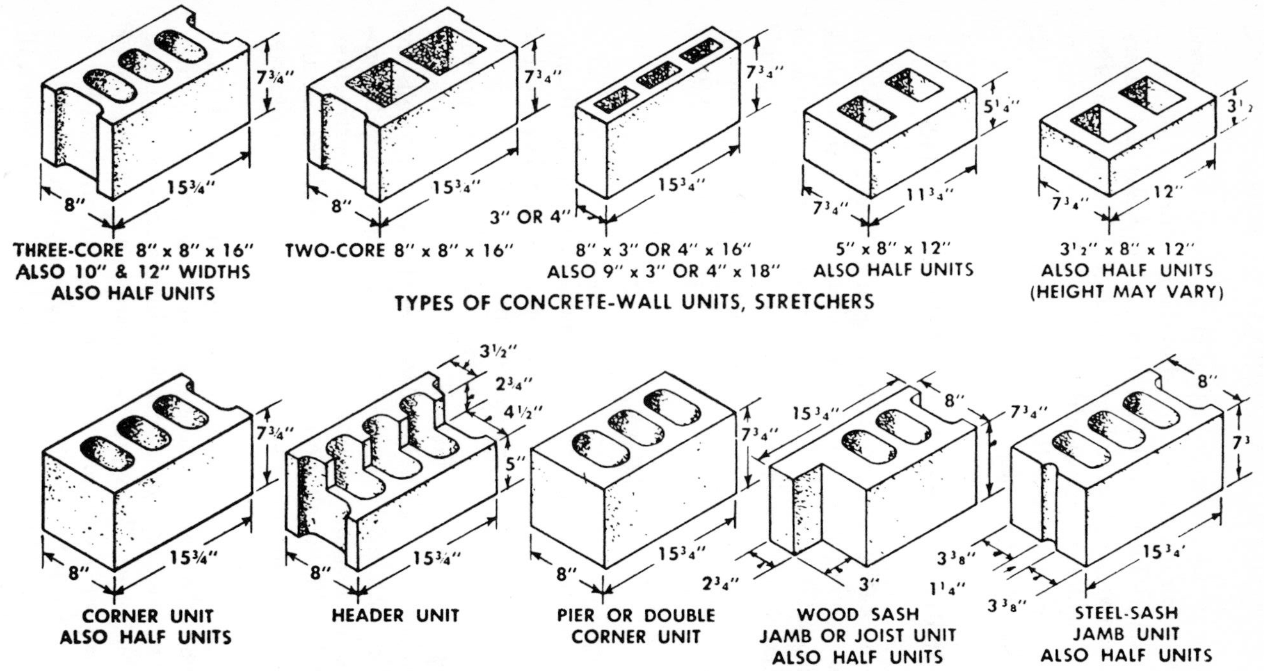

Fig. 4. Typical shapes and sizes of concrete masonry units.

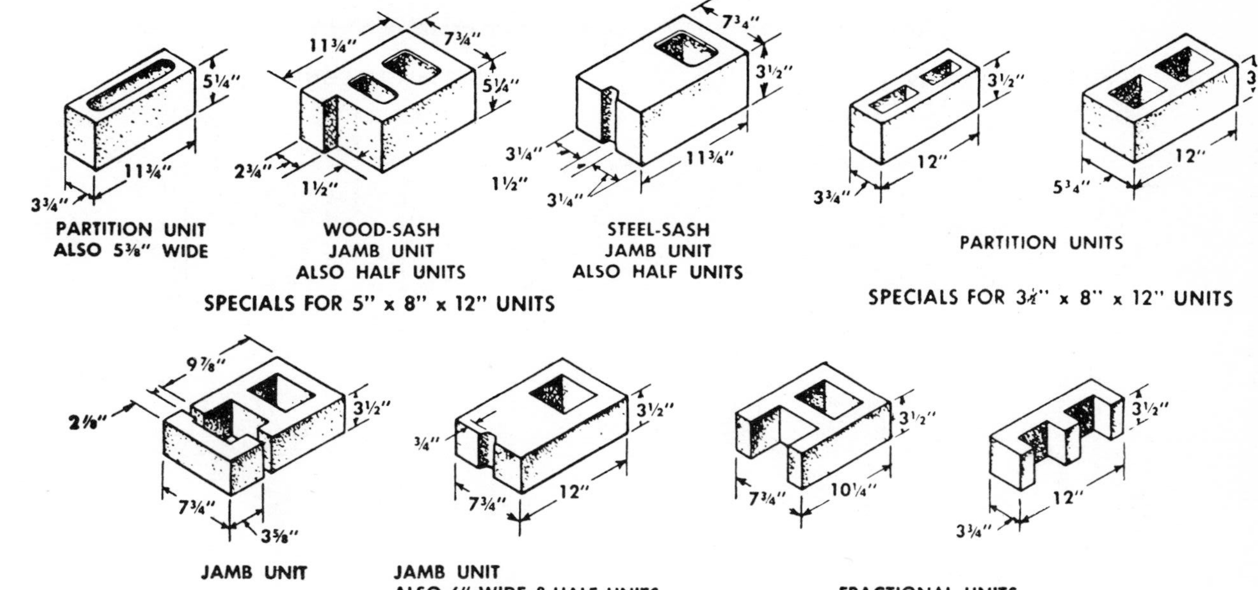

Fig. 4. Typical shapes and sizes of concrete masonry units (continued).

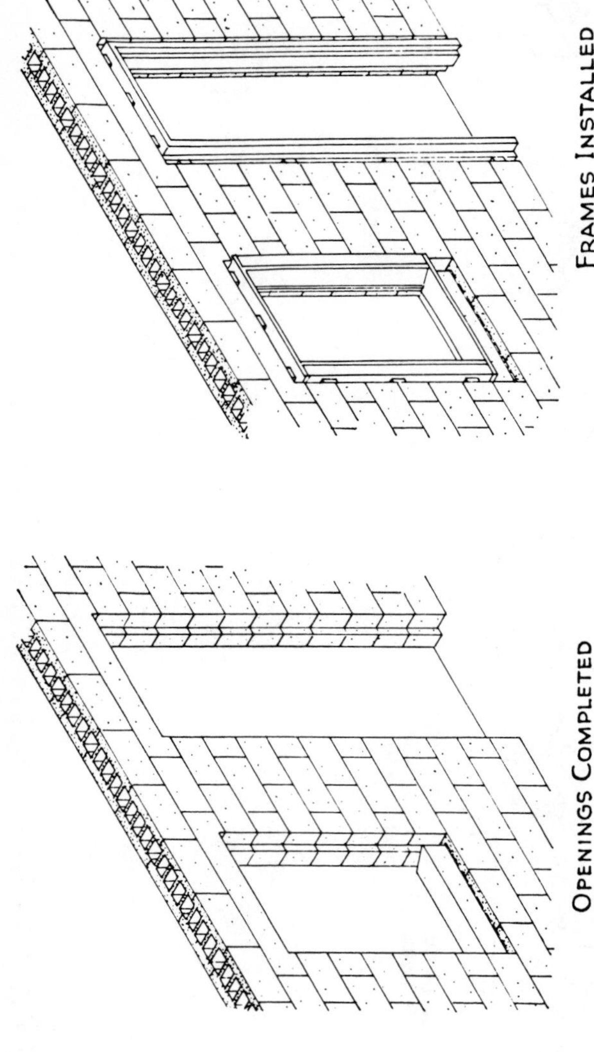

Fig. 5. Openings for windows and doors are built first—then frames are installed.

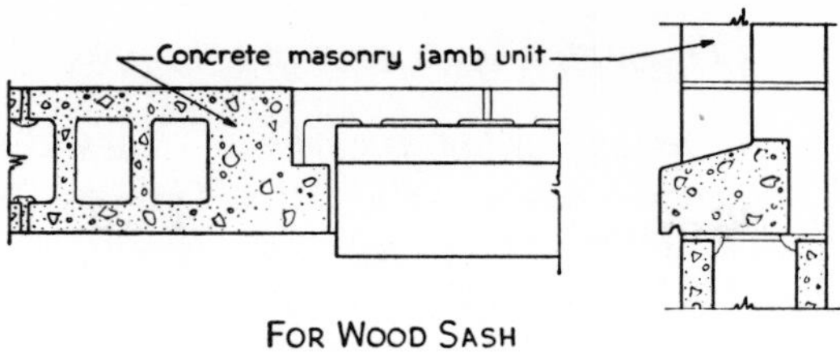

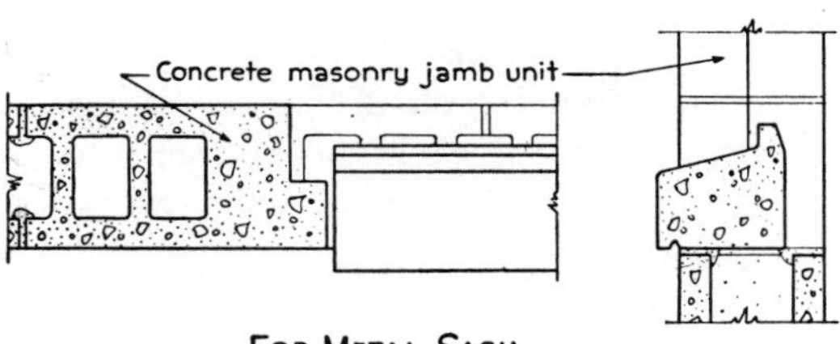

Fig. 6. Precast concrete sills.

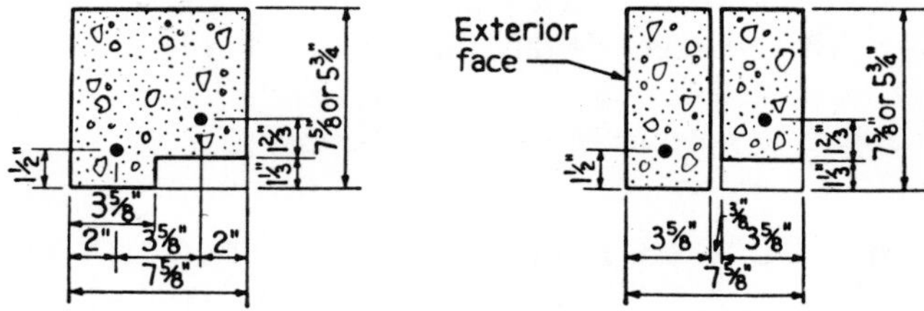

Fig. 7. One-piece lintel and split lintel

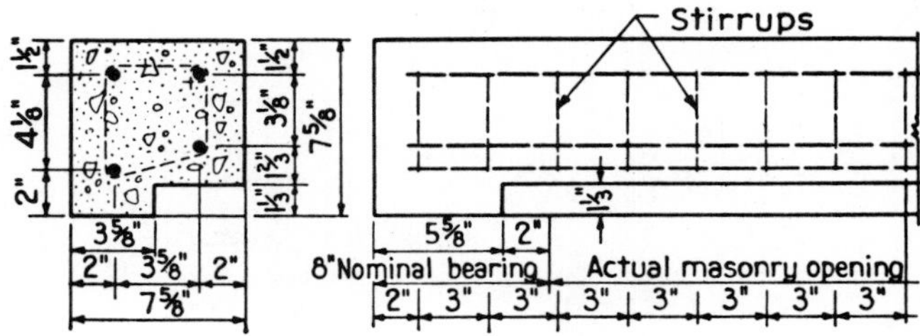

Fig. 8. One-piece lintel with stirrups

and floor loads. Designs for lintels shown in Tables 46, 47, and 48 are based on concrete having a strength of 2000 psi (140 kgs per sq. cm.). Split lintels should never be used to support combined wall and floor loads because it is difficult to design the inner section to have the same deflection as the outer section which carries wall load only. Differences in deflection of the two sections would probably result in cracks in the masonry wall. Split lintels are light in weight and easy to handle. The air space between the sections provides some insulation.

Reinforced concrete lintels should have a minimum bearing of at least 8 inches (20 cm.) at each end. Larger bearing areas are required for lintels having long spans carrying heavy loads. All but short simple lintels act as reinforced concrete beams and should be designed by an engineer.

Where it is desired to have lintels with a surface texture matching that of the concrete masonry wall, special cast-in-place or precast lintels can be made. Lintel block with depressed webs or without webs (Fig. 4) are laid end to end forming a channel. Reinforcing rods are placed in the channel and then it is filled with concrete. If the lintel is built in place, it must be firmly supported during construction. Another method is to use steel angles to support block over openings (Fig. 9).

METHODS OF INSTALLING HEATING DUCTS AND ELECTRICAL CONDUITS IN CONCRETE MASONRY WALLS

1. Cores are cut out of concrete masonry wall units to accommodate the heating ducts (Fig. 10).

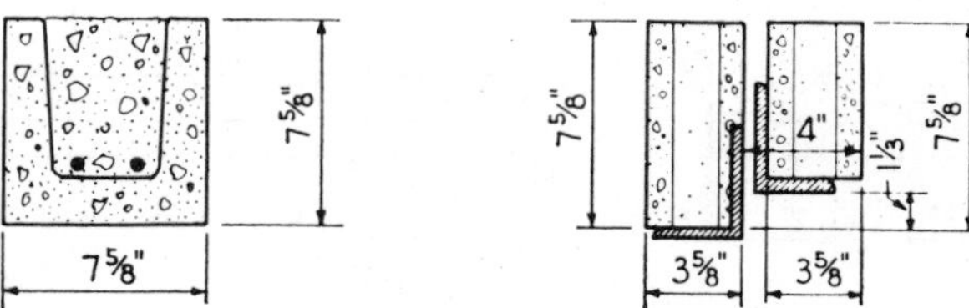

Fig. 9. Lintel block and steel angle lintels.

Size of lintel		Clear span of lintel ft.	Bottom reinforcement	
Height in.	Width in.		No. bars	Size of bars
5¾	7⅝	Up to 7	2	⅜-in. round deformed
5¾	7⅝	7 to 8	2	⅝-in. round deformed
7⅝	7⅝	Up to 8	2	⅜-in. round deformed
7⅝	7⅝	8 to 9	2	½-in. round deformed
7⅝	7⅝	9 to 10	2	⅝-in. round deformed

TABLE 46. LINTELS WITH WALL LOAD ONLY.

Size of lintel		Clear span of lintel ft.	Bottom reinforcement	
Height in.	Width in.		No. bars	Size of bars
5¾	3⅝	Up to 7	1	⅜-in. round deformed
5¾	3⅝	7 to 8	1	⅝-in. round deformed
7⅝	3⅝	Up to 8	1	⅜-in. round deformed
7⅝	3⅝	8 to 9	1	½-in. round deformed
7⅝	3⅝	9 to 10	1	⅝-in. round deformed

TABLE 47. SPLIT LINTELS WITH WALL LOAD ONLY.

Size of lintel		Clear span of lintel ft.	Reinforcement		Web reinforcement No. 6 gage wire stirrups. Spacings from end of lintel—both ends the same
Height in.	Width in.		Top	Bottom	
7⅝	7⅝	3	None	2—½-in. round	No stirrups required
7⅝	7⅝	4	None	2—¾-in. round	3 stirrups, Sp.: 2, 3, 3 in.
7⅝	7⅝	5	2—⅜-in. round	2—⅞-in. round	5 stirrups, Sp.: 2, 3, 3, 3, 3 in.
7⅝	7⅝	6	2—½-in. round	2—⅞-in. round	6 stirrups, Sp.: 2, 3, 3, 3, 3, 3 in.
7⅝	7⅝	7	2— 1-in. round	2— 1-in. round	9 stirrups, Sp.: 2, 2, 3, 3, 3, 3, 3, 3, 3 in.

TABLE 48. LINTELS WITH WALL AND FLOOR LOADS. (FLOOR LOAD ASSUMED TO BE 85 POUNDS PER SQUARE FOOT WITH 20-FOOT SPAN.)

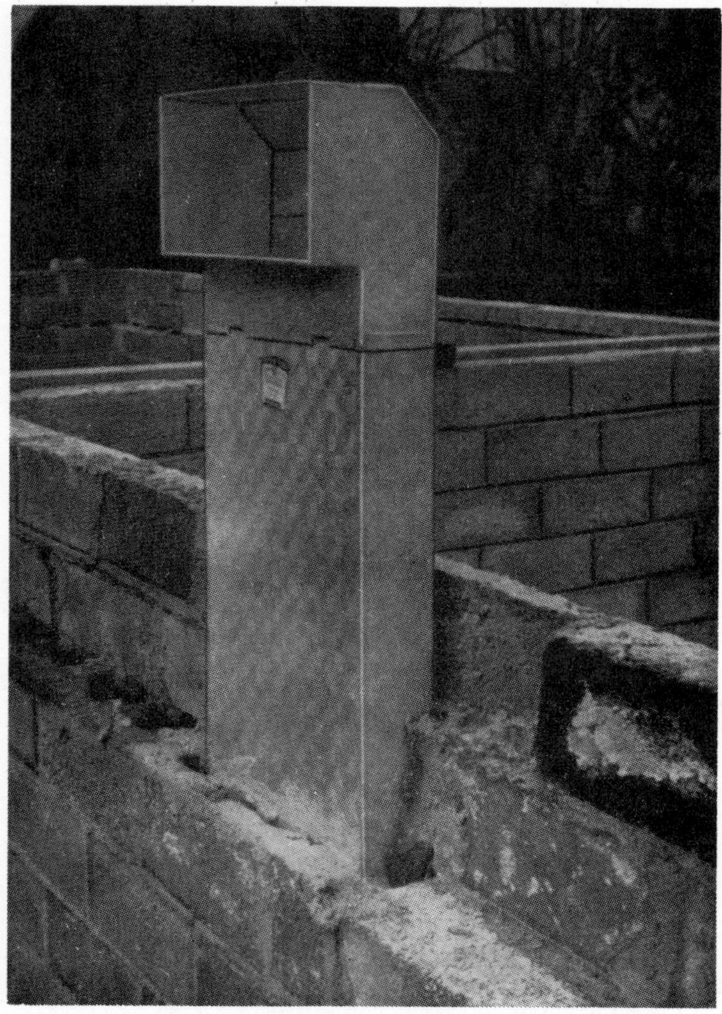

Fig. 10. Cores are cut out of concrete masonry wall units to accommodate the heating ducts.

2. Heating duct in exterior wall to be plastered direct on inside (Fig. 11).

3. Heating duct in interior non-load-bearing partition to be plastered direct on both sides (Fig. 12).

4. Typical method of installing electric conduit—concrete masonry wall furred and plastered (Fig. 13).

5. Heating duct in interior load-bearing wall (Fig. 14).

CONCRETE MASONRY WALL FINISHES

A wide variety of wall finishes are available with concrete masonry construction. The finish to use in any particular case will be governed by the type of structure in which the walls will be exposed and the architectural effects desired. Several popular finishes are described in this section.

SAMPLE PANELS

Regardless of which finish is selected, it is recommended that *sample panel walls* be constructed on all important jobs as a means of conveying to block producers, masons, and building contractors the grade of materials, quality of workmanship, and precise appearance desired in the finished walls. Such panels are much more effective than written words or photographs in defining and specifying the quality of work required.

Panels should be about 40 inches (100 cm.) long and at least four courses high and constructed of block of the same type, size, and surface texture as will be used in the finished wall. The units should also be laid in the same pattern with the same kind of joints as will be required in the finished work. If finished walls are to be painted, panels should also be painted.

Panels should be kept for reference until the construction is completed in a satisfactory manner.

WALL PATTERNS AND SURFACE TREATMENTS

Architects have worked out many interesting variations in

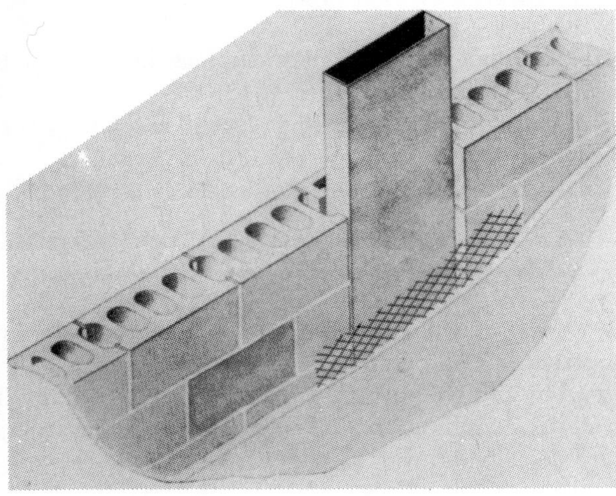

Fig. 11. Heating duct on inside wall will be plastered directly on inside wall.

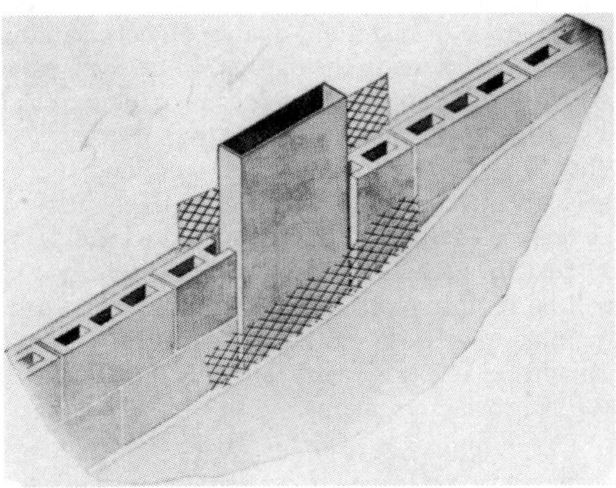

Fig. 12. Heating duct in interior non-load-bearing partition will be plastered directly on both sides.

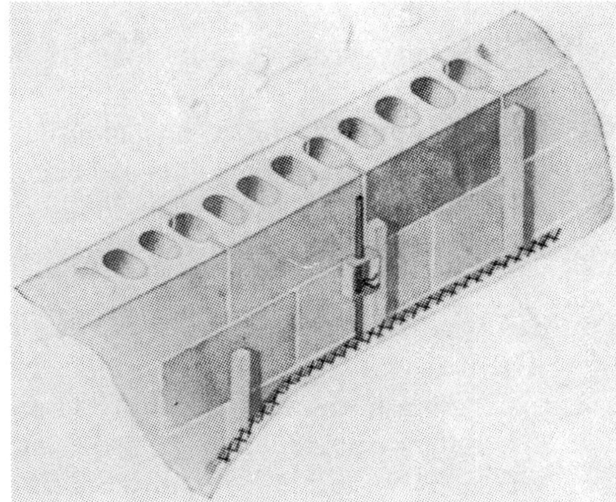

Fig. 13. Typical installation of electrical conduit.

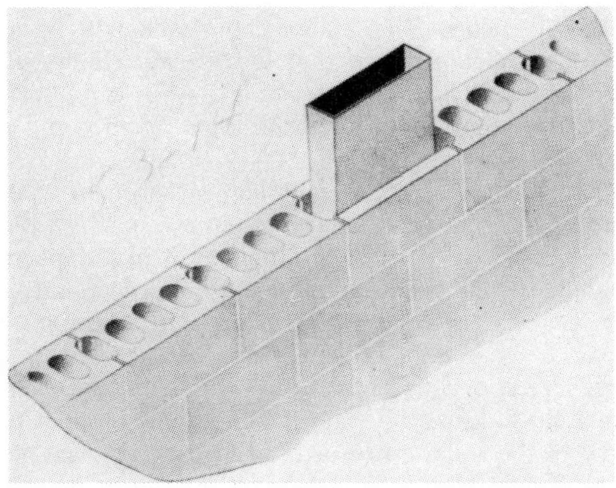

Fig. 14. Heating duct in interior load-bearing wall.

treatment of course heights and joints. The units may be laid in regular courses of the same height, or in courses of two or more different heights, or several sizes of units may be laid up in a prearranged ashlar pattern.

In some wall treatments all the joints are accentuated by deep tooling; in others only the horizontal joints are accentuated. In the latter treatment the vertical joints after tooling are refilled with mortar and then rubbed flush after the mortar has partially hardened to give it a texture similar to that of the concrete masonry units. In this treatment the tooled horizontal joints stand out in strong relief. It is well suited to buildings where it is desired to emphasize strong horizontal lines. When an especially massive effect is sought, every second or third horizontal joint may be tooled, with all other joints, both horizontal and vertical, rubbed flush after tooling and refilling with mortar.

Another variation in finish is obtained by extruded joints. An excess of mortar is used. Some of the mortar is squeezed out or extruded as the block are set and pressed into place. This mortar is not trimmed off but is left to harden in its extruded form (Fig. 15). This treatment is best suited to dry climates since the extruded joints may not be entirely weathertight.

Slump block (Fig. 16) are used to achieve special and unusual architectural effects. Slump block are made with a concrete mixture of such consistency that they sag or slump when removed from the molds, with the result that the irregularly faced units vary considerably in height, surface texture, and general appearance.

Split-block (Fig. 17) afford another variation in wall finish. They are used for facing fireplaces, chimneys, or the entire interior and exterior walls of the building. Split-block are made by splitting a hardened concrete unit lengthwise. The units are laid in the wall with the fractural faces exposed. Many interesting variations can be obtained by introducing mineral colors and by using aggregates of different gradings and colors in the concrete mixture. Split-block can be laid in simple broken joint patterns or in any of the other patterns used in concrete masonry construction. The fractured faces of the units produce a wall of rugged appearance.

Fig. 15. Extruded joints.

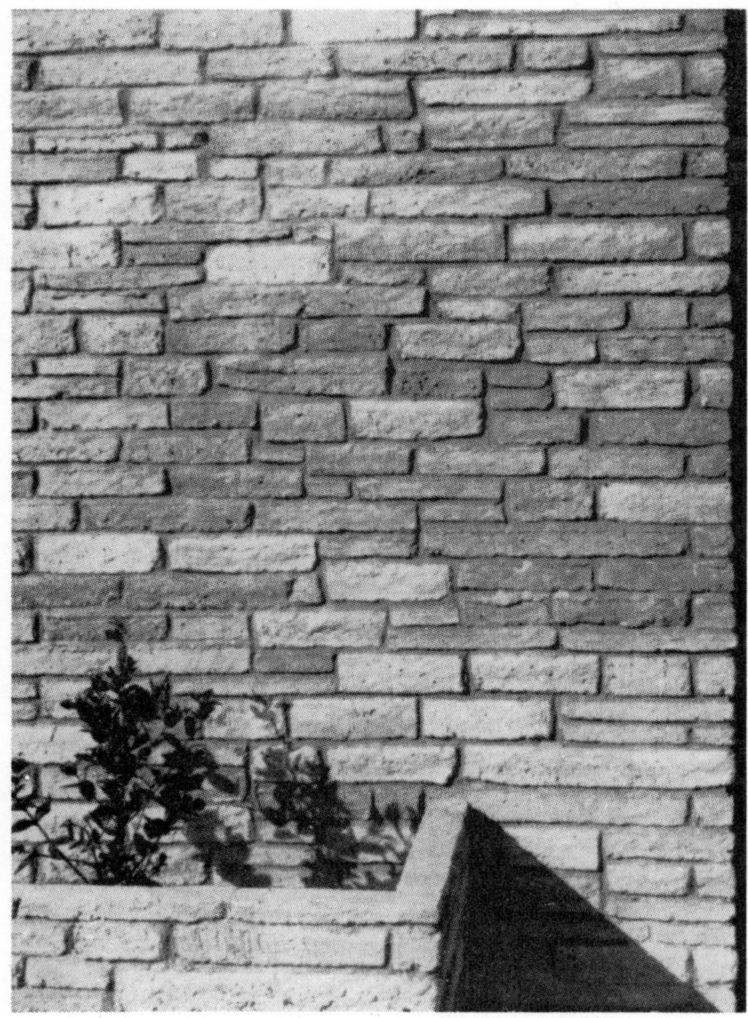

Fig. 16. Slump block laid in an ashlar pattern.

Fig. 17. Tooling mortar joints of concrete split-block masonry.

All block intended for use in exterior walls and which will not be painted should have low absorption, with joints carefully tooled for weathertightness.

PAINTED CONCRETE MASONRY WALLS

The growing popularity of concrete masonry and the demand for white or light-colored exterior surfaces has resulted in the increased use of portland cement base paints. Portland cement paint properly applied to concrete masonry walls serves two practical purposes—it provides attractive finishes and helps to make masonry surfaces weathertight.

Portland cement paint is sold in powdered form in a variety of colors and is mixed with water before applying. It should meet the requirements of the Federal Specification for Paint, Serial Designation: TT-P-21, Type II, Class A and Class B. Class A paint is used where the surface texture of the masonry wall is to be preserved. Class B paint contains a filler which gives the paint more body and is used to fill open porous surfaces.

Tests conducted on various types of paints on masonry walls have found that portland cement base paints are highly effective as weatherproofing and that they have a high durability rating.

The normal exterior concrete masonry wall treatment consists of two coats of portland cement paint. Where walls are constructed of dense block with weathertight joints, and paint is used only for its color, one coat of paint ordinarily will be sufficient.

One coat of portland cement paint is usually adequate for interior walls where weathertightness is not a factor. Surface texture as well as sound absorption values are better preserved when one instead of two coats of paint is used.

Portland cement paint should be applied to surfaces which are clean and free from oil, oil paint, dirt, or any substances which will prevent proper adhesion. Cracks or other wall imperfections should be cleaned of loose particles, dampened and filled with a stiff portland cement grout, and should be allowed to cure before painting.

The surface should be lightly and uniformly *dampened but not soaked* with water before painting is begun so that the wall will not absorb mixing water needed for proper hardening of the cement paint. A *garden pressure-sprayer* with a fine fog spray nozzle is recommended for this purpose (Fig. 18). All flashing, hangers, fasteners, trim, and other fixed supports should be in place before painting is started.

Portland cement base paint should be prepared by mixing with water in the manner and to the consistency recommended in the instructions furnished by the manufacturer. Frequent stirring is necessary to keep the paint powder in suspension. A shallow pan 4 to 6 inches (10 to 15 cm.) deep and 12 inches (30 cm.) or more wide provides a good container. In such a pan the paint can be stirred easily and quickly. When the pan is filled to a depth of only 2 or 3 inches (5 to 7.5 cm.) the paint can be stirred by the painter as he refills his brush.

Brushes (Fig. 19) with stiff fiber bristles not over 2 inches (5 cm.) long, such as scrub and fender brushes, should be used to scrub the paint into surface pores. Brushes should be designed to keep the hands from unnecessary contact with the paint, as tender or sensitive skin may become irritated by prolonged contact with cement paint. Typical brushes used in applying portland cement base paint are shown in Fig. 19: (1) ordinary scrub brush, (2) window brush, (3) brush with handle, and (4) fender brush. The use of rubber gloves is advisable in some instances.

The first coat, when scrubbed into the surface, will eliminate any small pinholes through which water otherwise might enter the wall. Mortar joints around each block should be painted first.

When the first coat has hardened sufficiently, usually not sooner than 12 hours, the second coat should be applied after first dampening the surface. After the painting has been started it should be continued to some natural stopping point such as corners, doors, belt courses, and the like. Frequent stirring of the paint is essential.

Paint should not be applied to frosty surfaces nor should painting be attempted if the temperature is likely to be below 40° F (4.5° C.) during the following 12 hours.

Fig. 18. Surface should be uniformly damp but not wet before painting.

Fig. 19. Typical brushes used in applying portland cement base paint.

Properly applied and cured, portland cement paint bonds to and becomes a part of the concrete masonry wall, sealing the mortar joints and block surfaces.

High winds, excessive heat, and strong sunshine will dry cement paint quickly and render it ineffective as a weathertight coating unless it is properly moist cured. Improperly cured portland cement base paints may chalk or dust. The first coat should, therefore, be kept in a slightly damp condition for at least 12 hours and the finish coat for 48 hours. Keeping the paint moist with a fine fog spray should start as soon as the paint is hard enough to resist damage.

Two-tone effects can be produced by applying first and second coats of different but harmonizing colors—as for example, a first coat of light brown and a second coat of cream. In this treatment the second coat is usually painted lightly over the first, touching only the high spots and being careful not to brush paint into the depressions. Another variation of this method is to rub off part of the second coat producing a mottled effect. A variety of other color combinations can be used depending on the skill of the painter and the decorative effect desired.

Only light pastel shades of portland cement base paint are recommended for painting exterior concrete masonry walls.

On jobs where a particular color effect is desired it is recommended that paint selection be determined by painting sample wall panels. This is important because the color of a painted wall will vary somewhat depending upon the kind of aggregate in the concrete block, the rate, and amount of absorption, the method of curing the paint and other factors. Sample walls should be constructed as previously described in the section on Sample Panels. The paint should be applied and cured in the same manner as will be used on the walls of the building. As an alternative for the sample panels, the paint can be applied to sections of the building wall.

Concrete masonry is an excellent surface for the application of other types of paints. Manufacturer's instructions for applying these paints should be followed. (*See* Chap. 52, Building Watertight Concrete Masonry Walls; *see also* Chap. 53, Miscellaneous Concrete Masonry Wall Jobs.)

Section 7

Brick Projects and Improvements

Brick is perhaps the most widely adaptable of our wall materials. For the poor man it will accept the humblest utilitarian role. From that it responds, all the way up the scale, to every demand made for higher degrees of quality in materials, workmanship, and design, lacking no merits that may be required of a material in the class of unlimited cost. It does not compete with stone or marble for the designer's favor, nor does it brook competition from them. At its best, it stands alone, no more to be compared with other materials than an iris can be compared with a peony. Each is comparable only with other members of its own family.

Chapter 54

Fireplaces, Barbecues, and Incinerators

The fireplace, the lineal descendant of the earliest known device for domestic heating and cooking, is today enjoying the greatest popularity in its long career. There was a time when the old fireplace was bricked-up or boarded-up to make a background for the new-fangled coal or wood-burning stove, but that age has passed. In all climates the practical fireplace is a necessary part of the modern home.

Not only is the fireplace serviceable and ornamental to indoor living but with the growth of outdoor living it is proving equally important as a garden accessory. All year around in the warmer climates, and during the summer in the northern portions of the country, the outdoor fireplace contributes to the sociability and ease of entertaining.

This chapter illustrates designs of fireplaces, both for the interior of the home and for outdoor use with correct details of construction insuring successful operation.

The building of a fireplace that is safe, efficient, and free from annoyance has been reduced to a science. The success of the fireplace inside and outside the house depends upon a number of factors. It must be safely constructed so that the roaring open fire will not endanger any abutting materials. It must be so planned that it will not emit smoke into the room it occupies, and it must give maximum heating efficiency. And may we remind you that the high fire-resistiveness of well-burned brick makes it the specified material for the chimney and the greater part of all fireplaces. The colors and textures of brick and tile permit them to grace the front and breast of fireplace and mantel in a manner admired by all.

The fireplace is properly a part of the furnishing of a room—a built-in feature. It should conform to the dominant architectural style and period (*see* Figs. 1 through 5). (*See* Chap. 7, Placing and Consolidating Concrete; Chap. 11, Finishing Concrete Slabs; Section 3, Brick Masonry; *also see* various chapters on tools and equipment.)

INDOOR FIREPLACES

It costs no more to build a successful *indoor fireplace* than to build it incorrectly. Fireplaces should be built in accordance with a few simple essentials of correct design to give satisfactory performance. From the standpoint of appearance and function, they should be of a size best suited to the room in which they are used. If they are too small, they may function properly but may not throw out sufficient heat. If they are too large, a fire that would fill the combustion chamber would be entirely too hot for the room and would waste fuel.

The location of the chimney determines the location of the fireplace, and too often the latter is governed by structural considerations only. A fireplace suggests a fireside group and a reasonable degree of seclusion; therefore, especially in the living room, it should not be near doors to passageways of the house.

The principal warming effect of a fireplace is produced by the radiant heat from the fire and from the hot back, sides, and hearth. In the ordinary fireplace, practically no heating effect is produced by convection (air current). Air passes through the fire and up the chimney, carrying with it heat absorbed from the room. The effect of the cold air thus brought into the room is particularly noticeable farthest from the fire. Heat radiation, like light, travels in straight lines, and unless one is within range of such radiation, little heat is felt. Tests made by the Bureau of Agricultural Chemistry and Engineering showed that about five times the amount of air required for even liberal ventilation may be drawn into a living room by the operation of a fireplace. Such excessive ventilation may cause chilling drafts. Persons located at advantageous points in the room will be comfortable under

Fig. 1.

Fig. 2.

Fig. 3.

Fig. 4.

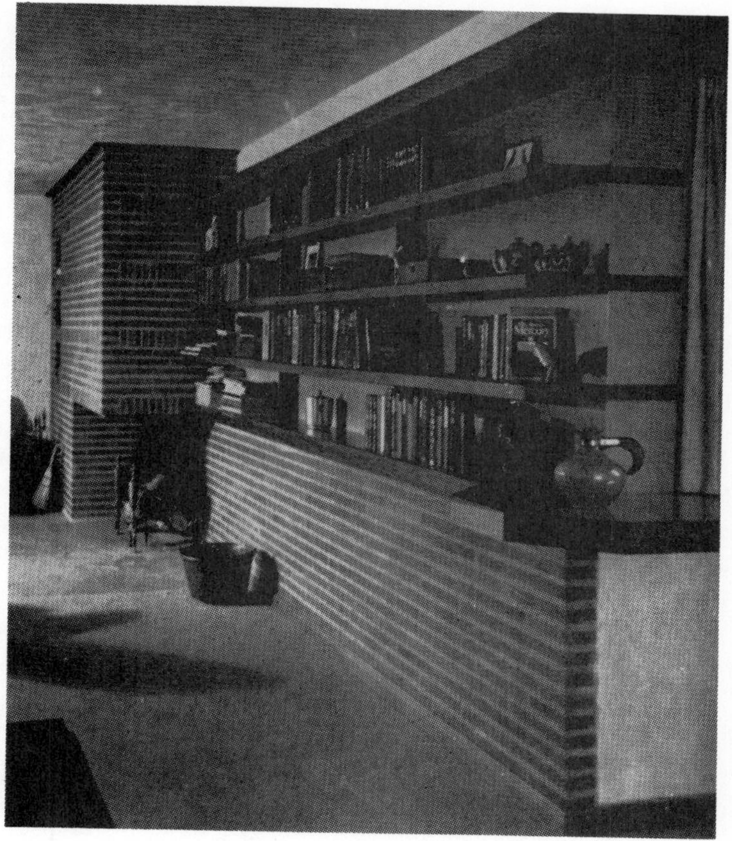

Fig. 5.

such conditions, but those outside of the radiation zone will not. Tests conducted by the bureau indicate that, as ordinarily constructed, a fireplace is only about one-third as efficient as a good stove or circulator heater. Nevertheless, it has a place as an auxiliary to the heating plant and for its cheerfulness and charm. In milder climates, fireplaces may suffice as the sole source of heat; also certain materials often wasted may be utilized for fuel. The disadvantages of the ordinary fireplace are lessened by *modified* fireplaces.

MODIFIED FIREPLACES

The modified fireplace (Fig. 6) shows at A, where air enters inlet; at C, air is heated as it rises; the tubes, T, are discharged into the room from the registers, B; and air is drawn into the fire at D, passing between the tubes and up the flue. In the fireplace shown in Fig. 7, the air is drawn in through the inlet, A, from the room that is being heated. The air is heated by contact with the metal sides and back of the fireplace. It rises by natural circulation and is discharged back into the room from the outlet, B, or to another room on the same floor or in the second story. Inlets and outlets are connected to registers that are located at the front of the fireplace. (*See* Fig. 8.) Registers may be located on the ends of the fireplace or on the wall of an adjacent room.

Modified fireplaces, as shown in Figs. 6 and 7, are units of heavy metal set into place and concealed by the usual brickwork or other similar units requiring no change in mantel design. The modifications are built-in standard parts of the fireplace, and only the grilles are visible (Fig. 8). One advantage of modified

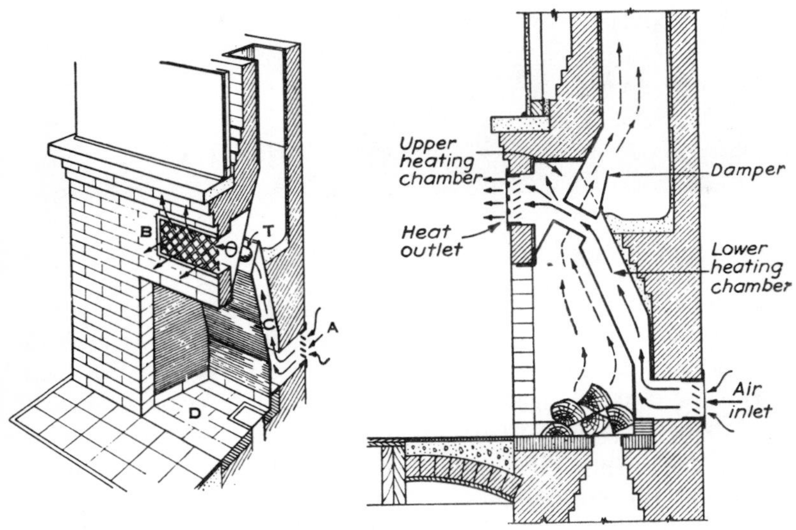

Fig. 6. Modified fireplace.

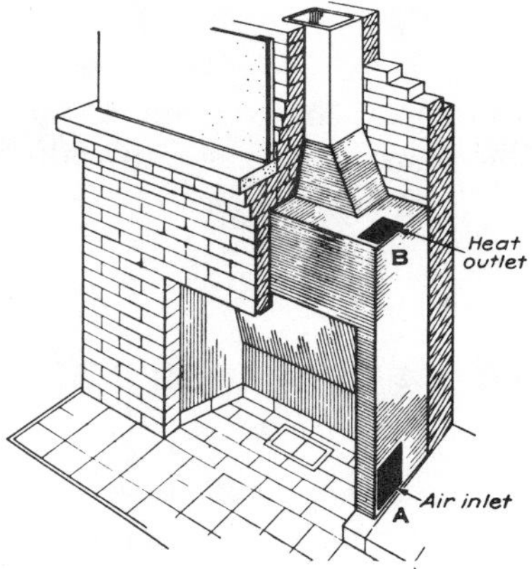

Fig. 7. Modified fireplace.

Fig. 8. The mirror has an interesting effect on the room. The opposite wall's reflection appears as a recess over the mantel.

fireplace units is that they have a correctly designed and proportioned firebox, manufactured with throat, damper, smoke shelf, and chamber, which provides a form for the masonry, thus reducing the risk of failure and assuring a smokeless fire. However, there is no excuse for using incorrect proportions, and the purchase of a foolproof modified unit merely to obtain proper proportions is questionable. Even a well-designed unit will not operate properly if the chimney is inadequate. Consequently, the standards for chimney construction, as set forth in the following information, should be adhered to with the modified unit as well as with the ordinary fireplace.

SELECTING AN INDOOR FIREPLACE

When selecting an *indoor fireplace,* one must consider the kind of fuel to be burned; also, the design should harmonize with the room in proportion and detail (Figs. 9 and 10).

Where cordwood (4 feet or 1.2 meters long) cut in half is to be used, a fireplace opening 30 inches (76 cm.) wide is desirable. Where coal is to be burned, the opening can be narrower (Fig. 11). Any opening less than 6 feet (1.8 meters) wide can be made 30-inches (76-cm.) high—a practical height for the convenient tending of the fire. Openings about 30 inches (76 cm.) wide (Fig. 12) are generally made with square corners. A high opening increases the likelihood of smoky fires. In general, the wider the opening the greater the depth should be. A shallow opening throws out relatively more heat than a deep one of the same width but accommodates smaller pieces of wood. Thus, one must choose between a greater depth, which permits the use of large logs that burn longer, and a shallower depth (Fig. 13A and B), which takes smaller-sized wood but throws out more heat.

For a small fireplace, a depth of 12 inches (30 cm.) will permit a good draft if the throat is constructed as outlined previously, but a minimum depth of 16 to 18 inches (40 to 45 cm.) is advised to lessen the danger that brands will fall out onto the floor. As a rule, a fireplace on the second floor should be made smaller than one on the first floor because the flue height is less (Fig. 14).

Unless a fireplace 6-feet (1.8-meters) wide is fully 28-inches (70-cm.) deep, the logs will have to be split and one advantage of the wide opening will be lost. Screens of suitable design should be placed in front of all fireplaces (Fig. 15).

A fireplace 30 to 36 inches (75 to 90 cm.) wide is generally suitable for a room measuring 300 square feet (27.9 sq. meters).

Fig. 9. The mantel is painted the same color as the walls and does not call attention to itself.

Fig. 10. Otherwise wasted space is used here for bookshelves and closet. This is a revival of early New England architecture.

Fig. 11.

Fig. 12. This small fireplace shows how well a plain brick front can be used in a small room.

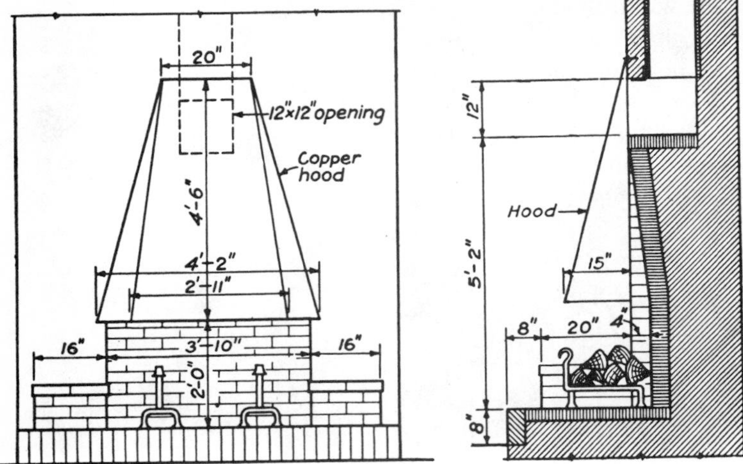

Fig. 13. This shallow fireplace with a copper hood, built as shown, emits considerable heat after the hood gets hot. The walls nearby should be of fire-resistant masonry.

Fig. 14. A shallow fireplace with a sloping back is used frequently in bedrooms.

Fig. 15. This fireplace makes artistic use of small stones and contrasts pleasingly with the log walls. Use screens to protect the upholstery on nearby furniture from sparks.

The width should be increased for larger rooms, but all other dimensions should be taken from Table 49 for the width selected.

The corner of a room often is the favorite location for a fireplace (Fig. 13). Fireplaces of the type shown in Fig. 13 are also built in corners. The photographs shown in Figs. 8 to 17, and Figs. 19 and 20 have been selected to illustrate various architectural effects, and they should help in the choice of a type suitable for houses of different designs. The essential elements of safety and utility should never be sacrificed for style.

INDOOR FIREPLACE CONSTRUCTION

The ordinary fireplace is constructed generally as shown in Fig. 17. It is essential that the flue have the proper area, that the throat be correctly constructed and have suitable damper, that the chimney be high enough for a good draft, that the shape of

Opening		Depth, *d*	Minimum Back (Horizontal), *c*	Vertical Back Wall, *a*	Inclined Back Wall, *b*	Outside Dimensions of Standard Rectangular Flue Lining	Inside Diameter of Standard Round Flue Lining
Width, *w*	Height, *h*						
Inches:	*Inches:*	*Inches:*	*Inches:*	*Inches:*	*Inches:*	*Inches:*	*Inches:*
24	24	16–18	14	14	16	8½ by 8½	10
28	24	16–18	14	14	16	8½ by 8½	10
24	28	16–18	14	14	20	8½ by 8½	10
30	28	16–18	16	14	20	8½ by 13	10
36	28	16–18	22	14	20	8½ by 13	12
42	28	16–18	28	14	20	8½ by 18	12
36	32	18–20	20	14	24	8½ by 18	12
42	32	18–20	26	14	24	13 by 13	12
48	32	18–20	32	14	24	13 by 13	15
42	36	18–20	26	14	28	13 by 13	15
48	36	18–20	32	14	28	13 by 18	15
54	36	18–20	38	14	28	13 by 18	15
60	36	18–20	44	14	28	13 by 18	15
42	40	20–22	24	17	29	13 by 13	15
48	40	20–22	30	17	29	13 by 18	15
54	40	20–22	36	17	29	13 by 18	15
60	40	20–22	42	17	29	18 by 18	18
66	40	20–22	48	17	29	18 by 18	18
72	40	22–28	51	17	29	18 by 18	18

TABLE 49. RECOMMENDED DIMENSIONS FOR FINISHED FIREPLACES. (LETTERS AT HEADS OF COLUMNS REFER TO FIG. 17.)

the fireplace be such as to direct a maximum amount of radiated heat into the room, and that a properly constructed smoke chamber be provided.

Dimensions

Table 50 gives recommended dimensions for fireplaces of various width and heights.

A well-designed and well-installed damper is essential in cold climates. If a damper is installed, the width of the opening (Fig. 17,J) will depend on the width of the damper frame, the size of which is fixed by the width and depth of the fireplace, and the slope of the back wall. The width of the throat proper depends upon the opening of the hinged damper cover. The full damper opening should never be less than the flue area. (Manufacturers of fireplace equipment are glad to provide information that may prove very helpful in the selection of a suitable damper for a given fireplace.) If no damper is used, the throat opening (Fig. 17,J) should be 4 inches (10 cm.) for fireplaces not exceeding 4 feet (1.2 meters) in height.

Footings

For information about *footings for chimneys* with fireplaces, see discussion under the heading of chimneys later in this chapter, under Outdoor Fireplaces. For chimneys without fireplaces, the footings should rest on firm soil.

Hearth

The *hearth* should be flush with the floor. If there is a basement, an ash dump located in the hearth near the back of the fireplace will be convenient. The dump consists of a metal frame about 5 × 8 inches, with a plate, generally pivoted, through which the ashes can be dropped into a pit below. In buildings with wooden floors, the hearth in front of the fireplace should be supported by masonry trimmer arches (Fig. 17) or other fire-resistant construction. Hearths should project at least 16 inches (40 cm.) from the chimney breast and should be of brick, stone, terra

Fig. 16. An adobe fireplace of the Mexican-Indian type, built especially with house walls of adobe. The logs are placed standing up, against the back of the grate to secure a high-licking flame.

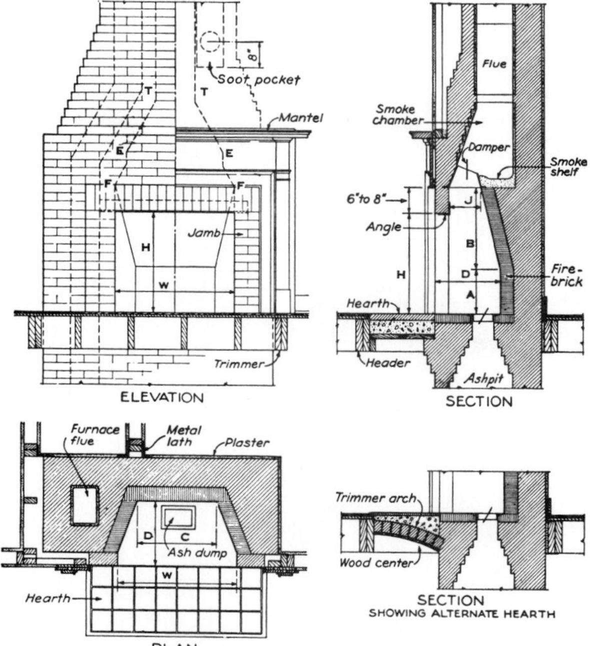

Fig. 17. Practical construction details for a typical fireplace.

cotta, or reinforced concrete not less than 4 inches (10 cm.) thick. The length of the hearth should not be less than the width of the fireplace opening plus 16 inches (40 cm.). Wooden centering under trimmer arches may be removed after the mortar has set, though it is more frequently left in place. Figure 18 shows a recommended method of placing floor framing around a fireplace. If a header is more than 4 inches (10 cm.) long, it should be doubled. Headers supporting more than four tail beams should have ends supported in metal joist hangers. Place the framing ½ inch (1.3 cm.) from the chimney because the masonry is 8 inches (20 cm.) thick.

Wall Thickness

The wall of fireplaces should never be less than 8 inches (20 cm.) thick, and if of stone they should be at least 12 inches (30 cm.) thick. When built of stone or hard-burned brick, the back and sides are often not lined with firebrick, but it is better to use firebrick laid in fireclay. If firebrick are laid flat with the long sides exposed, there is less danger of their falling out. They are generally placed on edge, however, forming a 2-inch (5-cm.) protection, in which case metal ties should be built into the main brickwork to hold the 2-inch (5-cm.) firebrick veneer in

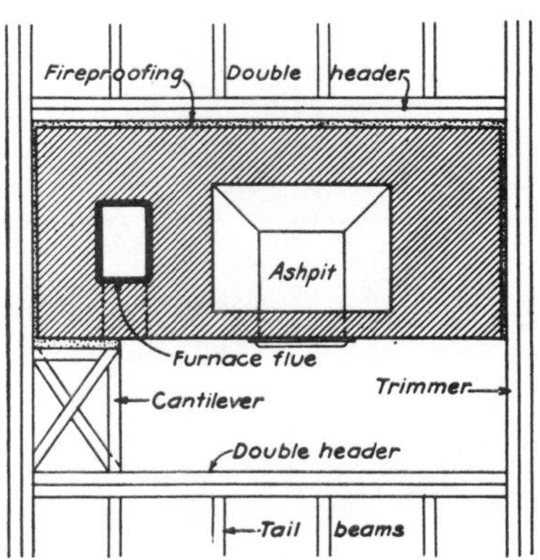

Fig. 18. Floor framing around a fireplace.

place. Thick metal backs and sides are sometimes used as lining. If a grate for burning coal or coke is built in, firebrick at least 2 inches (5 cm.) thick should be added to the fireplace back unless the grate has a solid iron back and is only set in with an air space behind it (Fig. 19).

Jambs

The *jambs* should be wide enough to provide stability and a pleasing appearance; they are frequently faced with ornamental brick or tile. For an opening 3 feet (90 cm.) wide or less, a 12- or 16-inch (30- or 40-cm.) width is generally sufficient, depending on whether a wood mantel is used or the jambs are of exposed masonry. The edges of a wood mantel should be kept at least 8 inches (20 cm.) from the fireplace opening. For wider openings and large rooms, similar proportions should be maintained.

Lintels

Lintels made of ½- × 3-inch (1.3- × 7.5-cm.) flat iron bars, 3½- × 3½- × ¼-inch (8.75- × 8.75- × .63-cm.) angle irons, or damper frames are used to support the masonry over the opening of ordinary fireplaces. Heavier lintel irons are required for wider open-

Fig. 19.

ings. Where a masonry arch (Fig. 20) is used over the opening, the jambs should be heavy enough to resist the thrust of the arch. Arches over openings less than 4 feet (1.2 meters) wide seldom sag, but sagging is not uncommon in wider fireplaces, especially where massive masonry is used.

Throat

The sides of the fireplace should be vertical up to the throat or damper opening (Fig. 17,FF). The *throat* should be 6 to 8 inches (15 to 20 cm.) or more above the bottom of the lintel and should have an area not less than that of the flue and a length equal to the width of the fireplace opening. Starting 5 inches (12.5 cm.) above the throat (Fig. 17,EE), the sides should be drawn in (Fig. 17,TT) to equal the flue area. Since proper throat construction is necessary for a successful fireplace, the work should be inspected several times a day during construction to make sure that the side walls are carried up perpendicularly until the throat is passed and that the full length of opening is provided.

Smoke Shelf and Chamber

The smoke shelf is made by setting the brickwork back at the top of the throat to the line of the flue wall for the full length of the throat. Its depth may vary from 8 to 12 inches (20 to 30 cm.) or more, depending on the depth (Fig. 17,D) of the fireplace. The smoke chamber is the space extending from the top of the throat (Fig. 17,EE) up to the bottom of the flue proper (Fig.

Fig. 20.

17,TT) and between the side walls. The walls should be drawn inward making a 30-degree angle with the vertical sides after the top of the throat (Fig. 17,EE) is passed, and they should be smoothly plastered with cement mortar not less than ½-inch (1.3-cm.) thick.

Damper

A properly designed *damper* (Fig. 17) affords a means of regulating the draft and prevents excessive loss of heat from the room when the fire is out. A damper consists of a cast-iron frame with a lid hinged so that the width of the throat opening may be varied from a closed to a wide-opened position. Various patterns are available, some designed to support the masonry over the opening, others requiring lintel irons.

A roaring pine fire may require a full-throat opening, but slow-burning hardwood logs may need only 1 or 2 inches (2.5 to 5 cm.) of opening. Regulating the opening according to the kind of fire prevents waste of heat up the chimneys. Close the damper during the summer to keep the flies, mosquitoes, and other insects from entering the house down the chimney.

In houses heated by furnaces or other modern systems, lack of a damper in the fireplace flue may interfere with uniform heating, particularly in very cold, windy weather, whether or not there is a fire on the hearth. When air heated by the furnace is carried up the chimney there is a waste of the furnace fuel, but a partially opened damper serves a slow fire of hardwood without smoking the room or wasting heated air from the main heating system.

Flue

The *area of lined flues* should be a twelfth or more of the fireplace opening, provided the chimney is at least 22 feet (6.7 meters) in height, measured from the hearth. If the flue is shorter than 22 feet (6.7 meters) or if it is unlined, its area should be made a tenth or more of the fireplace opening. The fireplace shown in Fig. 21 has an opening of 7.5 square feet, or approximately 1,080 square inches (.7 sq. meters), and it needs a flue area of approximately 90 square inches (580.6 sq. cm.); a rectangular flue, 8½ × 18 inches (21.3 × 45 cm.), outside dimensions, or a round flue with a 12-inch (30-cm.) inside diameter might be used as these dimensions are the nearest to commercial sizes of lining. (*See* Table 49.) It is seldom possible to obtain lining having exactly the required area, but the inside area should never be less than that prescribed previously. A 13- × 13-inch (32.5 × 32.5-cm.) flue was selected for convenience when combining with the other flues. If the flue is built of brick and is unlined, its area should be approximately a tenth of the fireplace opening, or 108 square inches (696.8 sq. cm.). It would probably be made 8 × 16 inches (20 × 40 cm.) (128 square inches or 825.8 sq. cm.) because brickwork can be laid to better advantage if the dimensions of the flue are multiples of 4 inches (10 cm.). (The principles of construction which have been detailed in our discussion of chimneys are also applicable to fireplace flues.)

Table 50 can be used in selecting the proper size of flue or in determining the size of fireplace opening for an existing flue. The area of the fireplace opening in square inches is obtained by

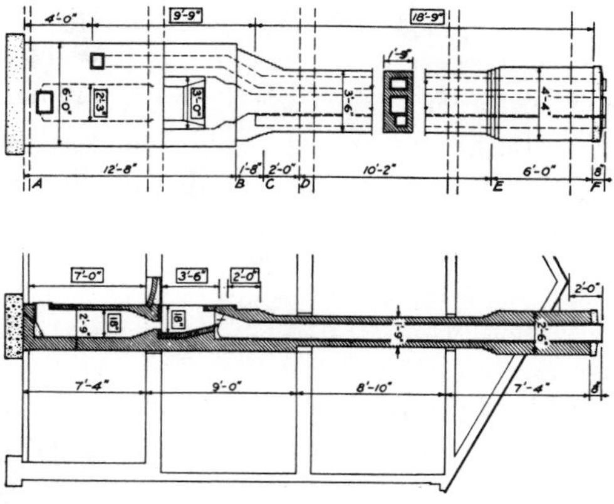

Fig. 21. Front view and cross-section of an entire chimney. The rectangular measurements show sizes of the voids or openings; the other measurements show outside dimensions of the brickwork.

Rectangular Linings [1]				Round Linings [2]			
Outside Dimensions (Inches)	Cross-sectional Area		Wall Thickness	Inside Diameter (Inches)	Cross-sectional Area		Wall Thickness
	Inside	Outside			Inside	Outside	
	Square inches:	*Square feet:*	*Inches:*		*Square inches:*	*Square feet:*	*Inches:*
4½ by 8½. . .	23.6	0.26	⅝	6.	28.3	0.29	⅝
4½ by 13. . .	38.2	.41	⅝	8.	50.3	.49	¾
7½ by 7½. . .	39.1	.39	⅝	10.	78.5	.75	⅞
8½ by 8½. . .	52.6	.50	⅝	12.	113.0	1.07	1
8½ by 13. . .	80.5	.78	¾	15.	176.7	1.62	1⅛
8½ by 18. . .	109.7	1.10	⅞	18.	254.4	2.29	1¼
13 by 13. . .	126.6	1.20	⅞	20.	314.1	2.82	1⅜
13 by 18. . .	182.8	1.70	⅞	22.	380.1	3.48	1⅝
18 by 18. . .	248.1	2.30	1⅛	24.	452.3	4.05	1⅝
20 by 20. . .	297.6	2.60	1⅜	27.	572.5	5.20	2

[1] All rectangular flue lining is 2 feet long.
[2] Round flue lining, 6 to 24 inches in diameter, is 2 feet long; that 27 to 36 inches in diameter is 2½ or 3 feet long.

TABLE 50. DIMENSIONS OF COMMONLY USED STANDARD COMMERCIAL FLUES.

multiplying the width (Fig. 17,W), by the height (Fig. 17, HH), both measured in inches.

OUTDOOR FIREPLACES

To provide recreation that every member of the family and friends will enjoy, there is nothing to equal an *outdoor fireplace.* This attractive, useful addition to the home and to outdoor living can be as simple or elaborate as individual taste desires and as economical or expensive as the budget permits. Various materials and designs likewise offer a broad choice to the homeowner. The designs shown in this chapter are readily adaptable to different garden, lawn, or landscape locations. They include every type from the simplest chimneyless, masonry-and-grill cookstove to the finest outdoor counterpart of a luxurious living room fireplace, complete with cooking and service facilities.

Location of Fireplace

If the slope of the ground in front of the fireplace is such that furniture cannot be comfortably used, some grading and construction should be done.

The fireplace may be put in a natural grove of trees. There, and also in the locations illustrated in Figs. 22 to 26, the design should be simple and in harmony with the surroundings.

The *fire hazard* from any of the designs shown is not great, particularly if nearby buildings are fireproof or if the fireplace is about 50 feet (15.2 meters) from the nearest building. One seldom builds a roaring fire; a fire burned down to coals provides the best cooking heat. Wood that crackles and snaps should not be used. A charcoal fire is excellent. Someone is usually present all the time the fire is burning and quick action can be taken in any emergency. The fire usually burns out of its own accord before the meal is over or soon after; but before leaving, be sure that it is completely out.

Construction Materials

Outdoor fireplaces may be built of brick, stone, concrete blocks, or a combination of one or more of these materials. The design and setting of your outdoor fireplace plus availability and cost are the factors that will finally influence any decision on the materials to be used. To be effective from a decorative standpoint, an outdoor fireplace should blend with its surroundings. Fieldstones or ordinary brick are ideal for a rustic informal setting; while concrete, smooth cut stones, or face brick express a certain degree of formality. Regardless, however, of the materials you finally select to use in the construction of your outdoor fireplace, always strive to achieve a naturally pleasing effect combined with an attractive masonry texture.

Ordinary *brick* is serviceable, economical, and easy for the amateur to handle. Inexpensive used bricks can usually be secured from local building wreckers. Concrete blocks can also be easily and quickly placed, and present a neat appearance.

At the expense of some spare time and labor, fieldstones can often be collected locally and used after selecting appropriate sizes and shapes. Stones of this kind are either stratified or unstratified. More common, and typical of the first, are the sandstones, limestones, and shales. These should be layered horizontally to assure a more desirable fireplace effect. Care

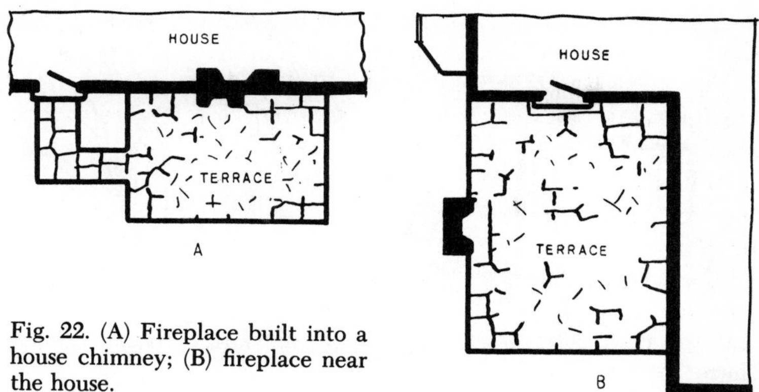

Fig. 22. (A) Fireplace built into a house chimney; (B) fireplace near the house.

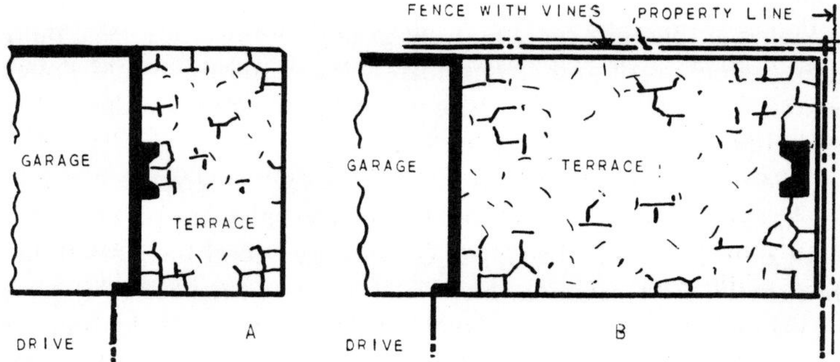

Fig. 23. (A) Fireplace near a garage; (B) fireplace at one end of a terrace on a narrow lot.

Fig. 24. A corner fireplace.

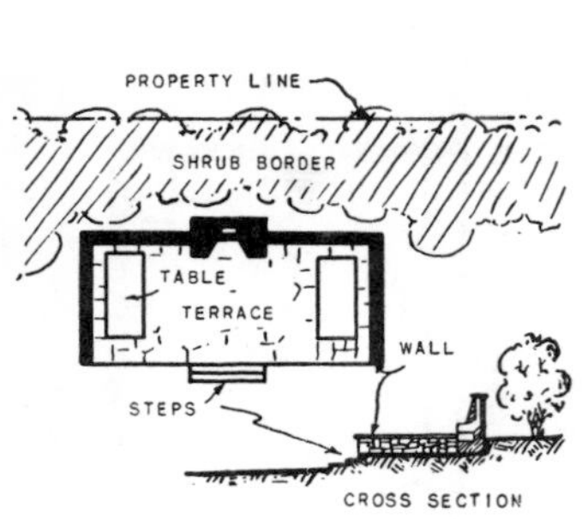

Fig. 25. Terrace above a sloping lawn.

Fig. 26. Terrace above a sloping lawn.

should be taken to choose stones that are not too porous, since they absorb water, and frost may cause them to crack, resulting in damage to your fireplace. Fine-grained sandstones resist damaging effects well and are preferred over limestones and shales, which flake or chip badly on exposure to heat and sudden temperature changes.

The unstratified type includes stones such as granite and lava rock. Careful selection is also the key to securing pleasing texture or effect with this type. Granite has good heat resistance but may flake and crack. Lava rock resists heat better.

When building your outdoor fireplace of any of these materials, guard against sharp angles, unevenness, and mortar joints that are too deep. Avoid having a structure that is an ungainly pile of stones and mortar.

To prevent damage from extreme temperature changes and from heat, be sure to line brick, concrete, or stone (with the possible exception of lava rock) with firebrick in the firebox of your fireplace. Add a flue lining to the chimney, too. Fireclay may be reached by the fire or the heat from it.

The various designs and plans shown on outdoor fireplaces can be modified with any original features that may suit your own requirements and preferences. There are, however, certain basic principles of outdoor fireplace design and construction that *must* be adhered to if the fire is to burn properly and do the work expected of it. You will get the most enjoyment out of your fireplace by following the accepted standards of design and construction given.

Until recent years, a major handicap in building an outdoor fireplace was the difficulty of locating essential metal parts, such as grills, doors, and grates. This is no longer a problem. Metal fireplace units and a wide variety of essential parts are now available. There are many ways you can vary the equipment and design of your outdoor fireplace by using these standard metal parts. Size and complexity of the fireplace you plan will determine the kind of top, door, grate, and other parts needed (Fig. 27). All of these parts may be bought separately. Some may be used to meet specialized needs, in place of the ready-built, all-metal units shown in Fig. 28. Some may be used along with the units when any extra utility feature such as an oven or incinerator is desired.

Your outdoor fireplace can be fitted with a heavy iron top just like those on old-fashioned kitchen ranges. It may have four holes or only two holes, complete with lids and lifter. A solid top or a half bar, half solid one is also available.

Grates may be obtained in different sizes and types for top and bottom of the fireplace (Fig. 28). There are bottom grates of standard bar type for use in burning wood as fuel, and a specially designed grate with smaller openings for use with charcoal.

All doors are strongly hinged to a sturdy frame that can be easily mounted in the masonry. The firebox or oven door of heavy cast iron is fitted with a spiral, heatproof handle. In the ashpit doors, a rotary slide vent provides draft control.

Additional equipment available includes a convenient generous-size, all-metal oven; cast-iron grate support bars; handy grate support lugs that fit into masonry; and long-handled wire grills for holding meats while they cook. With these easily installed items the construction of outdoor fireplaces has become a comparatively simple procedure. Even a novice can create an attractive fireplace by fitting brick, stone, or other masonry around the ready-to-use metal parts shown in Figs. 27 and 28.

Essentials of Outdoor Fireplace Construction

Basic types of outdoor fireplaces around which various improvements and modifications of design can be made are shown

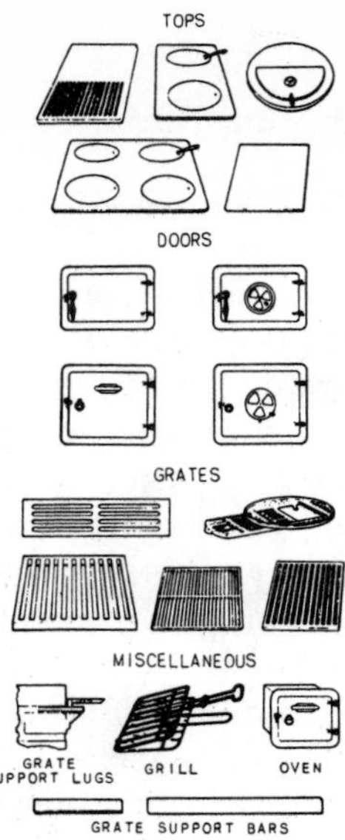

Fig. 27. Metal parts for any style of outdoor fireplace.

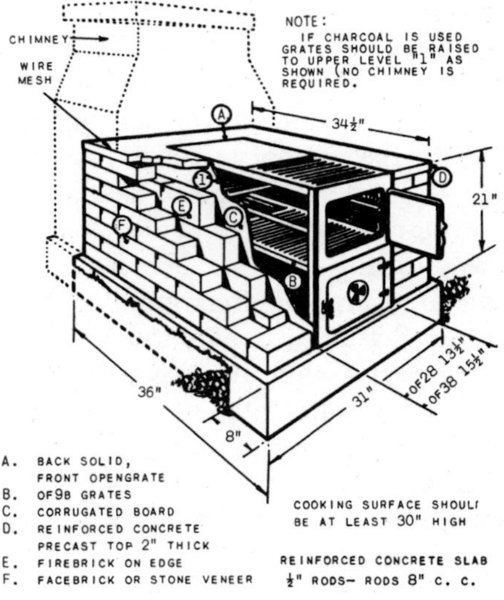

Fig. 28. Details of outdoor fireplace construction.

in Fig. 29. Both units consist of a firm foundation, sturdy walls constructed of brick or any other suitable material, a properly proportioned all-metal fireplace unit, plus a chimney if desired.

The first essential of a well-constructed and efficient fireplace is a suitably strong, solid foundation. The foundation should be made of concrete. Where subject to frost, provide either a reinforced concrete slab to ride up and down with rising and settling of earth, or a concrete or masonry foundation that extends below the frostline about 4 inches (10 cm.). Where not subject to frost, a firm bed of tamped ground, cinders, or gravel will usually

Fig. 29. Two outdoor fireplaces of simple construction.

serve. The concrete slab, at least 6 inches (15 cm.) thick, should be reinforced with metal bars or wire mesh. Reinforcing the foundation of an outdoor fireplace is of utmost importance, especially in localities where severe winter weather occurs. In regions where frost is not a factor, reinforcing may be eliminated. For general use, a heavy reinforcing mesh or crisscrossed bars 8 inches (20 cm.) on centers and 1 inch (2.5 cm.) from the bottom of the slab will suffice. In large units it is advisable to have two sets of reinforcing. One of these should be placed 1 inch (2.5 cm.) from the bottom and the other 1 inch (2.5 cm.) from the top of the slab. After pouring the concrete, be sure to tamp or work it around the reinforcing bars or mesh so there are no air pockets.

For a deep foundation, start with the base layer of concrete and rocks, then build up with a concrete mixture of 1 part cement, 2 parts sand, 4 parts coarse (about 1-inch, 2.5-cm.) gravel, plus water. For smoothing hearth and as ordinary brick mortar (not firebrick), use 1 part cement, 3 or 4 parts masonry sand, about one-tenth as much hydrated lime as cement, mixed with water until *mushy.* Ready-mixed mortar and cement requiring only the addition of water is available. A hearth exposed to hot sun while setting should be kept covered with moist burlap. For the reinforced concrete slab, use a mix of 1 part cement, 2½ parts clean sand, 4 parts gravel, plus water. For joining firebrick, use a fireclay mortar to which is added about 25 percent portland cement by bulk. The smooth floor of the ashpit should be level so the metal grill also will be level. After the metal unit is set, lay cement plaster on the floor of the ashpit, flush with the ashpit door opening in front and sloped upward about 1 inch (2.5 cm.) to the back. This serves to drain away rain or snow to prevent freezing and expansion. Some natural drainage also should be provided by banking dirt around the footing or building the fireplace on a small mound. If possible, always select a high spot for the location of your fireplace.

Either type of foundation should be at least 1 inch (2.5 cm.) wider on each side of the fireplace and 1 inch (2.5 cm.) longer at each end. These are minimum dimensions and may be extended as much as you wish. Extension of paved apron in front of the fireplace is especially desirable to provide a practical work area. (*See* Chap. 35, Design and Layout, and Chap. 44, Outdoor Home Improvements.)

The construction of a paved apron is similar in every respect to the methods employed for sidewalk or driveway construction. (*See* Chap. 35, Design and Layout; *see also* Chap. 44, Outdoor Home Improvements.)

Where a deep foundation of stones has been set in mortar, be sure that all joints are filled with mortar to prevent water from entering and causing damage from freezing and thawing. Additional directions for mixing and using concrete, laying a foundation, and procedures for bricklaying and other types of masonry work are previously described. (*See* Chap. 4, Mixing Concrete; Appendix V, Suggested Method of Laying Out a Foundation; Chap. 29, Bricklaying; and Section 2, Concrete Masonry.)

Walls and Firebox

The ready-built, all-metal fireplace units shown in Figs. 28 and 29 form a framework for the masonry and will keep the inner working parts of your fireplace in proper proportion. The unit shown in Fig. 28 is equipped with a removable top that is made in two sections, each 12 inches (30 cm.) square; one of these sections is of solid construction, while the other is made of evenly spaced bars. The two-section bottom grate can be placed at different levels for use with either charcoal or wood. The unit's frame is heavy angle iron. Doors and door frames are cast iron. The doors are 10 inches (25 cm.) wide and 8 inches (20 cm.) high. The complete unit is 21 inches (52.5 cm.) high, 26 inches (65 cm.) long, and 13½ inches (33.8 cm.) wide. This unit is available in ready-to-assemble form. The frame of the larger unit is constructed of heavy angle iron. Both the cast-iron bottom grate and the top grill are in two removable sections. The top is half bar, half solid. The bar-type grate adjusts to different levels for charcoal or wood fuel. Doors, which are 12 inches (30 cm.) wide and 8 inches (20 cm.) high, and door frames are of cast iron, with draft regulator in the ashpit door. All parts are easily assembled. The unit ready to install is 21 inches (52.5 cm.) high, 26 inches (65 cm.) long, and 15½ inches (38.8 cm.) wide.

These units have adjustable grates that can be raised close to the top grill when charcoal is used and lowered when wood is the fuel. This permits you to make more effective use of the heat, without waste.

If charcoal is to be used exclusively as fuel, a closely spaced bar grate is available for use in place of the regularly furnished bar type (Fig. 27). This can be inserted at the proper grate level to keep the small particles of charcoal from falling through until they have completely burned. A solid top section is also available to replace the front top grill of this unit. It provides a solid cooking surface that prevents smudging of pots (Fig. 27).

In the basic fireplace shown in Fig. 29, the outer walls may be constructed of brick. The inner walls are of firebrick placed on edge to conserve space and brick. These should be lightly butted with 1/16-inch (1.6-mm.) joints of fireclay mortar. This also applies to the space between firebrick and masonry. It is advisable to have the portion of the fireplace above the grates lined with firebrick. However, the walls, below the grates or surrounding the ashpit, can be made of common brick laid on edge. Common brick should be thoroughly wetted before laying up. The mortar joints should not exceed ½ inch (1.3 cm.) thick. Stones may be set with the mortar joints ½ to ¾ inch (1.3 to 1.9 cm.) thick. Before exterior joints of mortar set, rake them deeply with a stiff wire loop for rustic stone work, and flush for face brick. Place a coping or cap of flat stone, tile, or other material on top of the fireplace walls. This will prevent water from getting down between the firebrick and the exterior wall, where it may freeze and cause the masonry to crack. It also provides a smooth ledge or shelf for holding utensils and other cooking equipment.

In building any kind of fireplace, take care to provide proper allowances for the metal parts to expand and contract as the result of heating and cooling. When using a metal fireplace inner unit, this can best be accomplished by placing sheets of corrugated paper against the unit prior to placing the brick work around it. When the first fire is built in the fireplace, this corrugated paper will burn away and leave a space for expanding and contracting metal. Such a space will prevent cracked masonry and other damage due to changing temperatures.

Chimneys

A chimney is not always necessary. All that is required to make a fireplace of pleasing proportions and practical use are the walls around the all-metal units. However, if either wood or coal is the fuel to be used, the fireplace should have a chimney. If you are planning to burn only charcoal in the fireplace, no chimney is necessary. Suggested designs for a fireplace of this type are shown in Fig. 29.

Avoid giving your fireplace a top-heavy appearance. Keep the chimney a practical height. In most cases, this need be only a few feet. It is a good idea to have the chimney somewhat taller than the average person, or the top at least at eye-level. The chimney must be taller than this if trees, heavy shrubbery, or buildings are close by. If the fireplace is built against the side of a house, the chimney should rise at least 3 feet (90 cm.) above a flat roof or 2 feet (60 cm.) above a roof peak. If outdoor and indoor fireplaces connect to the same chimney, be sure to provide separate flues. The chimney on an outdoor fireplace is a comfort as well as a utility feature. It carries smoke away from the cooking area and improves draft. In an open-type fireplace, as in its indoor counterpart, a smoke chamber and a damper will prevent downdraft. To keep moisture out of the chimney, add a cap to the top, leaving smoke outlets at the sides. Install a wire-screen cap to prevent flying sparks. Make the outlet from the fireplace unit into the chimney at the rear. Better draft conditions will prevail if the connection into the chimney is smooth, with all square corners eliminated. The chimney should have a flue liner of firebrick. A good damper, while not necessary in most cases, will afford better cooking results by permitting better control of the draft. This is desirable for broiling, when the fire must be held to a bed of coals. Suggested designs and construction details for two fireplaces with chimneys are shown in Figs. 30 to 35.

Connecting Unit to Flue

Provide an opening into the flue from the firebox. This should be at least equal to half of the height of the firebox, measuring

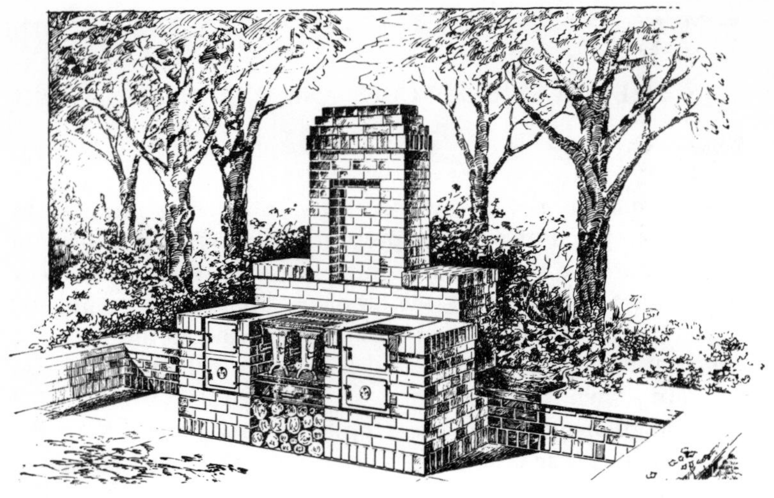

Fig. 30. An outdoor brick fireplace designed to meet the requirements of the most exacting outdoor chef.

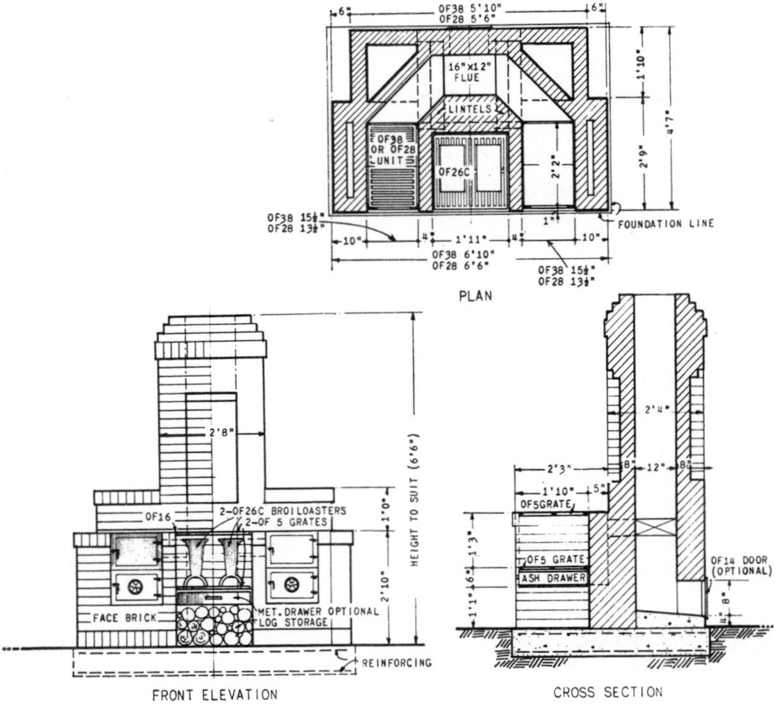

OF38 5'10"
OF28 5'6"
6"
6"
16"x12" FLUE
LINTELS
OF38 OR OF28 UNIT
OF26C
2'2"
1'10"
2'9"
4'7"
FOUNDATION LINE
OF38 15½"
OF28 13½"
10"
4"
1'11"
4"
10"
1"
OF38 6'10"
OF28 6'6"
OF38 15½"
OF28 13½"
PLAN
2'8"
OF16
2-OF26C BROILOASTERS
2-OF 5 GRATES
1'0"
2'10"
HEIGHT TO SUIT (6'6")
FACE BRICK
MET. DRAWER OPTIONAL
LOG STORAGE
REINFORCING
FRONT ELEVATION
2'4"
2'3"
8"
12"
8"
1'10"
5"
OF5GRATE
1'3"
OF5 GRATE
ASH DRAWER
6"
1'1"
OF14 DOOR (OPTIONAL)
8"
4"
CROSS SECTION

Fig. 31. Construction details of fireplace shown in Fig. 30.

Fig. 32. A complete outdoor living and dining room.

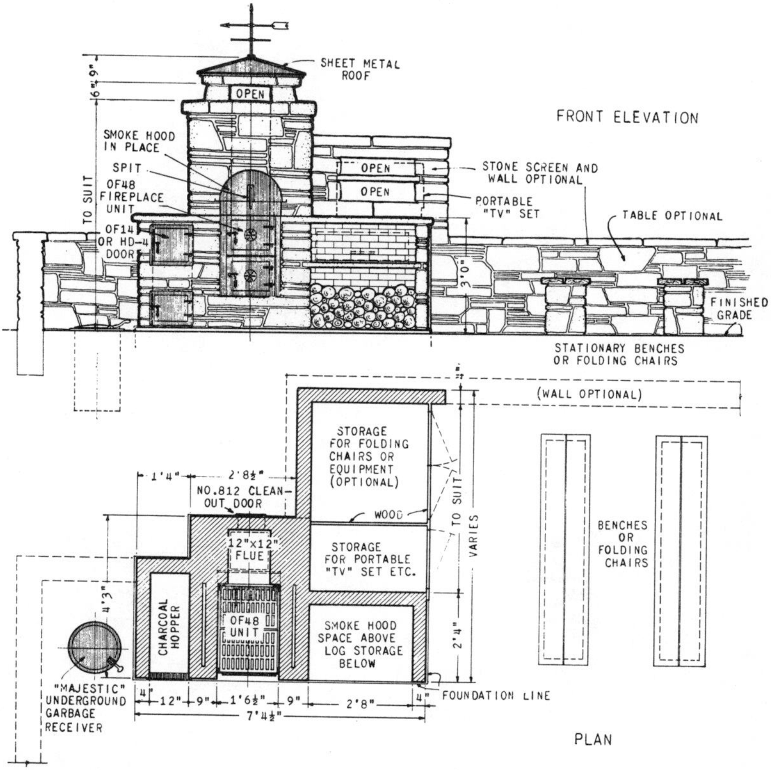

SHEET METAL ROOF
6'-9"
OPEN
FRONT ELEVATION
SMOKE HOOD IN PLACE
SPIT
OF48 FIREPLACE UNIT
OF14 OR HD-4 DOOR
TO SUIT
OPEN
OPEN
STONE SCREEN AND WALL OPTIONAL
PORTABLE "TV" SET
TABLE OPTIONAL
3'0"
FINISHED GRADE
STATIONARY BENCHES OR FOLDING CHAIRS

(WALL OPTIONAL)
STORAGE FOR FOLDING CHAIRS OR EQUIPMENT (OPTIONAL)
1'4"
2'8½"
NO.812 CLEAN-OUT DOOR
WOOD
TO SUIT
VARIES
12"x12" FLUE
STORAGE FOR PORTABLE "TV" SET ETC.
BENCHES OR FOLDING CHAIRS
4'3"
CHARCOAL HOPPER
OF48 UNIT
SMOKE HOOD SPACE ABOVE LOG STORAGE BELOW
2'4"
"MAJESTIC" UNDERGROUND GARBAGE RECEIVER
4" 12" 9" 1'6½" 9" 2'8" 4"
7'4½"
FOUNDATION LINE
PLAN

Fig. 33. Construction details of outdoor living room shown in Fig. 32.

Fig. 34. Another type of easily constructed fireplace.

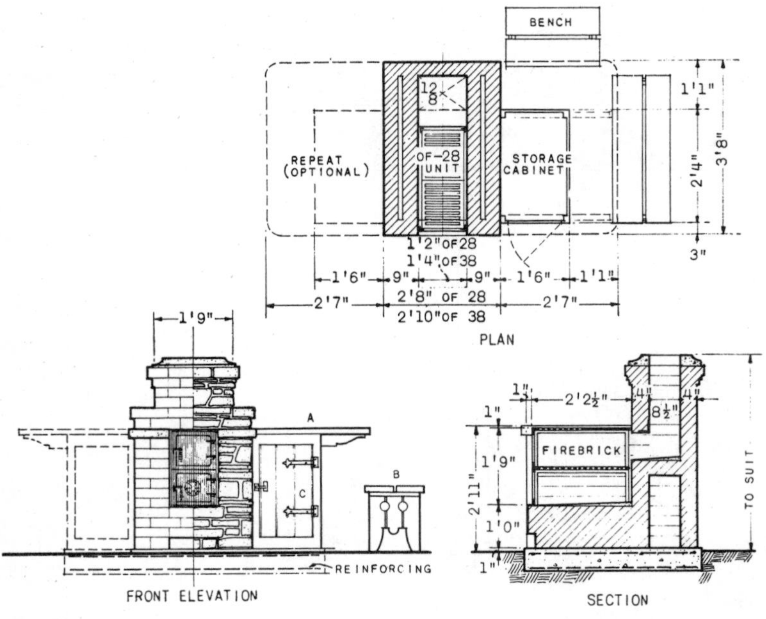

Fig. 35. Construction details of fireplace shown in Fig. 34.

from the top down, and should be at least equal to the area of the section of the chimney flue. It can be formed of firebrick or a section of flue tile laid horizontally.

Lintels of angle iron or bar iron should be used to provide support over openings. Measure the clear opening and add 4 inches (10 cm.) at each end for bearing. These lintels are available, cut to required size, from local building supply yards.

Waterproofing

It is advisable to waterproof the entire exterior of the completed outdoor fireplace. This adds to its life by sealing all porous portions, especially joints against water absorption. It not only protects the materials, but also accents and helps retain colors of the brick or stone. Be sure to clean all masonry surfaces before applying the clear, liquid waterproofing. If some cracks or holes are noticed in the masonry joints, fill these first and, when the structure is absolutely dry, apply the waterproofing according to the manufacturer's instructions. Your local supply sources can recommend commercial products for this purpose.

Barbecues

More and more people are living outdoors when weather permits. The building and use of garden fireplaces and barbecues has spread from the warmer climates, where they have long been in vogue, to all parts of the country. Many homeowners have improvised homemade fireplaces in their backyards to give them the comfort and joy of preparing and eating special outdoor meals.

Outdoor fireplaces (with or without spits for roasting) are frequently called barbecues. For occasional barbecuing parties where an outdoor fireplace is not available, dig a hole several feet deep and several feet larger each way than the size of the carcass to be roasted, then place stones in the bottom to retain the heat. A trench 30 inches deep, 36 inches wide, and 10 feet long (.75 × .90 × 3.5 meters) will accommodate about 400 pounds (181.4 kgs.) of beef. Build a fire ahead of time (about three hours) to heat the stones and bottom earth and accumulate ashes for banking.

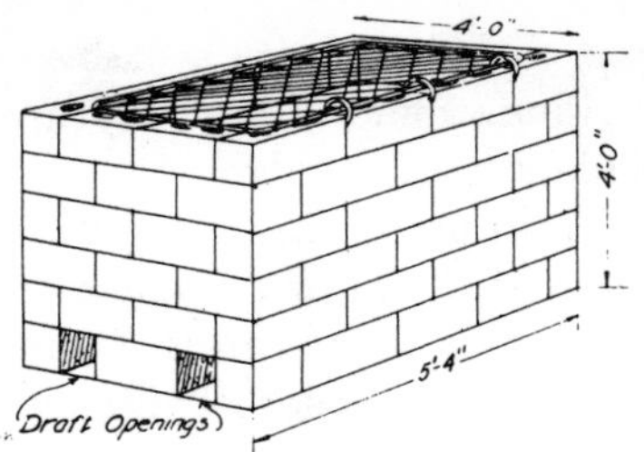

Fig. 36. Design for a simple concrete masonry incinerator.

Fig. 37.

INCINERATORS

A suggested design for making an inexpensive concrete or brick incinerator is shown in Fig. 36. To construct an incinerator, proceed as follows. Make an excavation 6 inches (15 cm.) deep upon which to lay the base. Assemble the base form and set it in place. (*See* Table 43 for recommended mixtures and proportions.) Place the concrete in the form, tamping it thoroughly. Level off the surface by means of a striking board resting on the edges of the form. Allow the base to harden twenty-four hours before removing the forms.

Concrete brick or block used for the walls are available at local dealers. (*See* Table 43 for recommended mortar mixes.) Add enough clean water to produce a plastic, workable mix. Lay the bottom course of masonry with half units at the corners, leaving draft holes at each end (Fig. 36). Place the succeeding courses of units by spreading a bed of mortar ½ inch (1.3 cm.) thick on each preceding course. Each unit being laid should be *buttered* on the ends to make well-filled vertical joints. Allow the mortar to harden for two weeks before using the burner.

Incinerator construction is more intricate than that of a simple fireplace, primarily because the water content of the refuse burned in incinerators necessitates a dehydration chamber. Also the increased draft desired dictates a higher chimney, which at the same time, adds to the more rapid dissipation of undesirable odors. In general, an incinerator has a suspended grate or plate above the fire and is so constructed that the flames and hot gases pass under and over the contents, first drying and then consuming the refuse. Figure 37 shows a practical backyard incinerator.

Chapter 55

Brick Improvements Around the Home

A large part of the pleasure to be derived from an outdoor living room comes from the planning and actual construction of its many features. The things you will want to plan and build will depend on your own tastes and the uses to which you want to put your home grounds. *Brick*, because of its warmth of color and its splendid texture for outdoor uses, is an ideal material for terraces, driveways, walks, walls, steps, and fences. (*See* Section 3, Brick Masonry.)

BUILDING A TERRACE

A paved terrace linking the house to the garden tends to draw the family outdoors. Such a terrace makes an ideal outdoor living room, dining room, and play area. Regardless of the size of the house or lot, a terrace can be built large enough for dining and lounging (Fig. 1). The addition of a well-proportioned terrace to the house will provide outdoor living facilities for many months of the year at a low cost.

Many kinds of brick and tile may be used in the construction of a terrace. A good grade of No. 1 hard-burned common brick, specially burned brick walk-pavers, or terrace tiles can be used in simple or elaborate patterns (Figs. 2 and 3). Suggested patterns for both tile and brick are shown in Fig. 4.

There are two ways of paving a terrace—it can be laid on either a sand base with sand-filled joints or on a concrete base with sand or mortar joints (Fig. 5). The sand-base method is easiest and requires a minimum of experience and equipment. A

Fig. 1. Old weathered bricks were used to build this terrace.

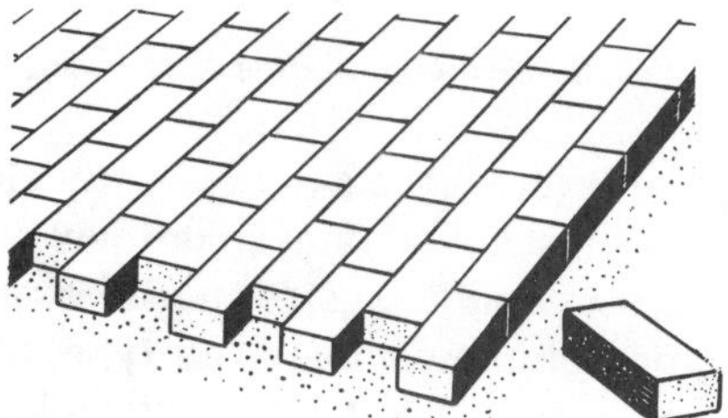

Fig. 2. Typical terrace brickwork.

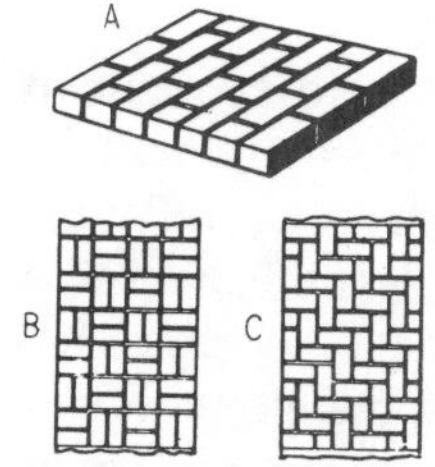

Fig. 3. Brickwork patterns.

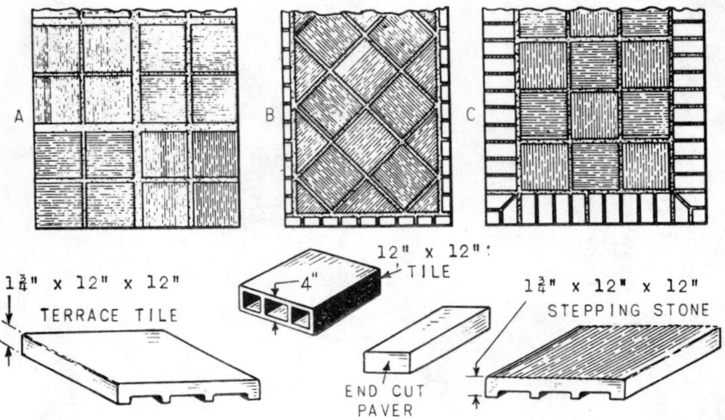

Fig. 4. Terrace tiles and typical patterns.

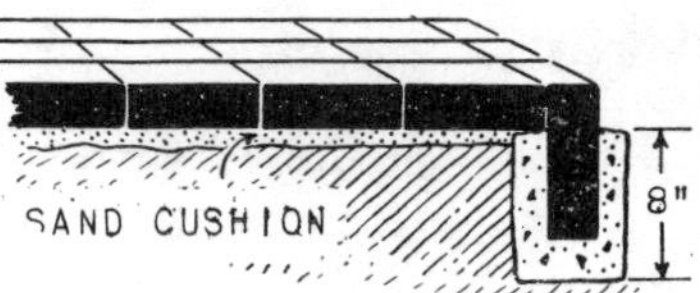

Fig. 5. Terrace laid on a sand base.

terrace can be laid level on the site or slightly elevated (Fig. 6). When a terrace is constructed on a slight elevation, a retaining wall consisting of three built-up sides must be constructed (Fig. 7). The construction of a low wall of this type, consisting of five or six tiers of brick, is similar to that described later in this chapter in the section on Garden Walls. The entire area inside the brick enclosure must be filled with earth before any of the terrace tile or brick is laid.

Whether the terrace is to be built at ground level or on a built-up elevation, excavate the soil to a depth of about 3½ inches (8.8 cm.) below the surface. With a spirit level make sure that the ground is fairly level. However, a slight slope away from the house should be made to allow for adequate drainage. If there is unevenness in spots, fill with fresh earth and tamp these spots smooth before attempting to lay any brick or tile.

If a terrace is to be laid on a portion of the lawn which is al-

Fig. 6. (A) Level terrace layout; (B) elevated terrace.

Fig. 7. Low wall, three-sided terrace arrangement.

ready established, make the excavation the exact width of the finished terrace. If it is to be laid on newly graded earth that has not yet been seeded, make the excavation approximately 1 inch (2.5 cm.) wider all around. Place 1-inch (2.5-cm.) boards on edge along all sides as a guide for leveling and to hold the brick or tile in place until the new lawn is well sodded. The boards can then be removed and the spaces filled with sand or dirt.

Cover the bottom of the excavation with 1½ inches (3.75 cm.) of sand carefully leveled to form a smooth, even surface. Lay the bricks flat on the sand in the desired pattern and as close together as possible, keeping the courses straight. As soon as all the bricks or tiles are laid, fill the spaces between them by spreading sand on top and sweeping it into all the joints. Spray the entire surface with water to pack the sand firmly and completely fill all the joints.

Where a more rigid or regular surface is required, use a 3-inch (7.5-cm.) base of concrete. Ready-mixed concrete is available at most building supply yards in bags of various sizes and eliminates the need for measuring the ingredients for a strong concrete mixture. It requires only the addition of water as directed by the manufacturer. Spread the concrete mixture over the area and lay the bricks in the manner previously described. The joints may be filled with sand but a grout fill is preferable for a terrace constructed by this method. A grout fill is made with ready-mixed cement mortar (also available in building supply yards) and requires only the addition of water (Fig. 8). Mix the mortar to the consistency of light cream and pour the fill into the joints until they are completely filled. To avoid mortar stains, brush the brick surface with raw linseed oil before grouting and smooth the fill flush with the surface of the brick. Spray the terrace with water twice daily after the grout has set, for two or three days, before using. The mortar or cement stains can then be easily washed off the surface.

Figure 9 shows a brick terrace and dutch-oven in a sunny spot near a family orchard. A brick paved terrace (Fig. 10) is an extension of the living room. Tucked neatly into its sheltered position, it may be used early in spring and late in autumn. The arrangement shown in Fig. 11 is ideal for hillside property. A chance to look at the surrounding view gives added pleasure to relaxing or dining on this elevated terrace. In a city garden, space has been reserved for an outdoor terrace (Fig. 12). Slopes are retained with walls which can also be used for seats. A hedge of laurel provides an attractive green background for the brick terrace and fireplace (Fig. 13).

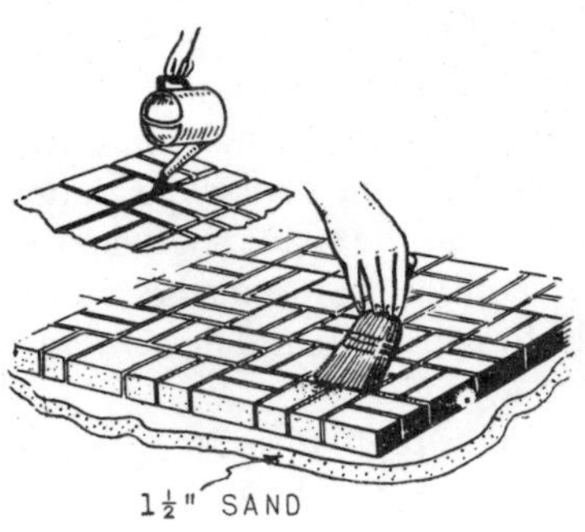

Fig. 8. Filling cracks with sand or grout.

Fig. 9. Brick terrace and Dutch oven.

Fig. 10. Brick paved terrace.

Fig. 11. Hillside terrace.

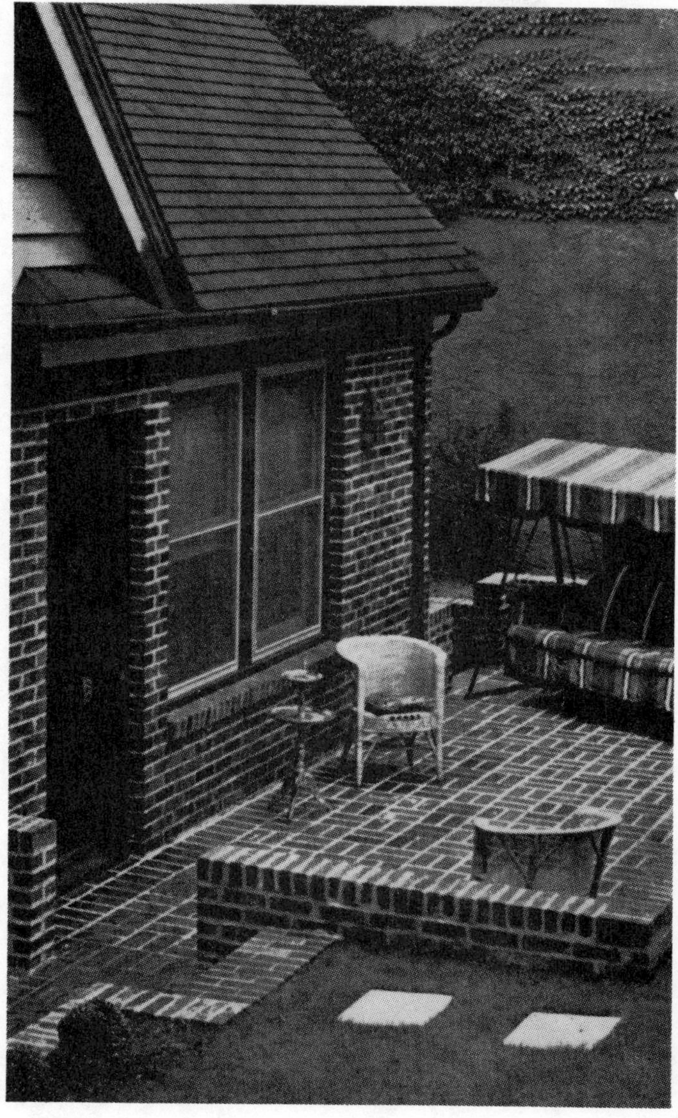

Fig. 12. Outdoor terrace.

Fig. 13. Terrace can be isolated with greenery.

BRICK GARDEN WALLS AND STEPS

Brick garden walls and steps add considerably to the attractiveness of the home grounds. Brick's soft, warm tones make a perfect foil for the varied greens of plants and vines that are grown at the base of a wall or on top of it. The slightly roughened texture of brick offers a good opportunity for many clinging vines to establish themselves securely.

Gardeners love to arrange perennials at the base of brick walls. The delicacy of blossom and leaf is shown to advantage in this situation. They like to plant a slope or terrace above a brick retaining wall, allowing trailing roses, heather, and old-fashioned rosemary and lavender to settle down on top of the wall in a picturesque manner.

The foundation can be built of brick and should be wider than the wall and deep enough to reach a firm base.

Next determine the bond or pattern of the wall. (*See* Appendix I, Glossary of Terms.)

CONSTRUCTION

There are many types of bond—common, English, Flemish, (Fig. 14) and dozens of variations thereof. If you plan an intricate pattern, it is wise to lay out one or two courses of brick dry, without setting them in mortar, to predetermine space. If the wall is to be only 4 inches (10 cm.) thick, common bond is the easiest to lay. Except where heavy freezing occurs, experience has proved the 4-inch (10-cm.) wall satisfactory. However, if there is more than 12 feet (3.7 meters) between corners, it is a good practice to strengthen the wall by using a pilaster (Fig. 15). A curved wall forms its own support, can be constructed without pilaster, and is stronger than a straight wall.

An inexpensive 8-inch (20-cm.) wall can be built on the all-rolok design. In all-rolok walls the stretchers are laid on the edge; every third course is a header course, with the brick flat. The headers are side by side (Fig. 16).

One simple variation of the common bond in a 4-inch (10-cm.)

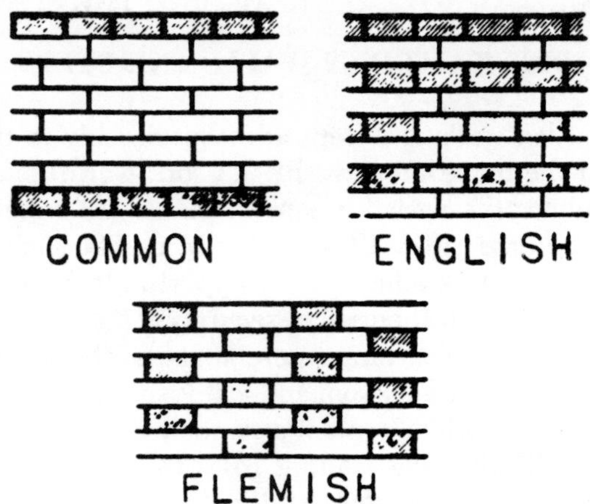

Fig. 14. Brick bonds commonly used.

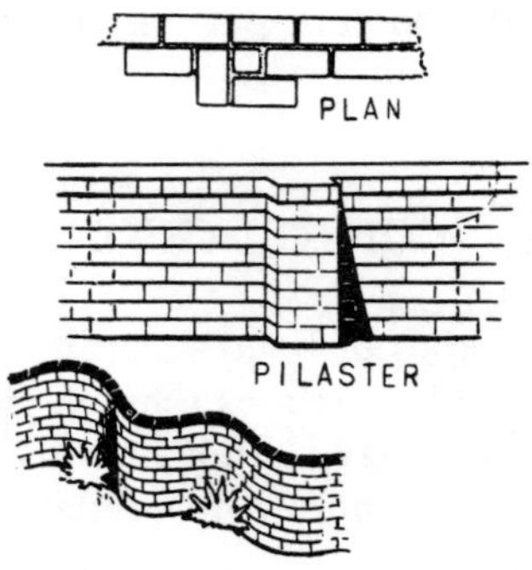

Fig. 15. Pilasters can be used to strengthen the wall.

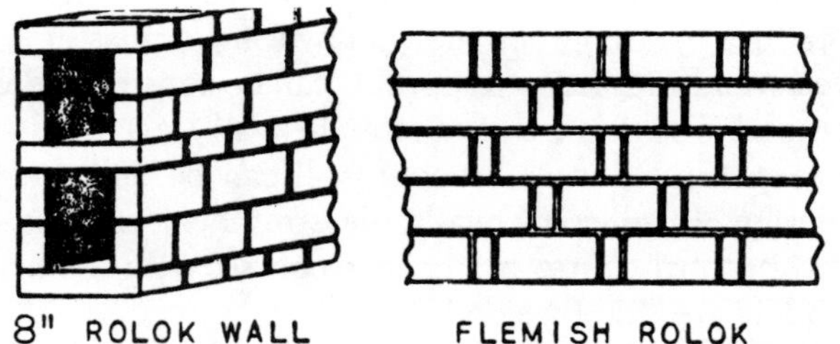

Fig. 16. Rolok walls.

wall construction is obtained by spacing three stretcher courses so that there is a 4-inch (10-cm.) space between bricks (Fig. 17).

In laying a wall be generous with your use of a guide line—do not trust your eye too much. Keep your mortar just wet enough so that it can be handled easily with a trowel (mortar mixture—1 part cement, ¼ part lime, 2¼ parts sand).

Wet bricks before laying them into the wall, as dry, porous bricks absorb too much moisture from the mortar. Wet bricks adhere to the mortar better. Water by sprinkling them with a hose for five minutes (Fig. 18).

In wall construction it is considered good practice to finish the joints on the exterior face. Three styles of jointing are diagramed in Fig. 19. Style A can be made with the edge of a board; style B with the handle of the trowel held down; and style C with the handle of the trowel held up. The B joint is preferred because of its water-shedding ability and the fact that each course of bricks will throw a horizontal line of shadow along the wall. All jointing should be done after the mortar has slightly stiffened.

SPLIT TILE AND BRICK WALL CONSTRUCTION

Split tile and brick wall construction as illustrated in Fig. 20 offers no problems. The square tiles are placed in equilateral triangles on top of the low brick wall. The manner in which tile fits against tile takes care of all stresses, but mortaring the joints strengthens the wall.

In building arches of brick, the common rule is to give them a rise of 1 inch for each foot (8.2 cm. per meter) of span. The mor-

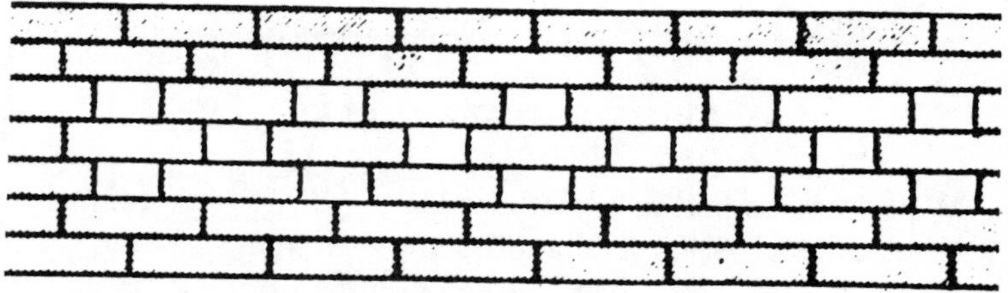

Fig. 17. Simple variation of the common bond.

Fig. 18. Wet bricks before laying them.

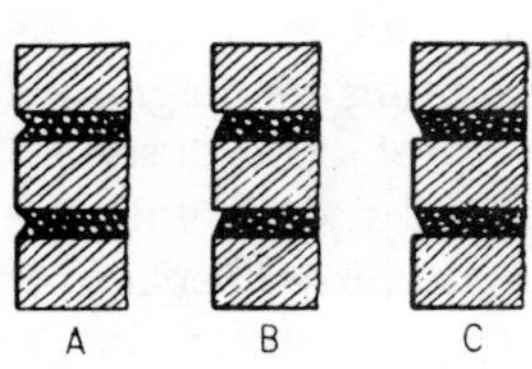

Fig. 19. Three styles of jointing.

Fig. 20. Split tile and brick wall construction.

tar joint is wider at the top, and wedge-shaped joints compensate for the curvature of the arch. Use wooden frames for support during construction (Fig. 21).

Figure 22 shows a standard method of *step* construction. The concrete base can be eliminated entirely and the solid bed used only as a form if the steps are tied to the foundation walls with steel reinforcing.

The treads of the steps should never be less than 12 inches (30 cm.) wide and should slope not more than ¼ inch per foot (2.1 cm. per meter). It is best to use grout to insure complete filling of the joints (*see* Figs. 23 and 24). (*See* Chap. 23, Structural Clay Tile Masonry.)

BRICK GARDEN WALKS

Walks may be laid in one of two ways—either on a sand base with sand joints, or on a concrete base with mortar joints.

In either case, No. 1 hard-burned common brick suitable for

Fig. 21. In building arches, use wooden frames for support during construction.

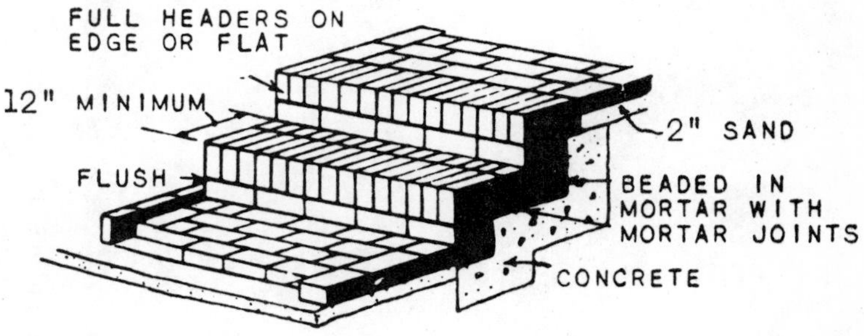

Fig. 22. Step construction.

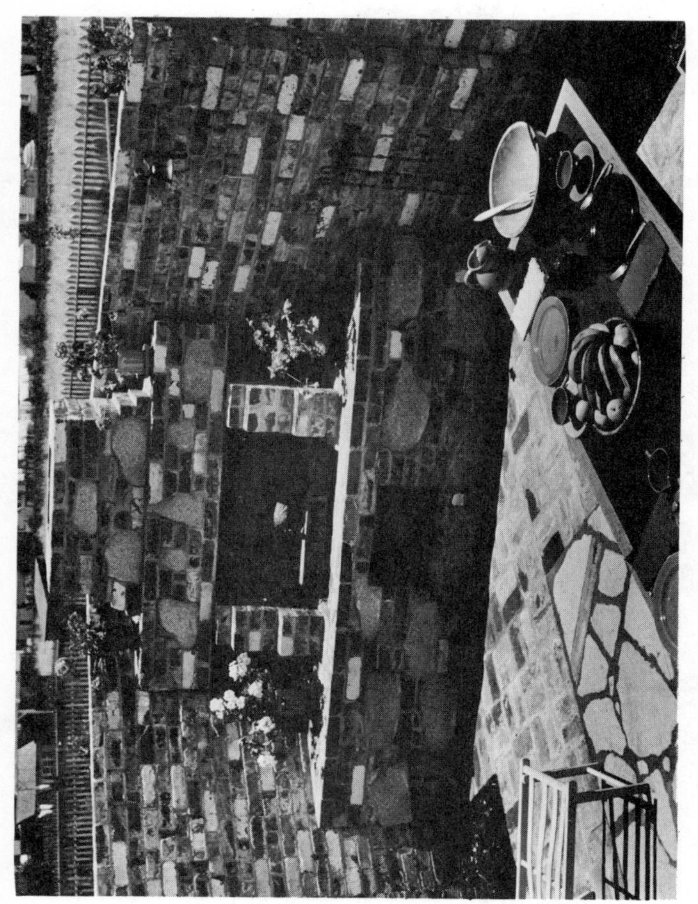

Fig. 23. A brick garden wall with a fireplace in the corner and a flagstone floor makes an ideal outdoor living room.

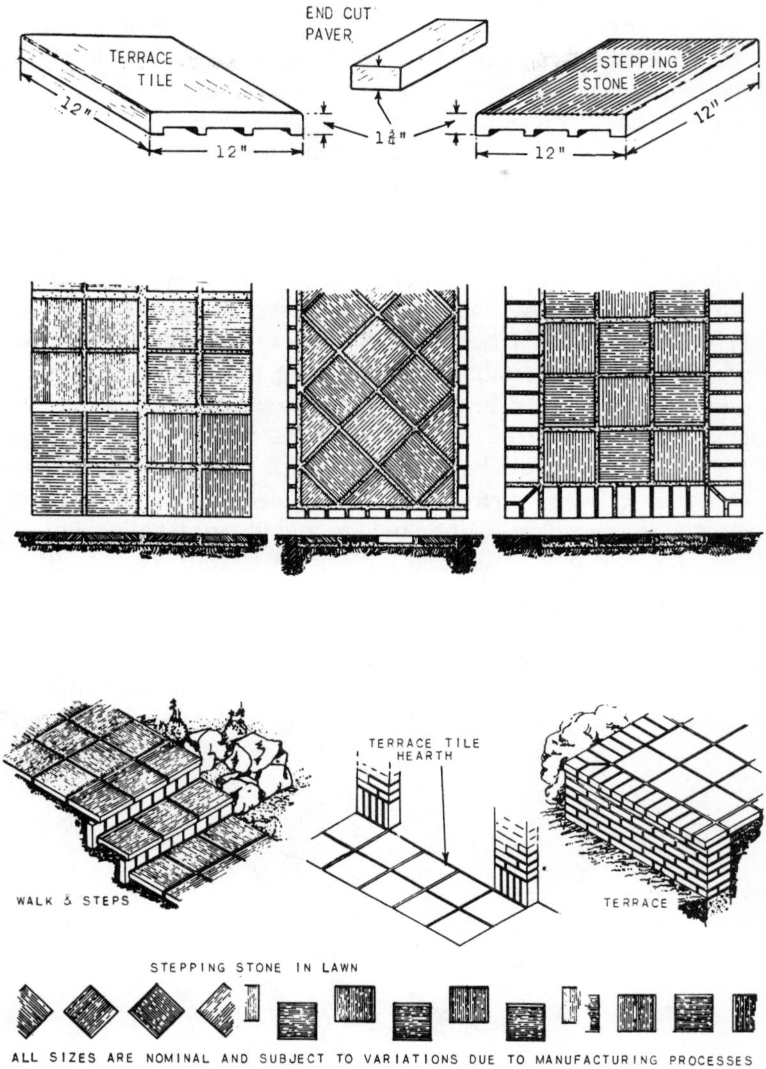

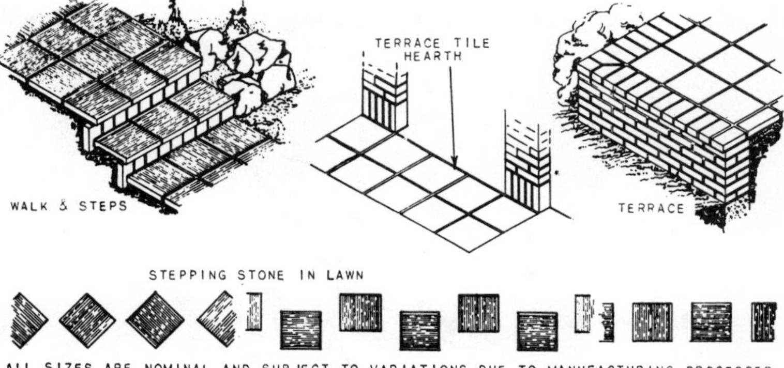

Fig. 24. Types of terrace tiles and how they are used. Note the varied patterns that can be made with these tiles.

sidewalk work is frequently used, although smooth-surfaced sidewalk paving brick is sometimes preferred.

If the bricks are to be laid in mortar, the services of a skilled bricklayer should be obtained, but if they are to be laid in sand, the work may be done by anyone who is handy, the only tools required being a level and a tamping block (Fig. 25).

The sand method is recommended for those who prefer a walk or terrace to be slightly irregular perhaps with grass growing between the bricks.

Excavate the soil to a depth of about 3½ inches (8.8 cm.) below the surface. If the ground is uneven and needs to be filled with fresh earth in certain places, puddle or tamp these smooth before laying the brick. If the walk is to be laid across lawn which is already established, make the excavation the exact width of the finished brick walk. However, if the walk is to be laid across newly graded earth which has not yet been seeded, the excavation should be approximately 2 inches (5 cm.) wider. One-inch (2.5-cm.) boards should be placed upright along both sides of the excavation, to be used as a guide for leveling and to hold the bricks in place until the lawn is well sodded, after which the boards may be removed and the spaces filled in with sand or dirt.

Cover the bottom of the excavation with 1½ inches (3.8 cm.) of sand carefully screeded (leveled) to form a smooth surface. Lay the bricks flat on the sand according to the pattern desired

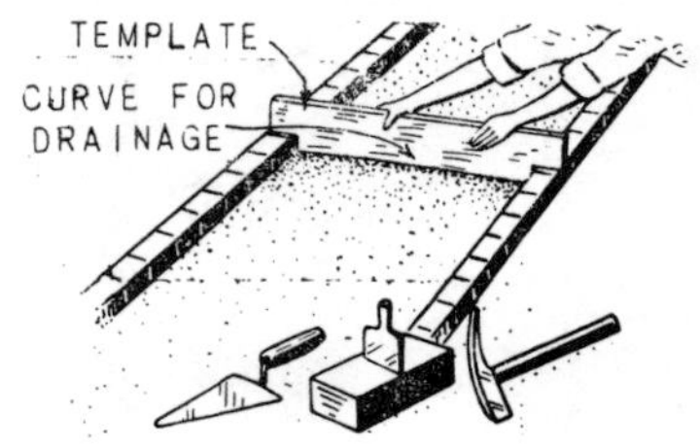

Fig. 25. The only tools needed to lay brick in sand are a level and a tamping block.

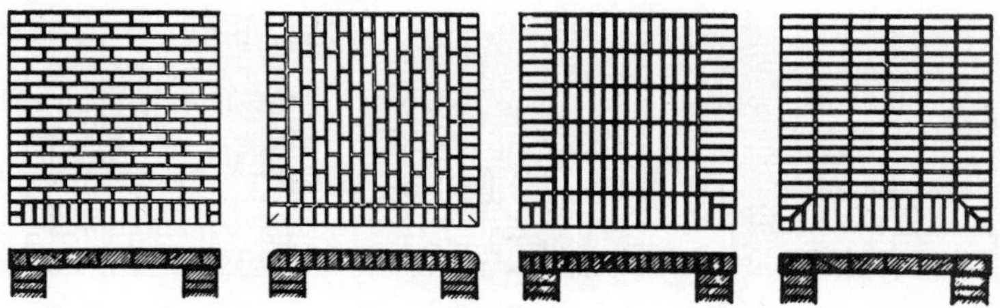

4" SLAB, BRICK ON EDGE MINIMUM 1/8" JOINTS, GROUTED FULL 3/8" DIA. RODS
HOOKED ENDS ALTERNATE RODS BENT, SPAN 6'-0", 100# LOAD.

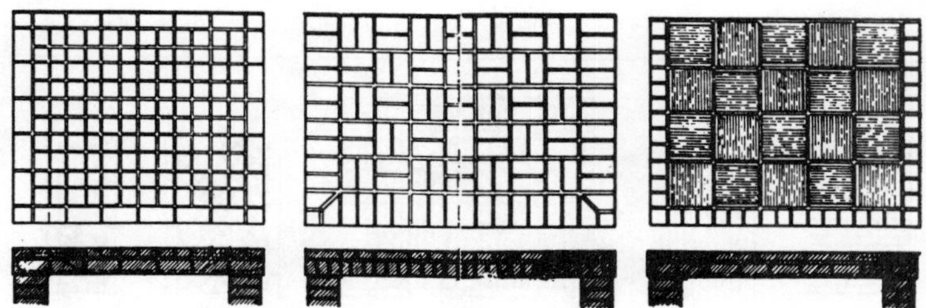

6½" SLAB, BRICK ON EDGE AN FLAT, BOND JOINTS ¾" WITH 3/8" DIA. HOOKED RODS
INTERMEDIATE JOINTS ½" WITH ¼" HOOKED RODS, GROUTED-SPAN TO 12'-0".

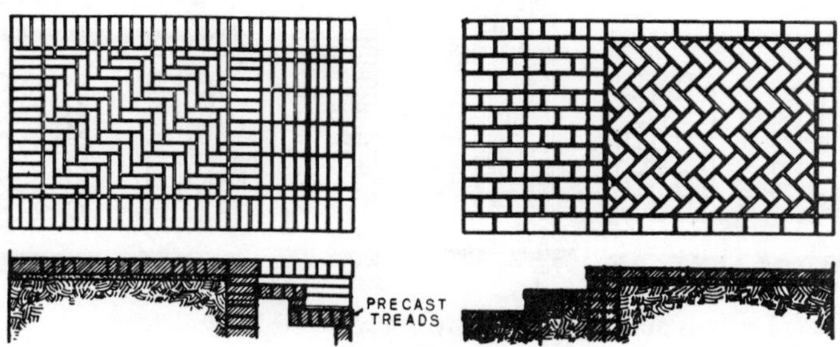

BACK FILL AND PUDDLE EARTH, IMBED WIRE MESH IN ¾" MORTAR BED, LET SET
PLACE BRICK IN PATTERN, POUR JOINTS WITH GROUT.

Fig. 26. Types of attractive brick porch floors and details of procedures employed.

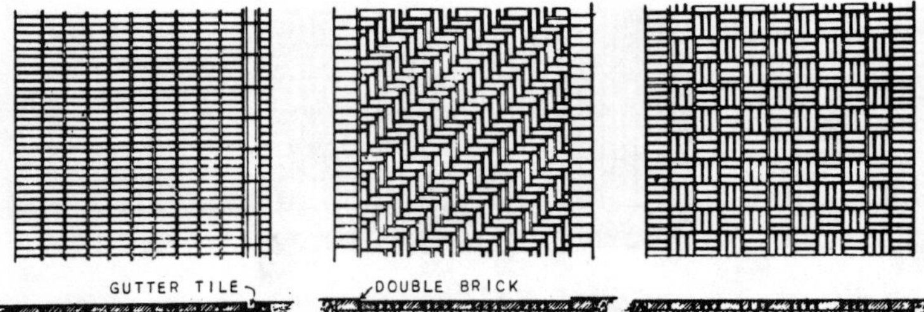
GUTTER TILE
DOUBLE BRICK
ESTABLISH GRADES AND CONTOURS OF DRIVEWAYS OR WALKS, SUB-GRADE TO BE UNIFORM, WELL PACKED AND SCREENED, APPLY THIN SAND BED, NOT LESS THAN 3/4" RICH MORTAR WITH WIRE MESH REINFORCEMENT IMBEDDED, LAY BRICK IN PATTERN, POUR JOINTS WITH GROUT.

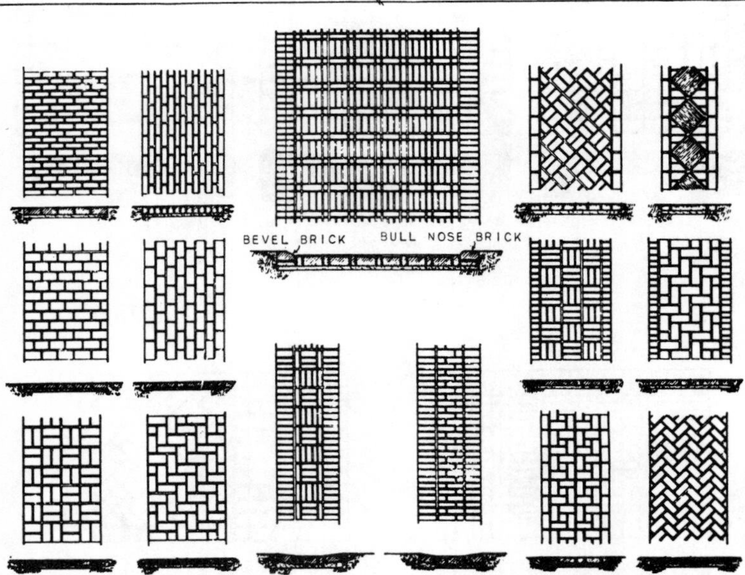
BEVEL BRICK
BULL NOSE BRICK

Fig. 27. Designs and types of easily constructed brick driveways.

Fig. 28. Brick garden walk and wall.

Fig. 29. Formal brick front walk.

and as close together as possible, keeping the courses straight. As soon as the bricks are laid, fill the spaces between them by placing a layer of sand on the walk and sweeping it into the joints with a broom. Spraying the walk with water will help to pack the sand firmly between the bricks so that the joints may be completely filled.

If a more rigid or regular surface is desired, a 3-inch (7.5-cm.) base of concrete is sometimes used and the bricks laid on a ½-inch (1.3 cm.) bed of cement mortar, the joints being filled with a dry mixture of sand and cement and sprayed. If a smooth-top brick is used, pour grout (thin mortar) into the joints and then tool it flat. Another method is to pack the subgrade thoroughly and apply a base of damp sand and cement mixed in the proportions of 3 parts sand to 1 part cement, leveling off to 2¼ inches (5.6 cm.) below the finished grade of the brickwork. Lay the bricks in the pattern desired, spray lightly, and fill the joints as previously described. This is an economical method of securing a finished job, and, when carefully done, has proved entirely satisfactory (Fig. 26).

Use a brick walk and terrace to carpet garden spaces under trees whose shade will not permit the growth of grass (Fig. 27). A brick garden walk and wall are practical as well as beautiful as shown in Fig. 28. Figure 29 shows a smooth, formally laid straight walk which extends from the front steps to the sidewalk.

Chapter 56

Brick Bonds and Patterns

Brick bonds are selected for many uses. Most bonds are for ornamental purposes. Permanent brickwork of all types must be laid on a foundation or footing of concrete. In laying brick on any type job, there are certain methods that are used to properly build a brick job. (*See* Section 3, Brick Masonry.)

A brick is a solid building unit of burned clay or shale. Brick are made for many uses, but mainly for building construction. Other uses are for fire brickwork, paving, chimney work, and lining retorts.

The brick used for building construction are generally of clay, shale, or clay and shale. The common brick are generally of clay or shale, having a natural face, made either by the stiff mud or sloppy mud process. The face brick are more generally made by the stiff mud process with smooth or rough textured surfaces made by special face scoring devices. Other surfaces of brick are ceramic and salt glazed. All brick are made also in special shapes for ornamental purposes, such as watertables, bull noses and jambs. Composition brick are those that are made of concrete and sand-lime. Sand-lime brick are sometimes used for facing in light shafts, due to their light colors.

CLASSES OF COMMON BRICK IN WALL CONSTRUCTION

Brick walls are built of common brick faced with natural or artificial stone, architectural terra cotta, face brick, or other facing material.

There are three classes of common brick used—severe-weathering, medium-weathering, and no-weathering. The severe-weathering are generally the hard, well-burned brick that run more evenly to class. The medium-weathering may be a mixture of well- and medium-burned brick, that might also be called *run of the kiln* class. The no-weathering are the soft, salmon or underburned brick. These brick should never appear on the weather side of walls as they will disintegrate when subjected to severe weather.

The severe-weathering are selected for heavy bearing walls. The medium-weathering are generally used for light construction.

The clinker is an overburned brick which has lost its shape, due to being in direct contact with the fire in the kiln. These brick are often used as face brick.

The quality of brick masonry is determined by three principal factors, namely—good quality of brick, mortar, and workmanship.

USING A MASON LINE ON BRICK JOBS

It is always advisable to use a *mason line* on all brick jobs that are 3 feet (91 cm.) or more in length. No good mechanic can lay brick on a straight wall without the aid of the line, as all brickwork (unless otherwise specified) should be laid straight, plumb, and level at all times. When a line is used, it will level and range or straight edge the brick at the same time, without disturbing the brick. Brick laid without a line must be straight edged with a plumb rule or *straight edge*, and in most cases the brick are disturbed, which is not desirable on a practical job, on account of using cement mortar. When the brick are disturbed after being laid, it prevents the bonding between the brick and mortar, and tends to make the walls leak. (*See* Chap. 26, Bricklaying Tools and Equipment.)

BUILDING A CORNER LEAD

All walls are laid up with a line attached to the corner *leads*. These leads are portions of the wall built up in advance, and act as a guide for the balance of the wall. On all good jobs, a foreman will lay out a gage stick so that all the bed joints for that particular portion of the job will have uniform bed joints. A *setting up* is a header and 5-6-7 stretcher courses on the face of the wall. The number of stretchers is determined by the local building code.

STORY POLE AND GAGE STICK

The *story pole* is a stick generally about 10 feet (3 meters) long or a story high. It is 1 × 2 inches (2.5 × 5 cm.) in thickness and width. The pole should have joint heights or brick gages marked on three sides and the sills, lintels, and frame heights marked on the fourth side. The window and door sills and lintels occur on the different levels. It is necessary to lay out on the pole so that the various thicknesses of brick joints will coincide with the sills, lintels, frames, and wall heights. (*See* Chap. 50, Laying Concrete Block, Fig. 19.)

Many jobs have more than one brick gage, and as various jobs may have different door, sill, and window heights, it is not possible to use the same pole.

The story pole is generally set on the water table on the outside of the job or on the first floor level on the inside, which is generally on the same level. The height of the windows and doors do not always match the joint heights so that the difference is made up by the thicknesses of the bed joints in the brickwork.

The *gage stick* is a short stick about 4 feet (1.2 meters) long and ¾ inch (1.9 cm.) square. It should have four different brick gage marks, one on each side. The purpose of gages is to be able to lay up brick courses in uniform bed joints. Where gage sticks are not used the 6-foot (1.8-meters) pocket rule is used, which requires much mathematical calculation and is slow in operation, and therefore tends to increase the cost of the job. All good jobs should use a gage stick. It is generally used when building corners and leads. The same gage stick should be used on both ends of the wall or job as this will insure an even and level wall. It should be used from the first course to the finish of the job.

BONDING OF BRICK IN WALL CONSTRUCTION

Brick bonds are selected for many uses. Most bonds are for ornamental purposes. Practically the only bond used in this country, structurally, is the American or running bond. There are certain principles in all bonds.

American or Common Bond

The *American* or *common bond* (Fig. 1) is composed of a header and 5, 6, or 7 stretcher courses on the face of the wall. This is called a setting up. The number of stretchers is determined by the local building code.

This bond is considered the strongest structural bond, because the brick overlap themselves by one half, lengthwise. The header serves to bond the various tiers together, or across the wall, depending on the thickness of the walls. The walls are of various thicknesses and are built to carry loads that are imposed upon them.

Each 4-inch (10-cm.) thickness of wall is called a *tier,* so that an 8-inch (20-cm.) wall has two tiers, a 12-inch (20-cm.) wall has three tiers, and so on.

The bond is used almost entirely in building construction, where ornamental or pattern bonds are used for the facing of the walls.

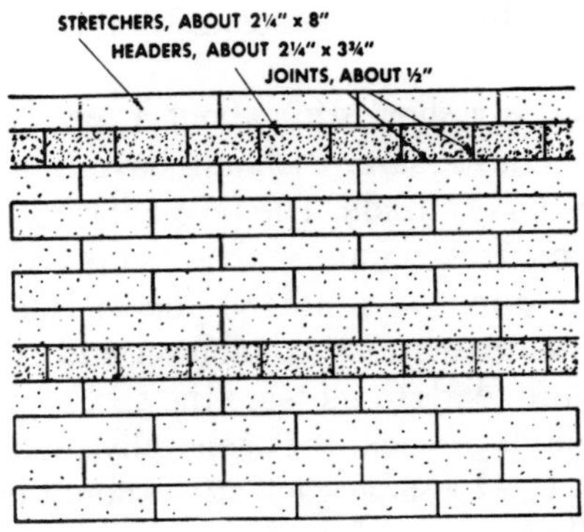

Fig. 1. American or common bond.

The English Bond

The *English bond* (Fig. 2) is one of the true fundamental bonds used in brick construction. As the name indicates, it is used very extensively in England and her colonies. It is also used in other parts of the world. In England it is used as a structural as well as an ornamental bond.

It is exceptionally strong across the width of the wall and weak lengthwise on the wall. Its weakness is also apparent on the face of the wall, because the brick overlap themselves by one-quarter length of the brick. The arrangement of the bond is that of alternate courses of headers and stretchers. In actual practice, the full headers are only used every sixth, seventh, or eighth courses in height. The other courses have snap headers or bats (half brick) to carry out the bond effect. This also speeds up the construction of the wall. The corners are started with a three-quarter brick, or a whole brick, on the stretcher courses. The strictly English method is to have a stretcher on the corner of the stretcher course and a closure on the header course.

Flemish Bond

The *Flemish bond* (Fig. 3) is a simple bond to maintain as it consists of alternate headers and stretchers on the same course. Like the English and Dutch bonds it may be started with either a three-quarter or whole brick on the corner. This is also a one-quarter lap bond and should be considered weak lengthwise on

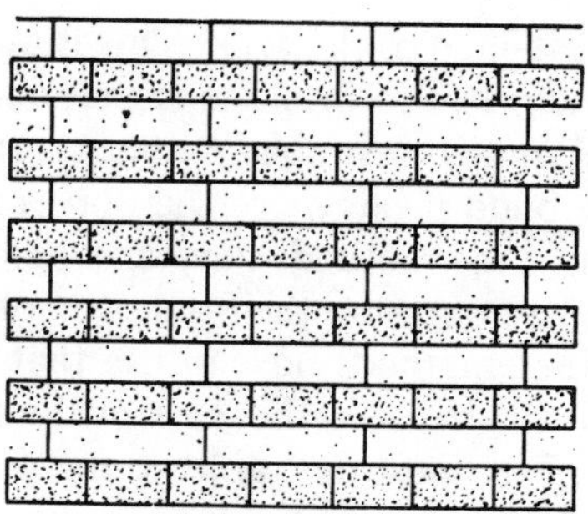

Fig. 2. English bond.

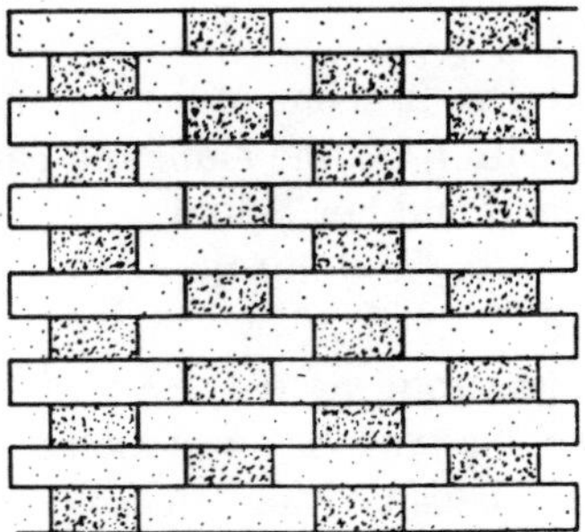

Fig. 3. Flemish bond.

the face of the wall. The true Flemish bond has single headers and stretchers on each course. It can also be changed with varied colored brick, such as red stretchers and black headers, or any other combination of colors. In cross bonding it is best to have the first two courses full headers and snap headers for the next 4-5-6 courses, depending on the local building code. The full headers should always be laid on two succeeding courses. This will only be 66 percent of transverse bonding, which is considered ample cross bonding on a 12-inch (30-cm.) wall, which is the average size of a wall.

Dutch Bonds

The *Dutch bond* (Fig. 4) is also called the English Cross bond. Its main feature is that the cross joints or perpends form a series of diamonds on the face of the wall. This is another of the true fundamental bonds used in brick construction. With the aid of varicolored brick many desirable patterns can be carried out. Like the English bond it has more than one method of starting the corner. Most of the methods have a stretcher course on one side and the header course on the other side of the same course. But there are other methods now in use that produce the diamond effect and still have the headers of the return corners on the same course. The most desirable corner for strength should have a full stretcher on the stretcher course, but this method will defeat the continuity of the diamond effect on both sides of the

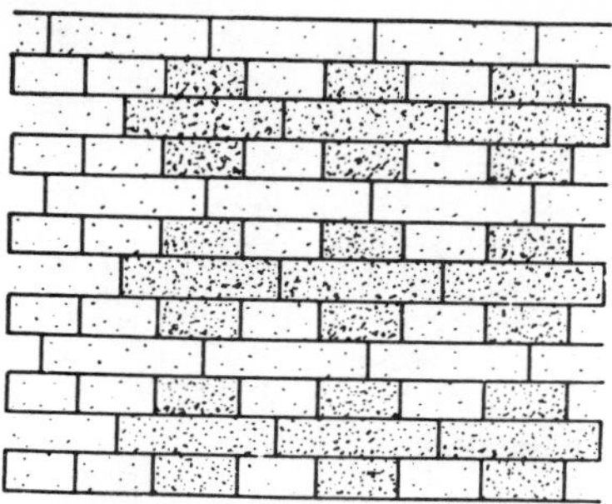

Fig. 4. Dutch bond.

corner. Whenever this bond is specified it should be laid out on paper so that the best effect can be produced. As this bond calls for headers on every other course, and as it would not be practical to lay full headers on every course shown, it is good practice to lay the full headers only on either the sixth, seventh, or eighth course, and put snap headers in between these full header courses. On the more important jobs, the cross joints are plumbed and marked to insure plumb joints and perfect effect of the bond.

JOINTS IN BRICKWORK

Jointing is the final dress-up of brickwork. (*See* Fig. 5.) A fairly good job may be made to look either good or bad by the final jointing. (*See* Section 3, Brick Masonry.)

PATTERN BONDS

Pattern bonds are strictly ornamental bonds, and should never be a part of the wall structurally. This is because of the absence of full headers in their make-up. Such patterns as the diamond units and their variations—herringbone, basket weave, and diagonal have no headers and can only be tied in with wall ties.

Most patterns have considerable cutting of brick and should

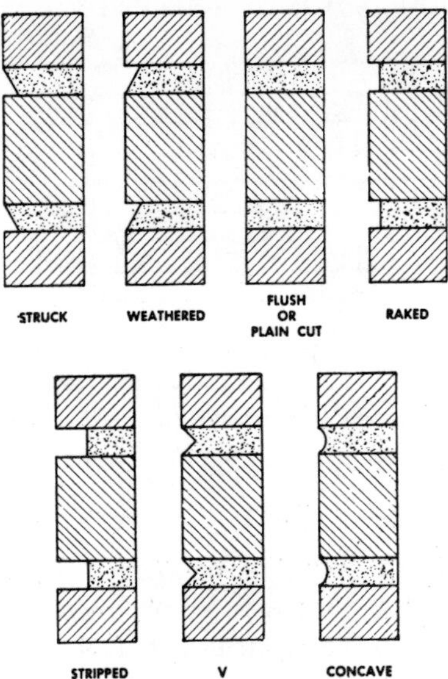

Fig. 5. Typical joints for brick masonry.

always be laid out on paper in full size. This is to enable the bricklayer to mark the exact size of the cut. This method may be longer due to the time required to draw out a portion of the pattern, but it can easily be made up when one considers that the cuts will be cut to the right size and the *cut and try* method which is often practiced in the trade will be avoided. The laying out of the patterns will also center the job more accurately. The unit patterns may be arranged to fit any particular portion of the wall by cutting or extending the units. The herringbone, basket weave, and diagonal patterns may also be laid on the *flat*, that is, with the bed of the brick faced up.

Running Headers

Continuous header courses are often used as ornamental patterns and should be considered as such. Whole header patterns should only be used in panels, as they are structurally weak lengthwise, due to less than one-quarter lap on their face.

In transverse bonding they can be used the same as for common bonding, and, due to the 100 percent of headers, any number of them can be used as full headers, but the full headers should occur only every fifth or sixth course in height. Snap headers (bats) can be used between the full headers on the face of the wall. In face brick construction this method would not only speed up construction, but would also reduce the cost of face brick as two headers can be made from a whole brick.

The header patterns can be used both with a continuous plumb joint or an overlapped bond effect. (*See* Figs. 6 and 7.) In estimating face brick always add 17 percent more when the full headers occur every sixth course.

Soldier Courses

All phases of brickwork that do not make possible the use of full header courses in part for the purpose of cross bonding may be considered pattern bond—including the soldier course. Due to their upright position in the wall they cannot very well be bonded into the wall of themselves, but must be made a part of a pattern. When two or more consecutive courses of soldiers occur on the face of any wall it presents not only a weak looking condition, but actually is weak, as they can only be held to the back wall by means of wall ties.

Soldier courses are mainly used as a watertable around the house at the level of the first floor and sailing or band courses at various levels to form part of the architectural design. They fit very well as flat arches over windows, doors, and other openings when laid on angle irons.

Soldier courses should always be perfectly plumb at all times. The eye can detect any slant or *out of plumb* in soldiers because of their upright position. When out of plumb they are called *drunken soldiers.*

Rowlok Courses

While *rowlok courses* cannot be classed strictly as a bond or pattern of themselves, they do form parts of patterns on the face of the wall. When rowlok courses are laid up as a part of a pattern, their height in relation to the regular flat courses often

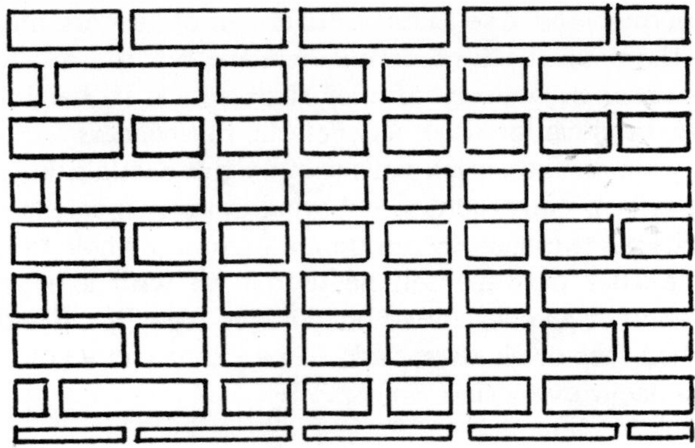

Fig. 6. Continuous plumb joint.

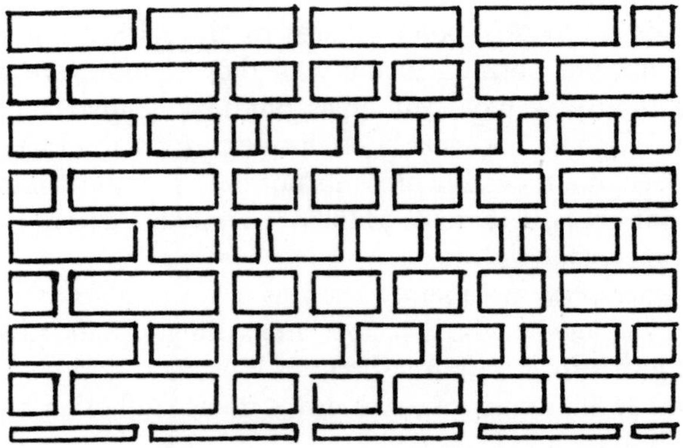

Fig. 7. Overlapped bond.

raises problems. One rowlok course should equal one and one-half flat courses or two rowloks equal three flat courses. Three rowloks should be the same length as a stretcher on the face of the wall so in laying out any band or border rowloks, their heights in the pattern should always be considered.

They are also used as band courses, continuation of sills, borders, parts of cornices, and as structural units such as sills, steps, and coping. Rowlok courses laid lengthwise across the wall can always be properly bonded into and made part of the wall structurally.

In arch construction the rowlok courses play an important part, as practically 90 percent of all brick arches have them in some design or other. Segmental, flat, or semi-circular (Roman) arches always have them, not only as part of the design but also as structural members.

Some architects specify the use of the *ideal all-rolok* wall which is composed of rolok headers and stretchers. This particular system has some merits, but is not generally used in all sections of the country.

Herringbone Pattern

The ***herringbone pattern*** is so called because it has the appearance of the bones of a herring. It is in proper form when the points formed by the end of a brick are laid at right angles against the sides of the second brick. It should be laid in a vertical position. It can also be laid sideways, but this is not recommended for good jobs. The herringbone pattern is also known as the zig-zag pattern. (*See* Figs. 8 and 9.) As this pattern has no headers, it has no mechanical bond with the wall. It can only be tied in with wall ties.

The uses of this pattern are many, but perhaps it is used mostly in panels, nogging in half-timber work, paving on stoops, porches, walks, and streets.

It makes a very acceptable design for paving, because there are no continuous joints. This will prevent any settling or cracking in any particular line, as may happen with any other pattern. When laid down as a porch, stoop, or approach pavement, they can be laid on edge or on the flat, but when laid on the flat, only those brick should be selected that have a uniform wire cut or pressed bed. Brick with holes or frogs could never be used in this manner. When used as a street pavement, it occurs at almost all street intersections.

In estimating brick for this pattern, the same rule is applied as for other brickwork. For each 4-inch (20-cm.) thickness of wall, there are $6\,^1/_6$ brick per square foot (.09 sq. meters) area. When

Fig. 8. Herringbone pattern.

Fig. 9. Herringbone pattern.

brick are laid on the flat for paving, one-third less brick are required, or 4 $^{1}/_{9}$ brick per square foot (.09 sq. meter) area.

Basket Weave Pattern

The absence of headers or any other mechanical ties makes strictly a pattern bond. It is called the ***basket weave***, block, or diaper pattern because it looks like the weave of basket material with each unit forming a square block. Alternate blocks are laid at right angles to the blocks adjoining them. This pattern can also be laid at a 45-degree angle and is then called the *diagonal basket weave pattern*. This pattern may be used as a watertable, continuous band course, portions of cornices, panels, and paving.

These blocks should be spaced so that three soldiers will equal one stretcher lengthwise and in height. It is important in its construction that both the vertical and horizontal joints are plumb and level, otherwise the job will look sloppy and lose its decorative value.

When used as a watertable it should be not over one block high, with a full header course above it to give a good tie in to the main wall.

This pattern makes an ideal paving design. It is very easy to lay down. It can be used on all types of pavements, such as stoops, porches, walks, and platforms. With the solid brick of the wire-cut or pressed kind the paving can be laid on the flat. This makes a very economical and attractive pavement. When laid on the flat there is a saving of one-third of the brick from the edge laying.

Diagonal Pattern Bond

The *diagonal bond* or *pattern* can be used in the same manner and for the same purposes as the other pattern bonds. In wall construction it is best used in panels, particularly where certain architectural designs are required.

This design is composed of ordinary straight stretcher courses laid at an angle of 45 degrees. These courses can only be tied to the wall by means of wall ties. Therefore, they should be considered weak and not be made part of the wall structurally. It is best to lay out a portion of the pattern in full size on paper in order to determine the proper sizes of the different cuts, in order to avoid the *cut and dry* method. The cross joints should line up and form right angles to the bed joints.

It can also be used as a paving design, but it is not as popular as the herringbone and basket weave patterns. When used for paving they can be laid both on edge and on the flat. For flat pavement, only the solid brick having no holes or frogs should be used. In estimating brick on the flat, consider one-third less than for brick laid in the usual way, that is, on edge.

Chapter 57

Brick Piers, Pilasters, and Arches

SOLID AND HOLLOW BRICK PIERS

A pier is a vertical shaft, either *solid* or *hollow*, constructed of masonry materials, usually supporting an arch, beam, girder, lintel, or other parts of the superstructure. The size and construction of the piers will be determined by the nature of the job, its height, and the load to be carried, and by local building code.

Hollow piers (Fig. 1) are mainly built for ornamental purposes as they can not carry any considerable weight. Since piers are of various dimensions in plan area, one of the best methods of estimating is to lay out model brick to cover the plan area shown.

Example: A solid pier shown on plan as 12 inches × 24 inches × 5 feet 4 inches (30 × 60 × 162.5 cm.) in height would measure 12½ inches × 25 inches (30.8 × 62.5 cm.) in plan if pre-modular conventional 8-inch (20-cm.) length brick are used or 11½ inches × 23½ inches (28.8 × 57.5 cm.) (actual size) with modular 7½-inch (18.8-cm.) length brick. In either case the plan layout would show that there are nine brick per course. Then estimate the number of courses required for the 5 feet 4 inch (1.6 meters) height, which is 24 courses using standard modular brick (3 courses plus 3 joints equals 8 inches or 20 cm.). The result is a nine brick course times 24 courses which equals 216 brick. (*See* Figs. 2 to 4.)

SOLID BRICK PIERS WITH BOND STONES AND TEMPLATES

Many *piers* require bond stones and steel templates to distribute the weight imposed on them. *Bond stones* are cut stones, generally made of limestone. They are the full size of the pier in

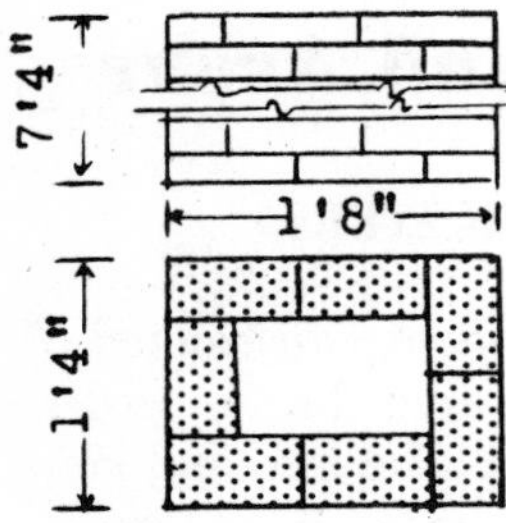

Fig. 1. Hollow pier.

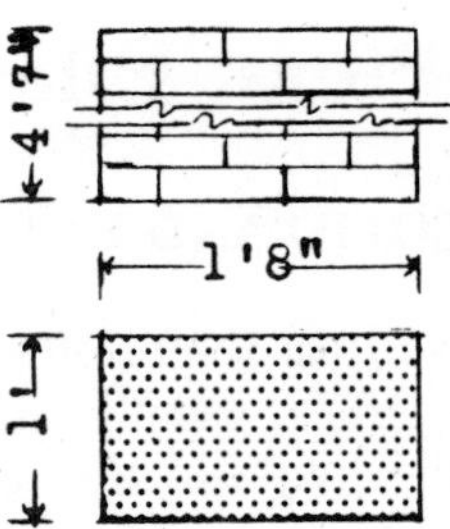

Fig. 2. Solid pier.

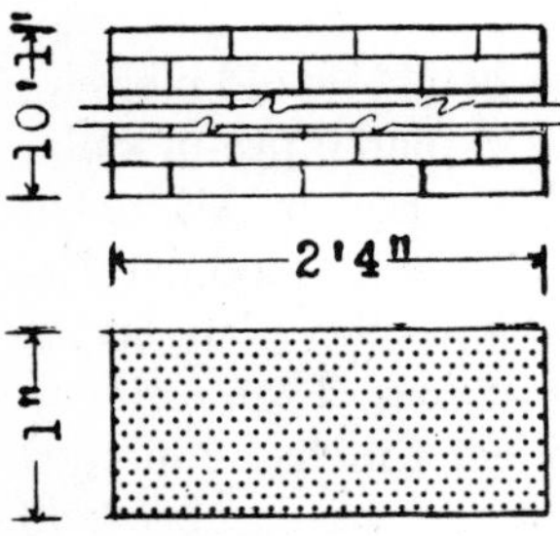

Fig. 3. Solid pier.

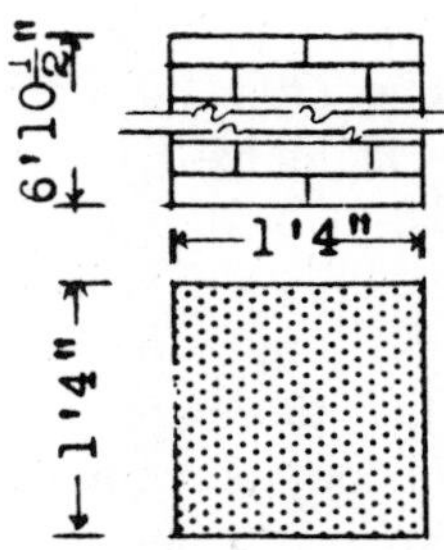

Fig. 4. Solid pier.

plan. The height of the stones should be in brick joint heights, usually about 2, 3, and 4 brick courses in height.

Steel templates are usually ¼ to ½ inch (.63 to 1.3 cm.) thick and are generally less than the dimensions of the cross-sectional area of the pier by about ½ inch (1.3 cm.) around the entire perimeter. When bedded in a tight bed of mortar, they are entirely concealed from view and the joints appear the same as the other bed joints.

The same methods of estimating the quantities of materials are used as previously described for Solid and Hollow Brick Piers, except that the various thicknesses of the bond stones should be deducted from the total height of the piers. (*See* Figs. 5 to 8.) Figures 5 and 6 are estimated by the brick per course method. Figures 7 and 8 are estimated by the cubic content method. Be sure to consult your local building codes.

SOLID BRICK PILASTERS

A *pilaster* is any vertical thickening of the wall structurally resembling a portion of a pier or support at any required points. These pilasters may be ornamented to conform with the design of the structure or left plain to appear as part of the wall. Some pilasters are built for appearance only. In general, however, pilasters are used to strengthen the walls. Pilasters are also called *wall piers* and *buttresses*. (*See* Fig. 9.)

Very often pilasters are built on a battered plane, that is, a diminishing thickness at the top. Then they are referred to as buttresses and sometimes called battered pilasters. They may also be battered on the sides, diminishing in width toward the top. All pilasters should be bonded into the wall and become part of it. The reveals or sides should be multiples of 4 inches or brick widths, 4 inches, 8 inches, and so on. The face should have nominal brick or half-lengths 8 inches (20 cm.), 12 inches (30 cm.), 16 inches (40 cm.), and so on. Sometimes a plan will call for an 8 × 20-inch (20- × 50-cm.) pilaster, but on the job it will measure 8½ × 21 inches (21.3 × 52.5 cm.) due to the mortar joints being added if pre-modular conventional 8-inch (20-cm.) length brick

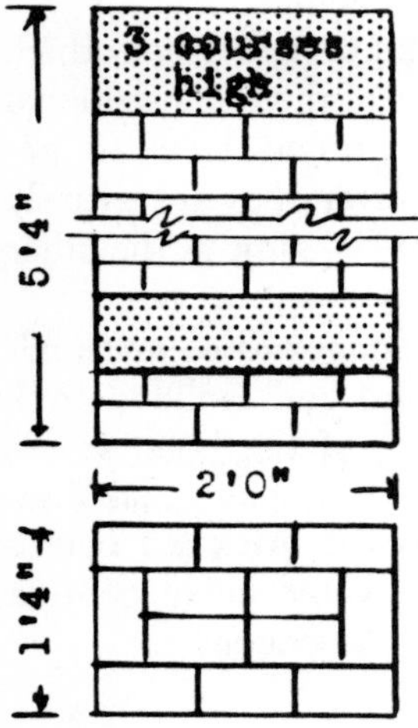

Fig. 5. Solid pier estimated by brick-per-course method.

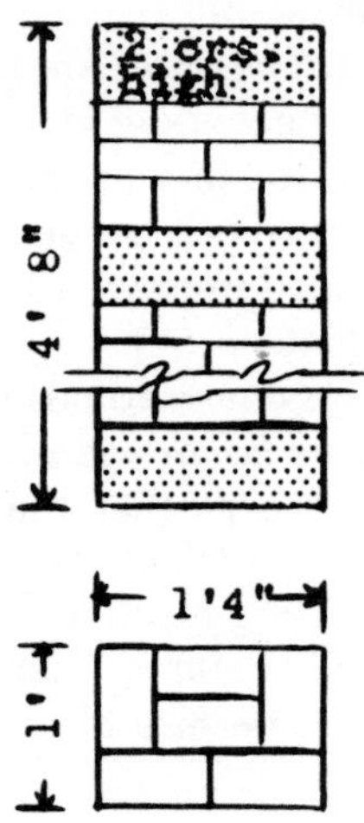

Fig. 6. Solid pier estimated by brick-per-course method.

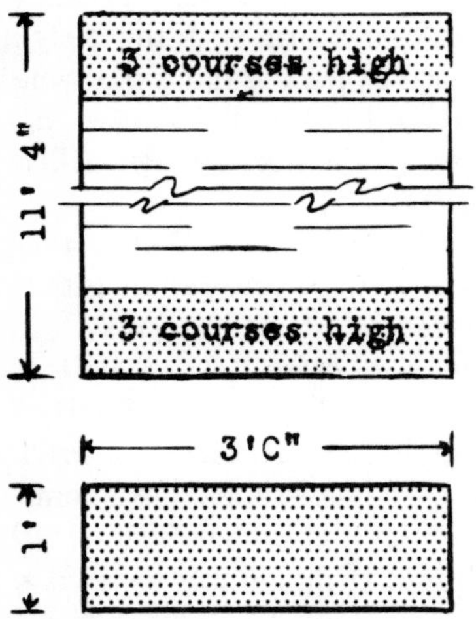

Fig. 7. Solid pier estimated by cubic content method.

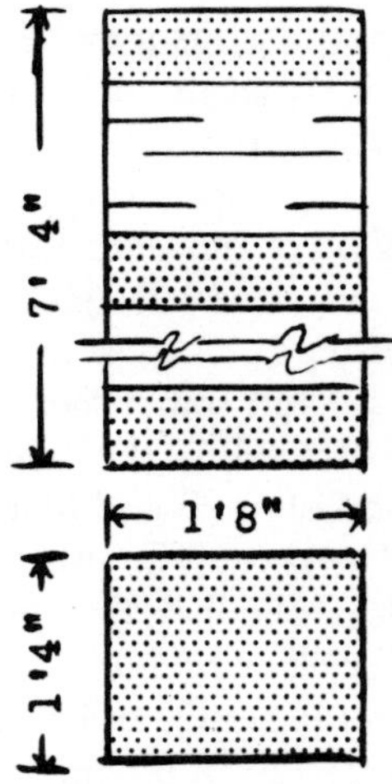

Fig. 8. Solid pier estimated by cubic content method.

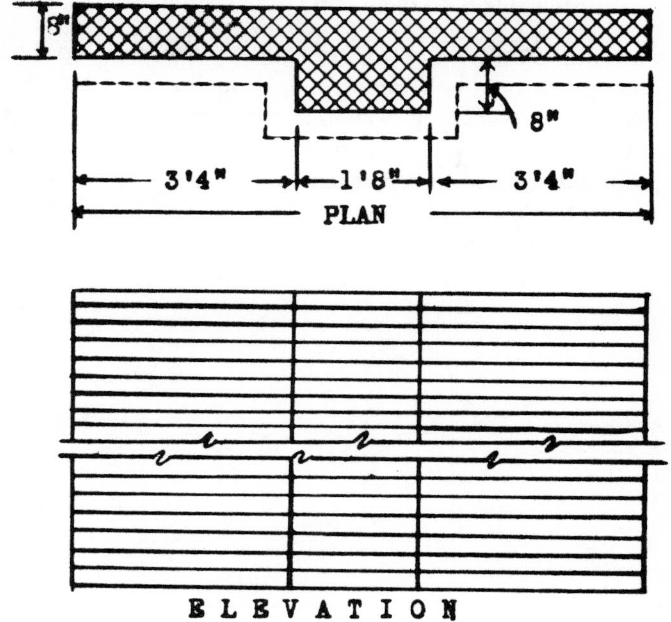

Fig. 9. Pilaster.

are used or 8 × 19½ inches (20 × 48.8 cm.) (actual) if standard modular sizes are used. Footings for pilasters should always be added to the wall footing. (*See* Chap. 41, Footings.)

USE AND PURPOSE OF BRICK ARCHES

When an opening is made in a masonry wall it is necessary to provide some means of spanning such an opening to support the superimposed masonry. Two methods have been employed by builders for this purpose—the lintel and arch. The use of the *lintel* which may be a beam, such as wood, stone, reinforced concrete, cast iron, steel, or reinforced tile. A lintel is placed across the opening and should be of sufficient strength to resist the vertical pressure of the weight it must carry. (*See* Chap. 8, Reinforced Concrete, Chap, 23, Structural Clay Tile Masonry, and Chap. 24, Stone Masonry.)

An *arch*, on the contrary, is a particular arrangement of stone blocks, architectural terra cotta, brick, or other material, put together along a curved or straight line, in such a way that they resist the load by balancing certain thrusts and counter-thrusts. Arches should have sufficient buttresses or side supports to resist the lateral and vertical thrusts. Many arches are built for architectural effect only, with the major weight carried by a lintel or relieving arch. Many terms are common to all arches.

Appendix I

Glossary of Terms

Absorption (of brick). Obtained by immersion in either cold or boiling water for stated periods of time. It is usually expressed as a percent of the weight of the dry brick.

Abutment. That part of a structure which takes the thrust of a beam, arch, vault, truss or girder.

Accelerator. Any material added to gypsum plaster that speeds the natural setting.

Acoustical plaster. A finishing plaster designed to correct sound reverberation, or reduce noise intensity.

Admixture. Act of mixing or the compound formed by mixing different substances together.

Adobe brick. A large clay brick, of varying size, roughly molded and sun dried. In certain sections of this country, a brick approximating paving brick size is known by this term.

Aggregates. Inert minerals such as sand, gravel, and crushed stone. The aggregates are divided into two sizes—fine and coarse.

Air-dried lumber. Lumber that has been piled in yards or sheds for any length of time.

Airway. A space between roof insulation and roof boards for movement of air.

Alligatoring. Coarse checking pattern characterized by a slipping of the new paint coating over the old coating to the extent that the old coating can be seen through the fissures.

Anchor. A piece or connected pieces of metal used for tying together two or more pieces of masonry materials.

Anchor bolts. Bolts to secure a wooden sill plate to concrete or masonry floor or wall.

Apron. The flat member of the inside trim of a window placed against the wall immediately beneath the stool.

Apron wall. That part of a panel wall between the window sill and the support of the panel wall.

Arch. A curved structural member used to span an opening or recess;

also built flat. (*See* supplementary definitions under kind.) Structurally, an arch is a piece or assemblage of pieces so arranged over an opening that the supported load is resolved into pressures on the side supports, and practically normal to their faces.

Arch (back). A concealed arch carrying the backing or inner part of a wall where the exterior facing material is carried by a lintel or other form of support.

Arch (basket handle). A three centered arch.

Arch (cambered). A flat arch with a slightly concave intrados.

Arch (catenary). An arch whose intrados or central line is a catenary curve.

Arch (cusped). One which has cusps or foliations worked on the introdos.

Arch (cycloidal). One whose intrados or center line is laid out to a cycloidal curve.

Arch (flat). One having a horizontal or nearly horizontal intrados and, in most cases, a horizontal extrados.

Arch (haunched). One in which the curve at the crown differs from that at the haunches.

Arch (horseshoe). One in which the curves are carried below the springing (also spring) line so that the opening at the bottom of the arch is less than its greatest span. A Moorish arch.

Arch (inverted). One whose springing line is above the intrados and the introdos above the extrados.

Arch (jack). Same as a flat arch. Also any arch doing rough work or one roughly built.

Arch (ogee). One having a reversed curve at the point.

Arch (pointed). One in which two curves meet at the crown at an angle, more or less acute. Ordinary two centered pointed arches are called lancet, acute, equilateral or blunt arches.

Arch (rampant). One in which the impost on one side is higher than on the other side.

Arch (relieving). One built over a lintel, or other similar closure or opening in a wall, and intended to divert the superimposed load above the opening of the piers or abutments on both sides, thus relieving the lintel or flat arch from excessive loading. Also known as a discharging arch.

Arch (round). One of semi-circular curvature and usually limited to one only slightly stilted, if at all, above the imposts, so that its general appearance is that of a semicircle.

Arch (rowlok). One in which the brick or other pieces of solid masonry material are arranged in separate concentric rings.

Arch (safety). Same as a relieving or discharging arch.

Arch (segmental). One in which the centers are below the angle made by the impost with the inner face of the abutment.

Arch (skew). One in which the axis and barrel form an oblique angle with the face of the wall.

Arch (splayed). An arch opening with a larger radius at one side of a wall than on the other side.

Arch (stilted). One in which the impost and architectual moldings, and the like, are notably lower on one side than on the other.

Arch (straight). Same as a flat arch.

Arch (straining). One used as a strut; as in flying buttress.

Arch (trimmer). An arch, usually of brickwork and of low rise, built between trimmers where a floor is framed around a fireplace or chimney breast and used for supporting the hearth.

Area wall. The masonry surrounding or partly surrounding an area. It also serves as a retaining wall.

Areaway. An open subsurface space adjacent to a building used to admit light or air or as a means of access to a basement.

Arris. A sharp edge forming an external corner at the junction of two surfaces.

Asphalt. Most native asphalt is a residue from evaporated petroleum. It is insoluble in water but soluble in gasoline and melts when heated. Used widely in building for waterproofing roof coverings of many types, exterior wall coverings, flooring tile, and the like.

Backfill. The replacement of excavated earth into a trench around and against a basement foundation.

Back filling. Rough masonry built in behind the facing, or between two faces; similar material or earth used in filling over the extrados of an arched construction. Also brickwork used to fill in the space between studs in a frame building.

Backing up. The operation of building up that part of a piece of masonry other than its facing.

Backup. That part of a masonry wall behind the exterior facing and consisting of one or more widths or thicknesses of brick or other masonry material.

Barge course. A course of brick, forming the coping of a wall, which is set on edge and transversely to the wall.

Base. The lowest part, or the lowest main division, of a building, column, pier or wall.

Basecoat. The plaster coat or combination of coats applied prior to the finish coat.

Base course. The lowest course of masonry of a wall or pier. A footing course.

Bat. A piece of broken brick.

Batter board. One of a pair of horizontal boards nailed to posts set at the corners of an excavation, used to indicate the desired level;

also as a fastening for stretched strings to indicate outlines of foundation walls.

Beam. A structural member transversely supporting a load.

Bearing. That part of a lintel, beam, girder or truss, which rests upon a column, pier or wall.

Bearing partition. A partition that supports any vertical load in addition to its own weight.

Bearing plate. A piece of steel, iron, or other material which receives the load concentration and transmits it to the masonry.

Bearing wall. A wall that supports any vertical load in addition to its own weight.

Bed. The prepared soil, or layer of mortar, on or in which a piece of masonry material is laid.

Belt course. Same as a string course.

Blank wall. One having no door, window or other opening.

Blisters. Protuberances on the finish coat of plaster caused by application over too damp a base coat, or troweling too soon.

Block. A unit in terra cotta or cement building, differing from a brick in being larger and, usually, hollow.

Block (hollow). A shape made of clay, terra cotta or other material fashioned with one or more openings in its body for lightness, and so on, whose net sectional area does not exceed 75 percent of its gross sectional area.

Blocking. A method of bonding two adjoining or intersecting walls, not built at the same time, by means of offsets and overhanging blocks consisting of several courses of brick each.

Bolster. A short horizontal timber or steel beam on top of a column to support and decrease the span of beams or girders.

Bond. The tying or bonding of the various pieces and parts of a masonry wall, by laying one piece across two or more pieces; the entire system of bonding or breaking joints as used in masonry construction. The mortar between brick is sometimes termed a bond.

Bond (course). The header course.

Boss. A Gothic ornament at the intersection of moldings.

Bracket. A superficial structure, usually in angles, forming a frame to support lath. Its main purpose is to save material and weight in ornaments or cornice.

Break. An interruption in the continuity of a plastered wall or cornice.

Brick. A structural unit of burnt clay or shale, formed while plastic into a rectangular prism, usually solid, the net sectional area of which is not less than 75 percent of the gross sectional area.

Brick and brick. A method of laying brick whereby the brick are laid touching each other with only mortar enough to fill the irregularities of the surface.

Brick (angle). Any brick shaped to an oblique angle to fit a salient corner.

Brick (arch). A wedge-shaped brick for special use in the voussoir of an arch; also a brick from an arch of a kiln which has been hard-burned and is therefore regarded as more suitable for certain kinds of brickwork.

Brick (clinker). A very hard-burned brick, so-called from its appearance and from the metallic sound when struck.

Brick (common). Any brick made primarily for building purposes and not especially treated for texture or color, but including clinker and over-burnt brick.

Brick (facing). A brick made especially for facing purposes, usually treated to produce surface texture or made of selected clays or otherwise treated to produce the desired color.

Brick (fire). One made of refractory clay which will resist high temperatures.

Brick (furring). A hollow brick used for furring or lining the inside face of a wall, usually the size of an ordinary brick and grooved or scored on the faces to afford a key for plastering.

Brick (gaged). A brick which has been ground or otherwise prepared to accurately fit a given curve. An arch brick.

Brick (hollow). A brick having one or more longitudinal perforations forming continuous ducts or channels, and having a net sectional area of 75 percent or less of the gross sectional area.

Brick (salmon). A relatively soft, under-burned brick.

Brick masonry. Principal properties or requisites of brick masonry are compressive and transverse strengths, resistance to fire, weathering, moisture penetration, heat transmission and sound transmission. Pleasing appearance is frequently an important consideration, particularly in exposed surfaces.

Brick nogging. The filling of brickwork between members of a framed wall or partition.

Brick veneer. A facing of brick laid against and fastened to sheathing of a frame wall or tile wall construction.

Brickwork. Any structure or structural part, made of brick and mortar.

Bridging. Small wood or metal members that are inserted in a diagonal position between the floor joists at midspan to act both as tension and compression members for the purpose of bracing the joists and spreading the action of loads.

Brown coat. Coat of plaster directly beneath the finish coat. In two-coat work, brown coat refers to the basecoat plaster applied over the lath. In three-coat work, the brown coat refers to the second coat, applied over a scratch coat. Brown coats are applied with a fairly rough surface to receive the finish coat.

Buckles. Raised or ruptured spots which eventually crack, exposing the lath beneath.

Bull-header. A rowlok brick laid with its longest dimension perpendicular to the face of the wall.

Bull nose. This term describes an external angle that is rounded in order to eliminate a sharp corner. Used largely at window returns and door frames.

Bull-stretcher. A rowlok brick laid with its longest dimension parallel to the face of the wall.

Butterflies. Color imperfection on a lime-putty-finish wall. Large variations which smear out under pressure of the trowel.

Buttering. Placing mortar on a brick with a trowel before brick is laid.

Buttress. A piece of masonry, like a pier, built against and bonded into a wall to strengthen the wall against side thrust.

Buttress (flying). A detached buttress or pier of masonry, at some distance from the wall, and connected thereto by an arch or portion of an arch, so as to assist in resisting side thrust.

Caisson. A foundation pier, either circular or rectilinear in plan, usually sunk to rock either by means of gravity, compressed air or by the open-well method.

Camber. A slight or upward curve of a structural member so that it becomes horizontal, or nearly so, when loaded.

Cap. The upper member of a column, pilaster, door cornice, molding, and the like.

Case mold. Plaster shell used to hold various parts of a plaster mold in correct position.

Casts. Finished products from a mold. Sometimes referred to as staff. Used generally as enrichments and stuck in place.

Catface. Flaw in the finish coat comparable to a pock mark.

Caulking. The operation or method of rendering a joint tight against water by means of some plastic substances such as oakum and pitch, elastic cement, and the like.

C/B ratio. The ratio of the weight of water absorbed by cold immersion (usually 24 hours) to the weight absorbed by immersion in boiling water (usually five hours). This ratio is also known as the saturation coefficient.

Cement plaster. Gypsum plaster made to be used with the addition of sand for basecoat plaster. Sometimes called neat or hardwall plaster.

Center. A timber framework or mold upon which the masonry of an arch, vault or beam is supported until self-supporting.

Check cracks. Shrinkage cracks in plaster still bonded to its base.

Chimney arch. The arch over the opening of a fireplace.

Chimney back. The back of a fireplace against which the fire is built.

Chimney bar. The lintel above the fireplace opening used for supporting the brickwork above.

Chimney breast. The front portion of a chimney which projects into the building from the face of the wall.

Chimney design. An integral piece of masonry from its foundation to top and may contain one or more flues and fireplaces.

Chip cracks. Similar to check cracks, except that the bond has been partially destroyed, causing eggshelling. Sometimes referred to as fire cracks, map cracks, crazing, fire checks, or hair cracks.

Closer. The last brick laid in a course; the end brick of a part of a course, fitted at the openings. A closer may be a whole brick or less in size.

Column. A pillar or pier of rather slender proportions which carries a load and acts as an upright support.

Common brick. (*See* Brick (common)).

Concrete. A mixture of two components, paste and aggregates.

Concrete plain. Concrete either without reinforcement, or reinforced only for shrinkage or temperature changes.

Coping. The material or member used to form a capping or finish on top of a wall, pier, or the like, to protect the masonry below by throwing off the water to one or more sides.

Corbel. That part of the masonry built outward from the face of masonry by projecting successive courses of the masonry.

Corbel out. To build out one or more courses of brick or stone from the face of a wall, to form a support for timbers.

Corner braces. Diagonal braces at the corners of frame structure to stiffen and strengthen the wall.

Cornerite. Metal-mesh lath cut into strips and bent to a right angle. Used in interior corners of walls and ceilings on lath to prevent cracks in plastering.

Counterfort. A buttress or portion projecting from a wall and upward from the foundation to provide additional resistance to thrusts.

Course. One of the continuous horizontal layers (or rows) of masonry units which, bonded together, form a masonry structure.

Cramp. An anchor for masonry, made of a short, flat bar of metal, with both ends turned down at right angles, and used for tying the masonry together by bedding the bent ends in holes provided in the masonry units.

Crawl space. A shallow space below the living quarters of a basementless house, normally enclosed by the foundation wall.

Crown. The top or head of an arch or vault.

Curtain wall. A non-bearing wall built between columns or piers for the enclosure of a building, but not supported at each story.

Damp course. A course or layer of impervious material in a wall or floor to prevent the entrance of moisture from the ground or from a lower course.

Deformed bars. Reinforcing bars with closely spaced shoulders, lugs or projections formed integrally with the bar during rolling so as to firmly engage the surrounding mortar. Wire mesh with welded intersections not farther apart than 12 inches (30 cm.) in the direction of the principal reinforcement and with cross wires not smaller than No. 10 may be rated as a deformed bar.

Dope. Term used by plasterers for additives to either accelerate or retard the set of any type of mortar.

Double-up. Plaster applied in successive operations without a setting and drying interval between coats.

Drip. Any projecting piece of material, member or part of a member so shaped and placed as to throw off water and prevent its running down the face of a wall or other surface of which it is a part.

Dry-out. Soft, chalky plaster caused by water evaporating before setting.

Effective area of brick masonry. The area of a section which lies between the centroid of the tensile reinforcement and the compression face of the structural member.

Effective area of reinforcement. The area obtained by multiplying the right cross-sectional area of the metal reinforcement by the cosine of the angle between its direction and that for which the effectiveness of the reinforcement is to be determined.

Effective depth. The distance from the center of gravity of tensile reinforcement to the compression surface of a structural member.

Efflorescence. Mortars which contain an excess of soluble salts will contribute to efflorescence of the masonry. Efflorescence can only occur when water penetrates the masonry, dissolves the salts and upon evaporation deposits them on the face of the wall. The surest preventative of efflorescence is to keep water out of masonry.

Eggshelling. Refers to the condition of chip-cracked plaster, either base or finish coat. The form taken is concave to the surface and the bond is partially destroyed.

Enclosure wall. An exterior non-bearing wall in skeleton construction, anchored to columns, piers or floors, but not necessarily built between columns or piers nor wholly supported at each story.

Enrichments. Any cast ornament that cannot be executed by a running mold.

Expanded metal. Sheets of metal that are slit and drawn out to form diamond-shaped openings. This is used as a metal reinforcing for plaster and termed *metal lath*.

Expansion joint. A bituminous fiber strip used to separate blocks or units of concrete to prevent cracking due to expansion as a result of temperature changes. Also used on concrete slabs.

Exterior wall. Any outside wall or vertical enclosure of a building other than a party wall.

Extrados. The upper or convex surface of the voussoirs composing an arch or vault.

Face. The front or exposed surface of a wall.

Faced wall. A wall in which the facing and backing are so bonded with masonry as to exert common action under load.

Facing. Any material, forming a part of the wall, used on the exterior as a finishing surface.

Facing brick. *See* Brick (facing).

Fat. Material accumulated on the trowel during the finishing operation and used to fill in small imperfections. Also a term to describe working characteristics of any type mortar.

Finish. Last and final coat of plaster. Used as the base for decoration.

Fire division wall. Any wall which subdivides a building so as to resist the spread of fire, but is not necessarily continuous through all stories to and above the roof.

Fireplace. An opening built into a chimney to contain an open fire and so designed that it will radiate heat into the room and deliver all smoke into its flue.

Fireproofing. Any material or combination of materials used to enclose structural members so as to make them fire resistive.

Fire-resistive material. (*See* Incombustible Building Material.) Improperly called Fireproof Material.

Fire stop. Any piece or mass of fire resistive material used for filling in the open spaces between wood framework or to close other open parts of a structure in order to prevent the passage of fire.

Fire wall. Any wall which subdivides a building so as to resist the spread of fire, by starting at the foundation and extending continuously through all stories to and above the roof.

Fisheyes. Spots in finish coat approximately ¼-inch (6.3 mm.) in diameter caused by lumpy lime (due to age or insufficient blending of material).

Flagstone (flagging or flags). Flat stones, from 1 to 4 inches (2.5 to 10 cm.) thick, used for rustic walks, steps, floors, and the like.

Flashing. The material used and the process of making watertight the roof intersections and other exposed places on the outside of the house.

Flue. The space or passage in a chimney through which smoke, gas, or fumes ascend. Each passage is called a flue, which together with any others and the surrounding masonry make up the chimney.

Flue lining. Fire clay or terra cotta pipe, round or square, usually made in all ordinary flue sizes and in 2-foot (60 cm.) lengths, used for the inner lining of chimneys with the brick or masonry work around the outside. Flue lining in chimneys runs from about a foot below the flue connection to the top of the chimney.

Footing. A masonry section, usually concrete, in a rectangular form wider than the bottom of the foundation wall or pier it supports.

Footing form. A wooden or steel structure, placed around the footing that will hold the concrete to the desired shape and size.

Foundation. The supporting portion of a structure below the first-floor construction, or below grade, including the footings.

Foundation wall. That portion of a load-bearing wall below the level of the adjacent grade, or below the first tier of floor beams or joists, which transmits the superimposed load to the footing.

Framing. Wood or metal members, such as studs, joists, and headers, to which lath is applied.

Frostline. The depth of frost penetration in soil. This depth varies in different parts of the country. Footings should be placed below this depth to prevent movement.

Furring. Wooden strips nailed over joists and rafters that are too far apart or crooked. Term also applies to strips attached to masonry to support lathing. This construction permits a free circulation of air behind the plastering, hence is used on walls in damp situations.

Girder. A timber used to support wall beams or joists.

Green. Describes wet or damp plaster.

Grounds. Guides used around openings and at the floorline to strike off plaster. They can consist of narrow strips of wood or of wide subjambs at interior doorways. They provide a level plaster line for installation of casing and other trim.

Grout. A mixture of cementitious material (cement, lime), sand and sufficient water to make a consistency that will flow without separation of ingredients.

Gypsum plaster. Gypsum formulated to be used with the addition of sand and water for base-coat plaster.

Hardwall. Term used for gypsum basecoat plaster. Regionally the term differs; in some cases it refers to sanded plaster, while in others to neat.

Haunch. The side of an arch about half-way between the crown and the abutment.

Header. A brick laid lengthwise across a wall and serving as a bond. A masonry unit laid flat with its largest dimension perpendicular to the face of the wall. It is generally used to tie two wythes of masonry together.

Heading course. A course of headers.

Hearth. The inner or outer floor of a fireplace, usually made of brick, tile, or stone.

Hollow wall. A wall built of solid masonry units laid in and so constructed as to provide an air space within the wall.

I-beam. A steel beam with a cross section resembling the letter *I.* It is used for long spans as basement beams or over side wall openings, such as a double garage door, when wall and roof loads are imposed on the opening.

Ideal wall. A hollow wall of solid brick, with one or both tiers of brick on edge and using solid brick bonding headers.

Inclosure wall. *See* Enclosure wall.

Incombustible (building material). Any building material which contains no matter subject to rapid oxidation within the temperature limits of a standard fire test of not less than 2½ hours duration. *Note:* Materials which continue burning after this time period are combustible.

Interior wall. Any wall entirely surrounded by the exterior walls of a building.

Intrados. The under or concave surface of an arch. The soffit.

Invert. The upper or concave surface of an inverted arch construction. The bottom half of a sewer.

Jamb. The side piece or post of an opening; sometimes applied to the door frame.

Joining. Point where two mixes on same surface meet.

Joint. The space between the adjacent surfaces of two members or components joined and held together by nails, glue, cement, mortar, or other means.

Joint cement. A powder that is usually mixed with water and used for joint treatment in gypsum-wallboard finish. Often called *spackle.*

Joist. One of a series of parallel beams, usually 2 inches (5 cm.) in thickness, used to support floor and ceiling loads, and supported in turn by larger beams, girders, or bearing walls.

Key. A wedge section of masonry placed at the crown of an arch, acting as a key.

Lacing course. A course of brick, or several adjacent courses considered collectively, inserted at frequent intervals, as in a stone wall as a bond course.

Lath. A building material of wood, metal, gypsum, or insulating board that is fastened to the frame of a building to act as a plaster base.

Lead. The building up and racking back, on successive courses, at a corner of a building at the time a wall is started.

Lintel. A horizontal structural member that supports the load over an opening such as a door or window.

Lintel (safety). A lintel of wood or other suitable material placed behind the main lintel or behind an arch; generally used in conjunction with a relieving arch.

Mantel. The shelf above a fireplace. Also used in referring to the decorative trim around a fireplace opening.

Masonry. Stone, brick, concrete, hollow-tile, concrete-block, gypsum-block, or other similar building units or materials or a combination of the same, bonded together with mortar to form a wall, pier, buttress, or similar mass.

Mastic. A pasty material used as a cement (as for setting tile) or a protective coating (as for thermal insulation or waterproofing).

Metal lath. Sheets of metal that are slit and drawn out to form openings. Used as a plaster base for walls and ceilings and as reinforcing over other forms of plaster base.

Mortar. A mixture of cementitious materials and aggregate, with or without the addition of plasticizers or other admixtures, reduced to a plastic state by the addition of water and suitable for use to bind masonry units together.

Neat. Generally, basecoat plaster, to which sand is added at the job.

Non-bearing wall. Any wall which carries no load other than its own weight.

On center (O.C.). The measurement of spacing for studs, rafters, joists, and the like in a building from the center of one member to the center of the next.

Panel wall. A non-bearing wall in skeleton construction, built between columns or piers, and wholly supported at each story.

Parapet wall. A dwarf or barrier extending above the roof.

Parging. To coat or plaster.

Partition. A wall that subdivides spaces within any story of a building.

Party wall. A wall used, or adapted for use for joint service by adjoining buildings.

Paste. Composed of portland cement, water, and air.

Penny. As applied to nails, it originally indicated the price per hundred. The term now serves as a measure of nail length and is abbreviated by the letter *d.*

Perm. A measure of water vapor movement through a material (grains per square foot per hour per inch of mercury difference in vapor pressure).

Pier. A column of masonry, usually rectangular in horizontal cross section, used to support other structural members.

Piers. Masonry supports, set independently of the main foundation.

Pilaster. An engaged pier, built as an integral part of a wall, and projecting slightly from either vertical surface thereof.

Piles. Long posts driven into the soil in swampy locations or whenever it is difficult to secure a firm foundation, upon which the footing course of masonry or other timbers is laid.

Plaster grounds. Strips of wood used as guides or strike-off edges around window and door openings and at base of walls.

Plate. Sill plate—a horizontal member anchored to a masonry wall. Sole plate—bottom horizontal member of a frame wall. Top plate—top horizontal member of a frame wall supporting ceiling joists, rafters, or other members.

Plumb. Exactly perpendicular; vertical.

Pointing. Pushing mortar into a joint after a brick is laid.

Post. A timber set on end to support a wall, girder, or other member of the structure.

Pulp. Term often used by the trade when referring to wood fiber or wood-fiber plaster.

Racking. The methods of building the end of a wall so that it can be built onto and against without toothers.

Raggle. A groove or channel made in a mortar joint, or in the solid masonry material, to receive roofing, metal flashing or other material which is to be sealed in the masonry.

Reflective insulation. Sheet material with one or both surfaces of comparatively low heat emissivity, such as aluminum foil. When used in building construction the surfaces face air spaces, reducing the radiation across the air space.

Reinforcing. Steel rods or metal fabric placed in concrete slabs, beams, or columns to increase their strength.

Reinforced brick masonry (R-B-M). Brick masonry in which metal is imbedded in such a manner that the two materials act together in resisting forces.

Reinforcement. Structural steel shapes, steel bars, rods, wire mesh, or expanded metal imbedded or encased in brick or other masonry to increase its strength.

Retaining wall. Any wall designed to resist lateral pressure.

Retarder. Any material added to gypsum plaster that slows up its natural set.

Return. Any surface turned back from the face of a principal surface.

Reveal. That portion of a jamb or recess which is visible from the face of a wall back to the frame placed between the jambs.

Roll roofing. Roofing material, composed of fiber and saturated with asphalt, that is supplied in 36-inch (90-cm.) wide rolls with 108 square feet (10 sq. meters) of material. Weights are generally 45 to 90 pounds (20 to 40 kgs.) per roll.

Rowlok. A brick laid on its edge. Frequently spelled *rolok.*

Rubble masonry. Uncut stone, used for rough work, foundations, backing, and the like.

Run. In stairs, the net width of a step or the horizontal distance covered by a flight of stairs.

Saddle. Two sloping surfaces meeting in a horizontal ridge, used between the back side of a chimney, or other vertical surface, and a sloping roof.

Salmon. *See* Brick (salmon).

Sand float finish. Lime mixed with sand, resulting in a textured finish.

Saturated felt. A felt which is impregnated with tar or asphalt.

Saturation coefficient. *See* C/B Ratio.

Scaffold or staging. A temporary structure or platform enabling workmen to reach high places.

Scratch coat. The first coat of plaster, which is scratched to form a bond for the second coat.

Screed. A small strip of wood, usually the thickness of the plaster coat, used as a guide for plastering.

Set-in. The amount that the lower edge of a brick on the outside face of a wall is held back from the line of the top edge of the brick directly below it. Also called *set-off.*

Sill course. *See* String course.

Sills. The horizontal timbers of a house which either rest upon the masonry foundation or, in the absence of such, form the foundations.

Skeleton construction. A type of building construction in which all loads are transmitted to the foundation by a rigidly connected framework of suitable material, with the enclosing walls supported by girders or by the floor at each floor level.

Skew. Inclination in any direction.

Skew back. That portion of an abutment having an inclined face, which is arranged to receive the thrust of an arch.

Skim coat. Last and final coat, referred to as such in some localities.

Sleeper. Usually, a wood member embedded in concrete, as in a floor, that serves to support and to fasten subfloor or flooring.

Soffit. The underside of an arch, floor, lintel, stair or other similar construction.

Soil cover (ground cover). A light covering of plastic film, roll roofing, or similar material used over the soil in crawl spaces of buildings to minimize moisture permeation of the area.

Soldier. A brick laid on its end so that its longest dimension is parallel to the vertical axis of the face of the wall.

Solid wall. A wall built of solid masonry units, laid contiguously, with the spaces between the units completely filled with mortar. Also walls built of solid concrete.

Sound transmission class (STC). A measure of sound stopping of ordinary noise.

Spall. A small fragment removed from the face of stone, brick or other masonry material by a blow or by the action of the elements.

Span. The distance between structural supports such as walls, columns, piers, beams, girders, and trusses.

Spandrel wall. That part of a panel wall above the top of a window in one story and below the sill of the window in the story above. Also, the space included between the extrados of two adjoining arches and a line approximately connecting their crowns.

Splash block. A small masonry block laid with the top close to the ground surface to receive roof drainage from downspouts and to carry it away from the building.

Springing line. A line marking the level from which the curve of an arch or vault rises from the upright or impost.

Square. A unit of measure—100 square feet (30.5 sq. meters)—usually applied to roofing material. Sidewall coverings are sometimes packed to cover 100 square feet (30.5 sq. meters) and are sold on that basis. A tool used by masons to obtain accuracy.

Stack (or Chimney). Any structure or part of a structure partly or wholly exposed to the atmosphere which contains a flue or flues for the discharge of gases.

Stair carriage. Supporting member for stair treads. Usually a 2-inch (5-cm.) plank notched to receive the treads; sometimes called a *rough horse.*

Story. That part of a building between any floor and the floor or roof next above.

Stretcher. A masonry unit laid flat with its longest dimension parallel to the face of the wall.

String course. A narrow, vertically faced and slightly projecting course in an elevation, such as window-sills which are made continuous. Also, horizontal moldings running under windows, separating the walls from the plain part of the parapets, dividing towers into stories and stages, and the like.

Stringing mortar. The name applied to the method by which a bricklayer picks up sufficient mortar for a number of bricks and spreads it before laying the brick.

Stucco. Most commonly refers to an outside plaster made with portland cement as its base.

Stud. One of a series of slender wood or metal vertical structural members placed as supporting elements in walls and partitions.

Suction. The power of absorption possessed by a plastered surface. *For example,* the basecoat must have suction in order to absorb the water out of the finish coat.

Sweat-out. Soft, damp plaster area caused by poor drying conditions.

Swedge anchor. An anchor bolt, threaded at one end and swedged or flattened in spots along the shank so as to produce greater holding power.

Table (water). *See* Water table.

Tail beam. A relatively short beam or joist supported in a wall on one end and by a header at the other.

Tapping. Setting a brick down on its bed of mortar with a light blow of the trowel blade or end of handle.

Temper. To moisten and mix clay, plaster, mortar and similar materials to the proper consistency for working.

Templet. A pattern to secure accurate and uniform shaping or spacing.

Termite shield. A shield, usually of noncorrodible metal, placed in or on a foundation wall or other mass of masonry or around pipes to prevent passage of termites.

Throat. The passage from the fireplace to the chimney.

Tie. Any unit of material used to resist the spreading of a wall, or the separation of the two solid parts of a hollow wall.

Tooling. Compressing and shaping the face of a mortar joint, usually with a special tool, other than a trowel.

Toother. A brick projecting from the end of a wall against which other wall is to be built.

Toothing. The temporary end of a wall built so that the end stretcher of every alternate course projects.

Trimmer. A beam or joist to which a header is nailed in framing for a chimney, stairway, or other opening.

Vapor barrier. Material used to retard the movement of water vapor into walls, and prevent condensation in them. Usually considered as having a perm value of less than 1.0. Applied separately over the warm side of exposed walls or as a part of batt or blanket insulation.

Vault. An arch or a combination of arches used to span a space.

Veneer. A facing of masonry material attached but not bonded to the backing.

Vermiculite. A mineral closely related to mica, with the faculty of expanding on heating to form lightweight material with insulation quality. Used as bulk insulation and also as aggregate in insulating and acoustical plaster and in insulating concrete floors.

Voussoir. One of the stones or pieces of other material used for forming an arch or vault.

Wainscot. The lower three or four feet of an interior wall when it is finished differently from the remainder of the wall.

Wall plate anchor. A machine bolt anchor, with a head at one end and threaded at the other, and fitted with plate or punched washer so as to securely engage the brickwork and hold the wall plate or other member in place.

Wall tie. Strip of metal used for tying a facing veneer to the body of a wall.

Water retentivity. Flow and resistance to segregation are factors affecting workability, which in turn are affected by the properties of both the cementitious materials and the aggregate.

Water table. A slight projection of the lower masonry or brickwork on the outside of a wall and slightly above the ground as a protection against water.

Withe or Wythe. A continuous vertical 4-inch (10-cm.) or greater section or thickness of masonry as the thickness of masonry separating flues in a chimney.

Wooden brick. Piece of seasoned wood, made the size of a brick, and laid where it is necessary to provide a nailing space in masonry walls.

Workability. An essential property of any mortar for masonry construction since it is only through this property that the mortar can be brought into intimate and complete contact with the masonry units, thereby incorporating the properties of the mortar into the masonry.

Appendix II

Suggested Details of Concrete Masonry Constructions

The construction details shown in Figs. 1 through 70 have been prepared in accordance with modular coordination of design. The grid lines are to scale of one inch equals one foot.

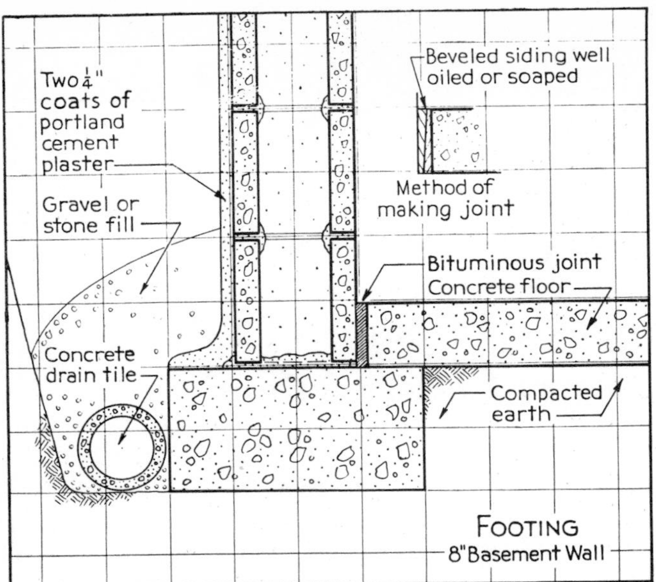
Two 1/4"
coats of
portland
cement
plaster
Gravel or
stone fill
Beveled siding well
oiled or soaped
Method of
making joint
Bituminous joint
Concrete floor
Concrete
drain tile
Compacted
earth
FOOTING
8" Basement Wall

Fig. 1.

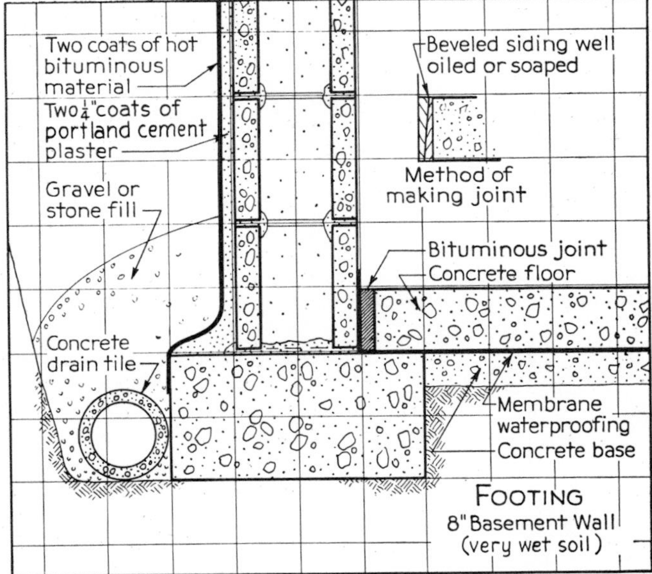
Two coats of hot
bituminous
material
Two 1/4" coats of
portland cement
plaster
Gravel or
stone fill
Beveled siding well
oiled or soaped
Method of
making joint
Bituminous joint
Concrete floor
Concrete
drain tile
Membrane
waterproofing
Concrete base
FOOTING
8" Basement Wall
(very wet soil)

Fig. 2.

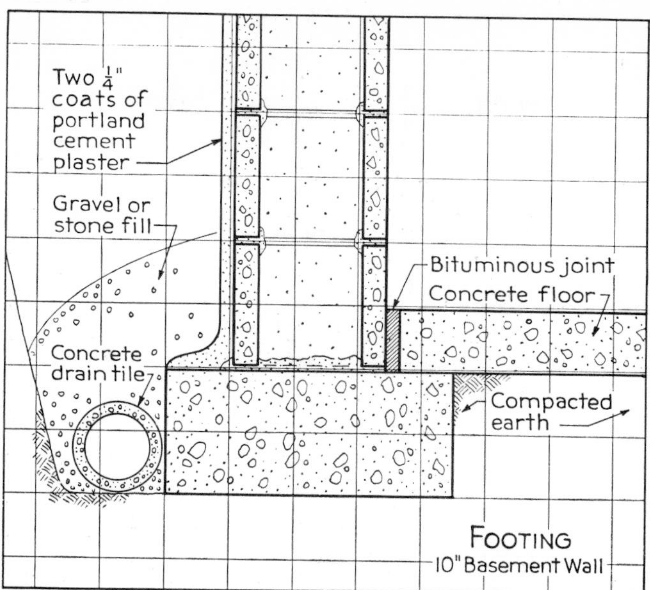
Two $\frac{1}{4}$" coats of portland cement plaster
Gravel or stone fill
Bituminous joint
Concrete floor
Concrete drain tile
Compacted earth
FOOTING
10" Basement Wall

Fig. 3.

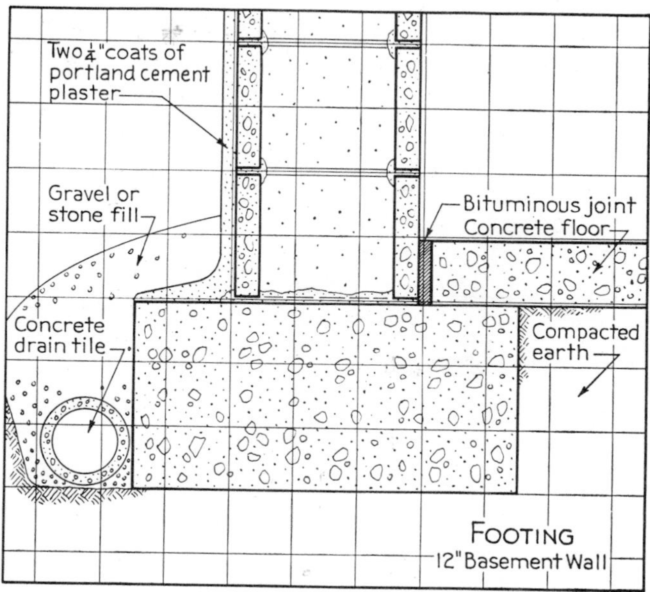
Two $\frac{1}{4}$" coats of portland cement plaster
Gravel or stone fill
Bituminous joint
Concrete floor
Concrete drain tile
Compacted earth
FOOTING
12" Basement Wall

Fig. 4.

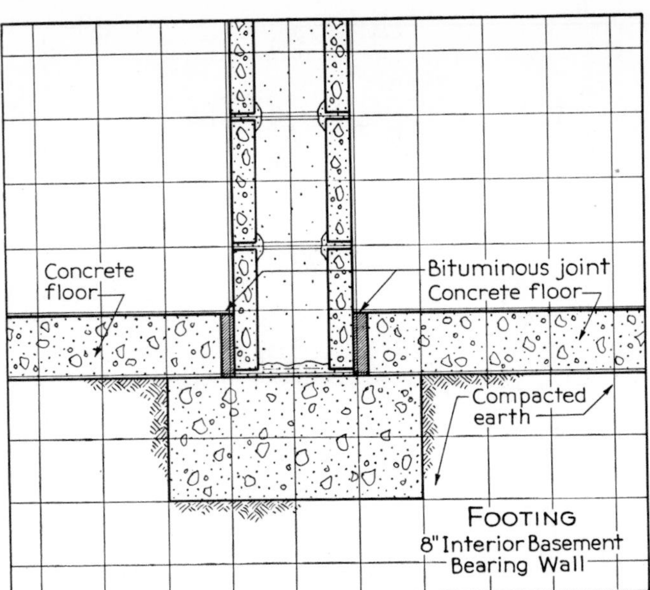
Concrete
floor
Bituminous joint
Concrete floor
Compacted
earth
FOOTING
8" Interior Basement
Bearing Wall

Fig. 5.

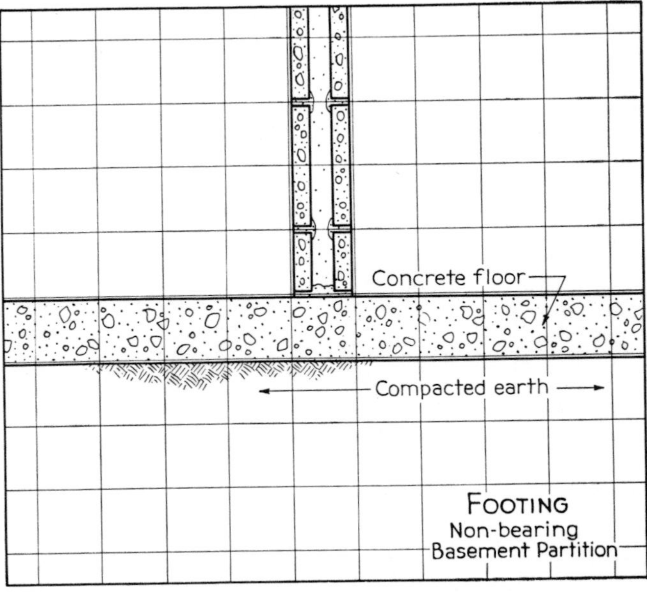
Concrete floor
Compacted earth
FOOTING
Non-bearing
Basement Partition

Fig. 6.

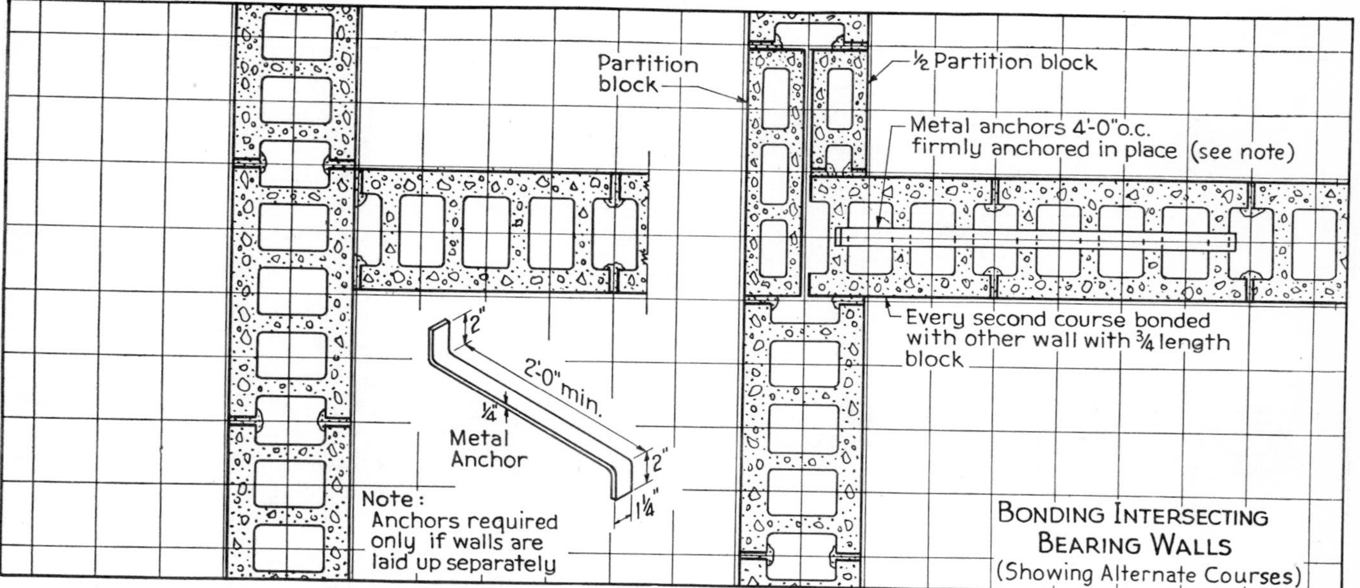
Partition block
½ Partition block
Metal anchors 4'-0"o.c. firmly anchored in place (see note)
Every second course bonded with other wall with ¾ length block
2"
2'-0" min.
¼"
Metal Anchor
2"
1¼"
Note: Anchors required only if walls are laid up separately
BONDING INTERSECTING BEARING WALLS
(Showing Alternate Courses)

Fig. 7.

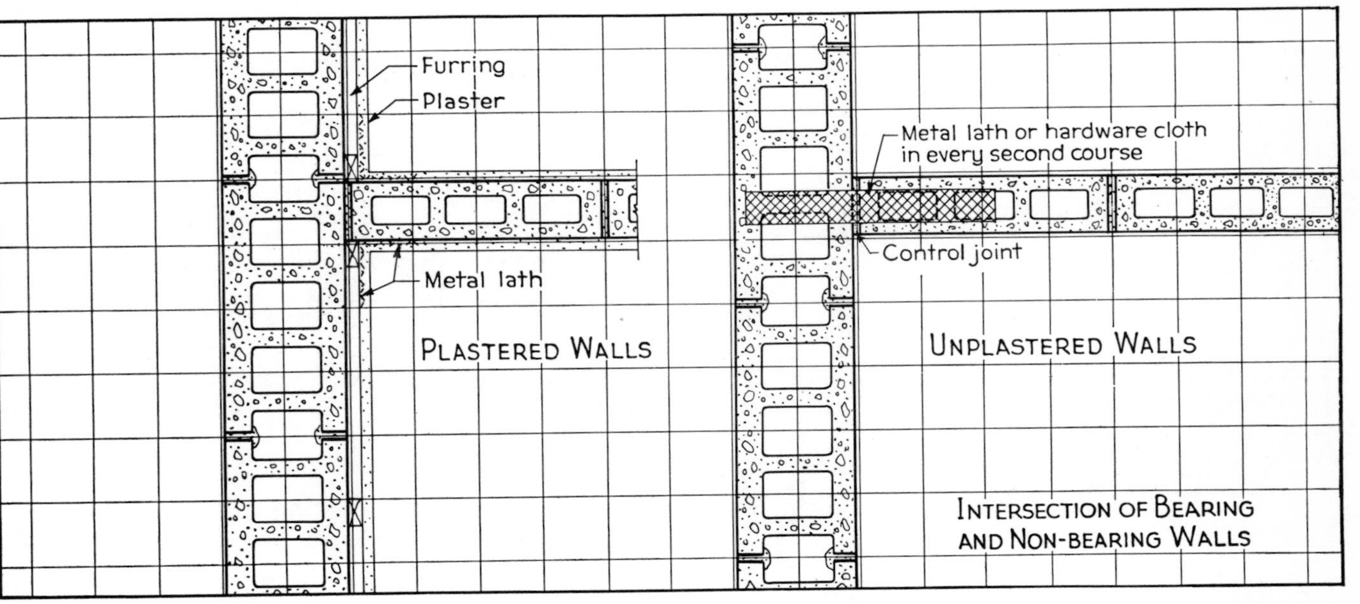
Furring
Plaster
Metal lath
PLASTERED WALLS
Metal lath or hardware cloth
in every second course
Control joint
UNPLASTERED WALLS
INTERSECTION OF BEARING
AND NON-BEARING WALLS

Fig. 8.

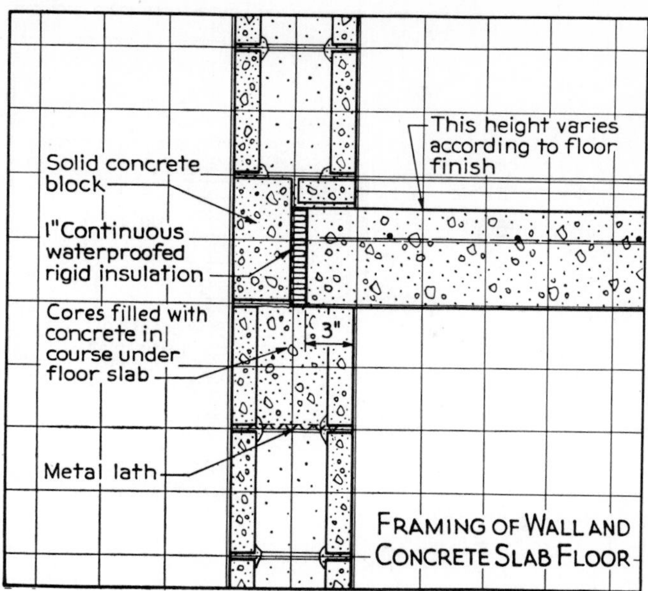
This height varies according to floor finish
Solid concrete block
1" Continuous waterproofed rigid insulation
Cores filled with concrete in course under floor slab
3"
Metal lath
FRAMING OF WALL AND CONCRETE SLAB FLOOR

Fig. 9.

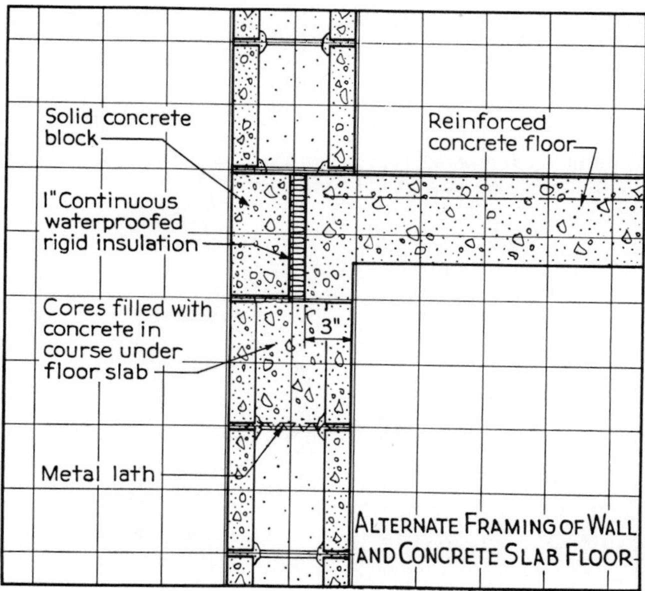
Solid concrete block
Reinforced concrete floor
1" Continuous waterproofed rigid insulation
Cores filled with concrete in course under floor slab
3"
Metal lath
ALTERNATE FRAMING OF WALL AND CONCRETE SLAB FLOOR

Fig. 10.

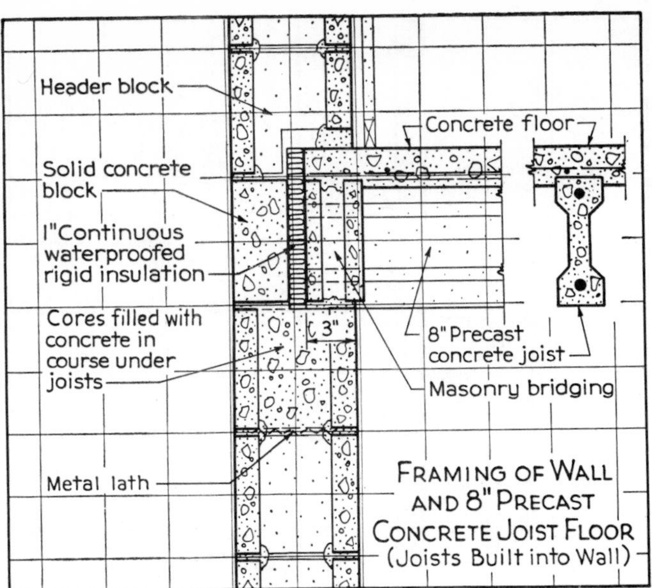
Header block
Solid concrete block
1"Continuous waterproofed rigid insulation
Cores filled with concrete in course under joists
Metal lath
Concrete floor
3"
8" Precast concrete joist
Masonry bridging
FRAMING OF WALL AND 8" PRECAST CONCRETE JOIST FLOOR
(Joists Built into Wall)

Fig. 11.

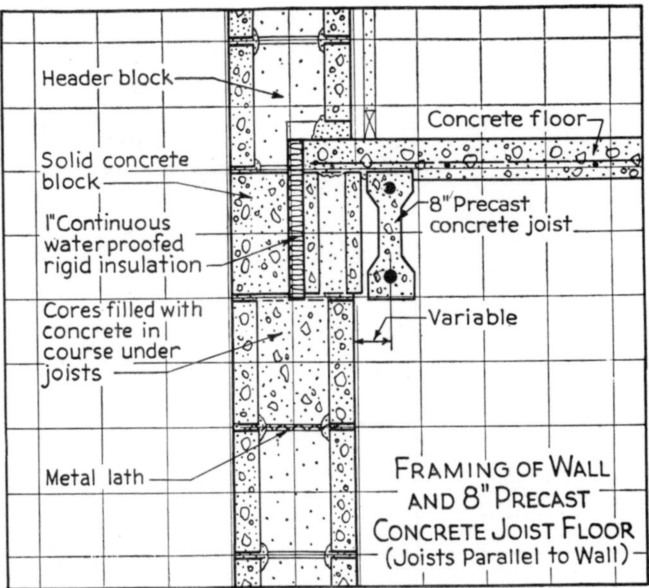
Header block
Solid concrete block
1"Continuous waterproofed rigid insulation
Cores filled with concrete in course under joists
Metal lath
Concrete floor
8" Precast concrete joist
Variable
FRAMING OF WALL AND 8" PRECAST CONCRETE JOIST FLOOR
(Joists Parallel to Wall)

Fig. 12.

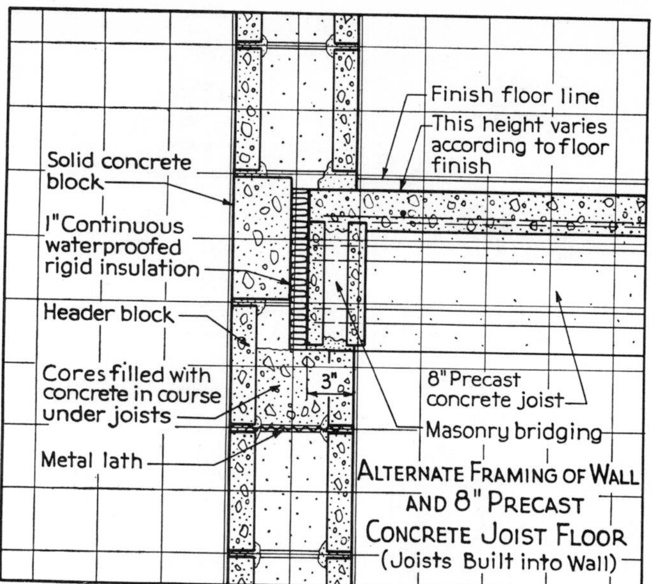
Finish floor line
This height varies according to floor finish
Solid concrete block
1" Continuous waterproofed rigid insulation
Header block
Cores filled with concrete in course under joists
3"
Metal lath
8" Precast concrete joist
Masonry bridging
ALTERNATE FRAMING OF WALL AND 8" PRECAST CONCRETE JOIST FLOOR
(Joists Built into Wall)

Fig. 13.

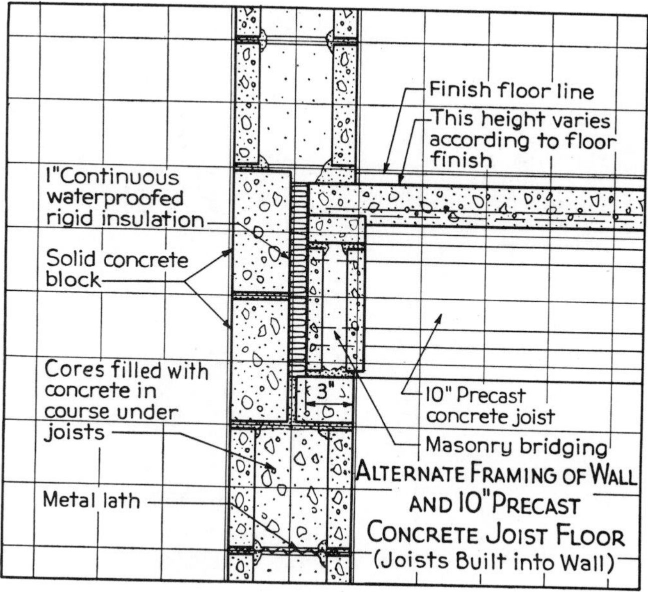
Finish floor line
This height varies according to floor finish
1" Continuous waterproofed rigid insulation
Solid concrete block
Cores filled with concrete in course under joists
3"
Metal lath
10" Precast concrete joist
Masonry bridging
ALTERNATE FRAMING OF WALL AND 10" PRECAST CONCRETE JOIST FLOOR
(Joists Built into Wall)

Fig. 14.

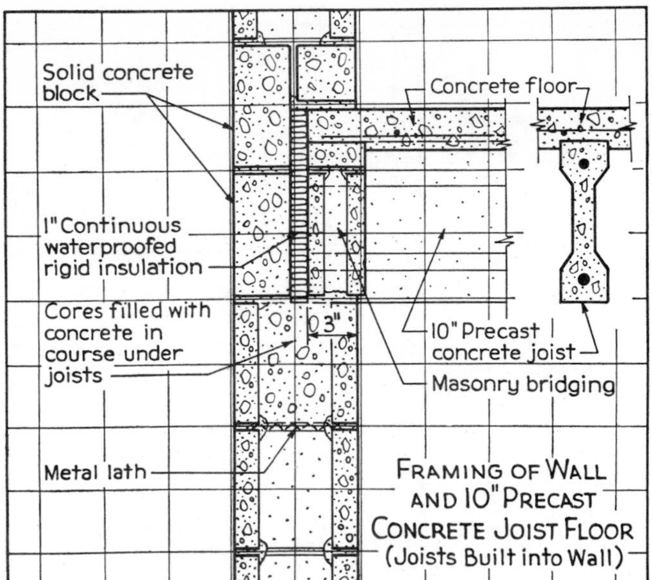
Solid concrete block
Concrete floor
1" Continuous waterproofed rigid insulation
Cores filled with concrete in course under joists
3"
10" Precast concrete joist
Masonry bridging
Metal lath
FRAMING OF WALL AND 10" PRECAST CONCRETE JOIST FLOOR
(Joists Built into Wall)

Fig. 15.

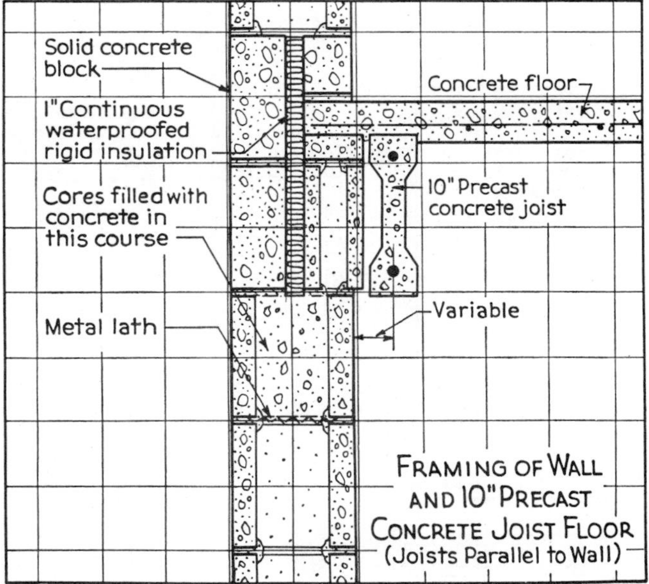
Solid concrete block
Concrete floor
1" Continuous waterproofed rigid insulation
10" Precast concrete joist
Cores filled with concrete in this course
Variable
Metal lath
FRAMING OF WALL AND 10" PRECAST CONCRETE JOIST FLOOR
(Joists Parallel to Wall)

Fig. 16.

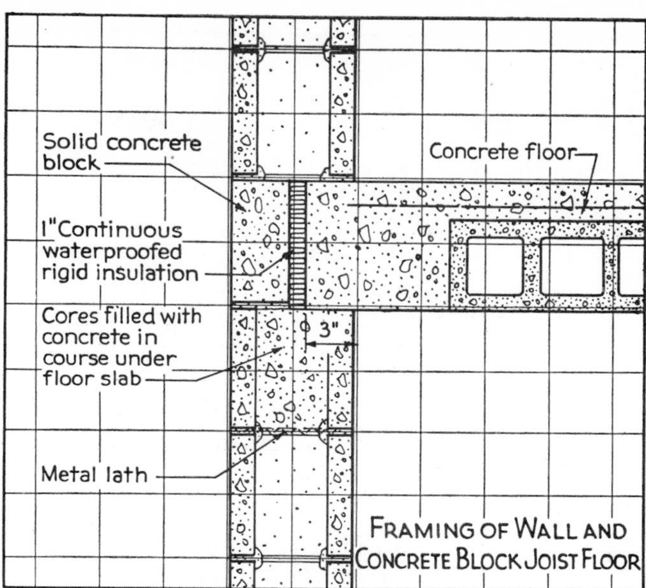
Solid concrete
block
1"Continuous
waterproofed
rigid insulation
Cores filled with
concrete in
course under
floor slab
Metal lath
Concrete floor
3"
FRAMING OF WALL AND
CONCRETE BLOCK JOIST FLOOR

Fig. 17.

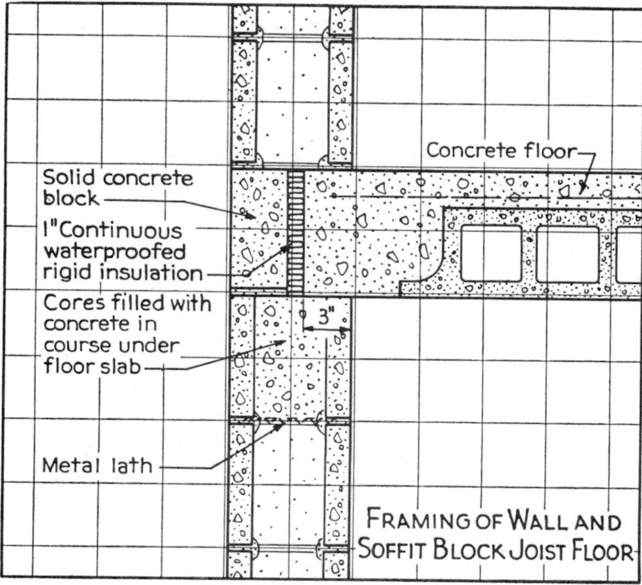
Solid concrete
block
1"Continuous
waterproofed
rigid insulation
Cores filled with
concrete in
course under
floor slab
Metal lath
Concrete floor
3"
FRAMING OF WALL AND
SOFFIT BLOCK JOIST FLOOR

Fig. 18.

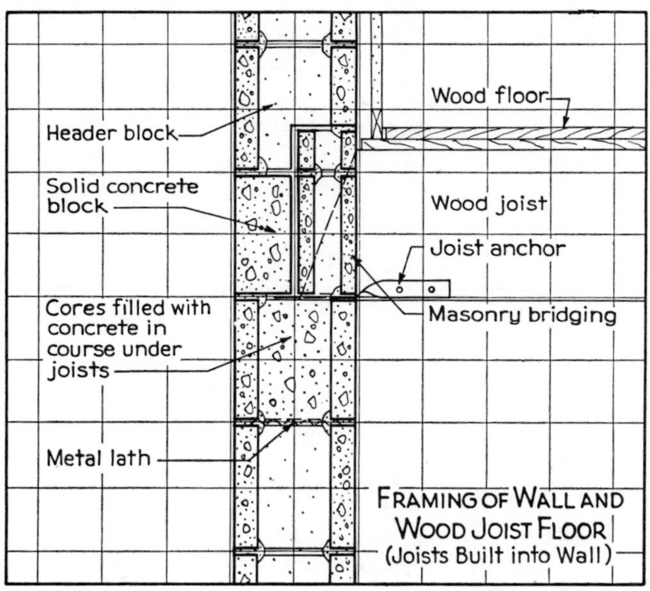
Wood floor
Header block
Solid concrete block
Wood joist
Joist anchor
Cores filled with concrete in course under joists
Masonry bridging
Metal lath
FRAMING OF WALL AND WOOD JOIST FLOOR
(Joists Built into Wall)

Fig. 19.

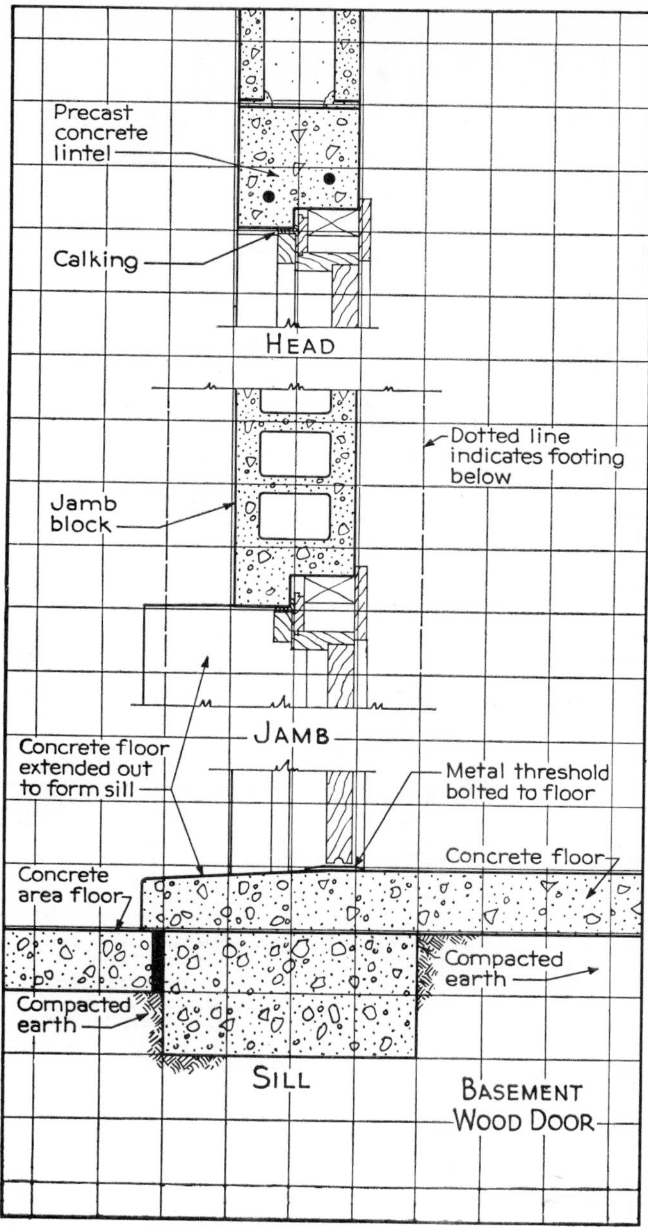
Precast concrete lintel
Calking
HEAD
Dotted line indicates footing below
Jamb block
JAMB
Concrete floor extended out to form sill
Metal threshold bolted to floor
Concrete floor
Concrete area floor
Compacted earth
Compacted earth
SILL
BASEMENT WOOD DOOR

Fig. 20.

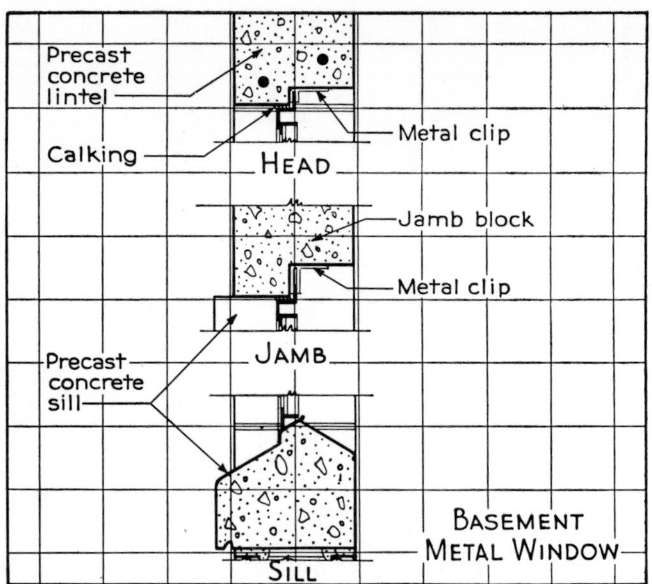
Precast
concrete
lintel
Calking
Metal clip
HEAD
Jamb block
Metal clip
Precast
concrete
sill
JAMB
BASEMENT
METAL WINDOW
SILL

Fig. 21.

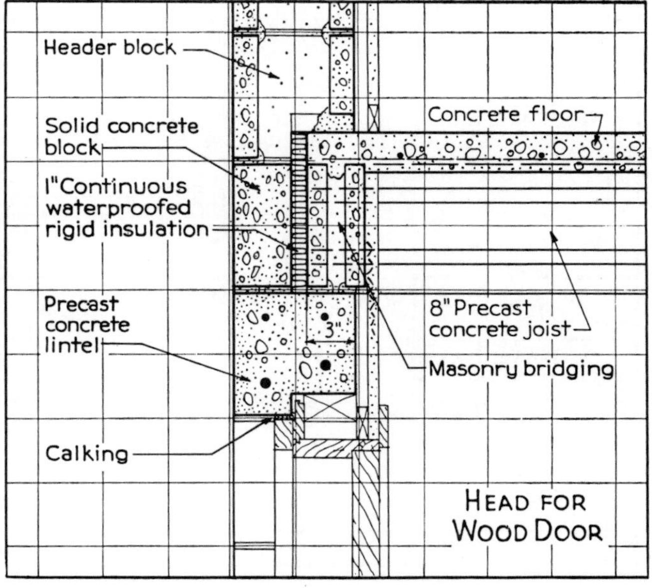
Header block
Concrete floor
Solid concrete
block
1" Continuous
waterproofed
rigid insulation
Precast
concrete
lintel
3"
8" Precast
concrete joist
Masonry bridging
Calking
HEAD FOR
WOOD DOOR

Fig. 22.

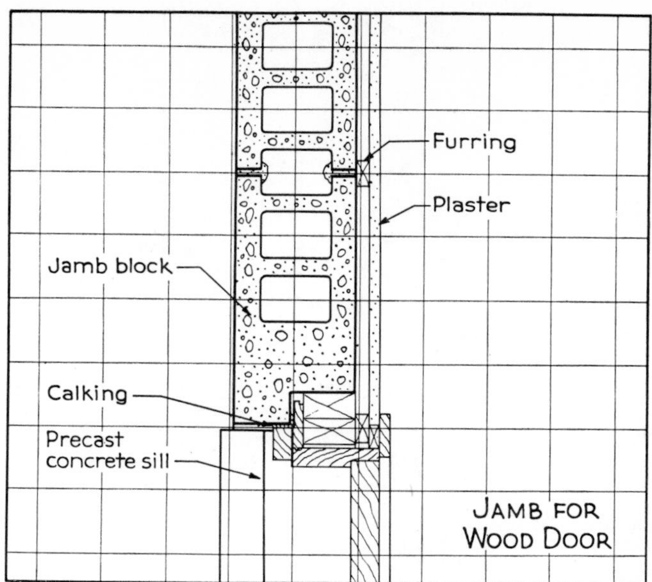
Furring
Plaster
Jamb block
Calking
Precast
concrete sill
JAMB FOR
WOOD DOOR

Fig. 23.

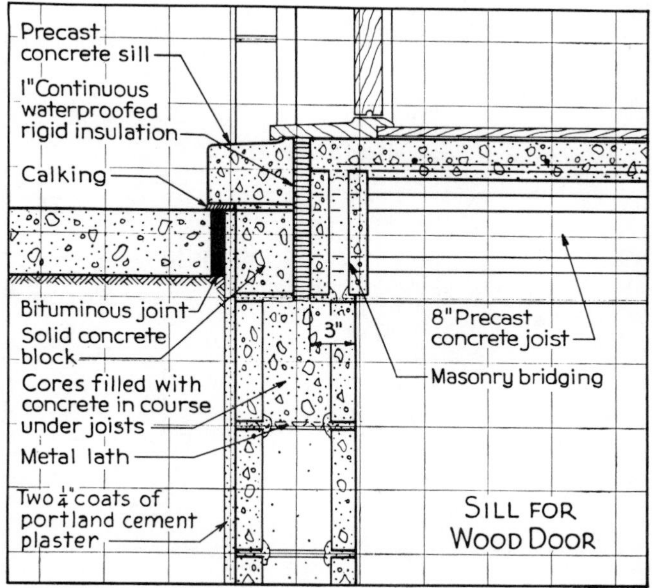
Precast
concrete sill
1" Continuous
waterproofed
rigid insulation
Calking
Bituminous joint
Solid concrete
block
Cores filled with
concrete in course
under joists
Metal lath
Two 1/4" coats of
portland cement
plaster
3"
8" Precast
concrete joist
Masonry bridging
SILL FOR
WOOD DOOR

Fig. 24.

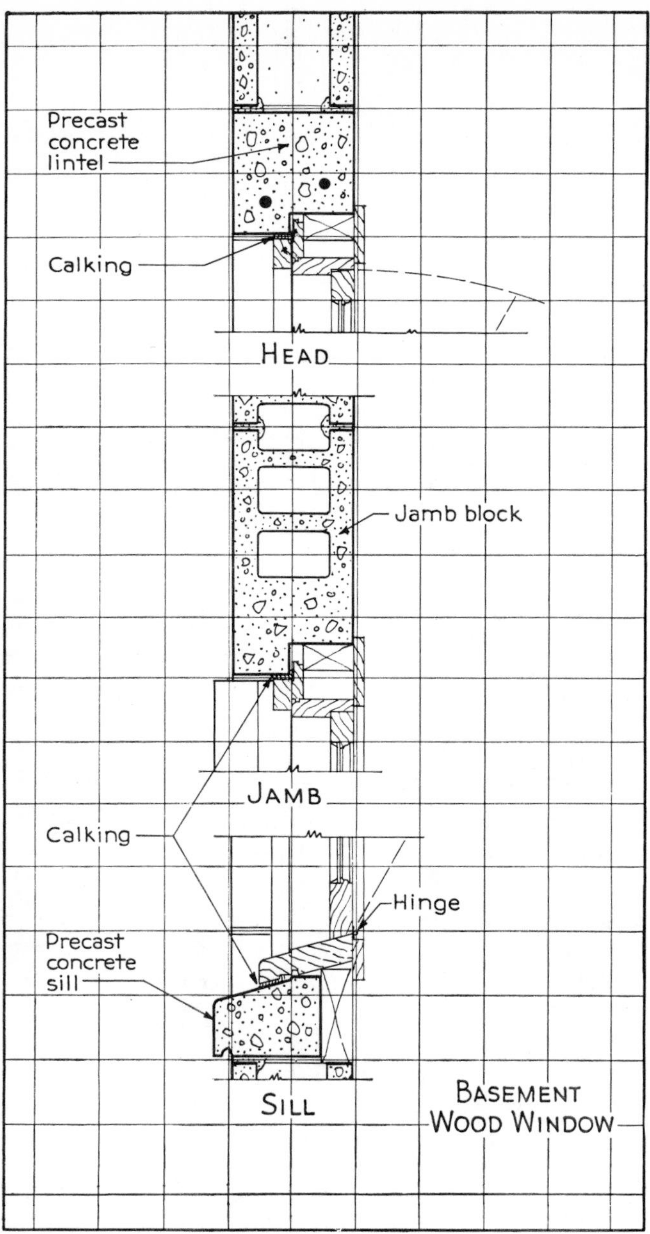
Precast
concrete
lintel
Calking
HEAD
Jamb block
JAMB
Calking
Hinge
Precast
concrete
sill
SILL
BASEMENT
WOOD WINDOW

Fig. 25.

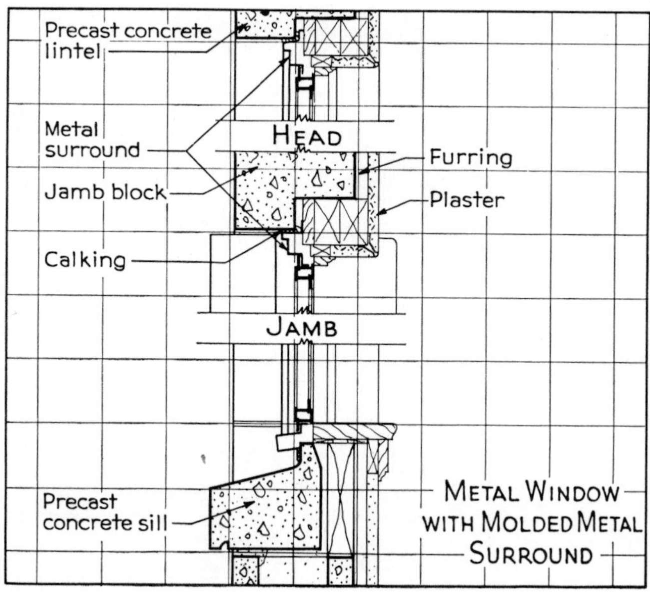
Precast concrete lintel
Metal surround
Jamb block
Calking
HEAD
Furring
Plaster
JAMB
Precast concrete sill
METAL WINDOW WITH MOLDED METAL SURROUND

Fig. 26.

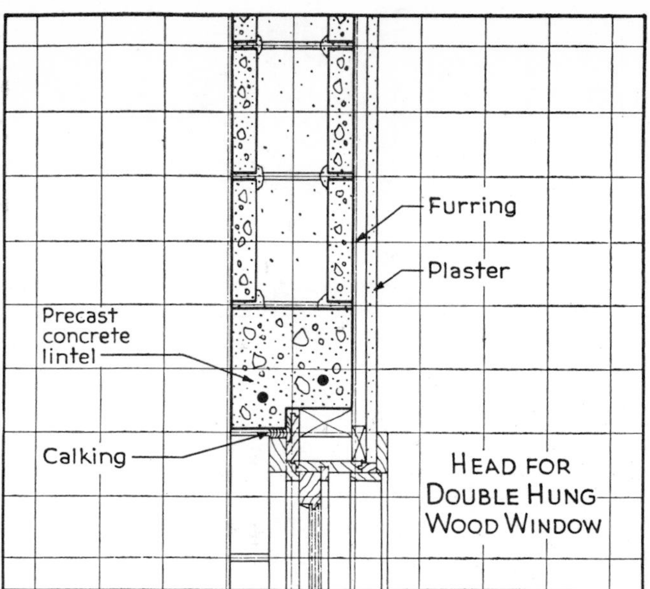
Furring
Plaster
Precast concrete lintel
Calking
HEAD FOR DOUBLE HUNG WOOD WINDOW

Fig. 27.

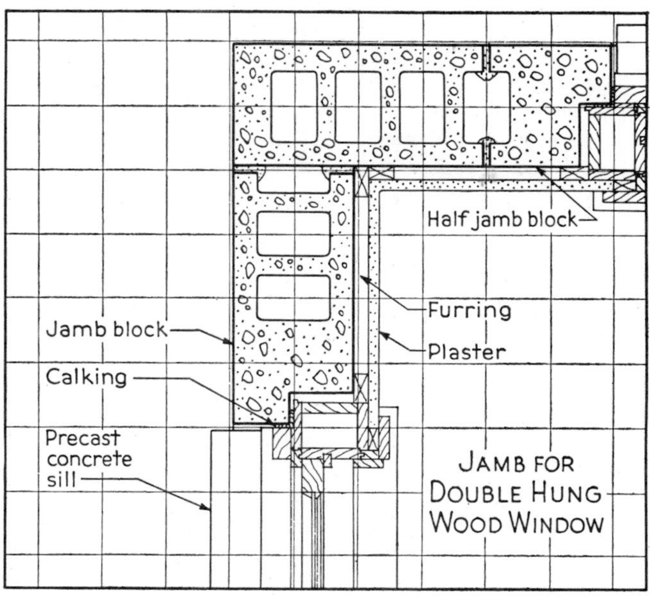
Half jamb block
Furring
Plaster
Jamb block
Calking
Precast concrete sill
JAMB FOR DOUBLE HUNG WOOD WINDOW

Fig. 28.

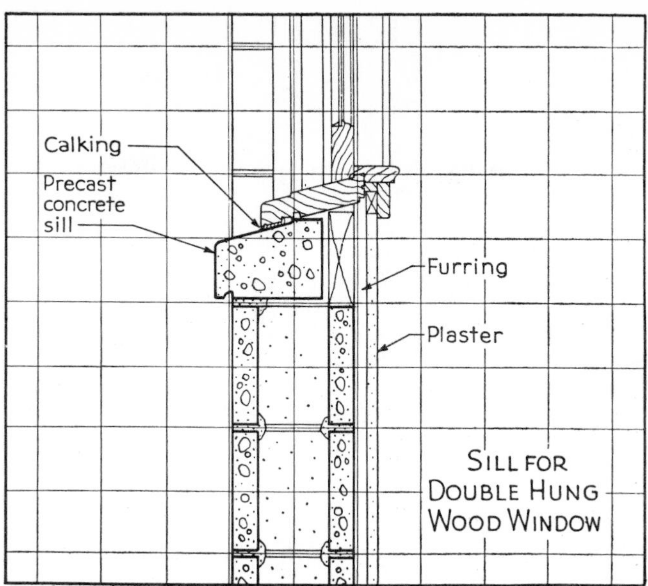
Calking
Precast
concrete
sill
Furring
Plaster
SILL FOR
DOUBLE HUNG
WOOD WINDOW

Fig. 29.

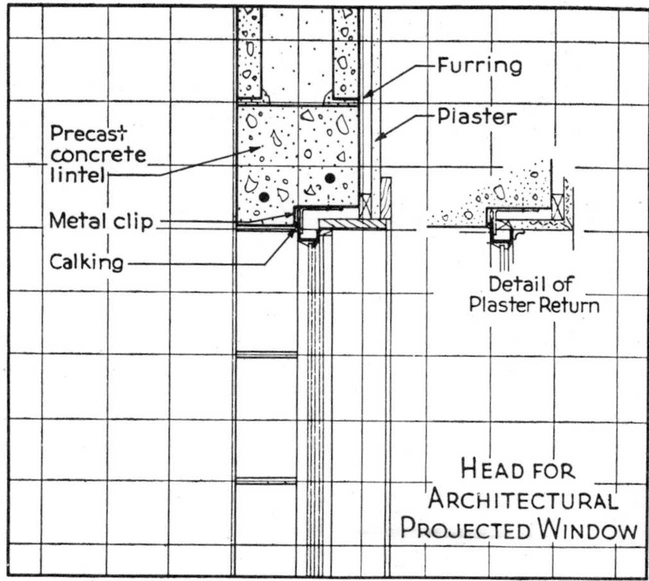
Furring
Plaster
Precast
concrete
lintel
Metal clip
Calking
Detail of
Plaster Return
HEAD FOR
ARCHITECTURAL
PROJECTED WINDOW

Fig. 30.

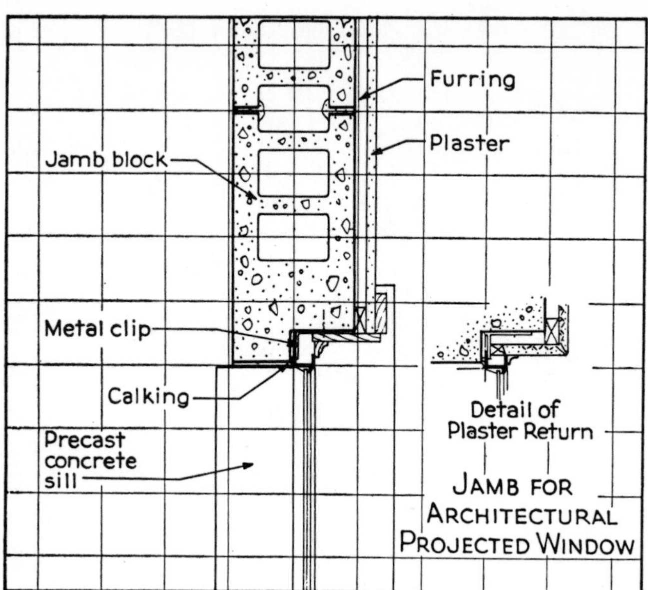
Furring
Plaster
Jamb block
Metal clip
Calking
Precast
concrete
sill
Detail of
Plaster Return
JAMB FOR
ARCHITECTURAL
PROJECTED WINDOW

Fig. 31.

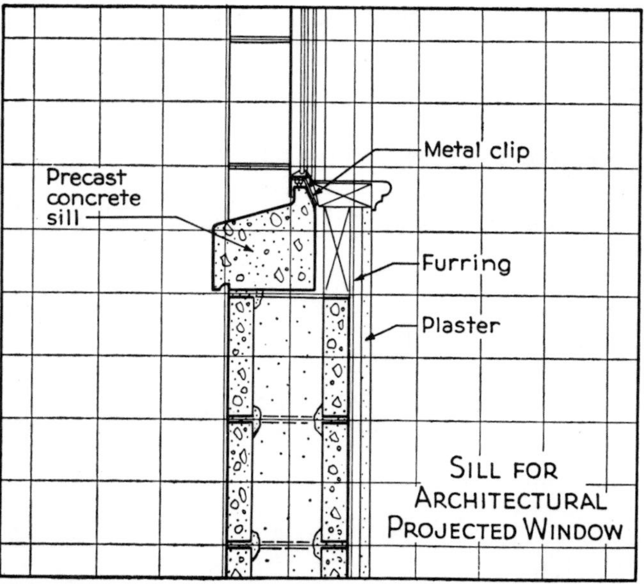
Metal clip
Precast
concrete
sill
Furring
Plaster
SILL FOR
ARCHITECTURAL
PROJECTED WINDOW

Fig. 32.

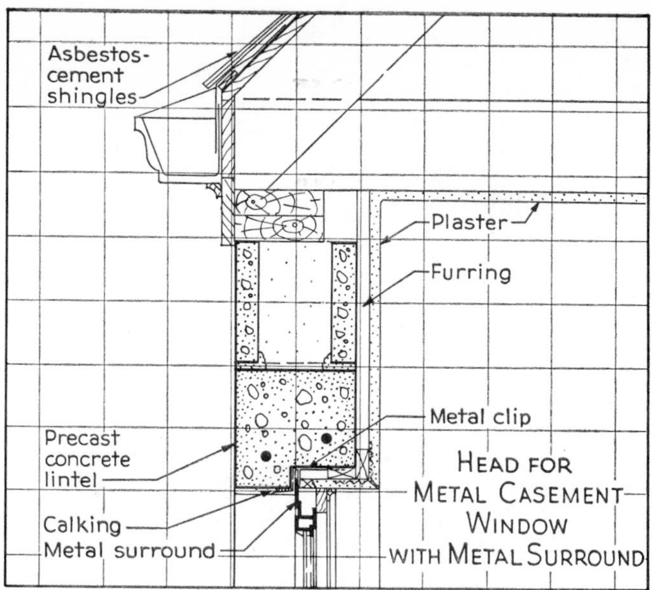
Asbestos-
cement
shingles
Plaster
Furring
Metal clip
Precast
concrete
lintel
Calking
Metal surround
HEAD FOR
METAL CASEMENT
WINDOW
WITH METAL SURROUND

Fig. 33.

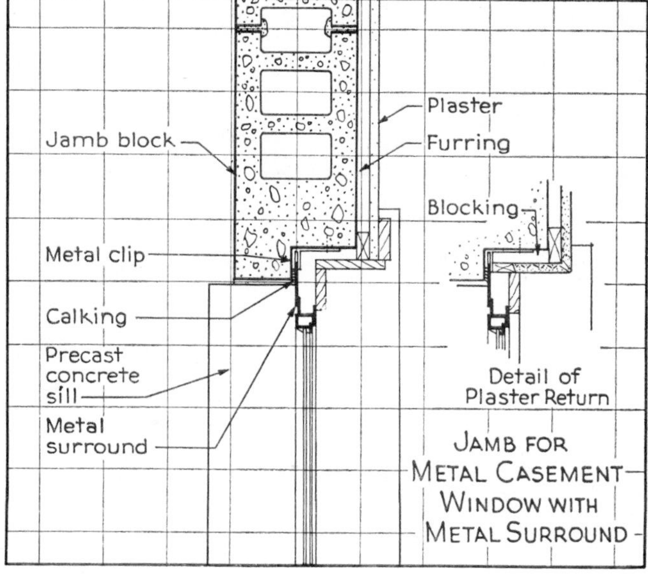
Plaster
Furring
Jamb block
Blocking
Metal clip
Calking
Precast
concrete
sill
Metal
surround
Detail of
Plaster Return
JAMB FOR
METAL CASEMENT
WINDOW WITH
METAL SURROUND

Fig. 34.

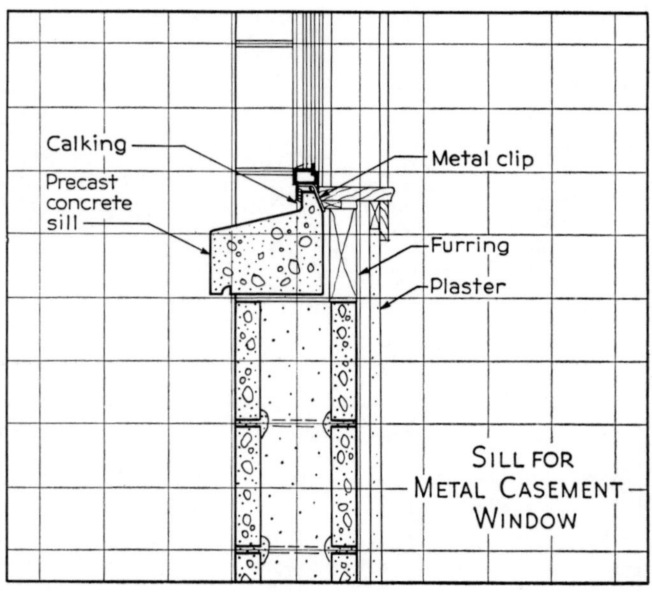
Calking
Metal clip
Precast
concrete
sill
Furring
Plaster
SILL FOR
METAL CASEMENT
WINDOW

Fig. 35.

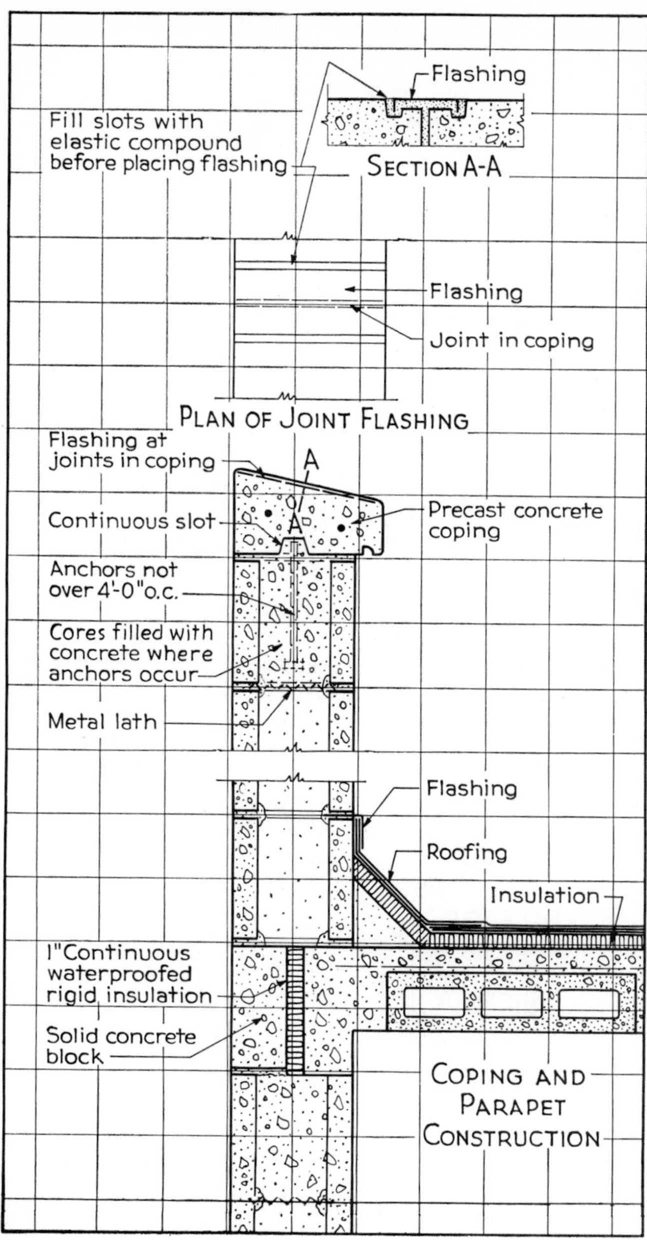
Flashing
Fill slots with
elastic compound
before placing flashing
SECTION A-A
Flashing
Joint in coping
PLAN OF JOINT FLASHING
Flashing at
joints in coping
A
A
Continuous slot
Precast concrete
coping
Anchors not
over 4'-0"o.c.
Cores filled with
concrete where
anchors occur
Metal lath
Flashing
Roofing
Insulation
1"Continuous
waterproofed
rigid insulation
Solid concrete
block
COPING AND
PARAPET
CONSTRUCTION

Fig. 36.

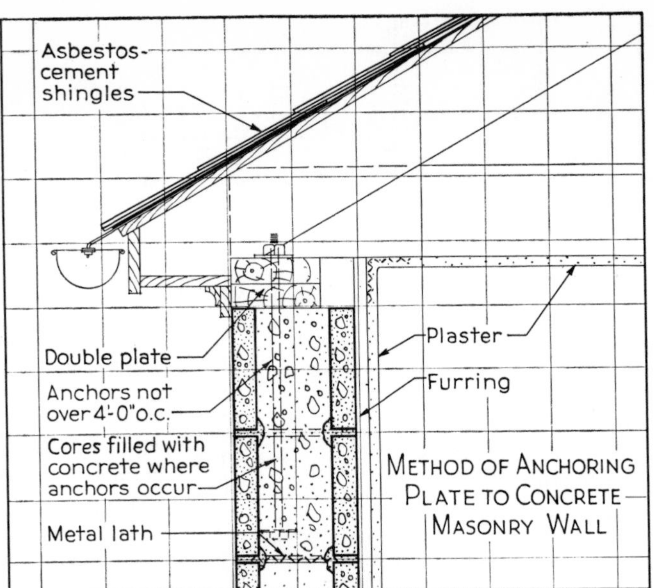
Asbestos-
cement
shingles
Double plate
Anchors not
over 4'-0"o.c.
Cores filled with
concrete where
anchors occur
Metal lath
Plaster
Furring
METHOD OF ANCHORING
PLATE TO CONCRETE
MASONRY WALL

Fig. 37.

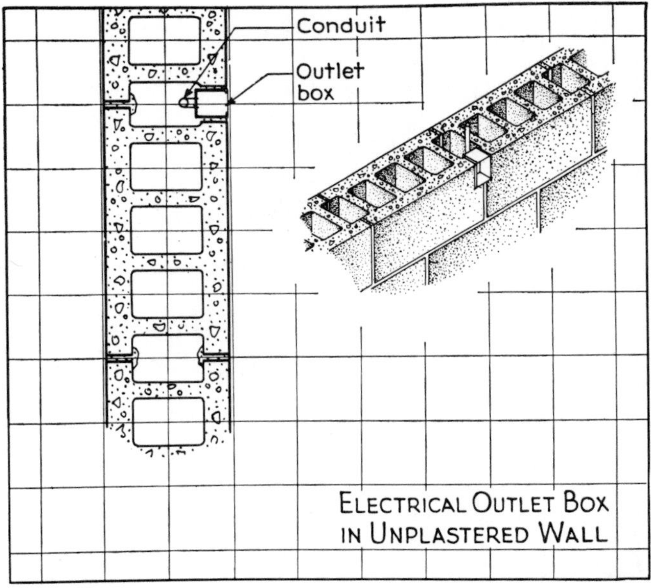
Conduit
Outlet
box
ELECTRICAL OUTLET BOX
IN UNPLASTERED WALL

Fig. 38.

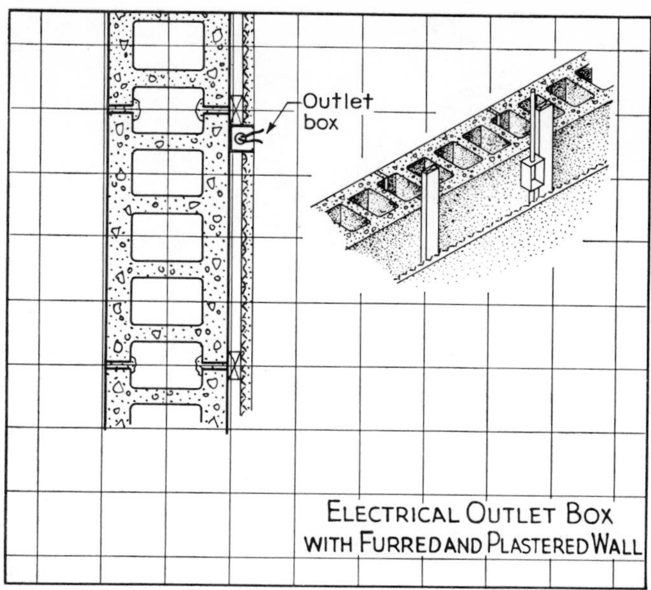
Outlet box
ELECTRICAL OUTLET BOX WITH FURRED AND PLASTERED WALL

Fig. 39.

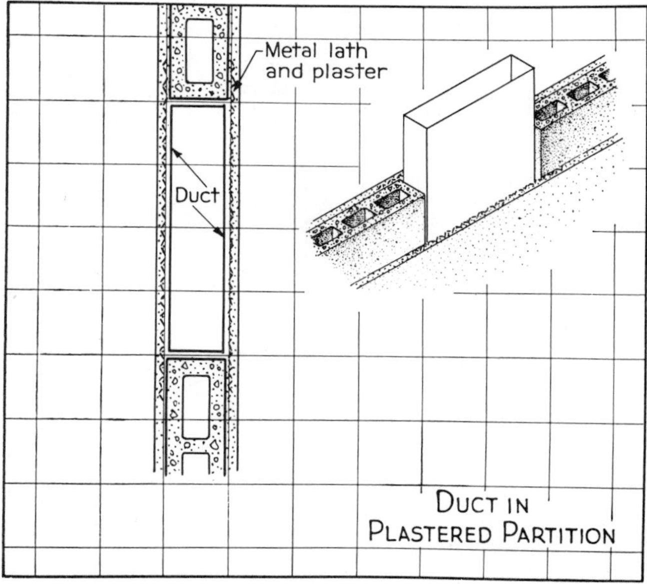
Metal lath and plaster
Duct
DUCT IN PLASTERED PARTITION

Fig. 40.

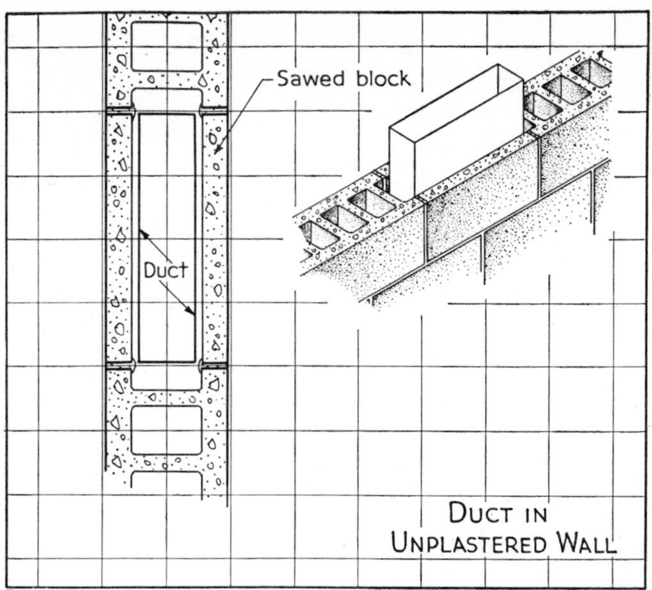
Sawed block
Duct
Duct in
Unplastered Wall

Fig. 41.

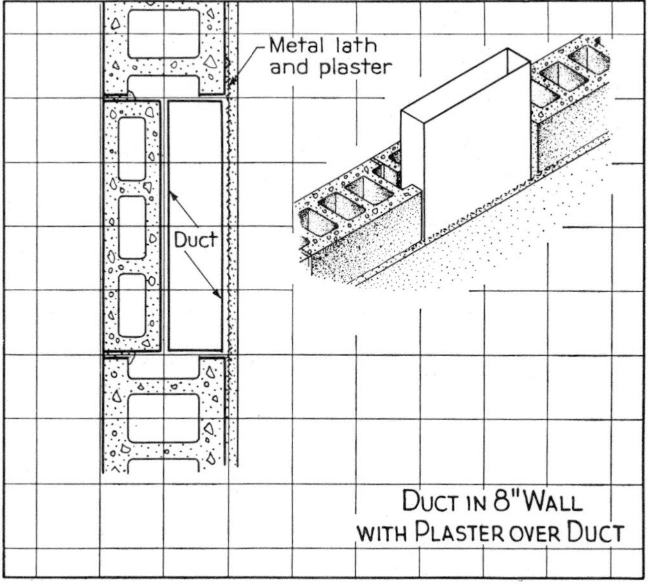
Metal lath
and plaster
Duct
Duct in 8" Wall
with Plaster over Duct

Fig. 42.

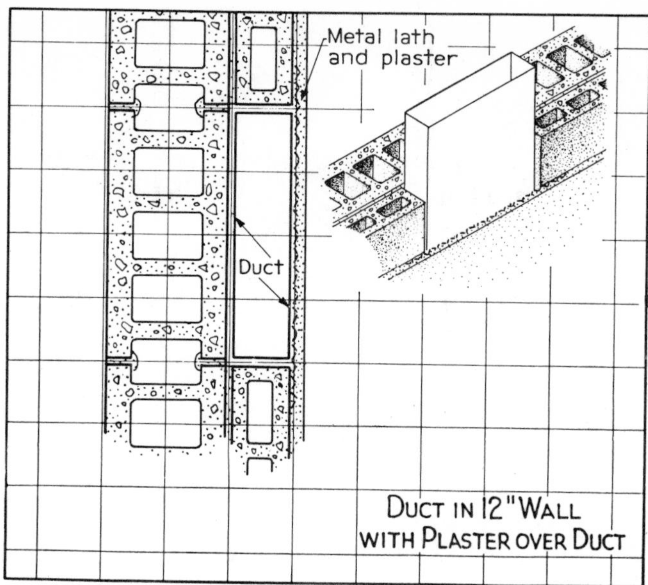
Metal lath
and plaster
Duct
DUCT IN 12" WALL
WITH PLASTER OVER DUCT

Fig. 43.

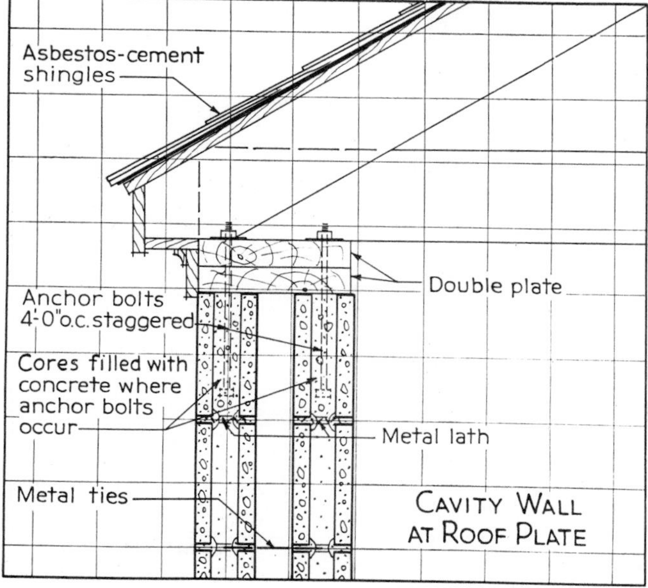
Asbestos-cement
shingles
Double plate
Anchor bolts
4'-0" o.c. staggered
Cores filled with
concrete where
anchor bolts
occur
Metal lath
Metal ties
CAVITY WALL
AT ROOF PLATE

Fig. 44.

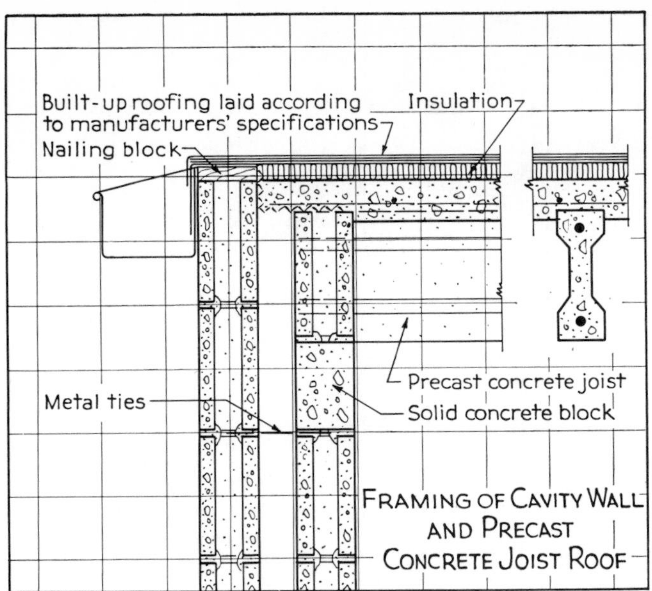
Built-up roofing laid according to manufacturers' specifications
Insulation
Nailing block
Metal ties
Precast concrete joist
Solid concrete block
FRAMING OF CAVITY WALL AND PRECAST CONCRETE JOIST ROOF

Fig. 45.

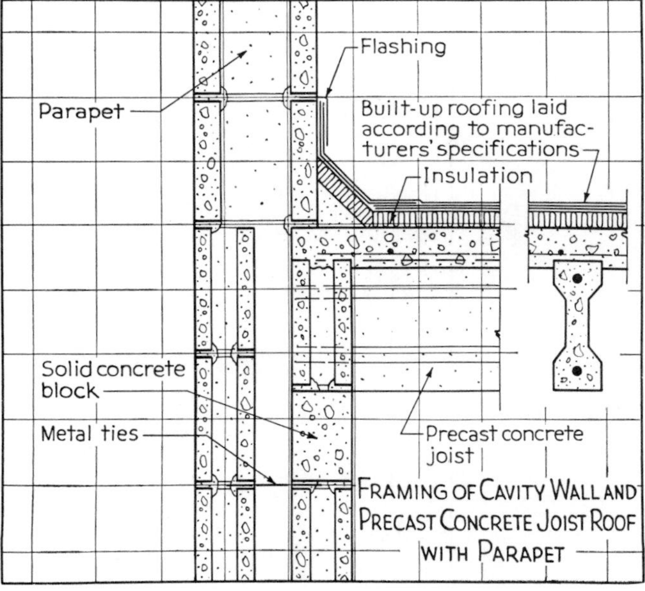
Flashing
Parapet
Built-up roofing laid according to manufacturers' specifications
Insulation
Solid concrete block
Metal ties
Precast concrete joist
FRAMING OF CAVITY WALL AND PRECAST CONCRETE JOIST ROOF WITH PARAPET

Fig. 46.

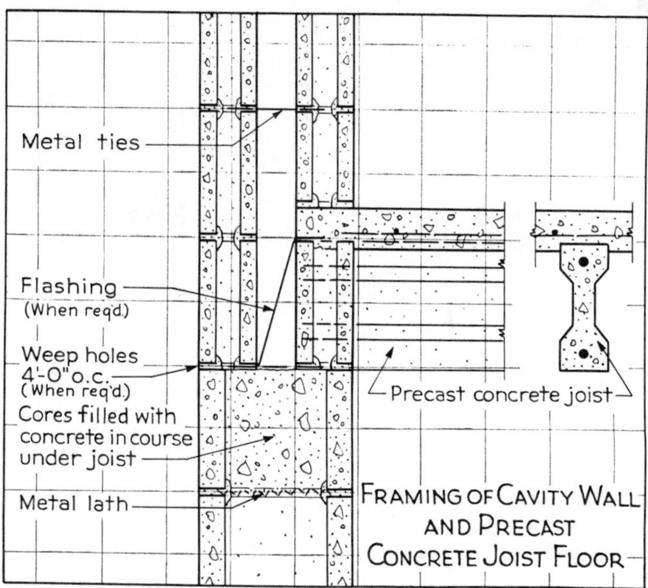
Metal ties
Flashing
(When req'd.)
Weep holes
4'-0" o.c.
(When req'd.)
Cores filled with
concrete in course
under joist
Metal lath
Precast concrete joist
FRAMING OF CAVITY WALL
AND PRECAST
CONCRETE JOIST FLOOR

Fig. 47.

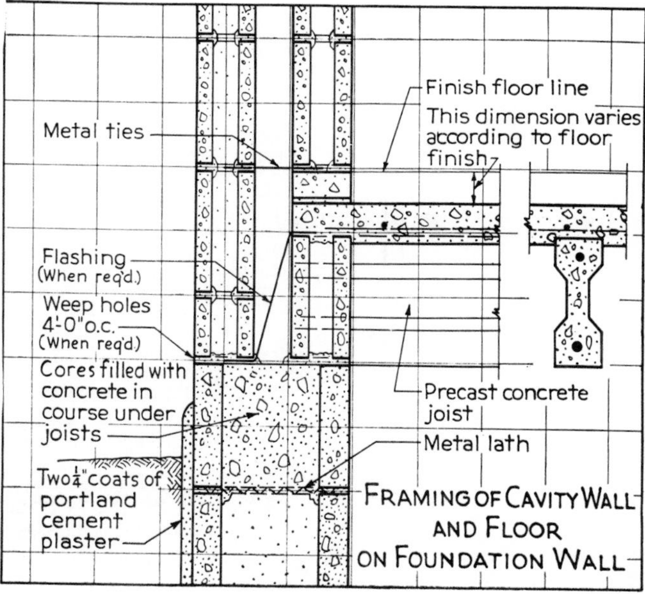
Metal ties
Finish floor line
This dimension varies
according to floor
finish
Flashing
(When req'd.)
Weep holes
4'-0" o.c.
(When req'd.)
Cores filled with
concrete in
course under
joists
Precast concrete
joist
Metal lath
Two 1/4" coats of
portland
cement
plaster
FRAMING OF CAVITY WALL
AND FLOOR
ON FOUNDATION WALL

Fig. 48.

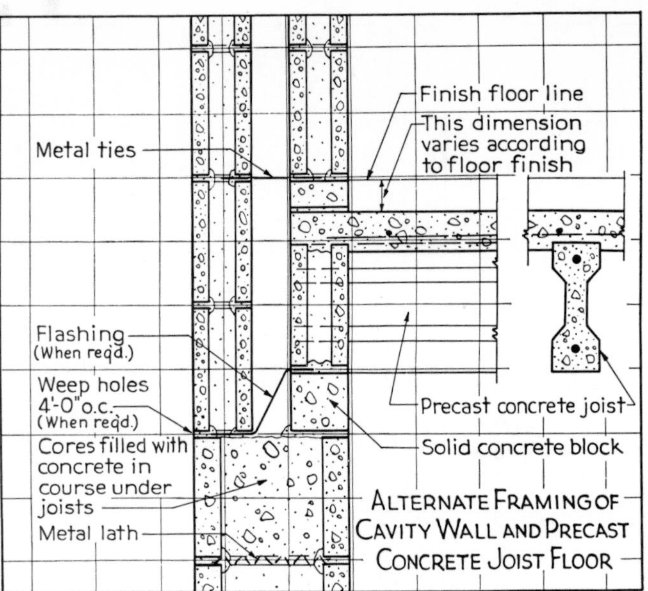
Finish floor line
This dimension varies according to floor finish
Metal ties
Flashing (When reqd.)
Weep holes 4'-0"o.c. (When reqd.)
Cores filled with concrete in course under joists
Metal lath
Precast concrete joist
Solid concrete block
ALTERNATE FRAMING OF CAVITY WALL AND PRECAST CONCRETE JOIST FLOOR

Fig. 49.

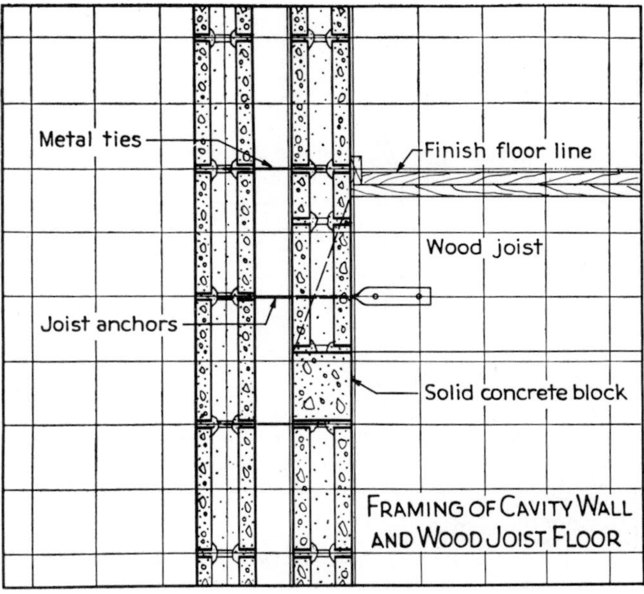
Metal ties
Finish floor line
Wood joist
Joist anchors
Solid concrete block
FRAMING OF CAVITY WALL AND WOOD JOIST FLOOR

Fig. 50.

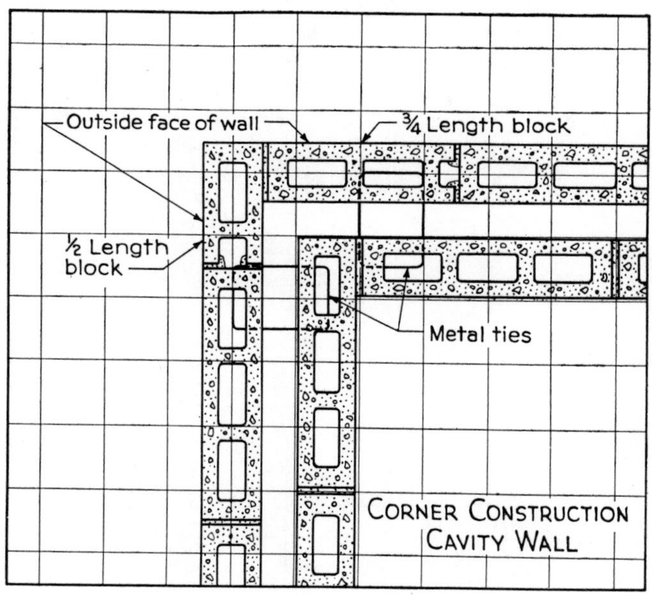
Outside face of wall
¾ Length block
½ Length block
Metal ties
CORNER CONSTRUCTION
CAVITY WALL

Fig. 51.

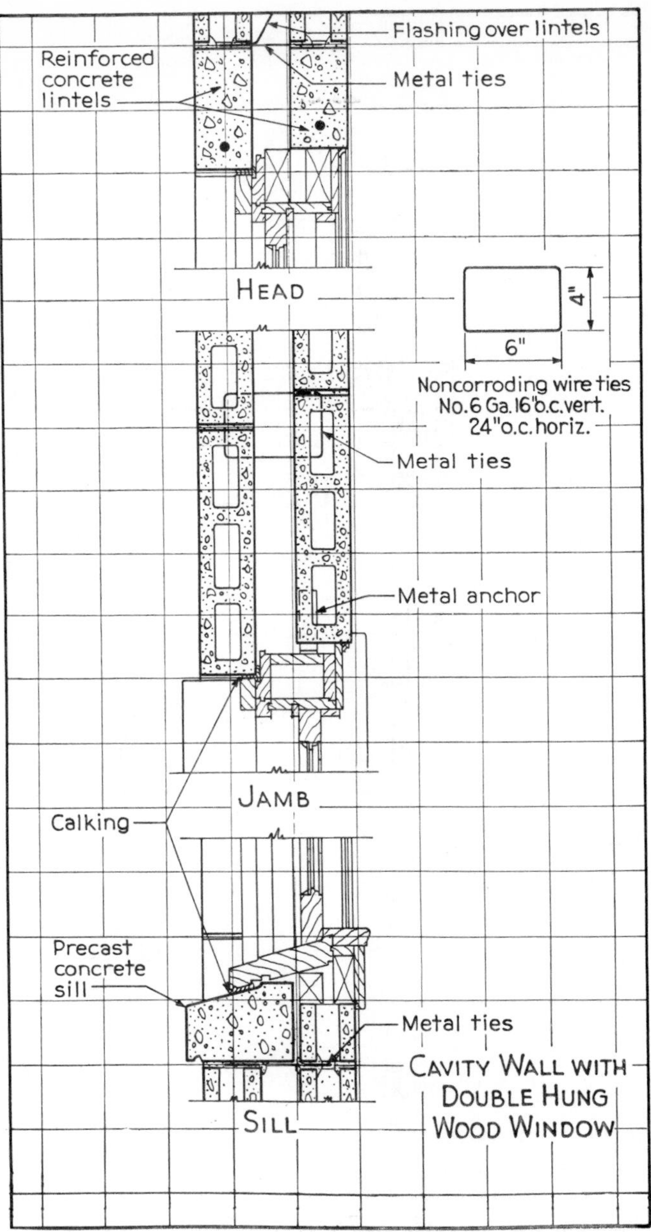

Flashing over lintels
Reinforced concrete lintels
Metal ties
HEAD
4"
6"
Noncorroding wire ties No.6 Ga.16"o.c.vert. 24"o.c.horiz.
Metal ties
Metal anchor
JAMB
Calking
Precast concrete sill
Metal ties
CAVITY WALL WITH DOUBLE HUNG WOOD WINDOW
SILL

Fig. 52.

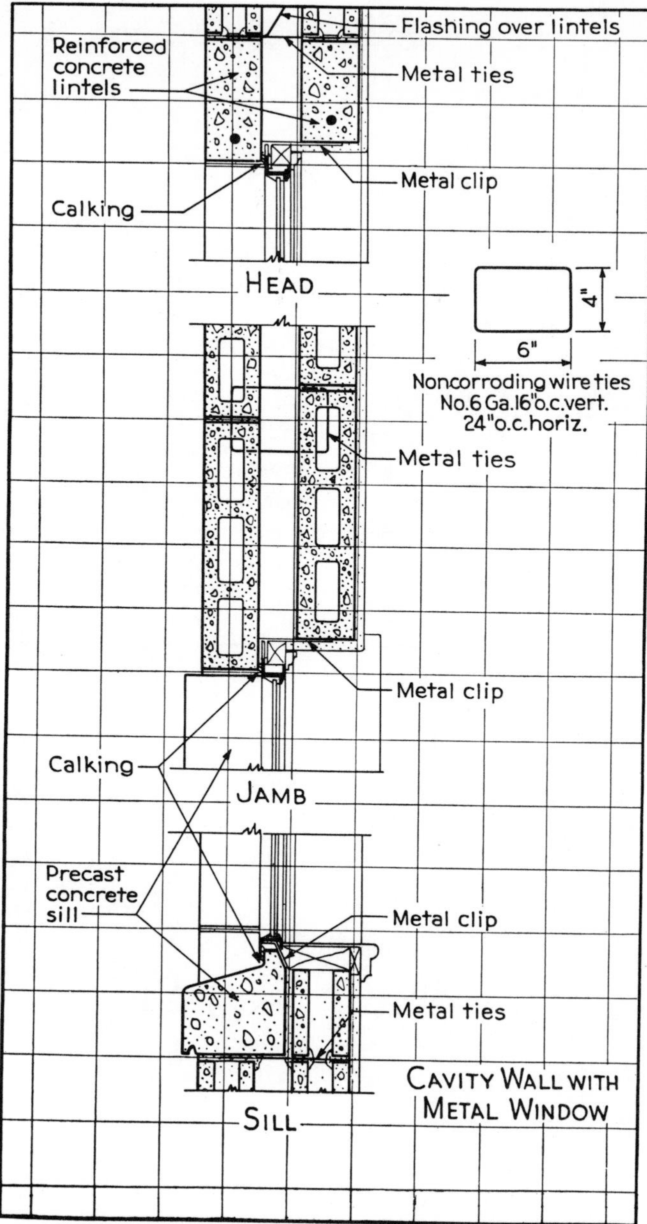

Flashing over lintels
Reinforced concrete lintels
Metal ties
Metal clip
Calking
HEAD
4"
6"
Noncorroding wire ties
No.6 Ga.16"o.c.vert.
24"o.c.horiz.
Metal ties
Metal clip
Calking
JAMB
Precast concrete sill
Metal clip
Metal ties
SILL
CAVITY WALL WITH
METAL WINDOW

Fig. 53.

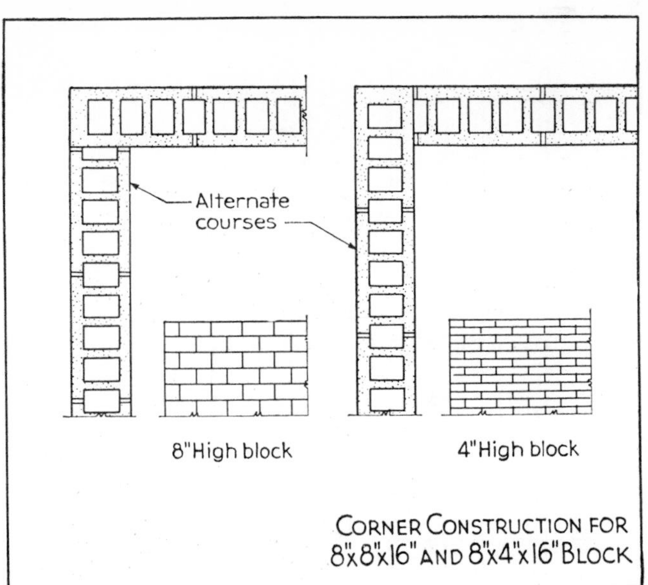
Alternate
courses
8"High block
4"High block
Corner Construction for
8"x8"x16" and 8"x4"x16" Block

Fig. 54.

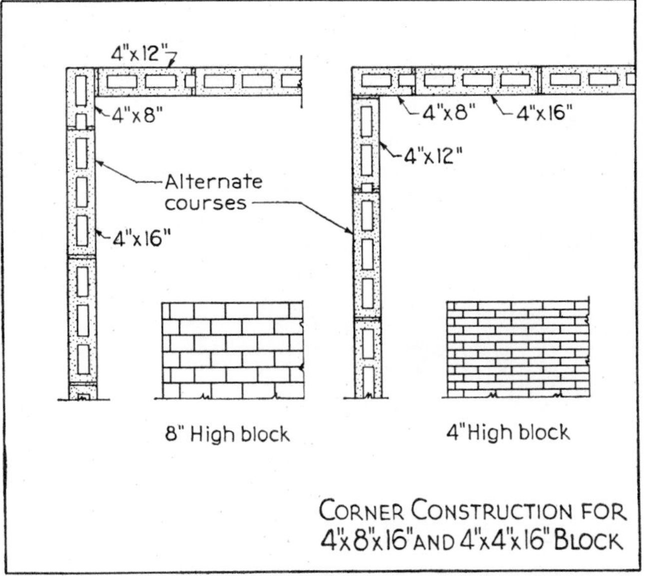
4"x12"
4"x8"
Alternate
courses
4"x16"
4"x8"
4"x16"
4"x12"
8" High block
4"High block
Corner Construction for
4"x8"x16" and 4"x4"x16" Block

Fig. 55.

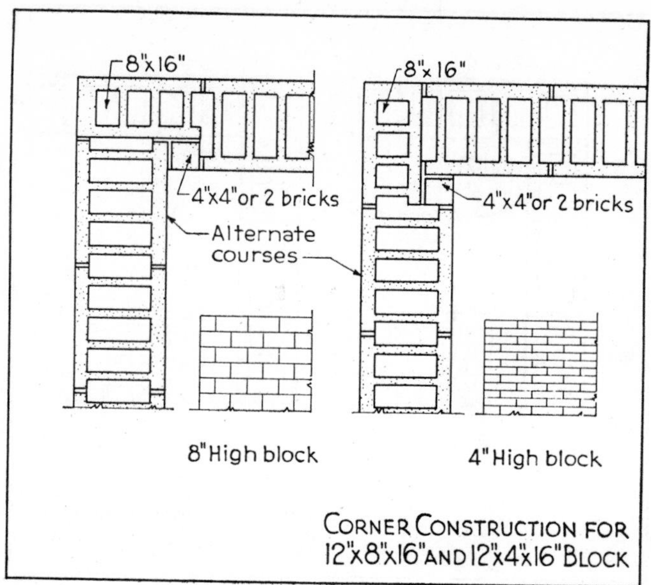
8"x16"
4"x4" or 2 bricks
Alternate courses
8"x16"
4"x4" or 2 bricks
8" High block
4" High block
CORNER CONSTRUCTION FOR
12"x8"x16" AND 12"x4"x16" BLOCK

Fig. 56.

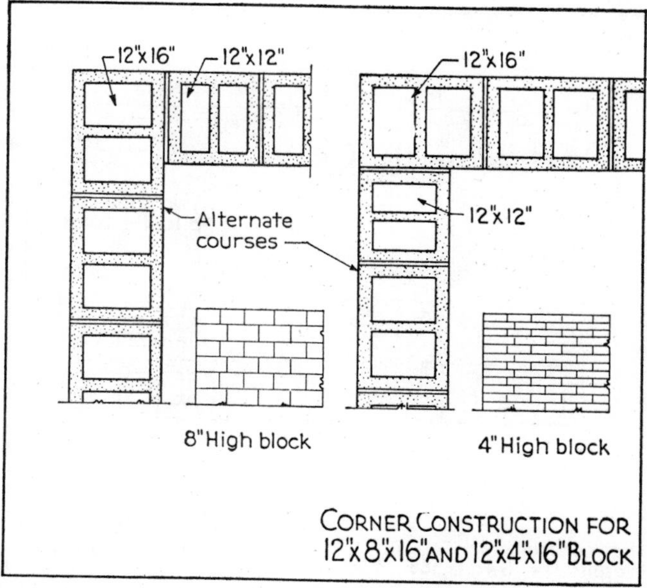
12"x16"
12"x12"
Alternate courses
12"x16"
12"x12"
8" High block
4" High block
CORNER CONSTRUCTION FOR
12"x8"x16" AND 12"x4"x16" BLOCK

Fig. 57.

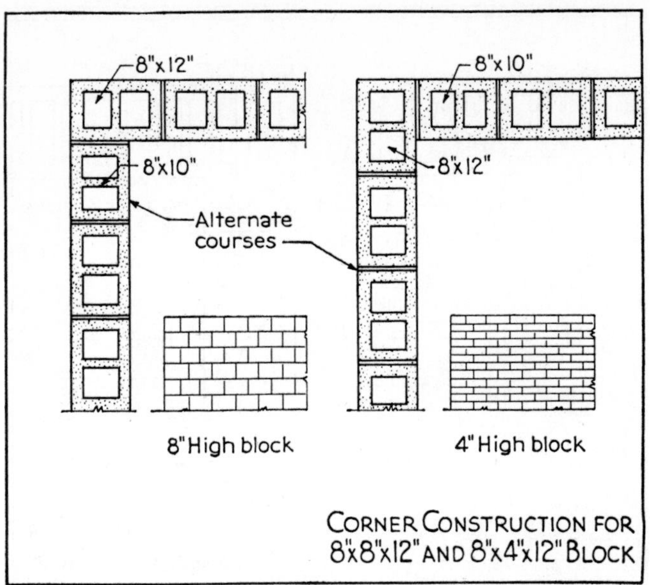
8"x12"
8"x10"
8"x10"
8"x12"
Alternate
courses
8" High block
4" High block
CORNER CONSTRUCTION FOR
8"x8"x12" AND 8"x4"x12" BLOCK

Fig. 58.

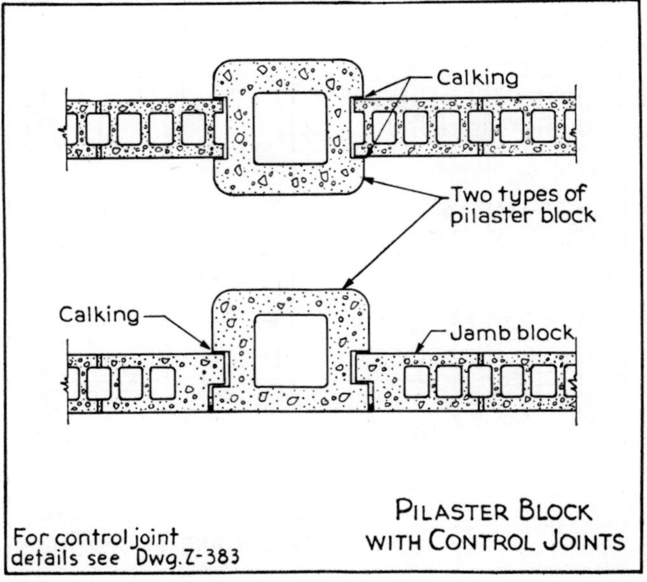
Calking
Two types of
pilaster block
Calking
Jamb block
PILASTER BLOCK
WITH CONTROL JOINTS
For control joint
details see Dwg. Z-383

Fig. 59.

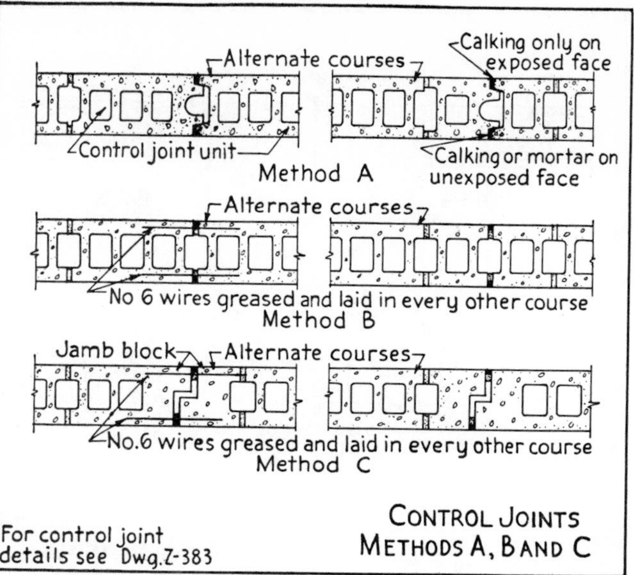
Alternate courses
Calking only on exposed face
Control joint unit
Calking or mortar on unexposed face
Method A
Alternate courses
No 6 wires greased and laid in every other course
Method B
Jamb block
Alternate courses
No.6 wires greased and laid in every other course
Method C
For control joint details see Dwg.Z-383
CONTROL JOINTS METHODS A, B AND C

Fig. 60.

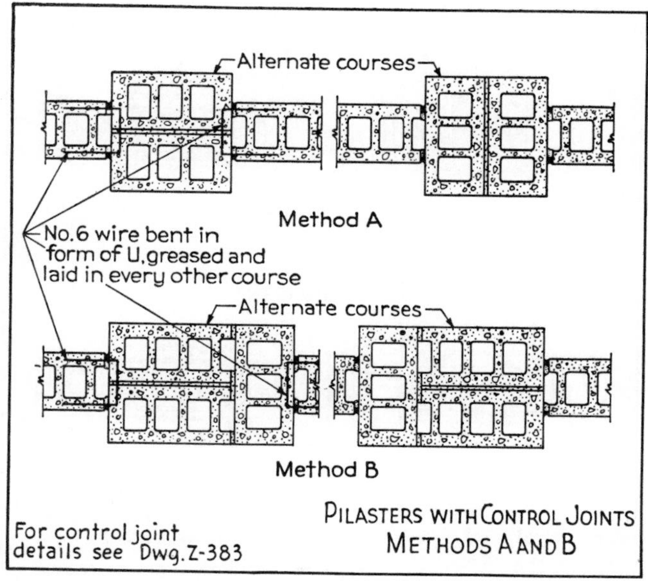
Alternate courses
Method A
No.6 wire bent in form of U, greased and laid in every other course
Alternate courses
Method B
For control joint details see Dwg.Z-383
PILASTERS WITH CONTROL JOINTS METHODS A AND B

Fig. 61.

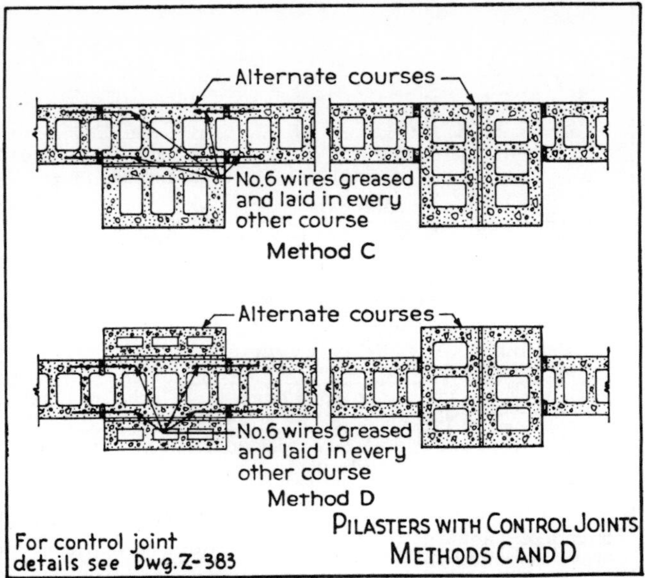
Alternate courses
No.6 wires greased
and laid in every
other course
Method C
Alternate courses
No.6 wires greased
and laid in every
other course
Method D
For control joint
details see Dwg.Z-383
PILASTERS WITH CONTROL JOINTS
METHODS C AND D

Fig. 62.

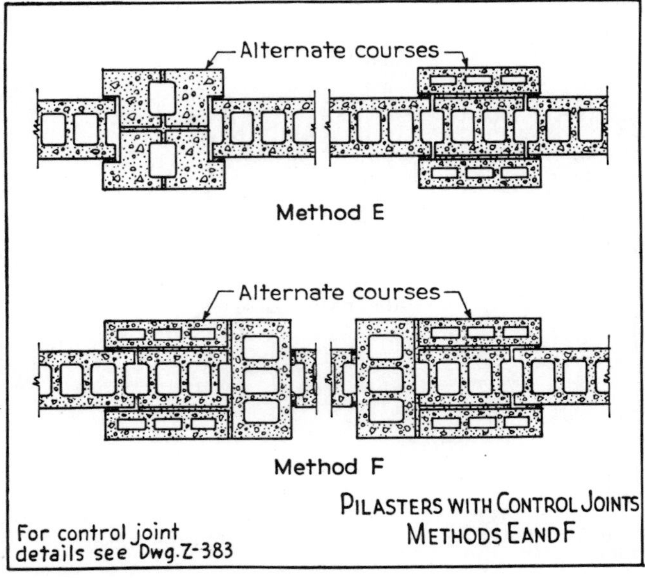
Alternate courses
Method E
Alternate courses
Method F
For control joint
details see Dwg.Z-383
PILASTERS WITH CONTROL JOINTS
METHODS E AND F

Fig. 63.

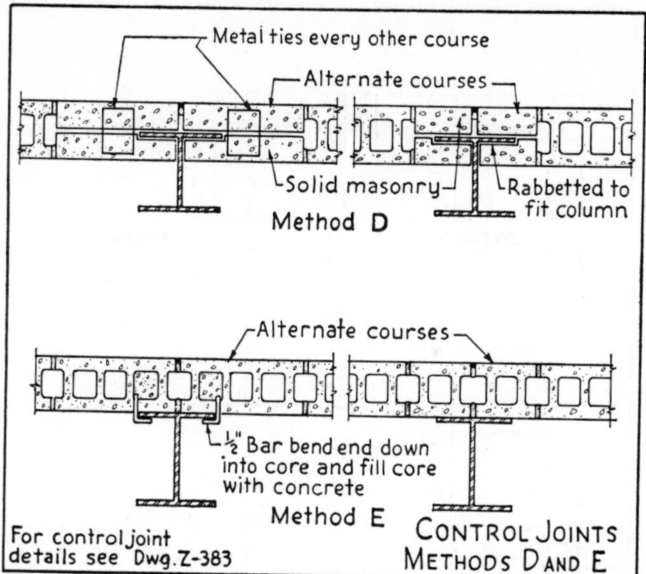
Metal ties every other course
Alternate courses
Solid masonry
Rabbetted to fit column
Method D
Alternate courses
½" Bar bend end down into core and fill core with concrete
Method E
For control joint details see Dwg. Z-383
CONTROL JOINTS METHODS D AND E

Fig. 64.

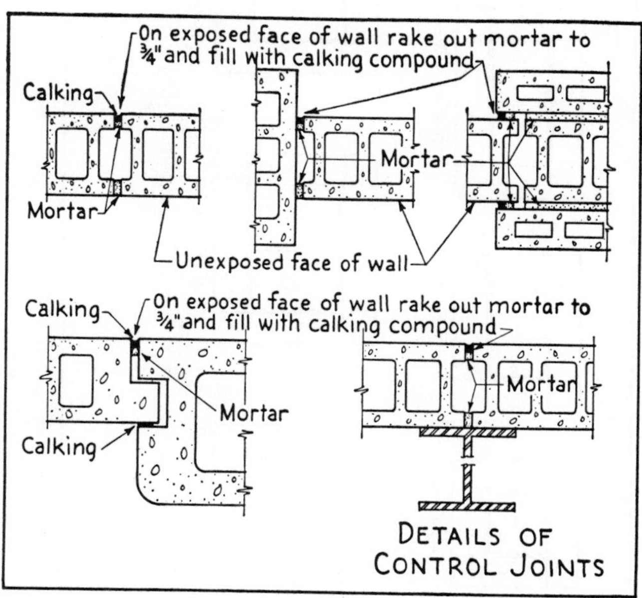
On exposed face of wall rake out mortar to ¾" and fill with calking compound
Calking
Mortar
Mortar
Unexposed face of wall
Calking
On exposed face of wall rake out mortar to ¾" and fill with calking compound
Mortar
Calking
Mortar
DETAILS OF CONTROL JOINTS

Fig. 65.

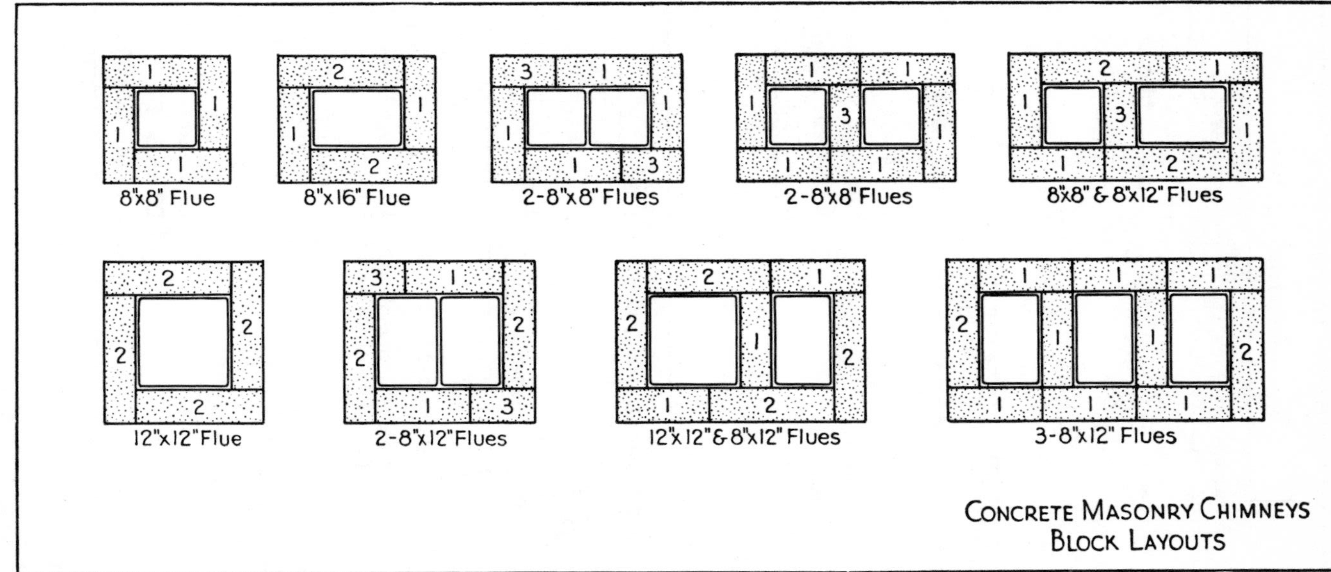
8"x8" Flue
8"x16" Flue
2-8"x8" Flues
2-8"x8" Flues
8"x8" & 8"x12" Flues
12"x12" Flue
2-8"x12" Flues
12"x12" & 8"x12" Flues
3-8"x12" Flues
CONCRETE MASONRY CHIMNEYS
BLOCK LAYOUTS

Fig. 66.

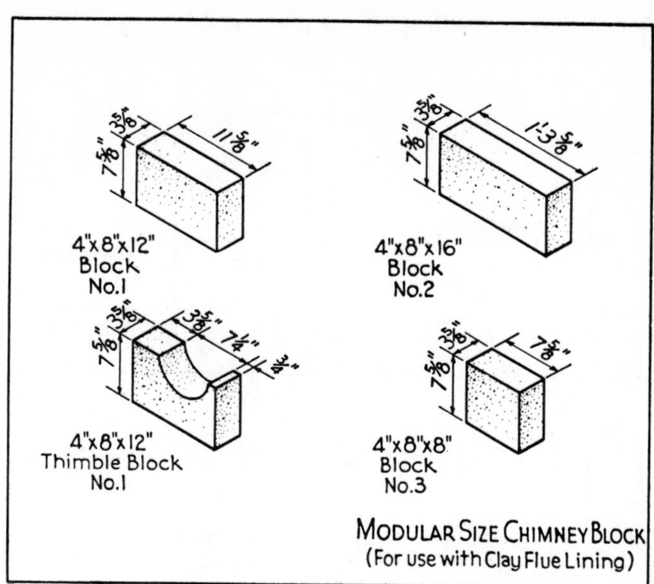
4"x8"x12"
Block
No.1
4"x8"x16"
Block
No.2
4"x8"x12"
Thimble Block
No.1
4"x8"x8"
Block
No.3
MODULAR SIZE CHIMNEY BLOCK
(For use with Clay Flue Lining)

Fig. 67.

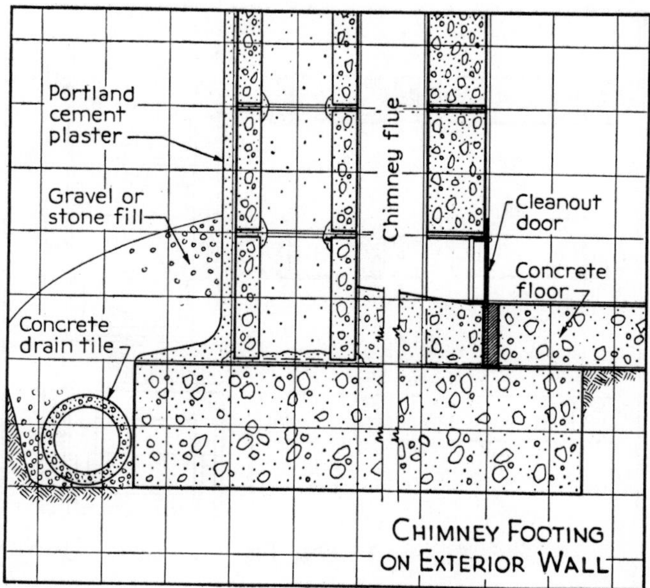
Portland
cement
plaster
Gravel or
stone fill
Concrete
drain tile
Chimney flue
Cleanout
door
Concrete
floor
CHIMNEY FOOTING
ON EXTERIOR WALL

Fig. 68.

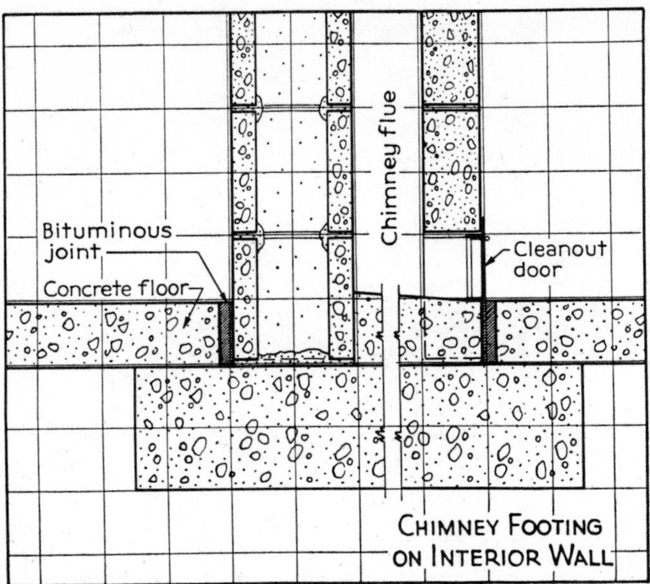
Chimney flue
Bituminous joint
Concrete floor
Cleanout door
CHIMNEY FOOTING ON INTERIOR WALL

Fig. 69.

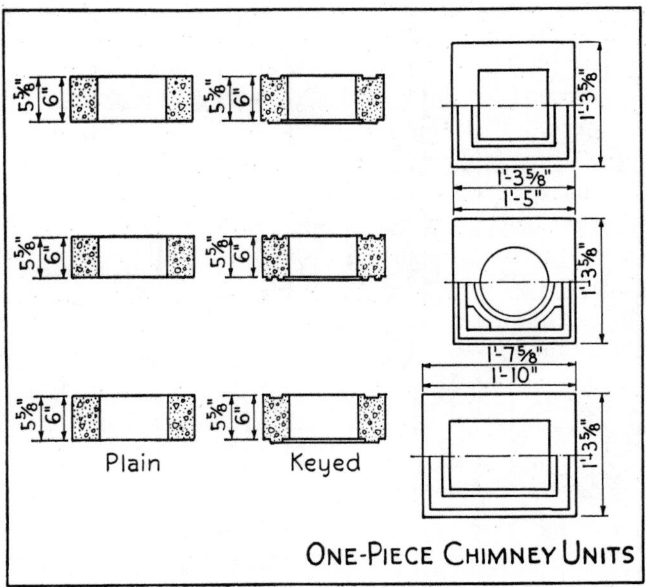
5⅝"
6"
1'-3⅝"
1'-5"
1'-7⅝"
1'-10"
Plain
Keyed
ONE-PIECE CHIMNEY UNITS

Fig. 70.

Appendix III

Patterns for Concrete Masonry

Exposed concrete masonry is being used more and more as a finished wall material for both exteriors and interiors of homes and other buildings. One reason for the increasing popularity of concrete masonry is that it can be laid up in a wide variety of interesting patterns, some of which are illustrated here.

Further variation of the patterns shown may be achieved by using different methods of finishing the mortar joints.

Another method of creating variations with the same patterns is by projecting the faces of some of the units from the overall surface of the wall. This variation can be handled as a definite geometric pattern, at random, or as an abstract pattern to accentuate certain architectural features of the building.

The structural strength and stability of load-bearing walls of 8- × 8- × 16-inch (20- × 20- × 40-cm.) units laid in running bond (Fig. 1) have been established by test. Recent tests have evaluated other patterns in relation to Fig. 1.

Several of the patterns illustrated require units of a size not produced in all areas. Local concrete masonry manufacturers should be consulted as to sizes they have available.

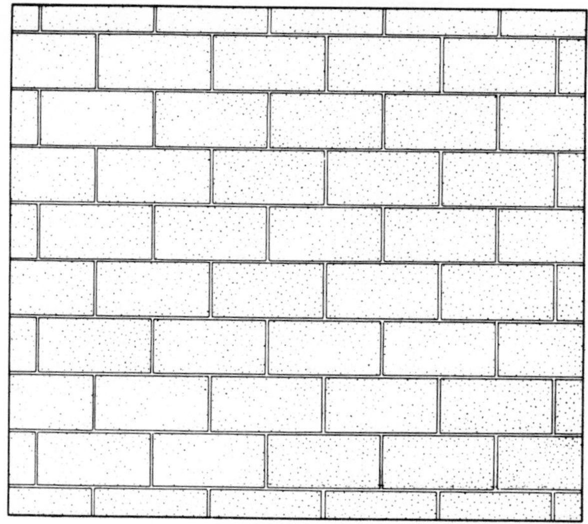

Fig. 1. Running bond, 8 × 16 in.

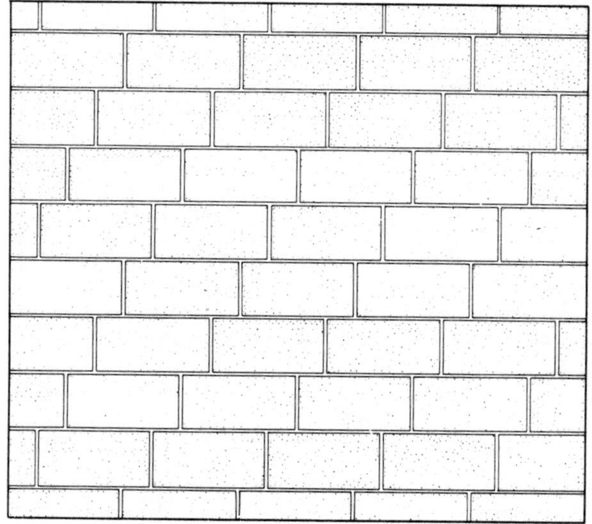

Fig. 2. Offset bond, 8 × 16 in.

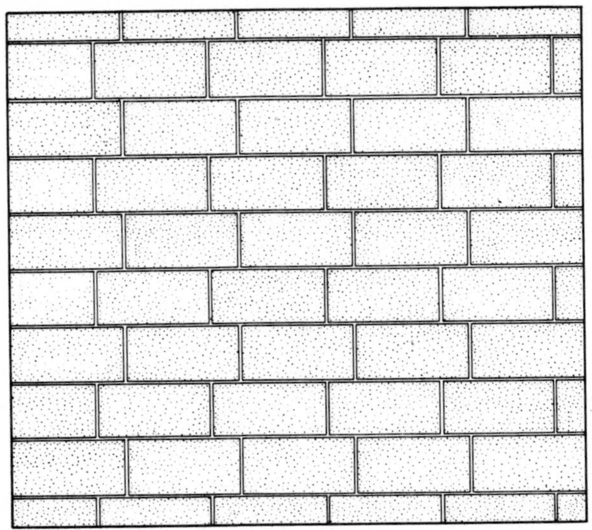

Fig. 3. Offset bond, 8 × 16 in.

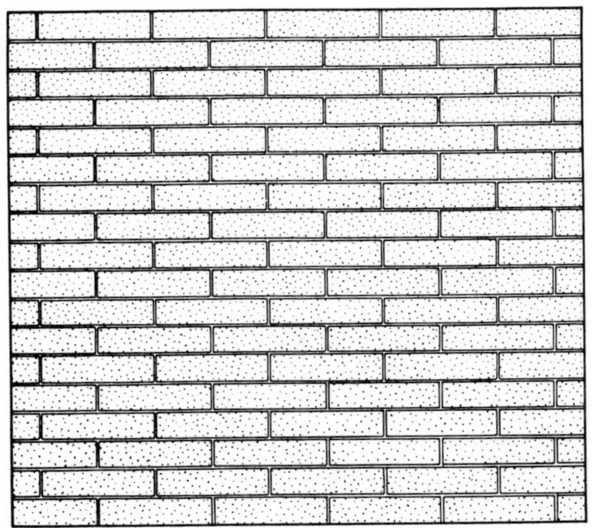

Fig. 4. Running bond, 4 × 16 in.

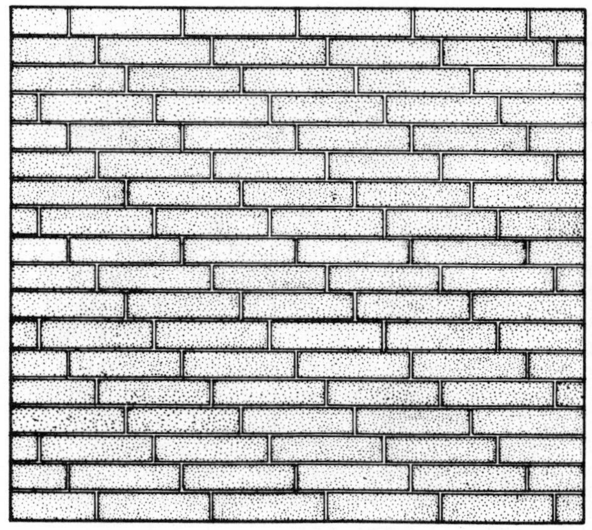

Fig. 5. Offset bond, 4 × 16 in.

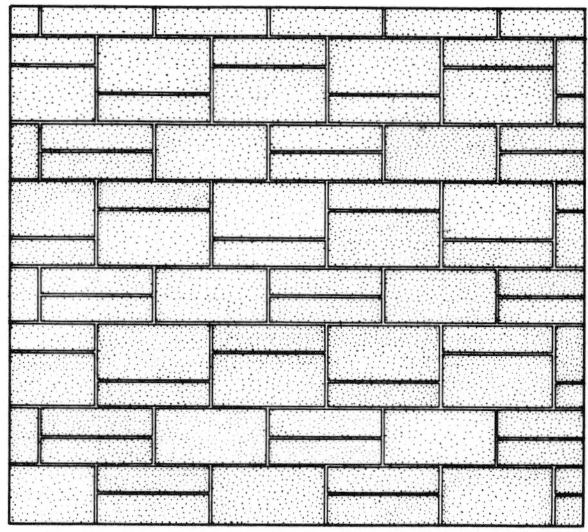

Fig. 6. Coursed ashlar, 4 × 16, 8 × 16 in.

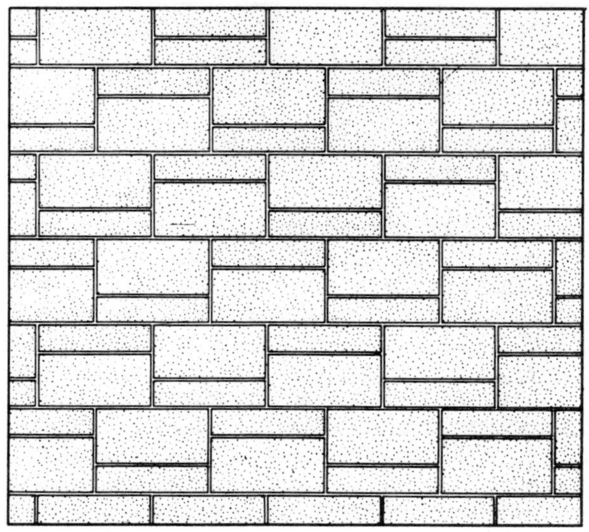

Fig. 7. Coursed ashlar, 4 × 16, 8 × 16 in.

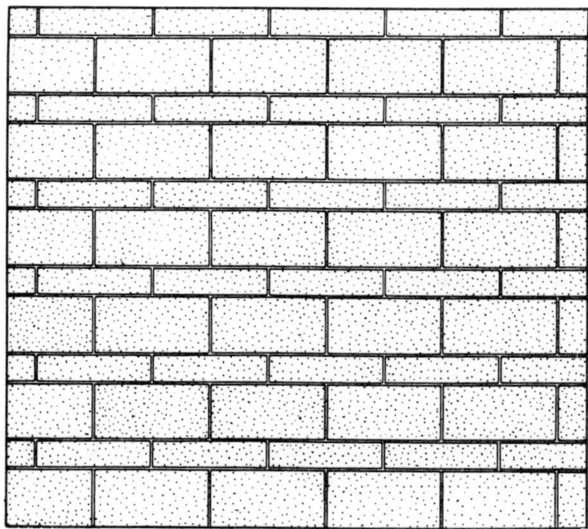

Fig. 8. Coursed ashlar, 4 × 16, 8 × 16 in.

Fig. 9. Coursed ashlar, 4 × 16, 8 × 16 in.

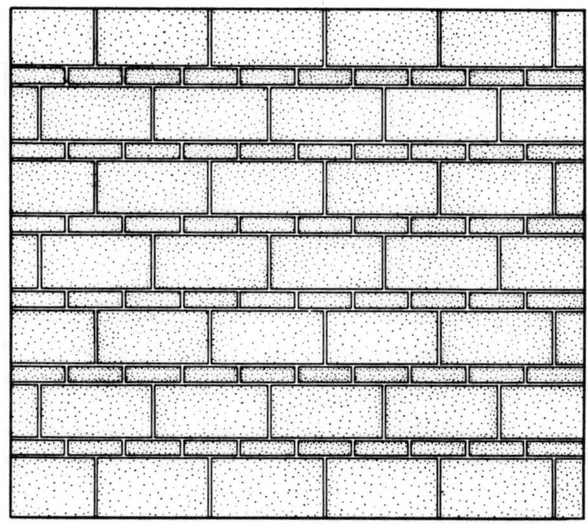

Fig. 10. Coursed ashlar, 8 × 16 in., brick size

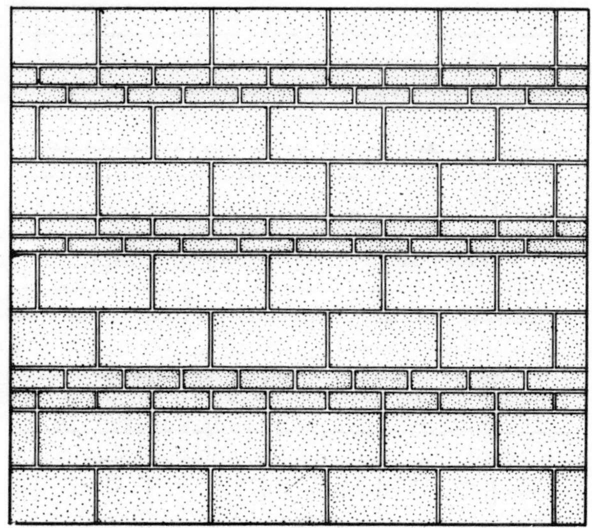

Fig. 11. Coursed ashlar, 8 × 16 in., brick size

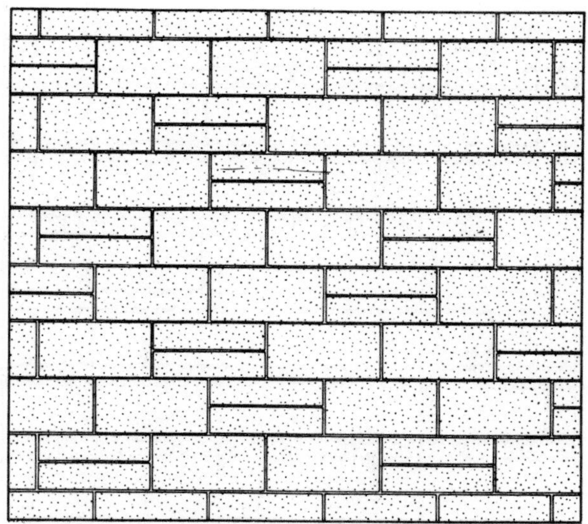

Fig. 12. Coursed ashlar, 4 × 16, 8 × 16 in.

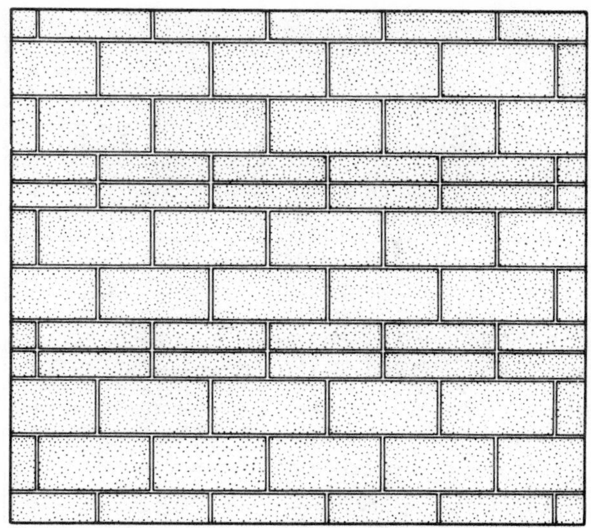

Fig. 13. Coursed ashlar, 4 × 16, 8 × 16 in.

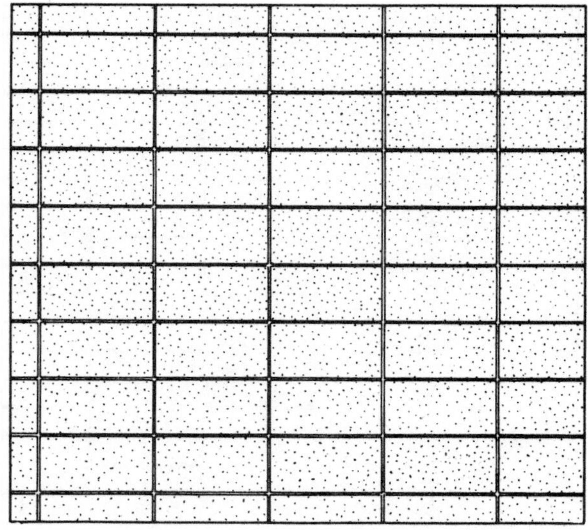

Fig. 14. Horizontal stacking, 8 × 16 in.

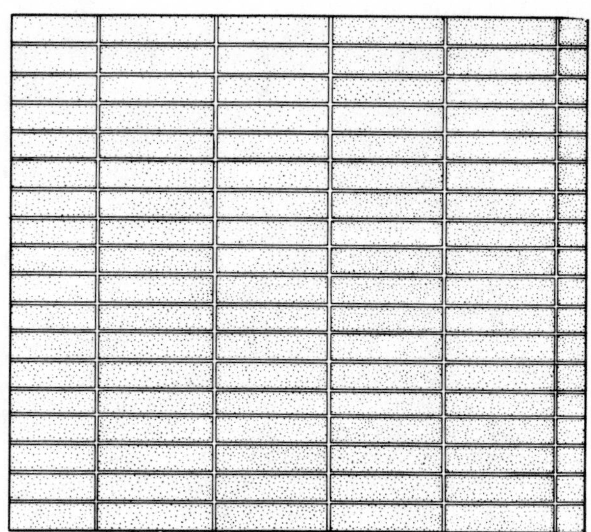

Fig. 15. Horizontal stacking, 4 × 16 in.

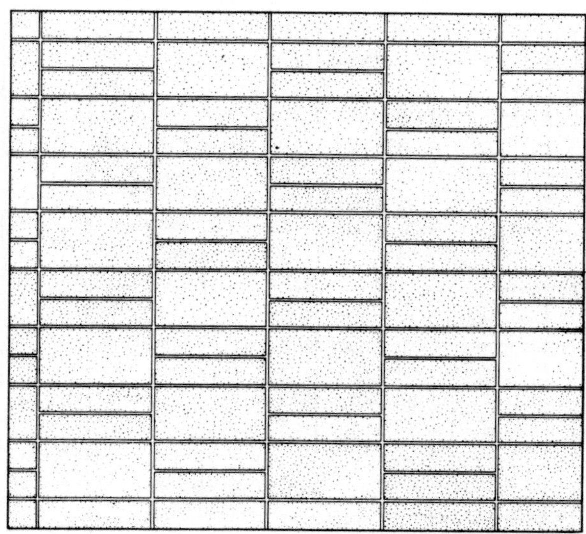

Fig. 16. Horizontal stacking, 4 × 16, 8 × 16 in.

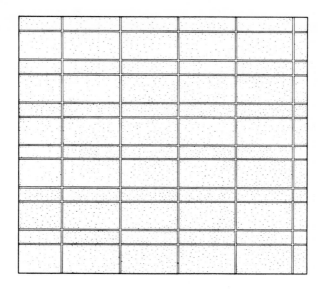

Fig. 17. Horizontal stacking, 4 × 16, 8 × 16 in.

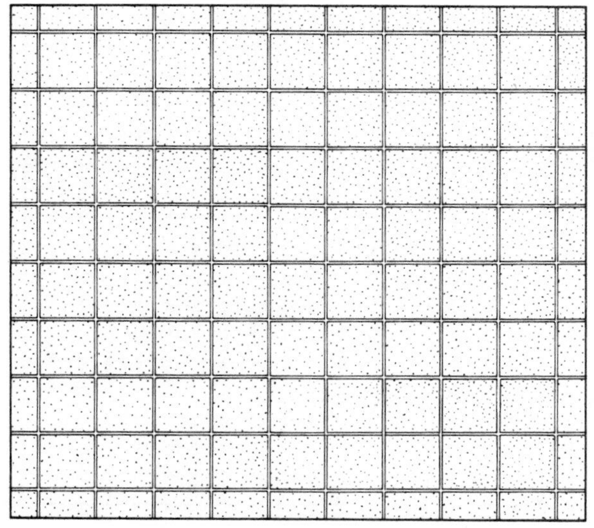

Fig. 18. Square stacking, 8 × 8 in.

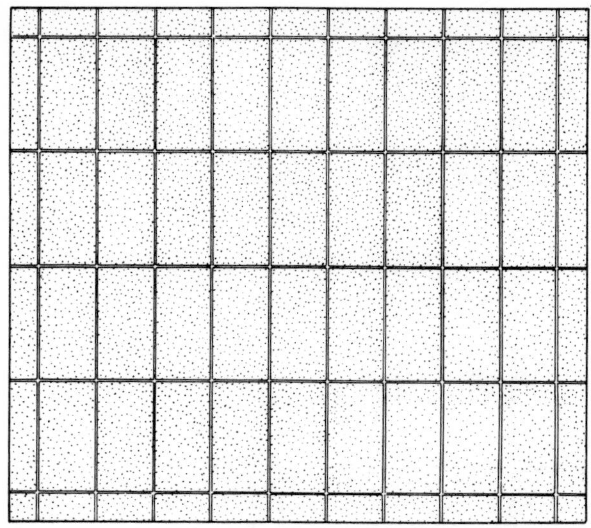

Fig. 19. Vertical stacking, 8 × 16 in.

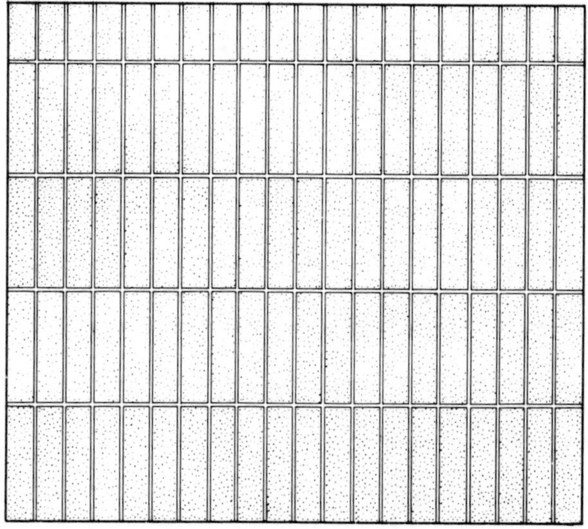

Fig. 20. Vertical stacking, 4 × 16 in.

Fig. 21. Diagonal stacking, 8 × 8 in.

Fig. 22. Diagonal bond, 8 × 16 in.

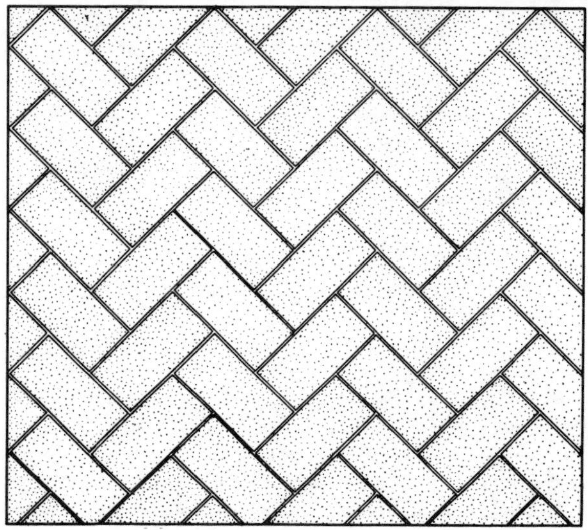

Fig. 23. Diagonal basket weave, 8 × 16 in.

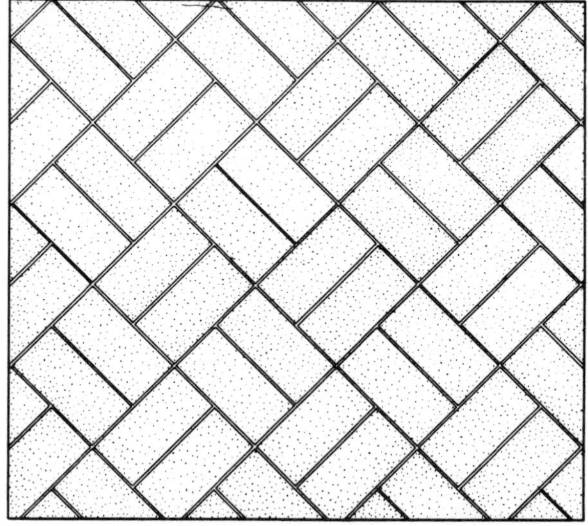

Fig. 24. Diagonal basket weave, 8 × 16 in.

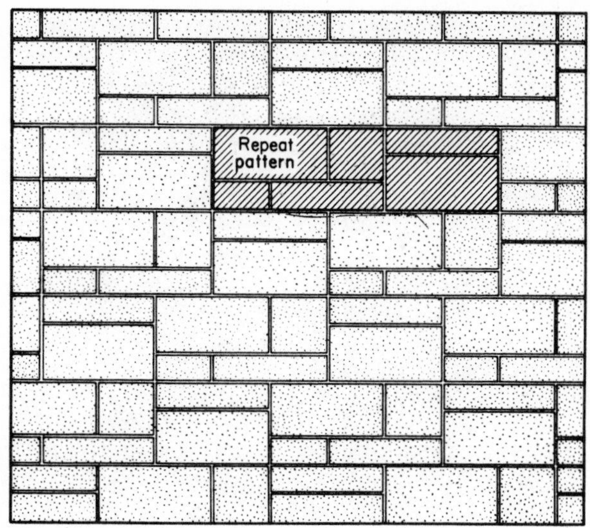

Fig. 25. Patterned ashlar, 4 × 8, 4 × 16, 8 × 8, 8 × 16 in.

Appendix IV

Tables

Analysis No.	1	2	3	4	5
Silica (SiO_2)	2.4	12.0	10.0	9.4	22.0
Iron (Fe)	0.1	0.0	0.1	0.2	0.1
Calcium (Ca)	5.8	36.0	92.0	96.0	3.0
Magnesium (Mg)	1.4	8.1	34.0	27.0	2.4
Sodium (Na)	1.7	6.5	8.2	183.0	215.0
Potassium (K)	0.7	1.2	1.4	18.0	9.8
Bicarbonate (HCO_3)	14.0	119.0	339.0	334.0	549.0
Sulfate (SO_4)	9.7	22.0	84.0	121.0	11.0
Chloride (Cl)	2.0	13.0	9.6	280.0	22.0
Nitrate (NO_3)	0.5	0.1	13.0	0.2	0.5
Total dissolved solids	31.0	165.0	434.0	983.0	564.0

TABLE A-1. TYPICAL ANALYSES OF CITY WATER SUPPLIES (PARTS PER MILLION—PPM) SUITABLE FOR MAKING CONCRETE.

Components			
Lime	**Silica**	**Alumina**	**Iron**
Cement rock	Sand	Clay	Iron ore
Limestone	Traprock	Shale	Iron calcine
Marl	Calcium silicate	Slag	Iron dust
Alkali waste	Quartzite	Fly ash	Iron pyrite
Oyster shell	Fuller's earth	Copper slag	Iron sinters
Coquina shell		Aluminum ore refuse	Iron oxide
Chalk		Staurolite	Blast-furnace flue dust
Marble		Diaspore clay	
		Granodiorite	
		Kaolin	

TABLE A-2. TYPICAL SOURCES OF RAW MATERIALS USED IN MANUFACTURE OF PORTLAND CEMENT.

Oxide	Range, percent
Lime, CaO	60-66
Silica, SiO_2	19-25
Alumina, Al_2O_3	3-8
Iron, Fe_2O_3	1-5
Magnesia, MgO	0-5
Sulfur trioxide, SO_3	1-3

TABLE A-3. OXIDE COMPOSITION OF TYPE I OR NORMAL PORTLAND CEMENT.

Type of portland cement		Compound composition, percent*				Fineness, sq.cm. per g.**
ASTM	CSA	C_3S	C_2S	C_3A	C_4AF	
I	Normal	50	24	11	8	1,800
II	Moderate	42	33	5	13	1,800
III	High Early Strength	60	13	9	8	2,600
IV	Low Heat	26	50	5	12	1,900
V	Sulfate Resisting	40	40	4	9	1,900

*The compound compositions shown are typical. Deviations from these values do not indicate unsatisfactory performance. For specification limits see ASTM C150 or CSA A5.

**Fineness as determined by Wagner turbidimeter test.

TABLE A-4. TYPICAL CALCULATED COMPOUND COMPOSITION AND FINENESS OF PORTLAND CEMENTS.

Type of portland cement		Compressive strength, percent of strength of Type I or Normal portland cement concrete			
ASTM	CSA	1 day	7 days	28 days	3 months
I	Normal	100	100	100	100
II	Moderate	75	85	90	100
III	High Early Strength	190	120	110	100
IV	Low Heat	55	55	75	100
V	Sulfate Resisting	65	75	85	100

TABLE A-5. APPROXIMATE RELATIVE STRENGTH OF CONCRETE AS AFFECTED BY TYPE OF CEMENT.

Kind of Work	Add U. S. Gal. of Water to Each One-Sack Batch if Sand Is			Suggested Mixture for Trial Batch			Maximum Aggregate Size
	Very Wet	Wet	Damp	Portland Cement	Sand	Pebbles	
5-Gallon Paste for Concrete Subjected to Severe Wear, Weather, or Weak Acid and Alkali Solutions							
		Average Sand		Sacks	Cu.ft.	Cu.ft.	
Colored or plain topping for heavy wearing surfaces; all two-course work such as pavements, walks, residence floors, etc.	4¼	4½	4¾	1	1	1¾	⅜"
		Average Sand					
Fence posts, flower boxes, garden furniture; work of very thin sections; all concrete in contact with weak acid or alkali solutions.	3¾	4	4½	1	1¾	2	¾"
6-Gallon Paste for Concrete to Be Watertight or Subjected to Moderate Wear and Weather							
		Average Sand		Sacks	Cu.ft.	Cu.ft.	
Watertight floors such as basement, dairy barn, milk house, etc. Watertight basement walls and pits, walls above ground, grain bins, silos, manure pits, scale pits, dipping vats, dams, lawn rollers, hot beds, cold frames, storage cellars, etc. Water storage tanks, cisterns, septic tanks, sidewalks, feeding floors, barnyard pavements, driveways, barn approaches, steps, porch floors, corner posts, gate posts, piers, columns, sills, lintels, chimney caps, etc.	4¼	5	5½	1	2¼	3	1½"
7-Gallon Paste for Concrete Not Subjected to Wear, Weather or Water							
		Average Sand		Sacks	Cu.ft.	Cu.ft.	
Foundation walls, footings, retaining walls, engine bases, mass concrete, etc., not subjected to weather, water pressure or other exposure.	4¾	5½	6¼	1	2¾	4	1½"

NOTE—It may be necessary to use a richer paste than is shown in the table because the concrete may be subjected to more severe conditions than are usual for a structure of that type. For example, a water storage tank ordinarily is made with a 6-gallon paste. However, the tank may be built in a place where the soil water is strongly alkaline, in which case a 5-gallon paste is required.

TABLE A-6. RECOMMENDED PROPORTIONS OF WATER TO CEMENT AND SUGGESTED TRIAL MIXES.

Water per bag of cement	Max. size aggregate (in.)	Pounds of aggregate	
		Sand	Coarse aggregate
5 gal.	¾	185	210
	1	175	240
	1½	170	280
	2	170	315
6 gal.	¾	245	255
	1	225	285
	1½	225	335
	2	220	380
7 gal.	¾	300	290
	1	280	330
	1½	270	385
	2	280	435

TABLE A-7. SUGGESTED TRIAL MIXES FOR CONCRETE USING COARSE SAND.

Size of aggregate	Trial Mixes			
	Mixing water* per sack of cement	Portland cement	Aggregates	
	U.S. gal.	Sacks	Sand Cu.ft.	Gravel or crushed stone Cu.ft.
Maximum size ¾ in.	5	1	2½	2¾
Maximum size 1 in.	5	1	2¼	3
Maximum size 1½ in.	5	1	2¼	3½

*Based on 6 gal. of water per sack of cement including water contained in damp sand.

TABLE A-8. RECOMMENDED CONCRETE MIXES FOR BASEMENT FOOTINGS, WALLS, FLOORS, AND STAIRS.

Thickness, in.	Area in square feet (width X length)					
	10	25	50	100	200	300
4	0.12	0.31	0.62	1.23	2.47	3.70
5	0.15	0.39	0.77	1.54	3.09	4.63
6	0.19	0.46	0.93	1.85	3.70	5.56

*Does not allow for losses due to uneven subgrade, spillage, etc. Add 5 to 10 percent for such contingencies.

TABLE A-9. ESTIMATING CUBIC YARDS OF CONCRETE FOR SLABS.*

Maximum-size coarse aggregate, in.	Air-entrained concrete				Concrete without air			
	Cement, lb.	Sand, lb.	Coarse aggregate, lb.*	Water, lb.	Cement, lb.	Sand, lb.	Coarse aggregate, lb.*	Water, lb.
⅜	29	53	46	10	29	59	46	11
½	27	46	55	10	27	53	55	11
¾	25	42	65	10	25	47	65	10
1	24	39	70	9	24	45	70	10
1½	23	38	75	9	23	43	75	9

*If crushed stone is used, decrease coarse aggregate by 3 lb. and increase sand by 3 lb.

TABLE A-10. PROPORTIONS BY WEIGHT TO MAKE ONE CUBIC FOOT OF CONCRETE.

Maximum-size aggregate, in.	Minimum cement content, lb. per cu.yd.	Maximum slump, in.	Compressive strength at 28 days, lb. per sq.in.	Air content, percent by volume
⅜	610	4	3,500	7½ ± 1
½	590	4	3,500	7½ ± 1
¾	540	4	3,500	6 ± 1
1	520	4	3,500	6 ± 1
1½	470	4	3,500	5 ± 1

TABLE A-11. GUIDE FOR ORDERING READY-MIXED CONCRETE FOR DRIVES, WALKS, AND PATIOS.

Maximum-size coarse aggregate, in.	Air-entrained concrete				Concrete without air			
	Cement	Sand	Coarse aggregate	Water	Cement	Sand	Coarse aggregate	Water
⅜	1	2¼	1½	½	1	2½	1½	½
½	1	2¼	2	½	1	2½	2	½
¾	1	2¼	2½	½	1	2½	2½	½
1	1	2¼	2¾	½	1	2½	2¾	½
1½	1	2¼	3	½	1	2½	3	½

TABLE A-12. PROPORTIONS BY VOLUME.

Characteristic	Significance or importance	Test or practice, ASTM and CSA designation	Specification requirement
Resistance to abrasion	Index of aggregate quality; warehouse floors, loading platforms, pavements	C131 C535	Max. percent loss*
Resistance to freezing and thawing	Structures subjected to weathering	C666, C671	Max. number of cycles or period of frost immunity
Chemical stability	Strength and durability of all types of structures	C227 (mortar bar) C342 (mortar bar) C289 (chemical) C586 (aggregate prism) C295 (petrographic)	Max. expansion of mortar bar* Aggregates must not be reactive with cement alkalies*
Particle shape and surface texture	Workability of fresh concrete		Max. percent flat and elongated pieces
Grading	Workability of fresh concrete; economy	C136 A23.2.2	Max. and min. percent passing standard sieves
Bulk unit weight	Mix design calculations; classification	C29 A23.2.10	Max. or min. unit weight (special concretes)
Specific gravity	Mix design calculations	C127 (coarse aggregate) C128 (fine aggregate) A23.2.6	
Absorption and surface moisture	Control of concrete quality	C70, C127, C128, C566 A23.2.11	

*Aggregates not conforming to specification requirements may be used if service records or performance tests indicate they produce concrete having the desired properties.

TABLE A-13. CHARACTERISTICS OF AGGREGATES.

Type of structures	Exposure conditions**					
	Severe wide range in temperature, or frequent alternations of freezing and thawing (air-entrained concrete only)			Mild temperature rarely below freezing, or rainy, or arid		
	In air	At water line or within range of fluctuating water level or spray		In air	At water line or within range of fluctuating water level or spray	
		In fresh water	In sea water or in contact with sulfates†		In fresh water	In sea water or in contact with sulfates†
A. Thin sections such as reinforced piles and pipe	0.49	0.44	0.40	0.53	0.49	0.40
B. Bridge decks	0.44	0.44	0.40	0.49	0.49	0.44
C. Thin sections such as railings, curbs, sills, ledges, ornamental or architectural concrete, and all sections with less than 1-in. concrete cover over reinforcement	0.49	—	—	0.53	0.49	—
D. Moderate sections, such as retaining walls, abutments, piers, girders, beams	0.53	0.49	0.44	††	0.53	0.44
E. Exterior portions of heavy (mass) sections	0.58	0.49	0.44	††	0.53	0.44
F. Concrete deposited by tremie under water	—	0.44	0.44	—	0.44	0.44
G. Concrete slabs laid on the ground	0.53	—	—	††	—	—
H. Pavements	0.49	—	—	0.53	—	—
I. Concrete protected from the weather, interiors of buildings, concrete below ground	††	—	—	††	—	—
J. Concrete which will later be protected by enclosure or backfill but which may be exposed to freezing and thawing for several years before such protection is offered	0.53	—	—	††	—	—

*Adapted from Recommended Practice for Selecting Proportions for Concrete (ACI 613-54).

**Air-entrained concrete should be used under all conditions involving severe exposure and may be used under mild exposure conditions to improve workability of the mixture.

†Soil or groundwater containing sulfate concentrations of more than 0.2 per cent. For moderate sulfate resistance, the tricalcium aluminate content of the cement should be limited to 8 per cent, and for high sulfate resistance to 5 per cent. At equal cement contents, air-entrained concrete is significantly more resistant to sulfate attack than non-air-entrained concrete.

††Water-cement ratio should be selected on basis of strength and workability requirements, but minimum cement content should not be less than 470 lb. per cubic yard.

TABLE A-14. RECOMMENDED MAXIMUM PERMISSIBLE WATER-CEMENT RATIOS FOR DIFFERENT TYPES OF STRUCTURES AND DEGREES OF EXPOSURE.*

Relative degree of sulfate attack	Sulfate present (as SO_4) in samples		Water-cement ratio
	Per cent in soil	Parts per million in groundwater	
Negligible	0.00 to 0.10	0 to 150	—
Positive (mild)	0.10 to 0.20	150 to 1000	0.50
Considerable	0.20 to 0.50	1000 to 2000	0.50
Severe	Over 0.50	Over 2000	0.45

*Adapted from Standards for Concrete and Reinforced Concrete (CSA A23).

TABLE A-15. RECOMMENDED MAXIMUM PERMISSIBLE WATER-CEMENT RATIOS FOR CONCRETE EXPOSED TO SOILS AND GROUND WATERS CONTAINING VARIOUS SULFATE CONCENTRATIONS.*

Air-Entrained Concrete *

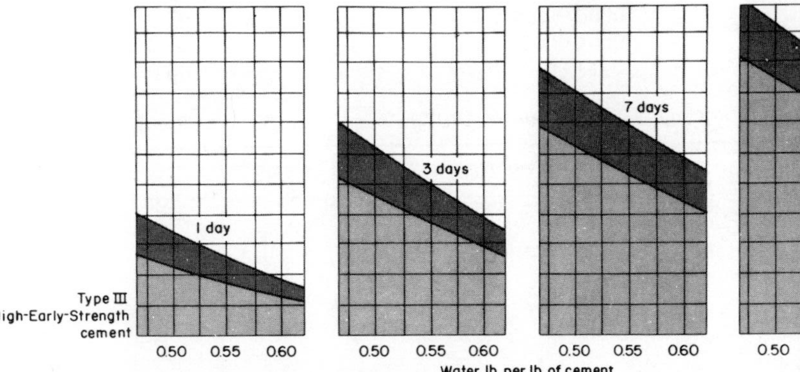

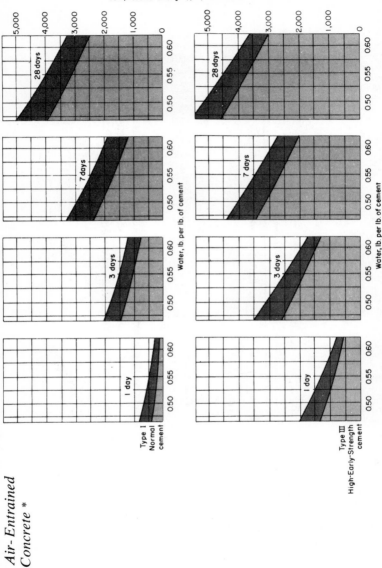

*Concrete with air content within recommended limits and maximum aggregate size of 2 in. or less

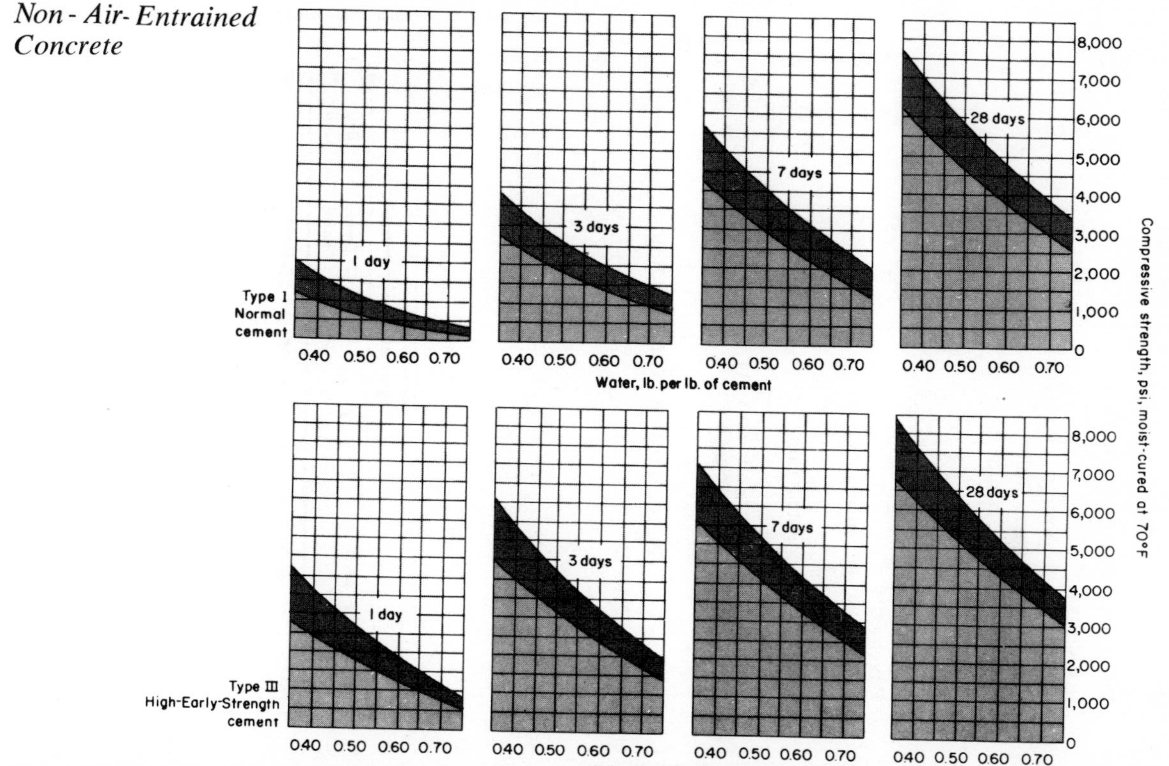

TABLE A-16. RELATIONSHIP BETWEEN WATER-CEMENT RATIO AND COMPRESSIVE STRENGTH FOR PORTLAND CEMENTS AT DIFFERENT AGES. (THESE RELATIONSHIPS ARE APPROXIMATE AND SHOULD BE USED ONLY AS A GUIDE IN LIEU OF DATA ON JOB MATERIALS.)

Types of construction	Slump, in.*	
	Maximum	Minimum
Reinforced foundation walls and footings	3	1
Unreinforced footings, caissons, and substructure walls	3	1
Reinforced slabs, beams, and walls	4	1
Building columns	4	1
Bridge decks	3	2
Pavements	2	1
Sidewalks, driveways, and slabs on ground	4	2
Heavy mass construction	2	1

*When high-frequency vibrators are *not* used, the values may be increased by about 50 per cent, but in no case should the slump exceed 6 in.

TABLE A-17. TYPICAL SLUMP RANGES FOR VARIOUS TYPES OF CONSTRUCTION.

SIZE OF BATCH	Pints of mixing water to add			
	Very wet sand	Wet sand	Damp sand	Dry sand
5 GAL. WATER PER SACK OF CEMENT				
1/2 sack	14	16	18	20
1/4 sack	7	8	9	10
1/5 sack (18.8 lb.)	5 3/5	6 2/5	7 1/5	8
1/10 sack (9.4 lb.)	2 4/5	3 1/5	3 3/5	4
6 GAL. WATER PER SACK OF CEMENT				
1/2 sack	17	20	22	24
1/4 sack	8 1/2	10	11	12
1/5 sack	6 4/5	8	8 4/5	9 3/5
1/10 sack	3 2/5	4	4 2/5	4 4/5

TABLE A-18. PINTS OF WATER TO ADD TO MIXES FOR BATCHES USING 1/2, 1/4, 1/5, AND 1/10 SACKS OF CEMENT.

TYPE OF STRUCTURE	Slump in inches	
	Minimum	Maximum
Massive sections; pavements and floors laid on ground.	1	4
Heavy slabs, beams or walls; tank walls; posts.	3	6
Thin walls and columns; ordinary slabs or beams; vases and garden furniture.	4	8

TABLE A-19. RECOMMENDED SLUMPS FOR CONCRETE.

Water per bag of cement	Max. size aggregate (in.)	Pounds of aggregate	
		Sand	Coarse aggregate
5 gal.	¾	185	210
	1	175	240
	1½	170	280
	2	170	315
6 gal.	¾	245	255
	1	225	285
	1½	225	335
	2	220	380
7 gal.	¾	300	290
	1	280	330
	1½	270	385
	2	280	435

TABLE A-20. SUGGESTED TRIAL MIXES FOR CONCRETE USING COARSE SAND.

Kind	Extreme fiber in bending	Compression perpendicular to grain	Compression parallel to grain $L/d \leqq 11$ ‡	Horizontal shear	Modulus of elasticity
Douglas Fir, coast region—No. 1 grade..........	1800	490	1500	150	1,600,000
Hemlock, west coast—No. 1 grade...........	1800	450	1340	125	1,400,000
Larch—common structural grade.	1800	490	1650	150	1,500,000
Pine, Norway—common structural grade......	1375	450	970	95	1,200,000
Pine, Southern—No. 1 grade.....	1800	490	1500	155	1,600,000
Pine, Southern Longleaf—No. 1 longleaf grade..	2125	570	1750	190	1,600,000
Redwood, Heart—structural grade.	1625	400	1375	120	1,200,000
Spruce, Eastern—structural grade.	1625	375	1220	120	1,200,000

†The working stresses given in this table are approximately 25 per cent greater than ordinarily used for permanent construction and for the grade and sizes (2-in. thickness or less) of lumber generally used for forms, because forms are temporary thereby reducing the effect of time yield. Basic data for this table were taken from **National Design Specifications for Stress-Grade Lumber and Its Fastenings,** 1950 Revised Edition, Recommended by National Lumber Manufacturers Association, Washington, D. C.

‡L = length of member in inches; d = least dimension of the member in inches.

TABLE A-21. SAFE WORKING STRESSES (PSI) AND MODULI OF ELASTICITY OF VARIOUS KINDS OF LUMBER FOR FORM CONSTRUCTION.

Actual unit sizes (width x height x length) in.	Nominal wall thickness in.	For 100 sq.ft. of wall				For 100 concrete units
		Number of units	Average weight of finished wall		Mortar*** cu.ft.	Mortar*** cu.ft.
			Heavyweight aggregate lb.*	Lightweight aggregate lb.**		
3⅝x3⅝x15⅝	4	225	3050	2150	4.3	1.9
5⅝x3⅝x15⅝	6	225	4550	3050	4.3	1.9
7⅝x3⅝x15⅝	8	225	5700	3700	4.3	1.9
3¾x5x11¾	4	221	3000	2150	3.7	1.7
5¾x5x11¾	6	221	4500	3050	3.7	1.7
7¾x5x11¾	8	221	5650	3700	3.7	1.7
3⅝x7⅝x15⅝	4	112.5	2850	2050	2.6	2.3
5⅝x7⅝x15⅝	6	112.5	4350	2950	2.6	2.3
7⅝x7⅝x15⅝	8	112.5	5500	3600	2.6	2.3
11⅝x7⅝x15⅝	12	112.5	7950	4900	2.6	2.3

Table based on ⅜-in. mortar joints.

*Actual weight within ±7% of average weight.

**Actual weight within ±17% of average weight.

***With face-shell mortar bedding. Mortar quantities include 10% allowance for waste.

Actual weight of 100 sq.ft. of wall can be computed by formula $W(N)+150(M)$ where:

W = actual weight of a single unit
N = number of units for 100 sq.ft. of wall
M = cu.ft. of mortar for 100 sq.ft. of wall

TABLE A-22. WEIGHTS AND QUANTITIES OF MATERIALS FOR CONCRETE MASONRY WALLS.

Types of windows	Masonry openings	Glass size	Masonry openings	Glass size	Masonry openings	Glass size
Double	2′0″x3′4″	16″x12″	2′8″x3′4″	24″x12″	3′4″x3′4″	32″x12″
	4′0″	16″	4′0″	16″	4′0″	16″
	4′8″	20″	4′8″	20″	4′8″	20″
	5′4″	24″	5′4″	24″	5′4″	24″
	6′0″	28″	6′0″	28″	6′0″	28″
	6′8″	32″	6′8″	32″	6′8″	32″
	4′0″x4′0″	40″x16″	4′8″x4′0″	48″x16″	5′4″x4′0″	56″x16″
	4′8″	20″	4′8″	20″	4′8″	20″
	5′4″	24″	5′4″	24″	5′4″	24″
	6′0″	28″	6′0″	28″	6′0″	28″
	6′8″	32″	6′8″	32″	6′8″	32″
	7′4″	36″	7′4″	36″	7′4″	36″
Casement	1′4″x3′4″	8″x25″	2′0″x3′4″	16″x25″	2′8″x3′4″	24″x25″
	4′0″	33″	4′0″	33″	4′0″	33″
	4′8″	41″	4′8″	41″	4′8″	41″
	5′4″	49″	5′4″	49″	5′4″	49″
	6′0″	57″	6′0″	57″	6′0″	57″
	6′8″	65″	6′8″	65″	6′8″	65″
Basement	Two light sash		Three light sash			
	2′0″x2′0″	8″x12″	2′8″x2′0″	8″x12″		
	2′8″	20″	2′8″	20″		
	2′8″x2′0″	12″x12″				
	2′8″	20″				

Note: Modular masonry openings shown above should also be used for metal window frames. It may be necessary, however, to provide metal surrounds to fit the metal frames into the modular openings.

TABLE A-23. MODULAR CONCRETE MASONRY OPENINGS FOR WOOD WINDOW FRAMES. (MASONRY OPENINGS ARE DIMENSIONED FROM JAMB TO JAMB AND FROM BOTTOM OF LINTEL TO BOTTOM OF PRECAST CONCRETE SILL. OPENINGS OF SIZES OTHER THAN THOSE SHOWN MAY BE USED BY KEEPING THE DIMENSIONS IN MULTIPLES OF 8 INCHES. GLASS SIZES SHOWN ARE FOR ONE LIGHT BUT ANY DIVISION OF THE SASH CAN BE USED.)

Number of block		Number of brick	Mortar* cu.ft.	Type of bond	
Stretchers	Headers				
97 (4x8x16″)	—	772	12.2	8-in. wall	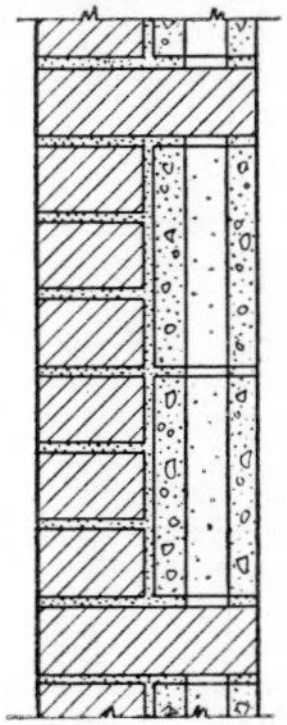 7th course bonding
97 (8x8x16″)	—	868	13.5	12-in. wall	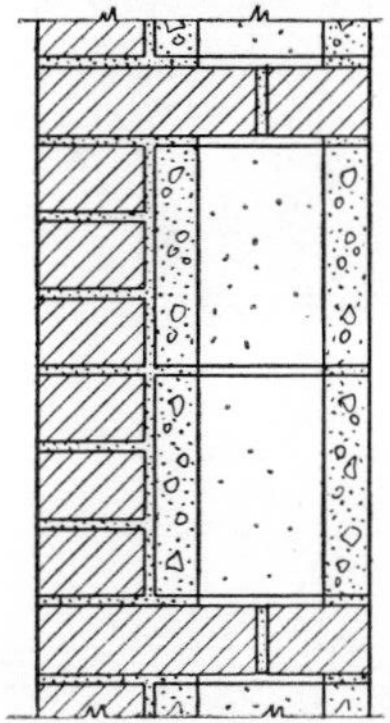 7th course bonding

TABLE A-24. NUMBER OF CONCRETE BLOCK, BRICK, AND MORTAR REQUIRED FOR 100 SQUARE FEET OF FACED WALL.

57 (8x8x16″)	57 (8x8x16″)	788	13.6	12-in. wall	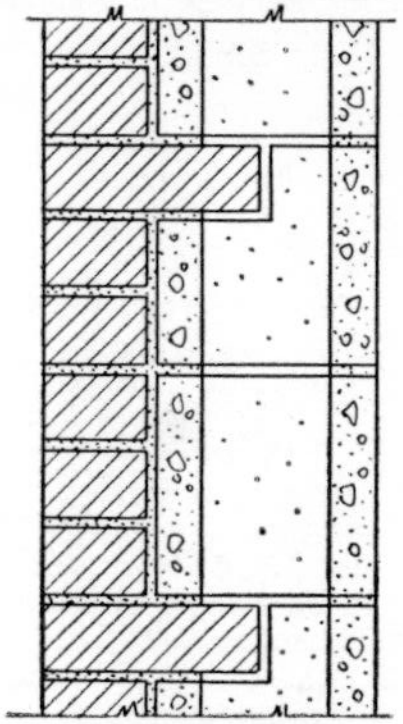	6th course bonding
193 (4x5x12″)	—	770	13.1	8-in. wall	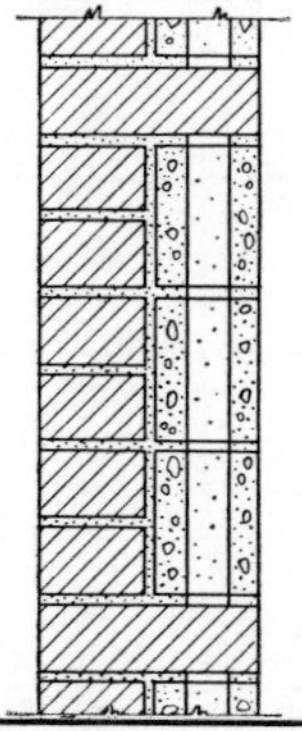	7th course bonding

*Mortar quantities based on ⅜-in. mortar joints with face-shell bedding for the block. Ten per cent included for mortar waste.

Specification, serial designation, and latest revised date	Minimum face-shell thickness, in.	Compressive strength, minimum, psi, average gross area		Water absorption, maximum, lb. per cu.ft. of concrete, average of 5 units	Moisture content, maximum, per cent of total absorption, average of 5 units
		Average of 5 units	Individual unit		
Hollow load-bearing concrete masonry units ASTM C90,1944†	1¼ or over:				
	Grade A*	1000	800	15	40
	Grade B**	700	600	—	40
	Under 1¼ and over ¾	1000	800	15	40
Hollow non-load-bearing concrete masonry units ASTM C129, 1939†	Not less than ½	350	300	—	40
Solid load-bearing concrete masonry units ASTM C145, 1940***†					
Grade A	—	1800	1600	15	40
Grade B	—	1200	1000	15	40
Concrete units; masonry, hollow Federal SS-C-621, 1935				Average of 3 units	Average of 3 units
Load-bearing units	1¼ or more	700	600	16	40
	¾ to 1¼	1000	800	16	40
Non-load-bearing units	Not less than ¾	350	—	—	40

*For use in exterior walls below grade, and for unprotected exterior walls above grade.

**For general use above grade where protected from the weather with two coats of portland cement paint or other satisfactory waterproofing treatment approved by the purchaser.

***Units with 75 per cent or more net area. The classification is based on strength and does not necessarily measure weather resistance.

†Tentative revisions to these specifications are shown in the 1950 Supplement to the *Book of ASTM Standards*, Part 3, pp. 347–349 incl.

TABLE A-25. SUMMARY OF PHYSICAL REQUIREMENTS FOR VARIOUS TYPES OF CONCRETE MASONRY UNITS.

		Compressive strength, minimum, psi, average gross area (brick flatwise)		Modulus of rupture, minimum, psi, (brick flatwise)	
		Average of 5 brick	Individual	Average of 5 brick	Individual
Concrete building brick ASTM C55, 1937†					
Grade A	—	2500	2000	450	300
Grade B	—	1250	1000	300	200

†Tentative revisions to these specifications are shown in the 1950 Supplement to the *Book of ASTM Standards*, Part 3, pp. 347–349 incl.

Basic wall construction*		Interior finish: Plain wall no plaster	½-in. plaster on: Wall direct	½-in. plaster on: ¾-in. furring with: ⅜-in. plaster-board	½-in. plaster on: ¾-in. furring with: ½-in. rigid insulation
Concrete masonry (cores not filled)	8-in. sand and gravel or limestone	0.53	0.49	0.31	0.22
	8-in. cinder	0.37	0.35	0.25	0.19
	8-in. expanded slag, clay or shale	0.33	0.32	0.23	0.18
	12-in. sand and gravel or limestone	0.49	0.45	0.30	0.22
	12-in. cinder	0.35	0.33	0.24	0.18
	12-in. expanded slag, clay or shale	0.32	0.31	0.23	0.18
Concrete masonry (cores filled with insulation)**	8-in. sand and gravel or limestone	0.39	0.37	0.26	0.19
	8-in. cinder	0.20	0.19	0.16	0.13
	8-in. expanded slag, clay or shale	0.17	0.17	0.14	0.12
	12-in. sand and gravel or limestone	0.34	0.32	0.24	0.18
	12-in. cinder	0.20	0.19	0.15	0.13
	12-in. expanded slag, clay or shale	0.15	0.14	0.12	0.11
Cavity walls (with 2-in. or larger cavity. Cavity not filled with insulation)	10-in. wall of two 4-in. sand and gravel or limestone units	0.34	0.33	0.24	0.18
	10-in. wall of two 4-in. cinder, expanded slag, clay or shale units	0.26	0.24	0.19	0.15
	10-in. wall of 4-in. face brick and 4-in. sand and gravel or limestone units	0.38	0.36	0.25	0.19
	10-in. wall of 4-in. face brick and 4-in. cinder, expanded slag, clay or shale unit	0.33	0.31	0.23	0.18
	14-in. wall of 4-in. face brick and 8-in. sand and gravel or limestone units	0.33	0.31	0.23	0.18
	14-in. wall of 4-in. face brick and 8-in. cinder, expanded slag, clay or shale unit	0.26	0.25	0.19	0.16
	14-in. wall of 4-in. and 8-in. sand and gravel or limestone units	0.30	0.28	0.21	0.17
	14-in. wall of 4-in. and 8-in. cinder, expanded slag, clay or shale units	0.22	0.21	0.17	0.14
4-in. face brick plus:	4-in. sand and gravel or limestone unit	0.53	0.49	0.31	0.23
	4-in. cinder, expanded slag, clay or shale unit	0.44	0.42	0.28	0.21
	4-in. common brick	0.50	0.46	0.30	0.22
	8-in. sand and gravel or limestone unit	0.44	0.41	0.28	0.21
	8-in. cinder, expanded slag, clay or shale unit	0.31	0.30	0.22	0.17
	8-in. common brick	0.36	0.34	0.24	0.19
	1-in. wood sheathing, paper, 2x4 studs, wood lath and plaster	—	0.27	0.27	0.20
4-in. common brick plus:	4-in. sand and gravel or limestone unit	0.45	0.42	0.28	0.21
	4-in. cinder, expanded slag, clay or shale unit	0.38	0.36	0.26	0.19
	8-in. sand and gravel or limestone unit	0.37	0.35	0.25	0.19
	8-in. cinder, expanded slag, clay or shale unit	0.28	0.27	0.20	0.16
	8-in. common brick	0.31	0.30	0.22	0.17
	1-in. wood sheathing, paper, 2x4 studs, wood lath and plaster	—	0.25	0.25	0.19
Wood frame	wood siding, 1-in. wood sheathing, 2x4 studs, wood lath and plaster	—	0.25	0.24	0.19

All concrete masonry shown in this table are hollow units. All concrete masonry wall surfaces exposed to the weather have two coats of portland cement base paint. Surfaces of all walls exposed to the weather subject to a wind velocity of 15 miles per hour.
Values based on dry insulation. The use of vapor barriers or other precautions must be considered to keep insulation dry.

TABLE A-26. COEFFICIENTS OF HEAT TRANSMISSION (U) FOR VARIOUS WALLS.

Appendix V

Suggested Method of Laying Out a Foundation

With surveying instruments, building lines and elevations of a new house can be laid out easily, quickly, and accurately. When they are *not* available, the right-triangle method is a simple way of laying out corners of the basement walls. This method is based on the fact that a triangle with sides 12, 16, and 20 feet long or of similar proportions, is a right triangle and the 90-degree angle, or right angle, is opposite the longest side. By applying this principle, building lines can be laid out perpendicular to each other. (*See* Fig. 1.) A simple method for setting elevation of batter boards *without* surveying instruments is shown in Fig. 2. (*See* Chap. 51, Concrete Masonry Basements.)

Right triangle method for laying out the foundation without use of surveying instruments.

1. Lay out a line representing outside face of basement wall in accordance with local ordinances.
2. Set stakes at *A* and *B* on this line locating two front corners.
3. Use nails in tops of all stakes for accurate location of all corners and other points.
4. Set stake *F* on line *A-B* 12 ft. from *A*.
5. Stake *E* is placed 16 ft. from *A* and 20 ft. from *F*. Angle *EAB* is a right angle.
6. Extend *A-E* to *D* for third corner of basement.
7. Locate *C* by an intersection of an arc described from *D* having a radius equal to *A-B* and an arc described from *B* having a radius equal to *A-D*.
8. To check accuracy of layout, *A-C* must equal *B-D*.
9. Set up batter boards outside limits of excavation.

Figure 1

16'-0"
12'-0"
20'-0"
A
B
C
D
E
F
These two diagonals should be equal in length
Cord lines directly over base lines
Base lines at outside face of basement walls

10. Tops of all batter boards are set at same elevation such as first floor level.
11. Stretch heavy cord tightly between batter boards directly over base lines thus establishing the building lines for construction purposes.

Setting elevations of batter boards without surveying instruments.

1. Set batter boards at one corner as at right.
2. Place hose as shown.
3. Fill with water until water level is at top of batter board *A*.
4. Mark water level at opposite end *B* and set board to mark.

Figure 2

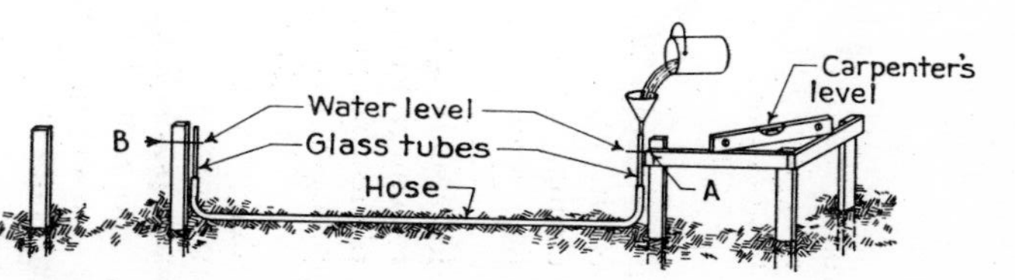

Index